Introduction to Personality and Psychotherapy

A Theory-Construction Approach

Houghton Mifflin Company Boston

Atlanta Dallas Geneva, Illinois
Hopewell, New Jersey Palo Alto London

Introduction to Personality and Psychotherapy

A Theory-Construction Approach

Joseph F. Rychlak

Purdue University

Printed in the U.S.A.

Library of Congress Catalog Card Number: 72-6887

ISBN: 0-395-14056-0

Acknowledgment is made for permission to reprint the following materials:

From the book *B. F. Skinner: The Man and his Ideas* by Richard I. Evans. Copyright © 1969 by Richard I. Evans. Published by E. P. Dutton & Co., Inc. in a paperback edition and used with their permission.

The Collected Works of C. G. Jung, ed. by G. Adler, M. Fordham, and H. Read, trans. by R. F. C. Hull, Bollingen Series XX, vol. 8, *The Structure of the Psyche* (copyright © 1960 and 1969 by Bollingen Foundation); vol. 9i, *The Archeytpes and the Collective Unconscious* (copyright © 1959 and 1969 by Bollingen Foundation); vol. 16, *The Practice of Psychotherapy* (copyright © 1966 by Bollingen Foundation); reprinted by permission of Princeton University Press.

From *Counseling and Psychotherapy*, by Carl R. Rogers. Houghton Mifflin Company, 1942. Reprinted by permission of the publisher.

From *Client-Centered Therapy*, by Carl R. Rogers. Houghton Mifflin Company, 1951. Reprinted by permission of the publisher.

From *On Becoming a Person*, © 1961 Carl R. Rogers. Reprinted with permission of Houghton Mifflin Company.

From *Verbal Behavior*, by B. F. Skinner. Copyright © 1957. By permission of Appleton-Century-Crofts, Educational Division, Meredith Corporation.

TO LENORE

PREFACE

Introduction to Personality and Psychotherapy: A Theory-Construction Approach surveys the major schools of personality and psychotherapy according to a standard outline per chapter, and then evaluates the content of these outlooks in terms of theory construction. Each theory is presented historically, with an effort to capture its development, the reasons for any changes in its content, and a detailed understanding of its full range of meaning. To promote this depth of understanding the theoretical rubrics of personality are extended to psychotherapy, where the student can see why they were initially advanced: to function helpfully in a living circumstance for both client and therapist. Finally, a comparative scheme of theory-construction issues drawn from the history of philosophy and science is offered to round out the student's grasp of the schools of thought, contrasting strengths and weaknesses of variations therein.

The area of personality theory is immense and confusing, and even the great thinkers in the field do not have a clear picture of one another. This multiplicity in outlook is compounded by the fact that many of the heavily-used secondary sources were written before the better, more thorough translations of Freud, Adler, and Jung were available and arrayed in proper sequence across the theorists' life spans, permitting a proper overview of developments and changes in their thought. Relying on secondary sources can confound the restricted and often slightly biased views of others with those of the original theorists. Thus in reporting from the original sources, I have tried to be meticulous in the citations, so that the serious student could look into the primary sources

for more detail. The reader will find this book thoroughly referenced and well indexed.

Years of experience have taught me that the student really cannot understand the classical personality theorists without also understanding their theories of psychotherapy. The ideas of people like Freud and Jung are easily misconstrued as simply titillating or mystical interpretations of the human condition when presented in the classroom without an opportunity for the student to see why such conceptions were considered essential in the consulting room. Though there has been a tradition of concern lest students being told about psychotherapy might begin practicing without adequate training and supervision, the complexity of modern times seems to negate this line of argument. If anything, a well-presented discussion of *several* theories of personality and psychotherapy can only help to sophisticate the college student so that he is not an easy target for some one, saving theory of mental health. This broadening, after all, is the purpose of education.

The conceptual scheme I offer has scholarly credentials and content recognizable to other sciences which might be applied to the teaching of this course. Modern psychology must be able to provide generalizations which coalesce with the thinking in other sciences if it is to be successful in its struggle to become an undisputed science. The best scheme and series of issues to unify personality theory would seem to be drawn from the history of philosophy and science. Thus, I give a detailed account of each theory and then consider it in light of a set number of theory-construction issues that all personality theorists have wrestled with at varying levels of clarity and sophistication.

Though I am committed to raising the status of personality theory and would like to develop an area of specialization in psychology which might be termed "theory construction," I am not so naive as to assume that all instructors will want to frame their courses around this emphasis. Many will want to use this volume in an introductory personality theory course, or an introductory psychotherapy course, and no more. And so, the reader will find that he can skip the theory-construction considerations altogether. These issues are set off in independent chapters so that *Introduction to Personality and Psychotherapy* is actually a theory-construction book within a personality and psychotherapy book. I would prefer that the instructor-reader see things my way and help to establish this emphasis, but only time will tell how accurately I have diagnosed psychology's needs on this score.

I have tried to make the non-theory construction chapters clear and straightforward. Each chapter is written according to a common framework; the student will always know where he stands in relation to the point of view under presentation. There are enough details and examples that he is not likely to feel that he is simply memorizing a string of terminology. I have also included diagrams of the more difficult concepts.

The theorists were selected for this volume on the basis of two criteria. First, they had to be major contributors to personality and psychotherapy. Second, they had to be an outstanding example of the various philosophical lines of development found in psychology. Fortunately, the combining criteria worked out to cover the most widely cited people in the area. Though some might quarrel with the inclusion of Kelly's constructive alternativism as a major school of thought, no one can question that his approach is a marvelous application of what I call a Kantian theoretical model.

Questions of space always nag the text writer,

and since I wanted to emphasize the specific theorists' writings I eliminated any forays into side issues or attempts to bring a school of thought up to date. An instructor may cover such topics in lecture. The present effort is devoted to theory *as written* by the founder over the years. We study his thought and try to do justice to its development.

I find that undergraduates genuinely want to learn what this book has to offer. *This* is what they think psychology is all about. They are not disturbed by the fact that psychology lacks empirical facts to back up everything it proposes. The undergraduates today are unusually insightful on the question of implacable scientific truth. They know from reading newspapers that modern scientists almost daily raise new objections to Darwin's evolutionary theory or Einstein's theory of relativity. They are already schooled in the attitude that scientific facts are never "true" for all time but only for as long as they describe and explain phenomena needing such conceptualization better than any other.

J. F. R.

ACKNOWLEDGMENTS

I would like to thank several people for their help and encouragement during the various stages of producing this volume. I am greatly appreciative of the biographical information provided by Gladys Kelly and Joseph Wolpe. Tom Stampfl not only gave me a candid overview of his life but helped immensely in making theoretical points clear. Carl Rogers generously provided me with material in prepublication form which facilitated bringing his still active and creative viewpoints up to date. Before his death, Carl G. Jung made available valuable information concerning certain influences on his thinking. George Kelly, my teacher and personal friend, exchanged letters with me over the years dealing with the theory-construction questions which so fascinated me. His was a great and generous intellect. Heinz Ansbacher not only substantially contributed to the structure my study of Adler would take, but he has continued to audit its progress over the years.

I would like to thank Jim Naylor for helping me find the time to do this book. Marvelous colleagues and friends like Jim Mancuso, Bob Hogan, Mark Stephens, and Dick Ingwell played an inestimable role in making me feel that this effort was worthwhile. I thank them for their bent ears and critical assessments. My students have probably done more to inspire me than anyone, and I would like in particular to thank Nguyen Duc Tuan for his scholarly support and personal friendship.

Clare Thompson, Dan Levinson, and Heinz Ansbacher kindly read portions of the manuscript, and I thank them for their valuable comments. I greatly appreciate the typing assistance of Carol Vester, Lorna Stewart, Joyce Von Dielingen, and Mary Sue Burkhardt. Finally, this book like my first book would never have seen print without the devoted assistance of my wonderful wife Lenore, not to mention the forbearance and sacrifice of my children, Steph and Ron.

CONTENTS

Introduction

A Framework for the Study of Man

To the beginning student, "What is personality?" is a simple enough question, straightforward and honest. Its answer should be easy to couch in uncomplicated terms. Yet, man has in one way or another been struggling to answer this question since he first became aware of that primordial something needing explanation—his identity. The question was probably first broadly phrased as "Who am I?" or "Why am I here?" In answering man was to forge human history, including the cultural belief systems which not only carried the meaning of such questions but determined the sorts of answers he would accept as significant. His assumptions about the nature of life, the structure of reality, the explanation of events, and the kinds of proof required for belief all combined to fix the boundaries of his plausibility. Those who feel that the question can be answered factually, by conducting empirical investigations, overlook the consideration that "facts" demand meaningful explanation; and it is in this realm that a variety of answers is possible. In a sense, then, the question has no answer if we expect *the* answer, but in a broader sense it does, for what this section points to is the inevitability of accepting *many* answers.

When we speak of "cultural belief systems" we refer to such broad conceptual units as national identities, theological outlooks, political convictions, the healing arts, the arts proper, and even that body of empirically verified beliefs known as science. Each of these products of history encourages a unique view and hence a unique answer to the question posed by this section. Indeed, these bodies literally encourage *one* answer—their answer—to the basic question. They imply no "grand design," but simply seek the recognition that meanings taken as assumptions encourage other meanings to develop consonant with these assumptions. All

1

theories are written for a purpose, and what determines unity of theory is unity of purpose. Where there is no goal acknowledged there is no unity among theoreticians. For our purposes, *all* belief systems of this sort are *theories*. A theory is a series of two or more schematic labels (such as descriptive words) which have been hypothesized, presumed, or even factually demonstrated to bear a meaningful relationship, one with the other(s). The "schematic labels" are the *constructs* of a theory. They are the carriers of meaning, the signposts of a theoretical terrain which, when brought together, indicate what each theory is "getting at."

Now, these signposts are not natural products of the terrain. They had to be constructed. Some of them are not even palpable. Why then believe in them? When we begin asking questions of this sort, we enter a realm of knowledge known as *philosophy*. Any psychologist who believes he can avoid this eventuality is courting ultimate ignorance. One of the fascinating aspects of philosophical study is that certain themes recur. Theoretical issues of a highly abstract nature—often called "metaphysical"—pop up again and again. Direct parallels of this sort occur in religious, political, and scientific theory. Although philosophical, these issues are not hard to understand, and they permeate our most banal theoretical beliefs—such as whether or not we can really *choose* to do anything in life. Are we machines, or are we people? What does the construct "person" imply that is absent from the construct "machine"? Not all psychologists acknowledge a genuine meaning in the construct "personality." Such theorists would find the question posed in this section, if not meaningless, then at least unsophisticated and outmoded. The question these theorists ask is not "what" personality "is" but "how" behavior "moves."

So, if we are sincere in asking our question we must take on the full challenge of the required answer. We need a scheme, a "prototype theory" which will define our particular assumptions and allow us to make sense of other theories in terms of it. Next, we need a decent sampling of personality theories to study. When we have our preliminary scheme and our sample theories, we can apply the former to the latter. When other "new" theories subsequently confront us we will use this prototype theory once again.

The assumptions of the prototype theory will be taken from history, using a scheme which mankind has put forward over the centuries. The sample theories to which this scheme will be applied are Freud, Adler, Jung, Sullivan, Dollard and Miller, Skinner, Wolpe, Stampfl, Rogers, Binswanger, Boss, and Kelly. These theorists are individual men, writing for the purposes of their particular attitudes and professional goals (cultural belief systems), and we must not overlook the influence of their life's unique course. Each account is therefore presented biographically, from the man's early to his mature writings. Relevant historical occurrences which played a role in his developing thought also appear in the appropriate context.

It would be incorrect to presume that universal themes cutting across these theoretical views do not exist. We turn next in this section to a series of such universal concerns phrased as additional questions, to which all theorists must respond in taking their stand. The constructs which we mention in light of these questions will frame our prototype or metatheory (overriding theory). What we acknowledge here is that theoretical constructs vary in abstraction, that is, in the extent of detail they include. The more abstract they are, the more details they leave out. Some constructs which are sufficiently abstract can *subsume* lower-ranging, more restricted constructs on the ladder of abstraction.[1] This makes it possible to array both Freud and Skinner under the *range of convenience* or scope of our more abstract metatheoretical conceptions. Although Freudian and Skinnerian theories are diametrically opposed on many lower levels, each can be positioned in relation to higher-level concepts so that they share meanings not previously apparent.

One of the possible definitions of personality is: "It *is* what causes it." This is another deceptively simple assertion; examined historically we must legitimately ask: what is a cause? Man's earliest formulations concerning the world were quaintly anthropomorphized accounts. Nature was made up of human-like gods and demigods having intentions, moods of vengeance or lust, hopeful aspirations, and so forth. Philosophy and thereby science is often said to have begun when Thales of Miletus (640?–546 B.C.) and his student, Anaximander (611–547 B.C.), began giving accounts of nature in terms of the basic "stuff" which presumably made it up—"water" or the "boundless" as their respective views expressed it. Heraclitus (540–480 B.C.) and Parmenides (515–456 B.C.) raised the issue of change, of whether anything really happened in this world of days and nights, and thus introduced a concern with the "fabric of movement" or impetus in events across time. Heraclitus was also instrumental in bringing another notion to the fore, the *logos* by which events flowed. The movement of time was patterned into a rational order which was *not* random. Based on this preliminary belief Democritus (460–370 B.C.) was later to say that there was no such thing as "chance" in the universe for everything is subject to patterned laws.

Aristotle (384–322 B.C.) was to take these conceptual models of substance, impetus, and pattern, and add to them the notion of a reason or a "that for the sake of which" events came about. The result was his profoundly influential theory of knowledge based upon what he called the "causes," plural since *four* such causes had to be isolated to show that one had a true grasp of his experience. In terms of theory construction, we might think of these as four "models" of description. A model is actually a kind of construct, used by a theorist to order his thinking about what he hopes to comment on. Sometimes a model is used *informally,* so that even the theorist employing it fails to appreciate its impact on his thought processes. It functions as an unnamed premise in his theory. For this reason, when dealing with something like "the personality," we must look carefully at the highly abstract hence easily overlooked meanings which a theorist sends our way as his "image of man." We invariably find this image in just how he goes about using the Aristotelian causes.

What are these four causes? The first Aristotle called the *material* cause, which was tantamount to Thales's and Anaximander's attribution of a pervasive substance to the world. In describing a chair we can say we know it is a chair because like most chairs it is made of wood, or iron, or marble; not many chairs are made of cotton or of ice cream. Another *cause* of the chair is the fact that someone or some machine "made" it, or put it together. This Aristotle termed the *efficient* cause, and we can see here the matter of flux and change which so fascinated Parmenides and Heraclitus. Events change, things are done, some form of energic propulsion seems evident in the flow of events. Chairs also take on certain patterned outlines; they meet our blueprint conceptions of what chairs "look like." Chairs look more like chairs than they look like tricycles or apple trees. This usage, drawn from the logos conception of Heraclitus and Democritus, Aristotle termed the *formal* cause.

It is important to appreciate that Aristotle did not advise *limiting* the number of causes used in describing the nature of anything. It is possible to have formless substances, as in a "blob" of mud, and even formless movement, such as the wafting of a breeze against our face. But mud can be shaped and baked into statues or dinnerware, and breezes can be elevated and patterned into an easily recognizable tornado. In like fashion, Aristotle believed, the enlightened physicist can bring to bear more and more causes to enrich his account of *natural* events.

But the cause which Aristotle himself seems to have added to this list is surely the most important for personality theory. Aristotle would have held that a rendering of the "causes" of the chair would not be complete until we had cited the "purpose" of the chair's existence. Another way of expressing this aspect is as the "goal" of the chair's existence, or "that for the sake of which" it now stands before us. Still another way of saying this is the "intention" of the chair's existence. This idea of a purpose or an intentionality in events Aristotle subsumed under his fourth cause— the *final* cause. A final cause is therefore "that for the sake of which" something is existing, is happening, or is about to take place. The "sake" for which a chair is constructed might be termed "man's comfort" or "laziness" or "utility in eating, writing," and so forth.

Of course, the chair does not *itself* decide to "come about" or "to be." The human being who obtained the wood (material cause) and made it into a chair (efficient cause) matching his physical needs (formal cause) so that he might live more comfortably (final cause) may be said to have a purpose or intention in his construction efforts. However, Aristotle was not above including such final-cause terms in his description of what today we call "inanimate nature." For example, in his *Physics* Aristotle (1952) theorized that leaves exist for the purpose ("sake") of providing shade for the fruit on trees, and he concluded thereby "that nature is

a cause, a cause that operates for a purpose."[2] Though mythological thinking had been dropped, the basic *teleology* of anthropomorphized accounts thus remained in early scientific theory. (*Telos* is from the Greek meaning *goal* or *the end* toward which events are aiming, moving, and so forth.) Aristotle was thus advocating a *natural* teleology, and when we substitute God for Nature we have a *deity* teleology. Such theorizing was to bring much heartache to science.

We now have a historically sound beginning for our metatheory. What if we were to look at our model personality theorists in terms of the Aristotelian causes? Would it help to array them, draw distinctions between them, and thereby gather sharper insight into what each was saying? The focus of this book evolves from a positive response to this question, and this scheme will be adapted for the analysis to follow in subsequent chapters. However, rather than using the classical terms material, efficient, formal, and final *causes,* dropping the designation of "cause" altogether seems most sensible, while retaining the core meanings of these constructions. Let us consider these the four *basic meaning constructs,* and define them as substance, impetus, pattern, and intention. Table 1 lists the four basic meaning constructs with appropriate examples.

Too many people today consider the term

Table 1
The Four Basic Meaning Constructs

SUBSTANCE CONSTRUCT:	The presumed underlying, unchanging essence of a thing at any given point in time. *Examples:* wood, cloth, flesh, carbon, ectoplasm, electron, or "matter."
IMPETUS CONSTRUCT:	The succession of events over time which are believed to originate or sustain motion. *Examples:* push, move, make happen, determine, or "cause."
PATTERN CONSTRUCT:	The style of organization and internal consistency of an object or other event in experience. *Examples:* personality type, blueprint, logical consistency, or design.
INTENTIONAL CONSTRUCT:	"That for the sake of which some line of movement or behavior is carried out." *Examples:* intentions, reasons, hopes, desires, expectations, or "just for the heck of it."

"cause" synonymous with the impetus construct meaning. There is a historical reason for this popular conception, which will be made clear in the discussion of the rise of modern natural science. For now we should simply be alert to the fact that when anyone asks "what is" *anything* our answers will have to be framed in terms of these basic meaning constructs. Even when we *induct* and make guesses about what we "see" in experience we frame such inductions as one of our meanings. Heraclitus's induction of a logos was clearly in the form of a pattern construct. Subsequent *deductions* from this logos construct by Democritus were then made, such as "since everything follows order there *is no chance* in the universe." Induction and deduction are ways of speaking about the ladder of abstraction and about how we use meaning throughout its levels.

ARE THEORETICAL MEANINGS BIPOLAR OR UNIPOLAR?

How might Aristotle account for a concept such as "theory"? Which of the basic meaning constructs can include this notion in its range of definition? Though one might argue that theoretical cogitation in the brain of a person takes place by way of electrical impulses fixed within *substantial* nervous tissue, a theory is more on the side of an ordered, *patterned* relationship among meanings, arrayed as premises and assumptions "for the sake of which" other hypotheses, beliefs, opinions, or conclusions can be reached. Theories are thus best defined in terms of pattern and intentional construct meanings (Aristotle's formal and final causes). Take the logician's syllogism, for example. We all know the "All men are mortal. This is a man. Hence, this man is mortal" sequence of reasoning called the syllogism. The initial assumption (All men are mortal) is the major premise, the secondary denotation (This is a man) is the minor premise, and the deduction made thereby is the conclusion. This has a pattern of meaningful relationship which extracts meaning implied in the premises and unites them by way of the conclusion.

An important insight here, and one that will recur in the subsequent chapters of this volume, is that the iron-clad relationship which the syllogism defines between its premises and its conclusion is *100 per cent determined*. That is, given this premise, and affirming it as we have done, there is *no other* conclusion possible: "This man *is* mortal." Theoretical propositions like "All men are mortal" may be considered to have two elements—an *antecedent term* (coming first as a subject term) and a *consequent term* (coming second as a predicate term). Now, logicians have made it clear that the meanings embodied in consequents follow necessarily *only* when the proposition's antecedent is affirmed. Only when we say "This is a man" does it follow that "This is a mortal." If we have reversed this order and *affirmed the consequent*, "This is a mortal," it would *not* have followed that "This is a man." Of course, one can reject the entire premise and say "All men are *not* mortal; there was at least one man who was divine." In such a case we enter into a debate or "dialectical" exchange. The term *dialectic* has many meanings,[3] but the major denotation here is opposition, bipolarity, the idea that meanings suggest their obverse. One defines the term "left" and *ipso facto* defines "right."

The earliest Greeks were much taken by the seeming dialectical nature of things. For example, Anaximander maintained that the elements of the universe were held together by an opposition—air is cold, fire is hot, and so forth. Heraclitus found oppositional "strife" to be the principle by which events moved over time. Empedocles (circa 493–433 B.C.) then argued that "love and strife" were the antagonists which moved events. But it was Socrates and Plato who raised the dialectic as a "method" in coming to know truth by way of error. Since truth and error are themselves essentially dialectical sides to the totality of events, there is no reason why—through dialectical discourse—two men could not "talk and learn."

The famous "dialogues" of Plato (1952) present the Socratic approach of "questions and answers" in which Socrates would pose a question for his student to take a stand on, and then defend the meaningful point in opposition to the student's. If the student chose A, Socrates defended not-A; if the student chose not-A, Socrates defended A. It was all the same to Socrates, for he did not think of himself as having any "true knowledge" to "communicate" from his head to the student's head. To use this dialectical method of questioning in order to manipulate a student's thought, or achieve advantage in debate with an opponent, is what Socrates termed *sophistry*. The early philosopher types who called themselves Sophists (Socrates learned his dialectical approach from them, in fact) used this method. The Sophists were thus insincere in their application of dialectical questioning. They used questions to manipulate and edge a conversation toward a predetermined end, which counters the open-ended, completely spontaneous spirit of dialectical opposition in meaning expression. If one points the dialectic toward a fixed pole of the bipolarity in meanings, he has already killed off that which is most precious in its use—the creative generation of alternative possibilities.

The point is, man's knowledge of experience is "all of a piece." There is a *one in many* or a *many in one* characteristic to meaningful knowledge, so that premises and conclusions generate new premises and conclusions which are all linked oppositionally one to another. By intellectually biting into this totality at *any* point and setting forth dialectically the human intellect can arrive at new insights which could not be predicted from the outset. Put another way: man can begin in *error* and come to know *truth*. By starting at one oppositional pole (error) and applying his natural dialectical reasoning capacity, man could in time arrive at the other pole (truth) because in a true sense the two poles—the "many"—were "one."

It was Plato's student, Aristotle, who first rankled at the "armchair" features of the Socratic dialectic, where two men talked and talked, often kidding themselves into believing that they were coming to know truth when in fact they were simply perpetuating error by way of personal opinion. Aristotle formulated the first "toughminded" position in philosophy, for he denied that it was possible to begin in error and come to know truth. These two sides of the coin are not necessarily united by dialectical opposition in the various meanings of language. Unfounded premises can only lead to unfounded conclusions. Aristotle did not deny that man *could* reason dialectically. In fact, he admitted that when under attack concerning our major premises we all must resort to a kind of oppositional defense of what we believe, because often there is no proof one way or the other. But just as often it *is* possible to proceed on sound premises, and in this case we should reason *demonstratively*. Aristotle then made a monumental distinction which will be relevant to our study of personality theory. As he put it:

Now reasoning is an argument in which, certain things being laid down, something other than these necessarily comes about through them. (a) It is a "demonstration", when the premises from which the reasoning starts are true and primary, or are such that our knowledge of them has originally come through premises which are primary and true: (b) reasoning, on the other hand, is "dialectical", if it reasons from opinions that are generally accepted.[4]

This important distinction between a dialectical and a demonstrative course of reason thus involves *only* the way in which we arrive at our major premises. Once our premises are in order, the syllogistic sequence reviewed above, including affirming the antecedent, is carried out. *All* men reason both ways, said Aristotle, and *all* men are therefore capable of the Socratic rumination if they wish to "play" with the bipolarities of meaning, taking an opinion of one sort or another. But if they wish to speak the truth, sound reasoners will shift to premises of a *unipolar* nature, or, as Aristotle called these premises: "primary and true." He meant by this either the form of tautological premise used in defining terms, such as "All bachelors are unmarried males," or, a statement which has been empirically established as a "fact." In the latter effort Aristotle founded biology, for he sought the observed truths of empirical reality rather than the *opinions* of verbal expression. A primary and true meaning is no longer bipolar; that is, it does not admit alternative possibilities (opinions). Such premises cannot be questioned.

As will be clear in subsequent chapters, whether or not one accepts the possibility of dialectical formulations in man's behavior dramatically alters the image of man he arrives at, as compared to exclusively demonstrative formulations. It was this latter, demonstrative view which took ascendance in the rise of natural science, a historical development of immense importance.

WHAT IS A SCIENTIFIC EXPLANATION?

Tracing the rise of modern scientific explanation in terms of our basic meaning constructs and the dialectical versus demonstrative reasoning strategies is a fascinating exercise. The Churchmen continued in Aristotle's vein to reason teleologically, shifting to a deity teleology. A common tactic here was to ask "What did God intend when He . . ." or "What is the intention of this natural act, as created by God?"[5] This emphasis on formal (God's plan) and final causality ("that for the sake of which" He created) was to place restraints on the empiricist who might dare to contradict the teachings of a theologically based physical explanation. Men were burned at the stake for such heresies, and Galileo (1564–1642) retracted his scientific theories concerning the earth's motion in relation to the sun rather than confront this possible eventuality.[6]

It is significant that Galileo was a *mathematician*. The dialectic as model for man has never done well when mathematics, which is surely the purest form of demonstrative reasoning of which man is capable, was in ascendance. Whereas the dialectician had seen the meaning of A in not-A, so that a contradiction in meaning is an invitation to learning, the mathematician held rigorously to his unipolar conceptions of single quantities totaling up with other single quantities to make a larger sum total which might appear bipolar but is not. Mathematicians begin with a proposition first suggested by Aristotle, known as the Law of Contradiction, which states: "A is not not-A." This mathematical emphasis was epitomized in the rise of British Philosophy, where Sir Francis Bacon (1561–1626) went several points "up" on Aristotle's toughmindedness and Sir Isaac Newton (1642–1727) fathered an empiricism far in excess of what the Greek mind could have conceptualized. There were *no* intentions in nature, said Bacon (1952); there was no rationality (logos) "for the sake of which" bones held up muscles or leaves shaded fruit.[7] As scientists, we must explain things *only* in material (substance construct) or efficient (impetus) cause terms—even if this means reducing terms on the ladder of abstraction below what they seem to be in the "natural" state observed by the eye.

Reductionism in science, then, means reducing pattern and intentional construct meanings to substance and impetus construct meanings. The natural scientist pared his causes to two, feeling that at the lowest substrate of reality he could find the materials and energic impetuses which moved events. Formal causes or pattern construct meanings were seen as "made up of" these lower order (less abstract) materials and energies. And since the final cause or intentional construct meaning suggests a certain creative arbitrariness in events—as if a God or *any artist* for that matter could actually select a "that for the sake of which" he created—this metaconstruct was relegated to theology and the arts. Bacon was especially instrumental in forming this division of the causes, and solidifying the modern scientist's emphasis on material and efficient causation. When the modern scientist speaks about defining his construct *operationally,* he means that he would like to reduce pattern and intentional construct meanings to the palpable substances as well as the observable energic exchanges which "get things done."[8] Who can point to an intention? This form of construct strikes the toughminded theorist as a return to the spiritual orthodoxy of the Middle Ages.[9] An operational definition is actually a "primary and true" tautology; the scientist is saying: "(the meaning of) X is (the measuring procedure) X" or simply "X is X, for the purposes of this study."

This reference to the demonstrative style of reasoning in empirical science is appropriate, for along with reducing our four causes (basic meaning constructs) to two, the British Empiricists—and particularly the mathematically inclined Thomas Hobbes (1588–1679) and John Locke (1632–1704)—simply *ignored* the fact that meanings were occasionally bipolar, and that man could thus reason dialectically. Hobbes analogized from mathematics to human thought and concluded that man's power of reason was "nothing but reckoning (that is, adding and subtracting) of the consequences of general names agreed upon for the marking and signifying of our thoughts."[10] Locke theorized that man's ideas were mental copies of his experienced reality—as the names of things which had a "primary and true" existence independent of his intellect. Ideas copied reality in a unipolar sense. The name "left" was a sign often occurring in relation to but entirely different from the name "right." Each language term was a unity having a circumscribed meaning which might be attached to or associated with other meanings in habitual fashion but never in that implicit identity sense of the dialectician's claim.

Thus, for the Lockean, each mental content (idea, word, label, memory) has a circumscribed meaning contained within it, as a box might contain some one thing. Such meanings began as simple ideas, which were indivisible (unipolar, atomic) units stamped on our minds by reality and then combined in a quasi-mathematical fashion to form more complex ideas. As building blocks for thought these simple ideas could only be given to man from experience, for as Locke said: "It is not in the power of the most exalted wit, or enlarged understanding, by any quickness or variety of thought, to *invent* or *frame* one new simple idea in the mind . . . nor can any force of the understanding *destroy* those that are there."[11] In short, man's intellect is on the "effect" side of the "cause-effect" tandem recognized as the efficient cause, or, as we shall call it: the impetus construct meaning. Man comes out exclusively demonstrative in reasoning capacity.

Over against this view, we have had philosophers down through history who view man as possessing an *active* intellect, one which could challenge a major premise fed into it from experience, reason dialectically to its opposite, and come up with an alternative plan of action (pattern construct) "for the sake of which" (intentional construct) he now behaved. This dialectical tradition is more likely to be seen in Continental Philosophy, where we have our phenomenological and existentialistic points of view taking root from a Kantian model of man's mind (although one could draw parallels here back to Plato). Unlike Locke, who viewed meanings as issuing "from below," from the input of efficient causes out of our experience, Immanuel Kant (1724–1804) stressed man's "categories of the understanding" which were like intellectual *spectacles* (pattern construct) framing in meaning "from above" (1952). Though he was distrustful of the dialectic as a method of arriving at complete truth, Kant believed that "free thought" was essentially dialectical. Unlike Locke, Kant argued that a man could and often did see the opposite implication of even simple ideas. To see "a tree, over there in my line of vision" implied to man the "possibility" that "no tree could be there, in experience." Affirming one proposition implied the other by dialectical definition.

The Lockean model provided the initial impetus in natural science and still holds sway in psychological theories of the so-called tough-minded variety. Newtonian physics is thus entirely Lockean in tone. However, twentieth century physics was to challenge this exclusive reliance on "empirical reality" as the necessary source of *all* knowledge. In a marvelously dialectical sense it is accepted today that light may be conceived as either a series of waves or as a series of discrete particles. A comparable arbitrariness is to be seen in theories of gravity, such as those of Whitehead and Einstein, which are basically incompatible yet predict empirical events equally well. There is no way —even in principle—to bring such theories together and the only ground for selection between them is of an aesthetic nature (see the discussion on affirming the consequence in science, p. 16). And Heisenberg's thought has deflected a modicum of Kantianism into the immutable reality accepted without question by the Newtonians as substrate to their mathematical explanations.[12]

A theorist is a *realist* when he believes that his constructs are mapped from a given reality independent of his conceptualizing mind. He is an *idealist* when he believes that the meanings contained in his constructs are provided more or less by his conceptualizing intelligence. Whereas the realist believes that man looks out onto a world having an independent existence, the idealist believes that man looks out onto a world of his own making. A distinction in philosophy between "abstraction" and "construction" parallels the realism vs. idealism issue.[13] To abstract implies leaving out details about what is "there," and this interpretation has become identified with realism. On the other hand, to construe requires that a contribution be made by a thinking intellect, and this interpretation has become identified with idealism. The psychologist who believes that all of his theoretical terms are, strictly speaking, "ab-

stracts" would surely be on the side of realism; whereas the psychologist who stressed the fact that he construed his data and thus was active in creating his picture of reality would be on the side of idealism. In modern usage the terms "abstract" and "construct" are used interchangeably, thereby glossing over the realism-idealism issue. We will also use them interchangeably, nevertheless aware of the historical difference in the nature of their meaning.

Unfortunately the terms objective and subjective are occasionally confused with realism and idealism. We shall see this in some of the personality theories considered in this volume. As we shall use the term, *objective* will refer to the case in which meaningful constructs and the theories which they sustain transcend the individual proffering them, so that they are clearly understood by all individuals who make the proper effort to understand them. Robert Oppenheimer (1956) used the term objective this way when he wrote: "The criterion of truth must come from analysis, it must come from experience, and from that very special kind of objectivity which characterizes science, namely that we are quite sure we understand one another and that we can check up on one another."[14]

A *subjective* theory is one which is somehow private, difficult to communicate, or impossible to generalize beyond the abstracter or construer in question. A common or uniform outlook is impossible when theory is subjective, because no one understands what the other fellow is talking about. A subjective position is reflected in the following statement: "Each individual has his own way of experiencing temporality, spatiality, causality, materiality, but each of these coordinates must be understood in relation to the others and to the total inner 'world.' "[15] The important lesson to be learned in defining terms this way is that a theorist is not referring to a palpable or "real" object when he uses the term objective. One *could* be an objective idealist, a theorist who contends that much of life's experience is "in the mind," yet communicate this experience in a generally understood fashion so that a truly scientific account might be rendered. On the other hand, simply believing that the world of reality "really exists" is no guarantee that one's account of it will be understood by others who also believe in a palpable world. Subjectives arise even in realistic accounts.

The most succinct way to summarize the essence of this section is to draw a distinction between what might be termed a Lockean and a Kantian "model." We will make considerable use of this distinction in the theory construction sections (i.e., Chapters 4, 8, and 12) of this volume. Figure 1 presents the Lockean model, which could also be termed a Democritan model. We have a triangle of increasingly abstract levels—in this case five, but there could be any number—from low to high (1 through 5). The structure is triangular to symbolize the

elimination of details in ascending the ladder of *abstraction* (in the case of Locke who was realistic in outlook "abstraction" is the proper usage). All of the numbers at any one level are the same, uniform, exactly like the others. The basic-level units (analogical to simple ideas) are numbered "1"; and these combine to form larger units (the beginnings of complexity) like "2"; and then "2" and "1" are both combined into the still more complex "3"; adding another level gives us "4" and so forth. Little things add up to or literally are the nature of bigger things. If we now ask "What is the meaning of a thing?" the answer would be: "Why, the kinds of little things of which it is constituted." Since it is assumed that all but the most basic constructs (things) are made up of building block constructs, to explain fully the meaning of a construct one must cite all of its subparts. Subparts must be broken down into subparts,

Figure 1
The Lockean Model

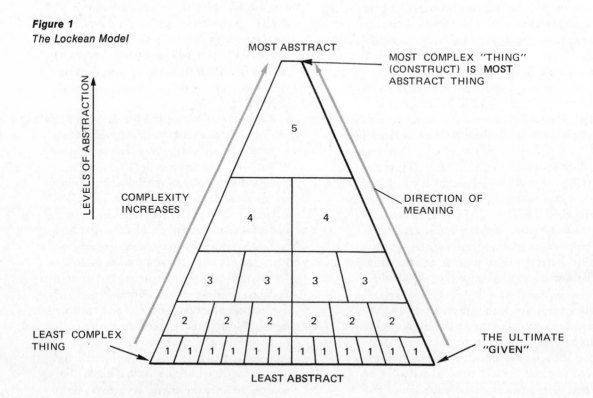

LEGEND: 1,2,3,4,5 = COMPLEXITY OF CONSTRUCTS

until one arrives at the root source where no further subdivision is possible (reductionism).

Note three things about the Lockean model: (a) meaning proceeds "from below." We can learn the meanings of one level only in terms of the levels below this level, until we come down to the final level; (b) the ultimate "given" in meaning is that point at which a level must be taken for what it is—an indivisible, irreducible, noncontradictory and unipolar substrate to all else; (c) increasing the levels of abstraction (from low to high) *always* increases the presumed level of complexity of the construct under consideration. The construct level "4" is more complex than that at level "3" and yet "4" is always less complex than "5." There is a unidirectionality between abstractness and complexity on this model.

Figure 2 is a triangular schematization of what we would like to call the Kantian model, which also could be considered a Platonic model. We have schematized Kant's categories of the understanding by having a pair of spectacles at the apex of the triangle. Kant held that we can never hope to know experience *qua* experience while looking through such intellectual spectacles. We never experience "things in themselves" (Kant called these *noumena*) but must deal with our sensory representations of things (*phenomena*) as organized by our spectacles (categories of the understanding). Take the ideas of "unity" and "plurality" (dialectical opposites), for example. Whereas Locke would have argued that such notions would have to be taught man, Kant argued that men are born with an *a priori* ability to know experience in terms of unities and pluralities. They must be taught the "word" signifying

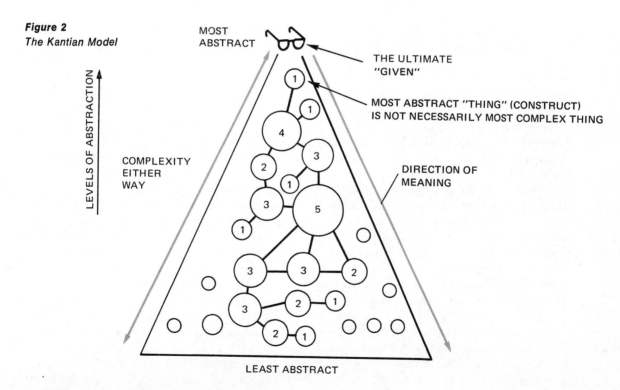

Figure 2
The Kantian Model

MOST ABSTRACT

LEVELS OF ABSTRACTION

COMPLEXITY EITHER WAY

THE ULTIMATE "GIVEN"

MOST ABSTRACT "THING" (CONSTRUCT) IS NOT NECESSARILY MOST COMPLEX THING

DIRECTION OF MEANING

LEAST ABSTRACT

LEGEND: 1,2,3,4,5 = COMPLEXITY OF CONSTRUCTS
(COUNT THE NUMBER OF CONNECTING LINKS)

unity or plurality, but the capacity literally to see this sort of distinction in events was not something that had to be learned.

Figure 2 presents a pyramid of abstraction or construction in which the numbers are not uniform as we ascend the levels of "leaving out details" (abstraction). At times a higher number (like "2") is at a more abstract level than a lower number (like "5"). What we are hoping to show here is that, though abstractness in the Kantian model is similar to that in the Lockean model, the levels of complexity are not viewed in quite the same way. Complexity is a function of the number of interlacing (patterning) constructs within a given theory.

Turning to the three points previously referred to, note that on the Kantian model: (a) meaning proceeds "from above." Before we can know what something means we have to know just what point of view (the spectacles) is being used to arrange and orient the abstractions or constructions below into some kind of order; (b) the ultimate "given" in meaning is not an irreducible substrate, but rather the particular nature of the abstract assumptions made by the point of view (the "kind" of spectacles being looked through). One cannot find the essential "facts" at the lowest level of abstraction in the Kantian model (which gives it an idealistic flavor); (c) increasing the levels of abstraction does not necessarily mean increasing complexity. Complexity and abstractness are not unidirectional. To tell how complex a construct is in Figure 2 you have to count the number of connecting links (meaningful ties) which a given numbered construct makes with other numbered constructs. This would mean that a "1" construct has only one meaning-creating connection, a "2" construct has two connections, and so forth. At just what level of abstraction these interconnections take place is irrelevant to the question of construct complexity.

For example, a complex theory of gene transmission in the germ plasm of animals might include "man" as one of its necessary components. Suppose that our gene theory were the "5" con-

struct of Figure 2 and our theory of man were the "4" construct. Since the concept of the gene seems to be a building block in the total organism, "man" might therefore appear to be more complex in "theory content" than the gene content taken alone might indicate. This is how the Lockean model would frame the issue. But the Kantian model says "no, not necessarily so." Complexity of theory and abstractness of theory are *not* the same things. One must look at the particular theory and see just what is being proposed before he can state the significance of one theory (gene) for the other (man). On the Kantian model, one can only understand complexity in terms of the constellation of meaningful factors—the connecting links of Figure 2—brought into play to achieve some purpose. Since it is always changing relations to any given theoretical construct, level of abstraction cannot be the sole criterion for the complexity status of a theory.

In fact, in Stimulus-Response (S-R) theory we have the clearest example of a *very* abstract yet a remarkably uncomplex theory of how stimuli supposedly get attached to responses. This S-R construct could well be the highest ranging number "1" of Figure 2, as it could be the lowest ranging "1" of Figure 1. This characteristic of a theoretical term which allows it to change levels of abstraction and hence alter meanings by changing the level of abstraction is termed *multiordinality*. That no theoretical term is really frozen into a level, although some terms are more capable of moving up and down the scale of abstraction than others, teaches us that we will *never* find the "top" of our ladder of abstraction. We will always be able to make further abstractions of current abstractions, so that higher-level theories will always emerge. This quality is termed the *self-reflexivity* of abstracts or constructs. The question for modern science is: Can we find a *substrate* to the ladder of abstraction, as was once supposed? Is there a final stopping point of matter (subatomic particles) or energic dispersions which we can measure without in any way influencing its nature? The Heisenberg principle suggests not, but the issue is far from closed.

Though many see an idealism in Kantian theory, he considered himself a "critical realist" in theoretical outlook. And although modern science has probably taken on considerably more of the Kantian outlook than it had in the nineteenth century, many Lockeans still stand in its front ranks. In psychology the academic centers are mainly Lockean while the applied centers receive a greater influx of Kantian thinkers. Finally, we should not disregard the fact that many scientists—in psychology and out—rely on *both* a Lockean and a Kantian model in their work. *Models* are ways of ordering an approach to the topic of interest. It is not inconsistent for the same theorist to use both models, depending upon the problem facing him and the likelihood that one or the other of these heuristic (schematic) devices will aid its solution.

ARE ALL THEORIES WRITTEN FROM THE SAME MEANINGFUL PERSPECTIVE?

The early formulations of natural science fixed man's attention to the outward, empirical side of things, which not only biased him toward "factual" accounts but actually started him thinking about things in a third-person fashion. He came to write his theory from this third-person perspective. *Perspective* denotes the standpoint or "slant" from which theoretical abstractions and meaningful relations between them (i.e., theory) are to be thought of, engaged in, or discussed. Natural science's perspective was *extraspective* (third-person). It formulated theories about "that" or "the object under observation." Any theory written from the point of view of the object of study was taken as anthropomorphization because it suggested a personified "first-person" view of events. The trick was to explain the overt, immediately apprehended series of events in a technically more correct fashion. This called for, as we have noted above, a reduction to the Lockean substrates of substance and impetus construct meanings.

When a theorist describes the flow of observable events in a common-sense fashion, his account is *phenotypic*.[16] Thus, if a person says "it is raining outside because the clouds gathered and opened up to release their moisture" we have a phenotypical description of precipitation. Although not in error on the common-sense level, this statement is technically incorrect. The natural scientist goes beneath such surface descriptions and renders a *genotypic* account. He thus explains the same event by way of atmospheric pressures, moisture evaporation, condensation, and so forth. This is a more dynamic, underlying description of the same event. In natural science the movement from common sense (phenotypic) description to technical (genotypic) description was accomplished on an exclusively extraspective basis, employing substance or impetus construct meanings. Indeed, natural science is 100 per cent extraspective in its formal theories.

In the twentieth century, however, thanks to the rise of psychology and psychiatry, a form of theoretical description arose which harkened back to the early days of mythological description. This style of theoretical usage was *introspective* in perspective. Introspective theory is written from a first-person slant; it deals with a "this, the self, ego, I, me" which is trying in some fashion to direct its behavior toward a goal, wish, or hope, or which is, in turn, avoiding some challenge, threat, or conflict. And when the introspective theorist begins formulating *his* dynamic, genotypic theory it is likely to come out clearly teleological, or at least quasi-teleological in meaning. He speaks of unconscious intentions, aspirations, life plans, and so forth. Never before had a "natural" science had to put up with such pattern and intentional construct meanings. It strikes the Newtonian as a return to the theological inquisitions of the Dark Ages, when science was repressed by such construct meanings. We shall find this problem recurring throughout this volume, as indeed it has recurred over the history of psychology's existence.

When one admits that theory can be written from two perspectives then it follows that the two accounts may differ yet *both* be true insofar as anyone can decide from actual experience. For example, an actuary's theory of behavior may be exclusively extraspective, ignoring the individual's point of view entirely. Just so long as he follows his empirical facts, an actuary can make a sound business of selling automobile insurance. He can determine the proportion of a population likely to suffer injury in accidents, adapt this to the number who drink intoxicating liquors while driving, and so forth. His comments about the drinking driver may even instruct us in a personality-related topic. However, the actuary's theory is not called upon to explain why the men and women about whom he makes predictions do in fact drink. All he need do is weed out the bad risks for his automobile accident policies. In fact, the actuary's view of man may negate any fanciful theory of personality genotypically accounting for why individuals "hit the bottle." But even though his theory works well for his purposes, an *alternate* theory written from the introspective perspective concerning such motivational questions may be equally valid. The introspective theory may not predict accidents as neatly as the extraspective theory, but it might give us several insights about why men and women *choose* to drink. The point is: although each type of theory takes a different stand on whether people can or cannot make choices about their future, they are probably *both* correct formulations within the confines of their purposes.

Troubles develop when a *formal* theory written from one perspective makes use of *informal* inferences gleaned from the other perspective. Formal theories are expressed very explicitly, with constructs interlacing in meaning to a precise degree. Sometimes such theories are called "systems." Informal theories are not nearly so explicit or all-embracing. Sometimes

they are encased in cultural *stereotypy*, such as when Freud once referred to his construct of "repression" as reflecting a Russian Censorship.[17] Many introspective theorists believe that although extraspective theory of the classical Lockean-Newtonian variety makes man appear to be a machine, the *reason* this happens is because in the experimental situation the subject is trying hard to find out what the experimenter is "doing." The subject falls back on *his* stereotype of the scientist, decides that he should cooperate with and meet the needs of a scientist out to do his job of precision, and hence he (the subject) literally makes himself appear more machine-like than he would otherwise.[18] If this pattern really occurs, then the informal (introspective) theory of the subject sustains in part the formal (extraspective) theory of the experimenter. As noted in the opening paragraphs of this section, empirical facts *do not* speak for themselves. Occasionally, we will have to become dialecticians and challenge the premises of our empirically based theorists to see if there is not an informal theory going unnamed in the supposed facts which support their formal theories.

A *typology* is, like our stereotype, a commentary on the *total* complex of behavioral tendencies we call "the person." These characterizations are really "sophisticated stereotypes," and we might call them *theorotypes* to capture the notion that they are not so rigidly or ignorantly held as are the stereotypes of everyday thought.[19] The proposition "Fat men are jolly" is a stereotype, whereas Freud's construct of an "oral personality" is a theorotype. Both of these designations are typologies. But it is also possible to study behavior on the basis of a trait theory. A *trait* construct would attempt to categorize on an "everybody to some extent" basis. For example, to study people on the basis of their intelligence or their dominance tendencies, we would not type people globally as either intelligent or not intelligent. We would probably want to speak of relative degrees of intelligence. We also think of people as "more or less" dominant than other people. A review of the history of personality study makes fairly clear that the usual progression has been for theory to move from typologies to trait theories.[20] The theorist has usually advanced a typology of some sort and then come to see that all people are more or less this way.

There is one other issue to be mentioned in this context of theoretical perspective. It concerns a distinction between two kinds of empirical study, popularized by Gordon Allport (1946) but first proffered by Windelband, who declared that the judgments of natural science are nomothetic while those of history are idiographic.[21] *Nomothetic* study of some phenomenon begins with the assumption that a theoretical abstraction can be made which has general applicability to several members of a given class. We can study the construct of dominance across a distribution of subjects in trait fashion. This approach would call for objectivity and would be highly suitable to extraspective formulations. Natural science is well-suited to nomothetic study, the use of large numbers of subjects, the application of mathematical statistics, and so forth. *Idiographic* study, on the other hand, emphasizes the uniqueness of historical events, the fact that a person or even a country passes through unique stages of development which may not be generalized to everyone or all countries on a more-or-less basis. This approach leads to subjective, idiosyncratic theory, often written from an introspective perspective. The psychoanalyzed client's life history may or may not reach out to touch each person's life in a trait fashion.

WHAT IS PROPER EVIDENCE FOR
BELIEF IN A THEORY?

The essence of demonstrative reasoning, and the point of Aristotle's distinction, is that dialectical plausibilities of the mind's eye cannot be accepted as sound proof. Aristotle was distinguishing between free theory (dialectic) and theory constrained by the demands of empirically based evidence. This question of evidence

is extremely important to any belief system, of course. It calls for a distinction between simply "theory" and the testing of that theory or "method." A *method* is the means or manner of determining whether a theoretical construct or proposition is true or false. Methods are the vehicles for the exercise of evidence. Dialectical discourse might generate truth, said Aristotle, but it might just as well generate error because it is limited to the plausibilities and opinions of a *cognitive* method. Something must be done in addition to finding common plausibilities among speakers. We must turn to the "primary and true" facts of experience in terms of what is today called a *research* method. It is thus possible to distinguish between two forms of evidence which issue from these contrasting methods: procedural and validating.[22]

When we believe a theoretical proposition because of its intelligibility, consistency with common-sense knowledge, or its implicit self-evidence, we are using *procedural evidence* as grounds for this belief. Common sense refers to the agreed-upon or accepted knowledge of a group, knowledge which is reflected in its culture and is no longer a source of contention among its members. Common sense need not refer only to the "sense of the common man." Different groups of individuals have different common knowledge, and this knowledge can change through innovation so that common sense changes over time. What strikes the theologian as plausible and rational may strike the physicist as absurd and ridiculous. Of course, the same man may walk within two spheres of common knowledge so that any given physicist may find it easy to accept both the theological and the natural science plausibility within its own particular context. Consistency here is not always possible, since both realms of knowledge rest upon unprovable assumptions which must be accepted on "faith." Moreover, if man is a dialectical animal then the fact that contradictions exist in one person is not to be interpreted as illogical (the law of contradiction is a demonstrative rule of thumb).

When we believe a theoretical proposition on the basis of observable consequences that follow a prescribed (predicted) succession of events which have been designed to test that proposition, we do so on the basis of *validating evidence*. The "trial run" in which we put our predictions to test empirically whether or not they hold water is called an *experiment*. The essence of validation is summarized by the phrase "control and prediction." The controls refer to the logical restrictions placed on one's interpretations of a sequence of events. If we hypothesize "All fat men are jolly," then as a beginning control we isolate a number of subjects varying in body weight relative to their size. This characteristic is the *independent variable*. We rule out men who are overweight or underweight due to recent factors such as illnesses, and we try to include a good sampling of individuals from all walks of life. Factors such as these are termed *control variables;* they are held constant or randomized across experimental conditions. When we have a good sampling of both fat and slender men we can begin thinking about some measure of "jolliness," which is our *dependent variable*. If our hypothesis is correct, we should find more fat men popping up high on our measures of jolliness than slender men.

This is essentially the logic of scientific method. Science follows an "if . . . , then . . ." sequence in which the "if" or antecedent statement is always one's theory and the "then" consequent statement is the prediction which follows from the theory. *"If it is true that fat men are jolly due to the genes which determine both corpulence and jolliness, then a sampling of men (and women) having varying body builds should find more jolliness among the corpulent than among the slender individuals surveyed."*

But note the flaw in this scientific proposition: the experiment which is done to prove it *affirms the consequent*. It was noted previously (p. 5) that logical necessity arises *only* when the antecedent of an "if . . . , then . . ."

premise sequence is affirmed. This relationship teaches us that the theories which explain empirical findings are *never* the only scientific theories "possible." No matter how much a scientist would like to claim exclusive rights to the empirical findings of his experiments, the truth is: *there are N (unlimited) potential theories to explain any fact pattern*. Scientific theories or "paradigms" as Kuhn (1962) has called them are never accepted or rejected entirely "on the evidence." Theories have a heuristic, organizing, "making sense" role to play, and scientists embrace them as long as they remain instructive and helpful to their interests. They will not accept a new one simply because it has empirical evidence in its support. But the scientist does at least make every effort to check his thinking against the empirical sequence of events we call experience, which usually has a sobering effect; it places limitations on the flights of fancy he might otherwise engage in. Moreover, if his theory is useful, by checking it against the empirical data a scientist provides us with the chance to *use* his knowledge in a practical way.

CAN WE STUDY THEORY WITHOUT DEMANDING RESEARCH METHOD SUPPORT?

The reader should now appreciate that, though the question of scientific validity is extremely important, theory and method play somewhat different roles in the development of knowledge. It is sometimes possible to have methodological (empirical) findings which one fails to understand, and it is surely possible to have theoretical understanding which one cannot prove methodologically (validate). As we have been using the term, "theory" is another way of speaking about thought—including belief, bias, conviction, and suggestion. Since the two sides of knowledge—theory and method—are *both* important, many psychologists believe that each merits careful attention. Methodological and statistical refinements do not constitute the totality of man's knowledge. Often we refine until the theoretical propositions put to test in our contrived experimental situations are just not worthy of study. They are uninteresting and fail to instruct us in what we want to know, which is something of ourselves, as *animal* beings caught in our peculiarly *human* situations.

It is therefore not only possible and desirable to evolve a way of thinking about theories *qua* theories in psychology, but it seems absolutely essential to do so if psychology is to advance as an instructive science. The proper attitude for the student of theory is not "What is truth?" but rather "How is this person going about formulating what he will consider the truth?" The sophisticated scientist is not interested in "the truth," but rather in "the truth thus far" or "the truth as I view it from my theoretical stance." An attitude of this sort must help strengthen the kinds of empirical study the individual will engage in when he turns from theory to methodological test. He will be just as suspicious of his evidence as he is of his theory. This is the proper scientific attitude. It is toughminded without being narrowminded.

WHAT IS PSYCHOTHERAPY AND WHY IS IT RELEVANT TO PERSONALITY STUDY?

If the question "What is personality?" is difficult to answer then "What is psychotherapy?" is doubly so. The two questions are not unrelated, however, since it is historical fact that many of our major personality theorists have come from the medical profession, or they have taken considerable interest in man's level of psychological health even as they were explicating his temperament, character, or "personality." These terms have been used to describe the "style" (pattern construct) of man's behavior. Temperament emphasizes substance construct meanings—such as when we say "She is a 'Smith,' and is easy-going like all the Smiths." The assumptions here are that something genetic is at play—a chemical determinant or whatnot. Character takes on the meaning of an evaluation of how the individual behaves regularly—as when we say "You can count on

good old Charlie; he is a trusted and true member of the community." All such judgments are forms of personality description.

When we speak about how this family behaves temperamentally and how that person can be counted on in a crisis, we enter into the general area of *individual differences*. We want to write theories about what makes some people differ from other people. Not all scientists have this interest; many view themselves as writing theories at a general or *vehicular* level. Theoretical propositions which employ vehicular constructs are those which tie together regularities in behavioral sequences (laws) *regardless of the particular content* of the behavioral sequence under study. These propositions and constructs hold at a high level of abstraction, and they therefore subsume (act as vehicles for) lower level constructs of a more specific and hence restricted range of convenience. The laboratory psychologist uses such constructs when he investigates and theorizes about concepts like reinforcement, stimulus generalization, hierarchies of response, and so forth. In fact, the construct "behavior" is vehicular in tone.

In contrast to the vehicular style of theorizing are *discriminal* constructs and propositions. Theoretical propositions which tie together discriminal constructs seek to draw a difference between *certain* behavioral sequences and other behavioral sequences. In this case the *content* of the behavior is all-important, and the discriminal construct does not have the abstract, broad range of convenience that the vehicular construct has. Personality theorists are drawn to such discriminal theorizing—at least, the classical personality theorists were. And one of the most dramatic forms of difference among people is the level of normalcy they reflect. There are "good" ways to be abnormal, of course, such as by excelling in a sport, having a popular personality, or achieving success in one's job. But such individuals are not causes for concern. A profession dedicated to studying them and helping them to achieve or be all the more popular does not seem to make sense. It is more important to help the negatively deviant—the criminals, mentally retarded, or insane—return to the fold of socially defined normalcy, or to help the average person excel in some fashion.

Many of those who took the first steps in modern science as personality theorists were members of the medical profession, men like Freud, Jung, Adler, Sullivan, Binswanger, and Boss. Others, like Rogers and Kelly, were clinical psychologists, a professional wing of psychology initially patterned to meet the needs of psychiatry. Though these men *were* healers, they did not confine their comments on man to the abnormal. How could they? A well-rounded theory of man was required if there was to be a place for the sick or abnormal man within the picture. The theories of Dollard and Miller, Skinner, Wolpe, and Stampfl are interesting extensions of vehicular theory into the consulting room. The contribution which these theories make to personality theory of a discriminal nature is consequently much less than we find the traditionalists making. This will all be made explicit in the chapters to follow, but for now two points are sufficient: first, it is not possible to grasp the full meaning of classical personality theory without also understanding the theories of psychopathology and psychotherapy within which they were framed; second, not all psychotherapists (nor their clients) are drawn to the therapeutic relationship for the *same* reason.

Of the three general motives for entering the field of psychotherapy, the first is *scholarly*. By taking his client's commentary in the therapy situation seriously and thereby attempting to teach him something about himself, Freud initiated the modern era of personality theory even as he founded the "practice" of psychoanalysis. Today, aside from their economic motivation, just as many individuals enter the profession of psychoanalysis out of an interest in people as out of a desire to heal the sick. Indeed, many clients who enter psychoanalysis do not think

of themselves as maladjusted, and many more would enter if they could financially afford it. This does not mean that everyone is a little sick and can use help; it indicates that one of the motives for psychotherapy is self-study: the individual wants to be educated—provided with insight—about himself.

Another motive we are likely to see in psychotherapy is *ethical*. Ethical study in classical philosophy dealt with all those aspects of life and behavior which were considered *good*, or valued by man.[23] Theology deals with the Absolute Good as embodied in the belief in a Supreme Being and thereby transcends considerations of "man" as such. Though *moral* has been used as the theological equivalent of *ethical*, in common practice these two terms are synonymous. There are undoubtedly many therapists who practice psychotherapy out of what can only be considered an ethical interest. They see in the nature of mental illness a reflection of the ethical injustices which have been wrought upon their clients, a situation which they hope to rectify; or they feel that the therapeutic benefits of the contact emanate from the "relationship," the coming together of two people in a certain way, with a proper attitude of mutual concern which is healthful.

The question naturally arises: "Is this the reason why clients seek therapy and pay their fees, to relate with someone in a certain way or to solve ethical problems?" Obviously, not all clients are so motivated, but evidence indicates that many are and that a desire to change or to grow toward self-realization represents at least one of the paying client's motives for therapy. People will enter psychotherapy to improve, to reform, and to grow better. They may seek a nonthreatening environment in which to examine themselves, in the company of a sensitive and genuine listener who takes a certain ethical stance in relating with them aimed at furthering this goal of self-realization. The client occasionally begins therapy with a definite problem, but in time this need for specific help evolves into something quite different. Along with insight, or possibly *rather* than the insight proffered by a therapist, many clients need—and actively seek—an examination of themselves *in their own terms*. They do not want to be interpreted so much as they want to be appreciated and accepted for themselves. Once such an atmosphere is made available to them, they tend to change and to grow under the weight of their own potential. Still other clients come to therapy to find a substitute for religion: a new faith, a different orientation from which they can find new meaning in life.

The final and most important motive of all today for both therapists and clients is the *curative*. People come to doctors to be cured of illness. When the illness is in their "minds" (translated by certain psychotherapists into "behavior"), then it is only natural that they analogize to physical illness and expect some kind of concrete assistance, manipulation, or prescription which might set matters straight. They come into therapy as "patients" in the true sense of that word, as passive recipients seeking help. Many people would no doubt love to submit to thought control from a competent physician, who would, through some form of medical device, cure their nagging psychological problems. If such a patient should enter into a form of therapy stressing one or the other of our remaining motives, he would have a rough time, at least at the outset. In time, however, if he also has or acquires some of the other needs—for self-insight, self-integrity, self-growth, and so forth—he may stay on and be lofted into another sphere of motivation. Suddenly, things seem different; he is going to the therapist for quite other reasons.

Whether or not these reasons will also lead to an eventual cure is an issue still in doubt. The insight approaches lengthen the time considered necessary to effect a cure. Is this not a mark against them as effective therapeutic measures? Relationship approaches seem to modify a person's outlook, but does this mean anything in his subsequent behavior, or are the changes merely "verbal" ones of no significance? Why

not then get to the heart of the matter, work directly on the so-called symptom and cure or change the behavior that is causing the trouble? The outcome here is less in doubt because therapists work on what is sick, atypical, or uncomfortable. Cure is the stated motive of those therapists who see therapy as a means of healing. As if in retort, the ethically motivated therapist often claims that this decision to change or control the behavior threatens the client's right to self-determination and hence self-growth. And the scholarly motivated therapist argues that merely changing or curing without providing insight into the nature of the abnormality cannot lead to lasting cures in any event.

So "What is psychotherapy?" is just as complex a question as is the other about the nature of personality. There is no answer to either of these questions without a full treatment of the related philosophical topics. We now have our prototype or metatheory on which to base chapters having to do with theory construction. The remaining pages of the Introduction outline the general plan of the chapters to follow.

The Plan of the Book

There are essentially three historical traditions in the field of personality and psychotherapy, and the present volume is organized around them. In Part One we begin with the first and probably still dominant tradition of psychoanalytic thought, though the term "psychoanalysis" belongs properly only to Freud. Theories of man could, of course, be traced to the earliest philosophies and theologies of recorded history, but it is generally acknowledged that what we know as modern personality theory begins with Freud's changes in the classical "medical model" of mental illness. Freud claimed to be studying man *scientifically,* and though we may challenge him on this point, surely no one can deny that his approach to the disordered psyche was somewhat different. He looked past the Gods, through the philosophical discourse, and found below the surface a *dynamic* psychology of the mind. Although they were not exactly his students, Adler and Jung followed to alter this dynamic psychology in their own unique ways. In terms of our major models, the analytical tradition must be considered a mixed Lockean-Kantian one, with Freud retaining a middle position throughout his life, Adler moving from an early Kantian to a clearly Lockean emphasis, and Jung retaining the most profoundly Kantian approach of the "founding fathers" of personality theory.

In Part Two we take up the second major tradition, which emphasized the empirical, observable facets of behavior. The dynamic *intrapersonal* becomes the *interpersonal* as behavior is seen as controlled "from without." Harry Stack Sullivan nicely bridges the distance between classical psychoanalysis and this tradition, moving as he did from an early analytical influence to what might be termed an eventual "Americanization" of his thought. We see in this Yankee spirit the heavy reliance on a Lockean model as promulgated by British Empiricism. In the behavioristic tradition of American academic circles we are then brought more fully into an almost "nonpersonality" style of thought in Dollard and Miller, Skinner, Wolpe, and Stampfl. That is, in the vehicular psychology of behaviorism the subtleties of a reflective and contemplative analytical psychology are dropped in favor of the view that "behavior is behavior" and "behavior is all." Pragmatic action and control are needed, rather than a continuing round of speculative imagination.

Finally, in Part Three we take up the third major force in personality and psychotherapy, which we have termed the phenomenological outlook. This view returns to the more Continental line of philosophy which has influenced psychoanalysis, and it is even more Kantian in tone than is the earlier dynamic psychology. At least, Rogers, Binswanger, and Kelly are clearly Kantian in outlook. There is some question

about Boss, but this difficulty in categorization is fitting since a major tenet of existentialistic thought is that we do entirely too much pigeon-holing today. The members of the phenomenological camp uniformly attack that natural science approach to the study of man so prized by behaviorists. Science distorts man's image, claim the phenomenologists; it forces his spontaneous and unique experience into a dehumanized portrait of the man-machine. We must recapture that phenomenally true side of life which our arbitrary theories of the universe have left out. We must put man back in center stage, allowing him to become that potential human person his existence harbors.

As the theories and the images of man which they prompt unfold in historical sequence we shall occasionally side-step into the knottier questions of theory construction. Is man free "to be" as the phenomenologists claim? Can he actually be controlled in the way that behaviorism claims is possible? Is Freudian thought physicalistic and mechanistic as many claim, or is there a hidden teleology in psychoanalysis? Questions such as these will be considered in separate chapters dealing with the broader implications of personality theory, the uniformity across these outlooks, and the essential differences in man's nature they imply.

A common "frame" will enable the reader to compare one view with another even as he is introduced to its constructs for the first time. Not only are the chapters aligned historically, but the presentation of each theory traces the originator's developing insights over the course of his life. We will now review the structural frame to be followed under the three main topics of our study: personality, psychotherapy, and theory construction.

PERSONALITY THEORY

A personality theory must answer four major questions. (1) What is the essential structure of personality? Or, if structure is to be disregarded, what are we to substitute? (2) On what basis does this structure act or behave? (3) Does this structure change over time, and if so, in what way? (4) How does one account for the variety of human behavior among different individuals? If we can answer these four questions to our satisfaction, then we have fairly well exhausted the possible meanings which any theory of personality might be expected to generate. Each section dealing with personality shall therefore take up these questions, in the following order:

Structural Constructs. Here we shall be interested in looking at the way in which the personality theorist has put man together. How does he sketch in the outline of his dynamically and spontaneously growing actor, or how does he construct the many details of his robot-like mechanism? What is the superstructure or the hull of the personality like, from his point of view, or does he reject superstructures altogether? Structural constructs, or their substitutes, will permit us to describe the nodal points of personality without necessarily being drawn into the question of how behavior takes place.

Motivational Constructs. Motivation is presumably what gets the personality structure underway, behaving, acting, responding, growing, or however the theorist chooses to describe this phenomenon. Sometimes the action is prevented from taking place due to a blocking within the personality structure, but this case would still involve questions of motivation. We shall see differences of opinion concerning the possibility of conscious vs. unconscious motivation.

Time Perspective Constructs. All humans change in certain ways over time, from birth through adulthood and old age. They change in physical appearance and stature, but they also change in psychological ways. Most personality theories attempt to say something about personality over time.

Individual Differences Constructs. Psychotherapists and personality theorists are prone to use discriminal constructs, and each of them has his own particular method of accounting for the uniqueness of personality. They usually settle upon a series of theorotypes drawing differences of one sort or another between people. This is *really* the summary personality term which each theorist has to offer. He looks at man, catalogues the style of behavioral differences he sees in some way, and then goes on to describe how each personality style "got to be that way" through development of substance, motivational, and time perspective constructs. In time, theorotypes become trait designations.

PSYCHOPATHOLOGY AND PSYCHOTHERAPY

When the review of the personality theory has been completed for a theorist, we shall move on to a consideration of his views on psychopathology and psychotherapy, staying entirely within his own language system. Common sense would dictate that there are three questions which must be answered in this context. (1) How does a personality "get sick" or "become maladjusted" or "begin behaving in an unrewarding fashion"? (2) How does the therapist go about curing, resolving, or controlling (changing) this condition? And (3) does he have any unique procedures in his approach distinguishing him from other psychotherapists? In order to answer each of these questions we shall organize the second section on each theorist around the following three subheadings: *theory of illness, theory of cure,* and *therapeutic techniques.*

Theory of Illness. Not all psychotherapists view mental illness as a sickness analogical to a physical sickness. Use of the term "illness" does not suggest that they should view it thusly, nor imply that they covertly view it in this fashion. This phrasing simply seems most realistic and honest because of its wide acceptability. Traditionally, people who sought psychotherapy were viewed as somehow out of sorts, short of potential, or lacking in sufficient insight or ability to perform at their maximum potential. To that extent all theories can come under an "illness" label, even though few believe that they are illnesses in the conventional sense. As we become more sophisticated in our use of the illness concept we shall be less likely to take its import at face value. Hence, under the illness subheading we will be reviewing the explanation of mental illness in light of the personality theory under presentation, showing how the theorist conceptualized this process.

Theory of Cure. The same general comments and admonitions apply here as in the "theory of illness" section just completed. However, the purpose of this section will be to review the ways in which a theorist claims or implies that a personality is righted following the application of an "illness" or "abnormality" label to it. What would a "therapeutic intervention" consist of?

Therapeutic Techniques. Under this subheading we shall review the specific techniques which a therapist has suggested to implement his theory of cure. Various therapists have become known for specific techniques of a "how to cure" approach, but just as often rather general proposals are made of a less circumscribed, technical nature. Sometimes a societal revisionism or even revolution may be the prescribed technique of cure. Whatever the case, we shall want to understand it properly, within the context of the broader theory of personality and abnormality.

STYLE OF THEORETICAL CONSTRUCTION

We come finally to the theory construction third of our presentation, which will be combined with other theorists in a special chapter. In this chapter we shall take up the technical nature of the theory, and hopefully provide continuity through comparison for the reader. This chapter will always proceed according to the following headings:

Kantian versus Lockean Models. We shall determine which of these classical models is employed by a theorist, or whether both might be used.

Demonstrative versus Dialectical Reasoning. The next theory construction issue will revolve around the employment of dialectical vs. demonstrative tactics. Although dialecticians tend to be Kantian in outlook, the reverse is not always the case.

Substance Construct Meanings. Here, we shall consider the theorist's use of constructs having a base in the palpable "stuff" of existence.

Impetus Construct Meanings. The question here centers on how much reliance does the theorist place on motion, the thrust of events over time, and so forth.

Pattern Construct Meanings. We move on to the emphasis on organization in theoretical description. Does the theorist rest his case with such patterned constructs, or does he go further to account for substrates in the substance or impetus sense?

Intentional Construct Meanings. We will next want to know how much reliance the theorist places upon purposive, self-directing, teleological aspects of behavior.

Motives to Therapy. Finally, we will move on to a discussion of the psychotherapy theory employed by the theorist, in light of our three motives.

Notes

1. Rychlak, 1968, Part I. 2. Aristotle, 1952a, pp. 276–277. 3. Rychlak, 1968. 4. Aristotle, 1952b, p. 143. 5. Leff, 1958. 6. Becker and

Barnes, 1952. **7.** Bacon, 1952, p. 44. **8.** Bridgman, 1927. **9.** Spence, 1956. **10.** Hobbes, 1952, p. 58. **11.** Locke, 1952, p. 128. **12.** Rychlak, 1968. **13.** Russell, 1959. **14.** Oppenheimer, 1956, p. 130. **15.** Ellenberger, 1958, p. 116. **16.** Brown, 1936, Ch. 2. **17.** Freud, 1954, p. 240. **18.** Based on findings of Dulany, 1961. **19.** Lippmann, 1946. **20.** MacKinnon, 1944. **21.** Cassirer, 1944, p. 235. **22.** Rychlak, 1968, pp. 74–79. **23.** Sidgwick, 1960, Ch. 1.

Part One
Mixed Kantian-Lockean Models in Classical Psychoanalysis

1

The Beginnings of Psychoanalysis: Sigmund Freud

Biographical Overview

Sigmund Freud was born on 6 May 1856 in the small town of Freiberg, Moravia (Czecho-slovakia). He was of Jewish extraction and proud of his heritage but never practiced the religion. His father, a merchant and a free-thinker, had been widowed, and Sigmund was the first child of the father's second wife. She was 21 years old at the time, and it is not sur-prising that Sigmund grew to be the apple of his mother's eye. He was a well behaved son, and he tells us in later years that he stood at the head of his grammar school class for the full seven years.[1] When he was about four or five years old his family relocated in Vienna, Austria, a more cosmopolitan environment and the city in which Freud was to live and work for the majority of his 83 years. As an adult he was critical of Vienna, but he also seems to have loved the city, for he would not leave it until forced to do so by the threat of hostility after the Nazis entered Austria in 1938. He finally gave in to the urgings of friends and emigrated to England where, on 23 September 1939, he died after suffering for almost two decades with cancer of the mouth and jaw.

As a young man Freud was undecided about what career he would pursue. He was more drawn to human than to "natural science" problems,[2] and for a time he gave serious con-sideration to the study of law. Thanks to in-spiration from Darwin and Goethe, Freud eventually settled upon the choice of medicine, but he was the first to admit that he was never a doctor in the usual sense of the term.[3] After entering premedicine at the University of Vienna in 1873 Freud found himself greatly attracted to the role of the "basic scientist." The primary stimulus to this role was provided by a commanding personality, a toughminded physiology professor named Ernst Brücke. Brücke once swore to follow the scientific canon that: "No other forces than the common physical-chemical ones are active within the organism."[4]

Working in Brücke's laboratory, Freud did many histological studies on the nervous system and devised a method of staining cells for microscopic study which earned him a minor reputation in his own right. Freud never experimented successfully, in the sense of control and prediction through design of a study. His view of science stressed rigorous observation. But events were to make a career as university scholar impossible for Freud. Only a limited number of positions were available, and Brücke had two excellent assistants ahead of Freud in consideration. Time had slipped by, and Freud's medical class had already graduated. He had also, in the meantime, met and fallen in love with Martha Bernays, the young woman who was to become his wife. Since income was now more than ever an important consideration, Freud talked things over with Brücke and decided to go on, complete his medical degree, and enter medical practice.

Before doing so he was fortunate enough—with the help of Brücke—to obtain a small traveling grant which permitted him to spend a year (1885) in Paris, studying under the famous psychiatrist Jean Charcot at the Salpêtrière. In 1889 he again returned to France, to observe the work of Bernheim in Nancy. Both Charcot and Bernheim were conducting experiments on hysterics with the use of hypnotism. Hysteria is a mental disorder in which the patient believes that he has lost some sensory (like vision) or motor (like walking) function, but he has not. His supposed lost function can be restored under hypnotic suggestion. Students of Freud often note that his contact with the French helped support him years later, when he began to deviate from the kinds of chemical-mathematical theories to which Brücke had limited his scientific explanations.[5]

After a short stay in Berlin, where Freud served a medical residency in neurology (which included the direction of a children's ward), he returned to Vienna to marry and to take up the practice of neurology. Today, his medical specialty would probably come under the heading of neuropsychiatry. Even before he had traveled to France, Freud had made the acquaintance of Joseph Breuer, a neurologist like himself but an older, more settled and successful practitioner in the Vienna area. Later, Breuer was instrumental in helping Freud to establish a practice in Vienna. He was important in the evolution of psychoanalysis as well, and we shall turn to Freud's professional relations with him in the next section.

Another important friend of Freud's in his early years as practitioner was Wilhelm Fliess, who had apparently been introduced to Freud by Breuer. Fliess was a successful nose-throat specialist who practiced in Berlin, thus accounting for the need to correspond through the mails with his friend in Vienna (though

Sigmund Freud

they also met fairly regularly to exchange scientific points of view). Fortunately, Fliess kept all of his letters from Freud, and this correspondence reveals the rather remarkable fact that virtually all of Freud's theoretical ideas had been sketched in over the period of 1887 through just after the turn of the twentieth century; the 1890s were particularly important. Freud observes that the "secret of dreams" was revealed to him on 24 July 1895.[6] His father died in October 1896, and his death seems to have exacerbated certain anxiety tendencies and psychosomatic problems (colitis) which Freud carried throughout life. Having by this time worked out a general approach to the study and treatment of neuroses, Freud began in 1897 his celebrated "self-analysis," from which we trace the verbal traditions now called a "psychoanalysis." This early work, done by a nonacademician, unrecognized and unappreciated by the broader scientific community, culminated in the publication of Freud's two great initial works, *The Interpretation of Dreams* (Vols. IV and V) and *The Psychopathology of Everyday Life* (Vol. VI). These books made their appearance in the 1900–1901 period, and they mark Freud's beginning as the father of psychoanalysis and, indeed, as the father of modern personality theory.

Freud was soon to attract a group of followers, among whom the more famous were Alfred Adler, Carl Jung, Sandor Ferenczi, Otto Rank, Karl Abraham, and Ernest Jones. He was not to hold the friendship of all of these men, and in fact, Freud's life is the story of a man with almost a penchant for rejecting or being rejected by those whose scientific views opposed his own. Breuer, Fliess, Adler, Jung, Ferenczi, and Rank—not to mention others— were to separate from Freud on more or less friendly terms; the separation with Adler was probably the most bitter. Psychoanalysis as a science has had and still has its difficulties in resolving theoretical disagreements among its advocates.

Freud made one trip to the United States, in 1909, at the invitation of G. Stanley Hall, who invited him and Jung to speak at Clark University. As he grew in stature and reputation he was also active in helping to establish the International Psycho-Analytic Association, with its accompanying professional journal, beginning as a small group of friends in Vienna and then spreading throughout the world.

THE BREUER PERIOD

In the period 1880–1882, while Freud was still in medical school, Breuer undertook the treatment of a 21-year-old woman who was bedridden, suffering from a series of hysterical symptoms like headache, loss of speech, visual distortions, and in particular, a severe contracture and anaesthesia of the right arm.[7] This woman was to become the patient in the celebrated case of Anna O. (a pseudonym). On a hunch, Breuer decided to use the hypnotic tactic which Freud later observed Charcot using. He found that when Anna was put under light hypnosis and taken back in time (time regression) she could recall the onset of her symptoms. The central feature of this symptom onset seemed to be that Anna was experiencing an emotion which she felt she could not express at the time. However, while in her hypnotic state Anna spontaneously relived her "pathognomic situation" and expressed all of the *strangulated affect* (Breuer's term) which had never before reached expression. To Breuer's complete surprise, with each hypnotic recall her symptom picture improved.

For example, Anna once relived an earlier pathognomic situation in which she was tending to her severely ill father. She was sitting in a chair next to his bed, and her mother was out of the house so that Anna doubtless felt a little frightened at the responsibility of looking after someone so close to death. Suffering from fatigue, and prone to what she called *absences* (state of waking somnambulism), Anna seems to have had what Breuer called a *waking dream.*[8] She "saw" a black snake coming from the wall next to her father's bed, ready to bite the dying man. Anna tried to fend the snake off, moving her right arm from the back of her chair where it had been resting. Apparently it had become slightly anaesthetic due to a lack of proper blood circulation, for when she tried to move it, she could not. Glancing at her hand, Anna was further abhorred by the fact that her fingers had turned into little snakes with her fingernails appearing to be like "death's heads."

Though she was unable to scream or otherwise express the fear and revulsion she felt at the time (pathognomic situation) Anna *did* do so under hypnosis and, as we have noted, this release led to an improvement in her condition. Breuer and Freud were later to call this *mental* reliving of a situation out of the past an *abreaction*. The physical expression of emotion was called *catharsis*. These terms have since been used interchangeably by psychoanalysts, but strictly speaking a mind-body dualism is involved here.[9] Now, Breuer was a toughminded scientist who favored the Brücke approach to science. Anna's tendency to fall into her "absences" Breuer ascribed to a constitutional, hereditary propensity he called the *hypnoid state*. He believed that some people are born with this tendency to "split consciousness" in a way which allows a set of ideas with an emotional component to continue its influence in the personality independent of the individual's self-control. Exactly what constituted an emotion (the physical state) and what constituted an idea (the mental state) was never made too clear in Breuer's theory.

In 1893 Breuer and Freud coauthored the *Studies on Hysteria* (Vol. II), in which they presented various cases of hysteria and two theories of its etiology. That is, by this time the two friends had begun their falling-out over the supposed reason for strangulating affect. Freud was finding in his practice that invariably there was some unknown (by the patient) *reason* for the splitting of consciousness.

What he saw at work was not simply some inherited, automatic hypnoid state. Rather, there was what he termed a kind of *defense hysteria,* in which the person invariably rejected some sexual implication in his behavior. Though he is polite enough in the *Studies,* acknowledging that hysteria may take two forms, Freud candidly observes: "Strangely enough, I have never in my own experience met with a genuine hypnoid hysteria. Any that I took in hand has turned into a defence hysteria."[10] In thus turning his attention away from the strangulated affect to the *strangulator* of the affect—the defensive counter to whatever was trying to reach expression initially—Freud made himself over into a new kind of physician. He was not *only* a healer, but a student of the workings of mind. He cured, as had Breuer, but this aspect of his work was secondary to his fascination for why sickness arose in the first place.

Personality Theory

STRUCTURAL CONSTRUCTS

DUALISM OF MIND VS. BODY

One of the first points we must appreciate in understanding Freudian theory is that it is built upon a mind-body dualism. Trained in the physiological laboratory of Brücke, Freud well knew that his mentor's hope was to circumscribe man in purely physical terms. He would have liked to achieve this feat, and in fact, thanks to the additional prompting of Fliess, he once attempted to write such an explanation of human behavior (the ill-fated *Project*[11]). He found it impossible to complete this theoretical presentation, and in time Freud was to note how useless physical explanations were for the proper understanding of the psychological side to man.[12]

Even though he relied less and less on physico-medical models of human behavior, and turned to the writings of anthropologists, archaeologists, and sociologists for inspiration, Freud continued to admit and even to stress the necessary tie-in of purely biological factors to human behavior.[13] Since there are several references to the potential efficacy of hereditary and biological theories in his writings, no one can honestly claim that Freud was a completely "psychological" theorist, even though his general outlook is more that of a logician than a student of structure (anatomist) or a cataloguer of incidents in observation (statistician-researcher). Freud's psychology is therefore very much a *content* approach. He takes more interest in the question "why" than in the question "how." His mental structural constructs are necessary preliminaries to what he wants quickly to get about describing—the *process, strategy, motives* of behavior.

THE EARLY MENTAL STRUCTURAL CONSTRUCTS: DEPTH EMPHASIS

We have already seen that Freud found himself on the trail of a strangulator in the psychology of hysterics. He seemed to find invariably that his early patients—most of whom were upper-socioeconomic-class women—were in the habit of defending themselves against the recall of a memory out of the past which was *still active* in mind, albeit from out of a region which was not located in "awareness." His first set of structural constructs was aimed at accounting for this observed phenomenon. He broke the sphere of mind down into three regions: the *conscious, unconscious,* and *preconscious.* In order to understand this model more clearly we will have to refer to what might be considered a motivational construct, the *censorship,* for it is this mechanism of defense which plays the role of strangulator in Freud's early theorizing. Figure 3 provides us with a schematization of his early structural model. We are now speaking of the *mind;* presumably, there is another region of our identity considered the *body* to which we are *not* now addressing our attention.

An interesting characteristic of Figure 3 is the stylized, dotted arc, moving an arrow

from left to right across points *1* through *9,* both originating and ending in the external world. It was fashionable in the late nineteenth century to pattern mental concepts on the "sensory-perception-motor" cycle of the reflex arc. Thus Freud in 1900 not surprisingly wrote: "Reflex processes remain the model of every psychical function."[14] If we now follow a mental excitation (stimulus) from its point *1* entry, note that it passes through consciousness into the second region of preconsciousness, on down into the lowest level of mind, the unconscious, before returning upward again through points 7 and 8 (censorship points) and issuing into motor action at point 9. Because we dip down into subterranean mental regions, far away from the external world and its immediate representative (consciousness), this model gives a sense of *depth* in mind.

Let us review briefly what Freud has to say about each of the constructs of Figure 3. *Consciousness* is defined as a "sense organ for the apprehension of psychical qualities,"[15] through which the individual is aware of sensory input (seeing, smelling, thinking about things seen), and also the awareness of "pleasure vs. unpleasure." Emotions (affects) are revealed through conscious awareness. Consciousness is therefore a relatively minor aspect of what we take to be the mental life of man. Consciousness does *not* rule the mind in Freudian psychology. It could never hope to do so, because for one thing it lacks the memory capacity to provide mental phenomena a sense of continuity over time. Freud included in his notion of consciousness only what we are presently aware of in our minds.[16] For centuries people had identified ideas in awareness with "thought," but Freud reversed this association and said in fact that "every psychical act begins as an unconscious one, and it may either remain so or go on developing into consciousness, according as it meets with resistance or not."[17]

If, therefore, you wish to grasp the nature of man's "true psychical reality," then you must understand his *unconscious.*[18] Freud actually

Figure 3
Freud's Early Mental Structural Constructs

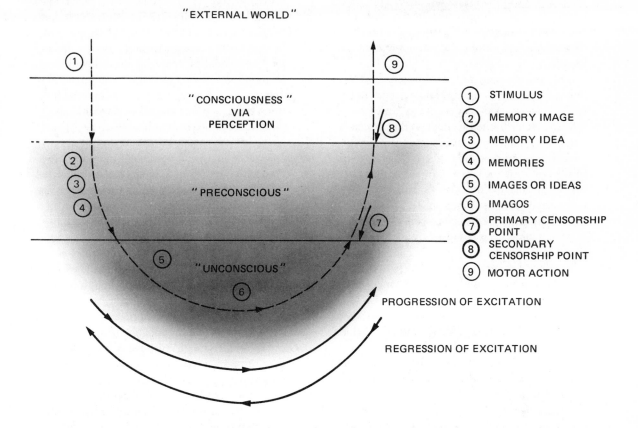

"EXTERNAL WORLD"

① STIMULUS
② MEMORY IMAGE
③ MEMORY IDEA
④ MEMORIES
⑤ IMAGES OR IDEAS
⑥ IMAGOS
⑦ PRIMARY CENSORSHIP POINT
⑧ SECONDARY CENSORSHIP POINT
⑨ MOTOR ACTION

"CONSCIOUSNESS" VIA PERCEPTION

"PRECONSCIOUS"

"UNCONSCIOUS"

PROGRESSION OF EXCITATION

REGRESSION OF EXCITATION

used this term in a general and a specific sense. In its general sense, unconscious merely meant all those psychic contents like thoughts, ideas, and images, which are not conscious at the moment but which might become so at any time (he sometimes included preconscious contents in this general usage).[19] More specifically and technically, however, Freud viewed the unconscious as an actual region in mind, one which was much larger than consciousness and which lived a mental life of its own. As Freud observed, "the unconscious is a particular realm of the mind with its own wishful impulses, its own mode of expression and its peculiar mental mechanisms which are not in force elsewhere."[20] Since it is a region outside awareness we can

only grasp its intentions by way of the practical effects noted in free fantasy (dreams) or mental slips of the tongue (parapraxes) which show another side to our nature; in short, we must *interpret* behaviors presumably under the sway of a region other than what we are currently aware of, if we are to grasp the unconscious.[21]

Man's basic hedonistic nature issues from his unconscious. The unconscious is also immune to the ravages of time, so that memory traces are *never* really permanently erased from our minds.[22] To appreciate Freud the reader must accept that we are all little babies, at this moment walking around with our psychic diapers intact, and whatever happened to us at the age of two or three is no less important to our present behavior than what has happened to us in the past hour. An "unconscious man" (or woman) exists within us, seeking expression and need satisfaction or the working through of problems long unresolved but not really forgotten.

The "unconscious man" within can show a line of reasoning, a strategy, and a persistence which is the mark of true mentality. In fact, there is often a hothouse effect, so that unconscious ideas proliferate and concoct completely new areas of interest and concern which are so foreign to "conscious man" (our awareness) that when such *unconscious derivatives* are manifested (such as Anna's snakes) their alien nature frightens the conscious personality into believing it has been possessed by another identity.[23] Unconscious man does not concern himself with reality very much, and he may reason in ways which appear illogical to the more conventional world of awareness.[24] Occasionally, the unconscious can even circumvent consciousness and make its wishes known directly to the unconscious mind of *another person*.[25] People can relate socially at a completely different level than the one they consciously believe is in operation.

Since emotions are revealed to us through consciousness, is it correct to speak of "unconscious emotions"? Strictly speaking, Freud would say no. There are no unconscious emotions *per se,* but there are unconscious ideas which in themselves relate to emotions. If these ideas begin to traverse our dotted arc in Figure 3 and threaten to seek motor action, then conscious awareness would reflect an emerging emotion to the personality.[26] Quite often the person is aware of a puzzling emotion even though he remains unaware of the unconscious idea which is pressing for motor action. This occurrence is common for all of us, such as when we feel moody, "jumpy," or "blue" on some given day without being able to understand why. Another often raised issue concerns the possibility of unconscious influences from antiquity. Did Freud think of the unconscious

only as a receptacle for ideas or images fed into the mind from external reality and then kept back from conscious awareness by the censor? Although this was surely his major emphasis, the truth is that Freud was influenced on this point by his famous associate C. G. Jung (see Chapter 3) into holding open the possibility of hereditary transmission of psychic contents.[27] If man were to receive influences from racial identities, then such mental contents would make themselves known in the unconscious (by way of the id[28]).

To account for that region of unawareness over which we often *do* have at least partial conscious control, Freud proposed the term *preconscious.* The preconscious region is made up of contributions from *both* the conscious and the unconscious, and it is the locus of censorship in the mind.[29] Psychic contents in the preconscious can therefore be gotten from the conscious or the unconscious, even though such contents may not be exchanged by the two regions of mind flanking the preconscious. Emotional feelings would probably arise as some unconscious idea sought expression by invading the preconscious. In most of the ordinary forgetful experiences we have—such as when we cannot recall the telephone number of a friend—we can see an example of a temporary loss to awareness of a psychic content which remains in the preconscious. Since the telephone number returns to our consciousness in time (an unconscious psychic content would not do this), we can refer to the forgotten number as "unconscious" only in that general sense to which we referred previously.

Notice in Figure 3 that a few memory images and ideas (2, 3, 4, 5, 6) are placed as psychic contents. Now, as these ideas or images would be carried back down to the region of the unconscious, it would be possible for them to continue on up again and achieve a motoric discharge in consciousness (we are overlooking the possibility of direct influence of one unconscious on another at this point). Assuming that a congeries of psychic contents were to seek motor action, there are *two* points at which this passage might be blocked through an act of censorship. Freud spoke of two points of censorship, one between preconscious and unconscious regions (primary censorship) and one between the preconscious and the conscious (secondary censorship).[30] Most of the *strangulation* of ideas or images took place at the primary point, but the secondary censorship was always possible.

This brings us to a final point concerning Freud's early structural constructs. Note in Figure 3 that moving from left to right, from stimulus to motor action along the dotted arc, was termed *progression* of mental excitation, whereas moving in the reverse direction was called *regression*. This is clearly a Freudian addition to the reflex arc concept, because our bodily reflex arcs—as witnessed in the action of the patellar knee tap—always move in the progressive direction (stimulus to response). In proposing a reversal to this direction, Freud was trying to account for the fact that sometimes ideas originating in the unconscious are experienced by the individual as literal stimuli in the environment—as visions or hallucinations. Anna's seeing a black snake was actually one such regression of an unconscious image moving in the reverse or regressive direction. She did not experience this image as an internal but as an external perception. What determines which way a mental excitation will move? This selection is up to the censor. If it blocks the progressive flow very aggressively, the process can be tilted in reverse, and then if in addition the unconscious very much desires to fulfill a wish, this reverse trend can culminate in a false input at the stimulus end of the dotted arc.[31] These states are not always abnormal, since all dreaming has this regressive character where we literally "think in pictures" by moving ideas backward to perceptions which are seen by the mind's eye as an image (a dream symbol). This concept of regression in mental life is to play a very important role in Freudian developmental theory. The concept of a progression is for all purposes dropped after its appearance in *The Interpretation of Dreams,* which appeared in

1900, and we shall have no further need of it.

THE FINAL MENTAL STRUCTURAL CONSTRUCTS: DYNAMIC EMPHASIS

As Freud continued his theorizing, he discovered that he could not deal with all of the personality machinations required in a thorough description of man with only the constructs of conscious, preconscious, and unconscious. These regions of mind allowed for the conception of depth adequately, but Freud needed theoretical constructs which ranged *across* the spatial or topographical levels of mind, and which could be seen as interacting *within* as well as between the levels of mind. Unconscious or preconscious mind did not oppose conscious mind, but certain identities within and across these regions opposed one another. This "clash and compromise" model fixed once and for all the *dynamic* flavor of Freudian psychology. Figure 4 presents a schematization of the final structural model of mind employed by Freud.

In order to maintain a continuity with our earlier schematization, assume that we have placed the egg-shaped structure of Figure 4 as a transparent template *over* the levels of mind of Figure 3. Note that now our combined schematization has an id, completely in the unconscious region, an ego, and superego stretching across all three levels, and an area of "repressed content" at about the spot of our primary censorship. The term *repression* now replaces censorship as a motivational construct, but it is the same essential idea of strangulation as first used in the Breuer model.

Down at the very depths of the mental structure of Figure 4 we find the *id*. It plays a role in the theoretical uniting of mind-body because our physical instinctual promptings for food, lust, self-enhancement, and so forth, first make themselves known there. The id is completely and unalterably an unconscious resident. We never can be in direct touch with it, even though there are aspects of the unconscious sphere of mind which are not id components. The id is entirely amoral and incapable of mak-

Figure 4
Freud's Final Mental Structural Constructs

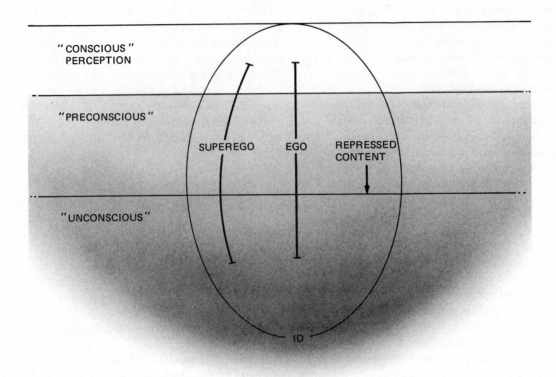

ing judgments like good vs. bad or just vs. unjust. It fulminates with greed, envy, and desire.
As Freud poetically defined it, "we call it a
chaos, a cauldron of seething excitations."[32] The
id is not concerned with realistic evaluation or
the demands of society, much less of logic. It
makes decisions illogically so that as id creatures
we might lust after someone and yet concomitantly be moved to kill the same person.[33]
Contradictions of this sort exist side by side in
the id, which has no conception of negation
and therefore is unabashed by inconsistency.[34]
Since it is entirely unconscious, the id does not
take cognizance of changes in time; it never
forgets as it never forgoes.[35]

Out of this unorganized, self-serving heritage

from nature there evolves a portion of mind devoted to reason, the evaluation of external conditions, and self-identity. It does not exist at
birth,[36] but as conscious awareness progresses
in the growth of a human being, the *ego* begins to be identified as an unchanging "permanent component" of the personality structure.[37] The contribution of muscular activity
to this process is very important, as the newborn
child begins to identify a difference between
himself "over here" in self-controlled movement
and the external world "over there."[38] Although the ego has contact across all three
levels of mind, its sphere is predominantly that
of consciousness.[39] Whereas the id draws its
basic coloring from instinctual forces, the ego

is shaped by conscious perceptions and contacts with the external world.[40] The ego is interested in meeting the demands of reality. It has a commitment there, literally an identity which is part of reality.

Since it emerges from the id, Freud viewed the ego as the "organized portion of the id."[41] Other succinct definitions of the ego include a "dominant mass of ideas"[42] and a "coherent organization of mental processes."[43] Due to his Darwinian outlook Freud assumed that what was first, earliest, or initially on the scene in life was basic to and determinative of all that was to follow in any particular realm. Thus, since the ego develops from the id, the id is primary; and it would not have happened that an ego evolved if this ego did not further the hedonistic goals of the id. The ego wants to placate the id, to achieve its ends. The point of divergence is merely over the strategy of how best to accomplish this end. As Freud said, "the ego stands for reason and good sense while the id stands for the untamed passions."[44]

Freud also expressed this difference in attitudinal outlook between the id and the ego in terms of what he called the *primary* vs. the *secondary* process in mind.[45] The id, coming earlier in time, operated according to a very primitive (primary) mental process, which sought immediate gratification through progression and motor action, or, if checked, reverted to hallucinatory actions by way of regression (see Figure 3). A baby might react in this way: spontaneously grabbing out for whatever it wants in life, or possibly even hallucinating a desired element (mother's breast) if the object were not immediately available. We might refer now to the censorship points of Figure 3. The ego's (secondary) process makes plain to the id's (primary) process that one cannot simply go out and take or do everything he wishes in life; nor is it profitable to hallucinate desired things in the environment because this loss of accuracy in the external world can lead to chaos for the organism in life. This checking of the id is, according to Freud, the reason why the core of man's being consists of

unconscious and often unsatisfied wishful impulses.[46]

In working out a proper strategy for need satisfaction the ego must actually serve *three* masters: the id (which may lust and want to kill), the demands of external reality (which may object to acts of rape and murder), and our next component of the personality, the *superego*.[47] We all realize that a certain "voice within" us—which we call our conscience—may well disturb us as we plan to do something in opposition to conventional values. In 1914 Freud said this "judgment from within" was due to a standard of how we ought to behave called the *ego ideal*.[48] When he later introduced the id construct (1923), Freud referred to the ego ideal as the *superego*. He did not make any real distinction between these terms, and we can view them as essentially synonymous.[49] The main point is that, as the id is organizing into the ego, a portion of this organization is solidifying into a superego (something which is ego but also beyond it as an ideal).

Now, as if to keep the roles of unconscious and id forces ever before our gaze, Freud goes on to stress that the superego, just like the ego, is ultimately a product of the id.[50] Many of the prohibitions on behavior which the superego advocates are stimulated in direct opposition to the id promptings.[51] Even so, due to this historic tie of the id to superego the id can occasionally harass the ego *by way of* the superego. The id always seems to have an advantage thanks to its rights of priority in the personality structure. Since the superego stretches from unconscious to conscious regions (See Figure 4), this id tie-in takes place in the unconscious. Hence, rather than opposing the id directly, in Freudian psychology the superego opposes the much put-upon ego. It is the ego which must somehow coordinate and compromise in order to keep the personality structure intact.

The superego is just as unbending and unreasonable as the id. It brooks no deviation from what it takes to be the rigid code of morals or propriety. It has, like the id, received an inheritance from the past in the sense of ethico-moral strictures. The id's inheritance is physical, the superego's is sociocultural, but both of these realms of mind seek to dictate to the ego. The superego dictates in a dual sense, for it not only tells the ego what it *"ought to be* like," but it also tells the ego what it *"may not be* like."[52] The seat of reason, accommodation to circumstance, and good judgment is thus seen only in the ego.

MOTIVATIONAL CONSTRUCTS

INSTINCT AND ENERGY

Although many of its interpreters stress the importance which *instincts* play in psychoanalysis, Freud actually made very little use of the terms "sexual instinct" or "instinctual impulse" in his earliest writings. It was not until about 1905, following his major work on dreams, that he turned to instincts as a major theoretical device.[53] By this time Freud was beginning to attract students, and in 1906 we find him active as the leader of the Vienna Psycho-Analytical Society.[54]

Freud was probably trying to bridge the gap between his mind-body dualism in formulating instinct theories. We say this because Freud constantly stressed two characteristics in referring to an instinct: (1) it is a stimulus from within the body and not from the external world, and (2) it provides a *constant* stimulus which cannot be avoided.[55] Instincts are probably precipitates of an earlier external stimulation in the history of mankind, which then became embedded in the physical nature of the organism by way of evolution. Freud defined his construct as follows: ". . . an 'instinct' appears to us as a concept on the frontier between the mental and the somatic, as the psychical representative of the stimuli originating from within the organism and reaching the mind, as a measure of the demand made upon the mind for work in consequence of its connection with the body."[56] Figure 5 schematizes this "bridge" role played by the instinct in

Freudian theory, and it also lists the four characteristics attributed to an instinct (source, aim, pressure, object).

Each instinct is said to have the *aim* of satisfaction, or removing the *pressure* (extent of stimulation) from its *source* (the point in the internal body area from which it emanates). If we have a "great need" for something, the given instinctual stimulus would be exerting great pressure upon us with the aim of achieving satisfaction, and the particular nature of our instinct (let us say it is to eat when hungry) would determine just how we would act (look for something to eat). Now, "the thing in regard to which or through which the instinct is able to achieve its aim" is the *object*.[57] This is a widely used, technical term in psychoanalysis which can refer to a person, an item of food, or a general, desired state of affairs. It can even refer to one's own person. Literally *anything* which might conceivably lead to the satisfaction of an instinct is an object.

Freud's theory of instincts embodies his hedonism. Need states arise as tensions in life, and they must be put back into a tone of relaxation or quiescence. Freud first came upon this homeostatic concept in the laboratory of Brücke, where it was termed the *principle of constancy*. This principle was first proposed by Robert Mayer in 1842, and then later popularized by such German investigators as Helmholtz and Fechner. As a follower of Helmholtz, Brücke advocated this principle,[58] and the early theory of Freud and Breuer made use of this idea as the *principle of neuronic inertia*: "If a person experiences a psychical impression, something in his nervous system which we will for the moment call the sum of excitation is increased. Now in every individual there exists a tendency to diminish this sum of excitation once more, in order to preserve his health."[59] Referring once again to Figure 3, we might say that the principle of neuronic inertia strives to account for the fact that sensory impressions, which come in by way of the "stimulus," *do* seek by way of mental images to either *progress* to motor discharge or *regress* to hallucinatory

Figure 5
Freudian Instinct as a Mind-Body "Bridge"

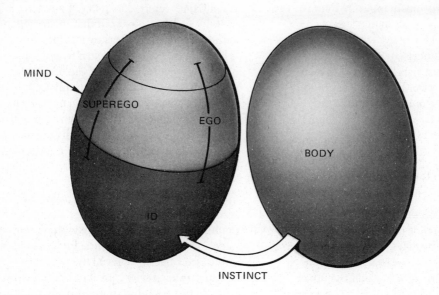

SOURCE:	LOCUS OF STIMULATION IN THE BODY.
AIM:	SATISFACTION OF STIMULATION OR NEED.
PRESSURE:	HOW MUCH DEMAND THE INSTINCTUAL STIMULUS IS MAKING UPON US AT THE MOMENT.
OBJECT:	THE PERSON, PLACE, OR THING IN THE ENVIRONMENT WHICH WILL SATISFY THE NEED (I.E., THE INSTINCTUAL STIMULATION).

(dream or real life) false perceptions. A built-in mechanism in the nervous system reduces excitations by way of discharge; and if this reduction cannot be accomplished, an unhealthy state of affairs (the "abreaction" phenomenon) is likely to result. The manner in which the mind succeeds—however effectively—in ridding itself of these states of heightened excitation is termed the *vicissitudes* of the instincts.[60] A vicissitude is a regular or irregular state of change in something, and Freud intended this to mean that instinctual promptings rise, fall, are distorted by defense mechanisms, and so forth, all with the *aim* of restoring equilibrium in the body-mind status of the individual.

Motivation may be defined in general terms as the "inducement to behavior stemming from provocation of a need in relation to a goal (object)." Freud's *object* was usually an item in the environment which could satisfy such a need, but the *aim* of instinctual satisfaction comes for Freud to mean *pleasure*. Psychoanalysis accepts this formula for motivation as basic to human behavior. Freud referred to this as the *pleasure principle,* which he defined as follows: "It seems as though our total mental activity is directed towards achieving pleasure and avoiding unpleasure—that it is automatically regulated by the *pleasure principle.*"[61] Historically, we can now identify the constancy principle with the pleasure principle as a homeostatic mechanism in mind to seek an even keel.[62] Freud did not believe man had an instinct to feel *pain*. At best, pain is a "pseudo-instinct" which has as its aim "simply the cessation of the change in the organ and of the unpleasure accompanying it."[63] Pain is thus merely another way of saying "loss of pleasure," and Freud has assigned the role of pleasure seeker (balancer) to the instinct construct. How many instincts (needs) does man have? Before we speak of Freud's theory of instincts as a whole, we must consider the *one* instinct (and need) he could never forgo in his conceptualization of man.

FREUD'S PROMETHEAN INSIGHT: THE SEXUAL INSTINCT

Freud's life-long conviction was that he had found the primary source of neurotic difficulties, and indeed the major wellspring of all human behavior, in man's sexual instinct. He had a rather stubborn attitude about the use of this term *sex* in his theory. Though its meaning seemed stretched out of proportion and he broke with certain of his followers rather than rename this instinct (Jung being the most famous example), Freud steadfastly refused to change this precise designation.

As he worked with his cases of so-called defense hysteria, Freud found that these patients were invariably *defending against* the conscious acceptance of sexual thoughts or impulses. We also have reason to believe that during his self-analysis following his father's demise, Freud resurrected his own sexual memories of having witnessed his mother in the nude while he was very young.[64] It is often difficult to separate *sex* from *pleasure* in psychoanalysis. Thus, Freud notes that "in man the sexual instinct does not originally serve the purpose of reproduction at all, but has as its aims the gaining of particular kinds of pleasure."[65] In the baby, for example, certain apparently nonsexual activities like sucking are pleasurably *autoerotic* (having the instinctual source of pleasure as the object of pleasure as well). Sucking in a baby may be compared to other behaviors like masturbation as *identical* forms of autoerotic activities, since in both instances pleasure is derived in the ac-

tivity itself. This derivation of pleasure from areas other than the genital regions of the body is sometimes referred to as *organ pleasure,* but Freud is quick to point out that the *reason* various organs have pleasure attached to them is because they satisfy a sexual instinct. Hence, other than genital regions of the body are sources of sexual instinctual stimulation.[66]

Freud coined the term *erotogenic zone* to signify any region of the body which might initiate a sexual stimulus. Literally *any* part of the skin can become an erotogenic zone, engendering the search for pleasure. It can be the mouth area (pleasure in sucking), the anal area (pleasure in defecation), or even the eye can serve as a sexual stimulant (pleasure in scopophilic "peeping").[67] In line with his view of a number of erotogenic zones, Freud made perfectly clear that he believed there were *many* sexual instincts, each contributing its components to the over-all state we think of as "sexual excitation."[68] There are also other than sexual instincts in the body, a theoretical view which Freud was never to reject.

The question naturally arises: If sexuality is fundamentally the search for pleasure, and if *all* instincts are based on the pleasure (constancy) principle, why distinguish between *sex* and *pleasure*? The best way to dramatize this point is to note that Freud named only one energy in the mind, which presumably afforded our mental structure (id, ego, sugerego across the levels of mind) the wherewithal to act. This energy was called *libido*, and it is defined variously as *"psychical desire,"*[69] all of man's "erotic tendencies,"[70] "sexual desire in the broadest sense,"[71] and "the motive forces of sexual life."[72] But probably the most complete statement of libido in his writings, and one which also gives us a good picture of Freud's use of "love," may be found in the following quote:

Libido is an expression taken from the theory of the emotions. We call by that name the energy, regarded as a quantitative magnitude (though not at present actually measurable), of those instincts which have to do with all that may be comprised under the word "love." The nucleus of what we mean by love naturally consists (and this is what is commonly called love, and what the poets sing of) in sexual love with sexual union as its aim. But we do not separate from this—what in any case has a share in the name "love" on the one hand, self-love, and on the other, love for parents and children, friendship and love for humanity in general, and also devotion to concrete objects and to abstract ideas.[73]

With an energy this all-encompassing there was probably no need for naming alternatives. Nevertheless, since there *are* other instincts than the sexual, one would have thought that Freud might have named an energy for at least one more such instinct. The fact that he never did is mute testimony that he continued to base his major motivational theories on sexual factors in the human personality. It is important to emphasize that libido is a *mental* energy. Libido is whatever it is that physically based instincts "turn loose" in the mind. Psychic libido is *not* identical to physical emotion. We must think of libido as that energy which is expended in the progressions and regressions of Figure 3. To round out this theory of how the mind works, Freud needed a term signifying that this mental energy had in fact been fixed upon or centered in certain mental ideas or images—whatever we might think of as the mind "doing." The term he chose to capture this fixing of libido onto a mental content was *cathexis*. Freud had first used this term in his *Project* as a physical concept, but noting his initial usage helps us to understand what he means in his later psychological theorizing. In the *Project* Freud said that a physical neurone (which is a "cell" in the nervous system) was "cathected" when it was filled with a certain quantum of physical energy.[74]

This idea of filling-up or occupying an item is what Freud retained when he later used cathexis in relation to libido as a psychical energy. Thus, to cathect an object now means that we fill it with libido in our mind's eye.[75] We occupy the image of a loved one or the memory of a longed-for state in our past with libidinal energy analogically to the way in which an invading army occupies a coveted region.[76] Cathexis, therefore, has the significance of a thrust, an entering, an occupation, or a fixing of interest on some *given object* by attaching libido to it or engulfing it with libidinal energies. Motives are therefore concerned with the libidinal cathexis of this or that object. Simply cathecting an object does not mean the individual will always seek to attain it in the external world. For example, if the id lusts for some object—let us assume it is a parent—then the ego can *anticathect* this investment of libido by opposing its own supply of libido to the id's cathexis.[77] Anticathexis, therefore, is another way of talking about strangulation, censorship, or repression.

One last point must be made concerning Freud's views on sex. He always held to the position that humans were bisexual. This theory was favored by Fliess, and Freud never rejected the notion, even though he did not develop it excessively in his formal theories. Fliess made use of the concept in a physical sense, arguing that both men and women are guided by a natural constitutional cycle of influence. Women show this in their menstrual cycles, and men can be shown to have something akin to menstruation in the engorgement of blood vessels in certain tissues of the nasal region; both sexes are thus governed by "periodic cycles" of physical influence.[78] Freud, on the other hand, gave his bisexuality a *psychological* interpretation, viewing masculinity as akin to "activity" and femininity to "passivity."[79] He even thought of libido as masculine in nature, because it was such an active agent of mental life.[80] He made the greatest use of bisexuality in his analysis of President Wilson, but most of his descriptions here are centered around Wilson's activity vs. his passivity toward his father.[81] Hence though we have here a bisexual theory, biological in tone, it is actually a psychological theory of how the mind thrusts and parries in interpersonal situations—in either an active or a passive manner.

Now that we have an understanding of some basic terms, let us run through the history of Freud's thinking on the role of instincts in human behavior. The first question which arises is: Just how many instincts are in the human animal? Freud believed that this was an empirical problem, one which could only be answered by tracing each instinct in turn to its ultimate *source* in the body.[82] The problem here, Freud noted, was that one is tempted to propose instinct upon instinct until every aspect of behavior is covered. For example, to explain "playfulness," one might propose that man has an instinct "to play." Yet, if we were to break this activity of playfulness down into its components, we might find that an underlying (genotypic) instinct entered into this activity in conjunction with one or possibly two other instincts. Indeed, only a small number of such underlying instincts may exist which can account for a myriad number of more complex behaviors.

Freud referred to these underlying, genotypic instincts as *primal instincts,* and the secondary, phenotypic variety he called *component instincts* since they were presumably made up of one or more primal contributions. Now, it is extremely important to note that, as a general theoretical strategy, *Freud was always to base the edifice of psychoanalysis on the interplay of two primal instincts, even though he implied that more than two were in effect.* He changed the names of these primal instincts over the years, but the fundamental opposition of two basic forces in the personality remains constant in Freudian thought. In fact, Freud maintained that instincts occurred in pairs of opposites, usually as we have seen in the case of bisexuality, taking an active and a passive opposition.[83]

Freud's first opposition of instincts was that of the *self-preservative instincts* (or *ego instincts*[84]) and the *sexual instincts* (or *object instincts*[85]). Recall that the ego was seen as the seat of reason in the personality. Whereas the id was guided initially by the pleasure principle,

Freud now argued that the ego comes to be guided by the *reality principle:* "This latter principle does not abandon the intention of ultimately obtaining pleasure, but it nevertheless demands and carries into effect the postponement of satisfaction, the abandonment of a number of possibilities of gaining satisfaction and the temporary toleration of unpleasure as a step on the long indirect road to pleasure."[86] Rather than permit the id to "act out" its cathexes overtly in *direct* motor action, the ego opposes itself to these impulses (anticathects) and seeks a gratification in pleasure realistically, by way of the reality principle. It works out various compromises (vicissitudes of sexual instincts) and utilizes the defense mechanisms in order to maintain harmony.

This was a rather nice "primal instincts" theory and it sufficed for several years. As we have already noted, Freud never coined an energy for the self-preservative instinct, even though he continually spoke of *energies,* implying that something other than libido was involved in moving the mental apparatus. But in actual practice, theoretical explanations were primarily based upon the libido. Since they had to be defended against, the sexual instincts were naturally more likely to emanate from the depths of the unconscious, where they entered mind by way of the id. Freud liked this kind of "depth" theory, and possibly it is for this reason that he was to drop self-preservation as the instinct in opposition to sexuality. In its place he introduced the construct of a "death" instinct. This addition was part of a masterful piece of theorizing, and the way in which he accomplished it was to base the death instinct theory upon two preliminary ideas: *narcissism* and the *repetition compulsion.* We will next turn to the development of his later instinct theory by way of these intermediate steps.

Narcissism. In Greek myth, Narcissus, the beautiful son of the river-god Cephissus, was supposedly the embodiment of self-conceit. He spurned the love of various nymphs even though they had great attraction to him. One such rejected maiden prayed to the deity that he might know what it meant to love and not be loved in return. A curse was put on his head and one day, leaning over a river bank for a drink of water, Narcissus was doomed to fall in love with his own reflection. He talked to it, tried to embrace it, lusted after it, and pined away until death without achieving gratification.[87] Freud was to take this theme of self-love and use it to alter his instinct theory. Problems were mounting due to the challenges of his detractors, some of whom—like Adler—wanted Freud to assign a more central role to conscious, reasonable, ego functions. Others—like Jung—felt that he was overstretching the meaning of libido, making it into an *elan vital*.[88] What Freud had to do was (1) explain ego functions (self-preservation) as a special type of sexual instinct, yet (2) avoid making the sexual instinct the *only* primal instinct in his theoretical armamentarium. In short, he deliberately set out to remove self-preservation from the list of *primal* instincts and to replace it with some other opposing force in the personality.

His first step was accomplished through his use of *narcissism,* a term which had been used by Paul Näcke and Havelock Ellis to describe a person who treated his own body as if it were a sexual object.[89] Rather than saying that the ego looked after self-preservation due to a primal instinct of this nature, Freud now claimed that the *ego is itself cathected* with libido from the outset. Thus, in evolving out of the id, the ego takes over its share of libido in the psychic structure and acts like a special instance of love—that is, self-love (narcissism). We can now draw the parallel between autoerotism and narcissism because they both refer to gaining sexual pleasure from an investment in our bodies as objects.[90] Freud referred to the libido invested in the ego as "ego libido" or as "narcissistic libido" and the libido eventually sent outward to others as "object libido."

We now have successfully done away with self-preservation as a *primal* instinct, even though the same kinds of self-preservative activities which the ego carries on continue as a secondary (*component*) instinctual manifestation. Self-care is self-love. But what do we now oppose to the sexual instinct and its pleasure principle? At this point, Freud went "Beyond the Pleasure Principle" (Vol. XVIII) and introduced one of his most controversial theoretical constructs as opponent to pleasure—the Death Instinct.

Repetition Compulsion. Not until roughly 1920 did Freud decide to change his theory of mental principles, to drop the reality principle as a major concept, and to substitute in its place an entirely new concept of mental functioning, the *repetition compulsion.* He had, of course, noted for decades that neurotics in psychoanalysis seemed to have a compulsion to repeat the dynamics of their case history in therapy, literally reliving their past conflicts during a session and bringing him as therapist into the action as participant. He was also struck by the fact that children are ever willing to repeat the same game or to hear the same fairy tale, over and over again. It was as if they were "working through" some anxious concern which preoccupied them, like the mystery of birth in their "hide-and-go-seek" endeavors. There are repetitive dreams and repetitive fantasies which everyone experiences occasionally, and historians have even noted that history tends to repeat itself.

Basing his argument on such points, Freud then concluded that, in addition to the pleasure principle in mind: ". . . there really does exist in the mind a compulsion to repeat."[91] Note that this is a mental or *psychical* principle. Freud now brings his two final primal principles together by a stroke of genius which ties them both back to his "constancy" idea. He observes that *an instinct is an urge inherent in organic life to restore an earlier state of things* which the living entity has been obliged to abandon under the pressure of external disturbing forces; that is, it is a kind of organic elasticity, or, to put it another way, the expression of the inertia inherent in organic life."[92] Instincts do not make things happen so much as they cause things to return to earlier states (the conservative nature of instincts). As in the case of the pleasure principle, a state of quiescence is achieved through sexual activity, thereby returning the organism to its even, homeostatic level. Life is a rhythm, expressed initially by Freud in the concept of the vicissitudes of the instincts. But the ultimate state of quiescence is death itself!

If we consider the matter biologically, even physical matter has a way of returning to a common, inorganic state. The Biblical reference of "dust to dust" captures this feature of cyclical repetition most succinctly (note here the Fliess "periodic cycle" influence on Freud). Thus Freud can say, in a biological manner of speaking, *the aim of all life is death.*[93] What he has succeeded in doing is to equate *both* a sex instinct and a death instinct on this matter of repetition: they both lead to a repeating of an identical state over time. Hence, we can now oppose our two instincts and view life as a vacillating rhythm of self-destruction (death) and self-perpetuation (life). He called the life-propelling instincts *Eros,* and they now take over the role of the older sexual instincts, including self-preservation by way of narcissism. Eros ensures that the final quiescence (death) will not come about too quickly. Man loves himself, so he looks out for himself and extends his stay on this planet. Eros also ensures that progeny will be forthcoming, as a by-product of the pleasure engendered from sexual relations between the sexes.[94] Opposed to Eros we now have another collection of instincts which have the *aim* of restoring man to an inorganic state, from which he presumably was begot centuries past. Freud called this master repetition compulsion the *Death Instinct* (he did not like the term Thanatos, which some of his advocates have used since). Grisly though they may be, the aims of Death are the satisfactions of the grave (repose, rest, and organic constancy).

If Freud has given some ground on his Promethean insight of sex as major motivator in man by recognizing the repetition compulsion, he has surely not given away an inch on the matter of hedonism, for *both* of his final instincts have the aim of a pleasurable outcome about them. As when he seemed to be identifying libido with pleasure, Freud here again seems to be identifying death with (pleasurable) satisfaction. He referred to this ultimate "reduction in tension" into the quiescence of death as the "Nirvana principle,"[95] but for all practical purposes as a theoretical device this is nothing more than a rephrase of the constancy principle and identical to the pleasure principle. Thus, in his final theory of instincts Freud has Eros and Death as the two primary instincts, entering conjointly into all manner of secondary or component instincts as witnessed in the byplay of ego, id, and superego machinations. This was called a *fusion* of instincts.[96] For example, sadism (a component instinct) would suggest a fusion of hostility (Death) and sex (Eros).[97] Ego functions such as pugnacity or other self-interest aggressivities could thus be handled as component instincts, made up of the primal instincts of Eros and Death. In fact, Freud stated clearly that his life and death instincts hardly ever appear in their "pure form" in human behavior.[98]

One might finally ask: Since Freud had libido as the energy of Eros in this final formulation of his instinct theory, did he ever name an energy in opposition to it? No, this was never to be the case. Even though he said that the Death Instinct can turn into a destructive instinct during wartime, and thus send out its hostile influences toward objects in the external world, Freud never sent a theoretical—to coin a word—"lobodo" outward to cathect such objects.[99] In the analysis of President Wilson he actually referred to the mixture of life and death energies without naming one of them, as follows: ". . . and the charge [i.e., quantum] of mingled libido and Death Instinct was again without outlet and remained repressed."[100] It seems certain that he *did* have an energy in mind for the Death Instinct, and his theory surely called for it, but Freud was not moved to raise other energies into the prominence which he had ascribed to libido.

Stemming from his initial theory of defense hysteria, down through all of his subsequent theoretical endeavors, Freud found it necessary to introduce several terms which described the unique behaviors of people. Since in most instances he was describing the behavior of abnormals, we have come to think of these as "defense" mechanisms. However, as the extension was made to normals and the "psychopathology of everyday life," we have come to think of these as simply "adjustment" or "mental" mechanisms. They are often defined *in terms of* energy expenditure, the blocking or rerouting of energies and so forth. In fact, one of the problems we face in trying to understand these *mental* devices is that they *are* so often presented as if they were part of the libido theory. Actually, there is a clear meaning for each mechanism which is easily grasped by any novice who lacks a knowledge of libido theory.

Repression. We have already introduced this concept as the historical descendant of the "strangulator" and the censorship. Repression was Freud's most basic mental mechanism, on which the other mechanisms are predicated. As Freud said, repression is "the corner-stone on which the whole structure of psycho-analysis rests."[101] We can define repression in two ways: (1) it is a countering of one cathexis by an anticathexis, or (2) it is the opposing of one idea in mind by an opposing idea. These are two ways of saying the same thing. One cannot grasp why one energy cathexis should oppose another cathexis unless he *also* understands that ideas are involved. Moreover, these ideas act as *intentions*, preparations for action which

come into conflict with one another. One aspect of the personality structure (id) intends one thing, and another aspect of the structure (ego) intends another.[102] When the more conscious level "wins out," we have a repression (anticathexis, in energy terms). When the more unconscious level "wins out," we have motor action or the "acting out" of an impulse which might well be considered antisocial in polite society.

The id impulses are usually the ones which undergo repression, although in theory contents in the unconscious regions of the ego or superego can also be put under repression. The deeper the level of mental functioning, the more certain we are that an anticathexis is truly a repression. In Figure 3, for example, the region of primary censorship is surely "repression." The region of secondary censorship in Figure 3 Freud would have considered more on the order of a *suppression*. What distinguishes suppression from repression is the extent of conscious control exerted in the anticathexis. We all know that we can consciously strive to keep something out of mind, to turn off a preoccupation, to stop thought or to think of something else in order to forget. Activities of this sort Freud termed suppression. Repression is entirely unconscious, and therefore when the repressed intentions of "unconscious man" are made manifest to us through analytical interpretations, we are repulsed by what we hear since they are ideas we do not identify as our own.

There are actually two stages in repression. The first, or *primal repression,* takes place during the time of the original conflict between ideas. This eventuates in what Freud called a *fixation,* a mental mechanism which we will take up in the next section, dealing with the stages of psychosexual development. Then later, when certain mental *derivatives* (outgrowths, promptings, vague recollections, symbolic expressions) begin slipping by the primal censorship (repression), a *repression proper* is carried on by the mind.

Displacement. Freud first used displacement to describe how it was possible to fool the censor, and in a dream formulation to displace the meaning of the dream onto an unrelated event or happening.[103] Having an unconscious hatred for our brother, we might displace this hatred in our dream onto a bobcat, which we track down and kill after a satisfying hunt. We never actually realize *consciously* that our victim is Bob or, short for our brother's name, Robert. Unconsciously we have killed our brother, but consciously only a derivation symbolized in a game animal has been done in.

Substitution. Humans can often find alternate objects in life. We can redirect our interests, for example, and find a new libidinal object if we are blocked from attaining our initial sexual choice. Freud observed that when an aging unmarried woman dotes over a pet dog, or when an old bachelor collects snuff boxes, the former has found a substitute for the marital partner she never acquired, and the latter has substituted a series of pretty boxes for the succession of beautiful women he never conquered.[104] Substitution is therefore a term referring specifically to the replacing of one object by another.

Sublimation. Freud defined this as follows: "The most important vicissitude which an instinct can undergo seems to be *sublimation;* here both object and aim are changed, so that what was originally a sexual instinct finds satisfaction in some achievement which is no longer sexual but has a higher social or ethical valuation."[105] This definition makes it appear that one cannot sublimate hostility or the Death Instinct. Actually, most of the instances which Freud uses to demonstrate sublimation *do* deal with sex or Eros, but it seems clear that he meant *any* (primal or component) instinct which is unacceptable to the superego could

be sublimated.[106] We do something of a "higher" good in sublimation, as when the young man who finds his sexual promptings "dirty" turns to art and becomes a talented painter.

Projection. Freud often noted that his disturbed patient—particularly the paranoiac (extremely suspicious tendencies)—would behave like a dreamer and assign internal mental excitations (perceptions) to the external world in the way we reviewed in Figure 3 (regression of mental excitation back to the stimulus). For example, the id might prompt the individual to feel hostility toward another person, but the superego would negate any expression of an angry nature. It is possible therefore to project one's own hostility onto another person and claim "I'm not hostile to him, but he is very irritated with me." Notice that the *nature* of the projected instinct remains the same—it is still hostility that we are dealing with.[107] Freud believed that the ability to project internal perceptions outward was a very primitive tendency in man, and that in point of fact, projection "normally plays a very large part in determining the form taken by our external world."[108]

Reaction-Formation. In working out the full theory of defense, Freud introduced a construct to account for those instances in which people seem to be arguing for or favoring some action, point of view, or intention in diametric opposition to what they *really* wish would occur. The young man who is so threatened by the thought of kissing a girl that he now professes a great "disinterest" in the opposite sex has probably been the victim of a harsh superego, which sees in sexual contact something "immoral." Wanting sexual contact badly insures that this lad will turn his *real* preoccupation into its very opposite, for as Freud said: ". . . there are motive forces in mental life which bring about replacement by the opposite in the form of what is known as reaction-formation. . . ."[109]

Rationalization. Freud's student and biographer, Ernest Jones, introduced the term "rationalization," which refers to the fact that a person often finds an acceptable (plausible, rational) reason to justify some action which is really prompted by a completely different (usually irrational, emotional) motive.[110] Thus, a housewife who unconsciously dislikes another woman in her circle of friends may find all manner of reasons for avoiding contact with this particular person. Her real reason is unconscious dislike (Death Instinct components), but her consciously stated reasons (rationalizations) may include that she is too busy to call the woman on a telephone, she is never free on the afternoons when this woman has a tea party, she was "sick" on the occasion when they were to travel together, and so forth.

Isolation. A disturbed person may sometimes be able to keep a rather horrible or frightening idea in mind. In order to account for this feature of mental life, Freud introduced the construct of *isolation,* by which he meant separating an idea from its emotion (affect).[111] Thus, a psychotic person might have a delusional belief that his stomach had turned into a huge snake and that it was eating him alive, or some such. The normal person would be horrified— on the order of Anna O.'s reaction—but this psychotic individual might continue to think about the delusion without showing a sign of emotion. Normals might occasionally isolate, such as in times of war when killing is required or when a parent tries to remove a child's badly mangled finger from a wire fencing, where it had become impaled in an act of play. We cannot always let our emotions get the better of us and must sometimes carry out a difficult task with a cool head even though it may appear unnatural to others.

The mental mechanisms of *introjection, identification, fixation,* and *regression* will be taken up in the next section, as we outline the stages of psychosexual development.

PSYCHOSEXUAL STAGES

Freud's earliest time perspective model had *four stages* in it, encompassing birth to young adulthood.[112] He tells Fliess in 1896 that each level must build on the earlier one, and that probably a quantitative measure of psychic energy is passed along from an earlier to a later stage. He then observes that if this energy is not forthcoming, if it does *not* move up from level A (ages 8 to 10) to level B (ages 13 to 17), then "the excitation is dealt with in accordance with the psychological laws in force in the earlier psychical period and along the paths open at that time. Thus an anachronism persists: in a particular province *fueros* are still in force, we are in the presence of 'survivals.' "[113] Freud's analogue of a "fuero" is from the Spanish term for an ancient law which protects a given province's legal privileges for time immemorial.

Since the unconscious is timeless, it follows that such personal fueros would dictate to us out of our own past. They would have demands to make and conditions to be met. Where do these demands come from? Why do they arise? Well, this would depend upon how one had lived, whether or not everything went smoothly from one stage of life to the next. Such things as primal repressions would surely mitigate against successful passage up life's ladder of development. As time went by, Freud not only worked out a series of psychosexual stages in human development, but he devised a way of explaining how some of these stages are not passed through completely, resulting in everything from minor personality variations to neurotic and even psychotic disorders.

He argued that such levels in mind were dependent upon the particular *erotogenic* zone of the body from which human beings obtained pleasure as they grew to adulthood. Sucking was said to be sexual, and therefore the mouth area was an erotogenic zone of primary importance to the baby. It follows that the "first" level of mind should in some way bear a meaningful relation to psychological factors centering around mouth-like activities. This is where libido issued from in the earliest stratum of mind; hence it would naturally retain that coloring if it were not advanced to a later period. Our mouth fuero would have oral dictates. Freud was to drop his first model of four levels in mind, and over the years we can actually count six or seven stages (sometimes called phases) in the development of the human being from birth to maturity. However, the first four, which are called the *pregenital stages,* are the most important in personality formation. Freud meant by "genital" the actual ability to reproduce, so that pregenital levels are those in which, although sexuality is manifested, genital (procreative) lust is not entirely possible. These psychosexual stages, to which we now turn, are not to be thought of as fixed clearly as to age level. There can be several months variation in age between any two people who pass through the same psychosexual stage.

ORAL PSYCHOSEXUAL STAGE

The child enters this world following birth in a completely unconscious state, dominated by the promptings of id instincts. At first, he does not draw a distinction between "others" and "self" (ego), but seeks in every way possible to obtain immediate (id) gratifications for his needs. He experiences an "oceanic feeling" of oneness and omnipotence, for the world is his oyster.[114] Desire is centered around "oral erotism" at this stage in life. When he has the opportunity to confront a source of food supply—as, the mother's breast or a bottle of milk —the baby literally seeks to devour it as a primitive savage might devour another person. This taking something physical into our body from an outside source Freud termed *incorporation.* The oral stage has the mouth as erotogenic zone. It is the first pregenital stage, and because of this emphasis on the physical in-

corporation of one body (mother's milk) by another (baby), Freud called it the "cannibalistic pregenital sexual organization."[115] He was making an analogy here to our primitive past, a tactic he will continue to follow in the phallic stage.

The oral stage is therefore primarily typified by taking in things from the external environment but also from within the psychic sphere itself. The ego forms out of the id and receives its libido from the id. In the same way that a child may take in his mother's milk, he also takes in libido from the id. We see in this the necessary mechanism for the beginnings of an ego structure. Hence, Freud said, the child in the first few months of life is in a state of *primary narcissism* (autoerotic). He is living according to the pleasure principle. If a bodily function is tension producing, through a physical reflex of some sort, he can remove the annoyance (defecation, urination); and if all else fails, he can resort to *wish fulfillment* at least to "see" what he desires in an act of fantasy (primary process thought). Wishfulfillments in fantasy are identical to dream mechanisms, and we know that through regression of libido in the dotted arc of Figure 3 we can create our own reality. Since there are no superego wishes to be met with as yet, the wishfulfillments of a baby in the oral stage are *all pleasant.*[116]

It is this "taking-in" propensity of the growing child in the oral stage which lays the foundation for *identification,* a mental mechanism that is not completely fulfilled until the phallic stage of development. Freud viewed this propensity to identify oneself with others in the external world as a more primitive mechanism than object choice, because to "take in" suggests a narcissism in mental functioning. Narcissism always precedes object choice in human development. An identification or a taking-in of characteristics from parents or other significant people is also a narcissistic activity. You are not sending cathexes *out* (object choice) when you identify, but rather you take behavioral patterns, attitudes, or beliefs *in*. You are making yourself like the external model. For this reason Freud occasionally referred to the oral period as the "stage of narcissism."[117] His student, Ferenczi, coined the term *introjection* for this taking of the object into the self.[118]

ANAL PSYCHOSEXUAL STAGE

Sometime around the close of the first year of life, when the child is first confronted with the need to meet the demands of polite society and learn to control his sphincters (urination, defecation), Freud viewed a shift in erotogenic zones, from the mouth area to the anus (and also to the urethra, our next stage). Whereas experience up to this time had allowed the child to take in, he is now called upon to delay certain gratifications (secondary process in thought), to live more along the lines of a reality principle. By this time the ego is being differentiated out of the mass that was the oceanic total of events, and as such the ego is confronted with certain annoyances. Freud said that when an instinct was not satisfied, we should speak of it as a *frustration;* the regulations put on the child by his parents to establish this frustration he called a *prohibition;* and the resulting psychological state of affairs in general he called a *privation.*[119] Hence, with the advent of the anal stage prohibitions and their resultant frustrations, states of privation must inevitably begin. This is therefore a difficult time for the child; and whereas the general tenor of the oral stage was passive and receptive, the tenor of the anal stage is aggressive and assaultive (Death Instinct prominent). In fact, Freud first referred to the personality in this phase as the "*sadistic-anal* organization, in which the *anal* zone and the component instinct of sadism are particularly prominent."[120]

The anal stage is still pregenital; but in the attitude of the mother as she trains her child for the toilet, there is an ever increasing source of potential difficulty in the clash of wills, both desiring to fulfill their own ends. The child finds that the mucous membranes of the anal region are a source of pleasure, and he might physically manipulate this region or "play" with fecal matter through retention, then rapid expulsion, and so forth. The mother may find such "games" disgusting and punish the child; or, she may be permissive and allow extensive manipulation of this sort.

URETHRAL PSYCHOSEXUAL STAGE

The urethra is the canal which carries urine from the bladder to the penis or to the vestibule of the vagina. Although he did not draw a hard and fast line between the anal and urethral stages, Freud did feel that an erotogenic zone contribution was made to pleasure ("sex" in the broader sense) from the urethra. We probably all pass through a phase where the anus is uppermost as contributor of libido and then another, briefer period in which the urethra takes the center stage in this role as source. This stage is still pregenital, and we are therefore speaking about the life period of roughly the third year or thereabouts, when major preoccupations of children focus on the retention or release of urine.

PHALLIC PSYCHOSEXUAL STAGE

We come now to the stage in which infantile sexuality takes a heterosexual turn, as object choices are sent outward toward a parent; even so, this is considered a pregenital stage. For Freud *genital* means literally reproductive, and phallus refers more specifically to the penis or clitoris engorged with blood. This development is possible even before reproductive organs have matured, of course, and in naming this level the phallic stage Freud wanted to stress that it was based on "not a primacy of the genitals, but a primacy of the *phallus.*"[121] One must accept that Freud begins with the premise that early in life *both* boys and girls highly value the *penis* (when erect, "phallus").

The phallic stage is begun late in the child's second or the third year in life.[122] Differences between the sexes at this point are nonexistent, and for all practical purposes "the little girl is a little man."[123] The boy discovers his pleasurable organ as the erotogenic zone shifts away from the anus-urethra to the penis, and he begins a period of active manipulation (masturbates) in order to gain pleasure from the new source; and the girl does precisely the same thing with her "small penis," the clitoris.[124] In fact, the girl senses a loss or a lack and very much envies her brother and other boys (called *penis envy*) for their superior organ, which doubtless exudes more pleasure as erotogenic zone due to its size.[125] Often the first reaction of the girl is to *deny* or *disavow* that she lacks a penis, but in time her psychology is greatly influenced by this fact.[126]

Ontogeny Recapitulates Phylogeny and the Origin of Society. Before going into what are called the Oedipal complexes of children, we will review Freud's theories on the origin of society, culture, or civilization (he did not make fine distinctions among these terms). As he matured, Freud found himself turning increasingly to the writings of anthropologists, sociologists, and other students of legal and religious origins like James Frazer, Herbert Spencer, J. J. Atkinson, and William Robertson Smith. He also read the works of Darwin and Lamarck. From Darwin and Atkinson as major sources, and doing considerable analogizing from his own personal clinical experience, Freud worked out a theory of how society and culture began. First of all, we must understand the Darwinian-Lamarckian theoretical rule that "ontogeny recapitulates phylogeny."

This rule states that in its *in utero* development from a fertilized egg (one cell) to a highly complex anthropoid the human being re-enacts the evolution of the entire animal kingdom. The human fetus passes through a state where it has a gill structure, suggesting a fish-like animal; later it develops a tail, and the distinction between human fetus and pig fetus is difficult to make in the early months

of gestation. There are those who challenge this theory today, but Freud at least was much taken by it. Indeed, the concept of a repetition-compulsion in life seems to have received its major strengthening in Freud's thought from this physical need for life to repeat its history in maturation.[127] By 1913 he was referring to the principle of ontogeny recapitulating phylogeny, and he announced that it was necessary to see this principle in operation mentally as well as physically.[128] Freud now contended that not only did people re-enact their *physical history* before birth, but they also re-enacted their *psychological history* after birth. The family setting, with its relations between parents and children, is thus viewed analogically to the origin of society as a re-enactment of our first social organization.

Theories of societal origin fall into two broad categories: those which stress the aggressive conquering or subduing of one people by another, or those which stress the more reasonable, cooperative, even loving side of human behavior.[129] Freud succeeds in using both views at different points in his theory. Basing his main argument on Darwin's theory of a *primal horde*, he argues that in the dawn of human society men lived in small groups under the complete subjugation of a single male. This "primal father" owned all of the horde's property, and the women of the group were his most prized chattel. He had unlimited power and sadistically exerted it, keeping all of his sons from the pleasures of sexual contact with the women in the group. If a son violated this prohibition, the father would either kill, castrate, or send him off into the wilderness to fend for himself. This naturally led to the practice of exogamy (seeking sexual objects as mates from outside one's kinship group), as the sons raided other groups and kidnapped their own complement of wives.

However, one group of sons eventually violated this pattern. A number of them who had been run off by the primal father returned as a smaller group of attackers with a common hatred. They were fearful of the old man, but through the strength of their number they succeeded in killing him off. Then, as many primitive groups are known to have done, they *literally* incorporated his entire person. They ate him in cannibalistic fashion, just as the baby now eats his mother's milk. The reason for eating the father (or a goodly portion of him) was that they hoped to "take in" or introject his strength. We might say that the sons cathected their father's body with the energy of the Death Instinct in killing him, but they *also* cathected him with libido in desiring his power. Hence, rather than taking him as a sexual object, they reverted to identification (incorporation) from object choice in the narcissistic oral fashion we have already discussed.[130]

The shock of having killed and eaten the old man presumably sobered them up enough so that now they realized that hostility breeds a return in kind and that no one can profit if the killing continues. Hence, they succeeded in doing what the primal father could not bring himself to do: they struck a rational bargain (sometimes called a social contract). They agreed to found what we now think of as families within the society, to cohabit only with the women of their families, and for *their sons* to limit their selection of wives from outside of the family (taboo of exogamy). Hence, neither the son nor daughter could properly expect to have sexual gratification (Eros) within their given family. As the generations slipped by, the killing of an actual human being was repressed, and the father's image was replaced by a totemic animal of some sort. Ordinarily, the animal could not be eaten except on certain ceremonial occasions, as a "sacrifice" to God. And this, now heavenly, God in the skies was also a deified projection of the primal father. Religious myths were then concocted to fill in the picture in other than patricidal terms; thus, Freud said, the real "original sin" was the killing off of the primal father.[131] With a common God and a common totemic animal the families which were organized into a culture (commonly

identified with a leader) would drain off hostility engendered within the group (Death Instinct) by directing it outward in wars on such other "societies" which also had evolved in the manner we have outlined.[132]

To weld this social theory to a single family, Freud now once again draws on Greek mythology in the tale of Oedipus. This famous myth runs as follows: Laius, King of Thebes, having been warned by the oracle that his newborn son would destroy him, had the child sent off to be murdered by a herdsman. Emotionally unable to kill the child, the herdsman merely pierced his feet and left him to die by the elements on a mountain. However, a shepherd rescued the boy and carried him to another region where he was reared by nobility, who named him Oedipus which means "swollen foot" (the foot is a displaced penis symbol in Freudian thought). In time, as he grew to manhood, Oedipus was to hear from the oracle that he would someday slay his father. Thinking his stepfather was his real progenitor, he left the region by chariot only to meet Laius on a narrow road. After a disagreement over the right-of-way Oedipus unknowingly killed his father. Later, thanks to the heroic act of solving the riddle of the Sphinx, Oedipus was made king of Thebes and thereby took Jocasta, his mother, as wifely queen. Years passed, and eventually the oracle made known the true relationship of mother and son to the two principles of our drama. Jocasta put an end to her life by hanging, and Oedipus blinded himself by puncturing the pupils of both eyes.[133] Freud now uses this term Oedipus to describe a *complex* (an "ideational content" or collection of ideas[134]) which both males and females carry about within their unconscious minds, and which they actually lived through as follows:

Male Oedipus Complex. In the case of the boy, along about his third year of life in the phallic stage, we find a re-enactment (repetition) of the primordial lusting for the female in the home (the mother). The boy senses pleasurable stimulations from his penis erotogenic zone, and he also has some inclination that this region is tied to mother in a physical way. Thus: ". . . he becomes his mother's lover. He wishes to possess her physically in such ways as he has divined from his observations and intuitions about sexual life. . . ."[135] Freud relied here on the role of intuition, and we can see the possible role of inherited mental contents from antiquity in the unconscious (see p. 32). For example, through the law of *talion* (animalistic retribution in kind), Freud argued that the child senses a countermeasure of hostility in the father for the cathecting of mother as object.[136] The son is lusting after the mother in the primitive horde re-enactment, and he senses the early prohibition with its threat of castration for those who violate the father's wishes. A *castration fear* is thus generated in the four-year-old child, by way of this intuitive grasp of the law of talion.[137] This establishes what Freud called the *castration complex* as an adjunct feature of the Oedipus complex. With each rise in the level of mother cathexis (the more libido the boy sends her way), there is a concomitant rise in fear lest the father emasculate the son. The ego is the most intimidated portion of the personality. It tries to head off the id, but as we know, the latter's needs are unreasonably insatiable. Things look increasingly bad for the boy.

When things are the blackest, and the fear is the greatest, a solution is found by the boy who essentially sells out his interest in his mother, reverts from object choice to identification, and rather than continuing his lust for mother, he takes in (introjects) the father's superego standards. Since the father's ideals also represent the cultural norm, the boy gets "civilized." The male conscience is born of fear. Although the son had had a warm feeling for his father before the phallic period, and he had doubtless begun to identify with the father somewhat out of this love, the final act of paternal identification is literally a matter of self-defense, born of fear. "Conform or be castrated"

is the civilizing rule. This is why Freud said that the superego is the "heir of the Oedipus complex."[138] In terms of libido theory, what happens is that a great wave of *anticathexis* sets in, which not only deflects the boy's interest away from the mother (represses his lustful id promptings), but from *all* members of the opposite sex (heralding the beginning of latency). Men do not recall their own lustful desires for their mothers because out of castration fear they have succeeded in putting this all down into the darkest regions of their unconscious. The ego triumphs by giving birth to the superego, but this is rarely a total victory. Virtually every man suffers some remnant of his Oedipal conflict. But if he does not resolve this issue pretty much as outlined, he is surely doomed to a life of neurosis.

Female Oedipus Complex. Some of his students have called this the "Electra complex," basing their analogy on the mythological tale of a slaying of a mother which was instigated and abetted by a revengeful daughter (Electra), but Freud specifically rejected this term and its mythological parallel.[139] Freud was uncertain in his theory of female sexuality, and it is fair to say that psychoanalysis is predominantly a theory of male psychology. He did not believe that girls experience the great fear of the mother that we witnessed of the father in the boy's Oedipal complex. The pre-Oedipal attachment of a daughter to her mother was far more important in the development of a girl, and it is only much later that a hostility and competitiveness with the mother might set in. Put another way, girls do not have a castration *fear* in their Oedipal complex, because they lack a penis which is under the threat of removal. What they do have is a *penis envy* and a basic sense of inferiority because they assume that they have *already been* castrated—either by nature, or by one of their parents (the mother is usually seen as this culprit after a period of time).[140]

The course of feminine development is now

seen as the result of just how the girl can work out the substitutes and sublimations of her "lost penis." The healthiest solution in the Freudian view is simply that the little girl find in her father's penis an adequate substitute, cathect it with libido, and thereby come in time to identify with her mother's role in the family. This gives us a certain parallel with masculine psychology, because this makes the little girl her father's lover. Many Freudians use this framework today, and say that there is a hostile competitiveness between the maturing girl and the mother, over who will *really* be the father's genital partner. They surmise that Freud believed this competition set up a comparable level of fear to the boy's, and that in this way the anticathexes of latency set in with roughly equivalent force for both sexes. Actually, though Freud *did* feel feminine identification was furthered in the competition with mother,[141] he *did not* formulate such a neat parallel with masculine identification in his outlook.

Freud's theoretical problem was that he did not have that mounting crescendo of fear on which to base the crystallization of the superego for the girl. He vacillated about just how much trouble this affords the female, noting that it does little harm if she does not fully resolve her Oedipal attitudes in one context,[142] but stressing in others that she really has a more difficult Oedipal maturation than the boy.[143] The major sublimation which the girl effects in time is to substitute a desire for a *baby* for a desire for a penis.[144] Both heterosexual desire and motherly love spring from the root of penis envy. The normal, healthy progression for the girl is thus: castration acceptance *to* penis envy *to* cathect father's penis and identify with mother *to* desire for a father-substitute's penis (i.e., husband) *to* desire for a baby.

But what about the superego as heir to the Oedipal complex? If girls do not have castration fear how can they get their superegos firmly in place? Well, they really cannot, and in Freudian psychology they do not. Speaking of women, Freud observes:

Their super-ego is never so inexorable, so impersonal, so independent of its emotional origins as we require it to be in men. Character-traits which critics of every epoch have brought up against women—that they show less sense of justice than men, that they are less ready to submit to the great exigencies of life, that they are more often influenced in their judgements by feelings of affection or hostility—all these would be amply accounted for by the modification in the formation of their super-ego which we have inferred above.[145]

Women sublimate less often than do men,[146] which would account for the fact that it is the man who has been the prime mover of civilization. Women, to be frank, are lesser creatures in the Freudian world view.

LATENCY PSYCHOSEXUAL STAGE

Both sexes eventually do "forget" (repress) their parental Oedipal attachments.[147] Thus, along about age six to eight and lasting until pubescence, which may make its onset from age 10 to as late as 14, we note a diminution of sexuality in the growing child. Freud called this the *latency* period.[148] The child renounces the infantile sexual aims and substitutes a feeling of "affection" for the lust he once directed toward the parent of the opposite sex to his own. In desexualizing his heterosexual attachments the child reflects the fact that his sexual instincts have been "inhibited in their aim."[149]

An important feature of latency concerns the growing hold which the reality principle has on the child's life. As this more realistic approach to life is being furthered by the ego through secondary process thought, the baser sexual promptings are redirected from the external world back into the personality structure itself, including members of the sex which look like the self. Thus, during the latency period the child begins turning to imaginative play (sublimated libido) with members of his own sex (projected self-image onto other humans "who look like me").[150] We again have the phenomenon of a reverting to the more primitive identification from object choice, as little boys solidify their identities as *males* and little girls as *females;* they "hate" the other sex (reaction formation) and wish only to play and be with members of their own sex (which means "with myself," via autoerotic use of libido). Object choice has been successfully eclipsed for the time being.

Freud did not believe that latency was an inevitable development in every person's life. He notes that in some life histories the latency period has been skipped entirely. He also stressed that the course of the latency period is not always uniform, and the cessation of sexual promptings might not be observed at every point along the way.[151] Some children, particularly depending upon their environmental stimulation, have incidents of overt sexual play during this latency period. However, by and large, the principle of a diminished sexuality is the case for children in this age span. One last point concerning latency: there is always the clear implication in psychoanalysis that a contribution is made to latency by biological factors. Freud referred to sexual development as a two-stage or *diphasic* process, which begins very early in life and is then interrupted by the latency period, before burgeoning forth again at pubescence. This diphasic process he referred to as a "biological peculiarity" of the human species,[152] but one which did not function unless it was nurtured in a certain sociocultural climate: "The period of latency is a physiological phenomenon. It can, however, only give rise to a complete interruption of sexual life in cultural organizations which have made the suppression of infantile sexuality a part of their system. This is not the case with the majority of primitive peoples."[153]

PUBESCENCE AND ADOLESCENCE

Pubescence is the period in maturation when humans begin to take on the mature physical characteristics of sexuality, including pubic hair, the production of semen in the male, and menstruation and enlarged breasts in the female. This period heralds the onset of genitality —true reproduction is now possible—and when this transformation in the body is completed humans enter the adolescent period, which is usually considered to fall between the ages of 12 and 20 years. Primitive peoples often have puberty rites, which ceremonially introduce the child into adulthood with much fanfare and recognition. Often, this is tied to a religious theme, as in the *bar mitzvah* of the modern Hebrew religion. But in the main the adolescent period is a time of uncertainty and stress for most individuals because of the rapidly changing demands being put upon the growing young adult, who sometimes feels neither fish nor fowl as he tries to work out his place in the scheme of things. Freud did not devote very much of his writings to adolescence *per se,* doubtlessly due to the fact that he had already fixed personality establishment by the time of puberty. One must always go back to the first five years if he is really to understand a personality system in Freudian terms.[154]

Puberty, said Freud, initiated the second step in the diphasic human sexual development. The sexual instinct now makes known the full strength of its demands.[155] Due to the changes in internal physical secretions of the various sexual hormones associated with pubescence, the actual amount of libido "accumulated" in the cathexes and anticathexes of the Oedipal resolution is increased.[156] What this amounts to is an exacerbation of the Oedipal conflict, which flares up again but in a somewhat modified form.[157] Unless a neuroticism is involved, the usual manifestation of this flare-up is that the young person falls in love with an older person of the opposite sex (adolescent "crush"),[158] a teacher, a cinema star, or a political figure. Adolescents are also noted for their sense of emotional commitment, and Freud would have viewed this characteristic as sublimation of libido into political causes, public demonstrations, or the desire to make this a better world.

In addition to the sublimation of libido

(Eros) in the sociopolitical criticisms of adolescence, we can also see a manifestation of the Death Instinct, in the *hostility* (component instinct) which adolescents often manifest. They are "angry" young men and women. Their hostility can also be channeled into antisocial behaviors like delinquency.[159] The opposite can also be seen in that sometimes all instinctual promptings are dismissed and repressed "out of sight," even to the point of reaction-formations like the pursuit of asceticism, vows of celibacy, the need for solitude, the attraction to mystical philosophies, religions, and esoteric cults—literally, a renunciation of the sensory or material world. But the average adolescent will, in time, find a substitute for his parental objects in the heterosexual dating and petting partners of the adolescent years. The adolescent will thus fall in love—probably several times—and eventually marry one of his heterosexual partners as he achieves adulthood.

Most modern theorists who have studied the adolescent stress the latter's reliance on his peer group. Although he did not address himself directly to the question of adolescence, Freud *did* place great stress on the role of group factors in man's behavior. Freud described man as "a horde animal, an individual creature in a horde led by a chief."[160] Freud analogized from the family once again and saw in the group leader a father substitute just as he had seen this projection in the God concept. Man takes in the values of the culture all the more because as he matures he finds with his "brother citizens" a common paternal substitute with whom to identify. In developing a group interest the adolescent is therefore merely reflecting the ingroup identification tendency which he will carry on for the rest of his life.

ADULTHOOD AND GENITALITY

Adulthood or the *genital phase* of psychosexual development is the period in which complete genital gratification can be realized in virtually any culture. Freud emphasized that the female's *second* phase in the diphasic sexual development had to be a feminine one, whereas initially she had been a "little man." To accomplish this shift the girl's erotogenic zone moves from the clitoris ("little penis") to the vaginal area proper, which occurs during and following pubescence.[161] As this takes place the maturing woman becomes increasingly passive (feminine) and receptive to the advances of the male, finding ultimate satisfaction in the possession of his penis as a lover, and the bearing of his child.

Freud was fully aware that the mere pursuit of genital gratification would never bring lasting happiness in adulthood. If two people marry and feel *only* sexual lust for one another (cathect one another with ample supplies of libido) this union will probably not last. Sexual gratifications, after all, result in a removal of cathexis as the lust is sated.[162] This is what we mean by romantic love or a passing affair. Freud therefore concluded that to last, a mature love must be based on *both* lustful desire *and* aim-inhibited lust or "feelings of affection," like the one we had for our parents in latency.[163] Quite often marriages are consummated under the initial drive of lust, and then in time a growing sense of affection (aim-inhibited lust) partially replaces this exclusively sensual zeal. If only aim-inhibited ties of affection were involved in the marriage, then the love would be platonic. Freud did not favor the platonic pattern for most people because instincts should be satisfied and a complete renunciation or aim-inhibition (aim-inhibited lust) is not consistent with this outcome.

FIXATION AND REGRESSION

Freud based his theory of personality and also mental illness on the particular way in which people passed through the psychosexual stages. Since the libido theory was developed concurrently with this developmental view of personality we must give the libido construct a bit more consideration at this point. What kind of energy is libido? How can we conceptualize it —as a liquid, a gas, or a solid? If we were to employ an appropriate analogy to describe libido we could not do better than to think of it as an electrical stream or river of energizing fluid without actual substance. In the most revealing passages on the fixation and regression of libido Freud makes a direct analogy with a stream of water or river bed.[164] He was fond of using the phrase "psychical damming-up," which he took from Lipps,[165] and the reader will find the modern Freudian referring to dammed-up libido as one way of expressing repression (cathexis dammed up by anticathexis).

Thus, libido energizes the personality structure in two ways: (1) there is always the suggestion of an electrical charge being carried through the organism in some fashion, and (2) it takes on hydraulic properties of force which we ordinarily associate with liquid. Actually, since libido is a construct which has no measurable referent in experience, the complete explication of its properties was never realized. One has the impression that Freud initially took it as an energizer which "might" someday be "found" or properly measured; but in time this seems to have become less important to him and in the end it is obvious that he is simply using the term libido to organize his thoughts in an analogical fashion.

Even so, Freud was always very emphatic on the importance of considering the role of such "quantitative factors" on behavior. Any single individual has just so much libido at his disposal. Since man does not have an unlimited supply of this precious mental fuel, that aspect of the personality structure which has relatively the most at its disposal can accomplish the most, get its needs answered the most, or keep mentally active the most.[166] The artist who sublimates libido into his art form must take it away from something else, and hence invariably his heterosexual adjustment will be tamed to an extent. Moreover, if libido is dammed up over time in the evolution of personality, then a psychosexual stage which has trapped this libido must necessarily have more to say about the ultimate coloring of that particular personality

structure, the style of behavior it will manifest, and so forth. Another way of putting this is that its fuero (see p. 45) makes a claim on today from out of yesterday.

This trapping of libido during a psychosexual stage is what we mean by *fixation*. Freud noted that the pathway to adulthood through the psychosexual stages is never without pitfalls, and various life circumstances can therefore cause a fixation or a psychical damming-up of libido at one or another of the psychosexual levels.[167] Although he once said that a heterosexual form of libido was not awakened until the second to the fourth year of life,[168] libido as the energy of Eros is surely active from the beginning of life: hence, a trapping or a fixating of libido might take place at any level in maturation. We have tried to schematize the concept of a "river of libido," emanating from a point at birth and moving on up to pubescence in Figure 6. Note that the river moves from the top of the figure to the bottom, passing through the various psychosexual stages, and that it has a number of "fixation pockets" which have gathered their own quota of libido, as if a river had lost some of its content via a small tributary, forming a pond or a small lake on its course along the lay of the land. Freud makes clear that fixation is related to *primal* repression, or the initial attempt to anticathect, so that the fixation points of Figure 6 are like the original strangulators of the Breuer-Freud model.

There are many reasons why the mind allows a modicum of libido to be attached to an earlier stage of development like this. Hereditary and constitutional factors can predispose a person to fixate,[169] but the strength of Freudian theory lies in his noting how various psychological factors can lead to this outcome. Some critics feel that the theory is too all-inclusive and indiscriminate on this point, since both traumatic situations in childhood[170] or tender situations in childhood[171] can lead to the fixation of libido at these earlier periods. A child who is completely rejected by the mother in the oral phase may fixate libido at this level, or the child who

Figure 6
Fixation of Libido and Regression

Figure 6 — Fixation of Libido and Regression

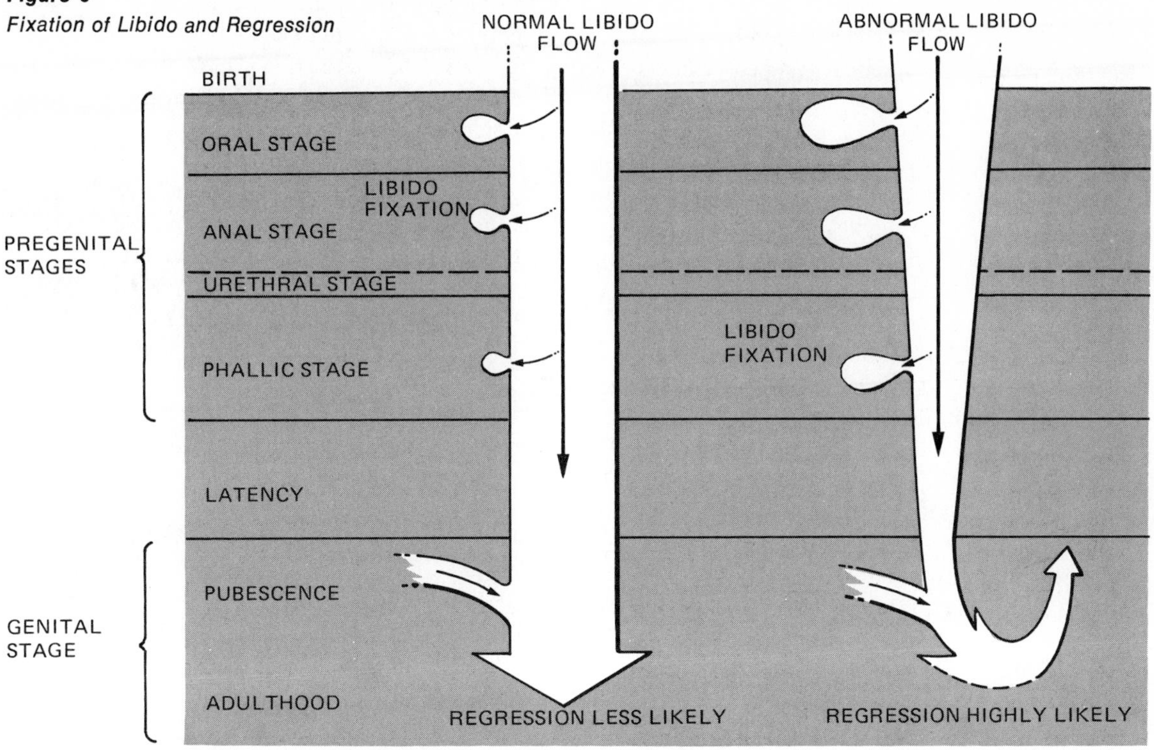

is overindulged by the mother with excessive "sensual sucking" may fixate.[172]

Possibly the matter can be clarified if we realize that a damming-up of libido (fixation) has the characteristic of a *frustration*. A need is not being met, an object has been cathected, but due to anticathexis the need is frustrated.[173] Thus, if a child is mistreated he can be thought of as frustrated, possibly even in the sense of wanting to strike back and to kill the rejecting parent, but being restrained in this id prompting (Death Instinct at root) by an anticathexis (which says unconsciously: "You cannot kill and hope to go on living yourself"). Alternately, a child who has been pampered and petted during one of the stages experiences frustration when he is finally called on to mature and to forgo these narcissistic pleasures. The anticathexis which the ego levels at the id

now has the quality of repressing autoerotic (pleasurable) impulses and might be thought of as the mandate to stop sucking his thumb or some such. Either of these frustrating situations can lead to a primal repression, hence fixation.

Note the two courses of libido outlined in Figure 6. Both examples have three levels of fixated libido, but the "abnormal" course has larger pools of libido being fixated, and consequently the stream of libido available at adulthood is considerably less. Pubescence adds a significant amount to both streams, as if there had been a confluence of rivers during this time, but even so, the abnormal individual simply has less libido to run on than the normal individual. This example should demonstrate that (1) virtually no one gets through development to adulthood without *some* minor fixations having taken place; (2) the greater the fixations (the more libido dammed up) and the *earlier* these serious fixations occur, the more abnormal an individual's subsequent adjustment is likely to be. Since he has less of the precious energy on which to run he becomes more vulnerable to life's experiences, which translates into the possibility that even more fixations are assured as he moves along through subsequent stages. The process feeds on itself, until such time when a frustration in adulthood completely reverses the flow of libido into what Freud called an involution or a *regression*.[174] That is, when the adult (or any age-level person for that matter) meets frustration in the present, this blocking turns the flow of libido around, as when a "stream of water . . . meets with an obstacle in the river-bed is dammed up and flows back into old channels. . . ."[175]

The completely irritated adult who "goes to pieces" in a temper tantrum or a crying spell is reflecting regressive behavior. The "hotheaded" teenager who is ready to engage in a fight at the slightest provocation is also reflecting regressive behavior. Recall that Freud had used this concept of regression in Figure 3's schematization as a return of "excitations" to the sensory input of the mind, to explain the origin of dreams and hallucinations (see p. 31). It was a comparatively easy matter to see in this process of a "reversal" in mentality the additional likelihood of a return to past times in the mind's eye. Note that the dotted arc of Figure 3 dips down into the unconscious regions. Since the unconscious is timeless any kind of dammed-up or choked-off libidinal development would have its fuero-like effects known down there, in the depths of our mental being.

Freud was fond of using as an analogy to mind the stratified levels of Rome, the "eternal city" which is constructed of layer upon layer, city ruin upon city ruin, open to all manner of archaeological excavation.[176] So too with the mind. No matter when something had taken place in the past it was open to study today because "the primitive mind is, in the fullest

meaning of the word, imperishable."[177] Freud employed the term topographical for these spatial layers in mind, and he spoke of *topographical regression* whenever he meant the return of libido across these levels. If an adult returns completely to an earlier psychical state and becomes infantile as a whole person his case would be *temporal regression*. And if only certain primitive methods of behavior are partially replacing the more mature methods which we ought to be using in the present, then this instance was considered *formal regression*. Practically speaking, Freud did not make much of this refinement in regression theory but stressed that all three are part of the same mechanism.

INDIVIDUAL DIFFERENCES CONSTRUCTS

ADULT CHARACTER OR PERSONALITY PATTERNS

Whether he called it a fuero or a Darwinian stage of ontogenetic evolution, Freud was much taken with the theoretical device of an earlier period influencing a present period. Literally *anything* which had happened in the past could act as a *prototype* influence on the present. This proclivity for a prototypical influence from the past is also reflected in Freud's explanation of personality—or *character*, which is the term he used. Since we *all* have fixated libido at one or another of the levels of psychosexual development, the amount and the level at which it was dammed up might well color the personality which we now exhibit as an adult. If *person A* has fixated a moderate amount of libido in the oral phase, while *person B* has done the same in the anal, then the differences in their style of behavior today should be in part traceable to the nature of the stages wherein their personalities were anchored to the past.[178]

Hence, by *personality* Freud means the working out of conflicts among the id, superego, and ego,[179] including the instinctual promptings which exert pressure on the mind; the repressions, sublimations, and reaction-formations of these impulsions;[180] and the kinds of compromises which can be worked out across the topographical levels of mind. Let us now review some typologies which Freud suggested might be observed among all peoples. Each of these followed the pattern we referred to in the Introduction of first being cited as a typology and then later moving to a trait designation (from the "anal personality" to "traits of anality" in all persons, more or less).

ORAL PERSONALITY

We might expect the orally fixated person to stress all those activities involving the taking-in of things from the external world, particularly by way of the mouth. Since he is therefore more likely to be influenced by than influence others, the oral personality is usually considered a passive, dependent, subservient personality type. He is more the follower than the leader. This fixation occurs during a rather carefree time of life. Hence, the oral adult character structure is more optimistic than pessimistic. Indeed, this individual is likely to be trusting, accepting, and even a little gullible. He has identified interpersonal love with eating, so that often this personality type does a lot of eating—which, of course, puts weight on him. The stereotype of the affable, chubby, pleasantly loquacious gourmand fits this personality type very well. "Everyone loves a fat man!" Think of how the Santa Claus image would suffer with each pound of weight the jolly little fat man would shed!

Since he relies so much on others the frustrated oral personality is prone to feel "blue" and depressed when things go wrong. If we were to stress the cannibalistic features of this phase (eating mother's milk), an oral type might be hostile, or "sadistic,"[181] but by and large the *main* suggestion of orality is passivity and acceptance of what the world has to offer. These people are more likely to be "lovers" than "haters," since the period at which they have fixated some libido is predominantly a time of gratification. They are also prone to identify

with people from whom they receive what are sometimes called *external supplies,* making them all the more likely to be interpersonally docile and conforming.

ANAL PERSONALITY

Freud named three characteristics of the anal personality, and we can see in each of these a persistence—or a remnant—of an attitude associated with bowel training. Thus, Freud said anal personalities have the characteristics of *orderliness* (concern over having cleaned the anus following evacuation, not "soiling" one's pants), *parsimoniousness* (wanting to hoard money and other valuable items, just as the child once wanted autoerotically to hoard and cherish its own fecal matter), and *obstinacy* (negativism engendered in parent-child relationship over the toilet training so that now the child refuses parental pleas to "go potty").[182] Recall also that the toilet situation is the *first* time our external world places definite requirements on us, intruding upon our autoerotic satisfactions, and asking that we begin laying down the outline of a superego in our personality. Fecal matter is, in a manner of speaking, the first *gift* which the child has for the parent, as something which he has created entirely from his own effort.[183]

In fact, feces can become a kind of economic barter between parent and child. If mother loves baby, baby gives feces when coaxed to do so on the potty; if mother rejects baby, baby withholds feces in retribution. For this reason Freud took fecal content in dreams as symbolizing something very valuable, as money,[184] or in the case of females it can symbolize a baby.[185] Misers are anal adults, for they want to retain money (derivative of feces). People who hoard just about anything have traits of anality. The anal personality is not so loving or passive as the oral personality. Anality can be a helpful personality tendency for those professions which demand an orderly approach, such as lawyers who must track down every last detail in making their case presentations. The anal per-

sonality is often asocial and selfish, but he is to
that extent self-sufficient, whereas the oral person, who is usually socially very engaging, can
become a clinging, dependent individual. The
anal person is thus more likely to emerge as a
leader than the oral type. Of course, excessive
anality can lead to overconcern with detail, a
narrow, constricted view of life, and a hostile
suspiciousness of the other fellow's point of
view which we can identify in the "Scrooge"
image of Dickens' *Christmas Carol.*

URETHRAL PERSONALITY

Freud noted that certain of his clients who had
suffered the humiliation of enuresis as a child
acquired a burning ambition to succeed in
life.[186] Rather than fighting through life's annoyances in the head-on manner of the anal
personality, the urethral character is likely secretly to envy the success of others and to look
for a quick success of his own. If he cannot attain easy success on the first attempt, he finds it
difficult to try again.[187] Thus, the urethral personality has built his competitiveness on a
strong underlying sense of inferiority ("You
can't even hold yourself back from wetting
your pants"), and though he strives to overcome this personal failing (react-formates) his
bid is often unsuccessful because he crumbles
when the going gets roughest. If he is a male,
he never really feels potent in the heterosexual
sense of being a "man's man."[188]

PHALLIC PERSONALITY

The phallic personality pattern developed by
an individual takes as its prototype the particular way in which the individual works through
the Oedipal situation. If the Oedipal situation is
completely unresolved, or greatly deviant from
the common pattern, then we would doubtless
be confronted with a neurotic adult. However,
partial fixations and the female's rather subdued working through of this level result in
personality predilections falling short of an actual neurosis. Since masturbation with an opposite sexed parent as object first emerges in
this psychosexual stage we would expect this

adult character type to value heterosexual sensual pleasure. This adult might be flirtatious,
concerned with looking attractive to the opposite sex, and even by that token appearing
rather self-centered and egotistical. The coquette and the "lady's man" would fall here.
The Don Juan stereotype captures the phallic
theorotype rather well. Heterosexual love is
more colored by lust than affection, and in fact
this character type is basically narcissistic. These
people may masturbate when tense or upset.

In some cases the male revolts against his
castration fears, and then we note in the adult
a revolutionary type of personality, who might
well generalize this tendency and violate social
conventions.[189] Often sexual promiscuity is a
major feature of such antisocial acting-out. Another phallic variant is the case of a female who
may refuse to accept the fact that she has no
penis. She may develop what Freud termed a
masculinity complex, and go on acting like a
male, retaining her aggressive clitoridal pleasure
and renouncing the passive vaginal pleasures of
femininity.[190] As an adult, she might be the
career woman who seeks her place in a man's
world. These types are sometimes referred to as
"castrating women" because the suggestion is
that they wish to take a man's penis for their
own (show him up at the office, defeat him in
a court case, and so forth). If the masculine
identification is extreme we might even witness
a homosexual tie, so that a greatly masculinized
woman might well find her sensual pleasure
playing husband to another female.[191]

Freud's psychological explanations of the
origin of homosexuality varied somewhat over
the years, and he was always careful to note
that genetic or hereditary propensities probably
contributed to this condition. His theory of female homosexuality is particularly unclear, but
we might take a look at the most common male
homosexual theory advanced.

Homosexuality begins in the phallic phase
for the boy, even though his actual decision for
a lasting homosexual adjustment is presumably
not made until around the onset of pubescence.[192] In order to explain homosexuality in

the male Freud made use of the now familiar theoretical device of reverting from object-choice to identification. Recall that interpersonal identification (which is an oral-stage mechanism) is considered more primitive than interpersonal object choice (which begins in the parental cathexis of the phallic phase). The homosexual boy is one who has been very close to and presumably pampered, doted over, greatly protected by a maternal figure. Rather than taking this mother as object in the phallic phase, thereby initiating the normal Oedipal complex, the male invert reverts from object choice and *identifies* with his mother. He thereby not only becomes feminized in his outlook, but he also seeks to re-enact the mother-son love pattern that he had enjoyed, playing the mother's part himself and using other boys as *his* substitute.[193] As he moves into latency, therefore, his sexual instincts may be less aim inhibited than normal boys. Other males are really projections of himself, and he seeks to cathect them with libido as stand-ins for himself. Homosexuality and narcissism are therefore related phenomena, because what the homosexual is seeking is a narcissistic self-love through loving himself in other males.[194]

LATENCY, ADOLESCENT AND GENITAL PERSONALITIES

Since the personality structure is finalized by the onset of latency—approximately age six years[195]—Freud had no need to evolve a latency or adolescent personality type. The important figures in our lives, our parents, siblings, related family members and hired helpers who had dealt with us in the formative years now act as *imagos,* against which we will be measuring the behavior of everyone we meet throughout life. An imago is thus a kind of "people prototype," and Freud observed that all of the person's later friendship and love choices "follow upon the basis of the memory-traces left behind by these first prototypes."[196] We thus re-enact (repetition compulsion of instincts) our very earliest patterns throughout life.

Some psychoanalysts do speak about the *genital character organization,* but this too is one of those unfulfilled pictures in Freudian theory. All this means, really, is that the person is finally capable of reproduction, and presumably can find in sexual relations the satisfaction which he had obtained earlier from the pre-genital erogenous zones. Of course, not all humans pass through the earlier levels smoothly enough to find sexual relations gratifying. Many women in particular find sex degrading and "dirty" due to the contents of their superego instruction as children. Interestingly enough, Freud viewed the sexual organs as "animalistic," as that part of human physiognomy which had not altered in evolution from its original shape in the state of lower existence.[197] Even so, he felt that heterosexual intercourse was an important aspect of human self-realization. Freud simply could not see the value of celibacy,[198] and the supposed love of mankind (altruism) which religious or socialistic political leaders often voiced he took to be a convenient smokescreen for the underlying hatred of an out-group.[199] He viewed altruistic love as *entirely* aim inhibited, derived basically from genital lust but not really a natural solution to the instinctual prompting. Freud once said that he could not see universal love as man's highest form of behavior, and then he added dourly: "A love that does not discriminate seems to me to forfeit a part of its own value, by doing an injustice to its object; and secondly, not all men are worthy of love."[200]

Psychopathology and Psychotherapy

THEORY OF ILLNESS

ANTITHETIC IDEAS AND COUNTERWILL

At about the time of his first publication with Breuer, and in fact, even before the Breuer-Freud "Preliminary Communication" on hysteria (1893) made its appearance, Freud put out a small paper under his name alone, entitled "A Case of Successful Treatment by Hypnotism."[201] In this what seems to be his very first attempt at explaining how a hysterical symptom like Anna O.'s anaesthetic arm might arise, Freud made use of a psychological theory without employing mental energies, though he did have a physical involvement (symptom) in the view. Freud begins by noting that there are two kinds of ideas which have an affect (emotion) or expectation connected with them: (1) *intentions* to do some specific thing in the future, and (2) *expectations proper,* which are ideas of what might actually happen to us in that future. The extent of affect attached to these anticipatory ideas is a function of how important the activity we are about to engage in is to us, and the amount of subjective uncertainty we have about the outcome. We are more emotionally involved in an upcoming school examination which will determine our future careers than we are about a tennis match we have to engage in this afternoon with a friend, whom we expect to trounce as usual in any case.

Now, this aspect of *subjective uncertainty* regarding the content of ideas we hold about our future performance is what prompted Freud to suggest the development of what he called *distressing antithetic ideas.*[202] To quote Freud's example of a distressing antithetic idea: " 'I shall not succeed in carrying out my intention because this or that is too difficult for me and I am unfit to do it; I know, too, that certain other people have also failed in a similar situation.' "[203] We all have such antithetic ideas as we undertake life's challenges; the normal person is able to suppress and inhibit them thanks to "the self-confidence of health"; but the neurotic unfortunately has lost his confidence and submits to their influence.[204] Freud was using the term *suppression* at this time, saying that neurotics are unable to suppress these antithetic ideas and consequently they end up losing motivation to try to succeed, they become depressed, and in some cases they even

do precisely the opposite of what they are really intending to do. It was as if a *counterwill* within the personality was making itself known by forcing the patient to do the opposite of what he or she was intending to do.[205]

Thus, Freud tells of a case of hysteria in which a woman (Frau Emmy von N.) made an uncontrollable clacking sound with her tongue and lips (hysterical tic). Freud was able to trace the origin of this symptom to a time when, exhausted with worry and fatigue while nursing a sick child, the woman told herself that she must not make any noise lest she disturb the sleep into which the child had just fallen. But in her exhausted state the antithetic ideas that she *would* make a noise took the upper hand and, in spite of her attempts to suppress it, she began to clack her tongue. Moreover, the symptom persisted and generalized so that she was embarrassed with its appearance in several situations having nothing to do with the daughter. Freud said the symptom had thus become fixated in her behavior for many years.[206] Charcot's famous student Pierre Janet had used a concept of the *fixed idea,* which is obviously similar to this treatment of the antithetic idea. Janet said that, due probably to some undiscovered physiological mechanism, certain people *dissociate* an idea and then this fixed idea operates on its own, outside of the control of consciousness.[207] Freud may well have been influenced here by the French, but his concept adds the important psychological explanation of how such ideas arise—namely, *as antitheses to intentions.*

We all have antisocial promptings of one sort or another which we consciously refrain from acting out, thanks to the healthy state of our ego control. Are these antithetic promptings over a life span lost to the mind? No, they are not: ". . . they are stored up and enjoy an unsuspected existence in a sort of shadow kingdom, till they emerge like bad spirits and take control of the body, which is as a rule under the orders of the predominant ego-consciousness."[208] We recognize the "shadow kingdom" of this quote as the unconscious mind. Thus mass hysteria among the clergy in the Middle Ages had seemed to be daemonic possessions: all of the blasphemies and erotic language which the religiously devout had laboriously suppressed now burst forth as the loss of ego identity in the masses generated a hypnotic effect (suggestion), releasing the control of consciousness and allowing the counterwill (system of antithetic ideas) to be expressed.

COITUS INTERRUPTUS AND CHILDHOOD MOLESTATION

Since antithetical ideas are intentions which we *do not* wish to carry out, they must bear some meaningful import in opposition to what we consider proper or acceptable behavior. They must be at odds with our conscious ego structures. Freud was fully aware of this conflict, and, as we have seen, in time he was to find that invariably a sexual experience was somehow involved in the mental dynamic. Two of his earliest sexual theories of illness are of historical interest because they are really somewhat more physically based than we ordinarily expect from Freud. Freud is searching about for a straightforward physical explanation of the relationship between the sexual incidents his patients are telling him about, and the resultant incidence of neuroses among such sexually aberrant life histories.

One of the complaints he often heard, especially from patients suffering an anxiety neurosis, was that they could not obtain gratification in sexual intercourse. A female patient could not achieve climax because she feared having children. A male patient became hysterically ill during a period when his wife had a physical illness and thus sexual intercourse was curtailed.[209] Freud referred to this sexual frustration as *coitus interruptus,* and he felt that possibly a kind of sexual *noxa* (harmful substance) was set loose in the body during the time when a sexual need (he did not speak of instincts at this time) failed to be gratified.[210] He did not always attempt to trace the psychic

factors which might have led to an inability on the part of some people to copulate successfully. Just *any* interruption was taken as a potentially harmful event, and he thought of this process in fairly mechanical, automatic terms. Though he believed that coitus interruptus was invariably a factor in certain neuroses, he was cautious enough to suggest that possibly a predisposing hereditary factor was also involved.[211]

The second sexual aberration theory which Freud entertained early in his career centered around the belief that neurotics had been molested or seduced into sexual activity before their physical apparatus had matured.[212] He had a series of patients who could recall an early childhood experience of having been either raped or at least sexually fondled by a parent, sibling, relative (uncle, aunt), or possibly a household servant.[213] Accepting these recollections, Freud felt that the premature introduction to sexuality might well have acted like a precipitator of the maladjustment he was then observing in coitus interruptus. Here again, the weight of explanation was on what had happened to the individual in the past. It was just an unhappy accident that the neurotic was molested as a very young child, and his present disturbance was therefore in large measure independent of a direct contribution by him.

The corrected infantile sexual theory was a remarkable example of how to win by losing, and it fixed for all time Freud's commitment to what we have called his Promethean insight. He could make this turnabout because one sees in Freud's speculations a growing weight being given to the role of fantasy (wish fulfillment) in mental life.[214] In his reformulation, the individual is no longer portrayed as an innocent bystander in life's sexual misfortunes. Freud now claims that recollections of seduction scenes are not copies of a past reality but rather the memories of *fantasies* indulged in during what we now call the early phallic phase.[215] While masturbating at this stage the child had fantasied the sexual rape or molestation, then repressed the entire affair following the Oedipal resolution. The memory of a fantasy was subsequently recovered while the patient was in treatment, and taken as fact. Sometimes this experience was indeed a factual recollection, but more often was fantasy confused with reality. The difference between fantasy and fact in the mental recollections of patients in analysis is always difficult to distinguish;[216] but this obscurity makes no difference because psychical reality is what counts, not what may or may not have *factually* happened outside of mind.[217] Thus, rather than rejecting his retrospective method because it had generated false memories, Freud now makes a virtue of the error, and through the concepts of fantasy and wish fulfillment, takes as evidence of infantile sexuality the fact that his patients remember so many *untrue* instances of sexual aberration in their early lives.

THREE-STAGE COMPROMISE MODEL OF MENTAL ILLNESS

Freud eventually settled on what we would like to call a three-stage compromise model of mental illness. His mature view of mental illness retained the kernel ideas of both coitus interruptus and the seduction-to-fantasy theory, added them to the original antithetic idea theory, and then proposed a *deflection* concept which could account for how neurotic (and psychotic) symptoms might arise. The coitus interruptus theory gradually evolved into what Freud called the *actual neuroses*—which were in turn then opposed to the *psychoneuroses proper*. The actual neuroses (neurasthenia, anxiety, and hypochondria) were presumed to be caused by a somatic (bodily) toxic factor, a *physical noxa* much like the one he had earlier attributed to frustrated copulation.[218] The psychoneuroses proper were those disorders (hysterias) which were due to what we will be calling a psychological cause via the compromise model. Since they were due to a physical toxic factor, the actual neuroses were considered unamenable to purely verbal psychoanalysis; the

physician had to prescribe definite changes in sexual routine in order to cure them.[219] Thus in his distinction between a physical (constitutional or hereditary) and a psychological cause of neurosis Freud was still confining *all* of his etiological factors to the sexual bodily sphere. The somatic toxic substance was not a foreign blood protein of undetermined origin, nor was it set loose by some unknown anomaly in the bodily structure. It was strictly a *sexual* function which led to the toxic substance being set loose, and we can see in this the earlier imprint of the coitus interruptus theory.[220]

The seduction theory, which initially had been rather mechanically and physically conceived, progressed—as we have noted, by way of fantasy—to a full-blown psychological explanation of illness in what is called an unresolved or improperly resolved Oedipal complex. Freud was very emphatic in calling the Oedipal the "nuclear" complex of every neurosis.[221] *All neurotics have unresolved Oedipal complexes.* In their present abnormal states the neurotics are re-enacting family situations which have never been properly sublimated, anticathected, or otherwise resolved. Recall that Freud referred to the initial stage of repression as *primal* (see p. 43). Then, later on the individual is forced to keep repressed material down through a continuing repression proper (sometimes called *after-repression* by his students). Neurotics find it impossible to keep Oedipal and other content-memories out of consciousness without also making it known overtly in a symptom. We will now review this process, using the schematization in Figure 7 as a point of reference for the three-stage compromise model of illness.

Note first of all that we retain the mind-body dualism. Symptoms of hysteria, like inactive body parts (Anna O.'s arm) or functional loss of sensation (blindness), are taken to be physical manifestations of psychical causes. The theoretical problem is to show how mind can influence body, and this is really the reverse of the problem Freud dealt with in Figure 5,

Figure 7
Freud's Three-Stage Compromise Model of Mental Illness

STAGE I: PRIMAL REPRESSION IN THE PREGENITAL STAGES

STEP A: Id Prompting (Wish)   STEP B: Ego Defends (Counterwish)

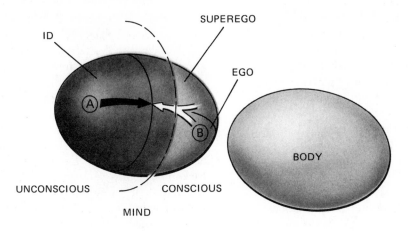

STAGE II: RETURN OF THE REPRESSED CONTENT FOLLOWING PUBESCENCE

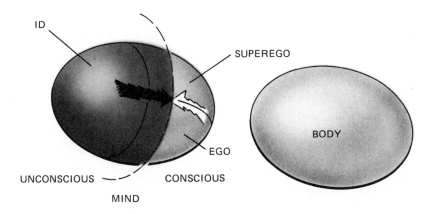

STAGE III: COMPROMISE DEFLECTION (CONVERSION) TO "SYMPTOMS"

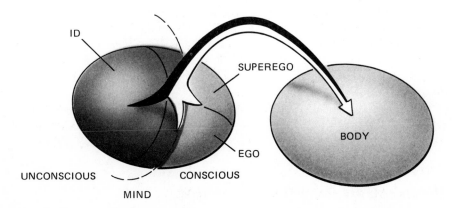

where he utilized the instinct construct to show how body can influence mind (see p. 37).

Stage I of Figure 7 takes place in the pregenital period of life. A hostile feeling for the father or a lustful feeling for the mother might once have occurred and been primally repressed in the child's early life. He represses such an id prompting or id "wish" (intention) using libidinal anticathexes from the ego and whatever aspect of the superego which has been formed by this time. In Figure 7 we have symbolized this repression by putting two steps in under stage I: step A would be the id "wish" and step B would be the countering, defensive "wish" of the ego *not* to carry out the illicit act. Two promptings in mind are opposed, checkmating one another for the time being. We have symbolized this clash in the stressed arrows of stage I, which meet in an unconscious region, probably at the primary censorship point of Figure 3. Stage I thus resolves itself into a *primal* repression, and if things have not been worked out too smoothly at this time (unresolved Oedipal), there would of course have been a concomitant fixation at this same age period.

The stage II of Figure 7 takes place at the close of latency, usually brought by the quantitative increase of libido following pubescence.[222] The inadequately repressed id fantasies (wishes, intentions) of a hostile or sexual nature are thus reinforced with a larger supply of libido in the diphasic completion of sexual maturity (recall that libidinal supplies of the sexual instincts find their entrance into mind through the id region). Freud spoke of this as the *"return of the repressed memories"* (of past fantasies, not necessarily factual happenings), and he noted that it was due to a failure of defense in the case of the neurotic.[223] With this return of repressed thoughts, a continuing repression proper is kept up by the ego, but even this fails. Note that the black arrow in stage II has passed the primary censorship point and is threatening to unload its content (lustful or hostile wishes) into conscious awareness.

Things are in a very bad way for the neurotic, who must express the content in some way but not be consciously aware of what it means. He cannot accept the lust for his mother or the death wishes for his father. But how to turn these "wishes" (intentions) out of mind before having to confront them and act them out in overt, conscious behavior?

To accomplish this feat, said Freud, humans are able to substitute one form of expression for another, thereby deflecting the course of an intention by way of compromise and satisfying both parties to a conflict. The two wishes "strike a bargain" and find some mutually expressive way to make themselves known. As in our step III of Figure 7, the arrow is deflected back into a bodily symptom of neurotic illness which in itself "expresses" the conflict and is party to both sides. Symptoms are thus always compromises[224] and also wish fulfillments.[225]

Precisely how this deflection is accomplished cannot be stated, anymore than we can say exactly how the instinct turns libido free in the mind. Freud called this process *conversion,* which he defined as "the translation of a purely psychical excitation into physical terms."[226] Thus it is that though a neurosis is actually acquired in early childhood, usually before age six, it ordinarily does not make its appearance until years later when a second wave of libido or a second frustration exacerbates the long-standing condition.[227] Freud's definition of a sympton was as follows: "A symptom is a sign of, and a substitute for, an instinctual satisfaction which has remained in abeyance; it is a consequence of the process of repression."[228] The symptom is, in a very real sense, a communication to the environment from the unconscious. It literally says something though the person is not consciously aware of what it is saying. Freud even referred to the *organ speech* of a hypochondriacal symptom.[229]

We might have considered our model in Figure 7 a four-stage model, since we have two "wish" steps in stage I; or, we might have considered stage II identical to stage III because Freud virtually identified "return of the repressed" with "symptom formation."[230] However, the alignment chosen meshes best with our earlier presentations of the Breuer model and the diphasic theory of sexual adjustment. Freud once speculated that this diphasic onset of sexual growth in man—its onset in two waves, with latency intervening—might "perhaps be the biological determinant of his predisposition to neuroses."[231]

We gain the greatest insight into symptoms by appreciating this dual aspect of their manifestation, and the fact that they are invariably compromises (at least, in the psychoneurosis proper) enables the analyst to assign the complete repressed meaning to them. We cannot hide our innermost conflicts from the practiced eye of the analyst. For example, one of Freud's female patients (Dora) suffered from a hysterical throat irritation which caused her to cough incessantly. He traced this physical symptom to an unconscious fantasy in which this 19-year-old girl had thought of performing an act of fellatio, thanks in part to her oral propensities (oral fixations) and doubtless also in part to her Oedipal desires for a penis of her own.[232] The repressed wish (intention) in this instance was probably something like "I would like to perform fellatio" and the repressing wish (counterwill intention) was probably "That is a disgusting thought which makes me sick." The only way to express both wishes here was to develop a mouth-throat involvement in which the oral zone of the fantasy could be partially realized but *also* the punishing wish could obtain gratification in the "sickness" of a sore throat and cough.

We have here a final development of the antithetic idea theory, because in every instance Freud considers from now on he finds a dual intentional involvement. He is convinced that at least certain "illnesses . . . *are* the result of intention."[233] But one never asks in a properly Freudian vein: "What does this symptom stand for?"; he really asks: "What *two* antithetical intentions does this symptom symbolize?"

DIFFERENTIAL DIAGNOSIS

Mental illness is regressive in character. There is a certain *primary* advantage in illness, because the individual can save a modicum of psychic effort by his "flight into illness."[234] He can be cared for and even obtain a secondary advantage (sometimes called secondary gain) from the fact that his illness will upset important people in his life, who in turn may give him extra consideration lasting beyond the period of illness. Thus, a daughter, feeling that her parents are giving too much attention to a sibling, "falls ill" and thereby obtains the spotlight in the home for some time.[235] Freud once compared neurosis to a monastery, as a place of refuge where people can flee when they feel too weak to face life's frustrations.[236]

Freud has a "quantitative" as opposed to a qualitative view of mental illness. He did not draw a hard and fast line between normal and abnormal, or between neurosis and psychosis within the abnormal designation.[237] People fall ill from the very same frustrations that normals bear up under.[238] How then does abnormality arise? Well, first of all we must recall that instinctual promptings cannot be avoided. They emanate from our internal physico-psychic economy, and unlike other stimuli in the environment we cannot flee from the stimulations of the instincts.[239] Hence, if at some point early in life we have fixated libido due to a frustration, and then later as adults suffer a frustration and regress even as we are evolving a mental illness, the nature of the illness will be colored by the (1) initial stage of fixation, (2) the amount of libido fixated initially, and (3) the extent of libido regressed following the second frustration in adulthood.

One of Freud's major theoretical devices for distinguishing one syndrome of illness from another centered on this fixation-regression model.[240] The deeper and more extensive the regression, the more likely that there is a profound disorder, so that by and large the *psychotic* regresses to a greater extent than the neurotic (see Figure 6). *Neurotic* symptoms of *obsessive-compulsivity* are traced to anal fixations; *hysterical* gullibility (taking-in) and other psychophysical reactions centering on the digestive tract (ulcer, alcoholism) are oral stage regressions, and so forth. Just as he could find a myriad number of personality differences in the partial fixation and regression theory, so too could Freud find ways of distinguishing between clinical syndromes in the reenactment of earlier (stage I) fixations of the more severe variety. Since this fixation-depth-of-regression explanation is used to cover both normal and abnormal behavior, it is almost better to distinguish between normal, neurotic, and psychotic adjustments on the basis of how the individual handles reality than on the basis of how deep or extensive his regressions are.

Everyone must confront frustration in life. We also all regress occasionally, and thus any of us might reveal in his regressive behavior the levels at which he had fixated (more or less) libido. But the difference between normal and abnormal regression centers around just what we are attempting to do in the process. The neurotic is running away from reality in his regressive attempts. Freud believed that the neurotic did *not reject* reality, or try to change reality; he merely fled into illness in his act of regression. The psychotic, on the other hand, *rejects* reality. He not only runs away into a regressive illness, but he then tries to reconstruct or alter his reality, to suit his personal fantasies (including fanciful, pleasurable content, or even hostile, threatening contents). The major distinguishing factor between levels of mental illness is the fact that psychotics entertain *delusions* (unrealistically false beliefs) and *hallucinations* (seeing, hearing, etc., things which are not there), whereas neurotics retain a better contact with reality. The *normal* personality combines the best, most constructive features of both clinical syndromes: "We call behaviour

'normal' or 'healthy,' if it combines certain features of both reactions—if it disavows the reality as little as does a neurosis, but if it then exerts itself, as does a psychosis, to effect an alteration of that reality."[241] In short, the normal person fights to keep in contact and to effect a constructive outcome, a change in the external state of things. He neither runs away from a challenge nor does he settle for a dream-world solution, even though he might regress and even act child-like from time to time.

ANXIETY THEORY

Freud based anxiety in the body, as a physical manifestation, and then over the years he attempted to show how it might arise in conjunction with a sexual involvement. The theoretical challenge here was to avoid letting anxiety take over the drive or energizing properties of the organism, in place of libido. Libido as a *mental* energy is what we want to keep in the forefront as the major determiner of man's behavior. How then can we tie a physical sensation into a mental phenomenon or give this physical sensation a mental representation?

Freud's first theory of anxiety was based upon a daring analogy between the physical appearance of sexual copulation and the physical appearance of an *anxiety attack*. After first noting that anxiety must lie in the physical sphere, Freud goes on to say that "*anxiety* has arisen by *transformation* out of accumulated sexual tension. . . ."[242] But at this point (roughly 1894) he has not yet introduced the *mental* concept of libido. Anxiety is a way of physical release, using primarily the mechanisms of breathing, to rid the body of physical stimuli which in themselves cannot be worked over psychically. By "working over" psychically, Freud meant something akin to abreaction. Anxiety could not be worked over mentally but had to be converted from one *physical* pathway into another. As physical sexual tension arose in the body of the anxiety neurotic, who could not for any of a number of reasons carry out an act of sexual intercourse (coitus interruptus), this mounting physical tension could be short-circuited (transformed) into a second physical pathway. Thus, in his anxiety attack, the neurotic manifested the clinical appearance of coitus—heavy breathing, dyspnoea, palpitation—because he was draining off one physical impulse by way of a common pathway in the body.[243] Freud said very clearly that, whereas hysterics convert a psychical excitation (fellatio fantasy) into a physical symptom (hysterical cough), anxiety neurotics convert one physical excitation (sexual tension) into another physical manifestation (anxiety symptom).[244]

Of course, we are speaking now about the case of anxiety in an *actual* neurosis. In the case of an *anxiety hysteria* (psychoneurosis proper), the individual could transform a psychical excitation (libido) into physical excitations (symptoms) along the lines of the compromise model in Figure 7. The earliest physical explanation of anxiety is dropped by Freud within three years of its appearance, and for a considerable length of time he referred to anxiety simply as "transformed libido."[245] Anxiety is now tied to libido, making it a sexual derivative of sorts. The libido has been repressed by the individual for various defensive reasons, and then subsequently converted into a dream with anxious content[246] or into a symptom just like any hysterical symptom.[247] This second anxiety theory was to give Freud some serious problems in time. First of all, it was difficult to explain the type of traumatic neuroses (sometimes called "shell shock") that followed World War II as always reflecting "transformed libido."[248]

The concept of repetition-compulsion, as a desire to repeat and to master the traumatic situation in the past seemed a more accurate description of what took place in these war neuroses than did an explanation basing its rationale on libidinal factors alone. Secondly, Freud had a number of students—Otto Rank as foremost example—who seemed desirous of putting anxiety in the place of libido, as a prime motivator in the organism. In the Freudian view, the neurotic does *not* move *primarily* to avoid anxiety, but rather to avoid facing up to the repressed mental content, which in turn is moved about in the mind by the mental energy of libido.

In 1925, some thirty-odd years after proposing his first theory of anxiety to Fliess in their exchange, Freud settled on the definition of anxiety as "a reaction to a situation of danger."[249] Symptoms of abnormal behavior are now seen as substitutes, as ways of avoiding facing up to a dangerous situation. And how are we signaled to begin developing our stage III symptom? By sensing the physical feeling (affect, emotion) of anxiety. As Freud said: ". . . the ego subjects itself to anxiety as a sort of inoculation, submitting to a slight attack of the illness in order to escape its full strength. It vividly imagines the danger-situation, as it were, with the unmistakable purpose of restricting that distressing experience to a mere indication, a signal."[250]

As Freud was to specify,[251] this interpretation removed anxiety from a restrictive *libidinal* tie. Anxiety need not relate only to the energy of the sexual instincts. Literally *any* situation of danger—real or imagined—could generate anxiety. Actually, only the ego can produce and feel anxiety in Freud's last formulation.[252] The id and superego were not in themselves open to this affective feeling. In fact, Freud's final view of "types of anxiety" parallels what he once called the "three tyrannical masters" of the ego, namely, "the external world, the super-ego, and the id."[253] Each of these sources of influence has its own intentions; they have things which they would like the ego as major personality representative to do, to be, to act out. The harried ego is thus in a constant state of diplomatic relations, trying as executive of the economic structure to avoid the most threatening consequences of any single vested interest. Anxiety is a physical feeling, something other than mind, primarily sensation, but cognitively bearing the stamp of expectation. When we are anxious we have that kind of feeling which suggests "What is going to happen now?" The physical feeling of fear is a more definite emotion, because it has affixed itself to an object.[254] We fear an automobile which is now bearing down on us, but the feeling is anxiety when we are going to the doctor for a check-up. The automobile is a clear danger; the doctor's examination may or may not result in some fearful diagnosis.

Paralleling the harsh masters of the ego, Freud spoke of three forms of anxiety,[255] but he also emphasized their basic similarity in signaling the ego of an impending situation of danger.[256] There is, first of all, the realistic form of anxiety, as when a young man knows that he is to go into battle tomorrow; he is safe for the night, but what of tomorrow? Such *realistic* anxiety takes its prototype from birth anxiety, which is obviously the first major threat of expectation we all experience.[257] Simply growing-up and taking leave of one's parents represents a realistic threat, and this too can be viewed as one of life's realistic anxieties.[258] The second type of anxiety deals with the ego-id relations, and it was termed *neurotic* anxiety. If one has an inadequately resolved Oedipal complex, then the materials which have been anti-cathected can always threaten a return to consciousness following puberty.[259] The thought "I wish mother were dead" might press forward to awareness in the teenaged girl, for example. As we have seen, such neurotic stirrings are often transformed or converted into symptoms.

The final type of anxiety, which takes us into the last topic of this subsection, Freud termed *moral* anxiety. Recall that in Freudian terms, the superego is formed out of fear—the fear of paternal retribution, and to a lesser extent, of maternal retribution. In the father's castration threat to the son there is a form of anxiety which serves as clear prototype of the conscience which the boy later forms. Freud said that castration anxiety develops into moral or "social" anxiety.[260] Hence, all of the moralistic teachings which are introjected by the child can later serve as grounds for calling down the ego as sinful.[261] Guilt is therefore a special

case of anxiety: ". . . the sense of guilt is at bottom nothing else but a topographical variety of anxiety; in its later phases it coincides completely with *fear of the super-ego*."[262]

CULTURE AS PRIME AGENT OF ABNORMALITY

Freud's theory of society and the ways in which man presumably becomes socialized through the Oedipal situation and the superego which has been built on fear and controls by anxiety makes him inevitably base the major cause of mental illness on the demands of civilization.[263] Culture advances thanks to the sublimations of sexual impulse, but people are constrained by this very same culture so that they cannot pursue the animalistic needs which continue to seek expression in acts of hostility and lust.[264] Freud said that he could not form a very high opinion of the way in which society attempts to regulate the problems of sexual life.[265] In most cases, he felt that the individual's superego was overly severe, and it did not adequately grasp the strength of the id promptings which the ego had to bear up under; more generally, the "cultural superego" (norms, values of the group) was too rigid and unrealistic, issuing commands which people find impossible to obey.[266] Thus, society, civilization, culture, and religion *all* melt into one at this point, constricting man by imposing unattainable standards on him. Freud's attitude toward the Golden Rule is interesting in this regard: " 'Love thy neighbour as thyself' is the strongest defence against human aggressiveness and an excellent example of the unpsychological proceedings of the cultural super-ego. The commandment is impossible to fulfil; such an enormous inflation of love can only lower its value, not get rid of the difficulty."[267]

The reason the superego can become so cruel and literally "wish" to destroy the ego, is that as the individual checks his outwardly directed hostility, he makes his ego ideal more *severe*. Freud noted that even ordinary morality has a rather harshly restraining, cruelly prohibiting quality about it in the thou-shalt-not's of formalized religion. Hence, to the extent that we *do not* express our basic natures (hostility, lust), our ego ideals must be elevated, and made more demanding, seeking a higher and higher standard by which to live.[268] Freud's assessment of President Woodrow Wilson's character, including his eventual nervous breakdown, was based in large measure upon such an elevated superego, with the attendant tie to the father as a representative of—and, in fact, identified with—God, who is now carried about from within as ego ideal.[269]

It follows, therefore, that Freud would favor a relaxation in the rigid strictures of religion and other social taboos. Not that he was in any way an advocate of sexual licentiousness and unbridled hostility. His own life was a model of probity and mature conformity to the niceties of polite society. Psychoanalysis as a world view is anything but a philosophy of revelry and instinctual release, which in most instances would be viewed as narcissistic and regressive in tone.[270] But Freud did argue for more insight into the nature of mental illness as a preventative measure, so that child-rearing practices might be better gauged to natural functions, and the excessive repudiation of even immoral dreams might not be continued as if they were tantamount to the overt act.

THEORY OF CURE

THE ROLE OF INSIGHT

If we believe that a neurotic is suffering from hidden meanings buried (repressed) deep in his unconscious, then our tactic of cure should be to provide him an understanding of these hidden meanings. Thus Freud's first theory of cure after his separation from Breuer stressed what has come to be called the *insight* of the client. As Freud then phrased it: "The principal point is that I should guess the secret and tell it to the patient straight out; and he is then as a rule obliged to abandon his rejection of it."[271] The general steps in providing client insight include

(a) determining when and why a decision for the flight into illness was made; (b) assuring the patient that a different pathway in life is possible and worthwhile; (c) stressing all the changes of a positive nature which have taken place in the patient's life since his act of primal repression.[272]

Freud viewed insight therapy as something different from most medical therapies. A physical therapy which could remove symptoms of illness through the application of chemical agents (pills, drugs) he termed a *causal therapy*.[273] Freud did not think of psychoanalysis as a causal therapy directed at symptom removal. There were no chemical agents to apply as a physical therapy, and consequently he said that in his *psychical therapy* he worked at symptoms from a more distant point of origin.[274] Even if a chemical were someday devised to alter libido levels and thus make a truly causal therapy available to medicine, Freud believed that psychoanalysis would have performed the necessary reconnaissance to say how it was that the libido became abnormally distributed in the first instance. A physical or causal therapy would *not* therefore invalidate his theory of illness.

FUNDAMENTAL RULE OF PSYCHOANALYSIS, AND FREE ASSOCIATION

To ensure that a properly insightful understanding would result, Freud asked his clients to be as free and open in their dealings with him as was humanly possible. He was, of course, trying to relax the level of client censorship, loosening the grip of the anticathexes. One day, a female patient criticized him for talking too much during the hour, asking questions of her, and so Freud simply sat back in his chair and let her speak. He found that he could gain as much insight into her condition by letting her do all of the talking during the hour as he could gain through questioning her directly. The main factor of importance was that she say everything which occurred to her, no matter how irrelevant or silly it might appear to her conscious judgment. Thus, open verbal expression and complete honesty are the hallmarks of the fundamental rule of psychoanalysis, and the procedure followed by the client has been termed *free association*.[275]

The usual free-association procedure is to have the client report what occurs to him, quite spontaneously. Naturally, the recounting of his symptoms will take considerable time. Gradually, he will also drift off into a recollection of past events, trailing back to childhood times. If he cannot "get started" during any one session, the therapist may cue him by returning to material improperly covered earlier, or possibly by taking an image or idea from one of his dreams or fantasies and asking the client what that might bring to mind.

Although we speak of "free" association, the fact that Freud believed he could in time come to guess or discern his patient's innermost repressions by encouraging him to express what *seem* to be spontaneous thoughts reflects his belief in *psychic determinism*. Such incidental and apparently irrelevant ideas as might pop into the mind during a reverie Freud did not take to be arbitrary or chance affairs of reason. As Freud said: "I cherished a high opinion of the strictness with which mental processes are determined, and I found it impossible to believe that an idea produced by a patient while his attention was on the stretch could be an arbitrary one and unrelated to the idea we were in search of."[276] Freud said that he believed in chance only in the realm of external events; in the internal world of psychical events he was an uncompromising determinist.[277] It is fundamental to the Freudian view that mental events press on to expression. The unconscious is said to have an " 'upward drive' and desires nothing better than to press forward across its settled frontiers into the ego and so to consciousness."[278]

RESISTANCE AND TRANSFERENCE

From the first, when he was using hypnotism, Freud noted that neurotics disliked having to look into themselves.[279] They sought in myriad ways to terminate or at least alter therapy, in hopes of maintaining the status quo in their lives. According to Freud's later theory of defense, any neurotic has two motives for initiating therapeutic contact—the one to be cured, and the one to avoid being cured (discovered, uncovered).[280] He called these defensive efforts during the therapy hour *resistance,* which in its broadest phrasing refers to *"whatever interrupts the progress of analytic work."*[281] This can range from breaking appointments or coming late for sessions, through subtle remarks to the analyst about a detractor's comments concerning psychoanalysis, down to actual "sudden cures" which provide the reason for terminating therapy.[282]

Resistance is often regressive in character. In reaction to the frustrating necessity of having to listen to the analyst's insightful comments, the ego may actually regress to a time in life when it had been better treated by the environment.[283] The nature of a client's past fixations will determine the style of resistance he will manifest.[284] Thus, an anal personality might begin obfuscating the recital of past memories in free association by becoming highly obsessive in his ruminations, insisting upon going over every minute detail, repeating material already covered, and so forth. An oral personality might regress into a state of dependency and "yes-doctor" the analyst, letting insightful comments go over his head by agreeing to everything the analyst says without *really* letting the insights make an impact.

One of the ways a patient can resist is to try to change the nature of the therapist-client relationship. Freud found that some of his clients began relating to him in a most unprofessional and often amorous manner. They asked him questions about his personal life, they wanted to know what kinds of books he read, or what he did with his free time. If he gave in to any of these diversions by answering such questions, he found his therapeutic results washing away. Once a female client threw her arms around his neck in an erotic gesture, and, as Freud later said, the "unexpected entrance of a servant relieved us from a painful discussion."[285] Freud did not attribute these love feelings to his personal charm. He saw in these maneuvers the re-enactments of *earlier* paternal affectional ties (repetition compulsion).

In thus projecting her genital lust from father to the therapist, the patient achieved two results: (a) she could re-enact her past "dynamic" thereby repeating attitudes and emotional impulses from her early fixations;[286] and (b) she could also increase the likelihood that the analysis would have to be terminated like a broken love affair, because how can the analyst—a married man, with many other such patients to treat daily—return such love?[287] We see in the patient's behavior a striking example of compromise in that, both instinctual needs (repetition compulsion) as the repressed wish, and defensive needs as the repressing wish are being symbolized in the "love affair" (to want the father genitally, yet not admitting that it is the father at all). Freud was to call this emotional involvement with the therapist *transference,* by which he meant: ". . . transference of feelings on to the person of the doctor, since we do not believe that the situation in the treatment could justify the development of such feelings."[288] The female patient was *acting out* her repressed images and ideas, now coming to consciousness, and diverted into sexual feelings for the therapist by way of a *father-imago.*

Thus through the imago prototype the patient can "replace some earlier person by the person of the physician."[289] This goes on all the time in the neurotic's everyday life. Even if he were to be hospitalized and given various nonanalytical therapies the real cure might be traced to the transference relationship. In fact, Freud noted that occasionally a neurotic will appear "cured" just so he will not have to face up to the real motives in his transference to the doctor.[290] The doctor thinks it is the pill which cured the patient, but it is the affection for the doctor which actually cures, as a re-enactment of the unresolved Oedipal drama. The imagos being projected onto the therapist by the client need not be *only* those of the parents. Freud notes that, in addition to father and mother imagos, a patient may use brother, sister, and other important figures out of the past to re-enact dramas long since repressed but not out of action in the psychic realm.[291] Hence, transference is the most powerful resistance which the therapist confronts, even though outside of psychoanalysis it may be bringing about rapid and superficial "cures."

The feelings transferred onto the therapist are not always positive in tone, of course. In fact, Freud said that it was virtually impossible for a patient to remain in psychoanalysis and continue in a positive state of transference throughout.[292] This ambivalence is due to the fact that our feelings toward past imagos are never "one way"; and due to the ambivalence involved, the negative features must inevitably show themselves. Furthermore, as the patient reveals more of his unconscious intentions (wishes), he is threatened by what he—with the help of the therapist—is learning about himself. In this situation anyone would become defensive or resistive.

Precisely when the *negative transference* will emerge is hard to say. Freud believed that one could sense its beginnings when the client's free associative processes began to be obstructed, when he could no longer concentrate, recall his dreams, or he refused to say aloud what did seem to be coming to mind privately.[293] The analyst begins at this point to *interpret* the nature of these positive or negative transferences. To interpret is to "find hidden sense in something,"[294] and in providing insight through analysis of the transference the therapist is trying to *overcome the client's resistance.* This naturally merely exacerbates the negative transference for a time, since the client is now all the more threatened by having to face up to his unconscious repressions. As time went by Freud began to think of overcoming resistance as the *most crucial* and wearying aspect of the psychotherapeutic process. Freud once defined psychoanalytic treatment as "a *re-education in overcoming internal resistances.*"[295] When repressed content is nearing awareness and is presented as an interpretation, we often witness the most vile forms of exchange between the participants of the relationship. Freud once summed it up vividly: "Resistance, which finally brings work to a halt, is nothing other than the child's past character, his degenerate character. . . . I dig it out by my work, it struggles; and what was to begin with such an excellent, honest fellow, becomes low, untruthful or defiant, and a malingerer—till I tell him so and thus make it possible to overcome this character."[296]

Although it need not always proceed in step fashion—sometimes both sides of the ambivalence emerge in the early sessions—the usual course of transference is from a positive to a negative state or *stage.* Freud believed that successful therapy called for a complete resolution of the transference phenomenon. The full implications of the transference onto the therapist must be made clear to the patient; hence, "At the end of an analytic treatment the transference must itself be cleared away; and if success is then obtained or continues, it rests, not on suggestion, but on the achievement by its means of an overcoming of internal resistances, on the internal change that has been brought about in the patient."[297] Many ex-patients who leave their therapists during the stage of a negative transference make up the most vociferous group of critics psychoanalysis has to face.[298] Even so, Freud did not favor avoiding such—what he took to be—necessities of the method; he did not think it advisable to use the transference-love to manipulate clients and thereby allow the hostile repressions to escape analysis.[299]

The therapist must also be careful about forming a *countertransference,* which involves the unconscious motives which the therapist might have acted out in his relations with the client.[300] If the therapist has not developed adequate insight into his own personality dynamics, then very possibly he will act out an imago of his *own,* using the patient as a substitute figure. This is one of the reasons Freud believed that a psychoanalyst should first be analyzed before undertaking the role of therapist himself.[301] Therapists, then, must resolve their own resistances first and thereby minimize their defensiveness in relation to their patients.

FINAL THEORY OF CURE

Thus far we have been discussing the general terminology which evolved in Freud's thinking about the nature of cure. His "final" formulation, as with all of Freud's other theories, will include a *libido* explanation. Freud always made the effort to explain things by way of the libido theory, even though he had fairly well explicated things in nonenergy terms. The final theory of cure may be summarized in six points.

1. The neurotic is someone with significant primal repressions (Figure 6), including those surrounding the unresolved Oedipal complex, and he thereby finds it difficult to relate interpersonally with others (leading to fits of regression due to the frustration). He does not feel loved in the present, and thus in each new person whom he meets there is a certain *libidinal anticipatory idea* which he has in mind.[302] This idea is usually at an unconscious level, and it might be something like "Won't you love and accept me?" or "Maybe now I can smooth things over and experience genuine love." In doing so, the neurotic is re-enacting his unresolved Oedipal complex, transferring onto others the imagos from out of his past.

2. The reason the neurotic gets sick is because his unconscious mental contents need liberation in the present.[303] His imagos and the ideas which surround them press toward consciousness and stimulate feelings for others in the present which are in reality feelings for others out of the past. In therapy, such transferences take three forms: (a) positive

transferences of an affectionate, friendly nature for the therapist *as himself*—a man having power, authority, a skill to be used in helping others; (b) positive transferences of an erotic, sexually lustful nature for the therapist as a surrogate for the imagos; (c) negative transferences of a hostile, death-wishing variety for the therapist as surrogate for the imagos. Now, it is on the basis of the suggestion which the *type a* positive transference affords that we can influence a patient to change. Freud said: "We readily admit that the results of psychoanalysis rest upon suggestion; by suggestion, however, we must understand . . . the influencing of a person by means of the transference phenomena which are possible in his case. We take care of the patient's final independence by employing suggestion in order to get him to accomplish a piece of psychical work which has as its necessary result a permanent improvement in his psychical situation."[304]

3. The individual must cure himself because only he can confront his unconscious, and resolve his own lack of communication between the two realms of mind. The therapist uses what power he has in the transference relationship to assist the client in this endeavor. A psychoanalysis is only a genuine psychoanalysis insofar as it has succeeded in removing the amnesia from a patient dating back to his second to fifth year of life, about the time in which the Oedipal conflict takes shape.[305] Transference is thus the *"true vehicle of therapeutic influence"* even though it is a major source of resistance.[306] This contradictory nature of transference is as it should be due to the compromise features of a neurotic's symptoms and the ambivalence of his behavior in general.[307]

4. Moving on to the specifics of therapeutic cure in terms of instinct-libido theory, Freud once again relied on the repetition-compulsion construct. He suggested that as the individual is passing through the psychoanalysis he develops what might be termed an *artificial* or a *transformed neurosis* within the four walls of the consulting room.[308] This is a miniature replica of the neurotic situation taken from his life history and re-enacted before the therapist's eyes (repetition compulsion). The real life neurosis is in this sense the prototype for the transformed neurosis which is presently unfolding in the imago transferences being sent the therapist's way. Freud occasionally referred to this miniature re-enactment as the *transference illness,*[309] a term which has led to some confusion because the artificial or transformed neurosis has since been called the "transference neurosis" by some of his students. Actually, the latter term is better reserved for a distinction which Freud made between those mentally disturbed individuals who can profit from therapy and those who cannot.

5. When we speak of positive or negative feelings being transferred to the therapist via imagos, we are *also* saying that libidinal or hostile cathexes are taking place (Eros or the Death Instinct). Shifting our emphasis to the energic type of explanation, we might say that psychoanalysis as a therapeutic method demands that the client be able *in fact* to cathect objects. If an individual could not cathect objects, he would be unable to develop a transformed neurosis within the transference relationship, and how then could we hope to provide him with insight as we worked through his resistances? We could not, really, and on this basis Freud distinguished between those who could and those who could not be treated by psychoanalytical method. People suffer from two fundamental types of neuroses: (a) the *transference neuroses,* which include anxiety neurosis, hysteria, and obsessive-compulsive disorders; and (b) the *narcissistic neuroses,* which include the schizophrenias and the more serious affective disorders like manic-depression. Today, we consider the latter disorders to be psy-

choses. The point Freud was making, however, is that any mental disorder taking on a narcissistic feature like this means that the individual has removed all libidinal cathexes from the external world and affixed them onto his own personality structure. This type of person regresses, builds his dream world, and simply breaks off all cathectic ties with external objects. He cannot be influenced because he has no libido to invest outside of his own identity.[310] The person suffering from a transference neurosis, on the other hand, *does* experience libidinal anticipatory ideas, he does cathect others, and he is amenable to the treatment. He is a perfect patient because he readily re-enacts his past by way of the repetition compulsion. In therapy, Freud said, "we oblige him to transform his repetition into a memory" which is *insight*.[311]

6. In more precise libido terms, the patient in psychoanalysis comes gradually to remove libido from object cathexes in the environment and from the symptoms he manifests in his body and to redirect this free libido onto his relationship with the therapist. The therapist takes on great significance because so much libido is invested in him (cathexis). The therapist's tactic is to make this additional libido available to the conscious aspects of the patient's ego and thereby to further a strengthening of the ego, thanks to its added quota of energy. Thus, as he works through the miniature neurosis with his client, the therapist does not allow further repressions, which as anticathexis would mean that the extra libido would be spent defensively. He literally helps the conscious aspects of the ego retain the precious mental energies set free in the transference relationship. Gradually, the "ego is enlarged at the cost of this unconscious."[312] The patient's ego is strengthened, it knows itself better, and it accepts itself for what it is despite the superego's former restrictions and admonitions.

EXTENT AND PERMANENCE OF CURE

Despite this rather comprehensive and encouraging theory of cure, Freud came in time to mute its more optimistic overtones. In a paper entitled "Analysis Terminable and Interminable," written in 1937, a few years before his death, he took a more cautious position on the extent and permanence of the cures which psychoanalysis could effect. His main reason for this growing pessimism seems to have stemmed from a belief that only those instinctual conflicts which were *actually active* in the transformed neurosis can be helped through analysis.[313] If some conflict is not manifesting itself in the present relationship—literally showing itself, being experienced by the patient in the "now"—then simply talking about it in *post hoc* fashion will not cure it. If a patient, for example, has severe death wishes for his father and the therapist gleans this insight quite accurately through the free associations of the patient, no amount of telling the patient about this death wish will lead to therapeutic cure *unless* the patient gains the insight during an actual sensation of the death wish in therapy—which means wishing the therapist's death! Hence, although this patient may have actually manifested many other conflicts in the transformed neurosis and received cures in the process thanks to the insights, he will never actually clear up the death wish conflict even though "intellectually" he has gained insight into it from the therapist.

Thus, we see an interesting repetition-compulsion feature in the theoretical life history of Freud. He began with the hypnotic method which took people back to a time when they were literally *within* a pathognomic situation and thereby cured them through a kind of emotional expiation (abreactive catharsis). Now, in his closing years, he once again said that the fundamental necessity for cure is something akin to this, an active rerun of the earlier prototypical situation, manifesting itself in the present. Just intellectually telling people will not work. We have to wait until such time as they feel prompted to re-enact their own special life drama. *Then* we provide them with the appropriate insight and remove the strangulator for all time.

A patient can never bring *all* of his past conflicts into the transference relationship as a transformed neurosis.[314] Nor can the therapist hope artificially to stimulate them by using various tricks to encourage, for example, the paternal death wishes by acting in some theatrically ingenuine way.[315] The backbone of psychoanalysis remains truthfulness and genuineness. All one can hope for, therefore, is to end a psychoanalysis on the best conditions possible. As Freud put it, "Our aim will not be to rub off every peculiarity of human character for the sake of a schematic 'normality,' nor yet to demand that the person who has been 'thoroughly analysed' shall feel no passions and develop no internal conflicts. The business of the analysis is to secure the best possible psychological conditions for the functions of the ego; with that it has discharged its task."[316] Because of this likelihood that aspects of our past conflicts have not actually been manifested (felt, experienced) in the past therapeutic relationship Freud advocated periodic reanalyses for even the practicing psychoanalyst. He felt that a practitioner should resubmit himself to analysis every five years or so, as a kind of continuing prophylactic against the menace of countertransference.[317]

SOCIAL REVISION

Freud was a "proper" man, and in no sense a revolutionary. His hope for the future centered not on sexual license, but on the insights which his *science* afforded modern man. In making unconscious factors conscious, he furthered the boundaries of the rule of reason.[318] Yet, it would appear that the most lasting therapy envisioned by Freud might be termed *preventative*. If mankind is instructed by the insights of psychoanalysis—as a patient *en masse*—then just possibly it will no longer need to sustain the level of repression which it now bears up under. Oedipal conflicts need not be so severe, superegos need not be so intractible, human understanding and mutual acceptance based upon something more honest and true than brotherly love may be fashioned. A gradual revision in the social structure is surely implied in much of what Freud has to offer mankind.[319] Sometimes, in removing repressions of the individual, a patient's life situation is made worse. He is forced to give up secondary gains and might thereby act out his irritation on society directly. Even so, said Freud:

The unhappiness that our work of enlightenment may cause will after all only affect some individuals. The change-over to a more realistic and creditable attitude on the part of society will not be bought too dearly by these sacrifices. But above all, all the energies which are to-day consumed in the production of neurotic symptoms serving the purposes of a world of phantasy isolated from reality, will, even if they cannot at once be put to uses in life, help to strengthen the clamour for the changes in our civilization through which alone we can look for the well-being of future generations.[320]

This is the ultimate therapeutic message of Freudian psychoanalysis. Freud is not a doctor "in the proper sense"[321] of being a physician for the individual. He is the teacher of mass man, the doctor of the body politic, and his cures transcend the individual or even an individual generation of men.

THERAPEUTIC TECHNIQUES

The relationship between therapist and client is commonly referred to as a *method* of therapy. Though we have occasionally employed this usage earlier in the chapter, at this point we will keep more strictly within our definition of method (see Introduction) as the vehicle for the exercise of evidence, and refrain from using *method* in the present section, which deals with therapeutic techniques. This usage would be appropriate for Freud because he believed that psychoanalysis was a scientific investigation in addition to a vehicle of cure. But not all of the therapists who practice psychoanalysis today agree, and many therapy orientations never propose to do the work of science within the four walls of the consulting room. We will refer to factors like the nature of the relationship and the various devices used to further therapy as *techniques,* recognizing that this does not imply any commitment by the therapist to use of a manipulative approach in his dealings with clients. Just as many styles of behavior are included in *personality,* so too manners of relating to the client can be called *techniques.*

EVOLUTION OF THE RELATIONSHIP

Freud began his practitioner's career as most neurologists of his day, using various physical interventions for the treatment of mental illness. Common physical techniques included sedatives, rest, massage, hydrotherapy (e.g., baths or stimulating showers), diet control, and change of routine. Freud's clients were predominantly of the upper socioeconomic classes,[322] and he could therefore send them off for a period of recuperation in a local resort spa. Of course, in extremely disturbed (psychotic) cases, he hospitalized the patient. What Freud did was gradually to define a new doctor-patient relationship as he evolved the psychoanalytical technique.[323]

As we recall, Freud began his search for the pathognomic (repressed) memory through the device of hypnotic time regression. His aim was to find the pathognomic situation in the past during which affect had been strangulated, and then to expiate it through cathartic release (the abreactive technique). The patient was asked to relax in a reclining or semireclining position on a sofa, and hypnosis was induced through the usual suggestions of drowsiness, falling off into a sleep, and so forth. As he used the approach with more clients, Freud found that not all of them could be put under

a sufficiently deep hypnotic state to ensure an adequate therapeutic outcome. In fact, several could not be hypnotized at all. Freud recalled that Bernheim (one of the French doctors he studied with) could invariably get a subject who had been under hypnosis to tell what transpired during that state by taking the subject's head in his hands and essentially "ordering" (strong suggestion) him to reproduce the supposedly amnesic content. When one day a difficult patient was not responding to the hypnosis instructions, Freud took her head in his hands, asked her to concentrate, and while applying a slight pressure he confidently asserted that she *would* recall when her symptoms had begun. Sure enough, the patient's recollections of the pathognomic situation were forthcoming, and he could thence encourage a certain amount of cathartic release.[324]

Freud referred to this approach as the *pressure* technique, and he used it with much success for some years, feeling that it had definite advantages over hypnosis because a client was conscious of his thought processes as he made his mental search. The focus of therapy was still on symptom removal during this stage of development. It was only a matter of time under this more conscious method of recall until Freud noted a strange and annoying development. He found that his clients were recalling all manner of trivia, apparently unrelated scraps of information which had no bearing on their neurotic symptoms. He did not dismiss these apparent irrelevancies, but drawing upon a psychic determinism view he considered them to be *screen memories* or *screen associations.*[325] These supposedly indifferent memories were covering up a more deep-seated complex of memories clustering around the pathognomic situation. Freud began to question his clients about screen memories, taking them even further back in time, until he hit upon the technique of free association. For a time, Freud used both the pressure technique and free association in combination, but by 1905 he had stopped touching the client entirely (a dangerous procedure, considering the matter of transferences). Thus today free association has emerged as the exclusive technique of the "classical" psychoanalyst.

VIEW OF THERAPEUTIC CHANGE

Freud was quite aware of the historic relationship psychoanalysis had with hypnosis, and by way of this tie, the possible criticism that he had cured people through suggestion. He defined suggestion as uncritically accepting the idea implanted in one's mind by another,[326] but he did *not* believe that this is what took place in psychoanalysis. He felt that the id promptings which lay at the root of a neurosis, thanks to the counterweight influence of the superego and the compromise effected by the ego, could not be so easily influenced. The id, after all, is illogical and refuses to evaluate any of its anticipatory ideas realistically. One might use a modicum of suggestion thanks to the positive transference of affection for the therapist as helper, but this kind of suggestion *to the ego* might or might not affect a change in the id sphere of mind. Anyone who practices psychoanalysis and formulates what Freud called *constructions* (the "constructs" of the Introduction) for his client knows full well that such theoretical suggestions are not completely accepted by the client.[327]

Freud argued that those who use the construct of suggestion never say what it is. From his point of view, suggestion was seen as based upon sexual forces in operation between two people. Its power in therapy results from the childlike dependency—the re-enactment of an infantile relationship—on the person of the therapist as surrogate for others. To understand the nature of suggestion we must first understand the nature of transference. Thus Freud's *goal* in therapy is to provide a certain type of relationship and thereby to learn something of the client's past history. He is not out to prove some obscure theoretical point in each case, and Freud observed: ". . . the most successful cases are those in which one proceeds,

as it were, without any purpose in view, allows oneself to be taken by surprise by any turn in them, and always meets them with an open mind, free from any presuppositions."[328] Freud said that he refused emphatically to make patients into his "private property," to force his own ideals upon the patient "and with the pride of a Creator to form him in our own image."[329]

The point is: *a neurotic is not a free man.* He is locked into his past like a character in a play. This past forces him to re-enact his unresolved Oedipal complex in the ever-recurring present. He is 100 per cent determined because his unconscious life is staging the scenes through which he must move. Thus, "analysis sets the neurotic free from the chains of his sexuality."[330]

CLIENT PROGNOSIS AND TRIAL ANALYSES

Freud believed that the ideal candidate for psychoanalysis was a person suffering from an inner conflict which he alone cannot resolve; he is therefore miserable and comes in virtually begging for help.[331] Anything which detracts from this ideal condition naturally darkens the prognosis. Thus, if he is forced into the relationship by relatives, if he is psychotic and imbued with the satisfactions of his fantasy world, if he is mentally retarded, brain-damaged or aged and senile so that he cannot concentrate on problems or deal with abstractions, the prognosis is not good. Children present a special difficulty, and in truth Freud was not much attracted to the role of child therapist. His famous case of Little Hans (Vol. X) was based upon the work of an intermediary therapist—the boy's father—who saw Freud and then carried the sexual insights to his five-year-old son in a most unabashed fashion. In general, Freud favored the conjoint treatment of child and parent, particularly since the conflicts which children are engaged in are invariably externalized, leaving the "internal conflict" aspect of a good prognosis unfulfilled.[332]

When a therapist takes a patient usually he is "buying a pig in a poke."[333] Freud favored a trial period of diagnostic assessment of from a few weeks to a few months during which the therapist can make his decision about whether or not he has affiliated with a patient with whom he can work effectively, whether the neurosis is of a narcissistic or a transference nature, and so forth. This trial period is quite flexible, and it may even be extended for quite some time, so that Freud often said people who are dropped as poor candidates for analysis are counted failures due to the trial analysis they have already completed. Freud admitted that his procedure took a long time, in some cases stretching over many years, but he could see no other way to resolve the more serious neurosis short of the superficial, suggestive cures which rely on manipulation and the authority of positive transference to suppress a symptom.[334]

INTERPRETATIVE TECHNIQUES IN DREAMS AND PARAPRAXES

It is fitting that Freud's first major works were *The Interpretation of Dreams* (1900) and *The Psycho-pathology of Everyday Life* (1901), because the fundamentals of his interpretative style are outlined in these two books. In the first he based the entire edifice of psychoanalysis on the *foundation stone* of dream interpretation,[335] and in the second he essentially justified the role of psychoanalysis as science by demonstrating that its insights referred to the most banal activities of our daily routine.

Dreams are phenomena in the psychic *not* the somatic realm of experience. They express a meaning, they say something, and though we think we do not know what their content signifies, at one level of awareness (unconscious), *we know full well*.[336] While asleep, all of those anticipatory libidinal ideas which we cannot consciously express due to their repression by the ego and the superego—which as a coalition might be thought of as the censoring agency—are given expression. Of course, in

order to get around the censorship, these ideas must be distorted in various ways so that their content is expressed through symbols which must be deciphered. Dreams have a *manifest* content or story line which often appears foreign and even odd to us because we do not understand their meanings. What Freud did was to translate this manifest content into what he called the *latent* content, which is the real meaning of the dream.[337] A stable translation, one which invariably could mean the same thing, Freud termed a *symbol*.[338] Thus, in general, elongated objects are taken to be masculine (penis symbols) and enclosed objects are likely to be more feminine (vaginal or uterine symbols). Man's use of symbols traces back to his most archaic thought form, and they can be seen in the various myths and religions of antiquity.[339]

A dream is fashioned out of *day residues,* which are the little bits and pieces of experience during the sleep day (day before night of dream) to which we have probably not fixed our conscious attention.[340] The dream is prompted by a *wish fulfillment,* of course, but we must keep in mind that this can be a lustful wish of the id, or it could also be the self-punishing wish of the superego. We must not make the error of assuming that by claiming every dream is a wish fulfillment Freud necessarily referred to a pleasurable outcome.[341] Freud relented on the idea that all dreams had to have a sexual content, but his wish fulfillment concept was retained to the end. This wish-fulfilling aspect of dreaming is achieved by way of what he called the *dream work,* and its fundamental way of expression is imagery. We do not dream in ideas, but in images, so that dreaming is like thinking in pictures. Freud once put it succinctly when he observed: "A dream is a picture-puzzle."[342] Dreaming also bears a psychological affinity to the process of hallucination in the behavior of psychotics.[343] Recall our "regression of excitation" to the stimulus-end in Figure 3. In fact, Freud was to say that "A dream . . . is a psychosis, with all the absurdities, delusions, and illusions of a psychosis."[344]

Since dreaming follows primary-process thought, Freud observed that the rules of conventional logic are suspended when we dream. Thus, we can *condense* many concerns or different people into a single dream image (symbol), and often *displace* the resultant product onto a seemingly unrelated activity.[345] For example, a young man who has doubts about his ability to succeed independently in life because he has always been subjugated by a strong paternal figure drives past a small carnival one afternoon. Snatching aspects of the carnival scenes as day residue, that night he dreams he is riding round and round on a carousel, but instead of the usual horse he is sitting on a bull which—free association later determines—has the heavy torso of his father. The dream is about important life issues, and the feeling of domination by a parent (latent content), but the young man recalls only something about having a good time at a carnival (manifest content which has been displaced to a pleasant experience).

A more general case of this human ability to combine several factors into one dream content is *overdetermination*. Freud believed that many dream images were more pregnant with meaning than was minimally necessary to make them occur in the first place.[346] Many more wishes squeeze into the same symbol than are required to express the symbol in the dream. Hence, it follows that no *single* interpretation of the manifest content can circumscribe all of the latent content which is actually being expressed.[347]

Dreams are actually the *guardians* of sleep, because if we could not express our unconscious mental preoccupations in some form, we would probably toss and turn all night long. If they occasionally disturb our rest, we must appreciate that they are merely carrying out a noisy duty for a good end, "just as the night-watchman often cannot help making a little noise while he chases away the disturbers of the peace who seek to waken us with their noise."[348] Since they always deal with our more important mental preoccupations, the interpretation of dreams provides the analyst with a *"royal road to a knowledge of the unconscious activities of the mind."*[349] The proper analytical attitude in dream analysis involves the following points:

1. disregard the manifest content as such, since this cannot possibly contain the unconscious material in itself;
2. present different portions of the dream content to the patient as stimulations for his free associations, call up the latent material by way of the substitute thoughts themselves without regard for how far this line of investigation takes you away from the dream itself;
3. do not suggest any direction to the patient, but through repeated dream analyses wait until the unconscious material suggests itself of its own accord.[350]

Freud gave his readers many practical hints to interpretation over the years. The following are examples. Dreams produce logical connections by simultaneity in time, so that things happening together are probably seen by the dreamer as somehow related. When a cause-effect relationship is suggested then the dream content is changed or distorted, as by a sudden shift in scene or the distortion of a face from one person into another's. If we dream that our mother's face changes into our wife's, then it is likely that we see an influence emanating from the former to the latter. We cannot express "either/or" in a dream, but instead link such alternatives with an "and" so that opposites can be combined into single images. Any time there is a condensation of dream figures, we must always suspect that the dreamer sees a similarity, identity, or possession of common attributes between the figures (father and bulls are *both* strong, if also a bit too stolid and demanding). A popular device used by the dreamer is *reversal,* or the turning into its opposite of some latent wish or image in the manifest content. Hence, we can never take a dream at its face value. All of these devices Freud referred to as the *means of representation* in dreams.[351]

In addition to the content of free associations and dreams, Freud found that he could glean insights into the motives of others through what he called *parapraxes,* or errors in behavior, "misactions" in which the person does something he is not intending to do. What happens when someone intends to say to his boss "Please sit down" and says instead "Please fall down," is that he is actually substituting the opposite of his intention—in this case, hostility for politeness.[352] Here again, the censoring agency is circumvented in a fleeting moment when our attention is caught off guard. The new bride writes a letter to her mother-in-law, beginning with "Dead mother" instead of "Dear mother," and the cat is out of the bag. Whether in spoken or written word, these are the notorious "Freudian slips" which tell us something of our unconscious wishes. The reason they are often humorous to other uninvolved people who observe us is that they know implicitly what our feelings actually are.[353]

SOME PROCEDURAL DETAILS

Although such techniques are altered considerably today by psychoanalysts, Freud had his patient lie on a sofa while he sat behind the head of the patient, out of direct sight.[354] This position reflects the influence of his earlier hypnotic and pressure techniques, but Freud also believed that it was wise to eliminate feedback to the client from his facial expressions. Also, he frankly admitted that he could not stand being stared at by other people for eight hours or more per day. He felt it advisable to tell the patient that therapy would take a long time—a year or more at the very least. His clients assumed an awesome burden in time commitment, for he met them several times a week—anywhere from two or three to five or six sessions weekly. As therapy wore on, the number of sessions could be reduced, depend-

ing upon how well the client was progressing. Another important burden to the client was entirely financial. Freud stressed that the analyst must treat money matters with the same frankness that he deals with sensitive personal topics. Money can be a tool of resistance for the client, who can use this excuse to terminate the contacts—particularly since the practice followed by Freud and his followers is to charge for every scheduled session, including those which a client misses (except under highly unusual circumstances). The only recourse is simply to state things clearly to the client at the outset and then to carry on without any further embarrassment. As Freud summed it up in any case, "Nothing in life is so expensive as illness—and stupidity."[355]

Freud saw his patients for the classical "50-minute hour." He was not much attracted to taking notes during the hour, preferring to do this sort of record keeping between patient appointments and at the close of the day. In the very earliest—including the first—sessions, Freud would simply turn the lead over to his client, and say: " 'Before I can say anything to you I must know a great deal about you; please tell me what you know about yourself.' "[356] Doubtless, many of these early sessions were spent in going over the details of the illness which prompted the client to seek assistance. Gradually, they would turn attention to dreams and other materials emerging in the free associations. Freud would begin instructing the client in the rudiments of psychoanalysis, even as early as the fifth or sixth session,[357] but he was decidedly opposed to the patient's independent reading and studying of psychoanalysis from books.[358]

Freud advised his patients not to make important decisions during the course of treatment —such as choosing a profession or choosing a marital partner.[359] His reason was to limit the possible chances of important errors in life due to the acting-out of unconscious impulses during the transformed neurosis. This suggestion may appear inconsistent with Freud's desire to refrain from living another person's life, but he viewed the admonition to *delay* important decisions as something quite different from the making of decisions *for* the client. In the lesser of life's decisions he definitely favored a hands-off policy for the therapist.

When he first began treating clients, Freud went quickly into an interpretation of their dynamics, but later in his career he cautioned against rushing the client. He favored waiting it out until the patient was "one short step" away from having the particular insight himself before making an interpretation for him.[360] Freud also dabbled in the setting of time limits to a therapy series—particularly since one of his students (Rank) made this a major technique variation. He admitted that at times the limit could be helpful, prompting the client to surmount his resistances by telling him there would only be "so many more" sessions before the relationship would be terminated. But he felt that one had to use this technique sparingly, and his reference to it as a "blackmailing device" obviously suggests that Freud did not think highly of it in any case.[361] Freud said analysis ended when the analyst and patient mutually decided to stop seeing one another. From the therapist's point of view, two general conditions have to be met before a termination is called for: ". . . first, that the patient shall no longer be suffering from his symptoms and shall have overcome his anxieties and his inhibitions; and secondly, that the analyst shall judge that so much repressed material had been made conscious, so much that was unintelligible has been explained, and so much internal resistance conquered, that there is no need to fear a repetition of the pathological processes concerned."[362]

Notes

1. Freud, Vol. XX, p. 8. 2. *Ibid.* 3. Jones, 1953, p. 28. 4. *Ibid.,* p. 40. 5. Wittels, 1924, pp. 29, 31. 6. Freud, 1954, p. 322. 7. Freud, Vol. II, pp. 38–39. 8. *Ibid.,* p. 38. 9. *Ibid.,* p. 8.

10. *Ibid.,* p. 286. 11. Freud, Vol. I, pp. 281–397. 12. Freud, Vol. III, p. 234; Vol. XIV, p. 168. 13. Freud, Vol. XIV, pp. 78–79. 14. Freud, Vol. V, p. 538. 15. *Ibid.,* p. 574. 16. Freud, Vol. XII, p. 260. 17. *Ibid.,* p. 264. 18. Freud, Vol. V, p. 613. 19. Freud, Vol. XV, p. 113. 20. *Ibid.,* p. 212. 21. Freud, Vol. XXII, p. 70. 22. Freud, Vol. XVII, p. 28. 23. Freud, Vol. XIV, p. 149. 24. Freud, Vol. XII, p. 266. 25. Freud, Vol. XIV, p. 194. 26. *Ibid.,* p. 80. 27. Freud, Vol. XXIII, p. 240. 28. Freud, Vol. XIX, p. 55. 29. Freud, Vol. XIV, p. 187. 30. Freud, Vol. V, p. 617. 31. *Ibid.,* p. 542. 32. Freud, Vol. XXII, p. 73. 33. *Ibid.* 34. *Ibid.* 35. *Ibid.,* p. 74. 36. Freud, Vol. XXIII, p. 240. 37. Freud, Vol. I, p. 323. 38. Freud, Vol. XXII, pp. 66–67. 39. Freud, Vol. XIX, p. 18. 40. *Ibid.,* p. 40. 41. Freud, Vol. XX, p. 97. 42. Freud, Vol. II, p. 116. 43. Freud, Vol. XIX, p. 17. 44. Freud, Vol. XXII, p. 76. 45. Freud, Vol. V, pp. 601–603. 46. *Ibid.,* p. 603. 47. Freud, Vol. XXII, p. 78. 48. Freud, Vol. XIV, pp. 93–94. 49. Freud, Vol. XIX, p. 28. 50. *Ibid.,* p. 36. 51. *Ibid.,* p. 55. 52. *Ibid.,* p. 34. 53. Freud, Vol. XIV, p. 113. 54. Nunberg and Federn, 1962. 55. Freud, Vol. XIV, pp. 118–120. 56. *Ibid.,* pp. 121–122. 57. *Ibid.,* p. 122. 58. Jones, 1953, p. 41. 59. Freud, Vol. III, p. 36. 60. Freud, Vol. XIV, p. 126. 61. Freud, Vol. XVI, p. 356. 62. Freud, Vol. XVIII, p. 9. 63. Freud, Vol. XIV, p. 146. 64. Freud, 1954, p. 219. 65. Freud, Vol. IX, p. 188. 66. Freud, Vol. XVI, p. 323. 67. Freud, Vol. VIII, pp. 168–183. 68. Freud, Vol. IX, p. 187. 69. Freud, Vol. III, p. 107. 70. Freud, Vol. XVII, p. 139. 71. Freud, Vol. XI, p. 101. 72. Freud, Vol. XXII, p. 131. 73. Freud, Vol. XVIII, p. 90. 74. Freud, Vol. I, p. 298. 75. Freud, Vol. XII, p. 74. 76. Freud, Vol. XIV, p. 234. 77. Freud, Vol. V, p. 605. 78. Freud, 1954, p. 324. 79. Freud, Vol. VII, pp. 219–220. 80. *Ibid.,* p. 219. 81. Freud and Bullitt, 1967. 82. Freud, Vol. XV, p. 123. 83. Freud, Vol. XI, p. 44. 84. Freud, Vol. XVII, p. 137. 85. Freud, Vol. XXI, p. 117. 86. Freud, Vol. XVIII, p. 10. 87. Gayley, 1965, pp. 188–189. 88. Freud, Vol. XXI, p. 118. 89. Freud, Vol. XIV, p. 73. 90. *Ibid.,* p. 134. 91. Freud, Vol. XVIII, p. 22. 92. *Ibid.,* p. 36. 93. *Ibid.,* p. 38. 94. *Ibid.,* p. 56. 95. From Barbara Low, in Freud, Vol. XVIII, pp. 55–56. 96. Freud, Vol. XIX, p. 41. 97. Freud, Vol. XVIII, p. 53. 98. Freud, Vol. XXI, p. 138. 99. Freud, Vol. XXII, p. 211. 100. Freud and Bullitt, 1967, p. 279. 101. Freud, Vol. XIV, p. 16. 102. Freud, Vol. VIII, p. 5. 103. Freud, Vol. IV, pp. 307–308; Vol. XIV, p. 305. 104. Freud, Vol. I, p. 209. 105. Freud, Vol. XVIII,

p. 256. **106.** Freud and Bullitt, 1967, p. 43. **107.** Freud, Vol. XII, p. 66. **108.** Freud, Vol. XIII, p. 64. **109.** Freud, Vol. XII, p. 299. **110.** *Ibid.,* p. 49. **111.** Freud, Vol. III, p. 58. **112.** Freud, Vol. I, p. 229. **113.** *Ibid.,* p. 235. **114.** Freud, Vol. XXI, pp. 67–72. **115.** Freud, Vol. VII, p. 198. **116.** Freud, Vol. V, p. 471. **117.** Freud, Vol. XXII, pp. 60–62. **118.** Freud, Vol. XVIII, p. 113. **119.** Freud, Vol. XX, p. 10. **120.** Freud, Vol. XVIII, p. 245; also see Vol. VII, p. 198. **121.** Freud, Vol. XIX, p. 142. **122.** Freud, Vol. XXIII, p. 189. **123.** Freud, Vol. XXII, p. 118. **124.** *Ibid.,* p. 118. **125.** Freud, Vol. VIII, p. 218. **126.** Freud, Vol. XXII, p. 118. **127.** Freud, Vol. XI, p. 97; Vol. XII, p. 82. **128.** Freud, Vol. XIII, p. 184. **129.** Becker and Barnes, 1952, Ch. V. **130.** Freud, Vol. XIII, pp. 141–143. **131.** *Ibid.,* p. 153. **132.** *Ibid.,* pp. 144–150. **133.** Gayley, 1965, pp. 261–263. **134.** Freud, Vol. IX, p. 104. **135.** Freud, Vol. XXIII, p. 189. **136.** Freud, Vol. XIII, p. 153. **137.** Freud, Vol. XIX, p. 144. **138.** *Ibid.,* p. 36. **139.** Freud, Vol. XXI, p. 229. **140.** *Ibid.,* pp. 229, 234. **141.** Freud, Vol. XXII, p. 134. **142.** Freud, Vol. XXIII, p. 194. **143.** Freud, Vol. XIX, p. 251; Vol. XXII, p. 117. **144.** Freud, Vol. XIX, p. 178. **145.** *Ibid.,* pp. 257–258. **146.** Freud, Vol. IX, p. 195. **147.** Freud, Vol. XIX, pp. 177–178. **148.** Freud, Vol. IX, p. 171. **149.** Freud, Vol. XVIII, p. 111. **150.** Freud, Vol. XII, p. 222. **151.** Freud, Vol. XVI, p. 326. **152.** Freud, Vol. XVIII, p. 246. **153.** Freud, Vol. XX, p. 37. **154.** Freud, Vol. XXII, p. 147. **155.** Freud, Vol. XVI, p. 336. **156.** Freud and Bullitt, 1967, p. 74. **157.** Freud, Vol. XVIII, p. 246. **158.** Freud and Bullitt, 1967, p. 74. **159.** *Ibid.* **160.** Freud, Vol. XVIII, p. 121. **161.** Freud, Vol. XXI, p. 228. **162.** Freud, Vol. XVIII, p. 115. **163.** *Ibid.,* p. 142. **164.** Freud, Vol. II, pp. 50–51, 170, 237. **165.** Freud, Vol. VIII, p. 118. **166.** Freud, Vol. XXI, pp. 103–104. **167.** Freud, Vol. VII, p. 235; Vol. XII, pp. 317–318. **168.** Freud, Vol. XVIII, p. 184. **169.** Freud, Vol. VII, p. 235. **170.** Freud, Vol. III, p. 163. **171.** Freud, Vol. XI, pp. 98–99. **172.** Freud, Vol. VII, p. 30. **173.** Freud, Vol. XII, pp. 61–62. **174.** Freud, Vol. XIV, p. 286. **175.** Freud, Vol. VII, pp. 50–51. **176.** Freud, Vol. XXI, p. 69. **177.** Freud, Vol. XIV, p. 286. **178.** Freud, Vol. XIII, p. 184. **179.** Freud and Bullitt, 1967, p. 43. **180.** Freud, Vol. IX, p. 175; Vol. XII, p. 190. **181.** Freud, Vol. XXII, p. 99. **182.** Freud, Vol. IX, pp. 169–170. **183.** Freud, Vol. XVII, p. 81. **184.** Freud, Vol. IX, p. 173. **185.** Freud, Vol. XVII, p. 82. **186.** Freud, Vol. IX, p. 175. **187.** Freud, Vol. XIII, p. 196. **188.** Freud, Vol. XXI, p. 90. **189.** Freud, Vol. XIX, pp. 91–92. **190.** Freud, Vol. XXII, pp. 129–130. **191.** *Ibid.,* p. 130. **192.** Freud, Vol. XI, p. 121. **193.** Freud, Vol. VII, p. 145. **194.** Freud, Vol. XII, p. 72; Vol. XIV, p. 96. **195.** Freud, Vol. XIII, p. 243. **196.** *Ibid.,* pp. 243–244. **197.** Freud, Vol. XI, p. 188. **198.** *Ibid.,* p. 133. **199.** Freud, Vol. XVIII, p. 110. **200.** Freud, Vol. XXI, p. 102. **201.** Freud, Vol. I, p. 116. **202.** *Ibid.,* p. 121. **203.** *Ibid.* **204.** *Ibid.,* pp. 121–122. **205.** *Ibid.,* p.124. **206.** *Ibid.,* p. 125. **207.** Janet, 1920, p. 324. **208.** Freud, Vol. I, p. 127. **209.** *Ibid.,* p. 185. **210.** *Ibid.,* p. 183. **211.** *Ibid.* **212.** Freud, Vol. III, p. 203. **213.** Freud, Vol. VII, p. 274. **214.** Freud, 1954, p. 193. **215.** Freud, Vol. VII, pp. 264–276. **216.** Freud, Vol. III, p. 168. **217.** Freud, Vol. XIII, p. 159. **218.** Freud, Vol. VII, pp. 278–279. **219.** Freud, Vol. XII, pp. 248–249. **220.** Freud, Vol. XI, p. 218. **221.** *Ibid.,* p. 46; Vol. XVII, p. 204. **222.** Freud, Vol. XII, p. 236. **223.** Freud, Vol. III, p. 169. **224.** Freud, Vol. I, pp. 248–251. **225.** *Ibid.,* p. 256. **226.** Freud, Vol. VII, p. 53. **227.** Freud, Vol. XXIII, p. 184. **228.** Freud, Vol. XX, p. 91. **229.** Freud, Vol. XIV, p. 199. **230.** Freud, Vol. XII, p. 76. **231.** Freud, Vol. XX, p. 37. **232.** Freud, Vol. VII, p. 51. **233.** *Ibid.,* p. 45. **234.** *Ibid.,* p. 43. **235.** *Ibid.,* p. 44. **236.** Freud, Vol. XI, p. 50. **237.** Freud, Vol. XIX, p. 204. **238.** Freud, Vol. XI, p. 50. **239.** Freud, Vol. XX, p. 156. **240.** Nunberg and Federn, 1962, pp. 100–101. **241.** Freud, Vol. XIX, p. 185. **242.** Freud, Vol. I, p. 191. **243.** *Ibid.,* pp. 192–193. **244.** *Ibid.,* p. 193. **245.** *Ibid.,* p. 257. **246.** Freud, Vol. IX, pp. 60–61. **247.** Freud, Vol. X, pp. 114–115. **248.** Freud, Vol. XVII, p. 210. **249.** Freud, Vol. XX, p. 128. **250.** *Ibid.,* p. 162. **251.** *Ibid.* **252.** Freud, Vol. XXII, p. 85. **253.** Freud, Vol. XII, p. 77. **254.** Freud, Vol. XX, pp. 164–165. **255.** Freud, Vol. XXII, p. 85. **256.** Freud, Vol. XX, p. 144. **257.** *Ibid.,* p. 93. **258.** *Ibid.,* p. 130. **259.** Freud, Vol. XI, p. 37. **260.** Freud, Vol. XX, p. 139. **261.** Freud, Vol. XXII, p. 62. **262.** Freud, Vol. XXI, p. 135. **263.** *Ibid.,* p. 124. **264.** Freud, Vol. IX, p. 203. **265.** Freud, Vol. XVI, p. 434. **266.** Freud, Vol. XXI, pp. 142–143. **267.** *Ibid.,* p. 143. **268.** Freud, Vol. XIX, p. 54. **269.** Freud and Bullitt, 1967, p. 42. **270.** Freud, Vol. XIV, p. 312. **271.** Freud, Vol. II, p. 281. **272.** Freud, Vol. XVI, p. 438. **273.** Freud, Vol. I, p. 100; Freud, 1954, p. 151. **274.** Freud, Vol. XVI, p. 436. **275.** Freud, Vol. XII, p. 134. **276.** Freud, Vol. XI, p. 29. **277.** Freud, Vol. VI, p. 257. **278.** Freud, Vol. XXIII, p. 179. **279.** Freud, Vol. I, p. 217. **280.** Freud, Vol. II, p. 268. **281.** Freud, Vol. V, p. 517.

282. Freud, Vol. XVI, p. 291. **283.** Freud, Vol. XI, p. 49. **284.** Freud, Vol. I, p. 266; Vol. XIV, p. 311. **285.** Freud, Vol. XX, p. 27. **286.** Freud, Vol. XVI, p. 290. **287.** Freud, Vol. XII, p. 167. **288.** Freud, Vol. XVI, p. 442. **289.** Freud, Vol. VII, p. 116. **290.** Freud, Vol. XII, p. 101. **291.** *Ibid.*, p. 100. **292.** Freud, Vol. XVI, p. 440. **293.** Freud, Vol. XII, p. 139. **294.** Freud, Vol. XV, p. 87. **295.** Freud, Vol. VII, p. 267. **296.** Freud, Vol. I, p. 266. **297.** Freud, Vol. XVI, p. 453. **298.** Freud, Vol. XXII, p. 156. **299.** Freud, Vol. XII, p. 166. **300.** Freud, Vol. XI, pp. 144–145; Vol. XII, pp. 117–118, 164. **301.** Freud, Vol. XXII, p. 150. **302.** Freud, Vol. XII, p. 100. **303.** Nunberg and Federn, 1962, p. 102. **304.** Freud, Vol. XII, p. 106. **305.** Freud, Vol. XVII, p. 183. **306.** Freud, Vol. XI, p. 51. **307.** Freud, Vol. XII, p. 107. **308.** Freud, Vol. XVI, p. 444. **309.** *Ibid.*, p. 454. **310.** *Ibid.*, pp. 444–447. **311.** *Ibid.*, p. 444. **312.** *Ibid.*, p. 455. **313.** Freud, Vol. XXIII, p. 231. **314.** *Ibid.*, p. 233. **315.** *Ibid.*, pp. 232–233. **316.** *Ibid.*, p. 250. **317.** *Ibid.*, p. 249. **318.** Freud, Vol. XVI, p. 435. **319.** Freud, Vol. XI, pp. 144–150. **320.** *Ibid.*, p. 150. **321.** Jones, 1953, p. 28. **322.** Ansbacher, 1959. **323.** Freud, Vol. XI, p. 144. **324.** *Ibid.*, pp. 22–26. **325.** Freud, Vol. VI, p. 43. **326.** Freud, Vol. I, p. 82. **327.** Freud, Vol. XVII, pp. 51–52. **328.** Freud, Vol. XII, p. 114. **329.** Freud, Vol. XVII, p. 164. **330.** Freud, Vol. XVIII, p. 252. **331.** *Ibid.*, p. 150. **332.** Freud, Vol. XXII, p. 148. **333.** *Ibid.*, p. 155. **334.** *Ibid.*, p. 156. **335.** Freud, Vol. XII, p. 170. **336.** Freud, Vol. XV, p. 100. **337.** Freud, Vol. IV, p. 121. **338.** Freud, Vol. XV, p. 150. **339.** Freud, Vol. V, p. 345. **340.** Freud, Vol. IV, p. 228. **341.** Freud, Vol. XXII, p. 27. **342.** Freud, Vol. IV, p. 278. **343.** Freud, Vol. XV, p. 129. **344.** Freud, Vol. XXIII, p. 172. **345.** Freud, Vol. IV, p. 279. **346.** Freud, Vol. II, p. 263. **347.** Freud, Vol. XIX, p. 130. **348.** Freud, Vol. XV, p. 129. **349.** Freud, Vol. V, p. 608. **350.** Freud, Vol. XV, p. 114. **351.** Freud, Vol. IV, pp. 314–327. **352.** Freud, Vol. VI, p. 59. **353.** *Ibid.*, p. 94. **354.** Freud, Vol. XII, pp. 133–134. **355.** *Ibid.*, p. 133. **356.** *Ibid.*, p. 134. **357.** Freud, Vol. X, p. 180. **358.** Freud, Vol. XII, pp. 119–120. **359.** *Ibid.*, p. 153. **360.** *Ibid.*, pp. 140–141. **361.** Freud, Vol. XIII, p. 218. **362.** Freud, Vol. XXIII, p. 219.

2

The Individual Psychology of Alfred Adler

Although Sigmund Freud wrestled with identical issues, no man in the history of personality study met the problems of physical vs. psychological explanation more directly than Alfred Adler. In order to appreciate the form of "medical models" which preceded his appearance on the historical scene—and against which he reacted—we will survey a handful of theorists, most of whom Adler specifically mentioned in his own writings. Individual psychology will then appear against the backdrop of this earlier tradition.

Medical-Physical Models of Human Behavior

HIPPOCRATES (circa 400 B.C.)

Hippocrates completely rejected the views of earlier Babylonian and Egyptian medicine, which held that disease was a punishment sent by a god who infected the individual with a worm or possibly a small stone. Diseases were due to "natural" causes, Hippocrates said, engendered by such factors as improper diet or unsafe climate. Additionally, *humors* in the body combined in various ways to result not only in illness but in temperamental variations as well: black bile, blood, yellow bile, and phlegm. Mixed in the proper proportions the humors favored the body with health, but an imbalance among them resulted in what today might be termed a mental (or physical) illness. For example, an excess of black bile could result in melancholia (depression) and yellow bile in preponderance heralded a choleric disorder (irritability and hostility).

A healthy, energetic person would have blood in ascendance, and an easy-going, slow individual would have phlegm as the ascendant humor. This humoral model was based to considerable extent on clinical observation: a sickly, cranky individual might indeed exude a yellow substance at some point—such as pus from a sore or mixed in sputum from a cough—whereas, a healthy individual with a ruddy countenance surely appears quite saturated with health-giving red blood. Turning to Hippocrates' structural model, we find him proposing an antithetical scheme of body type which he also observed bore a certain relationship with physical disease. On the one hand we have a person with a thick, muscular, physically strong body (*habitus apoplecticus*) and on the other a person with a thin, delicate, physically weak body (*habitus phthisicus*). When illness strikes these body types, the former is more likely to suffer from a cerebral "stroke" (apoplexy) and the latter from tuberculosis (phthisis).[1]

If we were to trace the history of physical medicine it would be easy to show that Hippocrates' humoral theory was to stimulate not only the elaborate study of the function of our hepatic (blood) system, including nutrition and immunology, but also modern endocrinology as well. His structural concepts stimulated the investigations of anatomy and physical maturation. Passing over several centuries and ignoring many details relevant to the study of man, we find in the eighteenth and nineteenth centuries the kinds of physical theories which Adler was to oppose.

FRANZ JOSEPH GALL (1758–1828)

An interesting extension of the structural model is found in the thought of the German anatomist and physiologist Franz Joseph Gall, a contemporary of the even more eminent French naturalist, Jean Baptiste de Lamarck (1744–1829). It was Lamarck who suggested that characteristics acquired by one generation might be transmitted to its progeny. Thus, a man and woman who train themselves into magnificent physical condition might favor their child with a physique far above average

from birth, for the inheritance by the child of characteristics acquired by the parents in their life span was considered possible. We cannot judge what role the thought of Lamarck played in the theorizing of Gall, but it is clear that he reasoned along similar lines.

Gall's theoretical system is known as *phrenology* (from the Greek *phrenos*, meaning heart of mind, hence, "study of the mind"). His idea was that personality characteristics are subject to direction from the brain. Whether due to inheritance or even actual practice (acquisition) of some given personality trait (called "faculties of the mind"), Gall believed that an enlargement in the brain's structure could be assessed externally by studying the convolutions of the skull. In the same way that an arm muscle becomes enlarged with exercise, a brain region specifically related to some personality tendency would enlarge through use, press against the skull during maturation, and thus form a "bump" which might then be detected by an observer. Gall claimed to have empirically established a number of such relationships between personality characteristics and head conformations.

For example, the faculty of "combativeness" was said to exist back and upward from the ear, along the side of the head. Gall claimed that he found members of the lower classes, masculine females, and hostile males reflected a perceptible bulging of the skull in this region. There were over two dozen such regions mapped out by Gall and his students, including such faculties as secretiveness and desire.[2] As with Hippocrates the clumsy beginnings of Gall's phrenology indicate a prototypic conception which was to culminate in today's theories of brain localization. We no longer seek to localize self-esteem as he did, but we are aware that visual processes are mediated by the occipital regions of the brain, auditory by the temporal regions, and so forth. There is a pattern of distribution in the physical structure of the body all right, but is this in any direct way related to personality factors of behavior?

CHARLES ROBERT DARWIN (1809–1882)

No single person has done more to underwrite physical theories of human behavior than the British naturalist, Charles Darwin (1952b). This remains true despite the fact that many theorists—including Alfred Adler—have used Darwinian rationales to support a kind of spiritual evolution (vitalism) in mankind as well as a physical evolution. Although theories of hereditary transmission were scanty and no Mendelian concept of the gene was then extant to support his explanations, Darwin succeeded in fixing a revolutionary concept of how mankind seemed to be advancing in his state of physical change from lower to higher animal. This idea of progress from a lower to a higher order had taken several centuries to catch hold in man's thought, for we had earlier believed ourselves to have descended from a Golden-Age or Garden-of-Eden existence which was far more advanced than our present state.[3]

Man, Darwin claimed, as any creature of nature, advanced simply because he had necessarily, albeit fortuitously, succeeded in evolving a viable constitution and pattern of behavior which suited him to the environment. Plants and animals which were unable to meet the demands of their environment simply did not last long in the centuries upon centuries of "organic evolution." There was no God's hand at play in nature. Even Lamarckian inheritance of acquired characteristics was not necessary as an explanatory principle. Darwin never completely rejected Lamarck, and in fact, for a period of time he relied rather heavily on the latter's concepts. But fundamentally the "survival of the fittest" (Herbert Spencer's phrase) accounted for progress in adaptation. After all, if an offspring is weak it will not survive, will not bear progeny, and hence through this process of natural selection an inept species of life will be lost to the earth.

What about self-direction, choice, selection, and the evaluations of morality? Darwin's writings reflect an ambivalence over questions of this nature. For example, in *The Descent of Man* (1952a) he argued that morality was probably viable to a social group because the tribe which had the spirit of helping one another among its members would be more courageous, obedient, and sympathetic.[4] During times of war, when under the threat of defeat and dissolution, such a society would doubtless sustain its identity over an enemy horde of selfish individuals. Hence, morality—the Golden Rule —would have survival value in natural selection. Yet, a few paragraphs later in the same treatise Darwin acknowledged the opposite side of the moral coin when he observed:

We civilised men . . . do our utmost to check the process of elimination; we build asylums for the imbecile, the maimed, and the sick; we institute poor-laws; and our medical men exert their utmost skill to save the life of every one to the last moment. There is reason to believe that vaccination has preserved thousands, who from a weak constitution would formerly have succumbed to small-pox. Thus the weak members of civilised societies propagate their kind. No one who has attended to the breeding of domestic animals will doubt that this must be highly injurious to the race of man.[5]

Thus a Darwinian rationale can support either side of social issues like rugged individualism vs. communal sharing or government control vs. laissez faire politics.[6] The problem facing us here stems from the adequacy or inadequacy of making an analogy between *physical* and *social* evolutions of the "natural" order. Can we draw such parallels in attempting to explain the nature of social institutions? Darwin apparently felt we could, for he took the "morality has vitality through natural selection" argument as sufficient rationale to use moral codes as a principle of conduct in his own life. He therefore rejected supernatural explanations altogether—though he had once considered becoming a clergyman—and ended his days an agnostic humanist.

CESARE LOMBROSO (1836–1909)

Combining the thought of Gall with the newer insights of organic evolution, the Italian criminologist Cesare Lombroso argued that criminal populations reflected more physical anomalies than normal populations. Specifically, the criminal "type" was said to have "atavistic" physical signs, signifying that a degenerate process or a reversion to earlier evolutionary stages had been at work. Signs such as low foreheads, jaws which jut out beyond the upper face, or small, beady eyes set well back into the skull were supposedly indicative of a "throwback" (animalistic) mentality and hence criminality. By 1900 the Mendelian laws of hereditary transmission had been rediscovered and popularized. This theory of dominant and recessive genes, permitting an occasional return of older forms to manifestations in a current population, offered a ring of plausibility to the atavistic conception. Lombrosian thinking has not stood up well under the weight of subsequent evidence, and it is generally rejected today.

ERNST KRETSCHMER (1888–1964)

It remained for the German psychiatrist Ernst Kretschmer to adapt certain earlier body-build typologies (of Rostan in France and Viola in Italy) and to elevate this approach to a science. Kretschmer defined three basic body types: *pyknics* (rotund, large visceral mass, "portly" physiques), *athletics* (large bones, heavy musculature, robust individuals), and *asthenic* (thin, linear, "delicate" types). Kretschmer also reflected the tendency cited in the Introduction to move from pure types to traits in that he had "mixed" typologies in his classificatory scheme (e.g., having the torso of an athletic type and the long, linear legs of an asthenic).

The point of this typology was to assess whether or not a relationship between body build and mental illness existed. Kretschmer therefore embarked on a series of empirical studies in which he compared body type to an independent diagnosis of a patient's psychosis. He used a fairly elaborate check list of signs which could help the observer categorize a patient, who stood nude before him. Kretschmer found in general that pyknic types were prone to cyclothymic temperaments (i.e., moodiness, feeling "up" and then feeling "down" or "blue"), and when they became emotionally upset they developed a manic-depressive psychosis. Asthenic types, on the other hand, were shy personalities who developed schizophrenia (retreat from reality, secretiveness, muteness) if they became ill.

Here again, one might ask: What is at work in this physical-to-social intermingling of concepts? If one has a slight physical build it is more likely that he was a late pubescent; hence, the probability of being introverted and possibly a shy "loner" is greater. The corpulent child, on the other hand, may be relatively more likely to enter into interpersonal relationships, if only as a follower and part-time confidant. Reasoning along these lines, critics point out that the body type might not determine the mental illness except in a very indirect—social learning—sense. Once mentally ill, a shy person is just more likely to be called schizophrenic by the diagnosing physician, since that is the presumed "nature" of schizophrenia—to be split off from reality and live in a world of one's own. And since a sample of more outgoing individuals is likely to reflect mood variations, manic-depressive diagnoses will be more prevalent among such a group of patients.

EMIL KRAEPELIN (1856–1926)

This German neuropsychiatrist might be called the "father of modern psychiatric diagnosis." Kraepelin took a number of clinical syndromes which had been named by others, and combining these with his own observations, proposed a scheme in 1883 which has survived in general outline to the present. Clinical typing is no longer considered vitally important in modern psychiatry, but thanks in part to the weight of convention—and in many instances thanks literally to legal statutes which call for a typing of patients "by law"—the practice of Kraepelinian diagnosis in mental disturbance has survived.

The classical Kraepelinian scheme is essentially as follows: the schizophrenic psychosis breaks down into four types: *simple* (distracted, blunted affect, asocial tendencies); *paranoid* (suspiciousness, delusions of persecution); *catatonic* (rigid and mute, or highly excited and assaultive); and *hebephrenic* ("silly," most deteriorated in personality of all subgroups). Originally, Kraepelin had an intricate subgrouping of the manic-depressive disorders, and he in fact devoted most of his personal efforts to this psychosis because he believed schizophrenia (or *dementia praecox,* as he called it) was incurable. In time, however, he simply lumped all mood disorders which had either *manic* (extremely excited, expansive and active behavior) or *depressive* (retarded, sorrowful, self-destructive behavior) features into one category. Although he occasionally acknowledged an etiological role for psychological influences, Kraepelin's fundamental theory was organic, emphasizing heredity and body chemistry. This period of medical history (1900–1911) also saw the identification of general paresis (a form of psychosis) as due to a syphilitic infection of the brain. Hence, any approach which promised to identify disease entities held great fascination for the academicians and practicing psychiatrists alike at the turn of the twentieth century.

WILLIAM H. SHELDON (1899–   )

Although not relevant as a precedent theorist for Adler, we would be remiss to neglect a review of William H. Sheldon's "constitutional psychology." This American psychologist-psychiatrist has taken the logic of Hippocrates and the scientific expertise of Kretschmer in theorizing the body build–temperament relationship to its ultimate. His theoretical statement is the clearest and most complete account

available in this general area of theoretical study.

Sheldon began with a reliance on hereditary factors by postulating a *morphogenotype* (gene-induced body form).[7] To observe the ultimate phenotypic manifestation of the morphogenotype, Sheldon felt it was essential to assess each individual along what he called three "primary components of physique." Here he relied upon a brilliant analogy to the *in utero* development of the human embryo. During cell division and multiplication, as the developing organism enlarges through the blastula and gastrula stages, three levels of cells can eventually be distinguished: the *ectodermal* or outer layer of the embryo, which eventually develops into the nervous system, sense organs, skin, and hair; the *endodermal* or inner layer of cells, which develops into the digestive system and other visceral organs; and finally, the *mesodermal* or intermediate layer of cells, which develops into the muscles, bones, blood vessels, and sex glands of the body. What Sheldon did was to parallel this tripartite breakdown of *in utero* embryonic dermal layers to a tripartite breakdown of the Kretschmerian variety thereby uniting internal with external factors.[8]

Thus, each individual is to be assessed along a primary component of physique termed *endomorphy* (digestive developments pronounced, so that physique is rounded, soft, and often corpulent, similar to "pyknic"), a primary component termed *mesomorphy* (muscular, strong, big boned, tough, similar to "athletic"), and a primary component of physique termed *ectomorphy* (thin, lightly muscled, fragile, similar to "asthenic"). The theory has it that everyone is influenced along all three dimensions thanks to his morphogenotypic, hereditary predilections, and that what we actually "type" someone as being is merely an overriding evaluation of all three factors at once. The primary components of physique therefore act as trait constructs, but when stressing one such factor we effectively have a typology.

Improving on Kretschmer's check-list rating procedure, Sheldon introduced the practice of having a subject photographed against a standard background in the nude, with pictures of him taken from the side, front, and back. He then worked out a reliable method of anthropometric measurement for each of the primary components—using such measures as ratio of one body part to another, and height to girth. Several indices for each component of physique are then collapsed into a single number, along a seven-point scale, with "1" a low and "7" a high score on the component in question. Hence, any given individual's combined ratings on all three components would read something like 7–3–1 or 2–1–6. Since the first number always refers to endomorphy, the second to mesomorphy, and the third to ectomorphy we would have here an endomorphic and an ectomorphic body type, in that order. This succession of three scores is called the *somatotype* (*soma* is Greek for body, hence "body type").

Sheldon also made use of ratings based on his photographs which are termed the "secondary components of physique." One such component is *dysplasia,* which is an inconsistent or uneven mixture of the primary components, much after the fashion of Kretschmer's "mixed" rating. Another is *gynandromorphy* (*g*-index), which is a rating of how much a subject possesses characteristics of the opposite sex. Feminine-appearing men would thus receive an elevated scoring.[9] Finally, the *textural* aspect (*t*-index) deals with the coarseness of skin and hair, the proportions of body build combined in an aesthetically pleasant or unpleasant fashion.

Basing his approach on an extensive review of the personality theory literature, Sheldon next devised what he termed were three "primary components of temperament," as follows: *viscerotonia* (people who love physical comfort, socially outgoing, complacent and amiable, tolerant and relaxed, love to eat and mix socially); *somatotonia* (assertive, physically active people, who love risk-taking, competition, and the assumption of command in social situations; can be ruthless, loud, and combative); *cerebrotonia* (people with restraint in action and emotion, a love of privacy, tendencies to impulsivity and unpredictability on occasion, and a hypersensitivity to pain). Sheldon found a significant relationship between: (1) endomorphy and viscerotonia (reminding us of Freud's oral type, Chapter 1); (2) mesomorphy and somatotonia; and (3) ectomorphy and cerebrotonia. He has also found some support for the Kretschmerian thesis we discussed above.[10] The same questions come to mind from reading Sheldon as arose in reaction to the theory of Kretschmer.

Modern Trends in Biochemistry and Psychopharmacology. As can be seen from the historical overview, the biological emphasis in personality has been placed on the Hippocratic body-types model rather than on the humoral model. We must appreciate the fact, however, that at some level these two models become one because the process which carries the development of one's physique along is chemical. Only an arbitrary distinction can be made between what is a physical-constitutional and what is a chemical theory of human behavior. Furthermore, we do an injustice if we fail to acknowledge the strong current of biochemistry which has continuously nourished the thought of psychologists.[11] For example, early in this century deficiencies of vitamin B were shown to lead to serious disorders, such as pellagra and beriberi, which in turn led to behavioral anomalies of a psychotic nature due to their harmful effects on brain metabolism. The work with the mentally retarded, in which administration of thyroid extract (an endocrine substance) led to improvement in cretinism (a form of mental retardation) has spurred all manner of chemical investigations into the nature of mental functioning.[12]

Thanks to the relative success of certain organic cures in mental illness, such as insulin-, Metrazol-, and electro-convulsive treatments, a continuing series of investigations in this area has based its theories upon organic models, such as correcting misfiring circuits in the brain, or wiping out unpleasant "memory banks" so that a patient can come upon life with a fresh start. A highly popular theory continues to center around some form of congenital or acquired physiological lack in the individual's organic functioning, one which allows the body to produce substances not ordinarily found in a healthy body—either as a byproduct via some harmful but yet undetermined process, or possibly more directly as an injurious "foreign substance."[13] Foreign proteins in the blood are often cited, and some even speak of a "schizophrenic serum."[14] It follows that if abnormal behavior is reducible to serums and blood physiology, personality will have such roots as well. We continue to wait for the chemical breakthrough which will isolate a physiological cause of mental illness, but we can already acknowledge a chemical breakthrough in the treatment of such disorders in recent decades.

We refer here to the remarkable success of relaxant or "psychotropic" drugs (tranquilizers, antidepressants). The number of beds occupied by mental patients has been drastically reduced thanks to the increased manageability engendered through use of a host of such "miracle drugs," which will not be listed since they multiply in number at an astonishing rate.[15] There seems little doubt about the significant contribution to the treatment of the mentally ill made by such drugs. Yet, how much this has to do with personality factors *per se* is debatable. A more directly related drug issue which has dramatically come to the fore in the latter half of the twentieth century involves the use of hallucinogenic drugs such as *mescaline* and *lysergic acid diethylamide* (LSD). Since the users of such drugs often cite as their reason the expanding of consciousness, or some related mystical experience of a quasi-religious nature, we must recognize a potential role for drug-induced states in personality theory.

Biographical Overview

Alfred Adler was born on 7 February 1870 in a suburb of Vienna, the son of Hungarian-Jewish parents. Few Jews lived in his community, and so Adler never acquired a strong cultural identity. Although he attended Synagogue as a boy, as an adult he considered himself a Christian.[16] Adler's father was a grain merchant, and though the family went through a period of financial setback, his earliest years were not made difficult by material want. He was the second son and third child in a family of six children (four boys and two girls). This proved highly significant in his life (and eventual personality theory) for he always seemed to live in the shadow of his older (first born) brother's successes. Though he was apparently fairly popular, a good singer, and a physically active child, Adler did not think of his childhood as a particularly happy time of life.[17]

He suffered from rickets while an infant, and his choice of a medical career in life stemmed from a near-fatal bout with pneumonia at the age of five.[18] After he miraculously recovered Adler resolved someday to become a physician. In his mature outlook, Adler believed that young people should be encouraged to make career or occupational choices early in life (by age 15).[19]

Adler was clearly his "father's son," and although he was to look back at his mother with understanding and acceptance in later years, he was not very close to her. He disliked staying home and spent many hours outdoors, trying to set records of accomplishment in children's activities which might compare favorably with his older brother's. Adler admitted that he brought much of his childhood misery on himself as a result of his great ambition.[20] He was only an average student, however. In time, true to his aspiration, Adler succeeded in attaining the medical degree from the University of Vienna in 1895, but he seems to have lacked a close mentor-student relationship with a professor to match Freud's tie to Brücke (Chapter 1) or Jung's tie to Bleuler (Chapter 3).[21] He did form an attachment to a group of student socialists in college, some of whom were Marxian, and Adler seems to have met his wife in this group.[22] Raissa Adler was from a wealthy Russian family, and she was much the enlightened, intellectual revolutionary of her time.[23] They were married in 1897 and had three daughters and one son.

Adler opened his first office as medical general practitioner in a neighborhood near the Prater, Vienna's famous amusement park. His patients were primarily of the lower social classes, and significantly, several of them were performers, artists and acrobats from the nearby amusement stands. Adler found that these physically skillful and often exceedingly strong performers had developed their outstanding abilities in reaction to a physical weakness or accident in childhood.[24] Although not documented with certainty, the initial contact with Freud apparently stemmed from a defense Adler made of Freudian theory in the public press. In line with his socialistic leanings, Adler was an indefatigable champion of the underdog. In 1902 he was invited by Freud along with others to begin a series of weekly meetings dealing with psychoanalysis. This is the group which eventually mushroomed into the Vienna and then International Psycho-Analytic Association. He was made the first President of the Vienna group in 1910. By the close of 1911 he had resigned his position and broken permanently with Freud.

The split with Freud can be credited to many factors, not the least of which was that Adler simply rejected the domination of a "second older brother." In 1907 he published his first major work, the study of *Organ Inferiority and Its Psychical Compensation*.[25] This was heavily flavored with physicalistic concepts, and we shall consider it in the chapter content to follow. Shortly thereafter he published a paper in which he introduced the concept of the "ag-

gressive drive." But as the years slipped by Adler became increasingly reluctant to think of human behavior in drive terms. He was developing a "social situational" conception of human behavior. Adler was particularly dissatisfied with Freud's insistence upon the omnipresent sexual instinct, and apparently the issue which brought their divergence in outlook to a "point of no return" was the Oedipal complex.[26] An unfortunate situation developed in which sides crystallized, and Freud was apparently prompted by the loyal supporters of his views to force Adler's hand in some way. His response was to write to the psycho-analytical journal which both men edited, saying that his name could no longer remain on the title page unless Adler's name was removed. Adler resigned and though Freud tried in a subsequent meeting of the Association to find some middle ground, the split was irreparable. This was probably the most acrimonious parting of the ways Freud ever had with a former associate.

Nine other members of the Vienna Psycho-Analytic Association left the meeting and the organization with Adler.[27] Individuals from this core established an Adlerian group which was initially called the "Society for Free Psycho-Analytic Research," an obvious jibe at Freud's authoritarianism.[28] Eventually they were to establish their own journal, and Adler's supporters were to increase and form into organizations all over the world. Shortly after the break with Freud, Adler discontinued his general practice and took up psychiatry as a full-time profession. It was 1911, and he was clearly his own man.

One of the first important influences on Adler's thought following the Freud period was a book published in 1911 by Hans Vaihinger, entitled *The Philosophy of "As If"*.[29] Vaihinger was a neo-Kantian admirer of Nietzsche, who took the spirit of Kant's ethical doctrine to "behave *as if* a God exists" and developed it into a concept of "fictions" of which Adler was to make use. Yet, we can see a drifting away from fictionalism in Adlerian thought over time, with a concomitantly growing emphasis on what he took to be the lessons of Darwinian evolutionary theory. Adler was to carry on a lengthy and congenial correspondence with Jan Christian Smuts, whose book *Holism and Evolution* appeared in 1926.[30] Adler's last book, *Social Interest: A Challenge to Mankind* (1964; published first in 1933), is heavily colored with evolutionary concepts.

It is actually possible to identify the period in his life when *social interest (Gemeinschaftsgefühl)* tipped the theoretical scales for Adler and literally recast his outlook. It was immediately following World War I. Adler had spent two years as a doctor near the Russian front. He was later in charge of a hospital ward which treated Russian prisoners suffering from typhus. He then returned to Vienna and worked in a military hospital setting. He also visited a children's hospital and saw the wretched effects of war from this heart-rending perspective. Returning to his followers after discharge, a definite change had come over Adler. He was always a good mixer and an optimistic, convivial, and affectionate friend. But now his energies were directed toward a single purpose: his theoretical approach was to be dedicated to the furtherance of "social interest." Man must fulfill the potential which evolution was nurturing within his very bosom and cultivate a sense of responsibility and care for his fellow man.[31]

This shift in emphasis, combined with Adler's unwillingness to associate his movement with a specific socialist political philosophy, was greeted with outcries of protest by many of his followers. The strong moralistic flavor of social interest seemed to wash away the earlier emphasis on subjectivity and relativism in the Vaihinger period. By 1925 considerable internal dissension had developed over these and other issues—culminating in an "old guard" vs. the "young Turks" confrontation which re-enacted the Freudian drama like a haunting replay of the past. At a heated meeting, in which the younger Adlerians clashed

with the old guard, Adler was moved, if not actively to support, then at least to do nothing which might contradict his more rabid young advocates. His older, influential followers, thus stymied by his reticence to defend their claims, left the auditorium and broke off from him much as he had broken off from Freud years before.[32] Doubtless Adler's personal nonauthoritarianism and sympathy with the underdog played a role in his actions, which cost him dearly for he lost the theoretical support in the Viennese academic circles that individual psychology might otherwise have enjoyed.

Meanwhile, the practical effects of individual psychology were being felt throughout Vienna. Following the war Adler held a minor political post, as a vice-chairman of a "workers committee," and through such contacts he made friends with certain officials of the Social Democratic

Alfred Adler

Party, which had taken power. Through one of these associates Adler succeeded in having an Individual Psychology Clinic attached to each of more than 30 of the state schools of Vienna.[33] These "advisory councils" were essentially child guidance clinics in which the entire family participated in counseling. Between 1921 and 1934 Adler and his students ran these clinics with such success that a noticeable drop in delinquency was recorded in the Vienna area.

In one sense, the loss of his older, scholarly, and pedantic followers spurred Adler to implement the kind of psychology he really favored, a psychology of "use" which today might be called "applied" psychology. Adler devoted himself to adult education, lecturing to groups of teachers and parents, in a very practical "conversational" fashion. His psychology has ever since been viewed by some as superficial and nontechnical. Of course, nothing could have upset Adler less than this charge. Unlike Freud, whose patients were predominantly from the upper social classes, Adler prided himself in being a psychologist for the common man as he took many clients from the lower classes as well.[34]

In 1926, Adler made his first trip to the United States. He later (1929–1930) spent one year as lecturer on the temporary faculty of Columbia University and then accepted a position as Visiting Professor for Medical Psychology at the Long Island College of Medicine—a position he held until his death. The situation in Vienna was deteriorating over this period due to the rise of fascism.[35] In 1934, after the Austro-fascists had come to power (they later closed his clinics), Adler left Vienna permanently and lived in New York with his wife.[36] His death came unexpectedly, on a European speaking tour. Adler was in the process of delivering a series of lectures at Aberdeen University in Scotland. The lectures were going extremely well, when following breakfast on 28 May 1937 Adler went for an accustomed stroll during which he suffered a heart attack (degenera-tion of the heart muscle) and died. Adler had lived 67 years.

Personality Theory

STRUCTURAL CONSTRUCTS

DUALISM, HOLISM, AND THE "LAW OF MOVEMENT"

The human organism is a *holistic* organism in the Adlerian view. One can understand interactions of mind-body only if he sees the totality of this process.[37] Constructs which seek to divide this holism fail to capture the truth due to their unwise arbitrariness. How then are we to think of mind? What differentiates mentalistic from nonmentalistic creatures? The factor of movement, answered Adler. Plants, for example, are *rooted* products of nature. Even if a plant could see that it was about to be ground underfoot by a stroller, it could do nothing to deflect the fatal end: "All moving beings, however, can foresee and reckon up the direction in which to move; and this fact makes it necessary to postulate that they have minds or souls. . . . This foreseeing the direction of movement is the central principle of the mind."[38]

Through what Adler liked to call the "law of movement"[39] mind and body are united. He argued that mentality may be seen in both physical *and* psychological actions of people. Adlerian structural constructs are thus intimately related to motivational (movement) constructs. As he once phrased it: "Movement becomes moulded movement—[i.e.] form. Thus it is possible to gain a knowledge of mankind from form, if we recognize in it the movement that shapes it."[40] Man is not a machine-like structure first and a moving system secondly, as when pushed by libido or somesuch. Man appears to have structure only because his behavioral movements take on the style (form) of what we have come to call "personality."

Adler was thus historically important to the

development of what is called *nonverbal communication* or *expressive movement* in interpersonal relations. He proposed that in man an *organ dialect* (*organ jargon*) could be noted in the way a man carried himself, the thrust of his jaw or the steadiness of his gaze.[41] Man speaks to us through his total mind-body, and the message so communicated can be guessed if we as observers simply appreciate the holistic nature of these two sides of the same coin.[42] One did not need a "depth psychology" to grasp what was being conveyed. Freud erred when he saw in the child-like manifestations of the adult—bed-wetting or retention of faeces—a *regression* to earlier times which had been prompted by the mind's unconscious eye. This was rather a continuing and unchanging physical expression of the organ dialect variety, expressing itself in the present as it had in the past.[43]

Adler did accept the distinction between a mind and a body in *animate* creatures. He agreed that some natural products with physical bodies lack minds, and the strategies of mental events are something different in kind from physical events. He viewed mentality in terms of *directed* movement. Purely physical actions lack goals, whereas psychic actions are predicated on and would be impossible without the projection of a goal. In 1914 he put into words the most basic law which his thinking was to retain throughout his mature years as theorist: "If we look at the matter more closely, we shall find the following law holding in the development of all psychic happenings: *we cannot think, feel, will, or act without the perception of some goal.*"[44] Since this principle of a goal direction distinguishes psychic from physical actions Adler cannot be labeled monistic. The monist would place emphasis on the *similarity* between mental and physical events.

GOAL ORIENTATION IN ALL PSYCHIC LIVING

The psyche, or the "soul" (Greek root of "psyche") as he sometimes referred to it,[45] was for Adler merely the *locus of movement,* set in the context of social ties as well as the individual's unique striving for advantages in life.[46] Adler's definitions of the psyche were thus likely to be framed in functional terms, as when he spoke of the psychic organs as: ". . . the evolution of a hereditary capability . . . for offense and defence with which the living organism responds according to the situation in which it finds itself."[47] Although this definition recognizes the role heredity plays in evolving the psyche, Adler was quick to point out that hereditary explanations fail to capture the true nature of the human soul (psyche).[48] Arguments from heredity turn our attention backward, to the fixedness of the physical past, rather than forward, to the uniqueness of the future. Hence, "It seems hardly possible to recognize in the psychic organ, the soul, anything but a force acting toward a goal, and Individual Psychology considers all the manifestations of the human soul as though they were directed toward a goal."[49]

Not only is man goal directed through his psychic living, but he never acts at cross-purposes with himself as Freudian psychology would have it. As mind and body can move in unison, conscious and unconscious psychic factors strive for the *same* ends.[50] Of course consciousness may conflict with unconsciousness over the means to these ends.[51] So-called unconscious psychic contents are poorly formulated intentions; they are "parts of our consciousness of which we have not fully understood the significance."[52]

The biological significance of consciousness in the human animal stems from the fact that it furthers the likelihood of a unified life plan.[53] The less an individual knows about his life plan the less effectively will he further the goals toward which it is impelling him. We customarily think of this as a case of being under the direction of the unconscious, but this does not mean that our conscious motives would "really" be opposed to this goal striving. If the man under unconscious direction could understand his entire personality correctly, he would know that there is no contradiction in ultimate goals (intentions) between the two spheres of the psyche even though it may on first blush appear to be that way.[54] The point of individual psychology is to teach people how to assess their *total* behavior, rather than easily succumbing to the plausibilities advanced by their conscious understanding.

STYLE OF LIFE

Adler believed that man was an animal who needed to frame his existence with meanings. Yet meanings are not natural concomitants of life's experience; they are applied to life by man's highly personal ideas.[55] Sometimes the meanings which we ascribe to our life situations are erroneous, so that errors result in our point of view.[56] Whether it stems from accurate or inaccurate meanings, the wise psychologist knows that *"a person's behaviour springs from his idea."*[57] One of the earliest and most important guiding ideas which the person formulates is the *prototype,* defined by Adler as the "original form of an individual's adaptation to life."[58] At a very early age, roughly between three and five years, the child assesses his life circumstance and then lays down a prototypical life plan of action.[59] This plan is rarely understood completely in consciousness, so most often one's prototype is unconscious, consisting of a goal and a relevant strategy for achieving that goal in the prototype. In fact, Adler once referred to the prototype as the "complete goal" of the life style.[60]

Once the prototype has been formulated, the child continues to ascribe the meanings contained therein to his life experience as he grows to manhood. He makes his own "law of movement" by constantly conforming to the dictates or implications of his life plan, the prototype. In drawing out this process of living according to a strategy, Adler experimented with various descriptive constructs. In 1913 he spoke of it as an *ego line.*[61] By 1914 he was speaking of the course of life as a *life line,* and then a *life plan.*[62] He later spoke of the graph

of life as a running path of development being carried on by the prototype.[63] It was not until the middle 1920s that he finally coined the phrase which has come to be most widely known in this facet of his theory: *style of life.*[64]

If the style of life was the totality of life's movement, then the *ego* was the "personality as a whole."[65] "Typing" people, trying to capture them as a whole with descriptive terms such as the oral personality, for Adler represented an ego terminology. There is surely more to the life of this individual than his presumed "orality." Yet the designation may well fit and may indeed communicate something about his personality.[66] Thus personality for the individual psychologist is roughly identical to an ego concept, and both in turn designate a totality of intermingling life traits which have been learned and obviously determined by such complex factors as the person's life opportunities, his prototypical life plan, his resulting law of movement, and the successes he achieved in reaching his goals.[67] If we now refer to *all* factors at once, we begin to use a life-style designation. But there are many instances when a more restricted term is satisfactory and a term like *ego* proves useful. Additionally, there is the strong suggestion that ego meant for Adler the understood (the conscious) psychic contents. The not-understood (unconscious) factors were also to be reckoned with in capturing man's life, of course, and when we do this we begin speaking in life-style terms.

Adler also used a concept of the *self,* but this was not precisely a structural construct. It enters into the theory more properly as a motivational construct, and we shall be taking it up later. When a theorist uses a self-construct structurally he ordinarily refers to a self-image, or possibly a self-identity. However, Adler specifically rejected the approach which reduced behavior to an individual's self-conception. Even though he viewed man as being moved by ideas and the meanings which they conveyed, Adler preferred to measure man by his actions, rather than by what he thought or said of himself. As he summed it up: "The only thing we can evaluate are his [i.e., a person's] actions. Thus, a person may consider himself an egoist, whereas we may find that he is capable of altruism and working with others. On the other hand, many people may consider themselves as real 'fellow men,' but a closer examination may show us, unfortunately, that such is not the case."[68] Note here the obvious stress Adler put on the conscious self-image. One gets a rather "light treatment" of the unconscious in Adlerian psychology. It is not a major concept, since it is viewed as the *lack* of something (understanding) rather than the positive assertion of a characteristic.

In order to clarify our thinking on the major structural terms of this section, Figure 8 pre-sents a schematization of the style of life. Note that an abscissa labeled the "span of life" runs from birth to maturity. The ordinate symbolizes increasing life experience, as the child moves from cradle out to the world. He eventually works out his *law of movement* as he gains experience. By roughly age five he has formulated a prototype which frames the meaning of existence and shapes his goals as a life plan. Let us say that the child of Figure 8 has adopted the prototype of being a "Peck's bad boy." For whatever reason, he has essentially decided to aspire to naughtiness. The prototype is symbolized as a scroll, with wavy lines running through it as if we were looking at a partly unfurled road map. The idea here, of course, is that the road map points

Figure 8
Style of Life

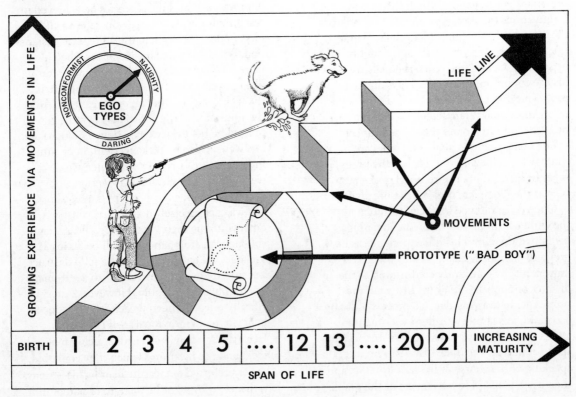

out the various "moves" which our individual child must make in order to retain his particular life style of being a "bad boy." As the individual in fact behaves according to his prototype, the wavy lines over the years act out the plan proposed by the prototype (labeled the *life line*). Adler was fond of referring to these life-line moves or strategies as the games people play in life.[69]

As an adult, the individual would naturally continue his life plan (prototype) by being a nonconformist, possibly a practical joker or even an asocial "individualist." If at any point along the way to maturity we "type" him in some such fashion, considering his personality as a totality, then this characterization would be an *ego* reference. His ego designations might thus change over time—as, from naughty child, to daring teenager, to nonconforming adult (see Figure 8). But the basic prototype would remain unchanged, even as he might shift to a new, previously unused strategy in the game of life. Indeed, Adler once observed that: "Very few individuals have ever been able to change the behavior pattern of their childhood, though in adult life they have found themselves in entirely different situations. A change of attitude in adult life need not necessarily signify a change of behavior pattern. . . . [The] goal in life is also unaltered."[70] Hence, when we step back and view the entire process, past, present, and future, prototype and law of movement, ego and life line, we capture the totality of Figure 8 in the phrase: *style of life*.

THE MEANING OF INDIVIDUAL: SUBJECTIVITY AND UNIQUENESS

In 1914 Adler summed up individual psychology as follows: ". . . I have called [my approach] '*comparative individual psychology*.' By starting with the assumption of the *unity of the individual*, an attempt is made to obtain a picture of this unified personality regarded as a variant of individual life-manifestations and forms of expression. The individual traits are then compared with one another, brought into a common plane, and finally fused together to form a composite portrait that is, in turn, individualized."[71] These traits of personality are acquired in maturation via the prototypical influence and are *not* inherited.[72]

Adler viewed each person as highly unique and in this vein he meant "subjective" when he used the term *individual*. In referring to the maturation and education of the school child he said: "There is always something subjective in the development of a child and it is this individuality which pedagogues must investigate. It is this individuality which prevents the application of general rules in the education of groups of children."[73] It is important to appreciate this subjectivity meaning of individual, because Adler also made great use of social or group factors in his theory. Since he felt it was impossible to get the individual's subjective point of view without having proper knowledge of the possibilities his social environment afforded him, Adler clearly stated that "Individual Psychology comes into contact with sociology."[74] But the focus of Adlerian psychology is always on the subjective life style, the totality of factors which go to make up the unique individual, rather than group factors as such. Men do not strive for "sameness."[75] Every life pattern which we see before our eyes *could* have been different.[76]

It was Vaihinger's concept of *mental fiction* which provided Adler with the construction he needed to capture the subjectivity of his theoretical outlook. Vaihinger had noted that *fictio* is taken from the Latin root meaning to invent, give shape, form, or construct.[77] Hence, the concept of a *prototype* is a direct translation of the fiction, though Adler also specifically used the terms *fictions* or *fictive goals* before he used the prototype phrasing to convey the same meaning.[78] Further, just as Vaihinger had claimed that the "real" world was not real, but merely appearing "as if" it were the way we wanted it to be, Adler argued that the individual behaves "as if" his life experiences were like the (fictional) prototype spelled them out to be.

Prototypes formulated the meridians and parallels of personal life maps, but maps can be wrong. A map which is in error as to the lay of the land is not only useless, it is dangerous. As he developed his theory of personality and especially psychotherapy, Adler became increasingly prone to refer to fictions in a pejorative sense,[79] as when he referred to the neurotic as being "nailed to the cross of his fiction."[80] Normals do not *lack* fictions, of course. We all have them; for instance, we believe that our country is the "best"—or the "worst"—on earth. Such consciously expressed beliefs, like the self-concepts described above, are likely to be *fictive* and hence erroneous.

Adler was never entirely committed to the completely relativistic outlook of Vaihinger. For Vaihinger, all beliefs were fictions, and one man's "error" was only an error because another man's "error" somehow gained the upper hand and convinced the first party that he was wrong. There was no "real world" on which to base absolutes, so that convention decided which fiction was "true." Adler, on the other hand, first thought of fictions as prototypes, then incorporated the prototype notion into his formal theory and subsequently referred to fictions as *discernible* errors. For a time, Adler even proposed a *counterfiction* construct which balanced the excessive claims that a given fiction might make. As he said: "This counterfiction consists of ever-present corrective factors and brings about the change of form of the guiding fiction [i.e., the basic prototype]. This counterfiction forces considerations upon the guiding fiction, takes social and ethical demands of the future in account with their real weight, and, in doing so, insures reasonableness."[81] This reference to the "social and ethical demands" should be kept in mind, for at this point in time (1912) Adler was willing to call these counter*fictions*. Following his return from World War I, however, he was not so ready to agree that all social demands are fictional. As we shall see, Adler was to find his absolutes in evolutionary theory.

MOTIVATIONAL CONSTRUCTS

ADLER'S EARLY USE OF ORGANIC CONSTRUCTS

Adler's first book, *Study of Organ Inferiority* (1907), was based largely on a medical model of abnormal behavior. The central thesis of the book was a kind of "Achilles heel" argument in which Adler contended that congenital or developmentally retarded (physical) *organ inferiorities* could lead to "a special tension in the psychical apparatus."[82] By *organ* Adler meant virtually any physically identifiable aspect of the human body, like the eyes, the leg muscles, or even the nerve tract developments leading from the kidneys to the urinary apparatus. In fact, Adler made a special study of the latter type of organ inferiority in children, noting that such individuals were more likely to develop enuresis than migraine headaches—assuming that a bodily disorder was to afflict them.[83] One breaks down at his weakest point. Adler cited over 50 cases in this study, and he tied the proclivity to enuresis to *hereditary* anomalies—although he later eschewed this case-citation form of theorizing.[84] In addition to the various organic inferiorities of the body which reflect themselves in symptoms (like enuresis) Adler felt that an invariable concomitant, synchronous *inferiority of the brain,* was associated with neurotic conditions.[85] This brain inferiority was a multiplying factor, since the combination of a heightened tension in the nervous system and a brain which lacked the potential to accommodate such rises in tension surely made a breakdown likely.

Adler found that not all children whom he suspected of having the necessary organic inferiorities (brain and related urinary weakness) actually developed enuresis. Some did exhibit this symptom, but only during certain times of the day or night. Others did not persist as enuretics but developed neuroses.[86] It was this belief in the multiplicity of response to organic inferiority which gave Adler his first inkling that the patient as an intentional *person* contributed something subjectively to the situation in which he found himself. Illness was not a simple cause-effect business.[87]

COMPENSATION

In order to explain the varied reaction to organic inferiorities Adler proposed one of his most important early concepts: *compensation*. Initially, he described this process in organic terms: "As soon as the equilibrium, which must be assumed to govern the economy of the individual organ or the whole organism, appears to be disturbed due to inadequacy of form or function, a certain biological process is initiated in the inferior organs. The unsatisfied demands increase until the deficit is made up through growth of the inferior organ, of the paired organ, or of some other organ which can serve as a substitute completely or in part."[88] For example, a child might be susceptible to inner ear infections. Having suffered through several of these illnesses—assuming no serious permanent damage to his hearing—he might develop such sensitivity to sound that this initial inferiority might evolve into an exceptional strength. Alerted to the finer nuances of sound or rhythmic variations he may grow up to be a talented musician.[89] Compensation, therefore, refers to a quasi-Lamarckian countering reaction to some deficit, either in the organ initially affected or in other organs which have retained the capacity to function. A man who develops a keen sense of hearing following the loss of his eyesight would also be compensating.

The response to organic inferiorities among potentially enuretic children is not uniform because compensatory activities vary among these children. The counter to the handicap explains the clinical variability; social—that is, interpersonal or psychological—counters (compensations) exist as well as the directly physical counters. As Adler said: "Enuresis can be overcome, except among feeble-minded children, if the child ceases to use the imperfection of his organs for a mistaken purpose."[90] By empha-

sizing the subjective goal direction of all behavior Adler succeeded in becoming a *psychologist* rather than merely a physicalistic or mechanistic theorist as were most of the practicing physicians of his time.

This transition in his development was a gradual one. Initially, the role of what we might term psychological strategies in behavior was subsumed by a kind of organic compensation of the brain in which Adler suggested that the brain simply increased proficiency due to the added size it might have attained in the process. This would be like the arm muscle of an originally puny teenager which swells into a powerful structure thanks to daily lifting weights. Here is how Adler captured this mechanical form of brain compensation in 1907: ". . . compensation is due to overperformance and increased growth of the brain. This strengthening of the psychological superstructure is shown by the successful outcome; its relation to steady exercise is easily guessed. . . . The psychological manifestations of such an organ may be more plentiful and better developed as far as drive, sensitivity, attention, memory, apperception, empathy, and consciousness are concerned."[91] This line of thought is not very original. It departs little from the theories we reviewed at the outset of this chapter, and in time he was to drop this conceptualization entirely.

ADLER'S SHIFT FROM ORGANIC TO SOCIO-PSYCHOLOGICAL EXPLANATION

Whether it was the influence of his student days or simply due to his growing experience as clinician, between roughly 1910 and 1918 Adler reflected a continuing move away from physicalistic constructs to the use of socio-psychological explanations. He specifically acknowledged parallels between his theory and Marx's social (not economic) theories.[92] In time, he came to speak against such historically important physical models as those of Hippocrates[93] and Lombroso.[94] He acknowledged Kretschmer's brilliance[95] but discarded his attempts to reduce human personality to internal chemical processes.[96]

Adler noted that a child who was born with a poor digestive system would receive a certain amount of pampering from his parents. The likelihood of his becoming a spoiled child, of learning to give up in the face of adversity, is doubtless greater than a child born with healthy internal organs.[97] Yet, what is at work here? Is the resultant personality *due to* the weak stomach, or is it the result of a complex interaction of the parental attitudes (they might have suppressed their overprotective impulses), the child's assessment of his situation in light of these attitudes, and the opportunities open to him for compensations in other spheres of life? In short, organ inferiorities are only *one* of many factors in the sociopsychological situation facing the child. Further, by now introducing the prototype construct Adler shifted the source of influence in a child's life from the *past* (humors, genes, body structure) to the *future* (the goal of the life plan in the prototype).

We can see how this developing change in Adler's thought came into conflict with Freud's thought. Adler was denigrating instincts and drives.[98] Although he flirted with drive theory at one point, even speaking of a *confluence of drives* and a *transformation of drives* into their opposite, only a few years later he began to reject all such concepts as too narrow.[99] By shifting his emphasis forward, to the *goal* of behavior, Adler could no longer see the value of energic systems which impelled the person or pleasure principles which supposedly directed him willy nilly.[100] Pleasure and displeasure are secondary factors, ways we talk about the individual's psychical state as he advances along the pathways of life in search of various goals. Rather than being determined by a physical state from his past, Adler now said: "The psychic life of man is determined by his goal."[101] Once the individual has framed his prototype he has locked himself into a means-end course of determined movement which is

inexorable, so long as the prototype remains unchanged.

Adler took as a major premise that *life itself was motion*. Though he used a homeostatic analogue in his initial theory of organ inferiority, he came to reject the conservation-of-energy model which Freud had used in conjunction with his *constancy principle*. If one relies upon a "dispersal of energy throughout a system" explanation, Adler said, one loses the *teleological* (goal-oriented) meanings so vital to the understanding of the human being.[102] A mechanical balancing of forces does not move man, rather man's own conceptualizations of his life situation: "We do not think of conservation of psychological energy because we know that the causality which we seem to meet was actually placed into the situation by the given individual himself. Man makes one thing the cause and another thing the effect. . . . The most important question of the healthy and the diseased mental life is not whence?, but whither?"[103]

This view is a direct rejection of the Freudian libido theory, though as we noted in Chapter 1, libido did play a directional role in psychoanalysis not unlike Adlerian goal concepts (cathexes fix goals for the individual; see p. 39). Although Adler made passing reference to libido in his earlier publications,[104] it was not long before references to some presumed, underlying energy system simply dropped out of his theory. What he substituted was a reference to the *creative power* of the individual.[105] Although Adler did not make this power a central *formal* concept of his theory, he considered creativity to be an aspect of compensation; the prototype is in one sense another way of expressing the fact that man conceptualizes his life situation, hence creates it anew over the course of life.

Creativity, unlike *libido*, is a psychological term with no physical analogue. When we observe an artist, painting *his interpretation* of a landscape, we can ask ourselves questions about his physical coordination, or his expenditure of caloric energy in getting the job done—the "how" of the finished product's accomplishment—but we can also simply ignore these factors and speak about the finished product itself. Why this interpretation of the scene and not another? What was the artist striving to create? What goal did he wish to achieve? This is the view Adler was to take, and he felt it was unnecessary to account for the movements in physical terms since what interested him was the style of that movement in terms of the goal sought by the individual.

THE ROLE OF FEELINGS IN MOTIVATION

A child's first creative act was said to be spurred by compensation,[106] eventuating in the creation of the prototype. But what triggers this compensatory reaction in the first instance? Initially Adler thought of compensation in organic, mechanical terms, but what about his later thinking, when the more psychological motivations might have been said to be operating?

Here Adler wrestled with varying motivational constructs before working out his popularly known point of view. While still under Freud's influence he had toyed with drive theory; in fact, he postulated two contradictory drives which were not so different from Freud's. Thus, Adler spoke of an *aggression* and an *affection drive*.[107] People have needs to express aggression, and yet they also have opposing affectional needs which they satisfy in tender interpersonal relations. This "drive" or "need" terminology did not last long, and about the time when he was writing of fictions Adler substituted the concept of a *will to power* for that of the aggression drive. Vaihinger was an admirer of the philosopher Friedrich Nietzsche, and Adler specifically mentions that his will-to-power construct was related to Nietzsche's.[108] Whether he really understood Nietzsche on this issue of power seeking is another matter. Nietzsche's use of the "will to power" and the "will to seem" (not unlike Vaihinger's "as

if") was *not* to be construed as a hostile, selfish exertion of one's individuality.[109] In the same way that Vaihinger's fictions were used positively and without an implied "error" connotation, Nietzsche's will to power was a manifestation of man's will to grow, to self-realize, to extend his personal scope. The general drift of Nietzsche's philosophy was that man has to develop and express his own identity because "God is dead" (as a concept worth cultivating), and man can no longer continue shifting his responsibility onto a superhuman power. Even though Adler would have agreed with this view, he uses the will to power in a somewhat negative tone, as heir to the old aggression drive concept.[110] In fact, he had it based in a reflexive response, as follows: "When not more than six months old the child is known to reach out for all objects and is unwilling to return them. Shortly after that, under the pressure of a will-to-power, it seizes hold of people who take an interest in him. Jealousy is the safe-guarding tendency accompanying this desire for possession."[111]

Adler did not think it desirable to cultivate this will to power in children, since he believed it a remnant of man's lower nature that might be best lived without. In the same way that he had opposed the affection drive to the aggression drive earlier, he now placed most of his emphasis on something in man's nature which might offset the uglier aspects of power striving. He spoke of the will to power as a "guiding fiction" (in a negative sense) and then noted that only when this is tempered by a "will to cooperate" will the individual avoid gross mistakes in living.[112] The concept of "will" was an improvement over "instinct," since it emphasized self-direction and the goal sought by the individual, but a full understanding of how this process might be initiated seemed to evade Adler.

Not until he had brought the emotions into central focus in his theory did Adler speak with greater clarity on the actual mechanics of compensation.[113] The purpose of emotions is to modify to the individual's advantage the situation in which he finds himself. They compress the life style into an accentuated, more vehement "movement" toward the goal, which is the reason a person's character and consequent life style is most clearly recognized when he is under a state of extreme emotion. The individual whom we refer to as "having quite a temper" tells us in his very loss of control how important the goal he is seeking is to him. If things do not go his way he becomes very angry and thus intimidates those around him into giving him his way as a sop to his outburst of temper.[114] A person's feelings put his body in shape to meet a situation in life. We "steel" ourselves with the affect of determination in order to get the job done. Even so, Adler rejected the notion that emotions were *produced*—in the sense of determined—by the body: "To a great extent, though they rule his body, they do not depend on his body: they will always depend primarily on his [i.e., a person's] goal and consequent style of life."[115] Adler firmly believed that one's emotions never contradicted his style of life.

Fixing now on those emotional feelings which might operate at the outset of a compensation, Adler proposed a duality which was reminiscent of his earlier opposition of aggression and affection needs. He named these emotions, which often worked in opposition to each other, *inferiority feelings* and *social feelings*. The feeling of inferiority is a conscious or unconscious recognition of physical or psychological insufficiency.[116] It may directly reflect an actual organ inferiority, or it may be due to a misunderstanding of personal worth. That is, some feelings of inferiority are based on an error in self-evaluation.[117] As children we all feel inferior because we *are* quite inadequate compared to older persons, and throughout life everyone continues to feel more or less incapable in the face of challenges.[118] An individual can begin to have an inkling of what his life status is even before he can consciously speak about it. He "feels" it though

he cannot state it. Once stated, it becomes conscious. To feel inferior is to be human,[119] and this is the root source of all psychic motivation for both normal and abnormal people.[120] Adler could now make the blanket statement that the single spur to action in compensation was a *"subjective sensation of inferiority."*[121]

Adler first thought of social feeling[122] as a countering sensation to selfish power strivings. In addition to seeking power (in response to inferiority feelings) the growing individual also has an inborn propensity to feel tender toward others, to empathize with them, and to seek contact with groups of people.[123] When we focus on the sensory experience, the actual "feeling," then the proper term is literally *social feeling*. However, when we begin to stress the cultivation of this feeling, the *goal* of social feeling among all men then the proper term is *social interest (Gemeinschaftsgefühl)*. Actually, Adler used the terms *social interest* and *social feeling* interchangeably so that practically speaking they are synonymous.[124] Probably the best definition of social interest is the following: "Social interest means . . . *feeling with the whole, subspecie aeternitatis*, under the aspect of eternity. It means a striving for a form of community which must be thought of as everlasting, as it could be thought of if mankind had reached the goal of perfection."[125]

FROM OVERCOMING TO FULFILLING
COMPENSATION

Adler's original conception of compensation was as an automatic, act-react phenomenon. Some physical or psychological "minus" served as a signal for a "plus" reaction. As such, a good catchword for early Adlerian theory would be "overcoming."[126] One did not submit to misfortune but overcame deficiencies precisely because they were there for the overcoming. Adler once put this in the form of a law to parallel his basic law of compensation: *"The fundamental law of life . . . is that of overcoming."*[127] Deficiencies can be overcome in either a positive (affectionate, socially concerned) fashion or in a more negative (power seeking, aggressively selfish) fashion. The ruthless businessman who seeks every shady advantage within the law may lack an admirable character, but we cannot overlook the fact that his predatory moves in the game of life might provide him with a sense of power to negate any "loser's psychology" that might threaten him. On the other hand, the saintly individual who gives his life to altruistic endeavors is occasionally the one who feels he must atone for a misspent youth. Both the businessman and the saint can thus be considered "compensators" though the forms which their compensations take are markedly different.

Adler's chosen task was to attempt some kind of rapprochement between these two manners of compensating inferiorities—the selfish way and the altruistic way. After he had moved on from the aggressive needs and the will-to-power constructs, Adler accounted for man's response to inferiority feelings by saying that we all set the highest goals for ourselves to overcome our greatest weaknesses. These goals may be very conscious or highly unconscious, and the direction which our overcoming takes is dictated by the nature of our inferiority. Furthermore, when we move to overcome we *strive for superiority,* we not only try to make up for our inferiority, we try to go "one up" in this or a related area of life.

Although the striving-for-superiority construct was meant to apply to all people, it often took on a negative connotation in Adler's writing (similar to the will to power), as when he observed: "This goal of complete superiority, with its strange appearance at times, does not come from the world of reality. Inherently we must place it under 'fictions' and 'imaginations.'"[128] Striving for superiority is thus one of those guiding fictions we have already mentioned.

To deal with the positive vs. negative aspects of superiority striving, Adler spoke of the extent of inferiority lying at the base of compensation. Thus, if a person felt he were *highly*

inadequate—much more than the average man felt about his capabilities as a person—then we say this individual is suffering from an *inferiority complex.* Adler defined this construct as "the gulf between an individual and his supernaturally high goal."[129] The more one was disappointed in his self-evaluations the more he would wish to overbalance the scales in the opposite direction. In fact, Adler called this desire *overcompensation,* and we can see in abnormal behaviors the clear stamp of this overreaction and excessive striving.[130] The "weakling" adolescent who begins a Spartan regime of body exercises so that he spends most of his time weightlifting, to the exclusion of most other activities in life, would be overcompensating an inferiority.

Not only is the counterbalancing compensation overdone in abnormal striving for superiority, but there is a concomitant rigidity and compulsiveness about it. Normal striving for superiority retains a certain degree of flexibility, so that if one avenue is blocked another can be substituted for it.[131] In some instances, the inferior individual may live out his superiority strivings so actively, as a life style, that it would be possible to speak of him as having a *superiority complex.*[132] Such a person constantly wants to be singled out as somebody special, and he makes exaggerated claims on others as well as on himself to be superior in every way. He carries a "Do you realize who I am?" emotional attitude (pride) with him into every social situation. Superiority and inferiority complexes are really two reactions to the same thing.

Adler's continuing problem as theoretician was how to distinguish between superiority strivings of an acceptable and those of an unacceptable nature. He thus brought the constructs of social feeling or social interest—as well as the *self* construct—in to round out his final formulation. That is, he began seeing the cultivation of social feeling—via striving for social interest as a uniform goal for mankind—as the natural antidote to the more selfish strivings for superiority. Even though he had named his approach *individual* psychology, the net result was that he placed himself firmly on the side of *social* factors in human relations: "That which we call social feeling in Individual Psychology is the true and inevitable compensation for all the natural weaknesses of individual human beings."[133] If it was human to feel inferior, then it was equally human to feel a sense of empathy for one's fellow man. Of course, community feeling had to be cultivated, for it was not so much an inborn instinct as it was an "innate potentiality."[134]

The cultivation of this feeling is precisely what Adler meant by social interest. We all must take an interest in cultivating the innate potentiality of social feeling. He had returned from World War I heartsick at the devastation men had wrought on one another because of selfish striving. The only antidote to this madness was social interest (*Gemeinschaftsgefühl*), which is a worthy goal because man strives not only for superiority but for *perfection*. Adler's last formulation thus placed the *striving for perfection* as the general case in all compensatory moves, with either selfish or altruistic strivings as special variants of this single form of movement.[135] In the final years of his life Adler contended that the power-grabbing and predatory actions among our fellow men were merely due to an overcompensated inferiority transferred into a kind of misfired striving for perfection. Such men had taken their *innate* prompting to perfect themselves as humans and perverted it to selfish ends. To define "innate," Adler reached back to his early interest in the physical side of man and emphasized the Darwinian theory of natural evolution.

Man is *by nature and through nature* evolving to a higher state of living. By cultivating social feeling as a goal for mankind (social interest) we are not therefore cultivating just another sociocultural *fiction*, nor even a counterfiction, but an "absolute truth."[136] As we noted previously, Adler did not retain the complete relativism of Vaihinger's "as if" philosophy. One was not behaving "as if" social feeling could be experienced or "as if" social interest could be cultivated. The superiority and power strivings are the fictions of mankind. Social feeling was a *fact* of life, one not to be taken lightly if mankind is to survive.

With this growing emphasis on the striving for perfection, "late" Adlerian thought began to take on a different coloring. The catchword became "fulfilling" or "becoming." Man is still overcoming feelings of inferiority, but he is doing so as *one family,* rather than *one person*. The family of mankind is evolving to a higher state, and each individual man has the moral responsibility to further this end, to raise the level of ultimate human perfection which nature had begun in organic evolution. The individual cultivates the total by improving himself as a single representative of that totality. The *self* therefore means the uniquely individualistic goal which we all have. Though the growth principle of Adlerian psychology is contained within social interest, this "growth for all" can only be achieved through individual acts of self-realization. The person must fulfill the potentials of mankind in his unique life style; hence: "It is the self which grows into life, which we recognize later on as creative power."[137] The self is creative because it represents the *goal* beckoning us to achieve our potential. As Adler said: "The most important question is: Who moves the mental life . . . and in which direction does he move it? The mover is always the self."[138] The fulfilling rather than the overcoming emphasis in later Adlerian theory is demonstrated in the closing lines of his last book, *Social Interest* (published posthumously in 1939):

Our present-day burdens are the result of the lack of a thorough social education. It is the pent-up social feeling in us that urges us to reach a higher stage and to rid ourselves of the errors that mark our public life and our own personality. This social feeling exists within us and endeavours to carry out its purpose; it does not seem strong enough to hold its own against all opposing forces.

The justified expectation persists that in a far-off age, if mankind is given enough time, the power of social feeling will triumph over all that opposes it. Then it will be as natural to man as breathing. For the present the only alternative is to understand and to teach that this will inevitably happen.[139]

THE GROWING RELIANCE ON DARWINIAN EVOLUTION

In roundabout fashion, the final formulation of Adlerian theory returned to its initial emphasis on man's physical stature by stressing organic evolution. Evolution was taking man someplace, and though Adler now put his emphasis on the evolution of social interest, he still did not quite become a full-fledged sociologist, a "supra-individual" theorist. He always stressed the individual physical being, as when he defined *culture* as: "The changes which the human race has made in its environment. . . . our culture is the result of all the movements which the minds of men have initiated for their bodies."[140]

What is really significant about Adler's Darwinism is that he always seemed to have considered it in teleological terms. We know from his biographer and personal friend, Phyllis Bottome, that Adler's belief in organic teleology was so basic to his thought that he took "progressive evolution" to be a proven scientific fact.[141] Evolution of new forms followed the aim and the will of the animal concerned. In 1910, for example, Adler argued that: ". . . a nutritive organ has followed the will and need of assimilation; touch, auditory, and visual organs have followed the will and necessity to feel, hear, and see; a procreative organ followed the will and necessity for progeny."[142] Adler rejected the survival-of-the-fittest aspects of Darwinism, scoffing at those who believed in a talion principle (Freud) or even a self-preservation principle.[143] The lessons of history proved that man was a pack animal;[144] he had to be part of a group due to his weak physical stature, as Darwin had theorized. Hence, the natural compensation for individual weaknesses was the evolution of societal forms.[145]

Adler felt that social feelings *per se* had emerged in evolution when man was made aware of his physical weakness and helplessness—particularly as this was reflected in his newborn offspring.[146] Thus *motherly love* plays an extremely important role in Adlerian psychology, because the mother is the first to respond to her child's weakness and must instruct him in social interest as he matures. So imbued was Adler with evolutionary theory that he came to define his entire approach in such terms: "The talking about social interest as belonging to the evolution of man, as part of human life, and the awakening of the corresponding understanding is today being attended to by Individual Psychology. This is the fundamental significance, its claim to existence, and this is what represents its strength."[147]

The great confidence which Adler came to place in his interpretation of Darwinian thought in his later years is nicely epitomized in the following quote. Overlooking Darwin's celebrated antiteleological theme of "natural" selection, Adler said in 1933:

The originators of the concept of evolution in the field of general organic life, such as Darwin and Lamarck, have pointed out that life must be understood *as movement toward a goal,* and that this goal—the preservation of the individual and the species—is attained through the overcoming of resistances with which the environment confronts the organism. Thus *mastery of the environment* appears to be inseparably connected with the concept of evolution. If this striving were not innate to the organism, no form of life could preserve itself.[148]

Having cast Darwin in a teleological light, Adler went on to argue against survival-of-the-fittest doctrine by claiming that the "striving to *master one's fellow man*" has been shown by individual psychology to be erroneous, "contradicting the concept of evolution."[149]

Men who justify selfishness by the predatory

aspects of evolution are simply not reading the lessons of evolutionary history correctly. Social organisms pass through stages of evolution much like physical organisms do.[150] Just as the physical body of man reacted to a situation of weakness and "evolved" into a higher form, the body of mankind must now react to its social weaknesses, like selfishness and hostility, and evolve to a higher form. Adler realized that he was describing a utopia. He was not referring to any present-day society, nor to any given form of religious expression.[151] God concepts and religious beliefs merely reflect the fact that all men *have* been made aware of what a perfect state of humanity might be—a "heavenly" state of interpersonal relationships.[152]

The good sense which evolution gave us tells us that what we must do is strive to create that ideal here on earth; we must appreciate that this insight is itself a product of evolution. We must be socially useful, for to act in opposition to the community is literally to *oppose* evolution.[153] It is this confident reliance upon the lessons of organic evolution which gives Adler his rationale for whatever socialistic commitments he had. His socialism was "loving," in contrast to the "angry" socialism of Marxian communism. He tells us:

The honest psychologist must therefore talk and work against poorly understood nationalism if it harms the community of all men; against wars of conquest, revenge, and prestige; against the drowning of the people in hopelessness due to widespread unemployment; and against all other disturbances of the spreading of social interest in the family, the school and the social life.[154]

MORALISTIC TONES IN ADLERIAN PSYCHOLOGY

Adler held what might be termed a "natural ethic," in that he believed man was naturally good, and the direction evolution was taking mankind was positive.[155] Though he was always ready to indict an individual for what were presumed to be "errors" in life style, Adler did not wish to judge people so much as he

thought it only fair to call a spade a spade. One's character reflected one's outlook on life, and if this outlook was antisocial or selfish then he wanted to be sure we understood where the individual psychologist stood on the matter.[156] Character was a social concept, so the effects of one's character must inevitably refer to one's style of relating with his fellow man.[157] The honest psychologist must surely know that he takes a position on the side of the single person *or* the group in interpersonal relations when he formulates his theory: "And so Individual Psychology stands on firm ground when it regards as 'right' that which is useful for the community. It realizes that every departure from the social standard is an offense against right and brings with it a conflict with the objective laws and objective necessities of reality."[158]

Adler was no apologist for the status quo. He made it quite clear that, though social structures rely on social feelings among individuals, the social institution must exist for the sake of the individual and not vice versa.[159] The courageous man, the man who could feel himself to be part of a whole communilty,[160] is also the socially progressive man.[161] People who strive for personal satisfactions without concern for others were *failures* in living.[162] The failure approaches life's challenges believing that cooperation will not help in their solution.[163] Paradoxically, the father of individual psychology called people who achieved compensatory gratification in a selfish—and completely "individualistic"—manner *cowards*. The coward is "like a person living in an enemy country."[164] How is it that such cowardice and selfishness arise in people? Adler usually traced these to the "errors" of his clients and others whom he considered to have lost courage (feeling with the total), or possibly who had never learned to feel courageous in the first place.

Sometimes a mistaken life style can spur the evolutionary advance of mankind. This happens when the harmful effects of an antisocial person, a selfish person, or a "spoiled" (pampered) person generate some kind of countering effort on the part of others to offset his negative influence.[165] Yet, fundamentally, it would be well if such errors would not be made. The lesson of evolution is that those aspects of life which are mistakes, hence ill-adapted to the environment, do not survive.[166] Thus Adler honestly believed that if we could educate man regarding those mistakes which turned him against evolution he would respond and come around to make the proper changes. The problem is one of making it clear to others, for: "If a man understood how he erred, stepping out of the way of evolution, he would leave this course and join general humanity."[167]

DEFENSE MECHANISMS OR MENTAL MECHANISMS

In 1913 Adler used the term *repression* to refer to the fact that some people work toward goals without being entirely clear on the means they were using to obtain them.[168] Such psychic contents were often seen in dreams, creating the emotional mood which was poorly understood in consciousness.[169] Later, Adler had little need for a concept of repression. He was in fact opposed to the supposed split in the psyche which Freud was postulating and hence in time Adler was to reject the construct of repression altogether.[170]

He did accept the concept of *identification*, though he felt it was essentially identical to the empathic promptings of social feeling.[171] Identification continues throughout life and is one of the bases for group formation. Sympathy is a partial expression of identification. In Adlerian terms, a boy identifies with his father only out of love and never out of castration fears, as Freud had suggested.[172] Adler felt it was incorrect to draw easy analogies from physics, about energies flowing back to infantile pathways, etc., and thus made no use of the *regression* construct—which he felt favored a *post hoc* conception of man in any case.[173]

The most fundamental and pervasive defense mechanisms in Adlerian psychology must be considered *compensation* and *overcompensation*, related concepts which we have already covered in some detail. The actual maneuvers (movements) in the game of life compensating for inferiority feelings would account for the kinds of individualized reactions which Freudian mechanisms tried to explain. One of the first enlarged explanations of a defensive type of compensation was what Adler called the *safeguarding mechanisms* or *tendencies* employed by an individual suffering from an inferiority complex. He meant the tendency on the part of certain individuals to be overly fearful of failure, sensitive to criticism, and avoidant of fictionalized "disgrace" in life.[174] Safeguarding might be seen in any of a number of behaviors. The individual might become habitually ill in order to avoid people or possibly slink about in a character structure of submission and defeat. In time, Adler was to rename this safeguarding tendency in terms of the individual's goal. That is, if one avoids a challenge which presents a goal, such as having to meet and get along with people by affecting the life style of a chronic grumbler, he would remove himself from the field of action. This avoidance mechanism, which Adler called *distance,* indicated the disparity between where one is and where the beckoning goal is.[175]

One who strives to widen the distance between himself and the goal, to avoid it, to make what Freud had called rationalizations in the face of the obvious, retreats from life. A graphic example of this mechanism was given by Adler's case of the woman who suffered from incontinence of urine and stool because she feared the responsibilities of marriage. As a child she was told by her mother that such afflictions would negate chances for marriage, and thus she used this device upon reaching maturity in order to place a distance between herself and the dreaded marital goal.[176]

Another term which Adler adapted to suit his theory was *protest*. This construct is related to overcompensation, and it means that individuals who feel unprepared for some desired goal in life overreact to their feeling of being denied by speaking about the goal too much, or trying in some way to carry it off in any case.[177] Although presumably any item of life might be protested against, Adler's major usage of this concept centered on the *masculine protest*. We shall return to this construct when we take up Adler's theory of neurosis, but for now let us think of it as a form of power struggle between the sexes.[178] In most cultures the man has been considered the superior. Anything associated with masculinity thus has certain advantages guaranteed by right of sex. Men have the advantages of a "double standard" sexual morality; they are permitted to live alone and to "sow their wild oats" in a way that women have never been allowed without considerable criticism. Some women therefore express masculine protest by taking on the values, manners, careers, and even attire of men. In Adlerian terms, the "career-woman type" who studies law, wears business suits, and refuses to be subordinated to any man is likely to be protesting masculinity.

Adler first emphasized this reaction in girls, but then noted that boys could easily become infected with this "poison" as well.[179] The complete "man's man" who thinks of women as silly little playthings to be put on a domestic shelf until needed sexually would also be expressing masculine protest. The main symptom of masculine protest is: ". . . a needlessly domineering attitude towards the opposite sex. It is always noticeably connected with a very ambitious style of life, with a goal of super-man or of a very much pampered woman."[180] Not all masculine-protesting women lack feminine mannerisms or heterosexual interests, though Adler considered lesbianism to be one form of masculine protest.[181] But almost as often one can find a highly feminine woman expressing masculine protest in her pampered and petted relationship with a harassed husband who finds himself continually under the thumb of his "sweet little tyrant." The negative attitude of the wife's constantly "lording it over" her husband defines the protest in this case. The pre–twentieth-century mechanism for the woman's masculine protest was in fact to make of her man a "gallant" slave, who bowed and scraped and catered to her every whim. Yet, Adler was much concerned about what he took to be the masculinizing trends of the women of his time. In a quaint pre-1928 observation he spoke ruefully of characteristic events: "At the present time, the masculine protest is rampant and widely displayed by women of all ages, who smoke, wear short skirts and short hair and do everything possible to approximate to masculine manners."[182]

TIME PERSPECTIVE CONSTRUCTS

GROWTH AND THE THREE PROBLEMS OF LIFE

Adler viewed the newborn child as a reflexive organism to whom environmental experiences "happen" automatically and mechanically. Since the infant has no ego identity at this time and hence no goal in terms of which the individual is striving, these early experiences are not especially important to his subsequent style of life. Somewhere beyond the first year, along about the time that the child begins to speak of himself in the first-person pronoun "I" we can expect the prototype to begin being formed.[183] The child can then begin assessing his situation in life, recognizing that it *is his* situation (ego identity). Hence, Adler's view of development reverses what many feel happens to us as we mature. Rather than victim to experience, *"nobody really permits experiences as such to form, without their possessing some purpose.* Indeed, experiences are moulded by him. That simply means that he gives them a definite character, being guided by the way in which he thinks they are going to aid or hinder him in the attainment of his final goal."[184]

No two children grow up under precisely

the same circumstances, nor do they make the same evaluation of their situation once their "I" (ego) awareness forms. One characteristic that all children do share, however, is the tendency to bifurcate evaluations, to divide everything they become aware of into opposites such as good or bad.[185] This *antithetic scheme* of apperception is carried on into adulthood, but it is particularly strong in childhood so that a child is more likely to err in his personal evaluation, thrusting himself to either extreme of judgment due to his lack of experience. If someone else is attractive he is likely to consider himself ugly, etc. It is thus extremely important to provide opportunities for the child to see that *everyone* has strong and weak points. Sexual identities should be established as quickly after ego identity as possible, particularly for the girl, in our culture, whose inferior role excites her wish to become a boy and hence makes her more vulnerable to masculine protest.[186] The child should be told at the age of two that he is a boy or a girl, that that sex can never be changed, and that little boys grow up to be men and little girls to be women.[187]

Sexual development undoubtedly begins early in life, and thus the child may begin to fondle himself sexually. However, this does not mean that he literally seeks to copulate with his mother, nor is he masturbating in the sense of an adult. Since this fondling is culturally inappropriate and a selfish indulgence at best, Adler favored discouraging the baby from this activity with as little show of concern or distaste as possible. If the child senses that we are overly concerned with his sexual play he will be more likely to continue these habits deliberately in order to gain attention.[188]

Since the prototype is finalized around the age of four or five, the child's ego identity is still not well established. This means that many of the experiences and subsequent strategies he incorporates into his life style are poorly articulated or possibly not verbalized at all. They would be "not understood" in Adlerian terms, hence unconscious. Adler felt that

Freud and Jung had taken these "wordless impressions" of childhood and misconstrued them, attributing to them the properties of instincts or inheritances from a racial unconscious.[189] Children are extremely dependent upon the parents for adequate preparation in life, and the parental challenge is to make a highly dependent creature independent yet considerate of others.[190]

Whenever Adler spoke of the problems or challenges of life which man must fulfill he framed them in terms of three problem areas: *occupational, social,* and *sexual.*[191] He felt that any problem of living could be subsumed by these terms, because human beings have certain inevitable ties. We are tied to the earth and in order to exist we must produce the necessities of life from natural products through work; we are tied to others in society as fellow creatures seeking common satisfactions in unique ways; and, we are tied to our history and the future of our kind by way of procreation.[192]

FAMILY CONSTELLATION AND BIRTH ORDER

Since everything hinges upon a child's life situation and his evaluation of this situation, the kind of character a child will develop must take root in the nature of the parental family constellation.[193] Such contingencies as the birth position of the child in the family, whether he is an only child or the only boy in a family with six daughters, must necessarily influence the kind of prototype he is likely to form.[194] One must never routinely evaluate birth order, but birth order does show definite trends.[195] In a multiple-child family, for example, the *eldest* or *first born* child often looks after his younger brothers and sisters, thereby becoming an extension of parental authority.[196] He not only becomes a great believer in power, but when he grows to adulthood he is more likely than other children in the home to have a conservative, conforming outlook, to be a "regular citizen" and a conventional individual.[197]

The *second born* child has a rather challenging position in the family constellation. Not only is his older sibling likely to be more adept at things than he, and also to have acquired certain authority advantages by rights of early possession, but the second born is also removed from the limelight role of being the "baby" of the family as younger children arrive. If he has any potential he can develop considerable talent in some aspect of life, as he works to outshine his older sibling's pace of achievement.[198] Unfortunately, this birth order can also foster an extreme ambitiousness, possibly even a jealous and predatory nature. In any case, we expect to see a lot of drive in the second born, and less authority-proneness than in a first born child. Third, fourth, and later children must be examined as a result of a combination of factors. What opportunities do they have to share a bit of the family spotlight? Are there older sisters, brothers, or both to outshine and compete with, and what are their particular skills?

It is not the number of children or the specific order so much as it is the *total* situation facing the child which must be understood. If the eldest child is mentally retarded, or for some other reason has adopted a very repressed personality, the second born might acquire the authority proneness which is thus left open for a more normal sibling to capture. If the time between sets of children is large, with a couplet of children much younger than an older couplet, the situation might resemble two separate "eldest vs. second born" dynamics emerging in the same family.[199] In some ways the *last born* or youngest child of the family has the most serious handicap of all to overcome in life, for he is the continuing baby of the family and thus most vulnerable to pampering.[200] Even as adults, such last born children may expect to have others do everything for them, and of course once out of the family context they can be rudely disappointed in life when they find that strangers do not give them special consideration. The *only child* is similarly likely to have received everything he

wanted in life without having to share and hence grow to maturity as a pampered child.[201] Even if he escapes this unfortunate turn of character, the only child is more likely to be an "individualist" as an adult than is a child with siblings.[202] Since Adler valued social interest, his writings make clear that he much favored families with more than one child. He felt it was excellent training to be brought up in a home with siblings where one learned the "give and take" so essential to communal living in general.

Adler once said that proper mothering demands two accomplishments: winning the child's trust through a show of love and redirecting this trust to other persons.[203] He contended that we can always see the contribution of bad mothering to the lives of failures, the neurotics, criminals, drunkards, and prostitutes of society.[204] There is no special skill or mystical power to the art of mothering. It demands interest and effort and is abetted by having a childhood in which such attitudes were passed onto the female by her parents.[205] In his final theory, Adler spoke of motherly love as an evolutionary product, one aspect of social feeling which is innately present.[206] He felt that the love was probably triggered emotionally, initially by the baby's helplessness, and then furthered by the baby's crying insistence to be cared for.[207]

If the mother is overly indulgent or protective, if she pampers her child and he accepts this goal in life as worthwhile, this might negate the organ inferiority and birth order factors already reviewed. A mother who rejects her child, who finds the womanly role distasteful and masculinely protests to be liberated from this wifely "chore," would doubtless also set a situational scene greatly relevant to the child's prototype formation. Adler was not trying to fix guilt by pointing to the nefarious role of bad mothering.[208] Possibly she was not trained for cooperation or her marital situation may be a source of unhappiness and great strain: "Moreover, it is not the child's experiences which dictate his actions; it is the conclusions which he draws from his experiences. . . . We cannot say, for example, that if a child is badly nourished he will become a criminal. We must see what conclusion he has drawn."[209] Adler was always careful to designate the individual child as a major source of the blame—or credit—for his eventual style of life.

Adler saw the father playing an enlarging role in the socialization of the child. He is secondary primarily because his influence starts later, but he is nonetheless important to the child's ultimate successes in life.[210] As Adler put it, "The task of the father can be summed up in a few words. He must prove himself a good fellow man to his wife, to his children and to society."[211] Adler was strongly opposed to the role of authoritarian for the father.[212] In fact, he was opposed to authoritarian family structures of any sort. If a father believed that he had special privileges as "breadwinner" he was making a mistake, because as a totality the family has common claims on such economic factors. The mother should not pressure him into being the family enforcer or punisher. If she does, then she admits that she has failed to win the child through social interest and love.

Adler spoke rather informally of stages or "epochs" in development, and he did not name explicit stages through which the individual supposedly moved while maturing to adulthood.[213] He looked at the process of maturation in somewhat more fluid, individualistic terms than Freud. In line with his emphasis on the moves in the game of life, Adler laid considerable stress on the useful role of *play* as a preparation for life. Making an analogy to lower animals who sharpened their predatory skills in playful activities as cubs or pups, Adler noted that humans cultivate their interpersonal skills through play as well,[214] and he preferred games which require cooperative

skills, or make-believe activities which fostered a productive goal with social interest. In fact, Adler was none too sympathetic with the telling of fairy tales to children. Fairy tales must be emphasized as "make believe" stories lest the child grow up hoping for the magic of these stories to provide him with an easy way out of life's problems.[215]

Adler's view of the universal *Oedipal complex* was an extension of the "preparation for future life" tendency we see in the games of children. He said that this was simply an attempt on our part to "play at" being fathers and mothers.[216] If a child did *in fact* develop an Oedipal complex in the Freudian sense, Adler would consider it an abnormal condition. One could not say that *everyone* went through a literal Oedipal situation as one phase of development. The pampered child, on the other hand, who has been coddled and petted by a mother who may find her own status in life unhappy and hence compensates by overprotecting her child, is likely to end up with the dynamics of the classical Oedipal complex.[217] Such a mother literally can stimulate the sexual appetites and fantasies of the child by her frequent hugging, kissing, and massaging of the child.[218] Very often the Oedipal pattern is seen in someone who is using distance. A daughter who has incestuous wishes for her father can attach herself to him, dominate him in time, and thereby use this supposed sexual "fixation" not only to receive many personal indulgences but to avoid meeting other males—men who could in fact fulfill the sexual promptings which she is really terrified to confront in a mature fashion.[219]

In rejecting the literal Oedipal complex Adler also rejected the Darwinian-Lamarckian theme of "ontogeny recapitulating phylogeny" on which it was based in Freudian theory (see Chapter 1). Here again, Adler proved selective in his acceptance of Darwinian concepts. For him a true Oedipal complex was tantamount to a mistaken life style, a "narrow stable" used by neurotics who had not been adequately prepared to meet one of the three major problems of life.[220]

Sometimes mistaken life styles were prompted by the relationships established with brothers and sisters in the home. Adler termed this *sibling rivalry*, by which he meant the striving for the spotlight in the home among the children, taking into consideration such factors as birth order, organ inferiorities, and parental attitudes as well.[221] Sibling rivalry is a natural extension of the need for each child to feel uniquely worthwhile, but it can be engendered and extended in families lacking social feeling to the point of a heedless competition or running warfare. A frequent outcome of sibling rivalry is a sort of "striving for naughtiness" in one or more of the children. If a first born, for example, is especially "good" then the only avenue open in the antithetical scheme of "good or bad" used by the second born is to try to be as naughty as possible.[222] Adler felt that one could always detect the nature and adequacy of a child's life style in the "transition" periods of life, as when a family structure suddenly alters with the birth of a new child, or the father has to shift jobs, or possibly the family changes locations.[223] Well-prepared children make these transitions smoothly and without overcompensation. Poorly prepared children are thrown in a crisis by such changes in routine.

THE ROLES OF THE SCHOOL AND TEACHER IN MATURATION

The child leaves the home context to attend school with a prototype well established (by age five). School experiences can help alter a prototype or at least add some features of more appropriate socialization to it by cultivating the child's social interest. Adler was one of the first thinkers to point out that school failures are often life failures as well.[224] Few school failures suffer from a physical variety of mental retardation, so when a child begins to dislike school or to fail in his subjects we can be fairly certain that he is beginning to give up on the problems of life. He would like to remove himself from the challenge (distance), even if this means being labeled "slow" or uneducable. Often, he substitutes naughtiness for academic effort, but this strategy of distancing himself from a challenge would not fool Adler. The school's responsibility is to help all children retain hope of overcoming their inferiorities.[225] Each child has a strong point which must be identified and given an opportunity to grow and thus bring him some modicum of personal satisfaction so that overcompensatory tendencies will not be needed.

Adler's emphasis on egalitarian values led him to criticize certain pedagogical devices, such as the track system where children are grouped according to their intelligence or facility for learning. He felt that this invariably led to a social-class grouping which worked against proper education.[226] Children from homes with more material advantages have had more experiences, wear better clothes, have been exposed to more educational adjuncts like books and magazines, hence they appear brighter and end up in the upper tracks of a grouped system. Adler was also opposed to children skipping classes because they were considered gifted.[227] The child who skips something and is therefore "ahead" of his natural peers adopts the psychology of wanting to skip and to achieve unreasonable goals in the future. Finally, Adler was distrustful of the intelligence quotient (IQ). He believed that children matured at different rates, and the risk of labeling a child as either "gifted" because of hastened maturation or "retarded" because of slower maturation was simply not worth the advantages gained by knowing a specific IQ. At the very least, neither the child nor his parents should be told the exact IQ score lest they use this knowledge to inflate or injure the child's ego identity.[228] As with the track systems which made use of them, Adler felt that intelligence tests greatly favored children from the upper social classes.[229]

Children should learn as much as possible

from their actual experience of doing things in school. They should learn the logic of life, not memorize information in rote fashion.[230] Adler favored letting children work along at their own rate, rather than trying to meet arbitrary standards, because they are individuals: "It is this individuality which prevents the application of general rules in the education of groups of children."[231] Not all children are suited to the classical programs of basic education particularly as they approach pubescence, and Adler looked favorably on manual training schools. Some children learn most effectively in coordination with their eyes, ears, and hands as they acquire occupational skills.[232] The ideal classroom is one which exists as a unity, where each child feels himself to be part of the whole.[233] Any form of discrimination, whether of race, creed, or social class is anathema to proper education. The teacher should also see that student rivalries and personal ambitions are kept within bounds. Without appearing contrived, the effective teacher must be able to give each child his occasional turn in the classroom spotlight.

One of the recurring controversies in education, particularly around the time of pubescence, is whether or not the school should provide children with sex education on a routine, formal basis. Continuing with his emphasis on the individualized approach, Adler did *not* favor the teaching of sex as an academic subject. The teacher can never know how each child is taking his words if he speaks to the class as a whole.[234] It is quite proper to teach the individual child whatever he wishes to know about sex, but only in response to his specific question. The home is really the proper place for sexual education.

ADOLESCENCE

Adler did not want to make anything special of adolescence, feeling that it would be too easy to emphasize the physiological changes and resultant dramatic alterations in physiognomy: "In fact adolescence is, for Individual Psychol-

ogy, simply a stage of development through which all individuals must pass. We do not believe that any stage of development, or any situation, can change a person. But it does act as a test—as a *new situation*, which brings out the character traits developed in the past."[235] At no other time in life is a person's life style so apparent as it is in adolescence. The challenge here is to become a finished person, to come up to the front of life's development and take on the pattern one will be following in his occupation, marriage, and social life throughout maturity. The child naturally feels this period as a test, the gnawing necessity of having to prove that he really is adult material.[236]

Adler felt that more concern should be shown in adolescence to the problem of occupational choice. We let sexual adjustment completely overcast the far more pressing problem of "What shall I do in life?" As we noted in the biographical overview, Adler believed that each person should settle on his occupational or career goal early in life—surely by early adolescence and preferably before the age of 15.[237] This bias follows from his view that only the individual who works toward a meaningful goal can find satisfaction in life. Occupationally disjointed people, or people with no given job aspiration, can hardly live socially useful lives. Adler felt that some people avoided career decisions because they feared the challenge of setting an aspiration; others secretly dreamed of having good fortune fall their way without personal effort.[238] The high school girl who dreams of "being discovered" as a movie star and the boy who hopes for a "lucky break" to move him ahead are courting disaster. The schools must therefore provide help with career decisions.

ADULTHOOD AND OLD AGE

Once into his twenties, the individual is considered an adult, and he has the task of harmonizing occupational goals with family and social goals. If sex was a preoccupation and concern in adolescence, it is doubly important to life now. Adler had to take a clear stand on the question of physical love or "sex," because Freud's sexual orientation continually stood in contrast to the social interest emphasis of individual psychology. In trying to sum up his attitude, Adler gives us a clear picture of what he took *love* to mean: " 'Love,' with its fulfillment, marriage, is the most intimate devotion towards a partner of the other sex, expressed in physical attraction, in comradeship, and in the decision to have children. It can easily be shown that love and marriage are one side of cooperation—not a cooperation for the welfare of two persons only, but a cooperation for the welfare of mankind."[239] Sex is not a power play, a subjugation of one sex (feminine) by the other (masculine).[240] It irritated Adler to hear people speak of marriage as an acceptable outlet for the satisfaction of a sexual "instinct." This was a drive psychology, a mechanistic interpretation of sex, and he felt it grossly underestimated the importance of love to man as a social animal. He was opposed to premarital sexual relations; he had seen too many unhappy outcomes from relationships founded on what is later recalled (especially by the male) as "easy virtue."[241]

The only proper way for a marriage to succeed is for each mate to be more interested in promoting the happiness of the other than in securing his own gratification. Adler also believed that for a full solution to the problem of love and marriage children are necessary: "A good marriage is the best means we know for bringing up the future generation of mankind, and marriage should always have this in view."[242] Since the intimacy required for a rich marital life must be regularly cultivated, the only proper marriage custom for man is monogamy.[243] People who enter into marriage with possible escapes in mind, such as promiscuity or divorce, are often those who have been pampered as children. Marital breaks occur "because the partners are not collecting all their powers; they are not creating the marriage; they are only waiting to receive something."[244]

Old age brings on special problems. The older person must step aside and allow new ideas and new directions to replace others. Unfortunately, the older person tends to be inflexible in his outlook. He becomes stubborn and loses the will to cooperate which is so essential to effective social living.[245] Even so, Adler felt that our civilization had not sufficiently considered the elderly. Too often we simply retire people to a drab existence, one which offers nothing but death as its final goal. We must care enough for our elderly to offer them a place in society. Religions, of course, provide the old person with a hope for the "life hereafter," which is a worthy goal if the individual has a faith. Actually, of course, religious beliefs are an extension of social interest in the Adlerian view.[246] The older person without a concept of the "hereafter" can therefore feel socially useful in some fashion, as working for the continued growth of mankind.

INDIVIDUAL DIFFERENCES CONSTRUCTS

Although his fluid view of living made "typing" according to some fixed scheme of development difficult, and in one sense, contrary to his major emphasis, Adler was aware of the need for personality theorists to generalize their insights. He therefore admitted to being a typologist of sorts.[247] Over the years Adler had occasion to type personality, sometimes in a technical but more often in an informal sense. He usually worked in the context of a clinical discussion, so that many of his suggested typologies were better suited to a psychotherapy or "diagnostic" scheme. However, we will combine Adlerian typologies of all varieties into our individual differences section in the interests of organization.

THREE TYPES OF WOMEN WHO FLEE FEMININITY
Adler once suggested that there were three types of women who really do not believe that woman can be equal to man. The first type

meets our theorotype of the "castrating" female. She spends her life proving that she is the equal or the better of any man. She wears the pants in the family, if indeed she ever does marry, and her inclinations are always to move into the domain of the masculine culture—have a career, enter politics, and so forth. A second type goes through life as a lackey—obedient and humble in relations with men, entirely content to resign herself to the fact that she is a member of the "weaker sex." The third type is like the second, except that she is unable to resign herself to this lesser role. She cannot fight like our first type, but rather drags herself through life appearing on the surface to be resigned, yet aggravated that she must play an arbitrarily decided second-class role in life.[248]

TWO APPROACHES TO PROBLEM SOLUTION

Adler respected the person who felt confident enough to speak his mind, to exert enough independence and aggression to seek out solutions to problems of living in a direct fashion. Those who used devious schemes, who withdrew passively and disliked "coming out" with their thoughts in preference to a halting manner, he found were habitually frustrating to both themselves and others. He once referred to the former type as the *optimists* in life. The *pessimists* were of the latter variety. Pessimists invariably look for the darker side of life because of an underlying inferiority complex; they cannot take life "head on" so they never seem to solve their problems.[249]

TWO STYLES OF FAILING IN LIFE

Adler's preference for the direct, aggressive manner of the optimist did not blind him to the fact that often a person can fail in life with something akin to this pattern of behavior. He once proposed to classify failures in terms of an active-passive dimension: "I have proposed a classification of difficult children which proves useful in many respects: into the more *passive* children, such as the lazy, indolent, obedient but dependent, timid, anxious, and

untruthful, and children with similar traits; and into a more *active type* such as those who are domineering, impatient, excitable, and inclined to affects, troublesome, cruel, boastful, liable to run away, thievish, easily excited sexually, etc."[250]

THREE TYPES OF CHILDREN LIKELY TO OVERCOMPENSATE

Although he spoke of compensation rather than overcompensation, Adler once typified three kinds of childhood situations which would be likely to generate pronounced reactions in the individual facing them. We think it best to term this a typology for the proclivity to *over*compensate, given Adler's eventual stress on the fulfilling aspects of compensation. Those most likely to overcompensate are "children who come into the world with weak or imperfect organs; children who are treated with severity and with no affection; and, finally, children who receive too much pampering."[251] Adler believed that neurotics were prone to be passive failures in life, retreating as they did to symptoms which might then be used as excuses for not confronting life (distance). Criminals, on the other hand, would be considered active failures because they aggressively seek to achieve their goals by taking, pushing others aside, hurting, and so forth. Regardless of the style chosen, all failures in life are due to a lack of social interest.

FOUR APPROACHES TO REALITY

We can also type the reactions which we have to others in interpersonal relations. Some individuals take a dominant or *ruling* approach. We always feel their presence because they invariably have something in mind for us to do—with them, for them, or directed by them. The second, which might be termed the *getting* type, is constantly leaning on us, borrowing or begging, asking us to help rather than ordering us, but in some way or another managing to have us provide them with something they want. A third type is the individual who is unavailable when problems arise. Adler thought of this as the *avoiding* type, who simplified his existence and avoids defeats by withdrawing from all challenge or responsibility. Thus far we have a series of rather unsuccessful life styles. Fortunately there is also the *socially useful* type in interpersonal relations. This type does not flee from us but struggles to overcome in union with us; he thinks more of giving than of receiving, and he is sensitive to our integrity as individuals so that he cannot subjugate his fellow man by being authoritarian.[252]

THE VARIOUS TYPES OF COMPLEXES

In 1935, Adler published a paper on the nature of complexes which will probably have to stand as his most thorough attempt to designate types or traits of personality. Adler viewed the *complex* as a simplification or schematization of the prototypical goal. It tells us what the individual is trying to bring about or "get" in life. There are literally thousands of types, and thousands more of the trait variations off of these basic types.[253]

As if to show that he could cite an unending series of complexes, Adler pointed to several examples which we can recognize as further descriptions of the life style.[254] Thus, an individual with an *inferiority complex* is telling us that he does not feel strong enough to solve life's problems in a socially useful way. The child with an *Oedipus complex* has been pampered and lets us know that his mother is the goal he cannot forgo. Some people have *redeemer complexes,* going through life trying to save or redeem others for some presumed drawback or failing. Others have a *proof complex,* because they are terrified of committing errors and hence want to intimidate us as well by constantly asking for immediate proof of anything we say.

Some people go through life with a *predestination complex,* either fearing nothing because they believe nothing can happen to them or failing to plan adequately because "it is all the same in the end anyhow." There is also the *leader complex,* frequently noted among geniuses and ambitious men. They stick to their guns and cut their own swath in life because they view themselves as "out front" in life. If their actual talent lags behind their desired goal they can become pitiful specimens. Many people go through life with a *spectator complex.* They want to be near the action of life, but they do not wish to participate or take the lead. Finally, there are those who oppose all change so that we may coin a *"no" complex.* Such people are either highly conservative and fearful of change or they must simply contradict whatever is said in their presence. It is as if they see something extremely advantageous and significant in disagreeing with others.

Psychopathology and Psychotherapy

THEORY OF ILLNESS

ACHILLES HEEL AND PSYCHOLOGICAL TENSION THEORY

Adler early postulated an "Achilles Heel" theory, including a synchronous "inferiority of the brain" concept which implied that a *psychic tension* was set up due to some physical inferiority of the body (see p. 99). The resultant *brain compensation* was initially treated mechanically, but in time Adler was to introduce the more psychological type of explanation. The point is: psychic tension is just as much an interpersonal as a physical phenomenon. Exactly "where" in the body we manifest our interpersonal problems is conditioned in part on our hereditary weak links—called *segment inferiorities*—but the fact that we *do* ultimately break down at these points (enuresis due to segmental inferiority in urethral region) must have a psychological (interpersonal) contributor as well.[255]

PSYCHIC HERMAPHRODISM AND NEUROTIC REVERSAL TENDENCIES

Children use *antithetic schemes* of apperceiving reality, bifurcating experience into black-white alternatives in what Adler considered to be a primitive and unproductive way of thinking. Neurotics continue to reason as children throughout life. They see the world as winners vs. losers, and then the strategy of the life game is to avoid losing. All of those traits of personality which appear weak—passivity, obedience, softness, fright, ignorance, tenderness—are relegated to the *feminine* role. And all of those traits appearing strong—greatness, riches, knowledge, victory, coarseness, cruelty, violence, activity—are elevated to the *masculine* role. It is within the resultant *fictional* bipolar divisions of all of life's activity that the neurotic lives. We can see in this division the mainsprings of *masculine protest,* which could of course be an attempt by either sex to gain the upper hand in life.[256] But Adler thought of this division between masculine and feminine in far broader terms than simply masculine protest.

He reasoned that everyone has the potential to behave as everyone else. In this sense, masculine and feminine proclivities of an active or a passive nature are the common substance of all behavior. We say that Jim throws a baseball "like a girl," and if Jim is a normal boy he laughs off this quip good naturedly even as he recognizes that his good mind and aggressive wit enable him to win in any classroom debate. The neurotic person, on the other hand, is unable to harmonize what he takes to be diametrically opposite tendencies in his nature—the one symbolizing power and the other symbolizing submission. If we say of a neurotic boy that he throws a baseball like a girl, he considers the comment a major threat to his security. He is upset and feels hostile toward us, and the next time he throws anything we had better take cover. This vindictive tendency among masculinely protesting male

neurotics is common. Adler named this tendency to split psychic contents into either/or along male-female lines *psychic hermaphrodism.*[257]

FALSEHOOD, FICTIONS, AND LIFE LIES

What distinguishes a neurotic from a normal person according to Adler is his carefully chosen style of life. Adler occasionally referred to the life style as a *life line,* as the course of movement over the years which we have already discussed in some detail in the sections on personality. The neurotic, however, is someone who lives a *life lie.*[258] Having divided his world into simple opposites, he now plays one side against the other, using cowardly excuses to avoid defeat and cheap tricks to gain advantage: "Act 'as if' you were lost, 'as if' you were the biggest, 'as if' you were the most hated."[259] If the child finds life a challenge, he can always cultivate the feeling of being hated by his parents—particularly if there is an element of truth in this assessment. Probably all parents go through a period when they tire of, and to that extent "reject," their child to a greater or lesser degree. There is no one living who has not received this kind of negative response from a parent, no matter how subtle its expression. But the neurotic life style capitalizes on this as a possible "out," an acceptable excuse for not confronting life's challenges. This individual can go through life saying he might have been something *if only* his parents had not hated him so.

The truth is, parents neither hate him completely nor feel love for a child every moment. He simply capitalized on a passing mood of irritation or disgust to fashion a prototype allowing him a cowardly way out. In fact, Adler viewed this "if" tendency as a common neurotic lament: "The discussion [in therapy] invariably reveals an accented 'if'; 'I would marry *if*'; 'I would resume my work *if*'; or 'I would sit for my examination *if*'; and so on. The neurotic has always collected some more or less plausible reasons to justify his escape from the challenge of life, but he does not realise what he is doing."[260] Life lies as life lines remain "not understood" or unconscious. But the neurotic more firmly than the normal individual lives by his fictions. He elevates himself into a god-like figure and then by skillfully avoiding challenges he sustains his deception. Whereas the normal never loses sight of reality, the abnormal virtually exists in a dream state, as if hypnotized by the grandeur he thinks is his. The neurotic is thus "nailed to the cross of his fiction."[261] He sets up imagined conflicts and achievements which he then struggles through and attains, all at the level of fantasy. Such *fictitious triumphs* sustain his cheaply won distinction as a human being.[262] They intoxicate him. He is the sort of person who corrects his friend's grammar after this friend has defeated him in a business transaction or a golfing match. Losing in one sphere he must come off the final winner in another.

Being chained as he is to a guiding fiction, the neurotic is prone to use *analogical thinking,* or the tendency to make analogies between the present and the past. As a reflection of their egocentricity, neurotics invariably see today's life circumstances as continuations or extensions of yesterday. The argument they have with us today is "just like" the arguments they used to have with their father. Hence, they respond to the present "as if" it were the past. We are suddenly in a drama not of our choosing, taking on attributes we never would assume if allowed to be ourselves.[263] In thus showing how the neurotic traps us by analogical thinking Adler was not trying to fix guilt. He preferred to speak of errors in living rather than of blame or guilt.[264]

One thing is certain: "Every neurotic has an inferiority complex."[265] Differential diagnoses of neurosis hinge upon the particular style selected by the individual to resolve this inferiority, but in *every* case the solution is one of a superiority striving. Therefore, every neurotic also has a superiority complex; he tries above all else to preserve his god-like fiction.[266]

Symptoms are the means by which the neurotic avoids solving life's problems without taking blame for the failure.[267] As Adler graphically expressed it: "The symptoms are a big heap of rubbish on which the [neurotic] patient builds in order to hide himself."[268] The most apparent and important neurotic symptom is the "advance backward." The neurotic gives us a flurry of activity to hide his retreat: "Neurosis is the patient's automatic, unknowing exploitation of the symptoms resulting from the effects of a shock. This exploitation is more feasible for those persons who have a great dread of losing their prestige and who have been tempted, in most cases by being pampered, to take this course."[269] Note in this quote Adler's emphasis on the *pampered* individual. He was to take an increasingly critical view of pampering as a major source of neurotic behavior over his years as therapist.

DIAGNOSTIC DISTINCTIONS IN INDIVIDUAL PSYCHOLOGY

According to individual psychology, the problem of diagnosis is to determine where a symptom is helping to take the individual. It is not a question of "where from?" but "whither?" the symptom leads.[270] Adler did not particularly advocate the practice of diagnosing patients preliminary to psychotherapeutic contact, but he did seem to feel that his psychology should be able to account for the major clinical syndromes.

Neurosis vs. psychosis. Adler took a quantitative view of the neurosis vs. psychosis distinction. The neurotic is a person who has a history of the life lie, seeking fictional goals, but he continues to meet a few of life's challenges. The psychotic, on the other hand, has completely failed in the three problem areas of life (work, love, society).[271] The psychotic withdraws to a dream world, concocts a delusional belief system, which is just a further extension of his fictional approach, and he also hears and sees things (hallucinations) which help him justify his failures and brings sympathy from others.[272] Although symptoms and hallucinations are painful in the short term, in the longer term a neurotic's or psychotic's suffering brings him more gain than loss. Anxiety, for example, can be used by the person to stimulate sympathy in others. He is so terribly fearful that we all must feel sorry for his apparent inability to shake off what he experiences as an impending danger.[273]

Mania. The manic individual is one who, faced with an extremely important and imminent decision in life, is hindered by a conflict in his outlook which deepens the underlying inferiority on which his life style is based. Rather than face up to the nagging decision, the manic individual moves to devalue reality and concomitantly to intensify the guiding life line which points to the fictive goal of superiority he has in mind.[274] He can thus poke fun at reality and simply assume that he is what he wants to be—an important person, an influential person, a person with vast insights or schemes. He is thus anticipating the fictive goal of superiority, making it *real* in his present illness.

Melancholia or Depression. The attitude of the person who succumbs to melancholia or depression in life is characterized by distrust and criticism. The decrease in social interest is apparent in his hesitating attitude. He does not wish to participate in activities, he is "blue" and pitiful because nothing in life has any meaning for him. If we knew more about such a person, we would find that he probably feels a continuing rage and is reproachful toward others.[275] He feels wronged and though he may seem to be blaming himself for something —saying that he is no good for anything, that he does not deserve to live—it is actually someone else against whom he rails. In fact, even a suicide carried out by a depressed person "always represents an act of revenge" leveled at the opponent, the supposed wrong-doing

party.[276] Rather than submit and cooperate, which would be for the depressed person a "final indignity," he leaves the scene of fictive conflict entirely even as he makes another person feel guilty for his self-destructive act.

Schizophrenia. This is one of the most severe forms of psychosis, where the individual has completely given up all hope of a victory in the real world. In his very dream state, which "splits him off" from reality, we can usually see his fictive goals being made manifest. Invariably, the schizophrenic will think himself a famous character in history or in the contemporary sociocultural scene. The more pathological the case the loftier the identity assumed, so that it is common among schizophrenics to believe that they are Jesus Christ (that is, "God" or a "Perfect Being").[277]

Paranoia. This disorder, often combining with schizophrenic symptoms, is typified by extreme suspiciousness and hostility—sometimes leading to physical harm being inflicted upon strangers who are unlucky enough to be brought into a paranoid's delusional (fictional) belief system. Adler felt that these individuals were probably advancing toward their place (goal) in society for a time, but then out of inferiority feelings and a complete disregard for the status of others they began to concoct imaginary schemes (fictions) which supposedly were the cause of their lack of courage to continue on toward the fulfillment of their aspiration.[278] The paranoid attack is likely to appear when the individual feels his social position is threatened.

Sexual Perversions. The individual who practices some form of sexual perversion reveals in this very action that he is not well prepared to face the challenges of love in this life. Rather than meet the problem, he *reverses* the customary sexual morality or the roles of the sexual partners. Basically, all perverts are highly selfish (lacking social interest). Personal gratification of lust is given precedence over a tender regard for the pleasure of a partner, so that in one sense perversions such as peeping, child molestation, and rape are variants of (selfish) masturbation.[279] Adler once defined masturbation as "the style of sexual life adapted to confirm isolation and to avoid love and marriage."[280] Exhibitionists are visual types who want to look or be seen "at a distance" rather than to confront sexual objects directly. The sadist achieves a feeling of superiority by sexualizing his hostility (lack of social feeling), and the willing masochist sexually revels in the power he can yield over the sadist.[281] The lesbian is expressing the ultimate of masculine protest,[282] and the male homosexual is often encouraged to take this role by a strong identification with a mother who gave him feelings of distinction and "difference" by dressing him in girl's clothing, and so forth.[283]

Alcoholism and criminality. Adler had the unique distinction among personality theorists of pointing to the many gains which supposed "losers" in life might actually seek to attain through what he once termed "a cheap success of notoriety."[284] People were self-defeating but not due to a death instinct or a wish for self-destruction. They were self-defeating as one of the moves in the life game, seeking a distinctiveness even if on the negative side of life.[285] The "town drunk," for example, attains a certain distinction by having achieved the goal of being a "monumental" drinker. He can also use this "curse" as a convenient excuse for not having done something with his life. This strategy is designed to win by losing in life.[286] The egocentric pattern among criminals is documented by the fact that so many of them delight in composing autobiographies.[287] They play at being Robin Hoods, but they merely delude themselves into overlooking the strong inferiority which lies at the root of their cowardice. Adler laid much of the blame for prostitution on a society in which the major sexual emphasis is on the male obtaining satis-

faction. The women who gravitate to prostitution do not relish the feminine role. They express their masculine protest by bartering with men for the highest dollar even as they despise their customers and take no satisfaction from the sexual experience itself.[288]

Obsessive-compulsivity. This disorder is often found among second-born family members, due to their inordinate ambition.[289] They have a compulsive need to be perfect, to keep clean, to get ahead, to escape criticism, and the like. Occasionally, a symptom such as the obsessive fear of germs may be used as a device to escape the necessity of being with people.[290] A hand washing compulsion is "always used as a means of avoiding sexual relations, and invariably gives the fantastic compensation of feeling cleaner than everybody else."[291]

Stuttering. The fact that a person who stutters does so on a selective basis, often losing the symptom when reciting, singing, or speaking to someone he loves, led Adler to conclude that the vital aspects of this disorder were interpersonal. For some reason, the individual has settled on this symptom to achieve the dubious but excuse-providing distinction of being somebody "special." Possibly his parents were overly concerned about his speech when he was a child, and he thus found it easy to gain their undivided attention by simply stumbling over aspects of his enunciation or delivery.[292] This was frequently the case in the life history of a pampered child. Possibly the stutterer discovered that he could irritate his parents or otherwise get back at them for imagined affronts through this device.

Sleep Disturbances. Adler was a firm believer that: "An individual who cannot sleep well has developed but a poor technique of living." [293] It therefore followed that any sleep disturbance would diagnose a life-style problem. Nervous insomniacs, for example, were seen as people who overvalue success yet lack the confidence to achieve their highly ambitious goals.[294] Adler saw a kind of body language (variant of organ dialect) in the sleep postures. One of his clients slept on his side, with his arms drawn up tightly against his body; Adler found that this man intensely disliked his profession.[295] Defeated people without initiative in life are prone to sleep with their bodies pulled up into a ball, like the fetal position, and they also like to pull the covers over their head.

THEORY OF CURE

SOME GENERAL CONSIDERATIONS

Adler once said that the first rule in treatment is to win the confidence of the patient completely, and the second is not to worry about success. The therapist who is constantly worried about his success will invariably forfeit it.[296] The aim of Adlerian psychotherapy is twofold. It proceeds from the assumption that the neurotic or psychotic has formulated a mistaken style of life, and to that extent his conception of reality is entirely out of focus. The therapist must thus first help him to achieve a reinforced and more correct view of reality. Secondly, he must confront the superiority mechanisms which are reflected in the power strivings and encourage the patient to—consciously and determinately—work on the cultivation of social interest (forgo his selfishness).[297] This dual strategy takes us into the matters of self-study (insight) and client-therapist relationships (transference).

First, however, we should consider briefly the general framework of the psychotherapeutic contact, as practiced by the Individual Psychologist. Adler believed that those who know enough about human nature to see the mistakes being made by others with unproductive life styles have the implicit duty to help the self-destructive individual rearrange his errant perspectives on life. [298] This is not to say that the therapist should force his therapeutic will

on others; the responsibility for a lasting change is placed squarely on the client's shoulders, with the therapist acting as skillful coparticipant.[299] He never promises a cure to the patient.[300] But Adler found in his practice that often a prospective client had heard of extended analytical treatments, lasting up to eight years only to end in failure. Such an individual deserves some prospective estimation. Adler was therefore in the habit of saying to his clients that, though length of therapy varied based in part upon the patient's willingness to cooperate, he did feel that at the end of three months they should note signs of improvement. He often added, to the client: "If you are not convinced after one or two weeks that we are on the right path, I will stop the treatment."[301]

THE ROLE OF INSIGHT

Adler believed most strongly in the importance of providing the neurotic client with insight into his condition. As he once summed it up: "The cure can only be effected by intellectual means, by the patient's growing insight into his mistake, by the development of his social feeling."[302] What Adler was emphasizing here is the fact that even social feelings must be cultivated by conscious intellectual effort, by making the decision to look out for and be interested in others. The strategy of the individual psychologist is to begin with the present life pattern of his patient, and then to work backward until it is clear to both therapist and client just what the latter's superiority goal entails.[303]

Adler's close association with teachers in adult education, and his founding of the individual psychology clinics in Vienna, combine with his emphasis on intellectual insight to give his theory of cure a kind of "educational" flavor. He was even wont to speak of the therapeutic task as a "re-education" of the neurotic in the art of living. [304] He did not refer to a formalized educational procedure, of course, but rather a kind of "corrective mothering" to be administered with curative goals in view. The neurotic had not been made to feel in empathy with a mother figure, who then transferred this community feeling outward to others. Hence, the therapist's role is literally "a belated assumption of the maternal function."[305] He must teach the neurotic the evils of striving on the useless side of life even as he somehow regains the neurotic's commitment to the community. This goal is not easy to accomplish because the neurotic has not only lived according to a mistaken life style for some years, but even when he begins to grasp the nature of his errors, he can always make use of the unconscious to obfuscate and demoralize the therapeutic effects.[306]

A typical neurotic ploy is to exacerbate a symptom picture when threatened. For example, as the life lie is being made clear to the patient his compulsive hand washing or his fear of height suddenly becomes "worse." Rather than be alarmed by this apparent "setback" Adler proved a genius at debasing the significance of the symptom. He often used humor, told little jokes, or made light of the symptom complaint with his attitude and countenance.[307] By acting this way, Adler was fixing his attention on the *goal* of the neurotic maneuver. Like the experienced mother who does not simply buckle under when the child begins to "act up" in a temper tantrum or feigned illness, Adler was not allowing the client to obtain a fictional triumph. He did not reject the client, he simply refused to let neurotic devices—including the "use" of the unconscious—throw the psychotherapy off the track.

Adler once referred to psychotherapy as an artistic profession.[308] He meant that one could not cite routine rules of thumb for its practice, but rather had to develop a proper style through continuing experience and self-critical efforts to improve. The best therapists are those who can "see with the other person's eyes, hear with his ears, and feel with his heart: one must identify with him."[309] In fact, if the therapist has gone through personal travail he can often do a better job. He is familiar with both the good and the bad sides of life on a firsthand basis, and he is therefore less likely to be misled by the neurotic's maneuvers.[310]

Adler realized that one's early interpretations in therapy often later turn out to be incorrect. This realization did not disturb him, for he pictured himself "in the same position as a painter or sculptor, who at the outset does whatever is suggested to him by experiences and skill. Only later on does he check his work, strengthening, softening and changing the features to bring out the correct image."[311] The cardinal rule of interpretation is: "A real explanation must be so clear that the patient knows and feels his own experience in it instantly."[312] The emphasis on *feeling* is of great importance here, for it was Adler's belief that a true insight *always aroused affect*.[313]

THE ROLE OF THE RELATIONSHIP

Unless he is completely removed from reality in a psychotic stupor, the patient in therapy always retains some vestige of social feeling or "group consciousness."[314] By confronting the client as an equal, by showing him "the interest of one man towards a fellow man" the therapist can engage his confidence via the group consciousness he has remaining.[315] Concern for others breeds a return in kind. Adler once called this *pedagogical tact,* by which he meant "the attitude of one man toward another, which is determined by a desire to raise the level of the other's feeling in a kind manner."[316]

Adler reversed the Freudian tables by having his concept of transference working in an opposite direction to that of classical psychoanalysis (see Chapter 1, pp. 71–73). Rather than transferring unhealthy features of the life style onto the therapist (transformed neurosis), Adler believed that therapy worked through the process of transferring healthy features of the relationship with the therapist back into the life style of the patient. Hence "the task of the physician or psychologist is to give the patient the experience of contact with a fellow-man, and then to enable him to transfer this awakened social feeling to others."[317] The therapist thus acts as a mediator between the selfish, secretive goal of superiority clung to by the neurotic and the broader community of fellow men.[318] Adler believed that many therapeutic approaches and even quacks gain their successes through this simple device of providing a disturbed person with a good human relationship, and then encouraging (mothering) him to approach life once again. Doubtless this is how some of the "miraculous" cures of the saints, Christian Science, or visits to Lourdes take place—by cementing the errant individual back to the group.[319] Even so, Adler refused to see the relationship *per se* as the vehicle of cure: ". . . we remain convinced that the cure of all mental disorder lies in the simpler if more laborious process of making the patient understand his own mistakes."[320] Insight was always to remain the *primary* vehicle of cure in individual psychology.

Insofar as one can speak of a *transference* as a feeling of warmth toward the therapist by the client, Adler claimed it was merely another term for social feeling.[321] But the notion that transference of sexual feelings onto the therapist is a necessary adjunct to therapy, leading to a positive and then a negative or resistive stage in the process struck Adler as preposterous. If a female client were to dream of having sexual relations with him, Adler asserted, rather than viewing this as a "love transference" he would see in it a caricature of the real emotion. This client would be running away from the genuine problems of love and marriage by concocting an impossible goal.[322] To frame this literally in sexual terms was to misunderstand the client's motivation.

It was Adler's view that classical psychoanalysis fostered sexual expressions by the client because of the analyst's penchant for viewing everything in the client's behavior as sexual from the outset.[323] As for individual psychology therapy, he felt that a *sexualized* positive transference was to be avoided at all costs.[324] Not only did the positive transference

reinforce the patient's feeling of inferiority, as he now submitted himself ("in love") to the presumed highly desirable and infallible analyst, but it also robbed the patient of his opportunities for ultimate independence and self-direction. One can understand the great length of classical analyses when he appreciates the fact that the patient is made to feel dependent and inferior—literally infantile—for long periods of time, all in the name of "positive transference."[325]

All neurotics behave negatively in therapy from time to time. One of Adler's female patients constantly nagged him to rearrange her therapy hour to suit her schedule.[326] He accepted this ploy, in conjunction with other symptoms, as a reflection of her masculine protest (bossing the analyst). But when a client "resisted" in the sense of refusing to look at his patent life-lie style, Adler considered this a lack of courage. The neurotic lacks the courage to return to the useful side of life, and hence he strikes us as resisting therapy.[327] A certain amount of this behavior is to be expected. However, if the therapist invariably faces deep resistance from *every* client he is probably behaving authoritarianly to encourage this reaction. Adler, of course, did not favor such authoritarian approaches, and he thus considered it improper to call every client a resister when it was the therapeutic style which was to blame.

THE ROLE OF SOCIAL FACTORS

Adler did not blame society for mental illness. Societies were not "sick" or in error; only people were. If people took care of their individual lives properly, with social interest, all of the "social ills" would take care of themselves. When community leaders begin capitalizing on social interest as a collective matter (many people as a whole) rather than encouraging it as an interpersonal phenomenon (two people in face-to-face relations), we will see the rise of nationalistic and imperialistic interests. Adler's socialism strained at power-grabbing and dismissed the presumed boundary lines of class or national origin. This also prompted him to reject the communism he saw taking hold in the world: "The rule of Bolshevism is based on the possession of power. Thus its fate is sealed. While this party and its friends seek ultimate goals which are the same as ours, the intoxication of power has seduced them."[328]

The point is, collective solutions—by definition—seek to manipulate people. The "group" is a fiction. What we need are *individual* solutions to man's problems, with a collective aspiration in mind—but this aspiration need never reach fruition. We are to be as the utopianist: undaunted by the fact that his society will never literally exist.[329] Once goals have been achieved progress stops, and it is in the *creativity* of an unfolding life that Adler put his faith. The neurotic has fixed his goal and now tries to make it real, literal, extant. The healthy man accepts his fluid position in life, looks to his goal of perfection for *all* men, and constantly works for an end he does not believe attainable in this life, even in principle.

THERAPEUTIC TECHNIQUES

THE STRATEGY OF THE RELATIONSHIP

Adler was opposed to hypnotism as an adjunct therapy, because the hypnotist essentially asks his client to forgo personal responsibility and self-direction.[330] The neurotic could easily begin using hypnotism as an excuse for not taking hold of things himself. Hypnotism seems to cure individual symptoms, and Adler believed it was a therapist's responsibility to do more in making the life lie clear to the patient.[331] There is also an authoritarianism in hypnotism. Adler even rejected that psychoanalytical remnant of the hypnotic method—the *couch*. His patients were free to sit, stand, or even to move about the consulting room if they wished.[332]

The therapist must keep three general goals in mind: (1) to see from his client's viewpoint; (2) to understand why he behaves as he does; and (3) to instruct the client in these features of his prototype and consequent life style.[333] If these three steps are followed, the subsequent implications for "what to do" in order to change will follow automatically because it is the ever-present system of mistakes in the prototype which continually frustrate the neurotic's chances for adjustment. Stating what a mistake *is* implies the alternative which can rectify it. The cultivation of social feeling is one aspect of this corrective action. Like the effective mother, the therapist must encourage his "charge" to advance on life at some point with self-confidence and a faith in other people.

THE TECHNIQUE OF COMPARISON

In arriving at the life lies used by the neurotic, Adler suggested that the therapist could use a technique of comparison.[334] After assuring himself that there is no specific organic deficiency, the therapist could actually begin this process of comparison by putting himself in the client's place, asking: "What goal might I be seeking by behaving the way this person is behaving?" Several aids can help to capture the feeling and attitudes of the client, for example, picturing his symptoms as analogical to organ dialects in that they express his outlook on life. Also, the way in which the individual presents himself on first contact, his handshake (demanding or tremulous), the chair he might select (close or far away), and his general posture (erect, slouching, haughty) all immediately communicate aspects of his life plan.[335]

As therapists, we are guessing at the life style of a client from the first contact. Though he made mistakes, Adler claimed it was not unusual for him to determine accurately the neurotic's life style on the first day of psychotherapy.[336] Sometimes the dynamics of a family problem—as between a mother and daughter —are so apparent that the clinician can be completely clear about the essentials in 10 minutes of contact with the principals.[337] Another aspect of comparison involves evaluating the degree of community feeling the patient manifests in his daily activity, based on the amount of time devoted to social relations, religious activities, political involvements, and so forth. A good picture of the recreational pursuits—whether solitary or outgoing—also offers clues as to the interpersonal status of the client.

The next major step, and the one which takes up a major segment of therapy, is to take the patient back in time, drawing out those psychological attitudes and physical handicaps which may have contributed to the formation of a prototype. The reason for calling this a "comparison" technique is that the therapist constantly weighs the implications of each bit of information against each other— the presenting complaint against the handshake, the outside activities against the memories of the past, and the combined effect of all four factors at once—until a single, overall prototype regularity is suggested.[338] If a preliminary overview convinces the therapist that the client is truly suffering from a neurosis, therapy moves into the interpretative phase. By this time, as a result of his pedagogical tact, the therapist should have established a relationship of trust with the client. A continuing comparison of life history data is now made with contemporary events in the client's life, and if the life-style interpretation of the therapist is correct, the insight afforded the client will be accepted because of its obvious instructiveness and usefulness.[339]

EARLY RECOLLECTIONS

Adler was convinced that "memories can never run counter to the style of life."[340] The only reason we have recollections is because the psyche is trying to further the life style by retaining what will cultivate its particular line of movement. Hence, in recollections which date from the first four or five years of life we can find the major fragments of the prototype formulated by the individual, a prototype which still directs his every move as an adult. Using the pampered child as one example, Adler once noted: ". . . if I suspect the life-style of a pampered child, I can invariably guess that the patient will recall something about his mother."[341] The solitary, defeated individual might well recall being lost and and alone in some large department store as a child. The timorous adult would be likely to remember the great fright he had in some childhood play experience, and so forth.

DREAMS

Adler also made use of the patient's dreams to elucidate the life style. Dreams reflect man's goal-oriented psyche in that they are always tied to what the individual desires in the future. In the same way that the neurotic strives to make his fictive goal real in the present, the dream encourages us to believe that we can see into the future and thus make our desires into realities.[342] The dream is stimulated by some frustration in life. We sense or know directly that what we want is slipping from our grasp, so the dream either "short circuits" our striving attempts by making it appear our goal is actually realized, or, it suggests possible moves that we might make in order to further subsequent goal attainment.[343]

An example of the first type is the dream of a shop owner who was once Adler's client. This neurotic woman suffered from a physical illness for a time, necessitating that she leave the shop under the direction of hired employees. One night she dreamed: "I enter a shop and find the girls playing cards."[344] Adler interpreted this dream as evidence that this woman literally hoped to find the "hired help" taking advantage of her absence in this fashion. This was the "future" she made "real" in her dream because she was a dictatorial employer, a martinet who simply did not want to believe that the business could go on as usual without her supervision.[345] An example of the second type of dream was the case of a jealous wife who dreamed that she saw a cat snatch a fish and run off with it. A woman then ran after the cat and recovered the fish. Adler interpreted this to show the jealous housewife that she was steeling herself in preparation for such a theft, so that when the occasion arose she would be ready to recover her husband.[346]

Adler believed that an acceptable psychology must account for dreams, since this is such a large part of mental life.[347] At the same time, he was careful to add: "The dream tells us nothing more than can be inferred from the other expressive forms as well."[348] Daydreams have the same self-deceptive quality as night dreams. Fantasy is an escape precisely because it allows us to paint a future state to our liking, one which denies the reality which we are likely to face.[349]

Dreams suggest the mood we want to feel: "Dreaming is a process of turning away, in sleep, from reality and common sense towards the individual's goal of superiority."[350] Freud erred grievously when he presumed that dreams could somehow tell us about a past reality.[351] The dream is a fiction, "a dress rehearsal, a trial performance of a step towards the fictive goal."[352] An adult who dreams—or who fantasies, for that matter—that he has had sexual relations with his parent is rarely stating a genuine sexual prompting from the past or the present. He is demonstrating by way of a metaphorical expression that he wishes to "subdue" his parent, to command the parent's complete affection and emotional subjugation. The parent may even stand as metaphor for someone else, as for authority in general, or possibly for all of mankind—whom the neurotic wishes to bend to his will.

We call these metaphorical devices *symbols,* said Adler, and he was none too pleased with the necessity of using them: "Metaphors are used for beauty, for imagination and fantasy. We must insist, however, that the use of metaphors and symbols is always dangerous in the hands of an individual who has a mistaken style

of life."[353] Take the case of a boy faced with an examination. The challenge is there, the problem is clear. He must study and prepare himself for the task, and then face it squarely and courageously. But if his style of life encourages retreat then he might well dream some night that he is in a war. He pictures the straightforward problem of an upcoming examination in a heightened metaphor—fear of death in war—and thus creates the mood he wishes to have, one which might enable him to flee the challenge which awaits on the morrow.[354] In the morning he develops a "sickness" and fails to attend school (distance).

The fact that dreams are designed to intoxicate us with power accounts for their renowned difficulty to understand. If we really grasped the reason for the dream we would effectively destroy the need for the dream: "The dream is a bridge between the present real problem and the style of life; but the style of life should need no reinforcement."[355] That is, only those styles of life which are selfish, devious, and unwilling to take a straightforward approach to life require dreaming as an adjunct deception. If one meets his responsibilities there is no need for dreaming: "Very courageous people dream rarely, for they deal adequately with their situation in the day-time."[356] Courageous people meet life with social interest and cooperation. One aspect of cooperation is seeing things the way most people do—in other words, with "common sense." If men lived according to common sense they would not need to dream, for "dreaming is the adversary of common sense" and vice versa.[357]

Although he carefully noted that one could not make easy generalities about dream interpretations, over the years Adler proposed a number of ideas on the likely meaning of dream patterns. Sometimes a person does not dream even though he is neurotic. The absence of dreams in this case indicates that the individual has established a neurotic situation which he does not wish to change.[358] Short dreams suggest that the present problems are such that the dreamer hopes to find a "short cut" between his present situation and the ultimate goal. Longer, more involved dreams imply a hesitating, procrastinating attitude in the life style, where security needs are excessive.[359] Dreams about dead people suggest that the dreamer has not yet buried his dead, and hence he is still under the influence of the lost ones.[360]

Dreams of falling, which Adler found to be the most common theme reported, invariably deal with the anxiety sensed by the individual who is losing his sense of worth. This dream content also implies a superiority feeling, the raising of himself "above" others.[361] Dreams of flying occur with regularity among highly ambitious types, who also want to raise their status above the crowd. Dreams in which the individual finds himself improperly clothed or naked reflect a concern about some personal imperfection or possibly a fear of being detected in some fraud. Sexual dreams may be seen in many lights. Sometimes they clearly suggest a poor preparation for sexual intercourse. At other times they reveal a retreat from the partner and a withdrawal to oneself.[362] They often have power overtones which transcend sexuality, as the dream mentioned above in which a parent is selected (metaphorically) as love object. One can never be certain what the dream means until he uses a broad base of comparison: "The interpretation of dreams is therefore always individual. It is impossible to interpret symbols and metaphors by formula; for the dream is a creation of the style of life, drawn from the individual's own interpretation of his own peculiar circumstances."[363]

GAMESMANSHIP TACTICS

Knowing as he did that neurotics sought to manipulate by their "moves" in the "game" of therapy, Adler was always alert to such maneuvers. He would not allow the neurotic to reinforce his power strivings by gaining an easy victory in the therapeutic contact. We have chosen to call these techniques "gamesmanship tactics," referring now to the approach he used in countering the moves of the client. For example, Adler once told of a 27-year-old woman who came to see him after five years of neurotic suffering and various unsuccessful attempts at previous therapy. She opened their first conference with: "I have seen so many doctors that you are my last hope in life." [364] Realizing that this neurotic woman was *daring* him not to cure her, so as to make him feel bound in duty to do so, Adler countered her superiority tactic with: "No . . . not the last hope. Perhaps the last but one. There may be others who can help you too."[365]

Another interesting vignette which Adler presented was his treatment of a case of melancholia (depression). Such individuals are often difficult to work with because they have retreated from life and seem very ill-disposed to make any new efforts at contacting others. Put another way, their social interest needs considerable recultivation, even if it has to be "pump primed" mechanically. Although slightly devious and manipulative, Adler felt that occasionally the therapist had to use a more "indirect" tactic with the melancholic. He often opened by saying to such a client: "Don't tax yourself, do only what you find interesting and agreeable these days." If the melancholic now says, "But doctor, nothing is agreeable to me," Adler would counter with: "Then at least . . . do not exert yourself to do what is disagreeable."[366] This has a certain novelty about it, which usually catches the patient unaware and sets the stage for Adler's next move in the game—which is to encourage a development of social interest.

Looking rather thoughtfully and a little doubtfully at the patient, Adler then suggests that he has a second rule he would like to recommend, but he is not at all certain that the patient can obey it. Nevertheless, if the patient could follow the rule Adler feels sure that he could be free of his melancholic symptoms in 14 days. Naturally, the patient now wants to know the second rule, which is: ". . . to consider from time to time how you can give another person pleasure. It would very soon enable you to sleep and would chase away all your sad thoughts. You would feel yourself to be useful and worth while."[367] If the melancholic individual were then to respond with something like "But how can you expect me to give others pleasure when I have none myself?" Adler would counter directly with "I see, then you will probably need four weeks to get back to your old self." If the patient instead responds "But who in this world gives pleasure to me that I should worry about them?" Adler applied what he considered was the strongest move open to him, by saying: "Perhaps you had better train yourself a little thus: do not actually *do* anything to please anyone else, but just think out how you could do it."[368] Adler also would occasionally ask the melancholic to bring the therapist pleasure by recalling and reciting his dreams during the therapy hour.

What is Adler doing here? We must not think of these examples as stylized attempts to treat people routinely. He honestly believes that by encouraging the individual to take an interest in others—*along with* the insight from the therapy contacts—in time a therapeutic outcome will be effected. The cultivation of social interest is tied to the correction of mistakes in any case, for the reason a person becomes ill is that he has departed from the useful side of life. He has retreated from this social side to a selfish fictional account of what life is all about, and thus is ignorant of the benefits which even mechanical attempts to assume an attitude of social interest might generate. In a sense, therefore, the "help others" gambit of the therapist is an aid to insight. As the client begins to feel the positive effects which Adler believed were bound to accrue from assisting others, he would be doubly impressed by the validity of individual psychology's broader teachings.

SOME PROCEDURAL DETAILS

Adler believed it was important to confront the patient or his family with a hopeful countenance—even when he had some doubts about the eventual success of the therapy.[369] Except for the grossest kind of physical abnormality, such as certain irretrievable forms of mental deficiency, the therapist should always consider a case amenable to treatment or at least worthy of a preliminary review. One can hardly demoralize the client at the outset and hope for great gains on the morrow. Adler had some definite things to say on the deportment of his followers: "The Individual Psychologist, unlike other psychotherapeutists, will avoid being sleepy, or going to sleep or yawning, showing a want of interest in the patient, using harsh words, giving premature advice, letting himself be looked upon as the last resort, being unpunctual, getting into a dispute, or declaring that there is no prospect of cure."[370]

It is important to get all questions of procedure cleared up and settled with the client from the very beginning. This would include such things as fees, the physician's pledge to secrecy, and the scheduling of appointments over the weeks.[371] The frequency of contacts varied according to the needs of the client, from daily through weekly or even monthly contacts. Adler believed that therapists should contribute some time without pay, and he stressed that we must never make the gratuitous patient feel inferior because of this arrangement. Payments were best made on a weekly or monthly basis, and Adler did not favor prepayment schemes.[372] Gifts proffered by a client should be declined in a friendly manner or at least put off until the termination of therapy. In no case should the therapist and his client mix socially during the run of therapy.

We have already mentioned that Adler could always skillfully debase a neurotic's symptom. This attitude of assured disdain had to begin from the very first contact, and be carried out in a friendly manner: "You must be as unprepossessed as possible toward the patient; avoid everything which could make him believe that you are sacrificing yourself for him."[373] Never appear perplexed, accept everything in a friendly manner, and devote yourself completely to the investigation of the life style. Finally, Adler believed in the advisability of using a series of fairly dramatic illustrations in making his point. If the therapist is too sober all he succeeds in doing is worrying the client needlessly, overvaluing the severity of the case, and establishing an authoritarian relationship. He must not make light of the client, of course, but the proper mood Adler sought was that of spontaneous cooperation in a joint effort which could assure success if they did not as therapist and client take themselves altogether too seriously. A hopeful person is not without a sense of happiness or lightheartedness, even in the face of some rather agonizing challenges.

Notes

1. Sheldon, 1944, p. 526. 2. Combe, 1851. 3. Becker and Barnes, 1952, Ch. 13. 4. Darwin, 1952a, p. 322. 5. *Ibid.*, p. 323. 6. Hofstadter, 1955. 7. Sheldon, Dupertuis, and McDermott, 1954, p. 19. 8. Sheldon, Stevens, and Tucker, 1940; Sheldon and Stevens, 1942. 9. Sheldon, Hartl, and McDermott, 1949. 10. *Ibid.* 11. Shock, 1944. 12. Alexander and Selesnick, 1966, Ch. 18. 13. Kety, 1960. 14. Bercel, 1960. 15. Alexander and Selesnick, 1966, Ch. 18. 16. Bottome, 1957, p. 26. 17. *Ibid.*, p. 27. 18. *Ibid.*, pp. 32–33. 19. Adler, 1964a, p. 148. 20. Bottome, 1957, p. 27. 21. Furtmüller, 1964, p. 331. 22. *Ibid.*, p. 333. 23. Bottome, 1957, pp. 46–49. 24. Furtmüller, 1964, p. 334. 25. *Ibid.*, p. 341. 26. Bottome, 1957, p. 75. 27. Ansbacher and Ansbacher, 1956, pp. 73–74. 28. Furtmüller, 1964, p. 345. 29. Ansbacher and Ansbacher, 1956, pp. 77–87. 30. Bottome, 1957, p. 84. 31. *Ibid.*, p. 121. 32. *Ibid.*, pp. 169–171. 33. *Ibid.*, p. 128. 34. Ansbacher, 1959. 35. Bottome, 1957, p. 224. 36. *Ibid.*, pp. 45–49. 37. Adler, 1958, p. 25. 38. *Ibid.*, p. 26. 39. Adler, 1964b, p. 74. 40. *Ibid.*, p. 95. 41. Adler, 1964a, p. 156. 42. Adler, 1958, p. 57. 43. Adler, 1964b, p. 47. 44. Adler, 1968, p. 3. 45. *Ibid.* 46. Adler, 1963, p. 166. 47. Adler, 1954, pp. 27–28. 48. *Ibid.*, p. 31. 49. *Ibid.*, p. 29. 50. Adler, 1964a, p. 163. 51. Adler, 1968, p. 229. 52. Ansbacher and Ansbacher, 1964, p. 93. 53. Adler, 1968, p. 229. 54. *Ibid.*, p. 228. 55. Adler, 1958, pp. 12–13. 56. *Ibid.*, p. 14. 57. Adler, 1964b, p. 19. 58. Adler, 1964a, p. 46. 59. Adler, 1964b, p. 229. 60. Adler, 1958, p. 59. 61. Adler, 1968, p. 126. 62. *Ibid.*, pp. 3, 6. 63. Adler, 1954, p. 73. 64. Adler, 1964a, p. 7. 65. Adler, 1964b, p. 244. 66. Ansbacher and Ansbacher, 1964, p. 216. 67. Adler, 1964b, p. 49. 68. Adler, 1963, p. xiii. 69. Adler, 1954, p. 86. 70. *Ibid.*, p. 18. 71. Adler, 1968, p. 2. 72. Adler, 1964b, p. 49. 73. Adler, 1930, p. 138. 74. Adler, 1964b, p. 42. 75. Ansbacher and Ansbacher, 1956, p. 180. 76. *Ibid.*, p. 194. 77. *Ibid.*, p. 78. 78. Adler, 1968, p. 229. 79. Ansbacher and Ansbacher, 1956, p. 98. 80. *Ibid.*, p. 246. 81. *Ibid.*, p. 144. 82. Adler, 1964b, p. 92. 83. Adler, 1958, p. 37. 84. Adler, 1968, p. 307. 85. *Ibid.*, p. 313. 86. Adler, 1958, p. 37. 87. Adler, 1968, p. 3. 88. Ansbacher and Ansbacher, 1956, p. 25. 89. Adler, 1963, p. 76. 90. Adler, 1958, p. 37. 91. Ansbacher and Ansbacher, 1956, p. 26. 92. Adler, 1954, pp. 34–35. 93. *Ibid.*, p. 147. 94. Adler, 1968, p. 336. 95. Adler, 1964b, p. 93. 96. Adler, 1954, p. 148. 97. Adler, 1968, p. 318. 98. Adler, 1964a, p. 47. 99. Ansbacher and Ansbacher, 1956, pp. 30, 38. 100. *Ibid.*, p. 121. 101. Adler, 1954, p. 29. 102. Adler, 1968, p. 41. 103. Adler, 1956, p. 91. 104. Adler, 1968, p. 143. 105. Adler, 1964b, p. 219. 106. *Ibid.*, p. 103. 107. Ansbacher and Ansbacher, 1956, pp. 34, 143. 108. *Ibid.*, p. 111. 109. Kaufmann, 1956. 110. Adler, 1968, p. 5; Adler, 1954, p. 128. 111. Adler, 1968, p. 150. 112. Adler, 1964b, p. 147. 113. Adler, 1954, pp. 133, 209. 114. *Ibid.*, p. 212. 115. Adler, 1958, pp. 29–30. 116. Adler, 1964b, p. 96. 117. Adler, 1954, p. 69. 118. *Ibid.*, p. 65. 119. Adler, 1964b, p. 98. 120. Adler, 1968, p. 100. 121. *Ibid.*, p. 81. 122. *Ibid.*, p. 9. 123. Adler, 1954, pp. 136–137. 124. Ansbacher and Ansbacher, 1964, p. 35. 125. *Ibid.*, pp. 34–35. 126. Adler, 1958, p. 15. 127. Adler, 1964b, p. 71. 128. Adler, 1968, p. 8. 129. Adler, 1954, p. 178. 130. *Ibid.*, p. 69. 131. Adler, 1958, p. 60. 132. Adler, 1964b, pp. 117–122. 133. Adler, 1964a, p. 31. 134. *Ibid.* 135. Ansbacher and Ansbacher, 1964, p. 30. 136. Adler, 1964b, p. 277. 137. Ansbacher and Ansbacher, 1956, p. 177. 138. *Ibid.*, pp. 177–178. 139. Adler, 1964b, p. 285. 140. Adler, 1958, p.

29. **141.** Bottome, 1957, p. 122. **142.** Ansbacher and Ansbacher, 1956, p. 57. **143.** *Ibid.,* p. 121. **144.** Adler, 1930, p. 117. **145.** Adler, 1954, p. 35; Adler, 1963, p. xi; Adler, 1958, pp. 263–264. **146.** Adler, 1930, p. 118. **147.** Ansbacher and Ansbacher, 1964, p. 38. **148.** *Ibid.,* p. 39. **149.** *Ibid.* **150.** Adler, 1964b, pp. 72, 103. **151.** *Ibid.,* p. 275. **152.** *Ibid.,* pp. 272–273. **153.** Ansbacher and Ansbacher, 1964, pp. 38, 69. **154.** *Ibid.,* p. 65. **155** Adler, 1964b, p. 48. **156.** Adler, 1954, p. 153. **157.** *Ibid.,* p. 133. **158.** Adler, 1930, p. 21. **159.** *Ibid.,* pp. 34–35. **160.** Adler, 1963, p. x. **161.** Adler, 1964b, p. 110. **162.** Ansbacher and Ansbacher, 1964, p. 56. **163.** Adler, 1958, p. 8. **164.** Adler, 1930, pp. 82–83. **165.** Adler, 1964b, pp. 103–104. **166.** *Ibid.,* p. 274. **167.** Ansbacher and Ansbacher, 1964, p. 37. **168.** Adler, 1968, p. 60. **169.** *Ibid.,* p. 223. **170.** Adler, 1964b, p. 16. **171.** Adler, 1954, p. 60. **172.** Ansbacher and Ansbacher, 1964, p. 42. **173.** Ansbacher and Ansbacher, 1956, p. 60. **174.** *Ibid.,* p. 109. **175.** Adler, 1968, p. 167. **176.** *Ibid.,* p. 118. **177.** Adler, 1964b. p. 192. **178.** Adler, 1954, p. 107. **179.** Adler, 1968, p. 72. **180.** Adler, 1964a, p. 42. **181.** Adler, 1964b, p. 64. **182.** Adler, 1964a, p. 68. **183.** Adler, 1954, pp. 73–74. **184.** Adler, 1968, p. 62. **185.** Adler, 1930, p. 144. **186.** *Ibid.,* p. 161. **187.** *Ibid.,* p. 221. **188.** *Ibid.,* p. 224. **189.** Adler, 1964b, p. 232. **190.** Adler, 1958, p. 59. **191.** *Ibid.,* p. 7. **192.** Adler, 1964b, p. 42. **193.** *Ibid.,* p. 149. **194.** Adler, 1954, p. 128. **195.** Adler, 1964a, p. 117. **196.** *Ibid.,* p. 101. **197.** Adler, 1968, p. 321. **198.** *Ibid.,* p. 322. **199.** Adler, 1964a, p. 96. **200.** Adler, 1968, p. 322. **201.** Adler, 1954, p. 127. **202.** Adler, 1968, p. 321. **203.** Adler, 1964a, p. 77. **204.** Adler, 1958, p. 123. **205.** *Ibid.,* p. 121. **206.** Adler, 1964b, pp. 44–45. **207.** *Ibid.,* p. 221. **208.** Adler, 1958, p. 123. **209.** *Ibid.,* pp. 123–124. **210.** *Ibid.,* p. 132. **211.** *Ibid.,* p. 134. **212.** *Ibid.,* p. 135. **213.** Adler, 1968, p. 62. **214.** Adler, 1954, pp. 81–82. **215.** Adler, 1930, p. 206. **216.** Adler, 1964b, p. 51. **217.** *Ibid.,* p. 21. **218.** Adler, 1930, p. 225. **219.** Adler, 1968, p. 11. **220.** Adler, 1958, pp. 54, 126. **221.** Adler, 1954, p. 127. **222.** Adler, 1930, p. 140. **223.** *Ibid.,* p. 150. **224.** *Ibid.,* pp. 12–13. **225.** Adler, 1963, p. 172. **226.** Adler, 1930, p. 104. **227.** *Ibid.,* p. 182. **228.** *Ibid.,* p. 171. **229.** Adler, 1954, pp. 100–101. **230.** Adler, 1930, pp. 112–113. **231.** *Ibid.,* p. 138. **232.** *Ibid.,* pp. 185–186. **233.** *Ibid.,* p. 173. **234.** *Ibid.,* p. 184. **235.** *Ibid.,* p. 209. **236.** Adler, 1958, p. 182. **237.** *Ibid.,* p. 243. **238.** *Ibid.,* p. 244. **239.** *Ibid.,* p. 263. **240.** Adler, 1954, p. 105. **241.** Adler, 1958, p. 277. **242.** *Ibid.,* p. 280. **243.** *Ibid.* **244.** *Ibid.,* p. 281. **245.** Adler, 1964b, p. 67. **246.** Ansbacher and Ansbacher, 1956, p. 461. **247.** Adler, 1964b, p. 127. **248.** Adler, 1954, pp. 112–113. **249.** *Ibid.,* pp. 142–143. **250.** Adler, 1964b, p. 129. **251.** Adler, 1930, p. 8. **252.** Ansbacher and Ansbacher, 1956, pp. 167–168. **253.** Ansbacher and Ansbacher, 1964, p. 72. **254.** *Ibid.,* pp. 74–79. **255.** Adler, 1968, p. 307. **256.** *Ibid.,* p. 22. **257.** *Ibid.* **258.** *Ibid.,* Ch. XX. **259.** Ansbacher and Ansbacher, 1956, p. 246. **260.** Adler, 1964a, p. 72. **261.** Ansbacher and Ansbacher, 1956, p. 246. **262.** Adler, 1968, p. 45. **263.** Adler, 1964a, p. 81. **264.** Ansbacher and Ansbacher, 1964, p. 302. **265.** Adler, 1958, p. 49. **266.** Adler, 1968, p. 30. **267.** Adler, 1958, p. 186. **268.** Ansbacher and Ansbacher, 1964, p. 198. **269.** Adler, 1964b, p. 180. **270.** Adler, 1968, p. 244. **271.** Adler, 1964b, pp. 13–14. **272.** Adler, 1968, p. 56. **273.** Ansbacher and Ansbacher, 1964, p. 303. **274.** Adler, 1968, p. 243. **275.** Adler, 1958, p. 259. **276.** Adler, 1968, p. 254. **277.** Adler, 1964a, p. 128. **278.** Adler, 1968, p. 255. **279.** Adler, 1964b, p. 201. **280.** Adler, 1964a, p. 75. **281.** *Ibid.,* p. 130. **282.** Adler, 1964b, p. 64. **283.** Adler, 1968, p. 188. **284.** Adler, 1964a, p. 39. **285.** Adler, 1958, p. 61. **286.** *Ibid.,* p. 62. **287.** *Ibid.,* p. 226. **288.** Adler, 1968, p. 336. **289.** *Ibid.,* p. 203. **290.** *Ibid.,* p. 207. **291.** Adler, 1964a, p. 105. **292.** Adler, 1930, p. 73. **293.** Adler, 1954, p. 143. **294.** Adler, 1968, pp. 166–167. **295.** *Ibid.,* p. 170. **296.** Adler, 1964a, p. 73. **297.** Adler, 1968, p. 15. **298.** *Ibid.,* p. 23. **299.** Adler, 1964b, p. 294. **300.** Adler, 1968, p. 43. **301.** Adler, 1964b, p. 294. **302.** *Ibid.,* p. 181. **303.** Adler, 1968, p. 13. **304.** Adler, 1964a, p. 20. **305.** *Ibid.,* p. 73. **306.** Adler, 1968, p. 228. **307.** Ansbacher and Ansbacher, 1964, pp. 192–193. **308.** Adler, 1968, p. 227. **309.** Adler, 1963, p. 162. **310.** Adler, 1968, p. 22. **311.** Adler, 1963, p. 1. **312.** Adler, 1964a, p. 74. **313.** Ansbacher and Ansbacher, 1964, p. 299. **314.** Adler, 1968, p. 152. **315.** Adler, 1958, p. 72. **316.** Adler, 1963, p. 162. **317.** Adler, 1964a, p. 20. **318.** *Ibid.,* pp. 73–74. **319.** *Ibid.,* pp. 40–41. **320.** *Ibid.,* p. 41. **321.** *Ibid.,* p. 73. **322.** Adler, 1968, p. 151. **323.** Ansbacher and Ansbacher, 1964, p. 217. **324.** Adler, 1964b, p. 289. **325.** Adler, 1958, pp. 72–73. **326.** Adler, 1968, p. 144. **327.** Adler, 1964a, p. 73. **328.** Ansbacher and Ansbacher, 1956, p. 457. **329.** Ansbacher and Ansbacher, 1964, p. 40. **330.** Adler, 1964a, p. 162. **331.** Adler, 1958, p. 47. **332.** Adler, 1964a, p. 88. **333.** Adler, 1968, p. 25. **334.** *Ibid.*

335. Adler, 1964b, p. 287. 336. Adler, 1968, p. 43. 337. Adler, 1963, p. 165. 338. Adler, 1964a, p. 72. 339. *Ibid.*, p. 72. 340. Adler, 1958, p. 74. 341. Adler, 1964a, p. 122. 342. Adler, 1968, p. 214. 343. *Ibid.*, pp. 219–220. 344. *Ibid.*, p. 217. 345. *Ibid.*, pp. 217–218. 346. Adler, 1964b, p. 84. 347. Adler, 1964a, p. 15. 348. Adler, 1964b, p. 262. 349. *Ibid.*, p. 242. 350. Adler, 1964a, p. 16. 351. Adler, 1968, p. 116. 352. Adler, 1964a, p. 16. 353. Adler, 1958, p. 103. 354. *Ibid.*, pp. 103–104. 355. *Ibid.*, p. 107. 356. Adler, 1964a, p. 164. 357. Adler, 1958, p. 101. 358. Adler, 1964a, p. 164. 359. *Ibid.* 360. Adler, 1964b, p. 263. 361. *Ibid.* 362. *Ibid.*, p. 264. 363. Adler, 1958, p. 107. 364. Adler, 1964a, p. 8. 365. *Ibid.* 366. *Ibid.*, p. 25. 367. *Ibid.* 368. *Ibid.*, pp. 25–26. 369. Adler, 1964b, p. 288. 370. *Ibid.* 371. Adler, 1968, p. 43. 372. Adler, 1964b, p. 295. 373. Ansbacher and Ansbacher, 1964, p. 192.

3

The Analytical Psychology of Carl Jung

Biographical Overview

Carl Gustav Jung was born in 1875 in a small Swiss village (Kesswil) but was relocated while an infant to the Rhine Fall near Schaffhaused where he spent his boyhood as the only child of a country parson. Churchmen were on both sides of Jung's genealogy—six parson uncles on the mother's side, and two paternal uncles as well—but his own father was really more attracted to philology and classical studies than to the ministry.[1] Economic necessity forced him to enter the ministry, and he married the daughter of his former Hebrew professor. Jung seems to have felt a greater overall attachment to his father.[2] Though his mother was the stronger parental personality in the home, he found her puzzling and even eccentric in manner.[3]

Jung's scholarly life began early, for when he was six his father introduced him to the study of Latin. Throughout later life Jung could read ancient texts, and this training doubtless helps to account for his historical approach to man. In a very real sense he was a classical scholar. When the family eventually moved to the more urban Basel from the Rhine Fall, Jung was roughly 12 years old. He had become a solitary person, physically large, active, yet secretive and prone to set his own daily routine. Going to school was never a particular joy for him. He disliked athletics, mathematics, and the competition for grades among classmates. Jung tells us that he deliberately settled for a second-in-the-class standing which he found "considerably more enjoyable"[4] than vying for first. Even so, his father's tutoring had put him ahead of the urban classmates he confronted in Basel, and this superiority led to a rather difficult hazing. He came to despise school, used sickness as an excuse to avoid attending, and for a time actually had a period of neurotic fainting spells of which he eventually cured himself through self-discipline.[5]

When he grew to young manhood Jung attended the University of Basel. He was interested in historical, classical, anthropological, and philosophical subjects but decided on medicine because it was a distinguished profession offering various alternatives for a career. Thanks to a selection he read by Krafft-Ebing, the famous German neurologist, Jung settled on psychiatry as a specialty which could combine his more humanistic and his scientific interests.[6] Following graduation from medical school Jung took a position at the Burgholzli Hospital in Zürich, Switzerland, serving under Eugen Bleuler, the noted psychiatrist who had coined the term *schizophrenia*. Bleuler was a professor of psychiatry at the University of Zürich, and Jung was also to hold a lectureship there, in conjunction with his studies on the nature of schizophrenia. It was at the Burgholzli Hospital, from 1900–1909, that Jung reached maturity as a scientist and became a world authority on the psychology of the abnormal and the normal individual. He furthered the technique of *word association* there, coined a term (*complex*) which played a central role in all of his later theorizing, and published his first book.

Jung immediately recognized Freud's genius, and he felt that his own studies had confirmed the undoubted existence of an unconscious sphere in man's mind. Their first meeting took place in Vienna in 1907, and it was memorable because Freud and Jung talked for 13 consecutive hours. In the method of word association Jung would ask a patient to respond to a stimulus word with the first word coming to mind. He then noted certain disturbances in the patient's word associations, such as a long response latency, a blocking of responding entirely, or a repetition of the stimulus word.[7] If

one repeated this procedure often enough he could gradually establish that certain words hung together, interlaced in the patient's associations, and formed a *complex* of ideas. Since these idea masses were invariably tied to emotional concerns Jung referred to them as "feeling-toned complexes."[8] The repressed memories and conflicts of the Freudian school were thus experimentally verified by the word association method. Free association and controlled association had common outcomes.

Jung did not come to Freud as a fledgling. He was a man who had made his own reputation, one which was in academic circles even more important (due to its acceptability) than Freud's. Further, Jung was too much of a loner and an independent thinker ever to play a submerged, student role to Freud. It is clear from early reactions that Jung, like Adler before him, was never completely sold on Freud's views, especially those on sex.[9] In 1909 they made their famous trip to Clark University in Massachusetts and it was this extended contact which led to their break.

There were three major reasons for this split. First, Jung was unable to accept the concept of libido as limited to sexual energy. As we shall see, Jung bases his energizing theory on a *principle of opposites,* and at one point he urged Freud to suggest an opposite energy to libido.[10] Since this criticism was necessarily a threat to the sexuality thesis, as we can recall from Chapter 1, Freud was adamant on the point. Related to this matter was the question of just how sex was to be interpreted symbolically. Did such unconscious dream symbols refer to a lustful interpersonal memory in *this* person's life, or was there something far more profound and even extraindividual about such symbols? Drawing on his classical studies, Jung argued that a "mother imago" cannot be tied to a single patient's life, for such mother symbols have made their appearance in too many and varied cultural myths to be seen so narrowly, as the reflection of a *personal* conflict.[11]

Jung wanted to include a *collective* aspect to the unconscious, and though Freud held to this view in principle he could not bend his thought to include this device more formally. The collective aspect of the unconscious would also demand an argument admitting inherited racial experiences, and Freud felt that he could not let this highly controversial issue take further attention away from the already notorious sexuality thesis. When Jung actually formalized these views in a book entitled *The Psychology of the Unconscious* he sealed his fate, for by his own admission this work cost him Freud's friendship.[12] The final major cause of their split stemmed from an incident on the trip to Clark University. Apparently the two men fell into analyzing one another's dreams— possibly as an exercise in mutual learning, although Jung hints that Freud actually referred to personal problems.[13] At a point during free association, Freud reneged with the observation that, were he to continue he would lose his authority in their relationship. This attitude took Jung aback, since he had been relating with respect but not as the lesser authority.

The relationship between the two cooled noticeably after the trip to America, even though Jung was by then the President of the International Psycho-Analytical Association (thanks to Freud's direct influence). Following a stormy convention of this association in Munich in 1913 when Jung's "heretical views" on the unconscious were the focus of debate, Freud and Jung went their separate ways. Though Jung was reelected to a two year term as President, future conventions during his tenure were made impossible by the developing World War I, and the two men never faced one another again. There ensued a very difficult period for Jung, during which he analyzed himself much as Freud had done (see Chapter 1). His only satisfactions at this time came from his wife's emotional support and their growing family. He describes this period, from roughly 1913 to 1917, as one of inner uncertainty and disorientation.[14]

It was as if he were being assaulted by fantasies from his unconscious, and he tried to hold them in check through Yoga and other means. He began to record these fantasies and eventually to work out a means of communication with his unconscious. He literally came to talk to a "person" within his identity, one he was to call the "anima."[15] Reminiscent of his childhood, he once again found that he had to conquer the hold this "person" had on his psyche; and by way of regaining his self-possession to "individuate" a new personality more representative of what he really was as a human being than the other.

After World War I Jung continued to attract a wide circle of followers. He once studied a group of Navajo Indians in America. He canvassed various tribes in field trips to North, East, and Central Africa. He spent time in the Sudan as well as Egypt and also embarked on a trip to India. In each of these

Carl Gustav Jung

ventures what Jung sought was further confirmation of his views on mankind. He thus not only saw his own patients and read widely, but he actually did the work of an archaeologist-anthropologist when the opportunity presented itself. On one occasion, while in America, he made a special study of black patients at the St. Elizabeth's Hospital in Washington, D.C. He became recognized as a scholar of the first rank, was awarded honorary degrees by eight universities, and was made an Honorary Fellow of the Royal Society.

Although he had actually spoken out against the rise of a war psychology in Germany as early as 1936,[16] some misunderstandings in other of his writings and an editorship of a German journal of psychotherapy which he accepted in 1933, resulted in Jung being criticized as a Nazi sympathizer.[17] Yet, as Jung himself noted, his books were burned by the Nazis, and he had it on good evidence that he was on the Nazi black list.[18] In time, it was established that not only was Jung unsympathetic to the Nazi cause, he provided significant aid to Jewish psychiatrists and psychologists who had fled the Nazis to settle in England. A thorough study of the entire matter cleared Jung's name without question, if any such exoneration were necessary.[19]

In addition to his academic appointment at Zürich, Jung once served as professor of medical psychology at the University of Basel. He remained a prolific worker and writer throughout his life, and his collected works are second in size only to Freud's. He spent the years following World War II putting together his finished thoughts on the archetypes, writing his autobiography, and meeting the requests of students and interested lay people to make his thoughts known. His students organized an Institute, and for a time his approach was referred to as complex psychology. However, the name Jung preferred and the one we shall use is analytical psychology. He died at Küsnacht, Zürich, in 1961.

Personality Theory

STRUCTURAL CONSTRUCTS

DUALISM OF MIND VS. BODY

In the *Psychology of Dementia Praecox* (Vol. 3), published before his meeting with Freud, Jung proposed that "the affect in dementia praecox favours the appearance of anomalies in the metabolism—toxins, perhaps, which injure the brain in a more or less irreparable manner, so that the highest psychic functions become paralysed."[20] This view was advanced very tentatively, while under the influence of Bleuler and other medical colleagues, but even so it has coaxed many into believing that Jung was a theorist who favored physical explanations of abnormal—hence, possibly all—behavior. Actually, if one reviews what he said about this speculation over a lifetime it seems clear that Jung was highly ambivalent, if not actually embarrassed about it altogether. In what is probably his final (1957) statement on the matter he took a moderate position, saying: "I consider the aetiology of schizophrenia to be a dual one: namely, up to a certain point psychology is indispensable in explaining the nature and the causes of the initial emotions which give rise to metabolic alterations. These emotions seem to be accompanied by chemical processes that cause specific temporary or chronic disturbances or lesions."[21]

Jung was in fact highly critical of his medical peers for their exclusive reliance upon physical explanations. He stated flatly that the psyche deserved to be understood as a phenomenon in its own right, and that there were no adequate reasons for thinking of it as a mere epiphenomenon simply because it had to rely on the physical functioning of the brain.[22] He did not believe that psychic factors had to be fitted into physical theories before they could be dealt with scientifically.[23] In the above quotes Jung gives emotional factors a prominent position in speaking about what might be termed "mental" illness. Unlike Freud, who theorized that mind *qua* mind was free of emotional content, Jung's psychology lumps both affective (emotional) and rational, intellectual contents into the mind from the outset. According to Jung, primitive man was ruled not by intellect but by a conglomerate of emotional "projections" which he ascribed to the world around him.[24] Thoughts simply "happen" to primitive man as they do to a modern man immersed in emotion, because neither individual recognizes that he is personally the source of the contents mentally projected onto existence in the emotive state.[25] As he recognized his emotional projections primitive man acquired a sense of personal consciousness and "directed thinking" was then possible.[26]

PSYCHE AS A REGION

In a classical Freudian psychoanalysis the structures of mind are relatively fixed in relation to the levels of mind, so that, for example, the id is constantly in an unconscious segment of the psyche. The id never leaves the realm of unconsciousness to take a self-directed turn around consciousness. It sends its derivatives (ideas or images) into consciousness by way of cathexes, which are themselves often symbolized to fool the conscious side of the ego; but the "id as an identity" remains rooted in the depths of the mind. For Jung, the psyche is a region, a kind of multidirectional and multitemporal housing within which identities of the personality like the ego can move about. In this case an id-like structure (complex) *can* move up into the conscious realm out of the unconscious and initiate behavioral manifestations to suit its own purposes.

Though Jung did not stress physical explanations of human behavior he did emphasize hereditary factors. However, his meaning here was more historical than physical. Man's heredity is psychic as well as physical in nature. We must not slight the former by relying too heavily on the latter. The mind-body problem was for Jung a pseudo-issue, a device which cer-

tain people could use to detract from the psyche's importance by saying "Oh, that's only a mental phenomenon, it's not real." Though the psyche is constituted of mental images it is not unreal. Jung argued that the psyche has as much validity and hence reality as the (physical) body events on which it is based.[27]

This psychical region of the mind has a history, hereditarily (historically) predetermined so that man begins life with *both* a physically ordered structure (hands work much the same for all men) and a psychically ordered structure (men reason and create meanings in much the same way). Further, man's psyche has evolved along a purposeful, teleological line.[28] If man were only an instinctual creature he would have no need of a psyche because a psychic act *modifies* reflexive or instinctual responses.[29] Neither is the psyche merely a reactive phenomenon, relying upon the external world to stimulate it and direct it; the psyche can and does infuse meanings onto reality from the outset, as well as give its own specific answers to those external influences which impinge upon it from the outside.[30]

We can see, therefore, that Jung's construct of the psyche is an all-encompassing one. As Jung said: "The psyche is not of today: its ancestry goes back many millions of years. Individual consciousness is only the flower and the fruit of a season, sprung from the perennial rhizome beneath the earth. . . ."[31] The contents of the psyche are also an unending source of creative "potentials" which give it anything but a homogeneous rhythm over time. In fact, the psyche is predicated on a "principle of opposites," which makes it so contrapuntal that any psychological claim about man substantiates its opposite as well.[32] All things are thus open to the psyche, and to discover what something means we must constantly attend to its obverse or opposite.

Figure 9 is a schematization of Jung's fluid psyche model. Note that the directionality from out of the past is suggested by presenting the psyche as a vortex (point 1). The "pri-

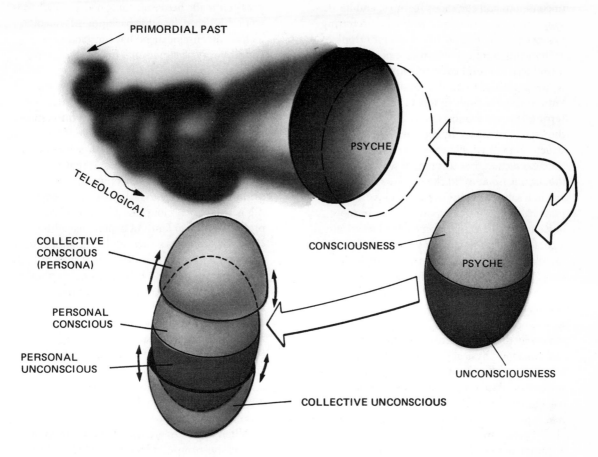

Figure 9
Jung's Psyche Model

PRIMORDIAL PAST

TELEOLOGICAL

PSYCHE

COLLECTIVE
CONSCIOUS
(PERSONA)

CONSCIOUSNESS

PSYCHE

PERSONAL
CONSCIOUS

PERSONAL
UNCONSCIOUS

UNCONSCIOUSNESS

COLLECTIVE UNCONSCIOUS

mordial past" would refer to man's roots in a primitive state, evolving as he did from a lower animal both physically and, of significance here, psychically. The purposiveness of man's psychic descent is noted in the teleological line of advance from the vortex, going "this" way and then "that" down through time. The "region" of the psyche within which Jung framed his personality constructs is the open-ended front of the vortex. Assume that a membrane (dotted portion of Figure 9) stretched across this open end and that for didactic purposes we can slide it off to give our typical egg-shaped diagram of the psyche at point 2. The psyche is now differentiated into two broad

regions of *consciousness* and *unconsciousness*.[33] As noted in the biographical overview, Jung believed that each of these two major subdivisions of the psyche could in turn be construed as having a collective and a personal aspect. We have schematized this at point 3 by a double set of egg halves, one of which (collective) can slide over the other making for a combined "collective psyche" and a combined "personal psyche" laying one over the other. These are not mutually exclusive regions, however. The contents of one can interpenetrate and interfuse with the contents of the other.

Even though we have allowed for the *collective conscious* in Figure 9, Jung never employed precisely this term. He did use the concept of a *collective psyche*[34] which combined unconscious and conscious features, and he also spoke of the *empirical psyche*[35] when referring to aspects of the personality one might think of as involving a collective consciousness. Jung introduced the term *collective unconscious,* but he never seemed to need a paralleling collective term in the conscious sphere of psychic life, preferring to cover ground in consciousness under the "ego" and especially the "persona" constructs, both of which we will be taking up in the next section. For this reason we have put the term *persona* in brackets along with the egg-half labeled "collective conscious." For all practical purposes these two are one. In the descent of man, as his brain evolved physically, a parallel evolution of the psyche was also taking place.[36] Subhuman man was a totally instinctual creature, responding mechanically and without the exertion of personal will. There was no awareness of a subjective identity, hence, no uniqueness among peoples. In the same way that man shares common instincts and common physical structures, he also shared a common, *collective* unconscious psyche. This form of unconsciousness was *impersonal,* it was supraindividual and to that extent *objective* (applying equally to all members of the class "human species").[37]

Jung liked to point to Lévy-Bruhl's concept of *participation mystique* as conveying what he was trying to capture in the collective unconscious construct.[38] The primitive individual sees nature as an undifferentiated mass of which he is part and parcel. He ascribes a daemonic power to certain mountains, he sees witches and devils in thunder storms or earthquakes, and plants and animals are taken as his peers, anthropomorphized participants in his personal world.[39] He conceives of his environment as such because in his state of unconsciousness the primitive is unable to grasp some of the most rudimentary distinctions between opposites like "subject" (I, me) vs. "object" (it, they). Another way Jung defined unconscious-

ness was: a mental condition in which all things are possible, and distinctions have not yet been made between, e.g., good and evil. It is from this broad "psychic background" of collective unconsciousness that consciousness (and by way of it, personal unconsciousness) must eventually emerge.[40]

To describe this process of consciousness formation Jung relied upon the construct of a *differentiation,* or a development of differences, the separation of parts from a whole.[41] Occasionally the term *discrimination* is substituted, but the idea behind either term is that from the global unity of the collective unconscious primitive man came to fashion an ever expanding island of consciousness. Consciousness is prompted by two kinds of experience, either of which promotes awareness of the subjective in an individual: when man is in a state of high emotional tension or when he is unconsciously contemplative of the collectively prompted ideas passing before him like vivid dream images.[42] Either state seems to jolt man into an act of differentiation, so that he might conceive for the first time that *"I* am having a state [of emotion] even though others are not" or "There is a vivid thought, hence here am *I* on whom it is making its impression" (or word feelings to this effect).

When opposites are teased apart into some kind of meaningful relationship of from "X to non-X" or whatever, man comes to "know" something. He learns, and the more he knows the wider does he expand his circle of consciousness.[43] By knowing things man also removes more of his unconscious projections from the environment and attributes them to his own identity.[44] Consciousness cannot project feelings or experiences, and it has little appreciation for the role of projection in human life. In fact, widening consciousness invariably spells a denigration of unconsciousness among human beings: "Because of its youthfulness and vulnerability, our consciousness tends to make light of the unconscious."[45] Yet, as the offspring of the unconscious our consciousness must always remain the smaller identity within the larger,[46] just as an island sits within the expanse of the sea from which it has emerged.[47] In fact, if man would only appreciate that the unconscious remains the ever-creative principle in his life[48] and that it can lead him in his endeavors in the same way that his automatic ("physically unconscious") instincts often help him to survive, he would be far better off.[49]

As consciousness arises and a subjective awareness is made possible, mental contents can be assigned to this "personal" awareness. Material once conscious in the Freudian sense can now be repressed. This is the *personal unconscious* realm of Figure 9, and we can recognize in it all of those features of unconsciousness which Freud had assigned to this construct. But contents of the collective unconscious are never repressed; they have never "been" at all. The personal unconscious is somewhat less "deep" in the realm of psychic unconsciousness than is the collective unconscious,[50] but we have indicated in Figure 9 that a complete parallel of the two realms of unconsciousness is possible because Jung always has the contents of the one mixing or uniting with the other.

THE "ADHESIVE MODEL" OF PSYCHIC STRUCTURE

Basic to Jung's theory concerning the structural identities of mind (psyche) is what might be termed an *adhesive model*. The contents of mind invariably accumulate and agglutinate into identifiable entities around some core preoccupation, like a fearful experience or the demands of a social role facing the individual. Jung first made use of the adhesive model in his inaugural dissertation for the medical degree in 1902 when he was trying to explain the "psychology and pathology of so-called occult phenomena."[51] How does it happen that a "medium"—a person who mediates between death and life—can seem to have a deceased loved one speaking through his or her (the medium's) vocal chords in conversation with the surviving relatives? Jung did not believe

there was always a conscious intent to deceive on the part of the medium. Drawing on the thought of both Bleuler and Pierre Janet, he equated such occult reactions with the "dissociative" reactions of hysterics and schizophrenics.[52]

Jung based his line of development on the fact that mediums so often call out to a presence which they supposedly "feel" in proximity during a state of concentration which is also emotionally charged. It is not unusual for the medium to ask this presence "Who is there?" and then, of course, to allow a reply by way of the medium's vocal apparatus. In asking this suggestive question while in an emotional state, Jung argued, an *automatism* was synthesized just as such automatic actions are synthesized in hysterical patients. This "identity from within" Jung termed variously a "feeling-toned complex" or a "feeling-toned train of thought."[53] All emotional reactions stimulate mental thoughts which form congeries of ideas called *complexes*.[54] The life of a complex is dependent upon the emotion attached to it; if the feeling-tone of the ideas constituting the complex is extinguished, so too is the complex as such.[55] We might retain the memory but not the complex.

Jung believed that most complexes formed in life quickly sink back with decreasing feeling tone into the latent mass of memories we all carry about in the personal unconscious. However, if it should encounter a related complex it might adhere to it, and then, thanks to its added size and import, it could begin intruding on consciousness. There is a "snow-ball" effect to be noted in complex formation, for the stronger is the complex, the more will it assimilate other contents in the psyche.[56] As it grows in strength it influences our life, by confounding associations on the word-association test, by causing parapraxes (slips of the tongue, etc.), or by showing itself in dreams. Whereas Freud believed the dream to be his royal road to the unconscious, Jung concluded: "The *via regia* to the unconscious . . . is not the dream . . .

but the complex, which is the architect of dreams and of symptoms."[57]

Although feeling-toned complexes are often triggered by emotional trauma[58] not all complexes are abnormal structural identities (recall that consciousness itself is stimulated by states of great emotion). The complex is merely the characteristic way in which the psyche expresses itself.[59] The psyche is teleological in nature, so complex formation always implies purposive action bent on achieving a goal, even if that goal is not consonant with the rest of the personality. People are not consistent in any case. The series of terms which we will now take up all fall within this adhesive model of psychic structures; most have the meaning of a "complex" but not all.

Ego. One of the first major complexes Jung named was the *ego complex,* which is usually shortened to simply *ego.* Consciousness is the necessary precondition for ego formation, but without a subjective ego to relate items to (meaning creation) consciousness would be unthinkable.[60] However, ego and consciousness are not identical. Important as it is in the ruling of consciousness,[61] the ego is not the only identity active in consciousness. The ego grows thanks to stimulations from the somatic as well as the psychic sphere; we form body images by way of direct physical sensations and from interpersonal experiences.[62] Another stimulus to ego formation is the feeling of success attained when something in life works for us. We attribute this success to our subjective identity: "I did that."[63]

The ego has a generic tie to what we will call the "self," and to that extent it has a role to play in connection with the unconscious (where the self is located as a potentiality). Jung dealt with the Freudian compromise model by suggesting that the unconscious can make projections onto the ego, which then acts as a mirror for all manner of unconscious manifestations.[64] He viewed these supposed ego-id compromises as forms of unconscious prompt-

ings projected onto the ego, rather than as ego-determined solutions. The ego's influence is thus kept *primarily* in consciousness in Jungian psychology. It is not free to do unconscious bargaining and is more the "moved-by" than the mover of unconscious processes.[65] The ego in Jungian psychology therefore plays a lesser role in the personality than it plays in the personality theory of Freudian psychology.

Persona. In addition to framing a subjective ego identity within consciousness we all acquire a series of patterned behaviors which make up what Jung called the *persona.* We have already referred to this term and it is entered in brackets on the collective conscious egg-half of Figure 9. Jung felt that the word *persona* met his theoretical needs perfectly, for it originally meant the "mask" worn by the actor in Greek drama.[66] In like fashion, we all wear facade masks as we perform our socially dictated roles in life, sometimes wondering where the "real me" begins and the "social me" leaves off. The implications of the collective (group) influence on the individual here is justification for considering the persona to be roughly equivalent to a "conscious collective." As Jung himself observed: ". . . what we said of the collective unconscious is also true of the persona's contents, that is, they are of a general [objective] character."[67]

It is virtually impossible to avoid masks in life. There are so many socially prescribed behaviors to be "proper" about, or demands to meet the expectancies of others as they look for certain behaviors from us ("Try to act like a Christian, will you?"); we are constantly falling back on these stylized patterns. Our parents, particularly fathers,[68] help to model many of these masks for us. Our masks are adjustment devices; they help us to get along in life, as when we adopt a fawning manner with a superior to impress him with our devotion to his interests.[69] As with the ego, the persona can carry unconscious projections and hence model for the ego some (even daemonic) factors out of man's depth; but conscious factors are always involved as well so that group fads, recognized sharing of viewpoints among the masses, etc., all find their focus in the persona.[70] The main danger in the persona is that we might identify with it and accept it as our real personality.[71] Conformers, timid defenders of banalities, the puffed-up and the bullies of the crowd are all prone to this mistaken identity.

Shadow. As man was evolving the corpus of behaviors which make up the ego and persona complexes another side to his personality was systematically ignored because he found it distasteful, inadequate, or evil. Such psychic contents often have a core of emotionality ("I failed and I'm miserable," "I have an urge to steal that wristwatch"), so if Jung was to be consistent he had to claim that they would form into a complex. He calls the nondeveloped aspects of the conscious personality the *shadow* or the *alter ego*.[72] As Jung phrased it: "By shadow I mean the 'negative' side of the personality, the sum of all those unpleasant qualities we like to hide, together with the insufficiently developed functions and the contents of the personal unconscious."[73]

The shadow is an inferior personality, a repressed, usually guilt-laden collection of behaviors residing in the uppermost layers of the personal unconscious.[74] It is located in the personal unconscious because it consists of the "other side" of behaviors that have been cultivated within consciousness. The shadow is not as finely differentiated as are the ego and persona, making it an agglutination of crude, bumbling, even confused behaviors which would shame us if it reared its uncivilized head in consciousness. Even so Jung believed it was important for man to make such repressions conscious.

Having presented the shadow as the negative side of our personality, in his typical oppositional fashion Jung asserted that occasionally the shadow has a *positive* aspect as well. The

more rare of the two possible situations occurs when for some reason an individual consciously espouses what is socially considered to be an unfavorable, even criminal or immoral, role in life. In this case the urges for behaving in a socially acceptable way, caring for the feelings of others, etc., would be repressed and formed into a "good" type of shadow.[75] Thus, even the sinner has a good side, although he has not developed those behaviors which are potentially altruistic and socially responsible. No one walks only one side of the street in Jungian psychology.

The second way in which a shadow can be said to have positive features is through a more sophisticated understanding of what factors go into evaluations like success, good vs. evil or socially acceptable vs. socially unacceptable. Surely these are often biased and short-sighted judgments pressed on the individual by the collective. The Victorian repression of sexuality can be seen as an instance of unnecessarily harsh judgment being placed upon a perfectly natural human urge. If the shadow of a Victorian individual therefore contained sexual promptings quite out of the ordinary, would this not be a reflection of honest, even necessary, human needs? In like fashion, Jung claimed, our shadows often contain the germ of "good qualities, such as normal instincts, appropriate reactions, realistic insights, creative impulses, etc."[76]

Self. If we continue our descent into the depths of the unconscious we might eventually come upon an identity—really only the potentiality of an identity—which is not precisely termed a complex, although it can assimilate the contents of the psyche which go to make up the ego, persona, and even the shadow. It therefore follows the adhesion model. This is the *self*, which in Jungian thought epitomizes the teleological nature of the psyche. Terms like totality, the center of the personality, and wholeness capture the basic meaning of self-hood.[77]

Jung once analogized to the ego in defining the self. He said that just as the ego is the subjective point of reference for consciousness, so too is the self the subjective point of reference for the totality of the psyche.[78] As such, the self is an ideal, something that not all men come to realize in their lifetime. This is why it is only a potential identity. One cannot become an individual unless he has first combined the influences of the historical past with the potentials and aspirations of the future. This point of subjective identity within the flow of time is the self.[79] The self is that which unites all opposites in the psyche, so that the self-realized individual finds it impossible to overlook any aspect of his nature, confusing persona with ego or rejecting the shadow as nonexistent. To quote Jung: "In the end we have to acknowledge that the self is a *complexio oppositorum*

precisely because there can be no reality without polarity."[80]

Personality. We now have four constructs all of which have something to say about the structure of personality. How do we put them together, and is some comprehensive definition of personality now possible? Figure 10 presents a schematization of Jung's view of personality. It extends the egg-shaped top of the vortex in Figure 9. We have dropped the "collective conscious" half of the egg in lieu of the complex of masks we now know to be the persona. The ego is set in the conscious sphere, the shadow sits near the line dividing consciousness and unconsciousness, in what we know as the personal unconscious. And the self is sketched in as a dotted circle down more deeply as *in potentia,* ready to emerge into a definite entity if conditions are right.

When Jung actually used the term *personal-*

Figure 10
The Psyche as Personality

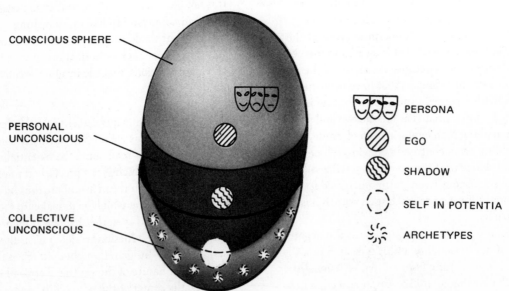

CONSCIOUS SPHERE

PERSONAL UNCONSCIOUS

COLLECTIVE UNCONSCIOUS

PERSONA

EGO

SHADOW

SELF IN POTENTIA

ARCHETYPES

ity his meaning was reminiscent of the self; for example: "I have suggested calling the total personality which, though present, cannot be fully known, the self. The ego is, by definition, subordinate to the self and is related to it like a part to the whole."[81] It would follow that if a self were to emerge in the individual, this subjective point of reference for the entire psyche would then contain much of the meaning of "personality." The question therefore, is not what is "the" (single) personality in Jungian psychology. We all have several personalities within our psyche, taking psyche to mean the functioning of part personalities like the ego, shadow, and persona.[82] A completely integrated (highly differentiated) personality, a total human being would be a self-realized human being.

THE "STYLIZED MEANING EXPRESSION" MODEL

In addition to the adhesive quality of psychic contents, forming around an emotive core, Jung constantly utilized what we might call the "stylized meaning expression" model of mental contents. The psyche is intentional by nature, and just as primitive man might anthropomorphize a rock by projecting his subjective reactions onto it, so too modern men have a tendency to express unconscious-to-conscious mental contents as *symbols*. Man is a symbolizing animal, which for Jung meant that he must ever create understandable (interpretable) psychic contents which have an intent, a meaning. Psychic expressions take on styles, so that in time we can come to know what is being expressed by recognizing the various stylistic manifestations.

Symbolism. Jung was adamant in differentiating between a symbol and a sign, arguing that Freud had blurred this important distinction. A *sign* is a mental content (image, idea) which stands as surrogate for some other mental content (its referent). When we use the word or character for number "7" as a sign we intend a short-hand designation for "seven things." Signs are translations of meanings; they are not active agents in the creation of meanings. However, if we now use the number "7" to express an alternate meaning, a meaning which was not originally intended by the mathematician when he selected this sign as a shorthand, we begin to get the idea of what symbolizing is all about. The number "7" might now symbolize "luck."

The great source of symbolic expression in Jungian psychology is the unconscious, and in particular, the collective unconscious. The capacity to symbolize is probably based upon some physical capability in man.[83] Symbols are less likely to appear as ideas; they are usually images which point beyond themselves to meanings which are still out of our grasp.[84] Language is the product of consciousness, and symbolic expression stems from our objective unconscious where specific idea thoughts are not generated. A symbolic image can combine with idea thoughts from the personal unconscious, of course, so that a complex can include both the image and the idea. But a symbol *qua* symbol is really on the side of an image, that is, pictorial rather than word contents. Symbols are usually analogues,[85] and they often express opposite intentions so we have to study an individual for some time before we can get the drift of his symbolic expressions.[86]

Dreaming is one of the ways in which a symbol is likely to make its first appearance. Since this symbolic manifestation is likely to have a collective influence behind it, a symbol can even express itself among large masses of people simultaneously. Our myths probably originate as extensions of dream reports or as "day dream" fantasies which capitalize on an inspirational prompting from a region man is not consciously aware of. Myths are never "made up" consciously; they arise from man's collective unconscious.[87] In primitive man, because thinking was simply happening, a myth was nothing more than the recounting of this dreamlike occurrence.[88] Myths can hold great truths for man, or they can mislead him entirely because the meanings contained are often two-pronged or oppositional.

In his study of the dream symbols of his patients Jung first began seeing parallels with mythological motifs. For example, a very young child would recite a dream to Jung which exactly paralleled some ancient and esoteric Persian myth. The child could not have been taught the myth, for very few people even knew of it who were not classical scholars. Further, in his travels and studies of primitive peoples in America or Africa Jung found that, though the content of a specific myth might change, the general story line was identical across cultural heritages which had no possible chance of contact. A common, almost instinctual, necessity for all men—including civilized man—to symbolize the very same theme in their myths seemed to exist. A good example is the hero-figure who comes from out of nowhere to save a tribe or a civilization during a time of drought, moral decay, and so on. Though the specific content of the redeemer figure might vary—he could have been a fish, lizard, man, man-bird, or God-man—the commonalities of the myths were striking in story line.[89] After considerable study and deliberation, and after he found such common manifestations in his own fantasies and dreams during his self-analysis, Jung adapted the Platonic-Augustinian term *archetype* in 1919 to account for such presumed expressions of a collective psyche.[90]

Many people incorrectly believe that Jung advocated a fixed or "universal" symbolism. Though he admitted that symbols had to take on a relatively fixed content in order for us to grasp their significance and to recognize them in different contexts—that symbols were relatively objective[91]—Jung was careful to point out that this necessity did *not* suggest a universal symbolism. He was very critical of Freud's tendency to ascribe a sexual significance to all elongated objects (male symbol) or enclosed places (female symbol).[92] Since the dream symbol is an unknown quantity at the root

source of meaning-expression, Jung opined that: "You get caught in your own net if you believe in fixed, unalterable symbols."[93] A sign can have a fixed meaning, but never a symbol.

The distinction between a *universal archetype* and a *universal symbol* may still be unclear. As a first step toward clarification, keep in mind that symbols are what we come to know in consciousness as images (possibly set within a complex of ideas as well). They are what dimly shines through the veil of historical dust from out of our collective past. The archetype, on the other hand, though recognized after much study by its theme, is *never* seen as an image. It stands behind the light, in the darkest reaches of the uconscious, and expresses its meaning by somehow directing the light thrown symbolically upon our conscious understanding. Hence, the symbolic contents may vary, but the theme or motif (archetype) under expression remains the same.

Archetypes. We will take up Jung's concept of instinct later, in the presentation of his motivational constructs, but it must be recalled at this juncture that the use of instincts to explain human behavior was a very common gambit at the turn of the twentieth century. Jung was no less attracted to this tactic than was Freud. If it is possible to think of the physical body as having evolved certain stylized ways of automatic behavior—called "instincts" to do this or that in a certain manner—then why is it not also possible for an evolving psyche to have its instinctual counterpart? And so Jung came to think of the recurring dream and mythological motifs as analogous to and based upon the instincts. He defined the instincts as *typical modes of action* and then added that the archetype might suitably be described as the *"instinct's perception of itself,* or as the self-portrait of the instinct."[94] Archetypes are thus typical modes of apprehending existence; they are stylized psychic behaviors reflecting the very essence of what the psyche means to accomplish, to learn, to express.[95]

Since they emanate from the deepest, collective regions of the unconscious, the archetypes are also called *primordial images,* as when symbols passed before the primitive's mind's eye preliminary to his myth making.[96] Here we begin having trouble distinguishing archetype from symbol, and universal from fixed-and-unalterable. For Jung now begins to use definitions of the archetypes as congenital pre-existent imagos[97] or inherited "form determinants."[98] Yet he also insists that these are not *inherited ideas,* for they lack the language structure which ideas must embody; it takes a cultural system of verbal contents (words) to have ideas, and the archetype transcends such consciously determined artifacts.[99] Now, it is easy to confuse idea (word content) with image (pictorial content) and to forget Jung's distinction between symbol and sign, which makes his entire point of view seem contradictory. What we must recognize is that Jung is saying the mind, in evolving and differentiating its nature over the centuries, has come to *function* in a certain way. The mind is not a complex mechanism which has stylized methods of expression built into it "from the outside" once it begins to function. The mind is rather a mechanism which has certain stylized methods of expression built into it "from the inside." Jung is looking at the nature of the mental mechanism itself when he speaks of archetypes, whereas the symbol is the means selected for external expression.

No one thinks of the human hand as a mechanism lacking a priori potentials. Hands are built in a certain way, with certain potentials for behavioral manifestation given to all those men who have them in normal working order. This hand paints a beautiful picture, and the delicacy of its movements gives us some inkling of what its owner's life has been like, while that hand is preoccupied with plunder and even murder, thereby defining an alternative possibility for the hand which might have been that of an artist's. The painting vs. the plundering are analogous to the specific contents of the mind: they can vary even though the structure of the hand making them possible does not. So too Jung sees the mind as having an inherited, a priori disposition to work in a certain way. It stylizes, orients for the future, and through its teleological nature must by definition frame ever new meaning from out of its depths. Asking why mind does this is like asking why the hand grasps. The psyche, Jung is saying, is not passive; it is an active agent in the framing of meaning. In differentiating what it "is" over the centuries, the psyche has evolved a set manner of expressing common human concerns or motifs. These themes, social situations, or preoccupations with the opposite sex are never seen directly as images (they work through symbols). We can even give these different archetypes names, but this does not make them something "put into" the mind. They are mind *qua* mind, expressions of the psyche in a stylized form without specific form content.[100]

Archetypes have a potentiality factor about them.[101] They must be beckoned forth by circumstance, and different archetypes operate in different lives. Jung once used the metaphor of a deeply graven riverbed to explain what he meant by the archetype.[102] Though nature has washed such beds into each of our psyches, not all of us experience their influence. Not until a mental thunderstorm of some nature empties its contents into all of the available channels will this deepened pocket make itself known as the shallow stream of mental activity swells into stretches of a mighty river, rumbling deep and quite out of its usual character. Possibly the most appropriate phrase Jung used to capture the meaning of archetypes was *"a priori* categories of possible functioning."[103]

Over the years, thanks to his study of dreams, mythologies, legends, religions, and even alchemy, Jung came to classify two broad categories of archetypes. First, there were the *personifying archetypes,*[104] which naturally took on a human-like identity when they functioned in the psyche. For example, there is the *anima* in man and its counterpart in woman, the *animus.* These are merely convenient designations for a number of interpersonal situations which mankind has experienced, particularly those between the sexes. Thus, the anima represents all of man's ancestral experiences with woman, and the animus represents all of woman's ancestral experiences with man.[105] The term *personification* was widely used by Jung; he believed that the most direct way in which the unconscious can influence us is through an act of personification.[106] When primitive man anthropomorphized a rock, projecting unconsciously his subjective contents onto objective elements, this was personification; and when we now dream of a "wise old man" that too is the personification of all of our inherited psychic experiences with wisdom, authority, cunning, and so forth.

The other category of primordial images Jung termed *transforming archetypes*. These are not necessarily personalities, but include typical situations, geometric figures, places, and ways and means that express the kind of transformation that might be taking place within the personality. We will be dealing with these archetypes (and their consequent symbols) of transformation when we take up Jung's approach to psychotherapeutic change. Jung identified a series of transformation archetypes like the circle, quaternity, and most important of all, the *self*. By and large, transforming archetypes emerge when the personality is moving for change and particularly that balancing change which will result in a "total" personality. Table 2 presents a list of Jungian archetypes.

Note that the shadow is an archetype. It will play an important role in psychotherapy, along with the anima. The ego and persona are not

Table 2
A List of Jungian Archetypes

Anima (including Soul, Life, Goddess, Witch)
Animal (various, as Horse, Snake, etc., including Theriomorphic Gods)
Animus
Child (including Child-God, Child-Hero)
Family
Father
God
Hermaphrodite (including Union of Opposites)
Hero (including Redeemer Figure, Mana Personality)
Hostile Brothers (or Brethren)
Maiden
Mother (including Earth Mother, Primordial Mother)
Order (or Number, Numbers 3, 4)
Original Man
Self (including Christ, Circle, Quaternity, Unity)
Shadow
Soul (including Mana)
Trickster (including Clown)
Wise Old Man (including Lucifer, Meaning)
Wotan (including Daemonic Power)

"It is no use at all to learn a list of archetypes by heart. Archetypes are complexes of experience that come upon us like fate, and their effects are felt in our most personal life."[107]

---

listed in the table because most of their content is conscious. As complexes framed within the unconscious, the shadow and the self are naturally more likely to express themselves (via symbols) archetypally. Jung always insisted that he had "discovered" the archetypes of Table 2. They were not "thought up" by him—as indeed it would be impossible to do—but rather identified and tentatively named only after years of painstaking research. One of the reasons he did not think it wise to memorize a list of archetypes was because new archetypes obviously might be discovered at any moment. Nor are the archetypes mutually exclusive designations. The Wise Old Man might appear in a dream as a wise old cockroach (Animal), or a clever clown (Trickster) who teaches us the clue to some puzzling problem. Fairy tales usually have interesting combinations of archetypal identities, and Jung often used such children's stories as examples of his theoretical outlook.

The best approach to an understanding of the archetypes is to take up these constructs as they emerge naturally in the Jungian topic under consideration. One term which we should know in conjunction with the archetypes first is *dominant(s)*. In some of his writings Jung seemed to use this term as synonymous with "archetype,"[108] but he also had in mind with this usage a special instance of archetypal manifestation. He seems to use it when stressing the actual functioning, the bringing to bear of an archetype into the stream of mental fantasy—as during a dream, reverie, or other forms of imagination. Thus, when archetypes are no longer potentialities but actualities underway as mental influencers, we may speak of them as dominants.[109] It is possible for such an engaged archetype to influence an entire group of people communally. The Nazi swastika, for example, served as a symbolic intermediary for a dominant. Since all who fell under its sway were subject to the meaning it was expressing we might even think of this as a kind of "daemonic" power of the symbol (dominant lying beneath).

MOTIVATIONAL CONSTRUCTS

INSTINCT AND ENERGY

Though constructs like instinct and energy strike many people as mechanical terms and thus nonteleological, for Jung these meanings were quite otherwise. Jung thought of life itself as an energy process, one which was always directed toward some goal. He said: "Life is teleology *par excellence*; it is the intrinsic striving towards a goal, and the living organism is a system of directed aims which seek to fulfil themselves."[110] Energies are therefore expended in relation to goals, presumably even in the physical sphere, but unquestionably so in the psychic sphere. And this is the sphere in which Jung took greatest interest. Teleological theories written about individuals imply *subjective* directionality, and in this way Jung made use of his *instinct* construct. Self-direction or subjective direction implies a capacity for willful choice or simply a *will* to express consciously.[111] Jung accepted this view of will which he believed was an ego function,[112] and in opposition to it he posed his instinct construct: "According to my view, all those psychic processes over whose energies the conscious has no disposal come within the concept of the instincts."[113] We say that our behavior is instinctive when it happens to us automatically.[114]

Jung rejected Freud's narrow definition of *libido* as the psychic energy of a sexual instinct. He acknowledged that medicine typically used the term libido to refer to sex, particularly to sexual lust; but Jung preferred to think of it in the sense first used by Cicero, as capturing "passionate desire," "want," "wish," or "excited longing."[115] In some of his translations Jung even used the term *hormé* (rather than libido), which is the Greek word for attack, impetuosity, urgency, and zeal.[116] Even though he occasionally fell into this usage,[117] Jung stated quite explicitly that libido was not to be hypostatized (made into a reality) and considered a psychic force.[118] Admitting that he was at fault for seeming to use it in this sense on occasion, Jung corrected his misconception by specifying that: "Technically, we should express the general tension in the *energic* sense as *libido,* while in the *psychological sense relating to consciousness, we should refer to it as value.*"[119] Introspectively, libido is perceived by the individual as the value-intensity of some psychic content. If we value something highly, it has a high concentration of libido attached to it; this is not to say that libido really exists as an energy, but it may be called an energy as a heuristic aide, to help us conceptualize how the psyche works. We have schematized Jung's views on psychical vs. physical energy in Figure 11.

Note the mind-body parallelism in Figure 11. Issuing from the mental region there is a psychic energy (libido) which in turn is experienced phenomenally by the individual as a value intensity (desire) which in turn goes into the mental activities of symbol formation, thinking, willing, and so forth. Issuing from the body region there is presumably a physical energy, which in turn exerts a certain force intensity on the formation of actions which we call behavior, the "doing" of things physically (including internal processes like digestion or breathing). At the extreme left side of Figure 11 we have the instinct construct which—as in all psychoanalytical theories—unites the mutual influence of mind and body within the personality. Jung makes it plain that instincts are partly psychic and partly physiological in nature.[120] But unlike Freud, who set libido loose in the mind by way of the sexual instinct and then explained all behavior on the vicissitudes of that libido, Jung has his instinctive counterpart (archetypes) built *directly* into the mind from the outset. Here is the heart of Jung's position:

Instinct is not an isolated thing, nor can it be isolated in practice. It always brings in its train archetypal contents of a spiritual nature, which are at once its foundation and its limitation. In other words, an instinct is always and inevitably coupled with something like a philosophy of life, however archaic, unclear, and hazy this may be. Instinct stimulates thought, and if a man does not think of his own free will, then you get the compulsive thinking, for the two poles of the psyche, the physiological and the mental, are indissolubly connected. . . . Not that the tie between mind and instinct is necessarily a harmonious one. On the contrary it is full of conflict and means suffering.[121]

What instincts "really" are we shall never know, for they are in large measure nothing but convenient labels for organic and psychic fac-

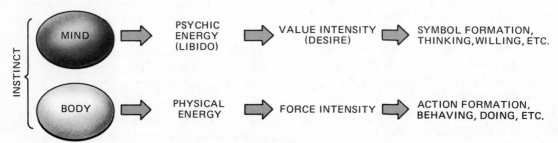

Figure 11
Jung's Views on Psychical vs. Physical Energy

INSTINCT

MIND ➡ PSYCHIC ENERGY (LIBIDO) ➡ VALUE INTENSITY (DESIRE) ➡ SYMBOL FORMATION, THINKING, WILLING, ETC.

BODY ➡ PHYSICAL ENERGY ➡ FORCE INTENSITY ➡ ACTION FORMATION, BEHAVING, DOING, ETC.

tors about which man must honestly claim ignorance.[122] But, insofar as there is a tie between the physical and the mental, Jung called upon the theorist to admit of more than simply one or two instincts at play in man's behavior. There is a sexual instinct, but even before it might come into play there is surely also a nutritive instinct in operation.[123] There are probably also self- and species-preservative instincts to be seen in man's behavior.[124] Jung did not accept the validity of a death instinct as such.

The psychic energy of libido can now be said to reflect itself in *any* of the instinctual ways.[125] An interest in cooking relates to our hunger, desiring protection from the elements results from an instinctive wish to live out our days, and so forth. Libido is therefore a construct which shades in meaning from an analogous physical energy to such concepts as psychological power, desire, aspiration—all terms which might well be used to describe the furtherance and enrichment of life. Bergson's concept of *élan vital* and Schopenhauer's concept of *Will* have much the same teleological connotation and it is thus not surprising to find that Jung equated his concept of libido with these more philosophical notions.[126]

Jung believed that we could use our subjectively perceived values as a kind of metric or measure of the libido potentially available in the conscious mind for expression.[127] We can get a relative idea of our personal (subjective) libidinal dispersion by asking ourselves how we "feel"—positively or negatively—about some aspect of life. If we happen to like some one activity, person, or place more than another, the reason is because there is more libido potentially available for the former than for the latter.[128] Unconscious value preferences also exist, but our egos cannot put themselves in touch with them. To get at the deeper preference values we must rely upon dream analyses, parapraxes, free or controlled (word) associations, and so forth.[129]

If our unconscious psyche begins to form complexes around a core of emotions which

reflect value preferences (indexing libidinal strength), then our egos might well sense this psychological intensity as a superhuman power "from within," or, if projected, "from without." Jung viewed the origin of religion in this sense. The primitive man often referred to a *mana* which he experienced as if sent his way by some god. Jung used mana as synonymous with libido in some of his writings,[130] but its special meaning was as the "extraordinary potent" reactions which primitives had to those symbols which emerged from their collective unconscious and were then projected onto an object in the environment.[131] When primitive man made a mountain into a god, the mountain was said to possess a *mana* which had medicinal powers, could save life, direct the course of the weather, and so forth. If the libidinal intensity was sensed as issuing from within the personality then a primitive might claim that he was possessed with the "spirit" of a god, and occasionally this was a devil-god. Thus, said Jung, religions are spontaneous attempts by man to come to know the truths contained within his psyche.

THE PRINCIPLE OF OPPOSITES

Basic to all Jungian thought on motivation is the *principle of opposites*. Not only does this principle provide the rationale for how change comes about in the personality, but it is thought fundamental to all psychic (and even physical) energy generation. As Jung once observed: "I see in all that happens the play of opposites, and derive from this conception my idea of psychic energy. I hold that psychic energy involves the play of opposites in much the same way as physical energy involves a difference of potential, that is to say the existence of opposites such as warm and cold, high and low, etc."[132] If repression was the cornerstone construct of Freudian psychoanalysis, then Jung's most basic conception was that of opposition. In fact, Jung believed that repression was a product of the psyche's oppositional tendencies. For any given intention or "wish" there is immediately suggested in the mind a wish *opposite* to it. Since for every "good" intention we have a corresponding "bad" one, it is only natural that certain of these intentions will have to be repressed.[133]

Although the principle of opposites remains the basic mover of behavior, by slightly modifying two physical science principles Jung made it appear—as Freud had before him—that libido behaved something like physical energy. The two principles borrowed from physical science were *equivalence* and *entropy*. Jung's theory did not initially contain these principles. He introduced them later and devoted a minimal amount of space to them, but in an interesting manner he capitalized on their meaning for his own purposes. Both equivalence and entropy are related to the principle of constancy, which Freud found useful as a theoretical device to unite the psychological and the physical. The principle of equivalence states that: ". . . for a given quantity of energy expended or consumed in bringing about a certain condition, an equal quantity of the same or another form of energy will appear elsewhere."[134] Jung then added significantly to this conception by claiming that as *opposite intentions* (wishes) are conceived in the psyche, potential energy is put at the disposal of *either* alternative. If we repress some "bad" intention which occurs to us as the other side of a "good" intention, then the former's libidinal quantum is not simply lost to the psyche when repression takes place. The repressed alternative has set loose a certain amount of "free libido" in the mind, even as the chosen ("good") alternative puts its libido to work by framing a conscious intention (we usually do what we think is right or "good" to do).

This free libido can constellate a complex in the psyche (adhesive model). It therefore happens that the more we deny our "bad" intentions and repress their contents without accepting them as having occurred to us, the more likely it is that free libido will flood the psyche with potential constellating power. By

the principle of entropy Jung meant an "equalization of differences" in the psyche, a tendency to vacillate more or less violently between the poles of opposition until a state of equilibrium is reached.[135] Entropy thus served as a homeostatic rationale for the psychic energy of Jungian psychology. Like the constancy principle, entropy implied that energies sought a common level, but before they equalized there often was a burst of energy release depending upon how far apart the original bifurcation of the two opposites (intentions, attitudes, biases, etc.) had been. Jung referred to the extent of disbalance in the psyche as *one-sidedness*.[136]

Note what has happened here: libido is seen to be generated by way of differentiation! As the teleological psyche frames an intention, differentiating the desired alternative ("I am going to help him with his work") from its opposite alternative ("I wouldn't help that bum out of this spot for anything"), libido is literally under spontaneous creation thanks to the act of discriminating between opposites. As we pull psychic opposites into independent contents we turn psychic energy loose as if we had split a mental atom. Freudian libido is not generated in this fashion, except in the sense of a certain rejuvenation which takes place at puberty (see Chapter 1). This is an often cited distinction made between the theories of Freud and Jung. But the truly important points to keep in mind are that Jung bases his energy ultimately on the principle of opposites, and that teleology plays a very central role in his view of mental activity. The *physical* principles of equivalence and entropy were certainly not premised on teleology, nor did they presume that opposites were necessarily involved in the energic redistribution which supposedly takes place.

COMPLEX FORMATION

Jung felt that the unconscious bore a *compensatory* or counterbalancing relationship with the conscious.[137] For any personality predilection, attitude, or intention differentiated in the

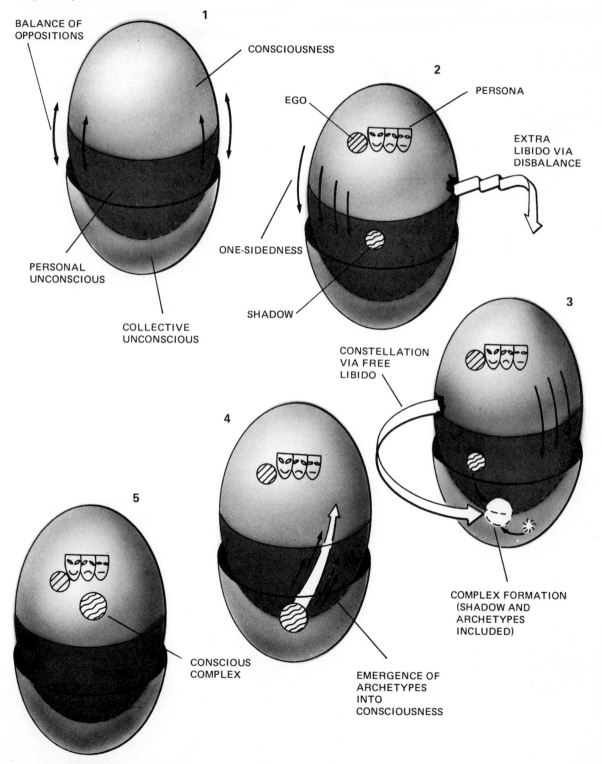

Figure 12
Jung's Complex-Formation Model

1

BALANCE OF
OPPOSITIONS

CONSCIOUSNESS

PERSONAL
UNCONSCIOUS

COLLECTIVE
UNCONSCIOUS

2

EGO

PERSONA

EXTRA
LIBIDO VIA
DISBALANCE

ONE-SIDEDNESS

SHADOW

3

CONSTELLATION
VIA FREE
LIBIDO

COMPLEX FORMATION
(SHADOW AND
ARCHETYPES
INCLUDED)

4

EMERGENCE OF
ARCHETYPES
INTO
CONSCIOUSNESS

5

CONSCIOUS
COMPLEX

conscious there was an off-setting and potentially balancing predilection to be found germinating in the unconscious—with its own quota of libido attached or else ready to be attached by way of complex formation. Figure 12 presents Jung's complex-formation model, broken down into five steps. Note first of all (step 1) that the unconscious should properly balance the conscious in what Jung sometimes called a "reciprocal relativity." If all is going well, then our arrow points indicate a free exchange of libido between consciousness and unconsciousness. The individual in this case would be acknowledging all sides of his nature, he would be aware of all intentions, promptings, etc., both those acted out overtly and those turned aside as unworthy of human action (other than repression, of course). Formation of a complex would begin with the one-sided development and recognition of only *certain* behaviors in consciousness (repression, denial, etc., of the lesser alternatives would now be the case). Assume that as the ego was forming, the "socially acceptable" behaviors were being organized into this "ego complex." Additionally, all of those pleasant mannerisms we "put on" in public—the politeness and cheeriness when we feel rotten, the feigned concern about the health of individuals we may fundamentally dislike—would be going to form our persona complex (masks). Since each of the "good" and "stronger" aspects of behavior had its opposite possibility, we can think of several behavior potentials which had *not* been incorporated into consciousness. We have symbolized this (step 2) by arrows pointing down into unconsciousness, with no counterbalancing arrows pointing back into consciousness. Many of these behaviors would of course go down and form into our *shadow*.

Gradually, if the individual loses touch with his weaker side, a state of one-sidedness (step 2) develops. Probably the most common way in which this can happen is when we identify our egos with our masks, when we think that the superficial face we show to others is

"really" who we are. We are then vulnerable to manipulation by the group, and we can easily deny our weak points, our selfishness, vanity, clumsiness, pride, and so forth. If we were to acknowledge these tendencies consciously rather than repressing and denying them, then of course the balance in the psyche would be restored, and the libido would no longer be free. It would be brought into consciousness and to that extent put to active use in offsetting our tendencies to personal overestimation and *inflation*.[138] To aid in the balancing, the unconscious as a compensatory mechanism in mind will actually prompt us if we begin to puff up with our own importance. The night of our greatest triumph as an actor or an athlete we might have a dream in which we suffer stage fright or lose an important athletic contest. The next morning we might remark to our friend how strange it was that we should dream of failure at precisely the time when everything is going so well for us. If only we knew! This dream could be an oppositional warning from the unconscious, an "alarm bell" which says: "Look, don't go overboard and think you are invincible just because you had this great triumph. You aren't so perfect, there is a side to your nature which is anything but admirable."

If some such adjustment in mental attitude is not made by the individual, greater onesidedness continues to develop, which means that more and more free libido is set loose in the psyche. The additional libido which is set loose by this vicious cycle is symbolized at step 2 by the phrase "extra libido via disbalance." Now, all of this free libido is eventually drawn into the unconscious, because the intentions to which it has been attached have not and are not consciously acknowledged. Jung is not arguing that all psychic intentions must be overtly *acted out* by the individual. If we have a socially inappropriate prompting, he is not saying that we must actually "do" the immoral thing which has occurred to us psychically. What we must do to avoid complex formation around such immoral actions is consciously to acknowledge them. This keeps their libido in consciousness where it can be used constructively, rather than going into unconscious complex formations.

If we do not have some means for acknowledging our shadow side, and if we continue to repress and to ignore the warning signs contained in our dreams or parapraxes (slips of tongue, etc.), then in time the free libido which constellates unconscious contents must necessarily form a large, potent complex of some sort. We have symbolized this at step 3. Note that as the complex forms, as the contents in the unconscious "agglutinate" like so many red and white corpuscles floating in the blood plasma, all kinds of mental contents may be included. Thus, a complex might include not only those sides of our nature we never "were," but also various archetypal identities can form into the complex by way of symbols; and this conglomerate might also bring the shadow into it as well. The shadow need not coalesce identities with the complex, but this representation in Figure 12 simplifies the diagram. Since the newly formed complex has considerable libido at its disposal, thanks to the extensive repressions and the one-sidedness of the individual, it can now emerge into consciousness (step 4). In a sense, the unconscious continues to operate compensatorily, because the aim of the complex is to express within consciousness those intentions never before realized or properly acknowledged by it. Thus, the arrows point from unconscious to conscious at step 4.

The upshot of all this is that at step 5 a newly emerged identity functions within consciousness outside of the control of consciousness. Neither the ego nor the persona have any control over the complex. Things are not necessarily in a very bad way as yet for the personality. We might simply begin noticing at this point that the individual is behaving "unlike himself"—in direct contradiction to his usual manner. The "man's man" (mask) may

cry easily, or the mild mannered school teacher (mask) might begin losing her temper at every turn. We have sketched the course of complex formation around the nondevelopment and repression of conventionally negative behaviors. But in theory, a subcultural deviant, like a delinquent or criminal who denies his better promptings, could also form a "good" or "guilt-laden" complex in time. The model should work with any coupling of behaviors, just as long as those behaviors are oppositional.

PSYCHIC DETERMINISM: CAUSALITY VS. SYNCHRONICITY

Surely the complex which emerges into consciousness, popping up from below as a cork might break water level if released from one's grasp beneath the sea, must be thought of as a completely self-contained, *determined* entity. Jung cautioned against the naive view that man is what he consciously thinks he is, as a personality: "The truth is that we do not enjoy masterless freedom; we are continually threatened by psychic factors which, in the guise of 'natural phenomena,' may take possession of us at any moment."[139] Such comments might make us think that Jung was a hard determinist—which in one sense is true. Along with Freud, Jung was a hard determinist in the *psychic* sphere. Not only are we motivated by unconscious personal forces in Jungian psychology, but the psychic inheritance from antiquity enters in to direct our fate to some degree. Racial-historical promptings within the collective unconscious that have been differentiated but denied consciousness *also* may form into a complex. Regardless of how a complex arises in consciousness, once it is "there" we can confront it and deal with it as if it were another personality within our personality.

We do not *have* to submit to our complexes any more than we have to be only one sort of conscious person in the first place. We can understand and admit to all of our attitudes, even the less desirable ones, yet ultimately direct our own fate by coming to know the unconscious ground plan written for us collectively—and then *modifying* it to suit our unique purposes. As Jung once said of himself: "I had to obey an inner law which was imposed on me and left me no freedom of choice. Of course I did not always obey it. How can anyone live without inconsistency?"[140] This paradoxical outlook makes Jung a hard determinist in the psychic sphere, but a soft determinist in the sphere of overt behavior. Even better evidence justifies the claim that Jung actively rejected the hard determinist's position. Probably more than any other psychoanalyst, Jung has wrestled with the problems of whether or not it is possible for the cause-effect principle to explain all that we know of human behavior. How can this deterministic view explain the strange and eerie experiences which we know as "psychic phenomena," like telepathy, clairvoyance or extrasensory perception?

For example, what do we say when a train ticket purchased in the morning on our way into the city bears the identical six-digit number which a cinema ticket purchased in the afternoon also bears? And then, upon returning home in the evening, we find a message to return a telephone call—once again, with the same six numbers![141] Well, we are prone to call such events "chance" occurrences, yet they have such meaningful impact that they can be among the most important "determiners" of our life's style. Take the case of a daughter who dreams of her mother's demise at the exact hour of the latter's unexpected death in an automobile accident. The impact of this "chance" experience is simply unexpressible for the person involved, yet cause-effect theories of physical science must dismiss these coincidences as happenstance and hence presumably of no theoretical consequence. Jung could not accept this shortsighted view, and as if to give such paranormal happenings acceptability he coined a term to cover them.

The term he selected was *synchronicity*, a difficult construct to define succinctly, but it may be thought of as *"meaningful co-inci-*

dence," "meaningful cross-connection" or *"acausal orderliness."*[142] These cross-connections are not cause-effects, but rather a kind of falling together or perceived similarity which cuts across the antecedent-consequent tactic of the physical science description. We have schematized Jung's view of synchronicity in Figure 13. Note that there are four arrows running from left to right: these represent a chain of cause-effect lines over time. The "time dimension" reference at the top of the figure represents a series of before-after, A-to-B causal connections over time. The inscription on the extreme left merely catalogues the series of four chained A-to-B causal connections which can be viewed as running parallel to each other. Now, synchronicity comes into play when we consider the crossconnections: S-to-S′. Rather than cause-effects, these interrelated and highly meaningful patterns emerge within the time series but not in a space-time sense. One happening (S) interlaces meaningfully with another happening (S′), neither of which can possibly be explained on the basis of before-after or proximity to one another.

We have symbolized the synchronistic pattern by showing three dotted circles. Thus, if a young woman experiences a sudden sense of alarm at 9:10 A.M. (S) on a certain day, only to learn subsequently that at precisely that instant (accounting for time changes) her fiancé had sustained a battle wound (S′) halfway around the earth from her, this would be an example of synchronicity. In this case the events were simultaneous, which can be thought of as the center circle of Figure 13. However, it is not necessary for the events to be precisely "synchronous" or simultaneous in time.[143] We might dream of a friend's good fortune after he had experienced some great success but had not yet found the time to contact us by telephone. Or, we might also dream of something which had not yet happened, but which will in fact take place some time later. In either of these cases the S and S′ connections of Figure 13 might vary over time, and tilting

Figure 13
Jung's View of Synchronicity

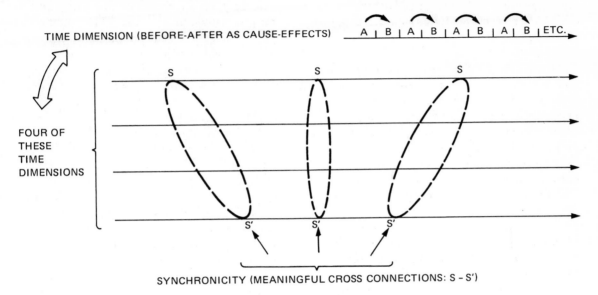

TIME DIMENSION (BEFORE-AFTER AS CAUSE-EFFECTS)   A | B | A | B | A | B | A | B | ETC.

FOUR OF THESE TIME DIMENSIONS

S   S   S

S'   S'   S'

SYNCHRONICITY (MEANINGFUL CROSS CONNECTIONS: S – S')

the dotted circle backward and then forward in time is our attempt to illustrate this conception of a pattern entirely beyond time factors. It is immaterial which way we think of the S and S' occurrences, for we do not believe that one "causes" the other in any case. Nor is it a matter of one S predicting the S', because the issue is not A-to-B causality.

ADJUSTMENT MECHANISMS

Repression vs. Suppression. Jung believed that repressions start as voluntary suppressions, that we actively try to keep something out of awareness, and then in time the boundary between consciousness and unconsciousness is crossed by the negative mental content and a repression results.[144] The reasons for repression are as varied for Jung as they were for Freud, but of course, Jung would not find quite so many sexual involvements in repressed material as Freud did.

Projection vs. Introjection. We have already discovered that Jung made extensive use of the *projection* construct. He viewed this as unconscious and automatic,[145] and in most cases it resulted when one individual transferred psychic contents onto another.[146] Only the unconscious can project, and this mechanism is one of the oldest in man's mental repertoire.[147] What we actually do in projection is to blur the distinction between subjective and objective experience. The "in here" becomes the "out there." *Introjection* is the other side of the coin, since it blurs or fails to differentiate between object and subject; in this case the "out there" becomes the "in here."[148]

Compensation, Balance, and Wholeness. Jung acknowledged that he had borrowed the term *compensation* from Alfred Adler, who had introduced the concept.[149] As we have already seen, the unconscious serves generally to compensate consciousness in Jungian psychology, but this term can also be used more specifically, as when Jung said the anima could compensate the persona.[150] This usage will become clearer when we discuss Jung's approach to psychotherapy.

Differentiation (Discrimination) and Opposition. These terms also relate to adjustment, for they are really aspects of many other mechanisms. To repress is to lose *differentiation* between consciousness and unconsciousness; to project is to fail to discriminate subjective from objective; to gain consciousness is to make oppositional distinctions; and so forth. As in Freudian psychology, adjustment mechanisms are not mutually exclusive constructs.

Identification, Possession, Numinous, Assimilation, and Inflation. In the classical psychoanalytical sense, Jung would accept *identification* as one type of introjection, and he even referred to it as "unconscious imitation" (taking in a parental attitude and making it our own).[151] However, when Jung used this term in his personal theorizing he was most often referring to imitations of one aspect of the personality identifying with another. For example, the ego might be said to identify with the persona or with the shadow-complex, if the latter were to emerge into consciousness. It is common in Jungian psychology to hear of the ego identifying with a complex.[152] Since the complex usually has an archetypal involvement, Jung also spoke of *"identification with the archetype."*[153] When this happens it is appropriate to speak of the conscious personality as being *possessed* by a foreign personality. To capture this idea of a power under which the individual falls Jung borrowed a term from Rudolf Otto: *numinosum.*[154] A numinous mental content is a dynamic agency which seizes control of the personality (including all members of a group) and directs it as a "power beyond reason." Anything from crowd hysteria to the heights of religious experience can be seen in Jungian terms as a numinous experience. Archetypal symbols are invariably found in these conditions.

It is at times like these that an *inflation* of the personality can take place.[155] Depending upon which psychic content the individual identifies with, he (his ego) can experience a *positive* or a *negative* inflation.[156] Identifying with shadow aspects of the personality which have combined with a daemonic archetype might lead the individual to overestimate his evilness, resulting in a depression, or possibly an elated reaction in which the individual thinks of himself as a master criminal. On the other hand, identifying with the persona aspects is likely to result in being swallowed up by the mood of the group, which in turn gives a sense of unrealistic power and an overestimation of personal worth. Another term which Jung sometimes used to describe a special kind of identification—really a "unification"—was *assimilation.* By this he meant the enveloping of one psychic identity by another, so that the engulfed identity was literally no longer differentiated in the personality. Thus, Jung said the self could assimilate the ego *in toto,* which of course, would *not* be a happy development for the personality.[157]

Progression vs. Regression. Jung took these terms from Freud but modified them to suit his own purposes. *Progression* was taken "as the daily advance of the process of psychological adaptation."[158] *Regression,* on the other hand, was the "backward movement of libido" that takes place when the individual is trying to recapture something important in his past.[159] Although he referred to something like it in a few of his writings, Jung did not really make use of the concept of *fixation.* Regressions happen all right, and libido is blocked resulting in a re-experience of early memories—even reaching back into the racial history—but this is seen somewhat differently because of the teleological interpretation of libido. If the libido flows backward, then it would seem a contradiction in terms to have a reverse teleology. Why then does regression take place? The reason for the return of libido is not to recapture pockets of "fixated" libido as Freud would have it; rather, the individual in regressing is attempting to rekindle a self-awareness that he had lost in the past.[160] In other words, the phenomenon of regression is a compensatory attempt on the part of the personality to return (regress) to that point in time when healthy progression was forsaken and a one-sided development began.

Constellation and Mobilization. By *constellation* Jung meant: ". . . the fact that the outward situation [external life circumstances] releases a psychic process in which certain [psychic] contents gather together and prepare for action. . . . The constellated contents are definite complexes possessing their own specific energy."[161] This definition obviously emphasizes the energic potential, the fact that a significant amount of libido is made available for an organizing of psychic contents. In terms of our adhesion model, however, we can say that the psychic meanings which are constellated have been mobilized into a single body of import or significance.[162] Jung will refer to the mobilization of the shadow or the mobilization of one's psychic virtues preliminary to self-realization.[163]

Individuation and Transcendence. These mental mechanisms will be considered in great detail under the psychotherapy headings. But we will now simply observe that in Jungian psychology the process of self-realization involves differentiating a totality called the "self" from all of the components of the personality, including the collective unconscious. This "process of differentiating the self" is termed *individuation.*[164] Life is teleological, and its most treasured goal is this final emergence of a completely total individuality. To accomplish this desired end, the individual must *transcend* what he is, consider what he is not, evaluate the pressures put on him by the collective to follow a predetermined plan, and

then emerge as a unique totality. Jung will use this term transcendence to describe the process whereby all of the opposites and group pressures are finally united in the personality.[165]

TIME PERSPECTIVE CONSTRUCTS

Though he followed in Freud's footsteps concerning the likelihood of stages or phases in development, Jung did not work out the elaborate psychosexual levels that we find in Freud. Freud's theoretical tactic was to explain the nature of adult behavior by finding those partial (or profound) fixations in the past which might account for present variations in personality. Jung was critical of what he termed such a reductionistic approach, because he felt that it failed to appreciate the teleological nature of the psyche.[166] If life is oriented toward goals in a purposive sense, then what does it add to retrace our theoretical steps in order to find the presumed meaning of behavior in the past? Even so, Jung did speak of some general periods in the life cycle.

PRESEXUAL PERIOD

Jung accepted as Freud had the Darwinian-Lamarckian principle that "ontogeny recapitulates phylogeny." He thus believed that children re-enacted in their growth of consciousness the prehistoric psychic birth which primitive man had achieved.[167] He even suggested that our true progenitors were not our parents but our grandparents.[168] Children are not born empty-headed or *tabula rasa,* said Jung. In fact mythological themes which belong more properly to the dream contents of a grown-up[169] appear in the dreams of three- and four-year-old children. Of course, in the very early days and months of life a child cannot report his dreams to us because he lacks consciousness as well as language.

We can say the child "knows" something for the first time when he has connected two or more psychic contents, thereby creating the initial meaning(s) in consciousness.[170] However, in order for consciousness to gain continuity the ego complex must begin forming, which requires a subject-object distinction ("there" is the world, and "here" is the me-ego). Only when the child begins to say "I" is there any perceptible continuity in consciousness. Life is a constant expansion of this realm of conscious knowledge. Jung did not believe that the sexual instinct was active in the presexual stage. This period of life is characterized almost exclusively by the functions of nutrition and (physical-psychic) growth.[171] It is a period of no real problems for the individual, because serious contradictions do not arise in this rather primitive state of consciousness.[172]

PREPUBERTAL PERIOD

This period sets in around ages three to five, depending upon the particular child and his tempo of development (which is a function of his heredity as well as environmental supports such as nutrition). The sexual instinct begins its germination in this period, and it is a time of rapidly expanding consciousness because the child will be entering school. Education is a major means of extending consciousness.[173] The prepubertal period remains a fairly carefree time of life, because one of the major differentiations which must eventually come about is not yet confronted: the evolution of an independence from the family.[174] The child is still heavily identified with his parental setting and many of the problems in life are thus answered for him thanks to what might be termed *dependency*.

Jung could never bring himself to believe in the legitimacy of incestuous desires on the part of all children. He felt the word incest had a definite meaning, designating an individual who could not link his sexual promptings to a proper object. But to apply this term to a child, who has not yet achieved mature sexual functioning was for Jung a gross misuse of language.[175] He did not deny that incestuous involvements with a parent were clinical truths.

He merely pointed out that in such cases the child was brought into an unnatural situation by the attitudes of his parents.[176] As to the fantasying of incestuous relations with a parent, Jung viewed these reminiscences as probably due to the repressed half of an intention which passed through the individual's mind while he was learning about sex. If we learn, around pubescence, that sexuality is to be exhibited in a certain way, the suggestion is easily made that we could perform this act with our mother (for a boy) or father (for a girl). The intention thus suggested is probably then repressed because of its inappropriateness, and it may return later as one of those false recollections which Freud made so much of. But we should not believe that we really had furthered such lustful fantasies as infants. Nor should we feel guilty about the incest reminiscence when it does occur later in life; we should merely acknowledge and accept it as the mind's ever-ready capacity to suggest possibilities, even unacceptable ones.[177]

PUBERTAL PERIOD

Puberty, of course, has its onset sometime between the tenth and the thirteenth year of life. Jung felt that most females leave their pubertal phase around age 19 or 20. Males were said to continue on to age 25 before they had seen the last of their pubertal phase.[178] Physiologically speaking, the estimates of a completed puberty are usually much earlier (ending in the middle teens). We note here a tendency on Jung's part to stretch the life span out considerably so that one does not consider himself "over the hill" in life nearly so early in analytical psychology as he might were he to fix on the infancy bias of classical psychoanalysis.

Due to the many challenges which face the individual in this period Jung felt that "true psychic birth" took place in the pubertal time of life.[179] Not only does the sexual instinct now place a major burden on the individual for gratification, but also there is the necessity of finding an appropriate work or career goal.

The range of social contact also extends and there are problems of adjustment to be resolved in establishing a proper identity among "gang" peers. All of these factors contribute to a differentiation of the person from his family. Parents may object to friends, proposed marital partners, or the choice of an occupation. Decisions have to be made, intentions have to be put into effect, and the child is faced for the first time with the likelihood of a one-sided development.[180]

YOUTH

The next period sets in at roughly 20 to 25 and runs to about 35 or 40. By this time the individual should have "cut his own swath" in life or he is in psychic trouble. For example, Jung felt that something like homosexuality is probably crystallized for all time in this period, due to the fact that a man was unable "to free himself from the anima fascination of his mother."[181] But for most of us youth is the time of marriage, the rearing of offspring, the purchase and establishment of a home, and the striving for a modicum of success in a career or occupation. In short, it is a time of increasing responsibilities and increasing consciousness (meanings, knowledge).

MIDDLE LIFE

At about age 40 we enter the second half of life, and now there is an entirely new psychic challenge for the individual, based in part on the fact that he has already lived this long, and in part on the fact that the meaning of life is not *only* on the side of consciousness. That is, in line with his opposition principle, Jung believed that man spends his first half of life enlarging consciousness by way of learning, acquiring possessions (including offspring) and experiences, investing himself in the world of affairs, and so forth. This is right and proper, but as he is fashioning this one side of his psychic nature he must inevitably be slighting the other side: *unconsciousness*. Thus, without turning his back on the realities of conscious-

ness, Jung said that the individual past middle life must *also* now further his knowledge of that inner nature which he has been neglecting. And the proper time to begin it is now, in middle life, where the rewards of an active growth to date are beginning to bear fruit. Children are now grown and leaving the nest he has provided them. Work has begun to pay off with positions of responsibility allowing for a modicum of delegation to other, younger people. Social demands are lessened. This is the beginning of a new life order.

OLD AGE

Once past age 60 or 65 we have to accept a time of life in which the term "old age" is appropriate simply because this is the reality of the life cycle. Jung took more interest in the psychology of the aged than any other major personality theorist. He believed that the older person must live by different ground rules than he had thus far been observing. He must never look back, but rather "look inward." He has a marvelous chance for individuation because he has now lived long enough to experience many different situations and their opposites. Jung believed that it was necessary for a balancing counterweight to express itself in the latter half of life because: "Man's values, and even his body, do tend to change into their opposites."[182] Physiologically the male becomes more feminine and the female masculine, and psychologically too there is a counterbalancing of psychic attitude by the anima or animus between the sexes.

Jung felt that in his experience a life directed toward a goal is in general one which is better, richer, and healthier than an aimless one, or one which is discouraged about its lack of a future. As he expressed it: "I am convinced that it is hygienic—if I may use the word—to discover in death a goal towards which one can strive, and that shrinking away from it is something unhealthy and abnormal which robs the second half of life of its purpose."[183] This is where the primordial image of a life after death plays such an important role in the life of man. If an older person were to consult Jung and complain of a depression or an anxious emptiness (loss of identity), Jung might well retort after a period of studying the patient: "Your picture of God or your idea of immortality is atrophied, consequently your psychic metabolism is out of gear."[184] The individual's archetypal prompting was being denied, and he had to pay the penalty of such repression. Thus it is that in Jungian psychology religious expressions are not taken lightly, as sublimated parental dependencies or the like, but rather are considered extremely important manifestations of the collective unconscious. In continuing the teleology which is life into an afterlife these archetypal symbolisms are to be cultivated, personified, and dealt with insightfully as legitimate aspects of our being.

IMMATURITY RATHER THAN FIXATION

Jung admitted that there was a tendency for all ages of man to look back to an earlier time in life when things seemed to be working out better for him. The teenager wishes that he could have that feeling of simple certainty and security which the protection of the parental home had afforded him. The married woman of 30 wishes she had the freedom of her teenage years. The aging man of 60 wishes he had the vigor of his 30s. All of these natural propensities for a replay of the life cycle are normal enough. Life is challenging, there are constant decisions and commitments to be made, and one might easily sentimentalize about a bygone day.

But if the individual had not actually freed himself from his childhood environment and his dependency upon parents, leading to an unrealistic attitude toward life in adulthood, Jung would have termed this *immaturity* rather than fixation.[185] Rather than a damming-up of libido into pockets of fixation this was taken to be a failure on the part of the individual to develop. One cannot block

the development of something which never was in the first place. Hence, as we noted before, the phenomenon of regression was for Jung a teleological attempt to return to an earlier time in life, and thereby to rekindle that opportunity for self-growth which had been overlooked or shunted aside by the individual.

INDIVIDUAL DIFFERENCES CONSTRUCTS

Jung was very sensitive to the problems of typing people, and he undertook the task with some reluctance. He felt that when one names a type he is speaking about statistical averages and not about people.[186] The danger in this is that the avid theorist may force his conceptions onto others in an arbitrary way, more to justify a theory than to capture the accuracy of the individual case. For his part, Jung wanted a scheme which could capture the obvious complexity in man yet also not lose the open-ended features of the psyche. He did not want to dictate man's condition for all time, but he was interested in the general problem of how it was that we came to type personalities in the first instance. Jung therefore turned to history, and he examined a number of earlier typologies to find some common thread that they might reflect upon. Thanks to his scholarly approach, Jung moves us in his book *Psychological Types* (1946, first published circa 1920) over the ages from the early Greeks like Plato and Aristotle, through the thought of churchmen like Tertullian and Origen, down to the more recent views of eminent psychologists like Friedrich Nietzsche and William James.

Running through this line of descent he finds that philosophers, theologians, and psychologists are citing a basically identical pole of opposition in man's mentality, or are themselves representatives of this pole in their cognitive activity. He then names this phenomenon the *introversion vs. extraversion* polarity in psychic attitude. Thus, for example, Nietzsche's Apol-

Ionian and James's tenderminded types are introverted in psychic attitude, and the converse typologies of Dionysian and tough-minded are extraverted.[187] This classification provided a continuity in analytical psychology with the typologies of history, but Jung also needed a way of explaining how the various psychic behaviors we know of as thinking, seeing, or feeling were arranged in man even preliminary to the introverted or extraverted style of carrying out such common psychic acts. Basing his line of theoretical development on the nature of the psyche as an active, differentiating, purposeful agent, Jung then named a series of what he called *functions*.

BASIC FUNCTIONS OF THE PSYCHE

Jung's construct of *function* can be conceived in two ways: as a psychological *or* an energic (libidinal) tendency to remain constant in order to judge the changing conditions of life. The basic idea is that, in differentiating opposites from among the myriad factors in experience (paralleling the rise of consciousness, of course), the psyche has to utilize a "set" number of activities or processes to make sense of experience. We need a system of coordinates within which to disassemble then reassemble the many sensations, feelings, hunches and ideas that we might possibly have about the world. In this sense Jung defined a *psychological function* as "a certain form of psychic activity that remains theoretically the same under varying circumstances."[188] Considered energically, a function was a constant libido expenditure, a means of keeping libido channeled into a fixed activity. If man needs some basic continuity in the psyche so that he might recognize changes by way of contrasts to these regularities, then how many such functions are necessary to cover all of his psychic needs? Since these needs are akin to structural elements of the mind we might have taken them up under our structural construct discussion. We did not do so because they were written specifically to account for individual

differences. Jung felt that four functions could well suffice in a description of man's basic psychic equipment, and he presented his argument succinctly as follows:

There are four aspects of psychological orientation, beyond which nothing fundamental remains to be said. In order to orient ourselves, we must have a function which ascertains that something is there (sensation); a second function which establishes *what* it is (thinking); a third function which states whether it suits us or not, whether we wish to accept it or not (feeling); and a fourth function which indicates where it came from and where it is going (intuition).[189]

Jung was laying down a theory of just what it takes for the psyche to advance teleologically upon experience. Since his view of man is one of a growing, expanding consciousness he wants to account for individual differences *in terms of* how that growth is *first* etched out. Rather than using the fixation-regression gambit, which must inevitably turn our attention to the past, Jung wants to keep his theory running ever toward the future. Hence, he must array his psychic functions—to account for those differences which eventually will emerge—at the very outset of life's journey. The functions are part and parcel of the psyche. In one sense they define the "psyche in action."

In theory, all four functions begin as conscious psychic activities,[190] but in short order we begin to rely on one or two rather than all four. Before we take up this matter of function selection let us give more extensive consideration to the functions as such. Note first of all that they are paired opposites, and two such pairs comprise the total model. Thinking is considered the opposite of feeling, and sensation is the opposite of intuition. *Thinking* is that function which allows for thought to take a direction, to begin with a premise then follow it through to a conclusion only to infer another premise, and so forth, in what we call "reasoning."[191] Thinking therefore permits us to understand the nature of things, to assess their meaning, and to infer their nature. Its opposite, *feeling,* can also be brought to bear in assessment. However, unlike directed thought, feeling is a process which takes place between the subjective ego and another mental content on the basis of *value.*[192] Does the ego like or dislike the item under consideration? If liked, a premise might be accepted without thinking. Thought demands evaluation by way of clear-cut statements, but feeling tones allow us to settle questions without deliberation. And so emotion and thought are anathema to each other.

Although opposites, thought and feeling were still considered *rational* functions by Jung.[193] We do not ordinarily view feelings as contributing to man's rationality, but considering them as acts of assessment or evaluation Jung makes a good point. Both thinking and feeling are concerned with judging the worth, truth value, significance or import of some psychic content for the individual. This includes a highly subjective factor of course, because what is valuable to one person may not be valuable to another. Thinking emphasizes truth vs. falsity or plausible vs. implausible, and feeling emphasizes like vs. dislike, or attraction vs. repulsion, but in either case the *point* of the function is to assess and thence decide on an alternative.

Our remaining pair of opposites Jung termed the *irrational* functions. He did not mean that they were contrary to reason but merely outside of the province of reason. They were not functions which had as their role the directed judgment and assessment of mental contents, but rather they made psychic material available so that such reasoning processes could be carried on. They are to that extent more on the automatic, reflexive side of mental life. *Sensation* is that psychological function which transmits physical stimuli to psychic awareness.[194] Sensation is essentially synonymous with "conscious perception." Seeing, hearing, touching, all of those psychic activities which

put us in touch with the world can be considered aspects of the sensation function. The inputs from our sense organs (sensation) provide the wherewithal for the ego to make a value judgment (feeling).

The *intuition* function Jung defined as "unconscious perception,"[195] thereby making it the opposite of sensation. In other words, just as consciousness takes in sensory data, so too can the unconscious automatically perceive the "inherent possibilities" of a situation as a kind of unconscious perception.[196] Sometimes the intuited input goes contrary to the sensory input, so that even though we might consciously perceive no danger in a situation our intuition tells us that something "bad" is going to happen. The fact that Jung accepted an intuitive function in man places him in a unique position among personality theorists, most of whom would attempt to reduce this intuitive sensation to "something else" in the psyche. Jung took intuition at face value, recognizing that yet undiscovered stimuli may account for these reactions which do seem to occur, synchronistically as it were.

We have to keep our conscious style of behavior internally consistent.[197] It would not do to jump about in consciousness from a thinking to a feeling to a sensation to an intuitive style of behavior. Not only would we be confused about ourselves, but our interpersonal relations would be strained to the limit; people would find us maddening. Thus only one function can be uppermost in consciousness at a time, and thanks to various chance factors we are all prone to differentiate that particular function into prominence which proves the most effective means of furthering consciousness. We further the one which seems to work best for us, termed the *primary* or principal function in a technical sense[198] or more informally simply "the most differentiated function"[199] or "the more favoured function."[200] The ego identifies with this function and it comes to color our consciousness, which in turn as an outward manifestation of behavior makes a typology possible.[201] Now, since the obverse of this primary function has characteristics in direct opposition to what is being favored, repression sets in to remove the particular opposite into the unconscious exactly as we have outlined the steps of complex formation in Figure 12.

Jung named this undesired opposite the *inferior* function.[202] Speaking in this depth fashion, of conscious vs. unconscious functions, it is now also correct to call the primary (favored) function the *superior* function.[203] The less-preferred psychic tendencies which are repressed coalesce into the shadow complex, and so the shadow takes on the character of our inferior function. This is all quite in line with Jung's principle of opposition and his claim that the unconscious complements consciousness.

What has happened to the remaining two functions as the superior vs. inferior functions are being differentiated across the levels of consciousness? Since they are not diametrically opposed to the most differentiated (primary, superior) function, these functions drop into an intermediate level of differentiated consciousness. They settle as poles of opposition just below consciousness in a kind of twilight position where they can come into play as supplementary or complementary functions for *either* the superior or the inferior function.[204] Jung termed these the *auxiliary* functions.[205] Customarily, *one* of the auxiliary functions is adopted by consciousness as a supplementary psychic process. It works in conjunction with the primary function and is therefore now considered a "secondary" function. The other auxiliary function may or may not then be repressed further into the unconscious to supplement the inferior function by forming into the shadow complex. In order to help the reader visualize the rather intricate relationships now under presentation Figure 14 schematizes the four functions.[206]

Note in Figure 14 that the primary function of thinking is at the highest point of differ-

entiation, dominating consciousness. We have not put the ego in here, but someone with this psychic constellation would surely consider himself a thinking type. The inferior function of feeling is represented down in the personal unconscious, where of course it could intermingle and form into complexes with the collective representatives (archetypes) as well. The shadow is not a part of the figure, but as we have already suggested, it would be identified with the inferior function. Across the intermediate levels of decreasing consciousness (which means decreasing levels of differentiation) we have our two auxiliary functions. Sensation is tilted up toward a higher level of consciousness to symbolize the fact that it has come to serve as a supplementary function to the primary function in the personality constellation. As such it can now be referred to as the secondary function. The tandem of thinking-sensation would now represent what we might call the "conscious personality" of this psyche. An individual with a primary function of thinking and a secondary function of sensation would surely have a precisely ordered, logical, and efficiently running mental style of coming upon the world. He would like to think things through and when he had to weigh arguments he would not want to rely upon hunches (that would be intuition); rather, he would constantly seek "the facts" (empirical observation via sensation). This conscious personality type might make a good detective, lawyer, or stock market analyst.

At the same time, depending upon how one-sidedly (repressively) he develops his "conscious personality," this individual could have a burgeoning impulse at times to cast logic to the winds and play a hunch which he "feels" cannot miss. This would tell us that his feeling-intuition functions were seeking to compensate his overt manner. This impulse might first make itself known in his dreams. If he does not respond to these promptings, then of course he might end up acting impul-

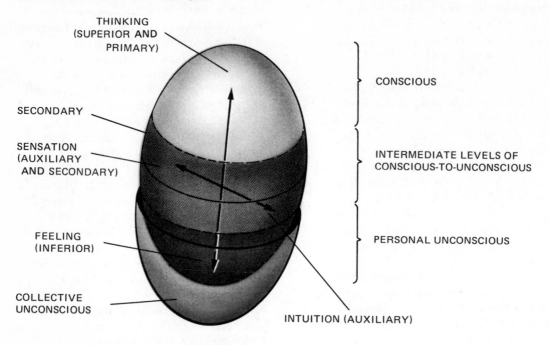

Figure 14
The Four Basic Functions of the Psyche

THINKING
(SUPERIOR AND PRIMARY)

SECONDARY

SENSATION
(AUXILIARY AND SECONDARY)

FEELING
(INFERIOR)

COLLECTIVE
UNCONSCIOUS

INTUITION (AUXILIARY)

CONSCIOUS

INTERMEDIATE LEVELS OF
CONSCIOUS-TO-UNCONSCIOUS

PERSONAL UNCONSCIOUS

sively, amazing himself with his foolishness yet unable to get hold of himself (in consciousness the complex operates under its own direction). In Jungian psychology the principle of opposites must always be satisfied.

Since either auxiliary can serve as the secondary function (we can have a thinking-intuition type rather than a thinking-sensation type), it is theoretically possible to classify people into eight distinct "conscious personality types" on the basis of Figure 14. Jung had something to say about these eight possibilities but we could carry this out even further because any one of these primary functions and its secondary (auxiliary) function can orient itself toward life in either an extraverted or an introverted attitudinal manner. This raises the possibilities of cataloging people into 16 different conscious personality types on the Jungian model. Jung did not go this far in his

writings, and in fact nothing would have interested him less than hanging such labels on people.

INTROVERSION VS. EXTRAVERSION AND THE PSYCHOLOGICAL TYPES

We have already noted how Jung came to identify the two major constructs of extraversion and introversion in his review of history. We can define these constructs in either psychological (attitude) or energy (libido) terms. The latter is the simplest in that extraversion may be considered an outward flow of libido and introversion an inward flow of libido.[207] This does not tell us much, actually, since it is the practical effect of the supposed libidinal flow which gives the concepts meaning.

The introversion-extraversion constructs take their basic meaning from the individual's preferred attitude toward the subject-object dichotomy which we have already discussed in the evolution of consciousness. As he is differentiating meaningful relationships and to that extent forging consciousness the individual can develop an interest in the subjective (the "I" pole) or the objective (the "that" pole) side of life. In referring to introversion and extraversion Jung ordinarily used the term *attitude,* and that is the procedure we will follow, though it is not a major construct as such. Just how much choice the person has in this attitude predilection is debatable. Jung hints that nature may supply the psyche with one or the other of these attitude styles and that an underlying physiological tempo may be the actual determiner of the course any one person will follow in the psyche.[208] Thus, in Jungian psychology environmental factors are given a more central role in shaping the individual selections of functions than they are in modifying the attitudes of introversion and extraversion. In fact, Jung felt that to try and change one's natural attitude into its opposite could be physically dangerous. At least, he found that in those few cases where people did try to exchange attitude styles they suffered from extreme physical exhaustion.[209]

Turning to the psychological characteristics of the extraverted type, Jung noted that such individuals value the objective pole of experience, so they rivet their attention to persons and things in their external environment.[210] The extravert wants to expend himself, to give himself to the object. His thinking tends to be concretistic and practical, he is not so likely to make abstractions and to play with ideas in an unrealistic sense. He likes to work himself into life and to take his self-identity from the interaction with concrete, no-nonsense, solid happenings. Current events therefore fix his attention, whereas historical events are considered important only as the record of the "dead" past. His morality may be quite conventional.

Rather than giving himself over to others, the causes of the moment, or the pressures of today, the introvert prefers to conserve himself and find within his own identity satisfactions comparable to those which the extravert gains by moving libido outward.[211] He likes to abstract and to play with ideas. Introversion can herald strength of inner character or it can herald timidity and a flight from the realities of life. The introvert is not impressed by the practicalities of current events. He adapts to his personal standards, and at times his morality may be quite other than that of his peers—either far above or seemingly below conventional standards. This inner conviction often gives him a stubborn, even childish appearance to others who might find him impractical, eccentric, or in other ways unusual. Jung was himself an introverted type, and he believed the twentieth century was an age of extraversion, a difficult time for the introvert to live.

By claiming introversion or extraversion was fixed by nature Jung may appear to have built a one-sidedness into his theory. This is not really correct, however, because the principle of opposites is brought to bear in the case of the attitudes just as it had been applied in the case of the psychological functions. Thus, if the superior function—whether by nature's prompting hand or otherwise—adopts an extraverted attitude then the inferior function offsets the tendency by adopting an introverted attitude.

Reaching back through history, Jung contrasted Plato (introvert) with Aristotle (extravert) and then later Kant (introvert) and Darwin (extravert).[212] Aristotle and Darwin surely placed considerable emphasis on the importance of external fact-finding, whereas Plato and Kant were more concerned with the functioning of universals or categories of the understanding *per se.* Jung also gave examples of personality types which combined his functions and the extraversion-introversion attitudes. A few examples might help the reader capture the flavor of Jung's outlook on personality classification.

Good leaders would be extraverted thinking types, and this personality is found more often among men.[213] Women are more likely to be extraverted feeling types; this personality reflects considerable reasonableness and concern for propriety.[214] The most reality-oriented personality of all is the extraverted sensation type; found most often among males, one might consider this personality hedonistic, for there is a great attraction to receiving pleasures through the senses such as eating, drinking, observation, mixing with others, and so forth.[215] Politicians, businessmen, and club-women are likely to have the extraverted intuitive personality, for this type is excellent at anticipating the politics of a situation and capitalizing on them for personal prestige, power, or advantage.[216] The absent-minded professor stereotype is subsumed in Jungian psychology by the introverted thinking type; these individuals can think individually hence reach genius status, or fumble miserably into a "quack" status.[217] When we hear the phrase "still waters run deep" applied to people, we capture the style of an introverted, feeling type —found most often among women.[218] The childlike, innocent person, responding almost impulsively to his felt emotions is the introverted sensation type.[219] Finally, the introverted intuitive type can range from the mystical seer at the one extreme all the way to the social crank or creative artist at the other.[220] Keep in mind that when we typologize a personality in this fashion we are doing so on the basis of its superior function. Obviously, all of these personality types have "other" personality potentials as well.

TRANSCENDENTAL FUNCTION AND THE MANA PERSONALITY

We have already seen how Jung spoke of transcendence in connection with his concept of individuation (see p. 157). He also viewed transcendence as an actual *function* of the psyche, along the lines of the four basic functions we have just discussed. The transcen-

dental function is concerned with man's tendency to combine consciousness and unconsciousness into a balanced totality,[221] and to that extent it stands for all unions of opposites within the psyche.[222] Jung referred to it as a "process of coming to terms with the unconscious"[223] or a "process of getting to know the counterposition in the unconscious."[224] As we have seen in the discussion of the four basic functions, though we might live by them they do not preclude the likelihood of a one-sidedness developing in the psyche. In order to balance off this one-sidedness we must turn around and confront the "other side" of our nature—and we do this by way of the transcendental function.

How do we achieve this confrontation with the unconscious? The transcendental functional process involves "a sequence of fantasy-occurrences which appear spontaneously in dreams and visions,"[225] which act as pacers of the individuation process in psychotherapy. If we were to take this discussion further it would carry us into Jungian psychotherapy, so let us now put the concept of transcendence aside until we once again pick it up in the relevant section. However, this would be the appropriate point at which to introduce a personality term which Jung uses and which we will also take up in the general context of individuation during psychotherapy. The *mana personality* is a kind of inflation of the conscious personality. Consciousness becomes puffed up in this personality constellation, and a denigration of unconscious forces is the result.

Primitives often acquire this sense of personal power in their tribal rites, and Jung noted that this is what Lehmann referred to in the phrase "extraordinarily potent."[226] In a war dance the primitive can work himself into a state of frenzy and literally feel the surge of power (mana) taking over his conscious senses as he dashes off to do battle. Jung argued that even the modern individual can lose his identity in the reality of the moment as a crowd member, and then in response to the collective promptings (archetypes) swell up into a self-proclaimed "superman." In fact, this is what occurred in the rise of Nazi Germany, where crowds not only fell under the sway of a Wotan (war god) archetype but the mana personality dominant (see p. 147) as well.[227] Another time when the individual is susceptible to inflating his conscious personality is during the individuation process.

"MAN IS MEN" IN HISTORY AND RACIAL IDENTITY

Since he extended the concept of individual differences beyond the individual to a consideration of differences between peoples as a group, Jung's broader views on the nature of racial identity and historical man are significant. Jung makes it clear that he cannot think of the life of a people as in any way different from the life of an individual: "In some way or other we are part of a single, all-embracing psyche, a single 'greatest man,' the *homo maximus*, to quote Swedenborg."[228] This collective man has a history, one which is "written in the blood" but also manifests itself through the individual so that it is the person who moves history rather than vice versa.[229] On the Jungian outlook, therefore, *man is men*. To differentiate between men we must at times differentiate between groups of men as a whole. Personality constructs cannot be limited to individual referents, even when speaking of one person's behavior. The term "race" for Jung has a very broad referent, combining not only physical (blood line) factors, but historical, sociocultural, climactic, and even theological considerations as well. For Jung, Christianity was just as much a part of European "races" as was their skin color or skull configuration.[230]

This is the reason Jung claimed that a Jewish psychology could not fully and completely appreciate the psychology of a European. He did not say that a Jew was incapable of understanding Europeans. He merely claimed that in order to do so the Jew would have to make use of a psychology written specifically for the European's unique nature. Jung's supposed anti-Semitism stems from a misunderstanding of what he was claiming about the psychology of collectives. Thus, Jung made the point that the Jewish people—due to a history of suppression by other "races" (nationalities, etc.)—had never acquired that tie to the land which the European had achieved. The Jews were unable to own land in many of the countries where they were allowed entry, making them fluid and mobile in both the material and the psychic economy. Even as they moved about without ties to the land the Jewish people were acquiring a high level of culture, so that Jung said they are more civilized as a people than are the Europeans. Now here is the point of confrontation between Freud and what Jung considered his Jewish psychology. Since the Jew is not as barbaric as the European he can look into his unconscious with less threat of a dangerous upheaval than can the European.[231]

Whether Jung is correct in his claims about the Jewish character and its supposed weakened tie to the land—particularly since the establishment of the Jewish state of Israel—is not nearly so important for our purposes as the recognition that Jung was applying a construct to a people in the same way that we are accustomed to apply such constructs to an individual. Jung was prone to do this in many of his writings. For example, he was critical of the tendency of the European man to ape the mental exercises of the Eastern man. Many people wrongly think that Jung advocated the study of Yoga or Zen Buddhism as a balancing tactic in their lives. Actually, Jung was opposed to the practice of Yoga for a European, because the latter's problem is not one which will respond to a greater control over consciousness—which is Yoga[232]—or the utter submission to the unconscious premises and promptings of Nature—which is Zen Buddhism.[233] European man must find his own "way" (Tao), because he has evolved a certain history, one which stamps his peculiar nature, and one which cannot be borrowed from another historical tradition: "Therefore it is sad indeed when the European departs from his own nature and imitates the East or 'affects' it in any way. The possibilities open to him would be so much greater if he would remain true to himself and evolve out of his own nature all that the East has brought forth in the course of the millennia."[234]

Modern man's plight in the Jungian world view is his one-sidedness. Not only was Jung a man of the West, but two savage world wars seemed to convince him that the problem of a denigration of unconscious psychic contents was becoming severe in the West. The rise of Nazism, the decadence in moral fiber, even the conflicting schools of modern art were seen by him as portents of the unconscious upheaval closing in on the one-sided materialism of Western society. Jung made it plain that he was not opposed to one-sidedness in principle, since only through complete commitments of this sort are great achievements brought about.[235] However, he also believed that it was a sign of high culture for diversities in outlook to balance one another. It was not desirable for everyone in a civilization to develop an *identical* one-sidedness,[236] which is what seemed to be happening in modern society according to Jung. By denying our darker side on a massive scale we ensure that reprisals from the unconscious in the form of collective complexes—including mana personality inflations—will take place. Jung even referred to this modern plight as the "sickness of dissociation."[237] This development was not irretrievably negative, however, since the beckoning counterbalance of modern complexes suggested a rebirth impulse. Modern Western man still has time to turn his attention inward and thereby not only recoup lost possibilities but extend his level of self realization.[238]

MALE VS. FEMALE PSYCHOLOGY

The final individual difference constructs to which we might refer in Jungian psychology concern masculinity and femininity. Consider-

ing the conscious personality first of all, Jung claimed that women were ruled by the *principle of Eros,* whereas men are ruled by the *principle of Logos.* Women are thus guided as conscious personalities by a capacity for relating to others. Eros signifies the binding, uniting, and also loosening and separating of portions from the whole. This capacity includes not only life-giving (birth) activities, but interpersonal contacts as well. Marital love for the woman is a union, not a sexual contract: "For her, marriage is a relationship with sex thrown in as an accompaniment."[239] A man's consciousness, however, is ruled by objectivity, interest in specifics, discrimination, judgment, and insight (which is why the thinking function is more often superior in the male). Logos signifies thought, cogitation, logic.[240] Judging from these conscious principles, it would follow that as a compensating manifestation the unconscious should present us with a contrasting psychological picture. And so it does.

Jung found rather early in his studies that male patients often reported feminine-like moods in their dream symbols, and conversely, women reflected opinionated masculine styles of symbolic expression. He viewed these as tied to the archetypal manifestations of the *animus* (Latin for mind) and the *anima* (Latin for "soul" or vivifying principle). The animus, which is therefore found in the unconscious of the female, arises at times in symbols to compensate for the female's conscious attitude as ordinarily exemplified in the principle of Eros. This is why women seem so puzzling to men. Though obviously reasoning on vague (unconscious) grounds, the woman seems perfectly certain in her animus-based conclusions.[241]

The man, on the other hand, is likely to develop a *mood* (rather than an opinion) of some sort when under the compensating activity of the anima.[242] When the "he-man" Army sergeant breaks down and "cries like a woman" under severe stress he is paying the price of one-sidedness and reflecting the anima possession under which he suffers at the same time. The anima plays a very important role in Jungian psychology, because not only is it an archetype which represents man's historical relationships with women in the past, and which to that extent compensates for his conscious personality principle of Logos, but it is involved in spiritualizing and life-giving symbolism as well. The symbols of life, birth, rebirth, rejuvenation, and so forth, are all likely to take on anima coloring.[243]

Psychopathology and Psychotherapy

THEORY OF ILLNESS

INCOMPATIBLE OPPOSITES, COMPLEX FORMATION, AND DISSOCIATION

The fundamental theory of illness used by Jung follows the model of complex formation we already outlined in Figure 12. Jung once said that he considered "normal" behavior to mean that an individual could somehow exist under all circumstances in life, even those which afforded him the minimum of need satisfaction.[244] Unfortunately, very few people can actually meet all of life's situations this handily, and therefore in analytical psychology the concept of normality is more of an ideal than an actuality. The truth is, we all develop more or less one-sidedly. The extent of disturbance we eventually suffer from will be a function of the number of incompatible opposites we generate in living, and how soon it is before we attempt to compensate for our lack of balance. Jung essentially defined mental illness in the following manner: "The vast majority of mental illnesses (except those of a direct organic nature) are due to a disintegration of consciousness caused by the irresistible invasion of unconscious contents."[245] He never fully rejected his early view that certain mental disorders—particularly those in the family of schizophrenias—might someday be traced to a metabolic toxin of some sort.[246] But Jung's unique theoretical contribution lay, as had Freud's, in the explanation of the functional disorders.

Jung traced the autonomy of complexes to their emotional core (feeling toned). He constantly stressed that emotions behaved as the more primitive thought processes once had for early men; that is, they are not willfully produced by man but simply "happen" to him. We can even see this happen to us, if under sufficient emotion, as when character traits which shock us emerge and we find ourselves foolishly jealous, dramatically vindictive, or histrionically injured by the setbacks of life.[247] If this sudden emergence of strange behaviors can happen to us in the normal state of mind, imagine what it must be like to fall under the control of a full-blown complex (or complexes). No wonder the paranoid schizophrenic feels he is under the control of identities other than his own—as if the devil or people from another planet were taking over his body! Insanity is thus an invasion from the unconscious of contents which are flatly incompatible with the aspirations and intentions of the ego. Therefore, the intentions of these shadow contents (complexes) cannot be *assimilated* into consciousness. By assimilation Jung meant accepting and integrating these formerly repressed contents with the more familiar elements of consciousness.[248]

When a complex is active within consciousness we are literally as if in a dream state, with conscious and unconscious factors interfusing. A highly dramatic example of this would be the multiple personality forms of hysteria, in which two or more personalities seem to take over consciousness in turn; actually, the original conscious personality (the one fashioned before the illness) remains out of direct contact with the emergent personalities (the ones formed via the illness). The latter, secondary personalities (complexes) obtrude on consciousness and literally push the original personality aside and keep it "in the dark" as in the Jekyll-Hyde conflict of the classic tale. In the same way less pervasive complexes as part personalities within consciousness can make themselves known to the ego even though the ego may feel they are not part of its identity. Or, the ego may not even be aware of the operation of a complex within consciousness, side by side with its very routine of behavior.

One sure way in which the ego *can* be made aware of a complex is through the mechanism of projection. Recall that only the unconscious can project! By putting its contents onto the external world, where the ego now takes them to be properties of "that" rather than "me," the complex finally opens an avenue for its own defeat. That is, by putting its constellated contents onto the world the complex makes it possible for the ego to enter into a relationship with the import of these contents. Take a dream for example, which is a rudimentary form of projection: by putting its contents into the dream the ego consciousness can—with the help of the therapist—come to know what "that dream" means "to me." By working this way in time an assimilation of the incompatibilities represented in the complex may be effected. As we shall see in discussing Jungian therapy below, other means of projection include artistic representations.

ROLE OF MORALS, EVASION, AND DENIAL

In trying to understand the nature of mental illness the analytical psychologist asks: " 'What is the task which the patient does not want to fulfill? What difficulty is he trying to avoid?' "[249] Jung viewed the Freudian super-ego as a collective body of ethical beliefs, analogical to Lévy-Bruhl's concept of the "collective representations"; he believed that such collective views, although not infallible and not always to be routinely followed, could often allow us to discover the basis for our judgments and decisions in life. If we were to reflect on the problem of "how ought we to treat one another?" for example, our collective symbols

would help provide the answer if given a chance to express themselves—as, by way of a dream analysis.

But now, when an individual for any of a number of reasons ceases to conform to the canons of the collective (superego), when he is being called back to balance for selfishness, let us say, but rejects the collective prompting, then a dangerous condition is likely to develop. In this case he would deny the collective prompting, as reflected in a dream, and then in time develop a neurosis due to his one-sided (selfish) development.[250] This is possible because the "other person" about whom he should be concerned is not only "out there" in the environment. He is also "in here," within the collective unconscious as part of the psyche. One cannot flaunt the moral promptings of the collective without paying the price of internal division and inviting the appearance of the "other identity" in consciousness as a complex. Recall that man is men. For this reason Jung could speak of clients who developed a neurosis for *want of a conscience*.[251] Denying a super-ego prompting is no small thing for Jung. For example he described the rigidly stylized behavior of an obsessive-compulsive as the surface appearance of a moral problem. The obsessive-compulsive patient must be meticulous and ceremonial in his overt behavior, because there is an internal struggle with evil underway in his psyche.[252] A "bad" conscience can be a heaven-sent compensation, if used in the interests of higher self-criticism.[253] It balances our natures and puts us back on the track of life.

Jung was critical of both Freud and Adler for miscalculating the spiritual needs of man. He felt that they had too readily fallen under the premises of nineteenth century science, and thus had become overly materialistic in outlook.[254] Man is morally responsible, he has an intellect which evaluates and strives for a "better" purpose in life no matter what that judgment of "better" is based upon.[255] In fact, Jung drew a parallel between the conception of "sin" and that of "repression." Once the human mind had invented a sin concept man had no recourse but to conceal or repress his sinful promptings.[256] And, since he invariably sees alternatives open to behavior which are sinful in nature, psychic bifurcation into conscious "propriety" and unconscious "shadow" factors is possible. These latter, repressed contents take on the coloring of a *secret,* which of course means that the individual nursing secrets is likely to be cut off from the rapport of his fellow men.[257] Secrets are divisive mechanisms which permit the repressed individual to shrink back from external reality and to that extent remove himself even further from the ethical tenets of his society. Thus, invariably evasion plays a central role in neurosis: "If we follow the history of neurosis with attention, we regularly find a critical moment when some problem emerged that was evaded."[258]

In this regard, it is fascinating that Jung believed an individual could fall into a one-sided mental illness because he had failed to live up to his inherent potential. Though myriads of individuals can exist without feeling out of sorts in the quagmire of collective opinions and collective routines, there are a number of people Jung called of the "higher" type, who for one reason or another in their lives have remained at a primitive level.[259] These would be potentially gifted types who have allowed an unnatural torpor to settle on their lives, and as a result of their narrowness in conscious outlook—a type of one-sidedness because they "could be" broader in outlook—they fall into neurosis. Jung referred to this type of disturbance as "a retarded maturation of personality."[260] Individuals of this type need to achieve self-realization and thereby fulfill their above-average potentials.

MEANING CREATION AND SYMBOLS IN ILLNESS

One of the reasons that a person becomes neurotic is because he lacks an adequate symbol or is no longer in touch with older collective archetypes, by way of a symbol, so that he finds life losing its meaning. Recall that for Jung a symbol was something in psychic life which expressed meaning, and in particular helped to formulate that which was inexpressible. Put another way, symbols act as *bridges* between the conscious and unconscious portions of the psyche. Since we cannot know our unconscious, and a complex is under its own guidance within consciousness, the only hope for balancing a one-sided condition in mind is the intermediary functioning of a symbol. When people lack such symbolic devices they are not only more likely to fall into illness, but they are also less likely to achieve a subsequent recovery. Figure 15 is a schematization of Jung's symbolic meaning-expression model, framed in libido terms.

The archetypes contain a store of libido all their own, called the *numen.*[261] Figure 15 shows archetypes with numen existing as potentials for expression nestled in the collective unconscious. Assuming that the conscious portion of the psyche—where we find the ego at the top of the egg-shaped figures—has developed one-sidedly due to a "retarded maturation of personality," how then might we hope for a balancing compensation to come about? If it were possible for an archetype to seize upon some *given* symbol (recall that archetypes take on various specific symbolic contents), then in expressing their meaning by way of a dream or fantasy symbol the ego could come to grips with the unconscious prompting and possibly begin an offsetting counterbalance. Thus, if an individual asks "What's the point of life?" or "Why was I born?" he might conceivably receive an answer to his question from out of his own psyche. That is, he could know the answer if he had a symbol to "cloak" it in.

Two cases are represented in Figure 15. On the left is the case of archetypal identities with stored libido (numen) releasing this libido in the act of compensation with the teleological goal of expressing the answer to the question posed ("Why am I living?"). However, since no symbol in consciousness is available through

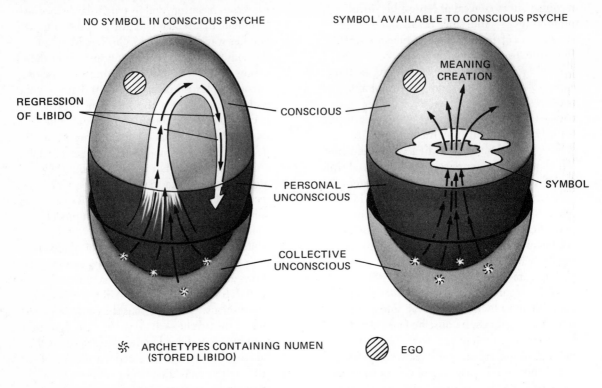

Figure 15

Symbols Create Meaning from Stored Libido (Numen)

NO SYMBOL IN CONSCIOUS PSYCHE

SYMBOL AVAILABLE TO CONSCIOUS PSYCHE

REGRESSION OF LIBIDO

MEANING CREATION

CONSCIOUS

PERSONAL UNCONSCIOUS

SYMBOL

COLLECTIVE UNCONSCIOUS

✵ ARCHETYPES CONTAINING NUMEN (STORED LIBIDO)

▨ EGO

which archetypal promptings in the form of libido release are expressible, the only recourse is for the libido to reflow or *regress.* Regression is not "giving up the compensation," but rather cycling back again to the roots of the collective in hopes of effecting a new rebirth.[262] On the right-hand side of Figure 15 is the case of a bridging symbol, so that now the libido released by the archetypes (numen) *does* achieve a conscious meaning expression—and to that extent it can serve to balance the one-sidedness of the psyche. A symbolic meaning creation has taken place, and the ego can grasp the symbol if it has a knowledge of how properly to interpret this symbol—the kind of knowledge that analytical psychology can provide.

Symbols which act in the way just outlined were termed *symbols of transformation,* because they transformed the libido from a lower to

a higher function in the psyche, they moved man along by offering him a chance to balance, and hence they emerge as a new identity thanks to his new-found insights.[263] Jung believed that man needs to symbolize in this fashion just as much as he needs to take in food and drink.[264] If we can no longer find meaning in the symbols of our forefathers, then we must find new symbols or risk falling out of touch with our roots—as embodied in our "primordial images," which define for us the very nature of our humanity.[265] This can be very dangerous.

Other symbolic expressions are to be found in Jungian psychology, and they do not all function as symbols of transformation. That is, as we can recall from our discussion of complex formation, an archetype can cement itself to contents constellating into a complex, and then make its appearance in consciousness known through its effects as an unconscious element. Once this complex has been projected onto an item or person in experience, the ego can then *identify* with this archetypal complex and lose its psychic independence from it. Put another way, the ego slips into unconsciousness by way of identification. Jung referred to this form of psychopathology as "identification with the archetype."[266] This invariably produces an inflation of the ego, for either good or evil in the life of the personality. The archetype comes to direct the ego, which is itself then said to be "possessed" by the archetype. For example, the psychotic murderer who thinks himself a great savior of mankind by senselessly killing a popular political figure might have fallen under the numinosity of a hero archetype, possibly constellated with the wizard archetype because of the supposed cunning involved in laying his murderous ambush. In this instance the poor, deluded ego would have no understanding of the meaning of its actions. It would have been the tool of a shadow complex dominated by the archetypal themes of salvation, retribution, and deviousness. Of course, not all outcomes of numinous experiences are so horrible. Anything which acts on the individual ego with a great intensity and urgency is numinous.[267]

NEUROSIS VS. PSYCHOSIS

Precisely "when" a neurosis will appear depends on the degree of one-sidedness evolved in living, and the consequent possibility of keeping the constellated complexes under repression. Jung did not feel that all neuroses had their beginning in the first five years of life. He approached each neurotic patient with the following question in mind: "What is this person attempting to avoid in his development or general life responsibility at *this* point in time?" Neuroses have a function to serve in the present, and we must not allow the patient to flee into his past and remain there safely in preference to confronting life in the present.[268]

Jung believed that the Freudians had been taken in by the maneuvers of an *adult* personality which, in its attempt to avoid responsibility, and due to its infantile character generally, had concocted preposterous sexual fantasies and projected these onto the past in an effort to evade the counterbalancing changes called for by the neurosis in the present. For example, after one of his female patients had "recalled" that her father once had supposedly stood at her bedside in an obscene pose, Jung remarked coolly: "Nothing is less probable than that the father really did this. It is only a fantasy, presumably constructed in the course of the analysis. . . ."[269] Yet even as the neurotic is retreating into regressive fantasy, the teleologically oriented quest for health has begun. The *neurosis* is two pronged, it consists of both an "infantile unwillingness and the will to adapt."[270] Through regression a rebirth, a "fresh start," is always possible. Thus neuroses do cleanse us, and they are not in themselves undesirable or meaningless diseases of the soul: "We should not try to 'get rid' of a neurosis, but rather to experience what it means, what it has to teach, what its purpose is. . . . We do not cure it—it cures us. A man is ill, but the illness is nature's attempt to heal him. . . . in the long run nobody can dodge his shadow unless he lives in eternal darkness."[271]

Jung then concluded that some people have the great advantage of being neurotic![272] If nothing else, this "inner cleavage" of a lesser variety can prompt a balancing of one-sidedness before a total inundation of the conscious by unconscious forces takes place.[273] When the latter takes place the result is a psychosis.[274] Jung's view of neurosis vs. psychosis was clouded by the fact that he did speculate on the possibility of a toxin in schizophrenia, suggesting that psychoses were qualitatively different from neuroses. However, due to his psychological explanations of all mental illness based on the stylized-meaning expression model (complexes, dissociations) Jung must actually be counted as holding to the quantitative view as regards neurosis and psychosis. He told us that he had seen many patients move from neurotic to psychotic states in their lives, and that claiming that they had actually been suffering from a "latent psychosis" while in the earlier, neurotic state[275] merely begs the question. Psychosis is thus an extension of the division of personality which begins with neurotic conditions. One finds that neurotic psychic contents are a bit more rational, so that they can be integrated into consciousness easier than can the contents of a psychosis.[276] The psychotic is like a sleepwalker, living out the most bizarre form of dream which has been put together by promptings from the darkest levels of the unconscious psyche. It is thus unfathomable, even to the psychiatrist.

Neurotics are therefore likely to have a better prognosis, because they can acquire insight (meaningful understanding) whereas psychotics cannot. Jung was a great believer in the efficacy of insight, even when dealing with the worst type of clinical syndromes.[277] He found that insight often softened the total impact of the psychosis. At the same time, he did not place much stock in the finer points of differential diagnosis for the functional disorders. He said that we are "not dealing with clinical diseases but with psychological ones."[278] The major discrimination to make is that of the clearly organic vs. the functional disorder, but after that it seemed pointless to go on categorizing patients.

THEORY OF CURE

GROWTH, BALANCE, AND SYMBOLIC
ASSIMILATION OF OPPOSITES

Over the years, Jung found that a certain percentage of his patients simply "outgrew" their problems. Even though he realized that time heals some wounds, what was unique in these cases was the fact that these people seemed to have evolved a new level of consciousness.[279] They somehow learned to live within life's

inner contradictions, and they did not assume that it was possible to solve every one of life's problems in any case. Jung himself came to understand that the greatest and most important problems of life are fundamentally insoluble—not because of man's ignorance but simply because of their nature. Life is dependent upon *polarities,* and the truly monumental difficulties carry this function of giving life a zest and a motive force (libido generation) for the future.[280] This does not mean one gives up on his attempts to resolve contradictions, but he recognizes the inevitability of two sides to any significant event or belief, he takes meaningful understanding from both sides, and he does not fall into the polarization trap of believing that only one side is "it" for all occasions and all times.

It is the polarization of seemingly incompatible opposites in the personality which brings on mental illness, so what therapists must do is to bring the two halves of the client's psyche back together again. This goal is very difficult to achieve because the two halves (conscious and unconscious) cannot easily make themselves cognitively known to one another. In a situation like this *any* confrontation—whether hostile and erratic or controlled and reasoned—is better than none. As Jung put it: "Every form of communication with the split-off part of the psyche is therapeutically effective."[281] Thus, the main strategy of analytical therapy is to effect a confrontation with the unconscious. This permits the individual to get to know aspects of his nature which he would never have admitted, and which therefore are at the root of his one-sidedness. Once admitted, a state of wholeness is possible.[282] If we can personify the shadow half of our psyche and come to terms with it then an assimilation is possible.[283] Jung referred to the defeat of the personified complex as a depotentiation—a "depowerizing"—of the unconscious (daemonic) forces of psychic life.[284]

Jung adamantly contended that merely providing the client with an intellectualized insight would not result in a cure.[285] The only way consciousness can be liberated from its possession by the unconscious forces is through a painful recognition and an experiencing of the the feelings which initially prompted the complex formation. This is no easy matter, and a risk is involved because one can lose his ego identity in the confrontation with the unconscious.[286] As we shall see, even the psychotherapist runs the risk of losing his mental health in the great effort which coming to terms with the unconscious demands. This is so because, though the confrontation begins with the shadow features of the personal unconscious, in time the client descends into the collective unconscious with tremendous effort not unlike a Faustian descent into the underworld.[287] All manner of fearful possibilities emerge as we come face to face with our primordial past, and hence admit to the influence it has exerted in our supposedly consciously directed lives.

The aim of psychotherapy is to convince the patient to give up the naive belief that life is exclusively the domain of ego consciousness and to find a new midpoint in the personality. This process begins with a recognition of the ego vs. shadow polarity and settles into an eventual balance at what we have labeled in Figure 16 as the "midpoint of the personality." The ego is not given preference in this balancing, nor is the shadow. As Jung said: "Assimilation is never a question of 'this or that,' but always of 'this and that.' "[288] One grows only by becoming whole.

To accomplish this feat of balancing the opposites Jung relied on two general tactics: symbol creation and verbal confrontation with the personified complex. Jung called his therapy a form of *hermeneutic* treatment.[289] The root of this term is from Hermes, the messenger of the Greek gods. Hermes thus brought information (meanings) to the gods from various sources. During the middle ages, theologians adopted the term hermeneutics to describe their efforts to extract all of the nuances of meaning from the Holy Scriptures. In similar fashion,

Figure 16
Centering of the Personality

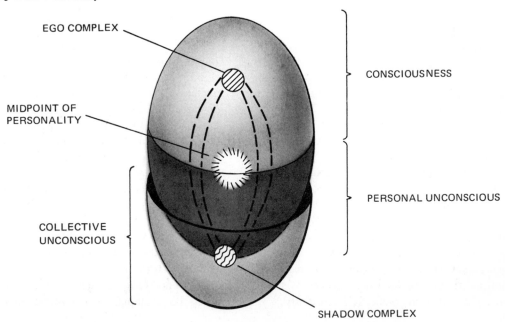

EGO COMPLEX

MIDPOINT OF PERSONALITY

COLLECTIVE UNCONSCIOUS

CONSCIOUSNESS

PERSONAL UNCONSCIOUS

SHADOW COMPLEX

the Jungian therapist helps his patient extract from his own unconscious all of those meanings which are potentially there, seeking expression through symbols of transformation in compensation for the one-sidedness of consciousness. Symbols therefore "compensate an unadapted attitude of consciousness."[290] They are an essential ingredient of the curative process, but they can cure only when experienced as a living phenomenon in psychic life.[291]

It is not enough to know the meaning of our dream and other fantasied symbols. We must confront the implications of the symbol and make a decision as to which side of the question we will live on, accomplished by literally turning the complex which troubles us into a person—if at all possible. By personifying our other half we can speak with it and hash out all of the attitudes it represents and come to some form of balanced overview which might well take both sides into consideration. As we already suggested, this solution is not always completely satisfying to either consciousness or unconsciousness; but then, that is the nature of life! Jung once referred to the course of analytical treatment as "rather like a running conversation with the unconscious."[292]

THE STAGES OF PSYCHOTHERAPY

In order to help his patient achieve a state of psychic balance, Jung admonished the analytical therapist to engender "a kind of dialectical process" in the therapeutic relationship.[293] By permitting a completely free and equal climate to emerge in the relationship between therapist and client spontaneous and open confrontations should emerge between participants. Not only did the relationship take on dialectical coloring, but the internal dialogue between conscious and unconscious contents was also viewed as dialectical in nature.[294] Jung insisted that the prime rule of his therapy was to consider each case uniquely and to afford a patient completely equal status in the two-person encounter.[295] Indeed, the therapist is constantly

"in therapy" with each client and can therefore make no claims to superiority except insofar as he has possibly carried his own personal insight a bit further thanks to his greater number of therapeutic encounters. But this experience is never to be used as a club over the client's head.

The course of analytical psychotherapy can be broken down into four stages. These are not clear-cut, nor is it necessary for an individual to carry out all four steps in order to achieve a positive outcome. In the opening sessions with a client the therapist witnesses the stage of *confession,* which for Jung was the goal of the cathartic method introduced by Breuer and Freud (Chapter 1). This was a reflection of the emotional side to mental upset, said Jung, and it reaffirmed his belief that intellectual insights were rarely effective without some involvement of the "heart" (emotion) as well. This form of cathartic release was probably identical to the expiation of guilt people had experienced for centuries in making religious confessions. Not that this would work for everyone, of course, but Jung felt that certain rather uncomplicated, simple souls can actually achieve a therapeutic benefit from regular use of the confessional (e.g., the Catholic sacrament.)

As the sessions slip by, the therapist will find his client moving on to matters which signify that he is no longer under the spell of confession. Jung termed this second stage *elucidation,* because it is now necessary to begin elucidating or making interpretations to the client regarding his past life and particularly regarding his present tendency to "transfer" various unconscious contents onto the therapist. In fact, one knows that he has entered the stage of elucidation when signs of the transference appear.[296] The client begins to have unusually strong (positive or negative) reactions to the therapist, who has himself done nothing to warrant such extreme emotional attachments. Jung had many things to say about the phenomenon of transference over the years. He began his theorizing rather traditionally, viewing transference as a special type of projection in which parental (maternal or paternal) *imagos* are ascribed to the therapist.[297] He also spoke of libido cathexes which had been fixed on the therapist needing to be removed and reinvested in the patient's personality structure by way of a resolution of the transference.[298] This is all a classical theoretical development. However, Jung was to expand on the construct and in time he even detracted from its importance in cure. As we know from Chapter 1, for Freud a transference was the *sine qua non* of psychotherapy. Jung, on the other hand, eventually made it plain that he did not think transference onto the doctor was a necessary precondition for therapy to take place.[299] Other forms of projection might serve the course of therapeutic insight equally well.

Jung begins to deviate from the classical view by stressing the interpersonal aspects of transference. The sexualized attempt at union with the therapist is *not* simply genital but rather a kind of caricature of the social bond which holds human society together.[300] The neurotic both wants to relate socially yet he would also prefer that we take the lead in the union for he fears taking responsibility. He thus assumes in the positive transference a highly dependent posture with a person through whom he senses the promise of a rebirth or renewal. He submits to the therapist as a slave to the master of his fate. Since regression also accompanies the projection of unconscious contents, there is often considerable infantile acting-out. In the Jungian view it is even possible for a patient to project *himself* as imago onto the therapist.[301] This intensified tie to the doctor thus acts as a compensation for the patient's faulty attitude toward reality.[302]

The aim of transference is clearly the re-establishment of rapport with reality, the dissolution of the split in the personality which has forced the neurotic into a continuing retreat from life. If the doctor and the patient lack mutual understanding, the dissociation from life is not likely to be restored. For this reason equality is paramount in the relationship. Once the patient realizes that he has been projecting onto the therapist the transference is resolved, and the stage of elucidation comes to an end. Before this can happen, however, any *countertransferences* which may exist must also be resolved and recognized as such by the therapist. It is inevitable that countertransferences will arise in the relationship because *"all projections provoke counter-projections."*[303] This is why Jung claims that the therapist is constantly working at his own therapeutic advance with each client he sees. Jung once observed that: "A therapist with a neurosis is a contradiction in terms."[304] This must be the case, because a sick therapist would have no ability to sense the unconscious projections which would be likely to pass between himself and the patient. The patient must have the prerogative of identifying countertransferences being projected by the therapist just as the therapist has this opportunity in the reverse direction.[305]

The third stage is that of *education,* in which the basic values of therapist and patient come to the forefront.[306] Since these values now belong to the individual client—and are not distorted reactions of an earlier time—it is possible to work with the often one-sided thinking expressed by the neurotic. One cannot have lived as an infant for years without oversights in personal education. Jung believed that Adler actually began his therapy at about this stage, whereas Freud had been content with ending his therapy at the close of elucidation. Jung agreed with the view that providing a person with insight was not sufficient, because we seldom get rid of an unhealthy state by simply understanding its causes.[307] The therapist must now help the client to educate himself in all those aspects of life which he found lacking. Jung did not offer any set recipe of training aids at this point. Whatever needs doing in the unique life history will have been made plain by this time in any case. The therapist will doubtless have to lend his moral support to the client, encouraging him as another person would encourage any friend to confront life.

For many cases these first three stages will suffice, and therapy would normally be terminated. However, occasionally a therapist will discover that he has a client whose problem is not amenable to a therapy aimed at normalization. These individuals have potentials beyond the average, and hence: "That it should enter anyone's head to educate them to normality is a nightmare . . . because their deepest need is really to be able to lead 'abnormal' lives."[308] When he has this kind of individual on his hands the therapist must move to the fourth and final stage of therapy: *transformation*.

SELFHOOD AND INDIVIDUATION VIA THE TRANSCENDENTAL FUNCTION

The stage of transformation is a completely unique rendering of psychotherapy, a view of the therapeutic process which no other major therapy has ever quite captured. It demands that we bring together many of the terms learned above, but now in a combined and interlacing way in order to make the single descriptive point of self-emergence or self-realization. The general process by which we accomplish this self-realization Jung called *individuation*. It is the first conscious inkling that we *do have* a shadow complex which triggers the individuation process. [309] In order to assimilate and integrate these shadow contents we have first to bring them into consciousness in a form which will allow us to confront them, and then ultimately conquer them lest they gain control of our being. One cannot argue the shadow complex out of existence or rationalize it into harmlessness.[310] The shadow provides a fundamental contrast to the conscious realm of personality (ego sphere), and to that extent it allows for the tension of opposites from which psychic energy—a valuable commodity—is generated.[311] Character is ac-

tually enriched through this constant interplay of a shadow prompting and the compensating measures we take. One never can be whole if he projects his shadow onto others. He must see it, confront it, and learn to live with it—even take strength and direction from an "interpersonal" association with it by way of personification.[312]

One might reasonably expect Jung now to claim that the shadow must be personified and confronted in the process of transformation. Yet, this is not precisely how the confrontation with the unconscious comes about. Rather, it is the anima, standing directly behind the shadow so to speak, and directing the shadow's actions in the psyche, which must be confronted in personified form.[313] Jung's usage of the term anima in this sense is captured in the following: "I have defined the anima as a personification of the unconscious in general, and have taken it as a bridge to the unconscious, in other words, as a function of relationship to the unconscious."[314]

Why does the anima complex now take on the meaning of our entire unconscious life, in place of the shadow? There are two reasons for this technical adjustment. First of all, Jung did not want the ego confronting and defeating the shadow during transformation because the shadow must continue to have a role in the psyche *following* individuation. Second, and doubtless more important, Jung had the anima stand as representative for the unconscious during transformation because this is what he discovered happened in his own case, during his personal self-analysis. In describing his self-analysis, Jung said that he was prone, when under a state of tension, to do something with his hands—to paint a picture, hew a stone, or record something (a fantasy) in writing. This creative prompting made his felt meanings and ideas concrete, hence most real, and he found that if he could put his symbolic promptings into a seemingly artistic product of this sort he could come to grasp their meanings much more readily. And so, he proceeded to do all of these things. One day, while he was writing down some fantasies which had been actively pressing upon his consciousness Jung was prompted to ask himself a question. Something happened then which brought home his theory of complex formation in a most dramatic and uniquely personal way; that is, a voice independent of his conscious control answered his query, as follows:

When I was writing down these fantasies, I once asked myself, "What am I really doing? Certainly this has nothing to do with science. But then what is it?" Whereupon a voice within me said, "It is art." I was astonished. It had never entered my head that what I was writing had any connection with art. Then I thought, "Perhaps my unconscious is forming a personality that is not me, but which is insisting on coming through to expression." I knew for a certainty that the voice had come from a woman. I recognized it as the voice of a patient, a talented psychopath who had a strong transference to me. She had become a living figure within my mind.

Obviously what I was doing wasn't science. What then could it be but art? It was as though these were the only alternatives in the world. That is the way a woman's mind works.

I said very emphatically to this voice that my fantasies had nothing to do with art, and I felt a great inner resistance. No voice came through, however, and I kept on writing. Then came the next assault, and again the same assertion: "That is art." This time I caught her and said, "No, it is not art! On the contrary, it is nature," and prepared myself for an argument. When nothing of the sort occurred, I reflected that the "woman within me" did not have the speech centers I had. And so I suggested that she use mine. She did so and came through with a long statement.

I was greatly intrigued by the fact that a woman should interfere with me from within. My conclusion was that she must be the "soul," in the primitive sense, and I began to speculate on the reasons why the name "anima" was given to the soul. Why was it thought of as feminine? Later I came to see that this inner feminine figure plays a typical, or archetypal, role in the unconscious of a man, and I called her the "anima." The cor-responding figure in the unconscious of woman I called the "animus."[315]

This remarkably candid account of his personal analysis gives us some firsthand knowledge of how Jung arrived at his finished theory and terminology. When adult males confront their unconscious, what better figure to stand in as representative for the unconscious than the "other half" of their sexual identity? It is obviously the animus which a female patient would confront in her transformation stage of therapy. Note also that it was a question—"What am I really doing?"—which first prompted the personified anima to make her appearance. This is similar to the theory of complex formation that Jung had used to explain the appearance of "spirits" in the voices of mediums which he had investigated for his inaugural dissertation for the medical degree. Just as the medium called up voices by posing the question "Who is with us?" or some such, so too did Jung encourage a personification of a living complex within his identity. Once "out in the open" of consciousness, the anima is found to have decided opinions on the nature of things. She tells Jung that he is doing something "arty," an aesthetic exercise which has no real meaning for him except as a form of pleasurable pastime. Jung does not accept this view, for if he did how could he come to self-realization? In denigrating his written fantasies the anima is essentially *resisting* the movement of individuation. Jung will have no part of this resistance, and counters with an argument of his own. In time, she accepts his vocal chords and responds to his counter with the logic of the female. And so it goes—the constant struggle of opposites, separated into polarized identities over the years and now coming to a confrontation by way of an internal polemic.

All manner of personal material emerges in the confrontation with the anima during transformation. The anima is a great threat to consciousness because in this internal polemic she *could* emerge as victorious combatant. If consciousness is to win out then it must press its case unflinchingly. Very often the shadow side of arguments are illogical and hence vulnerable as practical courses of action. Yet one must acknowledge their presence as *personal* views. That is, the client in therapy must come to know that the attitudes being expressed by the anima are *his* attitudes and yet he must appreciate that they need not be acted on completely even though there may be a modicum of truth in what they express.[316]

Many of the anima's arguments hit home, and they alter our conscious attitude significantly—toward our parents, our careers, our very selves. But since the anima is at this point necessarily one-sided we cannot submit to her pronouncements completely. We must depotentiate her lest we simply move from one type of one-sidedness (conscious) to another type of one-sidedness (unconscious). What we need is a balancing wholeness and therefore transformation is inevitably concerned with "educating the anima" (or the animus for the female).[317]

What is the vehicle of the process called individuation? Jung tells us that he asks a patient to take some aspect of a dream or possibly just any fantasied image which has occurred to him, and then to elaborate or develop it by giving his natural inclinations a chance to function: "This, according to individual taste and talent, could be done in any number of ways, dramatic, dialectic, visual, accoustic, or in the form of dancing, painting, drawing, or modelling."[318] He found that such "artistic" activity often diminished the frequency and the intensity of the dream or the fantasy from which the image had been selected. This is precisely what we would expect if the prompting from the unconscious were a form of hermeneutic symbol creation. Presumably, at some point along the way the anima is personified and specific issues are joined in the confrontation. By essentially reifying his fantasied symbols and by personifying the anima the

patient can challenge the collective promptings encountered therein and *individuate* a unique identity from among the collective forces which close in upon him. Thus Jung has referred to individuation as a "process of differentiation,"[319] or as the "process by which a person becomes a psychological 'in-dividual,' "[320] or, since it balances all sides including potentialities not yet realized we can think of it as the process "in which the patient becomes what he really is."[321]

Individuation is accomplished by breaking up the personifications—epitomized by the term "anima"—which are making themselves known in consciousness. The purpose of the dialectical process, the invitation to converse with another identity, is to bring these contents into consciousness, but then we must also break up these personifications for they are autonomous complexes with their own supply of libido (numen).[322] The reason we break them up is to make use of their libido stores in a healthy, balancing way. Libido set free by the anima (and other archetypes) can be utilized to form a connecting link between the conscious and the unconscious. It is the *transcendental function* which makes this connecting link possible, and it is the *self* as the symbol of unity which permits the libido to be constantly at the disposal of consciousness. We transcend what we had been, we unite all sides, and then we enter into a new personality constellation by way of the self-emergence. To demonstrate this process of individuation we must build on the model for symbolic-meaning creation in Figure 15 and the centering of the personality dynamic of Figure 16. Figure 17 combines these two features into a schematization of the individuation process.

We have our familiar egg-shaped psyche in Figure 17. Note first of all at point 1 that a one-sided development would imply that libido was regressing from consciousness to the unconscious, where it would be collecting into a shadow complex, and in time also combining with the anima archetype into a rather formi-

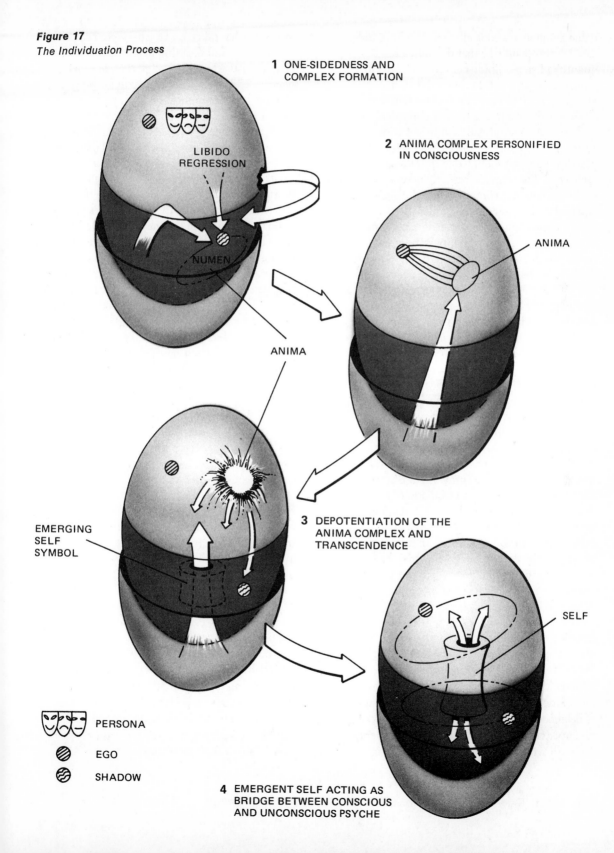

Figure 17
The Individuation Process

1 ONE-SIDEDNESS AND COMPLEX FORMATION

LIBIDO REGRESSION

NUMEN

2 ANIMA COMPLEX PERSONIFIED IN CONSCIOUSNESS

ANIMA

ANIMA

EMERGING SELF SYMBOL

3 DEPOTENTIATION OF THE ANIMA COMPLEX AND TRANSCENDENCE

SELF

PERSONA

EGO

SHADOW

4 EMERGENT SELF ACTING AS BRIDGE BETWEEN CONSCIOUS AND UNCONSCIOUS PSYCHE

dable autonomous constellation. We have indicated at this point (1) that the anima has a quantity of stored libido or "numen" as well. Our next step (point 2) shows the anima emerging into the conscious sphere where it confronts the ego in the kind of dialectical exchange we have already witnessed with Jung. At this point (2) the shadow is for all practical purposes included within the anima archetype. The anima is actually now equated with "unconscious contents," and the ego is equated with "conscious contents." By the time we reach the stage of transformation most of the persona factors would have been confronted and removed during elucidation and so forth, so we have not included the persona complex at point 2. The task now facing the ego, which has essentially invited the anima to a confrontation by asking it to assume a personified form, is to depotentiate the anima and thus balance the personality. Note that while the dialectical confrontation is going on at point 3 the self is beginning to take form, emerging as an archetypal symbol from the collective unconscious. If the anima *is* depotentiated, then its numen will be used by the emerging self to help center the personality at a region midway between consciousness and unconsciousness. If the anima is not displaced, then of course a self-bridge would not form. Assuming that the anima has been conquered, then at point 4 we would find a well-established self, with the ego still an identity within consciousness, and the shadow—which had now returned to the unconscious when the anima dispersed—occupying its place as counterpole to the ego in the unconscious.

The emergence of the self has some far-reaching consequences for the ego, which is in many ways displaced and itself defeated by the arrival of a new focal point for the personality.[323] The self is genetically tied to the inferior function, and it brings this feature of balance into prominence, thereby countering the superior function which the ego has identified itself with.[324] If the ego-dominated consciousness has taken on an extraverted coloring it must now find meaning in the introverted characteristics brought to light by self-emergence.[325] The self is also aimed at keeping channels of communication open to the shadow side of life, so that a balancing of conscious and unconscious mental contents can be maintained. This is all very upsetting and deflating to the ego, which in fact does not always give up its important position without a fight. There is often a dialectic carried on between the ego and the self, following that of the ego and the anima except that in the former case a complete destruction of one side or the other does not result.[326] The point is, our ego is a very biased, short sighted psychic complex. It has no proper appreciation of the historical antecedents of humanity. The self, on the other hand, takes a much larger view of things. In fact, Jung once referred to it as an "objective" ego, meaning that the self had a more transcending relevance, a more universal character.[327] The self originates in an archetypal prompting and then emerges into consciousness by way of a symbol. We have to recognize the self-symbol, or else the libido set free by the depotentiation of the anima, and the numen of the self archetype, will not be put at the diposal of consciousness to solidify the self-bridge. Jung termed a symbol which converts energy in this fashion a *libido analogue*.[328] Libido analogues canalize libido and change the form it takes—in this case, from formlessness in the archetype and from the form of the anima, to the form of the newly emerged self.

The most *positive* benefit of individuation—in addition to balancing the personality—is the widening of consciousness even as the individual becomes aware that he is never completely free of unconscious influence.[329] This is a typical Jungian paradox: we enlarge consciousness through recognizing the significance of the unconscious (especially the collective factors). Jung once defined the *transcendental function* as "getting to know the counterposition in the unconscious" and he gave an example of how some such insight could be mentally helpful in the following view: "A Christian of today, for instance, no longer ought to cling obstinately to a one-sided credo, but should face the fact that Christianity has been in a state of schism for four hundred years, with the result that every single Christian has a split in his psyche."[330] Thus, someone with a religious problem is not out of step with history. The collective schism for all Christians would simply be making itself known in his life and time.

The anima is not always defeated so easily in its battle with the ego as it is sketched here. When it is near defeat the anima can beguile the ego by appearing to depotentiate, only to have at this precise point in time a "substitute" archetype take its place with the expressed purpose of so fascinating the ego with its presumed skill that the ego will succumb to possession. In other words, the unconscious may tactfully lose one battle (anima vs. ego) in order to win the war of eventual personality control by bringing up a reserve archetype. We refer here to the *mana personality*. An inflation of the ego would usually come about as follows: at the point when the anima seems to be depotentiated several "insights" are made available to the ego. The ego feels it has conquered the unconscious and that now it knows a great deal about all aspects of the psyche. Sometimes these insights are frightening, so that Jung speaks of a positive or a negative form of inflation.[331] The ego becomes "drunk with power" over its success in forcing the anima to withdraw and seeming even to depotentiate. But if the ego takes such credit for the defeat of the anima, and particularly if the individuation process has taken the ego into mythological themes—which hold great fascination for man[332]—the ego might find itself identifying with the shrewd mana personality archetype which is likely to make itself known through a mythological symbol of some sort. When we speak of making pacts with a devil and thus acquiring daemonic power we are probably referring to a case of identification with the mana personality and the devil archetypes (combined). Manics or paranoids who strive to convince us that they have extraordinary power in business or political endeavors might seem almost correct at points in their arguments—since they often do have insights beyond the ordinary—yet something smacks of the extreme, the excessive, the overly "pat" in their urgent presentations, and we shrink back in doubt about whether to let them influence our lives. These are the mana personality identifiers.

The point is that an individual with a little bit of psychological knowledge can be impressed by his presumed power over the darker forces of life. As he denies the hold these darker powers have over him he in turn identifies with a mana personality symbol and, paradoxically enough, falls under their influence completely. If this domination takes place in psychotherapy we would witness the return of projection and to that extent new transferences onto the therapist would occur.[333] Since the patient often expresses supreme self-confidence about his ability to know what prompts him via the unconscious, if the therapist is naive about mana personality possession he may actually be fooled into thinking the neurosis has been cured. We often see patients leave therapy under this possession and vociferously acknowledge their great belief in the wonders of their particular insight. Jung cast a jaundiced eye toward these supposedly enlightened healers, many of whom have a social action program in mind to introduce to their group and "make this a better world."

The correct way in which to handle a mana personality is first to recognize it, and then second, to repeat the process already outlined in Figure 17, only this time with the aim of depotentiating the mana personality rather than the anima. The best defense here is simply to admit vulnerability to future promptings from the unconscious.[334] In this way, we differentiate the ego from the mana personality by way of personifying the latter and simply recognizing its numinous qualities. As Jung observes: "The mana-personality is on one side a being of superior wisdom, on the other a being of superior will. By making conscious the contents that underlie this personality, we find ourselves obliged to face the fact that we both know more and want more than other people. . . . Thus the dissolution of the mana-personality through conscious assimilation of its contents leads us, by a natural route, back to ourselves as an actual, living something, poised between two world-pictures and their darkly discerned potencies."[335]

The reference to a poised balance between two world pictures is the self, which has now once again emerged according to the Figure 17 dynamic. The ego falls to the background with this new focus of the personality. When conscious insights occur to it as lucky ideas, the ego no longer takes direct credit for them, but realizes how dangerously close it had come to an inflation.[336] The ego can no longer claim the central place of the personality but must be satisfied with the position of a planet, revolving about the sun.[337] Figure 17 attempts to present both the ego and the shadow as equal counterparts of conscious and unconscious psychic living, circling about the self at point 4 as if they were planets revolving about the sun. This representation is true to Jung's principle of opposites, even following individuation. As noted before, having depotentiated the anima—and possibly also the mana personality—the ego still needs its polar opposite against which libido shall be generated. The self acts as the continuing vehicle for the balancing of this dialectically generated libido, and the contrast provided actually vitalizes the personality as a whole.[338]

The question remains: Is it possible to individuate the personality in other than an analytical setting? Could a person self-realize in a general life setting, for example? Jung felt this was possible. In fact, he thought of the individuation process as "quickened matu-ration," a term he borrowed from G. Stanley Hall.[339] He meant that just as many people mature into a far-reaching wisdom over their life span, particularly in the latter half of the life cycle, so too does the individuated patient in analytical therapy acquire a vision of life beyond his years. He matures before his time, but he might have done so in any case.

SYMBOLS OF TRANSFORMATION IN MYTHOLOGY, RELIGION, AND ALCHEMY

We come now to an aspect of analytical psychology which has probably done more to promote the label of "mystic" for Jung than any other facet of his theory. Believing as he did that symbols cured through their molding of insight by way of canalizing libido,[340] Jung was fascinated by the many ways in which he found man attempting to rectify his one-sidedness through the manipulation of archetypal symbols—i.e., symbols through which an archetype may be seen expressing its particular meaning. The main archetypes of transformation discussed by Jung are the *quaternity* and the *mandala,* and we shall limit our consideration to these two because not only are they in a sense identical, but they subsume virtually all of the organizing, unifying, or balancing symbols which he discussed.

The word mandala is Sanskrit for "circle,"[341] and the quaternity reference has to do with geometrical figures having the property of being divisible by four, having four sides or four directions. If we contemplate the nature of a circle or a four-pointed (sided, etc.) figure it is easy to see that analogies to "totality" or "wholeness" are relatively easy to come by. Circles impel us to consider their centers, as we draw our eyes and attention "within" the circumference hence "inward" to the heart of the figure very naturally. Assuming now that the personality would need to symbolize a centering tendency or need, as stylized in Figure 16, for example, what more appropriate image might we select than *just this circle?* And so it is that in analytical psychology any circular, spherical, or egg-shaped formation which appears in dream or waking fantasies is taken to be a mandala symbol. Some common examples of mandalas are: wheels of various sorts, eyes, flowers, the sun, a star, rotation (including a swastika!), snakes holding their tails, enclosed places like courtyards, and whirling about centrifugally (like the dervish dances). Bringing mandala and quaternity symbols together, Jung said the most common forms of mandalas are the flower symbol (petals focusing our attention on the pistil) and the wheel symbol (spokes focusing attention on the hub), but he also noted that a frequent symbol for the mandala was the cross (focusing attention on the union of the four-sided structure).

The number four is a pervasive representative of quaternity symbols for Jung, and this holds for all numbers which are divisible by four. Thus if a patient dreams of four ugly witches, mixing a pot of some sort we might interpret it as an excellent example of a quaternity (four) and a mandala (the round pot) constellated into one dream theme. The "fourth point" invariably expresses a balancing effect on presentation of any number. One is single, two is only half-complete, three adds a tension calling for a complete coverage, but four gives us that well-rounded, spatially complete image as the four points of a compass (direction), the four sides of a box (complete enclosure), and so forth. Jung claimed that the primary colors of red, blue, green, and yellow reflected a quaternity, as did the early speculations on the nature of the universe in terms of the basic elements of earth, fire, water, and air.[342]

Jung observed that primitive peoples often insist upon a more "fantastic" explanation of birth than their own good sense would dictate. Thus, they might go on claiming that sexual intercourse has nothing to do with pregnancy, even in the face of their personal experience

or the education being proffered by a civilized man. Jung also underscored a phenomenon which any parent might find true of his child. That is, children not only seem to prefer a mythological explanation to a scientific or a "truthful" one, but they often simply fail to "remember" the latter explanation when it is made available by a parent. A seven-year-old child will not always give up his belief in the stork or Kris Kringle simply because a "modern" parent does not want his child believing in fairy tales and informs the child about the "facts" of life. Jung saw taking shape in this propensity for what might be termed the mythological explanation man's basic abstracting ability. Man is not an animal designed to fit his thought to the facts in any case. Put another way, if we must realize the self, which is not "real" (factual) but merely a possibility, then we must be permitted to develop a background of experience with mythologies of various sorts, as a kind of preparation for the eventuality of a symbolic expression in our lives. This is a vital process, one which needs practice, and one which might be termed "spiritual" because it is not concerned with the facts of reality in any sense whatsoever. As Jung summed its importance up: "Side by side with the biological, the spiritual, too, has its inviolable rights."[343] Hence the gremlin was a symbol of a modern myth, but the archetypes which went into its fashioning might have included the Trickster, Daemonic Power, and possibly even the Devil (Lucifer) (see Table 2).

Thus myths have a compensating role, just as dreams do. Myths arise from man's unconscious, and they often make their first appearance in the form of a dream.[344] Jung defined this feature of his theory as follows: "Mythology is a pronouncing of a series of images that formulate the life of archetypes."[345] Since archetypes express meaning about all manner of experience, it is possible to have mythologies reflected in science, religion, political ideologies, i.e., literally anything which man finds himself engaged in. We do not "make up" myths, they are like the primitive thought forms we mentioned above as "simply happening" to man independent of his conscious will.[346] The compensating balance which results when they make their appearance can actually be thought of as an elongated individuation process.[347] Interpreting the mythological symbol is thus a necessary adjunct of mythological individuation. Jung did precisely this with "flying saucers," a post–World War II phenomenon which he interpreted as the emergence of a modern myth.[348] Flying saucers were viewed as projected mandalas, put up in the sky by people needing a new balance within their psyches. In this age of science, when the old symbols (myths, religions) are losing their capacity to transform libido and thus balance the personality, a new symbol and its underlying myth is taking form. Since there is often a religious twist given to the saucer myth Jung took this to mean that man's spiritual needs were being projected in an effort to find a new significance for the non-material side of life in the modern age.

Jung in several contexts stated that the Catholic religion, with its wealth of symbolic rites and its liturgical dogma, held a decided advantage over the Protestant sects (of which he was once a representative) when it came to promoting individuated balance.[349] Religious belief systems excel the more rationalistic systems of thought because they alone consider *both* the outer and the inner man.[350] The appearance of a Papal Bull (an official document issued by the Pope) was for Jung a happy development, because this suggested that some of the older religious symbols might not be dying away completely.[351] Nothing is more dangerous to modern man than the disappearance of such symbols, for they act as the media for compensating archetypal expression. Furthermore, Jung held that people who deny the patent fact that they *are* often moved by what can only be termed a religious prompting are just as likely to slip into one-sided neurotic

states as are those individuals who refuse to admit in their religious devotion that they never doubt the validity of their beliefs.[352]

As to specific religious beliefs, Jung suggested that the concept of an eternal *soul* served a good purpose. In the first place, by believing in a hereafter the individual retains his teleological approach to life and thus maintains a sense of personal advance throughout his years on earth. Secondly, the average man's belief in a soul reflected the underlying "possibility" he harbored that a unity could be attained in the personality.[353] In this sense, the soul is the bridge which we can utilize to achieve that totality of personal being most men refer to when they speak of *God* (an archetype signifying unity).[354]

Since, as we know, individuation calls for the emergence of a self-symbol, religions might be expected to have engendered a self-symbol. And so they have: *Christ* is the symbol of selfhood, combining such opposites as God and man, inner and outer, divine and corporeal.[355] Christ also meshes with the Hero archetype,[356] balanced by the opposite fact that he was also a victim. We can see in the myth of a man made into a God the rise of the self, the realization of the most noble aspects of our human nature now personified in the figure of Christ. The symbolism of the Catholic Mass captures this in *transubstantiation,* which refers to the turning of bread and wine into the body and blood of Christ. In the same way that a man was transformed into God, a priest now transforms material of one sort into material of another, higher sort. The resultant sharing of this body by all the faithful in the act of communion brings about a totality which is in all essentials a direct parallel to individuation in psychotherapy. Thus Jung can say: "In this sense . . . we can speak of the Mass as the *rite of the individuation process.*"[357]

Jung had some very interesting, unusual views on the nature of religion and its mythology. He did not appreciate the decline in ritual symbolism and intricate dogma which had set in among the Protestant sects, and which was eventually to extend to the Catholic church. But there were aspects of dogma which he could *not* appreciate as well. One of these was the Augustinian view of the trinity (three persons in God),[358] which falls one short of a quaternity; Jung believed that for a complete totality we must have four identities represented in a God concept. Related to this was the issue of evil. Is evil an active principle in the world, as one might say that goodness is? If so, what is the relationship between God and the obvious existence of evil? Some of the early churchmen (Gnostics) had speculated on this problem, and they had accepted the fact that God was *both* good and evil in His impact on man. Later, St. Augustine and others defined evil in the negative sense as the "absence of good," but Jung could not accept this definition because it seemed an obvious denial of what we know to be the case.

Writing in his autobiography, Jung tells us that as a very young man he had the following insight regarding the God concept: "God is not human . . . that is His greatness, that nothing human impinges upon Him. He is kind and terrible—both at once—and is there-fore a great peril from which everyone naturally tries to save himself."[359] Jung was thus prone to refer to the "dark deeds of God,"[360] and his interpretation of the Biblical account of Job, who suffered though he was a good man, was that God simply had no appreciation of the supposed "evil" he was inflicting upon Job. God gives and he takes away, and from His vantage point there was no appreciation for the lamentations of Job. Thanks to His confrontation with Job, God decided to become man—that is, He sent His "Son" down to earth in the form of a man. This action not only gave God a view of life from man's point of view, but it solidified the totality of "man and God" which we now see manifest in religious rites (like the Mass). Job thus served as a vehicle for God's self-conscious development—in a sense, for God's individuation![361]

Coming back to the fourth point of the quaternity, if we now think about a complete totality in the God concept we might oppose the Son to the Father, and, in opposition to the Holy Spirit it would be appropriate to oppose the active principle of evil as personi-fied by Lucifer.[362] The Devil should round out our quaternity, but thanks to the Augustinian influence neither evil nor Satan are accept-able counterparts of the theological God con-cept. Yet, there was a time when theologians did speak of Christ as the brother of—and in some texts as even identical to—the Devil. It is probable that at a very early stage in the church, the real man named Christ vanished behind the emotions and projections that swarmed about him from peoples all over the world. It is often true in history that a given personality will act out in his life the uncon-scious promptings of an entire people. In the case of Christ, the historical man became the religious myth because it was *necessary* for such a projection to take place as a compen-sation from the collective unconscious.[363] Initially, the projection of a self-symbol (Christ) had the archetype of the Devil com-bined, but in time the opposites were made a bit clearer, and then two figures emerged.[364]

The early churchmen commonly spoke of an *Antichrist* coming to life, and Jung took this to stand for the shadow of Christ.[365] Gradually, thanks to the drift of theology the Devil and Antichrist symbols fell from potency (lost their numinosity), and the concept of the Holy Trinity was fixed ever more rigidly in the mind of Western man. However, as must inevitably take place in the act of indi-viduation, a tripartite identity was simply not satisfying because it did not fulfill all sides as a quaternity symbol would. Jung believed that, in dropping the Devil as one of the quaternity, it was only a question of time before the sub-stitution of the Blessed Virgin was accomplished as the new "fourth."[366] Thus, the trend to what is sometimes called Marianism in the Catholic church Jung took as evidence that a quaternity symbol of totality was not to be denied. Yet, for his part, Jung would have preferred the retention of the Devil as the fourth identity of the religious quaternity. He was wont to observe that even Jesus taught men to pray the *Our Father* in the most quizzical fashion by saying: " 'Lead us not into temptation'—for is not this really the business of the *tempter,* the devil himself?"[367]

Because he viewed religion as an important part of human living, and he was also willing to talk about religious beliefs in the way that he did, many people honestly feel that Jung believed in the existence of God as a *formal* hypothesis within his theory. Others think that he was deviously trying to bring psychology back to the older religious beliefs. Neither view is correct. Jung makes it quite plain that God is not real, for nowhere can He directly touch our lives. He *is* sensed as a "power within," but as we have already noted, such a numinosity could just as well be considered daemonic as divine.[368] Psychology is in no position to make metaphysical statements of this nature in any case. Analytical psychology can establish that the symbolism of psychic wholeness coincides with the God archetype, but it can never prove the existence or lack of existence of a true God.[369] Jung stated flatly that: "It would be a regrettable mistake if anybody should take my observations as a kind of proof of the existence of God."[370] Jung regarded the psyche as real, *not* the God-image as such.

In addition to his writings on mythological and religious symbols, the "mystic" charge has been leveled at Jung because he sought to explain the nature of alchemy. He often dealt metaphorically with the symbols of alchemy, leading critics to think that he had developed an esoteric view of some sort. Actually, boiled down to its essentials, the Jungian interpretation of alchemy is identical with the individuation theory we have been reviewing in terms

of mythologies and religions. Alchemy drew its roots from pagan beliefs, supplemented by borrowings from the Gnostics as well as the more conventional church dogma of Western history.[371] The alchemists are sometimes said to be the first scientists, because they emphasized knowledge rather than faith as a major value in the A.D. world.[372] However, Jung was to show rather clearly that in its early history alchemy was predominantly a religious movement. One could say that its prototype was something akin to transubstantiation. The alchemists drew an analogy to the transmutation of a natural, soiled, imperfect material state (bread and wine) into a spiritual state (body and blood of God) and claimed that they too sought to convert something baser (lead) into something higher and better (gold).[373] Occasionally this higher substance was taken to be quicksilver (mercury) because this remarkable material combined opposites into a "liquid-metal" state. Alchemists also sought the basic substrate to all things, thinking of it as a kind of divine prison within which the God spirit was confined; this was called *lapis* or the *stone,* or sometimes combined as the *lapis stone.*

Alchemists thus set out to find the secrets of matter, which they believed contained the "divine soul" (self-symbol) as a captive waiting for release. As Jung said of the alchemist: "His attention is not directed to his own salvation through God's grace, but to the liberation of God from the darkness of matter."[374] These men were extremely devout, and the aim of changing lesser metals into gold or quicksilver was not to acquire riches. If such a discovery could be made then we would have an empirical demonstration of the existence of God (knowledge not faith). During their pseudochemical work alchemists often had hallucinations and other hysteroid states in which complexes of various sorts would emerge and confront them in personified form. They projected their unconscious contents onto matter to such a degree that the product to be extracted from matter as a sublime substance was called *cogitatio* (having to do with thought).[375] A clear indication that an individuated self was being sought in the symbols of alchemy can be gleaned from the statement of Dorn, one of the famous alchemists Jung studied, who once proclaimed to his peers: " 'Transmute yourselves from dead stones into living philosophical stones!' "[376] In short, just as the patient in psychotherapy works through art forms to achieve individuation in the stage of transformation, so too did the alchemist work at his palpable materials in an effort (unknown by him) to find his unique identity. He looked outward to find what was really going on within him.

Alchemy as a spiritual phenomenon flowered through the Middle Ages, until roughly the seventeenth century when it began its decline thanks to the offsetting rise of modern natural science. The alchemists began to make a distinction between the more psychological (*mystica*) and the more palpable (*physica*) aspects of their study.[377] The older symbols lost their fascination, and men calling themselves alchemists were not striving for self-realization (via individuation) so much as they were literally trying to turn lead into gold. Materialism replaced spiritualism and this rather preposterous misconstrual of the original aims of alchemy brought on its current decline and disgrace.

MENTAL HEALTH AND MODERN MAN

Beginning around World War I and running through the rest of his life we note a mounting concern in the writings of Jung with what he termed the "sickness of dissociation" in the twentieth century.[378] One can see this splitting-up in the political and social conditions, the fragmentation of religion and philosophy, and even in the contending schools of modern art. Jung believed that man epitomized his psychic state in the art of his time, and rather than take this manifestation as *prima facie* evidence of a compensation and thus a healthy

move, he was frankly critical of the abstract, detached quality of modern art. The creations of a Pablo Picasso or a James Joyce did not enthrall him.[379] He felt the meaninglessness and the deliberate aloofness from the spectator or the reader in such art products expressed only too well what was taking place in the psyche of modern man.[380] The symbols of art are as far removed from significance in the life of man as are his fading religious and other mythological symbols. And for Jung when man loses his symbols he is unable to balance his one-sided state effectively. The irony of modern times is that, though we profess an almost devout religious belief in the "monotheism of consciousness" we are falling increasingly under the sway of the unconscious.[381]

Modern man cannot rid himself of autonomous complex possessions simply by denying them with a scientific critique from the vantage point of consciousness. An inflated consciousness is incapable of learning from the past, it cannot grasp the meaning of the present, and it is unable to lay the proper groundwork for a meaningful future because of the pseudo–self-direction it actually has. Speaking of the horrors of world war in the twentieth century, Jung observes: "Nobody realized that European man was possessed by something that robbed him of all free will. And this state of unconscious possession will continue undeterred until we Europeans become scared of our 'god-almightiness.' Such a change can begin only with individuals, for the masses are blind brutes, as we know to our cost."[382] In this rather vivid image we can see the collective Wotan emerging in the strutting of a Nazi "superman" or the submission of the individual to the demands of various social revolutions. Jung was not taken with collective solutions to what he viewed as a personal—that is, an individual's—problem. It is true to say that Jung favored listening to the collective promptings of the unconscious, to learn from what these group symbols had to say, but he rejected the reliance upon collective solutions which so many people have to make in the modern world. He once observed: "The steady growth of the Welfare State is no doubt a very fine thing from one point of view, but from another it is a doubtful blessing, as it robs people of their individual responsibility and turns them into infants and sheep."[383]

Lest Jung seem an arch-conservative and reactionary, we should realize that he had an ethical view of how man ought to behave which, if followed, would result in a social order of acceptance of variation and mutual respect for one's fellows. Jung termed behavior accepted from the group without a reasoned basis *moral* behavior. As we are growing our parents and other important social influencers provide us with the mores of the group, and we accept these principles emotively, based entirely on the feeling-toned fact that they are considered appropriate by all. In a sense moral behavior is instinctive or at least automatic. Ethical behavior, on the other hand, comes into play when we *reflect* upon our moral inclinations. Sometimes our automatic moral tendencies come into conflict with one another, and when we do not think about it we might overlook an inconsistency of this sort in our morally conflicting behaviors. At other times a conflict between our moral duties ushers in a severe test of our ethical judgment or "character."[384] It was Jung's firm belief that unconscious promptings, taken seriously and studied for what they portend, could function by way of our conscience to help us settle such ethical questions, and even more basically, to know precisely who we *are* as individuals. Through what he termed mediation and contemplation Jung believed that man could enrich his relationship with others.[385]

Unfortunately, modern man is too busy "doing things" to contemplate and introspect. One waits for empirical science to manipulate him to happiness in the twentieth century, he no longer turns inward and places his trust in the unconscious through fantasy, meditation, or self-discovery. Yet if he were to do that man could not go on projecting his shadow onto others.[386] The dissociation of modern times would thus be seen to exist not "out there" in the system or the establishment but "in here." If we really confront the personified evil which exists below awareness and assimilate it as *our self* (individuation) there would obviously be little need for the social reformers because everyone would see things more clearly and work to further rather than to hinder the changes necessary in collective living.

THERAPEUTIC TECHNIQUES

DIALECTICAL EQUALITY IN THE RELATIONSHIP

The "prime rule" of analytical psychotherapy is that therapy is a *dialectical* procedure, in which the individuality of the sufferer has as much right to existence as do the theories and individuality of the doctor.[387] The analytical procedure is dialectical in two ways: (a) the patient and therapist have equal rights in the dialogue,[388] and (b) the conscious and the unconscious square off on equal terms in their confrontation.[389] Real change demands openness and equality, with an opportunity for either side to prevail as regards an interpretation or a point of view.

As an exercise, Jung once showed how either the theories of Freud or Adler could be used satisfactorily to explain the dynamics of the same patient.[390] This admission has implications for client *resistance*, of course, because if the therapist admits that any of a number of theories can account for his client's distress, then when the client rejects his proffered interpretation of behavior how can the therapist claim this an act of "resistance"? It is therefore not surprising to find Jung claiming that analysts make entirely too much of resistance, which places him quite opposite to Freud, who stressed the overcoming of resistance as a major job of the analyst.[391] Jung insisted that his students take a self-critical attitude, and wear their theoretical prejudices lightly by not dismissing all patient counters as resistance.[392] Of his own practice Jung stated: "I am inclined to take deep-seated resistances seriously at first, paradoxical as this may sound, for I am convinced that the doctor does not necessarily know better than the patient's own psychic constitution, of which the patient himself may be quite unconscious."[393]

Jung realized that he had borrowed the dialectical procedure from the Greeks, and he said quite clearly that the strength of this approach lay in the fact that it encourages the emergence of a new point of view—a new synthesis—by giving initially equal weight to opposite points of view in the dialogue.[394] With this attitude toward the therapeutic encounter the analytical psychotherapist entered therapy with no preconceived goals or aims in mind. Jung acknowledged that suggestion played a certain role in all therapies, but he distinguished between conscious and unconscious suggestion. Conscious suggestion he took to mean following out a preconceived line of development or argument in making interpretations to the client.[395] Though the therapist cannot entirely avoid making unconscious suggestions to the client, he can and should avoid all such conscious forms of suggestion.

The therapist must be the model of a balanced individual if he is going to help his client. The client does not make himself like the therapist in a specific sense. He might value other things in life, or have a contrasting conscious type of personality. But on the issue of wholeness and totality there would be an identity between client and therapist, for this is what *self*-realization means. The therapist must show the way in his own adaptation, and Jung can thus say: "The great healing factor in psychotherapy is the doctor's [balanced] personality."[396] The so-called trans-

ference relationship is nothing more than a running series of projections sent the therapist's way from the unconscious of the client. Interpreting the origins of these imago projections is helpful, but this alone can never produce an attitude of healthy adaptation toward life in a teleological sense. By reducing today's relationship attempts to yesterday's imagos we constantly frustrate that which the patient needs most—a feeling of rapport with his fellow man.[397] And so Jung once again uses his bridge metaphor to say that in the human ties of the therapeutic relationship the abnormal individual can find his way back to the corpus of humanity. He need no longer deny, lie, sin, keep secrets or fight the mores of the group, for he has found the path from which he had strayed so long ago.

HERMENEUTIC TECHNIQUES OF AMPLIFICATION AND ACTIVE IMAGINATION

From his first reading of Freud's work, Jung took it as fact that free association was uncovering the same complexes which he had been uncovering in his experimental work using controlled word associations. Though evidence suggests that Jung used controlled associations in his therapy, particularly early in his career, he soon came to adopt the more open free association tactic.[398] In time he came to the conclusion that free association was not sufficient as the sole therapeutic device. Free association was an acceptable means of tapping the repressed complex, because mental associates are 100 per cent determined as links in the mind.[399] But it is also possible for the associations to lead us away from the present problem facing the client. We want to locate the complexes all right, but this could be done with any stimulus—as, beginning free associations from a line in a newspaper.[400] All roads lead to the complex in the psyche. But what we want in addition to this identification of the complex is a means of understanding what it is the unconscious wants us to do about our problems, the kinds of compensations to be made, and the change in conscious attitudes called for.

We can now appreciate more clearly what Jung meant by the "hermeneutic treatment of imaginative ideas."[401] Believing as he did that symbols are truly expressions of something we are trying to tell ourselves from out of a collective past, which is vital to our mental health as expressed, Jung did not think it wise to dismiss these messages as "covering-up" something else. He therefore rejected Freud's distinction between manifest and latent dream content, as follows: "The 'manifest' dream-picture is the dream itself and contains the whole meaning of the dream. When I find sugar in the urine, it is sugar and not just a facade for albumen. What Freud calls the 'dream-facade' is the dream's obscurity, and this is really only a projection of our own lack of understanding."[402] Dreams are not only or even primarily defensively constructed false fronts, hiding what they really mean to say. Dreams are fraught with symbolic meaning expression, and we must devise hermeneutic techniques not only to recognize the historical (collective) meaning which they represent but also to aid in forming a synthesis which might bring their message into the client's conscious outlook for today and tomorrow.[403]

There are two, somewhat related, hermeneutic techniques given prominence in analytical psychology. The first, tied more closely to free association, Jung termed *amplification*. He took this term from alchemy, where it referred to the fact that an alchemist would often let flow a series of psychic images and analogies while concentrating on his chemical studies.[404] Though he failed to appreciate what was occurring, the alchemist was in fact enlarging upon the context of some archetypal symbol which was expressing itself in his ritualized experiments and the theory he propounded to justify them. This tactic of "taking up the context" is precisely what Jung meant by amplification.[405] The client takes up

each salient feature of his dream, and then allows a flow of imagery to emerge by concentrating on some specific dream image. This is not identical to free association, because the client is not permitted to go from image to thought and then ramble on away from the dream images as such. For example, if a patient dreamed of a mountain scene, and then by concentrating on this dream image was reminded of a vacation last summer during which time he had a dreadful argument with his spouse, Jung would not consider it proper amplification if he were to go off and rehash his marital problems—letting the dream *per se* slip from view. This would be a freely associated identification of a complex or problem area, but what he would hope to do in amplification is find out what the unconscious is telling him. Concentrate on the mountain scene. What is happening? Describe it all in full detail, including any changes which might take place as you observe it unfolding.

If we were to follow this prescription for free fantasy, we might be surprised that our mind's eye will indeed begin to witness a scene of some sort, either limited to the dream as recalled or possibly even extending beyond it. The mountain might change its shape. Someone might begin falling down the mountain. We might find that from behind the mountain the sun was beginning to emerge, and so forth. Based on the recall of the dream and any additional action which might occur in the reactivated scene Jung could now help us establish the broader meaning of the dream symbols which have emerged. He might draw a parallel with the fantasied mountain scene and some relatively obscure Norse legend about mountain folk who had great strength of will.[406] This may strike us as doubly paradoxical because not only are we rather timid and unable to get hold of our life's circumstances, but we have always been ashamed of our Scandinavian lineage. In time, Jung would show us that this is precisely what our collective unconscious is trying to rectify via compensated dreaming, by essentially telling us to balance attitudes, to drop the one-sided timidity and advance on life even as we take pride in our national roots. The meaning of the dream is right there, in the manifest story line. One dream of this nature might not convince us, but if we were to have a series like this, all relating in some way to our problems and making the same point via the same symbolism, we might begin to take our unconscious seriously. This is the tactic of hermeneutics, and Jung was to extend the technique to go beyond simply a dream context as such.

This broader hermeneutic application he termed *active imagination,* which he defined as "a sequence of fantasies produced by deliberate concentration."[407] Once a theme emerges in active imagination it can continue for weeks and even months or years, possibly falling from view only to return again. Jung taught his patients to use this technique as a kind of barometer for the psychic state of balance, and he was known to diagnose the follow-up adjustments of his clients based upon the kinds of paintings they continued to come up with in active imagination after they had left him.[408] Jung believed that when we concentrated on our unconscious content productions in this fashion we literally charged them with more psychic energy and thus vitalized their symbolism.[409] In this way we ensure that symbols of transformation will solidify and effect a cure through balance.

INSIGHT, SYMBOLS, AND THE STRATEGY
OF INTERPRETATION

Jung once said that the psyche needs to "know" just like the body needs food—and not just any food or knowledge, but that which is appropriate and necessary for existence.[410] The symbol is the groping, usually analogical means by which the mind comes to know its new meanings.[411] Symbols are made up of cultural contents, used as analogies and metaphors, through which they can express meanings

never stated before. It is as if the archetypes were by nature dumb, and in order to express their compensating significance, they had to reach out and fix on whatever it was that the mind had learned in its particular culture. The cultural contents change and hence there are no fixed, unalterable meanings to be found in true symbolical expression.[412] Yet, surely within a given culture for a given period of time common symbolic meanings might emerge, recognized as meaningful by the entire collective.[413] The important point to keep in mind is that "Every symbol has at least two meanings."[414] One *never* exhausts the meaning of a symbol with a single interpretation. Take the supposed sexual meaning of a dream, for example. Must we assume that every sexual theme is aimed at a literal wish-fulfillment of a sexual prompting, or can there be other meanings to the *union* formed in copulation? Jung felt that there could indeed be, as in the frank eroticism of many coital symbols found in the staid artistic symbolism of the Middle Ages, where kings and queens were pictured copulating.[415] The symbolism here was not sexual lust, but the unity of the nation—a form of totality and wholeness. In like fashion, it is often the case that human beings symbolize their need for a return to social intercourse (relationship) with others by dreaming of sexual intercourse. The latter serves an analogical function for the former, so to speak.

Over the years Jung had many opportunities to proffer interpretations of symbolic content—both in dreams and other mythological, religious, and alchemical contexts. In order to give the reader some flavor of his style of symbolical interpretation we have listed a number of symbols taken from his works in Table 3. Note the decided lack of sexual allusions.

Coming now to the practical style of interpretation, Jung would usually begin by having his clients free associate to a dream image on the order of Freud's approach, to whom he gave credit as his teacher.[416] He departed from the classical free association procedure by voic-

Table 3
Some Jungian Symbolical Interpretations

Symbol	Interpretation
Albedo (Light)	consciousness[418]
Animal(s), aggressive	untamed libido[419]
Ascent, Climbing	sublimation, transformation[420]
Dark, Darkness	chthonic, i.e., concrete and earthy[421]
Descent	psychic setback, confrontation with unconscious[422]
Eye	consciousness[423]
Fish	unborn child (in utero)[424]
Gold	union of opposites[425]
Leftward Movement	moving to the unconscious[426]
Lightning	sudden, unexpected, overpowering psychic change[427]
Mercury, Quicksilver	uniting all opposites[428]
Moon	in man, unconscious; in woman, conscious[429]
Nigredo	unconscious[430]
Sun	in man, conscious; in woman, unconscious[431]
Theriomorphic snake, dove	male vs. female[432]
Tree	personality, especially growth of[433]
Water	unconscious or wisdom[434]

ing his own free associations in the dialogue, to supplement the thinking of the client's.[417] Since the therapist is in therapy and many symbols have a collective implication, his spontaneous ideas are just as legitimate as the client's. Furthermore, the Jungian analyst knows more about mythological and other historical symbols than the client, and we must bring out all such information from the objective psyche, if possible. Jung was also prone to report his own dreams to the client, particularly if these seemed relevant to their relationship. He once had a dream in which one of his female patients was standing at the balustrade of a castle. He had to look up at her, standing so high in the air due to the rise of the castle walls that he felt a crick in his neck as he fixed his gaze upward. This therapy series was not going well, and the next day he reported to his client that probably the reason it was not moving along was his fault. He had been thinking less of her than of other people, and

his unconscious was now trying to compensate for his conscious attitude of looking "down" on her by forcing him to strain in the opposite direction of looking "up" at her. The client admitted that she had felt this countertransference attitude on his part, and from then on the therapeutic relationship improved considerably.[435]

Jung agreed with Freud that no harm will be done if a therapist proffers his patients incorrect interpretations. In time, the unconscious will make our errors known. He should of course base his thinking on adequate samplings of unconscious data. Jung placed emphasis on analyzing a dream series, often running into the hundreds.[436] He told of a patient whose dreams reflected the water motif 26 times over a two month period.[437] Though "suggestion" may operate, by giving enough leeway and opportunity for self-expression the therapist ensures that only those suggestions which the patient is ready to accept in any case will be assimilated.[438] Hence, Jung did not lose sleep over the presumed certainty or fallaciousness of his interpretations. As he summed it up: "I do not need to prove that my interpretation of the dream is right (a pretty hopeless undertaking anyway), but must simply try to discover, with the patient, what *acts* for him—I am almost tempted to say, what is actual."[439]

Jung defined *dreams* in various ways, as "impartial, spontaneous products of the unconscious psyche, outside the control of the will,"[440] as "the hallucinations of normal life,"[441] or even as free associations, taking place without consciousness.[442] The emphasis here is obviously on spontaneity and autonomy. Basically, dreams have two functions: a *prospective* function, in that they help to prepare the dreamer for the following day,[443] and a *compensatory* function in that they balance off one-sided conscious attitudes such as Jung's condescension toward the client at the balustrade.[444] Jung took each dream as a kind of "self-portrayal," giving us in the conscious sphere of the psyche a look at—through symbols—the state of our psyche "as a whole." For this reason Jung believed *every* dream actor was representative of some aspect of the dreamer's personality needing balancing. A dream might compensate the conscious attitude without conscious awareness (by the ego), but ordinarily people need conscious understanding for a compensating balance to take place.[445] Jung also spoke of "big dreams," analogizing to the highly significant dreams which primitives report to their group as visions. The biblical story of Jacob's dream in which he saw the staircase to heaven would be an example of a big dream, for the significance of this imagery on his life—and hence on the life of other men—was monumental.

In approaching an interpretation of some dream the analyst should ordinarily consider two aspects.[446] First of all, enlarge on and come to know the context of the dream: Where is it set? What seems to be going on? How does the action proceed? Second, establish what compensation is being suggested by the unconscious. In studying the symbolical manifestations of the dream, Jung once observed: "Our position is more like that of an archaeologist deciphering an unknown script."[447] We will now review three dreams which Jung used as examples of his interpretation technique. They will provide an opportunity to see how his approach differed from that of Freud.

A favored example of a prospective dream mentioned by Jung in several of his writings[448] was told to Jung by a colleague who used to chide him about "making up" interpretations of dreams. One day the two friends met in the street and Jung was told the following dream: His friend is climbing a particularly steep mountain precipice. At first the ascent is very laborious, but as he moves upward it seems as if he is being drawn to the summit with ever greater ease. Faster and faster he climbs, in a state now of exhilaration and ecstasy, until it feels as if he is actually soaring to the top on wings. When he reaches the top of the mountain he seems to weigh nothing at all, and the dream ends as he steps off lightly into space. Jung advised his friend to be especially careful in his future expeditions because this was a rather ominous dream (particularly since the truth was that the man's marriage was going poorly and his conscious outlook was not a happy one at the time). The friend scoffed at this advice and rejected any thought that the dream was a message from his unconscious. A few months later he was observed to have actually stepped out onto space while descending a rock face, taking himself and a friend to their death below. The dream had him ascending and stepping up, the life actuality had him descending and stepping down. A Jungian could not dismiss this grim reflection of the principle of opposites as merely a coincidental happening.

Jung provided an excellent example of a compensatory dream in his case accounts. This dream was told to him by a young adult male.

The dreamer and his father are preparing to leave their home by way of a new family automobile. The father takes the wheel of the car but begins to drive in a very clumsy fashion. He moves the car forward with a jerk, then backward, zigs to the left and zags to the right until finally he succeeds in crashing the machine into a wall, damaging it rather badly. The dreamer is highly irritated with his father's behavior, and he proceeds to berate the parent only to find that his father is laughing—and obviously very drunk, a condition he had not noticed until after the accident. A classical Freudian interpretation of this dream would involve an Oedipal theme of some sort. In fact, the automobile, as an enclosed place might actually symbolize "mother," and the dream theme could be something like "this no-good bum is mistreating my mother, and he feels no remorse." In making this interpretation we would naturally be relying on the manifest vs. latent content distinction. Jung, on the other hand, took this dream at face value. The dream was aimed at taking the father down a peg or two: ". . . the unconscious resorts to a kind of artificial blasphemy so as to lower the father and elevate the son."[449] Knowing something about the young man helps us to make this interpretation of course, and in point of fact this young man did tend to overevaluate the merit of his parent. The dream was simply compensating for this attitude and asking that the conscious attitude be given more balance in outlook.

The final example of Jung's dream interpretation approach is the report of a 10-year-old girl, who Jung cautions had absolutely no possibility of ever hearing about the quaternity of God. This is important, because Jung here draws an archetypal parallel with biblical themes and thus presents us with the sort of evidence he accepted as an indication that an objective, collective unconscious existed in portions of the psyche. The little girl wrote the dream as presented in italics, and then Jung's comment follows to close this section.

Once in a dream I saw an animal that had lots of horns. It spiked up other little animals with them. It wriggled like a snake and that was how it lived. Then a blue fog came out of all the four corners, and it stopped eating. Then God came, but there were really four Gods in the four corners. Then the animal died, and all the animals it had eaten came out alive again.

This dream describes an unconscious individuation process: all the animals are eaten by the one animal. Then comes the enantiodromia [running to the opposite]: the dragon [matter] changes into pneuma [fog, spirit], which stands for a divine quaternity. Thereupon follows the apocatastasis [restoration], a resurrection of the dead. This exceedingly "unchildish" fantasy can hardly be termed anything but archetypal.[450]

SOME PROCEDURAL DETAILS

We might now end our consideration of analytical psychotherapy by considering what Jung had to say about the two-person contact in therapy. He did not believe in taking a detailed case history of the client from the outset, feeling that through free association one would get at the problems soon enough.[451] By and large Jung's view of therapy techniques was broad. He felt that all therapists are eventually forced into being eclectic, because no one will go on using that which is not effective just to be purist in outlook.[452] Any one of a number of theoretical outlooks (Freudian, Adlerian, etc.) could provide the rationale for understanding a patient's dynamics. Consonant with this realization, he played down the specific technique a therapist might use,[453] suggesting as we have already seen that the doctor's personality is more important than his particular therapeutic gimmick. He cautioned against trying to live the patient's life.[454] Jung approved of the patient modeling himself after the therapist, who had come to his level of adjustment by way of individuated effort. But if a therapist who had not acquired a broader understanding of the psyche wished to manipulate the life of another, a crisis would arise because it would suggest the functioning of a mana personality identification on the part of the therapist. Similarly, Jung was not attracted to group therapy approaches. He felt that group interactions merely prevent the individual from a painful confrontation with himself.[455] On the Jungian world view, all of our troubles flow from within, so it is merely a furtherance of the one-sidedness to pretend that we can rectify the situation by focusing on the outward, interpersonal situation.

Since he believed it to be a means for individuation, Jung was not above sending his Catholic clients off to the confessional where they might "cleanse their souls" through recognition of their shadow side.[456] By the same token, once balance of a sort was restored through communion Jung would not necessarily enter into a dialectical procedure with such a client. Anything which would aid in providing a meaningful balance for the individual would be acceptable to Jung: "If he [the client] can find the meaning of his life and the cure for his disquiet and disunity within the framework of an existing credo— including a political credo—that should be enough for the doctor. After all, the doctor's main concern is the sick, not the cured."[457] Of course, with the more sophisticated client it would be essential to carry on therapy through a dialectical tactic, on into transformation by way of individuation.

At the outset of therapy Jung saw his clients four times weekly.[458] As time slipped by and he moved ever more into the hermeneutic-synthetic aspects of the work he began cutting back the appointments to one or two hours per week. As this reduction in contacts was taking place Jung would be encouraging the client to analyze dreams for himself. He acted as consultant to the client's self-analyses. So long as proper assimilation was taking place there was no need for sessions more often than once weekly. Regarding the kind of patient he saw in therapy, Jung observed: "About a third of my cases are not suffering from any clinically definable neurosis, but from the senselessness and aimlessness of their lives. I should not

object if this were called the general neurosis of our age. Fully two-thirds of my patients are in the second half of life."[459] This is in striking contrast to the general characteristics of Freud's patients, who were considerably younger as far as we can judge. It seems clear that Jung's outlook on life was much different than that of Freud's, and his entire view of balance and of self-realization doubtless made it inevitable that he would carry a message well suited to the older person.

Notes

1. Jung, 1963, p. 76. **2.** *Ibid.*, pp. 24–25. **3.** Bennet, 1961, p. 14. **4.** Jung, 1963, p. 43. **5.** *Ibid.*, p. 31. **6.** Bennet, 1961, p. 147. **7.** Jung, Vol. 1, p. 166. **8.** Jung, Vol. 8, p. 96. **9.** Jung, Vol. 3, pp. 3–4. **10.** Bennet, 1961, p. 43. **11.** Jung, Vol. 5, p. xxiv. **12.** Evans, 1964, p. 89. **13.** Bennet, 1961, p. 40. **14.** Jung, 1963, p. 171. **15.** *Ibid.*, pp. 185–186. **16.** Jung, Vol. 9i, p. 48. **17.** Fromm, 1963. **18.** Bennet, 1961, pp. 58–60. **19.** Harms, 1946. **20.** Jung, Vol. 3, pp. 36–37. **21.** *Ibid.*, p. 272. **22.** Jung, Vol. 8, p. 8. **23.** *Ibid.*, p. 7. **24.** Jung, Vol. 11, p. 312. **25.** *Ibid.*, p. 83. **26.** Harms, 1946, p. 566. **27.** Jung, Vol. 8, p. 325. **28.** Jung, Vol. 5, p. 58. **29.** Jung, Vol. 9ii, p. 4. **30.** Jung, Vol. 4, p. 287. **31.** Jung, Vol. 5, p. xxiv. **32.** Jung, Vol. 16, p. 77. **33.** *Ibid.*, p. 90. **34.** Jung, Vol. 7, p. 279. **35.** Jung, Vol. 9i, p. 43. **36.** Jung, Vol. 5, p. xxix. **37.** Jung, Vol. 7, pp. 269–270. **38.** *Ibid.*, p. 204. **39.** Jung, Vol. 13, p. 45. **40.** Jung, Vol. 16, p. 170. **41.** Jung, 1946, p. 539. **42.** Jung, Vol. 16, p. 155. **43.** Jung, Vol. 8, p. 390. **44.** Jung, Vol. 13, p. 92. **45.** Jung, Vol. 9i, p. 280. **46.** Jung, Vol. 16, p. 177. **47.** Jung, Vol. 17, p. 52. **48.** *Ibid.*, p. 115. **49.** Jung, Vol. 7, p. 183. **50.** Jung, Vol. 15, p. 80. **51.** Jung, Vol. 1, pp. 3–92. **52.** *Ibid.*, p. 44. **53.** *Ibid.*, p. 97. **54.** Jung, Vol. 3, p. 67. **55.** *Ibid.*, p. 43. **56.** *Ibid.*, p. 63. **57.** Jung, Vol. 8, p. 101. **58.** *Ibid.*, p. 98. **59.** *Ibid.*, p. 101. **60.** *Ibid.*, p. 323. **61.** Jung, Vol. 9i, p. 276. **62.** Jung, Vol. 9ii, p. 3. **63.** *Ibid.*, p. 6. **64.** Jung, Vol. 14, p. 107. **65.** Jung, Vol. 11, p. 259. **66.** Jung, Vol. 7, p. 155. **67.** *Ibid.* **68.** *Ibid.*, p. 195. **69.** Jung, Vol. 9i, p. 122. **70.** Jung, Vol. 7, p. 291. **71.** *Ibid.*, p. 191. **72.** Jung, Vol. 10, p. 215. **73.** Jung, Vol. 7, p. 65.

74. Jung, Vol. 9ii, pp. 233, 266; Vol. 16, p. 124. 75. Jung, Vol. 9ii, p. 8. 76. *Ibid.*, pp. 266–267. 77. Jung, Vol. 11, p. 82; Vol. 12, pp. 41, 103. 78. Jung, 1946, p. 540. 79. Jung, Vol. 7, p. 190. 80. Jung, Vol. 9ii, p. 267. 81. *Ibid.*, p. 5. 82. Jung, Vol. 7, p. 194. 83. Jung, 1946, p. 294. 84. *Ibid.*, p. 336. 85. Jung, Vol. 14, p. 468. 86. Jung, Vol. 15, p. 104. 87. Jung, Vol. 4, p. 210. 88. Jung, Vol. 9i, p. 154. 89. Jung, Vol. 16, p. 124. 90. Jung, Vol. 11, p. 518. 91. Jung, Vol. 16, p. 156. 92. *Ibid.* 93. Jung, Vol. 4, p. 279. 94. Jung, Vol. 8, pp. 136, 137. 95. *Ibid.*, p. 137. 96. Jung, Vol. 7, p. 65. 97. Jung, Vol. 4, p. 315. 98. Jung, 1946, p. 368. 99. Jung, Vol. 5, p. 102. 100. Jung, Vol. 9i, p. 48. 101. Jung, Vol. 5, p. 181. 102. Jung, Vol. 15, p. 81. 103. Jung, Vol. 16, p. 34. 104. Jung, Vol. 9i, p. 37. 105. Jung, Vol. 7, p. 207. 106. Jung, Vol. 14, p. 106. 107. Jung, Vol. 9i, p. 30. 108. Jung, Vol. 5, pp. 390–391. 109. Jung, Vol. 8, p. 204. 110. *Ibid.*, pp. 405–406. 111. *Ibid.*, p. 182. 112. Jung, Vol. 9i, p. 319. 113. Jung, 1946, p. 565. 114. Jung, Vol 8, p. 206. 115. Jung, Vol. 4, p. 111; Vol. 5, p. 130. 116. Jung, Vol. 3, p. 190. 117. Jung, Vol. 5, p. 328. 118. Jung, 1946, p. 571. 119. *Ibid.*, p. 356. 120. Jung, Vol. 5, p. 139. 121. Jung, Vol. 16, p. 81. 122. Jung, Vol. 17, pp. 191–192. 123. Jung, Vol. 4, p. 127. 124. Jung, Vol. 7, p. 31. 125. Jung, Vol. 5, p. 431. 126. Jung, Vol. 10, p. 147. 127. Jung, Vol. 7, p. 46. 128. Jung, Vol. 8, p. 9. 129. Jung, Vol. 9ii, p. 10. 130. Jung, Vol. 5, p. 165. 131. Jung, Vol. 16, p. 6. 132. Jung, Vol. 4, p. 337. 133. Jung, Vol. 15, pp. 36–37. 134. Jung, Vol. 8, p. 18. 135. *Ibid.*, p. 25. 136. Jung, Vol. 3, p. 207. 137. Jung, Vol. 7, p. 175. 138. Jung, Vol. 9ii, p. 24. 139. Jung, Vol. 11, p. 87. 140. Bennet, 1961, p. 357. 141. Jung, Vol. 8, p. 424. 142. *Ibid.*, pp. 426, 427, 516. 143. *Ibid.*, p. 443. 144. Jung, Vol. 5, p. 58. 145. *Ibid.*, p. 59. 146. Jung, Vol. 10, p. 25. 147. Jung, Vol. 14, p. 107. 148. Harms, 1946, pp. 294, 582. 149. *Ibid.*, p. 531. 150. Jung, Vol. 7, p. 190. 151. Jung, 1946, p. 551. 152. Jung, Vol. 8, p. 98. 153. Jung, Vol. 9i, p. 351. 154. Jung, Vol. 11, p. 7. 155. Jung, Vol. 16, p. 15. 156. *Ibid.*, p. 262. 157. Jung, Vol. 9ii, p. 24. 158. Jung, Vol. 8, p. 32. 159. *Ibid.*, p. 33. 160. Jung, Vol. 16, p. 33. 161. Jung, Vol. 8, p. 94. 162. Jung, Vol. 9i, p. 267. 163. Jung, Vol. 9ii, p. 25. 164. Jung, 1946, p. 561. 165. Jung, Vol. 9i, p. 289. 166. Jung, Vol. 3, p. 187. 167. Jung, Vol. 10, p. 32. 168. Jung, Vol. 17, p. 44. 169. *Ibid.*, pp. 44–45. 170. Jung, Vol. 8, p. 390. 171. Jung, Vol. 4, pp. 116–117. 172.

Jung, Vol. 8, p. 390. 173. Jung, Vol. 17, p. 52. 174. Jung, Vol. 8, p. 390. 175. Jung, Vol. 17, p. 75. 176. *Ibid.*, p. 16. 177. Jung, Vol. 7, p. 25. 178. Jung, Vol. 17, p. 52. 179. Jung, Vol. 8, p. 391. 180. *Ibid.* 181. Jung, Vol. 9i, p. 71. 182. Jung, Vol. 8, p. 398. 183. *Ibid.*, p. 402. 184. *Ibid.*, p. 403. 185. Jung, Vol. 5, p. 284. 186. Jung, Vol. 9i, p. 87. 187. Jung, 1946, pp. 172, 374. 188. *Ibid.*, p. 547. 189. Jung, Vol. 11, p. 167. 190. Jung, 1946, p. 564. 191. *Ibid.*, p. 428. 192. *Ibid.*, p. 543. 193. *Ibid.*, p. 452. 194. *Ibid.*, p. 585. 195. *Ibid.*, p. 587. 196. Jung, Vol. 8, p. 141. 197. Jung, 1946, p. 514. 198. *Ibid.* 199. Jung, Vol. 12, p. 102. 200. Jung, 1946, p. 564. 201. Jung, Vol. 12, p. 102. 202. Jung, 1946, p. 563. 203. *Ibid.*, p. 426. 204. Jung, Vol. 12, p. 102. 205. Jung, 1946, p. 514. 206. Based in part on the Jacobi stylization, see Vol. 12, p. 102. 207. Jung, 1946, pp. 542, 567. 208. *Ibid.*, pp. 414–416. 209. *Ibid.*, p. 416. 210. *Ibid.*, pp. 417–419. 211. *Ibid.*, p. 414. 212. *Ibid.*, pp. 53, 389–390. 213. *Ibid.*, p. 436. 214. *Ibid.*, p. 466. 215. *Ibid.*, p. 457. 216. *Ibid.*, p. 464. 217. *Ibid.*, p. 484. 218. *Ibid.*, p. 492. 219. *Ibid.*, pp. 500–503. 220. *Ibid.*, pp. 508–509. 221. Jung, Vol. 7, p. 79. 222. Jung, Vol. 8, p. 90. 223. Jung, Vol. 7, p. 79. 224. Jung, Vol. 14, p. 200. 225. Jung, Vol. 7, p. 79. 226. *Ibid.*, p. 231. 227. Jung, Vol. 8, p. 225. 228. Jung, Vol. 10, p. 86. 229. *Ibid.*, p. 149. 230. Jung, Vol. 9ii, p. 97. 231. Jung, Vol. 10, pp. 13–14. 232. Jung, Vol. 11, p. 534. 233. *Ibid.*, p. 549. 234. Jung, Vol. 13, pp. 9–10. 235. Jung, Vol. 11, p. 493. 236. Jung, Vol. 13, p. 9. 237. Jung, Vol. 10, p. 140. 238. *Ibid.*, p. 141. 239. *Ibid.*, p. 123. 240. Jung, Vol. 14, p. 179. 241. Jung, Vol. 7, p. 205. 242. *Ibid.* 243. Jung, Vol. 9ii, p. 11. 244. Jung, Vol. 7, p. 55. 245. Jung, Vol. 17, p. 153. 246. Jung, Vol. 3, p. 253. 247. Jung, Vol. 9i, pp. 278–279. 248. Jung, Vol. 13, pp. 36–37. 249. Jung, Vol. 4, p. 182. 250. Jung, Vol. 16, p. 120. 251. Jung, Vol. 8, pp. 355–356. 252. Jung, Vol. 7, p. 179. 253. Jung, Vol. 11, p. 49. 254. *Ibid.*, p. 330. 255. Jung, Vol. 8, p. 244. 256. Jung, Vol. 16, p. 55. 257. Jung, Vol. 5, p. 207. 258. Jung, Vol. 7, p. 23. 259. *Ibid.*, p. 182. 260. *Ibid.* 261. Jung, Vol. 5, p. 232. 262. *Ibid.*, p. 398. 263. *Ibid.*, p. 232. 264. Jung, Vol. 13, p. 346. 265. *Ibid.*, p. 12. 266. Jung, Vol. 9i, p. 351. 267. Jung, Vol. 10, p. 462. 268. Jung, Vol. 4, p. 166. 269. *Ibid.*, p. 173. 270. Jung, Vol. 10, p. 169. 271. *Ibid.*, p. 170. 272. Jung, Vol. 11, p. 43. 273. *Ibid.*, p. 340. 274. Jung, Vol. 5, p. 370. 275. Jung, Vol. 3, p. 239. 276. Jung, Vol. 9i,

p. 278. **277.** Jung, Vol. 3, p. 247. **278.** Jung, Vol. 16, p. 86. **279.** Jung, Vol. 13, pp. 14–15. **280.** *Ibid.*, p. 15. **281.** *Ibid.*, p. 342. **282.** Jung, Vol. 14, p. xv. **283.** Jung, Vol. 9ii, p. 33. **284.** Jung, Vol. 13, p. 38. **285.** *Ibid.*, pp. 327–328. **286.** Jung, Vol. 11, p. 157. **287.** Jung, Vol. 13, p. 348. **288.** Jung, Vol. 16, p. 156. **289.** Jung, Vol. 7, p. 287. **290.** Jung, Vol. 13, p. 302. **291.** Jung, Vol. 16, p. 123. **292.** Jung, Vol. 7, p. 109. **293.** Jung, Vol. 16, p. 3. **294.** Jung, Vol. 12, p. 4. **295.** Jung, Vol. 10, p. 168; Vol. 16, p. 10. **296.** Jung, Vol. 16, pp. 61–62. **297.** Jung, Vol. 9i, p. 60. **298.** Jung, Vol. 4, p. 200. **299.** Jung, Vol. 7, p. 62. **300.** Jung, Vol. 4, p. 199. **301.** Jung, Vol. 7, p. 90. **302.** Jung, Vol. 16, p. 136. **303.** Jung, Vol. 8, p. 273. **304.** Jung, Vol. 16, p. 78. **305.** *Ibid.*, pp. 137–138. **306.** Jung, Vol. 7, p. 62. **307.** Jung, Vol. 16, p. 68. **308.** *Ibid.*, p. 70. **309.** Jung, Vol. 11, pp. 197–198. **310.** Jung, Vol. 9i, p. 20. **311.** Jung, Vol. 14, p. 497. **312.** *Ibid.*, p. 168. **313.** *Ibid.*, p. 452. **314.** Jung, Vol. 13, p. 42. **315.** Jung, 1963, pp. 185–186. **316.** Jung, Vol. 13, p. 42. **317.** Jung, Vol. 7, p. 201. **318.** Jung, Vol. 8, p. 202. **319.** Jung, Vol. 7, p. 152. **320.** Jung, Vol. 9i, p. 275. **321.** Jung, Vol. 16, p. 10. **322.** Jung, Vol. 7, p. 209. **323.** Jung, Vol. 13, p. 45. **324.** Jung, Vol. 12, p. 26. **325.** Jung, Vol. 11, p. 501. **326.** Jung, Vol. 14, pp. 544–546. **327.** Jung, Vol. 16, p. 199. **328.** Jung, Vol. 8, p. 48. **329.** *Ibid.*, p. 91. **330.** Jung, Vol. 14, p. 200. **331.** Jung, Vol. 16, p. 262. **332.** *Ibid.*, p. 15. **333.** *Ibid.*, p. 321. **334.** Jung, Vol. 7, p. 232. **335.** *Ibid.*, p. 235. **336.** Jung, Vol. 14, pp. 370–371. **337.** Jung, Vol. 12, p. 131. **338.** Jung, Vol. 8, p. 224. **339.** *Ibid.*, p. 290. **340.** Jung, Vol. 5, p. 141. **341.** Jung, Vol. 9i, p. 355. **342.** Jung, Vol. 11, p. 189. **343.** Jung, Vol. 17, p. 34. **344.** Jung, Vol. 5, p. 390. **345.** Evans, 1964, p. 48. **346.** Jung, Vol. 10, p. 443. **347.** Jung, Vol. 11, p. 196. **348.** Jung, Vol. 10, pp. 325–327. **349.** See Jung, Vol. 5, p. 441; Vol. 11, p. 353. **350.** Jung, Vol. 12, pp. 6–7. **351.** Jung, Vol. 9ii, pp. 174–175. **352.** Jung, Vol. 16, p. 46. **353.** *Ibid.*, p. 265. **354.** Jung, Vol. 9ii, p. 31. **355.** Jung, Vol. 11, p. 432. **356.** Jung, Vol. 9ii, p. 36; Vol. 11, p. 88. **357.** Jung, Vol. 11, p. 273. **358.** *Ibid.*, p. 59. **359.** Jung, 1963, p. 55. **360.** *Ibid.*, p. 62. **361.** Jung, Vol. 11, p. 406. **362.** *Ibid.*, p. 196. **363.** *Ibid.*, pp. 154, 432. **364.** Jung, Vol. 9ii, p. 72. **365.** *Ibid.*, p. 42. **366.** Jung, Vol. 11, p. 161. **367.** Jung, Vol. 9i, p. 214. **368.** Jung, Vol. 7, p. 237. **369.** Jung, Vol. 9i, p. 108. **370.** Jung, Vol. 11, pp. 58–59. **371.** Jung, Vol. 12, p. 343. **372.** *Ibid.*, p. 35. **373.** *Ibid.*, p. 297. **374.** *Ibid.*,

p. 299. **375.** *Ibid.*, p. 254. **376.** Jung, Vol. 9ii, p. 170. **377.** Jung, Vol. 12, pp. 403–404. **378.** Jung, Vol. 10, p. 140. **379.** Jung, Vol. 15, pp. 135–137. **380.** Jung, Vol. 10, p. 383. **381.** Jung, Vol. 13, p. 36. **382.** Jung, Vol. 12, p. 461. **383.** Jung, Vol. 10, pp. 200–201. **384.** *Ibid.*, pp. 454–455. **385.** Jung, Vol. 14, p. 498. **386.** *Ibid.*, p. 168. **387.** Jung, Vol. 16, p. 10. **388.** Jung, Vol. 11, p. 554. **389.** Jung, Vol. 12, p. 4. **390.** Jung, Vol. 16, pp. 113–114. **391.** Jung, Vol. 9i, p. 61. **392.** Jung, Vol. 16, p. 115. **393.** *Ibid.*, pp. 39–40. **394.** *Ibid.*, p. 3. **395.** *Ibid.*, p. 147. **396.** *Ibid.*, p. 88. **397.** *Ibid.*, p. 135. **398.** Jung, Vol. 4, p. 29. **399.** *Ibid.*, p. 16. **400.** Jung, Vol. 16, p. 149. **401.** Jung, Vol. 7, p. 288. **402.** Jung, Vol. 16, p. 149. **403.** Jung, Vol. 7, p. 80. **404.** Jung, Vol. 12, p. 277. **405.** Jung, Vol. 8, p. 285. **406.** Jung, Vol. 13, p. 348. **407.** Jung, Vol. 9i, p. 49. **408.** *Ibid.*, pp. 292–354. **409.** Jung, Vol. 11, p. 496. **410.** Jung, Vol. 13, p. 346. **411.** Jung, Vol. 14, p. 468. **412.** Jung, Vol. 4, p. 279. **413.** Jung, Vol. 16, p. 156. **414.** Jung, Vol. 4, p. 237. **415.** Jung, Vol. 16, p. 250. **416.** *Ibid.*, pp. 46–47. **417.** *Ibid.*, p. 44. **418.** Jung, Vol. 14, p. 77. **419.** Jung, Vol. 5, p. 328. **420.** Jung, Vol. 12, pp. 55, 60. **421.** *Ibid.*, p. 167. **422.** *Ibid.*, p. 60. **423.** Jung, Vol. 14, p. 53. **424.** Jung, Vol. 5, p. 198. **425.** Jung, Vol. 14, p. 111. **426.** Jung, Vol. 12, p. 184. **427.** Jung, Vol. 9i, p. 295. **428.** Jung, Vol. 12, p. 282. **429.** Jung, Vol. 14, pp. 53, 135. **430.** *Ibid.*, p. 77. **431.** *Ibid.*, pp. 53, 135. **432.** *Ibid.*, p. 76. **433.** Jung, Vol. 13, p. 194. **434.** Jung, Vol. 9i, p. 18. **435.** Jung, Vol. 7, p. 111. **436.** Jung, Vol. 8, p. 289. **437.** Jung, Vol. 16, p. 12. **438.** *Ibid.*, p. 47. **439.** *Ibid.*, p. 45. **440.** Jung, Vol. 10, p. 149. **441.** Jung, Vol. 3, p. 148. **442.** Jung, Vol. 4, p. 234. **443.** Jung, Vol. 5, p. 7. **444.** Jung, Vol. 8, p. 255. **445.** Jung, Vol. 10, p. 388. **446.** Jung, Vol. 16, pp. 152–154. **447.** Jung, Vol. 17, p. 154. **448.** Jung, Vol. 8, p. 81; Vol. 16, pp. 150–151; Vol. 17, p. 60. **449.** Jung, Vol. 16, p. 155. **450.** Jung, Vol. 9i, p. 353. **451.** Jung, Vol. 4, p. 29. **452.** Jung, Vol. 16, p. 88. **453.** Jung, Vol. 10, p. 159. **454.** *Ibid.*, pp. 456, 459. **455.** *Ibid.*, p. 471. **456.** Jung, Vol. 16, p. 16. **457.** *Ibid.*, pp. 16–17. **458.** *Ibid.*, p. 20. **459.** *Ibid.*, p. 41.

4

Theory Construction in Classical Psychoanalysis

The Mixed Kantian-Lockean Models of Classical Theory

The scientific style of explanation before the advent of the three "founding fathers" of psychoanalysis was almost exclusively Lockean. The medical-physical models reviewed in Chapter 2 (pp. 84–89) all rest on the assumption that some basic, underlying substratum of elements in man's physical being can account for why he behaves as he does. The Darwinian theory of evolution rests squarely on this view of man as a more complex assemblage of the factors making up the "nature" of lower organisms. Figure 18 schematizes what is sometimes called the "pyramid of life" in organic evolution.

At the lowest levels of life in Figure 18 we have the one-celled animals. Above these amoeba-like creatures we have in ascending order the sea urchins, fishes, amphibia, land crawling and then flying creatures. We move thence to mammals and the higher apes until, at the apex of our triangular hierarchy (the 5s of the Lockean model, see Introduction) we find the highest anthropoid, man. To round out the picture we should also include all of the extinct forms of life (such as the dinosaurs) as well as the presumed "links" between man and ape (such as the Neanderthal Man). But in broad outline, the "course of evolution" is "from below" in the Lockean sense, advancing ever upward to the "most complex" animal at the top of the pyramid. Adler was to concern himself with the question of whether or not this course of evolution took on a directional (teleological) quality. But all three of our theorists had to confront the heavy weight of theoretical bias issuing from the Lockean

Figure 18
The Pyramid of Life in Organic Evolution

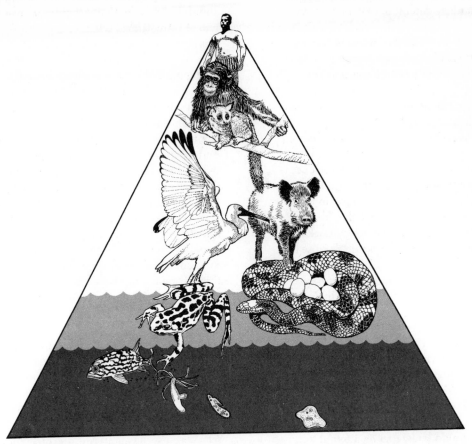

presumptions about organic life in the medical and biological sciences of their time.

There is in the theories of Freud, Adler, and Jung a decided tendency to *mix* Kantian and Lockean models. Freud begins the process by responding to the needs of his patients for (introspective) insight. Adler is probably the most Lockean of the three men, and Jung is clearly the most Kantian. There are three major theoretical issues to be considered in light of the mixed models employed by the founders of modern personality theory: extraspection vs. introspection, idealism vs. realism, and reductionism.

EXTRASPECTION VS. INTROSPECTION

Freud was greatly influenced by his teacher, Ernst Brücke, a toughminded Lockean of the old school who was convinced of an underlying physical-chemical substrate to everything in nature, including man's behavioral patterns (see p. 27, Chapter 1). Wilhelm Fliess was also committed to a biological approach, and —thanks to his influence—Freud once set out to write a traditional brand of psychology in his *Project for a Scientific Psychology*. In the opening paragraph of this document Freud states: "The intention [of the *Project*] is to furnish a psychology that shall be a natural science: that is, to represent psychical processes as quantitatively determinate states of specifiable material particles, thus making those processes perspicuous and free from contradiction. Two principal ideas are involved: (1) What distinguishes activity from rest is to be regarded as Q, subject to the general laws of motion. (2) The neurones are to be taken as the material particles."[1]

This remarkable preamble to an unfinished work clearly demonstrates that Freud understood what it took to write a "natural science" brand of psychology. This is the most beautiful expression of Lockean thinking in all of Freud's writings, but it was one that he could not build on. Freud found a purely Lockean formulation of things unworkable because he was trying to derive a picture of *mental* life in which he had to account for the *introspective* meanings people place on their life's circumstances. Freud would have preferred to remain within a Lockean frame of reference, for he was sincerely trying to raise his method of study to the level of natural science.[2] But he also found, and remarked to Fliess on more than one occasion, that he could not make sense of the neuroses based solely on the presumptions of an underlying physical-chemical substrate.[3] Freud knew that an attempt to explain "that" (the individual human being) extraspectively without taking "that" into account would be an arbitrary and worthless stretch of the imagination.

Thus, Freud created a role for the self-directed "person" to shape his own destiny thanks to those conscious or unconscious meanings which could never be captured extraspectively as "constituting" the chemistry of the body or as solely "coming from" experience in a unidirectional sense. The Kantian meanings "from above" are meanings infused by the intellect *onto* experience. To understand why the organism behaves in this sense we must slip on "that" person's Kantian spectacles (see p. 11) and view things the way he does. This approach shifts the locus of theoretical explanation from the extraspective to the introspective, and there is no doubt but that Freud was the first self-proclaimed scientist in history to make this theoretical shift. Philosophers, artists, and theologians were prone to theorize introspectively, but the natural scientist was schooled by the rigors of "empirical observation" to direct his theories outward, in third-person fashion.

Freud was not entirely Kantian, however. Kant had argued that without an a priori understanding of space and time man would be unable to organize his sensory impressions and thereby grasp the meanings of experience.[4] Freud could not accept Kant's claim that space and time were necessary concomitants of the human intellect. He found the unconscious portions of mind to be timeless, and in more than one of his writings he specifically rejected this Kantian view of the human intellect.[5] What Freud *did* accept in the Kantian model was its emphasis on the importance of man's personal contribution to the meanings he harbors in (conscious or unconscious) mind. As he said, "Just as Kant warned us not to overlook the fact that our perceptions are subjectively conditioned and must not be regarded as identical with what is perceived though unknowable [we never know things in themselves] so psycho-analysis warns us not to equate perceptions by means of consciousness with the unconscious mental processes which are their object. Like the physical, the psychical is not necessarily in reality what it appears to us to be."[6]

Adler did not clearly perceive this Kantian side to Freudian theory. Though he began theorizing on physical inferiorities and compensations within a strictly Lockean model, Adler's break with Freud was the occasion for a strong influx of Kantian thought by way of Vaihinger's "as if" philosophy (see Chapter 2). Adler consciously set out to include a more introspective view of man—epitomized in the highly subjective concepts of the prototype, life plan, life style, and so forth—and he named

Kant as the intellectual forebear of such theory.[7] At the same time, what Adler took from Kant was his "tougher side." That is, in distinguishing between "things in themselves" (noumena) and our sensory experience of such "perceived things" (phenomena), Kant was underscoring a potential for error in that man was able to *transcend* the real world (noumena based) in fashioning what was for him a "possible" world of speculative intellect (entirely phenomenological). Man has a creative intellect, forming things introspectively to meet his intentions, but some of his creations are flatly incorrect and "fictional" so that the *real facts* (noumena contributing here) are subverted. As a philosopher, Kant devoted much effort to a consideration of how man arrives at such error.

Jung was clearly the most Kantian of the founding fathers, and it would be correct to characterize him as a bridge to the phenomenological theorists of Chapters 9, 10, and 11. For present purposes, "phenomenology" may be defined as the study of how our experience is dependent upon (or not dependent upon) the nature of our Kantian spectacles. These spectacles *are* our "phenomenal reality" in opposition to the noumenal reality of "things in themselves." From an early age Jung was fascinated by Kant, whose thought is germaine to phenomenological theory, and there is little doubt that he much preferred the work of this German philosopher to the writings and outlook of the British Empiricist, John Locke.[8] Historically, two broad categories of phenomenology have emerged in psychology, both of which emphasize the introspective perspective. On the one hand the *sensory* phenomenologists, men like Wertheimer, Köhler, and Koffka, have translated the Kantian categories of the understanding into parameters for how man sees, hears, feels, and so forth, through his internal or external "sensory" receptors. This form of sensory phenomenology is reviewed in Chapter 9 (pp. 403–412). In contrast to this view is a *logical* phenomenology, in which the Kantian

spectacles are equivalent to the major premises of a syllogism. They are literally the predicate assumptions built into mental cognition from the outset which inevitably determine the kind of meanings which will be extracted through reasoning, inductions, deductions, and so on.

Jung can be considered one such logical phenomenologist (see Chapter 12, p. 514). His view of the archetype is precisely this—as a Kantian category of meaning which framed experience for man in what superficially appears to be a mechanical fashion but this is only because we fail to appreciate that archetypes are always intentional. They express new meanings for they literally seek to create some change in the state of meaningful affairs facing the individual (a new possibility). Kant had used "primordial image" in his *Logic,* but Jung seems to have taken this phrase as roughly synonymous with the "archetype" concept which originated with Jacob Burckhardt.[9] This entire treatment of a mind infusing its reality with meaning is decidedly Kantian, introspective, and phenomenological. Hence, it is no surprise to find Jung saying: "Although I have often been called a philosopher, I am an empiricist and adhere as such to the phenomenological standpoint."[10]

IDEALISM VS. REALISM

In shifting the locus of description to the introspective perspective we encourage an idealistic form of theory. Kant considered himself a "critical realist," holding that "things in themselves" really did exist even though all we can ever know is our sensations and perceptions of them. But many scholars have referred to Kantian philosophy as essentially idealistic. Although Freud began his career as a rather decided realist, he came in time to appreciate the role which a more idealistic approach to theory played in all sciences. In one of his last papers, referring to the modern physical theories, Freud said: "Our procedure in psychoanalysis is quite similar. We have discovered technical methods of filling up the gaps in the phenomena of our consciousness, and we make use of those methods just as a physicist makes use of experiment. In this manner we infer a number of processes which are in themselves 'unknowable' and interpolate them in those that are conscious to us."[11] So, not only did Freud accept the dictum that a person's psychical realm was built in part on his perception of things (psychical reality), but he also recognized that all science hinges upon a speculative contribution from a thinking human being.

It was Adler more than Freud or Jung who wrestled with this problem of idealism in human behavior. He—as Freud had occasionally done—tended to lump idealism and subjectivity into the same concept. Obviously, if the intellect contributes something to experience then it is possible for that contribution to be greatly slanted, selectively distorted—that is, subjective. This is the reason Adler embraced what we termed above the "tougher side" of Kant in Vaihinger's philosophy. Now, Vaihinger was a more thoroughgoing idealist than Adler. When Vaihinger spoke of "fictions" he was referring to something like a concept or a construct that all men employed to organize their intellect, as follows:

Fictio means, in the first place, an activity of fingere, that is to say, of constructing, forming, giving shape, elaborating, presenting, artistically fashioning, conceiving, thinking, imagining, assuming, planning, devising, inventing. Secondly, it refers to the product of these activities, the fictional assumption, fabrication, creation, the imagined case. Its most conspicuous character is that of unhampered and free expression.[12]

The question of subjective error is quite secondary here, since what Vaihinger addresses himself to is all the mental activity we refer to when we say that man idealistically contributes something to his experience which is not fixed, immutable, and real. There is an arbitrariness in the meanings man employs, for that is the basic nature of thought. Vaihinger would have

said that social interest was another one of those fictions which some men use to order life. Yet, as we saw in Chapter 2, social interest was for Adler no fiction but rather a fact of existence. Basing his argument on what he took to be the teleological course of evolution Adler said that all men could find the proper, the true, the real. At least, this is what distinguishes the normal from the abnormal man:

More firmly than the normal individual does the neurotic fixate his God, his idol, his personality ideal, and cling to his guiding line, and with deeper purpose he loses sight of reality. . . . The normal individual, too, can and will create his deity, will feel drawn upward. But he will never lose sight of reality and always take it into account as soon as action and work are demanded. The neurotic is under the hypnotic spell of a fictional life plan.[13]

Hence, whereas Vaihinger was clearly a logical phenomenologist in the style of Jung, Adler stopped short of the idealism this view engendered. Individual psychology thus takes into account man's subjectivity, the capacity he has for creating his own circumstances in life, but it tempers this relativism with the presumed directionality of organic evolution. The "real" is the direction underway in the course of evolution. We thus see a more Lockean emphasis in Adlerian thought at this point.

Jung was clearly the most outspokenly idealistic of the founding fathers. He often warned against the tendency to accept reality at its face value, as in the following: "Reality is that which works in a human soul and not that which certain people assume to be operative, and about which prejudiced generalizations are wont to be made."[14] Jung felt that the emphasis on materialism had made the modern intellect one-sided on the question of reality.[15] Existentialism as a philosophical counterweight to this realistic emphasis was thought by Jung to have arisen as a balancing historical movement (see Chapter 10). He was even skeptical about the use of the word "existence" by the existentialists, feeling that they might be falling into the same error they accused others of making.[16]

A rather unique aspect of the idealism-realism issue which Jung developed concerns the question of a "tabula rasa" versus an a priori conception of mentality. The phrase *tabula rasa* was first used by St. Thomas Aquinas, but its major identification is with John Locke's philosophy. It refers to the mind as a supposed "smoothed tablet," ready to receive imprints or inputs from the "real" environment. The Lockean conception of mind is a passive receptacle, a storing and collating mechanism which is ready for use at birth but lacking in any conceptualizing or "framing" capacities in the Kantian idealistic sense. Jung could not accept this Lockean view of mind. He argued that the mind is no less "blank" than the human hand, regarding its potential for use. We do not say that the hand is a mechanism ready to be acted on at birth. We think of the hand as a mechanism which can *itself act*. Nature has prepared the hand to "do," and although different hands may do different things, we can still appreciate that there is a contribution made to what is done by the hand itself.

In this way Jung argued that brains are fixed by heredity in a priori fashion, i.e., presumptive, coming before cognition as such. Brains are not shaped by inputs in this life span alone; they have also "evolved" out of the past efforts of man to adjust his mentality to experience. The brain evolved as the hand evolved. The hand is thus "by nature" ready to act in a certain a priori fashion, and the brain too is ready to behave in certain ways from the outset:

Hence the newly-born brain or function-system is an ancient instrument, prepared for quite definite ends; it is not merely a passive apperceptive instrument, but is also in active command of experience outside itself, forcing certain conclusions or judgments. These adjustments are not merely ac-

cidental or arbitrary happenings, but adhere to strictly preformed conditions, which are not transmitted, as are perception-contents, through experience, but are *a priori* conditions of apprehension.[17]

When Jung refers to the "preformed conditions" here he does not imply a deity teleology. He is not saying some Prime Mover put the mind into its present state. What he argues for is a human teleology. Man is men, because the individual man carries on with the physical structure (hands, feet, etc.) and the psychical structure (collective unconscious, archetypes, etc.) of his progenitors. Physical structures are not teleological in Jungian psychology. It is perfectly adequate to think of the body as a Lockean mechanism. However, the mind is constructed of somewhat different—or possibly somewhat more complex—features. This view makes Jung a *nativist* of sorts, because he allots man's heredity a role in the present functioning of mind. But we must not simplify this nativism. Jung's nativism is a *psychical* as opposed to a physical nativism. Moreover, he is a *teleological* nativist. Jungian racial theories are not of the old-line variety, as in the medical-biological theories reviewed at the outset of Chapter 2.

REDUCTIONISM

The style of theoretical development in the medical and biological sciences involved reducing the phenotypic description of a natural event to the genotypic factors which presumably underlie it. Invariably this amounted to finding a substrate energy which supposedly was the "real" cause of events—a chemical substance or a neuroelectrical impulse which somehow brought about the overt changes to be seen in behavior. This Lockean premise merged nicely with the Newtonian physics of the time. Truth was based on a realistic assumption of the nature of meaning. Hence, to render a completely true account of what "caused" anything it was necessary to cite these underlying "determinants." Freud wrestled with this brand of theorizing, and his agonies are plainly apparent in the Fliess correspondence.[18] In time, he was to settle on the "libido theory" as a kind of middle position, and as we saw in Chapter 1, Freud was always capable of explaining human behavior in either a completely psychological or a quasi-mechanical fashion (reflecting his mixed-model usages). He seemed to use libido analogues more frequently as the years passed, but there is an important distinction we will make between Freud's energic theories and those propounded in the broader "natural" sciences. The fascinating thing about Freud's wedding of Lockean substrate "forces" to the more Kantian psychological factors "framing-in" mentality is that he knew precisely why he formed the union:

. . . we must recollect that all our provisional ideas in psychology will presumably some day be based on an organic substructure. This makes it probable that it is special substances and chemical processes which perform the operations of sexuality and provide for the extension of individual life into that of the species. We are taking this probability into account in replacing the special chemical substances by special psychical forces. . . . I should like at this point expressly to admit that the hypothesis of separate ego-instincts and sexual instincts (that is to say, the libido theory) rests scarcely at all upon a psychological basis, but derives its principal support from biology. . . . It may turn out that, most basically and on the longest view, sexual energy—libido—is only the product of a differentiation in the energy at work generally in the mind. But such an assertion has no relevance. . . . Let us face the possibility of error; but do not let us be deterred from pursuing the logical implications of the hypothesis we first adopted of an antithesis between ego-instincts and sexual instincts. . . .[19]

Although he is discussing the opposition of an ego and a sexual instinct, Freud knew full well that he did not *have* to resort to energies or instincts *at all*. It was only the demands of biology as "mother science" which prompted him to theorize in this fashion. He used his instincts and energies in a peculiarly "human" way. It seems clear in this quote that Freud respected the Lockean substrate conceptions of his peers. He thus met the needs of the scientific community, spoke of energic substrates and instincts, and brilliantly combined the Lockean and Kantian models to father a new era in personality description.

Jung spoke out directly against the necessity of reducing psychological descriptions to "something else" lying beneath when he argued for the hermeneutic-synthetic form of explanation (see Chapter 3, p. 192). The effect of this mode of description in the case of man was to "reduce" a teleological organism to a substrate of mechanical routine. Using Wilhelm Wundt, the often cited "father" of experimental psychology, as a case in point Jung argued that Wundt was forced to reduce behavior to its physiological substrate because he failed to accept the significance of intentions in human behavior.[20] In the newly emerging physics of the period Jung could see that how a physicist's theoretical assumptions began the process of explanation often determined what it was that he might say about "natural" events. Wundt was a Newtonian realist but the new physics was far more idealistic in tone. Light could be seen as a series of individual particles *or* as a series of waves.[21] It was all up to the scientist's *intentions* in formulating the theory he had in mind. Jung could see that the older, Lockean assumptions of Newtonian physics were under attack from a familiar source: "Significantly enough, it is Kant's doctrine of categories . . . that destroys in embryo every attempt to revive metaphysics in the old sense of the word, but at the same time paves the way for a rebirth of the Platonic spirit. If it be true that there can be no metaphysics transcending human reason, it is no less true that there can be no empirical knowledge that is not already caught and limited by the *a priori* structure of cognition."[22]

However, Jung like Freud did translate his psychological insights into energic terminology.

And also like Freud, he refused to conceive of the libido as identical to the energic usages of the classical physical theorist. As we know from Chapter 3, Jung's energies (libido) are hormic—that is, teleological. We will return to this question later. For now we need only observe that Adler failed to see much difference between the typical physicist's usage of energies and the energic theories of Freud and Jung. Adler found their attempts to cement a "conservation of energy" principle to human behavior quite senseless. He loved to emphasize that a completely psychological examination of behavior would convince the unbiased observer that the individual person *decides* how much or how little so-called psychic energy is to be expended in this or that situation.[23] Thus, though both Adler and Jung were making identical teleological criticisms of the Lockean position, and as we shall see later even Freud's adaptation of energies bears the stamp of intentionality, there seemed to be little appreciation among the three giants of the task they shared. They did not grasp each other's theoretical intentions accurately!

Adler was clearly the least moved to meet the needs of conventional science. He stayed completely within the realm of psychological explanation—at least after his break with Freud. He once observed: "The study of instincts or urges will never enable us to understand the structure of an individual psyche: and it is interesting to note that psychologists who endeavour to explain the mind's working from such observations instinctively presuppose a style of life without noticing that they have done so."[24] Hence, Adler's psychology is far easier to grasp than is the psychology of Freud or Jung. He does not cloud issues with energic reductions of "common sense" understandings. He eschews the Lockean model at this point, even though he is not a complete Kantian in the sense discussed previously. He sees no need to give his psychology what he took to be the artificial sound of a natural science by recasting mentality into energic terminology.

Freud and Jung were far more conventional; they were striving to weld the older sciences to their newly emerging conceptions by retaining certain terminological ties—analogically, if in no other way. They spoke of energies, but if one reads them carefully it is clear that their energies were of a different type than the classical conceptions. Unfortunately, theories are not often read so carefully, and thus great confusion abounds about the meanings of Freudian and Jungian energies. Adler thus seems to have taken the clearest psychological tack here, even though he lost a certain prestige by not giving the classical "scientific" sound to his ideas.

Psychoanalysis and the Dialectical Side of Human Behavior

The clearest example Freud ever found that people do not act the way the Lockean model called for involved the law of contradiction. Freud discovered that people are simply not very logical: "The logical laws of thought do not apply in the id, and this is true above all of the law of contradiction."[25] In the dream life and in the unconscious generally, things both are and are not at the same time.[26] One can feel love *and* hate for someone at the same time. Something can be true *and* false in the psyche. Due to his personal introspective efforts, Freud was convinced of this oddity in mental life, and he tells us that he once had this "strange state of mind in which one knows and does not know a thing at the same time."[27] Though he accepted the Lockean substrate assumptions regarding energies, we doubt that Freud could ever accept Locke's view that simple ideas as *indivisible* units added up to more complex ideas in a quasi-mathematical fashion. Psychically speaking, when one deals with the content of ideas, *nothing is indivisible*. There is always the opposite meaning implied in those idea contents which have natural contradictories, as when "up" implies "down" or "truth" implies "falsity" (see the Introduction).

Thus Freud embraced a dialectical conception of man, beginning in his very first paper on antithetical ideas and counterwills, and extending through his typical ploy of opposing one personality identity (ego vs. id) or instinct (Eros vs. Death) with another to account for man's behavior. And, as can be seen in the extended quote regarding the ego vs. the sexual instincts in the previous section, the *essential* feature of Freud's energies is that *they behaved dialectically*. It was not merely the instinctual drive or its "energy" which provided the dynamics of motion for Freud, but *always* energy as stimulated and *then opposed* by another, oppositional (antithetical) energy which called for compromise in repression, projection, sublimation, or reaction-formation. Energies which are expended in physics never require "strategies" to manipulate countering censors by way of meaningful parapraxes. Demonstrative theories of energy make no allowance for such ploy and counterploy. Energies conceived demonstratively merely run off along the path of least resistance as true "conservation of energy" implies. In the Freudian unconscious there is trickery and deceit, bargaining and counterbargaining, until a synthesis which is satisfactory to all sides has been reached. But this synthesis is more akin to a struck bargain than to a dissipation of gases within a fixed region. We will have to keep this theme alive throughout subsequent sections, for to understand why Freud's energies performed this way it is necessary to take up the basic meaning constructs.

There are some excellent concrete examples of Freud dealing with what are clearly dialectical issues. In 1910, some 15 years after his antithetic ideas paper, Freud returned to this topic in a work entitled "The Antithetical Meaning of Primal Words."[28] The text was based upon the work of the philologist Karl Abel, and it delighted Freud for Abel had evidence to suggest that in the earliest known examples of human languages, such as Egyp-

tian, "there are a fair number of words with two meanings, one of which is the exact opposite of the other."[29] Abel contended that man's earliest mental concepts emerged as an undifferentiated total, which subsumed opposites, and only by guessing from context could one man understand what another man was referring to (note the "one" and "many" thesis implied here; see p. 6). Thus, the concept of strength doubtless first expressed the contrary ideas of strong vs. weak. It was this relationship between opposite meanings that man first captured in language as a single term. Meanings were thus bipolar and not, as Locke would have it, unipolar or indivisible! Freud also liked to use a writing style in his longer papers which took on a Socratic, dialectical tone. That is, Freud presented his case to an imaginary opponent, who countered with questions and challenges in opposition to his contentions.[30] In fact, Freud's basic writing style has this polemical feature in which he often raises objections "for the reader" before carrying on his line of thought.

Even so, Freud was unaware of the intellectual tradition within which he theorized, and he would in fact have rejected the "appellation" of dialectician. He equated dialectic with sophistry or senseless argumentation, motivated by more personal than scientific reasons. He makes this attitude clear in the following: "I have never been able to convince myself of the truth of the maxim that strife is the father of all things. I believe it is derived from the Greek sophists and is at fault, like them, through overvaluing dialectics."[31] These are strange words from a man who fought the resistance of the censor, broke with most of his former mentors and students, said of himself that he always needed an enemy to oppose as well as a close friend in whom to confide, stood against a generation of his fellow scientists confident in the belief that they were too threatened or constricted by their own sexual repressions to look objectively at the truth, and who spent the larger part of his life in dialectical exchanges, with patients, with students, and with the readers of his books. Only Freud, the man who could give the most banal acts an oppositional twist to set one's head spinning, could also in 1937 dismiss the dialectic with a cool sentence in a letter to R. L. Worall concerning Marxian theory: "As to the 'dialectic', I am no clearer, even after your letter."[32] Since Freud viewed dialectical analysis as sophistry, could it be that he did not wish to find the obvious parallels between his method and this classical method of coming to know experience? We shall never know, but we *can* at least take the position that Freud was a dialectician of major proportions in the history of thought.[33]

Adler was equally distrustful of dialectical strategies, and after he left the Freudian camp he positively opposed any oppositional type of theoretical formulation. In one sense this rejection of the dialectic is all the more remarkable for Adler than it was for Freud, because the founder of individual psychology was admittedly influenced by neo-Marxists. It is not unusual to find Marxian phrasings in Adler's early papers, as in the 1913 reference to "inner contradictions."[34] Adler frankly acknowledged parallels between his assessment of society and the writings of Marx and Engels,[35] though as we saw in Chapter 2, he rejected communism as a totalitarian, unsuitable philosophy for the advance of society.

The early Adlerian constructs of a neurotic's reversal tendencies[36] or attraction to antithetic formulations[37] are clearly in the vein of dialectical theorizing—reminding us somewhat of Freud's paper on antithetic ideas! The basic meaning of compensation—as a reaction to felt inferiority—is also dialectical in tone. Adler seems to have been aware of this dialectical approach in his theories of compensation[38] as well as psychic hermaphroditism.[39] While presenting the latter theory in 1911, Adler reasoned aloud for the compensating male: "The thought, 'I wish to become a man,' is only made tenable and only becomes bearable when joined to the contrasting thought:—'I might also become a woman' or 'I do not wish to become a woman.' "[40] Adler's subsequent theories of male vs. female protest can thus be viewed as stemming from this basic, essentially Marxian theme of a "contradiction between opposites." However, as time went on Adler found that dialectical theories were unfruitful and even harmful.

It is well known that it is difficult to rid ourselves of this manner of thinking; for instance, to regard hot and cold as opposites when we know scientifically that the only difference is a difference in degree of temperature. Not only do we find this antithetic scheme of apperception very frequently among children but we also find it in the beginnings of philosophical science. The early days of Greek philosophy are dominated by this idea of opposites. Even to-day almost every amateur philosopher tries to measure values by means of opposites. Some of them have even established tables—life-death, above-below, and finally, man-woman. There is a significant similarity between the present childish and the old philosophic scheme of apperception, and we may assume that those people who are accustomed to divide the world into sharp contrasts have retained their childish way of thinking.[41]

Dialectic led to error and hence was an unacceptable intellectual strategy, one which hopefully would be evolved out of existence in favor of a more straightforward, honest style of thought which did not require guile or trickery to twist reality into a selfish viewpoint. In the late 1920s Adler observed: "Individuals who do not regard their life's structure from a logical and objective point of view are for the most part unable to see the coherence and consistency of their behavior pattern."[42] This is a decided alteration in outlook for a man who had begun by championing the *subjective* reality of each individual. As he located his extra- or super-individual standard for reality in the teleological direction of evolution Adler found it increasingly easy to pass judgment on the supposed errors—dialectically arrived at, to be sure—of the individual human being.

Adler once named the dialectic as a procedure of motion in therapy, capturing the stylized movements of change over time but not in any way responsible for how this change came about; he discussed it as follows: "Dialectics in the sense of thesis, antithesis, and synthesis is, of course, found in our view as in the other social sciences. It becomes apparent most often when we are dealing with persons who expect to be spoiled by others (thesis). When they do not receive such treatment, they fall into hate and resentment (antithesis), until they find their way through to contribution, to general humaneness (synthesis)."[43] This example is improper as dialectic, because the thesis in this case (desire to be spoiled) is not truly an opposite or the contradiction of the antithesis (hatred for those who do not provide the spoiling). The true opposite would be something quite different (fear of being spoiled, for example). Moreover, the individual could easily endure both reactions without feeling a need to resolve any implicit contradiction in the example cited.

However, the point of such examples is to emphasize that Adler's image of man was *not* an organism fraught with internal contradiction. This is not man's natural state. We only find contradiction when the individual is selfishly trying to maintain a life style in opposition to what he either knows or *can* know is the proper (realistic) way in which to strive (that is, via social interest). This selfishness was first noted in the religions of mankind, and psychology would do well to reject it rather than to further it by acting as dialectical apologist for those who set themselves in opposition to evolution: ". . . the 'contradictory character' of man, as the deepest of Christian insights, first becomes evident, in our view, when the erring individual, on the road to initial improvement of his social interest, no longer can defend his error as strongly as before. The apparent contradiction in the neurotic does not lead to change in the neurotic attitude. As long as there is contradiction, only

one thing is certain: no change will set in."[44] The seeming contradictory nature of the neurotic is merely an artifact of growing social interest, which at one point makes the neurotic person seem doubt-laden. But to misconstrue this condition and somehow reify such inner turbulence as man's most basic nature is to confound the truth completely. This rejection of dialectical formulations merges nicely with Adler's growing Lockeanism in his final theories. He clearly saw the course of evolution as unidirectional, pointing to the demonstratively "true" direction, and he was not about to provide rationalizations for those who would deviate in the name of their supposedly self-contradictory natures. Individual psychology is thus less "dynamic" in its formulations than typical psychoanalytical or analytical psychologies.

Jung was without doubt the most conscious, thorough, and outspokenly sagacious dialectician of the founding fathers. He was philosophically the most well-read and sophisticated scholar of the group. He once said, "I see in all that happens the play of opposites. . . ."[45] Jung's catchword of "balance," and his logical phenomenology both rest on the view of a kind of individualized dialectic, at work within the psyche of each man. Referring to one of the most dialectical philosophers of history, Georg W. F. Hegel, Jung once opined that he had simply projected the subjective truths of his psyche onto the external environment.[46] Hegel had read his subjective dialectic into the movement of history, seeing the flow of thesis to antithesis and eventually a new synthesis as taking place objectively. Whether we agree with Jung's analysis or not, it is surely accurate to say that Jung's dialectic was introverted whereas the dialectic of Hegel was extraverted. Hegel and Marx sought their solutions for man's plight in the externalized world of historical and material forces. As we know from Chapter 3, Jung looked inward for man's solutions, and he was suspicious of such grand utopian designs, believing as he did that they were often based upon the projections of an individual under the sway (possession) of a mana personality archetype. Indeed, he once suggested that Hegel had megalomaniac tendencies in his distortion of objective reality.[47]

Jung's approach to the dialectic was more akin to that of Kierkegaard[48] (see Chapter 10). He thus viewed it as the grounds for all thought, as a subjectively necessary outcome of mental activity. There is no Kantian premise which mind takes on that cannot also be countered with an opposite position. In a sense, by affirming one point of view we *must* create its obverse, as an equally plausible alternative or possibility.[49] This is the nature of man's conceptualizing ability: "We name a thing, *from a certain point of view,* good or bad, high or low, right or left, light or dark, and so forth. Here the antithesis is just as factual and real as the thesis."[50] This inevitability is a bother and a problem for man, says Jung, because he naturally assumes that opposites are different and hence a decision must be made between them when both sides are implied.

That is, in the world of practical affairs it is often necessary to be consistent, which entails avoiding contradictions. The "law of contradiction" as a demonstrative logical principle thus appeals to us as "rational" men. Although external affairs may call for a one-sidedness of this sort, Jung did not believe that the psyche was best understood in terms of the law of contradiction. The *paradox,* for example, is one of man's most valuable psychical possessions.[51] It is only through an acceptance of paradoxes that we come anywhere near comprehending the fullness of life. Most of the paradoxes from which man has taken inspiration and gained new insights as regards the meaning of life stem from his religious views—as, in the belief of a Man God (Pharaoh or Christ), the Holy Trinity, and so forth. Since man has been undeniably drawn to such paradoxical beliefs, often holding them to his death, Jung felt it was only good sense to picture him in this dialectically framed fashion.

And yet, Jung bemoaned, the price one has to pay for this honest and objective description of man was the label of being a "mystic."[52] Jung's mysticism, as we have seen in Chapter 3, is a greatly overdrawn criticism usually advanced by demonstratively inclined critics who have no appreciation for what Jung was about. Viewed now in light of a dialectical logic, much of what goes by the name of mysticism—the directly unprovable, the use of nonmaterial constructs, the vaguely phrased analogue or symbol-expressing meaning just beyond our conscious grasp—can be understood and appreciated. If man is a dialectical as well as a demonstrative reasoner, then there is nothing "mystical" about those dialectically generated turns of mind which concoct fantastic ideas transcending reality, demonstrative logic, or empirical proof. Nor is it inconsistent to see the same person holding two or more contradictory views *at the same time!* Though Adler had no appreciation of this conception, surely Freud and Jung have a rationale for the multiple identities within the psyche (ego, id, superego, complexes, personae, and so forth) based simply on the view that meanings are bipolar. It is not that there are "little people" or homunculae populating the Freudian or Jungian psyche. Rather, there are multiple views—all possible—generated and thence interlacing within the single identity (the "one" among "many"). This is why we can argue with ourselves, see good points to both sides of an issue, and find it so difficult to make up our minds about what it is that we "really want to do."

Jung did not argue that the content of the belief systems held to by religions or alchemy were themselves "true." The psyche is real and its dialectically framed projections go to make up fantastic religious beliefs or megalomaniacal philosophies once they are projected onto reality by the individual or by an entire group of people. There are meanings expressed in these projections which may not be reducible to a demonstrative logic of the "primary and true," but this is no reason for dismissing their validity as *psychical* products. Thus, when the Catholic Church identified evil as the "absence of good," Jung was critical because this was a demonstrative—a unipolar—solution (see Chapter 3, p. 187). There was *only* good in the world, there was no active principle of evil. Experience had taught Jung that as a projection from the psyche the dialectical opposition of good and evil was essential, hence this one-sided demonstrative solution violated the most basic nature of man's psyche. After many years of study, Jung concluded that everything in the mind has at least two sides and sometimes several more as well. He even went so far as to say: "It is my belief that the problem of opposites . . . should be made the basis for a critical psychology."[53]

Substance Construct Meanings

Though he constantly emphasized that psychoanalysis has its biological underpinnings,[54] very early in his career Freud came to see that the mental sphere seemed to require concepts and study in its own right.[55] We have already documented his views on reductionism and the quasi-material "sound" he gave to libido as analogous to a fluid or hinting that it had a possible other molecular structure (gaseous, electrical). Freud once said that he hoped to capture the *action* of mind, and that he viewed structural aspects as a necessary instrumentality to this end. He then added:

It will soon be clear what the mental apparatus is [topographical structure]; but I must beg you not to ask what material it is constructed of. That is not a subject of psychological interest. Psychology can be indifferent to it as, for instance, optics can be to the question of whether the walls of a telescope are made of metal or cardboard. We shall leave entirely on the side the *material* line of approach, but not so the *spatial* one.[56]

Freud believed that everyone has the same innate disposition to perverse acts, so that we cannot account for them solely through transmission of an abnormal germ plasm or some such.[57] He rather emphatically held that no physiological or other chemical processes could account for the psychological findings of psychoanalysis.[58] For this reason Freud could give no clear role to the area of animal study for psychoanalysis.[59] As to anatomical structure, Freud had spent considerable time in such study while working for Brücke. After he had founded his own approach he remarked that though the medulla oblongata was a very serious and lovely object, which he had once dissected in great detail, "I know nothing that could be of less interest to me for the psychological understanding of anxiety than a knowledge of the path of the nerves along which its excitations pass."[60] What he *did* always admit through constructs like the "actual neuroses" and his recognition of obvious factors like brain damage and other toxic involvements, was that some forms of mental illness—probably as many as 50 per cent—could be seen as biological in origin.[61]

Though he was a dualist, Freud did not consider himself an advocate of what is sometimes called a "psychophysical parallelism." Some of his interpreters have used this term referring to his work, but Freud found this reference to a *parallel* invariably detrimental to psychoanalysis because it led to an identification of the "psyche" with "conscious mind" or simply "consciousness."[62] Since there were no parallels to be cited between conscious and unconscious levels of mind, he could see little benefit in speculating on the parallels between a physical and an exclusively conscious sphere of experience. For Freud, *mind* is what matters, and unconscious mind takes precedence over conscious mind.

Freud actually wished to be spared the necessity of having to concoct bodily constructs. What he did as a result was to accept the *instincts* (including the pleasure principle) as his basic connection between mind and body. As we documented in Chapter 1, this rather vague construct played a central—if changing—role in his theory precisely because it did lift him out of the biological and place him in the psychological realm. As he said: "Instincts and their transformations are at the limit of what is discernible by psychoanalysis. From that point it gives place to biological research. . . . We will not, however, leave the ground of purely psychological research. Our aim remains that of demonstrating the connection along the path of instinctual activity between a person's external experiences and his reactions. . . ."[63] Instincts are presumably fixed by nature, and they set energies free in the mind to run the structure. It is here, in the mental sphere, that Freud wished to do his theorizing.

As the father of organic inferiority, Adler is often mistakenly credited with having been a major advocate of substance constructs. He once said that he felt a little guilty for having paved the way for theories of heredity both in neurology and psychiatry.[64] Shortly after he had set out on his theoretical way by introducing the concept of the aggression drive Adler found that he invariably had to go beyond this construct in order to do his job as a psychologist. In 1908 he defined this construct as follows: "The aggression drive means to us a sum of sensations, excitations, and their discharges. . . . the organic and functional substratum of which is innate. As with the primary drives, the excitation of the aggression drive is set off by the relation of drive strength to demands from the environment."[65] This is a conventional medical-biological description of how man supposedly initiates behavior. The trouble is, Adler found that to explain what takes place in behavior it is essential to bring in directions, aspirations, and future orientations. Some men use their anger to bully others; they do not have "more" of this innate drive than anyone else. They simply find this a convenient instrumentality to achieve their ends. Adler thus came

to realize that he could tell more from the individual's assessment (prototype) of the socio-psychological situation than he could from such presumed substance-impetus propellers of behavior.[66]

Adler did not think that all attempts to relate physique or other organic factors to temperament were fruitless or meaningless. Although he at times criticized Kretschmer, who claimed that individual differences in personality might someday be traced to hormonal differences in the blood, Adler was also much impressed by such convincing demonstrations of the relationship between behavior and structure as the constitutional theorists advanced.[67] He said that Kretschmer's work in particular was a brilliant beginning to the understanding of how man's evolutionary advance can reflect the laws of movement which brought him to where he is today, albeit in a self-directed (teleological) sense. Returning to his Darwinian emphasis, Adler now adds the pattern construct meaning to a substance conception when he observes: "The plasticity of the living form certainly has its limits, but, within these limits movement has its own effect. In the stream of time this remains the same for generations, peoples, races. Movement becomes moulded movement—form. Thus it is possible to gain a knowledge of mankind from form, if we recognize in it the movement that shapes it."[68]

Coming back to the pyramid of life in Figure 18, Adler is now saying that one can see in the teleological direction taken by the "course of evolution" the exertion of what might be termed a will-to-evolve or, in his terms, to overcome by striving for perfection *framed within man's very physique*. Hence: "One must assume . . . that organic evolution has led to developments which we must regard as the differentiation of originally present potentialities of the cell. Thus a nutritive organ has followed the will and need of assimilation; touch, auditory, and visual organs have followed the will and necessity to feel, hear, and see; a procreative organ followed the will and necessity for progeny."[69] We have as human beings hands of a certain convolution because we have desired certain goals in life and behaved in a certain way (moved by reaching, grasping) in order to achieve these ends. The history of mankind's past movements is therefore written in the preformed shapes of our bodies as we come into existence. This is a clear substance usage in Adlerian thought, one which is virtually identical to the Jungian treatment of the preformed archetype in the *psychic* evolution of mankind!

That is, Jung's concept of the psyche as a racial inheritance (archetypes) is *less* dependent on substance construct meanings than is Adler's at this point. Moreover, Jung's concept of the psyche is as teleological as Adler's, a fact reflected in the following: "Just as, in its lower reaches, the psyche loses itself in the organic-material substrate, so in its upper reaches it resolves itself into a 'spiritual' form about which we know as little as we do about the functional basis of instinct. What I would call the psyche proper extends to all functions which can be brought under the influence of a will. Pure instinctuality allows no consciousness to be conjectured and needs none."[70] Since Jung clearly believed that it was not necessary to reduce the mental to the physical, and since he constantly spoke of the inheritance of archetypal prefigurations, it follows that he did *not* think of heredity only in organic (substance construct) terms. Jung was thus unwilling to confound psychological with organic factors; he once summarized his view as follows: ". . . anyone who penetrates into the unconscious with purely biological assumptions will become stuck in the instinctual sphere [as conventionally defined] and be unable to advance beyond it, for he will be pulled back again and again into physical existence."[71]

As Freud had done, Jung united the physical and the physiological through his *instinct* construct, which he defined less conventionally as "a very mysterious manifestation of life partly psychic and partly physiological by nature."[72] What distinguished the latter from the former? The presence of a teleology, as preformed by the Kantian a priori (the archetype): "An instinct does not apprehend its object blindly and at random, but brings to it a certain psychic 'viewpoint' or interpretation; for every instinct is linked *a priori* with a corresponding image of the situation, as can be proved indirectly in cases of the symbiosis of plant and animal."[73] When he next came to define *energy* Jung made it clear that his was something quite different than the physicist's conception.[74] He noted: "The idea of energy is not that of a substance moved in space; it is a concept abstracted from relations of movement."[75] In other words, as we look at the phenomenon of motion, energy as a theoretical term does not demand that we reduce such actions to a substantial entity "pushing" this or that about. Energy is merely a description of the *degree*—possibly quantitatively expressed—to which motion actually takes place. Substance meanings are thus irrelevant to an energic construct.

Although Jung was reluctant to emphasize substance construct meanings in his broader personality theory, he *did* certainly propose such a concept in his suggestion that schizophrenia might by caused by an unknown toxin. As we noted in Chapter 3, this was a very sketchy theory, but he referred to it in 1907[76] and again in 1956[77] when psychiatric research was beginning to suggest that psychotic-like states could be induced by the ingestion of a drug (mescaline). Thus, we would have to say that Jung was not above using a substance construct meaning on occasion. But even in this case, his final statement on the subject in 1957 emphasizes the psychological (feeling tones) rather than the physical forces *per se*: "To make myself clear, I consider the aetiology of schizophrenia to be a dual one: namely, up to a certain point psychology is indispensable in explaining the nature and the causes of the initial emotions which give rise to metabolic alterations. These emotions seem to be accompanied by chemical processes that cause specific temporary or chronic disturbances or lesions."[78]

Impetus Construct Meanings

Since he favored the Lockean reductionistic emphasis, Freud apparently believed that he had to underwrite his psychological explanations of mind with an energy concept. Though he did not use it in a physical sense throughout his career, the *constancy principle* (Chapter 1, p. 36) may be viewed as a contribution from Breuer which provided the substrate "impetus" to behavior by way of energy. Freud's peculiar twist, as we have seen, was to oppose *two* basic forces in dialectical clash and by way of compromise to effect a "dynamic" impetus in behavior. The constancy principle in itself would not be theoretically sufficient to explain the intricacies of Freudian psychology. The movement of a "blind" energy acting as substrate to all motion is better suited to the demonstrative line of descent, if we are to limit our description of behavior to this alone. Such blind energies might be said to come into conflict, but this would be an unnatural state of affairs in the demonstrative-Lockean world view. Freud found man to be a "clever work of fiction," a being fraught with contradictions and self-defeating actions, who was *never* likely to express his energic promptings in some fixed, mechanical way. Freud believed that if we remove the intrapersonal turmoil from the man we lose what is peculiarly human about him.[79]

Thus, the *real* Freudian insight always comes from the patterned "reasons for" libido expenditure, what is sometimes called "content" of Freudian mental maneuvers. Such contents are rephrased in energic terms but the *essential* meaning is never carried by the impetus con-

struct. Freud used an honest subterfuge in this rephrasing, a theoretical compromise of his own, to convince many of his followers that he was of a common mind with his Germanic "toughminded" background.[80] The energies of the body are surely demonstrative in tone: so many caloric units of energy taken in, weighed against so many caloric units expended in exercise, translates into so much weight (potential energy) gained or lost. The homeostasis of body functions is a beautiful example of a perfectly running Lockean theory. But this conception is not Freudian.

Why not? Why could we not think of intake calories of energy in food value and outgoing calories of energy in daily exercise as dialectical opposites, leading to a certain level of bodily weight analogical to Freud's symptom formation in the compromise model? Because in homeostasis we have: (1) a *fixed* and nonnegotiable ratio of the contribution made by the two parties in mathematical fashion, and to that extent no compromise at all; (2) the parties to the "compromise" have no bargaining power through strategy, so that an advantage cannot be won by either side, as is possible in Freudian psychology, where even a weaker party (less energy) might win a temporary or minor advantage; (3) the choice as to type of compromise—whether a dream, parapraxis, or symptom—is not possible, as is true of Freudian psychology. All of which goes to say that a standard (demonstrative) homeostasis model lends a mechanical, unintelligent coloring to the mental bargaining of an intrapersonal compromise. This is the very antithesis of the dialectical Freudian psychology, where guile, strategy, and timing all enter into the game of self-deception.

There is another way in which the impetus construct meaning can be seen in Freudian theory. This fundamental impulsion of mind is so basic to his entire theory that we can refer to it as the "big question" of psychoanalysis. We are referring to Freud's claim that the unconscious has "a natural 'upward drive.'"[81] Freud rests the edifice of psychoanalysis on the major premise which we might phrase as: *Unconscious mental contents seek expression.* If unconscious mental contents did not seek expression in consciousness—including motor action—then there would be no need for a counterwill or anticathexis (repression). Freud made it appear that this was a "natural" propensity for mental contents to seek expression, analogical to the tendency gases have to escape when released from containers. Some students of Freud continue to view this impulsion of the unconscious for self-expression in conventional (impetus) energy terms, but we are not confident that it is best understood in this manner and would like to return to the "big question" of psychoanalysis when we consider the intentional construct meanings.

In line with his indifference toward a proper natural science reductive explanation, Adler attacked the tendency to explain behavior exclusively on the basis of impulsion in many of his writings. He took the founder of behaviorism, John Watson, to task for overlooking teleological factors in human behavior.[82] The reflex arc conceptions, which had man a Lockean input-output creature were for Adler grotesque caricatures of the human condition (see Chapter 6 for an overview of behaviorism, pp. 283–290). Adler said the Watsonian psychology of "stimuli and reactions" was more suitable to biology and physiology than it was to human behavior in a social context.[83] Man is not moved by blind drives or energies which are outside of his intentional control. When Adler referred to an energy he spoke of a "creative energy," meaning the capacity the individual has to lay down his prototype and thence to carry it forward and make it into a reality. The energy is creative precisely because it is directional in nature, sometimes only vaguely understood or *intuited;* the point is that it must be viewed from the introspective perspective as a teleological construct.[84] The behaviorist's energies were blindly mechanistic because they were construed extraspectively, as "acting

upon" behavior rather than having behavior fashion them in directed ways.

Adler realized that the science of his day was heavily dependent upon methods which had been propounded almost exclusively on the basis of an impetus construct meaning. The concept of *lawfulness* in behavior, for example, was continually put forward by experimental psychologists like Wundt and Watson to buttress their theories of man as a mechanism. Adler felt that psychological experimentation in the laboratories broke the life style down into artificial units, and hence failed to teach us about personality as a totality, with its goal directedness intact.[85] And as for the lawfulness of behavior, Adler challenged the assumption that the kind of *necessity* we witness in natural events is directly comparable to the behaviors we witness in man: "It may be asserted that when a stone falls to the ground, it must fall in a certain direction and with a certain speed. But the investigations made by Individual Psychology give it the right to claim that in a psychic 'fall' strict causality does not play a role—only bigger or smaller mistakes which, after they are made, affect the future development of the individual."[86] By "strict causality" Adler means the automatic stimulus-response conception of impetus-motion over time. Adler has a distinctive view of determinism, and we shall return to it later.

Interestingly, Jung actually believed that Freud had succumbed to a Lockean fallacy, reducing everything seen "now" in behavior to something literally causing it in the past.[87] The existentialists of Chapter 10 make a similar criticism of Freud. Jung equated the Freudian reductive method of explanation with the reductive method of those psychologists like Wundt, who distrusted things actually seen empirically (secondary qualities) in favor of something "supposedly" more fundamental (primary qualities). Invariably, this more basic "something" was a substance or impetus construction; usually both meanings were used. Jung said that mechanists always bring substance construct meanings into their theories because something must "bump" something else to move it along, even if we get down to atomic structures in our reductions.[88]

Jung espoused what he called a *final-energic* view of impetus, in opposition to the *causal-mechanistic* view held by most psychologists. His theory of energy (libido) thus emphasized the directionality (teleological, hormic) properties of an entire field of changing conditions. In the causal-mechanistic view things seem to change by being essentially "bumped from behind" over time, thanks to the determinism of antecedent events (impetus construct). Jung felt this was a short-sighted and narrow conception of change, and he succeeded in taking this time element out of his explanation of psychic change. In the final-energic view psychical change results from a rearranging of events "all at once," in which case the total amount of energy is constant and never "used up," as it is in the antecedent-consequent bumping of events over time. Physical energies burn up by moving events over time in this fashion. But in the final-energic view energy is *not* the instrumentality for motion; it plays an important valuative role (libido is both teleological and indicative of the individual's value preferences). To underwrite this view Jung relied, as we saw in Chapter 3, on the principle of constancy, with its corollary principles of equivalence and entropy. Since this is a rather complex point we would do well to quote Jung at length on his view of change:

The causal-mechanistic view sees the sequence of facts, *a-b-c-d*, as follows: *a* causes *b, b* causes *c*, and so on. Here the concept of effect appears as the designation of a quality, as a 'virtue' of the cause, in other words, as a dynamism. The final-energic view, on the other hand, sees the sequence thus: *a-b-c* are means toward the transformation of energy, which flows causelessly from *a*, the improbable state, entropically to *b-c* and so to the probable state *d*. Here a causal effect is totally disregarded, since only intensities of effect are taken into account. In so far as the intensities are

the same, we could just as well put *w-x-y-z* instead of *a-b-c-d*.

The datum of experience is in both cases the sequence *a-b-c-d,* with the difference that the mechanistic view infers a dynamism from the causal effect observed, while the energic view observes the equivalence of the transformed effect rather than the effect of a cause. That is to say, both observe the sequence *a-b-c-d,* the one qualitatively, the other quantitatively.[89]

As causal mechanists we would observe the flow of psychic events, and be drawn to what is different over time, what has changed, the dynamism (impetus) of cause-to-qualitative-effect. As final-energic theorists we would be more impressed by how nothing has changed qualitatively except that redistribution has taken place. Harking back to the "many" and "one" thesis of the Introduction (see p. 6), we would note how the totality of energic forces has remained "one" among the many changes which seem to be taking place. What would draw our attention would be the *direction* of the changing psychic forces. Where does the pitch of *a-b-c-d* point to? What is the behavioral intent of the supposed energic "cause-effects"?

This extension of change to an entire region or system *without time* as a major principle of explanation places Jung squarely on the side of gestalt psychology and is a further reflection of his logical phenomenology (see Chapters 9, 10, and 12). The figure-ground constructs of a Kurt Koffka (1935) or the field theory of a Kurt Lewin (1951) are comparable attempts to substitute the one-in-many thesis (a pattern construct meaning) for the antecedent-consequent (impetus) view of causality (see Chapter 12, p. 512). Though we are anticipating the next section, it is propitious to observe that Jung's treatment helps us to grasp what he meant by *synchronicity*. Viewed from within the total energic system across time and even space, strange events which do not "make sense" as cause-effect (impetus) changes might be unfathomable due to our narrow view of the totality. If we could see the total picture and grasp how events are shaping up directionally, then what seems to be an acausal event may in fact be one of these patterned rearrangements of energy within the total system. Thus, even more so than Freud or Adler, Jung dared to go beyond the substance and impetus constructs to paint a picture of man with heavy reliance upon a sophisticated use of the pattern and intentional constructions.

Pattern Construct Meanings

We come now to a construct meaning which Freud employed repeatedly. Psychoanalysis is *post hoc* because Freud always sought some "style" or "pattern" of behavior from out of the past which could now enlighten us regarding the patient's psychological state in the present. Freud was cognizant of his approach to the study of clients, and he accurately traced this analytical method to his interlude with the French. He once observed that, whereas in Germany the clinicians were attracted to physiological interpretations of symptoms, in France the preferred technique was careful observation and classification of patient symptoms into a typology independent of physical constructs.[90] Freud referred to his French master, Charcot, in glowing terms which reflected this contrast in approach as follows: ". . . he [Charcot] can find no rest till he has correctly described and classified some phenomenon with which he is concerned, but that he can sleep quite soundly without having arrived at the physiological explanation of that phenomenon."[91]

Freud took strength from Charcot when he found it necessary to depart from the Lockean "substrate" explanation—at least in the sense of a physical substrate (he *did* retain the psychical substrate of energies). He let his natural curiosity take hold and ignored a medical-physical bias as he studied his clients through use of introspective constructs. It was not long until he was saying to Fliess in 1897: "Perverse actions . . . are always the same—with a meaning and made on some pattern which it will be possible to understand."[92] From this basic premise, Freud goes on to see infantile sucking at the breast as the prototype for adult sexual gratification,[93] sexual intercourse as the prototype for an anxiety attack, the mother figure as prototype for the selection of a mate by a man,[94] the universal symbol as prototype for the "given" conflict manifestation in a dream, and so forth. The prototype for the Oedipal situation is the original conflict in the primitive family, and the prototype for the transformed neurosis is the neurosis as then being worked through in real life. Everywhere we turn to in Freud we can see pattern constructs used as analogical templets, drawn from one phase of life and placed over another. The child is father (prototype) to the man in Freudian psychology as never before in history.

Freud really could not be considered the father of modern personality theory if he had not been so drawn to the pattern construct, which literally made him into a *discriminal* theorist. Personality as the style of human behavior demands a theoretician who is interested in defining certain replicable, internally consistent patterns in the behavior of others—especially from an introspective perspective. Freud's character types (oral, anal, etc.), which we now use in a trait sense, take their fundamental meaning from the pattern construct. Whereas his medical peers may have used a pattern construct in their extraspective diagnostic efforts—e.g., in the notion of a "syndrome" of tuberculosis or dementia praecox—Freud began a new era of theorizing by framing introspective propensities drawn from childhood and then re-enacted in adulthood as orality or anality. The breakdown of the personality into three distinctive features of id, ego, and superego is also primarily a pattern construct maneuver. In fact, therapeutic "insight" is essentially the grasping of a parallel by way of similarity between "this situation" in the present and "that situation" in the past. Freud's reductive attempts are primarily of this sort, and when Jung criticizes him for this proclivity we must keep in mind that this is quite a different reduction than the Wundtian attempt to explain mental contents by way of underlying physical mechanisms.

Freud may have been wrong in assigning *too* much meaning to the actions of people, but this is nevertheless the heritage of the psycho-analyst. He comes to know meanings held in that side of mind which the average person never confronts. He explains to his client something the client knows and yet does not know at the same time. Hence, except for some terminological refinements to make his thought clear, the analyst stays within the language content of his client. It is not even necessary to speak of mental energies (libido) to the client for him to gain an insight from psychoanalysis. What is the client intending to say or to do from out of the unconscious? That is what counts and what enriches the analytical literature with a psychology of man unlike any other in the history of thought.

It is from the Adlerian (Kantian) assumption that man is a meaning-creating animal that the reliance on pattern constructions flows. Adler's holism is tied to his pattern construct emphasis. Just as we have seen him arguing that movements take on forms in the substance of bodily physiques, so too does he argue that the behavior of an individual man in his unique life takes on a stylized pattern transcending any sort of (Lockean) analysis of details. As he said: "The style of life takes command of all expressive forms—the whole rules the parts."[95] We recognize in this treatment a variant use of the one-in-many thesis. As individual psychologists we would not build our understanding of behavior by the accumulation of many facts about the individual. We would, instead, make a guess about the totality of his pattern, and suggest the one overriding style in

order to grasp the connecting pattern of the many seeming unrelated events occurring in his behavior.

Some people have seen in this holistic emphasis a leaning toward gestalt psychology in individual psychology. Gestalt theory is, of course, fraught with the one-in-many thesis, and it is far more Kantian in tone than Adlerian theory (see Chapters 9 and 12). Although similar in this minor aspect, what differentiates Adler from the gestalt theorists is his reliance upon a teleology in the Darwinian theory he espoused. The completely phenomenological gestaltist would find it impossible to accept Adler's emphasis on the "mistakes" in perception made by those individuals who fail to follow evolution's lead. The gestaltist would find this moulding of one's intentions to that of evolution's direction an arbitrary act, a move to conformity on the individual's part rather than a truly and spontaneously arrived at impulse to totality.

Adler's patterned "one" meant the realities of the group, the hierarchy of organic life, and the very social "order" within which man moved. The gestaltist's "one" is more likely to focus on the totality of perception by the individual. This perception may be in line with the larger group, or it may be at variance with the broader "one." More importantly, the gestalt-phenomenologist could not view such deviations as "mistakes." Adler once observed that individual psychology differed from gestalt psychology in precisely this way; that·is, the former sought to provide a basis for determining the individual's (proper or improper) attitude in confronting life, whereas the latter failed to consider such factors as relevant.[96]

How is it that Adler found it so easy to accept the course of evolution as a standard against which to judge the mistakes of individuals? It seems clear that he came to this view as a result of his general tendency to see patterns in life, patterns of motion or substance "for the sake of which" things occurred. This notion implies a direction to events, a teleological standard for judgment purposes. If evolution is directional and the individual swims against its flow, then we have here a "mistaken life style." The problem which Adler never truly resolved is how to know precisely when to assign directionality to a "natural" pattern. That is, nature has many designs, many patterns which seem to us marvelously intricate and ingeniously fashioned. The pattern of a hurricane has something fascinating about it, even though it wreaks havoc, and no "rational" being—God or man—would *intend* to put such a plan into effect. The patterning of certain diseases in man takes on a "course" which the physician can follow and predict with relative certainty. Yet, is this to say that the succession of events characterized as measles or tuberculosis is working toward an end? Thus, simply having arrayed a pattern in natural evolution (Figure 18) is not sufficient justification for the imputation of a *teleology* in nature. Here is where Adlerian theory begins to make some rather debatable leaps.

It is one thing to assume that a human being has it within his power as natural product to direct his own behavior (human teleology). It is quite another to assume that in producing such an animal, nature has itself been working toward a goal (natural teleology). The most parsimonious explanation of the latter, natural teleology, is simply to view it as a projection of the human intellect onto nature. This is what "anthropomorphizing nature" *should* mean, although many toughminded psychologists feel that ascribing teleologies to the "anthrop-"—i.e., man—is *also* an act of improper anthropomorphization. The question we now pose and hope to answer in the next section is: Do we see teleologies in nature or does our teleologizing human intellect put them there? Adler's "two teleologies" clearly suggest that *both* human and natural teleologies are at play in the universe.[97]

We have already shown how Jung fell back upon a patterned construction in his view of energy. Not only synchronicity but the stylized meaning expression model which accounts for the framing of archetypes, personifications, and complexes can be tied directly to a pattern construct meaning. Freudian and Adlerian prototypes draw roots from the individual family unit, where life plans are put down or fixations weld a repetition-compulsion in the subsequent patterning of a life's dynamic. But Jung's "family" is much broader, extending the preformed and determining aspects of mental life to historical ties eons past.

The most difficult aspect of Jung's archetypal theory stems from his tendency to use phrases like "definite forms in the psyche" or "literally a pre-existent form" to describe them.[98] How is it possible for something which has a definite form *not* to be fixed? Is Jung not really talking about a "universal idea" after all? Jung staunchly rejects the belief in a universal symbolism (see Chapter 3). In terms of our basic meaning constructs, Jung seems to be thinking of his archetype as a "nonspecific form" or really a "formless form." Man's most basic experience is "one" across the centuries. Looked at objectively, the relations with the opposite sex, authority ties, or the finding of oneself as a unique individual within a herd of others are experiences that all men share for all time. In meeting these emerging demands of his humanity man has evolved a brain function called the "psyche" which takes on given "styles" of meaning expression but always in a teleological sense. It intends to express certain basic motifs when such an expression is called for; that is, when the energic dispersion we spoke of above has lost its balance. The *specific form* (pattern) which these motifs take on varies across cultures or "racial histories." The motifs are common patterns of expression because they define man's nature, yet their contents vary because man is a multipatterned animal. And so it is that Jungian psychology is a content psychology, one which seeks to identify the *common* meanings (the "one") in the variegated symbols (the "many") of mankind.

There is a parallel between the way in which Jung thought of archetypes and the activity presently underway in our study of theory construction. When we speak of basic meaning constructs as substance, impetus, pattern, and intention we do *not* claim that in each of the theorist's usages we have the *same* specific patterned meaning content being espoused. Freud's energic theory is not identical to Jung's, although there are similarities. The patterning of Sullivanian theory is dealt with extraspectively whereas classical analysis employed introspective patterned conceptions, and so on. Though we have some overriding notion of what substance or intention means, we do not have a "universal idea" here, since clearly, the thought (ideas) of our theorists varies. In the same way, when Jung speaks of archetypes he is speaking of common themes—such as our metaconstructs—which manifest themselves in various forms across cultures and racial identities. This is the insight of a historian, a man who could not subdivide knowledge into what was supposedly "science" and what was "non-science" even if this meant introducing or employing terminology certain to prejudice the case against him.

Jung was cognizant of the criticism he was open to by insisting upon speaking in mythological terms. Many advocates of analytical psychology urged him to play down his free use of astrological or religious allusions in making a point. But, just as Freud refused to water down the term "sex," Jung refused to mollify critics by denigrating what was for him an essential ingredient of man's nature. As he freely admitted: "I deliberately and consciously give preference to a dramatic, mythological way of thinking and speaking, because this is not only more expressive but also more exact than an abstract scientific terminology, which is wont to toy with the notion that its theoretic formulation may one fine day be resolved into algebraic equations."[99]

Intentional Construct Meanings

Although Freud's use of intentional construct meanings may be seen beginning with his *anticipatory* ideas paper, he made an even greater commitment to intentionality when he moved from the childhood molestation theory to the theory of a fantasied parental seduction (see Chapter 1). If a child is molested sexually before his physical apparatus has matured, and this experience in turn leads to neurosis, then no one can fault the adult neurotic now seated before the psychoanalyst. He has been the victim of an unfortunate occurrence quite independent of his own intentions. But if he is suffering today in part due to a lascivious wish (intended, hoped-for desire) held to in the past, then this is quite another matter. The illness has not simply "happened" to him in an impetus sense alone; he has contributed to it by way of his *purposive* behavior as a child. Freud spoke of the id or the ego as cathecting objects, and some of his interpreters have considered this process to be a mechanical way of fixing energies to environmental items. But in fact, from the very first Freud employed cathexis in an *intentional* sense. Thus, he said: "Tension due to craving prevails in the ego, as a consequence of which the idea of the loved object (the *wishful* idea) is cathected."[100] The ego, id, or superego intentionally cathects a wished-for object, and then "for the sake of" this cathected idea or image, it influences behavior of the total organism to achieve, possess, "get" the object so cathected; or, short of this, to effect the best compromise possible in negotiating with the other aspects of the personality structure.

Freud thus put self-direction back in the realm of scientific explanation which Bacon had much earlier helped to remove (see p. 7). He sums it up nicely in the following: "We seek not merely to describe and to classify phenomena, but to understand them as signs of an interplay of forces in the mind, as a manifestation of purposeful intentions working concurrently or in mutual opposition. We are concerned with a *dynamic view* of mental phenomena."[101] In this sense, Freud's teleology is exclusively introspective in tone whereas Adler has both an introspective (life plan) *and* an extraspective (course of evolution) teleological theory. Jung's teleology was more introspective than extraspective in tone, even though he viewed it as taking shape from generations past. Freud was a decided opponent of those who would view the "march of civilization" in quasi-religious terms. Because he was conventional or traditional in his view of science, Freud was more sensitive than Adler or Jung to the charge of being a teleological thinker. He once apologized for using teleological phrases in his writings.[102] He would have dismissed any suggestion that he formulated a teleological theory along the introspective perspective. Yet, in the following quote a rather clear argument for a human teleology is being voiced by Freud:

> According to our analyses it is not necessary to dispute the right to the feeling of conviction of having a free will. If the distinction between conscious and unconscious motivation is taken into account, our feeling of conviction informs us that conscious motivation does not extend to all our motor decisions. . . . But what is thus left free by the one side receives its motivation from the other side, from the unconscious; and in this way determination in the psychical sphere is still carried out without any gap.[103]

It was customary for Freud to refer to "free will" as an illusion.[104] But he did not reject the possibility of psychic self-direction in human behavior. We are never free of the unconscious influences in mind, so that a consciously "free" choice is psychoanalytically naive. *But there would be no point in providing insight to a client if self-direction were not possible.* As we have seen, the aim of all three of our

classical analytical positions is to set the neurotic free of his past, to provide him with fresh grounds on the basis of which he can direct his own fate. Having used the psychic determinism from out of the past in a constructive way, the analyst could hope indirectly to alter things in the neurotic's future.

In speaking of *determinism* we come to a point of agreement among the founding fathers. All three held to the view that psychic determinism arose because the individual was frozen into his behavioral pattern (including neuroses) by way of a (Kantian) prototype, archetype, or life plan. This view is entirely consistent with the rise of hard determinism in physical science. It was Newton's belief in a perfect God fashioning a perfect universe which led him to presume that events were entirely "lawful" and predictable. The upshot of this conceptualization is that the early psychoanalysts took the appropriate view of determinism —as tied more to pattern and intentional construct meanings than to substance or impetus meanings! Concepts of *physical* energy as used in the natural sciences do not have the meaning of inevitability clearly stamped into their conceptualizations since, as we know, they can oppose one another and thus divert or negate the action that either might have brought about alone. The "misaction" of a Freudian parapraxis would thus involve this kind of energy expenditure whether it was a compromise settlement between conflicting intentions, or merely a simple "misfire" in the mechanical apparatus of speech or behavior. What makes the misaction *meaningful* is *not* the energy expenditure but the conflicting intentions of the individual as reflected in his "slip of the tongue."

This is the only way in which our "big question" of the "natural drive upward" of the unconscious mind can be properly answered. The inevitability of Freudian mental activity seeking expression stems more from the *logical necessity* of an idea which *has to be expressed* than it does from the nature of an energy which seeks to expend its force or thrust. Even the seemingly passive act of "forgetting" in the Freudian sense is not as if an energy had been dissipated over time, like a gas rising into the stratosphere, taking our thoughts with it. To forget is to have one intention oppose another in an *active clash* at the unconscious level.[105] Both thoughts, ideas, or purposive intentions seek expression because that is the nature of *psychic* activity. Intentions seek their intended state independent of antecedent-consequent time factors. A "plan" if put into effect demonstrates this most clearly. The plan (pattern construct) is simply "there," free of time factors. When behavior is engaged in "for the sake of" this plan we have a clear teleology. Though the brain may work as physical mechanism through the expenditure of physical energy and the consequent motion of physical atoms (impetus), the factor of a logical necessity can be seen as issuing *not* from such forces but from the arraying of assumptions to conclusions to the meanings intending to be expressed thereby!

Freud was drawn to this very tactic of using what some have called "emotional syllogisms," as when he discussed paranoid projection developing from a proposition of the sort "*I* (a man) *love him* (a man)."[106] If we now provide the backdrop (Kantian) major premise here of "All homosexuals are mad" or "Only a filthy, degenerate subhuman could love a member of his own sex" we can see the *necessary* conclusion to follow if a man now senses "I love him." The implication, the flow of reasoning moves from the premises to a conclusion. The import is there without alternative *if* we really *do believe* the backdrop (Kantian) assumptions. Ideas are unyielding in their meaningful expression and show a "drive upward" as Freud suggested because that is what an idea "is." *Ideas express intents.* Adler and Jung would agree with this development entirely. It is a deterministic view of mind, framed introspectively, and clearly a human teleology. The determinism exists between premise, prototype,

life plan, or archetype and the *resultant* conclusions which flow once a "that for the sake of which" meaning has taken hold. This kind of theory borrows from the pattern (syllogistic style) and intentional (the premises "for the sake of which") construct meanings and *not* from the impetus construct meaning.

This is the only proper way to speak of a dualism in Freudian thought. The constancy principle was essentially an analogy, drawn from physical science and to that extent dealing with the *behavior* or flow of events *over time*. But when we speak of "mental" events, this time factor is unessential to an understanding of the *meanings* conveyed (see p. 217; also, see comparable discussion in Chapter 12, pp. 511–517). When we speak of ideas *intending* to express their meanings, we do *not* speak of ideas *acting* to express their meanings. An intention *has already* expressed its meaningful import. There is literally nothing left to say; our only alternative is to "be out with it!" Freud believed that such ideas were formed *unconsciously,* and then fought for natural expression in consciousness. However, when the censor (or ego) properly understood the implications—another term for intentional impact—of certain lascivious or hostile ideas there was an immediate flurry of compromise activity to deny such ideas the light of day (consciousness).

Adler added to this introspective teleological formulation his second *extraspective* teleology of evolutionary advance. He also added a strong theme of the "positive advancement" in life or the inevitability of progress which is sometimes called a *vitalism.* A vitalistic theory is not only teleological, suggesting that behavior is moving toward goals, but it also holds that the goals themselves continue to get better and better. Neither Freud nor Jung could brook such a positive conception, feeling as they did that man could just as readily lead himself downhill to perdition.

We might recall that Adler thought of man's psychic equipment as the *soul,* which he defined as a force "directed toward a goal."[107] Mentality is thus inseparably tied to goal orientation: "The goal of the mental life of man becomes its governing principle, its *causa finalis*"[108] (that is, intentional construct meaning). We might now ask: What is *the* goal or end toward which man's mentality (soul) is drawn? Adler would answer that it is *the* goal of *all* creatures on the face of the earth to develop, to adapt, and thus to strive continuously for a higher state of perfection as a life necessity.[109] There is nothing uniquely human in this, for: "This teleology, this striving for a goal, is innate in the concept of adaptation."[110] We are prone to speak of man's efforts in terms of a self-realization, which is why Adler considered the self to be man's goal—a projected end state toward which he was purposively striving.[111] In this sense "self" realization is "goal" realization. But we must never overlook the fact, in our zeal to think of man as something special on the face of the earth, that the *creative power* of all striving is literally due to the impersonal evolutionary progression seen in *all* organic life.[112]

This movement of organic life which we realize has a creative power or energizing quality about it is on the order of a cosmic principle, with its teleological directions written in the history of animal life (movement taking on form and direction). Hence, through the theoretical device of employing a concept of creative power or more simply "creation in life" Adler succeeds in joining the introspectively framed human teleology of man (self-realization) with the extraspectively conceived teleology of nature (directedness in the course of evolution). No one can say for certain just where evolution is leading us, or what the final end state will be like.[113] Religions attempt to predict in formulating their hopeful fictions about a life hereafter, but this merely teaches us that man must ever look to the future even in the throes of death.

Although Adler's was a very positive view of man's nature, the honest scholar must point out that his interpretations of organic evolution do not square well with Darwin's views. Although Adler gave short-shrift to the principles of "survival of the fittest" and "self-preservation," there is little doubt that Darwin took them seriously. The point of this Darwinian conception of natural selection is not that there is a *goal* (telos) toward which animal evolution is unfolding—even in the sense of a goal for better and better mastery over the environment (vitalism)—but rather that the relationship between an organism and its environment either *continues* to further life or does not.

When dinosaurs went down to extinction it was not because they had formulated an improper plan, or that nature had made "mistakes." The dinosaur was marvelously adapted to its environment. It just so happened that the environment changed. The animals who survived might in one sense be considered "lucky" rather than shrewd and effective planners for the future. This entire process of changing relationships between animal and environment can be thought of entirely mechanically, and thus precisely in opposition to the vitalistic position of individual psychology. Even so, by discrediting the extraspective, natural teleology of Adlerian thought we do *not* discredit his (and Freud's and Jung's) introspective *human* teleology. So long as man can reason dialectically from a meaningful input to its opposite, and thereby project an alternative "possibility" to be achieved in his future life style we can say that he is truly an intentional, self-directing animal. Whether he is getting better or worse—including making Adlerian mistakes—depends upon what it is we see him doing, the premises on which he proceeds, and so forth. But even though he may be steadily declining we can still see a teleology in his movements toward tomorrow's (ineffective, erroneous, "stupid") goal.

It was Jung's view that modern man was indeed developing (evolving) one-sidedly on the question of materialism and an overvaluation of consciousness (see Chapter 3). Hence he, like Freud, could not embrace such a potentially positive view of man as did Adler. We have already documented Jung's heavy commitment to teleological conceptions of mind. But there is one distinctive theoretical predilection he defended which gives his thought a uniqueness worth mentioning. Jung maintained that an item of behavior under theoretical description could not be properly described in both impetus and intentional construct meanings *at the same time*. He used the terms causality (impetus) and finality (intentional), but his position has considerable significance for our study of theory construction, as follows: "It is not possible to conceive that one and the same combination of events could be simultaneously causal and final, for the one determination excludes the other. There are in fact two different points of view, the one reversing the other; for the principle of finality is the logical reverse of the principle of causality."[114] Aristotle had never considered these meanings to be mutually exclusive (see pp. 3–5), nor have we treated them as such in the approach to the present volume. But Jung felt strongly enough about his teleology to argue for an unresolvable opposite between the two theoretical outlooks: "What to the causal view is *fact* to the final view is *symbol* and vice versa. Everything that is real and essential to the one is unreal and inessential to the other."[115]

Though we need not agree with Jung's conclusion here, we should see in this bifurcation the argument of a great dialectician, a Kantian and an idealist who cannot see his way clear to join hands with the demonstratively inclined Lockeans who wish to reduce everything to the substantive, measurable "hard facts" of reality which they presume is in flux before their eyes. Jung was more sensitive to the needs of conventional science than was Adler, but he also wished to capture the image of man he felt was alive in himself: "It cannot be disputed that, psychologically speaking, we are living and working day by day according to the principle of directed aim or purpose as well as that

of causality."[116] If Jung therefore poses the problems of impetus vs. intentional construct usages in somewhat harsher tones than are necessary, what he is trying to express is that man *cannot be limited* to a description only in impetus terms.[117] Man's peculiar intellect, his ability to reason dialectically and thus to weigh (judge) alternatives for the future is the wellspring of his finality as individual actor (human teleology) and his moral character.[118]

The Motives to Psychotherapy

THE SCHOLARLY MOTIVE AND PSYCHOANALYSIS AS METHOD

The fact that Freud was not greatly interested in becoming a "healer" has been well documented.[119] His delayed graduation from medical school, his interest in making "scientific" generalizations, his cautions about assuming responsibility for other people's lives in psychoanalysis, all testify to what Freud once said of himself: "You are perhaps aware that I have never been a therapeutic enthusiast. . . ."[120] After more than 40 years as psychoanalyst Freud could say that he had "never really been a doctor in the proper sense."[121] Of course, early in his career he stressed the primary importance of psychoanalysis as a therapeutic effort. In 1909 he spoke of the scientific insights as secondary to the therapeutic effects of psychoanalysis.[122] By 1916 he was saying that even if psychoanalysis proved to be an unsuccessful form of therapy, it would remain an irreplaceable instrument of scientific research.[123] In the mid-1920s he was acknowledging that the term "psychoanalysis" had changed in meaning from a primarily therapeutic orientation to a more broad and inclusive referent as "the science of unconscious mental processes."[124] And by the late 1920s Freud was rather confidently asserting: "In point of fact psycho-analysis is a method of research, an impartial instrument, like the infinitesimal calculus, as it were."[125]

How did this method work as a vehicle for evidence? In discussing how a physician might prove that something like "coitus interruptus" takes place in neurosis, Freud observes: "If, as a physician who understands this aetiology, one arranges, in a case in which the neurosis has not yet been established [i.e., symptoms fixed], for coitus interruptus to be replaced by normal intercourse, one obtains a *therapeutic* proof of the assertion I have made."[126] This early quote identifying proof a therapist could accept remained the basis for evidence in psychoanalytical methodology. Freud's so-called method relies heavily on the procedural evidence of the client. Yet, the accepting of client improvement (cures) as *necessarily* validating the therapist's theory of neurosis is a major weakness of the Freudian method.

It is clear that Freud considered proof a matter of "internal consistency." Just so long as a hypothesis hangs together internally and throws new light on old questions, we have good reason to accept its verity.[127] This approach is usually termed a "coherence theory of truth" in opposition to the "correspondence theory of truth" followed by the experimentalist who tries to array his hypothesis to meet an entirely independent series of prearranged empirical events leading to what we have called validating evidence. When we validate we keep our methodological steps entirely independent from our *and the subject's* procedural evidence. What we think about the flow of methodological steps makes no difference to the outcome. Though Freud felt that anyone using his method would arrive at the same findings he did,[128] the record of departed students and followers belies this conviction.

There are three crucial questions which might be put to Freud concerning his "scientific" method. The first concerns his interpretations of fantasies. How can we accept the supposed childhood fantasies as having *actually* occurred in childhood? Is it not possible that the Oedipus complex is merely the distortion of childhood relationships made by an adult,

who has sexualized his recall? To validate this claim more carefully, we might study children in the early years of life to observe, if possible, any indications of an Oedipal conflict. Since every child is said to pass through this complex we should be in a position to test this theoretical generalization. Yet, Freud did not favor this approach, feeling that the direct observation of children would yield no significant evidence because we never know quite how to interpret their behaviors and hence misunderstandings would result.[129] The only way to study the problem is through the cooperation of the client in a *post hoc* fashion.

When he discussed the more basic objection that an adult might be sexualizing his memories of the past, Freud noted that a sexual emphasis invariably emerged in the very process of reconstructing the past.[130] He also told of having tried to eliminate these memories of sexual fantasy from his patients' recollections of childhood, without success.[131] He had no alternative but to accept them as valid aetiological factors in neurosis.[132] Despite these justifications, we must honestly conclude that psychoanalysis is unable to distinguish between *falsified recollections* of a sexual nature (fallaciously remembering fantasying a parent sexually fondling us), and the actual sexual fantasies supposedly concocted in the infantile years (the fact of having *actually had* this fantasy years past). This distinction might make no therapeutic or practical difference, particularly since Freud argues that fantasies can cause illness. But scientifically speaking, this fundamental claim issues from the method, and it must be proven to everyone's satisfaction or eliminated as an item of knowledge.

The second question we might put to Freud has to do with the advisability of using an *ad hominem* argument so freely in dismissing the critics of psychoanalysis. Most of us are familiar with the old saw: "In psychoanalysis you are damned if you do and damned if you don't." Though it is probably an oversimplification there is surely a good deal of truth in the statement. The phenomenon of resistance is based upon an *ad hominem* attack against the client. We challenge his grounds and dismiss his arguments, no matter how plausible they might appear, as defensive rationalizations. The Freudian dialectical maneuver can even permit the analyst to take as positive evidence the contrary assertion to the one he suspects is true. For example, Freud notes that if he asks a patient the identity of a person in a dream which has been reported, the patient might easily answer something like "You ask who this person in the dream can be. It's *not* my mother." Due to this stress on negation Freud would take this as evidence to the effect: "So it *is* his mother."[133] Thus a "no" becomes a "yes." Now, since people are perfectly capable of doing precisely what Freud says they are doing—denying, repressing, resisting—it is entirely possible that he is *correct* as therapist to act the way he does. People *are* illogical and unreliable, so why not treat them accordingly through a dialectical logic? No one can object to this procedure as a part of therapy, or as a form of theory generation in discourse. *But is this an adequate methodological procedure for a science?*

The final question we have to raise deals with Freud's tendencies to use analogized parallels across the life span. Thanks to his frequent use of prototypes (pattern constructs) Freud made it appear that certain behaviors manifested in adulthood were *repetitions* of behaviors indulged in during childhood. Since the childhood behaviors came first, Freud took it as a maxim that their meaningful import was being repeated during the later period of life. An adult's belief in God was his attempt to repeat the narcissistic oceanic feelings of infancy. The meticulous adult was trying to recapture or resolve cleanliness training first confronted in childhood. By drawing prototypes in this fashion one could easily charge that Freud was prone to confuse a *characteristic* which two events have in common with the *essence* of the two events taken individually. Even if we

accept the fact that sensing a supreme being is identical to the state of narcissism experienced as an infant, or the concern for orderly routine is the same psychological reaction as experienced in early toilet training, it does not follow that what is common to the two events over time can account for the *complete meaning* of each.

We might rephrase this objection in terms of our basic meaning constructs. If adult pleasure and infant pleasure are identical in the meaning of *essence*—that is, the ultimate significance of both—then Freud's reduction of a belief in a God to the oceanic feeling is sound. But, is this really the same *type* of pleasure? One could easily argue that an infant's oceanic feelings are prompted by an *impetus* conception of pleasure. The infant "feels" pleasurable because his needs are being met, his sphincter expulsions and dietary wants are in no way frustrated from obtaining automatic gratification. Everything physically "good" simply "happens" to him, without his planning or maneuvering "for the sake of" a strategy. He does not risk himself hence he feels oceanically powerful and elated. But what of the adult, who sets out to achieve something great in life, even as Freud did in the face of tough opposition to his success? Are we to view the physical "feelings" of pleasure resulting from gaining a goal and experiencing success as directly comparable to the earlier feelings of the child? Insofar as they include the automatic sensations of that "good feeling" of happiness we might answer "yes." There is surely a comparability in this more restricted sense of an *impetus meaning*. This is what we mean by an identity in *characteristics* between childhood and adulthood.

But how valid is it to equate the *essential* nature of these two instances? Do we not need the additional contribution of an *intentional meaning* to characterize the adult situation more properly? The martyr or the hero in battle who sacrifices himself for his fellow man is living up to a system of intentions and beliefs which might well countermand impetus pleasure in many instances. The infant wants pleasure, and he does *not* seek it by way of an organized belief or moral system. He takes pleasure of *any* sort where and when he can find it, as do many adults. But the ethical or religious adult *denies* himself certain (impetus) pleasures—possibly including life itself—in order to obtain what is for him a more worthwhile pleasure defined by his ideals (intentions).

The scholarly motive did not play a leading role in Adler's commitment to the consulting room. As his biographical overview suggests, Adler lacked a scholar's temperament. He disliked having to write his theories down for publication, and he was not above purposely leaving ambiguous meaning in written presentations so that he could not be pinned down to a fixed phrase or a catchword at some later date.[134] Adler wanted a "psychology of use," and he stressed that "we musn't make our psychology too hard for people to understand."[135] He was not impressed by the Freudian and Jungian approaches, which made the patient a subject-collaborator in research.[136] Too often, he complained, the therapist lost sight of client needs as a result, and the scholarly motivation also multiplied beyond plausibility the number of supposed reasons for maladjustment. Adler was not in the business of finding excuses for neurotics, justifying their persistence in mistaken life styles.[137]

Adler did advocate the conducting of experiments along the lines of validating evidence, but he insisted that these be done in natural life settings.[138] Of what use was it for an experimental psychologist to design an apparatus to study some irrelevant point?[139] Although he did not concern himself with extensive controls, Adler did occasionally embark on empirical projects of his own. He tells of a survey tactic in the following: "I have occasionally attempted to make investigations in schools in such a tactful manner that no one

could possibly be hurt. On a sheet of paper on which no names appeared, answers were to be written to the following question: Has anyone ever lied or stolen? The general results showed that all the children confessed to petty thefts. . . ."[140] However, merely collecting data and submitting them to mathematical test did not constitute adequate science for Adler.[141] He felt that many investigators who were afraid of criticism fled to an artificial reliance upon mathematical reductionism in an effort to feel certain and secure.[142]

Adler now introduced therapeutic contact as a major method, essentially following Freud in the coherence theory of truth. He liked to emphasize clinical "guessing" about the future of the client as a form of prediction in the relationship. If the therapist-scientist really understands the client's life line then he should be able to guess or predict what he is going to do from day to day.[143] Here again, since the therapist judges success or failure, this method comes down to procedural evidence, and the same criticisms we made of Freud could be leveled at Adler. Adler's "method of comparison" (see Chapter 2) is a perfect example of procedural evidence, employing the coherence theory of truth.

Jung's motives for therapy placed high value on its scholarly aspects. During the early stages of analysis (confession, elucidation, education) Jung probably was more drawn to practical results than was Freud.[144] He did not feel that any one point of view was more valid in explaining the etiology of neurosis than another, and he constantly stressed that the client was present to be helped and not to prove the validity of a theorist's hypotheses. But Jung early in his career found what Freud had also experienced in working with clients—that simply curing people was not sufficiently rewarding as a career motive. He tells us that he had no desire to be passively transformed into a miracle worker, but rather: "I wanted to understand what really goes on in people's minds. . . . If only one did not have a scientific conscience and that hankering after the truth!"[145]

These are the motives of a true scientist, and we know from Chapter 3 that Jung's range as empiricist was breathtaking. Furthermore, he once employed "control and prediction" in an experimental situation. He compared the horoscopes of 483 marital couples, to see if astrology could predict successful combinations.[146] Jung failed to use an adequate control (comparison) group against which to judge his matched protocols, settling for a statistically determined "chance" estimate. Whether this was the reason for his failure is doubtful, but in any case the results of his study were negative—the pattern predicted by astrology was not confirmed by the sample to a statistically significant extent.

Undaunted, Jung went on to say that: "The statistical view of the world is a mere abstraction and therefore incomplete and even fallacious, particularly so when it deals with man's psychology."[147] He is, of course, correct in recognizing that mathematics rests upon a procedural evidence base in the same way that other theories begin in such plausible abstractions. But this is still the accepted scientific avenue, and Jung had to swallow the verdict of an uncontaminated (by experimenter or subject procedural evidence) verdict. He typically noted that the three "most important" signs predicted by astrological theory *did* seem to come together in a minuscule number of marital cases, too small for proper statistical test yet synchronistically meaningful.[148] These "chance" occurrences were for Jung still important: "Inasmuch as chance maxima and minima occur, they are *facts* whose nature I set out to explore."[149]

What is often detrimental to the development of personality theory in studies of this sort is not their hypotheses or their lack of findings, but the extent to which theorists like Jung will defend their questionable experimental designs and the resulting "trends." Obviously,

what Jung needed was another study of his best three signs in a subsequent sample, with an adequate control group chosen for better comparison. By haggling over the inadequacies of statistics to capture the subtleties of life all one does is upset those who are patiently and honestly seeking to validate theories before they proclaim them. This has led to much professional bickering among students of personality, and a refusal by many of them to test some of the more fascinating "folk beliefs," such as the legitimacy of astrological signs. Personality theory cannot flourish if the liberal thinker does not feel a greater responsibility to sharpen his methodological test, and the area surely cannot advance if the kinds of studies contemplated are limited by the arid simplicities of so-called laboratory techniques.

Jung made one spirited defense of procedural evidence in the clinical situation worth emphasizing for its brilliance. He begins with the proposition that personality psychology as we know it is made up of the confessions of singular—that is, individual—human beings.[150] We call this single individual a "theorist," but what he is doing in speaking about all people is to tell us something of himself. Freud told us something about ourselves even as he was confessing to highly personal facets of *his* personal psychology; Adler then came along to give us an alternative but equally true account of ourselves as he revealed something of *his* personal psychology; and so on with all subsequent personality theorists including Jung.[151] If an individual were totally different from every other individual, then we would have as many psychologies as we would people—or at least as many as there are people who would confess their insights as Freud and Adler had done. But such multiplicity (subjectivity) does not occur because: "Individuality . . . is only relative, the compliment of human conformity or likeness; and therefore it is possible to make statements of general validity, i.e., scientific statements."[152]

As we look around, broad ranges of human

experience overlap. Individualities (subjectivities) merge into commonalities (objectivities) so that we see Adlerian psychology uppermost in this *other* individual (besides Adler), Freudian psychology uppermost in that *other* individual (besides Freud), and so forth. It is even possible to see both Adlerian and Freudian themes in the *same* individual (movement from types to traits). And since this is the case, argues Jung, relying upon the plausibilities of an individual's procedural evidence in the therapy hour *can* be considered an appropriate method of arriving at scientific truths.

Though he has presented a superior defense of therapy as a method, Jung has surely minimized the case for an *incorrect* common belief which can be psychically held by many people (objectively). When all mankind believed the world was flat, their belief was objective. But if we think of "natural science" as an attempt to explain the universe independent of the psychic presumptions which seem plausible to the human intellect, then this belief is false as well. Science has constantly worked to remove man's biases from its *testing* procedures. In this way scientific truths have contradicted and negated the physical objectivities of the sort Jung is defending. In time, the newer scientific truths become absorbed into the common sense of all peoples, and they once again serve to prejudice the psychic outlooks of all concerned. Additional scientific evidence via validation may then be necessary to alter *this* corpus of objective belief. There is nothing sacred about scientific method. Defending something as being true because it is commonly (objectively) believed is still an *unacceptable scientific argument,* no matter how brilliantly Jung wages the defense.

ETHICAL THEMES IN PSYCHOANALYSIS

It is clear that Freud was a social revisionist and critic of civilization in general. He said that psychoanalysts were not social reformers, but the rigid manner in which the culture formulated strictures on sexuality forced them to speak out as critics.[153] The morals of passivity which engendered the Golden Rule were interpreted as stemming from strong reaction-formations to the underlying cruelty and violence which Freud accepted as a constituent of human nature.[154] For this reason Freud felt it necessary to align himself with the ego and try to soften the grip of the superego.[155] Freud thought of himself as the therapist of an entire culture; and his social criticism must be viewed in this light. He drew a parallel between the development of the individual and the development of the culture,[156] and he even spoke in terms of a cultural superego, handed down from past generations and operating very much like the superego of the individual.[157]

Freud was occasionally annoyed by those who, like Adler, wanted to account for man's "goodness." He lacked such an optimistic view of the march of civilization. Jung believed that Freud almost was neurotically pessimistic regarding mankind. Freud felt that one simply had to accept honestly the fact that man is a higher animal with id promptings which are quite beyond the ego's ability to control successfully, particularly since the ego is itself an extension of the id and "a separation of the ego from the id would be a hopeless undertaking."[158] However, if there is anything hopeful about man's innate goodness, it seems to be in the fact that he cannot act out evil promptings without guilt (moral anxiety) *if* he has the proper form of superego. Psychoanalysis confirms the Platonic saying that the "good" are those who are content to dream about the things which the "bad" really carry into action.[159] About as far as Freud ever went in acknowledging man's intrinsic goodness is contained in the following:

The ethical narcissism of humanity should rest content with the knowledge that the fact of distortion in dreams, as well as the existence of anxiety-dreams and punishment-dreams, afford just as clear evidence of his *moral* nature as dream-interpretation gives of the existence and strength of his *evil* nature. If anyone is dissatisfied with this and would like to be 'better' than he was created, let him see whether he can attain anything more in life than hypocrisy and inhibition.[160]

In contrast to Freud's negative view of super-ego promptings, Adler felt that the only hope for mankind lay in the affectively based judgments of the right, the proper, the good way to behave in relation to one's fellow men. Due to man's comparatively weak position in the animal kingdom, and as a natural compensation in the movement of organic evolution, a necessary feature of humanity is *collectivity*, the living in groups with its corollary necessity of caring for one another. Adler felt that many of those individuals who transgress this naturalistic ethic turned up in his consulting room as patients.[161] Since their eventual recovery of mental health was dependent upon a cultivation of that which they lacked—that is, social interest—it would be correct to say that Adlerian therapy tends heavily, if not primarily, toward an ethical motivation. The client may not wish to cultivate his better side, but the "facts of the case" as viewed from the therapist's perspective are that he *must* develop in this way if he wishes to return to normalcy. And the therapist cannot shirk his duty: "When we find an individual whose behavior pattern has rendered him incapable of a happy life, there arises out of our knowledge of human nature the implicit duty to aid him in readjusting the false perspectives with which he wanders through his life."[162]

This intrinsically motivated ethic does not mean that the therapist should—or can—do anything for the client, except encourage him to make an effort to rearrange his life style. The client must assume the burden of responsibility for change in full knowledge that he is free to select the course he wishes after being provided insight about what he has been doing to that point in his life.[163] It is this straightfor-ward description of the client's selfishness (lack of social interest) which gives Adlerian psychology an even more moralizing tone than its founder would have preferred. Adler tried to offset the harsher implications of his ethical approach by stressing *errors* (mistakes) rather than *sins*. He did not want to make people feel guilty when they behaved in egocentric ways.[164] He believed that man was born neither good nor evil,[165] but was a product of the environmental circumstances into which he was born and—most importantly—what *he* makes of them in framing a prototype. Since he makes himself he must cure himself. Adler believed that a simple rule of conduct dictated the satisfactions in life for all men: the individual must consider his fellows and adjust to their collective needs. Adler succinctly phrased his ethic: "When we speak of virtue we mean that a person plays his part; when we speak of vice we mean that he interferes with co-operation."[166]

Arguing as he did for the common good led to charges by critics that Adler advocated a repressive approach. It was as if he were saying that whenever a conflict arose between the individual and the group, regardless of the merits of the individual's case, the group must win out and be appeased. Adler took pains to answer this charge, noting that he did *not* advocate repression as a principle of adjustment, whether the individual's claim on the group was justified or unjustified.[167] When a claim on life was unjustifiable Adler believed that this lack of equity could be discerned by comparing it to the broader standard of community benefit. Once the evaluation was made, the individual who has a selfish or unjustified claim was not expected to repress anything. Rather, he was asked to *cultivate* (as a compensating measure) the social interest he has potentially open to him as a human being. The unfortunate aspect of human relations is that when one man gives in to his better promptings and allows an unjust advantage he enjoys to fade away without personal benefit he senses that he is playing the fool because how can he be certain that the "next time" when *he* is at the disadvantage he will be shown an equal regard by his fellow man? Why not therefore make our claims where we can and accrue what pleasure we can from the advantages of selfishness? Though a practical assumption for some, Adler viewed this as a justification for the narrow life view, rather than as a program for the future betterment of mankind.

We cannot advance as a race if we all assume by some Kantian definition that our fellow man is selfish; our very assumption determines what we shall do interpersonally, and if everyone thinks this way we will have the selfish world we literally create daily. Adler felt that Freud's mistake was viewing man as selfish by nature.[168] We have to see in the march of organic evolution a different side to man, the side which is taking him above these animalistic tendencies subsumed by the concept of an id. The steady movement of creative evolution is away from selfishness, even though the specifics of an ethical code cannot be circumscribed for all time. It is not some fixed ethical truth, but the striving upward that Adler emphasized as an ethical position. One need only look to his roots to see where he is going as an organic product. What we have *left* is precisely that side of our natures that Freud seems so intent upon retaining in his image of man.[169]

As we recall from Chapter 3, Jung relied rather heavily upon an ethical position in explicating the nature of maladjustment, as well as the steps one must take to overcome neurotic tendencies. If we would all look inward and admit to our shadow sides then this world would be much better, projections would be minimized, and a sense of personal humility would be substituted for the impersonalisms and hostilities detracting from modern life.[170] Though he never put it precisely this way, Jung felt the weighing of alternatives in dialectical reasoning meant that man constantly

faced a judgment in his behavior. Moreover, once man opts for what he takes to be the better of two alternatives, the "bad" side of his decision remains within his psyche as a future possibility for behavior (reduced to shadow status). As we have seen, unless these rejected possibilities are reconciled with the conscious personality a problem in adjustment (one-sidedness) can develop. This is the reason that religion is associated with cure in the Jungian view. Religions have aimed at restoring the balance through admissions of the shadow side to existence (sin, weakness, wrongdoing). Religions are naturally evaluative and moralizing because they reflect man's most basic dialectical propensities—to judge or to choose, both of which necessitate value distinctions which cannot be explained, as Freud has done, as merely dependency manifestations. Whereas Freud agreed with Shakespeare that conscience makes cowards of us all, Jung believed with Adler that conscience makes higher animals of us all, because it is only through our judgmental ability that we can submit our actions to a higher type of criticism.[171]

Jung once shocked a client by telling him that his problems stemmed from a lack of conscience.[172] Such an interpretation struck the client as not only too religious and nonscientific, but almost unprofessional as well. Jung was amused by this response, since it was his clear insight that if a man could become ill because of a harsh self-evaluation (Freud's rigid superego) it should be possible for him to fall ill because of a lack of that character which one ordinarily attributes to men of high standards and good conscience. Jung felt that Adler had seen this side of man more clearly than Freud.[173] By being sensitive to our own weaknesses—even "sins"—Jung argued that we would balance our shadow factors and thus be less likely to project them onto others. Here is a good summary statement of Jung's basic ethic:

If men can be educated to see the shadow-side of their nature clearly, it may be hoped that they will also learn to understand and love their fellow men better. A little less hypocrisy and a little more self-knowledge can only have good results in respect for our neighbour; for we are all too prone to transfer to our fellows the injustice and violence we inflict upon our own natures.[174]

CURATIVE MOTIVES TO PSYCHOANALYSIS

We have already documented the fact that Freud was—at best—a reluctant therapist. Freud had broader goals in mind than simply putting out the individual flames of neurosis which are kindled by the clash between cultural mandates and man's natural propensities for pleasure. Freud's "cure" is a long-ranged, broad-based program of understanding, demanding an intellectual grasp and a sense of tolerance if not humor concerning our common human plight. Freud was distrustful of the overly enthusiastic revolutionary with a program for curing men's problems overnight. Revolutions breed reactions, and the inevitable outcome of such zeal on both sides is suppression—if not in the present, then surely in the future.[175] Freud championed the individual man and defended a "new" God for mankind: *reason*.[176] We must drop the superstitions and illusions of yesterday, recognize that mankind slowly advances only through hard work and a willingness to face facts, and through rational efforts such as science there may yet be hope for the future. Though we might fault him for having an unworkable method of scientific investigation, we must see in this late nineteenth century rationalist whose thought could encompass man's irrationality, a monumental bravery and sincere honesty as he tried to interpret for us what he took to be the facts of the human condition.

Closely aligned with the ethical motives of Adler are his curative motives: ". . . the practitioner should either pledge himself to bring about a cure or not accept payment."[177] Because he did not think of the therapeutic rela-

tionship as primarily a scientific activity Adler was more prone to emphasize the necessity of effecting a cure. His emphasis on "how to" do therapy, using maneuvers we termed in Chapter 2 "gamesmanship tactics" (p. 127), might suggest a more instrumental than an intrinsic ethic of cure; but this is merely illusion, resulting from a superficial grasp of his closely aligned curative and ethical motives. Many of Adler's suggestions to the therapist are so directly tied to cure that they almost belong in a practitioner's manual of techniques. For example, Adler tells us at length how he notices and tells patients about their tendency to swallow gulps of air when anxious, giving them gastric disturbances of various sorts which only further their anxiety.[178] Therapy in this case is achieved by the simple expedient of the client being made aware of this tendency, countering it when the gulping begins, and then enjoying the benefits of a heightened sense of self-awareness. No "behavior therapist" (see Chapter 7) could do more for the client's symptom at this point. However, in traditional psychoanalytical writings such practical hints are not given prominence.

Unlike Freud, who viewed man's reason as the eventual source of social change Adler does not stress the march of society *qua* society. He did not pin his hopes for the future of man on sociocultural advance but rather on the physically based advance which each *individual* man carries along. A typical ordering of Adlerian priorities can be seen in the following: "The miracle of evolution is manifest in the perceptual endeavour made by the body simultaneously to maintain, complete, and supplement all the parts that are vital to it. . . . Here, too, the association of man—society —has acted helpfully and successfully."[179] It is in this sense that society is a compensatory— and the most important compensatory—factor for human weakness.[180] Man relies on man, but the *reason* for this interpersonal concern is rooted in organic evolution. Cultural values then emerge, but social interest is *not* a cultural product, something derived from man's reason and decision to behave in a certain way. Adler did not wish to see social interest put in the category of a sociocultural fiction. Man's social ethic of community feeling is a *fact* to be accepted as a "given," just as it is a fact that humans breathe. (Note the Lockean emphasis at this point.) Hence, in the Adlerian view, nature and *not* nurture (sociocultural factors) is man's teacher, showing him what direction he is going in. Man is a product of this organic nature, and in his higher state of development he produces a culture. The culture does not ride above his organic existence and somehow influence its direction. Man's direction on this earth is ready-made from out of his *cultureless* past. Hence, unlike Freud, Adler is no healer of society but of the *individual* man as organic reality. Treat the individual and the society will take care of itself.

We have already made the point that Jung was not primarily motivated by curative intentions. As he put it: "I should deceive myself if I thought I was a practising physician. I am above all an investigator, and this naturally gives me a different attitude to many problems. . . . I was a medical practitioner quite long enough to realize that practice obeys, and must obey, other laws than does the search for truth."[181] Jung stressed that analysis is not like a "cure," to which the individual submits and is then discharged healed.[182] Nor did Jung appreciate views which failed to see the client as an independent entity—literally a co-worker—in the relationship: "The patient is not an empty sack into which we can stuff whatever we like; he brings his own particular contents with him which stubbornly resist suggestion and push themselves again and again to the fore."[183]

Jung warned that a therapist should refrain from meddling with the psychology of his patient "like an overzealous saviour."[184] The best tactic is to avoid being directive and judgmental, and the therapist can help create such an atmosphere by adopting the Socratic, dialectical approach we have already outlined in Chapter 3.[185] Probably the clearest indication that Jung was not attracted to the role of healer can be seen in his view of the nature of human problems. To have problems was part and parcel of existence. As he once put it so well: "In the last resort it is highly improbable that there could ever be a therapy that got rid of all difficulties. Man needs difficulties; they are necessary for health. What concerns us here as therapists is only an excessive amount of them."[186]

Notes

1. Freud, Vol. I, p. 295. **2.** Freud, Vol. XX, pp. 57–58. **3.** Rychlak, 1968, p. 177. **4.** Russell, 1959, p. 241. **5.** Freud, Vol. XVIII, p. 28; Vol. XXIII, p. 300. **6.** Freud, Vol. XIV, p. 171. **7.** Ansbacher and Ansbacher, 1964, p. 51. **8.** Jung, 1963, p. 70. **9.** Jung, Vol. 7, p. 64. **10.** Jung, Vol. 11, p. 5. **11.** Freud, Vol. XXIII, p. 196. **12.** Ansbacher and Ansbacher, 1956, p. 78. **13.** *Ibid.*, pp. 246–247. **14.** Jung, 1946, p. 56. **15.** Jung, Vol. 8, p. 383. **16.** Jung, Vol. 10, p. 290. **17.** Jung, 1946, p. 377. **18.** Freud, 1954, p. 264. **19.** Freud, Vol. XIV, pp. 78–79. **20.** Jung, Vol. 8, p. 4. **21.** *Ibid.*, p. 229. **22.** Jung, Vol. 9ii, p. 76. **23.** Ansbacher and Ansbacher, 1956, p. 91. **24.** Adler, 1964a, p. 47. **25.** Freud, Vol. XXII, p. 73. **26.** Freud, Vol. VII, p. 61. **27.** Freud, Vol. II, p. 117. **28.** Freud, Vol. XI, pp. 153–161. **29.** *Ibid.*, p. 156. **30.** Freud, Vol. XXI, p. 21. **31.** Freud, Vol. XVI, pp. 244–245. **32.** Jones, 1957, p. 345. **33.** See Rychlak, 1968, for the sources of his dialectical bias, pp. 324–336. **34.** Adler, 1968, p. 227. **35.** Adler, 1954, p. 23. **36.** Adler, 1968, p. 143. **37.** *Ibid.*, p. 34. **38.** Adler, 1930, p. 145. **39.** Ansbacher and Ansbacher, 1956, p. 229. **40.** Adler, 1968, p. 92. **41.** Adler, 1930, p. 145. **42.** *Ibid.*, p. 63. **43.** Ansbacher and Ansbacher, 1964, p. 287. **44.** *Ibid.*, p. 289. **45.** Jung, Vol. 4, p. 337. **46.** Jung, Vol. 8, pp. 169–170. **47.** *Ibid.*, p. 170. **48.** Rychlak, 1968, p. 390. **49.** Jung, Vol. 9i, p. 109. **50.** Jung, Vol. 11, p. 305. **51.** Jung, Vol. 12, p. 15. **52.** Jung, Vol. 4, p. 339. **53.** Jung, Vol. 8, p. 125. **54.** Freud, Vol. XIV, pp. 78–79. **55.** Freud, Vol. XIX, pp. 216–217. **56.** Freud, Vol. XX, p. 194.

57. Freud, Vol. VII, p. 171. 58. Freud, Vol. XIV, p. 168. 59. *Ibid.*, p. 189. 60. Freud, Vol. XVI, p. 393. 61. Freud, Vol. XI, p. 224. 62. Freud, Vol. XIV, p. 168. 63. Freud, Vol. XI, p. 136. 64. Adler, 1958, p. 207. 65. Ansbacher and Ansbacher, 1956, p. 34. 66. *Ibid.*, p. 38. 67. Adler, 1954, p. 128. 68. Adler, 1964b, p. 95. 69. Ansbacher and Ansbacher, 1956, p. 57. 70. Jung, Vol. 8, p. 183. 71. Jung, Vol. 11, p. 516. 72. Jung, Vol. 5, p. 139. 73. Jung, Vol. 14, p. 417. 74. Jung, Vol. 8, p. 7. 75. *Ibid.*, p. 4. 76. Jung, Vol. 3, p. 97. 77. *Ibid.*, p. 253. 78. *Ibid.*, p. 272. 79. Freud, Vol. V, p. 621. 80. See Jones, 1953, pp. 41–43. 81. Freud, Vol. XXIII, p. 179. 82. Ansbacher and Ansbacher, 1964, p. 84. 83. Adler, 1958, p. 48. 84. Ansbacher and Ansbacher, 1964, p. 294. 85. Adler, 1954, p. 34. 86. Adler, 1930, p. 28. 87. Jung, Vol. 8, p. 19. 88. *Ibid.*, pp. 3–4. 89. *Ibid.*, p. 31. 90. Freud, Vol. I, pp. 134–135. 91. *Ibid.*, p. 13. 92. *Ibid.*, p. 243. 93. Freud, Vol. VII, p. 182. 94. *Ibid.*, p. 228. 95. Adler, 1964b, pp. 12–13. 96. *Ibid.*, p. 39. 97. Rychlak, 1970. 98. Jung, Vol. 9i, pp. 42–43. 99. Jung, Vol. 9ii, p. 13. 100. Freud, Vol. I, p. 361. 101. Freud, Vol. XV, p. 67. 102. Freud, Vol. XII, p. 247. 103. Freud, Vol. VI, p. 254. 104. Freud, Vol. XVII, p. 236. 105. Freud, Vol. III, p. 297. 106. Freud, Vol. XII, p. 63. 107. Adler, 1954, p. 29. 108. Ansbacher and Ansbacher, 1956, p. 94. 109. Ansbacher and Ansbacher, 1964, p. 31. 110. Adler, 1954, p. 28. 111. Adler, 1968, p. 126. 112. Ansbacher and Ansbacher, 1956, p. 177. 113. Adler, 1964b, p. 272. 114. Jung, Vol. 8, pp. 4–5. 115. *Ibid.*, p. 24. 116. Jung, Vol. 4, p. 295. 117. See Jung, Vol. 8, p. 281. 118. Jung, Vol. 4, p. 278. 119. Rychlak, 1968, Ch. VII. 120. Freud, Vol. XXII, p. 151. 121. Jones, 1953, p. 28. 122. Freud, Vol. X, p. 208. 123. Freud, Vol. XVI, p. 255. 124. Freud, Vol. XX, p. 70. 125. Freud, Vol. XXI, p. 36. 126. Freud, Vol. III, p. 104. 127. Freud, Vol. VIII, p. 178; Vol. XVIII, p. 122. 128. Freud, Vol. VII, p. 113. 129. *Ibid.*, p. 201. 130. Freud, Vol. X, p. 206. 131. Freud, Vol. XVII, p. 62. 132. *Ibid.*, p. 103. 133. Freud, Vol. XIX, p. 235. 134. Bottome, 1957, p. 171. 135. *Ibid.* 136. Adler, 1968, p. 297. 137. *Ibid.* 138. Adler, 1964b, p. 188. 139. Adler, 1968, p. 1. 140. *Ibid.*, p. 340. 141. Adler, 1964b, p. 86. 142. *Ibid.*, pp. 154–155. 143. Adler, 1930, p. 7. 144. Jung, Vol. 17, p. 93. 145. Jung, Vol. 4, p. 258. 146. Jung, Vol. 8, pp. 459–504. 147. *Ibid.*, p. 463. 148. *Ibid.*, p. 477. 149. *Ibid.*, p. 463. 150. Jung, Vol. 4, p. 334. 151. Jung, Vol. 7, pp. 40–41. 152. Jung, Vol. 16, p. 5. 153. Freud, Vol. XVI, p. 434. 154. Freud, Vol. X, p. 112. 155. Freud, Vol. XXI, pp. 142–143. 156. *Ibid.*, pp. 139–140. 157. *Ibid.*, p. 141. 158. Freud, Vol. XIX, p. 133. 159. Freud, Vol. XV, p. 146. 160. Freud, Vol. XIX, p. 134. 161. Adler, 1964b, pp. 210–211. 162. Adler, 1954, p. 23. 163. Adler, 1964a, pp. 73–74. 164. Ansbacher and Ansbacher, 1964, p. 302. 165. *Ibid.*, p. 307. 166. Adler, 1964b, p. 283. 167. *Ibid.*, p. 290. 168. Ansbacher and Ansbacher, 1964, p. 210. 169. Adler, 1964b, pp. 278–279. 170. Jung, Vol. 14, p. 168. 171. Jung, Vol. 11, p. 76. 172. Jung, Vol. 8, pp. 355–356. 173. Jung, Vol. 4, p. 87. 174. Jung, Vol. 7, p. 25. 175. Freud, Vol. XXII, p. 151. 176. Freud, Vol. XXI, p. 54. 177. Adler, 1968, p. 297. 178. Adler, 1964a, pp. 94–95. 179. Adler, 1964b, p. 72. 180. Ansbacher and Ansbacher, 1964, p. 213. 181. Jung, Vol. 4, p. 262. 182. Jung, Vol. 8, p. 72. 183. Jung, Vol. 4, p. 280. 184. Jung, Vol. 10, p. 159. 185. Jung, Vol. 16, p. 5. 186. Jung, Vol. 8, p. 73.

Part Two
Lockean Models in American Psychiatry and Behaviorism

5

An "American" Psychology: The Interpersonal Theory of Harry Stack Sullivan

Biographical Overview

Harry Stack Sullivan was born on 21 February 1892, the son of a Irish-American farmer eking out a impoverished existence in central New York state, and he died unexpectedly of a cerebral hemorrhage while traveling abroad, in Paris, France, on 14 January 1949. His childhood was not very happy. Not only were physical necessities minimally satisfied, but as the only surviving child of his parents (other children died in infancy) Sullivan seems to have been a lonely and solitary figure. He felt isolated from other boys in his early years.[1] His mother believed she had married beneath the "Stack" family level of her maidenhood, and Sullivan seems to have been emotionally closest to his father. He was brought up in the Catholic faith but left the church in his adulthood.[2] Somehow, the family seems to have put away enough money so that Sullivan could obtain a higher education. After first considering physics as a career, he entered the Chicago College of Medicine and Surgery, where he took the M.D. degree in 1917.

Sullivan reports that in 1915, while in medical school, he first studied psychoanalysis.[3] Apparently he also entered psychoanalysis as a patient in the winter of 1916–1917, receiving 75 hours of treatment or self-study.[4] Later Sullivan was to receive over 300 hours of training analysis from Clara Thompson, an eminent psychoanalyst. Upon receiving his degree, Sullivan entered the U.S. Army during the First World War. He worked at a Public Health Institute for a time and then later became a Veterans Bureau Liaison Officer at St. Elizabeth's Hospital in Washington, D.C.[5] It was here in the 1921–1922 period that he met and responded to the example of William Alanson White, superintendent of St. Elizabeth's and a leader in the "new psychiatry," along with men like Adolph Meyer who were attempting to explain mental illness in other than merely physical terms. White believed that psychiatry had much to learn from the social sciences of anthropology and sociology. Sullivan was eventually transferred from St. Elizabeth's to the Sheppard and Enoch Pratt Hospital in Towson, Maryland, where he also obtained an appointment as Associate Professor of Psychiatry at the University of Maryland School of Medicine.[6] It was at the latter hospital, sometime in the 1922–1923 period, that he instituted a new form of Receiving Service as an experimental ward, establishing himself as a leading authority on schizophrenia (particularly male).

By 1925 Sullivan was convinced that there was no adequate explanation of the schizophrenic process, even though he had read all of the major works on the subject, including those of Jung.[7] At about this time the American Psychiatric Association sponsored a series of colloquia (funded by the Rockefellers) on "personality investigation" with William Alanson White as Chairman. By now, Sullivan had become White's protégé, and he was assigned the role of secretary to these meetings. The first colloquium was held in December of 1928, and it brought together a host of eminent scientists, including Edward Sapir, W. I. Thomas, Gordon W. Allport, Harold D. Lasswell, Sheldon Glueck, L. K. Frank, Arnold Gesell, and David Levy.[8] The body of socio-anthropological theories which dominated this gathering has been referred to as the "Chicago School of Social Science," with traditions taken from Cooley, Mead, James, and Dewey, and the foremost proponents of which were Sapir, Lasswell, and Robert E. Park. A decided shift in tone in Sullivan's thought began with these contacts. He found a style of thinking here which proved highly compatible with his own budding outlook on the *interpersonal* aspects of mental illness.

At Sheppard and Enoch Pratt, Sullivan had emersed himself in the problems of treating schizophrenics. Finding the usual hospital routines inappropriate, Sullivan established a special form of "subculture" within the broader hospital confines by acquiring a separate and distinct ward of male patients, whom he surrounded with talented, well-trained male aides who acted as properly masculine models. Although he practiced individual therapy and even tried hypnosis with select patients, Sullivan's therapeutic efforts emphasized altering the environment for the schizophrenic on a 24 hour per day basis. Treatment was a full-time job, one which must be carried out within the framework of interpersonal relations and emphasize the total personality of each within the context of the group. As he phrased it: "The mental hospital became a school for personality growth, rather than a custodian of personality failures."[9]

Sullivan's thinking continued to take on a more "supraindividual" coloring over the years, and near the end of his life he spoke of himself as a social psychologist.[10] By 1929 the transformation from Freudian to "Sullivanian" thought seems to have been completed, but the specific terms we now associate with interpersonal psychology were not pulled together for many more years. He seemed to accomplish his best theoretical integration under the demands of a speaking or lecture series engagement. An important statement of his view of abnormality—*Personal Psychopathology*, written between 1929 and 1933—never reached print in his lifetime, at least partly due to Sullivan's fear that he might be "premature" in formulating his ideas.[11] Although Sullivan was to publish many articles, the only book which reached print during his lifetime was his *Conceptions of Modern Psychiatry* (1940). His other books and clarifications of his views —taken from lecture notes and electronic recordings of his talks—we owe to his students, particularly Helen Swick Perry, Mary Ladd Gawell, Martha Gibbon, Otto A. Will, Mabel Blake Cohen, and the generally acknowledged foremost expert on Sullivanian thought, Patrick Mullahy.

In 1929 Sullivan left Maryland and moved to New York City, where he took up the private practice of psychiatry and psychoanalysis on Park Avenue. He had noted in his hospital studies that schizophrenia was often presaged by an obsessive personality structure, and one of the expressed aims he had in moving to private practice was to study the obsessive form of neurosis. However, there was to be no report of these findings. Sullivan's reputation continues to hinge upon his initial competence in schizophrenia and the resultant personality explanations. He did much to advance psychiatry as a profession in the 1930s. Following White's death in 1933, Sullivan—with the help of Sapir and Lasswell—established and served as the first President of the William Alanson White Psychiatric Foundation.[12] The foundation was dedicated to an interdisciplinary approach to psychiatry, having training branches in both Washington, D.C., and New York City. Psychiatrists trained through this foundation are given a broad, sociocultural theoretical background in addition to their customary medical education. The resulting orientation has come to be called the "Washington School" of psychiatry even though the spirit of Chicago is most evident. In 1938 Sullivan founded the journal *Psychiatry*, which he edited until his death.

In 1941, Sullivan dropped all other clinical work to act as consultant to the U.S. Selective Service Commission, which was then making plans for improved psychiatric evaluations of its draftees.[13] This experience helped him formulate a series of lectures which we now have as the posthumous book: *The Psychiatric Interview* (1954). His germinative work on personality can be found in *Clinical Studies in Psychiatry* (1956), which is based upon a series

of electronically recorded lectures delivered to the staff of Chestnut Lodge, Rockville, Maryland, between 1942 and 1946. After World War II, Sullivan participated in the International Congress of Mental Health in London and the UNESCO Tensions Project dealing with the source of international conflict and misunderstanding. In 1948, the year before his death, Sullivan was active in forming the World Federation for Mental Health. He was on the executive board of this organization, and it was while he was traveling in connection with the business of this body that his sudden death occurred. He never married.

In attempting to cite the precedents for Sullivan's thought, we must begin with Freud and Jung. As we shall see, Sullivan used most of Freud's concepts, though he gave them significantly different meanings. His concept of "dissociation" goes back in psychiatry to Janet

Harry Stack Sullivan

(1920) and others. Jung's influence on Sullivan is seen in concepts like "personification" and the multiplicity of identities which form within the personality. We know that Jung once did a study of Afro-American symbolism at St. Elizabeth's while visiting America, and he apparently was assisted in arranging this sojourn by William Alanson White.[14] Sullivan's concept of "integration" seems to have roots in the theories of Adolph Meyer (1910). The predominant line of sociocultural theory we see reflected in Sullivan comes from Charles H. Cooley (1864–1929) of the University of Michigan, and more directly, from George H. Mead (1863–1931) of the University of Chicago. Mead emphasized the role of language in his theory of behavior, proposing that the spoken language plays a major role in man's development. Cooley emphasized the plastic nature of social evolution, in itself not reducible to physicalistic explanation.[15] Both theorists thus underscored the role of the "other person" in defining for an individual his personal characteristics. This *mirroring* action or "looking-glass self" emphasis can be traced to the concept of "sympathy" advanced by the Scottish economist and social philosopher Adam Smith (1723–1790), and it is much in line with what we have noted in the Introduction as the British Empiricist school of thought.[16]

Mead also coined the term "selective attention," a variant of which Sullivan used. There is also an area of agreement between Mead and William James, the father of Pragmatism.[17] It is within this context of philosophical outlook that men like Sapir and Lasswell labored. Robert E. Park was the major empiricist of this group, who probably more than anyone else gave Sullivan the "participant observation" thesis as well as a concern for the necessity of discovering laws in behavior, operationalizing terms, and so forth.[18] Sullivan even came to subtitle his journal *Psychiatry* as the "Journal for the Operational Statement of Interpersonal Relations."[19] W. I. Thomas (1951) provided grounds for speaking of behavioral patterns in "situations." Sullivan also cites the work of A. Korzybski (1921, 1924), and his mature theory is more akin to Korzybski than to his life-long friend Sapir (1921). Alfred Storch (1924) apparently provided background for his theories of archaic and primitive thought forms, and the anthropologist W. H. R. Rivers (1920) actually used terms we see in Sullivan like "unwitting" and "diffuse." Rivers also had a concept of the "protopathic stage" in thought. Dom. T. V. Moore (1921) was the first to use "parataxes," though he limited this concept to the thinking of the abnormal.

In his later years as theorist Sullivan began using the term "tension" which he adapted from A. M. Dunham, Jr. (1938), and he also made use of Lewinian (1935) "field" terminology although he made it perfectly clear in his writings that he was *no* Lewinian.[20] It is important to underscore the sources of Sullivanian thought at the outset because many people have believed he was more idiosyncratic in proposing terms than he actually was. Sullivan's style of theorizing was very much within the realm of a certain outlook on the nature of personality. He more than any other theorist in the first half of the twentieth century moved the locus of personality description to *inter*personal rather than *intra*personal aspects of human behavior. Though Freud, Adler, and Jung had all touched on this aspect of human behavior, they did not quite capture the *sociological* (supraindividual) meanings in the way Sullivan did.

Personality Theory

STRUCTURAL CONSTRUCTS

MIND VS. BODY AND THE ORGANIZING
ROLE OF PATTERN

As a budding theorist, Sullivan was convinced that psychology must accept the validity of man's cognitive (knowing) processes. In one of his first publications (1924) he even flirted with a form of human vitalism (teleology). By trying to reduce man's cognitions to a "brain physiology" the materialistic theorist ensures that a mind-body dichotomy will arise: "This is materialistic twaddle, and the succeeding mechanistic explanations are energized by the same old magical idea of mind and body, plus cultural accretions in the shape of 'disbelief' in dualism, the whole ensuing as monism."[21] Prior to 1925 when he began his more rigorous transformation, Sullivan was not disturbed by the thought that his theories might be dualistic —or pluralistic, for that matter.[22] Nor was he upset by teleological conceptions. As we shall see, there is some doubt whether he was quite so open to teleologies and dualisms in his final formulations.

The fundamental problem in Sullivanian thought was how to conceptualize an animal which has a physical side to it yet also has a psychic component. It is at this point that Sullivan seems to have leaned upon the conceptions of Adolph Meyer,[23] who pointed out that as animals advanced via evolution the one thing that typified their progress was increasing organization. The higher an organism becomes in the scale of evolution, the more complexly organized or *patterned* is his behavior. In man, a very important aspect of his behavior is the fact that he has language and to that extent can pattern a good deal more of his experience. Through language he can name things and "conceptualize" (organize, pattern) broad areas of knowledge. He can even conceptualize *himself* as an identity—an ego or a self!

Sullivan adopted this idea of a patterning into complexity, adding the very significant notion that *social unities* of an interpersonal variety are patterned as well. Sullivan was wont to define the pattern as follows: "*A pattern is the envelope of insignificant particular differences.*"[24] When energic motion takes on a form, the result is a pattern. The swirl of air, clouds, and water which we categorize as a hurricane is actually a patterning of many different energic forces. The amount of "difference" between one hurricane and another is insignificant, because if you see one hurricane, you can pretty certainly know when you see another. It is at this point—when we can slip all "hurricane concepts" into the same envelope (i.e., construct)—that we speak of the *pattern*.

In higher living organisms, not only do we have a physical patterning into bodily parts beginning with the basic unit of a cell and then encompassing organs, but we have increasingly complex units of description to deal with like speech functions, interpersonal relations, and so forth. Sullivan essentially asks why we call one sphere of patterned units the body and the other the mind. *Both* aspects of life share a common tendency to organize into patterns by way of identifiable energies or *an* energy. As suggested, Sullivan initially toyed with the idea of two energies (physical and hormic), but later in his development he spoke of the singular. Patterned energy resulted in discernible events and items in experience of increasing complexity. Though some of his interpreters have seen in this singular reference evidence that Sullivan was a monist on the question of mind vs. body, Sullivan actually disliked this label. He thought of himself as a more dynamic, interactive, pluralistic thinker than the term "monistic" seemed to suggest was possible.

The emphasis on patterning appears in his definition of memory, as "the relatively enduring record of all the momentary states of the organismic configuration."[25] Thought was defined as "organismic activity by the implicit functioning of symbols, themselves abstracts from the 'material' of life events."[26] Anything material which looks like "something" takes on a shape and to this extent is patterned; hence, Sullivan put his reference to such material in quotes. Even though Sullivan emphasized the role of language in thought, he did accept the possibility of "wordless thinking" through imagery.[27] His favorite construct was *referential processes*, by which he meant all those activities (energy transformations of a patterned sort) which we usually call our thoughts, mental pictures, or "mind's eye" view of things.

THE PATTERNING OF DYNAMISMS AND PERSONIFICATIONS

Just as the term "structure" is not entirely appropriate for Alfred Adler (see Chapter 2), it is only relatively appropriate for Sullivan, because he too wanted to view human behavior in a fluid, patterned, but ever-changing fashion. Sullivan carefully selected the term *dynamism* as his major "structural" term. He defined this construct as *"a relatively enduring configuration of energy which manifests itself in characterizable processes in interpersonal relations"*[28] and also as *"the relatively enduring pattern of energy transformations which recurrently characterize the organism in its duration as a living organism."*[29] The former definition emphasizes man's social side, but the latter could be used by any biologist or physiologist. The point of either of these definitions, however, is to stress that the flux and change of life fall into identifiable patterns. Because of a particular emphasis he was making in the context of defining "dynamism" on one occasion, some of Sullivan's interpreters have concluded that he meant "the" dynamism was the "smallest useful abstraction" for describing behavior or personality. This is not precisely true. Dynamisms as constructs can be very small relative to other dynamisms, or they can be vast conceptualizations.

For the biologist, who is analyzing matter into organized constituents, a cell might prove to be the "smallest useful abstraction" he chooses to use. Since the cell transforms energy for life processes it is clearly a dynamism, though in relation to the body we might consider it a *subdynamism*. Cells go to make up tissues and bones, which in turn constitute organs and skeletal frames, "totaling up to" the *dynamism* of a "man." A subsidiary or subdynamism can often carry on life even after the "total dynamism" comes to an end, as in the cases of hearts or kidneys which are trans-

planted from one body (dead) to another body (living).[30] Yet this explanation does not mean that in order to deal with dynamisms in his theory the theorist must think of a cell as "the" dynamism. He merely has to find some convenient level of abstraction with which to begin his job of description. The psychiatrist, for example, working on another theory—with different interests—might propose as his "basic unit" (in this sense we might say "smallest" but "basic" is clearer) something like the interpersonal situation. The interpersonal situation involves transformation of energy and so long as we can conceptualize this patterned interchange as a unit of analysis *it is a dynamism*.[31] The two broad categories of dynamisms[32] are the *zonal* dynamism, associated with physical activities like eating, drinking, excretion, sexual gratification (lust dynamism), etc., and the *interpersonal* dynamism, which is a very broad category ranging all the way from a "self" dynamism[33] through two-person interactions, groups, social classes, and even entire nations described as discernible units.[34]

Man is born with many of his zonal dynamisms intact (emotions like fear, anger, rage, grief, depression are all innately given dynamisms), but others, and in particular the interpersonal dynamisms, are subject to postnatal maturation or modification by way of learning.[35] Since acquiring language is an important aspect of maturation, dynamisms also include the signs and symbols made available by this growing experience with our native tongue.[36] Thus far, in speaking about a dynamism as an identifiable, patterned unit of whatever we are looking at or theorizing about, we have made it appear that only an observer —like a psychiatrist or a biologist—can fix such dynamisms. Actually Sullivan did not intend this. He believed that *everyone* could fashion dynamisms, for this is how indeed a self-dynamism or many of the attitude dynamisms (political "conservatism," let us say) arise. People pattern their experience all the time, and one of the *earliest* patternings we indulge in and then continue throughout life is what is known as *personification*.

Dating from about the period of his contact with the Chicago School of Social Science, Sullivan mused over the difference between "social" and other forms of human experience. He concluded: "It is approximately correct to say that experience is distinguished as social rather than extra-social when the 'external' objects which have important relation to it are invested by the experiencer with potentialities which are more or less human or anthropomorphic in character."[37] To anthropomorphize is, of course, to ascribe human-like characteristics to inanimate nature like rocks and trees and then to lower animals of all types. Sullivan was using the term anthropomorphic in a more basic sense, however, in that he meant we also assign human characteristics to other people and to ourselves! This is the essence of a *social* relationship. In time, Sullivan was to call this pervasive human tendency to assign humanity to the inanimate *and* animate features of life *personifying* (the action or process), which then resulted in a *personification* (the patterned item).

What occasionally confuses the student of Sullivanian thought is the fact that our personifications are also dynamisms.[38] We must remember that a dynamism need not "exist" in a palpable sense, even though energy is being transformed in order to bring it about—as in the fantasy products of a daydreamer. A personification can be entirely make-believe or *fantastic* (i.e., fantasied). Take, for example, the personification of a "boogeyman," which so many of us as children have related to interpersonally ("He's out there, and he's gonna get me!") in our frightened submergings beneath the bedsheets in a darkened bedroom. Or, the fantastic but happier personification of "Santa Claus." Extending this tendency, Sullivan held that God and related deity concepts were also *fantastic personifications* or *potent representations* of an anthropomorphized supreme being whom we can interact with and implore for guidance

or aid. Men also personify their airplanes and sailing ships ("she") and other possessions. Stereotypes of all sorts are personifications of a group of people taken *en masse*. Finally, social institutions or national identities are also personified, such as "Mother Church" or "Uncle Sam." Man is a personifying animal.

Sullivan believed that personification was first stimulated in life by the recognition that "my body" exists.[39] Knowing ourselves, we come to personify ourselves—distortedly and bizarrely as infants—and then in terms of this self-personification, we personify others.[40] It is not essential that a personification be an either/or matter. We can combine personifications into a single *complex personification* having seemingly incompatible elements. As children we learn to think of ourselves in terms of a *me* but also a *good-me*, a *bad-me*, and even a *not-me* (all of those items of behavior which we are "not like"). We also personify our parents into a breakdown of: *good mother, good father, bad mother,* and *bad father*.[41] The bifurcation of our mother's personification in particular acts as the basis for a series of what Sullivan called *eidetic people* which are retained throughout life. We can equate this term roughly with "imaginary people,"[42] "illusory people,"[43] or "past people."[44] Sullivan was here underscoring the fact that we all have a storehouse of personified images that we can bring up from out of the past and ascribe to others in a fantasied relationship. Often these eidetic people are based upon individuals in the past who have caused us anxiety. The teenaged anarchist who sees in the "establishment" an equation with his personified bad mother or father is engaging in an interpersonal dramatization in his zeal to "destroy the old order."

There is also something called a *subpersonification* in Sullivanian theory,[45] which refers to a number of "social roles" we don if they are to our benefit, even though we might not really believe that they accurately represent us. For example, as children we might "pretend" to be our parents, dress and talk like them and express their attitudes. Yet we would not *really* be personifying ourselves as representing these manners and points of view. Reminiscent of Adler, Sullivan spoke of these as being "as if performances" and "dramatizations."[46] Sometimes we can ape our parents' point of view and actually appear to be completely in line with their outlook, while in fact we are not. These Jungian-like masks which Sullivan acknowledged might be called "personae"[47] were what he meant by the subpersonification.

INTERPERSONAL RELATIONS, PERSONALITY, AND RESPONSIVE SITUATIONISM

Another step in Sullivan's fluid and complex conception of personality was a major patterning dynamism found in human behavior, the *interpersonal relation*. As spokesman for the Washington School of Psychiatry Sullivan could say (circa 1927): "The dynamisms of interest to the psychiatrist are the relatively enduring patterns of energy transformation which recurrently characterize the interpersonal relations—the functional interplay of persons and personifications, personal signs, personal abstractions, and personal attributions—which make up the distinctively human sort of being."[48] The unit of study is now the patterned totality of a series of "in-between" contacts going on between and within (personifications, eidetic people) the psychic identities we know as "people." It is thus correct to observe that by *interpersonal* Sullivan included what others might have said was *intrapersonal* phenomena.[49] A psychotic person, living in the world of dreams he has concocted, would still be in contact with his fantasies (fantastic personifications) in an interpersonal relationship.

To underwrite his view of interpersonal events Sullivan referred to the "situation," especially the *interpersonal situation,* but occasionally he spoke of a *personal situation.* Situations take on designs, they have imports or purposes, and whereas Sullivan had ascribed goal direction (teleology) to the human dy-

namism (the "man"), he now attributed this directedness to the situation, as follows: "The situation is not any old thing, it is you and someone else integrated in a particular fashion which can be converted in the alembic of speech into a statement that 'A is striving toward so and so from B.' "[50] Interpersonal relations can be *conjunctive,* such as when the participants come together in relative harmony, or they can be *disjunctive,* such as when the participants sense a pressure to separate or disperse.[51] The first situation facing a child, in which he behaves interpersonally, is the "me-you"pattern of a baby at the mother's breast. The *good* and the *bad nipple* would be a more accurate description of our earliest personifications than "mother."[52]

Man is literally always in some form of situation, "having commerce" with one or more "others" (imaginary or real people). Insofar as we can think of these situations we can freeze the processes of behavior into a structural terminology. Taking a hard look at the nature of human behavior in this sense, Sullivan found that he could not really separate the human "personality" from the "interpersonal situation" as such. Hence, he chose the only sensible alternative. He made *personality* into an interpersonal construct, paralleling the following definition of personality with the above definition of the interpersonal relation (circa 1933): ". . . personality is conceived as the hypothetical entity which manifests itself in interpersonal relations, the latter including interactions with other people, real or fancied, primarily or mediately integrated into dynamic complexes; and with traditions, customs, inventions, and institutions produced by man."[53]

When personality is such a broad concept, we invite the criticism, "You have lost the individual person! We all participate in common social situations, but we remain individuals; where is this idea in the definitions proffered?" In response to such criticisms Sullivan began a life-long denial that people *are* as individual as they flatter themselves to be. In fact, he liked to call this the *illusion of personal individuality*. Thus he observes: "For all I know every human being has as many personalities as he has interpersonal relations; and as a great many of our interpersonal relations are actual operations with imaginary people—that is, in-no-sense-materially-embodied people—and as they may have the same or greater validity and importance in life as have our operations with many materially-embodied people like the clerks in the corner store, you can see that even though 'the illusion of personal individuality' sounds quite lunatic when first heard, there is at least food for thought in it."[54] Sullivan is here using "individual" to mean *single*. Some theorists have emphasized individuality as an aspect or characteristic of *uniqueness*, and though he did not take this issue up directly, Sullivan accepted so-called uniqueness as the sum of interlacing factors in the situation for the individual (objective, subjective, fantasied, and so forth).

MODES OF EXPERIENCE, LANGUAGE, AND AWARENESS

When we speak of an individual's experience, we are of necessity looking at the flow of interpersonal events from the point of view of the person within those events.[55] How does he see the organized series of events? What are his successive levels of awareness or his " 'inner' elaboration of events"?[56] Sullivan termed these inner levels the *modes* of experience, and he outlined three such modes through which each of us passes—more or less—in the course of achieving adulthood: the *prototaxic, parataxic,* and *syntaxic* modes of experience.

The "raw feel" of life is first revealed to us on the basis of the *prototaxic* mode.[57] Our earliest memories are rooted in some such crude infantile recollection of a momentary state in which a particular discomfort or a fleeting satisfaction took place. Significant experiences of this preverbal period may emanate from various zones, such as the oral zone, where sucking reflexes brought satisfaction, or the anal zone, where tactile sensations brought great discomfort.

It is important to appreciate that Sullivan thought that the prototaxic mode—as well as the parataxic—would continue to preoccupy us at a somewhat lessened rate throughout life. We continue having such "preverbal" hence inexplicable experiences even after we have acquired language skills. Sometimes a highly important aspect of a social interaction is that our buttocks itched terribly but we could not scratch in public for fear of being considered vulgar and impolite. We laugh about such experiences later, even as adults, but they do color our relations with others. An intrusion of this sort could well put a different complexion on the way in which the "other" in the interpersonal situation regards us, as we seem inexplicably uneasy in his presence. By and large, all of those physiological reactions we sense throughout life as our bodily needs can be considered a form of prototaxic experience.[58] There are also initial attempts to conceptualize in the prototaxic mode. The earliest personifications like those of the good and bad nipples are formed at this time.

Along about the ninth month of life, the child begins to acquire language. He has had time by then to personify—both himself and then others. He has become aware that he possesses a voice, and he begins practicing sounds (babbling and cooing). He has also heard others speak and not infrequently has had considerable training in the expression of sounds—either as "baby talk" or as literal word training from parents (usually, the mother). The occurrence of the first word, or pseudoword (baby-talk word) signals the beginning of the *parataxic* mode of experience. In order to grasp fully the development of the parataxic and syntaxic modes we must now consider Sullivan's theory of *language*.

Sullivan believed that man communicated with others in two general ways: via gesture (nonverbal) and via language (verbal).[59] Nature provides man with the equipment to make vocal noises. It is the evolution of culture which then adapts these sounds into the phoneme units of the common language.[60] As we grow to maturity we adapt our vocal sounds to those of our parents, who act as models for us. Sullivan was adamant that words do not *carry* meaning in and of themselves but that they *evoke* meanings in the cognitive experience of a given person.[61] This point may seem obvious, but unfortunately too many people think that words "have" the dictionary meaning affixed to them in some definitive and intrinsic sense.

As technical terms referring to the contents of language Sullivan utilized two concepts, *signs* and *symbols,* both of which reflect his emphasis on pattern (recall that these are *also* dynamisms). A sign is defined as "a particular pattern in the experience of events which is differentiated from or within the general flux of experience."[62] Signs evoke meanings, as in the case of our seeing a road sign ahead which reflects a patterned configuration of light that we recognize and interpret as certain instructions. *We* experience the meaning, not the sign. This procedure of coming to know signs is increasingly complex, for the signs themselves combine into more and more complex (abstract) signs. Letters form into words, words into sentences, and sentences themselves are likely to be more or less intricate in the meanings which they evoke. To capture this complexity factor Sullivan proposed that: "Signs of signs we call symbols. Thus while signals [signs] are rather simply related to behavior, symbols are more complexly related, in that they refer to sundry signals which affect behavior."[63]

Signs and symbols (complex signs) make man's higher thought processes possible.[64] When we symbolize events, we relate them to other things, to thought forms, words, and other discernible parts of our experience, forming increasingly intricate webs of meaning.[65] To the extent that man relies upon word symbols to frame higher level abstractions we can speak of him as behaving increasingly symboli-

cally:". . . the infant behaves non-symbolically when he is taking nourishment from the breast; and the child behaves symbolically when he calls an inanimate toy 'kitty.' . . . Thus it is quite obvious that a great deal of what goes on by the time one is a year old, even if it is inborn, is very highly symbolic."[66] Sullivan felt that it was extremely difficult to distinguish between what is symbolic and what is not symbolic in behavior.

This is not to say that man is free from non-symbolized or poorly symbolized experience. Indeed, what Freud and the other analysts saw as an independent region of mind—the unconscious—Sullivan was to take as simply the remnants of our poorly symbolized prototaxic and parataxic experience. In other words, to the extent that man is symbolizing experience he is growing in awareness or "consciousness," particularly if he is following the rules of logic which culture designates as "common sense." Our parents thus not only model sounds and words for us, but they convey the cultural patterns of thinking which will now strike us as plausible. To the extent that a person is *not* following the culturally acceptable definitions and the logic advocated by the sociocultural milieu we can speak of him as being *autistic:* ". . . an adjective by which we indicate a primary, unsocialized, unacculturated state of symbol activity, and later states pertaining more to this primary condition than to the conspicuously effective consensually validated symbol activities of more mature personality."[67]

By *consensual validation* Sullivan meant (1) the ability to discriminate in experience sufficiently well so as to be able to assess what is a fact and what is not, and (2) the capacity to formulate communicable knowledge, to make our thinking clear to others and in turn have them make their thoughts clear to us.[68] Thus, as we come to adulthood we move from a primary state of preverbal experience (prototaxic mode) to one in which our language terms (signs, symbols) begin taking on meaning for us. But is this communicable meaning? If it is not, then we are still at an autistic level and not yet capable of consensual validation. We can now return to our consideration of the *parataxic* mode, and note that this is the time of life in which our first groping attempts are made to formulate signs (latter half of the first year of life). The child begins to ape the sounds of the parents, and he may at some point come out with "da da," never actually meaning what the proud father presumes he means, but insofar as he would affix a meaning to this sign we could begin to think of it as an autistic "word." What makes this baby word autistic is the fact that it is not communicable! Although we might now say the baby has a "private" word here, and Sullivan would occasionally refer to autistic symbols as "private words,"[69] actually he cautioned against viewing these language items as private. No word is entirely private, because all language signs and symbols are interpersonally taught to the child by an "other," usually the mother.[70]

Generally, autistic vocabularies are limited to noun forms, which begin in the *reverie processes* of the child as he begins to turn sounds, personifications, and interpersonal situations over in his developing cognitions. This process continues in the first half of the second year of life, which is still the period of the parataxic mode of experience. Just as we never lose the prototaxic mode of experience entirely, so too we never lose the autistic (uncommunicative) language signs and symbols that we have concocted in our early years. Nor do we lose the capacity to assign new autisms to experience, as witnessed most clearly in our dreams. Autistic disturbances of thought can be seen in all people to a greater or lesser extent, as when they "mix up" their language and say words to their listener having a confounded hence confusing meaning (*neologisms*).

Another way of referring to autistic intrusions of this sort is to call them *parataxic distortions,* although with this term we are probably introducing the idea of fantastic personifications as well. Sullivan believed that early man probably lived in a parataxic mode of experience. Rather than perceiving things accurately enough to achieve consensual validation, primitive man "prehended" his experience. Through *prehension* it was possible for man to approach life with a predetermined bias, to expect this or that to happen in this or that way even before the "happenings" took place.[71] This situation would be akin to our advancing on life heavily influenced by our hunches and other reverie processes, including all manner of fantastic personifications. Prehensions can serve a useful function if they align one with life in a way which brings about satisfactions. The child, for example, prehends the nipple-in-lips experience even before he has established clearly in mind that nipples exist independent of his own physical identity.[72]

Parataxic thought is thus highly intuitive, often disjointed, flying in the face of what we call logic and practicality. Because it relies upon autistic processes which are in large measure nouns, we can say that parataxic cognition is characterized by "thinking in stereotypes."[73] We do not have the suppleness or flexibility of later, more abstract thought. Overriding generalizations are not yet drawn by a child in the parataxic mode. Memory is also rudimentary; the parataxic reasoner is like a thinking machine with a poor memory bank.[74] He functions erratically and impulsively because he lacks the full range of recall from the past, or well-integrated projections into the future for that matter. Even so, the parataxic is a stage up the ladder of patterned organization from the prototaxic mode of experience.

The parataxic mode thus spans the preverbal to the early verbal stages in development. As this abstracting capacity continues to develop in the child (or the primitive), we witness increasingly complex and abstract symbols taking form and a style of thought emerging which allows for a consensus among all those who now move in this even higher mode of experience. Sullivan was to name this the *syntaxic* mode of experience. In the case of a child this mode is likely to emerge sometime in the second year of life, probably around the eighteenth month. Experience is now nicely framed in by a language system which has taken on syntax (orderly arrangement or pattern). As Sullivan put it: "I should stress that syntaxic symbols are best illustrated by words that have been consensually validated. A consensus has been reached when the infant or child has learned the precisely right word for a situation, a word which means not only what it is thought to mean by the mothering one, but also means that to the infant."[75] Now "da da" really does mean "father," which in turn designates a specific person or role in the familial structure.

Sullivan was eventually to drop the use of "unconscious" as a construct implying a uniform, meaning-laden aspect of mind in favor of other terminology we will be taking up below as well as the general picture of presyntaxic experience. In his view, the growing possibilities for awareness which consensually valid language afforded meant that man was growing comparably in his levels of consciousness: "When we are conscious . . . we are more or less completely under the sway of the processes of consensually valid communicative thinking that we have had to learn."[76] The so-called unconscious manifestations of behavior underscored by the Freudians were now taken as "eccentric symbol performances" rather than consensually meaningful expressions.[77] Or, they might include preverbal remnants from the prototaxic or parataxic modes as fantastic personifications.

THE DYNAMISMS OF PERSONALITY

It was Sullivan's view that all personality terms were mere hypotheses or inferences: "Persons (personalities) are the entities which we infer in order to explain interpersonal events and relations."[78] The student of personality is thus a participant in the process of assigning typologies to his object of study. He cannot stand off to one side in this study and use his sense or-

gans independently from within his *own* personality. The processes and the changes in processes that make up the data which can be subjected to scientific study occur not in the subject person nor in the observer, but in the situation which is created between the observer and his subject. This necessity to be a *participant observer* underlies Sullivan's entire approach to psychiatry.[79] Just as the field anthropologist cannot go into a strange culture and interpret it meaningfully without acknowledging his own cultural biases in the account, so too the psychiatrist must appreciate that his principal instrument for assessing others is his *own* personality.

A major division in Sullivan's theory is between that of the "self system" and the "rest of the personality."[80] The terms *self, self-system,* and *self dynamism* are used roughly synonymously, and Sullivan even combined an *ego* usage with this general designation. In 1931 he observed that the self: ". . . is built up of all the factors of experience that we have in which significant other people 'respond' to us. In other words, our self is made up of the reflections of our personality that we have encountered mirrored in those with whom we deal."[81]

The self dynamism is the central and most important dynamism in the personality. Its functions are to: (a) control awareness through whatever means it can, such as suppressing or repressing certain events;[82] (b) maintain interpersonal security and harmony so that the personality as a whole does not feel threatened or disintegrate entirely;[83] (c) control the direction of development which the personality is to take;[84] and (d) guard against change by forces outside of the personality which might disrupt the totality of factors making it up.[85] The self is, therefore, a kind of benign dictator, which seeks the best arrangement for all of the identities within its domain. It acts as a censor; it delimits what will be seen by the personality much as a microscope delimits the scope of inspection to the range of its tubular channel.[86]

The self is under formulation during our prototaxic mode of experience, and hence, though it is shaped by cultural forces via the parents, there is always an aspect of unique personification and autistic distortion about it. This is complicated by the fact that, in personifying himself the individual is *not* capturing his actual self. The *personified self*—that which we usually refer to when we say "I, me, my," etc.— is not the self we have been referring to thus far. The personified self is necessarily less inclusive than is the self-system.[87] The self-system must inevitably have inferred elements, including hypotheses which can only be made by a participant "other" in interpersonal relations with the individual who is being described. This is true because there are always things which the individual does not wish to know about himself. Indeed, the self's *duty*—it's *raison d'être*—is to hide these aspects of personality from the individual. A censoring agent which is established to deceive cannot be properly circumscribed by the individual under deception. So, we never know the complete workings of our self, even though we do personify ourselves.

One can see the development of two broad categories of personifications in Sullivan's theory, (1) personifications of ourselves and (2) personifications of other people. For our purposes, each of these types of personification can be thought of as examples of a structural construct. We have already mentioned the good-me and bad-me constructs. Combining these two into a single "self-image" would approximate what Sullivan meant by the personification of the self. We think that our relatively good and relatively bad points constitute the total of our self. The opposite of this self personification would be what we have already called the not-me. The not-me refers to states of affect which seem completely foreign to our natures, so that we might be experiencing a dreadful situation (e.g., a state of shock following the death of a loved one in an accident which was partially our fault) that makes us think "this is not happening to me." Personifica-

tions of others include the good and bad nipple, mother, father, and so forth. All of those fantastic personifications of institutions and inanimate objects would also fall under the designation of an "other" personification.

There are a few more of these "other" personifications worth emphasizing. Sullivan called an interesting one the *supervisory pattern*.[88] This is the imaginary and generalized other person to whom we are speaking when we deliver a talk or write something down. We write or speak to someone; we choose our words and formulate our thoughts in order to make our intentions clear (consensually) as if we were communicating to a *specific* "other." And, of course, not everyone in speaking or writing has the same image of what this other person is, so the choice of words, the level of argument, the clarity of presentation may vary. Sullivan made an effort to make his supervisory patterns clear to himself, noting on one occasion that his supervisory pattern was an "overprivileged juvenile."[89]

Another personification we have of a "generalized other" Sullivan referred to as *thee,* usually in the context of speaking about "thee and me" or sometimes "me-you patterns." The point he was making was that our language allows us to draw such distinctions, when in fact *no* person is completely separate from his *thee*.[90] We must appreciate that the other person in a true sense is *also* us (me). Furthermore, in coming together interpersonally, we bring to the relationship multiple me-you patterns from our past—which gets even more complicated because there are two or more people relating interpersonally so the fantasy involved in any social situation proceeds at a geometric rate.[91]

Sullivan liked to call the two-person interpersonal relation a "two-group."[92] Literally any interpersonal relationship in which two people were interacting (as opposed to one person fantasying with objects or his own make-believe people) would be a two-group. Sullivan put his emphasis on what social psychologists sometimes call the face-to-face group or, in the case

Figure 19
Sullivan's Conception of Personality

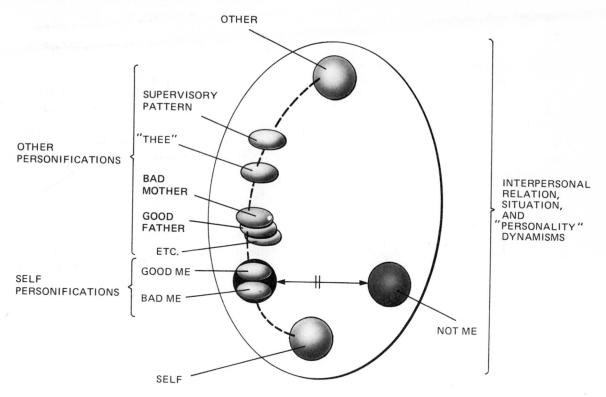

of family members and so forth, the primary groups. It was his belief that society was held together by the individual's overlapping memberships in such basic interpersonal groups.[93] But Sullivan went one step further than most social psychologists in demanding that we take the individual's fantasy productions into consideration. Figure 19 presents a schematization of Sullivan's conception of personality. Note that we have the entire interpersonal relation encircled, with the self and the other defining the extremes of the ellipse. On the left-hand side is a series of personifications, divided into self and other subgroupings. The self personification is made up of the good- and bad-me, and it is opposed to the not-me which lies over to the right-hand side of the interpersonal situation (relation). A series of other personifi-

cations are symbolized, running up the left-hand side of the interpersonal situation (relation), including just for demonstration purposes: good father, bad mother, thee, and a supervisory pattern. We must always keep in mind that the *same* scheme can be considered from the point of view of the other.

MOTIVATIONAL CONSTRUCTS

NEEDS AS ENERGY TRANSFORMATIONS IN SITUATIONAL INTEGRATION

Since personality is to be defined interpersonally, it is reasonable to expect Sullivan's theory of motivation to reflect this "supraindividual" flavor. He captures this view in speaking about the *integration* of a situation. We all have these *integrating tendencies,* based upon biological or cultural factors in our make-up.[94] To become integrated with others is to become involved with them, to exchange affective feelings in a reciprocal fashion, and thus to cement the interpersonal relationship. In a sense, the action of integrating situations is synonymous with "interpersonal relations."[95] It means that we *do* relate to others,[96] that we cement our ties to others,[97] but it also means that we "pull ourselves together" in the sense of having a self-identity and good feeling about ourselves.[98]

Sometimes a situation is integrated on the basis of negative feeling tones, so that interpersonal relations are then inharmonious, but as we shall see later, individuals have certain "devices" (dynamisms) which allow them to overlook unhappy aspects of the interpersonal situation.[99] There is usually more than one integrating tendency at work in cementing the relationship.[100] Also, it is possible for integrating tendencies to exert influence from outside awareness—outside the self-dynamism's purview.[101] What are the specific contents of these tendencies to integrate situations? Historically, the concept of a *need* has been used to describe their nature.[102] When someone senses what he considers a need in his personal make-up, whether that be for some physical gratification like food or some interpersonal gratification like "wanting to be liked," he is actually sensing a disequilibrium in his interpersonal situation. He is "out of integration." It is the alternation of needs with their gratifications which literally constitutes "experience."

Needs are sensed by the individual as a *tension,* which Sullivan viewed as the "potential for energy expenditure."[103] There are *three* types of tension and changes in tension level likely to be experienced by any of us: (a) the tension of physical needs (hunger, thirst, lust); (b) the tension of interpersonal needs (security, intimacy, love); and (c) the altered states of contrasting tonus and spontaneity we recognize as the difference between sleep and waking.[104] Sullivan did not attempt to name an exhaustive list of needs for the human being, though he was not above suggesting possibilities in both the physical and the interpersonal spheres. He spoke of the infant's needs to have oxygen, water, foodstuffs, a constant body temperature, freedom of movement, and an efficient organ system.[105] He also proposed a *power motive,* which he felt we were all born with, generating needs to acquire, gather, collect, achieve—as in the poetic allusion to a babe in the crib who sees the moon for the first time and automatically reaches for it.[106] The interpersonal needs for security, intimacy, and love (combined with lust) also play a prominent role in Sullivanian thought.[107]

How do needs (integrating tendencies) actually work? We know they herald energy transformation by way of tension, but how can we say they carry over into actual behavior? It was in dealing with this question that Sullivan was prompted to speak of drives, forces, and vectors. A *drive* is just another way of referring to the needs we have, except now we are emphasizing the motion rather than simply the disequilibrium.[108] The *force* is another way of speaking about the tension, for it implies to the individual that not only is there a potential for energy transformation (i.e., the tension) but that there is power to get the changes made once behavior is underway.[109] A need state is not merely a possibility for change, it is a positive force for change demanding some form of action through the expression of force. The concept of *vector* adds to this the idea of a magnitude and a direction which needs will take.[110] Needs are "more or less" in nature and they also suggest a direction to be taken in order to answer their prompting tendencies. Since the vectors map the direction which force will take interpersonally, Sullivan was prone to speak of *field forces* in his final theoretical formulations.[111] Figure 20 contains the various terms in a schematization of the integration of a situation.

Figure 20
Integration of a Situation

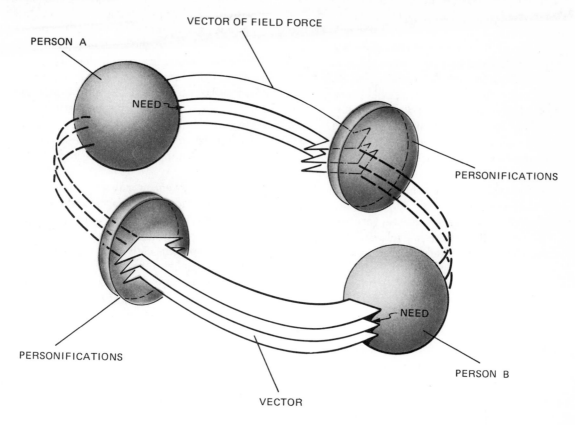

VECTOR OF FIELD FORCE

PERSON A

NEED

PERSONIFICATIONS

PERSONIFICATIONS

NEED

PERSON B

VECTOR

NEEDS = DRIVES, MOTIVES, TENSIONS — I.E., "ENERGY TRANSFORMATIONS"

Notice in Figure 20 that we have two persons (A and B), beginning to integrate an interpersonal situation. Various physical and psychological (interpersonal) needs emanating from the A and B identities assume a vector quality, pointing in the direction of the "other" (A toward B, and vice versa). We have subsumed the concepts of drive, motive, and tension under this general rubric of "need" and thus have emphasized that needs always presage energy transformations. Finally, note that one or more personifications are likely to intrude into the emerging situation, so that par-

ticipants A and B will be relating to several "others" (eidetic people or fantastic images of inanimate things) in the situation. This makes for a highly complex concatenation of the real and the unreal in all interpersonal relations.

EMOTION, SECURITY, SATISFACTION, AND ANXIETY

Emotional reactions—feelings—reflect the kinds of needs that are at play in the interpersonal situation. Sullivan held to what he called a "theorem" of reciprocal emotions,[112] which meant that integration is a reciprocal process in which the complementary needs of the participants in a situation are either gratified or aggravated. If John has a need to be mothered and Mary, his girlfriend, has a need to mother, then the resulting two-group will probably be well integrated. However, if either Mary or John did not feel complementarily about this matter of mothering, then we would not witness a happy interpersonal situation. John would feel Mary did not appreciate him, or Mary would not understand why John feels that she is overly possessive and so forth. If reciprocal patterns of behavior could not then be developed (some kind of altered relationship), the two-group would be dissolved.

Extreme or intense emotions are confounding elements in interpersonal relations, because the individual finds that he cannot function properly at this level of tension.[113] Another way of saying this is that extreme emotions become disjunctive forces. At one end of the spectrum we have an affective (emotional) state of "utter well-being" which Sullivan called *euphoria*.[114] At the other end of the spectrum we have the utmost states of extreme anxiety which are literally foreign to usual experience, such as awe, dread, loathing, and horror. Sullivan called the latter affective states the *uncanny emotions*.[115] Between these two ends of the tension dimension we have a continuum of varying levels of disequilibrium that the individual experiences as he wends his way through life. Complete euphoria is an ideal state of perfect equilibrium which is never realized in a literal sense.[116] But what we call "feeling good" or "pleasure" would surely approximate this emotional mood of satisfaction and security.

When the tension of an interpersonal situation is clearly physical in nature, Sullivan referred to this as a *satisfaction*.[117] Such things as meeting life's most basic needs to take in food, maintain oxygen, retain water, and so forth are all tied to satisfactions. In feeling hunger, we personify the refrigerator and integrate an interpersonal situation with it in order to relax the muscle tonus prompting us to seek

the satisfaction of eating.[118] When we are seeking friendships and integrating situations with human beings, Sullivan would not always consider this due primarily to a satisfaction motivation. Of course, the kinds of reactions we have are never either/or. The *forbidding gesture* of a mother, frowning at her son's antics when visitors are in the home, might lead to a termination of the misbehavior. As the son stops his "acting up," he may indeed sense a feeling (emotion) of well-being as his muscles relax now that mother is no longer irritated with him.

A bowel movement may seem like the most private experience in the world, yet the Sullivanian would point out that some of the most potent personifications in our personality system issue from the early toilet training relationship with mother. How we behave in the "toilet situation" was integrated and established as a style of personality many years ago. This is a particularly good example of how satisfactions are interfused with what might be termed the more "psychological" needs of *security* or *security operations*.[119] In our acts of integration with others socially we constantly face the threats of rejection, or we have the possibility of being surpassed by others in some way, being made to look foolish for our inability to "do the right things" or to compete with great skill. Hence, when Sullivan wanted to stress these more strictly social needs, he spoke of security rather than satisfaction as motivating the individual.

The need for security shades into what we might consider a need for *self-esteem* or *self-respect*. Sullivan even spoke of this as a "drive to maintain security," and essentially equated it with the power motive construct we mentioned above.[120] The self dynamism therefore protects us; it gives us the illusion that we are really brighter than we are or that our manner is not as irritating as some people have "jokingly" told us that it is. The stronger the self dynamism, the more likely it is that an individual will lack insight concerning his impact on others. This is why eminent people sometimes have decidedly eccentric mannerisms. They do not adjust (reintegrate) their interpersonal patterns because they have a sufficiently powerful self dynamism to retain security in interpersonal relations even with their —what other people take to be—atypical styles of behavior. But it is not only the great person who has a strong self dynamism. Even the psychotic can have a strong self, paradoxical as this may seem on first consideration.

If security is derived from interpersonal, sociocultural factors in human relations, then we need some way of conceptualizing how a person's behavior is molded into this or that cultural pattern. Over the years, Sullivan came increasingly to rely upon a construct of anxiety to serve this role in his theory. It is difficult to distinguish between *anxiety* and *fear* actually, and Sullivan admitted that probably in early life the infant could not distinguish between these two emotions very definitely.[121] However, the experience we call fear does have more specificity about it. We say we fear something when we have something specific in mind, which often permits us to plan action to counter the object and possibly to destroy it.[122] If we fear a snake, we can avoid places where snakes are likely to be found; or "seeing" a snake unexpectedly, we can crush it with a rock. Fear is thus a conjunctive force, and it often permits us to carry off an encounter with success. Anxiety, on the other hand, is more diffuse and vague. When we are anxious, we do not always know why we feel as we do. Or, if we become anxious in a situation, we might "lose our head" and actually become our "own worst enemy." Rather than destroying the snake, the anxious person tries to flee and blindly runs off a cliff or possibly stumbles into an entire nest of snakes just off the beaten path. Anxiety is thus a disjunctive force in interpersonal relations.

It is anxiety as an emotional reaction which takes us most directly into the theoretical explanation of interpersonal relations (personality). Anxiety is gradually distinguished from fear by the child, due probably to its more equivocal, diffuse nature[123] as well as the fact that it seems more oriented to his anticipations or expectancies.[124] How is anxiety first generated? Sullivan put it very succinctly in his "anxiety transmission theorem," as follows: *"The tension of anxiety, when present in the mothering one, induces anxiety in the infant."*[125] It can be taken as a universal presumption that anxiety is *always* triggered or evoked interpersonally (in the sense in which Sullivan uses this term[126]). When an infant is held at arms length and then given a slight drop through a loss of support, he will stiffen up and show obvious signs of *fright*. This is a fear reaction. However, when he becomes listless, cries plaintively, or even becomes apathetic due to a poorly integrated two-group of mother and child, we are witnessing the effects of anxiety.

The "mothering one" (actual mother, nurse, etc.) is thus the source of our first emotional awareness of anxiety. If she is relaxed and confident, loving and at ease in her contact with us, we have the feeling of euphoria. If she is in any way uncertain, unloving, or rejecting, we sense a *disphoric* state which Sullivan considered to be anxiety.[127] This combined "emotional linkage existing between the mother and infant" Sullivan called *empathy*.[128] Empathy is a remnant of the very primitive way in which men probably first related interpersonally. It is like what the sociologists call "contagion," i.e., a direct emotional stimulus as in the hysterical responses of crowds which get whipped up into a frenzy by a speaker. Sullivan now uses this direct emotional reciprocity to describe relations in a two-group. A child will feel in empathy with the feelings of its mother even before there is a language system or an awareness of other signs (forbidding gestures, for example) to influence the nature of his feelings. Even in the prototaxic mode of experience emotions permit a child to evaluate his situation, and to feel well integrated (conjunctive force) or poorly integrated (disjunctive force).

Some people retain this empathetic manner of integrating situations throughout life, but in most cases by the time the child is two years of age he no longer relies on sheer empathy to guide his actions.[129] It is probably most important in early childhood, which would run from roughly the sixth through about the twenty-seventh month of life or thereabouts. Since we are coming to know and define our selves at this time (good-me, bad-me, not-me), anxiety (loss of euphoria) has much to do with self-esteem or self-confidence. Sullivan came increasingly to define anxiety in terms of self-evaluations such as these. Here is a good example: ". . . anxiety is a signal of danger to self-respect, to one's standing in the eyes of the significant persons present, even if they are only ideal figures from childhood [i.e., eidetic people]; and this signal, other things being equal, leads to a change in the situation."[130]

Anxiety is often sensed in completely different emotional terms. For example, we may dislike someone and find reasons for avoiding him, yet the real reason may be that in some region of our personality (outside awareness, unconscious) he provokes anxiety. Hence, the self very smoothly puts into effect the security operation of "I find him a bore" or "His personality annoys me." Anger is frequently just a cover-up emotion for underlying anxiety: ". . . anger is much more pleasant to experience than anxiety. The brute facts are that it is much more comfortable to feel angry than anxious."[131] This indirect use of the anxiety construct led some of Sullivan's critics to accuse him of calling "everything" which has a disjunctive effect on integration "anxiety." He answered this charge by noting that several other emotions have equally harmful effects on integration as does anxiety, such as loneliness, envy, conventional prejudices held by people, or doctrines of sin and atonement.[132]

DEFENSIVE MANEUVERS, SELF-ESTEEM, AND THE SOCIALIZATION PROCESS

Thanks to the growing sensations of euphoria and anxiety the child can maneuver defensively in life. He can literally avoid noticing those behaviors which bring him a feeling of anxiety (loss of security). This *selective inattention* permits the self dynamism to lift awareness above the level where we actually can say that we "know" this or that about ourselves.[133] Our shoes are not shined, and this will bring disapprobation if mother notices, but the self-system selectively inattends and we somehow show up once again with scuffed shoes. Strange, how we could put on shoes and yet fail to notice their obviously sloppy condition until mother brought the matter up once again. Hence, Sullivan notes that when he is talking about selective inattention, he is "talking about things which you notice but never attend to—and they can be sentences or all sorts of things."[134]

If there is a defensive aspect to selective inattention, it is to avoid a lowering of self-esteem. But there is also a completely straightforward, nondefensive reason for this maneuver. Many of our activities demand rather complex, well-coordinated movements which would be impossible to carry off if we had to fix attention to every detail. For example, it is possible to drive a car with relatively little awareness of the many details, like shifting gears or constantly modulating speed. Though accidents sometimes arise because of such automatic procedures, many of us find ourselves driving an auto home from the office without being entirely aware of just how we got home so quickly. We were "lost in thought," but did we *really* fail to notice the road, the traffic, the demands of our responsibility? Probably not. Our driving was merely facilitated by selective inattention.

The important point for our long-term adjustment is just how smoothly selective inattention works and whether or not it excludes from awareness some rather important material which we could well use in improving our adjustment.[135] There is a natural tendency for the individual to selectively inattend to aspects of his behavior which embarrass him.[136] The girl who picks at her nose when tense "fails to notice" that she has this habit. Yet when it is pointed out to her, she can usually—after some soul-searching—find truth in the charge. Sometimes we selectively inattend in a period of heavy concentration or absorption, in what Sullivan called "brown studies."[137] We are so immersed in our thought or a conversation that later, when someone tells us about a certain highly important aspect of the situation which we did not find germane to our line of thought, it amazes us to wonder how we could have overlooked this significant matter.

A misperception of a situation is not clearly maladjustive until contents of experience have literally been *dissociated* from the self-system. Dissociation means that things have been entirely cut off from identification with the self.[138] No amount of soul searching is going to result in an awareness on the individual's part that he does indeed "do" this or "believe" that or "have" such a desire. Sullivan did not make an either/or distinction between selective inattention and dissociation, viewing the entire procedure as on a continuum, as follows: "It seems to me that the hierarchy of things that can happen about awareness of events begins with selective inattention and goes on to dissociation of events, with various degrees of awareness between, controlled largely by substitutive processes."[139]

The dissociative dynamism is ever-active and —a seeming contradiction—*vigilant*. It works by continuous alertness to all of those factors in awareness which might reveal its content.[140] When something in life is likely to reveal the dissociated contents, the self-system is capable of changing the topic of conversation, shifting the locus of concern, or simply dismissing the newly emerging factor as "boring." These devices are what Sullivan called in the above quote *substitutive processes,* for they act as di-

versionary events in substitution for the problem of living which is really at play. In a strange way, the stronger the self-system, the more smooth or *suave* (Sullivan's term) is dissociation, and the easier it is for a participant observer to see the effects of dissociated materials in the personality style of the affected person.[141] Thus, a man with dissociated homosexual impulses may take fleeting glances at the pants fly of another male. Sullivan called this movement of the eyes *unobserved alertness*.[142] The man with the dissociated homosexual impulse is not aware of his alertness; he does not observe himself glancing at or somehow pressing against the body of a male companion at every opportunity. He would be shocked and revulsed at the suggestion of an amorous intention on his part. But the sensitive participant observer can literally *see* this suave performance.

The interpersonal nature of the socialization process is underscored by Sullivan. We come to define our selves on the basis of *reflected appraisals,* which are the assessments of us made by significant people in our life.[143] In appraising us, others are of course also *personifying* us. The mother who has labeled (personified) her son as a "wild animal" or "bad boy," to be broken and subdued, ensures by her continuing reflected appraisals of him that he will come to view himself in precisely these terms. And furthermore, he will come to judge others in these terms: "It is not that as ye judge so shall ye be judged, but as you judge yourself so · shall you judge others; strange but true so far as I know, and with no exception."[144]

It is chronically low self-esteem which invariably calls out the dissociative processes, as well as other poor grounds for integration of situations such as exploitative attitudes toward others.[145] If the self-esteem is high, then we have a socially well-adjusted individual. Of course, things are never one way in personal adjustment, and this is the reason for speaking of the "me" as three persons. Behaviors which bring us euphoric feelings in life are personified into the good-me.[146] Behaviors which damage our self-esteem or which are foreseen to do possible damage to it "if we behave that way" are personified into the bad-me.[147] And the extremely unacceptable or bizarre behaviors enter into the "nightmarish personifications" of the not-me.[148] The not-me is usually in direct opposition to the values and knowledge of the self dynamism. It is completely foreign and associated with uncanny emotions because of its diametric opposition to what we know of as our self.[149] Whereas the good-me and bad-me are within consciousness—we can recognize our stronger and weaker points—the not-me is always outside of awareness,[150] usually seen in dreams, as a personification of some "other," but as we have already suggested above, in certain mental disorders it can also be personified in the waking state.

In forming these three self personifications, the individual relies upon cultural contents which are mediated by parental influence. Sullivan liked to use the adjective *significant* in referring to these mediators of the culture, whether he was referring to *parents*,[151] *people*,[152] *persons*,[153] or even *adults*.[154] Anyone who is thus important interpersonally "for us" and has to that extent "made us what we are today" is a "significant other." We usually carry our significant persons along with us throughout life as personifications. Though he did not like the term, Sullivan acknowledged that this was similar to Freud's *introjection*.[155] Much of the *guilt* we feel when we "misbehave" is due to these internally retained personifications of past (eidetic) figures, whom we have fantastically personified into bearers of the public morals.

The final point concerning Sullivan's view of socialization relates to his discussion of the *will* or *will power*. He found this concept unacceptable, an archaic term which assigns responsibility to the child even before he has an opportunity to develop a proper self dynamism.[156] It is the self which guides and directs awareness via dynamisms such as selective inattention and dissociation, relying in good measure upon *foresight* to effect change.[157] Yet this does *not* mean that we as individuals have a true freedom of choice to behave as we might choose.[158] This is an illusion, used by parents and educators in a misguided effort to single out responsibility for "the" cause or "the" fault of an undesirable situation.[159] The harm done when a parent assumes that the child "has a will of his own" is almost inestimable. Just as no one is completely individual, so too no one is completely free from the demands of others, the situation, or the reflected appraisals in the present and those in the past. Assigning a locus of control to the individual was for Sullivan just as wrong as assigning a fixed structure to the mind. So we must ever look beyond the individual to the social milieu if we wish to know what is happening within—even a single—personality.

THE ADJUSTMENT MECHANISMS

Sullivan referred to almost every one of Freud's constructs over the years, and so we should examine his modifications. It is easy to see how what Freud might have called *repression* or *repressed material* Sullivan considered dissociation or dissociated material.[160] He also felt that what was called repressed contents of mind were sometimes merely poorly formulated concepts and idea forms.[161] Recall that he believed thought without language was possible. Hence, it is equally possible to think of preverbal (parataxic) or nonverbal experience manifesting itself in dreams or other so-called "parapraxes" (Freudian slips). It is not that something has been pushed out of awareness so much as that something never had been properly framed for conscious expression to begin with. Sullivan simply could not accept a view of the mind turning in on itself via *antithetical* ideas in the way that Freud was so willing to conceptualize.[162] Whereas Freud was prone to see syntaxic meaning in mental blocks, slips of the tongue, neologistic words, and so forth, Sullivan questioned this antithetical strategy, claiming that parataxic distortions are syntactically *meaningless*.

Sullivan could find no evidence for *fixation* in his schizophrenic subjects.[163] He did think of human development in terms of stages, however. At certain crucial points along the way to maturity, while moving from one stage to another, a child might develop what Sullivan called a *malevolent transformation*.[164] This was a special form of dynamism, which crystallized some unhealthy pattern which then persisted in the person's behavior. Rather than being a fixation, the malevolent transformation would thus be a continuing pattern of maladaptive behavior. Hence, though Sullivan does not speak of fixation, he does refer to the "arrest and deviation of personality development."[165]

Consonant with this view of fixation, Sullivan thought of *regression* as the collapse of behaviors not yet fully learned, or the perseverance of previous stages now manifesting themselves when they should have already been passed through.[166] Regression is thus a common occurrence: ". . . in the course of the life of any child you can observe, practically at twenty-four hour intervals, the collapse, when the child gets thoroughly tired, of patterns of behavior which are not very well stamped in. . . ."[167]

Sullivan defined *sublimation* as "the unwitting substitution, for a behavior pattern which encounters anxiety or collides with the self-system, of a socially more acceptable activity pattern which satisfies part of the motivational system that caused trouble."[168] An unacceptable motivation is thus deflected and given only partial gratification in sublimation, as in the case of a woman Sullivan described who had sexual promptings for males she met, including some subliminal thoughts of being a prostitute. In time, through the mediation of a rather handsome preacher, she deflected her energies into "good works" aimed primarily at helping "fallen women."[169]

The concept of *identification* was handled by Sullivan in terms of a "feeling of familiarity" which exists between a mother and her daughter or a father and his son.[170] Parental interest and pleasure is stimulated when, for example, a mother sees her daughter excel at modern dance or a father observes his boy tossing a baseball around. The parents relive their own pasts in this way, and by applauding such efforts in their offspring, they ensure that the acceptable patterns will be culturally transmitted. Sullivan preferred the term *interiorization* to introjection. The child personifies and interiorizes the moral code which significant adults (parents, preachers) have advocated. Later, when he is about to do something which might transgress this code, he senses a "feeling of unpleasant anticipation" (guilt *qua* anxiety) which moves him to avoid the prompting and alter his course of behavior.[171]

Sullivan viewed *projection* as a special variant of foresight. Everyone projects in interpersonal situations because we all try to foresee what is about to happen.[172] If someone has a chronically low opinion of himself, then what we witness is a continuing projection of negative evaluations. The low self-esteem of a maladjusted individual makes it appear that he is projecting negative aspects of his self-system, but the truth is, he is projecting "what he is." Another probable cause of seeming projections is the fact that some individuals simply have not made adequate discriminations or differentiations between people.[173] A rebellious teenager might not have discriminated properly between the authority-subordinate relationship he has been experiencing with his father and the analogical but really *different* relationship of this sort he has with his teacher. Hence, he seems to be projecting elements from the father relation to the teacher relation, but rather than projecting he is simply failing to discriminate.

Sullivan's view of *compensation* was as a dynamism "by which simpler activities and implicit processes are substituted in lieu of difficult or impossible adjustment."[174] Going to the movies rather than doing homework would be a compensation. This is quite a different usage than we saw Adler develop in Chapter 2. Sullivan used *displacement* somewhat more conventionally, as the deflection of an emotion from one context to another. For example, the schoolboy who picks a fight with a peer on the way home from the classroom in reaction to his irritation with the teacher that day has displaced his hostility from the latter to the . former.[175] Finally, Sullivan also used *rationalization* in the familiar sense of "giving a plausible and often exceedingly inconsequential explanation" of some event rather than owning up to the real reasons prompting one's behavior.[176]

TIME PERSPECTIVE CONSTRUCTS

Sullivan outlined *six* preadult eras or "epochs" of development, and we will take them up in order.

INFANCY: FROM BIRTH TO THE MATURATION OF LANGUAGE CAPACITY

The newborn infant comes into the world in the state of experience we have called the prototaxic mode, and he has as his major "zone of interaction" the *oral* activities of breathing, sucking to eat, and so forth. This is what fixes his attention on the mother's breast in time and makes it likely that he will eventually personify this feature of life as his first discriminatory act (good vs. bad breast).[177] There are two ways in which anxiety now arises: through a violent disturbance in a zone of contact (injury to the mouth, for example) or through the manifestation of anxiety in the mother (loss of euphoria via empathy with the mothering other).[178] We have already considered how socialization proceeds—even before speech— through the guiding effects of anxiety on selective inattention and dissociation, the definition in time of the good-, bad-, and not-me.

Sullivan felt that the oral zone was the "main stream" for the evolution of the self, because it entered into so many of life's activities,

from eating and drinking to speech and sexual play.[179] The concept of a *zone* is thus simply that touchstone for all of the physical, chemical, *and* social activities which we engage in throughout life. Zones are intricately related to needs, which, of course, represent integrating tendencies. Dynamisms can thus be identified in connection with zones, and something like an oral zone is *also* an oral dynamism. When we stress the particular locus of a dynamism's influence, we are speaking of the zone, the region in which integration is literally being patterned.

Zonal definitions are not circumscribed by the specific anatomical structure which bears their name. For example, the oral zone includes the lower part of the face and the muscles of the mouth, throat, and larynx.[180] It also includes in the very young child the muscles controlling breathing, crying, and probably, to an extent, the auditory channels as well.[181] As we mature, a number of zones act as the locus of our life patterns, such as the retinal area, auditory apparatus, tactile receptors, kinaesthetic apparatus, urethral and anal zones, and the genital zone.[182] These zones mature and manifest energic transformations (dynamisms) which have hereditary components, yet they are patterned in large measure through interpersonal relations. Sullivan stretched his concept of zonal need to include a kind of "function" or "capability" pleasure in the delights of sheer growth. He once referred to the general term *zonal need* as the "need to manifest every capability that matures—what we see as the child's pleasure in manifesting any ability that he has achieved."[183]

Early learning begins in prehension (primitive perception). By about the sixth to eighth month of life the infant manifests facial expressions; in most instances, the child is rather well organized by the ninth month.[184] He can distinguish between fear and anxiety by this time, and he responds to the changes in his anxiety level in order to meet parental expectations. Language training is also beginning near the end of the first year of life, and he thus moves into the parataxic mode of experience in which autistic speech is the rule. It is very important for the child to acquire a sense of foresight in experience: "The comparatively great influence of foresight is one of the striking characteristics of human living in contrast to all other living."[185] Foresight demands an ability to evaluate not only factors in the present but what might be coming up next in life. Sullivanian theory emphasizes that a child can evaluate even *before* he has speech. He can judge what is likely to be taking place in the upcoming situation based upon how he *feels* (emotions, anxiety vs. euphoria) about it.[186] Later, he uses language to clarify his foresightful evaluations.

CHILDHOOD: FROM LANGUAGE TO THE MATURATION OF THE NEED FOR PLAYMATES

Much of what we mean by socialization is the restriction of personal needs, the willingness to forgo and adapt to the demands of others, and the acceptance of partial gratifications rather than full pleasures. This pretty well sums up what Sullivan meant by *sublimation,* and in his theory of development he saw this dynamism as taking shape during the first few months of life.[187] However, it is in the era of childhood that sublimation becomes a very prominent dynamism, thanks in large measure to the advent of language, the learning of "no, no" and "do this" or "don't do that." Mother and father are expanding their prohibitions, and the child must increasingly settle for less energic transformation than he would like to achieve in his zonal needs.[188] Gradually, sublimation is joined by identification, as the child comes to play "as if" he were mother or father.[189] The childhood era is a time of growing self-awareness, and the personifications of the self are increasing at a rapid pace (especially the good-me and bad-me). We are moving along now into the second and third years of life. Empathic controls are giving way to the controls of consensually validated language.

Hence, the prototaxic mode is being traversed, and early syntaxic experience enters the scene.

JUVENILE ERA: FROM PLAYMATES TO THE MATURATION OF THE NEED FOR ISOPHILIC INTIMACY

The next stage in development is defined broadly as "the years between entrance in school and the time when one actually finds a chum—the last landmark which ends the juvenile era, if it ever does end."[190] This is a time of continuing expansion in self-definition and knowledge for it covers much and sometimes all of our grammar school years. The personality really awakens for the first time in the juvenile era, and the self-system confronts the world as something truly existing for its own sake.[191] The child begins to appreciate that if he is to find a place in this scheme of things, he will have to become involved in many things which never before occurred to him. The world is no longer his oyster. The "spoiled" child finds that on the playground he must be considerate of others or be rejected.[192] Exclusion could be highly traumatic, for a child of this age period has a maturing need to associate with others of his age as playmates or *compeers*. The compeer is a friend who helps the child extend his range of capability in play and who acts as a buffer against the feelings of loneliness that might result if the child were isolated. There may be, and often are, more than one compeer in a child's life. He has bonds with these friends, but they do not assume the major importance that a very select person—the chum—will assume in our next stage of development.

The child in the juvenile era also learns the importance of *competition* in life. He finds that status in the group is a function of how bright one is in the classroom, how daring on the playground, or how expert in the misadventures of childhood pranks. He seeks to establish a *reputation* among his peers and thus tries to excel in some competitive endeavor of this nature. In fact, Sullivan used to equate the concept of a "juvenile person" with something like "habitually competitive" even if he were referring to an adult.[193] In order to ensure his status, and thereby protect his self-esteem, the juvenile attaches himself to certain "in-groups." Identification is thus furthered, for the child quickly equates himself with those he takes to be desirable—whether they be school achievers, delinquent or mischievous groups, or those with expensive and attractive clothes. Social stereotypy is a corollary aspect of this period, and the juvenile soon grasps the meaning of the more typical stereotypes like the "scheming Jew," the "indolent Negro," or the "ingenuine White Man."[194]

We might note at this point that Sullivan put more stress on the ages beyond four or five than the classical analysts did. He once said quite specifically that personality development continues beyond the age of 10.[195] In fact, one can never really say in Sullivanian terms that a personality is fixed, for what one "is" depends upon the social milieu in which he moves. Commonalities in behavior are to be noted, but these issue more from the sociocultural milieu than they do from some internally fixed structure called "personality."

Presumably the *Oedipal Complex* would take place around the late childhood to the early juvenile era of development (ages four through six). Sullivan did not deny that a seeming Oedipal situation existed in the male. He was not so certain about the female, and he once wrote a paper with the collaboration of his training analyst, Clara Thompson, in which the *Electra Complex* was specifically denied.[196] In time, it seemed to Sullivan that so-called Oedipal factors probably were misunderstandings made by analysts of some rather common tendencies in human behavior. For example, we have the man who actively compares his wife with his mother. Hysteroid people are likely to do this, probably because they are dependent, suggestible, and likely to seek mother substitutes as marital partners.[197] But this comparison need not be taken as evi-

dence that the grown man had literally desired his mother as he now desires his wife in the sexual (lustful) sense.

In order to make Sullivan's meaning clearer we will consider an important distinction he made about the way in which man finds himself attracted to other people or to his own body for that matter. First of all, recognizing that *philos* is Greek for love, Sullivan distinguished between this state and *eros,* which would refer more specifically to a genital factor in interpersonal relations. Lust (eros) is *not* identical to love (philos): "The tendencies to integrate lustful-erotic situations should not be confused with those which eventuate in love situations. The latter may survive indefinitely the loss of prospective sexual satisfactions or the integration of sexual situations with persons not in the love relationship."[198] The genital lust dynamism is not even matured at the period of life in which the classical psychoanalytical theory would have children lusting after their parents.[199]

We can now add some prefixes to our eros vs. philos distinction and speak about *autophilic* (self-love), *isophilic* (loving a member of the same sex), and *heterophilic* (loving a member of the opposite sex); or, alternatively, *autoerotic* (self-lust), *isoerotic* (lusting for a member of the same sex), and *heteroerotic* (lusting for a member of the opposite sex).[200] The point of this breakdown is to make entirely certain that we distinguish between love and lust, as well as the sex of the "other" sought in either situation. Early in life the child doubtless passes through what might be termed an autophilic stage, in which, as a result of a poorly defined awareness, he invests all love emotions in himself. Gradually, he extends his loving ties to parents as iso- (father) and hetero- (mother) philic ties. But these emotional ties are not to be confused with erotic attachments of a so-called Oedipal situation.

From the vantage point of the parent, a child is also something to be loved (not lusted). In addition, we have already noted that parents have a "feeling of familiarity" for offspring of their same sex. It thus happens that a mother is probably less accepting of her daughter's "antics" or a father is more quick to paddle his son for misbehaving than either parent would be if they were dealing with an opposite-sexed child.[201] The upshot of this feeling of familiarity is that children appear to be in conflict with the parent of their own sex because in point of fact the question of authority usually descends on them in this fashion.

PREADOLESCENCE: FROM ISOPHILIC INTIMACY TO THE MATURATION OF THE GENITAL LUST DYNAMISM

Sometime between the ages of eight and one-half and 12 years, a child moves into his preadolescence—assuming that he *ever* does—and this period is typified by the maturation of a need for *isophilic intimacy*. Sullivan occasionally referred to this time as an "isophilic stage" of personality development,[202] and he was not above speaking of it as a "homosexual age" in some of his earliest formulations.[203] It seems that as he came to distinguish more clearly between lust and love he dropped the reference to a homosexual stage *per se*. The point of isolating this life era is to underscore the growing need the young person has for an intimacy with someone, a bond of love (philos) which unites him to a member of the same sex on a far deeper level than he has ever experienced before with compeers. As Sullivan said of the preadolescent: "We can picture him as driven by the need for intimacy—just as lust will drive one when sufficiently unsatisfied—to look at practically everyone he came in contact with who was anywhere near his age as a potential friend, intimate, or chum."[204]

The same-sexed person he settles on is technically referred to as the *chum*. Preadolescence is clearly the era of the chum, and it waits on the maturation of a "capacity for intimacy" which is the highest manifestation of love.[205] When we love someone, we care more about his satisfactions and security than we do about our own comparable gratifications.[206] The preadolescent comes to trust and rely on his chum, to reveal his innermost secrets to him, and, in turn, to absorb all of the private views of this other. This makes a "true social orientation" possible for the first time in life.[207] The social tie is now an intimate one, and Sullivan defined intimacy as essentially a two-group in which near perfect equality is achieved across participants.[208] Up to this point much of the socialization experienced by the child has been in response to the anxiety vs. euphoria influences provided by the parents, or the predominantly autophilic pleasures attained in playing with compeers. But now the preadolescent is *giving* something to another and entirely committed to the interpersonal gratifications of another.

Thanks to the fact that he enters so centrally into the personality at this stage, the chum can act as a realistic "sounding board" for the preadolescent who brings him into life's very core. All of those autistic, or fantastic, ideas and personifications about oneself or others can now be tested against the thinking and experience of the chum.[209] If there is a serious distortion of facts about growing up or some uncanny feeling about an emerging impulse, the chum can allay potential fears of "being different" by noting that he too has experienced the same phenomena, that he does not see things quite that way, or that he would not worry about doing such and thus. Sometimes, particularly in later preadolescence (puberty period) when the lust dynamism begins to mature, transitory homosexual behavior may take place between chums. This is ordinarily nothing to worry about and can actually prove a healthy experience since it teaches both participants something about themselves in a shared and less distorted sense than might otherwise take place.[210] Of course, if this form of sexual release is continued—if the preadolescent era is not forgone and passed through—then a continuing homosexual pattern might well result.

Even when homosexuality is not practiced between chums this period of life can seem "abnormal" to the parent. Mothers sometimes witness their daughters having a terrible "crush" on another girl, being concerned about this other child's every move, change of friendships, and so forth. This relationship is sometimes complicated by more than one such intimate, though rarely do we find more than three people in a chumship triangle. Preadolescence is also the expanding "gang" age, so that patterns of leader or follower are formed.[211] When chums and other gang members are separated—as on vacations or due to squabbles—the parent witnesses periods of loneliness in the child. The wretchedness of feeling lonely is a direct corollary of being capable of feeling particularly intimate with another person.

EARLY ADOLESCENCE: FROM GENITAL LUST TO THE PATTERNING OF LUSTFUL BEHAVIOR

The time of puberty may vary considerably from person to person, but sooner or later the young person passes into pubescence and begins to feel certain definite "promptings" from a region that was formerly concerned with the elimination of wastes from the body.[212] Sullivan called this prompting feeling *lust,* or the "felt aspect of the genital drive."[213] Just as he was previously driven by the need for intimacy, the child is now driven by the need for lustful gratification. The problems which arise here are, of course, presaged by the fact that erotic is not necessarily philic love. Some adolescents, having been taught that sexual love is "dirty," shift their love style appropriately—from iso*philic* (same sex) to hetero*philic* (opposite sex)—yet cannot *also* acquire a hetero*erotic* tie. Others shift love style and readily acquire erotic drives for the opposite sex. Often it is possible to satisfy the genital lust dynamism without having *any* true sense of love for a sexual partner. If one party in sexual intercourse is satisfying love and lust, while the other is satisfying only lust, the outcome of this relationship is likely to be unhappy for one of the participants, if not both.

Sullivan noted that some people engage in sexual intercourse yet really do not concern themselves with the satisfactions of the other. Even as chronological adults, we witness people who "use" other people's bodies rather than their own hands in what might be termed *autoerotic masturbation.*[214] Such an individual has not really matured properly nor patterned his sexual responses in a social sense. He would surely not be "in love" and probably would have no particular need for intimacy. Sullivan felt that, as the last integrating tendency to mature, the lust dynamism was very powerful and could *not* be sublimated as easily as could other zonal needs (the zone here would be the genitals, of course).[215]

LATE ADOLESCENCE AND MATURITY

Sullivan tells us that: ". . . a person begins late adolescence when he discovers what he likes in the way of genital behavior and how to fit it into the rest of life."[216] There are many factors of educational and social class which enter into the person's decisions to seek gratifications of this or that variety. In certain cultures homosexual liaisons are tolerated, and, so long as this is acceptable to the group and the individual is not otherwise immature, we could not fault this level of adjustment. Not since the early years of its inception have we seen the rapid expansion of the syntaxic mode that we witness in late adolescence.[217] Higher education (college), marriage, and career occupations extend one's horizons and bring him ever more centrally into the fold of consensual validation, the "established" practices of social man and woman which eventuate in families, homes, parenthood, and all of the ensuing responsibilities of citizenship. It is the lot of the mature personality to learn "how to live" by way of *sublimatory reformulations,* which entails catching on to ways of gaining a good deal of, yet not complete, satisfaction.[218] Complete satisfactions can be degrading and uncivilizing to man, but if he has come through the years with a regard for others, the mature person should have learned enough to ensure a modicum of happiness in life. It is essential that a mature personality reflect a need for intimacy and collaboration with at least *one* other—and preferably, many others.[219]

INDIVIDUAL DIFFERENCES CONSTRUCTS

One does not find many personality typologies or traits in interpersonal relations theory, not the least of reasons being that Sullivan disliked reifying personality or psychiatric concepts.[220] His fundamental preference was for a fluid theory of man. The psychiatrist who likes to assign labels is probably showing us his personifications of the disease. For his part, Sullivan remarked that he would really rather typologize interpersonal relations than people's personalities.[221] Recall that Sullivan did not believe people were as "individual" as they usually flattered themselves to be. This attitude on his part stemmed from a belief that sociocultural factors carried the weight of influence in interpersonal situations. At the same time, Sullivan recognized that there were variations in the ways in which people integrate situations. Not only social class, racial, former national identities, but certain "styles" of behavior issuing from the developmental eras we have just reviewed did take place, leading to individual differences in Sullivanian thought.[222] Not all of these "arrest and deviations" need be malevolent, but as one might expect in the case of a psychotherapist, many of the personality types Sullivan construed did indeed have a slightly abnormal cast to them.

There is really only one major attempt in Sullivan's writings to define a series of types or "developmental syndromes," as he called them. In his 1940 book, *Conceptions of Modern Psychiatry,* he sketched a series of 10 such identifiable syndromes.[223] We will not devote much time to their study but will consider them in overview fashion as examples of the way Sullivan looked at people. The first five developmental syndromes were considered "autistic syndromes," issuing as they did from very early deviations in maturation. There are those who exhibit a *lack of duration* in their relationships, who never become intimate and really committed to others; they often show an inability to profit from experience and appear superficial or even psychopathic in behavior. There are *self-absorbed* people, who carry on fantastic reveries in order to pass through life without upset; we often say they are "escapists" or that they "live in dreams." The *incorrigible* type resists educative influences and integrates lasting situations only with those whom he considers his inferior. The *negativistic* person is just the opposite of the self-absorbed; rather than turn inward he looks outward but uses negation and contrariness to obtain visibility and even distinctions in life because sometimes his "griping" leads to real change. There is the *stammerer,* who uses this verbal "failing" in communication to defy and dominate others, who must "wait" until he decides when they may speak.

The next five syndromes are not considered autistic. They come on as a result of arrests and deviations in the order presented, dating from roughly the juvenile period through late adolescence. Recall that a chronic juvenile is likely to be competitive throughout life. Sullivan began here his nonautistic developmental syndromes by speaking of the *ambition-ridden* person, who has to compete with everyone on every silly and unimportant dimension of-life. The *asocial* person enters into two-group ties entirely at his own convenience. The *inadequate* person integrates situations on the basis of dependency upon an other or else he identifies with and gains strength through some "worthy cause." There is the *homosexual* person, who simply cannot integrate meaningful situations with members of the opposite sex; the degree of this tendency varies from the common "woman or man hater" to the more pronounced clinical syndromes in which lust can be satisfied only with members of the same sex. Finally, we have a rather broad category of behaviors which Sullivan lumped into the *chronically adolescent*. These individuals are driven by lust, and they never seem able to find the right sex object because, in fact, they lack the capacity for love (intimacy) and are often cynical in their outlook on life. We can place the Don Juan or "hymen hunter" types here, searching throughout life for a new conquest on the misguided belief that lust can satisfy needs for love.[224]

Underwriting all of his work, and dating from his earliest years as theorist,[225] the *one-genus hypothesis* underwrote Sullivan's continuing belief that human commonalities far outweighed individual differences. We have seen this tendency in his reluctance to emphasize individuality, as well as his dislike for typologizing people in general. But Sullivan claimed to be studying *all* men *all* of the time, even when he had psychotic individuals as subjects for his participant observation. Here is his final formulation of the one-genus hypothesis: "We shall assume that *everyone is much more simply human than otherwise,* and that anomalous interpersonal situations, insofar as they do not arise from differences in language or custom, are a function of differences in relative maturity of the persons concerned. . . . I try to study the degrees and patterns of things which I assume to be ubiquitously human."[226] This provides us with a natural bridge for considering the next major aspect of Sullivan's thought—his theories of illness, cure, and therapy.

Psychopathology and Psychotherapy

THEORY OF ILLNESS

THE GENERAL THEORY OF ABNORMAL BEHAVIOR

In line with the theory of classical psychoanalysis, Sullivan felt that mental abnormality was tied to personality in that the "sick" individual was limited in the kinds of behaviors he might exhibit.[227] These limitations were specifically concerned with the self dynamism, which for various reasons was incapable of securing the biologically necessary satisfactions of life.[228] This inefficiency of the self dynamism can often be traced to the fact that only one form of dynamism is used in attempts to relate interpersonally. Excessive use of such a *dynamism of difficulty* works as a multiplier of interpersonal inefficiency because the individual loses his flexibility and spontaneity.[229] We will have more to say of this later, but the point of Sullivan's definitions of mental illness is that a quantitative and continuous dimension extends from "normal to abnormal." Psychiatrists can even measure this dimension with various tests and name a point on a scale where a person will be diagnosed as "mentally abnormal"; but this point is arbitrary, singled out because presumably it is beyond there that the society will no longer tolerate the eccentricities of a member.[230]

As in his approach to personality, Sullivan did not want to rely upon organic, hereditary, or other constitutional factors to explain the nature of mental illness. He was attracted to the physical etiology thesis only in the case of a manic-depressive psychosis. But dating from his earliest contacts with schizophrenic patients, he remained convinced that mental illness—insofar as we can use this term—stemmed from inadequate or inappropriate interpersonal relations rather than from impersonal physical factors.[231] He was prone to speak of "difficulties of living" when referring to mental illness.[232]

In one of his earliest formulations, Sullivan stressed what he called the *warp of personality* noted in a developing individual, usually manifesting itself by about the juvenile era.[233] He was later to revise this critical period of life upward, in referring to the importance of a chum during preadolescence. But the fundamental point here is that a maturing child needs to have his asocial or poorly socialized (autistic, fantastic) views of the world *corrected,* both by interactions with compeers and especially through the intimacy of a chum. The next point Sullivan brought in to explain abnormality involved a person's self-esteem or confidence. Very often the individual withdraws into a dream world where he fosters autistic and unrealistic views of life.[234] This lowered confidence and withdrawal stems from a lack of parental empathy or negative reflected appraisals from significant adults.

As the maturing child feels his confidence waning, he begins to selectively inattend to and then to dissociate important aspects of his behavior needing rectification.[235] Rather than meet challenges the self dynamism has set on a course of avoidance, building security on foundations of sand. Hence: "We may say . . . as a generality, that healthy development of personality is inversely proportionate to the amount, to the number, of tendencies which have come to exist in dissociation."[236] One of the major sources of lowered self-confidence in our culture is the stringent taboo on sexuality.[237] Too many young people—especially young girls—are made to feel that sex is a "not-me" experience. Since the lust dynamism is extremely difficult to sublimate, the wretched tensions put upon the personality due to sexual taboos lead to eventual dissociation and the deterioration of adjustment.[238]

THE ROLE OF SOCIAL FACTORS

The previous section which emphasized socio-cultural teachings, combined with what we know of Sullivan's view of personality in a social context, prompts us to ask: Is the *person* mentally ill, or is the interpersonal situation—and, by extension, the *society*—the actual locus of abnormality? In 1931 Sullivan would have answered this as follows: "Some ten years' rather close contact with sufferers of schizophrenic disorders culminated in the firm conviction that not sick individuals but complex, peculiarly characterized situations were the subject-matter of research and therapy."[239] By the late 1930s Sullivan generalized this attitude to the social order as a whole.[240] And finally,

during the period of World War II, he put this supraindividual view most graphically: "The Western world is a profoundly sick society in which each denizen, each person, is sick to the extent that he is *of it,* of its blended vitality and debility, of its chances of dissolution or reorganization and recovering after a dangerous crisis."[241] We thus have an indictment of the entire civilization, prompted by the obvious madness of a world war. It was convictions such as these which generated Sullivan's active role in the international associations mentioned in the biographical overview of this chapter.

THE SYMPTOMS OF MENTAL DISORDER

Sullivan emphasized that a symptom is something which the patient "has," in the sense of "manifests," from his point of view in experience.[242] It is not for the psychiatrist to tell the patient what his symptoms are. The patient reflects something of his disturbance in behavior as a "sign." The psychiatrist cannot assume, however, that all signs are truly symptoms. As participant-observer he must pursue his diagnostic impressions and through skillful expertise come to establish that there is a true symptom underlying what seems to be a sign of neurosis. Not everyone who likes to straighten pictures on the wall (sign) is an obsessive-compulsive neurotic (symptom picture). Symptoms invariably show themselves when the dissociated experiences, cravings, or attitudes are completely out of balance with the self dynamism, leading to a collapse in the latter's capacity to restrain the dissociated materials. They appear in awareness as tics (involuntary muscle movements), seizures of emotions (uncanny), or the more dramatic forms of delusions (unfounded or distorted beliefs) and hallucinations (sensory misperceptions or apparitions).

One of the significant aspects of dissociation is that material which has been split off from awareness in this fashion does not simply "wait" there in limbo. It continues to integrate experience, to grow in influence as it increases in range and complexity.[243] This incubation factor means that what had once been dissociated as a relatively minor aspect of experience might some day return to awareness as a rather serious and all-pervasive system of energy transformation. It sometimes happens that a symptom makes its appearance at that point in time when the individual can gain some advantage through its arrival.[244] A man who is afraid of responsibility can believe that he has an uncontrollable impulse to kill himself and thus keeps his wife dashing about, looking after his affairs, because he must avoid all "risky" activities like crossing streets or driving a car.[245] This "secondary gain" feature of symptoms should not be overrated, but it is often an important reason for the appearance of dissociated material.

An even more ominous reason for the appearance of the symptom is when it appears as an *automatism*. This is invariably due to an active attempt on the part of the dissociated material—whether a tic, automatic writing, or a hallucination—to *integrate* some particular interpersonal situation.[246] The first manifestation of a hallucination is usually felt as an unpleasant or disturbing experience. The individual may have been dissociating highly self-deprecatory material—homosexual impulses or death wishes toward others, for example—and now finds the most horrible or repulsive accusations coming his way in the form of "voices." He then patterns these into identities: "The hallucinated utterances come rather quickly to be statements of particular illusory persons or personifications—God, the Devil, the President, one's deceased mother, and the like."[247] Delusions follow the same pattern, as they descend upon awareness as if from some other power, usually during a time of crisis to solve some problem in living. Sullivan called these *autochthonous ideas,* by which he referred to: "a content of thought, a matter of mind, which seems literally to have come from outside one, as if put there—that

is, one has no feeling of ownership or parentage."[248]

Another way of speaking about the more serious symptoms of mental disorder (delusions and hallucinations) is to note that they contain a heavy component of *parataxic* and even *prototaxic* distortion. Not only eidetic people but the not-me contents enter into delusions and hallucinations.[249] The increasingly disturbed individual draws back more and more into his autistic reveries and hence his referential processes become increasingly primitive.[250] If the resulting corpus of beliefs is poorly rationalized and autistic, we are likely to use the term *unsystematized* in describing this state of delusional mentality. *Systematized* delusions are better rationalized and hence more consensually plausible.[251]

An interesting feature of many delusions is that they take on the hue of epics or myths. Sullivan recognized that the psychotic individual is often histrionic in his autistic reveries. A revery is, after all, akin to a play in which we put ourselves on center stage to achieve some feeling of victory, revenge, depression, or sympathy. There is a rough analogy between the "personal mythology" of a psychotic—who is likely to see himself as the Emissary of Good and the psychiatrist as the Emissary of Evil—and some of the great mythologies of mankind.[252] But an analogy is *all* that this can be. Sullivan refused to believe that these tragic fantasies emanated from a racial unconscious.[253] Recall that he did not believe people were so terribly different. Hence, the "cosmic dramas" we see enacted in the depths of psychosis are universal to the extent that all men struggle with comparable life conditions.[254]

THE SYNDROME OF SCHIZOPHRENIA

Sullivan distinguished between two broad types of schizophrenia: (a) an organic, degenerative disease of insidious onset which was suggested by the traditional (Kraepelinian) view of *dementia praecox*; and (b) the disorder of *schizophrenia* proper, which is due to problems in living and comes on more or less abruptly in behavior even though it may be seen in potentia for years.[255] It is the latter form of mental disorder that we refer to in Sullivan's theory of schizophrenia. The Kraepelinian diagnostic category of "simple" schizophrenia, which often reflects this slow-developing, insidious onset, Sullivan considered dementia praecox and not a true schizophrenia.[256] Of course, as we discuss Sullivan's aligning of the diagnostic categories, we must constantly appreciate that he did not wish to reify and flatly rejected the "obsessional necessity for completeness" which drove men like Kraepelin (see Chapter 2, p. 87) to document each facet of a presumed illness in a detailed account.

Sullivan had found that the more abrupt a schizophrenic episode is, the more rapid the transition of behavior from normal to abnormal, the better the patient's prognosis for eventual recovery.[257] In broad terms, the depth of a regression (inadequate development) diagnosed the extent of disturbance. However, determining a schizophrenic's prognosis from his depth of regression was not a simple matter. The *hebephrenic* schizophrenic, for example, who regresses to an infancy level, often smearing his excrement about the walls of his room as he babbles incoherently, is probably not as deeply regressed as is the catatonic who assumes prenatal postures in what seems an "intrauterine regression."[258] Yet, the outlook for catatonia is more promising than it is for hebephrenia. Despite this technical problem over the depth of regression in schizophrenia, it is generally true that the schizophrenic regresses below the level of socialization, which puts him at least into the parataxic mode. This is why he seems so "crazy" to us, who occupy a more consensually valid world.[259] The onset of schizophrenia is usually noted between the fourteenth and twenty-seventh year of life.[260]

In Sullivan's view schizophrenia had two stages of development. In the first stage there was a rapid loss of faith in the self and the universe, with an excessive reliance upon dissociation as a way of solving the situation. The second stage was presented by Sullivan as follows: "The individual, with serious impairment of the dependability of his self and the universe, progresses into a situation in which the dissociated parts of his personality are the effective integrating agencies. . . . The result is a condition which I cannot distinguish by any important characteristic from that undergone by an individual in attempting to orient himself on awakening in the midst of a vivid nightmare."[261] This parallel between schizophrenia and sleep phenomena is a very central aspect of Sullivan's theory. He noted as early as 1927 that the schizophrenic's thought patterns were like a normal's reverie or dream processes, and it was his view that increasing knowledge of the sleep process should help us understand the processes of schizophrenia.[262]

The sleep theory aspects of schizophrenia might be considered the early "mechanics" of the disease. It appears that a "light sleep" is the vehicle whereby the person moving into a schizophrenic episode actually regresses. This is an initial attempt to reintegrate problems which had been poorly handled in development. As Sullivan put it: "When you effect contact with the intimate history of markedly schizoid people, you learn that at times which we would ordinarily say were times of unusual stress, these people underwent for quite extended periods a life that was more than half—sometimes nearly all—spent in a kind of light sleep."[263] If a deeper sleep had been possible at this time, then a satisfactory dissociation might have taken place. But in the light sleep of an individual developing schizophrenia, what is happening is that the poorly dissociated dynamisms (let us say homosexual cravings or hostile impulses) are simply not being taken out of the realm of influence. The self dynamism is not in control of awareness, because in fact light sleep keeps it checkmated as the poorly dissociated materials integrate more and more of his conscious life.

It is possible to see such schizophrenic states in the normal person: "An individual manifesting behavior when not fully awake would thus be clearly schizophrenic."[264] But in the case of a true *schizophrenic dynamism,* the dream state becomes habitual. The person literally lives in a dream state, often a living nightmare for all of those dynamisms which he wanted to dissociate now take control of his life from out of a region he has no awareness of—just as we "normals" lack awareness of our dream world.[265] It is thus possible to say that schizophrenia is a failure of the self-system, "a failure to restrict the contents of consciousness to the higher referential processes that can be consensually validated."[266] Things seem to "happen" to the schizophrenic. He cannot put the strange possessions he senses within his own identity into a proper perspective. A "profound puzzlement" is thus engendered, and from the stress of being unable to maintain dissociation comes a loss of control of great consequence within awareness (consciousness).[267]

So much for the onset of schizophrenia, but why is the self-system so inadequate in handling the seemingly profound dissociations called for in this life history? At this point we must return to our basic theory of illness. The "schizoid" personality type is invariably a shy, sensitive person who has been made to feel less than adequate by the reflected appraisals of significant adults.[268] He may be very dependent upon his parents—especially his mother—who really do not think of him as capable.[269] The sickness as such usually has its first stage onset in the juvenile to preadolescence era,[270] and the typical shortcomings of distorted life views are to be expected because the schizophrenic has not checked his thinking very carefully with either compeers or a chum. Sexual problems

are also a compounding factor. The normal homosexual cravings and interests of a boy in preadolescence or early adolescence are doomed to land the schizoid person in trouble as he carries these on beyond their appropriate age level.[271] It is correct to say that the schizoid personality has never really passed through the level of adolescence, so that a general immaturity in developmental pattern is the rule.[272] If we now add to this picture the failures in intimacy, and the consequent high tension developed because of the unanswered needs in this individual, it is easy to see how vulnerable the schizoid person is as he attempts to dissociate.[273] Little wonder that, when the break comes, it is like a "fragmentation of the mind."[274]

Returning to the mechanism of the disorder itself, Sullivan distinguished between the often cited variations of schizophrenia known as hebephrenia (grimacing, infantile verbal patterns), catatonia (posturing, muteness, rigidity vs. motility), and paranoia (prominent use of fairly systematized delusions). Once again, he did not think of these as "separate entities," but neither did he like the idea of referring to them as "mixed" diagnoses. Sullivan contended that when a schizophrenic dynamism emerged, when the self had been countered by the poorly dissociated systems, there was a rush of highly frightening (uncanny emotions) or otherwise peculiar occurrences in awareness. The *first* reaction of the individual at this point is catatonic in nature. He simply suspends all social habits and communication centers (muteness). If this continues to the extreme, a collapse into the despair of hebephrenia may be the case. However, if there has been a history of at least some intimacy with a person (chum) in preadolescence, the course of the disorder will be more along the lines of a living nightmare, with all of the consequent delusions and anxieties that any of us know from our own dream states. If the self-system is capable, it might formulate an "explanation" of the dissociated states. This would place the individual under the paranoid designation. The catatonic phase may be very brief, as the individual comes out of his "secretive shell" and presents us with a more or less systematized delusion of why he is being sought by a group of foreign agents or how he has been sent by God to bring the message of truth for all of mankind (paranoid symptoms).

The catatonic level is thus pivotal, falling roughly between the hebephrenic and the paranoid condition. As such, Sullivan concluded: "I would say that the catatonic is the essential schizophrenic picture."[275] The extent of consensual validation contained within the verbal products of the schizophrenic determines how "crazy" we consider him to be. If the schizophrenic is in a state of complete fright regarding the dissociated states, he can be extremely dangerous to himself and to others. The thoughts which trouble him reveal parataxic distortion, and if he tries to communicate these to us, he is likely to be further frustrated because what seems plausible to him is uncommunicative (autistic) to us. Precisely how he solves this *potpourri* of disjointed and inconsistent events gives us the "clinical picture" (syndrome) and the case history. Much of it is insolvable or "uninterpretable" for both the psychiatrist and the schizophrenic himself. Patients have, as we all do, autistic and uncommunicable signs and symbols which really can never be grasped in any case.

Many psychiatrists had spoken of a "pure" form of paranoia, in which the individual did not show the distortions of schizophrenia when presenting a highly systematized delusional belief—one that was so plausible we could easily believe it. However, Sullivan did not accept this as a significant possibility, remarking that in about 3,000 cases of paranoid schizophrenia he had seen only one individual who might be considered a "pure" paranoiac.[276] Every paranoid individual has been schizophrenic in the sense discussed previously, at least for a time. Paranoid individuals have a relatively strong self-system for a schizophrenic, which is probably the reason that we never see this syndrome appearing before preadolescence.[277] The older the patient, the more likely it is that he will be capable of at least some dissociation. The paranoid is essentially a schizophrenic who is aware of his inferiority as a person, passes quickly through catatonia, and then transfers the blame for his inadequacy onto sundry other people.[278] Occasionally such people can make the necessary adjustments to society during all of their lifetime, and thus some schizophrenics remain unidentified and unhospitalized. Were we to look more carefully, we might identify such people in our everyday world.[279]

OTHER CLINICAL SYNDROMES

Psychoses are usually divisible into the family of the schizophrenias, which we have been considering, and the *manic-depressive* disorders. Sullivan did not treat such cases in his experimental ward, and he admitted that he really had not formulated a complete theory concerning them.[280] In fact, noting that he was departing from his usual script, he was even tempted to accept a biological explanation for such mental disorders.[281] Assuming that a metabolic disruption of the physiochemical environment did not account for the regular cycles in mood these patients exhibited, Sullivan did proffer some possible explanations based on the style of interpersonal relations.

It seemed to him that *manic* individuals are those who try to sublimate extensively, until they eventually find it impossible to continue using this one dynamism as a cure-all.[282] Such an individual lacks the self-esteem to face an unhappy situation or to take setbacks in stride. When the pressure mounts to an unendurable level, the individual releases a torrent of activity aimed at integrating those aspects of experience that might heighten self-esteem. The manic thus proposes fantastic schemes at a frantic tempo, behaving as if he were one step ahead of a great wave of anxiety which is about to engulf him. Even so, the manic phase of this disorder is constructive in that integration is outward, toward others, and aimed at doing something about a miserable life situation.

In the case of *depression* we have quite another matter: "Depression is not a dynamism for the health-preserving release of integrative bonds which connect one to another. It is a chiefly destructive process. It cuts off impulses to integrate constructive situations with others."[283] Depression is thus heavily colored by divisive and even hostile emotions, and if the depressed patient directs this hostility inward, he can even destroy himself through an act of suicide.[284] The motive of this act of self-destruction is sometimes to punish some significant person in the patient's past.[285] It is, of course, possible and logically consistent that the same individual can manifest both a manic and a depressive energic transformation (dynamism) at different times, resulting in the hyphenation of the manic-depressive psychosis.

We now turn to the disorders which are considered subpsychotic, because they are less likely to manifest delusional or hallucinatory dynamisms. As we noted in the biographical overview of this chapter, Sullivan became convinced that schizophrenia and the *obsessive-compulsive* neuroses were etiologically connected. He often saw a preschizophrenic individual with obsessive symptoms slip into a schizophrenic break and then subsequently return to a nonpsychotic obsessional level.[286] He felt that obsessives regressed to a stage of autistic speech, just like the schizophrenic did. This is why their symptoms often include magical phrases, neologisms, and peculiar stylized tendencies of a verbal or behavioral nature.[287] The obsessive-compulsive person has a deep-seated sense of inferiority, and he often uses what Sullivan termed a "flypaper technique" to avoid being pinned down by circum-

stance or embarrassed interpersonally in any way.[288] Sullivan meant that when one talks to the obsessive, each time the conversation touches upon some area of concern which he has dissociated, the obsessive individual finds some way to shift the topic, misunderstand a question, belittle a major point as immaterial, or overemphasize a minor point as presumably important. Each time one takes a step to extricate himself from the confusion which descends on the relationship he finds himself "stuck" in an area of concern he had not even thought of or was interested in.

Of course, there is a negative return here and the self dynamism of the obsessive cannot always sustain the dissociations required. In time, a schizophrenic disorder can be the result. Sometimes an obsessive disturbance of this sort will forestall the development of a schizophrenic break, so that in one sense we could speak of obsessive-compulsivity as a "defense" against acquiring a schizophrenic disorder. But this is by no means a sure defense, as many times the obsessional neurosis is a guaranteed way station to schizophrenia. Sullivan did not feel that there was any real difference between the obsessional neurosis which progressed into schizophrenia and the one that did not.[289]

Mild depressions in which the individual suffers constant insomnia, debility, or physical complaints are what constitute *neurasthenia*.[290] Sometimes such patients are suffering from malnutrition or other physical deficiencies due to long periods of self-neglect. There is an element of hostility in these cases; patients nag others to death with their annoying, complaining manner. The *hypochondriac* is an individual who tries to integrate situations entirely on the basis of his supposedly failing state of physical health.[291] He has no other interests left but will relate interpersonally if someone humors him and lets him talk about his fantastic aches and pains. The *hysteric* also employs maladies for interpersonal contacts, but he is more likely to use these as excuses for why he does not live up to his potential.[292] Sullivan did not seem to feel that hysterics had quite the profound dissociations that characterize the psychoses. A multiple personality is, of course, a rather dramatic dissociated dynamism, but these cases are rare. In most instances, the hysterical activation (tic, grimace, arm movement) or inactivation (blindness, lameness, amnesia) are easily rectified through hypnosis. This proved to Sullivan that these disorders are closer to awareness than we might at first suspect. As he once summed them up: "What you see in the hysteric is . . . not a high-grade conflict between ideal structures and unregenerated impulses, but just a happy idea of how to get away with something."[293] A *fugue* state is when the individual actually lives out a dream, taking on an alternate identity much as we might do in a reverie while not losing contact with reality.[294]

We might now close our consideration of Sullivan's theory of illness with a few words on the syndrome known as *psychopathy*. In some of his earliest formulations Sullivan suggested that a psychopathic personality underlay schizophrenia.[295] The predominant characteristic of this disorder is an "inability to profit from experience,"[296] as well as a tendency to "say the right thing" and then presume that all is set right without having to prove oneself in actual performance.[297] Although psychopaths do not seem as bizarre or unusual to us as do the psychotics or the neurotics, Sullivan felt that this was a very serious deviation in development, probably beginning very early in life.[298] The psychopath uses language as the obsessive does—as a tool for self-defense. He tells others what they want to hear and what gets him off a "spot." He expresses regret about past misadventures, lays extensive plans for rectification in the future, but then somehow is always unable to fulfill expectancies when the time comes to act. Sullivan occasionally used the term *sociopath* as a synonym for the psychopath.[299]

THEORY OF CURE

THE NATURE OF MENTAL HEALTH

Sullivan did not like to use the term "cure" because he felt this remnant of medical terminology really had little meaning in the realm of personality.[300] Psychotherapy is closer to education than it is to the *medical* healing of sick individuals.[301] Sullivan said that in over 25 years of working with psychotherapy patients he had never found himself called upon to "cure" anybody.[302] The steps to mental health must be taken by the client, and he will reveal a spontaneous tendency to put his life in order if we only help him to make the proper examination and assessment of his situation. Sullivan was not above referring to this corrective tendency as a type of dyamism, as a *"drive toward mental health."*[303]

What then is "mental health"? We know from our review thus far that two major problems arise in the life of abnormals: an extensive dissociation *and* failing interpersonal relations as a result of the disjointed pattern of behavior which occurs when aspects of experience are not "in" awareness yet they do show up in behavior. It is therefore not surprising to find Sullivan emphasizing "balance" in speaking of mental health.[304] The disintegrated or poorly integrated personality must thus be reintegrated—rebalanced—before it can be said to be mentally healthy.[305] This rebalancing results in improved interpersonal relations and, to that extent, the state of living we all accept as "normal." Summing it up, Sullivan observes: *"One achieves mental health to the extent that one becomes aware of one's interpersonal relations. . . ."*[306]

THE ROLE OF INSIGHT

Sullivanian therapy is an "insight" approach much like that of the classical analysts. Sullivan even used the Freudian-Jungian term *imago* to refer to the eidetic personifications of the therapist by the client, personifications which become the focus of interpretation over the course of client contacts. Indeed, the psychiatrist will find that there are always three people in therapy: (a) the psychiatrist as imagined by the patient; (b) the patient himself; and (c) the psychiatrist himself, who is participantly observing and trying to get some clue as to what this imago to whom the patient is reacting may be like.[307] It is also possible for several imagos to intervene in the two-group therapeutic relationship, either alternatively or at the same time. As parataxic distortions they seriously detract from the proper functioning of memory to recall the essentials of past experience.[308] The psychiatrist must convince the patient that these personifications are natural remnants of his past, and that he must search to uncover the negative influences of these distortions in his life history. Therapy is thus an "uncovering process."[309] This is quite anxiety-provoking, and hence all of the interpersonal skills of the psychiatrist as an expert in human relations are required to reassure and support the patient as he makes this soul-searching effort.[310]

The easiest course for the therapist to take as educator is to begin with a client's selectively inattended behaviors and attitudes.[311] The patient thus comes to see a role for the psychiatrist independent of his imago projections onto the psychiatrist. Gradually, more central aspects of the case history are uncovered, interpretations are made in terms of parental involvements (loss of empathy leading to anxiety and the overreliance on dissociation as a mechanism of defense, etc.). Hence: "The goal of the treatment, including the ultimate complete resolution of the patient-physician relationship, dictates the gradual evolution of valid insight."[312] A patient's prognosis depends upon several factors in the interpersonal context. If he has a family which really wishes him to return to life outside the hospital, or a boss who is sensitive to his plight and willing to provide him time for a readjustment, then the prognosis is favorable indeed.[313] If the interpersonal context is hostile or unsympathetic to the patient, then the chances for eventual recovery are naturally bleak. The extent of personal deterioration suffered by a patient determines just how much communication we can have with him in therapy. If he is completely autistic, we cannot form a relationship and therapy becomes impossible.[314]

EXPANSION OF SELF

The course of therapy thus brings material which has been removed from awareness back into awareness. In accomplishing this reintegration, the therapist must confront the patient's self dynamism as a major obstacle to change. It was the self, after all, which initiated the dissociative process in the first place. There is nothing in the present circumstances which makes it any easier for the self dynamism to relax its vigilance and thus readmit what it still takes to be unacceptable aspects of experience back into awareness (bad-me, not-me). Sometimes it is necessary to enfeeble the self in some way, and though he did not live to see the complete impact of the "relaxant drug" therapies in the post–World War II period (see Chapter 2, p. 90), Sullivan's theory of cure was completely consistent with such a development. In fact, Sullivan tells us that he sometimes used alcoholic intoxication to relax and inhibit the "dissociating power of the self."[315] Intoxication seemed especially helpful in the case of a highly excited schizophrenic, who could usually relax and feel less threatened when "under the influence." Anything which permits the individual to relax his guard in this way can serve a therapeutic goal. Often, a vacation which allows one to "get away from it all" relaxes the individual enough to permit reintegration to occur quite spontaneously, and more than one incipient psychosis has probably been checked in this natural fashion.[316]

The paradoxical outcome of getting the self to relax and admit certain elements of past experience into awareness is that the self is strengthened: "Therapeutic results are the expansion of the self dynamism and the simplification of living which results from this."[317] The individual no longer needs to live a series of lies, to divert the others with whom he relates from exposing him, or to withdraw from communication with others out of a sense of anxiety. Another way of saying this is that consciousness is widened.[318] The self really integrates the dissociated impulses, so that now the person can admit, "Yes, I feel extreme shame whenever I feel sexually stimulated." Rather than behaving defensively, in reaction to diverse threats, the individual now assumes command of his life in a more confident sense. At this point we have the beginnings of a psychiatric cure, but there still may be a long road back to normalcy in the sense of a social cure.

SOCIAL FACTORS IN THERAPEUTIC CHANGE

Dating from his contact with the Chicago School of Social Science, Sullivan emphasized the need for *social* as well as *personal* adjustment.[319] It was not enough for the patient to understand some of the reasons for his unique motivations in life. Sometimes a patient will improve simply by being allowed to function for a time in a climate of acceptance and understanding. This "sympathetic environment" did more for an enhancement of self-esteem than any amount of intricate interpretation into the nature of one's illness could have achieved. Sullivan called this approach a "sociopsychological treatment," and though he did not say that all patients should be treated in this fashion, he did feel that considerably more emphasis should be placed on such factors.[320] In fact, he came to analyze the climate of the mental hospital much as the anthropologist might analyze the culture of a country. He spoke of the fixed *castes* which develop, placing the physician at the top of the social structure and the patients at the bottom. As for diagnosing patients: "Hospital classification of patients is in theory the segregation of patients on the basis of similarity of signs and symptoms."[321]

Sullivan felt that we need therapeutic communities, and he argued that something along the lines of the Civilian Conservation Corps for mental patients would be beneficial.[322] This would involve a community of people, all of whom had become victims of their social environment, working together to regain or cultivate the personalities necessary for a more effective life adjustment. After spending a period of time in such a milieu, the person could pass on into the more usual life experience which we all face. We see this "half-way house" philosophy in practice today in group efforts such as Alcoholics Anonymous and Synanon (ex–drug addicts), where a continuing social relationship can be maintained by the individual with others sympathetic to his problems.

THERAPEUTIC TECHNIQUES

THE TWO-GROUP RELATIONSHIP AND PSYCHOTHERAPY

The very same interpersonal factors which are a part of *any* two-group integration go to make up the psychiatric relationship.[323] Of course, in time—thanks to the accepting attitude of the psychiatrist—the therapy situation takes on a special significance, for the patient finds that he is completely free of restraint or constraint (within reason). Anything he wishes to say or do, so long as this is a constructive impulse (he is not permitted to harm the therapist or himself), the patient may express with impunity.[324] As a trained psychoanalyst, Sullivan was, of course, very familiar with all of the intricacies of *transference*. We find him using this term in 1925, and he even speaks of how certain schizophrenics have been known to effect a "transference cure."[325]

Essentially, Sullivan viewed transference as one variant of the general tendency for people to seek intimacy in interpersonal relations.[326] The only difference between the relationship with a psychotherapist and the relationship with any other individual is the intention of the two-group union. The patient submits himself to an expert in a subordinate role when he enters therapy; this is not the role he will always accept in seeking intimacy with non-professionals of his acquaintance. An expert is someone who derives his income and status from the use of information he is well versed in concerning some particular field—as interpersonal relations—to the benefit of others.[327] The client has a right to expect that this expert will help him in some way, and these are the general grounds on which he subordinates himself.[328] As therapy proceeds, it will become colored by the parataxic distortions of the client, and here again, much of what is called "transference" is merely a reflection of this tendency for people to color their interpersonal relations with autistic material of this sort (imago projections).[329]

The therapist works to make these interfering personifications known to the client, and this naturally provokes anxiety. Since anxiety detracts from successful communication by calling up autistic material or disorienting memory, it is not unusual for the client to *block* as he tries to answer a question. He cannot recall, or he has a significant lapse in his recollection. Too often, the classical psychoanalyst took this entirely natural and understandable reaction as a sign of purposeful evasion. The concept of *resistance* hinges on this questionable assumption of a deceitfulness on the client's part.[330] Sullivan did not share this easy ascription of a purposefulness in the client's behavior. He felt that anxiety was the root source of this problem in most instances, and the sophisticated interviewer must constantly be alert for signs of anxiety such as these. In fact, "When there is no regard for anxiety, a true interview situation does not exist. . . ."[331]

The client may become attached to and dependent upon the therapist. He may find it difficult to break off the interview, seek advice about innocuous aspects of his life, and otherwise make it plain that he considers the therapist-expert a special person in his life. This is also taken as transference by the classical analyst, but the truth is that clients have comparable ties to others outside of therapy as well. Sullivan did not discuss countertransference as such, but he did consider the role of the therapist as human being in therapy, and it is surely implied that the therapist too might be more or less prone to project personifications onto the client. Even so, Sullivan did not feel that every psychotherapist had to submit to a personal psychoanalysis or therapy series before he could hope to work effectively with clients. Although he had himself submitted to psychoanalysis, Sullivan contended that this was an intensely personal matter, for each aspiring therapist to decide on his own as to whether or not he needs therapy preliminary to entering the profession.[332]

THE PSYCHIATRIC INTERVIEW SERIES

Sullivan devoted considerable effort to a thorough consideration of the psychiatric—or therapeutic—interview. He defined the psychiatric interview as "a two-group in which there is an expert-client relationship, the expert being defined by the culture."[333] The therapist is always a participant-observer in this two-group. He demonstrates his expertise by taking the client through what are essentially four stages in the interview series: the *inception, reconnaissance, detailed inquiry,* and *termination.*[334]

The *inception* includes the formal reception of the client in the initial contact, the seating arrangements, and the initial inquiry as to the reasons for his coming to see the psychiatrist. Sullivan did not use the couch with his clients. He met them at the door, took a good look at their general appearance, indicated where they might sit, and then purposively avoided "staring" at them.[335] The interview began with general invitations being made by Sullivan to state as fully as possible why it was that the client came to see him. Sullivan did not like to take notes, feeling that he was too busy and attentive to interview properly and record his therapy impressions at the same time. We do know that he was one of the first to experiment with electronic recording of interviews and hence presumably there was a modicum of this sort of record keeping in his practice. In general, his approach to the client was very "structured," in that he believed one had to focus on the reason for coming to therapy. The client is there to learn about himself, and the therapist is not being engaged to putter about with his favorite theories of man. The effective psychiatrist must constantly keep three questions before himself: What is the client trying to say? How can we best phrase what it is we wish to say to the client in return? And what is the general pattern which emerges in what is being communicated and discussed?[336]

Having now decided that the client is indeed in need of psychotherapy, the psychiatrist would next move into the *reconnaissance* phase of the interview. This "transition point" is not clear or mechanical, of course. The inception phase may have taken more than one interview to traverse. The therapist simply finds quite naturally that he needs more information and thus goes into a survey of material ranging from questions about the client's educational level through some rather personal questions regarding his presenting complaint. We are now moving along over several days of interviewing, and the psychiatrist has taken a more active role. He does not act like a detective here, but more like the expert that he is in interpersonal relations.[337] The deeper one goes in this phase of interviewing the more it is true to say that he is doing "intensive" psychotherapy.

At this point the therapist may choose to use *free association*. Actually, Sullivan was relatively critical of those therapists who see in free association a "grand technique" and make of it the "all" of psychotherapy. Too often, the invitation to the client to say "every littlest thing that comes into his mind" merely results in autistic verbiage of no therapeutic merit.[338] Yet, many therapists go on chasing these verbal rainbows. Though he did use free association, he often found it more profitable to throw out possible hypotheses as interpretations rather than sit back and listen to a purposeless course of talk which had no discernible significance.[339] Sullivan felt that his psychiatric peers often derived pleasure from "getting lost in the schizophrenic woods with their schizophrenic patients."[340] He did not respect these histrionic types, nor did he believe that patients cared much for them. Too many psychiatrists have this juvenile propensity to have "fun" in their work.[341]

The legitimate reason for using free association arises when the client finds he has hit a snag in his recollections. At this point, the therapist does not go through any elaborate instruction in "how to" free associate. He merely says something like "Well, if that seems to have escaped you, why not just tell me what *does* come to mind when you think about this question?" Again, through a natural transition we move into a useful technique which helps us get some ideas about what the client is thinking when he cannot do this for us.[342] The better one's relationship with the client, the more trust and interpersonal intimacy achieved in the two-group, the less likely it is that such blocks will arise, and free associations will therefore not be required.

If we now continue to search with the client his past life, and begin pointing out to him how the parataxic distortions evident in his present interpersonal patterns might have arisen due to such and such a historical development in his life, we move into the *detailed inquiry* phase of psychotherapy. Ordinarily, before we move ahead into this more detailed and personal account we summarize for the client what the reconnaissance has taught us.[343] Sullivan was a great believer in summarizing, pulling things together, and keeping the course of therapy on a reasonable track. Occasionally he would interview a client for one and one-half hour periods (rather than the usual 50 minute hour), and he always spent the last 15 minutes summarizing what they had learned. The client comes to appreciate the expertise of the psychiatrist through this facility he has for organizing and bringing out the essential points in a clear and purposeful fashion. Occasionally, Sullivan asked the client to prepare a life chronology in writing, to help the recollected facts and fantasies to emerge in their proper sequence.[344]

At this point *interpretation* emerges as an ever more important aspect of psychotherapy. In line with his general outlook, Sullivan proved to be an active, direct, practical therapist. It was his feeling that what the client does not understand—particularly if he is a schizophrenic—he will not benefit from.[345] Theoretical formulations of too abstract and esoteric a nature are sure to go over the client's head. Interpretations must be founded on solid data, properly researched, and clearly presented to the client, at the time when understanding is most likely to follow. Timing is an extremely important facet of the interpretation.[346] We must make certain the client is prepared and ready to accept the interpretation before we ask him to accept it. Since most insights arouse anxiety in the client, a second vital aspect of interpretation is providing reassurance. As Sullivan put it: "Any question, and in particular, any explanatory statement—interpretation—that arouses anxiety is apt to prove worse than useless."[347] This is so because dissociative tendencies are triggered by the self when the anxiety level disturbs the client's euphoria.

Anything the therapist does or says in the therapy hour is taken by the client in greater or lesser terms as some kind of interpretation or judgment of what is transpiring in the two-group integration. Sullivan once said that there are roughly five different kinds of interpretations that we make as therapists.[348] There is the typical comment on the nature of the relationship, including the parataxic distortions of the client. There is the clarification we make in the extratherapy occurrences which the client reports on each day; thus, we might help him gain insight into the two-group integrations with his wife or employer. There is the extension into the past which we make, to show how eidetic people now confound the client's present patterns of behavior. There are also constructive attempts to be made for the future which we might help elucidate by drawing out the entire life complex for the client. Finally, there are all manner of emergency or crisis situations which arise both in and outside of therapy which we can use as material for our commentary on the client's personality tendencies. Sullivan liked to use a technique of interpretation he called "small contexts."[349] He circumscribed a small area of the client's life, and then used this relatively easy-to-grasp complex of events as the material for his interpretation. Making one such interpretation, he then moved into another small context, and so forth, rather than attempting to bring sweeping aspects of the client's life under the scope of an interpretation.

The client must cooperate in the therapist's endeavors, of course. Sullivan encouraged his patients to keep notice of any changes taking place in their physical state—such as fluctuations of mood or increases in muscular tension.[350] He also encouraged them to notice and report any marginal thoughts they might have concerning the material covered in the interview. Finally, he wanted them to say what they desired without fear or reticence. Gradually, due to the combined efforts of client and therapist, an unfolding insight can be expected. The therapist most often will form a clear statement of what seems to be the nucleus of the problem in living. He would then show the client how this explanatory theory serves to clarify and make sense of many different aspects of his behavior. The client would already have been aware that something had been interfering with his consciousness. In therapy he will be brought back to these parataxic distortions on many occasions, each time acquiring a better grasp and extending the control of awareness over the dissociated materials involved. Eventually, an expansion of the self occurs, and the client as known by others becomes the client as known by himself.[351] Dissociation has come to an end in the balance of personality we know as mental health.

At about this point in the interview series we move into the *termination* stage. The therapist begins by making a *final statement* to the client, summarizing again what they have learned together over the course of the interviews. He then draws from this the implications as a *prescription* of action, dealing specifically with what the client should avoid in life. Sullivan seems to have been more likely to disadvise than to advise his clients.[352] The therapist cannot tell people how to find happiness, but surely, based upon his knowledge of their past, he can make some worthwhile estimates as to what they should avoid in the future if they wish to prevent a recurrence. Next, the therapist makes a *final assessment* of the probable effects which the prescription might be expected to have upon the client's future life. Finally, there is the *formal leave taking*. One has the distinct impression in reading Sullivan that his clients were thoroughly schooled and well rehearsed as regards their life situation before he turned them loose to regain some semblance of life adjustment on their own.

DREAM ANALYSIS AND MISCELLANEOUS FACTORS

It follows from Sullivan's view of autism that so-called latent content of dreams is a highly dubious presumption made by the therapist who is taking parataxic material and "translating" it into consensually validated terminology.[353] Sullivan felt that this was another one of those games psychiatrists play with the lives of their patients, to keep themselves amused.[354] For his part, the therapist should be involved in more important and productive things than trying to guess what this or that dream symbol might "mean" to the client. He considered theories of dream symbolism to be far-fetched speculations. Sullivan did not, however, dismiss dreams as irrelevant to interpretations made during the detailed inquiry. The key to understanding a dream lies in its interpersonal nature: "Dreams are interpersonal phenomena in which the other fellow is wholly illusory, wholly fantastic, a projection, if you please, of certain constructive impulses, or of certain destructiveness, or of certain genital motivations, or something of that kind."[355]

The therapist, then, should consider the dream on its own level, without poking around for underlying latencies or presumed symbols. If he does this, then he shall find that impulses, which in waking life are dissociated from awareness, begin making their appearance. Dreams of an interpersonal sort are put on in a belated attempt to gain satisfactions which consciousness has not permitted. Dreams are literally portrayals of all that we are *not* in conscious life. We think of this as always on the side of lust and hostility, but the principle can be seen in the cases of those who dream very nice dreams: "Thus the dream processes of people who are full of hate [in awareness] will be found to include symbolic operations which actually have the purpose of releasing the tension of positive, constructive drive; this is one of the curious situations in which the nearest a person comes to warm human companionship is in his sleep."[356]

Sometimes the dream of one man can serve as a presyntaxic expression of gratification, sublimation, or compensation for an entire group of people.[357] When this happens, one man's dream becomes a myth, to be perpetuated by all men of a common identity who sense their needs being gratified in this parataxic operation. Hence, the dream always points to something, and a therapist who is willing to look with this intentional orientation can often see the outlines easily enough. He should not become lost in the details of "what this symbol means" but fix on the process, the movement and thrust of the action to see where it is taking the individual being enacted in the dream theme. The therapist can then clear up the significant details of the dream for the client by stripping them of irrelevancies and obscuring elements.

Sullivan had occasionally relied upon hypnotism in his work with psychotics,[358] but he seems to have eliminated this technique from his later work, and we do not hear anything about this tactic with neurotics. He believed in keeping the sex of the therapist and the client identical.[359] In his work with male schizophrenics he always emphasized the use of talented aides to work as assistants. He viewed these men as belated chums for his patients, who could help cultivate the intimacy and reality testing so necessary to proper development in the adult.[360]

Two therapeutic features which Sullivan introduced have continued to assume greater importance in the mental health field since his death: the "half-way house" and "communal sharing" tactics of reintroducing ex–mental patients to the community and maintaining them once there. Sullivan's technical style of "doing therapy" exhibits a strong regard for the necessity of reassuring the client, of not frightening him, of not using techniques to confuse or in any way demean him as a person.[361] He had a kind of Yankee "cracker-barrel," no-nonsense approach to therapy which afforded each client a dignity and importance even as it stressed that he submit himself to the expertise of another with a *practical* goal in mind. Sullivan's psychiatry was, as he intended, a uniquely American psychiatry.[362]

Notes

1. Sullivan, 1962, p. xxi. 2. *Ibid.*, p. xxxiv. 3. Sullivan, 1940, p. 178. 4. Sullivan, 1962, p. 312. 5. *Ibid.*, p. 5. 6. *Ibid.*, p. xv. 7. Sullivan, 1940, pp. 178–179. 8. Sullivan, 1962, p. xxvi. 9. *Ibid.*, p. 264. 10. Sullivan, 1964, p. xxxi. 11. Sullivan, 1962, p. 321. 12. Sullivan, 1964, p. xxviii. 13. Sullivan, 1956, p. xii. 14. Jung, Vol. 5, p. 102. 15. Hofstadter, 1955, p. 167. 16. Becker and Barnes, 1952, p. 536. 17. Sullivan, 1964, pp. xxii–xxiv. 18. Park and Burgess, 1921. 19. Sullivan, 1964, p. 196. 20. Sullivan, 1953, p. 35. 21. Sullivan, 1962, p. 142. 22. *Ibid.* 23. *Ibid.*, pp. 30–31. 24. Sullivan, 1953, p. 104. 25. Sullivan, 1940, p. 105. 26. Sullivan, 1962, p. 83. 27. Sullivan, 1953, p. 185. 28. Sullivan, 1964, p. 35. 29. Sullivan, 1953, p. 103. 30. *Ibid.* 31. *Ibid.* 32. *Ibid.*, p. 109. 33. *Ibid.*, pp. 164–165. 34. Sullivan, 1964, p. 325. 35. Sullivan, 1953, pp. 280–281. 36. *Ibid.*, p. 109. 37. Sullivan, 1962, p. 161. 38. Sullivan, 1964, p. 324. 39. Sullivan, 1953, p. 162. 40. *Ibid.*, p. 302. 41. *Ibid.*, p. 118. 42. Sullivan, 1964, p. 309. 43. Sullivan, 1940, p. 201. 44. Sullivan, 1954, p. 231. 45. Sullivan, 1953, p. 209. 46. *Ibid.* 47. *Ibid.* 48. *Ibid.*, p. 103. 49. Sullivan, 1964, p. 239. 50. Sullivan, 1940, p. 51. 51. Sullivan, 1964, p. 243. 52. Sullivan, 1953, p. 90. 53. Sullivan, 1962, p. 302. 54. Sullivan, 1964, p. 221. 55. Sullivan, 1953, p. 26. 56. *Ibid.*, p. 29. 57. *Ibid.*, p. 38. 58. *Ibid.*, p. 110. 59. *Ibid.*, p. 178. 60. *Ibid.*, p. 105. 61. *Ibid.*, pp. 106, 184. 62. *Ibid.*, p. 77. 63. *Ibid.*, p. 87. 64. Sullivan, 1962, p. 31. 65. Sullivan, 1964, p. 202. 66. Sullivan, 1953, p. 186. 67. Sullivan, 1940, p. 17. 68. Sullivan, 1964, p. 163. 69. See Sullivan, 1956, p. 221. 70. Sullivan, 1953, p. 182. 71. Sullivan, 1964, p. 19. 72. Sullivan, 1953, p. 76. 73. Sullivan, 1964, p. 311. 74. Sullivan, 1940, p. 92. 75. Sullivan, 1953, pp. 183–184. 76. Sullivan, 1940, p. 70. 77. Sullivan, 1962, p. 32. 78. Sullivan, 1964, p. 64. 79. Sullivan, 1962, p. 149. 80. Sullivan, 1954, p. 138. 81. Sullivan, 1962, pp. 249–250. 82. Sullivan, 1956, p. 4. 83. *Ibid.*, p. 92. 84. Sullivan, 1954, p. 142. 85. Sullivan, 1953, p. 192. 86. Sullivan, 1940, pp. 20–21. 87. Sullivan, 1954, p. 178. 88. Sullivan, 1953, p. 239. 89. *Ibid.* 90. Sullivan, 1956, p. 349. 91. Sullivan, 1964, p. 46. 92. *Ibid.*, p. 39.

93. *Ibid.,* p. 148. 94. Sullivan, 1956, p. 11. 95. *Ibid.,* pp. 69–70. 96. Sullivan, 1964, p. 83. 97. Sullivan, 1940, p. 80. 98. *Ibid.,* p. 224. 99. *Ibid.,* p. 277. 100. Sullivan, 1964, p. 72. 101. Sullivan, 1956, pp. 8–9. 102. Sullivan, 1953, p. 97. 103. *Ibid.,* p. 36. 104. *Ibid.,* p. 59. 105. *Ibid.,* p. 99. 106. Sullivan, 1940, p. 14. 107. *Ibid.,* pp. 263–264. 108. *Ibid.,* p. 47. 109. Sullivan, 1956, p. 7. 110. Sullivan, 1962, p. 5. 111. Sullivan, 1964, p. 244. 112. Sullivan, 1953, p. 198. 113. Sullivan, 1964, p. 234. 114. Sullivan, 1953, p. 34. 115. *Ibid.,* p. 315. 116. *Ibid.,* p. 37. 117. Sullivan, 1940, pp. 13–14. 118. *Ibid.,* p. 88. 119. Sullivan, 1964, p. 218. 120. Sullivan, 1940, p. 47. 121. Sullivan, 1953, p. 9. 122. Sullivan, 1964, p. 235. 123. *Ibid.,* p. 234. 124. Sullivan, 1954, p. 218. 125. Sullivan, 1953, p. 41. 126. Sullivan, 1964, p. 238. 127. Sullivan, 1956, p. 113. 128. Sullivan, 1962, p. 249. 129. Sullivan, 1940, p. 17. 130. Sullivan, 1954, p. 218. 131. *Ibid.,* p. 109. 132. Sullivan, 1964, p. 250. 133. Sullivan, 1956, p. 60. 134. *Ibid.,* p. 64. 135. *Ibid.,* p. 43. 136. Sullivan, 1964, p. 216. 137. Sullivan, 1956, p. 55. 138. *Ibid.,* p. 166. 139. *Ibid.,* p. 63. 140. Sullivan, 1953, p. 318. 141. Sullivan, 1956, p. 73. 142. *Ibid.,* p. 178. 143. Sullivan, 1940, p. 22. 144. *Ibid.,* p. 15. 145. Sullivan, 1953, p. 351. 146. *Ibid.,* p. 316. 147. Sullivan, 1964, p. 311. 148. *Ibid.,* p. 309. 149. Sullivan, 1953, p. 314. 150. *Ibid.,* p. 316. 151. Sullivan, 1962, p. 213. 152. Sullivan, 1940, p. 78. 153. Sullivan, 1964, p. 44. 154. Sullivan, 1956, p. 230. 155. *Ibid.,* p. 232. 156. Sullivan, 1940, p. 28. 157. Sullivan, 1953, p. 359. 158. Sullivan, 1940, p. 194. 159. Sullivan, 1953, p. 173. 160. Sullivan, 1956, p. 63. 161. Sullivan, 1940, p. 185. 162. Sullivan, 1956, p. 328. 163. Sullivan, 1962, p. 283. 164. Sullivan, 1964, p. 303. 165. Sullivan, 1953, pp. 217–218. 166. Sullivan, 1962, p. 196. 167. *Ibid.,* p. 100. 168. Sullivan, 1956, p. 14. 169. Sullivan, 1940, p. 126. 170. Sullivan, 1953, p. 218. 171. Sullivan, 1956, p. 232. 172. Sullivan, 1953, pp. 358–359. 173. Sullivan, 1956, p. 27. 174. Sullivan, 1962, p. 195. 175. Sullivan, 1940, p. 71. 176. Sullivan, 1953, p. 113. 177. Sullivan, 1964, p. 297. 178. Sullivan, 1953, p. 9. 179. Sullivan, 1940, p. 66. 180. Sullivan, 1962, p. 97. 181. Sullivan, 1953, pp. 122–123. 182. Sullivan, 1940, pp. 64–65. 183. Sullivan, 1953, p. 193. 184. *Ibid.,* p. 151. 185. *Ibid.,* p. 39. 186. *Ibid.,* p. 89. 187. Sullivan, 1964, p. 298. 188. Sullivan, 1953, p. 193. 189. *Ibid.,* pp. 208–209. 190. *Ibid.,* p. 227. 191. Sullivan, 1956, p. 123. 192. Sullivan, 1953, p. 228. 193. *Ibid.,* p. 233. 194.

Ibid., p. 238. 195. Sullivan, 1964, p. 265. 196. Sullivan, 1962, p. 204. 197. Sullivan, 1956, p. 215. 198. Sullivan, 1964, p. 72. 199. Sullivan, 1953, p. 294. 200. *Ibid.,* pp. 291–292. 201. *Ibid.,* pp. 218–219. 202. Sullivan, 1956, p. 164. 203. Sullivan, 1962, pp. 192–193. 204. Sullivan, 1956, p. 153. 205. *Ibid.,* pp. 105–106. 206. Sullivan, 1940, pp. 42–43. 207. *Ibid.,* p. 42. 208. Sullivan, 1956, p. 157. 209. Sullivan, 1953, p. 249. 210. *Ibid.,* p. 256. 211. *Ibid.,* pp. 250–251. 212. *Ibid.,* p. 263. 213. *Ibid.,* p. 295. 214. Sullivan, 1954, p. 171. 215. Sullivan, 1953, pp. 259–260. 216. *Ibid.,* p. 297. 217. *Ibid.,* p. 298. 218. *Ibid.,* p. 234. 219. *Ibid.,* p. 310. 220. Sullivan, 1956, p. 193. 221. Sullivan, 1962, p. 262. 222. Sullivan, 1940, p. 77. 223. *Ibid.,* pp. 77–86. 224. Sullivan, 1953, p. 280. 225. Sullivan, 1962, p. 224. 226. Sullivan, 1953, pp. 32–33. 227. Sullivan, 1962, p. 297. 228. Sullivan, 1940, p. 22. 229. Sullivan, 1956, p. 359. 230. Sullivan, 1953, p. 6. 231. Sullivan, 1962, p. 261. 232. Sullivan, 1953, p. 314. 233. Sullivan, 1962, p. 190. 234. *Ibid.,* p. 221. 235. *Ibid.,* p. 279. 236. Sullivan, 1940, p. 47. 237. Sullivan, 1962, p. 206. 238. Sullivan, 1956, p. 34. 239. Sullivan, 1962, p. 261. 240. Sullivan, 1940, p. 175. 241. Sullivan, 1964, p. 155. 242. Sullivan, 1954, p. 183. 243. Sullivan, 1962, pp. 327–328. 244. *Ibid.,* p. 107. 245. Sullivan, 1956, p. 258. 246. Sullivan, 1940, p. 139. 247. *Ibid.* 248. Sullivan, 1953, p. 360. 249. *Ibid.,* p. 361. 250. Sullivan, 1956, p. 337. 251. Sullivan, 1940, p. 157. 252. Sullivan, 1956, p. 332. 253. Sullivan, 1940, p. 152. 254. Sullivan, 1962, p. 99. 255. Sullivan, 1940, pp. 148–149. 256. Sullivan, 1956, p. 309. 257. Sullivan, 1962, p. 239. 258. *Ibid.,* p. 165. 259. *Ibid.,* p. 164. 260. Sullivan, 1953, p. 325. 261. Sullivan, 1962, p. 243. 262. *Ibid.,* p. 149. 263. Sullivan, 1956, p. 190. 264. Sullivan, 1962, p. 278. 265. *Ibid.,* p. 218. 266. Sullivan, 1956, p. 182. 267. *Ibid.,* p. 187. 268. Sullivan, 1962, p. 219. 269. *Ibid.,* p. 327. 270. *Ibid.,* p. 190. 271. *Ibid.,* p. 327. 272. *Ibid,* pp. 327–328. 273. *Ibid.,* p. 160. 274. Sullivan, 1940, p. 142. 275. Sullivan, 1956, p. 313. 276. *Ibid.,* p. 305. 277. *Ibid.,* p. 154. 278. *Ibid.,* p. 146. 279. *Ibid.,* p. 358. 280. Ibid., p. 284. 281. *Ibid.,* pp. 287–288. 282. *Ibid.,* pp. 290–291. 283. Sullivan, 1940, p. 102. 284. *Ibid.,* p. 25. 285. Sullivan, 1956, p. 298. 286. Sullivan, 1964, p. 231. 287. Sullivan, 1956, p. 29. 288. *Ibid.,* p. 271. 289. *Ibid.,* p. 257. 290. Sullivan, 1940, p. 104. 291. Sullivan, 1956, p. 78. 292. *Ibid.,* p. 216. 293. *Ibid.,* p. 204. 294. Sullivan, 1953, p. 323. 295. Sullivan, 1962, p. 110. 296. *Ibid.*

297. Sullivan, 1956, p. 229. **298.** *Ibid.*, p. 360.
299. Sullivan, 1954, p. 196. **300.** Sullivan, 1956,
p. 228. **301.** Sullivan, 1962, p. 281. **302.** Sullivan, 1954, p. 238. **303.** *Ibid.*, p. 106. **304.** Sullivan, 1962, p. 280. **305.** Sullivan, 1956, p. 168.
306. Sullivan, 1940, p. 207. **307.** Sullivan, 1954,
p. 231. **308.** Sullivan, 1940, p. 115. **309.** *Ibid.*,
p. 94. **310.** Sullivan, 1964, p. 331. **311.** Sullivan,
1953, p. 346. **312.** Sullivan, 1940, p. 208. **313.**
Sullivan, 1962, p. 158. **314.** *Ibid.*, p. 183. **315.**
Sullivan, 1940, p. 219. **316.** *Ibid.*, p. 224. **317.**
Ibid., p. 98. **318.** Sullivan, 1956, p. 360. **319.**
Sullivan, 1962, p. 348. **320.** *Ibid.*, p. 269. **321.**
Sullivan, 1940, p. 227. **322.** *Ibid.* **323.**
Sullivan, 1954, p. 53. **324.** Sullivan, 1940, p.
206. **325.** Sullivan, 1962, pp. 37, 44. **326.** *Ibid.*,
p. 283. **327.** Sullivan, 1954, p. 11. **328.** *Ibid.*,
p. 16. **329.** Sullivan, 1956, p. 200. **330.** Sullivan,
1954, p, 219. **331.** *Ibid.*, p. 107. **332.** Sullivan,
1940, p. 214. **333.** Sullivan, 1954, p. 17. **334.**
Ibid., pp. 39–41. **335.** *Ibid.*, p. 60. **336.** *Ibid.*,
p. 50. **337.** *Ibid.*, p. 78. **338.** Sullivan, 1940, p.
190. **339.** Sullivan, 1956, p. 48. **340.** *Ibid.*, p.
328. **341.** Sullivan, 1953, p. 295. **342.** Sullivan,
1954, pp. 81–82. **343.** *Ibid.*, pp. 85–87. **344.**
Ibid., p. 89. **345.** Sullivan, 1956, p. 370. **346.**
Ibid., p. 225. **347.** Sullivan, 1940, p. 97. **348.**
Ibid., p. 191. **349.** Sullivan, 1956, p. 244. **350.**
Sullivan, 1940, pp. 200–202. **351.** *Ibid.*, pp.
233–237. **352.** Sullivan, 1954, p. 213. **353.**
Sullivan, 1962, p. 91. **354.** Sullivan, 1953, pp.
338–339. **355.** Sullivan, 1940, p. 69. **356.** Sullivan, 1956, p. 105. **357.** Sullivan, 1953, p. 339.
358. Sullivan, 1962, p. 101. **359.** *Ibid.*, p. 289.
360. *Ibid.*, p. 253. **361.** Sullivan, 1956, p. 366.
362. Sullivan, 1940, p. 176.

6

Behavioral Learning in Personality and Psychotherapy: Dollard and Miller

Before we can properly appreciate the theoretical approach of John Dollard and Neal E. Miller to personality and psychotherapy we should survey the background positions of the more important figures in what is usually called learning theory—a branch of which is *behaviorism*.

Historical Overview of Learning Theory and Behaviorism

IVAN PETROVICH PAVLOV (1849–1936)

One of the fundamental constructs in this theoretical line is the *conditioned reflex* or *conditioned response*, as it has come to be known. It was the Russian physiologist, Ivan P. Pavlov (1927), who first demonstrated that natural or spontaneous responses could be "conditioned" or "made conditional upon" the appearance of an unnatural stimulus. When a light or bell is presented with or slightly before some food is placed in a dog's mouth, a dog's salivating tendency becomes attached to the light or bell after several such pairings of the unrelated stimulus with the food stimulus. The theoretical language which issued from this work labeled the food an *unconditioned stimulus* and the natural tendency to salivate when food is present an *unconditioned response*. The arbitrary alternative stimulus of a light or bell is considered the *conditioned stimulus* and when it reliably elicits salivation we speak of that behavior as a *conditioned response*. Stimuli and responses which are conditioned are thus manipulated, controlled or nonspontaneous alterations of a natural course of events due to experimental intervention.

This procedure, which was crystallized by

1902, has come to be known as *classical conditioning*. Pavlov believed that conditioning could be achieved only through physiological changes taking place in the brain. His theory begins with the assumption that man's higher nervous system has the capacity to form "temporary nervous connections" on purely physical grounds. The agent which could cement these connections was termed a *reinforcement*. Food, for example, is a natural reinforcer of such bonds, because it restores the body and re-energizes it through chemical action. The human organism will continue to perform a certain behavior if that behavior somehow rectifies a chemical disbalance which initially resulted through the energic expenditure to move, i.e., "behave." We thus learn to act based upon inborn and unlearned responses which have survival value depending upon how they serve to enhance our status as living beings.

The Pavlovians were also to establish that both response and stimulus *generalization* took place in human learning. For example, a dog conditioned to salivate to a bell of a certain level of cycles per second (e.g., 1000) would *also* salivate, though perhaps to a lesser degree, to values approximating this level (e.g., 500 to 1500). This would be an example of stimulus generalization. Similarly, other responses were found to develop in relation to the conditioned stimulus, responses which were not specifically reinforced (perhaps not only salivation but a slight head-turning propensity). This is called response generalization. It is possible, through repeated reinforced or nonreinforced trials in the classical conditioning procedure, greatly to reduce the range within which such generalizations occur or to eliminate them entirely (so that the animal would respond only to 900–1100 cycles, or eliminate the head turning). This is called stimulus or response *differentiation* (or *discrimination*).

A variant conditioning procedure which was introduced by the Pavlovians was so-called *instrumental* conditioning (named by Hilgard

and Marquis, 1940). In classical conditioning, the animal does not really have to carry out any particular behavior before it is reinforced. Just as soon as it sees the food the animal has seen the reinforcement which is probably forthcoming no matter what happens. Or, in many of the studies, food (powdered meat) was placed directly into a dog's mouth so that there was an immediate reinforcement upon sensing (seeing, smelling) the "reinforcer."

In the 1920s, some of Pavlov's followers began experimenting with a new conditioning procedure. They first sounded a bell or flashed a light (unconditioned stimulus) and then flexed a dog's leg (unconditioned response), following this sequence up with a bit of food (reinforcement). Although the experimenter had to flex the dog's leg initially, to bring it up from the surface on which the animal was standing, in time the dog came to lift the paw quite spontaneously when the bell was sounded or the light was flashed. It was as if the animal were automatically anticipating the reward to follow leg flexion. Hence, the term "instrumental" suggests that a conditioning sequence depended upon the animal's response. The dog must "do" something (an instrumentality) before a reinforcement will be presented.

EDWARD L. THORNDIKE (1874–1949)

Our next prebehavioral theorist is Edward L. Thorndike, an American, as are all of the remaining men we will consider in the tradition. Thorndike's early work on animals actually predated Pavlov's, and he drew a series of laws from his experiments which are of central significance to all learning theories. Although we need not review all of his laws, the *law of effect* should be considered. This law underscored the fact that certain responses get "stamped in" and others get "stamped out" of an animal's—or a human being's—repertoire of responses, based upon their consequences. In its first version, the law of effect held that responses were *connected* to the situations in which they appeared if their consequences were satisfying to the organism.[1] If the consequences were discomforting, the law of effect held that the connection between the situation and the response would be weakened. After conducting studies with humans Thorndike revised the law of effect by noting that annoyance does not weaken the connections between a situation and a response as much as satisfaction strengthens it. Annoyance simply allows an alternative response to take place.

Thorndike also put another major idea into this intellectual tradition in his *law of exercise,* or use and disuse, which first suggested that mere repetitions of a response in a given situation would strengthen the connection whereas prolonged disuse of a response in a given situation would weaken the connection. After some work with humans Thorndike admitted that mere repetition strengthened a person's response little, if at all. Repetition required what he called a *confirmatory reaction* in order for the person to learn the connection between situation and response. The confirmatory reaction was the result of the individual establishing a "set" toward obtaining a particular goal and then subsequently confirming it through reaching the goal.[2] To explain how satisfactions or confirming reactions worked to cement a connecting link between situations and responses, Thorndike took a modified biological position.[3] He suggested that some kind of hedonic physical satisfaction doubtless heralded the confirmatory reaction and also suggested that man could gain satisfaction from an on-going sense of control over situations as they were continually arising.[4]

JOHN B. WATSON (1879–1958)

Our next historical figure is clearly the father of *behaviorism.* John B. Watson coined this term and initiated this rigorous outlook on the nature of psychology while completing his doctoral studies and working as an instructor at the University of Chicago, where he studied with John Dewey, among others. The essential point of behaviorism was that psychology had to stop trying to find its data from "within awareness," and thus it must reject the introspective methods of Wundt and Titchener and devote its attention only to observables: "The rule, or measuring rod, which the behaviorist puts in front of him always is: Can I describe this bit of behavior I see in terms of 'stimulus and response'?"[5] In thus describing something observable the behaviorist changed psychological experimentation from the somewhat fruitless introspective examination of sensations and emotions to a more dynamic demonstration of how behavioral sequences actually change through environmental influence.

By limiting himself to observables Watson could, in 1913, erase the distinctions between "higher and lower" animals that most philosophically inclined psychologists had accepted as patently obvious until that time: "The behaviorist, in his efforts to get a unitary scheme of animal response, recognizes no dividing line between man and brute."[6] Although he made some effort to apply and extend Thorndike's laws of learning, Watson gradually relied almost exclusively on the conditioned response to explain behavior. Indeed, one can see an identity in the way behaviorists speak about the *response* and what they mean by *behavior;* that is, both conceptions are motile, under the control of a stimulus, circumscribing all that can be said about animal or human psychology, and depending upon reinforcements. Watson clearly viewed psychology as a natural science, one which needed no assumptions about consciousness or mental events to explain the succession of stimuli and responses which were the proper object of its study.[7] He introduced an important theoretical distinction between the *external* response and the *internal* response, saying that what we consider to be thought (mental activity) is actually a form of subvocal speech, in which we covertly manipulate the muscles of our speech apparatus and related structures.[8]

In drawing out how behavior is determined by the empirically demonstrable environment rather than by inborn features of the body, Watson helped fix the terms *shaping of behavior* and *habit* into the vocabulary of all psychologists.[9] Watson did not deny that physical equipment surely limited what one could do, given certain factors in the environment. So long as pianos are made according to a standard size, the man with a small hand will find it difficult to become a great pianist. Physiology is also important since, after all, one cannot behave effectively if his response *repertoire* (a term Watson also helped introduce) does not function properly.[10] When we are sickly or handicapped by nature there is a serious limitation placed upon our potential. Even so, the *major* source of behavioral variety continues to be the influences which enter the life cycle following birth. This famous quote epitomizes Watson's outlook:

I should like to go one step further now and say, "Give me a dozen healthy infants, well-formed, and my own specified world to bring them up in and I'll guarantee to take any one at random and train him to become any type of specialist I might suggest—doctor, lawyer, artist, merchant-chief and, yes, even beggar-man and thief, regardless of his talents, penchants, tendencies, abilities, vocations, and the race of his ancestors."[11]

Human behavior involved aligning a series of stimulus-response sequences (considered now in the sense of numberless Thorndikian connections or Pavlovian associations) into habits (fixed sequences). Watson thus viewed man as coming into the world as an *"assembled organic machine ready to run."*[12] The environment takes this machine and shapes it or molds it according to the particular responses which are positively or negatively reinforced into *habits*. It is the scientific duty of psychology

to establish laws and principles for the *"control of human action."*[13] Man is thus fundamentally a responder, he is not a creator of aspirations or goals toward which he can direct his own behavior. Watson believed that those who place a mentalistic control in man "get lost in the sophistry of 'foresight' and 'end.'"[14] What then is personality? It is the *"end product of our habit systems."*[15]

EDWARD CHACE TOLMAN (1886–1961)

Not all men who considered themselves behavioristic in outlook followed Watsonian lines. Edward C. Tolman became the foremost spokesman of his time for those behaviorists who would like to have seen a more complex formulation of behavior than the input-output mechanism of Watsonian behaviorism. Tolman spent time studying with the gestalt psychologist, Kurt Koffka (Chapter 9), and he became convinced that something more than a simple, unidirectional stimulus-to-response circuit was involved in human learning. Drawing on the writings and inspiration of William McDougall (1923a, 1923b), a nonbehavioral social psychologist who had called for purposive descriptions of behavior,[16] Tolman named his approach to psychology *purposive behaviorism*. Tolman did not mean to imply that lower animals or man for that matter were teleological organisms.[17] He felt that purpose could be directly observed, as when an animal, facing several trial and error alternatives relative to some end (such as a food box), is seen to follow the "more efficient of such trials and errors with respect to getting to that end."[18]

Tolman argued that there must be mental processes which *intervene* or *mediate* between the stimulus input and the response output.[19] These "coming between" variables, which Woodworth (1929) had termed S-O-R or "organismic" variables, are thus given a central role in purposive behaviorism. The organism does not simply respond to the environmental stimuli in an automatic fashion. It formulates a kind of "cognitive map" which it can later use in memory to direct its present behavior. The animal in the maze learns a *significate* or a visual image giving the general layout of the physical properties of the maze. In addition, as the animal traverses this recalled layout a series of *signs* orient it in relation to the goal which is being purposively sought (the food box). Tolman then combined all of these features, the significates, the signs, the means-to-ends purposive behaviors which were thus made possible, into the single theoretical construct of the *sign-gestalt*.[20]

In the evolution of learning theories Tolman's sign-gestalt sequences of means-to-ends have been incorporated under the general rubric of *expectancy*. Tolman frequently spoke of his "means-end–readiness" constructs as expectancies, held by the animal in probabilistic fashion toward one goal or another.[21] He also suggested regarding expectancies, that: "To some extent, rats, and to a large extent the higher animals, seem capable of expecting not merely simple, and single, direction-distance correlations but also successions or hierarchies of such correlations."[22] This important concept of a *hierarchy* of expectancies—which probably flows from Watson's concept of a "repertoire of response"—has since been of central importance as a means of conceptualizing the sum of all behaviors going to make up animal or human behavior.

CLARK LEONARD HULL (1884–1952)

It remained for Clark L. Hull to raise behaviorism and learning theory to what is probably its highest level of expression. Hull was eminently influential in the tradition not only because of the extensive and detailed experiments he and his students conducted to support their views, but because he provided a kind of philosophical-theoretical background for the thinkers who followed Watson's lead. Building on Tolman's intervening or mediating approach to learning, Hull formulated a highly sophisticated and intricate theoretical

system to explain the nature of learning (1943, 1952). For our purposes, only a few aspects of this theory need consideration.

First of all, it is historically important to appreciate that Hullian theory rests upon a *drive-reduction* interpretation of reinforcement. That is, learning is not held to take place unless a response, which has been continuously associated with a stimulus, is followed by some form of drive or need reduction. This is essentially identical with the Pavlovian-Watsonian tradition. In his first formulation, Hull (1943) spoke about this reinforcement as involving a definite drive reduction or drive gratification. For example, the animal learns in classical conditioning to make a response in relation to a stimulus because of the gratification of a food drive when powdered meat is placed in its mouth. After several years of study Hull modified the specific reference to a drive *per se,* in favor of a *drive stimulus.* It takes time for drives to result in a hedonic gratification, as in the case of hunger where several minutes elapse in the processes of ingestion, digestion, and absorption before the organism achieves a sense of revitalization. Obviously, reinforcement must follow a given response fairly quickly in order for a stimulus-response connection to be strengthened. It therefore seems plausible that a reduction in the stimulations—or a part of them—which herald a drive's presence—not total drive reduction—might well account for how stimulus-response bonds are cemented (reinforced). Hence, once food is in the mouth of an animal, the stimulus value of a drive is doubtless reduced because the animal has learned that such preliminary alterations of a drive stimulus herald the certain gratification of a need. This softened the Watsonian mechanistic position considerably, even as it pitched behavior toward the goals being sought rather than simply being conceived of as due to automatic reflexes.

In time, this goal orientation of behavior became a major feature of Hullian theory.

Hull in no way implied a teleology, and indeed, he was less attracted to expectancy constructs than Tolman. However, he did introduce a concept of the *fractional, antedating goal reaction* or *anticipatory goal response* which attempted to account for the fact that behaviors are often learned which are not specifically consummatory—in the sense of leading directly to reinforcement—yet they *are* vital aspects of the learning process.[23] For example, a rat running a maze in which he must turn left in order to reach the food box (goal) may begin running closer to the left-hand wall before making his turn; or, he may begin a series of head turnings to the left, even before he comes to the point at which he must turn. Tolman would have considered these purposive moves on the animal's part, as it was adapting to ongoing signs along its significate-expectations. Hull, however, preferred to consider these responses "fractions" of the eventual complete goal response (turn left and eat)—fractions which in turn provoked a further stimulus to register on behavior, the *goal stimulus*.

This theoretical innovation extends the mediation conception of Tolman and Woodworth to say that some stimuli "intervene" between an input and an output because they have literally been generated by a fraction of the total output. A fraction of the output (a response) thus can generate a type of new input (an intervening stimulus). These "new" stimuli, which have been produced by fractional responses, Hull called *pure stimulus acts*. They were "pure" in the sense that their only role was to guide the course of behavior along the route to eventual reinforcement. They could not result in gratification through stimulating the consummatory responses. These latter, broader response patterns included the fractional antedating goal reactions (running to the left, head turning) plus all of the physical behavioral responses needed to consummate the behavioral sequence (chewing, swallowing, and so forth).

Two important theoretical concepts flow from Hull's treatment of fractional antedating goal reactions and their consequent goal stimuli. First of all, this characteristic accounts for *secondary reinforcement*. The *primary* reinforcement would imply a decided drive reduction, of course—or at the very least, a sense of immediacy as when we literally have food in our mouth. However, it is possible to see how goal stimuli more and more removed from this consummatory act can take on reinforcing properties of a "secondary" sort. Thus, the tendency to run along the left wall or the slight head-turning of the rat can themselves function as pure stimulus acts leading to the (primary) reinforcement. The animal has learned that this or that sequence of events antedates the goal attainment, hence its behavior is furthered by the appearance of these "secondarily" reinforcing features of the environment. A better example of secondary reinforcements of this type, often used to explain human motivation, is the easily demonstrated fact that people work long hours to acquire bits of paper and metal called "money." They do so *not* because there is any intrinsic value in these objects (they cannot be eaten, hence cannot themselves gratify needs in a primary sense), but because they act as types of goal stimuli, as secondary reinforcers heralding the eventual satisfaction of basic needs (money buys food, clothing, extends one's power, and so forth).

Second, picking up from where Tolman had begun, Hull acknowledged that animals learned *many* behaviors which might gain the achieved goal object in their series of learning trials. The organism never learned just one "habit" (stimulus-response regularity) but a host of such habits forming a *habit-family hierarchy*. The habit which a given stimulus or complex of stimuli was most likely to evoke stood at the apex of this hierarchy, as the "most probable" response(s) to occur. However, given that this response could not be made, or given that this response were to be made several times without eventual reinforcement taking place, an alternative response, lower in the probability of occurrence at the outset, could move up the hierarchy to "most probable" response.

BURRHUS FREDERIC SKINNER (1904–)

Having considered Hull's elegant attempts to raise behaviorism to the status of a theoretical science, we will end our review of prominent figures with a consideration of B. F. Skinner, a neobehaviorist who not only found the S-O-R model inappropriate for psychology but disparages all attempts to build systems or to theorize about what is supposedly taking place "inside" the organism.[24] Skinner took the Pavlovian-Watsonian admonitions to deal with observables to their logical limit, even though he was not attracted to a "physical reflex" psychology. In his now classical *The Behavior of Organisms* (1938) and the papers which followed shortly thereafter, Skinner gradually turned his attention away from classical conditioning to that form of behavioral control Hilgard and Marquis had termed instrumental conditioning.

Skinner observed that classical conditioning was a "stimulus produced" form of behavioral regularity. A specific and clearly known stimulus (e.g., food powder) is paired with a response under conditions in which it serves as a reinforcer of the "other" stimulus (the bell or light) in relation to the spontaneous response (in this case, salivation). Knowing the specific stimulus, the experimenter can treat the behavior under his control in a physical reflex sense—that is, he can see that it is *elicited* (drawn out or evoked in a way which does not bring the animal's behavior into the picture at all). Nothing the animal might "do" will alter what eventually "happens." The unconditioned stimulus (food) is also the reinforcer, so everything gets aligned quite rigidly and automatically.

It was Skinner's feeling that this form of conditioning was not typical of most of life's learned behaviors. Responses of animals or men are not elicited through such iron-clad successions of events. Rather than being elicited, most behavioral responses are actually *emitted* or sent forth by the organism in relation to certain consequent environmental factors which either "reinforce" the behavior emitted or fail to do so. In this case, what the animal "does"—his response—is central to obtaining reinforcement. If a bear, roaming the woods, turns over a log and is rewarded thereby with a nest of insects, this consequence (insects as reinforcement) will ensure a subsequent repetition of log-turning (the response) by this particular animal. The behavior (log-turning) which "operates" on the environment to produce a reinforcing effect Skinner termed the *operant*. Hence, *operant conditioning* focuses on the response and asserts that responses followed by reinforcers are likely to be manifested again, and the more we reinforce these responses (operants) the more frequent will they be manifested. Whereas the classical conditioner of behavior looked to the "size" of the response eventually conditioned (as the amount of saliva secreted), or the rapidity with which this response is made as conditioning is carried out (how quickly salivation begins following flashing of the light), the operant conditioner focuses on the frequency of conditioned responses (the number of log-turnings over a fixed period of time) as the proper measure of degree of behavioral conditioning achieved.

Note what has happened here: Skinner dismisses as irrelevant for his purposes the time honored behaviorist concern with "the" stimulation of a response (Why did the bear roll the first log over?). This means that he also is not called upon to speculate about the nature of drives or needs as Watson and Hull had done before him. Such speculations are risky at best, dealing with presumed variables going on "within" the organism. As Skinner once phrased it: "I don't see any reason to postulate a need anywhere along the line. . . .

As far as I'm concerned, if a baby is reinforced by the sound made by a rattle, the sound is just as useful as a reinforcer in accounting for behavior as food in the baby's mouth."[25] Thus, we might characterize the position Skinner takes on reinforcement as an *empirical law of effect*. As we have already seen, Thorndike had stipulated the law of effect in a general way, and subsequent developments were to tie this law to presumed drive reductions of this or that need. Skinner then stated that "whatever" stimulus he can *empirically observe* following a response that serves to increase the likelihood or rate of that response's subsequent emission he will accept *prima facie* as a "reinforcement stimulus" or a "positive reinforcement." If the observed stimulus following a response inhibits this likelihood of occurrence, such as spanking a child following some misbehavior, we can speak of a "negative reinforcement." But what and how something is to be taken as a reinforcement is for Skinner an entirely empirical matter.

By emphasizing the "subsequent effect" of a behavioral response in this fashion Skinner picked up a theme introduced by Tolman. That is, Skinner speaks of these subsequent affairs as *contingencies,* by which he means "the conditions which prevail at any given time and which relate a bit of behavior to its consequences."[26] Skinner also takes a molar view of responses, preferring to think of them as *classes* of behavior rather than one-to-one reactions.[27] An operant is thus a "class of responses," and though he does not speak of hierarchies Skinner clearly achieves the same multiplicity of behavioral description in this use of a class construct as Tolman and Hull had achieved in their hierarchy constructs. One does not learn a single response when he finds that rummaging through the kitchen can lead to a tasty snack, he learns a host of potentially rewarding responses. It is thus the case that operant behavior is far ranging and greatly adaptive.

At the same time, precisely which way behavior will go and how specific it becomes is to be determined by the "response-reinforcement contingency." Skinner extended Watson's concept of *shaping* behavior to include what he has called the *method of successive approximations*—a method of behavioral control which is presumably at work in all of our lives each day. The idea here is gradually to arrive at a desired (or, randomly decided) behavior in the organism by taking it in stages of shaping. The animal trainer who patiently rewards his dogs as they approach a stool, until he has them up on the stool and then jumping from it, then through a hoop and so forth, is demonstrating the method of successive approximations. With each movement toward the desired behavior he slips his dog a bit of food as a reward, and the likelihood of the animal repeating this behavior is thereby increased, until the proper sequence is one day aligned and—at a signal— the dog will carry through the entire "act" before seeking his reward at the hand of the trainer. In the same way, Skinner argued, man is controlled by his environmental circumstances. We are all shaped each day, behaving this way or that contingent upon the reinforcements which emanate from our environment. To change ourselves we must first change our environment, for: "Men will never become originating centers of control, because their behavior will itself be controlled, but their role as mediators may be extended without limit."[28] The nonteleological heritage of behaviorism is thus kept intact. We must look to sources outside the individual man to find observable reasons (shaping circumstances) for why he behaves as he does.

The Learning Theory Approach to Personality and Psychotherapy of John Dollard and Neal E. Miller

The two men we now turn to were uniquely equipped to achieve the task they set themselves—that is, to unite the physical and behavioral with the social and psychiatric sciences. It is rare to find the breadth of scope each man had personally achieved in theoretical outlook. Dollard brought the knowledge of ethnology, sociology, and anthropology to the partnership. Miller brought the knowledge of experimental psychology, physiology, and animal experimentation. Dollard was the field investigator, Miller the laboratory experimenter. Dollard leaned in the direction of the social sciences, and Miller leaned in the direction of the natural sciences. Yet both men had first-hand experience with psychoanalysis. Dollard and Miller are transitional figures in the history of personality theory, more historically important than literally "founders" of a school. They paved the way for the behavioral therapy approaches of Chapter 7, though their stated objective and major achievement was to show how theories of man might be brought together into an enriched overall picture.

John Dollard was born in Menasha, Wisconsin, on 29 August 1900 and grew up in this small town set in rural surroundings before attending the University of Wisconsin. He took his B.A. degree from Wisconsin and then did graduate work in sociology at the University of Chicago where he earned the M.A. (1930) and Ph.D. (1931) degrees in this academic specialty. It is of some interest to note that Dollard's intellectual stimulation thus came from the very same Chicago School of social thought which was infusing Harry Stack Sullivan with an outlook on man. In the 1931–1932 period Dollard was in Germany, as a research fellow in social psychology, and it was there that he received training in Freudian psychoanalysis at the Berlin Psychoanalytic Institute. In 1932 he returned to America as assistant professor of anthropology at Yale University. In 1933 he moved into the newly formed Institute of Human Relations at Yale, where he was to form his working collaboration with Neal E. Miller. Some appreciation of Dollard's versatility can be gained from the fact that he was carried on the staff rolls of three departments at Yale (anthropology, sociology, and psychology) before retiring to professor emeritus status in 1969.

Dollard's professional studies have ranged with his career interests. He did a classic field study in the 1930s, dealing with the role of the black man in a southern community, which quickly established his talent for combining personality and sociocultural factors into an overall analysis.[29] He was a consultant to the Secretary of War during World War II and published works on the psychological aspects of fear, including those associated with battle.[30] He seems to have become increasingly interested in psychotherapy during this time. Dollard did in fact train psychotherapists and for many years carried on a moderate private psychotherapy practice. In addition to his work with Miller he has published books dealing with the practical aspects of psychotherapy as well as the assessment of human motivation.[31]

Neal E. Miller was also native to Wisconsin, born in the more metropolitan city of Milwaukee on 3 August 1909. He attended several universities, obtaining his B.S. from the Uni-

John Dollard

versity of Washington in 1931, M.A. from Stanford University in 1932, and his Ph.D. from Yale in 1935. During the period of 1932–1935, while completing his doctoral studies, Miller served as an assistant in psychology at the Institute of Human Relations. In the year following his completion of his doctorate, Miller obtained a traveling fellowship which sent him to Vienna, where he studied psycho-analysis at the Vienna Institute of Psycho-analysis. Although his training and research interests were in animal study and Hullian neobehaviorism, this experience with psycho-analysis laid the groundwork for his eventual collaboration with Dollard. Clark L. Hull was at Yale during this period, and during the year 1938–1939 he held a series of Monday night gatherings with members of the Institute of Human Relations and others. Miller was an active participant in this group. Indeed, in time Miller became an important influence on Hull, encouraging him to change his interpre-tation of reinforcement—from requiring that a drive be reduced, to requiring that merely the drive stimulus be lessened. Miller's excellently conceived researches were making this point increasingly clear to all those interested in Hullian theory.

Miller retained his academic affiliation with the Institute of Human Relations until 1942, when he left to direct a research project for the U.S. Army Air Force during World War II. He returned to Yale in 1946 and continued his distinguished work there until 1966, when he accepted an appointment as professor of psychology and head of the Laboratory of Physiological Psychology at Rockefeller Uni-versity. As the latter appointment might sug-gest, Miller's interests in his maturing years as researcher and theorist centered more and more on the physiological correlates and sub-strates of reinforcement. Miller has published extensively and importantly for several years, in addition to his collaborative efforts with Dollard.[32] He was to be honored by his fellow

psychologists, who elected him President of the American Psychological Association in 1949, and in 1965 he was awarded the U.S. President's Medal of Science.

The collaboration of Dollard and Miller was the natural outgrowth of the spirit en-gendered by the Institute of Human Rela-tions. In 1939, the Institute's staff combined to publish what has become a monumental example of interdisciplinary study, in their monograph entitled *Frustration and Aggres-sion*.[33] The point of this work was to analyze the general phenomena of frustration and aggression in terms of stimulus-response psy-chology, psychoanalytical theory, and the findings of sociology and anthropology. Following this, Dollard and Miller were to do two books together, from which most of the material of Chapter 6 will be drawn, *Social Learning and Imitation*[34] and *Personality and Psychotherapy*.[35]

Neal E. Miller

Personality Theory

STRUCTURAL CONSTRUCTS

BEHAVIORAL MONISM AND MENTAL ACTIVITIES

It should be clear from our review of behaviorism that theorists in this general tradition do not accept self-directing mentalistic concepts in their descriptions of man. Dollard and Miller are no exception to this rule, eschewing teleological concepts for what they consider the superiority of the reinforcement principle.[36] Man can make *only* those responses which he has learned, and he makes them *necessarily* when the stimulus conditions are appropriate.[37] Purposive behavior is not really possible, although by using more precise terms we can account for such—in common parlance terms—"mental" tendencies quite adequately.[38] Hence, to speak of a mind vs. body dualism in this neo-Hullian approach to personality is really beside the point. All behavior, whether inside the organism's skin or outside it, is essentially the *same* thing.[39]

One does not find the mind vs. body type of discussion in the works of Dollard and Miller. Unlike the nonacademic therapists discussed thus far, there was no need to confront the medical biophysical models in performing the theoretical integration these theorists set themselves. One does see a possible "dualism vs. monism" issue in the matter of how behavior is brought about in life. Dollard and Miller are particularly distrustful of an easy reliance upon nativistic positions. They feel that if one attributes behavioral tendencies to inherited instincts he forfeits a certain amount of scientific inquisitiveness.[40] It is always very tempting to simply say "Person X is different from person Y because they have different native instincts."

The same applies for those theories which rely upon principles of organic maturation.[41] Though they do not deny that physical limitations and physiological developments (e.g.,

sexual promptings at puberty) enter into the range of behaviors one must consider in describing personality, Dollard and Miller emphasize the malleability, alterability, and learnability of human behaviors rather than focusing upon such more sterile conceptions. We can best capture their attitude by describing their approach as a "behavioral monism." The theoretical challenge is thus: How can we retain the insights of Freud while recasting them in more scientifically acceptable terms? Hence, their stated goal is "to combine the vitality of psychoanalysis, the rigor of the natural-science laboratory, and the facts of culture."[42]

THE FUNDAMENTAL ORGANIZATION OF BEHAVIOR: ATTACHMENTS, STIMULI, AND RESPONSES

Since the aim of this integrative effort is to redefine and hence clarify the Freudian terminology,[43] one might expect that concepts like id, ego, and superego would represent the basic structural constructs of the present chapter. Though in one sense true, the larger truth is that the specifics of Freudian thought are quite secondary to what Dollard and Miller attempted to say as unique theorists.

What are the basic constituents of "personality"? Though their 1950 book is entitled *Personality and Psychotherapy,* and one can find several definitions of psychotherapy within its pages, there is no clear-cut definition of what a "personality" is, independent of the general assumption that it is part and parcel of "behavior," and behaviors are different across people due to their environmental experience, social class, and general cultural influences. However, if we contemplate the most important theoretical usages it is not difficult to point to what are in our terms structural constructs of personality.

A term which Dollard and Miller use frequently, albeit in a somewhat informal sense, is "attaching," or the *attachment* of one element of experience with another; for example, the attaching of words to important features of the environment,[44] the attaching of anxiety to acts or language sentences,[45] the attaching of certain responses to certain cues,[46] the attaching of correct emotional responses to habits or verbal cues,[47] and even the attaching of words to words in higher mental processes.[48] Now, we can see in this "hooking-up" concept a theoretical descendant of the *association* or *connection* constructs which have been used by behaviorists since the time of Pavlov, Thorndike, and Watson.

The most fundamental structural constructs, however, remain the *stimulus* and the *response*. One might assume that these two terms must of necessity be a single unit. Stimuli cannot be stimuli unless they stimulate responses, and, in turn, responses must respond to stimuli. Yet a given stimulus can either now, or through learning at some time in the future, stimulate *any of a number* of responses. Since we can think of stimuli on the one hand and their attached or detached responses on the other, it is therefore correct to view these as independent theoretical terms. In their 1941 book, Miller and Dollard made clear that they were not using these terms in the traditions of reflex psychology. Stimuli were not considered as *only* those literal energy exchanges taking place in the real environment, and responses were not *only* those muscular contractions or glandular secretions that the early associationists and behaviorists had sometimes made them out to be. Relying on the observable, functional tactic of explanation Dollard and Miller then defined their terms as follows: "A response is any activity within the individual which can become functionally connected with an antecedent event through learning; a stimulus is any event to which a response can be so connected."[49] They did not consider this definition circular, since it rests ultimately on observably demonstrable facts. Hence, in their 1950 book they once again rest their definitional case with: "We shall call anything a stimulus that seems to have the functional

properties of a stimulus and anything a response that seems to have the functional properties of a response."[50]

The point is, if we can show that a behavioral or environmental antecedent *A* is tied in regularity to behavioral consequent *B,* we have a stimulus-response regularity or habit.[51] If we now wish to speak about how such habits become regular occurrences in our behavior we are *ipso facto* speaking about *learning.* Theories of learning attempt to explain how such habits are established, sustained, and eventually changed. Reverting to the language of Thorndike's connectionism, Miller and Dollard opine: "What . . . is learning theory? In its simplest form, it is the study of the circumstances under which a response and a cue stimulus become connected. After learning has been completed, response and cue are bound together in such a way that the appearance of the cue evokes the response. Everyone remembers to stop at a red light when driving an automobile."[52]

A *cue* is thus an antecedent event which takes on stimulus properties.[53] Cues determine when we will respond, where we will respond, and which particular response we will make.[54] Cues do not have to occur singly or in isolation. It is possible for a *patterning* of cues to take place, so that a complex network of stimulations can happen all at once, often giving qualitative differences to the stimulations of experience. Getting down to the specifics of their concept, Miller and Dollard note that "stimuli may vary in two respects: in strength and in kind."[55] The cue of a flashing red light is different from the cue of a delicious aroma emanating from the kitchen. Each signals a different kind of response.

What we "do" about the stimuli or how we "behave" in relation to them depends upon the kinds of responses we have in our repertoire. Behavioral responses are highly complex structural affairs. Recognizing the role of heredity in this structuring of responses, Dollard and Miller speak of an *innate hierarchy of response* which any organism brings into the world. This concept of a hierarchy refers to the probability with which a given response will be elicited—and consequently the ease with which it is "learned"—in relation to any given stimulus or complex of stimuli.[56] A baby, for example, has as one of its most probable (called *dominant*) responses to any potentially annoying stimulus the "cry." If a diaper pin pricks the infant he responds with a scream of pain and the crying pattern so familiar to any parent. In time, other responses to annoying stimuli of this sort will be learned (the older child will learn to remove a pin from his flesh if it is pricking him), yet this crying "potential" will always remain as a *weak* response in the hierarchy. Since the responses in the hierarchy are a function of the stimuli which elicit them, these probabilities are continually changing as we mature, depending upon the situation in which we find ourselves.[57] Thus, as a child approaches adulthood the probability that he will cry in public decreases as the behavior is relegated lower positions in his hierarchy of response, though in certain situations like public funerals we might still be highly likely to show our crying responses because it is more socially acceptable.

RESPONSES BECOME STIMULI: MEDIATION, LABELING, AND LANGUAGE

As Tolman and Hull had done earlier, Dollard and Miller found it advisable at this point to modify the more simple construction of a stimulus-response regularity, particularly regarding what seems to happen between the input and the output of observable behavioral regularities. Man is capable of learning responses to stimuli easily enough, but he *also* seems perfectly capable of turning previous responses into subsequent stimuli, so that he can retain information from his teachers (responses) which serve him well in later years (as stimuli). It is this recognition and the experimental data which supported it that led Dollard and Miller to distinguish between *instrumental acts* as responses and *cue-producing responses* as responses, as follows:

An instrumental act is one whose main function is to produce an immediate change in the relationship to the external environment. Opening a door, lifting a box, jumping back on the curb are examples of instrumental acts. A cue-producing response is one whose main function is to produce a cue that is part of the stimulus pattern leading to another response. Counting is a cue-producing response.[58]

Man has a marvelous ability to "restimulate" himself by making use of former responses which we now will call *cue-producing responses,* though the term *response-produced stimuli* conveys the same meaning and was used by Dollard and Miller in their first formulation.[59] We might conceptualize it as follows:

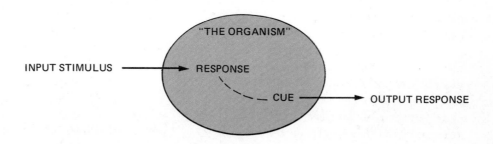

The instrumental act or, as it is sometimes referred to, the "instrumental response" is obviously the actual, overt, *output response*. If man were nothing but an instrumental responder then each stimulus input would go over directly into an output. Some behaviors do indeed proceed in this way, such as the reflexive-type physical connection of a tap on the knee leading to a knee jerk (Patellar reflex). Even more psychological behaviors are of this nature, such as when a husband, sighting his marital partner in a compromising situation with another man, "reflexively" strikes out at his rival. But man also responds through the intervention of cue-producing responses and hence he is a far more intricate organism than this.

There are two kinds of cue-producing responses: *verbal* (words, numbers) and *nonverbal* (sensory recollections, images, moods, and so forth). If the cue-producing response can be formulated in verbal terms, then it can be used by the individual in place of making his own instrumental responses, as when we ask another person to bring us a glass of water.[60] Nonverbal cue-producing responses can provide an intervening series of cues, as when we do not recall the name of a street in trying to locate a friend's house, but by simply driving along in our automobile we can locate his home with little difficulty through recalled visual cues.

Instrumental responses aligned in a sequence of from "stimulus" to "response" and no more would mean that no other alternative would be possible in a line of behavior. But: "A series of cue-producing responses is not limited in this way. It is possible for certain cue-producing responses that have been associated with the goal to move forward in the sequence and provide cues that have a selective effect on subsequent responses. Hull . . . calls these *anticipatory goal responses* [fractional, antedating goal reactions] and presents a rigorous deduction of how they could make the

adaptive combination of habits more likely to occur in a novel situation."[61] This capacity for problem solving is a great improvement over the kind of blindly determined problem solving known as *trial and error*.[62] The human being can acquire an *insightful* solution to his problems thanks to his capacity for extensive use of cue-producing responses.[63] He can make finer *discriminations* between patterns of stimulation in the environment and thus come to more subtle solutions of the problems facing him.[64] It should be clear that we are now speaking about how man thinks and reasons.

If man uses such "higher mental processes"[65] to modulate his behavior, does this not force us into a teleological position extending beyond the traditions of behaviorism and S-R psychology? Dollard and Miller would suggest that we can retain the integrity of S-R theory by realizing that the concept of *mediation* can account for how it is that cue-producing responses work. Hence, a *transfer of learning* (making an earlier response in a later or different situation) is often possible thanks to the fact that cue-producing responses mediate between inputs and outputs.[66]

Language must surely play a major role in the learning and use of cue-producing responses. Dollard and Miller have stated: "Language is the human example *par excellence* of a cue-producing response."[67] This would be on the side of a verbal cue-producing response, of course. To account for language acquisition, Dollard and Miller speak of the learning of labels or the process of generalizing labels to other situations as one of *labeling*. A label is thus a "verbal cue-producing response."[68] In other terms it is possible to speak of verbal *signs* or *symbols*, which are equivalent constructs in this theory.[69] Certain signs or symbols are nonverbal, like a country's flag or the display of wealth in wearing opulent jewelry, but the verbal symbol—word-forms—plays the most important role in higher mental processes. Dollard and Miller observe: "Most human thinking is done in words and sentences"[70] and: "Words and sentences play an exceedingly important role in human reasoning."[71]

As we mature, we learn to match words (signs, symbols) to important features of the physical and social environment.[72] Once we have attached it to the proper feeling state, the word "love" becomes a cue-producing response of major significance for most of us. Complexity is introduced through the patterning of these words into sentences and sentences into various thought forms known as *logic,* or the use of proper reason to eliminate contradictions and confusions.[73] Furthermore, language is the natural storehouse for all of those effective problem solutions that culture has eked out of experience for generations past.[74] The natural role of culture is to aid in the transmission of those artifacts and living styles which have proven successful across the span of time.[75]

FREUDIAN STRUCTURAL CONSTRUCTS AS
LEARNING THEORY TERMS

What have Dollard and Miller to say of the classical Freudian structural constructs? They never discuss the *id,* though one can surmise that the hedonism of a reinforcement principle relying upon drive reductions would probably suffice. There is a fairly extensive treatment of the unconscious vs. conscious aspects of experience, some of which has relevance for the id construct. That is, Dollard and Miller acknowledge that an uncultivated, uneducated, human being lacking in "proper" labels might well reason illogically and impulsively carry over his promptings to action without the intervention of moral values or social conventions.[76] Such an uncouth creature could well be considered an id-dominated person.

The *unconscious* "mind" is the total of behaviors carried over into action without an intervening label of some sort which would identify them for the individual who simply "acts out" instrumentally without insight.[77] Often, such unverbalized (unlabeled) experiences take place before the child has

learned to talk effectively. Hence, it is natural to find early experiences accounting for life's later difficulties. We do not forget or repress our early experience so much as we simply cannot recall what has not been properly labeled. If we do have adequate cue-producing responses to utilize as mediational aides, we can speak of *conscious* behavior.[78] Consciousness is thus closely related to the higher mental processes and problem-solution capacities of the insightful and cultural variety which we have considered previously.

Consciousness bears a close affinity to the *ego* in the view of Dollard and Miller, since the ego is also described in terms of the capacity which the individual has to deal with life through higher mental processes.[79] In fact, there is more concern expressed about *ego strength* in the learning theory translation than there is about the ego *per se.* One can assess ego strength by evaluating the extent of preparation an individual has had to confront life—both in his familial setting and his broader contacts with school and related social outlets. When training in these preparatory aspects of life has been scanty, we can speak of "a weak ego or a poor sense of reality."[80] If the consciousness is weak, and there are many unlabeled aspects of experience entering behavior, it follows that the ego would be submerged and something akin to an id domination would be the result. Dollard and Miller have, on at least one occasion,[81] used the phrase "unconscious wish" in describing a personality pattern. This usage is quite proper in a classical Freudian framework, but it is somewhat unclear how an unlabeled and unconscious stimulus could represent a "wish," unless of course we are dealing with unlabeled images of some sort, as in a dream. We might thus "see" ourselves visually in a dream situation even though we have never put this preoccupation into actual words.

The *superego* is the result of cultural modeling and training. We are taught the rules of personal cleanliness, and then building upon those conditioned traces of acceptable behavior, first pressed upon us in the toilet training situation, we evolve increasingly complex rules of "proper" behavior.[82] All of those familiar emotions we experience when we transgress social boundaries, like guilt, fear, and anxiety, are controlling mechanisms to make us hew the line valued by the culture. This is not meant in the sense of repression, of course, because *any* collective identity of people, from a gang of delinquents to an entire nation, must inevitably have its rules of conduct laid down if it is to survive as an entity.

MOTIVATIONAL CONSTRUCTS

THE NATURE OF DRIVE, MOTIVATION, AND REINFORCEMENT

In order for a stimulus-response attachment to be retained for any length of time it must be *reinforced.* Dollard and Miller put forth the *principle of reinforcement* in lieu of Freud's pleasure principle.[83] It is acceptable to speak of reinforcements as *rewards,* but we will use the former more technical term.[84] Before we can properly define reinforcement we must first consider the *drive* construct to which it is closely related.

A drive is a strong stimulus which *impels action,* and literally any stimulus can become a drive if it is strong enough.[85] The drive is what "stimulates" behavioral responses to get into motion. When this happens, we speak of motivation. To be motivated is to be under drive, ready to act, and there is really no clear distinction between these terms except that a motive can probably combine several different drives into an overall state of readied motility.[86]

The two broad classes of drives are *primary* or *innate* and *secondary* or *learned.* Primary drives include such feelings as pain, the sexual urge, or the desire to take a breath of air.[87] Secondary drives occur when a previously neutral cue stimulus has gained the functional capacity to stimulate an organism to re-

spond.[88] Once a habit has been established, drives also increase the tendency for the habit to be performed.[89] Indeed, it is the reduction in the drive which originally establishes the habit, and the continuing drive-reduction then sustains the stimulus-response regularity (habit). This brings us back to the reinforcement principle underwriting Dollard and Miller's theory:

. . . the following relationships between drive and reinforcement are clear: (1) a prompt reduction in the strength of the drive acts as a reinforcement; (2) reinforcement is impossible in the absence of drive because the strength of stimulation cannot be reduced when it is already at zero; and (3) the drive must inevitably be lower after the reinforcement so that unless something is done to increase it, it will eventually be reduced to zero, at which point further reinforcement is impossible.[90]

The "heart" of reinforcement is thus the occurrence of a "prompt reduction in the strength of a strong drive stimulus."[91] When the sun's glare becomes strong enough to motivate us to move into the shade, the reduction in the annoying stimulus which results is itself a reinforcement of the habitual movement being formed—that is, to seek the shade when annoyed by the sun. Dollard and Miller admit that there may be other forms of reinforcement, and rather than haggle over the matter, they choose to say that so long as at least *some* reinforcements operate through sudden reductions in drive stimulation their theoretical fabric remains intact.[92] They want to further their theory without having to pass on the ultimate nature of all reinforcements.

Since reinforcements depend upon drive stimuli, they too can be considered *primary* or *secondary.* The gratification achieved by eating when hungry or the reduction of painful tensions in defecation are both examples of "primary reinforcement," resting ultimately on innate response tendencies. But most of man's motives and his habit system itself are taken from his sociocultural environment. The drive for success can take on proportions far exceeding that necessary to sustain life. Since wealth signifies power in the social hierarchy, all of the accouterments of wealth known as *social status* (nice home, good clothes, automobiles, memberships in the better clubs) begin taking on secondary drive properties which means they take on secondary reinforcement potentials as well.

It takes a rather high-level animal to work for the distant reinforcements of a "pay day." Several experiments on both lower animals and humans have shown that *immediate reinforcements*—given immediately following the response being rewarded—are more effective to habit formations than are *delayed reinforcements*. The greater the delay between a response and its reinforcement (usually called the *latency*) the more difficult is it to establish a stimulus-response connection. Folk wisdoms such as "A bird in hand is worth two in the bush" and "Don't count your chickens before they hatch" capture the idea that one is better off with reward *now* than dreaming about what might or will be "tomorrow." The principle that immediate reinforcements are more effective than delayed ones is called the *gradient of reinforcement*.[93] Another aspect of this principle, which accounts in a way for the cue-producing responses Hull had called the *anticipatory goal response* is that there is a more active tendency to respond the closer one comes to goal reinforcement. The goal is ever more present as one gets closer to pay day, and though a worker may have felt "down" during the week, the day when he receives his check he is cheered by the prospect, and he works with renewed vigor.

Thus, thanks to man's higher mental processes he is capable of working toward the more distant or "delayed" reinforcements. Lower animals lack this capacity (relatively speaking, since even chimpanzees have been trained to work for poker chips which have been associated with food on earlier learning trials), and

hence they cannot show the "delay of reward" potentials that man constantly demonstrates in his behavior. When we speak of learned drives which work by motivating an animal for the future we are referring to *incentives*.[94] The *goal* is that cue-produced response or incentive which man has learned to work toward after the fashion of a delayed reinforcement.[95] If reinforcements were always automatic and reflexive, after the fashion of Pavlov's dogs, then man would not be capable of the long-range (delayed) activities which sustain him.

Are we ever aware or primarily *conscious* of the fact that we have been or are being reinforced? Dollard and Miller would respond: "According to our hypothesis, all reinforcements have a direct automatic strengthening effect on immediately preceding responses. Thus the primary effect of a reinforcement is always unconscious. In addition to this primary effect, it is possible for a reinforcement to have other effects that are mediated by verbal responses."[96] There are actually three levels of consciousness involved in reinforcement. First of all, there is the case of verbal labeling and mediation, in which the person would be conscious of his motivation. The boy who is cutting a lawn for pay and decides he has had enough of the hot sun sustains his drive level by reminding himself: "I'm getting five dollars to do this job." Second, a nonverbal mediation may occur, such as in the pleasant visual reverie the boy may have, seeing himself purchasing a desired motorcycle without actually saying (labeling) he intends to do so. Finally, the drive and its goal response may be completely unlabeled and unmediated, so that a direct instrumental response is made with a following reinforcement occurring entirely outside of consciousness. The boy may be cutting the grass for reasons other than money; for example, a pretty daughter of the homeowner who employed him may be providing unconscious motives quite out of the realm of financial gain.

How is it possible for reinforcements to

intrude themselves in this fashion at an unconscious level? To account for this fact Dollard and Miller rely on the related constructs of *generalization* and *discrimination*, representing *secondary* or *learned* generalization. For example, if the child is taught the word "sharp" in relation to kitchen utensils which can cut and injure him (knives, slicers, etc.), he can later be taught to avoid other "sharp" objects as well (broken glass, sheared metal, etc.) thanks to the mediation of this language sign. But there is a *primary* or *innate* form of generalization as well. If a pattern of cues is learned as a stimulus to certain responses, closely related patterns of cues will spontaneously elicit the responses as if the original stimulus were calling forth the action. If on a mushroom hunt we strike a bonanza of mushrooms in a certain type terrain, it is natural for our hunting responses to occur in a comparable topographical region the next time we go out. In fact, the more a terrain matches our original "good luck area"—even if we haven't named it such (no verbal cue-producing responses are involved at all)—the more likely will it be that our hunting will begin again. The mushroom hunting response will be *least* likely to occur in countryside which is highly *unlike* our bonanza area. This demonstrates the *gradient of generalization,* or the fact that the less similar a stimulus situation is to the original stimulus situation, the less probable is it that a transfer of response will take place.

Thus far we have been speaking of cue or stimulus generalization, but it is also possible to see in behavior the generalization of responses. This kind of phenomenon is not cited heavily by Dollard and Miller; in most instances, when they speak of responses generalizing they usually mean by way of some mediation from "input stimulus to cue-producing response to output response." But one can also see in the acquisition of learning a tendency for closely related responses to generalize to the same stimulus. In learning to write (response) some children also learn to stick their tongue out of the side of their mouth (response) at the same time, as a kind of tension-sustaining mechanism. Later, remnants of this tongue response can generalize to all writing activities, so that some people even as adults make odd facial expressions (grimaces, lip-biting, and so on) when they write. There need be no significance attached to these mannerisms. They may merely be the remnants of response generalizations (from moving hand, to moving body, to moving tongue, etc.).

Of course, the permanence or transitoriness of a response which has been elicited by a cue generalization is a function of the reinforcement which follows. If a college freshman at his first mixer asks *every* available young woman for a dance he may find that not all of his potential partners (cue stimuli) will agree to his request (response). In time he may learn that *certain* girls, with certain mannerisms as he approaches them, signal reasonably clearly that his chances for success are good. Unless he has a very strong ego and does not mind being rejected, before long he will learn to *discriminate.* He will no longer simply respond to the stimulus pattern of girl-as-potential-dance-partner but girl-as-probable-dance-partner. Discrimination is thus a further aspect of generalization. Much of what goes on in the name of *rehearsal* or *practice* is this interlocking procedure of generalization vs. discrimination learning.[97]

If a habit continues to be manifested but fails to bring reinforcement at least some of the time it will gradually *extinguish* and not occur when the stimulus conditions are proper. With 100 per cent failure our boy seeking a dance partner will be seen to "give up" (though he may not have mediated this consciously via a cue-producing label) and spend his time talking with male cronies at the mixer. He might stop attending dances altogether, particularly if this lack of popularity reflects itself in his dating behavior generally. It is not that he has forgotten how to dance or how to ask young women out. To *forget* is to lose a behavior as a result of spending a long interval of time during which the response is not practiced, such as when we do not recite a poem for months. But: "Extinction occurs when a response is practiced without reinforcement."[98] The rapidity of extinction depends upon the level of drive stimulation experienced (how badly the boy feels the desire for feminine company) and the number of times the habit has been reinforced in original learning (how many acceptances he initially obtained when he first set out to ask girls to dance). Interestingly, even after a response has been extinguished it can recur "from out of the blue." One night, after several months of nonattendance at the mixers our young man shows up and "tries again." Even he is surprised that he had this impulse to return at the last minute. This reappearance of an extinguished response after an interval of time is called *spontaneous recovery*.[99] The fact that it takes place demonstrates that extinction does not destroy a habit but merely *inhibits* it.

Unlike forgetting, where there seems to be a loss of the cue-to-response connection, in extinction the inhibited response seems to be replaced by an incompatible response in the hierarchy of responses. But the connection to the older habit remains and can be manifested after a period of time quite spontaneously. If one wishes to keep a response from reappearing in this fashion the incompatible response must be very effective—that is, reinforcing. In *not* going to dances the young man must find greater pleasure than he did when he was attending. Since solitary hobbies are rarely that rewarding, it is easy to see how the older responses might spontaneously recur. For this reason extinction is ordinarily not the best way to remove a response from the most probable levels of the response hierarchy. More effective results, if more unpleasant, can be achieved through the use of *punishment*. If the young man had not been simply politely declined when he asked potential partners to dance or

girls to accompany him on dates but was in addition ridiculed in some fashion, then his sudden reappearance at the Friday night mixer would be much less likely.

Even though reinforcement makes a response more likely to recur and punishment usually makes it less likely to recur, the two mechanisms are really not so different. It is the *end* of punishment which strengthens the avoidance response associated with it.[100] When a child is spanked for an improper act, the reason he continues to avoid that act is because with each (verbal or nonverbal) cue-produced "thought" of it his anxiety mounts. He knows it is "going to bring trouble and pain" if he continues, but the contrary notion—of "being good"—reduces this mounting state of fear, and therefore he is immediately reinforced by avoiding the behavior which had been punished. Hence, punishment is also sustained by a drive-reducing reinforcement (fear reduction).

This discussion of punishment rests upon a major theoretical conception in the evolution of modern learning theory. It took some time (1939) before one of Hull's more brilliant students, O. H. Mowrer, clearly worked out the hypothesis that certain drives—like fear—can be both stimuli to behaviors *and* self-sustaining reinforcements to that behavior when their level of stimulation is reduced. Fear is the most important drive construct employed by Dollard and Miller, probably because it adapts so well to the explanation of abnormal behavior. There is no real difference between their views of fear and anxiety: "When the source of fear is vague or obscured by repression, it is often called *anxiety*."[101] As a learnable drive, fear (anxiety) can be attached to previously neutral cues—including language labels. The ultimate source of fear is innately determined by the physiology and neurology of the body; but in human learning it is extremely difficult to separate the innate from the learned aspects of fear.[102] Fear is also highly resistant to extinction, and it assumes drive proportions as easily as it impels the individual to manifest "trial and error" behavior.[103] When this activity hits upon a reduction in fear, the drive diminution is immediately reinforcing and thus sustains the response which led to it.

It is important that drives actively stimulate the organism to behavior. A term which is often confused with drive is that of "need." When we say there is a need in the organism we usually imply that a drive needs reduction. However, some deficits in the organism are not *ipso facto* drive producing. Take the case of carbon monoxide poisoning, for example. Although we need to escape the inhaling of carbon monoxide, there is no innate drive to do so, and an individual can be accidentally killed if he finds himself inhaling the gas.[104] The same goes for eating a well-rounded diet. Though we all need adequate vitamins and minerals, many people suffer from various deficiencies even though they eat large amounts of food. Dollard and Miller use *many* drive constructs to explain behavior, of course. Fear is simply a major concept. Since drives are learnable, virtually anything which can be taught can take on drive value. Such learnable drives provide Dollard and Miller with their major tools for the explanation of sociocultural behaviors. For example, they speak of learned drives to "connect" (make meaningful ties in experience), to be logical, reasonable, and sensible, and to *not* fear things which are harmless.[105] But the major learned-drive construct in their outlook—the drive to imitate others—stems from their early collaboration.

THE ROLE OF IMITATION IN HUMAN LEARNING

One of the major causes of the cohesiveness in behavioral patterns witnessed in a given sociocultural identity is that of *imitation*, defined as follows: "Imitation is a process by which 'matched,' or similar, acts are evoked in two people and connected to appropriate cues. It can occur only under conditions which are favorable to learning these acts. If matching,

or doing the same as others do, is regularly rewarded, a secondary tendency to match may be developed, and the process of imitation becomes the derived [i.e., learned] drive of imitativeness."[106] The child who is given love and attention in the home when he matches his behavior to that of his parents—by coming to the dinner table on time, eating with the proper utensils, etc.—will acquire a drive to imitate others outside the home as well. This process is tantamount to socialization.

There are two major types of imitation to be noted in human behavior. One is simple copying, in which case individual A consciously tries to bring his behavior into line with a model, individual B. In this case, individual A has to have a certain amount of insight to know precisely when his responses are consistent with those of the model. Children rehearse their language sounds (phonemes) with such insight and thereby copy the verbal expressions of adults quite by design.[107] However, there is a type of imitation in which the model responds to environmental stimuli with insight but the imitator does not. This is termed *matched-dependent* imitation, a term which captures the idea that the imitator is dependent upon the model to carry out the correct instrumental response if he is to be reinforced. Leaders emerge as leaders in life because they have insight into the behavioral sequences which bring rewards. And their followers often "blindly" imitate them in this behavior, behaving in a matched-dependent fashion.

If one now extends this general logic to the verbal and nonverbal styles of behavior in a sociocultural context, we can explain a large range of behavior. Children conform to the patterns of their parents, even before they properly grasp why it is important to do so (matched-dependent). They accept parental religious views and come to have an outlook on life consistent with the social class in which they are reared. In time, a change in outlook can take place. The child in school may adopt the behavioral patterns of a different social class, and the direction this takes defines aspiration in terms of *upward* or *downward* social mobility. Ordinarily, there is a strong learned drive to strive upward in the social structure.[108] The ambitious child from a working-class background wants to "get ahead," to advance himself through education and become a professional person because as he ascends the social hierarchy the reinforcements of life are ever more assured. Hence, we note a common emphasis on being with "one's own kind" or "not marrying beneath one's station" in the larger culture. Social levels and, indeed, national identities seem to be the result of this tendency for man to imitate the "best" among his fellow men—which means the most rewarded and successful models available.[109]

There is a form of similarity in behavior which is *not* imitation which Miller and Dollard call *same behavior;* they mean by this that two or more people can be stimulated by the same cue at the same time, neither one copying or matching the other. In going to a football game, for example, many people act the same way as they ascend the stands, take their seats, and cheer for their favorite team in unison. Although imitation may be a factor here, it is not *essential* that we see this behavior as imitative. It is possible to view this regularity as merely "same behavior," which has been learned in the past without imitative aids.[110]

An interesting secondary motivation which seems to spring from imitation is that of *competition* or *rivalry.* If person A not only imitates person B but tries "to go him one step better," B may return this innovative advance in kind. Both individuals now seek to outdo the other. Gradually, this behavioral sequence can acquire drive status, and competitive motivation is established.[111] Humans in particular seem to have this motivation to compete because they have the ability to retain cue-producing responses in the form of words and sentences. Such anticipatory goal responses as "plans" are significant aspects of this competi-

tive process. A *goal* is essentially a cue-producing response, a form of improvement in reinforcement attainment mediated and hence generalized into the future.[112] Planning and foresight are other ways of speaking about the capacity which man has to project "into the future" by way of mediating cues and ensure that more reinforcement will be forthcoming.[113] Such capacities to orient the self in terms of the future can be trained into a growing child, and from every indication this is a vital aspect of successful living. When a drive of this sort is established we sometimes speak of the individual's *aspirations* or *hopes* that he will gain the goal in question.

Finally, a very important behavioral tendency which is essential for the proper functioning of human collectives stems from a special type of copying. We refer here to *empathy* or *sympathy,* which Dollard and Miller define as copying the "other person's" feelings or responding with appropriate signs of emotion to his mood.[114] Because we can sympathize or empathize with others, we are able to put ourselves in their place and respond accordingly as a "fellow man." One has no sympathy for "the enemy," since he is construed as outside of one's personal group designation or definition.

FRUSTRATION AND CONFLICT IN HUMAN BEHAVIOR

Life rarely goes along smoothly. Sometimes there is a high state of drive in the organism but the response which is called forth by this (innate or learned) drive is blocked. When this happens we speak of *frustration.*[115] The hungry person, arriving in town too late to find a restaurant open is confronted with one of life's frustrations. The poorly educated, working-class man who is thrown into unemployment with each dip in the economic cycle suffers a life-long round of frustrations as he loses economic power and can never see himself "getting ahead." Frustrations can mount, one on another, so that the "losers" in life often are pressed into a drastic frame of mind by their string of "bad luck." One of the predictable outcomes of a frustration, easily noted in researches on lower animals as well, is that frustration stimulates innate anger responses in living organisms. Block a child's approach to attractive toys and he will kick your legs trying to get around your obstructive body. Nature has seemingly provided an assertive response, high in the innate hierarchy, to attack and hence remove the *barriers* to goal attainment.

There is an extension of this frustration concept, one in which the barrier results from the fact that incompatible responses are being triggered at the same time in a given situation. This is called a *conflict*. In 1931, the gestalt psychologist Kurt Lewin (see Chapter 9, pp. 407–410) described three types of conflict in which people were likely to find themselves.[116] Though he did not use stimulus-response terminology to make his case, Hull (1938) and Miller (1937) later translated these three types of conflict into learning theory terminology. Considerable experimental work was then conducted by the Hullians, much of it by Miller (1944), to provide evidence in support of their terminology. Today, rather than a gestalt theory the conflict theory is one of the major bulwarks of stimulus-response theory.

We have already noted that goals are often cue-producing responses which mediate a person's aspirations for upcoming reinforcements. If we drop this restrictive usage and simply consider any given stimulus or pattern of stimuli in the behavioral environment as possessing a positive (reinforcing) or negative (punishing, fearful) aura, then we can consider these stimuli as goals. To sight a water fountain when thirsty is to see a goal with positive incentive properties. To avoid the drafty corner of a room is to withdraw from a goal having negative incentive properties. We have already discussed the *gradient of reinforcement* (p. 299).

Dollard and Miller used the term "gradient" because the learning theorists have measured the level of motivation exerted by an organism in relation to positive or negative goals—such as the amount of physical effort expended by the rat pulling various weights toward a goal—and this level of motivation has been plotted as a curve measuring changing values over various distances from the goal. It has thus been proven that—all other things remaining equal—the organism will exert great effort to flee from an imminent unpleasant situation, but this motivation drops off fairly rapidly as distance is put between the organism and the feared goal. The approach gradient, on the other hand, is relatively "flatter," that is, though we become more motivated to approach a desired goal as we grow closer to it, this increase is not dramatically greater than what it was at some distance from the goal. We have a more steady impulsion in this case, and, even when we are far away from the *desired* goal our motivation is fairly strong when we begin moving toward it.

This contrasting influence of approach and avoidance gradients on behavior can be made clear in a practical example of what is called the *approach-avoidance* conflict (also called "ambivalence"). In this case, the *same* goal has both a positive and a negative incentive (or valence) for the organism.[117] A good example is the necessity of our having to see the dentist for a toothache. In this case, we would be caught in the conflict of *approaching* the goal (dentist's office) out of a desire to end our pain, yet also suffering an *avoidance* motivation to flee the goal (dentist's office) due to the undoubted intermediate pain we would suffer at his albeit therapeutic hands. Since the avoidance motivation is relatively lower than the approach motivation when we are far away from the dentist's office, it is not difficult to make the telephone call to arrange for an emergency appointment, to get into our automobile, and to begin our drive to his office. However, as the proximity to the ambivalent goal increases our avoidance motivation rises ever rapidly, eventually outstripping our motivation to approach. By the time we park our automobile and begin ascending the stairs to the dentist's office we are much more motivated to flee than we are to be treated. What we actually do depends upon several factors. One of the important variables in the eventual outcome here is just how painful our toothache is (drive to avoid pain). Another motivation, which can fuse with this one, is the concern we have generally built up as a secondary drive to keep our physical appearance attractive, and hence, to avoid losing teeth through negligence. Such drive factors can summate and decide the outcome in favor of our seeking dental aid if they become strong enough. It is obvious that proper labels, acting as cue-producing responses, would be important here. One must be able to plan, to project desired goals, and to sustain an immediate pain for a longer term, delayed reinforcement. Sometimes there is considerable vacillation at some "point of decision" or "choice point." We might be seen walking to and fro outside of the dentist's office, on the sidewalk below, making up our mind. Strictly speaking, of course, according to this theory the human being does not determine his own fate. He can only do what the stimuli conditions make it possible for him to do, so what happens is up to the drive summations already mentioned.

A second major conflict is that of the *avoidance-avoidance* variety.[118] In this case, the individual is forced into a situation where two goals face him, neither of which he has any approach motivation toward, the case of being "caught twixt the Devil and the deep blue sea." The young man who has just been conscripted into the military forces of his country and is asked to choose between service in the infantry or the field artillery when either alternative is for him a horror of boredom and inconsequential life delay faces the avoidance-avoidance conflict. Such conflicts can become very severe because the individual perceives nothing as positive in settling upon an alternative. It makes little difference how near or how far

he is from the goal, though doubtless "getting away from it all" helps anyone who is caught up in this form of conflict. In fact, there is a decided tendency for individuals in avoidance-avoidance conflicts to escape in various ways. Men who desert their families, potential draftees who flee the country rather than face prison for refusing to serve in the armed forces, or even the abnormal individual who chooses to live in fantasy are all demonstrating the same basic tendency to remove themselves from what they perceive to be intolerable life situations.

The third general case of conflict is that of *approach-approach*.[119] In this case, the individual has to select either of two goals, both of which provide approach motivations. Once a move is made toward either of the two goals, since there is no avoidance motivation in the picture it is easily resolved, because as we know, the closer we are to one positive goal than the other, the higher is our motivation to attain that goal. If we are standing on a street corner, trying to decide which of two movies we should see that evening, and it really makes no difference to us since both are worth seeing and we will probably go to the one we do not see tonight another time, this would be a fair example of the approach-approach conflict. Any whim or related motivation which would move us closer to one or the other of the movies would doubtless decide the issue. For example, suppose that we looked up the street and saw a candy shop a half-block from our street corner. If we now stroll the few steps to get our favorite chocolate, this slight proximity advantage for one movie over the other would doubtless determine our choice for that evening, since our motivation would now be slightly higher for "this" movie than for "that" movie.

Quite obviously, the approach-approach conflict is not a very serious matter and in fact, we might question whether it is a "conflict" at all. We often settle such matters in life by simply tossing a coin! What is more true to life is the fact that decisions of this sort are usually like *double approach-avoidance* conflicts, in that each of two goals has some positive *and* some negative incentive value. Rather than the single goal of a dentist's office, we now think in terms of our movie theaters as each having both an approach and an avoidance gradient feature to them. The negative incentive at this point in time is at least something like "well, if we see this movie we won't see that one."

FREUDIAN ADJUSTMENT MECHANISMS AS
LEARNING THEORY TERMS

We now turn to a number of Freudian adjustment mechanisms to see how Dollard and Miller have redefined them in terms of learning theory. The mechanisms of *fixation* and *regression* will be put off to the "time perspective constructs" section which follows below.

Repression, Suppression, and Inhibition. The term *inhibition* in general learning theory means that a response is prevented from occurring or continuing even though its customary stimulus may be taking place. In their broader theory Dollard and Miller strongly emphasize inhibition in an "overt" sense, meaning that they think of it as the prevention of overt acts (instrumental responses), as opposed to the inhibition of cue-producing responses. Here is how overt inhibition is defined: "Overt inhibition will be used by us to refer to the prevention of instrumental responses by strong conflicting responses that are not under verbal control. Thus a patient is sexually inhibited when he is unable to perform normal sexual responses."[120] Inhibitions thus stop actions, whereas the matter of repression takes us into the realm of "thoughts"—that is, labels and other forms of cue-producing responses.

When, for various reasons, the individual lacks cue-producing responses (labels, mediational signs, language words, or sentences) we speak of the cause as *repression*. As Dollard and Miller state it: "*Repression* refers to the automatic tendency to stop thinking and avoid remembering."[121] There are different kinds of repression in behavior. In discussing these differences we use the term "inhibition" in an alternative sense to that of overt inhibition. We now mean a tendency simply to "stop thinking" as a learned response. If one stops thinking and avoids labeling, he can eventually suffer from three forms of repression.[122] The first involves inhibition of the responses labeling a drive. For example, a person may be frustrated and angered yet fail to label his emotional state properly; he just thinks he is "feeling poorly," which could mean anything. Second, there can be an inhibition of the responses which produce a drive. If someone thinks "I'm not dirty" each time he senses a rising sexual urge in relation to a member of the opposite sex, he can readily inhibit the eventual cultivation of his sexual mood. One can "lose the mood" or deny any genuine emotion if a competing, inhibitory cue-producing response of this sort arises (possibly via an early training that sex is dirty).

The third type of repression involves the inhibition of a response which mediates the drive. This is roughly opposite to our second type of repression. It sometimes happens that what goes on in mediation actually generates a "new" drive of its own, and thus adds something to a life situation which was not there before the mediation came about. For example, if two men are arguing yet controlling their anger responses, all may proceed in civilized fashion. But if one or both should suddenly respond to the situation with the cue (i.e., attitude) "This man is insulting me," an entirely new situation is created by this—even erroneous—cue-producing response. The new drive of anger now leaps into the picture entirely on the basis of a mediated label. If one or both stopped thought at this point (not going on with the "insult" rumination) a repression would result—a repression which might help divert thought to other matters and thus avert a nasty ending to the argument.

This teaches us something about repression:

it need not always be a bad thing, and, in theory, it should occasionally "work" to the betterment of personal adjustment. Dollard and Miller take a more positive view of such inhibitory tactics in the handling of human affairs than had the classical psychoanalysts. Societies have always taught their members to avoid painful topics, to "be civil," or to present themselves as socially mature and not impulsive in their relations with others.[123] When this process of stopping thought and avoiding remembering is done by conscious design, we can speak of *suppression*. Suppression is a normal human response, employed effectively by religious institutions and helpful to self-control for all humans so long as it is not used to deny reality.[124] Repression is, therefore, merely the automatic, unconscious counterpart of suppression.

Identification. This adjustment mechanism is an aspect of imitation, whether of the copying or the matched-dependent variety.[125] As children, and later as adults, we tend to take on certain customary patterns of behavior through imitating our parents, friends, and other members of our society.

Projection. The attribution of personal motives to others is like its reverse, taking in such motives through identification.[126] Dollard and Miller note that we all learn to expect fellow members of our society to react in roughly the same way that we do to different experiences (same behavior). This makes empathy and sympathy possible, and we help guide our interpersonal relations through such knowledge.

Reaction-Formation. The capacity to respond with "opposites" is probably the outgrowth of language learning. Dollard and Miller note that many studies on word associations have found antonyms to be a frequent type of response to word stimuli.[127] Now, if for some reason an individual feels a rising anxiety in relation to certain thoughts, feelings, or other

behaviors he is manifesting, he can make use of this training to profess or believe the opposite. If one senses hatred for another individual, he has all the more reason to reject this fearful reaction by asserting "I like him very much." In this sense, then, to react-formate is to deal with motivations by moving to their opposite expression.

Rationalization. We are taught to have logical explanations for anything we do. The drive to be logical makes us feel uneasy when involved in a behavior which we cannot explain or which seems irregular by common standards. Hence, there is strong motivation to justify what we do, to find "good reasons" for our behavior even though the actual motivation may be unconscious (unlabeled). This is rationalization.[128] The young man who feels driven to smoke a cigarette and frequently dashes off to buy a pack at the local tobacco store, overlooking the pack he has lying in clear view on his dresser top, may rationalize by saying he needs cigarettes. But we, knowing a voluptuous young woman dispenses these articles in the nearby store, could cite alternate motives for the frequent emergency trips.

Displacement. The displacing of emotions such as love or hostility to sources other than the original stimulus pattern is explained in terms of generalization. For example, a woman who feels great hostility for her mother, though unable to recognize this source of her feeling because she has not labeled it properly, may express hostility toward all older women.[129]

TIME PERSPECTIVE CONSTRUCTS

Although Dollard and Miller do not present their views on development in terms of Freud's stages of psychosexual development (Chapter 1), one can see the effects of Freudian theory in their general outlook. They speak of the four critical training situations in development as feeding, cleanliness, sex, and anger.[130] We shall take up their comments on these four situations and then turn to their views on fixation and regression.

THE FEEDING SITUATION

The newborn infant is completely dominated by desires for immediate (instrumental, pleasurable) reinforcement. Hunger, thirst, pain, and fatigue are the primary drives of major importance, and the child's helplessness in the face of these stimuli makes early life quite a difficult experience: "Infancy, indeed, may be viewed as a period of transitory psychosis. Savage drives within the infant impel to action. . . . The higher mental processes (the Ego) cannot do their benign work of comforting, directing effort, and binding the world into a planful sequence."[131] As infants we are frustrated easily and, hence, the likelihood of conflict formation is great. Dollard and Miller therefore advocate a highly permissive treatment of young children, until such time as they have the mental equipment (language terms) to deal with problem solutions.[132]

High in the innate hierarchy of response is the instinctive pattern to root for the mother's nipple, to suck and take in nourishment. This is the basis for a child's first social contact, and the feeding situation is the premiere learning situation of life. When reinforcement is not forthcoming the child's innate response is to cry. If the child is left to "cry himself out" he may learn that there is nothing he can do about circumstances, hence the experience may foster a developing tendency to passivity and a distaste for "trying something new" in later development.[133] The mother or mother-surrogate is extremely important in establishing a child's basic outlook on life. She is the first representative of "society."[134] A child who is generally ignored and given minimal care can grow into an adult compulsively driven to seek social contact, who cannot stand being alone because of the anxiety which solitude generates.[135]

Since the infant lacks verbal cue-producing responses in the first year he cannot label his conflicts, and hence they become unconscious aspects of behavior.[136] Language learning probably stems from the matched-dependent imitative behavior children manifest.[137] Infants rehearse their crying patterns, responding to their own voices with variations of the cry. In like fashion, and possibly as a generalization from this self-stimulation, the infant begins taking on and rehearsing the vocal sounds of his family members. The child's rate of language acquisition is dependent upon his sense of drive reduction in relation to verbalizing aspects of experience. A mother who lovingly responds to the child's primary drive needs gains the child's attention and then can gradually bring his interest to bear upon more and more of the surrounding environment through seeing, feeling, and speaking about things with her offspring.

CLEANLINESS TRAINING

If the feeding situation had certain potentials for the attachment of fear to it, the toilet-training situation is literally fraught with such potentials. Negative parental attitudes toward the child can result in the delay of attaining proper cleanliness attitudes; the child is most sensitive to rejection during periods of stress—and the toilet situation presents many. But often even a loving and accepting parent can forget that the child must learn a complex behavioral task here, and without the proper verbal skills to facilitate acquisition of the habit.[138] This is at least one important consideration in deciding when to begin toilet training: Can the child verbalize his needs in this area?

Many personality patterns generalize from toilet-training habits. A well-managed relationship, beginning in the feeding situation and then continued and complicated at the child's natural pace and rate of language acquisition can lead to a cooperative personality picture. Such children learn that social cooperation can be fruitful and helpful, even though it is not always easy. When a child is punished for mistakes in this area of learning he attaches anxiety cues to the very presence of his parents and can thus become devious and furtive, seeking every opportunity to escape from his parent's sight.[139] The implications for subsequent character formation here are obvious. It is also possible for the child to become overly meticulous regarding his personal hygiene and thereby generalize this pattern as rigidity and scrupulosity to all of life's concerns. This is what Freud was presumably getting at in his reference to "a 'Superego' or unconscious conscience."[140] Such individuals may grow into highly conforming, guilt-ridden adults.

EARLY SEX TRAINING

Dollard and Miller note that the sex drive is far from man's most salient drive stimulus. As primary drives, pain, hunger, and fatigue outrank sex; and even secondary drives like anxiety, ambition, and pride can prove stronger motivations than sex in behavior. What then is the reason for the predominance which sexuality has attained in the motive patterns of mankind, so well documented by Freud? Dollard and Miller would reply: "Sex seems to be so frequently implicated because it is the most severely attacked and inhibited of primary drives. Even though relatively weaker, sex can exert a strong pressure which produces great activation in the organism and great misery if blocked for long periods. In no other case is the individual required to wait so many years while patiently bearing the goading drive."[141] The taboos of religion and other sociocultural institutions such as marriage and the family pattern all combine to focus restrictive pressures on the individual to bear up under his drive state. Hence a relatively unimportant drive in the scheme of things—so far as the economy of the body is concerned—becomes a major source of concern. Indeed it would not be too difficult to conclude that the secondary

drive aspects of sex (what Freud called the taboos) are more important to patterned behavior than the primary, physiological drive of lust.

So-called "infantile sexuality" would be for Dollard and Miller simply a natural outcome of the reinforcement achieved when, for example, the child discovers that fondling his penis brings a pleasurable sensation. There need be no more significance attached to this act than the fact that the child tugs at his ear and, here too sensing a tickle or pulling feeling, continues to play with his ear for a longer period. If the parent who witnesses the child fondling his penis interprets this as sinful or dirty and punishes the child accordingly, anxiety can be attached to the genital sphere. In later years, when a prompting to masturbate may arise around pubescence, the conflict of sex vs. anxiety can present a serious adjustment problem.[142] Such concerns can be carried on into adulthood and can adversely affect the individual's marital adjustment as well. The masturbatory taboo is the first of the important sex taboos our particular culture exerts on our behavior.

Another early taboo which each of us experiences stems from the sanctions Dollard and Miller call *sex typing* of personality.[143] Historically, the sex *roles* have been apportioned so that men are expected to act in one way and women in another. The growing child soon learns what "boys do" and what "girls do" in the way of games, activities, and interests. Clothes differ, and all of the training received aims ultimately to prepare the child of a given sex for the "proper" role he will someday fill as a man and husband or woman and wife. Mothers who "baby" and overprotect their male child may rear a timid, fearful, essentially effeminate young man. Rather than emphasizing the boy's masculine character such a mother may keep his sexual identity uncertain. If a child's sex typing is unclear it is all the more probable that he will learn to relate his sexual promptings to a person of his own sex. It is in this way that sexual "deviation" may be considered a product of learning.[144]

After sex has been typed and the proper taboos against masturbation and homosexuality have been learned, the child is vaguely led to expect that sexual reward is to be forthcoming from the opposite sex. If he has been severely punished for earlier masturbatory activity, each sexual prompting toward the mother or a sister will generalize the anxiety in the male child, and hence we can witness what Freud called *castration anxiety* and the *Oedipus complex*.[145] This matter is often complicated by the fact that the father may be jealous of the child, who now seeks close contact with the mother, possibly even including wanting to sleep with her.

Dollard and Miller's view of the *Oedipus complex* emphasized the contribution parents made to this interpersonal conflict. The father becomes jealous of his son's masturbatory attraction to the mother and makes a hostile projection onto the offspring, which is picked up by the child who can actually interpret it in terms of castration anxiety.[146] Occasionally the tales of school friends about parents emasculating their children reinforce the child's anxiety. The female Oedipal has similar roots: closeness to the father and a resulting jealous reaction by the mother. Dollard and Miller accepted the view that some little girls feel they have been castrated in life, probably by their mothers. The Oedipal conflict is eventually resolved as follows: "Anxiety which was once attached only to the masturbation impulse is now attached to the heterosexual approach situation [e.g., toward mother in the boy]. If the anxiety is made very strong it can produce a certain relief in the intensity of the conflict. This is the so-called 'resolution' of the Oedipus complex. When anxiety is greatly dominant over approach tendencies, the conflicted individual stays far from his goal and but few of the acquired elements in the sexual appetite are aroused."[147] Since Dollard and Miller do not feel that everyone passes through the Oedipal complex in coming to maturity, their theory is not nearly so reliant as was Freud's on this construct.

TRAINING IN ANGER CONTROL

The final critical training situation concerns how the growing child manages his anger responses (used synonymously with hostility). As we should recall from the discussion earlier in this chapter, anger drives are stimulated by the innumerable and unavoidable frustrations which arise in life. Infants have very low frustration tolerance, easily scream, kick, vent their hostility in the flailing of arms and so forth. An important aspect of socialization is the learning of how to manage such virulent emotions, for they are naturally destructive and unproductive. Indeed, toilet training is greatly bound up with concurrent learning of how to curb anger. Dollard and Miller note that the punishing of rebellious children is one of the oldest patriarchal codes in our culture, once incorporated into the early Connecticut Blue Laws to the extent that a father could even kill his disobedient son.[148]

From the point of view of a learning theory, it is important to know why the individual expressing anger is doing so. What is the cause of his frustration, and can anything be done about this aspect of the situation? Too often, unfortunately, the parent will punish his child without an assessment of this source. The point of anger is, after all, to mount aggressive behavior against some barrier to his drive reduction. The stuck door irritates him, and he throws an aggressive shoulder into this obstruction and clears his passageway. If aggressive or hostile responses never result in such positive reinforcement but rather lead to repressive punishment, what is the outcome? As in other instances cited above, the child learns to attach anxiety cues to the very feelings of anger, and we have what Dollard and Miller call an *anger-anxiety conflict*.[149] Each time the individual senses a rising anger he also senses apprehension, hence the anger is repressed (inhibited).

The opposite approach, of course, might result in a completely selfish and uncontrolled individual. The person who feels it is perfectly all right to lose his temper when he wishes, to throw temper tantrums in public, and to expect others to make allowances for these immaturities would be one who had never learned to cope with (suppress, inhibit) his anger drives. Such an individual would doubtless have found these extreme emotional displays a highly effective means of achieving drive reductions of all sorts. One can easily summon the image of the "spoiled brat" holding his breath or knocking his head against the floor (inwardly directed anger) as his harried mother fumbles nervously in her purse for the money to buy him the ice cream sundae he really should not be eating before dinner. If such a child does not achieve self-controls he will hardly become a paragon of social sensitivity and cooperation as an adult.

There are many reasons why children feel extreme frustration, of course. The child may sense parental indifference or rejection. Another common source is *sibling rivalry*,[150] when a child displaced somewhat in the home by a younger brother or sister, feels a natural jealousy, which is simply anger toward another. Children can compete for parental affection. They are immature and hence very "basic" creatures; they often tease and torment one another to an unbearable degree. Skills vary across children, and any excellence in one child is potentially a source of frustration to another. Parents must be sensitive to these factors and try to offset the more extreme forms of anger-display by meeting the underlying causes rather than expecting the child to repress the anger through punishment.

As the individual moves up through adolescence and into adulthood, and then on through life in general, many factors both within himself as a person and in the culture as structured must inevitably frustrate him. Dollard

and Miller note that the most likely source of this frustration is the growing recognition that a desired upward mobility in the culture will *not* be achieved. The little boy grows up to learn that he lacks the ability to become a major league baseball player. The little girl matures into a pretty woman, but hardly the talented "movie star" she had dreamed of becoming. The middle-aged man comes to see that he will never get that promotion or receive an invitation to join that country club, which would clearly stamp him the success he desperately wants to be in life. Sometimes we cannot state the reasons for our lack of upward mobility; we blame it on "luck" or "not knowing the right people," and this makes it all the more galling. Entire groups feel the grip of social prejudice and discrimination, which keep them "in their place" and forever outside the pale of the Promised Land.

AGE GRADING, FIXATION, AND REGRESSION

A maturing child's life is measured in terms of how far advanced he should be, considering his age. Thus, the bladder and bowel training should be completed by *this* age, the first word should be uttered by *that* age, and walking should be mastered by *such* and *thus* age. Differences of a few months in chronological age come to have immense significance in the lives of young children. The point is: culture tends to *age grade* patterns of behavior in a fairly clear fashion.[151] Both the parent and the child can assess rate of development. From this metric of what is or is not "more mature" (advanced) behavior a strong learned drive is established. Hence, Dollard and Miller suggest that the drive to "get ahead" via upward social mobility may be a generalization of the drive to "grow up."

Since behaviors can be arrayed in this hierarchical fashion, from childhood to adolescence, to maturity, Freudian conceptions of *fixation* can be conceived as the retention or easy return of a behavioral pattern below that of the current level of development. A strongly reinforced habit, for example, which has never really been put far down in the hierarchy of response, can return at an inopportune moment and make the individual appear to have *regressed* in his behavior to an earlier point of fixation. In order to make this process clearer we would do well to consider the usual course of learning.

Recall that children come into the world with an *innate hierarchy of response* (see pp. 294–295). We now know that this hierarchy becomes arranged and rearranged many times, based upon the history of reinforcement, extinction, and punishment in the individual's course of life. The innate hierarchy is thus eclipsed and altered thanks to the new learning which goes on in development.

At any point in time the individual's response repertoire is arrayed in what we may now call his *initial hierarchy of response*.[152] The very first initial hierarchy was the innate hierarchy, and Dollard and Miller use the term "initial" to emphasize the constantly changing qualities of the response hierarchy. What changes it is confrontation of a *learning dilemma*.[153] Learning dilemmas result when the responses most likely to occur in the response hierarchy *do* occur, but they are *not* followed by reinforcement. The man who has learned that when the engine of a car will not turn over properly one should pour a little gasoline in the carburetor or dry off the sparkplugs performs these behaviors when facing the stimulus of a balky engine. But what if his "tried and true" remedies fail to work? He then faces a learning dilemma and must somehow rearrange the hierarchy of response until he hits upon a successful (reinforcing) response. This triggers a series of trial and error attempts, until he corrects the problem or finally calls in a mechanic (at some financial loss, the negative incentive of which kept him from making this response in the first place). If he discovers a solution without professional assistance the next time he confronts a similar situation the response which "worked" (was reinforced) will

rapidly generalize, which essentially means that it has moved up in the response hierarchy. The changed order of probabilities in the hierarchy is called the *resultant hierarchy of response*.[154] The terms "initial" and "resultant" thus merely indicate which side of a changing hierarchy of response we are considering.

The point of *age grading* is that as we become mature certain responses are less likely to be elicited by certain stimuli. Bladder control is a basic example. Thanks to years of effort we learn to inhibit urinating while wearing clothing, yet some situations may permit an adult to be forgiven if he were to soil himself. Uncontrolled giggling in church or at communal political gatherings would not ordinarily be acceptable behavior, but it would be far more understandable if the offenders were a pair of 10-year-olds than two 35-year-olds. The potential always exists for anyone to "break up" over some ridiculous issue and go into silly laughter. But when this occurs we are likely to label it childishness and—in Freudian terms—*regression*. To regress is thus to return to an earlier habit, usually in response to the frustration of a current habit.[155] The earlier habit may be fixated, which means that it has been given enough reinforcement in the past to make it more likely to appear than some other, more appropriate (age-graded) response.

Immature behavior can also be triggered spontaneously, from stimulus input to response output without intervening cue-producing responses. This is characteristic of the young child. He is impulsive, fails to think about things, and behaves more through direct instrumental responses than anything else. When, as adults, we face severe frustrations (fears, anxieties) a comparable return to impulsive, "childish" behavior is likely to be noted in our behavior. Hence, a regression occurs in two senses. We return to earlier habits, and these habits are themselves age graded *much* below where we ought to be functioning. When people become hysterical or act "like animals" in panic, we are witnessing this most severe of all regressions, to directly triggered instrumental behaviors of the most base variety.

INDIVIDUAL DIFFERENCES CONSTRUCTS

When theorizing at the level of behavior and in the manner of Dollard and Miller, typologies or trait concepts have little relevance. Furthermore, from their perspective Freud did not properly examine the specific constituents of his personality components (id, ego, and superego) in a properly scientific manner. Speaking of defense mechanisms rather than personality types but reflecting their general attitude concerning categorizing how and why people differ, Dollard and Miller observe: "In the absence of a detailed analysis in terms of motive, stimulus, response, and reward, the sheer fact of 'defense' is all that could be noted [by Freud]; with this analysis available, the defense becomes intelligible in terms of a general theory of behavior. It is precisely the function of scientific theory to take such orphaned notions and give them a conceptual home."[156]

The point is: stimulus-response analyses can be applied to *all* other theories of personality. We could just as well redefine and reanalyze the constructs of Jung or Adler in learning theory terms. The typologies and traits of behavior which have emerged from the latter theorists could be given a more properly scientific conceptual home. To expect learning theories themselves to propose typologies is thus to misconstrue their role. Dollard and Miller do, of course, make certain generalizations about behavior. We have already reviewed the sources of behavioral trends above such as hostility, passivity, the immature personality, and so forth. They are also not above using such phrases as the "affirmative personality," when discussing the fact that children must be brought up with sufficient confidence to express appropriate aggressiveness.[157] But

these are all merely examples and informal designations to make their thinking clear to us.

If there is any single theoretical device which Dollard and Miller might favor to account for individual differences it would be the use of a social (including class-level) construct, along the lines we have already considered in the previous section. Culture accounts for such behaviors as social attitudes, dress, religious convictions, and so on. There is a fascinating complexity among the peoples of the world, as well as the peoples within any given sociopolitical identity. Delinquent gangs have their normative style of behavior, influencing the individual in certain predictable ways, and so do the religious callings of minister, priest, and rabbi. To find the "individual" we must look at that intersection point where social roles and heritages meet, adding there a modicum of "unique" or "accidental" habit formation due to the specific experiences of the person under description. Since they aim their strategy of description at observables, the theory of personality which issues places more emphasis on the overt products of cultural training and imitation than on the covert intricacies of an internal world of interpretation and fantasy.

Psychopathology and Psychotherapy

THEORY OF ILLNESS

THE STUPIDITY-MISERY-SYMPTOM CYCLE

Abnormal behavior is learned behavior, which means that it serves a drive-reducing function in the personality.[158] The theoretical task facing Dollard and Miller was therefore to capture this process even though it might overtly seem that a neurotic or psychotic is suffering anything but the pleasure of a drive reduction. Even when the drive being reduced is fear or anxiety, in the case of an abnormal it quickly reappears to torment the poor soul trapped in his condition. How could such self-defeating behavior come about through learning, especially since it seems to contradict the very nature of the learning process—which presumably should generate some form of improved life circumstance for the human organism?

Dollard and Miller emphasize that the misery of the neurotic is genuine. There is no doubt that many people who present themselves to psychiatrists and psychologists are living a nightmarish existence, made all the more terrifying by the fact that nothing they do seems to help.[159] They are caught in some form of round-robin life cycle which cannot be broken and seems ever worse with the passage of time. Dollard and Miller speak rather succinctly of neurosis in terms of *stupidity, misery,* and the resultant *symptoms.* Since there is a circular aspect to this learning of neurosis we have simply hyphenated terms and will now present that part of their theory involving the construct of a "stupidity-misery-symptom" cycle.[160]

By speaking of the neurotic as "stupid" Dollard and Miller do not mean to disparage his intellect. The neurotic is a person with strong, unlabeled, emotional conflicts,[161] particularly of the approach-avoidance variety.[162] He is driven to do something with a mounting desire and yet also driven *not* to do that very thing out of a rising sense of anxiety. As the drives which impel him in both directions increase he is put in an unspeakable state of misery, as if caught in the tendrils of an unconscious network of thorns. The processes of repression (failure to label, lack of cue-producing responses) lie at the heart of this unconscious conflict. The neurotic is stupid because he has no language terms to identify the problem, hence he cannot discriminate and, for example, mistakenly generalizes old responses to new situations. He treats all authority figures as if they were the father who earlier in life rejected him and

thus "acts out" a learned pattern to inappropriate cues.[163] And in this acting out we can often see the symptoms of neurosis and psychosis.

The symptoms, along with the misery which they seek to abate, are what usually bring the client into therapy. Dollard and Miller do not feel that the symptoms are "the" neurotic disorder but merely the overt manifestation of the underlying conflict needing resolution: "The symptoms do not solve the basic conflict in which the neurotic person is plunged, but they mitigate it. They are responses which tend to reduce the conflict, and in part they succeed. When a successful symptom occurs it is reinforced because it reduces neurotic misery. The symptom is thus learned as a habit."[164] Although literally *any* repressed (unlabeled) emotion can cause a neurotic's misery, the most common explanation proffered by Dollard and Miller is anxiety (vague fear). For example, Dollard and Miller tell of a woman who was unable to walk or even stand because she could not flex her knees. From what could be discerned from a study of the case, they felt that the extreme conflict about sexual intercourse this woman had acquired lay at the heart of this symptom. She desired intercourse yet had great anxiety about submitting to it. Hence, when her lower extremities "stiffened up," the problem over "what to do" in this approach-avoidance conflict was solved and the anxiety reduction this afforded (avoiding sex but also "solving" a wretched and anxiety-provoking problem) served as reinforcement to the symptom.[165]

Over the long range the symptom proves self-defeating.[166] But since the neurotic has not labeled the conflict and hence cannot recall its origins, the outlook is bleak. Furthermore, simply removing the symptom without confronting the underlying conflict will not help. If a symptom is suppressed or inhibited by punishment or hypnotic suggestion the drive level being managed below the surface is going to rise, which in turn will increase the misery and lead to the learning of new symptoms.[167] Usually, the neurotic settles on those few symptoms which bring the most consistent reduction to his drive levels, and hence we have the emerging patterns of so-called "clinical" *syndromes*.[168] There is also an admitted *secondary gain* (secondary reinforcement) from "having a neurosis" since people do empathize and feel sorry for him in his predicament.[169]

Why do certain people become neurotic? We do not find Dollard and Miller speculating on the likelihood of inherited proclivities, but doubtless any handicap in life can provide a potential reason for the development of neurosis. The fact that a daughter is being reared by a father who very much wanted a son would doubtless increase the chances that a behavioral disorder would develop in the girl, especially if her mother cannot offset the paternal attitudes in relation to the child. This is surely an example of inheritance, though it has nothing to do with built-in neurotic disposition. Hence, to answer the question Dollard and Miller say: "Our answer is that neurotic conflicts are taught by parents and learned by children. . . . Out of confused instructions to parents, combined with the character faults of parents themselves, arise the situations in which children are put in severe conflict. . . . even if one granted the existence of a science of child rearing, it would still be necessary to get the correct rules into the habit systems of whole generations of parents."[170]

Dollard and Miller accept the general tenets of Freudian psychology about the evil effects of a too harsh superego or conscience: "It is hard to say whether a morbid conscience is a worse enemy of life than a disease like cancer."[171] It would follow, therefore, that extremely high parental standards before adequate labeling is possible would not bode well for the future adjustment of a child. All children are particularly vulnerable to the formation of conflicts. Children cannot understand the world, and they cannot control their emotional reactions.[172] Therefore, even the well-meaning

parent may find that one of his children is developing abnormal trends. A certain aspect of this process must be recognized as due to the unusual circumstances of early life, and Dollard and Miller do not intend to blame parents in blanket fashion.

Frequently the person developing a neurosis has some glimpse of his problem, some inclination suggests the conflict situation to him. However, since this developing cue immediately triggers anxiety the response to "stop thought" is produced and thence reinforced by the resultant reduction of the triggered fear drive. The individual literally "knocks out" connections which might have removed his stupidity.[173] Now the individual is more stupid, which means he more easily generalizes his neurotic responses to different situations, which in turn makes him more miserable as more people find him annoying, which in turn exacerbates his symptom, and so forth. Anxieties pile on anxieties, and he finds that he is caught up in a behavioral sickness which is "utterly mysterious and uncontrollable."[174] Dollard and Miller classify all such responses as stopping thought, or stopping talking, or triggering fear when a situation faces one, or even acting excessively dependent rather than taking on responsibility as *obstructive* or *avertive responses*.[175] Rather than learn to solve his conflict, the individual who responds obstructively simply digs a deeper pit of misery for himself.

DIFFERENTIAL DIAGNOSES IN LEARNING
THEORY TERMS

The *neurotic's* basic approach-avoidance tendencies are between thinking and repression on the one hand, and goal responding and behavioral inhibition on the other.[176] Though the individual's capacities are probably equal to the life challenge facing him, neurosis makes a coward of him: "The neurotic starves in the midst of plenty; a beautiful woman cannot love; a capable man cannot fight; an intelligent student cannot pass his examinations. In every case the contrast is sharp between capacity to enjoy and opportunity to enjoy."[177] The *psychotic* is so preoccupied with internal stimulation that he rejects reality.[178] One witnesses *delusions* and *hallucinations* in his behavior, each of which intertwines with *fantasied* stimuli. This is because cues must be "attached" to the instrumental responses which appear in a person's overt behavior.[179] Where such a connection is weak, so that habits of thought can be learned simply within the realm of the cue-producing responses as mediators (images and ideas), we speak of "living in a dream world." Since this fantasy realm is not reality oriented it offers an inviting escape opportunity to the conflict-laden individual. Drive reduction is being attained for some especially strong drives, and it is therefore difficult to break into this pattern.[180] Dollard and Miller do not consider the psychotic amenable to their form of therapy.

Delusional beliefs are explained along the lines of rationalization. In the same way that we find "good reasons" for our behavior we can—when extremely conflict laden and developing abnormally—find a socially acceptable reason for why we fail in life. At first it is that our school teachers do not like us; they seem to have it "in" for us. Later, our employers and then our friends are also against us. They are jealous of our attractiveness, or the fact that we are so honest in our relations with others, and so on. In time, we suspect that a grand plot has been laid against us, and the elaboration of this "scheme" might take on fantastic intricacies, making us seem to an observer as the most important person in the world (which to us, would be no erroneous observation). Now, we search around to find why we are so important. Could it be that we are not whom we thought we were? Maybe our "so-called" parents really are not our parents after all. And so it is that psychotics enter the hospital with delusional beliefs of self-importance which seem fantastic distortions of the learning process. But this is possible because such beliefs have been hatched entirely within fantasy.

Often a psychotic combines his delusional beliefs with actual sensory perceptions. Dollard and Miller explain such hallucinatory phenomena in terms of generalizations which have been motivated by extremely strong drives, so that it is difficult to see the commonality which suggests seeing or hearing something to the psychotic. We all know that when under the heightened drive of fear it is not unusual to "see something move" or to "hear an unnatural sound" in a vacant house or along the pathway leading past the graveyard. Doubtless there is some stimulus for our "normal" form of hallucination, like the rustling of leaves. But we interpret such cues differently, as a result of our uneasiness (heightened drive state). It is the same with the psychotic, although in his case the cues are even more remote and possibly entirely within fantasy. If the drive state is strong enough an image which is retained in memory might easily be called into "sight" where it could compete with incompatible responses being elicited by cues in the external environment.[181] Dollard and Miller note that in societies where the expression of visions is more acceptable the frequency of hallucination increases tremendously, all of which suggests that learning is at the heart of this subtle process.[182]

Alcoholism and *drug addiction* are sustained by the temporary reduction in anxiety which they afford.[183] Experiments have shown that alcohol produces a temporary, direct reduction in fear and conflict misery. An anxious individual who would become intoxicated would be reinforced to drink again due to his improved state. Dollard and Miller note that alcohol is probably more effective in the removal of inhibitions (instrumental responses, overt "doing" of some formerly feared act) than it is in the removal of repressions (starting to think about formerly avoided topics). Hence, alcohol does not aid in acquiring insight (labels, cue-producing responses).

The *phobia* or unnatural fear of some object, person, or situation is also a learned pattern of anxiety increase and reduction.[184] The housewife who has narrowly escaped death in an automobile accident might subsequently find it impossible to drive the family automobile to the market. Soon *all* automobiles and (generalizing) even buses and bicycles cause her to break out in a cold sweat and breathe rapidly (anxiety). By avoiding the fear-producing cues she can sustain her composure, and hence this phobia is learned as an obstructive habit.

The *anxiety attack* is one of the most direct manifestations of the general case in which anxiety mounts to a dramatic conclusion and then subsides abruptly following a swoon, pseudo–heart attack, or a complete loss of control via a "fit" of some sort.[185] The individual feels certain that his world is about to come apart, and the pressure of an anticipated terrifying climax is almost unbearable. The terror we witness in a panic of this sort is admittedly difficult for learning theories relying on reinforcement as a substitute for the pleasure principle to explain. Dollard and Miller frankly admit to theoretical problems in this area, specifically concerning the immediate effects of such states on the behavior preceding them. How is it that the anxiety continues to mount so rapidly and painfully? Punishment would dictate suppression. Since no one really knows enough about the role of painful stimuli in the neuroses, Dollard and Miller conclude that there is not sufficient evidence to reject their reinforcement thesis at this point in historical time.[186]

The *obsessions* (thoughts forcing themselves on the person) and *compulsions* (acts forcing themselves on the person) are explained very much like phobias.[187] That is, if we are forced to think something or to do something even though it is against our conscious desire, the fact that we *are* engaged in some activity means that we are *not* engaged in something else. The woman who has an unconscious approach-avoidance conflict over sexual promiscuity can avoid thinking about it by feeling compelled to count her heartbeat five or 10 times each hour of the day.[188] The clinical pictures of *hypochondria* and other so-called *psychosomatic* illnesses are doubtless related phenomena. The individual who is constantly worried about his health has probably succeeded in avoiding many other of life's genuine concerns. Although a little miserable he is greatly sheltered.

This secondary gain is also apparent in the clinical picture of *hysteria*.[189] The person who is caught up in the morass of unconscious conflict can sometimes flee into a total amnesia, in which he completely breaks off connections with an intolerable life situation. No doubt this process has a precursor, a form of mediating trial and error in which the individual had not exactly planned anything but did say something angular, as: "If a person blanked out, no one could blame him for not getting the job done." In like fashion, hysterical symptoms of blindness, the loss of motility, or the activation of muscular spasms (tics) may all be directly instrumental responses which can be reinforcing if followed by anxiety reduction. This automatic feature of hysteria is critical because though the person may have contemplated things in the fashion described above, if he *consciously* put some such plan into action for himself we would have a case of *malingering* (feigning illness) rather than true hysteria.[190]

Though Dollard and Miller do not take up the psychoses in detail, they do single out *paranoia* for some consideration.[191] This mechanism is an extension of projection, and it often has a feature of reaction-formation about it. The individual with a homosexual urge can repress this due to the anxiety it arouses and then express overt disgust for all such what he now considers subhuman beings. In time, since the conflict is engendered by attractive individuals whom he meets or sees in the newspapers, he can attribute homosexual motives to all such people as a form of class or caste. For example, the claim that a government agency is being overrun and hence perverted by homosexual administrators may represent a kind of paranoid projection (delusion) of unconscious conflicts.

THEORY OF CURE

PSYCHOTHERAPY AS THE TEACHING OF LABELS AND DISCRIMINATIONS

If neurotic behavior is learned, then psychotherapy should become a matter of unlearning old habits and eventually learning new habits.[192] Dollard and Miller view the psychotherapist as a kind of teacher or coach, who works to improve the client's pattern of living: "In the same way and by the same principles that bad tennis habits can be corrected by a good coach, so bad mental and emotional habits can be corrected by a psychotherapist."[193] Hence, to be successful, psychotherapy must first provide conditions under which neurotic habits can be examined, identified, and then unlearned; secondly, it must facilitate the acquisition of more fruitful patterns of behavior, which will extend beyond the consulting room into life generally.[194] This defines the two phases of psychotherapy. In the first, or *talking phase,* the therapist and client work to remove repressions and thus to restore the client's higher mental processes.[195] In the second, or *performing phase,* the client must be supported and encouraged to apply his gains in actual performance changes outside the therapy hour.[196]

A basic aspect of therapy concerns the learning of proper labels, so that conflicts can be identified by the client and in turn, proper discriminations be made. Some help is gained from the outset due to the permissiveness of the therapist. Through his accepting, nonjudgmental manner he guarantees that the client will not be punished for anything he

thinks or says in the therapeutic situation.[197] Since the client is reluctant to speak openly, making the therapy contact itself a form of approach-avoidance conflict, this reduction in the avoidance gradient feature of psychotherapy is immediately beneficial. The client feels free to release further higher mental processes in recollection. Due to the harmful effects of past repressions, many new words and sentences must be learned: "The neurotic is a person who is in need of a stock of sentences that will match the events going on within and without him. The new sentences make possible an immense facilitation of higher mental processes. With their aid he can discriminate and generalize more accurately. . . . By labeling a formerly unlabeled emotional response he can represent this response in reasoning."[198]

The acquisition of proper cue-producing responses greatly enhances mediation. The therapist can point out, for example, that the frigid wife is at least in part unresponsive to her husband because she has failed to see a difference between this marital partner and her father. It had never occurred to her before, but the husband's behavior is often identical to that of her now deceased father. Over the years she has come to react to the husband in the cold manner which she had earlier reserved for her moralistic father, whom she had disliked. As the cues are rehearsed in the dialogue with the therapist, this woman begins to view her husband in a new light. If the therapist were now to add something like: " 'Enjoying sex with your husband is expected and permitted,' the word 'permitted' could serve as a cue for all the responses that had already been attached to it and would tend to make [her] . . . free to respond to sex activity as she had previously responded to other 'permitted' activity."[199] This interplay of discrimination and generalization continues throughout the talking phase of psychotherapy.

Often certain key labels play a highly significant role in this learning process. For example, if the patient who had always considered himself "loyal and dependable" were told (relabeled) by the therapist that his seeming loyalty and dependability were really signs of an immature "dependence" on others, then he would see his entire behavioral pattern differently. He could then generalize the usage of this label and better discriminate when he was being overly dependent in other social situations as well. He was the "good old reliable" helpmate to friends due to the fact that he was too frightened to express his own desires when they conflicted with others because he could not risk losing the friendships. Hence, he was constantly being taken advantage of and left to wonder why others were treating him so badly. If the relabeling is not instructive in this fashion, then in time it will simply be ignored by the client with little positive or negative effect. Therapist *interpretations* (relabelings) then must be reinforcing to the client or they will drop very low in the latter's response hierarchy.[200]

An important verbal discrimination cue is the simple dichotomy of past vs. present.[201] Sometimes a client could be cured rather easily if he were to make a single attempt to do what frightens him. If the handsome young man who is terrified to ask a young woman for a date were to make even a fumbling effort, he could surely experience the success his distorted fantasy life had convinced him was impossible. Based on past failures in probably irrelevant circumstances—such as not having been selected as a member of athletic teams or elected to student government offices —he has come to be convinced that he lacks the masculinity and popularity to be considered attractive to females. But if the therapist can emphasize that yesterday's failures are *not necessarily* relevant to today's successes, anxiety might be reduced, allowing the approach motivation to take over. He might be made to feel that this is a "fresh start" in a new situation. With success in achieving the first date—and the usual help of the young

woman to set her handsome young man at ease —the avoidance responses which had kept him immobilized could easily *extinguish* and effect a cure. This example demonstrates a general rule which Dollard and Miller make. Since the avoidance gradient rises more rapidly as we approach the goal than does the approach gradient, it is better to encourage advancement toward the goal by *reducing the avoidance motivation* than it is by increasing the approach motivation.[202] To have encouraged this young man to "be a man" and "get in there and *make* the girl respond to you" would have been the wrong tactic, for it would have done little to reduce the avoidance motivation (probably would have raised it) and instead would have threatened the client's masculinity concerns all the more by challenging him to prove himself.

With the first steps toward successful change the client also learns to anticipate further steps. He learns an anticipatory sense of "hope," which may possibly even be labeled as such by the therapist.[203] Cures also issue from the fact that various behaviors are inhibited as changes take place which lead to a more satisfying form of drive reduction. Symptoms which have been sustained by anxiety drive reduction lose their potency as sex or achievement drives begin being reinforced. Of course, in order for the latter to occur we must move into the second phase of psychotherapy. New or altered labeling would have no benefit if this did not transfer behavioral change into the life circumstance: "According to our theory of the matter, the matter of 'trying out something new' is quintessential to a therapeutic result. Mere verbal change will not suffice."[204] The point is: if generalization from words to action does not occur, therapy has not occurred.[205] As Dollard and Miller put it: "We conceive of therapeutic results . . . as strictly related to and dependent upon the external conditions of reinforcement in the life of the person."[206] It is not what one knows but what he *does* that counts.

It is tempting to draw a direct parallel between the Dollard and Miller discussion of what is usually called "insight" in therapy and the kind of insightful interpretations Freud made. This is even furthered by the fact that Dollard and Miller state that they are describing "essentially the psychoanalytic technique for adult neurotic patients."[207] Yet, the differences which emerge in this approach are so dramatic that they demand special consideration. The parallels to classical insight are clear, but the differences in outlook on the function and even necessity of insight outweigh the similarities.

First of all, insight begins in the grasp which the therapist has of the client's problems. He must identify the neurotic habits of his client and then gradually label them so that the adjustments and changes may follow.[208] Classically, this has meant a kind of self-study, a review of the past in which the client describes his early life to the therapist in great detail. In doing so, he sometimes rekindles old emotions, emotions which have gone unrecognized (repressed) or improperly labeled. It is important to stress that labeling does include the identification of feelings, along with other promptings to instrumental action: "We emphatically do not take the stand that mere labeling can be important if it is not immediately linked with the emotional, instrumental, and other responses which are being manifested and *changed* in the relation between patient and therapist."[209]

If the therapist points out the neurotic conflict or suggests a more appropriate label, and the resulting "insight" is helpful to the client, the potential for change in the latter's behavior is great. In fact, the procedure which is learned can take on drive characteristics, so that the client imitates the therapist as model and furthers the process on his own: "In some cases the patient will know immediately that he has created a valuable new sentence because

drive reduction (insight) occurs at once."[210] The client finds that he can predict his own behavior now.[211] He is no longer the slave to his emotions that he was earlier. Self-control and self-direction are finally within his grasp.[212] This procedure is formalized into a habit in time, one which we might designate as learning to "stop and think."[213] Rather than immaturely responding instrumentally to an input stimulus the client now properly mediates with cue-producing labels of greater accuracy and relevance.

Thus far the parallels with Freudian psychotherapy are clear. It would seem to be a straightforward translation of classical psychoanalysis into stimulus-response terminology. However, Dollard and Miller's great emphasis on change in overt behavior make clear that "insight" is not an understanding of one's behavior in terms of some *particular* view of personality. Taking up the matter of the clinical history first, they observe "that recovery of the past is not useful *per se* but only to the extent that past and present conditions are actually different and that the contrast between them is vividly made, either spontaneously by the patient or with the aid of the therapist."[214] Whereas Freud's *post hoc* approach could eventuate in dynamic insights which might have to be suffered graciously, Dollard and Miller wish to emphasize that the historical recollection acting as insight is merely an *instrumentality* to the present change it may afford.

Even more fundamentally, the necessity of classical insight as a historical reconstruction leading to greater self-understanding is called into question: "While highly advantageous, we do not feel that the reconstruction of the past is an absolute necessity for therapeutic advance. The therapist may be able to set up a strong presumption that present-day neurotic habits have been learned without being able to specify the learning conditions in detail."[215] The client gains a sense of conviction when he has the chance to take his past life and essentially place it alongside his present life. But is the value of this historical survey the truth gleaned or the conviction achieved? Dollard and Miller emphasize the latter.[216] Hence: ". . . it should be made perfectly clear that *significant therapeutic effects can also be produced in other ways without any improved labeling or 'insight' on the part of the patient.* As has already been pointed out, we would expect the general reassuring and permissive attitude of the therapist to produce a considerable reduction in fear. This reduction in fear should generalize from the therapeutic situation to the rest of the patient's life and thus reduce somewhat his conflict, misery, and motivation for symptoms."[217]

It is this highly pragmatic view of "insight," as a kind of instrumentality in the therapeutic process, which makes Dollard and Miller the *bridge theorists* to the behavioral theories of Chapter 7. Though still cloaked in the older terminology of therapist interpretation and client insight, theirs is a new vision in the history of psychotherapy. Change comes about in the present, and no matter what one *says* about why the initial or resultant patterns of behavior array themselves as they do, the processes of change have a relevance all their own. The next historical step is to drop the emphasis on the client's past entirely and focus only upon what is taking place in the changing present. Dollard and Miller did not go quite this far, presumably because they were hoping to unite psychotherapy approaches under one theoretical language rather than trying to strike off on an approach entirely different from that known to their time. But the seeds were sown, and an even more action-oriented, pragmatic psychotherapy was to follow (see Chapter 7).

RELATIONSHIP FACTORS

Dollard and Miller view the therapist and the client as co-responsible for cure. The client must not feel that the therapist will make him well by administering a pill, dispensing advice, or providing reassurance.[218] Neither will the therapist make decisions for the client when it comes time to apply the special insights gleaned from therapy.[219] The patient must work hard, beginning with a detailed review of his background, and the therapist must make it as easy as possible for him to begin reviewing delicate areas and anxiety-provoking recollections. Dollard and Miller feel that mere catharsis, which presumably means telling others about one's "sins" or mistakes, can rarely be therapeutic.[220] If one makes guilt-laden confessions without ensuing punishment, then anxiety may be reduced. But for lasting and genuine benefit the lengthy "working through" or practicing of relevant words and sentences must be followed up by actual overt behavioral changes.[221]

The client constantly generalizes emotional responses to the therapist and the therapy situation. Since the therapist is comparable to former authority figures in the client's life history like parents and teachers, "power vs. submission" features may begin to show up in therapy. Freud referred to these as *transferences*. Dollard and Miller do not see anything particularly unique about such generalizations, feeling that they are everyday phenomena.[222] Generalization is automatic, and from the outset of therapy the client begins transferring both facilitative and obstructive responses to the therapist.[223] On the positive side he transfers his training in being sensible, self-critical, orderly, and logical. The motive to please others, particularly those in authority, is also generalized to the therapist. Therapy could not proceed without these generalizations. On the negative side he transfers patterns of dependence and fearfulness which have remained fixated in his response hierarchy since childhood.

Not all of the feelings the client has toward the therapist are erroneous generalizations from the past: "If the therapist is hasty, stupid, cruel, or uncontrolled, he will earn real emotional reactions from his patient."[224] What does the therapist do with those warm, loving reactions engendered in the client by his manner—be they transferred generalizations or simply true responses to his manner? He capitalizes on them and puts them to use as a positive force in therapy. If the client thinks highly of him, this affection can be used at the right time to encourage the client to make some needed change—not in a deceitful or authoritative manner but in the sense of one person caring for another. If too much client-dependency is built up by this use of a therapist's reinforcing capabilities, then near the very end of therapy the appropriate interpretations can be made to the client.[225]

A more vexing problem involves what Freud called the *negative transference* and the *resistance* which this usually signifies to therapeutic advance. The client begins missing sessions, arguing with the therapist, criticizing his insights, and so forth. Dollard and Miller did not accept these phenomena in the same sense as Freud. They failed to see any intentionality in resistive behavior: "The therapist is frequently inclined to feel that there is something diabolically purposive in these emotional interruptions, that the patient is somehow cunningly 'resisting' him. He should refuse to accept such a view of the phenomenon. He should, instead, understand that the emotional responses in question are generalized *automatically* to the therapeutic situation because the strength of avoidance reactions to unconscious emotion has been reduced."[226] As the source of these resistive and critical tendencies, Dollard and Miller note that most of us have learned a drive for "independence" and self-direction, so that when we seem to be submitting to the direction of another we automatically respond with a certain negativism and self-expressiveness.[227] Since the neurotic often has this dependence-independence conflict, when he begins to improve the therapist is most likely to note his positive movement being accompanied by more negative self-sufficiency.

The therapist must be prepared to see these developing changes in the proper light. It would be a great mistake to punish the client for assuming responsibility. Although they do not discuss it in specific terms, Dollard and Miller do make clear that *countertransference* (unconscious generalizations to client by therapist) works against proper conflict designation and accurate labeling.[228] The merits of transference are thus twofold. On the one hand, thanks to his generalization of unconscious (unlabeled) conflicts and their accompanying emotions onto the therapist, a kind of immediate arena for the enactment of neurotic habits is possible. The therapist can use these automatic responses in his job of teaching the client about himself. On the other hand, by not losing his composure or attributing nefarious intentions to his client the therapist gains enough respect and even affection to use his ties to the client as a direct means of reinforcing behavioral changes in the second phase of therapy.

NORMAL BEHAVIOR

Though "normality" is hard to define, Dollard and Miller suggest that a person who is meeting his drive stimulations relatively well, has not repressed (failed to label) major areas of experience, and is not suffering the misery of avoidance is what we mean by the "normal person."[229] There are many reasons why people can fail to maintain this normal pattern, some of which lie far beyond any possible hope of their control—as in the very social conditions which surround them. Many times a therapist feels inadequate to help his client, who may simply require so many tangential skills in order to adjust more adequately that no amount of behavioral insight is going to help. He cannot change because the changes needed are based on skills not easily attained: "Perhaps the resources of schools where speech, manners, 'charm,' and [social] class traits are taught should, when needed, be added to those of the therapist's."[230]

One of the unfortunate but true realities of the psychoanalytical technique is that it is itself "class-linked," a therapy for the wealthy, verbal, and sophisticated members of our culture. Too often a therapist in this theoretical persuasion begins to make interpretations of others from lower social-class levels and completely misses the mark because of his ignorance of social differences.[231] Dollard and Miller note that there are two general errors in the social sciences. The "sociologist's error" is to assume that a study of class and social situations *per se* can account for everything in behavior, thereby giving short shrift to constitutional and other unique factors in personality. The "psychologist's error" is to place too much emphasis on constitutional and unique habitual patterns and to dismiss sociocultural factors as minor and secondary. Based on their experience, Dollard and Miller suggest that: "The favorite error of therapists is *not* that of sociologists!"[232]

THERAPEUTIC TECHNIQUES

THE SELECTION OF PATIENTS

If psychotherapy is to be successful, then the therapist must be especially careful about the kind of patient he accepts. Dollard and Miller list a series of points in this selection process.[233] Obviously, a first consideration is the nature of the presenting problem. It has to be one resulting from past learning and not based on organic deficiencies. The prospective client should also be suffering misery—the more the better!—because this is what motivates him to seek professional assistance. The history of a symptom or syndrome picture is important to evaluate, because the longer a symptom has been reinforced the more difficult it will be to remove it. The prognosis will be more favorable if the prospective client has "much to live for." An individual trapped in the repressed economic conditions of the lowest classes cannot be considered a good bet for successful behavioral change.

Prospective clients should also have certain minimum social skills, such as speech which is recognizable, the capacity to relate to others in a reasonable way, and so forth. The therapist cannot be expected to take over the basic functions of a parent. Ordinarily, if a person can use language reasonably well he has attained the minimal level of competence needed for therapy, assuming he is not psychotic. This rules out the mentally retarded. Further, if the fundamental social training of trying to be reasonable and logical in discourse has not been accomplished, then individual psychotherapy cannot be carried out to a successful conclusion. Habits of an obstructive sort which specifically deny the efficacy of therapy are also negative signs. The abnormal who does not accept his eccentric condition, the rigid moralist who considers any talk of human motives sinful, or the social revolutionary who views psychotherapy as a technique of subjugation against deviating political philosophies are all examples of poor subjects for successful behavioral psychotherapy. Finally, practical matters like the physical health of the client or the ease with which he can meet therapy appointments must be considered in accepting patients.

FREE ASSOCIATION, INTERPRETATION, AND THERAPEUTIC SUPPRESSION

Dollard and Miller describe the practical procedures in therapy along classical Freudian lines. Thus, a technique of importance in the first (talking) phase of therapy is that of *free association*, which is a condition of learning imposed upon the client: "The rule of free association is not a mere invitation to speak freely. It is an absolute obligation which is the foundation of the therapeutic situation. It is a compulsion which has some of the rigor of any compulsion. This rule defines the patient's work which is to drive ruthlessly through to the pronouncement of sentences which may evoke sickening anxiety."[234] Material forthcoming in the free associations enlightens the therapist about the nature of the problem, the unlabeled emotions, and so forth. Even if he wished to, the therapist could not elicit such information because he does not know the proper questions to ask. The point is: free associations are not actually "free" but follow lawful regularities.[235] They emerge because they must emerge, as a patient gives in to a kind of compulsion to talk about what preoccupies him.

The therapist is trained to listen to this flow of verbal material without in any way imposing an a priori hypothesis on what he is hearing. His goal, based upon learned drives to give a complete account, to be logical, and to judge the appropriateness of a response, is eventually to propose a thorough and rational verbal account of the patient's life.[236] Gradually, hypotheses based on what the client is saying in free association are put into words by the therapist. Commonly cited cues like blocked associations or "slips of the tongue" are all noted and taken into account in forming hypotheses. When these hypotheses have received considerable support from the client's verbalizations, the therapist proffers them as his *interpretation*. The skilled therapist does not offer hunches. He waits until he has strong evidence before proposing a label or teaching a discrimination to the client. Dollard and Miller speak of using *successive approximations* in the interpretative technique, by which they mean the therapist must constantly refine his hypotheses to match the succession of facts which emerge over the course of therapy.[237]

Observations made in the situation of psychotherapy are a kind of "natural history," even though they lack the controls of a purely scientific experiment.[238] The neurotic individual will transfer feelings in the transference relationship and this focused dynamic can be observed by both the therapist and the client as time slips by. It is important for the client to begin rehearsing the labels and sentences being proposed by the therapist.[239] Often, the client will pick up this procedure of self-insight through a form of matched-dependent

copying of the therapist. But if he does not, Dollard and Miller feel that the therapist should resort to *interpretative prompting*,[240] or the continued use of suggestions to the client, such as: "Could this feeling you speak of really be anger and not fear?" Not only does the therapist here suggest labels, but he also instructs the client in the process of self-examination and self-labeling.

Though Dollard and Miller do not devote great space to *dream interpretation,* they acknowledge that dreams can be profitably used as a kind of extension of the processes involved in free association.[241] A dream involves: ". . . private, imageal responses which produce cues. These cues are what are 'seen' as the dream. Since they are private responses they are less likely to have strong anxiety attached to them and are likely to be 'franker.' "[242] In other words, we may see ourselves doing things in the dream which seem quite in contrast to our customary behavior. These deviations from common pattern are entered into the successive approximations of the interpretation, which in turn can be rehearsed by the client and thence used as cue-producing responses for subsequent discriminations as repression drops from sight and the individual gains better control over his own behavior.

In the second phase of therapy the patient is expected to begin making actual behavioral changes. One of the sources of courage here is the therapist himself—as a model to be emulated (imitated) by the client: "Since he has a great deal of prestige, his calmness, courage, and reasonableness are imitated by the patient, who thus tends to become calmer, more courageous, and more reasonable."[243] One of the procedures they recommend in bridging the gap between talking about behavior and doing new things is to use a series of graded tasks.[244] For example, a young man who is concerned about his masculinity and who is not entirely certain that he had adequate heterosexual drives might be taken through a series of graded efforts beginning with the practice of masturbation while contemplating intercourse with sensuous females (possibly using pictures of inviting women). In time, his interest in the opposite sex would be stimulated, and thence he and the therapist would plan a series of strategies to begin dating women—possibly beginning with group activity so the responsibility for entertaining his companion would not fall entirely on the client's shoulders. Double-dating might then be the next step. Finally, the young man would be brought up to solitary dating and complete sexual adjustment—culminating in sexual intercourse with a female either before or after engagement or marriage (a choice left to him and his cultural values to decide).

Dollard and Miller recognize that one of the major vehicles of cure in the later stages of psychotherapy must be *suppression,* or the conscious delimitation of thoughts by the individual.[245] Whereas free association tended to open up recall and widen the range of mental processes, suppression must now close off the behavioral habits of rumination and compulsive insight-seeking. It works as follows: "In order to suppress a train of thought a person must take his attention off the stimuli which are producing this train of thought and turn his attention to some other cues which produce an incompatible train of thought. . . . As attention is turned to new cues, these cues produce different responses, and these responses in turn produce new and different motivation—that to accomplish the task to which the person is addressing himself."[246]

Dollard and Miller wisely recognize that the individual who is constantly mulling over memories, labels, and statements of presumed insight is the sort of person who will never change. He has acquired a secondary habit of thought which can itself insulate him from action. Self-study must constantly be pitched at the changes which should be made in light of new insights. Hence, suppression is particularly useful as a technique of cure *late* in therapy: "In psychotherapy, as elsewhere, suppression should be used when the patient knows what to do but lacks the ability to get into action. Suppression is particularly necessary in the phase of 'trying out in the real world' the new plans that have been made in the period of free association. Eventually the patient must abandon brooding and reflection, form a dominant plan, make a decision to act, and put the plan at hazard. Only thus, as we have shown, can he achieve real reduction of the drives which have been producing misery."[247]

THE TERMINATION OF THERAPY

There is no rule about the timing of therapy termination. In discussing one case Dollard and Miller refer to an interpretation which was formulated in the *nineteenth hour;* it is obvious that they consider psychotherapy to be a long term affair—at least for some clients.[248] It seems clear that the patient should not attempt to terminate therapy until "the baneful effects of repression are lifted."[249] This would involve a weakening of fear in the avoidant motivation of the underlying conflict. Most importantly, the client should not be considered "cured" until he is innovating responses in his outside life and getting significant rewards for them.

We noted previously that self-study must be pitched toward actual behavioral change. Continuing in this vein, Dollard and Miller hold that for successful treatment to be sustained after termination the client should learn a habit of self-study.[250] A planned period of time should be set aside by the ex-client when he first senses that problems are forming. Then, depending on his predilections, he should have some means of exploration whereby responses for study will be forthcoming. He might, for example, write down a series of points. What seems to be the problem? Is this really the problem, or could it be something else? When did it start? What seem to be the factors involved? How does he feel about this or that aspect? Questions such as these are brought into the open and then dealt with in turn. A program of rectification should be planned even as the nature of the difficulty is being worked out. Dollard and Miller view this procedure as the logical heir to Freud's original self-analysis (see Chapter 1). It differs from ordinary reasoning in that the client makes use of the knowledge he has gleaned about human behavior from psychotherapy.[251] Training in this procedure should be considered a routine aspect of psychotherapy: "It is theoretically possible that special practice in self-study might be given during the latter part of a course of therapeutic interviews. The patient might be asked to practice solving particular problems and the therapist could act as a kind of control."[252]

Notes

1. Thorndike, 1898. 2. Thorndike, 1933, p. 66. 3. Thorndike, 1943, p. 33. 4. *Ibid.*, p. 22. 5. Watson, 1924, p. 6. 6. Watson, 1913, p. 158. 7. Watson, 1924, p. 8. 8. *Ibid.*, p. 15. 9. *Ibid.*, pp. 77, 79. 10. *Ibid.*, p. 11. 11. *Ibid.*, p. 82. 12. *Ibid.*, p. 216. 13. Watson, 1917, p. 329. 14. Watson, 1924, p. 84. 15. *Ibid.*, p. 220. 16. McDougall, 1923a, p. 288. 17. Tolman, 1960, pp. xvii–xviii. 18. *Ibid.*, p. 14. 19. *Ibid.*, p. 414. 20. *Ibid.*, p. 135. 21. *Ibid.*, p. 29. 22. *Ibid.*, p. 97. 23. Hull, 1952, Ch. 5. 24. Skinner, 1950, 1936b. 25. Evans, 1968, p. 10. 26. *Ibid.*, pp. 19–20. 27. *Ibid.*, pp. 17, 19. 28. Skinner, 1957, p. 460. 29. Dollard, 1937. 30. Dollard, 1942, 1943. 31. Dollard and Auld, 1959; Dollard, Auld, and White, 1953. 32. For a selective overview of Miller's work see: 1944, 1948a, 1948b, 1951, 1957, 1959, 1961, 1963, and 1964. 33. Dollard, Doob, Miller, Mowrer, and Sears, 1939. 34. Miller and Dollard, 1941. 35. Dollard and Miller, 1950. 36. *Ibid.*, p. 187. 37. *Ibid.*, p. 277. 38. *Ibid.*, p. 270. 39. *Ibid.*, pp. 5–6. 40. Miller and Dollard, 1941, p. 290. 41. Dollard and Miller, 1950, p. 62. 42. *Ibid.*, p. 3. 43. *Ibid.*, p. 337. 44. *Ibid.*, p. 119. 45. *Ibid.*, pp. 146, 249. 46. *Ibid.*, pp. 216, 309. 47. *Ibid.*, p. 311. 48. *Ibid.*, p. 326. 49. Miller and Dollard, 1941, p. 59. 50. Dollard and Miller, 1950, p. 69. 51. *Ibid.*, pp. 15, 50. 52. Miller and Dollard, 1941, p. 1. 53. *Ibid.*, p. 16. 54. Dollard and Miller, 1950, p. 32. 55. Miller and Dollard, 1941, p. 22. 56. Dollard and Miller, 1950, p. 36. 57. *Ibid.*, p. 37. 58. *Ibid.*, p. 98. 59. *Ibid.*, p. 56. 60. *Ibid.*, p. 99. 61. *Ibid.*, pp. 110–111. 62. *Ibid.*, p. 37. 63. *Ibid.*, p. 109. 64. *Ibid.*, p. 53. 65. *Ibid.*, p. 98. 66. *Ibid.*, p. 105. 67. *Ibid.*, p. 122. 68. *Ibid.*, p. 101. 69. *Ibid.*, pp. 56, 119. 70. *Ibid.*, p. 100. 71. *Ibid.*, p. 113. 72. *Ibid.*, p. 119. 73. *Ibid.*, p. 120. 74. *Ibid.*, p. 103. 75. Miller and Dollard, 1941, p. 26. 76. Dollard and Miller, 1950, p. 220. 77. *Ibid.*, p. 198. 78. *Ibid.*, p. 250. 79. *Ibid.*, p. 130. 80. *Ibid.*, p. 122. 81. *Ibid.*, p. 398. 82. *Ibid.*, pp. 140–141. 83. *Ibid.*, p. 9. 84. *Ibid.*, p. 29. 85. *Ibid.*, p. 30. 86. *Ibid.*, p. 33. 87. *Ibid.*, pp. 30–31. 88. *Ibid.*, p. 78. 89. *Ibid.*, p. 31. 90. *Ibid.*, p. 40. 91. *Ibid.* 92. *Ibid.*, p. 42. 93. *Ibid.*, p. 187. 94. *Ibid.*, p. 81. 95. *Ibid.*, p. 55. 96. *Ibid.*, p. 214. 97. *Ibid.*, p. 117. 98. *Ibid.*, p. 49. 99. *Ibid.*, p. 51. 100. *Ibid.*, p. 75. 101. *Ibid.*, p. 63. 102. *Ibid.*, p. 69. 103. *Ibid.*, pp. 72–78. 104. *Ibid.*, p. 30. 105. *Ibid.*, pp. 318, 335, 412. 106. Miller and Dollard, 1941, p. 10. 107. *Ibid.*, p. 11. 108. *Ibid.*, p. 188. 109. *Ibid.*, p. 197. 110. *Ibid.*, p. 92. 111. *Ibid.*, p. 149. 112. Dollard and Miller, 1950, p. 87. 113. *Ibid.*, pp. 114, 219. 114. *Ibid.*, p. 93. 115. Dollard, Doob, Miller, Mowrer, and Sears, 1939. 116. Lewin, 1961. 117. Dollard and Miller, 1950, p. 355. 118. *Ibid.*, p. 363. 119. *Ibid.*, p. 365. 120. *Ibid.*, p. 221. 121. *Ibid.*, p. 220. 122. *Ibid.*, pp. 211–213. 123. *Ibid.*, p. 200. 124. *Ibid.*, p. 453. 125. Miller and Dollard, 1941, p. 164. 126. Dollard and Miller, 1950, p. 181. 127. *Ibid.*, pp. 184–185. 128. *Ibid.*, p. 177. 129. *Ibid.*, p. 323. 130. *Ibid.*, p. 132. 131. *Ibid.*, p. 130. 132. *Ibid.*, p. 131. 133. *Ibid.*, p. 132. 134. *Ibid.*, p. 133. 135. *Ibid.*, p. 134. 136. *Ibid.*, p. 136. 137. Miller and Dollard, 1941, p. 81. 138. Dollard and Miller, 1950, p. 138. 139. *Ibid.*, p. 139. 140. *Ibid.*, p. 141. 141. *Ibid.* 142. *Ibid.*, p. 142. 143. *Ibid.*, p. 143. 144. *Ibid.*, p. 144. 145. *Ibid.*, pp. 145–146. 146. *Ibid.* 147. *Ibid.*, pp. 146–147. 148. *Ibid.*, p. 149. 149. *Ibid.*, p. 148. 150. *Ibid.*, p. 150. 151. *Ibid.*, p. 91. 152. *Ibid.*, p. 36. 153. *Ibid.*, p. 45. 154. *Ibid.*, p. 36. 155. *Ibid.*, p. 171. 156. *Ibid.*, p. 337. 157. *Ibid.*, p. 152. 158. *Ibid.*, p. 7. 159. *Ibid.*, pp. 13–14. 160. *Ibid.*, p. 223. 161. *Ibid.*, p. 281. 162. *Ibid.*, p. 359. 163. *Ibid.*, pp. 248, 306. 164. *Ibid.*, p. 15. 165. *Ibid.*, p. 169. 166. *Ibid.*, pp. 224–225. 167. *Ibid.*, pp. 385–386. 168. *Ibid.*, p. 195. 169. *Ibid.*, p. 238. 170. *Ibid.*, pp. 127–128. 171. *Ibid.*, p. 141. 172. *Ibid.*, p.

130. **173.** *Ibid.*, p. 19. **174.** *Ibid.*, p. 225. **175.**
Ibid., pp. 266, 270. **176.** *Ibid.*, p. 399. **177.**
Ibid., p. 318. **178.** *Ibid.*, p. 425. **179.** *Ibid.*, p.
338. **180.** *Ibid.*, p. 237. **181.** *Ibid.*, p. 180. **182.**
Ibid., p. 181. **183.** *Ibid.*, p. 377. **184.** *Ibid.*, p.
158. **185.** *Ibid.*, p. 17. **186.** *Ibid.*, p. 190. **187.**
Ibid., p. 164. **188.** *Ibid.*, p. 17. **189.** *Ibid.*, p.
165. **190.** *Ibid.*, p. 167. **191.** *Ibid.*, p. 183. **192.**
Ibid., p. 7. **193.** *Ibid.*, p. 8. **194.** *Ibid.*, p. 25.
195. *Ibid.*, p. 235. **196.** *Ibid.*, p. 331. **197.** *Ibid.*,
p. 248. **198.** *Ibid.*, p. 281. **199.** *Ibid.*, p. 311.
200. *Ibid.*, p. 333. **201.** *Ibid.*, p. 307. **202.** *Ibid.*,
p. 362. **203.** *Ibid.*, p. 316. **204.** *Ibid.*, p. 319.
205. *Ibid.*, pp. 332–333. **206.** *Ibid.*, p. 342.
207. *Ibid.*, p. 235. **208.** *Ibid.*, p. 306. **209.** *Ibid.*,
p. 304. **210.** *Ibid.*, p. 286. **211.** *Ibid.*, p. 299.
212. *Ibid.*, p. 279. **213.** *Ibid.*, p. 300. **214.** *Ibid.*,
p. 315. **215.** *Ibid.*, p. 317. **216.** *Ibid.*, p. 318.
217. *Ibid.*, p. 321. **218.** *Ibid.*, p. 267. **219.** *Ibid.*,
p. 276. **220.** *Ibid.*, p. 246. **221.** *Ibid.*, p. 334.
222. *Ibid.*, p. 261. **223.** *Ibid.*, pp. 262–266. **224.**
Ibid., p. 273. **225.** *Ibid.*, p. 277. **226.** *Ibid.*,
p. 274. **227.** *Ibid.*, p. 293. **228.** *Ibid.*, pp. 274–
275. **229.** *Ibid.*, p. 431. **230.** *Ibid.*, p. 345. **231.**
Ibid., p. 419. **232.** *Ibid.*, p. 421. **233.** *Ibid.*, pp.
233–237. **234.** *Ibid.*, p. 241. **235.** *Ibid.*, p. 252.
236. *Ibid.*, p. 254. **237.** *Ibid.*, p. 284. **238.** *Ibid.*,
p. 6. **239.** *Ibid.*, p. 280. **240.** *Ibid.*, p. 253. **241.**
Ibid., p. 282. **242.** *Ibid.*, p. 256. **243.** *Ibid.*, p.
395. **244.** *Ibid.*, p. 350. **245.** *Ibid.*, p. 445. **246.**
Ibid., p. 448. **247.** *Ibid.*, p. 458. **248.** *Ibid.*, p.
317. **249.** *Ibid.*, p. 349. **250.** *Ibid.*, pp. 431–
442. **251.** *Ibid.*, p. 431. **252.** *Ibid.*, p. 438.

7

From the Laboratory to the Consulting Room: Skinner, Wolpe, and Stampfl

Dollard and Miller set the scene for a dramatic shift in the conceptualization and treatment of neurotic behavior. Though they did not speak of "behavior therapy" their emphasis on the instrumentalities of the therapeutic relationship certainly presaged the newer attitude: "Behavior theory emphasizes the great importance of being certain that the groundwork of new habit is laid while the therapist still has some influence. Perhaps most therapists already instinctively follow this injunction of behavior theory. If so, they should continue to do what they are doing and put this condition of therapy yet more consciously and systematically into effect."[1] The systematic and conscious attempt to effect conditions was precisely the aim of the behavioral therapies.

When Dollard and Miller argued that "the direct removal of a symptom (without treatment of its cause) produces an increase in drive and throws the patient back into a severe learning dilemma," they retained that element of Freudian outlook which kept them merely transitional theorists.[2] To the complete behaviorist a symptom can be taken as "the illness," as the observable maladaptive behavior to be removed. Why therefore quibble about underlying causes (conflicts)? Surely this aspect is not a parsimonious addition to the hard facts of the case. Furthermore, if stimulus-response psychology can *subsume* Freudian psychology and thereby account for all of those factors which psychoanalysis explained, why not take the next logical step and drop the analytical translation altogether? Why not approach therapy *strictly* on behavioristic principles? Most experts feel that Skinner and Lindsley (1954) actually coined the phrase *behavior therapy*. For those who dislike using "therapy," R. I. Watson's (1962) phrase *be-*

havior modification has proven worthwhile. There are countless people to be identified in this area, but only a few can be mentioned in the limited space of an introductory personality text.

The tie that binds behavioral approaches together is the fact that they all claim rationale based on laboratory experimentation. There is no common formal "personality theory," though there is a definite image of man in these views. There is a marvelous—and sometimes zealous—spirit of empirical flexibility among these men. The old therapy prescriptions have all been challenged and in large measure rejected. Nothing is sacred except the spirit of empirical investigation. Within a remarkably short span of time the behavioral approaches have become a major force in the field of (psycho?) therapy.

In the present chapter, we will deal with the three approaches most often cited as behavior therapies, those of B. F. Skinner, Joseph Wolpe, and Thomas G. Stampfl.

The Technique of Operant Conditioning: B. F. Skinner

BIOGRAPHICAL OVERVIEW

Though he is not a psychotherapist in the usual sense nor even a personality theorist, it is essential to grasp Skinnerian thought to understand its influence on behavioral fields in modern times (see p. 288 for initial comments on Skinner).

B. F. Skinner was the major heir and advocate of behaviorism in the latter half of the twentieth century. His comments on man as a behavioral organism have surely been of monumental significance (see, for instance, 1971). He has been revered and emulated by a number of highly talented psychologists, and yet no psychologist since Freud has been more maligned by those who find his style of thought distasteful.[3]

He was born on 20 March 1904 and reared in the small railroad town of Susquehanna, Pennsylvania, though his parents (of English-American lineage) later moved to the larger city of Scranton around the time he was attending college. Skinner's father was a lawyer, a cultivated and ambitious man who seems to have felt that life did not afford him the opportunity to show the talent he actually possessed. Though he wrote a widely used text on Workmen's Compensation Law, he impressed his son as a man who bitterly considered himself a failure.[4] Skinner's mother was an attractive, intelligent, emotionally strong woman who seems to have complemented her husband well and established what many would consider an old-fashioned, hard-working family climate so typical of the American Protestant family at the turn of this century. The Skinners were to name their first son Burrhus (maiden name of his mother) Frederic. A second son died of a cerebral aneurism at the age of 16. There were no daughters. Skinner's childhood was typified by much activity, a love for the outdoors, a penchant for building and making things, and a great attraction to school work.

Skinner attended Hamilton College in Clinton, New York where he majored in English. He did not take any courses in psychology as an undergraduate student. He did not consider himself a typical student of the times, for it seemed to him that few of his fellow students had intellectual interests in anything except the typical fraternity activities and athletics. Though he joined a fraternity he did not enjoy the experience. He was also not a particularly talented athlete. Skinner resented the school's restrictive rules and the pressures to conform. Students were required to attend daily chapel, and Skinner had long since dismissed his belief in a God. By his senior year he was known as a rebel and had begun writing for student publications criticizing the school administration. One memorable editorial attacked the honorary scholarly society, Phi Beta Kappa.

Skinner was also working at his desired profession of novelist and poet, and he began submitting poems to literary magazines. Following receiving a Bachelor of Arts degree in 1926 his plan was to give writing a serious effort. He built a small study in the attic of his parents' house and set to work. By his own evaluation, the results proved disastrous for he could not discipline his creative spirit and frittered away his time. Before a year had passed by he took an assigned writing job in which he abstracted court decisions for an additional year and published them as a volume dealing with labor-union grievances in the coal industry. There followed a brief stint of "bohemian living" in Greenwich Village, a trip to Europe, and then a return to the United States to enter graduate school in psychology at Harvard in the fall of 1928.

Through a Herculean effort, he made up for his lack of psychology background even as

he moved toward the Master's degree in two years (1930) and the Doctoral in another (1931). Skinner remained at Harvard for the next five years, doing various researches as a National Research Council Fellow and then as a Junior Fellow in the Harvard Society of Fellows. He took his first teaching position at the University of Minnesota in 1936, where he was affiliated until 1945, at which time he moved to Indiana University as Chairman of the Department of Psychology. In 1948 he was invited to join the Psychology Department at Harvard, where he was to enjoy several decades of international recognition as one of the foremost psychologists of his time. Skinner married in 1936, the year of his first teaching position and fathered two daughters—the second of whom received considerable publicity for having spent her first two and one-half years in the "air crib," which her father designed to control the environment of an infant so that clothing was unnecessary, temperature and humidity kept constantly comfortable, interesting toys were readily available, and so on. Hundreds of children have since been reared in this fashion, which removes the necessity of mundane and routine care, freeing the mother to spend time with her baby in more blissful circumstances than diaper and tousled clothing changes.

We have already reviewed Skinner's primary constructs in Chapter 6, with the following terms being most significant in his outlook: *emitted responses, operants, contingencies, classes of responses,* the *shaping of behavior,* and *the method of successive approximations.* One of the most fundamental insights Skinner (1956) was to gain in his early years as researcher was that behavior did *not* require a reinforcement on every occasion (trial) in order for it to be seen continuing in the organism's (rat's, pigeon's, then man's) response repertoire. The drive-reductive behaviorists of this time were of the opinion that behavior could not be stabilized at some constant level unless reinforcements occurred following *each*

B. F. Skinner

performance of the conditioned response (100 per cent reinforcement). Skinner was to find that even when responses are administered less than 100 per cent of the time, in either periodic or aperiodic *time intervals* or *response ratios*, the organism will manifest learning. A stable level of responding can then be graphed as a kind of standard against which we can begin shaping to demonstrate behavioral manipulation.

To prove his point Skinner constructed apparatus of various sorts, but the one which now bears his name (*Skinner Box*) consists essentially of a container (cage, four walled box) in which an organism can be placed, one wall of which has a bar or lever protruding near a receptacle which catches ejected food pellets (reinforcements). If we were to place a rat in this apparatus and wait a period of time, eventually through sniffing about the rat would move the lever and thus eject a pellet of food into the food trap. Based on operant conditioning principles, it would soon be possible to establish a lever-pressing response, particularly if we were to begin by using 100 per cent reinforcement (have the apparatus controlling food pellets release one each time the bar is depressed). This is termed a *schedule of reinforcement*, and we can then vary it into an interval or ratio schedule if we so desire. For example, we could set the apparatus to eject a pellet every fifth depression (*fixed ratio*) or every fifth, then every third, then back to every fifth depression (*variable ratio*), effectively rewarding only some of the rat's lever-depressing responses. Similar manipulations could be made on a time schedule, having the apparatus eject a pellet each minute (*fixed interval*) or every one minute, then two minutes, then back to one minute time intervals (*variable interval* schedule). Depending upon the distribution of reinforcements the rat would probably "strike a level" of responding "so many times" per unit time. Moreover, altering the schedule of reinforce-ment will cause the rat to alter this level of responding accordingly.

Skinner could now define his concept of reinforcement entirely on such empirical grounds of changing behavior: "By arranging a reinforcing consequence, we increase the rate at which a response occurs; by eliminating the consequence, we decrease the rate. These are the processes of operant conditioning and extinction."[5] Skinner thus took issue with formulations like Dollard and Miller's, hinging as the latter do on a distinction between primary and secondary drive learning. The internal drive is a superfluous theoretical construction. Regardless of what one wishes to name as presumed internal states of the organism, it is experimentally clear that *behavior is attached to stimulus consequences*. In time, Skinner increasingly emphasized what he called the *contingency* of an operant response, which was another way of speaking about the consequences of an operant response—whether or not its emission will lead to reinforcement. A *program* is a series of such changing contingencies, resulting in the manipulation of behavior or the control of behavior. Tolman had used the term "contingent implications" in speaking about the means-end aspects of learning. Hull's anticipatory goal response concept would also carry this general meaning of the influences on behavior of a consequence of that behavior.

To clarify this, take the case of hiring an employee. If we were to ask him "Will you do this work for 100 dollars?" we are essentially dealing in hypothetical contingencies. What are the conditions in this potential employee's response history that might cause him to see the sum of 100 dollars as a reasonable reinforcement for the emission of his work responses? Obviously, this would depend upon past experience, which is another way of saying the typical operant level of work-responses and the financial amount to which he has typically responded contingently in the past.

Almost anything can serve as a contingent reinforcement. This is simply an empirical question (*empirical law of effect*). Some people work more for status than money, particularly when the salaries are all quite high in the kind of work they do (executives, for example). Others need signs of affection and care from their employer, in a dependent fashion. It is not our role as operant conditioners to speculate about why this or that reinforcement "works" for the individual. The point is: regardless of what reinforcement we may single out, the principles of operant conditioning will remain unchanged.

Man is an animal constantly oriented to the reinforcing consequences of his behavior. Much of what we mean by the "fruits of culture" as contained in literature is really a matter of making explicit the contingencies of reinforcement following varying behaviors. A poker player, for example, can increase his chances of winning through study of the probabilities of the game as recorded in a book on the subject.[6] He could also learn these probabilities over time by direct experience. It would all be the same in the end. But, much frustration and financial loss might be averted through a judicious investigation of the contingencies involved in drawing to an inside straight.

When behavior is controlled through some form of punishment, loss, or pain following operant responding Skinner refers to this as aversive stimulation. Since psychologists use the terms *punishment* and *negative reinforcement* to describe aversive controls Skinner proposed the following distinction: "You can distinguish between punishment, which is making an aversive event contingent upon a response, and negative reinforcement, in which the elimination or removal of an aversive stimulus, conditioned or unconditioned, is reinforcing."[7] Thus, if a child is spanked following some misbehavior he has been punished. If the child is now made anxious each time he is in the "misbehavior" situation, and by leaving it feels a sense of relief through reduced

anxiety, this would suggest negative reinforcement. The reinforcement is still on the side of a "good" contingency, but it is carried along by the fact that previous learning has made some stimulus pattern anxiety-provoking. Skinner is a staunch critic of all aversive stimulation tactics to control behavior. Research across the animal kingdom has shown that it leads to negative side effects, making it inferior to controls through positive reinforcement. Rather than using aversive stimulation, Skinner suggests that extinction (removal of reinforcement) or the positive reinforcement of responses incompatible with the undesired responses be employed.[8]

Over his long and highly successful career as researcher and teacher Skinner put these principles and beliefs into practice—both in the practical world of education and child rearing and also in the fantasy world of fiction. While teaching at Minnesota he wrote a utopian novel entitled *Walden Two* (1948). It is the story of a brilliant but somehow threatening genius—a psychologist—who is the main force behind the establishment of a near-ideal subculture. The community of Walden Two is "behaviorally engineered" along operant conditioning lines, with group dependence upon a series of changing, empirically verified set of scientific findings and principles that are put into effect by highly trained planners and managers (who are themselves recruited from the general populace of Walden Two). Skinner frankly admitted that the book was written as a form of self-therapy, in which he was striving "to reconcile two aspects of my own behavior represented by Burris and Frazier,"[9] the two major figures, a professor of psychology named Burris (Burrhus) who tells the story, and the founder of Walden Two, a psychologist named Frazier (Frederic?). These two are not exactly on good terms at the outset of the story, but by the book's close Burris moves from visitor to resident of Walden Two.

Although Skinner never lost his conviction

that Walden Two communities were within the realm of possibility[10] and he expanded on the design of cultures in other writings,[11] his innovations were never realized in the quite literal fashion of founding a utopia. Other ideas were to be put more or less into concrete form. We have already mentioned the air crib, the prototype of which can be seen in *Walden Two* (1948). During the years of World War II Skinner worked out a fairly practical means of guidance whereby pigeons, trained operantly to peck at objects projected onto a screen (such as small ship models), could be used in an air-to-ground guided missile.[12] The pigeons were to be placed within a projectile of this sort and to act as a homing device. Though never used operationally, it shows the willingness of a highly creative person to put what he later joked was a "crackpot idea" into operation.[13] Probably the most practical and productive innovation for which Skinner can be given major credit (though Sidney L. Pressey must also be recognized as an early progenitor of the idea[14]) is the "teaching machine." The practical strategy of the widely used programmed instructions based upon operant conditioning principles has established a place of lasting honor for Skinner in this sphere of endeavor.[15]

Skinner's major academic works have been the following: *The Behavior of Organisms: An Experimental Analysis* (1938); *Science and Human Behavior* (1953); *Schedules of Reinforcement* (with Ferster, 1957); *Verbal Behavior* (1957); *Cumulative Record* (1959); *The Technology of Teaching* (1968); *Contingencies of Reinforcement: A Theoretical Analysis* (1969); and *Beyond Freedom and Dignity* (1971). He received several honors in recognition of his work, including the Distinguished Scientific Contribution Award of the American Psychological Association and the President's Medal of Science. His many students have carried on his work, and his impact on psychology and the image of man which it portrays has been tremendous.

Yet, the curious aspect of this impact is that Skinner pointedly set out to avoid playing the "theorist," much preferring to confine his activities to the control and manipulation of behavior. He once observed: "When we have achieved a practical control over the organism, theories of behavior lose their point."[16] Why quibble over which drive is being reduced or what behavior is being repressed when one has direct operant control of the organism? The basis of Skinner's polemic here rests on the "inside vs. outside" dichotomy of behavior which Watson had introduced (see p. 285). For Skinner, the term *theory* often means "an effort to explain behavior in terms of something going on in another universe, such as the mind or the nervous system."[17] He rejected this form of theory and since stimulus-response psychology is heavily invested with this tactic, he could not consider himself an S-R psychologist.[18] On the other hand, Skinner did feel that he was a theoretician in the sense of formulating an overall theory of human behavior combining many facts into a general picture.[19] In this sense, it would be fair to say that the weight of history forced Skinner ever more into a role as theorist and even "social philosopher."

This growing necessity of having to expand his commentary doubtless stemmed initially from the reaction Skinner witnessed to *Walden Two* (1948). Though he tried to express his strong sense of humanity in this work, many readers were appalled by the seeming "mass manipulation" of the human spirit. Skinner felt that he was being misunderstood, for he at no time viewed his utopia as a kind of Brave New World.[20] The citizens of Walden Two were happy. Aversive stimulation was virtually nonexistent, and both the basic and the aesthetic needs of life were amply reinforced. Skinner felt that his critics had confused the democratic political ideals of America with the intent of the book, and that the only thing wrong with his utopia so far as he could tell from their criticisms was that someone (Frazier) had "planned it that way."[21] The role of social philosopher was to descend upon his shoulders thanks to a series of debates he subsequently engaged in with his friend Carl R. Rogers (Chapter 9). Rogers specifically reacted against the seeming disregard of the "person" in Skinner's outlook, and he also questioned the "control and manipulation" of people as the proper role for the science of psychology. The following passage from an article of Rogers' in which he speaks about an exchange he had with Skinner shows both Skinner's intellectual consistency and the extremes to which he was willing to go in order to defend his theory of behavior:

A paper given by Dr. Skinner led me to direct these remarks to him: "From what I understand Dr. Skinner to say, it is his understanding that though he might have thought *he chose* to come to this meeting, might have thought he had a purpose in giving this speech, such thoughts are really illusory. He actually made certain marks on paper and emitted certain sounds here simply because his genetic makeup and his past environment had operantly conditioned his behavior in such a way that it was rewarding to make these sounds, and that he as a person doesn't enter into this. In fact if I get his thinking correctly, from his strictly scientific point of view, he, as a person, doesn't exist." In his reply Dr. Skinner said that he would not go into the question of whether he had any choice in the matter (presumably because the whole issue was illusory) but stated, "I do accept your characterization of my own presence here."[22]

It is this side of Skinner that we must neither overlook nor misunderstand. Though he always speaks of the consequences of behavior and the contingencies of reinforcement, Skinner staunchly defends the antiteleological position of behaviorism. He observes: "Operant behavior, as I see it, is simply a study of what used to be dealt with by the concept of purpose. The purpose of an act is the consequences it is going to have."[23] Would this not imply that rules could be abstracted from past

behavior and used in the present as a means of self-direction (teleology)? Well, though rules may be abstracted and plans surely can be made (Frazier was a great planner), this does not establish the fact of a *self*-direction: ". . . when a man explicitly states his purpose in acting in a given way he may, indeed, be constructing a 'contemporary surrogate of future consequences' which will affect subsequent behavior, possibly in useful ways. It does not follow, however, that the behavior generated by the consequences alone is under the control of any comparable prior stimulus, such as a felt purpose or intention."[24]

Those who argue for self-direction must inevitably defend internal stimulation as the control of their external manifestation of behavior. As a behaviorist, Skinner is unable to accept this. Scientific experimentation has proved beyond doubt that men respond to environmental manipulation. The argument that there is some form of self-identity—a person, ego, or whatever—directing behavior from the inside is simply the last ditch stand of an outdated ideology.[25] As Skinner sees it: "Men will never become originating centers of control, because their behavior will itself be controlled, but their role as mediators may be extended without limit. . . . 'Personal freedom' and 'responsibility' will make way for other bywords which, as is the nature of bywords, will probably prove satisfying enough."[26] This does not mean that man will forego progress in his state of living: "I take an optimistic view. Man can control his future even though his behavior is wholly determined. It is controlled by the environment, but man is always changing his environment. He builds a world in which his behavior has certain characteristics. He does this because the characteristics are reinforcing to him. He builds a world in which he suffers fewer aversive stimuli and in which he behaves with maximum efficiency."[27]

And so we have the paradox of a seeming humanist who believes in the progress of civilization and the future of man, yet who can find no use for the "person" in his psychology: "As far as I'm concerned, the organism is irrelevant either as the site of physiological processes or as the locus of mentalistic activities."[28] This is what many take to be Skinner's "black box" or "empty organism" conception of the organism, a way of expressing the issue which Skinner frowns upon and which was attributed to him by others.[29] There are surely mediating processes at work in the organism, which is a physical reality, but they cannot be observed and hence are a poor choice as the basic data of a psychology. Skinner sticks to his empiricism, and he has won many battles simply by demonstrating the obvious role which operants and their contingent reinforcers have upon the nature of animal and human behavior. And here is where psychotherapy or "behavior modification" enters. Though not a therapist, Skinner's views have worked well in the clinical manipulation (cure) of patients. We now turn to some examples of operant conditioning in a therapeutic setting.

THEORETICAL CONSIDERATIONS

THEORY OF ILLNESS AND CURE

Though they do not deny the occasional physical-biological involvement, by and large the view of operant behavior therapists is that maladaptive behavior is no different than any other behavior, once reduced to the learning principles which sustain it. Somehow, based upon his life experience to date, the psychotic individual has been conditioned by the environment to respond (operantly) in a way considered incorrect or inappropriate by the broader society and the culture it has promulgated. Customarily, this results in a pattern of no reinforcement, behavior under the control of aversive stimuli (punishments, negative reinforcements), or the complete rejection of external stimuli by the "psychotic" in favor of his own dream world. Social expectations enter

to damn him as lazy, bad, "crazy," or "possessed by the Devil," none of which helps him to adjust his operant level to life in a more realistic fashion.

There is another very significant aspect of mental illness to which behavior therapists point.[30] Once labeled as "sick" or a "mental patient" the expectation established for the troubled person by his environment is that he must submit to the contingencies of his new role. The so-called "secondary gain" features of mental illness are considered a part of this role, but there is much more as well. The "good patient" is not troublesome but rather passive and willing to accept the direction and manipulation of his caretakers. If the broader culture is organized to get the inadequately behaving members of society "out of sight" and under "lock and key" this is a reasonable role for the abnormal individual. But if efficient psychotherapy or behavioral therapy is the goal, this capitulation of self-assertiveness and self-control is anything but beneficial.

The broadest phrasing of the operant therapist's view of maladaptive behavior is that two things have gone wrong: (1) adaptive behaviors have never been learned; (2) maladaptive behaviors *have* been learned. The problem facing the therapist is therefore to identify maladaptive behaviors in an individual's repertoire and *remove* them through operant techniques. Concurrently, more adaptive responses should supplant them. There is little or no need for an extensive review of the client's past life, though the more information one has concerning the maladaptive patterns the easier it is to arrange a program of operant conditioning for the client. Psychological tests or interviews are used only in this pragmatic fashion of identifying the symptom picture as clearly as possible and thence arranging circumstances for a change in behavior. Though informal insights doubtless occur to the client, there is no attempt to make cure dependent upon the extent of self-understanding a client may have.

INDIVIDUAL TREATMENT CASES

Let us assume that a mother brings her eight-year-old son to a behavior therapist with the complaint that, though he once talked reasonably well and often enough, since beginning school around age six he has deteriorated in speech and is now virtually mute. He was held back in first grade for another year because of his muteness. Physical examinations and consultations with medical specialists have been to no avail. The behavior therapist might spend several sessions reviewing the case history with the parents and then, after careful planning, institute a program of operant conditioning. First, he would ask that the parents simply take the pressure off of their son to speak, since all they are doing is attaching aversive stimulus cues to the speaking situation in any case. Next, he would ask that the boy be brought in to see him over a series of half-hour to one-hour sessions. Having determined from the parents what their son prefers in the way of sweets, he would have on hand in the therapy room (which might be equipped with several games, construction toys, and so forth) an ample supply of—let us say—chocolate candy. Now, therapy would begin.

At the outset of the first hour the therapist might or might not tell the child something about what it is they hope to accomplish together. More than likely he would simply introduce the boy to the "play room" and permit him to select any toy or game that struck his fancy as a means of passing the hour. If the boy seemed to want it, the therapist would enter into the play. At the first sign of vocalization—a throat clearing, a grunt, or possibly merely a movement of the lips—the therapist would slip the boy a chocolate. With each subsequent approximation (method of successive approximation) to speech the boy would receive an additional piece of candy. The reinforcement level can of course be increased when word sounds are emitted (two pieces of chocolate). After a very few such meetings (three or four), the child will begin saying a few words to his therapist.

The therapist might alter contingencies in some fashion. For example, he might compliment (reinforce) the boy for his progress in speech and work out some arrangement whereby instead of chocolates little plastic chips can be collected over the therapy hour with each word or sentence the therapist notes him using. At the end of the hour these chips can be turned in for "prizes," such as model airplanes or picture books which the therapist has determined are among the boy's most prized possessions at home. The therapist may now instruct the boy's parents how to operantly reinforce the child's behavior in the home setting. Rather than showing concern—hence attention and thereby reinforcement—for muteness, he instructs the parents to ignore the child when mute but to make every reasonable show of attention when he does speak (or grunt or move his lips, for that matter). In this fashion, the operant level which has been "primed" in the therapy session can be transferred to the life setting proper.

The final phase of therapy would then demand an environment in which reinforcement for speaking would be arranged for the child. Friends who are supportive and nonthreatening should be brought into the home, with the same schedule of ignoring muteness and responsiveness to speech efforts followed. Gradually, this circle of environmental manipulation can be extended. The behavior therapist may wish to speak to the boy's school teachers and to make recommendations along the above lines to them as well. The results have been shown to be quite successful through use of this technique. Note that the therapist works to *extinguish* the mute response and to *operantly reinforce* the speech response. Behavior therapists emphasize that there is little or no evidence to support the claim that a "symptom substitution" or replacement of one disorder (such as muteness) with another (such as bedwetting) is likely to take place.[31] Hence, Skinner proposed that the claim that an "underlying reason" must be confronted before lasting cures result is simply another one of those unsubstantiated superstitions which therapists have accepted without proper study.

Operant techniques can be used in the modification of much more serious behavioral problems. Let us assume that we were to visit a large all-female "locked ward" of some hospital (where patients are unable to manage for themselves without constant supervision and protection). Women would be sitting around in heavy wooden chairs, gazing blandly into space or looking furtively about. Some would be lying on couches or on the floor. Others might be nervously pacing about, mumbling to themselves, often grimacing and waving their hands in the air. Hardly a likely source of patients for psychoanalysis! Assume that we were to pick one of these women as a potential therapy *subject* (the terms client and subject are often synonymous to the behavior therapist). The woman selected had shown no particular change in behavior for over two years. She is 40 years of age, has been diagnosed as schizophrenic, and has been hospitalized for over five years. She sits all day long, staring into space or gazing at the television set. This is the fourth and seemingly last admission to the hospital in her life, for it appears unlikely that she will ever be discharged as "in remission" again. Even her family has begun to give up hope that she will ever be able to return home. She had never married, since her strange behavior had begun manifesting itself early in high school and boys were disdainful of her.

What kind of therapy can we provide this wretched person? Skinner and his associates devised a procedure which has brought more than a score of such people back to a level of living they had not experienced for some time.[32] The principles involved emanate from earlier experience with lower animals in the "Skinner Box." The therapist would bring this highly abnormal patient into a specially prepared cubicle. She would be seated in a comfortable chair, facing a panel on which from one to four levers would protrude (depending upon how intricate the reinforcement program is). There would probably also be a row of lights, one for each lever, and a screen on which pictures could be flashed (possibly from within the apparatus, so it would have the appearance of a television screen). Finally, below each lever there would be a container box into which small items like bits of candy or cigarettes could fall. The patient might show little interest in this panorama of unlit lights, darkened TV screen, and slot-machine-like arrangement of levers all beckoning her to respond. She might simply sit there unmoved and stare at her knuckles or some such.

However, in time, out of curiosity—particularly if the therapist reaches over and pulls one of the levers and a bit of chocolate falls into one of the trays below—the patient will pull a lever. Sometimes it is necessary to place a patient's hand on the lever and begin the process by depressing it for her. These early responses are rewarded, possibly on a 100 per cent basis, but ratio schedules (reinforcing one of every three pulls) can also maintain an operant level. Variations can be introduced in the procedure. For example, instead of candy or cigarettes the patient may find that pulling a lever causes an aesthetically pleasing landscape picture to flash on the screen. Since there are several levers some form of problem solution can be introduced into the task. The lights can be made to flash, and a different color will occur with each lever. It might now be necessary for the patient to learn that only when red is followed by blue light flashes will a reinforcement be forthcoming. It is possible to make problems of varying difficulty, and the therapist can even introduce a second patient into the procedure later on and have the two women work cooperatively to solve their joint problem.

Several investigators have used this behavioral modification technique, finding it remarkably effective in reviving a patient, bringing him out of a dream world and enabling him once again to function with fairly appropriate verbal contact.[33] The patient described above no longer sits around the ward and stares into space. She talks, listens to others and makes her wants known. The psychologist now extends his operant tactic outward, into more and more of her daily routine. Nurses, psychiatric aides, and indeed the entire staff of the hospital is instructed to use praise and attention to reward desired behaviors and to ignore those more bizarre patterns which had previously brought attention and signs of concern to this woman. In time, with additional instruction given to her parental family members, it may even be possible for this woman to return to her life outside the hospital. Just as with the boy who would not speak, the self-reinforcements which accrue to a person as he advances on life will work to continue the recovery so mechanically begun in the quasi-Skinner Box of the hospital. Through behavioral manipulation we have "pump primed" the woman's behavior and now hope to see her take over in life the way everyone else does.

THE THERAPEUTIC COMMUNITY AND SOCIAL REVISION

Since the operant behavior therapist believes that an individual's environment "shapes" his behavior for the most effective outcome a total, "community approach" to cure should be put into operation. Skinner has noted that too often our institutions for the mentally ill are based upon ineffective and even improper contingencies.[34] Aversive stimulation (threats, beatings, confinement) and poor tactics, like providing the troublemaker with all of the attention of the hospital attendants, is more the rule than anything else. A totally redesigned community—not exactly a Walden Two but with this overview approach in mind—is the obvious answer.[35]

One of the most interesting applications of Skinnerian thought to a large scale treatment of this sort has sometimes been called a "token economy."[36] Since a community cannot be put into a Skinner Box, why not use the same principles *in vivo*? Why not make the "good things of life" in the mental hospital contingent upon a patient's performance? By designing an appropriate token, either circular or rectangular like the modern "credit card," and assuming the cooperation of an entire hospital—or at least one or two large wards in that hospital—therapists can begin a designed program of behavioral manipulation and improvement. The first step would usually involve some form of determination about just what the typical behavior of patients is. Do they engage in activities, attend group functions, meet schedules for meals, and so forth? What is the incidence of bed wetting? Do any patients take weekend leaves? Naturally, the general rate of turnover—hospital discharge—would be a significant measure of overall efficiency as well.

A therapist could now institute the practice of reinforcing all those behaviors he takes to be generally oriented toward personal adjustment both within and outside of the hospital social milieu. For example, each time a patient makes his bed, cleans himself, gets through the night without wetting his bed, or shows an interest in another patient's welfare, he can be issued a token. The level of reinforcement can be varied by having different colored tokens represent more or less value. When a patient now wishes to watch television, he might be required to give up a token to do so. If he wants to purchase cigarettes or candy at the hospital store, this too would be contingent upon possession of tokens. The limitations on what should be reinforced and for how much is left entirely to the ingenuity of the therapists who supervise such a program. The psychologist does not walk about administering tokens for all patients, of course. Though he may participate if he wishes, it would also be possible for him to act as a consultant to the general staff—the nurses, attendants, etc.—who would do the actual dispensing of reinforcements.

VERBAL CONDITIONING AS PSYCHOTHERAPY

The final aspect of psychotherapy to which Skinnerian thought applies is that of "talking" therapy. Can we view spoken words as operants on a par with actions like reaching for a glass of milk? Skinner would answer yes to this question, with the proviso that strictly verbal behavior is "behavior reinforced through the mediation of other persons."[37] Vocalizing is not essential, since literally: "Any movement capable of affecting another organism may be verbal."[38] A nonverbal response affects the behavioral environment in some way, such as when we put a glass of milk to our lips; a verbal response operates (operant) on the behavior of another person. Skinner worked out a series of technical terms to describe how verbal behavior in the form of "words" influences other people when we use them—such as the *mand* (Stop) or the *tact* (Hello)—but there is no need to elaborate on this scheme for present purposes.

More to the point for present considerations is that Skinner gives language a central role in behavior without acknowledging a truly *meaningful* side to it. It was essential for Skinner to develop this thesis, because as a behaviorist if he were to accept language as truly expressive of meanings he would be picturing man purposively saying something or intending that something be expressed. "To mean" takes Anglo-Saxon roots from "to intend" or "to wish." This usage clearly implies a teleology. Here is how Skinner deals with the technical problem even as he acknowledges the relationship of purposiveness to meaning: "It is usually asserted that we can *see* meaning or purpose in behavior and should not omit it from our account. But meaning is not a property of behavior as such but of the

conditions under which behavior occurs. Technically, meanings are to be found among the independent variables in a functional account [of verbal behavior], rather than as properties of the dependent variable. When someone says that he can see the meaning of a response, he means that he can infer some of the variables of which the response is usually a function."[39]

What is the result of this analysis? It confronts us with the picture of men speaking, none of whom is under stimulus control of what they are speaking about. There are words being vocalized, leading to other words being vocalized, but the control of what is being said has nothing to do with the meanings the participants may think they are expressing. In the same way that emitted behaviors of a nonverbal nature are under the control of their consequences, verbal statements are under the control of the effects they have on other people—which is another way of saying the consequences are to be noted in interpersonal behavior. We can now better understand why Skinner was willing to put his behavior under the "person-less object" characterization in his exchange with Rogers. He could not be intimidated by this characterization because this is his formal stand on *all* behaviors, including that of Rogers.

Hence, according to Skinnerian theory, a classical therapist using psychoanalysis is not "providing insight" through meaningful interpretations. He is verbally manipulating the emitted responses of his client because he has himself been shaped to emit responses in a certain fashion. His training has conditioned him to say certain things when the client says certain things. He is *not* an originating source of control in the relationship any more than the client is. Each has his own level of operant behavior, speaking about this or that topic at one or another level of emission rate. It *is* possible to change the class of responses being emitted (change the topic, bring out more "healthy" responses and extinguish the "un-healthy") or the rate of their emission. Hence, the nature of psychotherapy as the nature of speech itself is identical to verbal conditioning. Effective therapy involves efficient manipulation of the verbal behavior of a client. But first, we must manipulate the verbal behavior of the therapist, making him over into a kind of "social reinforcement machine."[40]

The line of research which has buoyed up this view of psychotherapy began in the now classical study of Greenspoon (1954). The basic design called for a period of time in which the subject is asked to emit verbal responses, with no limitation placed on the class of responses he emits. For example, the subject is asked to sit with his back to the experimenter and to state aloud all of the words (given singly, not in sentences) which occur to him quite spontaneously. It is possible after a period of time (let us say 10 minutes) to get an "operant level" measure of the classes of responses he typically emits. Of all words emitted, what proportion are nouns, adjectives, singular or plural references, and so forth? Electrical sound recording of a subject's responses makes this dissection of the total words emitted into classes a simple matter after data have been gathered. In the next step, the therapist selects a class of verbal responses (Greenspoon used "plural nouns") and operantly reinforces just these words for a 10-minute period. The reinforcement used by the experimenter might be a simple "mmm-hmm" or possibly the word "good." Each time the subject says a plural noun, the experimenter follows it with the verbal reinforcement stimulus. Finally, a closing 10-minute period is recorded in which the subject relies again on his own devices, stating words without reinforcement.

What did Greenspoon find? The verbal class "plural nouns" showed a significant increase in operant level between the first and the third periods of study. He had effectively manipulated the subject's behavior, and the even more fascinating aspect here is that he claimed to have done this without the subject's knowledge. Asking the subject what had happened afterwards made no difference to the findings as to whether or not his operant level was changed. It was no accident that Greenspoon had selected the "mmm-hmm" reinforcement, for during this period of historical time the "nondirective" approach to psychotherapy advanced by Carl Rogers (Chapter 9) was receiving considerable attention in psychology. Rogers was claiming that he did *not* control or direct in any way the lives of his clients. His entire strategy was to turn over direction of therapy to the client, and one of the encouraging expressions that he used in this regard was "mmm-hmm" (in the sense of "Yes, I see . . . please go on . . ."). Now, here was Greenspoon and several other operant conditioners who followed with variations on his design, claiming that the "mmm-hmm" was not so noncontrolling after all.

There is no need to go into the variations on the Greenspoon design which were to follow.[41] Suffice to say that the operant view or model of psychotherapy became one of having a therapist—himself operantly trained—manipulate the behavior of his client through well-placed reinforcements in the chain of verbal emissions (operants) being made by the client. Though this has tremendous implication for all forms of so-called insight (meaningful) therapies, in point of fact the technique of verbal conditioning as pseudo-insight is not widely used as a behavioral therapeutic tactic. The reinforcing of personal insights is not in the traditions of behaviorism, since what the client says about his behavior may or may not be behaviorally tied to what he actually does in a real life performance. Any "insights" thus sent the client's way are pitched to some definite behavioral adaptation. Rummaging around in the past is eschewed in favor of laying down specific programs of action for today and tomorrow.

Techniques Based on the Principle of Reciprocal Inhibition: Joseph Wolpe

BIOGRAPHICAL OVERVIEW

Joseph Wolpe's parental family immigrated from Lithuania to the Union of South Africa around the beginning of the twentieth century. He was born on 20 April 1915 and recalls the closeness of his early family life. His people were orthodox Jews, and though they were not extreme in the keeping of religious observances, Wolpe was heavily imbued with a religious outlook as a child. He was particularly close to his maternal grandmother, who encouraged him to read the Hebrew theologian and philosopher, Maimonides. This grandmother passed away when Wolpe was 16, and by his early university days the theistic orientation she had fostered began to leave her grandson. By the time Wolpe had extended his reading from Kant, through Whitehead, Moore, and Russell, as well as immersing himself in his medical subjects, he had abandoned the belief in God.

Wolpe's father was a bookkeeper. His mother was a level-headed person who managed her four children (including two daughters) as efficiently as she took care of finances. The father was a man of unassailable integrity, who developed increasingly liberal or left-wing political views as the years passed. One has the picture of a very stimulating household, with cross-currents of old world religion and a growing emphasis on the need for change in the modern world.

His childhood years were happy ones for Wolpe. He enjoyed school, was a voracious reader by the age of eight, and in his teen years became fascinated with chemistry, a development which he felt led him into the profession of medicine. He enjoyed music but did not regularly listen to classical music until he was past age 20. The visual arts were late interests as well. As a boy he did not especially appreciate the scenic factors of the environment, but he did have an uncanny sensitivity to aromas and odors. In his mature years he developed a strong interest in painting, and he also came to love the beauty of sculpture and Persian rugs.

In 1948 Wolpe was married, and in time fathered two sons. This was the year in which he also took the MD degree from the University of Witwatersrand, where he subsequently retained an association for the next decade as a lecturer in psychiatry. Although initially attracted to Freudian theory, Wolpe rejected psychoanalysis because of its lack of empirical support in scientific researches. Near the end of his medical school days he had begun a careful study of the works of Pavlov (see

Joseph Wolpe

Chapter 6). Though he did not accept Pavlovian theory he was drawn to the elegance of such research procedures. At about this time a friend introduced him to the work of Hull (see Chapter 6), and here Wolpe found a theoretical formulation within which he could work—even though in time he adapted the empirical findings to his unique style of thought. Another source of influence was the work of Jules H. Masserman (1943), who had done considerable work on the role of conflicts in cats. Wolpe dismissed Masserman's theories, which drew on Freudian terminology, but adapted his experimental tactics to suit a more behavioral view of neurosis.

In the years 1946–1948 Wolpe studied the role of counterconditioning—what he called "reciprocal inhibition"—in cats who had developed an experimental neurosis and then were "cured" of the affliction.[42] This was actually a continuation of the experimental work he had initiated in partial fulfillment of his MD thesis (1948). Based in large measure on the findings of these researches, Wolpe took up the private practice of psychiatry as a behavior therapist in Johannesburg.

In the year 1956–1957 Wolpe was awarded a Fellowship at the Center for Advanced Study in the Behavioral Sciences at Stanford, California. He used this time to pull together his ideas on behavior therapy in his now classical book: *Psychotherapy by Reciprocal Inhibition* (1958). Feeling the need for more time to pursue the experimental implications of his theories, in 1960 Wolpe accepted an appointment as Professor of Psychiatry at the University of Virginia School of Medicine. Coming to a new land was a challenge, but Wolpe had found that he increasingly disliked the political climate of South Africa. His brother, a lawyer who had been imprisoned there for political reasons and effected a spectacular escape to England, had since taken up a new career as academic sociologist. Wolpe thus considered immigrating to England feeling that was his natural environment. However, his

position in America allowed him to contribute more to his area of interest than any other move, and he never joined his brother in England. In 1965 he again changed academic affiliations, to the Health Sciences Center, School of Medicine of Temple University. In the meantime, he had lectured on behavior therapy throughout the world, acquired many followers, and established himself as the foremost spokesman for behavior therapy of his time.

Unlike Skinner, Wolpe's medical education and Hullian predilections kept his theorizing close to the physical structures of the body. He is more ready than Skinner to speak of the *necessary* role of neurones in learning, and physiological terms enter into his writings quite regularly. Wolpe's theories invariably focus on the functioning of observables or the potentially observable structures and functions of the body. Wolpe is adamantly nonteleological in the best traditions of rigorous behaviorism. Here is how he once dealt the death blow to mentalistic conceptions:

Between a stimulus and the responses that follow it there must be an unbroken network of causally related events, potentially observable by an outside beholder, no matter whether or not some of the neural events have correlates in the consciousness of the subject. Any contents of the subject's consciousness would be *in parallel and not in series* with their neural correlates, and would in essence constitute the unique reaction of a specially placed observer (the subject) to these neural events. Thus, an image of which I am not conscious now will appear in my imagination if appropriate stimuli activate certain of my neurones. It can have no independent existence apart from the stimulation of these neurones. Within my nervous system, a *potentiality* which includes the evocation of this image may be said to exist, but *only in the same sense as it may be said that my nervous system harbors the potentiality of a knee jerk given the stimulus of a patellar tap.* If the relationship of images to the nervous system is so conceived, all talk of "mind structure" becomes nonsensical.[43]

LEARNING THEORY AND THE PRINCIPLE OF RECIPROCAL INHIBITION

Wolpe considers *learning* to have taken place when "a response has been evoked in temporal contiguity with a given sensory stimulus and it is subsequently found that the stimulus can evoke the response although it could not have done so before."[44] Even if the stimulus could have evoked the response earlier but now does so with greater regularity and strength, learning has taken place. In this definition Wolpe takes a Watsonian-Hullian view of responses as evoked and not emitted. The *response* is a "behavioral event" standing as consequent to a *stimulus* or pattern of stimuli.[45] And *behavior* is essentially a "change of state or of spatial relations to other things."[46] When such shifting relations freeze into what Hull once called a *"persisting state of the organism"* Wolpe would say that a *habit* or a recurring manner of response to stimulation has been learned.[47]

This process of shifting relations between stimuli and the responses which they evoke is dependent upon *reinforcement* which Wolpe defined as the strengthening of functional relations.[48] Reinforcements are the result of two circumstances: (a) a certain closeness or *contiguity* must exist between a stimulus and its response, with reinforcement following closely behind or concurrently with the response; and (b) a drive reduction must be involved. Wolpe distinguished between a need and the drive which mediates it as follows: "Whatever the mechanisms involved, need conditions, being antecedents of neuro-effector responses, are stimulus conditions to these responses. But between the stimulus conditions and the effector responses *there intervenes excitation of neurones in the central nervous system;* and to this excitation the term *drive* may usefully be applied."[49] Needs are thus the ways we have of speaking about sensory stimulations of various sorts: "Every sensory stimulus . . . has the essential characteristic of a need."[50] We can often show that certain needs are correlated with the amount of activity or motor discharge (drive) an organism exhibits, but this is not a perfect relationship by any means. So-called primary needs—for nourishment, sex, etc.—are different from other needs only in the sense that they tend to stimulate stronger responses when the organism is deprived of them.[51]

Since the drive is stimulated by a need, the nature of the drive is more akin to a response than a stimulus (which is the emphasis Dollard and Miller had given it). Though Wolpe does not state it precisely this way, the drive state is likened to a mediating series of electrical responses, carried by the nervous system, the *reduction* of which "stamps in" the stimulus-response contiguities occurring in the animal's molar (external) behavior. There is no intentionality (teleology) involved, but Wolpe is attempting to account for the actual processes within the organism that make for learning. He therefore does not dismiss the organism as irrelevant to his theory, as did Skinner.

The most important drive concept of Wolpe's theory is *anxiety,* which he defines as "the automatic response pattern or patterns that are characteristically part of the given organism's response to noxious stimulation."[52] The anxiety construct is used to explain the disruptive effects on learning of noxious stimulation, as well as the phenomenon noted by Dollard and Miller (Chapter 6) of a reduction in anxiety leading to the stamping-in of a response due to the reinforcing qualities of such a reduction. There is a slight disclaimer, as when Wolpe noted in his original work: ". . . the argument of this book will not be affected if it should turn out that the onset of anxiety is all-important to its learning and its reduction of no moment at all. There are some apparently undeniable instances of learning reinforced by conditions of drive increment [rising anxiety] instead of drive reduction."[53]

Wolpe found in his researches that the direct effects of noxious stimulation were enough to produce the symptoms of an experimental neurosis.[54] For example, a cat would be placed in an experimental cage and given five to 10 severe grid shocks, each of which was immediately preceded by a "hooting sound" lasting two or three seconds. The animal soon developed signs of crouching, trembling, heavy breathing, and striving to escape; when blocked the cat urinated and defecated out of apparent terror. These symptoms were soon brought on when the hooting sound was presented even before shock could be administered (on the order of Pavlovian conditioning and Hull's fractional antedating goal reaction). Generalization of the "neurotic" pattern was noted in other situations and with other noises; when exhibiting anxiety the animal's eating pattern was disrupted.

It is this inability to make one response (eating) while another is in ascendance (anxiety) which lies at the heart of Wolpe's explanation of both neurosis and therapy. Hull had pointed out that behavior is not only "learned" or put into habit regularities through reinforced practice (repetition of response), but there also seems to be a natural *inhibition* of responsivity with repeated trials. Anyone who has to repeat some behavior over and over again, even if it is pleasurable to begin with, knows that in time a sense of fatigue or boredom comes on which motivates him to stop performing. Hull named this fatigue-associated state *reactive inhibition*. Wolpe speculated that it was probably due to some form of substance produced by the muscles which acted on the neurones at their synaptic connections to other neurones.[55] This form of inhibition is not what seems involved in the fact that Wolpe's cats could not both eat and reflect anxious behavior at the same time. To explain the latter form of behavior Wolpe borrowed a construct from the neurologist

Sherrington (1947) and wedded it to a concept used by Hull.

Hull had found a type of inhibition occurring which was not simply due to repetitive fatigue but seemed a matter of *conditioned inhibition*.[56] When a response is forced to *cease* by some competing response, the stimuli associated with the cessation of this response act as conditioned inhibitors. If a cat is hungry and about to approach the food tray when Wolpe sounds the hoot and then administers the shock, the anxiety responses occasioned by the noxious stimulation are thence conditioned to the stimuli of the sound and the electrical discharge. Furthermore, the food responses which ceased as the anxiety responses were being learned are themselves inhibited. We have a response acquired (anxiety) and a response inhibited (eating), both of which have been learned through conditioning. It is this form of conditioned inhibition which Wolpe now employs as a principle of explanation.

However, as if to underscore his greater reliance on neurophysiological terminology, Wolpe seems to have adapted a physically-based concept used by Sherrington to his theory, as follows: "The term *reciprocal inhibition* was first introduced by Sherrington . . . in relation to the inhibition of one spinal reflex by another, such as occurs when stimulation of an ipsilateral afferent nerve causes relaxation of a vastocrureus muscle contracting to a contralateral stimulus. Its use may be expanded to encompass all situations in which the elicitation of one response appears to bring about a decrement in the strength of evocation of a simultaneous response."[57] Reciprocal inhibition thus deals with the weakening of old responses by new ones: "When a response is inhibited by an incompatible response and if a major drive reduction follows, a significant amount of conditioned inhibition of the response will be developed."[58] By not eating (inhibition) but seeking to escape from the noxious stimulation the animal reinforces its neurotic pattern through the reduction in anxiety to follow. The trick is to reverse this process.

And so Wolpe reasoned that if he wanted to inhibit the anxiety responses, a reasonable program to follow would be to present food in a *less* anxiety-provoking situation than the original one, where the naturally competing response of eating might be more likely to be elicited. For example, experimenters might begin feeding the animal outside the experimental room, where the strength of generalization is weaker, hence fewer signs of extreme anxiety are noted. Once the animal was capable of eating in this situation it could be brought into the actual experimental room, then closer and closer to the original cage as it came to eat while under a gradually decreasing level of anxiety. In this fashion, a "cure" of the experimental neurosis was attained. Wolpe named this technique *systematic desensitization*.[59] He had systematically desensitized the animal to the anxiety-provoking stimulus.

THEORY OF ILLNESS AND CURE

Wolpe's personal practice and the techniques derived therefrom have focused on neurotic behavior, which he defines as *"any persistent habit of unadaptive behavior acquired by learning in a physiologically normal organism."*[60] Since all men are under causal determination, to speak of a neurotic as someone who wants to be sick or who derives "secondary gain" from his illness strikes Wolpe as absurd.[61] The core of neurotic behavior is essentially those autonomic patterns we have labeled as anxiety responses. Wolpe makes no distinction between anxiety and fear, since the physiological processes are identical.[62] Making an analogy to animal studies, Wolpe proposed that the neurotic's behavior may have developed from conflicts in life, forcing him into behavioral quandaries and inconsistencies or that it may be the direct effects of noxious

stimulation such as punishment or any of life's "tough breaks." As an autonomic response pattern anxiety has some rather peculiar characteristics. Once underway as a free-floating state it can be attached to any number of extraneous, irrelevant stimuli. For example, Wolpe tells of a man who had eaten onions while in a state of anxious emotional upset. The anxiety sensed at this time attached itself to the feeling of abdominal distention, and henceforth whenever he had overeaten or had similar gaseous conditions of the intestinal tract he experienced the earlier emotion of anxiety.[63]

Anxiety reactions are also "additive," so that mild fears generated in one context can be summated with mild fears generated in another, snowballing anxiety into something quite serious.[64] Wolpe also suggested that as an autonomic response anxiety is not so subject to reactive inhibition as are responses tied to the muscular activity of the more voluntary aspects of the central nervous system. Finally, of course, we have the feature of anxiety which acts as a drive. Sometimes people are propelled into self-defeating neurotic patterns because the anxiety drive-reduction achieved is "worth it" over the shorter span of experience. A person who has neurotic fears of illness may ignore ominous physical symptoms months on end simply because the thought of seeing a physician is so anxiety provoking that some other thought which suggests that he does *not* need a check-up reciprocally inhibits any move to the physician's door. Anxiety feeds on itself in this fashion, and one does not require fanciful "dynamic explanations" to account for the greater majority of neurotic illness. The theory of cure which now is invoked in opposition to the neurotic habit is best summed up by Wolpe:

If a response antagonistic to anxiety can be made to occur in the presence of anxiety-evoking stimuli so that it is accompanied by a complete or partial suppression of the anxiety responses, the bond between these stimuli and the anxiety responses will be weakened.[65]

THREE STEPS IN BEHAVIOR THERAPY

Wolpe has discussed what are essentially three steps in the therapeutic process. The *first* involves a careful elucidation of the stimulus conditions which acted as antecedents to the clinical picture.[66] The therapist must learn about the client's earlier experience not because he wants to fill in the outlines of a personality theory, but because he has to know as explicitly as possible the nature of the abnormal pattern, the kinds of stimuli which bring it about, and the circumstances under which it seems to vary. In a real sense, he is performing a "stimulus-response analysis" of the client's behavior from the outset of their contact.[67] Wolpe typically uses a detailed interview at this point, including questions about parents, siblings, school performance, and developing sexual adjustment. Each of these areas has been shown relevant to the development of anxiety in neurotic patients. Of course, the presenting problem will usually dictate the direction this clinical anamnesis will take.

It is essential to be accurate about what stimuli have been at work in the production of a neurosis, because the tactics to follow will be dictated by what this turns up. For example, one of Wolpe's female clients complained of a powerful urge to flee a feeling of being "closed in" when engaged in conversation with others. On first blush this seemed to be some form of claustrophobic response to social situations, but upon more detailed questioning Wolpe was to find that this woman felt trapped in an unhappy marriage.[68] This information put a new interpretation on the case and dictated alternative therapeutic tactics. To assist his diagnostic efforts Wolpe makes use of various paper-and-pencil devices as when he asks the client to assess his general level of anxiety in a quantifiable fashion, isolate the

sources of his fears, and estimate his level of self-sufficiency.[69] Another rather unique way in which Wolpe assesses a client's emotional status is to school him in using units of measurement called a *sud*, for "subjective unit of disturbance."[70] The client is asked to think of a scale of 100 points (suds), with the top point being the "worst fear" imaginable and the zero point representing "absolute calm." By using this measure routinely, in time the therapist can simply ask his client "How many suds would you say are involved in that scary situation?" and the client retorts with immediate clarity "Oh, about 50." The client also usually contributes spontaneous sud estimates as therapy proceeds.

The second step of therapy concerns the proper preparation of the client. The client is likely to begin blaming himself or other people for his present state. Often, he is made more anxious with the thought that he is "crazy" after all. Wolpe insists that the proper attitude for a behavior therapist is to be objective and nonjudgmental.[71] Since behavior is determined by circumstances in the neural and external environment, little is gained by trying to find the more obscure objects of "blame" for a behavioral problem. Of course, if someone in the *present* life circumstances is frustrating the client or in other ways involved in his neurosis then proper actions will have to be taken to change the nature of the relationship. But the more removed, obscure analyses so typical of psychoanalysis are unnecessary. It is not unusual for Wolpe to provide his clients with a brief discussion of the nature of reinforcement, using as an example the "burnt child."[72] A child is burned while touching a big, black, hot, coal stove. Later, his anxiety concerning big, black objects which stand in the room is generalized to the black bureau in the bedroom and so forth. The point of this "structuring" is to teach the client that anxiety reactions are automatic and—whatever their cause—amenable to the sorts of tactics he will soon be engaged in. Wolpe might even tell his client something about the experimental studies on which his techniques are founded.[73]

Despite this preparation, some clients need to be told directly in clear-cut fashion that: (a) they are not insane; (b) their neurotic responses are not all that unusual, and the therapist understands them quite well; and (c) there is no point in forcing themselves to "face" their fears because invariably these concerns have nothing whatever to do with character building. Neurotic symptoms are forms of "penance unrewarded by blessings."[74] This is an area generally known as the "relationship" between client and therapist. Since Wolpe does not believe that therapeutic effects issue from the relationship *per se,* he does not consider this issue formally. He was once treating a client and had to leave town for a time. A substitute therapist was arranged, and therapy proceeded quite satisfactorily during his absence.[75] If transference were an essential aspect of the curative process this kind of interruption would have been harmful to continued progress. There is no denying that a "relationship" may form with the client along the lines of conventional psychotherapy. The point Wolpe makes is that the behavior therapist does not curry any such tie more than, let us say, the usual doctor of internal medicine does. Whatever benefit accrues to therapy as a result of the client's faith in or affection for the therapist is taken as just so much additional benefit.[76] Wolpe would explain relationship gains as due to reciprocal inhibition in any case.

The final step of therapy is to design the proper strategy which will counteract the neurotic pattern and then put this program of change into effect. We shall now consider three therapeutic techniques Wolpe employed.

ASSERTIVE TRAINING

Some clients need instruction in how to express feeling in the life situation (*in vivo*). Wolpe refers to this as *assertive* responding, which has the connotation of aggressivity but is not to be taken so narrowly in this context. Assertive behavior includes the expression of friendliness and affection as well as irritation and hostility.[77] Certain people are brought up to consider themselves "fair game" to the intrusions of others. They have overemphasized social niceties, so that when someone pushes in ahead of them in a queue, though they sense the hostility we all do they would never think of complaining. The woman who expressed an unhappy marriage through claustrophobic feelings of being "closed in" is a case in point. Wolpe found that he had to deal with her problems through assertive training. He had to reassure her that she could make just demands on her husband, and after the specifics of the case had been worked out in the interview, he made recommendations about what she might say or do in certain situations relating to her husband. A useful technique here is that of *behavioral rehearsal,* by which Wolpe means a kind of role-play situation in which he takes the identity of some person who has been giving the client difficulty through impositions of one sort or another.[78] For example, if the woman finds herself going into a depression right after breakfast and Wolpe decides that this is due to the husband's behavior during the meal he might set up a behavior rehearsal scene. He takes the part of the husband and thus rehearses her in how to be more assertive with her mate. It might be quite difficult for her to say something like "Well, for goodness sake, *must* you constantly grumble about every little item in the newspaper? I find this very annoying, morning after morning." There is an important rule to follow in using this tactic: *"Never instigate an assertive act that is likely to have seriously punishing consequences for the patient."*[79]

Sometimes a passive individual gains an advantage when pressured by a more aggressive person by constantly staring at the latter's forehead, rather than making eye contact. People find this tactic very annoying, and the client may find himself more in control of the superior-inferior relationship than he had been earlier. Another such "lifemanship" tactic is to open a conversation with something like "Mr. Johnson, is there anything wrong? You seem a little upset (pallid, depressed) today?" Such an opening gambit, showing concern and social grace yet obviously putting one's opponent at a disadvantage in the ensuing conversation has helped more than one individual who has been under the thumb of a bully.[80]

The point here is not to make a client manipulative and insincere. He is to use such tactics in self-defense. It is also hoped that he will speak up when a proper *positive* emotion grips him as well. People with free-floating anxiety may find a reciprocal inhibition *in vivo* taking place when they say "My, that's a pretty dress you have on today" or "I really want to thank you for helping me with those packages yesterday." Expressions on all sides of the emotional spectrum are called for in *certain* cases. One does not urge these measures on all clients, as if they were a panacea for human relations. They are prescribed and developed in response to a specific need. Wolpe lists some of the common *hostile* assertive responses he teaches as being: Please don't stand in front of me; you have kept me waiting for 20 minutes; do you mind turning down (up) the heat; your behavior disgusts me; I can't stand your nagging; how dare you speak to me like that. On the more *commendatory* side he lists such remarks as: You look lovely; that was a clever remark; I like you; I love you; that was brilliantly worked out; what a radiant smile.

SYSTEMATIC DESENSITIZATION

Wolpe found that he could remove fears from his clients' behavioral repertoire by systematically increasing their anxiety responses in conjunction with antagonistic relaxation responses.[81] The detailed interview at the outset of therapy establishes the specific stimuli—social situations, actually—which evoke the anxiety. In the case of free-floating anxiety, where there has probably been a subtle form of anxiety summation, the specific stimuli may be unclear. But usually the client can differentiate between *some* situations which are more upsetting than others. He can use suds to help the therapist rank-order a series of life situations which frighten him. Let us assume that a young college man has come to Wolpe for treatment concerning an extreme fear he has when taking examinations. He becomes so anxious that his grades suffer for he is unable to concentrate in the testing situation. After a detailed clinical interview Wolpe finds that this anxiety pattern is not limited to school examinations but extends to all kinds of evaluative situations. For example, this young man is afraid to see doctors and dentists. He is gripped with uncomfortable tension when a policeman looks his way. He does not like to be asked directions by a stranger and simply having people look at him is mildly upsetting. Without going into the detail that Wolpe would at this point, a complete picture of the anxiety reactions would be specified and then rated as to sud units.

Wolpe now has the anxiety responses identified as a first step, but what response antagonistic to them shall he induce in the client? Wolpe was to find the relaxation exercises of Jacobson's *Progressive Relaxation* (1938) very useful in this regard. Jacobson had demonstrated that autonomic responses like pulse rate and blood pressure could be diminished through what he called "deep muscle relaxation." In adapting these exercises to therapy Wolpe found that roughly six interviews of 30 to 50 minutes duration are required. The client is told that in order to counteract his emotional anxiety he must master a skill in muscle relaxation. Wolpe might begin muscle training by having the client grip the arm of his chair with one hand while leaving his other relaxed. Can he sense the difference between the tense hand and the one which is relaxed? Good, then they can proceed to other muscles of the body in this fashion. How limp can he make his arms if he places both hands in his lap and simply relaxes for a few minutes? From here, they may go to the muscles of the shoulder and the neck, for these are particularly important indicators of tension level.[82] Tenseness in the facial and tongue muscles are usually easy to identify as reflecting level of anxiety. From here, they might go to the larger muscles of the back, abdomen, and thorax, and then end with a consideration of the feet and legs. Through careful study and some practice at home between sessions a client can acquire the skill of relaxing his deeper muscles quite readily.

In some instances, Wolpe may be preparing a client for hypnotism at this point. Hypnosis is closely related to relaxation, of course. Wolpe's approach to hypnosis is strictly empirical; he uses it only when a subject seems especially prone to the phenomenon of suggestion and has immediate benefit. Hypnosis is not essential for systematic desensitization to work, though Wolpe does use it in about 10 per cent of such cases.[83]

The next step involves constructing an *anxiety hierarchy*, based on the data of the interview, the objective instruments, and the help of the client: "An anxiety hierarchy is a list of stimuli on a common theme ranked in descending order according to the amount of anxiety they evoke."[84] Anxiety hierarchies can be arrayed as relaxation training is being carried out. When all of the sources of anxiety have been identified, the therapist arranges a hierarchy according to some central theme. In the case of the college student, Wolpe might construct one around the "taking of examinations," but he might also construct one around the theme of "being examined by physicians or dentists" and even one of "being scrutinized by others."[85] Here is a hierarchy built around examination fears, based on one of Wolpe's actual cases:

(Greatest Sense of Anxiety)
1. On the way to the university on the day of an examination.
2. In the process of answering an examination paper.
3. Before the unopened doors of the examination room.
4. Awaiting the distribution of examination papers.
5. The examination paper lies face down before . . . [client].
6. The night before an examination.
7. One day before an examination.
8. Two days before an examination.
9. Three days before an examination.
10. Four days before an examination.
(Least Sense of Anxiety)[86]

Not all clients would arrange precisely this hierarchy of from most-to-least anxiety reaction concerning the taking of examinations. Some might find the situation of having the examination paper lying face down before them more anxiety-provoking than—as in this case—feeling upset on the way to the university to take the examination. After we have constructed two or three (possibly more) such hierarchies and have prepared the client in muscle relaxation, the next step in systematic desensitization is to—through fantasy—place the client in the least anxiety-provoking circumstance (four days before an examination in the above example), encourage him to imagine that he is now at this point in the hierarchy and then to apply his relaxation skills until he feels perfectly calm.

Feedback from the client is important in these fantasied or hypnotically induced states. If under hypnosis, Wolpe has the client lift a finger when he is sensing any anxiety at all. If the finger is not lifted, this tells the therapist that he is completely relaxed, and for this stimulus situation at least anxiety has been successfully inhibited. In the case of imagined scenes the client may use this finger technique as well, but Wolpe found that even verbalization of the sud unit does not detract from the effectiveness of relaxation. Hence, when the client says "zero suds" he is feeling perfectly calm at whatever step in the anxiety hierarchy the therapist has been placing him. Once Wolpe had achieved this initial desensitization, he would move the client up to the next level (three days before an examination), and so forth, until gradually the most anxiety-provoking situation could be imagined without anxiety.

The therapist must exercise clinical skill in the application of such a technique. The scenes cannot be experienced for extended periods. The usual practice is to have the patient relax for a period of 15 seconds or so before inducing the scene for five to 10 seconds.[87] This brief enactment of a particular scene may be repeated several times. The more anxiety experienced by the client the shorter the scene presentation. Wolpe notes that prolonged exposure to highly anxiety-provoking scenes (as in a phobia) can lead to exacerbation of a symptom.[88] The number of scenes presented during a desensitization session also varies. In some cases only one or two exposures seems justified. In others, particularly in the advanced stages of therapy, as many as 30 to 50 presentations of five to seven seconds duration each may be encouraged. Some patients can be moved up from one scene to another in the same session. Others require concentration on one scene per session. A desensitization session ordinarily can be completed in from 15 to 30 minutes, and the length of therapy varies from as few as six to possibly 100 or more sessions. Wolpe once administered 100 sessions to a client who suffered a severe death phobia.[89]

An interesting feature of this technique is that spacing of sessions does not seem to affect outcome. As a rule, clients are scheduled for two or three sessions per week, but even when sessions are massed on the same day (when for instance a client must travel long distances to therapy on a weekend) or carried on once monthly positive results can be noted. Wolpe has shown that the rate of symptom removal

follows a clear deceleration pattern in curves of learning regardless of the time factor.[90] Very little improvement occurs between sessions.

Wolpe's technique revolutionized the practice of psychotherapy. Extensions and variations of the systematic desensitization tactic were to proliferate following Wolpe's appearance on the historical scene. Though the facts of conditioned inhibition and counterconditioning had been known for years, and John B. Watson had actually induced and then removed a fear of phobic proportions in a child using a comparable procedure,[91] it was Wolpe's example which more than any other fostered the development of the "noninsight" or "nondynamic" psychotherapies so prevalent in the latter half of the twentieth century.

Occasionally a client is not a good subject for hypnotism nor can he "imagine" situations well. In such cases the therapist may have to plan an anxiety hierarchy which can be desensitized *in vivo*. For example, airplane phobias can be worked out by systematically taking an individual closer to the airport, and then on a plane, which could well be rented and simply taxied about for a time, and so forth. Gradually, increasing approximations to flight might be engaged in on the airstrip, until an actual take-off and immediate return to earth is accomplished. Lazarus (1961) has extended the desensitization tactic to group application, working with a number of people at once, all of whom suffer from claustrophobia, agoraphobia, or sexual phobia. One highly ingenious tactic employed by Wolpe is to use an electrical (faradic) shocking device, much on the order of commercial "shocking machines" in amusement parks. Carnivals often have such an attraction, where an individual can test his mettle and see how much electroshock he can sustain. Wolpe has his subjects sustain such a shock, to the most painful point they can muster. At the zenith of their pain, he has them say "calm" and then immediately discontinues the shock. The word "calm" conditions to the feeling of relief. Subsequently, when in a life situation that is anxiety provoking, the client finds that by saying "calm" his conditioned relaxation reciprocally inhibits the anxiety he is sensing.

AVERSION THERAPY

The final technique we will consider as an example of reciprocal inhibition is not specifically a Wolpean innovation, nor was it especially popularized by him alone. He rarely considered it the first choice treatment in his own practice, except possibly in the case of drug addiction.[92] However, Wolpe has given considerable space to a discussion of this technique of *aversion therapy,* and hence we include it here. Aversion therapy or "avoidance" counterconditioning was probably first used in the control of alcoholism by Voegtlin and Lemere (1942). The treatment consisted of giving the alcoholic a nausea-producing drug, such as emetine, followed by consumption of a favored alcoholic beverage. Vomiting as a response to the emetine was thus conditioned to the taste of alcohol, and after 10 sessions of this nature it was not unusual for an individual to become severely nauseous at the smell or taste of alcohol alone. Recasting this general strategy, Wolpe viewed the process of aversion therapy as one in which an undesired response (drinking, gambling, food obsessions, etc.) is presented following the stimulus of a strong avoidance response (in the example cited, avoiding nausea). The avoidance response thus reciprocally inhibits the undesired response (avoiding nausea means avoiding drinking). The avoidant stimulus which Wolpe used in his work was electric shock.

To cite examples of this technique, Wolpe once successfully treated a woman with rheumatic heart disease who was obsessed by the thought of certain particularly harmful foods. From time to time she would lose control and go on "eating sprees" which threatened her physical health. The therapy tactic here involved making a list of all of the items of food that figured into her obsession. Electrodes were then attached to her forearms, and the woman was asked to close her eyes and to imagine each of these foods in turn, signalling with her hand when she achieved a good image. Ten faradic shocks of rather uncomfortable intensity were then administered per session for a total of five sessions. Following the second session Wolpe noted improvement and when therapy was terminated after five contacts the results were complete and lasting.[93] In another instance, a compulsive gambler was treated by Barker and Miller (1968) while actually participating in his favored game of chance. A special "one-armed bandit" was arranged in the hospital, and, as was his practice, the patient stood before this slot machine for a three-hour period. He withstood 150 shocks over this period of time, and by the end of his second three-hour period he had begun losing any desire to play. The shocks were administered during all aspects of the gambling activity, from the insertion of coin discs to receiving pay-offs. By the end of 12 hours this patient was sufficiently cured of his gambling to refrain for 18 months. A relapse at that time was easily countered by six hours of "booster" treatment.

One of the more ambitious applications of aversion therapy has been its use with homosexuals. Both emetic substances and electrical shocks have been used as the avoidant-producing stimuli.[94] Assuming that a therapist were to treat a male homosexual, the first step would be to assemble a number of pictures of men—including nudes—and to have the client array them as to preference value (though a specific hierarchy is probably not necessary in all cases). The therapist might then have the client take an emetic substance just before being presented with slide projections of the men he had found sexually stimulating. An alternative method would be to shock him as he observed the picture. The therapist might have a device whereby the patient would press a button to keep the picture of a male on the screen for a certain length of time, and the longer he would gaze at this sexual object the more severe would the shock become. In time, the sexual response stimulated by the masculine nudes would be reciprocally inhibited by the avoidant response to shock.

Clinical experience has shown that such avoidant techniques will not be successful unless the client is *also* exposed to the pleasant stimulation of heterosexual stimuli. Hence, we would have a session in which the client would be shown seductive pictures of females, in varying stages of attire including completely nude presentations. Sometimes a behavior therapist will increase the likelihood of pleasurable sexual stimulation in gazing at females by injecting his clients with 10 milligrams of a male hormone (*testosteronum propionicum*).[95] As attraction to the female increases, the client will be urged to practice masturbation in relation to female pictures, elaborating as much as possible through the use of fantasied imagery. This combined tactic of aversion with strong approach training is a good example of just how flexible the behavior therapist must be if he is to help his client. Those who would castigate him for indulging "sadistically" in shocking clients do not properly understand or accept the ground rules on which he operates. In every instance, his measure of success rests firmly on the well being of his client.

THE ROLE OF RECIPROCAL INHIBITION IN
ALL FORMS OF PSYCHOTHERAPY

We have not circumscribed all the approaches Wolpe and his followers use. For example, Wolpe uses certain drugs and even carbon dioxide as adjunctive therapy devices to relieve anxiety symptoms.[96] Taken along with all of the other approaches to psychotherapy, the panoply of behavior techniques which eventuate in successful cures forces one to ponder what all of these methods of cure have in common? It seemed to Wolpe, as he mulled this

question over, that reciprocal inhibition was more the common denominator than the variant "gimmick" some took it to be. What the so-called insight therapies have in common is that a private interview is conducted in which the patient confidentially expresses his innermost emotional reactions to a skilled expert who shows an interest in him and then proffers certain "explanatory information." Hence, claimed Wolpe: "If, in a patient, the emotional responses evoked by the interview situation is (*a*) antagonistic to anxiety and (*b*) of sufficient strength, supposedly it will reciprocally inhibit the anxiety responses that are almost certain to be evoked by some of the subject matter of the interview, and therapeutic effects will occur."[97]

This brings us back to the matter of transference. Although Wolpe dismisses this factor as central, he has noted that certain patients having a strong positive emotion toward him occasionally begin showing improvement even before the specific techniques of cure were settled on.[98] Such quick forms of "transference cure" could easily be seen as the direct results of reciprocal inhibition. Cures noted among clients placed on waiting lists may well stem from the fact that they now feel something is "going to be done," and this renewed emotional confidence can serve to inhibit anxiety.[99] Indeed, reciprocal inhibition can explain cures—even those induced by drugs—to greater theoretical satisfaction than can alternative theories explain the cures of behavior therapy.[100] Rather than superficial and secondary, behavior therapy may be said to "change personality" if by personality we mean the totality of a person's habits.[101] Symptom substitution is rarely the result, and then only when improper consideration has been given to specific autonomic responses.[102] Hence, Wolpe leaves us with a confidently expressed challenge to consider the likelihood that reciprocal inhibition is an overriding principle of explanation in the cure of *all* neuroses.

The Technique of Implosive Therapy: Thomas G. Stampfl

Not everyone who preferred the behavior therapy approach departed significantly from the lead of Dollard and Miller. One final example of a behavior therapist presents us with a thinker who did not reject the "spirit" of Freudian thought even as much as did Dollard and Miller.

BIOGRAPHICAL OVERVIEW

Thomas G. Stampfl was born in Cleveland, Ohio, on 28 December 1923. He is of German-Austrian lineage, both of his parents having immigrated to the United States from Austria. Stampfl's father was a printer by trade, a strict disciplinarian but a devoted father. His mother was the warmer parent, very supportive of her children and a hard worker. The family religion was Roman Catholic, and Stampfl has maintained an association with the more liberal, progressive wing of this faith. Stampfl was the tenth child, with eight sisters and a brother preceding him; one sister died in infancy. The brother was 10 years his senior, an outstanding athlete whom Stampfl found himself trying to compete with despite the large disparity in age.

As the youngest child Stampfl received considerable attention in the family. His youth traversed the "Great Depression" years of the 1930s, but fortunately his father's trade was in demand and the family remained economically self-sufficient. Stampfl rebelled against his father's authoritarian ways, causing some friction in the home, but no actual physical punishment resulted. He took up the hobby of magic and sleight-of-hand as a boy; he also became a superior gymnast during high-school years. But his main interests were intellectual pursuits.

The impact of the depression years contributed to Stampfl's decision while in high school to become a printer. But events were greatly to alter his life. He graduated from high school in 1942, during the period of World War II. In March of 1943 he volunteered for the Army paratroopers, eventually earning the rank of Staff Sergeant in the 82nd Airborne Division. Stampfl was wounded in the Battle of the Bulge and hospitalized for three months in England before returning to America where he was eventually discharged.

With the help of the GI Bill (government-supported higher education) Stampfl was able to think seriously of a career in psychology, an interest which slowly developed during his maturing years. He attended John Carroll University in Cleveland, receiving his B.A. in 1949, and then subsequently earning his M.A. (1953) and Ph.D. (1958) degrees at Loyola University in Chicago, Illinois. While in Chicago Stampfl also took courses in Rogerian client-centered counseling. He was particularly inspired and helped by Elaine Dorfman and Eugene T. Gendlin. In the meantime, he had developed great interest in the learning theory of Clark Hull and had also worked for a year in psychoanalysis, with special emphasis on Fenichel. His major clinical professor, Frank J. Kobler, convinced Stampfl of the necessity of basing clinical work on laboratory investigation. Later, he found intellectual stimulation in the two-factor theory of O. H. Mowrer and the general outlook on abnormality represented in the work of Maslow and Mittlemann (1951). His highly varied, integrative educational background included both the classroom and the consulting room.

From 1952 to 1954 Stampfl held the position of Director at the Newman School for Severely Mentally Retarded Children (Chicago). It was there that Stampfl began to note how important the expression of emotion was to a child's personal adjustment. Over the years, working with various neurotic and psychotic children in play therapy, Stampfl found that children seemed to "whip up" emotion in their play. This often took on gruesome prospects, as boiling a parent in vats of acid, sending siblings off to burn in hell, and so forth. Therapeutic results were more likely to take place when such emotional displays were generated by the child than when they were not in evidence. Stampfl was fully aware of Freud's early abreactive techniques. He believed that the early psychoanalytical efforts in the Breuer period were probably closer to what therapy really amounted to than were those of the later "couch" period—which became enmeshed in the more debatable aspects of insight.

Stampfl had married in 1950 shortly after beginning graduate school, and as he worked his way through the graduate years he decided to return to his home town of Cleveland, where he accepted a position as Chief Psychologist in a Catholic Child Guidance Clinic. He also

Thomas G. Stampfl

began an association with John Carroll University as instructor, and over the next dozen years or so was to build his clinical acumen, take the Ph.D. degree, and formulate the essentials of "implosive therapy." He fathered two children and eventually relocated in Milwaukee, Wisconsin, where he became professor of psychology and Director of Clinical Psychology Training at the University of Wisconsin (Milwaukee). During an academic hiatus in the 1960–1966 period he was in private practice as a psychotherapist.

As he perfected his therapeutic approach Stampfl felt increasingly that he needed more empirical justification for its effectiveness. In part due to this need Stampfl returned to academia on a full-time basis to take up further study of *avoidance conditioning,* with rats as his subjects of study. Stampfl never denies the possibility that "dynamic" factors in neurosis may trigger a symptom picture of some sort (as an "anxiety" reaction); however, the strictly therapeutic principles on which his therapy rest do *not* require a dynamic explanation. Hence, Stampfl's belief is that the best source of evidence for implosive therapy is in experimentation on lower animals. Stampfl is quite "toughminded" on the question of research, though his broader outlook is flexible and open to alternative explanations of the neurotic process. One senses the honest effort to keep all sides of psychology open in his writings. The scientific base is clearly the laboratory, but the clinical setting has much to reveal as well.

THEORETICAL CONSIDERATIONS

LEARNING THEORY AND THE PRINCIPLE OF EXPERIMENTAL EXTINCTION

The principle of learning which Stampfl uses to explain his therapeutic effectiveness is *experimental extinction.* Though all behavioral therapists make use of this construct to some extent, Stampfl raised it to its highest level, building on the earlier work of O. H. Mowrer. Mowrer was one of Hull's students, and he more than anyone developed the thesis that *reduction in anxiety* could serve as a reinforcement.[103] As the presentations of Chapters 6 and 7 have demonstrated, this concept has been of inestimable value to the explanations of symptom formation. Mowrer has a theory of neurosis and cure well worth study in its own right.[104] Space allows consideration of only one small aspect of Mowrer's work relevant to Stampfl's, a classical paper entitled "Learning Theory and the Neurotic Paradox" (1948), in which he demonstrates his considerable ability to parallel animal study with human behavior in an instructive fashion.

Mowrer drew an analogy between various types of rat experiments and the form of vicious circle in which the neurotic finds himself daily. One such experiment went as follows: picture a long "runway" type of cage in which there are essentially three separate areas of floor space. Referring to the floor of the cage in left-to-right spatial terms we might speak of area A, area B, and area C. Additional features of the cage include electrical grids set into the floor of areas A and B so that a shock can be given to any rat in these areas of the runway. Area C, on the other hand, lacks a grid and thus can always be considered a "haven" area if the experimenter turns on the electricity over the floor areas A and B.

The experiment which Mowrer designed involved placing a rat on the floor area we have termed A, and then after a brief period of time (during which the rat sniffed about the runway walls and so forth) electrifying the grids over areas A and B. The rat naturally responded with vigorous exploratory behavior to the painful stimulus of the shock. In dashing about, rats (several animals were put through the apparatus) quickly learned to find area C where relief from pain was forthcoming. The reduction in pain presumably acted as a *primary* reinforcement to the learning of the sequential responses "run from A to C by way

of B." Additionally, reasoned Mowrer, there were surely *secondary* reinforcements which could have contributed to this learning sequence. Upon reaching the C area there was probably a reduction in pain (primary reinforcement) but *also* a reduction in fear anxiety (secondary reinforcement). If this is true, then possibly one could sustain the running "from A through B to C" even though we might stop applying electrical shock to the floor of area A.

This is what Mowrer did and, as expected, the rats continued to run out of area A, over to area C. But in so doing, they also ran across an area B *which had its electrical grid on!* The rat was thus actually shocking itself as it ran from a quiescent area A, across a live grid on area B, to the area of conditioned anxiety reduction, area C. This paradoxical outcome was, said Mowrer, analogous to the neurotic who constantly keeps his symptoms alive due to the recurring anxiety which he creates for himself. Mowrer found that he could eliminate this self-punishing behavior only when he had placed a block between the B and C areas in the second phase of his study. When blocked from proceeding to area C, and hence forced to dash back to A, the rat rapidly discontinued its self-defeating behavior—usually on one trial. Why did this happen?—presumably because the response of running to anxiety *extinguished* thanks to the barrier which forced a more realistic learning to proceed.

It was out of researches such as these that Mowrer fashioned his two-factor theory of learning. He proposed that some forms of learning can be considered *problem-solving* activities, mediated by the central nervous system and tied to the skeletal musculature of the body making responses in this domain under what we usually call "voluntary" or conscious control. An alternative form of learning, however, is *conditioning*. In this instance the responses are tied to the smooth musculature and visceral tissues of the autonomic nervous system. Conditioned responses are thus *not* under voluntary control. Fear or anxiety reactions, depressions, the pain of guilt or the delight of love, all such emotional reactions on which a "lie detector" (polygraph) relies to catch us up in spite of ourselves can be considered conditioned responses (literally, "conditionable" because they are part of our innate equipment). In Mowrer's study, the reason neurotic behavior is self-defeating or "stupid" (*re* Dollard and Miller, Chapter 6) is because it is mediated by the conditioned responses of the autonomic nervous system. Problem-solving behavior is called for but cannot take place until the autonomic responses are first extinguished in some fashion. Once we have removed the grip of the latter on our behavior we can expect the former to find a more suitable level of adjustment.

THEORY OF ILLNESS AND CURE

Stampfl then put together the two-factor theory of Mowrer with his observations of children in play therapy, whose behavior mounts to a frenzy at times and then seems to improve dramatically. He recalled the early successes of Freud and Breuer with the abreactive technique (pp. 28–29). An old truism among practicing psychotherapists warns that a therapy session has not gone well unless the client has actually invested some emotion in the hour. It makes no difference whether this emotion is affection, fear, or anger. Just so there is an investment of feeling. Taking this conviction further, Stampfl wondered: Could the affective factors mediated by the autonomic nervous system run their course and eventually extinguish in emotionally provoking circumstances which do *not* lead to punishment? What if, instead of trying to calm the client, we were to encourage an expression of the pent-up feelings he is too terrified to feel?

An *implosion* is a "bursting inwards," in contrast to the outward bursting of an explosion. Hence, implosive therapy implies that emotive reactions are erupting, but their expression is "internal to" the individual's self-

identity, that is, within his imagination or fantasy. Emotion is displayed, but action is entirely at the verbal level, supplemented greatly by imagery. In other words, *primary* reinforcements or punishments do not follow re-enactment of emotionally arousing scenes. When he defines his approach, Stampfl places emphasis on the potentially unifying aspects it affords: "Implosive therapy (IT) is an approach which incorporates formulations inherent to dynamic systems of treatment re-translated and reapplied in terms of learning principles; dynamically oriented clinicians need not relinquish their fundamental conceptions of the human situation to use it."[105]

The theory of illness on which implosive therapy rests is essentially as follows: For any of a number of reasons—including all of the typically Freudian explanations—the individual has been emotionally conditioned (via autonomic nervous system) to some stimulus in his environment. Whenever this stimulus comes into view—through imagination, a dream, or actual experience—he is gripped with a sense of mounting anxiety (fear). As this level of anxiety increases it acts as a portent of the horrible things which are likely to happen. Stampfl notes that Freud's final formulation of anxiety as a "warning signal" is very apropos. Rather than permitting the anxiety state to reach complete expression the individual has learned to do something which will lower the level of anxiety. This "something" is what we know as either a host of defense mechanisms or the symptoms of neurosis.[106] Such behaviors are aimed at avoiding the impending doom which the autonomic responses suggest are about to take place. Probably the most common defense mechanism is what Freud had called *repression*.[107] The individual learns to forget what raises his anxiety level, and when this forgetting results in lowered anxiety he finds himself in a situation of sustaining ignorance, much along the lines of Dollard and Miller's "stupidity."

Symptoms, on the other hand, are simply the

more dramatic and personally harmful extensions of this mechanism for reducing anxiety. Technically we would call them "conditioned avoidance responses."[108] The person with a phobia sees the feared object—be it a high place, a closed-in space, a snake, or speck of dirt—and he is gripped with anxiety until he puts distance between himself and the feared stimulus. Or, if this stimulus has "come to mind," he must get it out of mind by doing something to remove the preoccupation. The compulsive must wash his hands to counteract his horror over dirt. The obsessive must hum a "lucky tune" or repeat some magic formula which seems to calm him for a time. Hysterical body tics and even paranoid delusions can all be learned methods of reducing such anxiety promptings. An interesting feature of Stampflian theory holds that the symptom may have "symbolic" ties to the origin of the neurosis. When the stimulus arises and a symptom reaction occurs, a host of unknown or forgotten (repressed) thoughts, memories, and images are *redintegrated*.[109] To redintegrate is to re-open or re-enliven past cues of an anxiety-provoking nature. This is the reason anxiety seems to snowball when the neurotic is placed in a threatening situation. The claustrophobic is responding not only to the present cues but to other long-forgotten cues as well.

This teaches us something about neurotic symptoms. The reason they are retained in a behavioral repertoire is because they effectively offset the return to mind of a host of other even more fearful stimuli. The claustrophobic flees the elevator stimulus, with its four walls pressing in on him, long before he begins to recall the more dynamic memories of a fear that he was being abandoned by his parents and "buried" in the blankets and bed clothes of his infant crib (crib symbolizing rejection). Hence, the level of anxiety experienced by an individual in any given situation is a rough measure of the *relevance* of this situation to his neurosis. Relevant situations redintegrate more anxiety than irrelevant situations.

This is why Stampfl feels that: "The symptom usually tells us what the patient is avoiding."[110] If we press the neurotic in the general area of the symptom and block his attempts to flee, in time a series of meaningful cues will emerge to tell us more and more about what has provoked his neurosis in the first place. It is thus possible to distinguish between two types of cues in neurosis: first, the *symptom contingent cues,* which might be something so simple as the sight of a tall building; second, the *hypothesized conditioned aversive cues,* which relate to what we have been calling the symbolic or dynamic meaning tied to the neurosis. The former essentially redintegrate the latter.[111]

The dynamics of symptom formation and redintegration can be demonstrated by reviewing one of Stampfl's earliest cases, concerning a young man who suffered from a compulsion to make certain his radio was turned off before going to sleep at night.[112] He came to Stampfl, complaining that he found it necessary to check this fact as many as 50 times per night before he could doze off. Pulling out the electric plug did not help, and the symptom seemed to be getting worse. When asked what he felt might happen if the radio were left on the young man replied that he experienced a subjective feeling that something terrible or catastrophic would happen—possibly a fire which would consume him in its flames. Rather than reassure him or teach him to relax in proximity to radios, Stampfl instructed this young man to go to bed that night imagining that the radio was actually on, or to turn it on so that he was certain it was alive with electricity. Then, he was to lie in bed and imagine that a spark from the radio produced a tiny flame which would get bigger and bigger, until the room would become engulfed in a general conflagration and he would be burned up. Stampfl encouraged his patient to imagine this entire scene as vividly as possible and to experience fully the anxiety it would provoke.

In the next therapy session this young man reported that he had followed Stampfl's instructions, and, though the image of the fire was fearsome, he had found great relief from his compulsion immediately following it. He was able to fall asleep without the recurring round of radio checks. Further, he told of an interesting phenomenon which had happened at the height of the imagined fire. He heard his father's voice calling to him, over the roar of the flames. He had not mentioned his father up to this time, and Stampfl was to learn on subsequent questioning that the boy's father had been a stickler for security measures in the home. Such things as lights left on, dripping faucets, or running electrical appliances sent the father into a rage which invariably resulted in punishment of the hapless child who was the cause of the oversight. At the very least, the father would devote much time to lecturing his children on the horrifying consequences of such careless acts.

Though Stampfl did not feel insight to such factors was essential for a cure, he did accept the likelihood that a Freudian or Adlerian analysis of this family structure could well account for the boy's symptom. This boy may have sensed a death wish on the part of the father; the father wanted his son dead but expressed it through an obsessive preoccupation with "safety" procedures (reaction formation). Even if this were the dynamic cause of the case, the practical factor which sustained the symptom today was the fact that by checking his radio the young man could gain a sense of protective relief from mounting anxiety ("I will not die"). This reduction in anxiety sustained the abnormal pattern and *also* prevented a redintegration of the broader clinical dynamics (father hostility, rejection, the need to defend the self, the need to make the father guilty for his hostility by killing the self in a fire, and so on).

By encouraging the boy to experience his anxiety when no punishment resulted—a fire did not start—Stampfl found that the autonomic reactions quickly extinguished. After a few such practiced self-destructions this young man

lost his radio compulsion completely. There was no "warning sign" to begin the compulsion at bed time because permitting anxiety full expression interrupted the triggering mechanism. This is the essential theory of cure: "The fundamental hypothesis is that a sufficient condition for the extinction of anxiety is to re-present, reinstate, or symbolically reproduce the stimuli (cues) to which the anxiety response has been conditioned, in the absence of primary reinforcement."[113] Extinction follows, and the symptom is removed. Even though Stampfl believed that psychodynamic factors were often involved in neurotic conditions, the point of his therapy is that one need not base a cure on such "insights."[114] The insight is secondary to the cure, which can be thought of in entirely mechanical, learning-theory terms. One possible exception to this rule of cure is in the cases of somewhat more severe behavioral disturbances. In such cases, it is more likely that implosive tactics will have to be supplemented with the insights of a psychodynamic approach.[115] It is, of course, difficult to separate insight from what is happening to the client during the implosive procedures. If the young man hears his father's voice calling him, regardless of what the therapist may do formally, a certain amount of soul-searching recollection (accompanying redintegration) will doubtless take place.

THE STEPS OF IMPLOSIVE THERAPY

Out of his early successes of the sort described above and considerable experience with various types of client, Stampfl worked out a procedure of therapy which took the form of seven steps.[116] These are not to be followed mechanically and deviations or additions are allowed according to client needs. But the steps do provide a framework for study.

1. *Symptom Study*. The first step in therapy entails a careful study of the symptoms. The therapist attempts to identify as many of the symptom-contingent factors as he can. What

things frighten the patient? When is he likely to feel the most anxious? What sorts of things relieve his feeling of discomfort? It is usually possible to determine that a symptom has been successful for some time, and that only recently has a symptom failure led to the redintegration of the more speculative, conditioned aversive cues.[117] This would result in more severe discomfort due to the exacerbation of anxiety, and hence the client would come to therapy for relief.

Stampfl did not feel the therapist must accept only what the client told him regarding the nature of the symptom. Though he focuses on symptom removal, the therapist can make appropriate "guesses" about what is involved in the neurotic condition.[118] A classical psychoanalytical hunch on the part of the therapist may come in handy. This does not mean that a therapist must provide his insight—as a therapist—to the client in order for him to be cured. But he might press a client in some area based upon his professional hypotheses concerning the underlying conditioned aversive cues which prompt his symptomatology. For example, if an excessively prudish woman comes in with a handwashing compulsion he might actively speculate about why this symptom originally arose. If in clinical discussion with the client he surmises that this woman has a problem with sexuality, he may suspect that her concern about cleanliness may date back to a time when she manipulated her own genitals and felt the abhorrence of "sin" intermingled with the physical thrill of sexuality. She might even have been thinking of her father as sex object at the time. He notes that each time he approaches the topic of sex in the interview, and particularly masturbation, this woman (she may be married or unmarried) becomes very uneasy. He puts this down as one of the areas in which anxiety will have to be provoked, since the very fact that the topic increases anxiety is *prima facie* evidence that the area of sex is tied to the area of "being clean."

2. *Training in Neutral Imagery.* Since imagined scenes will be crucial to therapy it is desirable to spend some time training a client to formulate imagery. Stampfl views images as hypothetical constructs which the therapist presumes the client is actually "seeing" or experiencing in his own psychological sphere.[119] It is possible, of course, to check on the client's imagery through verbal means, and one can also measure emotional changes through use of galvanic skin response measures, heart rate, breathing rate, and so forth, to prove that an autonomic response consistent with imagination is taking place. At this point a therapist would be teaching the client to imagine predominantly pleasant or neutral stimulus situations. Not everyone is skilled at imagining situations, and some people cannot be treated in this fashion at all. But for the majority of the cases, having a client imagine scenes from his hometown or the faces of people from his present or past life can help him develop this facility. This procedure may take only a portion of one session or it may require a few sessions to prepare the client for visual, sensory, and even auditory imagination. It is not unusual for implosive therapy to begin with actual deconditioning procedures after two clinical interviews, a portion of one such interview having been given over to imagery preparation.[120]

3. *Introduction of the Avoidance Serial Cue Hierarchy (ASCH).* Based upon his study of the symptoms in the clinical interview, the therapist may arrange a hierarchy of avoidance images in serial order at this point. The technical term for this arrangement is the *avoidance serial cue hierarchy (ASCH)*, which runs serially from the least to the most anxiety-provoking situations in a person's experience.[121] The client need not be told about the particular steps of this hierarchy, since some highly upsetting scenes may be depicted at its apex. For example in the case of the woman with the handwashing compulsion a therapist might

begin at a very low level of anxiety, introducing scenes of witnessing dirt, then muck and mire; gradually, the greater anxiety-provoking scene of putting her hands into the filth might be called out. Then she might picture her hands festering from germs due to the filth—and possibly now including gore—when implosion would be induced. At the very highest levels are the scenes of actual masturbation, with horrified discovery by loved ones or neighbors, possibly even sinful denunciation by ministers or even supernatural figures (Judgment Day) included. At this point in therapy the scenes are merely arrayed by the therapist for future reference. It is also possible that a scene will be suggested by subsequent events—as in the client's spontaneous reactions—while actual implosion is underway.

4. *Scene Presentation.* The next step involves placing the client, as fully and realistically as possible, in each of the scenes the therapist has arranged for him, working up the *ASCH*. It is not unusual for the therapist to prepare his client for this procedure by explaining in fairly simple terms the avoidance-conditioning model on which it rests. He should make the point that in order to extinguish anxiety it must first be stimulated and experienced fully. Hence, as the therapist begins to introduce the least frightening scenes he encourages the client "to experience as much anxiety as possible."[122] The client is also encouraged to concentrate attention on the sensations of anxiety *per se,* since some of the reason anxiety snowballs may be because the anxiety responses themselves act as secondary cues to further anxiety stimulation. As he comes to know (problem solving) what anxiety stimulation is like and as the autonomic responses extinguish, there is less and less likelihood that the recurrent "vicious cycle" in the future will be triggered. In other words there is an assumption that as clients ascend the *ASCH* a generalization of extinction is taking place from the least to the most anxiety-provoking

situations. The fact that not *only* symptom-contingent cues are used in the *ASCH* is made plain in the following quote, which also adds some insight into what constitute the most frightening scenes:

The cues found most anxiety eliciting usually center about the expression of hostility and aggression directed toward parental figures, retaliation for aggressive acts by the patient with cues depicting various degrees of bodily injury, and those related to experiences of rejection, deprivation, abandonment, helplessness, guilt, shame, and sex. Oedipal, anal, oral, sibling-rivalry, primal scene, and death-wish impulse themes are worked into the hypothesized ASCH, along with the introduction of "acceptance of conscience" cues and other areas somewhat neglected by psychodynamically oriented therapies.[123]

By *acceptance of conscience cues* Stampfl refers to the nagging sense of sinfulness people feel for behaviors in which they have indulged (Mowrer also develops this in his "integrity therapy" approach, 1961). Rather than reassure them and teach them that they are wrongfully upset about such superego problems, Stampfl places them securely in the guilt-laden situation and calls out the appropriate anxiety. This image might be a courtroom scene with all of the relatives present and a great deal of descriptive rendering of just how evil the person has been.[124] The court might then find the person guilty and punish him in some way, such as by hanging or the electric chair. This theme is continued through to the very act of execution. As suggested previously, for a religious involvement the individual might come before God, where a full confession and punishment might be part of the scene—possibly closing with a horrible vision of bubbling in the fires of hell! Of course, these scenes would probably be at the very top of the *ASCH*.

5. *Scene Repetition to Anxiety Reduction.* The role of therapist in this implosive process is to

describe the scenes in as complete and realistic detail as possible. The naive observer might feel that the therapist is simply trying to "scare the Devil" out of the client—by any means. But this would be a great misperception since the point of the therapy is to deal with *relevant* scenes. The therapist has no desire to punish the client, only to help extinguish the cues which are clearly related (symptom contingent) and those which are peripherally related (conditioned aversive) to the vicious cycle of neurosis.[125] If clients were being punished or lastingly upset by the procedure, they would not return. Actually, the relief obtained from the first few sessions is noticeably helpful to the client, so he continues the treatment as he continues painful dental or medical treatments.[126]

Scenes can be presented and elaborated for as long as 10 minutes. The autonomic responsiveness (perspiration, breathing rate, etc.) dictates the success which a particular scene is having in arousing anxiety, and each scene is presented until anxiety reduction is achieved. For example, an acrophobic patient (fears high places) would be initiated by simply looking at a high building, off in the distance. The therapist would emphasize the height of the building until the patient could visualize this aspect clearly. Next, the patient would walk toward the building, closer and closer, then enter, ascend the stairs, higher and higher, until he came to the very roof. Each scene along the way would be detailed to give him the greatest sense of realism. The therapist would sense his expected reactions and describe them in terrifying detail. For example: "You feel that ripple of fright down your arms as you climb the stairs. It is getting harder to breathe as you ascend, and your heart is beating so rapidly that you think it will burst. You feel that wrenching in the pit of your stomach and want to vomit. You stop, full of perspiration, and grip the bannister. You feel faint. Now you do vomit, and as you see the vomit spilling down the stairwell you picture yourself

falling. Your foot slips, and dangles dangerously over the edge of the stairwell." And so it goes, a rather grizzly prospect for anyone, yet especially upsetting for someone who fears height.

6. *Elaboration of the Symptom Contingent Cues to Hypothesized Conditioned Aversive Cues.* It is at about this point that psychodynamic material, or simply extravagant and unreal scenes, may be introduced. The acrophobic might be taken up onto the roof, led to the edge, dropped over it and squashed on the pavement below in as gory a scene of bone-crunching, blood-spurting reality as the therapist can muster. Great attention must be paid to details in this description since the client should experience emotion to its fullest *without* primary negative reinforcements (punishment) taking place.

7. *Training the Patient to Manage His Own Therapy.* A unique feature of implosive therapy is the practice of having the patient work through the scenes of his *ASCH* at home between sessions with the therapist. This form of "homework" speeds up the process of extinction and also permits the client to use implosive tactics *in vivo,* as we saw in the case of the radio compulsion.

SOME FINAL CONSIDERATIONS

Although the clearest demonstration of implosive therapy occurs in treating a phobia, an anxiety state, or possibly an obsessive-compulsive neurotic, Stampfl does not feel that his technique must be confined to such cases. This approach can be used to treat a host of symptom pictures, and the actual limitations of the approach depend more upon the astuteness of the therapist in isolating the symptom than they do on the inherent nature of the therapeutic procedure. For example, a depressed individual may experience a modicum of anxiety reduction through avoiding various past scenes in his life which he found very traumatic. He sensed guilt for some action years back, avoided it through repression, and now the "pangs of conscience" assault him. Or, he sensed rejection by loved ones, repressed these thoughts and the hostility they aroused, and now this hostility is turned inward as a form of self-depreciation. By having him now confront an *ASCH* built around his self-degradations (the court scene described above) or built around scenes of great hostility and killing, it is possible to extinguish the anxiety which has been attached to either of these underlying reasons for his depression. Experience has taught Stampfl that situational cues having dynamic import usually center on any one of the following designations: aggression, punishment, oral, anal, or sexual material, rejection, bodily injury, loss of control, acceptance of conscience, and autonomic or central nervous system reactivity.[127] Hence, regardless of what the syndrome diagnosis is, any case having such features can be approached through the implosive technique.

Though many of the *ASCH* scenes are based directly on the symptom, and Stampfl also recommends that one might begin implosion by using a traumatic situation from out of the client's past or possibly one of his recurring dreams, it is not essential that every scene be historically true. The client does not have to believe or accept every scene as directly based on his life to benefit from the implosive experience.[128] An admission from the client that material introduced into the scenes actually applies to him is unnecessary. Unlike Wolpe's hierarchy, which is constructed with the client's assistance and judgment of relevance, the Stampflian hierarchy is arrayed and even altered spontaneously based upon the therapist's clinical judgments. Scenes may last for several minutes, or they may be changed within a minute—possibly through the introduction of new features into the action which is taking place. One is looking at a fear-provoking snake in the scene. He is then made to approach it in imagery, to pick it up, to place it

around his neck. Now the snake bites him, tears out an eyeball, and the blood gushes down his cheek as the snake thrusts itself into his cranial cavity, and so forth. Precisely how rapidly the therapist develops a scene in this fashion depends upon the clinical cues of the patient, his physiological reactions, and his general demeanor.

Overcoming *resistance* to therapy is rarely a major factor because the benefits of the procedure are immediately felt by the client. A therapy series rarely lasts beyond 30 hours.[129] There are certain personality types which are least amenable to the procedure. Stampfl notes that someone with an extremely rigid superego often rejects the imaginary scenes based on moral principle. Others with various character disorders resist the procedure because they cannot sustain any form of discomfort at all. Psychotic patients also prove difficult cases as a result of their general disorientation which detracts from proper cooperation.

Finally, implosion can be an adjunct to otherwise successful insight therapy. It has been used successfully in cases where, following a period of one year of insight therapy, some nagging symptom, such as an anxiety attack, has persisted at a much reduced level. The client has improved dramatically, but still occasionally suffers from some remnant anxiety. Implosive tactics can be introduced even at this late date to extinguish such self-sustaining or free-floating feelings of anxiety.

Notes

1. Dollard and Miller, 1950, p. 350. 2. *Ibid.*, p. 168. 3. Skinner, 1967, p. 412. 4. *Ibid.*, p. 387. 5. Skinner, 1963a, p. 506. 6. *Ibid.*, p. 513. 7. Evans, 1968, p. 33. 8. *Ibid.*, p. 35. 9. Skinner, 1967, p. 403. 10. Evans, 1968, p. 46. 11. Skinner, 1961, 1971. 12. Skinner, 1960. 13. *Ibid.*, p. 36. 14. Pressey, 1926. 15. Skinner, 1968. 16. Skinner, 1956, p. 231. 17. Evans, 1968, p. 88. 18. *Ibid.*, p. 20.

19. *Ibid.*, p. 88. 20. Skinner, 1948, p. 53. 21. Rogers and Skinner, 1956, p. 1059. 22. Rogers, 1963, pp. 271–272. 23. Evans, 1968, p. 19. 24. Skinner, 1963a, p. 514. 25. Skinner, 1957, pp. 458–459. 26. *Ibid.*, p. 460. 27. Evans, 1968, p. 107. 28. *Ibid.*, p. 22. 29. Especially Boring, 1946, p. 177. 30. Ullmann and Krasner, 1965, p. 22. 31. Eysenck, 1952; Rachman, 1963. 32. Skinner, Solomon, and Lindsley, 1954. 33. Ullmann and Krasner, 1965. 34. Evans, 1968, pp. 41–44. 35. *Ibid.*, p. 44. 36. e.g. Atthowe and Krasner, 1968. 37. Skinner, 1957, p. 14. 38. *Ibid.* 39. *Ibid.*, pp. 13–14. 40. Krasner, 1962. 41. Krasner, 1965. 42. Wolpe, 1958, p. 37. 43. *Ibid.*, p. 16. 44. *Ibid.*, p. 19. 45. *Ibid.*, pp. 3–4. 46. *Ibid.*, p. 3. 47. *Ibid.*, p. 5. 48. *Ibid.*, p. 20. 49. *Ibid.*, p. 8. 50. *Ibid.* 51. *Ibid.* 52. Wolpe, 1960, p. 88. 53. Wolpe, 1958, pp. 23–24. 54. *Ibid.*, p. 43. 55. *Ibid.*, p. 26. 56. *Ibid.*, p. 28. 57. *Ibid.*, p. 29. 58. *Ibid.*, p. 30. 59. *Ibid.*, p. 139. 60. *Ibid.*, p. 32. 61. *Ibid.*, p. 33. 62. *Ibid.*, p. 34. 63. *Ibid.*, p. 35. 64. *Ibid.*, p. 63. 65. *Ibid.*, p. 71. 66. Wolpe, 1969, p. 23. 67. *Ibid.*, p. 22. 68. *Ibid.*, p. 142. 69. *Ibid.*, p. 28. 70. *Ibid.*, p. 116. 71. *Ibid.*, p. 55. 72. *Ibid.*, p. 57. 73. *Ibid.*, p. 58. 74. *Ibid.*, p. 60. 75. *Ibid.*, pp. 244–245. 76. *Ibid.*, p. 13. 77. *Ibid.*, p. 61. 78. *Ibid.*, p. 68. 79. *Ibid.*, p. 67. 80. *Ibid.*, p. 70. 81. Wolpe, 1958, p. 139. 82. Wolpe, 1969, p. 103. 83. *Ibid.*, p. 123. 84. *Ibid.*, p. 107. 85. *Ibid.*, p. 118. 86. *Ibid.*, p. 117. 87. *Ibid.*, p. 127. 88. *Ibid.* 89. *Ibid.*, p. 131. 90. *Ibid.*, pp. 134–135. 91. Watson and Rayner, 1920. 92. Wolpe, 1969, p. 200. 93. *Ibid.*, p. 204. 94. Freund, 1960; Feldman and MacCulloch, 1967. 95. Freund, 1960, p. 317. 96. Wolpe, 1969, Chapter IX. 97. Wolpe, 1958, p. 193. 98. *Ibid.*, p. 194. 99. *Ibid.*, p. 198. 100. Wolpe, 1960. 101. Wolpe, 1969, p. 277. 102. *Ibid.* 103. Mowrer, 1939. 104. See especially Mowrer, 1961. 105. Stampfl and Levis, 1967a, p. 497. 106. Stampfl and Levis, 1968, p. 34. 107. *Ibid.* 108. Stampfl and Levis, 1967b, p. 24. 109. *Ibid.* 110. Stampfl, 1966, p. 14. 111. Stampfl and Levis, 1969. 112. Stampfl and Levis, 1966. 113. Stampfl and Levis, 1967a, pp. 498–499. 114. *Ibid.*, p. 499. 115. Stampfl and Levis, 1968, p. 33. 116. Stampfl and Levis, 1967b, p. 26. 117. Stampfl and Levis, 1968, p. 32. 118. Stampfl, 1966, p. 19. 119. Stampfl and Levis, 1969. 120. Stampfl, 1966, p. 15. 121. Stampfl and Levis, 1967a, p. 500. 122. Stampfl and Levis, 1967b, p. 26. 123. Stampfl and Levis, 1967a, p. 501. 124. Stampfl and Levis, 1969. 125. *Ibid.*, p. 101. 126. *Ibid.*, p. 100. 127. Stampfl and Levis, 1966. 128. *Ibid.*, p. 10. 129. Stampfl and Levis, 1967a, p. 502.

8

Theory Construction in Sullivanian and Behavioristic Thought

The Drift to a Lockean Model in American Academic Psychology

The advance of astronomy, physics, chemistry, and biology since the beginning of the seventeenth century has heralded a remarkable wave of technical and mechanical progress for mankind. It hardly seems necessary to document the great hold which modern "natural" science has on the academic intellect—particularly in America where, as we have seen in the previous three chapters, the rise of an empirical psychology has resulted in an image of man departing in significant ways from analytical conceptualizations. Dollard and Miller once noted that the direction psychology is taking with increasing methodological sophistication is toward "the status of a natural science."[1] The rise of behaviorism and thence all learning theories was a profound attempt to keep psychology within the realm of the natural sciences. Sullivan's changing theoretical style was also pitched in this direction, although not to the extent of the behaviorists. Now, in its advance, natural science has repeatedly disproved or at least cast doubt on much of what earlier men had accepted without question. Skinner has properly said that as science advances "it strips men of fancied achievements,"[2] such as when Copernicus and Darwin altered man's role in the universe by making him just another animal on a minor planet.

One of the major "fancied achievements" which behaviorism was to strip from man was the belief that he had power over his behavior through self-identity. Up until John Watson's time (p. 285) psychology had been predicated in large measure on an *introspective* principle. The aim of psychological study was to describe through a *method* (a way of establishing proof) of introspection how we experienced sensations of color, tone, and so forth. The concept of a *mental event,* which somehow predetermined psychological experience in the Kantian sense was routinely accepted. Here is how one early introspectionist defined his area of study: ". . . psychology is the science of mind—of the mental life and mental development of the individual man."[3] The introspective method relied upon self-observations, a kind of looking at oneself as an object of study which Hugo Munsterberg once defined as the "internal microscope of attention."[4]

However, not all introspective methods wound up supporting introspective theories! One could describe a physical sensation of some sort which seemed to be taking shape in awareness without relying on an introspective theoretical perspective. The sensation is felt happening to one "here," no question of that; but it is "happening to" one "from over there." Such a mechanistic account may have little to say on the self-identity which experiences the actual (Kantian) *phenomena.* As we shall see in Chapters 9 and 10, a phenomenologist is always introspective *as a theorist.* An introspectionist might or might not write a truly introspective theory, even though his method of pressing evidence is introspective. We know from the Introduction that it is essential to distinguish between methods and theories in this way. Even so, it is likely that if a psychologist feels that introspective methods are useful he will be more open to the possibility of introspective theories as well. Events were to discredit introspection as a method, due in large measure to its ultimate reliance on procedural evidence.[5] Watson carried on a vigorous attack against the introspective method, elevating the more extraspective approaches of conventional science in his dictum: "Psychology as the behaviorist views it is a purely objective branch of natural science."[6]

The practical effect of this rejection of an introspective *method* was that introspective *theory* was also considered less than scientific.

Natural science had never called for an introspective formulation of events, of course, since admittedly no "psyche" existed in inanimate events. But can we capture an organism *with* a psyche—a means for knowing, grasping, understanding—without formulating things introspectively in our theories? The behaviorists and learning theorists who followed their lead have consistently answered yes. When Skinner studies man's language capacities he proceeds as follows: "I think an analysis which deals with verbal behavior without appealing to mental concepts such as meaning is a step in the right direction."[7] *Meaning* as a concept takes roots from the Kantian-like glasses, which frame, organize, make possible, and so forth. As a Lockean extraspectionist, it strikes Skinner as unparsimonious and even "mystical" to impute a meaningful understanding to the organism "over there," under his empirical observation (extraspection). We have seen some rather striking examples of a meaningless course of human behavior in Chapter 7, such as Skinner's self-characterization as automaton (p. 334) or in Wolpe's claim that mental events run parallel to rather than in series with overt behavior (p. 342). We might now add a third even more classical example, drawn from the writings of Hull who was quoting from Albert P. Weiss, a prominent behaviorist peer:

We may start with the assumption that every drop of rain in some way or other gets to the ocean. . . . Anthropomorphizing this condition we may say that it is the *purpose* of every drop of rain to get to the ocean. Of course, this only means that virtually every drop *does* get there eventually. . . . Falling from the cloud it may strike the leaf of a tree, and drop from one leaf to another until it reaches the ground. From here it may pass under or on the surface of the soil to a rill, then to a brook, river, and finally to the sea. Each stage, each fall from one leaf to the next, may be designated as a *means* toward the final end. . . . Human behavior is merely a complication of the same factors.[8]

What do Skinner, Wolpe, Weiss, and Hull have in common, as they impute this "acted upon" rather than "acting" image to man? Quite obviously, they each rely upon our Lockean model to an *exclusive* degree. As Skinner once said: ". . . I short-circuit Kant by going back to the British Empiricists."[9] Though Skinner did not accept Locke's "idea" construct, he did favor the latter's claim that it was language *per se*—as opposed to a "mind"—which made reasoning possible for the human being.[10] Words are thus items of verbal behavior which mediate input experience into output behavior. Wolpe cites the writings of J. S. Mill concerning such linkings of antecedents to consequents.[11] Dollard and Miller state as a fundamental tenet that: ". . . language and other cue-producing responses play a central role in the higher mental processes. This should be contrasted with the approach of some philosophers who seem to believe that language is a mere means of communicating thoughts which somehow 'exist' independently of speech rather than an essential part of most thinking and reasoning."[12] Among the behaviorists covered only Stampfl is open regarding the possibility that man can reason or "wish" in ways which might transcend merely verbal mediation.[13]

If man is a product of his inputs, mediated in part by past inputs called language, then his environment and social milieu would be an important source of his behavioral patterns or his "personality." It is in this sense that H. S. Sullivan gravitated ever more to an extraspective, Lockean frame of reference. Though Sullivan was not a behaviorist, the Chicago School of Social Science which influenced him took strength from the same British Empiricist sources that had fed the behaviorist movement. John B. Watson was at the University of Chicago when he launched his attack on introspection as scientific method. Sullivan once admitted that in his earliest theoretical attempts he relied on "faculty" psychology which stemmed from a Kantian ap-

proach that turned the "categories of the understanding" into supposedly inborn "faculties of mind." The rise of empiricism in modern psychology was directed in large measure against the "outmoded" faculty psychology of the nineteenth century. Sullivan toyed with his "preconcept" notion at the time but as we know from Chapter 5 he was to drop this neo-Jungian conception.[14]

However, as he came to emphasize operational definitions and to assume the more extraspective attitude of the Chicago group, Sullivan gave up attempts to account for such unobservable and *private* mentalisms.[15] When Sullivan viewed man from the outside, in his social milieu, he found that man is more the product of the inputs than of the inwardly conceived perspective that he might have emphasized from *his* (introspective) perspective. This is why Sullivan harangued so against those who would see themselves as "unique" individuals.[16] An operational science is oriented to what is "common" and observably provable! When Sullivan briefly used the language of field theory he did so because for him a field was an observable event, a matrix of patterned energy exchanges which could be objectified.[17] This was not a truly phenomenological usage, as we shall see in the theories of Part Three.

Sullivan's conception of language is consistent with behaviorism. Language is a matter of manipulating signs, which are themselves summative inputs from the culture (Lockean model). Symbols are merely "signs of signs."[18] The mind *qua* mind is passive and receptive. Man does not repress actively, as Freud held. He simply overlooks and dissociates (loses connections with) aspects of his experience. Thought is dependent upon input and never *creates* meaningful input: "Thought, for our purpose, is organismic activity by the implicit functioning of symbols, themselves abstracts from the 'material' of life—events."[19] Sullivan rejected purely mechanistic conceptions of man. He felt that *both* psychoanalysis and behaviorism were more mechanistic in tone than was his own brand of psychology. We will return to this question when we discuss the impetus construct meaning.

Demonstrative Reasoning and the Yankee Spirit

Although H. S. Sullivan never took up the question of dialectical vs. demonstrative reasoning these factors are built into his approach. Some of his students have even cited the gradual drift of his theories away from the dialectical formulations of classical analysis.[20] He felt that the dichotomies of love vs. hate or aggression vs. passivity made more theatrical than scientific sense. Sullivan specifically rejected Freudian analyses of "colliding thoughts" (antithetical ideas), suggesting that: "Instead of another thought having collided with the thought that was being expressed, what seems more nearly the case usually is that consciousness has been disturbed, and what was being said is no longer there."[21] Hence, as he shifted his emphasis from intrapersonal to interpersonal description Sullivan's theory lost that internal dynamic quality that dominated the Freudian and Jungian line. He is much closer to Adlerian theory on most points (except that he is a true social theorist, as we shall show, whereas Adler was not).

Sullivan had great faith in the common-sense rationality of man. He reflects a decidedly demonstrative image of man in the following, where he is speaking of how man responds to difficulty: "It is my opinion that man is rather staggeringly endowed with adaptive capacities, and I am quite certain that when a person is clear on the situation in which he finds himself, he does one of three things: he decides it is too much for him and leaves it, he handles it satisfactorily, or he calls in adequate help to handle it. And that's all there is to it."[22] There is no internal wrenching and compromise in this account of man. The Freudian-Jungian

complexities, based upon a dialectical formulation, have given way to the clarity and simplicity of the Yankee spirit of pragmatism and good sense.

Sullivan was not blind to the oppositional in behavior. His treatment of dissociations and dreams often reflect the "counterpoint observations about life."[23] He also had an Adlerian suspicion that dialectical maneuvers were often nothing more than the defensiveness which an individual manifested—an individual who did not wish to think about something which was anxiety provoking. He called this a *not* technique or process and observed: "The patient thinks a great deal about what is not the case. This is greatly tributary to security, for anything *is* but *one* thing, but *is not* an infinity of other things. One can proceed, therefore, by the not-processes to contemplate innumerable formulations, thereby easily avoiding the *one* formula that would be illuminating —and anxiety-laden."[24] A dialectician would surely find this capacity to think about what something "is not" a reflection of the dialectical reasoning capacity in man. Sullivan is mute regarding such refined philosophical precedents.

In many ways the behaviorists were even more within the Yankee spirit than was Sullivan. All such tendencies to think of what a thing is not or to turn an input meaning into its opposite would be seen by men like Watson and Hull as independent Lockean bits of behavior which had been somehow learned in the past as "generalizations" from what was the focus of learning. Opposition is not germane to meaning on the behavioristic view since, as we have seen, meaning is itself a superfluous conception. Whether we affirm, negate, qualify, or oppose items in awareness is all a function of our past training (inputs). Dollard and Miller say: "It seems possible that responses involved in reaction formation are favored by the fact that our verbal training produces an especially strong association between words that are antonyms."[25] Thus, when we are taught certain words such as "boy," "up," "right," and "good" as children we are virtually always being reinforced for "girl," "down," "left," and "bad" at the same time. It is this associative bond which accounts for oppositional ties in language and not any implicit tie, as the dialectician would have it.

The behaviorist has typically gravitated to a position of *realism* in line with his demonstrative style of thought. The behaviorist identifies idealisms with mentalisms as "inside" factors having no explicable tie to observable events. Consequently, idealisms are presumed to be erroneous, even primitive forms of explanation. The Lockean input is viewed as a "primary and true" item, even though it may not copy reality correctly or the reality copied may be influenced by cultural beliefs which have no substance themselves (religions, myths, and so forth).[26] The cybernetics machine is a perfect example of the model for man advocated by neobehaviorists. Cybernetics is derived from the Greek word meaning "steersman," and this science is concerned with steering, controlling, directing, and communicating information.[27] This "information" is not meaning-laden of course. That is, what the cyberneticist takes as information usually comes down to the extent of control a message has over a receiver via a sender. How much can an input "message" alter the eventual output action? The more changes the more the information sent into the mechanism.

Through use of feedback circuits (considered "primary and true" by the machine in that they are never dialectically questioned) the machines can "read" the layout of a terrain and behave accordingly. They can locomote, bump into things, back up (via feedback information), move on to new locations, etc. Today's huge computers and the so-called "thinking machines" which perform remarkable feats of mathematical calculation are also of the same general type. Norbert Wiener, the "father of Cybernetics" once reminisced: "I have often said that the high-speed computing machine is primarily a logical machine, which confronts different propositions with one another and draws some of their consequences. It is possible to translate the whole of mathematics into the performance of a sequence of purely logical tasks."[28]

The important point for our purposes is to recognize that cybernetics machines *do* reason but *only* demonstratively. "True and primary" principles are fed into them as program formats and scoring data. These are never questioned in a dialectical manner by the machine. Through the use of feedback and a memory bank the machine then proceeds to reason according to the premises fed into it by the program format. In short order the machine arrives at a conclusion, based upon the data submitted by the operator. This conclusion does not always provide a clear answer to the question, but the machine does as well as any man could do in the circumstance, probably a lot better. Yet, machines do not formulate those Freudian-Jungian "possibilities" transcending their program formats that we see in dreams. They do not state opinions (unless by opinion we mean a certain statistical level of probability). They do not create (unless we mean that they extract all fixed-possible combinations from a mass of data fed to them). And, most human prerogative of all, they do not commit errors of logic once the data have been put into them accurately (barring any mechanical failure). Not making an error is merely the other side of not creating anything new. Behaviorism views "error" as essentially "lack of control," and we might even say "lack of information." If all variables were known and were under proper control there would be no error! There is no active principle of error in behaviorism, no Jungian-like prerogative to "do wrong."

Behaviorists see dialectical strategies in thought as "techniques of influence or control" rather than as spontaneous characteristics of human nature. Recall from the Introduction that Socrates viewed the dialectical technique of discourse as entirely spontaneous, and to direct it consciously to some preconceived end would constitute sophistry (p. 6). Yet Dollard and Miller draw no real distinction here: "'Failure to understand' is the essence of the Socratic method of teaching. To each answer of the student the teacher poses a further question which tells the student that there is something missing in his response and motivates him to continue responding."[29] By putting "failure to understand" in quotes Dollard and Miller indicate that this device can be used as a didactic technique, a facilitator of input of which the teacher *really* wishes to inform (in the cybernetic sense) the student. Socrates would consider such a predecided, manipulative attempt sophistical. This tactic of asking prearranged questions, always one step ahead of the student, is also what Skinner made use of in his "teaching machines." The machine poses a question, and if the student answers it correctly he is moved along to new material and new questions. If he answers it in part, the "programmed instruction" develops knowledge further through additional questions. If the student misses the question entirely the machine requests that he go back to his studies for more information (input) and then try the question sequence once again. And so it is that, in paradoxical fashion, what Socrates would have considered improper (sophistical) use of a dialectical tactic has come to serve a most important role in modern education.

Although the dialectic has no *formal* role to play in behavioristic theories, one can find many references to such factors in the informal comments made by these thinkers. For example, Wolpe tells us that he once made a conscious effort to devise a technique of cure based upon his finding "a response that was theoretically the diametric opposite of anxiety."[30] Since Stampfl is willing to use "dynamic" formulations one would expect that he might find dialectical formulations to his liking. Yet, true to behavioristic form, when he recognizes a potential role for dialectical reasoning he translates this opportunity into a demonstrative premise. For example, in discussing dream distortion and the absence of (demonstrative) logic in dreams, Stampfl suggests that these irregularities are due to early conditioning (input) experiences which have been retained since the earliest, hence most sketchy moments of self-awareness.[31]

The most extensive and fascinating examples of dialectic are found in the literary and biographical writings of Skinner. In *Walden Two* (1948) Skinner has his hero, Frazier, who planned the ideal society, say at one point: "We take no pleasure in the sophistical, the disputative, the dialectical."[32] He is referring to the fact that in Walden Two man is not set against fellow-man in competitive fashion. In another context, where the psychologist Frazier confronts his philosopher-antagonist, Castle, we find a most searching analysis of demonstrative vs. dialectical reasoning hidden beneath an exchange dealing with personal freedom to behave:

[Castle has just said:] ". . . I *know* that I'm free."

"It must be quite consoling," said Frazier.

"And what's more—you do, too," said Castle hotly. "When you deny your own freedom for the sake of playing with a science of behavior, you're acting in plain bad faith. That's the only way I can explain it." He tried to recover himself and shrugged his shoulders. "At least you'll grant that you *feel* free."

"The 'feeling of freedom' should deceive no one," said Frazier. "Give me a concrete case."

"Well, right now," Castle said. He picked up a book of matches. "I'm free to hold or drop these matches."

"You will, of course, do one or the other," said Frazier. "Linguistically or logically there seem to be two possibilities, but I submit that there's only one in fact. The determining forces may be subtle but they are inexorable. I suggest that as an orderly person you will probably hold —ah! you drop them! Well, you see, that's all part of your behavior with respect to me. You couldn't resist the temptation to prove me wrong. It was all lawful. You had no choice. The deciding factor entered rather late, and naturally you couldn't foresee the result when you first held them up. There was no strong likelihood that you would act in either direction, and so you said you were free."

"That's entirely too glib," said Castle. "It's easy to argue lawfulness after the fact. But let's see you predict what I will do in advance. Then I'll agree there's law."

"I didn't say that behavior is always predictable, any more than the weather is always predictable. There are often too many factors to be taken into account. We can't measure them all accurately, and we couldn't perform the mathematical operations needed to make a prediction if we had the measurements. The legality is usually an assumption—but none the less important in judging the issue at hand."[33]

This key exchange of the novel contains an excellent contrast between man's intellectual and behavioral functioning. The dialectician would see in the very fact that the novel is carried along by *clashes* of this sort evidence that drama—as life itself—is a dialectical affair.[34] Such considerations aside, however, he would then point to the strategy of this scene as proof of how *both* Frazier and Castle reason dialectically. Castle says he is free. Frazier denies it. Castle picks up a pack of matches and says he has at least two alternatives—to hold or to drop the matches. Frazier, falling back on the demonstrative tactic, claims he has just one (primary and true) alternative—and then, when Castle seems to go against his first tentative prediction, Frazier claims that very opposition as evidence for his demonstrative views. Castle went against the prediction because of the "feedback" that this was "Frazier's prediction" and he was out (programmed) to "prove Frazier wrong." Hence, he countered Frazier thanks to the "later" feedback information.

The dialectician would claim that Frazier was himself reflecting a dialectical strategy in making his points so smoothly and effortlessly. Indeed he was being sophistical since literally *nothing* Castle could do would have removed him from pin-pointing demonstrative logic. For example, when Frazier had said "You will, of course, do one or the other," if Castle had tossed the matches up in the air, negating the two alternatives (hold or drop) put to him, he would not have saved the day. Frazier could simply say this was an example of Castle's behavior "with respect to me." Since Frazier has the prerogative here of the extraspectionist, thereby construing circumstances to meet *his* theoretical perspective there is no way out of this dilemma except to realize that one can always find more than one theory to account for a fact pattern. The dialectician would see great evidence in this exchange for his image of man. Yet, there is no convincing another theorist if the latter also has his concepts locked into place.

There are other strictly biographical accounts of the dialectic in Skinner's writings. He tells of an exchange he once had with the eminent philosopher and mathematician, Lord Alfred North Whitehead (1861–1947). The point of their exchange was quite similar to the fictionalized account already presented. It seems that Skinner once sat next to Whitehead at a banquet and naturally fell into conversation with him concerning the nature of science. This was in 1934, and the youthful Skinner was admittedly flushed with the excitement of behaviorism, arguing that in time man's behavior will be completely accounted for by the environmental factors which determine it. Whitehead apparently found some things lacking in this program for a science of behavior. Skinner gives us this account of their closing positions:

He [Whitehead] agreed that science might be successful in accounting for human behavior provided one made an exception of *verbal* behavior. Here, he insisted, something else must be at work. He brought the discussion to a close with a friendly challenge: "Let me see you," he said, "account for my behavior as I sit here saying 'No black scorpion is falling upon this table.' "[35]

How might a dialectician view this exchange? He would be intrigued by the fact that Whitehead reached for an improbable "something" to have fall on the table—a black scorpion—not to affirm but to negate! This sentence is not to be taken as an example of directly communicated information. It is to be seen as an attempt to say "Only man, with his dialectical ability to affirm or deny any proposition expressed, would feel it necessary to prove a point by saying what is obviously the case—that something highly improbable to begin with is *not* taking place." Yet, this is not what the demonstratively inclined Skinner was to make of the statement. After mulling it over, Skinner was to cite what he presumed *was said* and not what did not need saying! He thus analyzes this statement to find the probability in it that the black scorpion response was a metaphorical allusion to behaviorism.[36] Hence, the demonstrative reasoner finds Whitehead saying: "I'm afraid that behaviorism just isn't going to be accepted at this table today." Either interpretation can be considered the correct one, and it is not for us to decide which or whether both meanings were involved.

Finally, Skinner has presented an even clearer example of what the dialectician means by altering experience via self-initiated language oppositions in an account of his behavior as a boy. He tells of a time when he lost a watch which he had just been given by his family. Feeling quite unhappy about the loss, Skinner went out into the woods along a creek, where he and his friends had built a club house, in order to contemplate his situation. As Skinner put it: "I was miserably unhappy. Suddenly it occurred to me that happiness and unhappiness must cancel out and that if I were unhappy now I would necessarily be happy later. I was tremendously relieved."[37] Though he tells us this in passing and goes on to describe how he eventually found the watch and even was moved to consider this a religious life event for a fleeting period, the point of significance

for the dialectician is this oppositional cast to Skinner's own reasoning processes. Down through the ages men have responded similarly at low points in their life, often going forward with renewed faith in the future to found political causes or religions. Is this a mere accident, or does the oppositional side of man's reasoning potential reflect a *basic* capacity to think dialectically? The demonstratively inclined theorist would probably scoff at this "anthropomorphization" of a purely natural act, observe that happiness and unhappiness do follow empirically over time, and that it made good sense (demonstrative logic) to reason as Skinner did. Here again, how one solves the problem of description stamps him as leaning in one or the other of our two reasoning-style directions.

Substance Construct Meanings

Sullivan did not emphasize substance construct meanings in his theorizing. Recall from Chapter 5 that only in the case of manic-depressive psychoses did he suggest that some form of metabolic explanation might be useful.[38] More generally, the body-based constructs of his professional peers were taken by Sullivan to be prototaxic in meaningful import.[39] That is, they were too far removed from psychological factors to be instructive. Sullivan therefore concluded that: "The proper language of biology is not adequate to psychiatry and any attempt to make sense of interpersonal events and relations in strictly biological terms is foredoomed to 'neurologizing tautology,' obscurantist reifications, or circular reasoning."[40] Sullivan wanted to write his theory in terms which could be communicated as genuine psychological events. He found the sociopsychological, interpersonal event to be meaningful and capable of instructing us in human behavior, and that is what he tried to further in his theory.[41]

In its effort to remain within the pale of natural science, behaviorism was to embrace the substance meaning in terms of a Lockean reduction to the substrate conceptions of a bodily neurone and a physical drive of some sort. Pavlovian reflexology was thus a great boon to behaviorism, tied as it was to the observable input-output sequence of the identifiable neurone. The arc of electrical impulse could be mapped, and it was only a step from there to think of the intricacies of behavior as increasingly complex combinations of these identifiable units of electrical current all totaling somehow into the machine-like animal known as man. When he defined behaviorism Watson paid proper respect to its reliance upon substance meanings: "Behaviorism . . . is, then, a natural science that takes the whole field of human adjustments as its own. Its closest scientific companion is physiology."[42] Man was to be thought of as *an assembled organic machine ready to run"* at birth.[43]

We have already covered the evolution of drive theory over Chapters 6 and 7. This must now be appreciated as a Lockean reductive attempt, entirely in line with the broader natural sciences of history. The problems of drive-reduction theory have continued to plague neobehaviorists. Following his collaboration with Dollard, Miller conducted a series of intricate and highly creative studies on the relationship between brain physiology and learning in rats and cats. He identified areas in the brains of these animals which, when stimulated by electrical currents following an overt response like bar pressing, led to a continuation of that response. It thus appeared that the electrical impulse acted as a reinforcement, and one could easily see here a potential empirical basis for behavior theory. However, at some of these points the animal might press one bar to activate the "reinforcement center," only to press another which previously had been learned as a means of discontinuing this electrical stimulation. Miller observed that it

was as if the brain system concerned "responded with pleasant sensations at first, which continue to increase until they become unbearable . . . contrary to the drive-reduction hypothesis."[44]

Although he did not reject the drive-reduction thesis as a result of such studies, in his subsequent formulations Miller did speculate more along the lines of Thorndike's "confirming reactions," including the possibility of central perceptual processes of the sort Tolman might have suggested (see Chapter 6). He proposed a "go mechanism" which might be energized by some unconditioned stimulus, as in the classical conditioning paradigm, or possibly triggered by the "removal of a discrepancy between an intention and an achievement."[45] Though the latter formulation might be said to have teleological overtones, Miller retained his behavioristic convictions by viewing all such central processes of the brain's physiology as *mediated* phenomena. In his Presidential Address to the American Psychological Association, Miller summed up his view of the brain:

We no longer view the brain as merely an enormously complicated telephone switchboard which is passive unless excited from without. The brain is an active organ which exerts considerable control over its own sensory input. The brain is a device for sorting, processing and analyzing information. The brain contains sense organs which respond to states of the internal environment, such as osmotic pressure, temperature and many others. The brain is a gland which secretes chemical messengers, and it also responds to such messengers, as well as to various types of feedback, both central and peripheral.[46]

Though surely more dynamic than the earlier formulations of brain operation, we can still recognize in this description a kind of cybernetics machine, intermingling feedbacks from contact with the environment and combining physiological factors to sort and process—that is, mediate—information. But in no sense can it be viewed as actively conceptualizing the environment in a Kantian way or reasoning to the opposite of its input and thence projecting an alternative possibility quite at variance with what might be mediated in a straightforward sense. Behaviorism is clearly showing progress in its theories, and what is more important for a science of psychology, it is upholding its traditions of empirical observation. The behaviorist modifies his theory only when empirical data dictate a change. He may be conservative in his willingness to speculate, but only because he values staunch evidence above the flash of a so-called insight.

Skinner's great commitment to such "observables" led him to *forsake* a reliance on substance construct meanings in his theory. Skinner's successful foray into a completely outside-the-organism psychology has demonstrated that drive theory may be an unnecessary appendage to the style of thought so typical of the behaviorist. As noted in Chapter 7, Skinner once defined *theory* as "an effort to explain behavior in terms of something going on in another universe, such as the mind or the nervous system."[47] Based on his empirical studies, Skinner concluded that such formulations were unnecessary.[48] In fact, said Skinner, even if someday an investigator were to discover an "arrangement of molecules" to account for how inputs become outputs in the brain or elsewhere in the body, we would still need to study the question of schedules of reinforcement in the customary manner. The former knowledge would not provide us with the latter. Skinner thus does not reject his traditions. He merely adapts the Lockean model to behavioral substrates without taking this a step further into the realm of physical substrates.

Stampfl did not feel that a drive-reduction theory was essential to the explication of implosive therapy.[49] However a stimulus becomes bonded to its response, the essentials of implosive therapy remain the same. Clearly, the behavior therapist most committed to the drive-

reduction thesis is Wolpe. He saw learning as the process of establishing functional connections between neurones, based upon physiological mechanisms taking place in the body;[50] he spoke of a "fatigue-associated substance" which might account for the decrement of a response in experimental extinction;[51] and, his interpretation of anxiety as a noxious stimulus bears the heavy imprint of physiology.[52] It is therefore not surprising to find him defining systematic desensitization as a "physiological state inhibitory of anxiety [which] is induced in the patient."[53] It could well be that Wolpe's training as a physician and a nonanalytical therapist cemented his Lockean views most firmly to the substance construct meaning. He is highly realistic in outlook. His admirable series of empirical researches on the nature of reciprocal inhibition also bear the stamp of physiological mechanisms.[54]

Impetus Construct Meanings

Early in his career Sullivan criticized the classical analysts—specifically Jung—for their use of "hydraulic" conceptions.[55] He was referring to libido theory and reacting to what he took to be the "mechanical" way in which human behavior was being portrayed. Rather than an interpersonally dynamic affair, observable to the eye, the analysts turned man inward, responding to the pushes and pulls of a pseudo-fluid of some sort. Sullivan felt this was no better than the reliance of the behaviorists on a conditioned-reflex psychology.[56] He referred to both Pavlov[57] and Watson[58] in less than flattering terms, suggesting that they were simplistic in their approach to behavior, basing it on a theoretical fiction. He opined: "There is no simple stimulus-response situation."[59] At the same time, Sullivan did not disregard the impetus construct meaning in his view of man. Actually, as a Lockean theorist, he was very much dependent upon the (extraspectively conceived) flow of behavior taking place before the "participant observer's" eyes.

This flow, which included personality descriptions, amounted to the "relatively enduring pattern of energy transformation" rather than to specific factors such as dominance, fixations, or even stimuli and responses. Sullivan was not drawn to a study of what is called individual differences in human behavior. As a social psychologist, he had other interests: "We will attempt . . . to study human similarities. And we will not study people as such, but what they do, and what can be fairly safely inferred as to why they do it."[60] As Sullivanians we study the flow, the *common* impetus to action which is suprapersonal and therefore a determiner of the behavior for all individuals who behave in "this situation." This vehicular tendency is another bond cementing Sullivan to the behaviorists.

We find Sullivan steadily increasing his reliance on energic constructs over the years. Terms like *tension, vector, field force, habit,* and *drive* take on greater importance in his maturing thought. And although he may have rejected the seeming biological inwardness (reflex arc) of behavioral conditioning theory, he was not opposed to a reinforcement theory in principle. Sullivan appreciated that, given our biological equipment, we require certain physical gratifications, like the satiation of thirst or hunger, which act as reinforcements to unite the elicitation of a behavior to a specific social stimulus. He even spoke of "cultural conditioning" at one point.[61] In the latter case, however, cultural learning cannot be reduced to the satisfactions of a physical need. Even the lust dynamism cannot be used as an associating agent because it matures too late in life. Sullivan thus called for the acceptance of a "power motive" in man, which was based upon the sense of self-esteem gained when one achieved something valued in life— often meaning that there was an interpersonal feature in the achievement. This emphasis on man's need to achieve as well as to satisfy physi-cal wants is in line with Sullivan's theoretical aim to retain a modicum of purposiveness and futurity in his account of human behavior.

Since the time of Bacon the theoretical challenge for all "toughminded" theorists has been to explain behavior in impetus construct terms. Initially, the tie to substance constructs was also retained. Beginning with their original ties to body chemistry and physiology, the empirical learning theorists fanned out to study myriad factors in learning paradigms which did not require drive-reduction accounts to sustain the explanation. The growing reliance on an empirical law of effect was clear proof that substance construct meanings were not as essential to the "flow of events" in behavior as was the impetus construct meaning. Of course, it was usually taken as a Lockean "given" that there were physical processes in the bodily structure which would eventually account for how input stimuli become attached to output responses. Miller's brain research is decidedly in this vein. But the history of behaviorism has been one of moving away from a necessary tie to substance construct meanings to an almost exclusive *formal* theoretical tie to the impetus construct (as we shall see later, all of our construct meanings are informally brought into play).

The idea of a "stimulus" which can bring about—singly or in combination with other stimuli—a "response" or a host of such responses is surely the *sine qua non* of an impetus construct meaning. Man has always been impressed by the fact that there is a flow to time, that events move from seeming antecedents (the befores) to consequents (the afters) in predictable ways.[62] It is extremely important to appreciate that *time* is a major factor in behavioral theory. Time catalogues change in observable events. We can "see" something taking place "over there" (extraspectively) if we observe long enough. In fact, one might say that "behavior" equals "change over time" in the classical learning theorist's most fundamental conceptualization. Phenomenologists like Jung (see Chapter 4, p. 217) and the gestalt-existentialistic group (see Chapter 12, p. 512) seek to account for aspects of behavior with time parcelled out of the account! This is literally impossible for the learning theorist, as he bases everything on the flow of (input) events—present or stored in a memory bank from out of the past.

In line with the Baconian proscriptions for natural science to explain things without intentional meanings the behaviorists have come to base their determinism exclusively on the view of antecedents attaching to consequents over time in what they like to call a "lawful" manner. Thus, Dollard and Miller say, in speaking about their notion of an innate hierarchy of response, that the "stimulus causes the subject to make the correct response on the first trial."[63] Wolpe opens his book with the following presumption: "Everything in this book rests on the fundamental assumption that the behavior of organisms, including human beings, conforms to causal laws just as other phenomena do."[64] Skinner says: "As a determinist, I must assume that the organism is simply mediating the relationships between the forces acting upon it and its own output, and these are the kinds of relationships I'm anxious to formulate."[65] Skinner's view here is based on an impetus form of determinism, so that behavior "gets started" at some point (birth or some time *in utero*) and is then carried forward by the pressure of events shaping or conditioning it over time. Directionality has been dropped, but the inevitability of a "before" pushing an "after" has been retained.

Of course, if events are lawfully related in this fashion, then we do not have to assume that the organism altering over time—that is, "behaving"—is in any way self-directed. Here is how Wolpe puts it:

The behavior therapist takes it for granted that human behavior is subject to causal determination no less than the behavior of falling bodies or of growing plants. For example, a man pauses at crossroads, undecided along which of two routes to proceed. The route that he eventually takes is the inevitable one, being the resultant of a balancing out of conflicting action-tendencies. The strength of each action-tendency is essentially a function of the incipient reactions evoked by impinging stimuli, internal and external, whose effects depend primarily on the character of previously established neural interconnections—that is, on pre-existing habit structures.[66]

Note the striking compatibility of *this* formulation with the "constancy principle" style of thought which we said was *not* typical of Freud (see Chapter 4, p. 215). And as for consciousness or self-awareness in human behavior, Skinner had this to say:

It doesn't make any difference to me whether things are conscious or unconscious; the causality in behavior does not depend upon awareness. Awareness is something imposed upon us—we become aware of what we are doing and why we are doing it because society insists that we talk about these things. Society says, "Why are you doing that?" or "What are you going to do next?" and the child learns to look around and find something to talk about in reply. In that way he becomes a self-conscious person. The curious thing is that it is society that makes the individual observe himself—he has no reason to do so otherwise. There is nothing in a nonsocial environment which would ever generate awareness.[67]

When Skinner and other behaviorists speak of awareness they mean essentially "what is conscious" to the person. Behaviorism's determinism is thus essentially beyond consciousness, resting on the assumption that the "laws of nature" fix what happens in human behavior just as they fix the course of a growing plant. A frequent error in theoretical understanding is to equate the "nonconscious" determinism of behaviorism with the "unconscious" determinism of a psychoanalytical theory. This is a false comparison, of course, because in the

Freudian conception there is something in addition to simply a natural law "determining behavior." There is a decided strategy being worked out, an intention being fulfilled or countered in some way. Behavioristic determinism is truly *blind* (lacking intentional construct meaning); psychoanalytical determinism is *directed*.

The behaviorist sustains his great faith in a hard determinism by the fact that in his empirical researches he is constantly proving that behavior is manipulatable and predictable. And it follows that only a determined behavior could be predicted! Wolpe's entire theoretical approach hinges upon the "lawful facts" he first established on researches with cats, and he observes thereby that "modern therapy is applied science; and behavior therapy could not enter the world of science before there was a sufficient foundation for it in the basic studies of the experimental laboratory."[68] Stampfl moves to prove his point through study of lower animals and affirms that "conditioning principles" shape behavior, hence presumably are at work over the human life span in directly comparable ways to rat laboratory demonstrations.[69] And, as we know, the rationale of Dollard and Miller's Freudian translations all hinge upon experimental results.[70] With this large body of empirical findings who can doubt that behavior is determined and determined in a way demonstrable from outside of the person's awareness?

Without in any way denying the value of experimentation, the thoughtful student of theory must at this point observe that behaviorists—and indeed most rigorous psychologists to date—have seriously *confused their methods with their theories!* When natural science deals exclusively with inanimate or subhuman events the extraspective account which results is well suited to an impetus construct meaning. Events "over there" are taking place across time. Antecedents press on to move consequents. This can even be demonstrated in experimentation, another extraspective formulation. Thus in evolving the scientific *method* as a sequence of independent-to-dependent variables (IV-DVs) the emphasis was completely on the impetus construct meaning. The "cause" of events was seen as *only* this "fabric of movement" conception. There was great compatibility between this *method* and the "blind" physical *theories* which underwrote them. This compatibility has continued into modern psychology where the distinction between what is theory and what is method has been blurred.[71]

If our IV-DV methods are based upon the same (impetus) metaconstruct as are our S-R theories, then what is to prevent us from slipping between these two—actually identical—conceptions as we reason along? This would be a natural mistake, but one having immense consequences for the image of man who is under study in our experiments. It is thus not surprising to find Skinner crossing wires, as follows: "As an analyst of behavior, I want to relate the probability of response to a large number of independent variables, even when these variables are separated in time and space."[72] Technically, one does not relate responses to independent variables but to stimuli. But by uniting the IV-DV sequence of events with the S-R sequence of events we can interchange meanings at will, and if the outlook which we have is a realism, this "finding behavior predictable" can give us a great sense of conviction. We measure the real world, which is lawful, and prove to our satisfaction that man is determined in literally every study that we conduct.

An even more harmful result of this confounding theory with method arises when a theorist proposes some construct having for him the meaning of *other* than an impetus construct. When he then designs his study in IV-DV terms, he finds that any experimental results accruing to his view *automatically* lend direct support to the impetus S-R conception. Indeed, many psychologists equate *all* research findings with S-R theory, as witnessed by the fact that they speak of "S-R laws" when they should be speaking of "IV-DV laws." This *S-R bind* is so persuasive that many humanistically inclined psychologists have been demoralized regarding experimentation, feeling that it is impossible to change the "mechanical" image of man which research studies generate *by their very nature*. The S-R bind is thus based upon a confusion of what is evidence (IV-DV impetus regularities) with what is a theory (S-R impetus regularities).[73] We must appreciate that establishing the former does *not* support only or even primarily the latter. We must look to the meanings being conveyed in the theory and interpret them in light of the research findings at their own level. If we then give them an S-R interpretation, we must realize that this is simply another theory about what is taking place over time and nothing more. There is no added validity to this interpretation because it happens also to bear an impetus meaning.

In confining his theory to the impetus construct meaning, the behaviorist effectively becomes a *vehicular* theorist. The so-called "principles of learning," such as reinforcement, extinction, generalization, and even drive reduction, are framed vehicularly. Wolpe's challenge to consider reciprocal inhibition the general explanation for all therapeutic cures is merely an extension of this vehicular strategy.[74] The upshot of this state of events is that in relying on impetus construct meanings in this way the behaviorist can capitalize on the self-reflexivity of his S-R concept to subsume *any* lower level designation of change or "behavior." Since behavior is by definition a flow of events *over time* we can readily admit that *all* behavior has implied impetus meanings. This is why it is correct to say that S-R concepts are the most abstract designations in psychology! Literally anything in experience is potentially a stimulus or a response in the sense that we customarily use these words. The question remains: Are there also *other* meanings worth acknowledging in a time-bound behavioral sequence?

Pattern Construct Meanings

Sullivan was so taken with this metaconstruct that "patterning" is a tempting catchword to typify his theoretical style. The "envelope of all insignificant differences" (dynamism) holds virtually every idea he had to express.[75] His early use of preconcepts or his imago-like personifications are in this vein. Field forces are patterned, so that the "me-you" and the "two-group" integrations take on specifiable characteristics.[76] Notions such as balance, conjunctive vs. disjunctive, or "system" are all based on this construct meaning. Even the modes of experience as typified by language development carry the implication of a gradual patterning into a consensual mode which makes possible the science of psychiatry as a vehicular endeavor. When Sullivan thought of the man-animal as human, thanks to cultural inputs, he was thinking of the patterned ways in which this higher animal behaves. Man can remember more and learn more than other animals, thanks to the signs and symbols which take on and hold a pattern of significance for him. And his very intellect is a syntaxic organization of events (consensually valid) which cannot themselves be reduced to the prototaxic and parataxic organizations of the physical sphere.[77]

Since the technical goal of learning theory is to compress all descriptions of behavior into the impetus construct, the *formal* usage of patterned meanings is not significant. Even when patterns or plans are mentioned, the "basic" meaning emanates from the underlying impetus factors. Discussing the theoretical style of gestalt psychology, which emphasizes the pattern meaning construct (see Chapter 9), Dollard and Miller observe: "We maintain that any specifiable attribute of the environment, which the gestalt psychologists or other students of perception discover as a consistent basis for discriminations, can be used in the stimulus, or cue position of a stimulus-response formula."[78] And so it is that invariably when a pattern construct meaning is employed in learning theory we find it being represented as a stimulus rather than as a response factor. Responses are patterned, of course, and it would even be possible to think of a series of patterned responses taking place in response to a single cue—as, the stylized movements of a hurdler in response to the sound of the starter's gun. But such patterns are said to be the final stage of a refined series of learned responses which themselves had been initiated by discrete stimuli and then brought together through learning. Once a pattern has been coalesced it can generalize *in toto* but the stress on the learning of a pattern is usually thought of as the product of patterned stimuli.

Both Pavlov and Hull had discussed *patterning* in roughly the following terms: "If a response is reinforced whenever two or more cues occur in combination but not when these cues occur separately, the response will tend to be elicited by the combination but not by its separate elements. . . ."[79] A child learns, as he matures, that only when mother "says no" and "looks stern" need he really be concerned about discontinuing his "naughty" behavior. A simple "no" without the expression is probably nothing to be worried about because mother is not yet really angry with him. Such patterns are important to thought, and they serve as important cue-producing responses for the process of *discrimination*. A man who takes the wrong turn on his way to his new job in a strange section of the city soon gets his bearings. He receives a positive reinforcement from the layout of the streets only when his course takes him efficiently to the office. If he is easily confused at some point, he takes special pains to discriminate "this" turnoff (stimulus pattern) from "that" turnoff (stimulus pattern).

Language is an important instrumentality here. The child learns to speak about things—including his "awareness" of why he did what he did—through his interaction with others in the culture (note Skinner's remarks concerning awareness in the previous section). Just as in the examples of a mother saying "no" while in a certain mood, the child should be able to learn a kind of personal patterning of this sort in what we call "thought." As Dollard and Miller put it: ". . . we would expect just as much complex patterning in a person's responses to the words in sentences that he says or thinks to himself as we observe in those that he hears other people say."[80] The process of thinking or mediating by way of cue-producing stimuli is thus heavily colored with pattern construct meanings. These Lockean combinations are quite different in essence from the Kantian patternings by way of meaningful categories (the spectacles). Rather than conceptualizing—that is, bringing meanings to bear—the patterns of behavioristic mediators are constitutive, built up, and at best simply mediators of inputs into outputs. The cue-producing responses are thus combined in various ways, patterned into sentences, and so forth. What we know of as the "meaning" of language is for the behaviorist the kinds of responses which such patterned mediators elicit. This analysis would be more in line with a Hullian theory, but Skinner's view of language as emitted responses is also closely tied to the stimulus examples provided by the language community: ". . . many . . . responses would never have been emitted except under the special encouragement of the literary community, which . . . provides sensitive examples of verbal behavior."[81]

In presenting their technique of self-study, Dollard and Miller made much of the necessity for plans, the stopping to think and to arrange mediators properly so that living is accomplished with greater efficiency.[82] Plans, as any strategy for reaching an objective, can surely be subsumed by the pattern meaning construct, which draws major significance from such blueprint conceptions. The mature individual responds properly to a well-ordered sequence of stimuli, for as Dollard and Miller note, adults must plan.[83] Children are impetuous and unpredictable precisely because they do not process input stimulation through proper, planful mediation, to a more sound output of behavior. Though he does not view it in such terms formally, Skinner's "schedules" of reinforcement are on the side of a pattern construct meaning. Note that the behaviorist's *hard determinism* thus also relies on the (scheduled) patterns of regularity seen in nature. A "law" as a theoretical construct (not simply the cataloguing of a methodological finding) is on the side of a patterned regularity, which is of course the idea Sullivan had in mind when he spoke of dynamisms as patterned energy transformations.

We come now to a sensitive area in the thinking of the learning theorist—particularly those in this school who take a very tough-minded approach. The difficulty arises in the extraspective vs. introspective sphere of learning, and it touches on both the pattern and the intentional construct meanings which may or may not be functioning in learning theories at an *informal* level. This discussion will be extended in the next section, when we take up intentional construct meanings, but for now we will focus on the matter of whether or not there is such a thing as the introspective planfulness of behavior in the behaviorist's account. Skinner has taken special pains to counter any such suggestion. If men reasoned as the philosophers say they reason, then presumably they would attack problems with an idea of what they wish to accomplish—their plans or blueprints for what they intend to bring about. In the realm of science they would pose hypotheses, make predictions, and then seek validating evidence much as we have claimed they do in the present volume.

This is a philosophical analysis, introspectively framed and based upon a Kantian image of man. As such, it "stacks the deck" against the rugged empiricist who says "nonsense" to such anthropomorphized accounts. In a remarkable paper on how he approached the study of behavior entitled "A Case History in Scientific Method" (1956) Skinner presents us with the sort of disclaimer the behaviorist makes to allusions of self-directed planfulness. After noting that the only "plan" he had as a clue from Pavlov was to "control your conditions and you will see order," Skinner goes on to cite five so-called unformalized scientific principles which he followed in his work:

1. "When you run onto something interesting, drop everything else and study it."[84]
2. "Some ways of doing research are easier than others."[85]
3. "Some people are lucky."[86]
4. "Apparatuses sometimes break down."[87]
5. Capitalize on "serendipity—the art of finding one thing while looking for something else."[88]

What do these five "principles" which guided Skinner's career as a scientist have in common? They ultimately dissolve into happenstance, accident, or chance occurrence. Skinner is saying that he—as a behaving organism—had no introspectively conceived plan (except for the Pavlovian admonition) and that his discoveries were all brought about strictly through impetus factors. Things "happened" and Skinner, with his Pavlovian eye open for order, "found it." Hence, he summarized his general approach as scientist in the remarkable conclusion to follow:

I never faced a Problem which was more than the eternal problem of finding order. I never attacked a problem by constructing a Hypothesis. I never deduced Theorems or submitted them to Experimental Check. So far as I can see, I had no preconceived Model of behavior—certainly not a physiological or mentalistic one, and, I believe, not a conceptual one. . . . Of course, I was working on a basic Assumption—that there was order in behavior if I could only discover it— but such an assumption is not to be confused with the hypotheses of deductive theory. It is also true that I exercised a certain Selection of Facts but not because of relevance to theory but because one fact was more orderly than another. If I engaged in Experimental Design at all, it was simply to complete or extend some evidence of order already observed.[89]

It is essential for Skinner to discredit philosophical accounts of how man reasons because basic to his point of view is that man is incapable of such (Kantian) self-direction. Of course, even as we speak about Skinner's "point of view" we ensnare him in *our* conceptual model. Skinner denies that models are relevant, and yet here we conceive of him as a man using a model! There is no way to avoid this eventuality, and the best we might do for a theorist like Skinner is to acknowledge that we have here an "anthropomorphic bind" to parallel the "S-R bind" which he applies so neatly to methodological findings. Based on the orientation of this volume we have to see in Skinner's Pavlovian admonition and selective orientation to the facts a kind of *informal theoretical model* (pattern meaning construct) being pressed.

A related issue of importance involves what is called the difference between response-response or R-R laws in psychology and the "more basic" S-R laws emerging from the psychological laboratory. We have already pointed out that laboratory findings are *not* S-R, but rather IV-DV regularities. However, assuming now that we make the error in logic of confusing IV-DV empirical findings (method) with S-R theory, what does R-R lawfulness imply? It was the behaviorist Kenneth W. Spence who introduced this distinction into the learning theory literature. Framed in terms of *methods* of scientific investigation, Spence's distinction actually hinges upon a theory of lawfulness. Here is the distinction as taken from Spence:

. . . R = f(R) laws, describe relations between different attributes or properties of behavior; they tell us which behavior traits are associated. This type of law is investigated extensively in the fields of intelligence and personality testing, and the laws that have been discovered have formed the basis of much of our technology in the areas of guidance, counseling, and clinical diagnosis. These empirical R-R relations also form the starting point for theoretical constructs of the factor analysts. . . .

The second class of laws, R = f(S), relates response measures as the dependent variable to the determining environmental conditions. There are really two subclasses of laws here, one relating to the environmental events of the present and the second to events of the past. The first subclass includes the traditional laws of psychophysics, perception, reaction time, and emotions. . . . Insofar as the behavior at any moment is a function of environmental events that occurred prior to the time of observation one is dealing with laws of the second subclass. The most familiar instance of this kind of relation is represented by the so-called learning curve which relates the response variable to previous environmental events of a specified character.[90]

Several toughminded characteristics appear in this quote. The attitude previously expressed by Dollard and Miller, concerning the reducibility of gestalt terms to S-R terms, is reflected. The confounding of S-R with IV-DV impetus construct meanings is also easy to identify. There is a realistic interpretation of meaning pervading the distinction, implying that S-R laws are getting at the "real" facts which R-R laws are not, and one is therefore not surprised when Spence opines: "These R-R laws represent only one small segment of the total framework of a science of behavior, and unfortunately not a very basic one at that."[91] As a vehicular theorist, Spence sees the more discriminal interests of the clinician or the school counselor—trying to determine why one person should be fearful of life's challenges while another is not—as "less basic" than the interests of a laboratory psychologist who nails his concepts down to the Lockean substrates of reaction times and perceptual regularities which can be graphed and pointed to. The notion of a "lower versus higher level law" has permeated laboratory psychology since the time of Watson, and it draws its plausibility from the Lockean model.

The Spencian distinction was given great credence in psychology, where it has also been termed the difference between a "correlational" (R-R) and an "experimental" (S-R) approach to scientific psychology.[92] How are we to think of this distinction in theory construction terms? Leaving aside methodological considerations at this point,[93] there is merit in considering the theoretical constructs which might emerge from either the R-R or the S-R tactic in the study of personality. Clearly, the S-R law would borrow from the impetus construct meaning. The R-R law, on the other hand, would draw its meaning and significance from the pattern construct. When we learn that a person's self-evaluation is related to the school grades he earns, with the more confident child earning on the average a higher grade-point, what has this "R-R law" told us? It has identified a patterned relationship, extending a meaningful tie from the comments made about self to the grades made in class. We cannot say whether the low self-opinion determines the low grades or the high self-opinion is a function of the higher grades; or, for that matter, whether grades and self-judgment are both functions of yet another factor in life. The complete pattern has not yet emerged. Since much of what interests us in life takes on significance only when a total pattern *has* been formed, it seems that Spence may have been a bit too harsh in his judgment of the R-R law.

Another common application of the pattern construct in theories of learning is in the *hierarchy* construct. We saw Dollard and Miller, Stampfl, and Wolpe all make great use of this concept. In Stampfl's *ASCH* or Wolpe's anxiety hierarchy the response was uniform—fear or anxiety throughout. In Dollard and Miller's treatment, however, a more general use of pattern meanings was involved. The very "structure of personality" was seen as an interlocking network of habitual patterns, all more or less likely to take place. The return of earlier patterns constituted regression. What is more, even the most probable patterns of behavioral emission were to be judged against a sociocultural standard of "age grading."[94] A patterned hierarchy is fixed by sociocultural forces to establish proper or acceptable behavior for an individual based upon his chronological age. This brings us to the final point of importance in the present section.

How can social preferences making for such things as language usage, the age grading of responses, and other cultural artifacts arise in the first place? Can we really account for such differences on the basis of impetus meanings alone? Pushing the problem of individual differences up a notch to "cultural differences" really does not resolve our dilemma of how to account for discriminal behavioral concepts. It is a truism that, eventually in their line of theoretical development, *all S-R psychologists become social psychologists!* They *must* move in this direction, for the vehicular utility of the S-R impetus conceptualization breaks down in the rarified atmosphere of abstraction, and one finds it impossible to say "why" John Doe differs from Sam Doakes. One has to fill in such differential accounts with "input differences" which have been ready made by a cultural environment. It is therefore no accident that we find an affinity between the thought of Sullivan and the behaviorists.

The only difficulty with this cultural gambit is that we still face the problem of explaining how giggling in church may be accepted as childishness in a young person but doing so at a more advanced chronological age might stamp an adult as severely unstable. Can the judgments of polite society about what is "proper" be subsumed entirely by the impetus construct meaning? Who arrays the age grading which Dollard and Miller point to, and why? How is it that so-called lower animals lack the inhibitions to scratch and otherwise relieve themselves of such physical discomforts whenever and wherever they find the occasion arising—but man does not?

It would seem that culture, like personality itself, borrows much from the pattern construct meaning. Man seems to be a stylizing animal, having great promptings to meet the needs of others or to "conform" to patterns of behavior which his group considers meritorious. Dollard and Miller have taught us that this potential for imitative behavior is the basis of group solidarity and continuity. But is this not something more than simply receiving and mediating inputs? Imitation may well imply a bit more active process, one involving constant *evaluation* of behavior to see if it is "good," "proper," "the 'in thing' to do," and so forth.

Though learning theorists do not say precisely how the culture has arrived at its valued orderings of behavior, presumably a Darwinian advantage exists in this array. Cultures which organized in this fashion seem to have been the ones to survive. Continuing his interest in the social forces which move man, Skinner eventually spoke of what he called *paleobehavior*: "I've become interested in what I privately term 'paleobehavior,' the evolution of the behavior of civilized man over hundreds of thousands of years. On the surface it seems to be a kind of accidental programming of very subtle contingencies. When behavior is established it is transmitted to other members."[95] Again, we have accidental advance. Frazier of Walden Two capitalized on his knowledge of such contingencies to shape his utopia. But how can man have such an insight if he is nothing but a mediator? Is there not something unique about human intelligence, separating it from the lower forms of animal life as reflected in the value structures of culture? Such talk is likely to irritate the behaviorist, for he senses in it some medieval theological longing on the part of those who voice it to return to their gods. The old buga-

boo of teleology closes in on him once again, taking us all into the next section.

Intentional Construct Meanings

We noted in Chapter 5 that Sullivan once used a concept of teleology but dropped it because of its vitalistic overtones.[96] It was one thing to claim man was goal directed but quite another to believe that he was somehow spiritually endowed. Though man was drawn to self-improvement and mental health, Sullivan did not feel he was in any way assured of a world in which things were *necessarily* getting better and better. There is a continuing ambivalence in Sullivan's writings about whether or not man has any real power to direct his own fate in the sense of a goal-striving teleology. He saw teleological arguments as resting on the assumption that "the goal is supposed to cause, in a certain curious fashion, the phenomena discussed."[97] Since his view of cause-effect was on the side of patterned impetus (dynamisms) meanings he could not really see how man could be conceptualized in this teleological fashion. A goal cannot "draw" man; he expends energy to "get to" it over time.

Sullivan conceded that people make decisions in their lives.[98] They do have a conception of something called an intention or a purpose. This intentionality in behavior permits an orientation for the future and foresight. The theoretical problem arises when we ask: "Is this anything other than a patterned dynamism which in turn has been given to the individual by his interpersonal environment?" If it is not, then we do not need the additional meaning of "that for the sake of which" in our theoretical account. The classical analysts, believing as they did that environmental inputs could be distorted by mind through a dialectical opposition thereby manufacturing an alternative not really gotten from experience, seemed to need this additional intentional phrasing. But did the more demonstrative theorist, Sullivan, need it? It seems that Sullivan never really settled this to his satisfaction. Here is how he mulled over the problems involved:

I touch here on what I believe is the most remarkable of human characteristics, the importance exercised by often but vaguely formulated aspirations, anticipations, and expectations which can be summed up in the term, foresight, the manifest influence of which makes the near future a thoroughly real factor in explaining human events. I hope that you will resist the idea that something clearly teleological is being introduced here; I am saying that, *circumstances not interfering,* man the person lives with his past, the present, and the neighboring future all clearly relevant in explaining his thought and action; and the near future is influential to a degree nowhere else remotely approached among the species of the living.[99]

We must conclude that Sullivan did not want to use an intentional construct in anything other than an informal, time-oriented sense. In fact, he came to think of the word "goal" as a cultural artifact. Culture conditions us to think of our behavior "in terms of" (a variant of "for the sake of") a goal which we are working toward; or, simply the "why" of a task we are about to undertake.[100] Sullivan wanted to employ the term goal as a kind of patterned signal which helped bring about patterned actions. This gives Sullivanian theory an automatic, mechanical flavor even though its author thought of himself as a dynamic and nonmechanical theorist. Man reasons to the future, but this is more a question of probabilities than creative expression in the classical sense of self-realization. As Sullivan observed: ". . . we project the future by juggling with past symbolizations, understandings, and present formulations in terms of probable future events."[101] This is a Lockean intellect, mathematically combining the "primary and true"

(that is, unquestioned) inputs into the best projection of a probable outcome.

A continuing thorn in the side of the behaviorist is the hostile reaction he must sustain by those who simply cannot accept the image of man as portrayed in the examples we have cited from Skinner, Wolpe, and Hull. Somehow the dignity of man seems to have been shorn from him in the behaviorist's account. What is the crux of the issue? It would seem that in collapsing all of man's behavioral movements into the impetus construct the behaviorists have made him into a passive responder—passive in the sense that he cannot initiate a course of action. Put in terms of the basic meaning constructs this says that man cannot *intend,* plan, aspire, or aim for a goal. In short, the critics of behaviorism—sometimes called "humanists"—simply cannot give up their teleological views of man in order to conform to the natural science style of theoretical description.

How successfully do the learning theorists account for teleological meanings in their theories aimed at removing this element? Hull's anticipatory goal response or Tolman's sign significate were probably formulated to deal with this matter. Miller's subsequent "go mechanism" seems aimed at the same general issue of how organisms prepare to achieve even before reinforcement is available. Each of these conceptions emphasizes the *mediational* aspects of human behavior. In the same way that a cybernetics machine might have programs which had been written and put into them by the man who runs them, each living organism may be said to have received training from the environment "in past experience." Now, as new information concerning a goal comes into view, the rat or the man can respond to these new cues in terms of his earlier cognitive map, or learned reactions that a goal is about to loom into sight. Hence, all of those behaviors which seem to be self-directed and oriented to the future goals in life are really simply learned responses, combining past learning with present circumstances just as a cybernetics machine can solve new problems based on earlier programming. The machine has no self-identity, and it surely does not aspire or "plan," except in the sense of the programmed (mediational) aide it has to order tomorrow's problems as efficiently as it has done today. Hence, the machine lacks real control. It cannot have intentions, from which alternatives arise. To be consistent, then, neither does man.

Skinner achieved an even more subtle "capturing" of the intentional construct meaning under the impetus construct meaning. Pavlov's conception of the reflex was completely fixed in the structure of the body. The S-R construct was first written around this highly mechanical conception of an input stimulus, exciting a neurone which sent a wave of electrical potential to the spinal cord, and thence to an output neurone which innervated muscles and glands to respond in a fixed way. This physically based construct was eventually modified to a far more supple conception; the ordering of antecedents and consequents into regularities (habits) with necessary ties to muscles and glands was dropped by many behaviorists altogether. Skinner stood at the forefront of this disengagement. But what is not always appreciated is that, by placing his emphasis on the operant as behavior which *produces* effects rather than behavior which is stimulated to occur, Skinner necessarily focused on the *intentional* aspects of behavior. He acknowledged as much when he observed: "Operant behavior, as I see it, is simply a study of what used to be dealt with by the concept of purpose. The purpose of an act is the consequences it is going to have."[102] Now, in speaking of the consequences of behavior—or the contingencies of reinforcement—the operant conditioner is of course speaking about behavior extraspectively. He is not saying that the organism under description has an awareness of behavioral contingencies. Or, if he does have an awareness, as in the case of Castle's sense of self-direction (p. 369), this is merely a kind of mediational device which facilitates responding. Presumably, the *real* factors controlling Castle's behavior as he dropped the matches are *in the environment*.[103]

Yet, if we were to apply Skinner's theory to behavior in an introspective fashion, then we would have a truly "purposive behaviorism" along the lines which William McDougall (1923a) had called for in psychology. Skinner is closer to Tolman than he is to Hull. He has put intentionality—however informally and covertly—back into his description of man. As experimenters and operant conditioners interested in man's behavior, we stand off to one side and observe men extraspectively. If we wish to make people work faster, we first get a base rate at which their output normally takes place. Then, with a keen eye to other factors in their environment, we determine empirically just what may step up their production. Financial increases may work, but we find that simple recognition, such as a the "Best Worker of the Month" award, stimulates considerable additional output. Though the expense is minimal—a certificate and possibly a ticket to a ballgame or a dinner for the worker's family —the production rate has risen markedly for the entire plant. Hence, we have manipulated or controlled the operant rate through reinforcement. What is the reinforcement? What is this thing called "best worker"? What is involved in status? Such questions are irrelevant to the operant conditioner at this point. Presumably these are previously conditioned inputs from a culture which defines the worker's values. There is no need to answer all of these removed issues in order to show the validity of operant conditioning.

The humanist, on the other hand, would want to know more about the nature of the reinforcement which the operant conditioner is manipulating. Is it not possible that in this case, unlike another where production is modified by a common economic stimulant (say, 10 cents per hour bonus for production), we are manipulating something unique? Is not "best" something a person could aspire to and achieve?

The fact that a manipulation of this sort is so economical for the employer—costing him one certificate and a night "on the town" for one worker rather than 100 bonuses of 10 cents per hour—would surely confirm that something uniquely human is at play. Rats and cats could hardly be motivated in this fashion. The behaviorist might then respond by noting that rats and cats could indeed be manipulated in this fashion, if they had a language, and if their resultant culture had conditioned them to work harder when they are challenged to do so competitively.

Language thus becomes the agent of mediation, on the order of IBM cards which enter the organism's memory bank as programmed instruction to facilitate the emission of responses. The humanist would respond with acceptance of language as an important variable. He would then point out that *if* man can reason dialectically, *then* he can also turn the tables on his input, reason from what "is" or "has been" true in the past, and project a new "ought" or "possibility" into the future. This intention or projected goal can then be sought —and achieved. By giving people an opportunity to be recognized as "best" the operant conditioner might stimulate a person who has never before been recognized, who has been defeated in life's contests since childhood. But now he has a new chance to prove himself. He thus turns out more work through an extreme effort to make his goal a reality, if only for one month. Would this not be a different kind of person than the one portrayed by behaviorism? The retort by the behaviorist would be along the lines of Frazier's argument: that is, this "new chance" is itself an input manipulation by the operant conditioner, hence it determines what this "life's loser" does in any case. There is no escaping the fact that behavior is an antecedent-consequent affair (S-R bind).

In speaking of mature behavior Dollard and Miller observe: "The adult must be responsible for others. He must take painful thought. He must stop and plan. He must live more in

his mind and less in his muscles, more in the future and less in the present."[104] In other contexts they speak of man's ability to anticipate danger, to make plans, to reward himself for accomplishing such plans, and even to control his thoughts to some degree.[105] In clearly recognizing the importance of futurity, the ability to reason from the "now" to the "future" *for the sake of* a plan which can be put into action, Dollard and Miller are surely in agreement with the humanist's image of man. Man must take responsibility. Yet, how then can we also say that he lacks a true sense of identity and that he is moved along like a raindrop by natural laws and no more? The typical rebuttal here is Hull's goal gradient or otherwise mediational theory, as in the following: "Through their capacity to mediate learned drives and rewards, verbal and other cue-producing responses enable the person to respond foresightfully to remote goals."[106]

Wolpe and Stampfl have acknowledged that the steps in their hierarchies (anxiety, *ASCH*) —at least some of them—do not have to be accepted by the client as having actually taken place in his life for therapy to work.[107] If this is true, then obviously even manufactured cues can help cure neurosis. But is not a manufactured cue much like the "possibility" of a projected goal toward which man might be said to strive? And how is it that a nonjudging intellect can array hierarchies of "greater or lesser" in the first instance? Does the mediational construct really capture the meaning of a judgment? The humanist would deny that it does.

The extent of teleological "sounding" commentary in Skinnerian writings is truly remarkable. Though he views man as controlled and not controlling, Skinner observes: "If you are faced with two courses of action, check off all possible foreseeable consequences before making a choice."[108] Skinner has often wondered why his readers react so negatively to *Walden Two* (1948), opining: "Apparently the main difficulty is that my good life was planned by someone."[109] Though he does not consider it in terms of our basic meaning constructs, this interpretation is probably the correct one. Frazier is the only citizen of Walden Two who has achieved a gratifying goal which singles him out within his own identity (for he gets no group recognition) as a successful creator of something. But humanistically-inclined readers who cannot identify with Frazier find the controlled environment of Walden Two—however idyllic it might be—demeaning their dignity as self-directing human beings.

And what does one make of Skinner's views on the march of science, except as a teleological—if not a vitalistic—pronouncement when he says: "The growth of science is positively accelerated, and we have reached a breathless rate of advance."[110] Recognizing his optimism about the future, Skinner remarks: "I take an optimistic view. Man can control his future even though his behavior is wholly determined. It is controlled by the environment, but man is always changing his environment. . . . He builds a world in which he suffers fewer aversive stimuli and in which he behaves with maximum efficiency. . . . he will be more effective in the future, and so on."[111] As an example of Skinner's personal environmental manipulation he tells of a special clock affixed to his desk lamp; he uses it as follows: "The clock runs when I'm *really* thinking. I keep a cumulative record of serious time at my desk. The clock starts when I turn on the desk light, and whenever it passes twelve hours, I plot a point on a curve. My record begins many years ago. I can see what my average rate has been at any period. When other activities take up my time, like lecturing, the slope falls off. That helps me refuse invitations."[112] Though he personally emphasizes luck and happenstance in his career success,[113] the humanist would find it hard to overlook the pattern construct meanings in this highly unique plan for productivity. And, the fact that he continues to behave "for the sake of" his knowledge of hard-thinking time over the

years implies an intentionality in his personal behavior that Skinner's formal theory denies to all men. Once again, the Skinnerian retort would be put clearly and fairly: "I regard myself simply as an organism responding to its environment. This is my environment. It's designed to bring out my verbal behavior with maximal efficiency."[114]

In what is sometimes said to be his "major statement" on the question of man's capacity for self-direction, the book entitled *Beyond Freedom and Dignity* (1971), Skinner probably made the most obviously teleological statements of his career. In fact, he seemed to be equating the concept of a contingency of reinforcement with the intentional construct or "final cause" as it was termed in the Introduction (p. 4). Take the following statement, for example:

The process of operant conditioning presumably evolved when those organisms which were more sensitively affected by the consequences of their behavior were better able to adjust to the environment and survive. Only fairly immediate consequences could be effective. One reason for this has to do with "final causes." Behavior cannot really be affected by anything which follows it, but if a "consequence" is immediate, it may overlap the behavior. A second reason has to do with the functional relation between behavior and its consequences. The contingencies of survival could not generate a process of conditioning which took into account *how* behavior produced its consequences. The only useful relation was temporal: a process could evolve in which a reinforcer strengthened any behavior it followed. But the process was important only if it strengthened behavior which actually produced results.[115]

As Darwin had speculated before him (see p. 86), Skinner now views this process of operant conditioning as having evolved through natural selection—blindly, nonteleologically. A contingency is essentially an "event" over a time period, *following* an earlier "behavioral event." This is not the way in which intentions (or "final causes") have been traditionally viewed. An intention is more like a "before," or a premise (bias, point of view, expectation, or aspiration) which predetermines the "outcome" to follow. In other words, some things in life are reinforcing contingencies only because a man has previously projected them as goals: "I want to win this game, so I am playing hard. I won. It is great, and I'll try hard again." But the reverse may not prove reinforcing: "I don't really care to win this game, so I'll play it in a relaxed fashion. I won. So what? I won't try any harder the next time." Although a simple example, if we begin thinking of a man's values which direct his behavior in similar fashion, we can see that a contingency which "seems" to follow the event (in this case, the winning of the game) when we are viewing it extraspectively actually has been put into effect (introspectively) *before* the contest has run its course.

It is confusions about the nature of a contingency such as this that many feel are at the root of Skinner's confidence about controlling behavior. Is behavioral control which relies on a man's stated aspirations or value systems a matter of control along an *impetus construct meaning,* or is it control along an *intentional construct meaning?* Is the man whom we control by helping him meet *his* valued aspirations under our control in a *literal* sense, or is he merely cooperating with us in order to gain advantages he knows full well could be going another way? An excellent summary of Skinner's quizzical view of man's capacity for self-advancement, albeit indirectly by way of scientifically discovered environmental changes which he subsequently arranges to change himself, is:

Man has "controlled his own destiny," if that expression means anything at all. The man that man has made is the product of the culture man has devised. He has emerged from two quite different processes of evolution: the biological evolution responsible for the human species and the cultural evolution carried out by that species. Both of these processes of evolution may now accelerate because they are both subject to intentional design. Men have already changed their genetic endowment by breeding selectively and by changing contingencies of survival, and they may now begin to introduce mutations directly related to survival. For a long time men have introduced new practices which serve as cultural mutations, and they have changed the conditions under which practices are selected. They may now begin to do both with a clearer eye to the consequences.[116]

The Adequacy of Stimulus-Response Translations of Freudian Theory

A reasonable question at this point is: How adequately have Dollard and Miller represented the *meaning* of Freudian psychology in making their translations to learning theory? What happens when a Kantian formulation is pressed into a Lockean framework, or when an intentional construct is subsumed by an impetus construct? An impartial survey of the effects would surely support the conclusion that a good deal has been lost, shifted, and otherwise distorted in the translation. Consider the constructs of *repression* and *unconscious* mental events, for example. Dollard and Miller define these constructs in terms of a *lack* of something—a lack which eventually results in the "stupidity" of the neurotic individual. Repression is thus the inhibition of cue-producing responses which mediate thinking—and thinking is done at the conscious level.[117] The unconscious is the unlabeled or unverbalized.[118] Lumping these two ideas together, Dollard and Miller then state: "According to Freud . . . the repressed, or unconscious, is the unverbalized."[119] Though one can see some truth in this claim, he would have to keep in mind that Freud would mean here literally "vocalized" or "vocalizable" rather than what is formed in language terms (which is what Dollard and Miller mean by verbal labels). Just as we have seen learning theories interpret error as the lack of something—control—so too do they interpret unconscious behavior as lacking in something—verbal controls! Freud, on the other hand, saw *no* lack of anything in unconscious behavior—except in the sense that the individual was not in contact with unconscious contents.

If thinking is truly a question of manipulating labels or cue-producing responses, then how would the learning theorist explain Freud's views when he states *"the most complicated achievements of thought are possible without the assistance of consciousness."*[120] There is literally *no* difference between unconscious and conscious aspects of the mind in classical analytical theory, except in the very vital sense that some aspects of mind are kept out of awareness. Freud also left the question open about whether other than repressed contents could be contained in the unconscious regions of mind. In answering the challenges of Jungian psychology, with its archetypal inheritances from antiquity, Freud clarified his position on what is repressed and what is unconscious as follows: "We have learnt from psychoanalysis that the essence of the process of repression lies, not in putting an end to, in annihilating, the idea which represents an instinct, but in preventing it from becoming conscious. . . . Everything that is repressed must remain unconscious; but let us state at the very outset that the repressed does not cover everything that is unconscious. The unconscious has the wider compass: the repressed is a part of the unconscious."[121] This makes it possible for the Freudian to say that, just as consciousness may "take in" experience and formulate a sphere of information and even self-identity ("conscious man") so too can the unconscious have a sphere of impressions and an identity ("unconscious man"). Conceptualization is not limited to consciousness; the unconscious lacks nothing, and indeed the unconscious has a

far more accurate grasp of the psyche than does consciousness.

Probably the most graphic description of how conscious and unconscious mind works was given by Freud in a minor paper entitled "A Note Upon the 'Mystic Writing-Pad.' "[122] What Freud did there was use as a model the writing procedure often seen in children's playthings whereby a thin sheet of paper is laid over a waxed board which is grey or black in color. Over this we have a heavier, transparent, celluloid sheet entirely covering the thin "middle sheet." Both the thin paper and the celluloid are attached to the waxed board at one end of its usually rectangular form. If we now use a stylus and write upon the celluloid, this pressure forces the thin middle sheet slightly into the waxed board and it fixes there so that a message can be recorded. When, however, we wish to erase the written material, all we need do is lift the thin paper and celluloid (which acts as a protection for the thin paper) jointly, pulling them both away from the waxed background. It is now possible to write something new on the pad with our stylus. However, if we keep the waxed board in mind, we must be aware that the original impression, which passed through the light of day however fleetingly, remains permanently imbedded. It is in some comparable way, said Freud, that the "perceptual apparatus of our mind functions."[123] Consciousness deals only with the recorded meaning of the thin sheet; unconsciousness deals with the waxen impressions—though, of course, it can combine these in all of the active ways that consciousness activates thought.

This is another way in which Dollard and Miller have altered man's Freudian image to suit their stimulus-response image. In claiming that repression is due to the lack of labels or cue-producing responses, they make it a *passive* affair. Yet it is clear that Freud thought of repression in an active, intentional sense.[124] Repression does not arise until a cleavage has developed in the psyche. There must be some inner tension of opposition, with one wish implying a given aspiration (indulge lust) and a conflicting wish implying otherwise (reject lust). Hence, says Freud, *"the essence of repression lies simply in turning something away, and keeping it at a distance, from the conscious."*[125] Repression is never a passive business, and it goes on continuously as the disparity between what the person knows and yet "does not know" is continually resolved in the compromises of dreams, parapraxes, or neurotic symptoms. Furthermore, the cleavage on which repression rests invariably comes down to an ethical or moral conflict. There is some personal prompting, but a countering force of social convention or religious teaching keeps the individual from doing or thinking something without guilt. Morals and ethics are clearly on the side of intentional construct meanings. They state commandments or principles "for the sake of which" the individual is supposed to behave.

A related point here involves the nature of neurosis. Dollard and Miller have the neurotic made stupid by the lack of mediational aids repression has brought about. Freud's neurotic is hardly stupid, as the following quote from Freud demonstrates: "The more important portion of the mind, like the more important portion of an iceberg, lies below the surface. The unconscious of a neurotic employs the conscious portion of the mind as a tool to achieve its wishes. The convictions of a neurotic are excuses invented by reason to justify desires of the libido. The principles of a neurotic are costumes employed to embellish and conceal the nakedness of the unconscious desires."[126] We might say that the neurotic is not so stupid as he is consciously uninformed about what he *really* is after in life. One side of his identity (unconscious) uses the other, lesser important side (conscious). Rather than stupid the unconscious is cunningly wise.

It is this intelligent—literally *mental*—side of human motivation that behavioral translations have eclipsed. Take the matter of *anx-iety,* for example. Thanks to the skillful way in which they employ anxiety as a major motivational construct, the behaviorists have made neurotics (and all troubled or threatened individuals) appear to be moved to behave as they do in order to *avoid anxiety*. There are countless neoanalytical therapists today who would agree with the statement: "Neurotics behave as they do to avoid anxiety." Theorists of all persuasions have misunderstood Freud on this point, viewing his reference to a "neurotic anxiety" as confirmation of this view. Yet, as we know from Chapter 1, what motivates the neurotic is a *libidinal* involvement, a fixation which has persisted and which relates to a "danger situation" having the meaning of lascivious desire for a parent, fear of bloody reprisal in castration, and so forth. Indeed, since only the ego can experience anxiety, it is the unconscious side of this mental identity which *allows itself* to experience a slight amount of the anxiety which would take place if the "full truth were known" (see p. 67). It is the what is known and yet not known which motivates the human being—*not anxiety!*

Saying that neurotics are moved to avoid anxiety is like saying the reason we leave a railroad track with a train bearing down on us is because of that feeling of fright we sense based on our awareness of the impending danger (this would be Freud's "realistic" anxiety). Is it really the anxiety which moves us or our capacity to reason "for the sake of" a possibility in our immediate future—the likely possibility that if we do not move off the track we will surely die a wretched death? Freudian theory emphasizes the latter meaning, relegating anxiety to an instrumental role as warning sign, whereas behavior theory must make it appear that it is the anxiety *per se* which causes the behavior observed. Anxiety is extraspectively identifiable—we can show its effects on a polygraph—and whether we use humans or subhuman animals the theory written can be quite similar, hence the "wedding" of Freudian and behavioral thought. Yet, the image of man carried by one view is drastically different from that of the other.

This passive, directionless translation of Freudian mixed-model concepts into a strictly Lockean formulation has to be considered the major failing of Dollard and Miller's attempt to unite personality theory with the laboratory. The counter to this criticism which the learning theorist might make is: "Well, granted, my meanings may not be precisely those which Freud had proposed, but so long as I can account for the same behavioral observations in my theory which he accounted for in his, is this not proof that my theory is superior? Why not use a scientifically validated theory rather than a clinically supported theory, based on procedural evidence?" Though this argument has a certain appeal at first blush, we must ask ourselves if the stimulus-response theory, which here shows us excellent *integrative* functioning as a theory, would have *generated* the meaningful hypotheses about man which Freudian theory did? Could a Lockean strategy really comprehend a dialectical formulation such as reaction formation, or "knowing and not knowing at the same time"? This seems highly doubtful. Just as certain idiomatic phrases cannot be translated from French to English without great loss, so too the fundamental meanings of psychoanalysis will ever elude the stimulus-response conceptions. If this were not true, there would be no point to differentiating between our basic meaning constructs. The underlying difficulty here stems from the fact that one cannot *mean* pattern-intentional when he speaks exclusively in substance-impetus constructs!

The Motives to Psychotherapy

THE DECLINE OF SCHOLARLY MOTIVES

There is no doubt that Sullivan was always very sensitive to the needs of conventional science. He was articulate about the distinction between what we have called validating and procedural evidence, as in the following: "Utility of a [theoretical] conception may be said to hinge on its providing a ground for successful prediction of events, and for the construction of crucial experiments. Its plausibility of application to facts of observation already at hand is not a scientific sanction if the hypothesis cannot be *tested*. The therapeutic 'test' is no test at all."[127] One cannot rely upon the acceptance by the patient of an insight as necessarily proving the personality theory correct,[128] for there are always five different theories to explain and cure the same problem in living when five different therapists are involved as analysts of the causes.[129] Hence, Sullivan believed that we need *both* clinical and experimental study before we can establish a proper theory of man.[130] This attitude separates him clearly from Freud, who viewed his therapy as a scientific method of equal status to laboratory investigation.

Sullivan was not a naive or rabid empiricist. His very emphasis on the necessity of a psychiatrist to become part of what he is observing shows that Sullivan was a sophisticated empiricist: "There is no such thing as 'objective' observation; it is participant observation in which you may be the significant factor in the participation."[131] Even so, Sullivan clearly wanted to move psychiatry away from the older "case history" tactic of the classical analysts to a more modern, empirical, evidential approach. He once remarked that men who are "philosophical types" do not make good therapists, because they find the schizophrenic patient only too happy to philosophize (talk, talk, talk) rather than actively work to change what he is doing.[132] He had little patience with the highly intellectualized analyst, who spent inordinate amounts of time looking for theoretical subtleties in the client's history.[133] He once said: "I have never felt entitled to torture patients by the month to find out something that interested me but was of no special moment to them—if only because I do not think that anything can be learned by doing it."[134] This is the comment of a pragmatist, a man who is more interested in effectively removing a symptom than in learning "supposed" truths about why it is the symptom arose in the first place. He was well aware that a psychiatrist could effect cures without understanding everything that was happening in a scientific sense.[135] We therefore conclude that Sullivan's motives to therapy were not *primarily* scholarly.[136]

It is Dollard and Miller among our behaviorists who acknowledge the greatest role for psychotherapy as a means of gaining worthwhile knowledge about human behavior. They observe: "If psychotherapy were used only as a way of curing neurotic persons, it would have a real but limited interest to students of human personality. The psychotherapeutic situation, however, provides a kind of window to mental life. Advanced research students in psychology are taught the rudiments of the therapist's art so that they may sit at this window."[137] Such observations are naturalistic and hence uniquely important to personality study.[138] Furthermore, abnormals have much to teach about the behavior of normals.[139] This general acceptance of the consulting room as an extension of the laboratory was not to be seen in the behavioral theorists who followed in Dollard and Miller's wake.

Wolpe thus views his role as that of applied scientist. He has established his principles of behavioral change, and now moves to the clinical setting in order to put that knowledge into effect. Stampfl moves in the same direction. Though he is ready to admit that dynamic factors may have been involved in the origins of neurosis, the most effective way to remove symptoms once formed is to fall back on learning principles and animal experimentation.[140] The Skinnerians take a comparable position. Behaviorists thus do not view themselves as detectives, searching for clues to new insights regarding the human condition. They are *doing something* to their clients, effecting

changes in their behavior as efficiently as their previous scientific researches have made it possible to do.

CURATIVE MOTIVES AS UPPERMOST

Sullivan's major research efforts were pitched at his unique approach to the healing (improving interpersonal relations) of the schizophrenic. His research ward, his creative analysis of the hospital as a social milieu, the advocacy of halfway houses and early intervention, all point to what seems to be Sullivan's major motive—that of cure. One can see this motive burgeoning in the 1930 period, when Sullivan had parted ways with classical analysis. He summed it up in a typically Sullivanian sentence, as follows:

Either you believe that mental disorders are acts of God, predestined, inexorably fixed, arising from a constitutional or some other irremediable substratum, the victims of which are to be helped through an innocuous life to a more or less euthanastic exit—perhaps contributing along the way as laboratory animals for the inquiries of medicine, pathology, constitution-study, or whatever—*or* you believe that mental disorder is largely preventable and somewhat remediable by control of psycho-sociological factors.[141]

Sullivan held that a patient should have a definite expectation of improvement when he enters psychotherapy.[142] People are not in consulting rooms to further the selfish goals of the therapist. Speaking to therapists, Sullivan once said: "There is no fun in psychiatry. If you try to get fun out of it, you pay a considerable price for your unjustifiable optimism."[143] Those therapists who frequent cocktail parties and stroke their—often bewhiskered—chins with supposed wisdom as they make "profound" comments or who write case histories up for popular consumption to gain cheap prestige or notoriety were objects of scorn to Sullivan.[144] He felt there were entirely too many such "juveniles" sitting in therapists' seats.[145] Psychiatry cannot be indifferent to its clients. In the post-war years, Sullivan was to pitch his by then internationally acclaimed school of psychiatry in the direction of helpfulness to those in need: ". . . that is what we strive for in psychiatry of the Washington School: a rational system as to what can be done about anyone anywhere who is not living as well as he seems capable of living with his fellow man."[146] This commitment to action is one of the clearest manifestations of the character of the man who once said: "I am very much more interested in *what can be done* than in what has happened."[147] The analytical study of man had moved into a new age, in a new land, with a Yankee tempo of movement, change, and controlled improvement.

Most behavior therapists assume that they have been hired to do a job in therapy, and they hope to accomplish this goal as professionally and effectively as possible, in as little time as is necessary.[148] The behavior therapist does not need six months of free associations leading back to a client's earliest years in order to propose a program of change. He is usually on the road leading to change within a half-dozen sessions. He takes cure as his *major* responsibility. As Wolpe once expressed it: "The *raison d'etre* of psychotherapy is the presumption that it can overcome certain kinds of human suffering."[149] For a therapist to say, as Freud did (p. 75), that his therapy would occasionally make a client worse seems to the behavioral therapist a contradiction in terms and an admission of failure.

Behavior therapists are wont to call for experimental evidence to decide which therapy is the best to apply. As Wolpe expresses it: "Success is the yardstick by which alone comparison can be made with other modes of psychotherapy."[150] If Freudian therapy is "good" therapy, then let us compare the outcome of patients seen within this framework and patients seen within the framework of systematic desensitization or some such behavioral tactic. This challenge is almost flaunted by some be-

havioral therapists, so convinced are they that therapy means cure and only cure and especially since the evidence from such empirical tests is very favorable to behavioral therapies! Since we do not test the "dynamic insights" generated by one therapy versus the other (scholarly motive), analysis has little opportunity to gain ground on this score. Assuming that Freudian insights have been instructive to *all* men and that Freud has gleaned these theories from his consulting room contacts, this side of "success" should be an object of our attention. Such an argument strikes the behavior therapist as a *non sequitor,* since he feels the proper place for empirical study is the laboratory and not the consulting room.

ETHICAL THEMES AND MANIPULATION OF BEHAVIOR

Ethical themes are prominent in Sullivanian thought. In Chapter 5 we reviewed his theories on social revision, his desire to liberalize attitudes toward sex, and his general feeling that Western society in the World War II years was a "profoundly sick society" needing basic reorganization.[151] His views on the nature of man, whether he was capable of willful behavior, would also be relevant to this topic. Problems of conscience were ascribed to the culture. That is, Sullivan felt cultural values —often issuing from religious beliefs—foisted guilt on the individual actor.[152] Religions were not so different from delusions, said Sullivan, except that many people participated in them and thus helped systematize such beliefs.[153] Much of religious mythology can be traced to the autistic and preverbal attacks on the problems of living advanced by powerful historical figures. Such religious leaders introduced a modicum of parataxic distortion into the cultural lexicon, so that myths of a consensually understood nature were manufactured.[154] These are not in themselves harmful, particularly since they are often based upon the call for intimacy in human relations. But there *is* one aspect of religious conviction which can prove harmful to humanity: "the illusion that we have a more-or-less all-powerful . . . will."[155]

Although gains in character can be seen from this belief in a personal will, the losses in feelings of guilt for "wrong" actions engendered by this belief far outweigh such positive features. Sullivan could not convince himself that there was any such force as a will in the personality,[156] and he concluded: "There seems to be very little profit in psychiatry from dependence on any such idea as the mysterious power of the will."[157] Rather than furthering such outmoded thought, Sullivan called for an assessment of behavior in terms of field forces, interpersonal vectors, and sociopsychological variables of all sorts. Man must search for group solutions, extending even to international relations. Thus, Sullivanian theory has a close affinity for ethical motives as an extension of the basic prompting to cure unhealthy situations in living. Sullivan thus became a moralist and social critic of great influence in the post–World War II years. His untimely death doubtless cut this phase of his illustrious career as healer-to-mankind short.

The question of ethics is very complex regarding behavior therapy, since such "behavioral" issues are taken as the extension of a science and no more. We will need to develop this general topic in some detail. The behaviorist's logic in applying his science runs something like this: (1) experimentation has established certain lawful relationships between the independent variable (IV) and the dependent variable (DV) in laboratory studies; (2) for all practical purposes the IV is the stimulus (S) and the DV is the response (R); (3) the S is what ordinarily controls the elicited R; or, Rs which are emitted are controlled by their consequences; (4) all behavior is thus shown empirically to be controlled—that is, determined—behavior; hence, (5) insofar as change is possible in psychotherapy it too must be controlled change, initiated by the therapist—who effectively manipulates an IV or S—and

aimed at altering the behavior of the client—viewed now as DVs or Rs; (6) *conclusion:* therapy is a *process of means to ends* rather than a question of ends *per se.* When ends come into the picture they becloud the issue, for *any* therapist *must* control the behavior of his client! Empirical proof of this via the IV-DV sequence of validation establishes this beyond question.

Based on this train of reasoning, the behavioral therapist devotes himself to removal of a client's symptomatology, and he demonstrates empirically that this form of cure does not result in relapses, secondary symptoms, or otherwise harmful outcomes. Sometimes his willingness to innovate behavioral change makes him appear highly unconventional or immoral by customary standards, though objectively no one can cite adequate grounds for this charge. At other times he is seen as almost "fascistic"—the charge Castle was to hurl at Frazier—or at least power hungry in his zeal to influence the lives of others. There are roughly three kinds of ethical questions which seem to confound the objective approach which the behavior therapist is likely to feel he is taking in his curative techniques. We shall discuss these in turn.

1. Is it right to remove a symptom without confronting the issues which prompt it? A person's anxiety is often due to some mistreatment he has suffered at the hands of unthinking or uncaring parents. The accidents of life scar us all, and in a case like this we have no qualms about removing anxieties or guilt feelings. But what about other instances, in which the anxiety might have its source in an *improper* behavior which the client had indulged in. What if the client is not blameless after all? Are we still to remove the unwanted emotions without confronting the ethical issues that prompted them? Stampfl is the only behavior therapist who seems to touch on this question, dealing with problems of conscience acceptance as he does.[158] More fundamentally, we might ask how fair this ethical question is to the behavior therapist? Presumably, the dynamic theorist like Freud would, in exploring the compromise solutions and defensive maneuvers of the neurotic, provide a thorough insightful account of how guilt might stem from actual "death wishes" for a parent and so forth. But he too must inevitably take a position on the merits of this reaction—as Freud did, in fact, viewing harsh superegos as extremely important to the etiology of neuroses.

Dollard and Miller accepted the Freudian thesis, indicated in the following: "It is hard to say whether a morbid conscience is a worse enemy of life than a disease like cancer, but some comparison of this kind is required to emphasize the shock produced in the witness when he sees a psychotic person being tortured by such a conscience. Enough is known now to convince us that we should make the humble-seeming matter of cleanliness training the subject of serious research."[159] Hence, separating behavioral from dynamic therapies on a charge of this nature is not an easy matter. Doubtless just as many behavior therapists discuss the ethical concerns of the client with him as do the dynamic, insight therapists, and just as much harm or good can result from the removal of symptoms through either procedure. Though his formal position does not embrace introspective concepts *per se*, the behavior therapist views moral and ethical training as important sources of labels for mediation in behavior. He can hardly be blind to the necessity of dealing with such matters in an informal manner. Finally, therapists who are also physicians—as is Wolpe—emphasize that the doctor is there for the aid of his client. Refusing to treat a client's anxiety on ethical grounds would be like refusing to heal a syphilitic on moral grounds.

2. *Is it correct to violate convention in effecting therapeutic cures?* One of the charges sometimes leveled at the behavior therapist stems from his willingness to work actively with his client in designing changes which will counteract his symptoms. In a sense, the Stampflian implosive techniques are an example of such extremes. Although in fantasy, having people imagine horrible things happening to themselves or to others can occasionally be taken as ethically upsetting or demeaning. Wolpe has actually noted that some of his clients find it morally objectionable to use assertive tactics *in vivo*.[160] Is it proper to play the gamesmanship tactic of "one up on you" with fellow human beings (see Chapter 7, p. 347)? Wolpe usually tells his client at this point that there are three ways to approach life. In the first instance we can run roughshod over everyone and not care what happens to our fellow man. The other extreme would be to completely submerge oneself to the desires of others. Finally: "The third approach is the golden mean, dramatically conveyed in this fuller quotation from the Talmud: 'If I am not for myself, who will be for me? But if I am for myself alone, what am I?' "[161] Although an informal appendage in his therapy technique, it is interesting that this quotation bears a certain dialectical intonation. In any case, we must reassure our client that sticking up for his just rights does not make an immoral monster of him.

But Wolpe takes his therapist role even further than this. In treating cases of religious scrupulosity, he has given his clients books with an antireligious content.[162] The dynamic explanation of Freud's concerning the nature of religion could hardly be considered proreligion, of course (see Chapter 1). But, in a kind of behaviorally engineered spirit of change, Wolpe has even seen it as his role to encourage or help male clients with sexual problems to seek extramarital affairs with lovers or prostitutes when the wife is unable or unwilling to assist in the relaxation procedures. As he once put it: "Perhaps there will some day be a 'pool' of accredited women who will sell their services to men with sexual problems. At present there seems to be no other recourse than to seek out a regular prostitute—and it is usually no easy matter to find one who is both personally appealing and able to muster enough sympathetic interest to participate in the therapeutic program."[163] This concept of a "therapeutic extramarital relationship"[164] is open to the criticism now under consideration. However, Wolpe is moved to such extremes only when the marital partner is unable to assist. Furthermore, who can honestly say that a marriage without sexual compatibility is worse than a marriage with sexual adjustment brought about by extramarital training in systematic desensitization?

Doubtless the behavior therapist is not alone in his use of atypical techniques to resolve a client's neurotic problems. Some of the clients of a psychoanalyst also carry out extramarital affairs, or they come to therapy in the throes of such complex human relationships. The analyst can use such case history material as grist for his interpretative mill. Though he does not go out and arrange sexual liaisons for practical outcomes, the limitations which the analyst urges on his clients—such as not to marry or change occupations (see Chapter 1) —are sometimes just as ethically difficult to sustain as the behaviors the Wolpian might suggest. After all, Wolpe is not advising divorce as a routine solution, an outcome which is likely when copulatory problems in the marital relationship are left unattended. So, here again, we would not wish to differentiate clearly between behavior and dynamic therapists. Our last point, however, does bring up a clear theoretical divergence in outlook between the behaviorist and the humanist in what they consider to be the role of a therapist in the control of his client's life.

3. *Should all psychotherapists control the behavior of their client, and can they avoid doing so even if they try?* By far, the greatest sense of confusion over the ethics of psychotherapy enters when psychologists begin speaking of the *control* of human behavior. Psychol-ogy is often defined as the science which aims at controlling and predicting behavior. What more plausible demonstration of this science can we have than the case of a psychotherapist, controlling his client's behavioral responses back to a more pleasurable state of living? Yet, there are those therapists who take violent offense at the suggestion that they wish to control anyone's life, least of all the life of their client. What is the problem here? Confusion arises from the fact that the term "control"—and its frequent phrase-partner "prediction"—are used as if bearing a common meaning, yet three usages are constantly intermingled. Before we can appreciate the ethical issues involved, it will be necessary to review these different usages.

The first usage of *control* might be considered as a *theory of knowledge*. Validating evidence hinges upon the phrase "to control and predict," in the sense that we array controlled circumstances (IVs) and then make specific predictions to their expected effects (DVs). In this sense, as a science psychology deals with the control and prediction of behavior. The realist usually interprets control to mean a *literal* grasp of the antecedent (which he takes as the S rather than the IV), and then moving the value of this variable either up, down, or both up and down some scale of measurement in order to witness changes in the consequent (which he takes as the Rs rather than the DV). The impetus meaning is clearly given precedence in this "grasp and manipulate reality" interpretation of control. The idealist theorist is more likely to view control in the sense of *logical* control. The reason we manipulate the IV is to prove a point, much as we modulate our thought in debate. We state premises in debate. We propose experimental designs in research. We then draw other inferences, make observations, and reach a conclusion in debate. Likewise, we draw inferences, make observations (and measurements) and come to some statistically significant level of confidence in our research findings. We see the application of a pattern construct meaning in this usage of control. The control meets a plan—from premises to conclusion in the "flow of logic"—and measurement is only an aid to this patterned flow.

A second usage of "control and prediction" is found in psychology, usually among behaviorists or learning theorists. This usage stems from a fact we have already acknowledged, namely: "All behavior has an impetus meaning implied by definition." Behavior moves over time, hence it can be categorized as antecedent and consequent. If we now view antecedents as *controlling* consequents, then any behavior which can be seen over time is theoretically under the control of something and if we knew just "what," it could be predicted with accuracy. We might call this usage a *language of description,* since the point of this usage is further to describe the details of behavior. If we say "Jane is hostile," since we are in a time-bound universe, what we are doing in this sense is predicting that the next time Jane gets a chance to behave, her behavior will be patently hostile. Or, if one person is speaking and a second listening, the stimulus-response psychologists will sometimes claim that the former is controlling the latter's behavior or that a reciprocal control is in effect. Skinner once included as techniques of control education, seduction, moral suasion, and threats of force; he even hinted that the "tyranny of the beautiful woman"[165] may be so conceived. It is obvious that in these instances we are using terms to further explicate other terms, but we have done so vehicularly. Literally *anything* expressible in S-R terms becomes a "controlled" sequence of antecedent-to-consequent over time. These are theoretical descriptions, but not everyone would agree that being moved by a woman's beauty is comparable to acting in the face of threats of force. The discriminal theorist would wish to split some hairs here, and doubtless he would find this usage unacceptable.

This problem comes home with full weight when we consider our final usage of control and prediction—as a *method of social influence.* We refer here to the claim made by many behavior therapists that they see it as their role to control and presumably predict the course of their clients' lives. A succinct yet almost classical attitude of this sort is expressed in the following:

A science of psychology seeks to determine the lawful relationships in behavior. The orientation of a "psychology of behavior control" is that these lawful relationships are to be used to deliberately influence, control, or change behavior. This implies a manipulator or controller, and with it an ethical and value system of the controller.[166]

We note our method vs. theory fusion here —the presumption that demonstrating lawful relationships between IVs and DVs is only the preliminary to the manipulation of Ss and Rs in the application of science to follow. Furthermore, the decision to move from the first sentence to the second, from study of laws to their application, is not itself considered an *ethical* decision. There are those who would consider the decision *at this point* to be made upon ethical grounds. Ethics do not come in after the fact, as a sort of "rule stipulation" as to what we shall do to manipulate a person one way or another. The question of "what is good" for people is at the basis of all ethics, a term used by the Greeks to apply to man's character as opposed to his intellect.[167] Throughout history there has been disagreement on the matter of just what this "good" represents, how it is to be known, and who is to receive its benefits. It would be helpful to get these two sides in this dispute clearly in mind—usually said to be involved with the distinction between *intrinsic* and *instrumental* value.

On the one side, we have had over the centuries ethical philosophers who believed that each man holds within him the rational—sometimes called the intuitive—power to know the *good* implicitly and to carry out ethical obligations for their own sake as a matter of duty. There is no calculation from means to ends on this view; the *good* is not the pursuit of happiness so much as it is the fulfilling of duty which thereby makes one worthy of happiness. Immanuel Kant reasoned in this tradition when he argued: "Act so as to treat humanity, in thyself or any other, as an end always, and never as a means only."[168]

On the other side, we have had ethical philosophers who believed that the only thing men seek is happiness—sometimes phrased as "pleasure rather than pain"—and that they decide on what is good in the particular case by referring to *this* end. The goal of "general happiness" for oneself and one's fellow man is what defines the good of any present act of behavior. The British utilitarians Jeremy Bentham and John Stuart Mill reasoned in this tradition when they argued that pleasure is what people pursue in life and that the greatest pleasure over pain for the greatest number of people is the foundation of ethical obligation. Man does not have a sense of moral intuition which guides him, nor can he be counted on to do the *good* things through rational cogitation; it is the ultimate pleasure or pain associated with the observance or violation of moral rules which directs man's behavior.

Now, invariably, when the advocate of operant conditioning speaks of controlling behavior he presumes an instrumental interpretation of value. Viewing himself as the scientist, accruing lawful relationships in behavior, he tells himself as in the quote above something like "I must use my knowledge to help others, to help as many people as I possibly can." The greatest good for the greatest number is the criterion against which he thus judges his behavior. Moreover, he is likely to emphasize the control of behavior through "positive shaping"[169] rather than through so-called aversive stimulation or punishment. Skinner is noted for his rejection of aversive

controls, preferring to use positive reinforcement because of its proven utility—its tendency to make more people happy more of the time. He observes rather half-heartedly: "If we knew as much about negative reinforcement as we do about positive, I suspect we would find that it can be rather effective in shaping behavior, but at the moment it isn't very effective, and the negative by-products are still in evidence, so I am opposed to it."[170] This is a technical acknowledgment, but it is clear from his discussion that Skinner wishes to maximize positive reinforcement.[171] He speaks fondly of his followers in these terms: "When operant conditioners get together, there is never any criticism or bickering. Everyone tries to be helpful. They practice positive reinforcement, and it is a wonderful thing."[172]

The operant conditioner, viewing all behavior as controlled behavior anyway—a fact he has proven to his satisfaction through the IV-DV tactics of validation—therefore finds it common sense to manipulate behavior in therapy. And if he tries to use a positive form of manipulation, then he cannot understand why anyone who is knowledgeable about the findings of psychological experiments could object. The matter of intentionality, of the fact that a person is being controlled "for the sake of" another person's purposes, seems to him quite beside the point since everyone controls everyone else all of the time anyhow. In short, the behaviorist is wont to *shift meanings* back and forth between control as a theory of knowledge (his experiments), as a language of description (the way he speaks about the flow of events over time), and the decision *he then makes* to deliberately influence other people. Psychotherapists who take an intrinsic position on the nature of value say to him: "You are making a decision for others which you deny that they can make for themselves. *They* are 100 per cent determined, but you feel with your great knowledge of behavior that you can reason for them. You are actually assuming an ethical stance in relation to them, even as you deny that this is the case." When Skinner finds his critics irritated over *Walden Two* (1948) and observes that the only problem seems to be "that my good life was planned by someone,"[173] he is unknowingly dramatizing the fact that people do not want manipulation planned by others and also that he cannot really sympathize with the merits of this criticism. This is simply beyond his ken as theorist. It is not a legitimate point of his philosophy!

Yet the problem arises: How can we *empirically* assess what is *good*? Let us assume that we wish to manipulate the behavior of a pigeon. We are going to drop kernels of food each time the pigeon takes a step in some way and gradually, over time, through the method of successive approximations, teach him to walk a "figure-eight." This form of behavioral shaping has been achieved several times, and Skinner himself has "taught" pigeons to do remarkable things. An intrinsic ethical thinker might ask why have we selected a figure-eight to shape the pigeon's walk. Why not a circle or a diamond-shaped pattern? When it comes to human behavior, such questions are not silly. People want to know the *grounds*—"that for the sake of which"—a decision of this sort is made. If we have the devices to shape a person's behavior into "group dependency" or "self dependency," what should we do? Do we want people to be highly dependent on one another, to mix and spend time with one another? Or would we prefer a society in which people live more inwardly and individually, relying upon others for solace and support only during times of unusual difficulty? If Skinner or others have done research to prove that group dependency is a much more satisfying and efficient form of life and then proceeded to control us into believing and acting this way also, what do those of us who value individuality, social reserve, and solitude have to say? We argue that he has made an ethical decision on two counts: (1) to control us, and (2) to control us into *his* form of preferred behavior, based on *his* scientific findings.

But, cannot science empirically establish the *good*? As we reviewed in the Introduction, the scale of measurement of an experimental test must be predetermined in order to validate. This means that when we turn to the test of an ethical proposition, we must agree at the outset upon what will constitute a positive or negative outcome at the criterion end of our "control and prediction" sequence (theory of knowledge). We can then decide upon an experimental design and test the hypothesis; for example: "Group dependency is to be favored over self dependency because it leads to a happier and more fruitful life for all concerned" (instrumental ethic). But here is the rub. By defining happiness and the essentials of a fruitful life we must inevitably *rely upon ethical considerations at the outset,* even before we have nailed down our criterion measurements operationally. This *criterion problem* is insurmountable, and it signifies that all attempts to validate ethical hypotheses must ultimately beg the question. If a man tells us that he has empirical evidence on which to base his decisions as to how he will control us, we can be sure that this evidence rests upon premises which themselves have included debatable value decisions. Value decisions cannot be circumvented—including the decision to control others in the first instance. This is not to say that controlling others in some way *is* unethical. If we go to a psychotherapist and wish to have some annoying anxiety removed from our behavior, we might well have every expectation that the doctor will control us into no longer feeling as we do. The position one takes on the first two questions above merely defines *his* ethical value system. One cannot decide the issue for everyone. Some therapists do not wish to control their clients at all (see Rogers, Chapter 9). The only generality important at this point is that ethical issues are involved!

An important aspect of behavioral control has to do with the matter of *awareness* in the subject being manipulated. If one knows that he is being controlled, he can presumably be less vulnerable to unwarranted influence. Skinner has observed, concerning what the individual can do to defend himself against unwarranted controls: "The best defense I can see is to make all behavioral processes as familiar as possible. Let everyone know what is possible, what can be used against them."[174] This would seem to be a recognition that even positive shaping can be used to get a man to buy an automobile he cannot quite afford, convincing him in the process that he is a true success because everyone who "is" anyone has such an automobile and is in debt just as he is! Though he does not discuss such outcomes, it seems entirely possible to shape "happy" people caught up in a materialistic rat race. Of course, in judging materialism this harshly, we too are letting our values color our judgment. But surely the more aware we make our general populace the more likely that everyone can decide questions of control for himself. If this is the case, are we not acknowledging that intentionality *is* an aspect of human behavior? Well, to the behaviorist the answer would be "no" because he would consider the input knowledge about control possibilities to be mediational aids rather than proof that people can direct their own behavior.

The question of awareness has entered the picture in another way since the early work of operant conditioning in verbal situations. Dollard and Miller found the Greenspoon "mmm-hmm" experiment (see Chapter 7, p. 340) to be evidence that client insight might be achieved simply by the fact that a therapist covertly encourages one form of verbal emission rather than another. However, since Greenspoon's early work, other investigators have presented evidence to show that only when the experimental subject becomes aware of the experimenter's premise—the tactic of verbalizing "mmm-hmm" following every noun or every adjective stated by the subject—does real learning or the most effective learning take place.[175] If the subject does not "catch on" to this experimental premise, he is not likely to learn "as predicted." It comes down to: Is a subject being conditioned or is he cooperating with the experimental hypothesis once he catches on to it? Looked at in terms of theory construction issues, the Kantian model receives more support in these awareness findings than does the Lockean model. Looking through his Kantian glasses—cognitive or conceptual frames of reference—the subject who arrays (pattern construct) factors properly is the subject who is seen changing (impetus construct).

Here again the toughminded behaviorist is not prepared to forsake his Lockean model. He takes the findings on awareness as evidence of the role of mediation in learning. Awareness of the "response-reinforcement contingency" is thus simply another aspect of the stimulus complex which makes a reinforcement possible. The lesson for the student of personality is: all experimental findings are subject to interpretation! Data *never* kill a theory dead because, as we know from the Introduction, for any fact pattern unfolding before our eyes there are literally N possible theoretical explanations which might account for it. Furthermore, as has often been the historical lesson, tomorrow's data collections may well swing the pendulum back in the direction of the Lockean model on this question.

Notes

1. Dollard and Miller, 1950, p. 8. 2. Skinner, 1957, p. 458. 3. Ladd, 1899, p. 121. 4. Munsterberg, 1900, p. 1. 5. See Rychlak, 1968, Chapter VIII. 6. Watson, 1913, p. 158. 7. Evans, 1968, p. 15. 8. Hull, 1937, p. 2. 9. Evans, 1968,

p. 15. **10.** Skinner, 1957, p. 448. **11.** Wolpe, 1958, p. 4. **12.** Dollard and Miller, 1950, p. 100. **13.** Stampfl and Levis, 1967b, p. 25. **14.** See Sullivan, 1962, p. 4. **15.** Sullivan, 1964, p. 209. **16.** Sullivan, 1953, p. 10. **17.** *Ibid.*, pp. 367–368. **18.** *Ibid.*, p. 87. **19.** Sullivan, 1962, p. 83. **20.** See Sullivan, 1964, p. xxvii. **21.** Sullivan, 1956, p. 329. **22.** Sullivan, 1954, p. 24. **23.** Sullivan, 1956, p. 74. **24.** Sullivan, 1940, pp. 187–188. **25.** Dollard and Miller, 1950, p. 184. **26.** *Ibid.*, p. 421. **27.** Rychlak, 1968, p. 291. **28.** Wiener, 1954, p. 154. **29.** Dollard and Miller, 1950, p. 310. **30.** Wolpe, 1958, p. 73. **31.** Stampfl and Levis, 1969, p. 95. **32.** Skinner, 1948, p. 122. **33.** *Ibid.*, pp. 257–258. **34.** See Rychlak, 1968, Chapter XI. **35.** Skinner, 1957, p. 457. **36.** *Ibid.*, p. 458. **37.** Skinner, 1967, p. 391. **38.** Sullivan, 1956, p. 287. **39.** Sullivan, 1953, p. 110. **40.** Sullivan, 1964, p. 63. **41.** Sullivan, 1962, p. 108. **42.** Watson, 1924, p. 11. **43.** *Ibid.*, p. 216. **44.** Miller, 1957, p. 1277. **45.** Miller, 1963, p. 95. **46.** Miller, 1961, p. 753. **47.** Evans, 1968, p. 88. **48.** Skinner, 1950. **49.** Stampfl and Levis, 1969, p. 87. **50.** Wolpe, 1969, p. 219. **51.** Wolpe, 1958, p. 26. **52.** *Ibid.*, p. 34. **53.** Wolpe, 1969, p. 91. **54.** *Ibid.*, p. 99. **55.** Sullivan, 1962, p. 102. **56.** *Ibid.*, p. 297. **57.** Sullivan, 1964, p. 298. **58.** Sullivan, 1962, p. 142. **59.** *Ibid.*, p. 166. **60.** Sullivan, 1953, p. 26. **61.** Sullivan, 1940, pp. 13–14. **62.** Rychlak, 1968, p. 120. **63.** Dollard and Miller, 1950, p. 38. **64.** Wolpe, 1958, p. 3. **65.** Evans, 1968, p. 23. **66.** Wolpe, 1969, p. 55. **67.** Evans, 1968, pp. 7–8. **68.** Wolpe, 1969, p. 4. **69.** Stampfl and Levis, 1969, p. 88. **70.** Dollard and Miller, 1950, p. 63. **71.** Rychlak, 1968, pp. 215–220. **72.** Evans, 1968, p. 12. **73.** Rychlak, 1968, p. 57. **74.** Wolpe, 1969, p. viii. **75.** Sullivan, 1964, p. 324. **76.** *Ibid.*, p. 296. **77.** Sullivan, 1962, p. 142. **78.** Dollard and Miller, 1950, p. 34. **79.** *Ibid.*, p. 209. **80.** *Ibid.*, p. 100. **81.** Skinner, 1957, p. 96. **82.** Dollard and Miller, 1950, p. 414. **83.** *Ibid.*, p. 314. **84.** Skinner, 1956, p. 223. **85.** *Ibid.*, p. 224. **86.** *Ibid.*, p. 225. **87.** *Ibid.* **88.** *Ibid.*, p. 227. **89.** *Ibid.* **90.** Spence, 1956, pp. 16–17. **91.** *Ibid.*, p. 9. **92.** Cronbach, 1957. **93.** See Rychlak, 1968, pp. 103–110. **94.** Dollard and Miller, 1950, pp. 90–91. **95.** Evans, 1968, p. 105. **96.** Sullivan, 1962, p. 31. **97.** Sullivan, 1953, p. 51. **98.** Sullivan, 1940, p. 193. **99.** Sullivan, 1953, p. 369. **100.** Sullivan, 1956, p. 8. **101.** Sullivan, 1964, p. 202. **102.** Evans, 1968, p. 19. **103.** Skinner, 1971, p. 67. **104.** Dollard and Miller, 1950, p. 314. **105.** *Ibid.*, pp. 324, 441, 445. **106.** *Ibid.*,

p. 219. **107.** Wolpe, 1969, p. 109; Stampfl and Levis, 1969, p. 99. **108.** Evans, 1968, p. 109. **109.** *Ibid.*, p. 47. **110.** Skinner, 1957, p. 459. **111.** Evans, 1968, p. 107. **112.** *Ibid.*, p. 104. **113.** *Ibid.*, p. 103. **114.** *Ibid.*, p. 65. **115.** Skinner, 1971, p. 120. **116.** *Ibid.*, p. 208. **117.** Dollard and Miller, 1950, p. 10. **118.** *Ibid.*, p. 136. **119.** *Ibid.*, p. 198. **120.** Freud, Vol. V, p. 593. **121.** Freud, Vol. XIV, p. 166. **122.** Freud, Vol. XIX, p. 227. **123.** *Ibid.*, p. 232. **124.** Freud, Vol. V, p. 604. **125.** Freud, Vol. XIV, p. 147. **126.** Freud and Bullitt, 1967, p. 106. **127.** Sullivan, 1962, p. 141. **128.** *Ibid.*, p. 151. **129.** *Ibid,* p. 207. **130.** *Ibid.*, p. 197. **131.** Sullivan, 1954, p. 103. **132.** Sullivan, 1962, p. 289. **133.** *Ibid.*, p. 35. **134.** Sullivan, 1956, p. 270. **135.** *Ibid.*, p. 368. **136.** Sullivan, 1953, p. 167. **137.** Dollard and Miller, 1950, p. 3. **138.** *Ibid.*, pp. 6, 98. **139.** *Ibid.*, p. 5. **140.** Stampfl and Levis, 1967a, p. 498. **141.** Sullivan, 1962, p. 270. **142.** Sullivan, 1954, p. 16. **143.** *Ibid.*, p. 10. **144.** *Ibid.*, p. 12. **145.** Sullivan, 1953, p. 295. **146.** Sullivan, 1964, p. 262. **147.** Sullivan, 1956, p, 195. **148.** Dollard and Miller, 1950, p. 275. **149.** Wolpe, 1969, p. 18. **150.** Wolpe, 1958, p. 204. **151.** Sullivan, 1964, p. 155. **152.** Sullivan, 1962, p. 232. **153.** Sullivan, 1964, p. 80. **154.** Sullivan, 1956, p. 348. **155.** Sullivan, 1953, p. 173. **156.** Sullivan, 1940, p. 191. **157.** Sullivan, 1953, p. 301. **158.** Stampfl and Levis, 1969, pp. 107–108. **159.** Dollard and Miller, 1950, p. 141. **160.** Wolpe, 1969, p. 19. **161.** *Ibid.* **162.** *Ibid.*, p. 257. **163.** *Ibid.*, pp. 77–78. **164.** *Ibid.*, p. 77. **165.** Skinner, 1955, p. 549. **166.** Krasner, 1962, p. 201. **167.** Sidgwick, 1960, Chapter I. **168.** *Ibid.*, p. 274. **169.** Evans, 1968, p. 42. **170.** *Ibid.*, p. 34. **171.** *Ibid.*, p. 72. **172.** *Ibid.*, p. 111. **173.** *Ibid.*, p. 47. **174.** *Ibid.*, p. 54. **175.** Dulany, 1961; Spielberger and DeNike, 1966.

Part Three
Kantian Models in the Phenomenological Outlook

9

Applied Phenomenology: The Client-Centered Psychology of Carl R. Rogers

Since the view of personality examined in the present chapter takes root in phenomenological and gestalt psychology, we will first review several important predecessors of Rogerian thought. Phenomenology and existentialism have common philosophical ties as well, so the survey of existentialism in Chapter 10 (pp. 443–446) will continue the present review.

Background Factors in Rogerian Thought

EDMUND HUSSERL (1859–1938)

Husserl is often called the "father of phenomenology" even though he was not the first to speak of phenomena, nor was he the first philosopher to refer to his outlook as phenomenological (that distinction belongs to Hegel). Yet he did more to define the issues and to stimulate the general phenomenological point of view than any other theorist.

Kant had divided the world into two spheres: the *noumena* (what something is "in itself," independent of our sensations) and the *phenomena* (our sensory knowledge of "things" in the external world). Though he believed that noumena existed, Kant argued that we could never know such "things in themselves" directly and that, in fact, our mind through its categories of the understanding framed in the noumenal world. Husserl's philosophy originates in this distinction between noumena and phenomena. He felt that no matter how prepared we are to be empirical, all we can ever know "immediately" is our phenomenal experience. Hence, in the last analysis science is based upon *intersubjectivity*, i.e., the approximation to objective agreement which individual subjects can arrive at from the perspective of their unique *phenomenal* worlds. As Husserl said of phenomena: "Everything that in the broadest sense of psychology we call a psychical phenomenon, when looked at in and for itself, is precisely phenomenon and not nature [i.e., noumenal existence]. . . . A phenomenon, then, is no 'substantial' unity; it has no 'real properties,' it knows no real parts, no real changes, and no causality; all these words are here understood in the sense proper to natural science."[1]

The natural scientist can properly define things materialistically and see events in terms of antecedent events pushing consequent events along in a mechanistic fashion. But if we realize that natural scientists are human beings, and to that extent "subjects" dealing with their phenomenal experience, then surely we must appreciate that to describe *them* in terms identical to those of inanimate life would be a gross mistake. Man, said Husserl, is directed by *intentionality,* and the fundamental intention of all men is to relate their subjective grasp (phenomena) to an objective referent (noumena). We need a new language of description and with it a new *method* of scientific investigation if we are to capture the human condition.

What sort of method is this to be? Husserl devoted much of his life to working out a proper phenomenological method, one that would capture experience as known by the man subjectively "within" phenomenal experience. Since the question of independent, noumenal existence is irrelevant (who can know it?), the phenomenological method must capture the *essence* of meaning. This "essence" is the conceptual significance of the words we use to describe our phenomenal world through an act of intuition; it involves the immediate, unbiased knowing of what is going on in our phenomenal experience.[2] This method is not precisely "introspection," because the introspective psychologists of Husserl's time felt that they were studying the body's *real* or noumenal

processes. Phenomenology does not deal with "being there," since the question of existence always founders on the noumenal-phenomenal dichotomy.[3] Hence, to the question "What can phenomenology teach us?" Husserl would have answered:

Phenomenology can recognize with objective validity only essences and essential relations, and thereby it can accomplish and decisively accomplish whatever is necessary for a correct understanding of all empirical cognition and of all cognition whatsoever: the clarification of the "origin" of all formal-logical and natural-logical principles (and whatever other guiding "principles" there may be) and of all the problems involved in correlating "being" (being of nature, being of value, etc.) and consciousness. . . .[4]

Husserlian phenomenology is completely idealistic in tone. Since the scientist can only be objective through an exercise of his subjective cognitions, he must have a means of investigating his personal phenomenological experience even as he looks out into the world for his more materialistic, mechanical explanations of the world. This requires that the scientist study his consciousness, and every act of consciousness is "consciousness of" something.[5] Thus, consciousness is basically intentional; it seeks to know things beyond itself. We must have a way of confronting consciousness as a process itself and studying that process in as unbiased a fashion as possible. We must reflect and clarify how we become "conscious of" events in experience.[6] We are not studying "that" but "this," our very beginnings as conscious, intelligent beings. Hence, Husserl can say of his proposed science: ". . . we meet a science of whose extraordinary extent our contemporaries have as yet no concept; a science, it is true, of consciousness that is still not psychology; a phenomenology of consciousness as opposed to a natural science about consciousness."[7]

Kant was alert to the seeming fact that man is able to turn his mental attention to himself

—to reflexively study his own mind as a process. If man has machine properties, then unlike other machines in nature this man-machine can turn back on itself and observe its own parts as they are at work. To describe this process Kant introduced the term *transcendental*. We transcend when we go beyond the usual functioning and see things as they happen from the vantage point of an observer outside the usual pale of activity. Husserl borrowed this construct to speak of his method of personal study as "transcendental phenomenology." The individual turns into himself to study the organization and function of his phenomenological experience.

The success that Husserl achieved in these phenomenological studies is debatable. His career seemed more a critical introduction to the establishment of a phenomenological method than an actual demonstration of the fruits of that method. He presented insights into the nature of consciousness, particularly as it relates to the dimension of time, but one cannot point to a uniform body of knowledge in this area as one can point to a body of knowledge in gestalt psychology—an approach to psychology which acknowledged the role of phenomenological description.

THE GESTALT PSYCHOLOGISTS: MAX WERTHEIMER (1880–1943), WOLFGANG KÖHLER (1887–   ), AND KURT KOFFKA (1886–1941)

When psychology began as an independent branch of science, a major preoccupation of its first proponents was sensation and perception. How does man come to know his environment through his senses, and what constitutes an adequate explanation of his higher mental processes? Watson's emphasis on the more fluid aspects of behavior was not in vogue during the last few decades of the nineteenth century and the first decade of this century. The "founding fathers" of experimental psychology, Wilhelm Wundt and Hermann von Helmholtz, were trained in physiology and physics. They took it as their role to explain human behavior in the general style of all natural scientists which meant finding the underlying substrate of energies (atomic structures, ultimately) which *really* moved events.[8] This actually amounted to a quest for the noumena! The entire strategy of psychological study was thus pitched at the breakdown of experience into the elemental properties of sensation, the nervous impulses being carried along by individual neurones, and the physical structures of the sensory apparatus (eye, ear, tactual receptors).

Many young men entering the field of psychology could not accept this form of material reductionism, which seemed bent on ignoring the totality of human experience. Looking back, Köhler spoke of the excitement generated when an alternative to the reductionistic approach was first advanced: ". . . it was not only the stimulating newness of our enterprise which inspired us. There was also a great wave of relief—as though we were escaping from a prison. The prison was psychology as taught at the universities when we still were students. At the time, we had been shocked by the thesis that all psychological facts (not only those in perception) consist of unrelated inert atoms and that almost the only factors which combine these atoms and thus introduce action are associations forged under the influence of mere contiguity. What had disturbed us was the utter senselessness of this picture, and the implication that human life, apparently so colorful and so intensely dynamic, is actually a frightful bore."[9] The man who was to father this "new look" was Max Wertheimer (1945).

In 1912, one year before Watson's epic call for a behaviorism (Chapter 6), Wertheimer published his classic paper on *phenomenal movement,* or more simply, the *phi-phenomenon.* Essentially, this perceptual phenomenon accounts for our seeing motion based solely upon the temporal displacement of perceived objects in our visual field, even when no actual external movement is taking place. The most obvious example here is the motion picture, but we can generalize this emergent property of moving points to note that melodies emerge as total impressions from individual notes combined in certain tempos. The point Wertheimer was making and the criticism which his students and collaborators, Köhler and Koffka, were to continue throughout their eminent careers was: "we can never find these qualities of experience in reductive experiments." Thus, the meaning of *gestalt* is that of the "total, whole, essential nature of." Just as Husserl argued that an essence cannot be found in reality, so too the gestalt psychologists argued that man is an organizing animal, one who arranges an incoming physical (distal) stimulus into a unique totality at the level of phenomenal experience (proximal stimulus). Man does as much to reality in shaping experience as reality does to man.

Thus the first major reaction to an elementistic psychology, or a mechanical psychology, occurred in the field of perception. Gestalt psychology takes root in perceptual study, though its founders were to extend their descriptions to higher mental processes, personality description, and even social organization.[10] And in doing so they specifically advocated the use of phenomenology, which they defined as follows: "For us phenomenology means as naive and full a description of direct experience as possible."[11] The emphasis on naive description is important, for the gestaltists were reacting to the strictures of reductionistic experimental psychology, in which introspective study was based upon a "trained introspection." When we preselect what we wish to introspect about, the gestaltists were saying, the resultant product is often a perversion of true phenomenal experience.

For example, science teaches us that some things are sensations and other things are realities. A cloud may appear threatening to us as it approaches from across the sky, but this threat is not really being "seen." The cloud is just a collection of liquid material particles.

It has no intrinsic quality of threat. Yet, says Köhler, to the primitive mind a phenomenal experience of threat *is* perceived directly in the cloud.[12] The primitive has no science to tell him otherwise. He can only perceive what he perceives, and hence the natural environment is experienced in quite other terms than it appears to modern man. Indeed, Köhler once suggested that modern man could not be completely naive about his phenomenal experience, so biased had his perceptions become thanks to the influence of natural science.[13] The primitive belief in spiritual forces such as "mana" (see Jung, Chapter 3) can thus be taken as a directly perceived *phenomenal* experience.

Making an analogy to physical science the gestaltists spoke of a "field" of vision, organized into a molar totality and acting as a gestalt. Though it was a constantly changing field, the relative properties within the field of vision remained somehow constant and obeyed certain laws of organization. The subparts of the total were *articulated* and distinct, yet the overall effect could not be predicted from a study of the parts! Over a period of years the gestaltists named a series of laws which described how this *phenomenal field* was organized, as follows:

Law of unit formation and segregation. Uniform stimulation produces a cohesive field, whereas inequality in level of stimulation produces articulation in the field.[14] A circle or ring would be an example of the very cohesive field, unbroken by articulated inner parts. If we now begin drawing lines through the circle, making it into a cartwheel design, we are increasing the complexity of articulation. Generally, the geometric form which has the most cohesive properties is the one which is most likely to emerge in vision and the easiest one to retain in memory.

Law of closure. If we perceive a straight line, it remains as such until it may begin to curve and return to its point of origin—at which time there is great cohesive pressure to "close" the line into an actual figure of some sort.[15] Thus, a circular line which is not completely closed into a ring will be perceived as a closed ring by the average person, especially if he merely glances at the seemingly incomplete figure. Closed areas are more stable than open areas because they have the cohesiveness of a uniform field or subfield.

Law of good shape. The shapes which emerge perceptually—as in closure—will be those which have the best balance and symmetry.[16] An unbalanced, asymmetrical figure is not cohesive and will not be perceived ("seen") so readily as a nicely balanced figure.

Law of good continuation. Straight lines or the contours of geometric figures seem to follow their natural propensity to continue as they "are." A curve will proceed in the direction of its arc, an ellipse will continue as an ellipse, and so forth.[17] In addition this principle can be seen in a melodious tune which continues in the direction which previous notes have taken it. There is a certain "demand" placed upon the melody to flow in the line of best continuation.

Law of proximity and equality. Items in the perceptual field which are equal or similar in nature will be grouped together, as will items which are simply placed close to one another.[18] In viewing this series of dots . . . . we are prone to see three groups of three dots, rather than nine dots in a row. Dispersing lines within this collection of dots would result in our organizing the lines *and* dots as differentially articulated aspects of the total phenomenal perceptual field (proximal stimuli).

These laws of organization are not mutually exclusive categories of description. They can interact, as for example when a good continuation might take precedence over closure. In point of fact, the gestaltists recognized that all of the laws of organizing the proximal stimulus could be subsumed by the single law of *pragnanz,* which states that the "psychological organization will always be as 'good' as the prevailing conditions allow."[19] By "good" the gestaltists meant regular, symmetrical, simplified, pristine, and perfect articulation. Furthermore, it is possible to speak of such figures only if we also consider the "ground" on which they rest. A closed circle, for example, closes as a cohesive figure set against a background of cohesiveness. The contour of the circle is defined inwardly, so that the only way we see *any* figure—the circle or our friend John—is as a figure framed-in by a ground. We can thus name another all-embracing *law of figure-against-ground formation:* ". . . if two areas [of the perceptual field] are so segregated that one encloses the other, the enclosing one will become the ground, the enclosed the figure."[20] When we now add that this figure will tend to be as simple, well articulated, cohesive as is possible, we have rephrased the law of pragnanz in figure-ground terms.

Using the laws we have just reviewed, plus some others which we need not go into, the gestalt psychologists began to extend their style of thought to include all manner of human behavior—from human learning to personality organization, and from the structuring of creative intelligence to the structuring of social groups. Indeed, Wertheimer proposed that the actual motions of the molecules and atoms of the brain, insofar as they moved about, conformed to the patterns of gestalt principles. As molar processes, both the actions of physiological structures and the very way in which we go about thinking are *isomorphic* —that is, identical as to form.[21] This principle of isomorphism was the supreme gestalt response to the reductionistic theories of Wundt and Helmholtz. In a real sense, isomorphism claimed an *identity in pattern* for the phenomena (thought) and the noumena (the swirling of atoms and molecules in matter).

In this sense gestalt psychology takes on a nativistic tone. The view is based on the belief that certain patterns within nature literally do exist, and man does not "learn" to perceive things as they are or to think about things as he does, so much as certain innate tendencies within the patterned natural processes of perception and thinking themselves dictate just how these activities will be carried on. Experience *can* influence figure-ground relations, of course, but usually this tendency to think in a certain way is given spontaneously by nature—much in the way that our hearts and livers function in a given way from the outset.[22]

A conceptualization of man as an ego system, set within the social environment, was also developed by the gestaltists analogically to a figure-ground relationship. As Koffka said: ". . . the Ego seems to behave like any other segregated object in the field."[23] It senses disbalances in the phenomenal field and gravitates to situations of balance to relieve motivational tensions (pragnanz). The emotions, sensations of pain and pleasure, wishes, desires, and all needs are to be seen as peculiarly ego functions. Now, in seeking gratifications of these field-produced phenomena the ego must relate itself to a host of environmental (ground) factors. Above all, the ego finds itself immersed as a subunit within the broader units of family, neighborhood, social class, nation, and so forth. And each of these concepts is to be seen itself as a figure upon an ever broader ground. To gain some feel for how the gestaltist might speak about group formation we might turn to Koffka: "Groups are more or less closed, with more or less defined boundary lines. Consequently, the more closed they are, the more difficult it is to introduce new members into them. . . . It seems that the degree of closure and of resistance to innovations vary directly with each other. Thus the rural group is more conservative than the city group."[24] Koffka went on to break down group formation into the articulated subunits of leader, follower,

class levels in the social hierarchy, and so forth.[25]

KURT LEWIN (1890–1947)

Though he was not an orthodox gestalt theorist, Kurt Lewin, as the founder of "field theory" in psychology, received considerable stimulation from the work of Wertheimer, Koffka, and particularly Köhler—all of whom were his colleagues for a time at Berlin University.[26] Lewin took the concept of a perceptual phenomenal field and drew it out into a view of the *life space,* the total psychological environment which each of us experiences subjectively. This construct embraced needs, goals, unconscious influences, memories, and literally anything else which might have an influence on one's behavior.[27] Lewin formulated the equation $B = f(LS)$, or "behavior is a function of the life space." This must be viewed as an alternative description of behavior to the one proffered by the behaviorists, who viewed behavior as a function of the "external stimulus." The life space is like a phenomenological membrane coming between man and the external world. Rather than seeing behavior as an *incoming* process of stimulus-to-response, Lewin emphasized that behavior takes on "field properties" as an outgoing process of organization and interpretation.

The life space is thus a phenomenal field.[28] In order to predict an individual's behavior accurately we must know the patterned structuring of the total life space. In defining the articulation and resultant structure of the life space Lewin did not fall back upon specific laws of organization as the classical gestaltists did. He and his many students worked out a number of alternative concepts, some of which directly overlapped orthodox gestalt theory, though others did not. One such concept was the *level of aspiration.*[29] Lewin's field theory emphasized that human behavior was directed toward goals and that man set his own expectations for what would be taken as a success or a failure experience in life. For some—even talented—students, a grade of "C" is considered successful attainment while others would be as crushed by this "low grade" as if it had been an "F." The former have acquired the habit of setting low levels of aspiration for themselves, while the latter have come to project high levels of aspiration—at least in this one sphere of possible achievement.

The course of action one might follow between where he stands at this moment and the direction and distance of his goal was termed the *path* or *pathway*. Since the life space included influences from the past and also took future life expectancies into consideration—aspirations or goals are by definition "ahead" of us in time—it was possible to speak of the *directedness* of behavior. If a goal had attractive features it has a *positive valence*; if it was threatening or distasteful it has a *negative valence*. As we noted in Chapter 6 (p. 304), Neal Miller's researches on conflict were initially stimulated by the theoretical discussions of Lewin, who combined his positive and negative valences into the various types of frustrations a person might experience in having to decide between positive, negative, and both positive and negative goals. Such valences were not to be conceived—as Miller was eventually to do—as somehow assigned to the goals by a human being separated from the goal in question. The goal is "in" the person's immediate perception. Returning to Köhler's example above, just as the primitive sees threat *in the cloud,* so too does a positive or negative valence (power of attraction or repulsion) exist *in the object as experienced via the life space!*

If behavior is the result of a total life space, functioning constantly in the present, combining features from the past, and projecting a directedness into the future, then identities within this field other than the "person" might influence the action to be observed. For example, if we pass by a mail box on the way to our place of work each morning that mail box is *not* quite the same item in our life space each morning. On the morning when we have no letter to drop it is merely a potential obstacle to our free stroll, like any other object—a tree, a post, or whatever. But on those mornings when we have a letter to mail—and especially when it is a particularly important letter—the mail box takes on quite a different status. Rather than something to be stepped around, the box literally beckons us to use it (it has great positive valence). Phenomenologically speaking, it has taken on what Lewin called a *demand character,* so that it would be as correct to say that the "box brought us to it" as it would be to say "we went to the box." It is only man's egocentricity as the focus of interest in his phenomenal field (life space), which makes the latter description of behavior the correct one. Yet the field forces in his life space play no favorites. The stresses and strains of disbalance when one aspect of the field beckons must be thought of as acting in a molar fashion to attain a new balance (pragnanz). The person is merely one figure among other figures on an environmental ground.

Lewin hoped that a system of mathematics would eventually be adapted to aid in the prediction of events taking place in the life space. He specifically advocated the use of topological geometry, a nonquantitative geometry which seemed potentially useful in the handling of structural and positional factors in the life space. Actions in the life space were not always identical to those seen in the *foreign hull,* which is what Lewin called external experience, the palpable reality (a derivative notion of the noumena). Sometimes the shortest distance between two points in phenomenal experience is to move *away* from the goal, as any girl knows who has "played hard to get" with a boyfriend. But how to measure this kind of complex psychological behavior with mathematical precision was quite another matter; though Lewin advocated its development for this purpose the refinement of topology for field theory was never realized.

In conceptualizing just how the life space was organized Lewin fell back upon the differentiation and articulation theoretical models of the gestaltists. Thus he spoke of *regions* within which aspects of the individual's life could be distinguished, with more or less permeable membranes differentiating them. Someone with an active religious life "on Sundays" but rather unscrupulous business ethics throughout the week would be a person with no internal *communication* between regions. In moving from one life area to another, such as going from a school to a home setting, the individual was said to *locomote*. And, as an aspect of the total life space, the individual was himself a differentiated region. Motivations central to the personality were themselves figures on the ground of a total person. So, even within the individual there was articulation and differentiation of molar processes. At the lowest level, where differentiation was thought to cease, we can speak of the *cell*—a kind of a modified substratum theoretical conceptualization which put Lewin closer to the Wundt-Helmholtz line than was true of the classical gestaltists. Of course, Lewin did not contend that one had to reduce personality description to these smallest common denominators in order to render an appropriate scientific account. He remained a true molar theorist to the end.

At the upper reaches of organization we can begin speaking of the social group. Actually, during the last decade of his life Lewin was moving away from personality theorizing toward the role of social theorist. He probably did more for the establishment and development of social psychology than any other theorist in the history of psychology. In 1939 he coined the phrase "group dynamics," and in the early 1940s he established the Research Center for Group Dynamics at the Massachusetts Institute of Technology (MIT) (later moved to the University of Michigan following his death). He and his students performed the first controlled studies of leadership, in which they contrasted democratic, authoritarian (autocratic), and laissez faire types of group leadership.[30] The model which underwrote this new area of group dynamics had the typical gestalt emphasis on totality, organization of roles, and the resultant channeling of hostile tensions outward to scapegoats, and so forth. Lewin also worked on propaganda and the role of prejudice in the control of human relations. Indeed, his life work always bore the stamp of relevancy and practical application. Yet he was fond of observing: "There is nothing as practical as a good theory."[31]

Thanks to his open mind and practical approach Lewin and his associates (Ronald Lippitt, Leland Bradford, and Kenneth Benné) initiated the group encounter activity which has come to be known as T-groups (Training groups) or "sensitivity training."[32] In 1946 the researchers from MIT were holding a summer workshop aimed at training leaders to become engaged in countering racial and religious prejudice. The project was sponsored by the Connecticut State Inter-Racial Commission, and it eventually led to the creation in 1947 of the National Training Laboratories. The workshop brought together some 41 hand-picked professional educators or social agency workers, about half of whom were minority group members from the black and Jewish segments of the population. The strategy of the workshop was to begin with open discussion among participants and then to reach a group consensus if possible on various social issues such as the nature of prejudice, its causes, and how to counter it. A research staff recorded the group interactions and then reported on their observations during evening sessions at which Lewin was present in his capacity as researcher. Apparently some of the subject-participants also attended these evening reporting sessions, which were conducted on the campus of Teachers' College, New Britain, Connecticut. When the point of view being expressed by the research psychologist conflicted with that of a subject-participant's recollection of what had taken place that day a kind of spontaneous "group dynamic" took place in the often heated discussions which followed.

Rather than discourage such commentary from his subjects, Lewin encouraged it and thus literally began a "second study" of group interactions following feedback from earlier interactions. This was quite a unique circumstance, in which a subject under study could "come back at" those who seemed to be formulating information about his performance—not all of which he agreed with. Also, he was to develop new insights regarding his impact on others in the open group discussion. As a result, the Lewinian investigators were to find a more personalized, emotional reaction emerging in the evening session. Literally, the gathering had become "group therapy," with tremendous potential for personality change among the participants. Lewinian advocates were to refine this tactic of group confrontation into a device for the promotion of social change. As we shall see later in the chapter, Carl Rogers picked up on the importance of such "encounter" groups for therapeutic purposes. Therefore, though he was not a psychotherapist, Kurt Lewin has left us with an extremely important legacy having far-reaching implications for the healing of social ills.[33]

OTTO RANK (1884–1939)

Along with Adler and Jung, Otto Rank is generally considered one of Freud's most talented and important coworkers. Unlike these, Rank was not a physician. He joined the psychoanalytical circle while still a young man of roughly 18 years. He served as the secretary to the Vienna Psycho-Analytical Society while attending the University of Vienna. He was to stay with Freud for approximately 20 years, until the appearance of his first major book, *The Trauma of Birth* (1922–1923). As he had been moved to do in other instances (see Chapter 1), Freud parted with his younger colleague—though the split with Rank was

not nearly so bitter as were others. This separation between teacher and student became a symbolic manifestation of Rankian theory, for Rank's entire outlook is colored by this necessity for man to express his own will, to shift for himself, and to accept the necessity of being an independent person.

Rank left Vienna in 1926 for Paris, followed by several trips to America, and then in 1935 he moved to the United States permanently. He died in 1939. While in America Rank became quite influential in the area of social work, where he and his major student, Jessie Taft, helped promote what has been called the "functional" school—as opposed to the "diagnostic" school—of social case work. Essentially, in Rank's view a social worker takes a dynamic approach to the client and, through relatively short term therapy contact, effects a cure by helping the client to exert his own will, to assume responsibility for his own life. Diagnosis or problem definition is thus secondary to the actual change in living. It was while he was the Director of the Rochester Guidance Clinic that Carl Rogers came into contact with the philosophy of treatment reflected in Rankian social work, and we shall see definite parallels in the two outlooks.

It is essential that we grasp Rank's convictions regarding the purpose of psychotherapy. He never tired of emphasizing that the therapy relationship is for the client and *not* the therapist. If the latter insists upon pressing his pet theories onto his client, generalizing from past clients to the human being now facing him, he can never cure what is "wrong" in the life of a neurotic. Hence, says Rank: "In each separate case it is necessary to create, as it were, a theory and technique made for the occasion without trying to carry over this individual solution to the next case."[34] The effective therapist learns the speech pattern of his client, as well as the particular point of view regarding the world expressed within that individualized idiom.[35] It is the spontaneity and the uniqueness of the therapeutic relationship which is the precious aspect of therapy—and that which cures—rather than the fanciful, high-blown theories of the therapist.

The central problem facing the neurotic is the problem of every one of us, as we grow to maturity. We must learn to express our personal *will* and thereby take command of our own life. If we fail to attain this independence from mother and father, we will go through life subjugated and miserable, hating those who repress us and hating ourselves for not willing positively. By "giving up" the neurotic does express a form of will, one negative in nature —he opts for flight from responsibility. When he feels thoroughly defeated, the neurotic enters therapy and sees in the therapist a figure symbolizing all that is positive in the sphere of will exertion. That is, the neurotic projects his positive will onto the therapist. This is what Freud meant by "transference," said Rank. But there is an ambivalence in all of this, for the neurotic would truly like to become a positive-willing person himself. He tends to put this time off, of course. One can see glimmerings of a client's more positive will when he "stands up" to the therapist and argues against this or that interpretation made in the course of the analysis. Freud incorrectly referred to this as "resistance,"[36] considering it an impediment to therapy. For Rank, resistance is the very heart of *successful* therapy, for it signals the fact that the client—long subjugated by the wills of others (parents, peers, teachers, etc.) —has finally begun to express his own *positive* will.

Of course, the time it takes for a client to come to this stage of resistance in therapy varies. If the therapist treats him as if he were a slave to his past, to the mistakes of his childhood, and all of the time is spent in therapy searching about for these long-forgotten "fixations," a client might never take command of his life. Even worse, the client's occasional "resistances" are likely to be crushed by the authority of the therapist. Rank once observed that therapy is like a battle, a dynamic clash between participants, but it is a battle which *the client must win!*[37] The therapist simply aids in this process of finding independence. An innovation which is usually credited to Rank—at least in the sense that he developed this tactic to its fullest extent—is setting a definite time for the *termination* of therapy. A host of "short term therapy" approaches have evolved from this general strategy. However, as a theoretical development Rank viewed the termination as the high point and most crucial phase of therapy. He drew direct parallels between the anxiety generated in the client at this point and the "separation anxiety" the child experiences in being born (birth trauma), in leaving mother to attend school as a child, in leaving the family to take up his own life as a young adult, and so forth.

These are the clear acts of commitment we all must make to life. By degrees, in growing to manhood and thus expanding our consciousness we all take on the responsibility of self-direction, which means we exercise our positive will function. Rank found his clients reliving all of these separation situations during the end stages of therapy. In their dreams he saw birth symbols and came to view therapy termination as a form of *rebirth*—paralleling the religious acts of baptism which have for centuries been acknowledged as "being born again." As such, particularly since the client plays a major role in directing his rebirth, Rank saw this experience as a *creative* act. In the Rankian world view man is constantly creating his own reality. Here is a definite tie to phenomenology! Just as man must perceive by way of phenomena he must believe in things by way of illusions—points of view which are more or less socially acceptable. Hence, says Rank: "The individual often lives better with his conception of things, than in the knowledge of the actual fact, perhaps is able to live only with his own conception of things."[38] It is not important that we discover the "real facts" of how the person became neurotic. It is of quite secondary concern that we have a unifying, single theory of the neurosis. What is important is the decision on the part of a neurotic to create his own cognitive-phenomenal world and to live it with willful commitment from day to day. When he has made this move, the neurosis ends.

There are other influences on Rogers' thought which could be detailed, as Lecky's (1945) "self-consistency" construct or Snygg and Combs' (1949) view of the "phenomenal self." However, the major drift of phenomenal theory has been captured in the men reviewed to this point, and we can turn to Rogerian thought with sufficient background for a proper understanding.

The Client-Centered Approach to Psychotherapy and Human Relations: Carl R. Rogers

BIOGRAPHICAL OVERVIEW

Carl Ransom Rogers was born 8 January 1902 in Oak Park, Illinois, a suburban community in the metropolitan area of Chicago. He was the fourth of six children, five of whom were males. His father was a civil engineer and contractor who achieved considerable success in his profession, so the family was financially secure throughout Rogers' childhood and young manhood. When he was 12 Rogers' parents bought a large farm 30 miles west of Chicago, and it was in this essentially rural atmosphere that the founder of client-centered therapy spent his adolescence. Though the family was self-sufficient and inwardly dependent upon each other, one does not get the impression of actual joy and lightheartedness among the members.[39] For one thing, the parents, although sensitive and loving, were devoutly and rigidly committed to fundamentalist religious views—at least, the mother was. Rogers' parents seemed to foster independence and "common sense" in their chil-

dren, offering them opportunities which might stimulate growth whenever possible. Rogers could never recall having been given a "direct command on an important subject" over his span of maturing years.[40]

Rogers was a dreamy boy who loved books and spent much time in solitary pursuits. He could read before he attended grammar school, which prompted the school authorities to start him in the second grade, and he remained a top student throughout his preparatory years. All of the children participated in farm chores, and Rogers was often up at 5 A.M., milking several cows before breakfast. Summers were spent cultivating the fields and learning to be responsible; the family's most central belief was that hard work could straighten out any of life's problems. Rogers attended three different high schools and did little dating. He seemed a rather lonely person who felt that his next older brother was favored by their parents.[41] Even so, Rogers drew strength from and even sought a "very positive kind of aloneness" at times in his life.[42]

Rogers attended the University of Wisconsin, the school which both his parents and three siblings attended. He selected scientific agriculture as his initial field and roomed in the Young Men's Christian Association (YMCA) dormitory. He became active in various Christian youth groups. During his sophomore year, following a conference of such young people who had as their motto to "Evangelize the world in our generation," Rogers decided to drop agriculture and study for the ministry. A major event at this point changed the direction of his life: in his junior year he was selected as one of 10 students from the United States to participate in a World Student Christian Federation Conference in Peking, China. He was gone for more than six months and had an opportunity to witness a broad range of human behavior in cultures far different from his own. The experience liberalized his outlook, and on the ship enroute he first seriously entertained the thought that "perhaps Jesus was a man like other men—not divine!"[43] From this point onward his letters home carried a different tone, one which was to upset his parents; but partly because of the geographical distance between parents and their son, the emancipation was achieved with a minimum of emotional upheaval.

Though his religious views had altered, Rogers was still drawn to Christian work. He had, in the meantime, begun corresponding with a young lady whom he had known since childhood in the Oak Park area. By the time of the voyage to China a decided romance had blossomed. Upon graduation from college Rogers opted to attend Union Theological Seminary, a liberal religious institution quite at variance with the fundamentalism of his youth. Against the advice of both their parents he and Helen Elliott were married in August of 1924, just before setting off for New

York City and a life of their own. It was in a course at Union Theological Seminary that Rogers was first extensively exposed to psychiatrists and psychologists who were applying their skills to individuals needing help. Realizing the commonality of the ministry and the mental health professions, Rogers began taking psychology courses at Teachers College, Columbia University, which was located across the street from Union Theological Seminary. His entire outlook on life began to change. In about his second year of graduate study a group of students put together a seminar on "Why am I entering the ministry?" in which instructors were not permitted to structure the course. As a result of this early group experience and the soul searching which was to follow, most of the participants including Rogers "thought their way right out of religious work."[44]

He then turned to psychology and over the next few years managed to keep himself, his wife, and their first-born child together on modest fellowship stipends. There was no "single," outstanding figure in his education, and Rogers was to look back somewhat thankfully that he never had a mentor to defend or to react against as he came to intellectual maturity.[45]

After taking the Ph.D. in clinical psychology in 1928, Rogers accepted a position with the Rochester Society for the Prevention of Cruelty to Children. He was to remain in Rochester, New York, for the next 12 years, a highly productive time in which he developed his approach to the treatment of both children and adults in what was then called *non-directive therapy* and is better known today as *client-centered therapy*. It was there that he came into contact with social workers who were greatly influenced by Otto Rank. He heard Rank speak in a workshop and though not impressed at first gradually began to see the value of these new conceptualizations. Educated in an eclectic theoretical atmosphere, with fairly heavy doses of Freudian theory, Rogers needed a few years to find that therapist

Carl R. Rogers

insights—even when acceptable to the client—often failed to help the client materially alter his life style. The Rankian emphasis on shifting creative self-definition to the client began to cement with Rogers' heavy personal commitment to the ideals of individual choice and freedom.

Rogers found the typical brand of psychology reported on in the professional meetings of the American Psychological Association (APA) too far removed from his interests as a clinical psychologist to become active in that organization. Consequently, he turned to the professional organizations of the social workers and held both state and national offices in this wing of the helping professions. Later, he was to be very active in the American Association for Applied Psychology (AAAP), a splinter group of psychologists who had organized to press their interests in a more practical form of psychology. He became president of AAAP, and later he played a central role in bringing the APA and AAAP together into a single organization which is known today as simply the APA. Rogers served as the president of the APA and received its Distinguished Scientific Contribution Award in 1956. He also played a leading role in forming the American Board of Examiners in Professional Psychology (ABEPP), a group commissioned by the APA to protect the public from malpractice in the areas of clinical, counseling, and industrial psychology. Rogers tired of professional activities *per se* and withdrew from them as his interests ranged beyond psychology to education, industry, and social issues of all sorts.

While in New York Rogers founded a new Rochester Guidance Center and had his first experience with interprofessional tension with psychiatry over the fact that he—a psychologist—was to direct what appeared to be a medical facility. Working with children and their parents in psychotherapy seemed no more medical than psychological to Rogers—and to thousands of psychologists since—so a professional confrontation ensued which Rogers "finally won."[46]

In the closing years of the 1930s Rogers published a book on the *Clinical Treatment of the Problem Child* (1939), and as a result of this highly successful work he was offered a position as full professor at the Ohio State University. Though reluctant to accept due to affection for the new guidance center, Rogers had always found the idea of an academic affiliation very attractive. He had lectured at Teachers College for a summer and found the experience rewarding and broadening. Hence, with the encouragement of his wife, he moved to Columbus, Ohio.

It was while at Ohio State that Rogers achieved his initial world-wide recognition. He brought to the academic setting a new kind of practicality and direct study of what clinical psychologists do as psychotherapists. He was one of the—if not *the*—first clinicians to work out a scheme for the study of the interpersonal relationship which evolved during therapy. He attracted numerous talented students, and a series of breakthroughs in clinical research began to issue from Ohio State University. To order his thoughts concerning a proper client-therapist relationship Rogers wrote the manuscript of *Counseling and Psychotherapy* (1942), a clear and thorough statement of how the therapist should proceed if he hopes to engender changes in the client. By this time he had also completed his family—a son and daughter—and life seemed to be settling into another phase of successful achievement.

In 1944 Rogers spent the summer teaching a course at the University of Chicago, and out of this contact came an unusual offer. He was given the opportunity to establish a counseling center at the University of Chicago, using those practices and procedures he felt were necessary without encumbrances from other sources of influence in the academic or professional community. Rogers took up these duties in the autumn of 1945 and established a center in which professional staff, graduate students, clerical help, and related faculty members worked as complete equals. Rogers was then working out the details of what he has called the "helping relationship," and in his major work, *Client-Centered Therapy* (1951), he provided a first statement of the theory underlying his approach to interpersonal relations. This book and a paper written subsequently[47] provide the two primary theoretical statements of his career, although there are many less technically oriented papers which add to these fundamental statements. A collection of the latter papers were published under the title *On Becoming a Person* (1961). The Chicago period was once again highly successful, as the non-directive approach was being shown empirically to be as effective a method of psychotherapy as any other approach.[48] Rogers not only had an outlook on therapy and a theory of personality formulation and change, but he constantly sought to prove the merits of his thought empirically. It was this interest in research and a desire to extend his approach to the highly abnormal person that took him away from Chicago to the University of Wisconsin and an unpleasant period of his professional life.

Returning to his undergraduate university in 1957 was naturally a sentimental occasion for Rogers. A seemingly excellent position was arranged for him which carried joint appointments in the Departments of Psychology and Psychiatry. Unfortunately, things did not turn out as he had hoped. He initiated a large scale research project on the schizophrenic patient which involved a staff of 200 and extensive arrangements with a local state hospital, but problems developed among the staff—not all of whom had a point of view amenable to client-centered philosophy. Data mysteriously disappeared, and considerable tension mounted, but after much heartache among all concerned the project was completed.[49] It was not an entirely successful piece of research. The abnormals showed little improvement, and little evidence supported the contribution of a course in client-centered therapy over and

above the typical hospital routine (which was modern and efficient in its own right).[50] However, other aspects of the study supported the fact that therapists with the proper client-centered outlook engendered more improvement in their patients than did therapists who lacked the proper outlook.[51]

It was not such tepid research findings which discouraged Rogers at the University of Wisconsin. What destroyed his confidence in that school's psychology department and in all such "typical" programs of education in that period of psychology's history was the narrowly restrictive and punitive approach taken to the education of aspiring doctoral candidates. Rogers found that the graduate student in psychology was given an extremely detailed form of preliminary (predoctoral) examination, which usually meant that he had to devote himself entirely to so-called scientific courses which in fact required him to memorize vast amounts of minutiae. As a result, some of the most talented clinicians and creative individuals left the program in disgust. Rogers claimed that only about one graduate student in seven ever attained the degree under this rigid, laboratory-oriented program.[52] In a "passionate statement" of dissent for the then current trends of graduate education in psychology Rogers fired his parting shot and resigned from the Department of Psychology at Wisconsin.[53] Shortly thereafter he resigned from the Department of Psychiatry as well, for in 1964 he took a position with the Western Behavioral Sciences Institute (WBSI) of La Jolla, California. He was once more out of an academic setting—foregoing his professorship and tenure at a university for the third time in roughly two dozen years.

The WBSI acted as a bridge for Rogers, since after a few years of affiliation with this organization, which was devoted to humanistic studies of the interpersonal relationship, he helped found a new group which is called the Center for Studies of the Person, also located in La Jolla, California. A developing interest in the needs of the group, organizations, school systems, and indeed, the common problems of mankind were to preoccupy him. He became a major spokesman for the use of encounter groups (T-groups) in resolving human tensions.

Personality Theory

STRUCTURAL CONSTRUCTS

MIND-BODY, PHENOMENAL SUBJECTIVITY, AND THE WISDOM OF ORGANIC EVIDENCE

The question of mental vs. physical events does not enter Rogerian theory, since his initial assumption is that mind and body are united by a *phenomenal field* which combines all of man's experience in a highly unique and even subjective fashion. Figure 21 contains a schematization of the phenomenal field.

Note that a number of experiential processes flow toward the phenomenal field. A dotted plane separates experiences which are customarily subsumed by the terms "mind" and "body," but in this case all are represented equally in the phenomenal field at the right. The specific experiential processes will be referred to as we unfold Rogerian thought, but for the present what is important is that the phenomenal field is composed of a gestalt which combines factors emanating from the entire organism. The firing of neurons in central nervous system activity, or the chemical exchanges going on in physiological and biological processes like digestion are *not* part of the phenomenal field.[54] This is why they are placed outside, to the left of the enlarged cone-shaped extension of the phenomenal field.

In this sense Rogers circumvents the customary issues of "physical determinants of behavior" even as he gives a central role to the bodily processes in his theory of behavior.

Those theorists who seek atomistic physical causes of behavior rarely provide us with a satisfactory theory.[55] The reason a physicalistic theory is almost useless to the phenomenologist is that physical processes "bear" phenomena. A physical illness like an upset stomach heralds a disturbance, and to that extent it is represented in the phenomenal field. But the patient cannot through introspective effort become "aware" of the physiological processes which have gone awry. Diagnosis and treatment by an expert other than the individual is called for in such circumstances.

It is quite another thing when we speak about phenomenal fields, for now we enter a realm of *meanings* and *values* which do express themselves *in* the physical process. Hence the phenomenal field: ". . . includes all that is experienced by the organism, whether or not these experiences are consciously perceived. . . . only a portion of that experience, and probably a very small portion, is *consciously* experienced. Many of our sensory and visceral sensations are not symbolized."[56] In making the latter comment Rogers underscores the fact that, though our chemicophysical processes do not enter our field of experience directly as meaningful reactions, *what they portend* may indeed be symbolized or fail to be symbolized. A *symbol* is thus a cognitive reflection of some state of affairs in the life of the individual.

A frustrated person who feels the tension of irritation course through his body as someone whom he finds obstructive enters a room is thus symbolizing—making aware—his frustration. It would be possible for an individual to feel such irritation organismically, yet fail to symbolize the emotion he is experiencing properly. He might find that a certain person causes him to feel uncomfortable, or he might not really "notice" a person who enters the room. As a physical organism the spontaneous responses would be identical across such instances. But the significance of a phenomenal field here is that *in principle* the import of

Figure 21
Rogerian Uniting of Mind-Body in the Phenomenal
Field

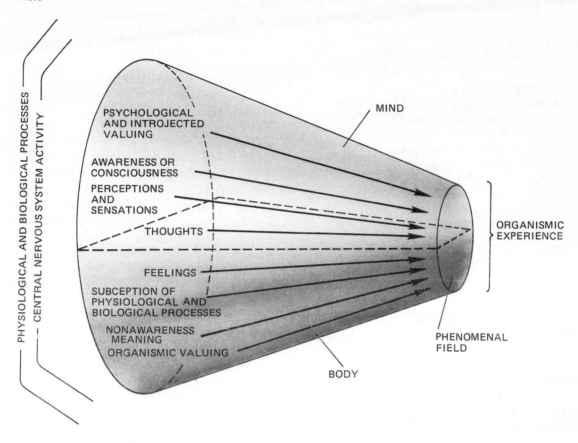

this emotion could be symbolized. We will never "feel" our neuronal activity or the digesting of our food. But we do "feel" excited, bored to tears, in love, out of love, sick, and so forth. The former are aspects of physical functions, but what makes the latter *meaningful* is the patterned import of the feelings in terms of the total life situation.

This brings up a further characteristic of the phenomenal field: it defines what is for the individual *his* subjective reality.[57] "Man lives essentially in his own personal and subjective world, and even his most objective functioning, in science, mathematics, and the like, is the result of subjective purpose and subjective choice."[58] This introduces not only subjectivity but also *teleology* to Rogerian theory, for the phenomenal field is organized around goals. Behavior is thus a goal-oriented activity, organized by the phenomenal field and carried out as a total gestalt.[59] What we call objectivity is thus a special case of "intersubjectivity." It is literally impossible for us to know another person's phenomenal field, and indeed we rarely know all of our own experiential phenomenal field. The more open and unafraid a person is to experience all that he "feels" in relation to the changing circumstances of life, the more likely that he will know himself—that is, his phenomenal field—and feel free to communicate this to another.[60]

At this point Rogerian theory introduces the view that our total organismic experience is *wiser* than our so-called intelligence or mental functioning *per se*. After all, if cognitive symbolization is a prerequisite for consciousness and if some potentially meaningful things can be denied symbolization, then we might all learn something by simply turning our attention openly and honestly to our feelings! We might learn something of ourselves in this process. How is it possible for the "organism as a whole" to have information about things which consciousness lacks? Well, says Rogers, there seems to be a process of *subception*[61] which permits us to make discriminations and hence effectively "know" things emotively which intellectually we do not yet perceive! Rogers defines subception as "a discriminating evaluative physiological organismic response to experience, which may precede the conscious perception of such experience."[62]

Thus man's very organic processes can instruct him, often dealing with subtleties of which the intellect falls short. In his first book on the nature of emotive, organismic learning in psychotherapy Rogers sounded the note he continues to express throughout his career: "They are learnings with deep emotional concomitants, not learnings of intellectual content, and hence may or may not find clear verbal expression."[63] We cannot always express the grounds for the evaluations being felt through organic processes. We know what we like and do not like, what we hope will happen and what frightens us as a possibility. At least, we *can* know such things if we give our organic feeling tones a chance to operate freely, and then "listen" to what they suggest. Hence, Rogers speaks of an "organismic valuing process."[64] We can always assess things in light of our "personal organic evidence."[65] There is wisdom in such evidence.[66]

THE SELF AS A CONSCIOUS ASPECT OF THE PHENOMENAL FIELD

One of the most important experiences that is open to man is self-learning. Rogerian theory is sometimes referred to as self-theory because of the importance placed on coming to know oneself accurately and thoroughly as a complete person. The terms *self-concept* and *self-structure* are both used to describe the self, with slightly different emphases. The *self-concept* refers to the conscious self-definition we give to ourselves when we speak of "me," or "I."[67] We are dealing here with phenomena—with our phenomenal fields—but only with certain aspects of it since other people come into our experiential field as well. The term *self-structure* is a more technical reference, used when speaking about individuals from an external frame of reference.

The self is thus a *conscious* portion—or at least a *potentially conscious* portion—of the phenomenal field.[68] We are not always aware of ourselves as an identity as we go through the day; we may "lose ourselves" in work, for example. But, given the right circumstance, we can always fix consciousness on self-identity and come up with some rough estimation of "who we are." This is not always the case with an abnormal person. To capture the fluctuating nature of the self Rogers relied upon the figure-ground concept. When the self emerges into awareness we have a "figure" on the "ground" of experience, just as any experience now in awareness may be said to take on figure properties: ". . . most of the individual's experiences constitute the ground of the perceptual field, but they can easily become figure, while other experiences slip back into ground."[69] Figure 22 presents a schematization of the self as an organized subportion of the phenomenal field. Note that we have taken the tip of the cone-shaped figure in Figure 21 and turned it outward in Figure 22, so that the phenomenal field now takes on an elliptical shape.

Figure 22

The Self as a Conscious Aspect of the Phenomenal Field

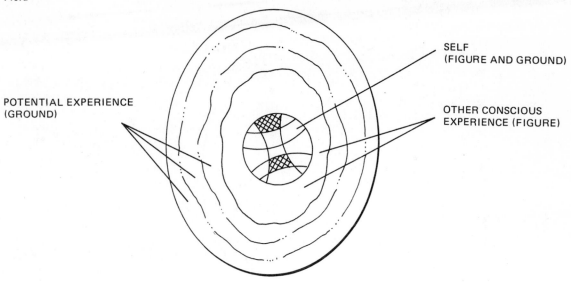

SELF
(FIGURE AND GROUND)

POTENTIAL EXPERIENCE
(GROUND)

OTHER CONSCIOUS
EXPERIENCE (FIGURE)

In the very middle of Figure 22 is the "self," which is also an organized configuration of subparts, set within the broader context of experience known as the phenomenal field. There may be other-than-self aspects of consciousness within awareness at any point in time, indicated as "other conscious experience." Finally, there are potential experiences which might come to the fore as figure in the phenomenal field given the right circumstances. Figure 23 reflects the case in which a person may be so aware of the presence of others in his phenomenal field that he may completely lose himself as figure in the interaction. Yet, he is always potentially retrievable as a "self-identity."

Now, since his experience may *go beyond* what the person knows intellectually, it follows that what he takes to be himself, his experience, his preferences in life, may be off the mark. The self-concept is therefore a series of hypotheses which the person holds about himself and which may be true or may be false. Only in the sense that such hypotheses take on organization is there a "structural construct"

in Rogerian theory. Actually, Rogers is diametrically opposed to all personality theories which see man fixed into structures. He prefers to think of human behavior in fluid, process terms. Yet, in the sense that we now consider the term we find Rogers saying: "We may look upon this *self-structure* as being an organization of hypotheses for meeting life—an organization which has been relatively effective in satisfying the needs of the organism"[70] [italics added]. We may think of this organization as a "self-gestalt."[71]

MOTIVATIONAL CONSTRUCTS

ORGANISMIC ENHANCEMENT AS LIFE'S
MASTER MOTIVE

The most fundamental truth about human life is that the organism strives to maintain, further, and actualize experience.[72] Rogers found from his earliest days as therapist that when given a chance the individual would spontaneously initiate a positive course of action.[73] He

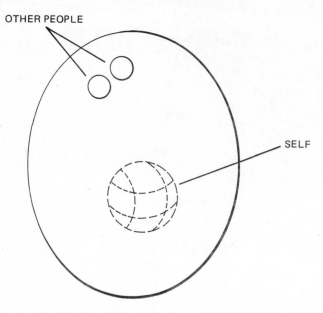

OTHER PEOPLE

SELF

would seek to know more about himself and his world, to encourage others in this regard, and thereby to enhance the phenomenal field within which he lived. As we have already seen, this *organismic enhancement* takes on a directional tendency, so that all behavior which is expressed is goal oriented.[74] The very nature of life, says Rogers, is directional: "The directional trend we are endeavoring to describe is evident in the life of the individual organism from conception to maturity, at whatever level of organic complexity. It is also evident in the process of evolution, the direction being defined by a comparison of life low on the evolutionary scale with types of organisms which have developed later, or are regarded as farther along in the process of evolution."[75] This evolutionary theme is a subtle point in Rogerian thought which we must keep in mind.

Rogers employs a concept of *need*, which he defines as "physiological tensions which, when experienced, form the basis of behavior which appears functionally (though not consciously) designed to reduce the tension and to maintain and enhance the organism."[76] Man's sense of need is thus rooted in his physiology, though what is specifically need-generating in life is influenced by cultural factors, the unique life experience of the individual, and so forth. But when behavior does eventuate, moving the organism to seek a goal which bears an organized relationship to its needs as contained within the phenomenal field, it is the *currency* of such factors which determine behavior: "Behavior is not 'caused' by something which occurred in the past. Present tensions and present needs are the only ones which the organism endeavors to reduce or satisfy. While it is true that past experience has certainly served to modify the meaning which will be perceived in present experiences, *yet there is no behavior except to meet a present need*" [italics added].[77]

The import of this currency factor in human behavior is that we do not have to dig back into a distant past in order to find out why the individual is behaving as he is this day. The individual can know "right now" why he behaves as he does. Emotional tones accompany and facilitate need satisfaction by helping the organism to attain its goals.[78] The more intense an emotion is, the more significant is this behavior and this goal to the individual. There are both pleasant and unpleasant emotions, heralding satisfaction or exciting frustration, as the case may be. But by paying careful attention to these organismic reactions the individual can often learn something about himself that he has not yet grasped (or "symbolized"). This capacity to attend to the organism is vital in Rogerian theory, for it so happens that the *needs of the organism* are not always consonant with the *needs of the self*.[79] The organized subportion of the phenomenal field we know as the "I" may not have it as a goal to enhance the organism by moving it in the directions spontaneously "felt" (emotions) to be the natural, correct ones.

This takes us into what Rogers calls the *valuing process*. In defining his self-concept an individual acquires certain preferences, expressed ideals, feelings of commitment to, and so forth.[80] Often a value is sensed directly by way of "sensory or visceral reactions."[81] We know instinctively or intuitively that "this I like" or "I have never really felt right doing that sort of thing." Many of our values are straightforward cultural accretions, handed to us by family members. We know what is "right" and what is "wrong" in behavior. We come to value a certain view of religion or political life. The trouble is: sometimes what we sense viscerally does not coincide with what we tell ourselves consciously. When this happens we witness a confrontation of the needs of the organism with those of the self. Faced with such a personal inconsistency, we are forced to ask ourselves "What do I really believe in anyhow?"

The reason we invariably ask ourselves this question is that, along with a need for organismic enhancement and growth, the individual has a need to be *self-consistent*: "The only channels by which needs may be satisfied are those which are consistent with the organized concept of self."[82] In other words, since the self-concept is organized (see Figure 22), it will not simply accept perceived differences and contradictory bits of evidence concerning its nature. The brave man who feels frightened when called upon to act senses an organismic truth which his self-concept may simply deny. Not all organismic functioning is thus "listened to" by the individual. Only that experience which seems consistent with the self is readily furthered.

The possibility of self-inconsistency is immediately threatening to the individual.[83] We like to think of ourselves as "complete," as a unified individual with one general outlook on life. If we change in any way, this "completed structure" alters to some degree over time. To think of ourselves as a highly fluid "process," receiving constant inputs rather than being a finished product is upsetting, particularly since such inputs often contradict what we had assumed our completed identity to be. Yet Rogerian theory is saying precisely this: the self is never finished, it is a constant process of change within spells of seeming identity. Hence, it is correct to say that *both* the organism and the self are pitched toward actualization—that is, growth, enlargement, enrichment and diversity.[84] One does not move in this direction without sensing ever-recurring periods of inconsistency. When this happens, new tensions develop and a sense of needing to be "whole"—self-consistent—once again is renewed. We see here a special application of the law of pragnanz.

CONGRUENCE VS. INCONGRUENCE AND POSITIVE REGARD

It is freedom from inner tension which indexes the extent of psychological adjustment achieved by the individual. As Rogers expressed it in his first theoretical statement: "We may say that freedom from inner tension, or psychological adjustment, exists when the concept of self is at least roughly congruent with all the experiences of the organism."[85] An individual who does things which he claims are really not "his" intention to do or who is not certain why he should feel so upset about something he really does not "care" about is obviously poorly adjusted. He has some consciously symbolized picture of himself (self-concept) which is at variance with how he behaves. It is this *congruence* between feelings and self-identity which Rogers now develops as a major term. The concept is defined as follows: ". . . when self-experiences are accurately symbolized, and are included in the self-concept in this accurately symbolized form, then the state is one of congruence of self and experience."[86] A more personalized definition would be: "The term 'congruent' is one I have used to describe the way I would like to be. By this I mean that whatever feeling or attitude I am experiencing would be matched by my awareness of that attitude."[87]

To be incongruent is thus to be "out of kilter" with oneself. Such a state might have devolved quite accidentally, via the natural course of maturation and the acceptance of parental values. Or one might literally foster such a condition by adopting a facade, refusing to be open to experience, "playing a role," and so forth. There is a range of congruence-to-incongruence, so that the extent of inner tension (psychological maladjustment) can vary. In its more extreme form the state of incongruence can be quite harmful to proper organismic functioning: "This state is one of tension and internal confusion, since in some respects the individual's behavior will be regulated by the [organismic] actualizing tendency, and in other respects by the self-actualizing tendency, thus producing discordant or incomprehensible behaviors."[88]

Thus, in a real sense, the directionality taken by the self-concept strains against the spontaneous organismic actualizing tendency. The person is striving to become something that he intuitively feels is unnatural for him.

This calls for a modification, a return to the proper inclination and in most cases it is achieved. We call this a *change in personality,* but the altered course is more accurately seen as a *growth,* for the individual aligns his actualizing potentialities rather than allowing them to work at cross-purposes. What has changed is the inner alignment. A fixed structure has not been altered. Rather, a process has once again begun to flow forward.

In elucidating the factors necessary for the individual to maintain congruence, Rogers hit upon what he called *positive regard* in human relations. This is defined as follows: "If the perception by me of some self-experience in another makes a positive difference in my experiential field [i.e., phenomenal field], then I am experiencing positive regard for that individual. In general, positive regard is defined as including such attitudes as warmth, liking, respect, sympathy, acceptance."[89] Based on the work of one of his students,[90] Rogers was to add to his enhancement principles and the need for self-consistency, a "need for positive regard" which each person is said to possess.[91] We cannot have a feeling of self-regard—a sense of personal acceptance—unless we feel positively toward our entire organism and accept it for *what it is* rather than merely what someone has told us it is. Preliminary to congruence is the feeling "I am worthy" or "I can be what I feel myself to be without shame or apology." The person without such positive self-regard is likely to develop an incongruent personality pattern. And when this occurs we witness defensiveness.

DEFENSIVENESS VS. SPONTANEITY IN HUMAN BEHAVIOR

The individual is made defensive by a growing sense of *anxiety,* which in turn heralds a disparity between the concept of self and the total organismic experience pressing through to awareness.[92] An attitude at variance with the symbolized belief system begins to take on a figure status from out of the darker ground reaches of the phenomenal field. In order to maintain the picture of self as symbolized, the individual now begins several maneuvers which are comparable to the classical defense mechanisms. Rogers occasionally employed a term from classical psychoanalysis in this context. He spoke of *introjection* when he was referring to the fact that we "take in" values from others, usually our parents, and thus make it appear that these are our personal values when in fact they may or may not be.[93] He also used *repression* but gave this construct a uniquely Rogerian interpretation: ". . . it would appear that there is the organic experience, but there is no symbolization of this experience, or only a distorted symbolization, because an adequate conscious representation of it would be entirely inconsistent with the concept of self."[94]

This notion of a *distorted symbolization* is central enough to be considered a Rogerian mechanism of defense. It is closely related to what Rogers sometimes called *denial,* and both of these concepts rely somewhat on the concept of subception (see p. 418). A good summary definition is: "When an experience is dimly perceived (or 'subceived' is perhaps the better term) as being incongruent with the self-structure, the organism appears to react with a distortion of the meaning of the experience (making it consistent with the self), or with a denial of the existence of the experience, in order to preserve the self-structure from threat."[95] For example, if a college student thinks of himself as a poor scholar but earns an unexpected grade of A on an examination, he can retain his low level of positive self-regard by distorting the symbolized conceptualizations of this success experience by saying "The professor is a fool" or "It was pure luck." Rogers would occasionally refer to such distortions as *rationalizations.*[96]

The final Rogerian mechanism which can be used defensively deals with *locus of evaluation.* Each person acquires values in life; the locus of this valuation bears directly on the responsibility which an individual will take for his behavior. What is the source of a person's values? Rogers observes: ". . . an internal locus of evaluation, within the individual himself, means that he is the center of the valuing process, the evidence being supplied by his own senses. When the locus of evaluation resides in others, their judgment as to the value of an object or experience becomes the criterion of value for the individual."[97] A "mama's boy" who never manages to untangle himself from mother's apron strings would be putting his locus of evaluation into her identity. He would think as mother thinks and value what mother values. Though it would be difficult to see how organismic enhancement or self-enhancement might be achieved in this forfeit of independence, the young man would attain a short-term advantage by shifting his locus of evaluation from his self to his mother. She would be deciding things for him, freeing him from the responsibility of making choices in life. To that extent, this maneuver would represent a type of defense.

Running through Rogerian thought on the matter of defensiveness is an opposition between the status quo and spontaneity. An individual caught up by defensiveness is not truly free to be a spontaneous self. He lives by preconceptions and distorted assessments of what it is he really wants to be. This need not refer to "evil" behavior. Occasionally the child actually subceives "I like hitting baby brother on the head" but denies this symbolization in awareness because he thinks of himself as a "good boy." But it is just as possible for a child to subceive the warmly emotional feeling of "I want to tell baby brother of my love for him" and yet fail to do so because of his self-concept as a "tough little boy who does not act sissified." The "repression" of a positive experiential prompting proves, said Rogers, that it is not derogatory or evil perceptions *only* which are denied to awareness.[98] Indeed, the relative goodness or badness of an experiential prompting is irrelevant. It is the consistency or inconsistency of an experience with the self-concept which determines whether or not it will be made conscious (denied symbolization or distorted).

TIME PERSPECTIVE CONSTRUCTS

Although Rogers did not devote much effort to development *per se,* he did attempt to sketch the process of maturing in terms of his personality constructs. He began with the assumption that a human infant is a valuing animal. The child enters life with a "clear approach to values."[99] Thus, the organismic experience of hunger is negatively valued. Food is positively valued, as are security and an urge for new experience. Pain, bitter tastes, and sudden loud noises are negatively valued by the infant organism. This "organismic valuing process" is never fixed into a rigid succession of events. It is constantly responsive to experience, promoting whatever tends to actualize the organism, and halting what fails in actualization. Since only the child can know his personal phenomenal field, he has greater potential awareness of what reality is for him than anyone else.

The valuing process thus is a regulatory system which keeps the organism on the proper course of need satisfaction.[100] In a true sense the infant creates his world. He may be picked up by a well-meaning adult, who would like to show him love, but if the infant perceives this as a fearful individual then the threat *is reality* for the child. As Rogers said: ". . . the effective reality which influences behavior is at all times the perceived reality."[101] Rogers felt it was a fruitless procedure to attempt to catalogue the supposed equipment which a child carries with him into the world, such as the various reflexes. He considered these peripheral factors for a personality theory, since regardless what inborn structures may be present they all serve the goal of organismic enhancement.

Out of a general tendency for organismic

actualization the child gradually differentiates a self-concept. He grasps an identity and senses a locus of evaluation, as a result of the interactions between the growing child and his parents or other guardians. The specific nature of this relationship will of course be reflected in the child's awareness of self, the unique emphases he gives to his personality and so forth. There is no specific designation that one can give to the *personality,* and we find Rogers quite purposefully avoiding the use of this term in conventional ways. To speak of personality is to speak of a totality including phenomenal fields, self-concepts, the relationships one has and has had with others, and so forth. It involves one's entire life, the developing changes and the present changes which result from a continuing process of evaluation and movement on to the next, most enhancing situation or state of affairs.

If all went well, the self-enhancement would parallel organismic enhancement, and a "fully functioning person" would be in formation.[102] This is an unlikely probability for most individuals. As self-awareness emerges the individual develops a need for positive regard, which may be learned or may be innately given to all humans.[103] Not only does the child acquire a need for positive regard from others, but he develops a need for self-regard as well. He turns this process of evaluation in on his own identity. It is the fact that a child wishes to keep his self-concept in line with the projected positive regard of others that creates all sorts of problems for the maturing individual. The problems stem from the discrepancy between what the organism senses immediately as positive and valuable and what others (parents, teachers) accept as worthy of positive regard. Adults in the child's experience make their positive regard for the young person *conditional.* They express warmth and acceptance only when he meets their conception of what he ought to be. They are unable to provide him with *unconditional positive regard,* which means that he would be accepted exactly as he "is."

Language enters here as well. The young person must symbolize (name, develop a system of ideas about) his experience. In line with our discussion of the defense mechanisms, the individual is likely to symbolize only those valued behaviors and attitudes which his parents and other adults consider valuable. When this valuation goes against what the organism may prefer he has a *distorted symbolization*. Rogers was a great believer in the superiority of learning by actually experiencing things, rather than by simply being told or "taught" them. A parent who expresses his own views of things, yet allows his child sufficient latitude to test out a position at variance with the parental view—in the long run—encourages a more congruent adjustment in his offspring. As Rogers once put it, the parent might sincerely say to the child: "I can understand how satisfying it feels to you to hit your baby brother (or to defecate when and where you please, or to destroy things) and I love you and am quite willing for you to have those feelings. But I am quite willing for me to have my feelings, too, and I feel very distressed when your brother is hurt (or annoyed or sad at other behaviors), and so I do not let you hit him. Both your feelings and my feelings are important, and each of us can freely have his own."[104]

By behaving in this manner the parent does not allow a "phony" relationship to develop. He quite honestly accepts the child's misbehavior even as he makes it clear why he too as a person cannot brook it without personal upset. The child might respond to this attitude with: "I enjoy hitting baby brother. It feels good. I do not enjoy mother's distress. That feels dissatisfying to me. I enjoy pleasing her."[105] Granting this emotional succession it follows that the child would opt for *not* striking his brother, even as he does not distort the hostile emotion he *does* feel. An important feature here is the *locus of evaluation,* which is obviously placed within the self-concept and not in the parental identity. Rogers feels this encourages taking responsibility and furthers

the growth-as-enhancement process which human development actually is.

INDIVIDUAL DIFFERENCES CONSTRUCTS

Rogers is opposed *in principle* to pigeon-holing people into personality classifications of any sort. He once said: "The client is the only one who has the potentiality of knowing fully the dynamics of his perceptions and his behavior."[106] In the Rogerian view each person "writes his own" theory of personality description without prompting from others. He is free to choose descriptive labels which strike him as organismically valid. To foist our concepts on others is to do violence to the fundamental Rogerian outlook. This is why non-directive or client-centered theory has always lightly treated the question of personality constructs. In his first book on individual therapy Rogers avoided the question of a "personality theory" altogether, only to be criticized later because his views failed to proceed from a "coherent" formulation of this sort.[107] This interested and amused Rogers, who felt that such formulations were unnecessary until and unless clear phenomena call for explanation.

One therefore looks in vain for a series of theorotypes in Rogerian psychology. At the same time, there is no question but that generalized commentaries on certain types of adjustment, and even definite personality traits, can be identified in Rogers' writings. With full appreciation for his theoretical position we will now review a handful of the more informal constructs used by Rogers to account for individual differences.

Dependent vs. Independent. A rather clear theme in Rogerian writing deals with the matter of whether or not the individual person takes on an independent or a dependent pattern of behavior. We can see decided Rankian influences emerging here. Speaking about the most difficult client for his therapy approach to deal with, Rogers notes: "The attitudes which most frequently seem to be ineffectively handled are those which might be called 'aggressive dependence.' The client who is certain that he is incapable of making his own decisions or managing himself, and who insists that the counselor must take over, is a type of client with whom we are sometimes successful, but not infrequently unsuccessful."[108] When he discusses the kind of client best suited for his therapy, Rogers suggests that he should have achieved a reasonable level of independence.[109] It seems clear that this dimension of personality has great significance for Rogers, and it relates to the question of *locus of evaluation*. A dependent person surely does not and often cannot assume responsibility for the locus of evaluation which has been framed internally. He looks outward for standards and introjects uncritically.

Self-Ideal vs. Self. In some of his researches Rogers has employed a concept of the ideal self or self-ideal, which he defines as: "the self-concept which the individual would most like to possess, upon which he places the highest value for himself."[110] In other words, the ideal self is a goal toward which the individual is oriented and—if all things were equal—one to which he aspires. There may be conditions which he perceives as denying him this goal, but in principle if the self and self-ideal could be brought into the same identity, the self would definitely be enhanced. Of course, the self-ideal can change over time.

Rogers and his students have made use of a rating procedure adapted from Stephenson's Q-technique (1953) to measure this relationship between self and self-ideal concepts. The procedure followed is quite simple. A patient about to enter therapy sorts a number of statements which may or may not describe him accurately, as a person. Each statement is printed on a separate card, and it might read "I feel pleased to meet other people" or "Rather minor things tend to upset me." There is no fixed type of statement. The main point is that a patient must sort these cards according to certain statistical assumptions (approximating a normal distribution), usually on a seven-point scale from "Like Me" to "Not Like Me." Having completed this sorting (taken as the conscious self-concept) the patient re-sorts the same cards into the scale of "Most Like an Ideal Person" and "Least Like an Ideal Person." The definition of what ideal means would of course be made clear to the sorter ("someone you think would be near perfect and like whom you would want to be"). The two sortings can then be statistically intercorrelated and even factor analyzed. Rogers' studies have usually employed a simple correlational measure indicating to what extent a self-concept and an ideal-self concept are identical. The assumption is: the greater the positive correlational value, the more highly a person thinks of himself. Patients have been shown to acquire higher correlations between these two sorts following psychotherapy than the correlational values they reflected before therapy.[111] Rogers has therefore used this as a measure of therapeutic improvement.

Vulnerability. "Vulnerability is the term used to refer to the state of incongruence between self and experience, when it is desired to emphasize the potentialities of this state for creating psychological disorganization. When incongruence exists, and the individual is unaware of it, then he is potentially vulnerable to anxiety, threat, and disorganization."[112] Hence, just as we can draw distinctions between people on the basis of how similar they are to their self-ideals, so too can we speak of the differences in degree of vulnerability to maladjustment that people are likely to have.

Mature Behavior. It is also possible to think of individuals as more or less mature in their behavior. "The individual exhibits mature behavior when he perceives realistically and in an extensional [i.e., flexible and alert] manner, is not defensive, accepts the responsibility of being different from others, accepts responsibility for his own behavior, evaluates experience in terms of the evidence coming from his own senses, changes his evaluation of experience only on the basis of new evidence, accepts others as unique individuals different from himself, prizes himself, and prizes others."[113] This abstract conception gives us a succinct picture of what Rogers' personal "ideal type" might represent.

Fully Functioning Person. This phrase is a special case of the maturity construct. However, since Rogers does name this ideal person as a worthwhile goal for mankind we could do no better than end our consideration of his individual differences concepts by citing his definition: "It should be evident that the term 'fully functioning person' is synonymous with optimal psychological adjustment, optimal psychological maturity, complete congruence, complete openness to experience, complete extensionality, as these terms have been defined. . . . The fully functioning person would be a person-in-process, a person continually changing."[114] Further, the fully functioning person is: ". . . more able to live fully in and with each and all of his feelings and reactions. He makes increasing use of all his organic equipment to sense, as accurately as possible, the existential situation within and without. He makes use of all of the information his nervous system can thus supply, using it in awareness, but recognizing that his total organism may be, and often is, wiser than his awareness."[115]

Psychopathology and Psychotherapy

THEORY OF ILLNESS

MALADJUSTMENT AS THE CLASH OF
ORGANISMIC VS. SELF ENHANCEMENT

The needs of the organism are not always identical to those of the self. The organism in this sense seeks enhancement via an actualizing tendency even as the self-actualizing tendency is operating.[116] The organism is thus responsive to the actual visceral promptings, the emotions which define for the person what he "is" in any given situation at any given time. However, if the self has been defined through distorted symbols, if the person consciously thinks of himself as a "me" in opposition to the spontaneous feelings of the organism, the resultant incongruence leads to increasing tension within the personality structure. Rogers defines *psychological maladjustment* as existing when the personality system "denies to awareness, or distorts in awareness, significant experiences, which consequently are not accurately symbolized and organized into the gestalt of the self-structure, thus creating an incongruence between self and experience."[117]

Since behavior is current, the individual could presumably turn his attention to the feelings which prompt him and, through a movement from subception to conscious perception, discover his more true being. However, what happens in practice is that an individual becomes increasingly threatened. *Threat* is a state of anticipation due to the subception of an incongruence between self-structure and experience.[118] When this incongruence is very close to awareness the individual senses anxiety. Before anxiety can overwhelm the individual he is likely to become increasingly defensive, and thus stiffen his behavior to close out even more experience than before. He is driven to deny and distort his symbolized values all the more. The young man who subceives a homosexual impulse becomes all the more "touchy" about jokes implying he is sexually interested in his male companions, he reacts with disgust at the effeminacy of certain men, and so forth. So long as a defensive separation of emotion from conscious intellect can be sustained this young man will be capable of functioning. However, it is likely that in time so much insincere deception will take place that a behavioral problem of severe proportions will develop.

It is when the self-structure is subceived as

discrepant from experience, hence incapable of meeting either organismic or self-needs, that the individual seeks help in the form of therapy.[119] The extent of behavioral disorganization which results from such inconsistencies varies, but the main point of abnormal behavior is that the individual can no longer value himself with positive self-regard. Indeed, he finds with each passing day that he really does not know himself. It is difficult living with a stranger; the individual senses internal opposition to what he consciously feels he is striving to be. Put another way, the individual has lost communication within his personality system, and this state of affairs affects his relations with other people as well. As Rogers sums it up: "The emotionally maladjusted person, the 'neurotic,' is in difficulty first because communication within himself has broken down, and second because, as a result of this, his communication with others has been damaged."[120]

THE IRRELEVANCY OF DIAGNOSTIC DISTINCTIONS

In the same way that Rogerian theory dismisses categorizing people into preselected, hence arbitrary and unnatural, designations of personality so too does it argue that diagnosis is unnecessary. Since our behavior is presumably caused by the ever-recurring present, how can anyone really tell us what we "have" as a problem in the way that a physician can tell us what our biological sickness is? As Rogers observed: "Behavior is caused, and the psychological cause of behavior is a certain perception or a way of perceiving [present circumstances]. The client is the only one who has the potentiality of knowing fully the dynamics of his perceptions and his behavior."[121] Any changes in perception which can be effected must be accomplished by the client himself.[122] So, why diagnose, categorize, and run the risk of once again distorting what the client can spontaneously know if he simply turns in on himself and re-establishes a proper

inner communication between feelings and conscious ideas? Anything which might pressure or control a *client*—the term Rogers prefers to the more passive designation, *patient*—is thus to be shunned.

Rogers does speak in broad terms of neurotic and psychotic behavior. A *neurosis* can actually represent the more spontaneous side of experience, a prompting from the organismic side of life to accept some attitude which is at variance with the self-attitudes. The person says "I don't know what has come over me. I just can't concentrate on my studies yet I know how important they are to me. All my life I have wanted to be an engineer, just like Dad." The question is: Are these engineering goals reflective of a true, organismic valuing or are they introjected and distorted values? The individual is merely aware of a symptom: he cannot concentrate; he cannot sleep, etc. The thought that he should so work at cross-purposes with what he wants stymies the neurotic. As Rogers notes: ". . . the neurotic behavior is incomprehensible to the individual himself, since it is at variance with what he consciously 'wants' to do, which is to actualize a self no longer congruent with experience."[123] At other times a neurosis may represent the defensive maneuvers of the individual to avoid becoming aware of his lack of self-consistency. All of the defense mechanisms discussed above may enter here.

When such efforts to sustain an incongruence in the personality lead to *excessive* distortions in reality, then we can begin speaking of a *psychosis*. An example of a mild distortion of reality might be when the individual refuses to accept responsibility for some misadventure in life which was clearly his fault. He senses this guilt organismically (emotively) but denies it, asserting "that was not due to anything I did." If this insincerity continues and extends into all aspects of life, rather than preserving the brittle structure of the self in time a complete split from reality might result. Now the person says "Other people are always blaming me. Everyone seems to be out to 'get' me, maybe to kill me" (paranoid delusion). Other forms of escapist fantasies can then intrude, so the thoroughly disjointed personality now basks in some preposterous insight: "They want to capture and torture me because I'm really the reincarnated Jesus."

An individual who has slipped over the brink of rationality to this extent might begin hearing voices or seeing images as well (hallucinations). Since the phenomenal field is organized by all factors active from moment to moment, it follows that perceptual distortions can become great if the falsification somehow holds things together. If we inwardly feel that things are about to explode with terror, then "seeing" an evil figure lurking about with clearly hostile intentions helps us to account for our extreme anxiety.[124] During this entire course of deterioration the individual's relations with others suffer. One cannot speak of neurosis and then psychosis without thereby speaking of interpersonal relationships. Rogers makes quite clear that, to the extent one individual in an interpersonal relationship is incongruent, the relationship suffers in that it encourages incongruity in the "other"; it distorts the nature of the true interpersonal experience; and it seriously handicaps any form of genuine communication emerging.[125] Incongruence breeds incongruence! Fortunately, through proper interpersonal relations this process can be reversed.

THEORY OF CURE

THE NATURE OF A HEALING RELATIONSHIP: THE CLIENT-CENTERED HYPOTHESIS

From the first, Rogers approached counseling and psychotherapy with the view that a therapist's responsibility is to provide a climate which furthers the self-directed change of his client. It is the client who must change, and the therapist must trust him to do so. In his earliest phrasing of what he then called the "therapist's hypothesis" Rogers wrote: "*Effective counseling consists of a definitely structured, permissive relationship which allows the client to gain an understanding of himself to a degree which enables him to take positive steps in the light of his new orientation.*"[126] The key word in this statement of therapist values is *relationship*. Rogers made clear that all must be subordinate to the establishment of a "free and permissive relationship" having the characteristics of warmth, acceptance, and freedom from coercion.[127] Certain limitations had to be placed on the client—that is, he could not physically assault the therapist—but these "structurings of the relationship" between client and therapist were to be minimal. In his second and more extensive treatment of the topic, Rogers was to expand this therapist hypothesis into what he now called the *client-centered hypothesis,* as follows:

. . . we may say that the counselor chooses to act consistently upon the hypothesis that the individual has a sufficient capacity to deal constructively with all those aspects of his life which can potentially come into conscious awareness. This means the creation of an interpersonal situation in which material may come into the client's awareness, and a meaningful demonstration of the counselor's acceptance of the client as a person who is competent to direct himself.[128]

Over the years, since first expressing this client-centered hypothesis, Rogers has moved gradually toward a growing openness in the therapist to reveal *himself* as a person. There is good reason for this developing change, and we now want to capture this shift in theoretical emphasis. In the earlier formulations the relationship was pitched entirely in the direction of the client's identity: ". . . the relationship is experienced as a one-way affair in a very unique sense. The whole relationship is composed of the self of the client, the counselor being depersonalized for purposes of therapy into being 'the client's other self.' It is this warm willingness on the part of the counselor to lay his own self temporarily aside, in order to enter into the experience of the client, which makes the relationship a completely unique one, unlike anything in the client's previous experience."[129] Rogers was careful to emphasize that there should be no evaluation of the client by the therapist (to parallel his dislike for diagnosis in general), no probing, no "interpretation" of what the client is supposed to be doing, and "no *personal* reaction by the counselor."[130]

The relationship is thus *client*-centered because it is the client who needs to reopen his inner communications between organismic and self evaluations. Since these blocked communications influence his behavior interpersonally as well as intrapersonally, the therapist simply reverses the process of illness beginning with accepting and respecting the client *as he is,* which in turn prompts him to value himself in somewhat different terms.[131] It is not that the therapist *controls him* into accepting himself, that he "positively reinforces" or otherwise subtly influences him to change. He simply asks the client to take a more responsible attitude in a unique human relationship, one which places no prerequisites or demands on him. Whatever he is, wants to be, wants not to be, and so forth, is perfectly acceptable to us. We trust him to know organismically who he is and what he wants to do in life. Although not the whole answer, part of the therapeutic cure stems from the fact that a client will likely introject this accepting attitude of the therapist.[132] The client senses something like: "If this other human being can accept me as I am, even with my self-doubts and inner contradictions, why can't I accept myself?" An attitude of this sort is often the first step toward change.

As the individual increasingly puts himself in touch with his organismic values, and rejects those of the self which are distorted and not genuine, he is becoming increasingly congruent. We might say that the congruence *in* the relationship between therapist and client

has led to congruence *within* the client's personality system. Well, if it is true that interpersonal congruence breeds intrapersonal congruence, then it follows that what we have been limiting to the therapeutic situation may have broader applicability. Rogers was to develop precisely this view of things, and in his mature formulations he therefore speaks of a tentative "law of interpersonal relations," as follows:

Assuming a minimal mutual willingness to be in *contact* and to receive communications, we may say that the greater the communicated *congruence of experience, awareness,* and behavior on the part of one individual, the more the ensuing relationship will involve a tendency toward reciprocal communication with the same qualities, mutually accurate understanding of the communications, improved *psychological adjustment* and functioning in both parties, and mutual satisfaction in the relationship.[133]

This general attitude of proceeding interpersonally has occasionally been termed the *helping relationship*,[134] and it is also a significant aspect of what is called the *process equation* of psychotherapy.[135] The basic point of these designations is that one person in a relationship—be that therapeutic or simply social—intends that there should come about in another person "more appreciation of, more expression of, more functional use of the latent inner resources of the individual."[136] The Rogerian world view has every man a therapist for every other man. Therapy is life and life is therapy, both involving a succession of relationships with others—relationships which can either make or break the participants who enter into them. Indeed, it is better to speak of a *facilitator* than a therapist in interpersonal relations of this general scope.

At this point in Rogerian thought we must reassess the nature of client-centered therapy as originally conceived. If the therapist is himself 100 per cent congruent, without facade and completely accepting of his organismic valuing processes, what does he then do when feeling the definite prompt to thrust himself *personally* into the relationship? How can he both keep a one-way relationship focused on the client, and yet be himself an entirely congruent human being? He cannot. And so it is that we witness in the development of Rogerian thought an increasing willingness for the therapist to reveal himself as a person in the relationship. One can see this gradual shift in Rogers' writings, and it is particularly prominent in his later work with the basic encounter group. Thus, we find Rogers saying of his own behavior in one encounter group: "When a young woman was weeping because she had a dream that no one in the group loved her, I embraced her, kissed her, and comforted her."[137] He also notes: "If I am currently distressed by something in my own life, I am willing to express this in the group."[138]

This change in manner across over some 30 years does not make Rogers inconsistent. He admits quite frankly that his manner in the group differs from that in the individual psychotherapy session, yet he is quick to affirm: "I believe that in no basic philosophical way does my approach differ from that which I have adopted for years in individual therapy."[139] This basic philosophical outlook remains that of a client-directed focus of attention, concern, and acceptance.

INSIGHT AND TRANSFERENCE

One of the clear implications of the client-centered approach as initially conceived by Rogers was that each client should be left to find his own explanations for why he suffers from this or that psychological maladjustment. Only the client can know what subjectively moves him, and one does him no favor to convince him otherwise. This does not mean that Rogers rejected a concept like *insight,* of course, which he defined as "the perception of new meaning in the individual's own experience."[140] An insight permits the client to understand new relationships of cause and effect or to see the pattern of his behavior in a new light. Yet these are emotive learnings as well, and in fact the most significant insights to be gleaned from the relationship cannot be clearly expressed verbally. Nevertheless, "insight is a highly important aspect of counseling treatment, and as such deserves the closest scrutiny."[141]

Since the classical analytical theories make much of the relationship in terms of transference and countertransference, Rogers had to take a position on these constructs. The caressing and kissing of clients could easily be taken as an instance of countertransference, for example. Since Rogers rejects—even in principle—the foisting of what he takes to be arbitrary theories of personality onto patients he does not have to concern himself with such questions on the more abstract plane. However, on the more practical plane Rogers has discussed the issue of transference in terms of client-centered counseling. He has admitted that phenomena of a transference nature seem to take place in client-centered therapy but at a much reduced level when compared to that of psychoanalysis. As he put it in 1951: "Thousands of clients have been dealt with by counselors with whom the writer has had personal contact. In only a small minority of cases handled in a client-centered fashion has the client developed a relationship which could in any way be matched to Freud's terms."[142]. Rogers meant that surely infantile attitudes are not transferred onto a therapist who presents himself as another human being, face-to-face and entirely open in his contact with the client.[143] There is plenty of feeling in the relationship, but the realistic approach and equal status of client and therapist prevent the sort of distortion and projection which the analytical couch situation seems to foster.

Hence, if a true transformed neurosis (see Chapter 1) develops in the relationship, it is the result of a mishandling of the client-centered approach rather than a necessary out-come of the interpersonal pattern. If the client expresses affection, love, or hostility toward his Rogerian therapist the latter merely accepts these feelings as genuine organismic reactions which can be expressed and further clarified without any recrimination.[144] Possibly the therapist deserves the reaction. He may have been incongruent enough surreptitiously to seduce his client even as he told himself that he was being completely open and non-direc-tive. His manner may lead to irritation on the part of the client, who finds him an authori-tarian or simply a bore. But what has this to do with some esoteric theory about how a present pattern must of necessity be re-enacting a much earlier pattern of behavior? Behavior exists in the present situation, and the evaluat-ing organism is the source we must turn to rather than some quaint, highly intellectual-ized account. We fix on the present relation-ship, make all feelings and attitudes clear, avoid incongruence, and in time things begin falling into place for the client who begins to construct his *own* theory of why he has certain problems.

Just how much a therapist should reveal himself as a person in therapy was a slowly developing question for Rogers. In 1941 he thought in terms of a one-way relationship, focused *only* on the client's individuality. This had changed by 1959 to the view that some-times one should and even must speak out *as a person* in the relationship. This would be espe-cially called for if the therapist found himself focusing on his personal emotions rather than the client's.[145] What is his organism trying to express? Why does he feel this way and can he really help the client by remaining silent about his prompting mood? Surely his feeling must be adversely affecting the relationship since he is clearly no longer congruent in the interper-sonal contact. By 1970 Rogers was prepared to be as open as his organismic valuing process spontaneously suggested, to the point of vent-ing great anger and irritation to other members of the encounter group.[146]

PSYCHOTHERAPY AS A PROCESS OF CHANGE

Due to Rogers' great desire to keep therapy free and open one notes a decided emphasis in his writings on the therapist rather than the client. As client-centered therapists we do not wish to judge or evaluate the client, but we have rather decided ideas about the proper manners and attitudes which a therapist should manifest. In the early writings the emphasis is on the more "selfless" style of therapist interaction: "In client-centered therapy the client finds in the counselor a genuine alter ego in an opera-tional and technical sense—a self which has temporarily divested itself (so far as possible) of its own selfhood, except for the one quality of endeavoring to understand."[147] The thera-pist behaved like the "client's other self," help-ing him to perceive his phenomenal field more openly and accurately.[148] This was vitally im-portant to cure, for it was the client's self which was badly distorted and out of kilter with the organismic valuing process. Hence, psychotherapy was defined in these terms: "Psychotherapy deals primarily with the or-ganization and functioning of the self. There are many elements of experience which the self cannot face, cannot clearly perceive, be-cause to face them or admit them would be inconsistent with and threatening to the cur-rent organization of self."[149]

The therapist acts as a companion, as an acceptant alter ego who helps the client work his way through a dark forest of misunderstand-ing and confusion.[150] By making this passage the client comes to experience himself in new ways, even as he rejects the older ways of self-definition.[151] In a very real sense psychotherapy is a "learning of self."[152] Of course this learn-ing would not take place if the proper rela-tionship were not formed. From the outside psychotherapy might be defined as the "alter-ation of human behavior through interpersonal relationship."[153] It was when he attempted to name the essential elements in this relationship that Rogers made it most clear that he put more trust in attitudes than formal theories. One cannot teach psychotherapy in textbooks. Every research study he conducted convinced Rogers the more that "personality change is initiated by *attitudes* which exist in the therapist, rather than primarily by his knowledge, his theories, or his techniques."[154] Hence, whether we call him therapist or teacher, the true *facilitator* of change is a person with the ability to relate to others as outlined above.[155]

Now, it is possible to conceptualize this *process of change* within the client as he benefits from the correct form of relationship. Figure 24 is a schematization of the general course which this process takes. At point 1 is a badly put together self-gestalt. The pieces simply do not fit well, as they are distortions of the real organismic functioning. Some aspects have not yet become figure since they are being denied symbolization out of fear or threat. This inadequate self-gestalt retains its weak organization only with the greatest effort and rigidity on the part of the individual. At point 2, the poorly articulated gestalt loosens during the course of therapy. Elements which were denied symbolization in the past may now be brought forward and examined in considerable detail as figures. In time, as feelings are properly symbolized and a "reorganization of self" is effected, the individual arrives at point 3—with a more natural and spontaneous self-gestalt.[156] He now perceives and subceives more accurately. He accepts the locus of evaluation as within himself.[157]

While trying to capture the point 2 process of change in psychotherapy Rogers was to work out a "seven-stage process of cure" which eventually devolved into a research scale which was employed by members of his research group.[158] The specific points on this seven-step scale are not relevant for our purposes, but we might note the general scheme as an example of Rogerian thought. The first stage is fixity

Figure 24
The Process of Change in Figure-Ground Terms

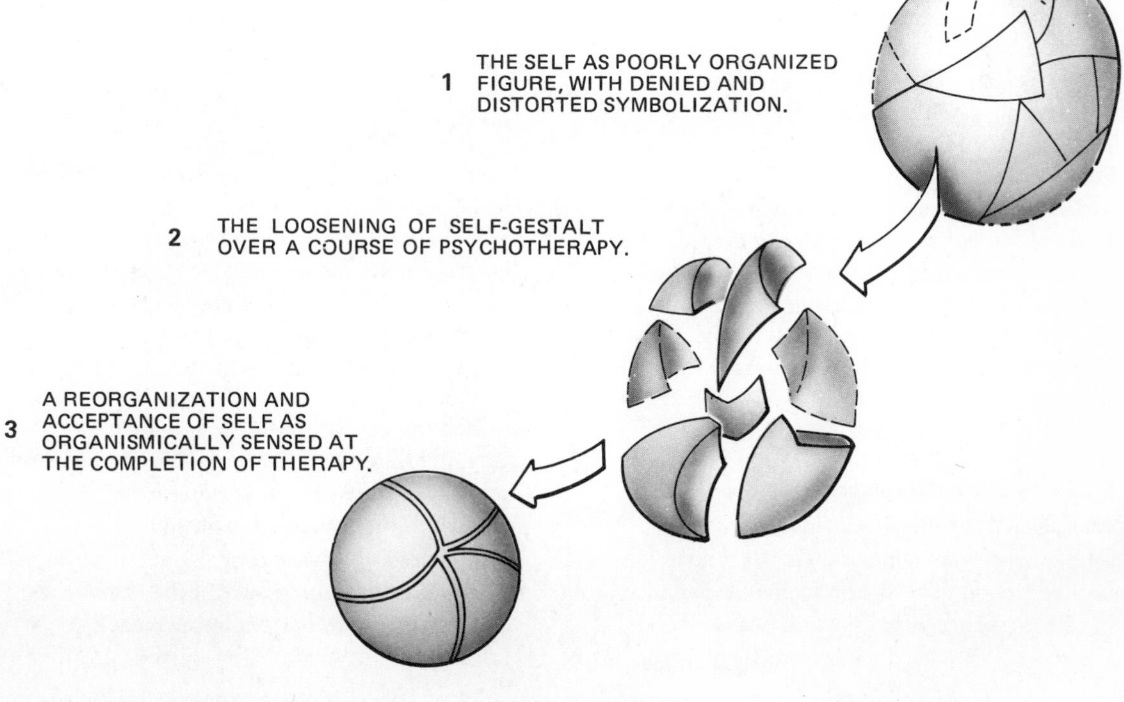

1 THE SELF AS POORLY ORGANIZED FIGURE, WITH DENIED AND DISTORTED SYMBOLIZATION.

2 THE LOOSENING OF SELF-GESTALT OVER A COURSE OF PSYCHOTHERAPY.

3 A REORGANIZATION AND ACCEPTANCE OF SELF AS ORGANISMICALLY SENSED AT THE COMPLETION OF THERAPY.

and remoteness of experience as the individual does not even recognize existing feelings. He is rigid and unbending, often unwilling to admit a personal problem of any sort. Other people may be blamed. Gradually, in stages two and three he begins to become aware of himself as a feeling-organism, sensing himself as he is. A gradual relaxation then sets in at stage four, as the individual senses the contradictions existing between his feelings and experience as he has come to know it. As a result of his confidence in the accuracy of his feelings the individual begins to trust his spontaneous reactions. By the fifth stage feelings of great import well up to surprise the person. He is fascinated by this process of spontaneous change and usually seeks to understand the meanings of these feelings. In the effort to be more exact he also senses the natural implication about what ought to be done.

Occasionally a feeling tone fails to make itself known very clearly. It may become "stuck" and fail to progress into a fully meaningful experience. A working-through of such partially-known feelings is necessary at this point until, along about stage six they "come unglued" and flood the person's awareness with their full import. The individual experiences no fear as he now begins organizing these feelings and cognitions into a new organization (step 3 of Figure 24). He is now fully aware of the locus of his feelings and of the evaluations which they imply. He no longer thinks of himself as an object, to be moved about by others or by circumstances, but he takes the responsibility of self-direction. Subjectivity is no longer a threat. In the final or seventh stage the client becomes a fully functioning person.

In order for this process of therapy to proceed Rogers noted that certain conditions must be present. First, two people must be in *contact*, which means that there is communication between them. One of them, the client, must be *incongruent* though he may experience this incongruence as anxiety and not see the

actual problem. The other person, the therapist, must be *congruent* in the *relationship*. Further, the therapist must be experiencing *unconditional positive regard,* which is defined as follows: ". . . if the self-experiences of another are perceived by me in such a way that no self-experience can be discriminated as more or less worthy of positive regard than any other, then I am experiencing unconditional positive regard for the individual."[159] This attitude is tantamount to acceptance, the prizing of another as a fellow human being, and related descriptive terms which Rogers has used in other contexts. Another requirement is that the therapist experience *empathic understanding* of the client from the latter's internal frame of reference. Empathy is seeing another person's point of view without forgetting that his subjective feelings in their entirety can never be known. Finally, for therapy or the "process of change" outlined above to be successful the client must himself perceive the unconditional positive regard and the empathic understanding of the therapist, "at least to a minimal degree."[160] These are the attitudes of importance, and they override the particular orientation or personality theory which the therapist employs.

MENTAL HEALTH: THE CHARACTERISTICS
OF A THERAPIZED INDIVIDUAL

Over the years, Rogers wrote extensively about the benefits of counseling or therapy for the individual. However, due to the extent of this literature we will only consider selected aspects of these writings as examples of what Rogers understood to be mental health.

In his earliest papers, as he was working out the essentials of a relationship, Rogers stressed the necessity for the individual to perceive himself as a total organism more objectively.[161] This does not mean he sees himself as an "object," something acted upon and manipulated. Rather, it implies a more willing, honest, and open acceptance of the emotive prompting. Another aspect of the mentally healthy person is that he loses his self-consciousness as he acquires a greater sense of selfhood.[162] Neurotics are symptom-laden because they are self-conscious; they are continually on guard and sensitive to the reactions of others. A healthy person does not concern himself with the rigid steps or rules that others hold out as bait or reward for what they want him to do. Healthy interpersonal relations are not characterized by such manipulations.

A healthy person is not entirely without defensiveness. Threats will naturally arise, and even the most self-enhanced individual will from time to time exhibit a certain defensiveness.[163] But the mentally healthy person is more aware of his defensiveness. He may wish that he were less so about some issue, and he may viscerally respond to his deviousness when he does opt to be less open. If more openness in life were the rule it would be easier for all of us to drop our defensiveness. But the point here is that so long as we recognize when we *are* being defensive then we have not slumped to the level of the first stage of the process of change, where the individual is unaware of his feelings. Hence, in defining mental or psychological adjustment Rogers was to say: "Optimal psychological adjustment exists when the concept of self is such that all experiences are or may be assimilated on a symbolic level into the gestalt of the self-structure."[164]

Awareness thus continues to be the central concept in Rogerian definitions of mental health. The mentally healthy person is open to experience, trusting in his organism, accepting of his subjectivity as an evaluating person, and willing to be a process of change.[165] Taking a phrase from the existential philosopher, Sören Kierkegaard, Rogers said that to be fully functioning is "to be that self which one truly is."[166] This state necessitates dropping facades, moving away from rigid compunctions, meeting experience as it is and not doing things simply to please others, accepting responsibility for self-direction, and moving ever toward new aspects of life with an acceptance of others and a trust in one's self.[167] These are the essentials of what Rogers was finally to call *existential living,* a concept which combines his phenomenological approach and his emphasis on the changing processes of life. Existential living is thus to live with "a maximum of adaptability, a discovery of structure *in* experience, a flowing, changing organization of self and personality."[168] An individual following this advice would live fully, "in the moment,"[169] and from moment to moment as a fully-functioning person.

AN EVOLUTIONARY THEME AND A NATURAL ETHIC

If man relies upon his spontaneous organismic functioning, what is there in a formal theoretical sense to convince us that he will truly opt in the constructive, self- and other-enhancing fashion that Rogers claims is likely to take place? Can we accept the client-centered theory on face value simply because it has been expressed in these more positive terms, or do we need a technical basis for believing that the organic wisdom will truly unite men? Though it is not given prominent status in his earlier writings, one can find a decided evolutionary theme in Rogerian thought, one which becomes more pronounced in his later comments on the nature of interpersonal relations.

In basing his concept of mental health on the organismic valuing process Rogers is, after all, saying that man's physical organism has a decided stake in his future. Phenomenologically speaking, the process of cure is a *natural* one. In other words, cure is "in nature" and not "in the constrictions put on nature" by men who feel they know better than nature what affects it. This strong existential theme emerges ever more centrally in Rogerian thought. Thus, he noted in 1951: "From an external point of view the important difference [following reorganization of the self] is that the new self is much more nearly congruent with the totality of experience—that it is a pattern drawn from or perceived in experience, rather than a pattern imposed upon experience."[170] The reorganized self is thus more settled within the *natural processes* of the universe; it is one of these processes and must be appreciated as such. Hence, by changing during psychotherapy the individual is actually moving back "into nature" as a spontaneous process once again. We see this attitude clearly in the following: "Thus the therapeutic process is, in its totality, the achievement by the individual, in a favorable psychological climate, of further steps in the direction which has already been set by his growth and maturational development from the time of conception onward."[171]

Client-centered therapy is thus not a form of human engineering or a method of controlling nature to meet an arbitrary end. The only end which is acceptable to Rogers is that spontaneous state of uncontrolled—literally "natural"—living. In 1959 he stated: ". . . psychotherapy is the releasing of an already existing capacity in a potentially competent individual, not the expert manipulation of a more or less passive personality."[172] We now begin to see what Rogers takes to be man's capacity for self-enhancement. As congruence is fostered both intrapersonally and interpersonally, the potentials for a broadened experience are of necessity enhanced since people do not need to act defensively, to "turn off" sincere promptings. If nature prompts, why should man deny this prompting? Based upon more than 30 years of experience as therapist and consultant, Rogers in his mature statements began to see that *all* men move in the same general direction of enhanced experience, provided that they are allowed to be free in their relationships: ". . . there is an organismic commonality of value directions."[173] These common value directions are of such kinds as to enhance not only the in-

dividual and the members of his community but also *"to make for the survival and evolution of his species"*[174] (italics added).

Rogers has seen men in various countries, in therapy or encounter groups with therapists of quite differing personalities, all moving toward the common organismic values which he outlined in such detail. Putting this commonality in natural terms, he observed: "I like to think that this commonality of value directions is due to the fact that we all belong to the same species—that just as a human infant tends, individually, to select a diet similar to that selected by other human infants, so a client in therapy tends, individually, to choose value directions similar to those chosen by other clients."[175] When people are free to choose they choose alike, and the valued goals selected are "goals which make for his own survival, growth, and development, and for the survival and development of others."[176] This is to say that *in any culture, at any time in history,* the mature individual would opt for these very same values.[177] Thus, Rogers defends a *universal natural ethic,* rooted in the very fabric of organic life and transcending cultures. He makes this plain in the following excerpt:

Instead of universal values "out there," or a universal value system imposed by some group—philosophers, rulers, priests, or psychologists—we have the possibility of universal human value directions *emerging* from the experiencing organism. Evidence from therapy indicates that both personal and social values emerge as natural, and experienced, when the individual is close to his own organismic valuing process. The suggestion is that though modern man no longer trusts religion or science or philosophy nor any system of beliefs to *give* him values, he may find an organismic valuing base within himself which, if he can learn again to be in touch with it, will prove to be an organized, adaptive, and social approach to the perplexing value issues which face all of us.[178]

THE EARLY TECHNIQUE EMPHASIS: NON-DIRECTIVE THERAPY

Thanks to the great interest he took in the nature of a relationship and the resultant attention paid to the therapist's manner, Rogers frankly admitted that his early writings were heavily technique oriented.[179] This emphasis was a paradox of sorts, because the value system on which his approach was based *rejected* all attempts to manipulate or control the lives of a client. Yet the great stress placed on a therapist's approach (how often he spoke up in the interview, whether he interjected himself as a person into the discourse or not, etc.)

seemed to impress some of Rogers' interpreters as shrewd clues for "how to" manipulate a client most successfully. Rogers was merely trying to demonstrate the essentials of an effective therapeutic relationship, and he had developed a series of scoring procedures on the basis of which recorded interviews were broken down for empirical study. It was thus possible operationally to define the difference between a *directive* therapist and a *non-directive therapist*. Table 3 presents such a distinction, as drawn from his research findings.

Now, if one wished to acquire a client-centered or, as it was then called, a non-directive approach to the relationship he *could do* those things which Table 3 suggests a non-

Table 3
Frequency of Techniques Used by Directive and Non-Directive Approaches[180]

Directive Counselor-Therapists	Non-Directive Counselor-Therapists
Most Frequent	*Most Frequent*
1. Asks highly specific questions, delimiting answers to "yes," "no," or specific information.	1. Recognizes in some way the feeling or attitude which the client has just expressed.
2. Explains, discusses, or gives information related to the problem or treatment.	2. Interprets or recognizes feelings or attitudes expressed by general demeanor, specific behavior, or earlier statements.
3. Indicates topic of conversation but leaves development to client.	3. Indicates topic of conversation but leaves development to client.
4. Proposes client activity.	4. Recognizes the subject content of what the client has just said.
5. Recognizes the subject content of what the client has just said.	5. Asks highly specific questions, delimiting answers to "yes," "no," or specific information.
6. Marshals evidence and persuades the client to undertake the proposed action.	6. Explains, discusses, or gives information related to the problem or treatment.
7. Points out a problem or condition needing correction.	7. Defines the interview situation in terms of the client's responsibility for using it.
Least Frequent	*Least Frequent*

directive therapist *in fact did.* This led to an overemphasis on technique *per se,* and it is from this aspect of his career that Rogers earned the reputation of the "mmm hmm" therapist. One of the least directive or "leading" statements a therapist can make is simply to nod his head or murmur an encouraging "mmm hmm" as if to say "yes, go ahead, I am listening" to the client. Although most of his advocates stressed the client-centered values of this procedure, some viewed this tactic as a highly efficient instrumentality, a subtle way of controlling the client's talk. As we have already seen in Chapter 7 (p. 340), the classical study by Greenspoon (1955) proved that one could indeed verbally condition a subject through such subtle factors as a nod of the head or an "mmm hmm."

The Rogerian tactic is thus to turn over as much lead as possible to the client in individual therapy. Given a good listener and accurate communication, the client-centered hypothesis holds that an individual will come to solve his own problems as he reorganizes his self-structure. The therapist simply facilitates the process.

Rogers has been seen to "validate" individuals as persons, whether individually or in an encounter group. By this is meant that the therapist responds to others with questions or comments that show immediately his respect for their presence, their view, and their problems.[181] Only when the therapist can *trust* others is this kind of interpersonal validation possible.[182] If he nods his head and says "mmm hmm" or makes a more extensive comment bearing on the present relationship, the client-centered therapist is not covertly seeking to manipulate anyone. He wants to be as spontaneous and natural in the situation as possible. He continues to *avoid interpreting* the client's behavior in terms of pet theories about human behavior that he might subjectively hold.

GENERALIZED PRINCIPLES FOR INTERPERSONAL BEHAVIOR

The interpersonal concern for the "other" should not be limited to therapy. Rogers extended his view of the relationship to all manner of interpersonal and even institutional situations. An effective facilitator in the classroom sets an open climate, helps group members to settle on their goals, trusts the participants (students) to direct their own self-enhancement, and becomes a participant learner within the total process.[183] Rather than viewing his role as that of filling the heads of his students with facts, as in the "mug and jug" view of learning, Rogers sees the teacher as a resource person for the student body. He shares himself with his students, recognizes and accepts his own limitations (congruence), and encourages the expression of emotions as well as intellectual insights in the classroom. He organizes and helps make things available, but he does not forfeit trust in others for a kind of military regime or an obstacle-course tactic. Learning is another natural process, and it will be entered into spontaneously if the learner is provided the appropriate climate.

Rogers emphasizes that the learner must see the relevance of the material he is expected to acquire. One of the poorest tactics for a teacher to use is threat-induced instruction. When the self is under threat a rigid defensiveness, which is anathema to learning, is the result. By reducing threat and encouraging spontaneity new experience can be perceived and differentiated. Learning is greatly enhanced when the student can share in the responsibility of the classroom, including the decisions as to course content and even his eventual grade in the course.[184] Self-evaluation is one of the most important things we must learn in life, and yet how many teachers view this as one of the skills they must help the student acquire? Rogers feels deeply that effective education like effective therapy must teach the participant about himself and life as a process. Hence, he draws the parallel: *"To my mind the 'best' of education would produce a person very similar to the one produced by the 'best' of therapy."*[185]

This would seem to make every teacher a therapist. Yet an even more fundamental truth is that *every man is a therapist!* Much of Rogers' later papers are taken up with discussions of how congruence can be promoted in various interpersonal settings. For example, parents must be congruent in their relations with their children and acquire that sense of trust which will permit the child at a certain time in life to be a separate person.[186] Every member of a family must be allowed the dignity of separation from time to time, with the freedom to have solitude and his own preoccupations. Rogers is not seeking a world of handholders with smiling faces who place the group above the individual. In fact, his view is that one cannot be creative unless he has the capacity to accept the feeling "I am alone."[187] The creative individual hopes to communicate with others in time, but in order to be capable of independent thought he must retreat to a psychological if not literal "corner" in life from time to time.

Rogers has proposed a few rules which might facilitate congruence in interpersonal relations. For example, what if a family discussion or a labor-management arbitration were to follow the rule: "Each person can speak up for himself only *after* he has first restated the ideas and feelings of the previous speaker accurately, and to that speaker's satisfaction."[188] If all group participants honestly followed this rule, says Rogers, improved communication would necessarily result. Not that an easy solution would then follow; but at least one side would not be manipulating the other, forcing it to support predetermined prejudices, and so forth. This is what we mean by "validating the other person." Rogers feels that even organizations and nations might consider some such principle in facilitating the changes necessary within their identities.[189] It is unfortunately true that sometimes the individual person changes, but the institutional framework within which he lives and works *does not.*[190] This is one of the reasons that Rogers became heavily involved in the encounter group, a technique which he felt could change (cure?) institutions.

THE BASIC ENCOUNTER GROUP

Rogers' approach was somewhat more revealing and open in the encounter group than with individuals. The basic philosophy of congruence and relationship remain the same, but encounter groups have demands of their own which require special techniques.

There is really no adequate definition of an encounter group. The first such groups were essentially post mortems on Lewinian researches (p. 409). These evolved into an attempt to treat several individuals together in what is tantamount to "group therapy." The number of clients in a contemporary encounter group can vary from three or four on up to as many as 15 or 20, but the most common average from six to 10. Some group therapists have taken strictly Freudian views of illness and cure, and the level of interpretation in such approaches is virtually identical to interpretations in individual therapy. Other group therapists have relied more on gestalt psychology or Lewinian "small group" theory to provide the rationale for what goes on when people get together, motivated by an interest in self-knowledge and greater facility for relationships. Rogers finds himself trying to maximize everyone's freedom in the groups which he conducts: "In an encounter group I love to give, both to the participants and to myself, the maximum freedom of expression. . . . I do *trust* the group, and find it often wiser than I in its reactions to particular situations."[191]

Encounter groups are customarily held at a somewhat removed hotel, motel, or resort area.

They may continue for a few days or as long as a week. The group sessions may take up a half-day, an entire day, or it is not unusual for so-called "marathon" groups to last for 24 and more hours, with participants actually sleeping together in catnap form. There are various rationales for each of these approaches, but the essential point is that in time a peculiar phenomenon emerges in which the identification among members is strengthened and the false faces "come off" or at times are "ripped off" by fellow participants. One group member is likely to inform another of how he feels about him, in both positive and negative terms, and it is very difficult avoiding being "sensitized" to one's impact on another in such situations.

As in his approach to teaching, Rogers does not wish to lead, to assign tasks for the group, or to lecture to them (unless asked about something as a resource person); everyone shares responsibility for what is accomplished or not accomplished.[192] He opens the group with a minimum of structure and then listens to others—validating each in turn.[193] He hopes to make the climate of the group psychologically safe, so that no one will feel threatened and real learning can proceed. It is vital to accept the group and each individual within the group as they now *are*. The leader never pushes the group. At the same time, the facilitator can choose to commit himself or not commit himself to what is taking place. Rogers has been known to walk out of a gathering and go to bed when the group is behaving superficially.

Rogers does speak of *resistance* in the group, whereas his writings on individual therapy devote little space to this general topic. He noted: "I am willing to accept silence and muteness in the individual, providing I am certain it is not unexpressed pain or unexpressed resistance."[194] It would appear that if a group facilitator does sense resistance in a group participant and then expresses this feeling to the participant he would essentially be *interpreting*

or "providing insight" to that client. Rogers would have no argument with this usage. He would emphasize that the focus of his comments in the group would be on *present* behavior, and in particular on how that behavior communicates to him. He is prepared to say "I don't like the way you chatter on" to a participant, but: "I do not want to attack a person's defenses because that seems to me to be judgmental."[195] By focusing on a specific behavior and the present relationship he circumvents the kind of distortions in symbolization that might result.

The approach to discussion of how the group as a whole seems to be going along is the same. By studying people he can isolate leaders, indicate what direction the group attitude is taking, and so forth. The Lewinians called this "group process" and studied it in great detail. Rogers said: "I make comments on the group process very sparingly. It seems to me such comments make the group self-conscious. I think they slow the group, make the members feel that they are under scrutiny."[196] Rogers does not use planned group exercises in the sense of scheduled activities. There are many encounter leaders who seem to feel this or that tactic *must* be used if a group is to prove satisfactory. Such prearrangements are too mechanical and "gimmicked" for Rogers' taste. But if a facilitator spontaneously thinks of role playing, bodily contact, psychodrama, or various other exercises to promote group interaction, their performance will be natural and acceptable. Rogers has used all of these techniques.[197]

When a group begins to coalesce and people loosen up enough to say what they feel, a host of potential problems arise. Many psychologists reject basic encounter groups because of the harm they can do people, no matter how experienced and alert a facilitator might be about the emotional clashes which result. Rogers admitted that he had known participants who developed psychotic breaks following their encounter group sessions.[198] However, he felt that these were rare enough occasions to be worth the risk, considering the thousands of people he had seen helped by their encounter experience.

Rogers cited several characteristics of certain encounter group facilitators as *nonfacilitative*.[199] In general, Rogers was suspicious of the person who appears to be exploiting the purposes of the group, using it for his subjective needs. Facilitators who manipulate the group, make rules for it, or covertly direct it toward preconceived ends are not recommended. The histrionic facilitator, who judges success by how many participants weep, is also to be avoided. Rigid facilitators, who have some "one thing" to accomplish like "drawing out the basic rage in everyone," are not going to help a group become what it otherwise would. Rogers would not recommend a facilitator who has such severe personal problems that he has to turn the center of attention in the group on himself at all times. He also did not favor the type who proffered "dynamic" interpretations at every turn. He considered this person too authoritarian.[200] Finally, he did not advocate a facilitator who withheld himself from personal emotional participation in the group—which would be the other side of completely dominating the group with personal "hang ups." It is often the "expert" type who keeps aloof, feeling that he can analyze the group processes or the "dynamics" of the participants by remaining on the sideline.

Notes

1. Husserl, 1965, p. 106. 2. *Ibid.*, p. 110. 3. *Ibid.*, p. 116. 4. *Ibid.* 5. *Ibid.*, p. 90. 6. *Ibid.*, p. 91. 7. *Ibid.* 8. Rychlak, 1968, pp. 222–223. 9. Köhler, 1961a, p. 4. 10. Koffka, 1935. 11. *Ibid.*, p. 73. 12. Köhler, 1961b, p. 209. 13. *Ibid.*, p. 10. 14. Koffka, 1935, p. 126. 15. *Ibid.*, p. 150. 16. *Ibid.*, p. 151. 17. *Ibid.*, p. 153. 18. *Ibid.*, pp. 164, 166. 19. *Ibid.*, p. 110. 20. *Ibid.*, p. 192. 21. *Ibid.*, p. 62. 22. *Ibid.*, pp. 209– 210. 23. *Ibid.*, p. 319. 24. *Ibid.*, p. 665. 25. *Ibid.*, p. 666. 26. Marrow, 1969, p. 8. 27. Lewin, 1935. 28. Marrow, 1969, p. 37. 29. Lewin, Dembo, Festinger, and Sears, 1944. 30. Lewin, Lippitt, and White, 1939. 31. Marrow, 1969, p. 128. 32. *Ibid.*, pp. 210–214. 33. See especially Lewin, 1947. 34. Rank, 1968, p. 3. 35. *Ibid.*, p. 4. 36. *Ibid.*, pp. 104–105. 37. *Ibid.*, p. 179. 38. *Ibid.*, p. 172. 39. Rogers, 1967. 40. *Ibid.* 41. *Ibid.*, p. 345. 42. *Ibid.*, p. 376. 43. *Ibid.*, p. 351. 44. *Ibid.*, p. 354. 45. *Ibid.*, p. 376. 46. *Ibid.*, p. 360. 47. Rogers, 1959. 48. See Rogers and Dymond, 1954. 49. See Rogers, Gendlin, Kiesler, and Truax, 1967. 50. *Ibid.*, pp. 79–81. 51. *Ibid.*, pp. 83–85. 52. Rogers, 1967, p. 370. 53. See Rogers, 1970e. 54. See Rogers, 1959, p. 197. 55. Rogers, 1951, p. 487. 56. *Ibid.*, p. 483. 57. *Ibid.*, p. 485. 58. Rogers, 1959, p. 191. 59. Rogers, 1951, p. 491. 60. *Ibid.*, p. 496. 61. After McCleary and Lazarus, 1949. 62. *Ibid.*, p. 507. 63. Rogers, 1942, pp. 174–175. 64. Rogers, 1951, p. 522. 65. *Ibid.*, p. 524. 66. Rogers, 1970f, p. 2. 67. Rogers, 1959, p. 200. 68. Rogers, 1951, p. 491. 69. *Ibid.*, p. 483. 70. *Ibid.*, p. 191. 71. *Ibid.* 72. *Ibid.*, p. 487. 73. Rogers, 1942, p. 18. 74. Rogers, 1951, p. 491. 75. *Ibid.*, pp. 488–489. 76. *Ibid.*, p. 491. 77. *Ibid.*, p. 492. 78. *Ibid.*, pp. 492–493. 79. *Ibid.*, p. 493. 80. *Ibid.*, p. 498. 81. *Ibid.*, p. 501. 82. *Ibid.*, p. 508. 83. *Ibid.*, p. 516. 84. Rogers, 1959, pp. 196–197. 85. Rogers, 1951, p. 513. 86. Rogers, 1959, p. 206. 87. Rogers, 1961, pp. 50–51. 88. Rogers, 1959, p. 203. 89. *Ibid.*, pp. 207–208. 90. Standal, 1954. 91. Rogers, 1959, p. 208. 92. *Ibid.*, p. 204. 93. Rogers, 1951, p. 523. 94. *Ibid.*, p. 505. 95. Rogers, 1959, p. 205. 96. *Ibid.*, p. 228. 97. *Ibid.*, p. 210. 98. Rogers, 1951, p. 508. 99. Rogers, 1970c. 100. Rogers, 1959, p. 222. 101. *Ibid.*, p. 223. 102. Rogers, 1961, p. 191. 103. Rogers, 1959, p. 223. 104. *Ibid.*, p. 225. 105. *Ibid.* 106. Rogers, 1951, p. 221. 107. *Ibid.*, p. 15. 108. *Ibid.*, p. 213. 109. *Ibid.*, p. 228. 110. Rogers, 1959, p. 200. 111. Rogers and Dymond, 1954. 112. Rogers, 1959, pp. 203–204. 113. *Ibid.*, p. 207. 114. *Ibid.*, p. 235. 115. Rogers, 1961, p. 191. 116. Rogers, 1959, p. 203. 117. *Ibid.*, p. 204. 118. *Ibid.* 119. Rogers, 1951, p. 192. 120. Rogers, 1961, p. 330. 121. Rogers, 1951, p. 221. 122. *Ibid.*, p. 222. 123. Rogers, 1959, p. 203. 124. *Ibid.*, p. 227. 125. *Ibid.*, p. 236. 126. Rogers, 1942, p. 18. 127. *Ibid.*, pp. 87–89. 128. Rogers, 1951, p. 24. 129. *Ibid.*, p. 208. 130. *Ibid.*, p. 209. 131. *Ibid.* 132. *Ibid.*, p. 518. 133. Rogers,

1959, p. 240. **134.** Rogers, 1961, p. 40. **135.**
Rogers, 1970a. **136.** Rogers, 1961, p. 40. **137.**
Rogers, 1970f, pp. 20–21. **138.** *Ibid.*, p. 17.
139. *Ibid.*, p. 3. **140.** Rogers, 1942, p. 174.
141. *Ibid.*, p. 175. **142.** Rogers, 1951, p. 201.
143. *Ibid.*, p. 200. **144.** *Ibid.*, p. 203. **145.**
Rogers, 1959, p. 214. **146.** See Rogers, 1970f,
p. 16. **147.** Rogers, 1951, p. 40. **148.** *Ibid.*, p.
208. **149.** *Ibid.*, p. 40. **150.** *Ibid.*, pp. 112–113.
151. *Ibid.*, p. 222. **152.** *Ibid.*, p. 519. **153.**
Rogers, 1953, p. 48. **154.** Rogers, 1970a, p.
202. **155.** Rogers, 1970d, p. 470. **156.** Rogers,
1951, p. 77. **157.** *Ibid.*, p. 210. **158.** Rogers,
1961, pp. 132–151. **159.** Rogers, 1959, p. 208.
160. *Ibid.*, p. 213. **161.** Rogers, 1951, pp. 40–
41. **162.** *Ibid.*, p. 135. **163.** *Ibid.*, p. 195. **164.**
Rogers, 1959, p. 206. **165.** Rogers, 1961, pp.
115–118. **166.** *Ibid.*, p. 166. **167.** *Ibid.*, pp. 169–
175. **168.** *Ibid.*, p. 189. **169.** *Ibid.*, p. 285. **170.**
Rogers, 1951, p. 194. **171.** *Ibid.*, p. 196. **172.**
Rogers, 1959, p. 221. **173.** Rogers, 1970c, p.
439. **174.** *Ibid.* **175.** *Ibid.* **176.** *Ibid.*, p. 440.
177. *Ibid.* **178.** *Ibid.*, p. 441. **179.** Rogers and
Hart, 1970, p. 520. **180.** From Rogers, 1942,
p. 123. **181.** Rogers, 1969a, p. 63. **182.** *Ibid.*,
p. 75. **183.** *Ibid.*, pp. 164–165. **184.** *Ibid.*, p.
91. **185.** *Ibid.*, p. 279. **186.** Rogers, 1961, p.
325. **187.** *Ibid.*, p. 356. **188.** *Ibid.*, p. 332.
189. *Ibid.*, p. 180. **190.** Rogers, 1970b, p. 297;
Rogers, 1970h, p. 5. **191.** Rogers, 1969a, p. 73.
192. *Ibid.*, p. 144. **193.** Rogers, 1970f, pp. 5–10.
194. *Ibid.*, p. 10. **195.** *Ibid.*, p. 16. **196.** *Ibid.*,
p. 19. **197.** *Ibid.* **198.** Rogers, 1970g, p. 4;
Rogers, 1970h, p. 3. **199.** Rogers, 1970f, pp.
23–25. **200.** *Ibid.*, p. 20.

10

Existential Analysis or Daseinsanalysis: Binswanger and Boss

Existential Philosophy

Existentialism as a movement in philosophy dates from the first half of the nineteenth century, when Sören Kierkegaard (1813–1855) reacted critically to the all-embracing intellectualism of Georg Wilhelm Friedrich Hegel (1770–1831). The spirit of this movement was then advanced by Friedrich Nietzsche (1844–1900), but it was not until a series of brilliant people, most of whom read, admired, or actually studied with Husserl (see Chapter 9), began speaking of *Being, Ontology* (study of being), and *Existence* that the movement really took shape. These were individuals such as Karl Jaspers (1883–   ), Martin Heidegger (1889–   ), and Jean-Paul Sartre (1905–   ). There are other important thinkers, like Gabriel Marcel (1889–   ), who advanced existentialism, but we will focus on those existentialists whose theoretical innovations had direct relevance to psychology.

Existentialism as a view of the world is *not* a uniform philosophy. Although central to the development of this view, both Jaspers and Heidegger have specifically denied that they are "existentialists." These men disagree on major points and meanings for the same terms change within their writings. Yet, existentialism is a peculiarly *modern* philosophy which speaks for large segments of the world's populace; it has something to say about contemporary man's *predicament* (a term often employed) as he advances into the twenty-first century. Will he make it? Is it all worth it? Does he really have the "answers," philosophical or scientific, to enrich life as he once dreamed he might? Can he discover or create that which he must know to "truly be"? These are the questions to which existentialism addresses itself.

It is possible to isolate a half-dozen terms which best represent this point of view. The writings of Kierkegaard and Heidegger are probably more relevant to personality and psychotherapy than those of any other. These two thinkers have had the most direct influence on modern psychology.

ALIENATION

As the last philosopher who attempted to write a "world view," embracing the totality of history as well as mankind's current status, Hegel played an important role in the birth of existentialism. A rather distinctive idea which he proposed was that each of man's creations are capable of an independent existence once they have been formed. An artist's painting or the writings of an author are really "there" in existence independent of his control. If the artist and author change their views —their judgment of what is beautiful or worthy of literary mention—their creations remain as originally conceived. Furthermore, the creations may take on meanings never intended by the creators! More than one creation has been known to come back and haunt its creator as in the fictional case of Frankenstein's "monster." Not only the works of major artists and authors, but even the most humble statements and activities of everyday life can have a similar effect—as a letter written in haste, an "act" of seemingly justified revenge, and so forth.

Hegel referred to this "alien existence" of created objects, ideas, or actions as *alienation*.[1] He also spoke of an *estrangement* between the creative mind and its creations. Kierkegaard was to take this idea of an alienation and apply it to the various attempts to describe the essence, nature, history, and even scientific status of man. Central to his philosophy was the Christian's relation to his church. Too many Christians, said Kierkegaard, look to the established writings of their church and to the customs of the group (church body) for their

faith. These dogmatic writings and manners are often meaningless rituals which have become alienated from the living spirit of faith. Nietzsche launched a similar attack against the established philosophies of his time. He stressed that if a thinker has to align his thought with earlier restrictions then he is bound to be alienated from his own intellectual promptings.[2] How can today's man answer today's questions by immersing himself in yesterday's assumptions?

Heidegger noted how words can be substituted for living things, and hence the existential truth can be subverted (alienated) and manipulated by facile language.[3] We can actually live out a life of untruth, making it all seem plausible and "real." Sartre has said as much about modern psychology, which bases its assumptions about man not on the living, phenomenological reality but rather on the strained mechanical analogies of natural science.[4] Sartre greatly developed the idea first suggested by Kierkegaard—that group pressure by way of national identities has become so great in our time that everyone alive lives in self-alienation. We cannot be who we are because of the immense and subtle pressures to conform, to be as others would have us be and as everyone around us is.

AUTHENTICITY

Kierkegaard was the first philosopher to point out that man becomes inauthentic if he lets the group or culture define him (self-alienation). Modern concepts of the Mass Man, who sells himself out by submitting to what the "system" says he ought to be, take root in Kierkegaard's attack on the staid and lifeless rituals of the Christian Church.[5] Nietzsche spoke of the "Will to Power" (see Chapter 2) as man's fundamental capacity to be self-creative and hence authentic. If man bases his life on what he *is* (thinks, feels, desires) then he cannot be self-alienated or self-estranged. Man's conscience urges him to be free, to be himself, and guilt is that reaction to his rejection of this instinctive desire to be free of others' conceptualizations.[6]

Jaspers elaborated on this opposition of authentic vs. inauthentic being in his philosophy. He referred to *Dasein* as "being there" or, literally, the objective fact that we do materially exist.[7] Nature automatically determines that we exist in this sense. But another realm of existence which Jaspers termed "being oneself" demands action on our part before it is made real. To be oneself requires effort, personal decision, and the selection of alternatives which create what one "is" in his own life style. The group cannot provide this being oneself for us. It can set limits on what we might be, and the point is not to reject all of its admonitions about what life "is." But the human individual must further what he is capable of being through his *own* efforts.

For Heidegger, authenticity is fulfilling one's possibilities.[8] That is, we can *become* what we aspire to be. As humans we can see a "potential being" ahead of us and work to "be" that unique self. The term *Dasein* as used by Heidegger includes this possibility, this tentative projection of what "might be" in the future. We also realize that our possibilities are not endless. Other human beings have established certain prescribed ways of doing things. We can go along with the established routine without question—which would make us inauthentic—or we can evaluate, embrace, discard, and affirm our own sequence of possibilities, ways of living which when realized in our life style would make us authentic.[9] No one can be completely free of group impositions. The authentic person thus synthesizes the imposed and the self-willed to reach a pattern of existence (*Dasein*) which is uniquely his own.

SUBJECT VS. OBJECT

Kierkegaard noted that when man permits himself to live inauthentically as a being who is defined by others, he comes to think of himself as an *object* rather than as an individual human being or a *subject*.[10] Subjective knowledge is not the same as objective knowledge. The objective facts may show what man is, but how he got to be that way, the internal examinations, the passionate feelings, the wretched decisions which men have exerted to press themselves along history's way may be entirely hidden to the objectivist. When man looks inward and decides in an ethical sense what he "ought" to be and then *lives that life*, he makes "possibility" a reality. However, when he looks at another man and proclaims what this other man ought to be, his proclamation remains in the realm of mere possibility.[11] We cannot force a (possible) reality onto another, said Kierkegaard, at least not an ethical reality. Yet, by considering him *and* ourselves as existing within an "objective reality" we are more prepared to accept such forced prescriptions.

We therefore accept as correct all statements which are predicated on some sweeping generalization such as "the Church teaches" or "science has found" or "all good citizens agree" because we think of ourselves as one of a collection of objects. Truths discovered scientifically by experimentation with animals or other nonhuman subjects apply to us because our subjectivity is an illusion. Beliefs and convictions framed by other times and other people apply to us because we are "all the same." Kierkegaard speaks out against this what he termed a "leveling" process by emphasizing the subjectivity of man's existence. Jaspers observes that if one allows modern science to define what he is then he is confounding the objective realm of *being-there* with the subjective realm of *being-oneself*. Since the former can never arrive at the latter, Jaspers calls for a transcendence of objectivity because it is falsifying (alienating) man's subjective realm of true existence.[12]

Heidegger's treatment of the subject-object dichotomy is similar to Kierkegaard's, except that he introduces a concept of *nothingness*. Inauthentic existence is the everyday world of "anyone" or "everyman." We see ourselves as part of this objective mass, this faceless crowd of objects which move about like ants conforming to the prescriptions of science, church, country, and so forth. To "be" is something and yet "to be nothing" is also a part of this world of meaningless routine. Heidegger does not view nothing as the opposite of being. The individual (subject) who is truly *being* emerges from the background of nothing like a figure emerges from the ground (see Chapter 9). For a subject to experience his individuality he must separate himself from the nothingness of his daily life. He must negate an easy identity with the objective mass and subjectively affirm who he is.

COMMITMENT, ACTION

The very essence of man's spirit is *activity*.[13] One must strike off on his own path to fulfill the possibility he has subjectively decided upon. Hence, Kierkegaard said: "To be human is not a fact, but a task."[14] Nietzsche was in agreement that man must "leap" into life. Passion accompanies such commitment, said Nietzsche, but this does not mean that the committed man is irrational. Reason and emotion are not antithetical.[15] Reason helps us to control our passions, but without passionate *commitment* we are lifeless automatons. If one is simply "going through the motions" of life he is not committed, not really existing. He is a figment of someone else's possibility.

Jaspers claims we must commit ourselves to a course of action, in light of our historical time and personal situation.[16] Heidegger notes that some men flee from this need for subjective affirmation into the anonymity of mass movements and other popular fads.[17] Sartre has brilliantly drawn out this tendency of man to give up in the face of a need for affirmation and to deceive himself through "bad faith" by letting himself down and not acting to realize his possibilities.[18] The thrust of existentialism is thus to put the individual "at the center" of life. He cannot flee and say that he

behaves as he does because of his social climate, nationality, or race. He must recognize that even when he refuses to choose, to act, to commit himself to a direction in life he *has already chosen*. There is no escaping the existential predicament.

ANXIETY, DREAD, DESPAIR

The existentialists are wont to use terms like anxiety, dread, and despair to capture inauthentic man. Kierkegaard spoke of anxiety as resulting from self-alienation, which transforms into despair as the "sickness unto death."[19] Nietzsche spoke of fear as the negation of the Will to Power.[20] When man avoids commitment and suffers alienation he is afraid, even though such fear is not overt. Indeed, we can assuage anxiety by losing ourselves in Mass Man and thereby gain a sense of boredom instead. Boredom masks the anxiety beneath, which in turn could reveal man's empty life. As Heidegger observed: "Anxiety reveals nothingness."[21] Both Kierkegaard and Heidegger recognize that before man can "be," before he discovers that being-oneself which Jaspers spoke of, it is often necessary for him first to sense anxiety. Out of the nothingness of dreaded anxiety man begins to fashion his unique self. Anxiety is thus a prelude to self-affirmation, the movement from alienation to being-oneself.

ABSURD

The last term we wish to underscore as representative of existentialism is "absurd." The usages vary here, having either a positive or a negative connotation depending upon how the term is employed. Kierkegaard used the term "absurd" to say that when the individual looks subjectively inward, he may find a conviction based on incongruity and contradiction which would be completely unacceptable to objective reason. All truth is subjective. It is flatly absurd to think of a God who has been born, grown up, and died, exactly as other human beings have done and are doing. Yet, subjectively considered, it is the absurdity of this occurrence which makes it subjectively believable.[22] Those things which are simply "too much" for rational, objective, and plausible evidence to embrace may subjectively lend a sense of conviction because of that very fact. Paradoxes and absurdities thus carry great weight as evidence.

Sartre intends an alternate meaning for absurd, which has a more negative connotation. He views absurdity as a quality of existence, as literally pervading all of man's experience. We have the absurdities of death, bringing to end nature's highest creations.[23] We have the absurdities of clashing moralities, where opposed sides are drawn along a line of armed conflict aiming to demolish one another in the name of their God (who is often the same). We have the absurdities of birth, in which advantages are partitioned according to class or race. And the more complex life becomes the more absurd does it become. We can see in this rather pessimistic summation an increasing need for each person to ferret out his stand on existence and to thrust himself into life along a more honest and authentic course.

Existentialism as a Theory of Man and Psychotherapy: Binswanger and Boss

BIOGRAPHICAL OVERVIEW

Two men have formed the nucleus of existential applications to personality and psychotherapy, both Swiss in national origin, Heideggerian in philosophical outlook, and both initially trained in classical (Freudian, Jungian) approaches to psychoanalysis. In the chapter sections to follow we will review the customary topics by interchanging the thought of these two men, providing contrasts where called for. The actual founder of existential analysis or *Daseinsanalyse* (after Heidegger) was Ludwig Binswanger, who was born in Kreuzlingen,

Switzerland on 13 April 1881. There was a tradition of medicine in his family, and Ludwig decided to follow it, taking the M.D. degree from the University of Zurich in 1907. He studied under Jung for a time and also took an internship with Eugen Bleuler (see Chapter 3).

In 1911 Binswanger succeeded his father as director of the Sanatorium Bellevue at Kreuzlingen, a position he held for over four decades during which he earned an international reputation. Although he studied with Jung, the major therapeutic interest among the Swiss in the first decade of this century was Freudian psychoanalysis. Binswanger became active in this area of psychiatry and gradually cemented a personal friendship with Freud—who visited him in 1912 when Binswanger was ill.[24] Gradually, however, Binswanger became disenchanted with Freud's penchant to explain behavior in what seemed

Ludwig Binswanger

to be extraneous and distorting concepts of energies, psychic systems, and so forth. There followed a period of reading and study during which Binswanger became interested in the philosophy of Heidegger. By the 1920s he had worked out a view of man which he felt was more accurate than Freud's. Binswanger delivered a lecture in Vienna on the occasion of Freud's eightieth birthday, in which he attempted to contrast psychoanalysis with a more existential view.[25] The paper was not well received by the Freudians, and not until recent times has existential thought made inroads on the classical analytical position.[26] Binswanger and Freud remained on good personal terms through all of their disagreements.[27] In 1956, Binswanger stepped down from his directorship of the Sanatorium Bellevue, though he continued to study and write until his death in 1966.

Our second existentialist, Medard Boss, also graduated from the medical school of the University of Zurich. He was born in St. Gallen, Switzerland, on 4 October 1903 and is currently professor of psychotherapy at Zurich, as well as the director of the Institute of Daseinsanalytic Therapy there. Boss also studied Jung, Bleuler, and, of course, Freud. Though he was to disagree with the founder of *Daseinsanalyse* (translated as "Daseinsanalysis") on certain points, Boss acknowledges that he was initially stimulated to study Heidegger by the writings of and then personal contacts with Ludwig Binswanger.[28] Boss became a close personal friend of Martin Heidegger as well. He has written more extensively than Binswanger and has also lectured in the United States. For many years Boss was the president of the International Society for Medical Psychotherapy. Boss uses the term *Daseinsanalysis,* but we can consider this translation interchangeable with *Daseinsanalyse,* both of which are synonymous with "existential analysis."

Medard Boss

Personality Theory

STRUCTURAL CONSTRUCTS

THE CENTRALITY OF PHENOMENAL MEANING FOR MAN AS BODY-MIND GESTALT

To a confirmed phenomenologist, the problem of mind vs. body is a pseudoproblem, resulting from natural science splitting up experience to meet its particular needs. Binswanger emphasizes that man "is and remains a unit."[29] We do not divide him into a body and a psyche but recognize that each such component of life is merely a different aspect of the same thing. What the existentialist finds interesting is the problem of being or, more technically, of *ontology* (the study of being). Binswanger noted: ". . . the mind-body problem is not an ontological problem, but a problem of scientific knowledge, a purely theoretical problem. 'Theory' therefore is called in for help in 'solving' this problem. No theory, however, can really 'solve' it. . . ."[30] This arbitrary division is thus another manifestation of a theory becoming alienated from the very human being it has set out to understand. The scientist poses a *phenomenologically untrue* division of body vs. mind, and then must wrestle with further "theoretical" constructs to patch up what is already a bad job of description.

It is this truly *un*natural division of man into a material and an immaterial sphere which leads to the *reduction* of phenomenal experience to the so-called more scientific substrate of organic matter.[31] But when we do this we have reduced a *subject* to an *object* or made a "thing" out of a phenomenally experiencing being.[32] Yet Boss notes: "Without a subject nothing at all would exist to confront objects and to imagine them as such. True, this implies that every object, everything 'objective'— in being merely objectivized by the subject— is the most subjective thing possible."[33] If we simply contemplate our existence for a time, it soon becomes clear that the phenomena of our very being are not separate from us, as if we were subjective bodies "having" objective experiences. We *are* our experience. We do not "have" ideas, for example; we *are* our ideas.[34] When we stand before a beautiful tree, we do not face it with our consciousness or perceive it with our eyes or brains. The tree is simply "there," it existentially presents itself to us as we experience it for what it is.[35]

This is not to deny that brain processes go on as we experience relating to the tree, coming to know it as its being dictates. We must acknowledge that retinal images and taste buds can be isolated and shown to "function" in predictable ways during experience. Yet, what have such things to say ontologically? According to the existentialists, very little indeed. Phenomenologically, what is most important is the recognition that *meaning* and not simply function is what is uppermost in experience. As Binswanger said: "What we perceive are 'first and foremost' not impressions of taste, tone, smell or touch, not even things or objects, but rather, meanings."[36] Boss then adds: ". . . man cannot see, hear, and smell because he has eyes, ears, and a nose; he is able to have eyes, ears, and a nose because his very essence is luminating and world-disclosing."[37]

Hence we may speak of the "body" as existentialists, but we recognize in this merely a partial realm of existence, one which has no real significance for phenomenal experience. The scientific truths about brain function, the chemical actions of the nervous system, etc., may well be valid, but quite forthrightly the meanings of existence are not themselves to be found in chemical substances or biological processes; indeed, the concepts of "instinct" or "libido" or "drive" are considered equally meaningless as descriptive terms for experience —regardless of their *facticity* (the "given fact" that man "has" instincts as he "has" ears).[38] Binswanger refers to the bodily sphere of experience as the *Eigenwelt*.

EXISTENCE, BEING-IN-THE-WORLD, AND DASEIN AS ENDOWED OR DISCLOSED

The core theoretical constructs employed by our existentialists are *existence, being-in-the-world*, and *Dasein*. These terms cannot be defined independently of each other, and for practical purposes we should think of them as variant ways of expressing *being* if not synonyms. The human experience of being takes on a quality all its own when we think of it from our personal frames of reference. Being literally *transcends* (i.e., mounts, goes beyond, overrides) all of the other qualities of experience such as colors, the size and weight of materials, the feelings of emotion, and so forth.

To clarify this stance we will review an argument which was first made by Hegel and later adapted by Heidegger concerning the nature of being.[39] It runs as follows: Suppose we were to explain the "being-ness" of one of nature's most common items, the chunk of earth known as a *rock*. If we now ask "Is the rock's being-ness due to its color?" the answer would be "no, its being is not due to its color." Comparable questions about the rock's shape, its material substance, its weight, and so forth would similarly be answered in the negative. A rock's being or not-being is not quite any of these qualities—even when we put them into combinations (gestalts). Stripped of all its qualities, therefore, we would still have failed to capture the "is-ness" of the rock. Even more paradoxical, after all of the qualities had been removed from the rock we would have *nothing*. Heidegger as Hegel before him thus observed that "being and nothingness" are closely related. Hegel viewed these as opposites, and Heidegger viewed these as partial identities as well as independent states of existence.[40]

One might say: "But this is surely nonsense. For all practical purposes and insofar as it is possible to prove anything, a rock *is* the sum of its qualities, which I perceive and name as a 'thing.' When the properties are not there the rock does not exist and there is no such concept as 'being' to be concerned about." Granting this retort for a rock, what does one say in response to a person's *self-examination*? If we simply and honestly look into our own *phenomenal* experience, what do we learn about *our* being? Is it not true that even as we grow to adulthood and change coloring, size, personal attitudes, and ambitions, we somehow sense a continuity of having-been, of being-now, and of being-in-the-future? And is there not (for some) a spiritual sense of continuing on with this identity even beyond the grave, a compulsion to feel this futurity even though we may know scientifically that it is unlikely?[41] What do we say about such human experiences? Are they to be dismissed as quaint illusions, or are we to attempt an ontological study of them in their pure form?

The existentialists have obviously felt the latter study to be important. Science has taught us to ignore such highly personalized, subjective truths. Yet, the language of science has probably alienated man from his most basic and pure experience. The ways in which Bin-swanger and Boss deal with this question of being, as something beyond simply the palpable and observable qualities, constitute the variations in *existential analysis* they each advocate. There is a fundamental divergence in the emphasis placed on the approach to the study of existence. Binswanger emphasizes the ways in which experience is made possible or *endowed* with meaning by man's most basic ways of looking at and thinking about it. Boss, on the other hand, emphasizes the meaning *disclosed* to man by existence, as if it were not so much how man "looks at" but how existence "reveals itself," that is what matters. This contrast in views will become clearer as we move through the more technical terms of the theories.

Turning to Binswanger first, a major structural construct employed in his version of existential analysis might be called the *a priori ontological structure*.[42] A priori signifies "coming before," and ontological structure means the kind of beginning assumptions, basic slant on things, or, as Binswanger also called them, the *world-designs* which an individual presumed. These are not to be thought of as inherited ideas, nor is Binswanger interested in the number of such ontological structures a person carries with him *per se*—though he does comment on this facet in his theory of pathology.[43] The ontological structure is more like a matrix of meanings, which begin from the outset of experience to frame an individual's existence. The human organism begins to formulate experience, creatively "putting it together" in a meaningful way as things happen. There are various ways in which the existential analyst can come to recognize a person's most basic presumptions: "Language [i.e., what a person says about life], the poetic imagination; and—above all—the dream, draw from this basic ontological structure."[44]

Boss is none too pleased with this interpretation of how one's "being-in-the-world" is said to take place—as if it were framed in by an overriding abstraction coming before concrete experience.[45] For Boss, being-in-the-world is not predicated on anything. Such being is always a concrete occurrence: "Fundamentally, 'being' always means 'coming forth and lasting.' How could any such coming forth and lasting be possible without a lightened realm into which this happening can take place?"[46] In other words, it is not so much a question of how we premise via world-designs before we "go at" life, but rather how life is revealed to us through concrete examples of living. Boss views life as if it were ever emerging under the rays of a torch or flashlight, carried by the living person. The rays are actually his immediate awareness of experience, the structured phenomena of life. As Boss notes: "The very word 'phenomena,' however, is derived from *phainesthai*, i.e., to shine forth, to appear, unveil itself, come out of concealment or darkness."[47] Hence, for Boss a *phenomenon* is "that which shows itself."[48] Binswanger would say that the "phenomenon" is found most directly in the language expression of an individual as a world-design.[49] Boss would point out that the phenomenon is just as likely to claim the person's being as it is to be claimed by his world-design presumptions about being.[50]

Both men agree on the fundamental immediacy and meaningfulness of experience. Binswanger does not attempt to explain away or reduce the "now" of experience to an a priori "something" which makes the now possible. He and Boss accept the reality of existence as a *being* (sein) *there* (da), as a right-now happening which must be studied in its own terms and not taken out of context into an artificial realm of "theory." Hence, we have the *Dasein* (there-being) as being-in-the-world or existing concretely. There is also the idea here of man as a different aspect of nature than, for example, the inanimate structures and the subhuman creatures. Binswanger has noted the "distinction between human existence (*Dasein*) or being-in-the-world, on the one hand, and nature on the other."[51] Boss defines Dasein in terms of his light analogy, which he

calls *lumination,* and emphasizes that the "there" (da) of Dasein is a luminated happening.[52] Lumination may thus be equated with *disclosing,* and whereas Binswanger's emphasis is on how the a priori ontological structure *endows* existence with meaning, Boss emphasizes the meaning-disclosing features of Dasein, Boss's definition is as follows: "*Dasein,* thus being essentially and primordially of a disclosing, i.e., luminating, nature, shines forth at any given time. But—as with every kind of 'light'—its lumination varies as to color and brightness."[53]

The fact that lumination varies emphasizes that Dasein or being-in-the-world or existence takes on different features. Binswanger thinks Dasein is experienced in both a temporal and spatial sense. The primary aspect of "temporalization" is intentional, pitched toward the future, even though a sense of the past and the present are always experienced as well.[54] Certain structural arrangements of Dasein are fixed, or *thrown* as the existentialists call it.[55] For example, we are born into this world with certain physical equipment, into cultural environments with given beliefs, and hence to an extent our existence is defined for us or "limited" by circumstances beyond our control. Existence is also fixed somewhat by preceding happenings, by the *historicity* of Dasein.[56] The term historicity signifies that various forms of existence *can* be worked out by those individuals who have premised life's meaning before us with various world-designs. When we study history we learn about the actual outcomes of this potential for Dasein to be frozen into historical precedent. Historical precedents are thus one way of speaking about the thrownness of Dasein; there is a facticity about the history of a people which any one person being born into this group must recognize. Social values and other world-views are examples of such historicized aspects of Dasein.

Dasein is at all times a gestalt totality. Boss says: "There are *myriads* of *different* modes of human relationships and patterns of behavior toward what is encountered, all of them constituting man's *one* fundamental nature, i.e., his unique way of being-in-the-world as the disclosing, luminating realm of world-openness."[57] Though we can speak of the individual's Dasein, we must not forget that an aspect of "being there" is "being with" others.[58] We are not cutting up existence into individual private worlds when we speak of Dasein. Binswanger likes to speak of the three "worlds" (*welt*) of existence: (1) *Eigenwelt*: the self-world of inner feelings and affections, including all of those experiences we think of as "within" the body sphere; (2) *Umwelt*: the environment or "world around" us, including both animate and inanimate features of existence; and (3) *Mitwelt*: the social world, the world of one's fellow men, including all of those things we refer to when we speak of "society."[59] Boss has noted: "The world of Dasein is essentially Mitwelt."[60] Once again, these three worlds are all "one" in the Dasein, and we refer to them individually only for purposes of communication. Dasein is always to be conceived as a gestalt.

If Dasein is thrown, then we must also appreciate that it is open to *possibilities* as well. Binswanger notes that being means "being-able-to-be," thus emphasizing that man finds his most *authentic* existence in achieving his potentials or possibilities.[61] Indeed, the very notion of temporalization—Dasein as moving across time—is dependent upon the fact that man does try to live authentically by fulfilling a better tomorrow. An inauthentic existence would result if he simply gave into the thrown aspects of existence, if he did not try to fulfill those possibilities which suggest themselves to him.[62] Boss warns that man can fall prey to the "anonymous, unauthentic mentality of 'tradition,' to 'authoritarian commands' foreign to him."[63] There is always a kind of interplay between the thrown features of Dasein and the open possibilities. The fact that man commits himself to change and growth by

way of fulfilling possibilities is what the existentialists mean by *care*.[64] Man furthers his existence by caring for what is disclosed to him and by extending his time horizons to reach goals he sees create a "better" existence than he now confronts. If man did not care he would not rise above yesterday's thrownness, he would not *transcend* the givens of today and move on to the possibilities of tomorrow.

DASEIN AND IDENTITY

Now that we have reviewed the nature of being and the global view of Dasein which existentialists advocate we might ask: "Is there a concept of self or personal identity which is used to explain personality?" This question may be answered with both a no and a qualified yes. That is, strictly speaking the existentialist, like any convinced phenomenologist, is opposed to categorizing experience according to some arbitrary preconception (see Chapter 9). To name a "self" in the personality means we must speak about the self vs. the environment or the "external world" confronting the self. This structural split is *not* acceptable. Freud is thus taken to task for having split up the unity of experience into an id, ego, and superego.[65]

Technically speaking, no *formal* designation as the "self" exists in existentialism, even though the term is used as an identity construct.[66] Hence, we might simply use the term *identity* to refer jointly to that aspect of the Dasein which other theories have classified as a self, person, human being, the I, the Me, a man, and so forth. All such designations can be found in the writings of existentialists as designations of identity. The pictorial role of identity in the Dasein, schematizing the contrasting emphases of Binswanger and Boss, is shown in Figure 25.

Point 1 of Figure 25 is a figure-on-ground arrangement, with the global figure labeled "Identity" and the entire complex (of global figure and dashed line arrows) labeled the

Figure 25
The Dasein and Identity Terms

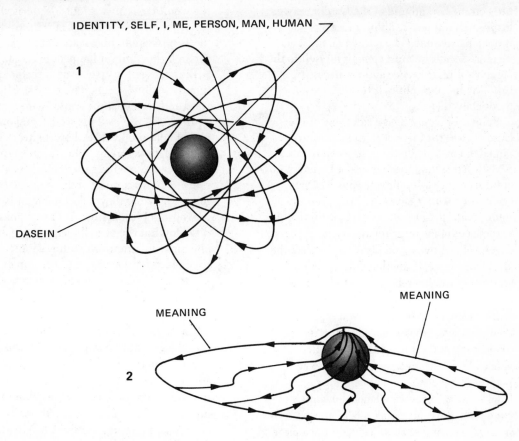

IDENTITY, SELF, I, ME, PERSON, MAN, HUMAN

1

DASEIN

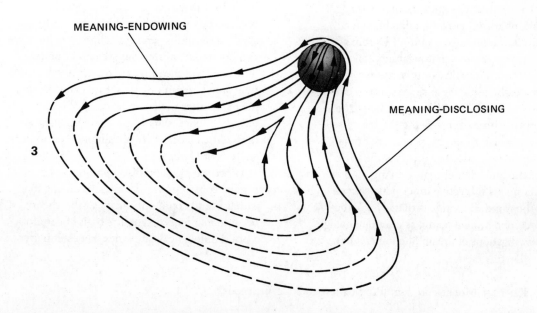

MEANING

MEANING

2

MEANING-ENDOWING

MEANING-DISCLOSING

3

"Dasein." It is not unusual for the existentialists to speak of the self as a form of emergent (figure) on the background of the Dasein, so we begin with this tactic.[67] This process of identity is not a passive one. The individual must act, he must decide, he must commit himself to the facticity of his existence and the necessity of fulfilling his possibilities if he is to live authentically.

Point 2 in Figure 25 is a side view of the Dasein, with the identity portion arbitrarily pulled out away from the gestalt complex as a whole, stretching the "fabric" of Dasein without disturbing the totality of point 1. Once again, the *identity* aspect of Dasein is not "other than" the Dasein. We might think of it as the locus of meaning relations within the Eigenwelt, Mitwelt, and Umwelt. Indeed, the arrows of Figure 25 are the multidirectional aspects of meaning relations that phenomenal experience makes available to the identity within Dasein. At point 3 we can see the different emphases placed on the role of meaning in the stretched Dasein advanced by Binswanger and Boss. Note at point 3 that the moving outward, "away from identity" arrows are labeled *meaning endowing*. Binswanger takes his stance at this point of meaning-relation, viewing the a priori categories which the individual manifests as endowing existence with certain meanings.

Boss, on the other hand, takes his stance within the "luminated realm" of Dasein as such and emphasizes that meanings "move inward," toward identity. In this case we speak of *meaning disclosing* because we want to emphasize that man is *within* being, hence he endows it with nothing. Being discloses itself *to* man, as man shines his peculiarly human light onto the world, and others shine their light onto him. Rather than viewing man as projecting his subjective inner perspectives onto the world, Boss argues that: ". . . the 'essence' of a human being, as phenomenological investigations of dream phenomena have

shown time after time, is of quite a different kind: man 'ex-ists' in the very literal sense of the word. He is always 'outside'; he is with the people, animals and things of the world he meets; just as a light can appear as such only through the things it happens to reveal."[68]

Binswanger thus places us at the point of lumination projection, where the self looks outward and "comes at the world" with certain a priori "givens," as if we were fixing on the lens of a flashlight to see how it affects the pattern of light before us.[69] Boss stands out in this light and analyzes the immediately appearing, meaningful items that make themselves known as they reflect the light back to the source of lumination.[70] The emphasis is different, but the overall picture is a cohesive one, since to luminate requires a source of luminosity (endowing) and a region or object to receive the rays and thence reflect them back (disclosing).

There remains the question of conscious vs. unconscious behaviors to consider in this context of an identity. Here again, the existentialists do not accept the classical distinction. All one can examine is man's experience, and to divide it up in some fashion, calling the dream world unconscious and the waking world conscious, strikes the existentialist as another one of those arbitrary divisions of experience made to meet a theoretical prejudice. Harking back to the mind-body problem, how is it possible for natural science to define consciousness as a "function" of nervous systems or brains? The realms of meaning are drastically different here, and one can never capture man's existential experience in physiological or chemical terms.[71] Hence, why speak of consciousness in the first place? Why not simply refer to the analysis of Dasein?

What the existentialists point out concerning the conscious vs. unconscious distinction is that Freud could only arrive at this theory because *he* proceeded on the basis of certain a priori ontological categories. He essentially viewed existence as a matter of "being contained" within separate, non-open structures.[72] He did not see man as living outwardly, in a world openness. Thus Freud could break up the gestalt totality of man into an "unconscious man" and a "conscious man," since two "things" can "be contained" within one structure (the psyche).[73] This does not mean, of course, that the existentialists deny the phenomena Freud described as reflecting unconscious processes. They simply take them "as disclosed" and explain them in different ways. For example, the thrown aspects of existence may be seen as unconscious phenomena.[74] The individual who accepts direction from others and never questions what is taking place in his existence is essentially "being lived" in a so-called unconscious fashion.

Another form of unconscious behavior stems from having a restricted or constricted *world-design* or *world-outlook*. These terms are other ways of expressing the a priori ontological category or categories being employed by the individual.[75] They have also been termed the *key* or *key-theme* employed by the individual in his approach to the world (meaning endowing).[76] For example, one of Binswanger's clients viewed the world as either entirely harmonious across time or on the verge of complete collapse. Hence, when one day her skate heel collapsed at a skating rink she interpreted the event as a negation of her entire world. There was a break in the continuity of existence, and she had no offsetting ontological category (of the "unexpected" or "chance" event) within which to endow this experience with a meaning other than "my world has collapsed" or some such. She lost consciousness over this seemingly innocuous incident. The "cause" of the fainting was not some repressed and hence unconscious conflict or wish but the even more basic factor of a *limited horizon* along which to transcend due to the restricted ontological category (i.e., continuity) on which she proceeded to live.

MOTIVATION AS THROWNNESS, PITCH, AND THE
FULFILLING OF POSSIBILITIES

Since mind cannot be reduced to body, it follows that motivation as a human experience within Dasein cannot be reduced to physical energies or libidos. All such physical substrates to human behavior are an aspect of the thrownness of Dasein.[77] There is no attempt to reduce the more psychological aspects of Dasein to such "elements," although occasionally the term "energy" may be employed merely in the descriptive sense of effort being expended by the individual.[78] Boss takes a similar view of how man's mood, passion, or affect might color his Dasein and to that extent alter his very being. He speaks of such moods as the *pitch* of Dasein being luminated, as follows:

An individual's pitch at a certain moment determines in advance the choice, brightness, and coloring of his relationships to the world. In a mood of hunger, for instance, he perceives totally different things than when he is in an anxious mood, or when he is in love. He also discloses quite different qualities and meaningful connections of the things he perceives in these respective moods.[79]

The pitch of Dasein, its attunement with the moment, cannot be explained by reducing it to a function of the nervous system or a gland. Even if nervous system and glandular differences parallel our emotional states, this says nothing about Dasein. We do not *have* emotions any more than we *have* ideas; we *are* our emotions just as we *are* our ideas. *Emotions* therefore reflect the state of attunement or being in tune with our existence as a whole; they also reflect the particular manner in which we are experiencing Dasein at the moment.[80] Since the Dasein is meaning disclosing we will find our emotions "out there," in what we are doing and in what others are doing, rather than "in here," lurking among the atoms of body chemistry.

The major motivational concept employed by existentialists doubtless stems from their basic view of man as a future-oriented being, drawn to the *possibilities* which Dasein offers as a result of this capacity to transcend and grow. Binswanger says: "The [subhuman] animal has its environment by the grace of nature, not by the grace of freedom to transcend the situation."[81] Man, on the other hand, can be many things—a hunter, business man, lover, and so forth—all in one span of time or at various times over his life.[82] This is actually what "being" is all about, for existence would indeed be ludicrous if man did not capitalize on his potentials. Put another way, existence would then be *meaningless* for man would have sunk into *nothingness*. Hence Boss says: "In reality, man exists always and only as the myriads of possibilities for relating to and disclosing the living beings and things he encounters."[83]

If Dasein is thrown and assumes a pitch from time to time, how can we suggest that man is free to choose one manner of behavior over another? The existentialists have probably devoted more time to this question of freedom and choice than any other group of thinkers in modern times. Essentially, the answer to our question is that man must face up to the fact that Dasein *is* thrown. This is the "facticity" of Dasein, and to deny it would be to deny existence. Man's freedom begins "in the commitment of the Dasein to its Thrownness."[84] Having accepted the facticity of Dasein's thrownness, man can oppose himself to the seeming unalterability and causal rigidity of his past, project those possibilities which remain open to him through this comprehension, and then work to attain goals through action, effort, and commitment. A possibility is merely a suggestion that might or might not reach actuality. One can never know whether a possibility can be an actuality until he makes

the decision—he chooses—to see it through to goal attainment. It is precisely here that man rises above his lower-animal state, for the animal is not aware of its thrownness, hence it cannot project a possibility into the future for attainment. It is blind to the past (thrownness) as well as the future (possibility).

Boss emphasizes that to recognize and accept the disclosed possibilities of one's Dasein and thereby assemble them in a unique and free fashion is the very heart of authentic living.[85] Too many people are so invested in the views and life styles of others that they cannot see real possibilities for themselves. Hence, they live other people's lives, they live inauthentically! It takes courage to live authentically, for then we permit ourselves to express whatever in our pitch (mood) of Dasein is being disclosed. The pitch of Dasein makes claims on us. We feel this way or that about what we are doing, who we are relating to, and what sort of person we are. Feeling this way, what is suggested in our mood? A change? Can we change our occupation, turn our backs or at least say no to our so-called friends, and become the sort of person that we now are not? This is the beckoning challenge of Dasein, the claim that it makes on us through suggested possibilities at every turn. And Boss concludes: "Man's option to respond to this claim or to choose not to do so seems to be the very core of human freedom."[86]

EXISTENTIAL VS. NEUROTIC FORMS OF ANXIETY AND GUILT

Of course, not all people opt for freedom and attempt to transcend their circumstances to achieve a future possibility. Even those who do can see yet another possibility which was not attempted, a further possibility beckoning from tomorrow's Dasein. In speaking about just why possibilities are or are not achieved or furthered by the individual Binswanger and Boss have emphasized the concepts of anxiety and guilt respectively, even though at a certain level these constructs seem identical.

Binswanger thus distinguishes between what he calls *existential anxiety* and what we may term *neurotic anxiety*. All anxiety stems from difficulties in the world (Mitwelt, Umwelt, Eigenwelt) as experienced by the individual—as when our world seems shaky, about to collapse or vanish completely.[87] Anxiety often begins with a feeling of *uncanniness,* such as when things begin happening which seem unfamiliar to our world as known earlier.[88] Gradually, this loss of grasp increases until our threat is strong enough to speak of it as *dread* (*Angst*).[89] And when the dread is fixed upon something definite—when a man suddenly realizes that his work performance has slipped below minimal standards—we can speak of *fear.* Anxiety thus moves from an amorphous quality through uncanniness to a heightening level of dread and then into a state of fear.

How does anxiety arise in the first instance? Binswanger makes it plain that part of "being" in a "world" is concerned with the likelihood that this world will fade into *nothingness.* It is this basic "loss of world" that he calls *existential anxiety.* This form of anxiety is not an emotion, it is not felt in a heightened, tremulous state of terror with perspiring hands and quaking voice. Binswanger once described a bland, laconic client as "a burned-out crater" and added that this state was not a feeling or an effect "but an expression of *existential* anxiety, that is, of the draining of the existence, and of its progressive loss of 'world.' Of course, loss of world is accompanied by loss of self. Where the existence is no longer in a position to design the world freely, it also suffers the loss of the self."[90] Existential anxiety is thus the source of feeling bored, empty, void. Binswanger speaks of this as the "nothingness of anxiety," for it petrifies Dasein into a state of immobility, narrowing horizons and forcing it into ever more difficult and rare possibilities of growth.[91] Recall that "being and nothingness" are related concepts. Hence, everyone is motivated to enrich Dasein and thereby avoid the nothingness of existential anxiety.

The other form of anxiety, which is *neurotic* in tone, is also likely to be experienced by all of us from time to time, but it is more an unpleasant sensation we usually identify as feeling "anxious," "upset," "jumpy," and so forth. Those individuals who develop a neurosis invariably arrive at this level of derived anxiety by way of their world-designs. A common reason for this is *constriction* of world-design: "The emptier, more simplified, and more constricted the world-design to which an existence has committed itself, the sooner will anxiety appear and the more severe will it be."[92] Healthy people have a broad-ranging world-design. If one aspect of their world does not go well, they can move on to another for they have alternatives at hand. The constricted person, however, as the young woman who relied solely on "continuity," has only one aspect and hence must surely sense a loss of world (anxiety) more readily.

Although Boss refers to anxiety as a mood, or the pitch of Dasein, he develops the themes we are now considering under the construct of *guilt.*[93] That is, we can distinguish between an *existential guilt* and a *neurotic guilt* on almost the same grounds that we have distinguished between these two forms of anxiety. By existential guilt Boss is referring to a primary or basic *debt* that man has, to carry out possibilities in existence and thus further his potentials.[94] If we think of all of those things which "need doing" in life, which have to be accomplished in order for Dasein to be enlarged and enriched in meaning openness, then we must surely recognize that man senses a basic indebtedness to his future. Our futures always make demands of us, and not until we breathe our last do we stop being aware of the possibilities of existence. Also, as we noted previously, with every act, every choice, we must of necessity reject other possibilities which might be open to fulfillment. This too puts us behind the flow of events as we wonder and ponder "Have I done the right thing?"

For this reason Boss views man's basic life

situation as one of guilt. If being and nothingness are two inevitable aspects of existence, then being and guilt are also in necessary tandem. And here we can speak of the *conscience* in existentialism: "Man is aware of existential guilt when he hears the never-ending call of his conscience. This essential, inevitable being-in-debt is *guilt*, and not merely a subjective *feeling* of guilt."[95] As existential anxiety is not "simply" an emotion, existential guilt is not "simply" a feeling. We are down to the basics of existence here. Neurotic guilt, on the other hand, is a form of derived guilt in which the individual has suffered the misfortune of having been reared in a given environment.[96] This is more the result of historical accident. Some people are born into situations which generate abnormality, and others are not. But existential guilt is something we all must experience, and woe to the psychotherapist who fails to distinguish between these two manifestations of guilt. Neurotic guilt can exacerbate existential guilt, but the reverse is not true.

PSYCHODYNAMICS AND THE ADJUSTMENT MECHANISMS

If Dasein cannot be split into conscious and unconscious regions, or into the subdivisions of ids, egos, or superegos, then surely it cannot be made into a "past" which now psychodynamically influences the "present."[97] For Boss, "defense" means that the individual is unwilling to become aware of a certain world-relationship which is under lumination.[98] The more he tries to defend himself against this lumination, however, the more certain that the individual will adhere to it, be involved with it, and become unable to free himself from its import. He really cannot escape it · through defensive maneuvers and in no case can he "hide" his real character from its world-openness. The theories of Freudian adjustment mechanisms all presuppose some arbitrarily reductive, divisive breakdown of existence.

Take, for example, Freud's concept of *introjection*. Boss sees an entirely different phenomenon here: "Wherever so-called introjection is observed, nothing has been taken *in*. On the contrary, a human existence has not yet taken itself *out* of and freed itself from the original being-together undividedly and undiscriminatingly with somebody else."[99] Phenomenologically, many of Freud's mechanisms must be seen in this more direct and clearly discernible fashion. Rather than calling something *repressed*, we would be more accurate to say that an aspect of existence is unable to become engaged in an open, free, authentic, world-disclosing relationship.[100] One does not *project* into Dasein, but finds there what experience means as he luminates existence.[101] Who is to say that a subject's Dasein is a projection of "something else"?

Although Binswanger agrees with Boss in this general matter of defense and so-called mechanisms of adjustment, he is more likely to use language that smacks of these meanings—often in an informal sense and occasionally with apologies.[102] For Binswanger, a defensive behavior is one made in reaction to existential anxiety.[103] So-called defenses are merely one way of speaking about world-designs. For example, if the individual endows his world with the meanings of "solid certainty vs. holes of uncertainty" then he might well "take in" in order to fill the areas of phenomenal emptiness. Such taking-in can be termed *introjection* or *identification* for a practical clinical purpose.[104] Binswanger makes similar informal references to regression, repression, and projection.[105] He has rather severe reservations concerning *sublimation*, however, since it implies that something higher literally "comes out of" something lower—and this is essentially a reverse form of the reductive tactic which existentialism has found untenable.[106]

One genuine "mechanism" (in the sense of a stylized behavior tactic) can be laid at the feet of the existentialists, and that is what might be termed "trusting to fate." To believe that *fate* will somehow enter into one's existence and decide alternatives for one is an escapist device that many people use.[107] Such individuals relieve themselves of existential anxiety by saying "Oh well, no need to feel beaten by things, it was my destiny to be here and you can't argue with your fate."

TIME PERSPECTIVE CONSTRUCTS

DASEIN'S HISTORICAL DEVELOPMENT

The existentialists have not worked out an intricate scheme for the description of development. Their feeling is that Freud and others emphasized development because of the latters' great reliance on biology,[108] which specifies growing, physical maturation, and so forth. However, since Dasein is a historical totality including the past, present, and future (temporalization) temporal generalizations are possible.

At birth, each of us is thrown into existence with certain givens, such as our sex and other possible strengths or weaknesses in physical structure.[109] The initial person of great meaningfulness for the child is the mother. The child must come to know existence—the meaning of life—through his being sheltered and loved by the mother. If the mother is not open and luminating, the child's earliest world-designs are likely to be narrow and constricted.[110]

The existentialists frankly admit that we cannot really say what the original world-designs of an individual were like, since they were preverbal. Of the earliest formulations of one of his clients, Binswanger says: "If we knew the infantile arch-form of the father theme, we would probably recognize in it the seeds of all possibilities which we found developed and utilized in the later variations."[111] It is such archforms which literally constitute the formation of the Eigenwelt (body, identity), Umwelt (other than body, environment), and Mitwelt (other bodies, society). Although these three aspects of world constitute a totality, early experience begins to demarcate and can even fix impermeable boundaries between

them.[112] If an infant senses anxiety due to the uncanniness of a shaky world in relation to the mother, he might stop taking in his milk. This would establish a boundary between the Eigenwelt and the Umwelt—for at this age the Mitwelt of other people would not be as clearly relevant as self vs. not-self. Most offspring do not fix boundaries of this sort, of course, but they do learn to recognize the three aspects of existence as they are living and being lived by it.

THE TASK OF LIFE

If there is one theme to be emphasized in the existentialist's view of what development constitutes it is that an individual must advance on life, extend his Dasein, and assume responsibility for meeting its possibilities. He must achieve *independence* from the thrownness of rigid nature, paternal direction, and those related factors which take decision and choice out of the individual's hands. The major life theme is thus one of *dependence-independence*. Though they refer to stages merely informally,[113] ample evidence suggests a "mature vs. immature" existential life pattern.[114] Boss says: ". . . the child's world must die and give way to ever more grown-up ways of behavior."[115]

Major shifts in the nature of Dasein take place at important points in life. Probably the first and most pervasive alteration of Dasein occurs while language is being acquired. The very concept of "phenomena" in existentialism rests upon language capacity, for as Binswanger has observed: ". . . it is in language that our world-designs actually ensconce and articulate themselves. . . ."[116] Of course, many thrown aspects of Dasein are already "given" in the language structure which the child acquires. But language is also a preverbal possibility of Dasein, even in the infant, for "understanding something *as* something, marking it, spotting it, denoting it, indicating it, necessarily presupposes language, even though the perceived characteristic of the thing cannot be named as yet by audibly perceptible names."[117] Hence, the existentialists would reject any suggestion that experience is the result of language or that language makes Dasein possible. Language is vital to phenomenal experience, but Dasein contains a basic and primary possibility for language expression.

Another major shift in Dasein occurs at the time of school. The possibility of forming friendships increases at this point, and henceforth the Mitwelt increases in importance. Boss likes to emphasize that "being" means primarily "being with" others, as well as things.[118] At puberty there is a fantastic extension of horizons as Dasein holds the possibilities for sexual and love relationships. Identity problems are quite common during adolescence, and it is in this sense that Binswanger is likely to use the term "identification" to say that a meaning relation to peers is cemented during the teenage years.[119] This gradual shift from family to complete independence is furthered over adolescence until adulthood. The adolescent has by now elaborated his world-designs and luminated existence in his own, subjective fashion. So-called "fixations" would represent the inability for Dasein to move forward. Dasein can become "stuck" and not mature properly. The Freudian Oedipal conflict is one such immature pattern, in which dependency upon a parent is the major feature.[120] The existentialists do not agree with the sexual interpretations advanced by Freud. However, by adulthood the healthy individual has usually met the sexual possibilities in life. On the other hand, if he has opted for a life of religious celibacy this would *not* be considered abnormal.[121]

THE ROLE OF RELIGION

Binswanger and Freud had one of their most fundamental disagreements over man's religious inclinations. Freud thought of religion as an adult type of dependency. Man was trying to extend his paternal feelings into a cosmic principle—a "father in the sky." Binswanger argued that this seemed to be another one of those reductions which Freud was so fond of, reducing one thing (religion) to another (paternal fixations). Binswanger tells us of his retort to Freud: ". . . I found myself forced to recognize in man something like a basic religious category; that, in any case, it was impossible for me to admit that 'the religious' was a phenomenon that could somehow be derived from something else. (I was thinking, of course, not of the origin of a particular religion, nor even of religion in general, but of something that I have since learned to call the religious I-thou relationship)."[122]

Freud dismissed such talk as essentially an emotional and personal wish on the part of Binswanger to defend religion. Whatever the case, though existential analysis may view other behaviors as immature and dependent, the cultivation of religious I-thou unions with others and even a phenomenally sensed Supreme Being is *not* considered an immature adult pattern.[123]

INDIVIDUAL DIFFERENCES CONSTRUCTS

Since the existentialists are particularly sensitive to the alienating possibilities of "theories" which supposedly capture why Dasein is as it is, they naturally are reluctant to name a host of theorotypes. What one means by types such as the anal, oral, and so forth is that a given and restricted world-design has taken hold of the individual.[124] Anality, for example, may be true of miserly people, compulsive people, and so forth. This world-design is probably along the lines of viewing the world as a hole, to be filled up.[125] This "filling" premise makes possible the eventual clinical picture of "anality," since the former preoccupation colors the latter. Subsequent "fillings" also take place, as when we call this person a compulsive hoarder of money, affection, ideas, and so forth.

Of course, in order to communicate their theories the existentialists must make generalizations. We have already seen how they speak about what is tantamount to a dependent vs.

an independent Dasein pattern in the growing child. They also speak of tradition-bound people, who are thrown by the attitudes and beliefs of the inauthentic "everybody" rather than by the authentic views peculiar to themselves.[126] We might therefore accuse them of doing precisely what they find objectionable in Freudian theory. However, the thrust of their theory is clearly to retain a higher level of abstraction than classical analysis and to leave a broad range of detail for the subjective description of a Dasein's "case history." Hence, their very concept of individual differences is more "individual" than is the case in classical analysis.

Psychopathology and Psychotherapy

THEORY OF ILLNESS

CONSTRICTED DASEIN

The personality structure most prone to abnormal adjustment is that one which proceeds on only a few a priori ontological categories. The Dasein becomes vulnerable because everything is staked on one world-design.[127] Existence therefore "shrinks" and the individual's perspective narrows and shortens. Binswanger observes: ". . . the freedom of letting 'world' occur is replaced by the unfreedom of being overwhelmed by a certain 'world-design.' "[128] The individual may often press a kind of "idealization" in the one or two ontological categories of his world view. He may expect all things to be perfect, everyone to love him or to behave as he fantasies the way in which people "ought" to behave. If in the course of life he finds people acting differently, he concludes in his simple, rigid either/or way that the Mitwelt is *not* compatible with the Eigenwelt.[129]

This constriction of Dasein may also take place "across time," resulting in a temporally

"stuck" Dasein.[130] When this happens, the individual's sense of development into the future is hampered because he cannot move forward (become unstuck) by projecting possibilities. Hence he fails to gain a sense of achievement or advance because his world is essentially a replay of yesterday—again and again.[131] Rather than extending and growing, the being of the abnormal is ever drifting into thrownness.[132] The self is therefore not authentic. It is alienated from its potentials and can no longer transcend the circumstances in which other individuals find new possibilities. The outcome of such an existence is a decidedly dependent and even immature human being.

LACK OF AUTONOMY AND INDEPENDENCE

Although the practical outcome of an abnormal existence is constriction of Dasein, the *reason* for this shrinkage is the failure of the individual to opt for an authentic existence. As indicated previously, the abnormal individual has surrendered himself to the thrown aspects of Umwelt and especially Mitwelt (until such time as he may reject Mitwelt altogether in the fantasies of a psychosis). The existentialists do not "blame" this so much on the molding capacities of parents and other external influences in the child's life as they do on the individual's own actions. Boss observes that: ". . . in the strict sense of the term, no event in the life history of a person can ever be the 'cause' of neurotic symptoms. Personal experiences merely initiate inhibitions against fully carrying out all possible interpersonal and interworldly relationships."[133]

This stance places the major responsibility on the individual to "move beyond" the difficulties of his environment, where due to an unloving parent, for example, he might not have felt he could explore his Mitwelt with impunity. But to continue blaming his inability for extending world-relations in the present on this unhappy childhood experience is simply to misconstrue the nature of his abnormality. The problem exists in the *present* behavior, in the unwillingness to commit oneself authentically to current existence. For this reason the existentialists think of mental illness as "self-chosen unfreedom."[134]

The point of "growing up" is that we must learn to transcend, which includes rising above the difficult experiences of life, and carry out our potentials by authentically committing ourselves to the new avenues which the future opens up. Some people have more difficult times than others, but if one clinically examines the life history of abnormals he often finds that they have permitted rather minor setbacks to defeat them. It is the subjective interpretation of life that counts.[135] Hence, the abnormal person retains a kind of childlike existence.[136] He is immature and incapable of accepting his own authentic impulses as we all must in maturing to adult status. Boss once analyzed a nine-year-old boy who was terrified of police dogs and concluded that the boy "could not achieve a free relationship to his own impulsive and sensual possibilities of relating, nor to the realms of being which show themselves in the light of these possibilities."[137]

Binswanger has noted that many abnormals vary the "fate" defensive maneuver to project a certain amount of inauthentic futurity. Thus, through emphasis on superstition, luck, and magic the immature person can hope to offset doom by performing some rite, saying certain words, carrying a potent charm, and so forth. Normal manifestations include knocking on wood, lucky numbers, rabbit's feet, but an overreliance on such devices suggests that an *existential weakness* has developed: "By existential weakness we mean that a person does not stand autonomously in his world, that he blocks himself off from the ground of his existence, that he does not take his existence upon himself but trusts himself to alien powers, that he makes alien powers 'responsible' for his fate instead of himself."[138] The various forms of mental illness are thus extensions of this tendency for a surrender of the self to others,

to circumstance, to a world-design which limits authentic growth.

DIFFERENTIAL DIAGNOSIS

Since the existentialists are critical of the relation of the classical medical model of disease to Dasein, they are reluctant to "diagnose" their patients.[139] This aspect of treatment seems yet another reductive attempt to explain existence in terms of alienated concepts.[140] On the other hand, they do not deny the legitimacy of clinical pictures and over the years they have offered a number of explanations of the so-called clinical entities. *Symptoms* are forms of communication, announcing the existential problem in which the individual is trapped.[141] Often the symptom is just as much a possibility as is any other form of behavior. It may offer a "way out" of an intolerable life circumstance.[142] It often conceals a world-relation which the individual does not wish to be open about.[143] Ultimately, the diagnostic picture emerges in a *social* context. Boss has observed that: ". . . no psychopathological symptom will ever be fully and adequately understood unless it is conceived of as a disturbance in the texture of the social relationship of which a given human existence fundamentally consists, and that all psychiatric diagnoses are basically only sociological statements."[144]

The existentialists view *neurosis* as an increasingly serious extension of the constriction of Dasein and the self-surrender of autonomy and independence. This self-chosen unfreedom moves into *psychosis* when the degree of surrender is complete enough so that the individual lives completely within fantasy, which means that literally a "new *form* of being-in-the-world" has come about.[145] We cannot judge this world by the presumptions and standards of our world. Take the *hallucination,* for example. When the psychotic sees or hears something that we cannot it is erroneous to claim these are "unrealistic" occurrences.[146] These are just as legitimately part of his Dasein as seeing a "real" person is in ours. The discernible reason for the hallucination, of course, is the complete surrender in psychosis to a reification of the forces under which the individual feels himself thrown (directed). The abnormal now literally has strange people telling him what to do or judging the merits of his behavior. He listens to these admonitions, or he runs away from them to the extent that he can. He never succeeds in ridding himself of the hallucination so long as he accepts the thrownness of Dasein on which they rest.

Hallucinations are accompanied by *delusions* (false beliefs), and here again we must not dismiss the essential nature of this phenomenon by saying it is "unrealistic" from the outset. Binswanger in particular emphasized that the delusion—especially persecution—is central to all psychoses. By surrendering so completely to others and concocting some reified hallucinatory images and voices to direct his existence, the psychotic *must* inevitably come to hate his directors as enemies.[147] They are plotting against him. They are critical of him, spreading lies about him. He is being destroyed. In curious fashion, the self-destruction is genuine, for: ". . . where there is delusion there can no longer be any genuine self. To speak of a 'delusional self' would be a contradiction *in adjecto*."[148] In time, the psychotic loses all sense of distinction between "inside" and "outside," between what he is as a self in existence and what the world is as another aspect of that existence.[149] When that happens, the psychotic has slipped completely into a thrown state. He cannot transcend for he is literally "nothing." Neurotic anxiety is compounded by existential anxiety, and the future is bleak indeed.

We will now examine some of the classical clinical pictures which the existentialists have mentioned, in order to illustrate their approach to "diagnosis."

Ulcer cases. The world-relation typical of an ulcer patient emphasizes seizing, overpowering, and taking possession of the environment so that everything is robbed of its individuality.[150] The considerable concealment of this demolishing pattern among ulcer patients renders its manifestation inward. The person may appear to be unaggressive, even passive, but the somatic realm behaves in the style which typifies the Dasein's true structure. Food is grasped, cut up by the teeth, and plunged into the stomach and intestine, where it is literally "demolished" by an overabundance of motility, hydrochloric acid, pepsin, and the enzymes of the pancreas.[151] As a byproduct of this world-disclosing pattern the symptoms indicate actual intestinal damage known as "peptic ulcer."

Hysteria. The hysterical patient is far more open than the ulcer case in expressing his symptoms, which always reflect an extremely immature, passive world-design.[152] The hysteric may complain of physical aches and pains which do not exist in the literal sense of the ulcer patient. The hysteric asks to be cared for by making his hypochondriacal complaints. He somaticizes his interpersonal relationship because he cannot break himself free from an almost "organic bond" with others. Hence, he dramatically reveals symptoms of tremor, limp extremities, or blindness because he cannot carry his Dasein forward authentically. He slips into amnesia and "other" identities because he is unable to assume the responsibility for his own—his self.

Phobia. Phobias protect the individual from losing hold of his world entirely. So long as the individual can fix a sense of fear (specific anxiety) on some clear identity in experience —dogs, germs, heights, etc.—he avoids total collapse of world into nothingness and existential anxiety.[153] He can thus continue to exist under the direction of his phobia—avoiding this and that terrifying experience, possibly supplementing his fears with magical rituals.

Sexual Abnormality. The sexual abnormal invariably reveals a specific concealment and restriction of the possibility for loving.[154] The "peeper" does not wish to participate. He would rather continue in the immature pattern of "just looking." The homosexual cannot give himself sexually to an opposite-sexed partner, hence he foregoes this experience by continuing his masturbatory pattern on into same-sexed contacts. In every instance of an abnormal sexual tendency we can find the time in development when an individual so "afflicted" has not accepted the responsibility of committing himself to the possibilities of his maturing status in life.

Obsessive-Compulsive Neurosis. The obsessive ordinarily will accept as his own responsibility only those aspects of life which are open to pure, conceptual thought. His world-design is predicated by this highly intellectualized view.[155] By behaving this way the obsessional patient avoids the possibility of investing himself in the more intimate, emotional world relationships that we all confront in life. The existentialists do not deny the Freudian "anality" concept, but they see in this relation a kind of fear developing of one's creature, emotive, nonintellectual side. Fearing to be "quite that human" the obsessive begins to deny possibilities and to approach life in a more idealistic, superhuman, intellectual vein.

Schizophrenia. Binswanger has referred to this disorder as a complete "emptying of the personality."[156] The self of Dasein no longer exists as the schizophrenic literally retreats from the world of his fellow-men (Mitwelt) into *autism*.[157] Though he has retreated, his experience continues to be dominated from other than self, as his elaborate delusions and hallucinations become the controlling factors in —and "one" with—his existence. Binswanger pointed to two general steps in the schizophrenic process.[158] In the first phase the individual seems to be aware of considerable inconsistency in existence, which arises because he is not projecting his own life course. In the second phase inconsistencies are split into what is right and what is wrong, or what things are like and what things should be like. Following this split, the schizophrenic continues to pursue the right or the "should be" alternative which he has staked all to attain. He therefore greatly misperceives the other side of existence and becomes entirely incapable of adjustment because he relentlessly pursues his subjectively defined "shoulds."[159] In time, the rigid and inaccurate edifice crumbles.

Manic-Depressive Psychosis. The manic-depressive patient jumps from one world-design to another, thrown into each one yet never freely committed to any.[160] In this sense he is confronted by a somewhat different form of inconsistency than the schizophrenic. The manic-depressive patient seems ever to be coming round to a new view which might salvage his existence. He flits from one prospect to another, never settling on one for a stable approach to the future. His spirits rise then deflate. He is thrown "between worlds." The melancholic aspects of this clinical syndrome suggest a person constantly disappointed because things did not "work out" for him. Rather than taking events into his own hands in authentic fashion, the depressive patient has surrendered to others whom he blames when his plans fail to materialize after all.[161] The melancholic person also may feel considerable personal guilt for not having taken command of his life, and sometimes these guilt reactions take the form of self-destructive tendencies.[162] Suicide, however, is another of those avoidant trends where, rather than solving problems, the individual is defeated most finally by them.

THEORY OF CURE

THE SEARCH FOR AUTHENTICITY
AND VIEW OF INSIGHT

The question of mental health in existentialism settles on essentially three points, each of which contributes to the picture of authenticity. The mentally healthy individual is *free to choose* and hence transcend,[163] *mature* in outlook[164] and *independently responsible*.[165] The general "goal" of psychotherapy is thus to help the "unfree" and childishly dependent person become a genuine human being. Boss views this goal as helping him to accept his "debt" to existence, so that he will let all his possibilities of world relating emerge.[166] This will in turn permit a greater extension of Dasein and an enlarging of self. Through phenomenological study of the individual's experience the therapist helps him to arrive at some understanding of his *present* circumstances. Binswanger seeks to find "the particular world-design, the being-in-it, and the being-self corresponding to it."[167] Boss is seeking the "immediately accessible essential meaning and content of all immediately perceptible phenomena."[168]

The focus is thus on self-understanding or "insight," but this is of an immediate, current nature: "How are we existing in the present? What are our assumptions about life? What does experience disclose to us when we give it a sincere chance to express itself?" These are the kinds of questions to be answered, not some involved and far-removed obscurities such as "Where is the fixation-point in this life history?" As we might surmise from their attitude concerning reductive explanation, the existentialists dislike genetic explanations.[169] This does not mean that they avoid examining the client's life history in therapy. They make a very thorough analysis of the client's Dasein, from the earliest years, including fantasy products. But what is being sought is not "the" explanation for what now "exists" but rather the historical grasp of Dasein. In helping the client to grasp the meaning of his existence in its historical totality, the existential analyst always stays within the language of phenomena.[170] The therapist speaks in terms of verbal contents introduced by the client rather than trying to press alienating theoretical concepts onto him.

Several factors account for a cure. First of all, the individual comes to view his experience in greater perspective. He regains a *future* orientation as he comes to understand that he has been allowing possibilities and opportunities to slip by him due to the immobility of Dasein.[171] Transcendence and self-growth demand that the individual have something to aim for, a goal which can be brought into reality through committed action. It begins as a possibility, but the next step is to make this a reality. This is where the relationship with the analyst enters, and we will consider this special topic in the next section. Once the individual begins taking command of his life, however, he is on his way to being cured.[172] Binswanger notes that often we can rely on a client's conscience at this point. The client feels guilty about foregoing his self-direction. Conscience is thus a kind of "calling back" to authenticity.[173]

Hence, the existentialist may not be so ready to dismiss or explain away the client's guilt feelings. As we have noted before, to feel guilt is normal. Existential guilt is a major experience of all men. If we now confuse this form of guilt with guilt over "something else" and thereby teach the client that he need *not* feel guilty, what are we doing? The existentialists feel that classical Freudian analysis arbitrarily decides which phenomenal experiences they will take at face value and which they will explain away in this fashion. Existential analysts take *all* phenomenal experience at its face value, seeking the meaning for present existence of all moods and emotions.

As the client begins to respond to his feelings, sees possibilities in his future, and makes attempts to achieve his possibilities independence increases in his life style. Boss makes it clear that no therapy is successful until the client shows such changes outside the therapy hour.[174] When this comes about—and no specific length of time can be generalized for all clients—existential analysis has been successful.[175]

RELATIONSHIP, TRANSFERENCE, AND RESISTANCE

The existentialists emphasize the patient-therapist relationship. Binswanger speaks of the therapist as "the post to which existence clings while adrift in the whirlpool, from whom it expects aid and protection as a sign that some interhuman relationship is still possible."[176] The severely disturbed person needs to be "rescued" by someone else.[177] Boss emphasizes that these are *genuine* relationships, and any love expressed by the client for his analyst is therefore "love of the analyst himself, no matter how immature and distorted it may appear because of the limitations of perception imposed on the patient by his earlier relationship to his real father."[178] The existential analyst is at all times kind and reassuring, respectful of all that emerges from a client's Dasein, and he is basically permissive.[179] Of course, this permissiveness does not mean that the existential analyst is passive, allowing the client to direct therapy entirely to his whim or satisfaction. Permissiveness encourages an openness in the client, so that now for possibly the first time in his life he can "live out" his true being in relation to the therapist as a fellow human being.

The existentialists accept the clinical facts of transference *and* resistance, but they interpret them quite differently from Freudians. The client truly loves his therapist who is a source of last ditch help in meeting his predicament. Through a permissiveness and an encouraging interpersonal relationship the client can begin revealing himself. The nature of this interpersonal relationship may begin taking on a childish father-son coloring but only because the client is immature.[180] Nothing is "transferred" in this relationship. If the therapist accepts the role of father and somehow—possibly through his own misperceptive countertransferences—encourages such a pattern he is sure to engender hostility or *negative* transference in his client.[181]

What is properly called for here is *not* a continuance of the world relationship in which the client's Dasein has become stuck but a furtherance of his possibilities to be on a more adult level. Boss observes that if the male analyst is aware of the childlike nature of a neurotic's Dasein he will never confuse the erotic demands of his female patients as "grown-up sexuality."[182] He will appreciate that these arise from a childlike longing to be loved and cared for as a small daughter. What this comes down to, therefore, is that in psychotherapy the client must eventually "live out" or "act out" those world-designs which are ever active in his Dasein. The existential analyst makes these known through proper interpretations and thereby encourages the client to begin advancing on life through a more appropriate world-design—which is worked out through phenomenal self-study.

This is a difficult course to follow, and the client does not accept it without resentment. It is positively terrifying for many. At this point the client often evidences *resistance,* which is interpreted as extreme reluctance to assume responsibility for change or the meeting of new responsibilities.[183] It is here that the therapist must demonstrate his greatest compassion and skill, to help the client overcome his flight from responsibility. Beginning in a small way, within the therapy hour, at first on an entirely verbal level, the client can begin projecting possible courses of action in light of what Dasein is revealing to him. Then, he must take his first steps outside the hour. As he fails and is moved to retreat only the strength of a bond with his therapist saves him. The existential analyst is completely committed, even to the extent of going to the client's home during times of crises to provide support and encouragement.[184]

Because of this commitment the existentialists have been accused of formalizing their "countertransferences" into their therapy—literally becoming too involved in their client's lives. Boss rejects this interpretation and observes that a decided healing agent in the relationship as manifested by the therapist is *psychotherapeutic eros*. This is not like any other love relationship in man's experience, not like a parental, romantic, friendship, nor even a religious love for others. It has a flavor all its own: "Genuine psychotherapeutic eros . . . must be an otherwise never-practiced selflessness, self-restraint, and reverence before the partner's existence and uniqueness."[185] If the therapist does not or can not feel this love for a particular client, he should remove himself from the case. Boss frankly admits that he has done this on more than one occasion.[186]

THERAPEUTIC TECHNIQUES

COMPARISON TO CLASSICAL PSYCHOANALYSIS

Since Binswanger and Boss began their professional careers as orthodox Freudian-Jungian psychoanalysts, their techniques are appropriately compared to the more classical approaches. Technically, the existentialist approach opposes all doctrinaire therapeutic aids as potential alienators of the client from his genuine experience.[187] For example, the methods of free association (Freud) or amplification (Jung) invariably take the client away from what he has experienced phenomenologically to find some abstruse connection far from the given which is then said to be the "real" point of concern. This often serves to contort a true symbolic expression into something which it is not—such as when the analyst finds sexual objects behind fantasies by waiting until the patient suggests something sexual in free association.

At the outset of therapy the client is required to be absolutely and unreservedly open in the relationship.[188] Honesty and candidness are valued in this approach just as they are in classical analysis. If the patient prefers he may lie down, but this position is not essential.[189] Existentialists follow most of the customary procedures of classical analysis; the therapist generally listens silently and tries as best he can to enter into the meaning-disclosing relationship of his client.[190] It is not unusual for him to employ the free association procedure, although not in the rigid, doctrinaire fashion described above. This is merely a convenient way to encourage the client to begin a verbal review of his world.[191] As the client goes along the therapist may question in order to clarify and gradually the clinical history begins to take shape.[192] It is at this point that interpretation is employed to further client insight.

The point of the interpretation is to clarify a world-design, although it may be some time before such insights are possible. Existential analysis can take anywhere from one to five years, although presumably there are shorter contacts with certain highly effective clients.[193] But when an interpretation *is* advanced we find no particular preference given to historical contents.[194] That is, in line with their deemphasis of genetic explanations of neuroses, the existentialists do not feel that some "one dynamic" must be confronted with each client —as in having to analyze the unresolved Oedipal conflict. Furthermore, the so-called "deep" interpretation is not so likely to be made by an existentialist therapist because he sees these depth efforts as reductive attempts. Hence, the interpretations are probably more at the level of "common sense." A good example of Boss's interpretation, made to a female patient and bearing the content of what the classical analyst would consider Oedipal material, is: "Perhaps those feelings toward me that came over you, and that you had for your father in that dream, and your wish to have pretty clothes and to be attractive, are still far too big and unmanageable for you. I don't think the little girl, who you really are, can yet even begin to cope with such feelings. Perhaps it will be best if you don't do anything, or start wanting to do anything, without first asking the little girl within you if it's all right with her."[195]

This is a particularly good example because

we can see the immaturity view of neurosis reflected in the "little girl" reference. There is no intricate superstructure of personality theory here to bring into an interpretation. We are concerned as existentialists with the person's ever-present world, hence interpretations are made in terms of the present life setting. There is also a form of challenge put to the client, to begin meeting the possibilities revealed in Dasein.[196] Boss observes: "The Daseinsanalyst often asks his patients, 'Why not?' thereby encouraging them to ever greater tests of daring. 'Why is it that you don't dare to behave in such-and-such a manner during the analytic session?' is a question which is often asked in place of the usual analytic 'Why?' "[197] Of course, we should not put the "why not" to a client too early in the analysis, for this would place undue pressure on him to act. But it is apparent that with his great commitment to the client (psychotherapeutic eros) and the gentle pressure that he can put on him to begin trying things, the existential analyst must take a highly active role in therapy.

DREAM INTERPRETATION

The existentialists make use of dream interpretation, and in fact Boss (1958) has devoted an entire volume to the topic. Consistent with their broader view, the dream is seen as a legitimate aspect of Dasein. Binswanger views it as entangled in the Eigenwelt, reflecting a certain amount of confusion and self-forgetfulness.[198] In our dreams we mean to act, but seem immobilized by the passing of visual events.[199] Binswanger observes: "To dream means: I don't know what is happening to me."[200] Boss is critical of Binswanger because of the passive role he assigns to the dreamer.[201] It is thus to Boss whom we turn for a thorough explication of dreaming from the existentialistic viewpoint.

Boss emphasizes that: "We *have* no dreams; we *are* our dreaming state. . . ."[202] The dream state is simply one side of life, a completely subjective experience which can, for example, present us with new perspectives on the experience of time and space.[203] Events change rapidly, and we move backward and forward in time; there are distortions, but this does not make the dream a product of some unreal "other" world. Our waking and our dreaming lives are continuous so that what happens in the dream theme *per se* has relevance to Dasein.[204] We do not take dream contents and term them "symbols of something else." We take them in the phenomenal reality, at their own level, and then explore the meaning as expressed for the individual.[205]

Boss distinguishes between objective and subjective dream interpretation.[206] Freud approached the dream objectively, hoping to isolate a theme common to all dreamers. Hence, if a man dreamed he was plowing a field, Freud's sexualized theory would suggest *ipso facto* that the plow was "really" a penis and the furrow which it parted was "really" a vagina.[207] Though any dream can be made to conform to such an objective regularity, examined subjectively—i.e., in terms of the individual's unique life history—the meaning might be dramatically different. This plowing theme might signify a prompting to begin picking up life again, forging forward into the future and meeting responsibilities no matter how effortful the work might be.

Most of what Freud and Jung have called *symbols* Boss would view as reflections of the luminating Dasein, visual contents reflecting a given world-design. For example, the person may dream that he was a "thing," rather than a person. This would suggest that he is being made aware of his inability to act in his waking state.[208] He is not a human being but an inanimate, inert "something." The terror dreams of children often involve wild animals or strange creatures. As with the phobic behavior, we can view these as fearful reactions to certain newly discovered sensuous or hostile possibilities that the child is just becoming aware of. A man dreams that he sees his brother lying dead, in a casket. The brother had been killed in a traffic accident. Boss interprets this *not* as a covert death wish for a sibling but as the projected softer, loving side of life, a side he had been turning his back on in his egotistical devotion to business matters.[209] The dream is telling him that he is killing off his humane side in the vain pursuit of material wealth. Dreams of teeth are invariably connected not with sex but with precisely what is phenomenally suggested by the tooth function.[210] That is, we seize, grasp, get ahold of and devour with our teeth. Hence, the dream reflects this form of world relationship.

Note the uncomplicated approach to dream interpretation here. There is no claim made of a dream censor, distorting what "is" into what "is not."[211] Dreams merely supplement the rest of our experience. In a true sense, they alert us to possibilities developing in life.[212] This is where their use in therapy is particularly relevant. When the therapist is expressing his "Why not?" attitude to the client, he is doubtless not just thinking up things for his client to accomplish. He is, rather, basing his question on material which has been suggested by the client's dream. The person's childishness can be brought out in a dream,[213] but also the person's suggested "better side" can be implied in the dream content.[214] By discussing the dream content and drawing the implications therefrom the existential analyst can find something vitally meaningful to his client from which to begin a new approach on life.

Notes

1. Heinemann, 1958, p. 10. 2. Kaufmann, 1956, p. 70. 3. Blackham, 1959, p. 93. 4. *Ibid.*, p. 143. 5. Heinemann, 1958, p. 35. 6. Kaufmann, 1956, p. 213. 7. Heinemann, 1958, p. 64. 8. *Ibid.*, p. 91. 9. Blackham, 1959, p. 98. 10. Heinemann, 1958, p. 36. 11. Blackham, 1959, p. 9. 12. Heinemann, 1958, p. 65. 13. Blackham, 1959, p. 19. 14. Heinemann, 1958, p. 39. 15. Kaufmann, 1956, p. 203. 16. Blackham, 1959, p. 58. 17. *Ibid.*, p. 91. 18. Sartre, 1956, p. 48. 19. Heinemann, 1958, pp. 36–37. 20. Kauf-

mann, 1956, p. 163. 21. Heinemann, 1958, p. 98. 22. *Ibid.*, p. 43. 23. *Ibid.*, p. 116. 24. See Freud, 1960, p. 286. 25. Binswanger, 1963, pp. 149–181. 26. See Freud, 1960, p. 431. 27. Binswanger, 1957. 28. See Boss, 1958, p. 10. 29. Binswanger, 1958, p. 231. 30. Binswanger, 1963, p. 209. 31. Binswanger, 1958, p. 200. 32. *Ibid.*, p. 193. 33. Boss, 1958, p. 51. 34. Boss, 1963, p. 82. 35. *Ibid.*, p. 83. 36. Binswanger, 1963, p. 114. 37. Boss, 1963, p. 140. 38. Binswanger, 1963, p. 99; Boss, 1963, p. 230. 39. See Rychlak, 1968, pp. 286–287. 40. Boss, 1963, p. 36. 41. Binswanger, 1963, pp. 2, 183. 42. *Ibid.*, p. 250. 43. *Ibid.*, p. 119. 44. *Ibid.*, pp. 224–225. 45. Boss, 1963, p. 39. 46. *Ibid.*, p. 41. 47. *Ibid.*, p. 28. 48. *Ibid.*, p. 70. 49. Binswanger, 1958, p. 200. 50. Boss, 1963, p. 218. 51. Binswanger, 1958, p. 232. 52. Boss, 1963, p. 39. 53. *Ibid.*, p. 183. 54. Binswanger, 1963, pp. 5–6. 55. *Ibid.*, pp. 130–131. 56. *Ibid.*, p. 174. 57. Boss, 1963, p. 233. 58. *Ibid.*, p. 55. 59. Binswanger, 1958, p. 224; 1963, p. 72. 60. Boss, 1963, p. 55. 61. Binswanger, 1958, p. 303. 62. Binswanger, 1963, p. 116. 63. Boss, 1963, p. 68. 64. Binswanger, 1963, p. 213; Boss, 1963, p. 45. 65. Binswanger, 1963, p. 171. 66. *Ibid.*, p. 67. 67. Ibid., p. 100. 68. Boss, 1958, p. 183. 69. Binswanger, 1963, p. 174. 70. Boss, 1958, p. 108. 71. Boss, 1963, p. 89. 72. *Ibid.*, p. 92. 73. Binswanger, 1958, p. 326. 74. Binswanger, 1963, p. 219. 75. *Ibid.*, p. 31. 76. Binswanger, 1958, p. 223. 77. Binswanger, 1963, pp. 99, 311. 78. *Ibid.*, p. 117. 79. Boss, 1963, p. 41. 80. *Ibid.*, pp. 113–114. 81. Binswanger, 1958, p. 198. 82. *Ibid.*, pp. 197–198. 83. Boss, 1963, pp. 182–183. 84. Binswanger, 1963, p. 116. 85. Boss, 1963, p. 47. 86. *Ibid.*, p. 271. 87. Binswanger, 1958, p. 205. 88. *Ibid.*, p. 280; Boss, 1963, p. 121. 89. Binswanger, 1958, p. 280. 90. Binswanger, 1963, p. 337. 91. *Ibid.*, p. 299. 92. *Ibid.*, p. 112. 93. Boss, 1963, p. 100. 94. *Ibid.*, p. 270. 95. *Ibid.* 96. *Ibid.*, p. 271. 97. *Ibid.*, p. 108. 98. *Ibid.*, p. 97. 99. *Ibid.*, p. 127. 100. *Ibid.*, p. 120. 101. *Ibid.*, p. 126. 102. See, e.g., Binswanger, 1963, p. 250. 103. *Ibid.*, p. 323. 104. Binswanger, 1958, pp. 280–281. 105. Binswanger, 1963, pp. 250, 321, 324. 106. *Ibid.*, p. 175. 107. *Ibid.*, p. 300. 108. *Ibid.*, p. 196. 109. Binswanger, 1958, p. 271. 110. Boss, 1963, p. 35. 111. Binswanger, 1958, p. 225. 112. *Ibid.*, p. 270. 113. See Boss, 1963, p. 250. 114. *Ibid.*, p. 126. 115. *Ibid.*, p. 266. 116. Binswanger, 1958, p. 200. 117. Boss, 1963, p. 215. 118. *Ibid.*, p. 245. 119. Binswanger, 1958, pp. 280–

281. **120.** Boss, 1963, p. 200. **121.** Binswanger, 1963, p. 183. **122.** *Ibid.* **123.** See Boss, 1963, p. 260. **124.** Binswanger, 1958, p. 318. **125.** *Ibid.*, pp. 218, 310. **126.** Boss, 1963, p. 96. **127.** Binswanger, 1963, p. 112. **128.** Binswanger, 1958, p. 194. **129.** Binswanger, 1963, p. 254. **130.** *Ibid.*, p. 116. **131.** Boss, 1963, p. 178. **132.** Binswanger, 1963, p. 115. **133.** Boss, 1963, p. 248. **134.** Binswanger, 1963, p. 118. **135.** Boss, 1963, p. 173. **136.** *Ibid.*, p. 242. **137.** *Ibid.*, p. 178. **138.** Binswanger, 1963, p. 290. **139.** Binswanger, 1958, p. 230. **140.** *Ibid.*, pp. 330–331. **141.** *Ibid.*, p. 213. **142.** Binswanger, 1963, p. 260. **143.** Boss, 1963, p. 145. **144.** *Ibid.*, p. 56. **145.** Binswanger, 1958, p. 201. **146.** Boss, 1963, p. 85. **147.** Binswanger, 1963, pp. 263–264. **148.** *Ibid.*, p. 336. **149.** *Ibid.*, p. 311. **150.** Boss, 1963, p. 144. **151.** *Ibid.* **152.** *Ibid.*, pp. 143–145. **153.** Binswanger, 1958, p. 205. **154.** Boss, 1963, p. 186. **155.** *Ibid.*, p. 183. **156.** Binswanger, 1958, p. 363. **157.** Binswanger, 1963, p. 288. **158.** *Ibid.*, pp. 252–254. **159.** *Ibid.*, p. 254. **160.** *Ibid.*, p. 143. **161.** Boss, 1963, p. 209. **162.** *Ibid.*, p. 210. **163.** Binswanger, 1963, p. 218. **164.** Boss, 1963, p. 160. **165.** *Ibid.*, p. 210. **166.** *Ibid.*, p. 271. **167.** Binswanger, 1958, p. 327. **168.** Boss, 1963, p. 285. **169.** Binswanger, 1958, pp. 334–335. **170.** *Ibid.*, p. 330. **171.** *Ibid.*, p. 295. **172.** *Ibid.*, pp. 224–225. **173.** Binswanger, 1963, p. 318. **174.** Boss, 1963, p. 254. **175.** *Ibid.*, p. 210. **176.** Binswanger, 1963, p. 292. **177.** *Ibid.*, p. 348. **178.** Boss, 1963, p. 125. **179.** *Ibid.*, pp. 198, 234, 253. **180.** *Ibid.*, p. 124. **181.** *Ibid.*, p. 240. **182.** *Ibid.*, p. 258. **183.** *Ibid.*, pp. 79, 150. **184.** *Ibid.*, p. 20. **185.** *Ibid.*, p. 259. **186.** *Ibid.*, p. 260. **187.** Boss, 1958, p. 119. **188.** Boss, 1963, p. 19. **189.** *Ibid.*, p. 62. **190.** *Ibid.*, pp. 61–64. **191.** *Ibid.*, p. 192. **192.** *Ibid.* **193.** See Binswanger, 1963, p. 272; Boss, 1963, p. 147. **194.** Binswanger, 1963, p. 30. **195.** Boss, 1963, p. 22. **196.** *Ibid.*, p. 196. **197.** *Ibid.*, p. 248. **198.** Binswanger, 1963, p. 231. **199.** *Ibid.*, p. 319. **200.** *Ibid.*, p. 247. **201.** Boss, 1958, p. 129. **202.** Boss, 1963, p. 261. **203.** Boss, 1958, pp. 47, 89. **204.** *Ibid.*, pp. 80, 127. **205.** *Ibid.*, p. 158. **206.** *Ibid.*, p. 120. **207.** *Ibid.*, p. 158. **208.** *Ibid.*, pp. 155–156. **209.** Boss, 1963, p. 265. **210.** *Ibid.*, p. 267. **211.** Boss, 1958, p. 103. **212.** *Ibid.*, p. 130. **213.** Boss, 1963, p. 200. **214.** *Ibid.*, p. 204.

11

The Psychology of Personal Constructs: George A. Kelly

Biographical Overview

George A. Kelly was born in America's heartland, the flat, expansive state of Kansas on 28 April 1905. Kelly was an only child, and his mother doted on him. His father was a Presbyterian minister and farmer who was forced to give up his ministry for reasons of health but did occasionally follow his calling on a sporadic basis over the years. Kelly was born in a farm home and began his education in a one-room elementary school. He later attended high school in Wichita, Kansas, living away from home much of the time after he was 13 years old. Kelly's parents were devoutly religious in a fundamentalist sense, and they were always working to help the needy in any possible way. His mother made pastoral calls on the sick, and his father was active in his faith even when he was not leading a church congregation of his own. The family was hard-working and frowned on frivolities such as dancing or card-playing. However, as the only child Kelly was afforded considerable attention, and his school attendance away from the family home provided him with a scope he might not otherwise have had.

Kelly attended Friends University for three years, where he was active in debate and music. His last year of undergraduate work was spent at Parke College, where in 1926 he received the B.A. degree in physics and mathematics. Kelly was not certain what he wanted to do with his life at this point. He first considered a career in aeronautical engineering and even worked at this fledgling profession for a brief period but found that his interests were moving toward education.[1] In rapid succession he worked at a labor college in Minneapolis, taught speech for the American Bankers Association, and then conducted an Americanization class for future citizens. It was while he was teaching at a junior college in Sheldon, Iowa, during the winter of 1927–1928, that Kelly met Gladys Thompson, who later became his wife. Mrs. Kelly was teaching high-school English, but both she and George coached dramatics in the same building. This work in theater was to prove extremely important to Kelly's eventual theory of behavior.

Kelly's professional development took a major turn in 1929, when he was awarded an exchange scholarship. He spent a year studying under Sir Godfrey Thomson—an eminent statistician and educator—at the University of Edinburgh. Kelly earned a Bachelor's degree in Education during this period, but in the process he developed an interest in psychology. He returned to the United States from Scotland in 1930 to enter the State University of Iowa as a graduate student in psychology. In 1931 Kelly was awarded the Ph.D. based on a dissertation dealing with common factors in speech and reading disabilities. He had, in the meantime, begun work in physiological psychology and developed a speculative theory on the nature of what he called "transient aphasia."[2]

The Stock Market collapse and subsequent depression had settled on America by this time, and Kelly's career did not seem especially promising as he took up a position with the Fort Hays Kansas State College. He had recently married. Times were difficult, and though Kelly's home life was a source of personal happiness—he was to father a daughter and then a son—he soon decided to "pursue something more humanitarian than physiological psychology."[3] Kelly threw himself into the development of psychological services for the state of Kansas. He was the major force in establishing a program of traveling psychological clinics, which not only served the entire state but permitted his students to obtain practical field experience. Kelly never distinguished between what in psychology was science and

what was application. His early writings dealt with such practical issues as training and treatment, but Kelly was an inveterate experimenter and creative thinker. He was beginning to piece together his innovative approach to therapy.

Kelly first turned to Freud when he dropped physiological psychology.[4] He found that Freudian interpretations often helped his clients, but he also noted that other theoretical statements worked as well to provide "insight" and thence a "cure" for some disturbance.[5] He was also reading Moreno and Korzybski over this period of time, theorists who emphasized language and the importance of man's dramatic or role-playing capacities. By 1939 he had begun using a form of role play in his therapeutic approach, as well as the technique of fixed-role therapy.[6]

Kelly often said that a major influence on his life was the onset of World War II. He entered the Navy as an aviation psychologist and

George A. Kelly

was placed in charge of the program of training for local civilian pilots. Later he went to the Bureau of Medicine and Surgery of the Navy in Washington, D.C., and remained in the Aviation Psychology Branch until the war's end. In 1945 he was appointed Associate Professor at the University of Maryland. The war had brought considerable demand for the training of clinical psychologists, as U.S. veterans were returning *en masse* with all forms of personal problems. Indeed, World War II was doubtless the single most important factor in evolving the profession of clinical psychology. Kelly was to become a major figure in this evolution—working with medicine, psychiatry, and related professions to spell out a proper role for psychology in the healing sciences. In 1946 he was moved into national prominence, as Professor of Psychology and Director of Clinical Psychology at the Ohio State University. Carl Rogers had already left Ohio State for Chicago, and Kelly, along with his brilliant clinical colleague Julian B. Rotter, during the next 20 years built this program in clinical psychology into one of the best in the country.

Kelly completed his major theoretical work at Ohio State. His students helped to refine his thought, conduct experiments in support of it, and at the end of a decade of hard work the *Psychology of Personal Constructs* reached print (1955a & b). The only other volume of Kelly's work appeared posthumously, under the editorship of a former student, Brendan Maher (1969). Kelly spent the last decade of his life disseminating his insights. He held visiting professorships at several universities in the United States and lectured at various research congresses and institutions of learning all over the world. He acquired followers and admirers on both sides of the Iron Curtain. In 1965 Kelly left Ohio State to take the Riklis Chair of Behavioral Science at Brandeis University. He was in the process of putting his many papers together into a volume when he died in March of 1967.

Personality Theory

STRUCTURAL CONSTRUCTS

BODY VS. MIND THEORETICAL FORMULATIONS AND CONSTRUCTIVE ALTERNATIVISM

Kelly based his approach to psychology on a single philosophical assumption: *"We assume that all of our present interpretations of the universe are subject to revision or replacement."*[7] He did not mean to formulate an entire philosophical system but called this attitude *constructive alternativism.* For Kelly the world of man was a world of meaningful *interpretations* or points of view rather than a world of frozen "givens." It is not that we "make up" the world to suit our fancy. Events must be handled in such a way that our interpretations "fit" them. Kelly stated his position rather concisely: "The universe is real; it is happening all the time; it is integral; and it is open to piecemeal interpretation. Different men construe it in different ways. Since it owes no prior allegiance to any one man's construction system, it is always open to reconstruction. Some of the alternative ways of construing are better adapted to man's purposes than are others. Thus, man comes to understand his world through an infinite series of successive approximations."[8]

The distinction between "mental" and "physical" events troubles theorists only because they think of the problem in these terms at the outset. Yet, literally, "any event may be viewed either in its psychological or in its physiological aspects."[9] Events in the real world do not belong to any one discipline or any one scientist. The medical man cannot claim "mind" as his province simply because a physical theory underwrites much of the bodily functioning. Nor can the psychologist claim that his area of study is out of the realm of physical theory. Kelly did not feel that a resolution could be reached by somehow uniting the realms of mind and body, nor did he think that a dualistic assumption placing these two theories of events "side by side" made much sense.[10] He thought it most useful simply to acknowledge the fact that these are two different ways of making experience meaningful. Men devised these theories, and hence we can look at reality through each of these interpretations independently—at least for the time being. Whether or not it is possible to formulate a single theory of reality Kelly left open—arguing that *if* this were to take place it would happen at a very distant point in the future.[11]

Hence, without denying the possibility of a single theory of experience Kelly took the view that for the foreseeable future it made best sense to proceed with theories of an intermediate, even "miniature" nature. He spoke of his psychology of personal constructs in these terms, expecting that it would one day give way to better formulations which might say more sweeping and lasting things about the reality of experience.[12] Thus for Kelly, the issue of mind vs. body is a pseudoproblem, one which evaporates when we properly grasp the nature of science and theorizing.

EVERY MAN A SCIENTIST: THE HUMAN
ORGANISM AS A PROCESS

Kelly was opposed to those theories of human behavior which viewed man as fundamentally inert, as a fixed structure being moved by something other than his very nature. Too many psychologists have accepted the view that man's evolution has already ceased.[13] For Kelly, what man "is" must still be seen as an open question for he continues to alter, change and move *by definition:* "For our purposes, the person is not an object which is temporarily in a moving state but is himself a form of motion."[14] Hence, man is a behaving *organism* steeped in the *process* of movement which is pitched toward the ever recurring future events taking place in his life. Kelly stated flatly that:

"All behavior can be construed as anticipatory in nature."[15] Behavior is man's way of posing questions about life.[16] The individual comes at life with an active intellect, which is the controlling feature of man's mind.[17] Man is not under the control of events, but controls events based upon the questions he asks and the answers he finds.

As man finds his answers and poses new questions he is constantly changing outlooks. At least, this is possible for man even as it is possible to freeze into a single outlook and hence effectively turn one's back on change. Man can *learn* or he can avoid learning.[18] There is nothing special about the learning capacities; they are simply another way of talking about the processes of organismic functioning. A *person* is thus an organismic motion, a network of posed questions and answers sought along various pathways into future experience.[19] For this reason Kelly can say: ". . . every man is, in his own particular way, a scientist."[20] Kelly once remarked that he was amazed to see the contrast between personality theories espoused by a psychologist to explain his *own* behavior and to explain the behavior of his experimental subjects.[21] In his own case the psychologist was likely to speak about his hypotheses, the predictions he is formulating into an experimental design which he will subsequently put into effect, and so forth. The hapless subject, on the other hand, is described in terms of a kind of blind determinism, a reinforcement history which pushes him onward like some unwilling and unthinking blob of protoplasm.

Running through the very heart of Kellyian psychology is this continuing polemic waged against those theories of personality which deny the subject or therapy client the same status afforded the scientist. Kelly insisted that a personality theory *must* account for *all* men— those under study but also those who study and report on the "findings" of a science of man. For his part, *personality* was defined in terms of the organismic processes already mentioned, as "a course of events that keeps flowing along."[22]

THE BASIC NATURE OF CONSTRUING AND CONSTRUCTS

Man looks at life, notes a series of recurring events which seem somehow repetitive and then "places an interpretation" upon this predictable aspect of his experience.[23] This process of interpretation and prediction is termed *construing*, and it bears the meaning of both an abstraction from events and yet also involves conceptualizing subsequent events based upon this earlier abstraction. These events or the "facts" of experience are real enough, but each man sees them from his own particular slant. Different people do not always see the same meanings in the same fact pattern. Construing is a temporal process, so that: "To construe is to hear the whisper of the recurrent themes in the events that reverberate around us."[24]

This process is uniquely *bipolar*. That is, when one affirms the commonality of events which he has observed recurring over time he must *also* negate some other aspect of that experience. To say "Redheads tend to be hotheads" is *also* to say "Non-redheads tend to be level-headed." Construing is thus *never* a unidimensional proposition.[25] Indeed, *thought* is only possible because man can and must dichotomize experience into *similarities* and *contrasts*.[26] Meaning takes on this bipolarity, and when we speak of the products of thinking or of construing we are referring to this *relationship* between what things seem "like" and also "different from." This is how Kelly now arrives at his definition of the *construct*: "In its minimum context a construct is a way in which at least two elements are similar and contrast with a third. There must therefore be at least three elements in the context. There may, of course, be many more."[27]

Constructs are like "transparent patterns or templets" which man has created (i.e., construed) in order to "fit over" the recurring realities of life.[28] They begin in abstraction and generalization, but they are also imposed upon subsequent events so that man influences his psychological experience as much as events have influenced him.[29] Since the construct is a product of the construing process Kelly refers to these as "working hypotheses,"[30] "interpretations,"[31] "predictions,"[32] "pathways of movement,"[33] and even as "appraisals."[34] His point is that the construct is an identifiable, patterned structure or style of viewing life which we, as students of personality, can identify in others and in ourselves. It is not essential that a construct be named.[35] Kelly presumed that children began formulating constructs even before they could speak. Some of our constructs are so difficult to put into words that we may find it necessary to pantomime them. For example, poking a forefinger under a nose, to slightly raise the head can signify "being uppity" or "stuck up." This is a construct, even though we might not add the symbol (word) "uppity" to the visual act.

Of course, just saying "uppity" makes it appear that we have named our construct in terms of a commonality of behavior—as seen in people with inflated self-conceptions, for example. This would not quite capture what Kelly meant by a construct. To be specific, we must name *both* ends of the construct dimension in order to define it properly. Here is how Kelly expressed it: "We do not explicitly express a whole construct if we say, 'Mary and Alice have gentle dispositions but neither of them is as attractive as Jane.' We would have to say something like this, if we were to express a true construct: 'Mary and Alice are gentle; Jane is not.' Or we might say, 'Jane is more attractive than Mary or Alice.' "[36] Kelly referred to these two ends of the construct dimension of meaning as the *poles* of a construct. Each construct thus has a *similarity pole* and a *contrast pole*.[37] A construct says how two things are alike (similar) and also different (contrast) from a third thing. Kelly rejected the term "concept" because he felt that it merely considered the similarities among things, and he never wanted to overlook that saying what something "is" implies what it "is not."

When we come to name our constructs we are free to choose the most cryptic and vague designations we might spontaneously arrive at. This is what Kelly meant by the *personal* construct. One can never know what a person's language means until we know a good deal about how he is construing events.[38] This is not to say that we lack group constructs or common constructs which everyone grasps quite clearly. But as a personality theorist Kelly was attempting to show how individuals arrive at their uniqueness. What appears objectively to be the same experience for everyone concerned is often something entirely different. Constructs are usually named on the basis of their similarity pole. In Kelly's example above, for instance: "The construct of *Mary-like-Alice-unlike-Jane* is likely to be symbolized in the person's thinking simply as *Mary* or *Mary-ness.*"[39] Our construct of "uppity" suggests

that we see people commonly (similarity pole) as having this characteristic but that there are others who are *not* seen this way. Of course, just what the contrast pole may be named is up to the individual who is doing the construing. One person may contrast "uppity" to "just plain folks" while another person may contrast "uppity" to "poor folks." The point of a psychology of personal constructs is to find what the individual *personally* means when he applies the constructs he does to create his life.

Figure 26 presents a schematization of two "construing minds," A and B, ordering the identical life events from different perspectives. Note that one "templet" or construct is stylized as a square (mind A) and the other construct as a triangle (mind B). This indicates that the specific constructs may vary yet the events brought under the aegis of one or the other construct may be identical. These two people (minds A and B) might find it difficult to communicate the facts of the life events being construed. On the other hand, other constructs can come into play or the constructs presently being employed by an individual can alter their

Figure 26
Alternative Constructions of the Same Life Event

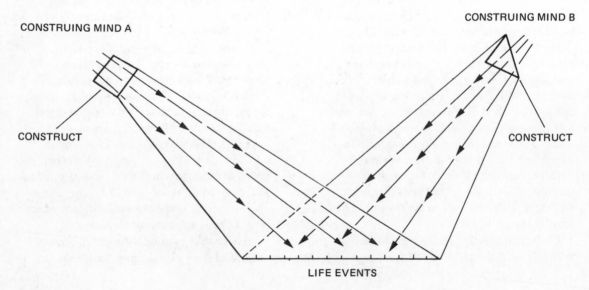

CONSTRUING MIND A

CONSTRUING MIND B

CONSTRUCT

CONSTRUCT

LIFE EVENTS

structure and meet with the perspective of his peers. Man is not locked into his construct system unless he believes that he is. The square thinker can take on a triangular slant for variety or in a "let's pretend" sense. When he does, the kinds of meanings which will issue in the life events under construction will have changed somewhat. He will see things differently. The construct which he now may "end up with," how he may *reconstrue* the life events of Figure 26, is an open question. Rather than a square and a triangle, if both minds assume the other's perspective we might end up with two circular constructions of the same life events. This is what *constructive alternativism* signifies. Man should constantly seek to find a "better fit" between his perspective and the demands of life—which often includes the points of view of others.

COMMON CHARACTERISTICS OF CONSTRUCTS

Since constructs are not only abstracted from but imposed upon events—ordering them and determining the meanings of one's experience —they can be called *controls*.[40] A construct can lock us into a fixed course of action. Constructs are real, and they capture real events. Although the reality of a construct is not necessarily the reality of a factual element under construction, the person behaves in terms of his construct and *not* the factual elements.[41] A divorce lawyer hearing a husband and wife recount the "facts" of their declining marital relationship soon realizes that people are not simply "lying" about what happened. With each hurt a predicted recurrence of the offending partner is put to test again and again, convincing the husband or wife of the other's loss of affection. Neither seems to see that by not accepting the viewpoint of the other they have effectively doomed their relationship. A reconstruction is required, but the time seems past when it might have been possible.

Life would be an intolerable series of inconsistent events if man could not perceive regularities and thereby formulate constructs. The tendency is to order life around one's controlling constructs. Man tends to systematize his constructs by removing contradictions between them, resulting in what Kelly called a *construction system*.[42] Cultural stereotypes are special cases of this systematization. We do not analyze those times when a black man is industrious, a Catholic is flexible, or a Jew is shy and suggestible. We allow our prejudiced (controlling) views to freeze us into the stereotypes of lazy blacks, rigid Catholics, and aggressive Jews. Even such fixed constructs can help us anticipate events, of course, so long as our predictions are not always invalidated. If it is possible to see laziness, rigidity, and aggressivity in *any* man, then finding these qualities in our ethnic prejudices should not be too difficult. Furthermore, how we behave in relation to blacks, Catholics, and Jews could easily bring about the kind of behavior we predicted from the outset. Constructs can become self-fulfilling prophecies.

When our construct systems are arrayed into higher- or lower-order ranges of constructs we can speak of their *ordinality*.[43] A *superordinate* construct *subsumes* a *subordinate* construct. The former is more abstract than the latter, and it thus can take the latter into its *range of convenience*.[44] For example, a construct such as "loyalty" may be superordinate to the less abstract concepts of "working unselfishly" and "doing what's asked." The range of convenience is the scope of a construct's relevance. In Figure 26 the life events subsumed by the squares or triangles would define the range of convenience for these constructs. If life events fall outside a construct's range of convenience they are *not* opposites of the construct but are simply irrelevant to the dichotomous construct being applied which already has its opposite built in.[45] The individual may apply his loyalty construct *only* to the family sphere. Family members should be loyal to one another. In extrafamilial matters, however, the construct may not be applicable. Once outside of parental and sibling relations the range of convenience for this construct ceases.

A construct can move up or down the ordinal scale, subsuming other contexts of the construction system or otherwise extending its range of convenience. For example, we can *dilate* our construct by broadening the perceptual field within which we make it applicable.[46] The loyalty construct can be extended beyond the family setting. Sometimes this extension of a construct's range of convenience is *loose,* so that the meaning is not always as clear.[47] What the person considers loyalty in the family context may be applied in his job situation more as a kind of "subservience" to his wishes than simply loyalty. The loyal person may be perfectly willing to tell his friend something distasteful. Yet, if a subordinate tells a superior something upsetting about the job he may feel his workers are not "being loyal" to him in the way his family is loyal. In the home setting the family relationship might be entirely open and free, with no fear of speaking one's mind. Yet, in this case a man may consider his workers unloyal when in fact he has switched loyalty meanings between home and office. This is what Kelly called a *loose* construction. To loosen construct meanings is not always bad, since it leads to creative insights at times.[48] When we loosen we apply a "rubber-sheet templet" to experience and thereby shift our frame of reference.[49] It would be best if we did this consciously, as an active experiment whose new perspective might give us an idea.

It is also possible to *tighten* constructs, to freeze them into rigid definitions. Tight constructs lead to unvarying predictions.[50] They help us to bring our thinking around to where we can possibly get a yes-or-no answer. The person who applies a tightened construct to his stereotype would make it perfectly clear to himself that "now, if it is true that red-headed people are hotheaded then this red-headed man who is talking with me will lose his temper. Let's see if he does!" Here is a clear-cut prediction, and the results can be stipulated. The loosened thinker would simply muddle along, possibly "recalling" angry comments of this man even though there was nothing unusual about his tone or behavior during the discussion. Tightening stabilizes constructs and facilitates their organization. Superordinate constructs are difficult to develop if the lower-order constructs which they subsume continue to be vague and unstable (loose).[51] If every man is a scientist then tightening is obviously an important aspect of experimentation—making thinking clear, projecting a clear hypothesis for confirmation or denial, and so forth.

Tightening also relates to the *permeability* of constructs. By this Kelly meant the relative capacity for a construct to embrace new elements.[52] A permeable construct is not necessarily loose. In our example of "loyalty" a loose construct was *impermeable*—it was incapable of being extended from the home sphere to the job sphere of life without stretching its meaning. Impermeable constructs which are tight, as in the case where someone says "That is clearly a chair and all one can do is use it as a chair," are also possible. Such a person would be less likely to see the myriad possibilities of chair functions, as ladders for reaching, props against doors, barricades for children's games, and so forth. Such a person's thought would take on an impermeable coloring: "You are either right or you are wrong, now which is it?" In contrast to such impermeable constructions, Kelly noted: "A construct is permeable if it is open to the addition of new elements, or elements beyond those upon which it has been explicitly formed."[53] The permeable construct admits situational differences. A ladder is not a chair, but given certain situations where no step ladder is available we can substitute a chair, or even a table, for a ladder. Here is the beginning of supple thought, responsive to circumstance. Like anything else, it can lead to difficulty if constructs are too impermeable and hence interfuse with one another to a great extent. Here permeability may shade into looseness.

A highly impermeable construct which freezes its elements into *only* its unique range of convenience Kelly termed a *preemptive construct*.[54] The black-or-white form of thinking which is so typical of the rigid person reflects this extreme form of impermeability. On the other hand, a construct which permits its elements to belong to *other* realms concurrently, even as it fixes definite qualities for present purposes, Kelly called a *constellatory construct*.[55] Our stereotyped thinking models above provide examples of constellatory thinking. Once someone is called "Jew-like," for instance, even though he in fact is a Christian, the qualities of a Jewish stereotype would be immediately constellated to him. "If Jew-like, then aggressive, pushy, materialistic, and so forth." The preemptive thinker would say "Only Jews are Jew-like." A construct which leaves its elements open to construction in all other respects is termed a *propositional construct*.[56] The propositional thinker is likely to engage in conscious elaboration of a permeable construction system, for he reasons that "it is conventional to view all Catholics as rigid and authoritarian, but let's see if things can be restricted this easily." The propositional thinker is thus open to new evidence, willing to take an altered view on an experimental basis, and to this extent, he represents an opposite end of the continuum from preemptive and constellatory thinkers.[57]

There are other terms of descriptive importance used by Kelly. A *comprehensive* construct is one which subsumes a wide variety of events, whereas the *incidental* construct has a much narrower range of convenience.[58] A construct could be made more comprehensive through dilation, of course. The opposite tendency to focus a construct and thus restrict its range of convenience is called *constriction*.[59] It is possible so to constrict the range of convenience of a construct that it will apply to a very limited aspect of life. Presumably, something like a profound religious experience which has taken place "only once" in life might be delimited by a highly specific, constricted construct. The feelings and impact of this single experience might not be applicable anywhere else in life. A *regnant* construct is a form of superordinate construct which subsumes many other constructs and helps to color their meaning.[60] Regnancies are thus comprehensive constructions, and they help us to simplify our thought by allowing a broad range of convenience. When they are impermeable they are likely to become preemptive and constellatory.[61]

CONSCIOUS, UNCONSCIOUS, AND THE SELF AS A CORE ROLE CONSTRUCT

We have already noted that not all constructs are verbalized. Kelly accounted for the "conscious vs. unconscious" mind conceptions of classical analytical theory in terms of this capacity for man to formulate templets which are not put into words. So-called unconscious mental contents, as seen in dreams, represented preverbal constructs which continue to exert an influence on experience.[62] Strictly speaking, Kelly did not want to use this distinction: "We do not use the conscious-unconscious dichotomy, but we do recognize that some of the personal constructs a person seeks to subsume within his system prove to be fleeting or elusive. Sometimes this is because they are loose rather than tight. . . . Sometimes it is because they are not bound by the symbolisms of words or other acts. But of this we are sure, if they are important in a person's life it is a mistake to say they are unconscious or that he is unaware of them. Every day he experiences them, often all too poignantly, except he cannot put his finger on them nor tell for sure whether they are at the spot the therapist has probed for them."[63]

Kelly was opposed to thinking of an entity called "self" or "ego," but he did say that we all have some construction label in terms of self-identity: ". . . it is quite appropriate to refer to a given person's self-construct, or to a class of constructs which can be called personal self-constructs."[64] Here again, we are likely to formulate our self-construct around what we see as a core of similarity about our behavior. We are "sincere" or "athletic" or "nice" in all of life's circumstances; at least, we believe ourselves to be consistent across many time-bound life events. It might surprise and even hurt us to discover that what we consider "nice" behavior another person calls "passivity," but that is how life goes. The point is: we do formulate constructions of our own behavior based on our experience, and these self-constructs exert the typical *control* on what we do as we move through life.

Why do we formulate a self-construct in the first place? It happens quite spontaneously as we mature, passing through interpersonal relations. Indeed, to construe another person is often to construe oneself.[65] We are prone to see ourselves as "like" others yet "different" from people at the opposite end of our construction. At times, we are as selves on the "different" end of the dimension. We see "dirty people" as a commonality, implying that we are at the other end of this dichotomous construct dimension—that is, clean people. The meanings which issue here are tied somehow to the "role relationship" we have with other people. Kelly once thought of calling his approach "role theory."

Kelly's use of "role" should not be equated with the usage often employed by sociologists and social psychologists. A role in the latter sense refers to a series of behavioral prescriptions, laid down by the culture and then filled by people who play the role of physician, father, teacher, mother, and so forth. For Kelly, the *role* is defined by the individual. It is a *process* whereby the individual construes the construction processes of another or others, and based on his understanding of what they are doing *in relation to him,* carries out an interpersonal activity.[66] Once we see our fellow

man as a construing being and take an interest in the way in which our behavior is being viewed by him we can enter into a *role relationship* with him.[67] The essential consideration in determining a role construct is that it be "based upon one's interpretation of the thinking of the other people in relation to whom the role is enacted."[68]

It is *not* necessary for the other people in relation to whom one is formulating role constructs to make this affair conjoint.[69] The other individual need not enter into a role relationship with the construing person. Hence, role constructs can be gross distortions.[70] The beautiful young woman who finds one day that her pleasantries to a rather innocuous young man "down the block" have led the latter to construe an intricate and involved love affair between them finds herself the victim of the unfortunate lad's colorless and lonely life. Yet, insofar as this fantasied love affair entered into the young man's behavior—eventuating in a highly embarrassing scene when he sees his "girlfriend" on the arm of another—we can speak of his delusional system as a kind of role relationship. In most cases, of course, the role relations of people are more realistic and interpersonally accurate than this. Most of us learn to "read" the intentions of others more correctly.

Now, when we speak of the self as a construct we actually refer to a special case of the role construct. Kelly indicated that there are unique *core role constructs,* which define our relationship to other people.[71] We behave in relation to these as if our very life depended upon them—as in one sense, it does. The early Christians, for example, who went to their deaths rather than renounce their faith were behaving in terms of their core role constructs, viewing their fellow Christians as brothers in God. A more mundane example might be the person who construes himself as an "individualist." If he senses that others are—in their construction of him—"putting him into a mold," he might react quite angrily and stubbornly to any suggestion that he compromise or accommodate his views to those of the group.

MOTIVATIONAL CONSTRUCTS

MAN AS A PROBLEM-SOLVING ANIMAL: FREEDOM VS. DETERMINISM IN BEHAVIOR

Since Kelly begins with the assumption that human beings are processes in constant change he does not think of motivation as a form of propulsion. There is no frozen psychic structure to move. Hence, we need no mental energies to "run" the personality system.[72] Kelly specifically rejects such terminology, as well as the time-honored term "drive" which has been used so prolifically by the learning theorist.[73] He was not sympathetic with the views of learning being advanced in the academic centers of his time, which he felt had man little more than the tail end of an unplanned reinforcement history.[74]

Rather than some hedonistic principle based on the satisfactions of energic expenditure or instinctual reinforcements, Kelly said that man found his rewards in the prediction and anticipation of events.[75] It is not the reward but the *solution* which brings man his satisfactions.[76] There is nothing special about this outcome. Motivation is not a topic which should give the psychologist much concern, and in fact he can dismiss it from his vocabulary altogether.[77] If we look to man as a problem solver, an active process of construing events in order to predict and control them, then both "learning" and "motivation" fall into line without special treatment. For Kelly, change was a question of *reconstruction*.[78] When an individual's construction system confronts new life events and yet is not helpful or applicable, a change is called for. When newly formed constructs are inconsistent with older constructs, a change is called for.[79] Of course, the human does not always change. He develops *habits,* which Kelly defines as "a convenient kind of stupidity

which leaves a person free to act intelligently elsewhere."[80] Or, he literally avoids changing due to the secondary factors operating on him, such as the lack of comprehension that change is possible or the threatening possibilities which changing behavior implies.

It is on the basis of constructs as controls that Kelly develops his conceptions of *choice, freedom,* and *determinism.* Since a construct projects its meaning onto reality, the range of convenience and the significance of the construct are important controls. If these constructs prove to be impermeable the individual becomes "locked into" their import in an unvarying, controlled, determined sense. Superordinate constructs are naturally the most significant "determiners" of behavior, for they subsume many lower level constructs and thus have a broader range of convenience and influence.[81] To become free of this superordinate control the individual must either reconstrue his circumstances or otherwise alter his most superordinate constructions. By placing a new control over his outlook he can achieve freedom. Indeed, freedom and determination are two sides of the same coin: ". . . determinism and freedom are two complementary aspects of structure. They cannot exist without each other any more than *up* can exist without *down* or *right* without *left.* Neither freedom nor determination are absolutes. A thing is free *with respect to something;* it is determined *with respect to something else.*"[82]

If we are to see behavioral change we must alter the "respect to something" which freezes a person into his present pattern. As we have noted, this amounts to some form of construct alteration. Kelly was sensitive to the charge that his theory of freedom and determinism as a relationship between superordinate and subordinate constructs might be seen as an overly "intellectual" account of man's behavior.[83] His typical response to this criticism was that man's construing of events is *not* limited to verbalized symbols. Furthermore, conative (striving) as well as cognitive (knowing) behaviors fall under the range of convenience of one's construction system. Intellectual explanations would seem to be limited to verbalized (symbolized) and cognitive explanations, which is clearly *not* the tactic selected by the psychology of personal constructs.[84] Actually, Kelly did not like to think of his view as a cognitive one.[85] He did not believe the term signified anything worthwhile for the personality theorist.

THE C-P-C CYCLE AND THE CREATIVITY CYCLE

Two important concepts used by Kelly clarify how constructs and construction systems can change. The first is the *C-P-C cycle,* which involves a sequence of construction in which *circumspection, preemption,* and *control* follow in that order and lead to a choice which precipitates the person into a particular situation.[86] By *circumspection* Kelly meant that the individual deals with the issues facing him as regards some problem in a propositional fashion. Recall that a propositional construct leaves its elements open to construction in all other respects. It is "open to alternative hypotheses." Hence, at the outset of the C-P-C cycle the individual mulls over the various possibilities facing him, looks at his problem this way and that way, until he finally preempts! That is, he fixes on some "one" and "only this one" definition of the problem. When Hamlet mulled over his situation, including his father's death, his mother's behavior, his uncle's attitude, and so forth, he was dealing circumspectively with a gnawing issue. However, when he finally settled on the critical point, "To be, or not to be; that is the question . . ." Kelly argues that Hamlet preempted other possibilities, other "middle grounds" short of murder or no-murder.[87] A definite control was fixed to Hamlet's future behavior once he decided which of the preemptive alternatives open to him he would follow. Kelly notes that the final C of the C-P-C cycle could just as well be termed a "choice" as a "control" feature of the cycle.[88] Due to the dichotomous nature of thought the human being is always free to choose in the

direction of a construct pole that he believes will further his construction system—his prediction and control of subsequent events.[89] Once the choice has been made, then the control settles in, and an act of behavior is *determined.* And so it happened in the gloomy "destiny" of Hamlet that he was to kill his uncle.

The second way in which we can observe a sequence of events taking place in the process of construction leading to change Kelly termed the *Creativity Cycle.* In this case, the succession of events follows a loosening-to-tightening of constructs.[90] A person who has tight constructs cannot easily be creative, for he is unable to go beyond the bounds of his rigid blueprint. The creative person, on the other hand, is one who can allow his constructs to stretch —he can often play with them, or "try them on for size." Indeed, it is this "what if?" or semiplayful attitude of the Creativity Cycle which differentiates it from the C-P-C Cycle. In the latter case, the individual is engaging in a succession of events which *will bring him to act* in a personal way.[91] In the Creativity Cycle there may be no appreciable personal commitment. In the C-P-C Cycle we witness behavior which might be termed "involved" or "committed." Something will issue "one way or the other."

EMOTIVE TERMS AND THE PSYCHOLOGY OF PERSONAL CONSTRUCTS

Kelly thought of *emotion* as behavior which was either loosely defined[92] or not a word-bound construction.[93] A person's *feelings* are inner events needing construing.[94] It may be that a construct is already at play, drawn from preverbal experience. Or possibly what the individual calls an emotion is the "other side" of some consciously expressed construct. How we "feel" may be the other side of how we "know." By and large, however, emotional expression is loose expression.[95] The individual is unable to state precisely or reliably what is his attitude toward some aspect of behavior. We only make sense of emotional factors in behavior when we stipulate more precisely what is taking place in the construction system. Take *humor,* for example. Jokes are neat reconstructions, associated with quick movements and unexpected outcomes due to a reversal in our expectations.[96] The pompous and officious general stumbles on his way to the rostrum and in his subsequent blushing and stammering proves to his snickering troops that he is a human being after all.

Kelly defined *threat* as awareness of an imminent comprehensive change in one's core role constructs.[97] One is threatened to the extent that what he feared was about to take place looks as though it is really coming about. Threats are unhappy predictions we make. We are certain that we have some terrible disease, so we arrange to see our physician. With each solemn "look" on the physician's face we grow increasingly apprehensive, for we feel convinced that he is finding that we are as ill as we have predicted we are. *Stress* is a more removed phenomenon, a kind of awareness of potential threat.[98] But when actually threatened the person is just about convinced that something is going to happen in his life which will have far-reaching implications.[99] He is going to have to do some reconstruing. Things look shaky, or scary, or simply "incomprehensible."

At times like these we witness *signs of emotion.* The person may perspire, he may tense up or possibly flee from the threatening situation in a headlong panic. When the mounting threat is not clearly verbalized we might witness an abnormal behavioral pattern emerging as an "unconscious" manifestation. Because it is difficult to retain in memory what is unstructured people have a hard time remembering what is happening to them when under various levels of threat.[100] This is another way of saying that while under threat we are not likely to construe things effectively because we are waiting to see "what will happen to me."

Kelly thought of this "loss of structure" as *anxiety.*[101] The anxious individual is one whose constructs do not seem to apply to the events which he senses about him. Kelly used to refer facetiously to this state as being "caught with his constructs down."[102] Under such circumstances the individual cannot predict; hence, he cannot solve any of his problems. The affective state of *fear* is at least a more focused state, in which some imminent incidental construct has loomed up in one's path to suggest that impending change is likely to take place.[103] We suffered anxiety above, as we watched our physician, knowing not what he might find but predicting that whatever it is, it will be terrible. When he now fixes a specific diagnosis (incidental construct) which is "serious" and demands immediate treatment we begin to suffer *fear.* The advantage of fear is that with the stipulation of a given illness we have already begun a process of reconstruction. We can now set about following our physician's directions for cure. Of course, if our illness is incurably fatal, anxiety will not abate. Here is something—death—so incomprehensible that nothing within our present construction system subsumes it. At this point, what problem solution we arrive at depends upon many factors, including our views on the meaning of existence and afterlife.

Another realm of emotive behavior which most clinical schemes emphasize is that of aggression or hostility. Kelly had a specific way of viewing these terms, which are often used interchangeably. For him, *aggression* was tantamount to an active elaboration of a perceptual field.[104] The person acts aggressively when he seeks to extend the scope of his construction system. He may employ the C-P-C Cycle in fixing a definite course of action or fall back on the helpfulness of the Creativity Cycle. If he procrastinates or devises experimental tests which are simply out of the question (fantasied "wishes" for example) then Kelly would call this individual *passive* in behavior. We are all more or less passive in our life styles

—exhibiting active elaboration in some spheres and greatly reduced elaboration in others. When one is aggressive he is more likely to threaten other people than when he remains passive. Our moves to know, to elaborate, to "find out" upset the gentle routine of others, who may actually misunderstand our intention and consider us hostile. But we need not necessarily be hostile simply because we are aggressive.

We are only *hostile* in Kelly's terms when we insist upon finding true the predictions we made in the face of contradictory evidence.[105] As Kelly observed: "The trouble with hostility is that it always attempts to make the original investment pay off. It is unrealistic."[106] The hostile person freezes his constructs into impermeability. He "knows," and no matter what evidence life offers him to the contrary he will persist until he finds confirmation for the predictions made. A hostile parent will punish a child who does not produce the kind of behavior the parent thinks he is motivating. It is the "child's fault," not his, even though closer examination may show that the parent was insensitive to the child's construction of events. Hostile people do not much care about what others think, which is why they are often so difficult to live with. Whereas the aggressive person responds to the "give and take" of interpersonal relations, the hostile person permits only one outcome—*his* predicted expectation. The hostile person thus punishes or "hurts" others for not behaving the way he expects them to behave, and he can do this in a *passive sense*—by not hearing what they say to him, by "forgetting" some important appointment, or by overlooking some vital aspect of life which could have saved others a lot of pain if it had been mentioned.

Another emotional tone often alluded to in theories of behavior is *guilt*. Kelly defined this as a perception of apparent dislodgement from one's role structure.[107] The guilty person is thus one who has done something which either is, or seems to be, in direct contradiction with his self-image, around which the core role constructs coalesce. This is what *conscience* or *superego* represents in the psychology of personal constructs. Note that this dislodgement of guilt still represents "threat." We are threatened by guilt just as readily as we are by anxiety—and indeed it is sometimes difficult to separate anxiety from guilt. The point is, in guilt the individual feels he has somehow transgressed or *sinned*.[108] He has violated what is most sacred to him, what defines him most centrally as a human being. The guilty man often feels alienated from others, for, in transgressing his core role constructs and to that extent contradicting his self-image, he has also violated his relations with others. This is so because the self-construct is always defined via interpersonal relations.

THE DEFENSE MECHANISMS

Kelly did not favor a "defense mechanism" approach to the description of behavior, even though he did comment on some of these classical concepts. Kelly viewed the so-called mechanism of *repression* as the result of the suspension of constructs by the individual, who possibly could not resolve their contradictions or who was so gripped by the threat of imminent change that he failed to construe when he might have.[109] *Incorporation* represented a willingness on the part of a person to see other people like himself.[110] *Identification* or *introjection* results when we take over constructs which our group—including family members—have already been using.[111] *Regression* is due to behavior which is predicated upon either preverbal or at least highly immature constructions of life.[112] *Projection* would be a special form of hostility, in which the person insists upon naming what another's motives are despite all evidence to the contrary. *Reaction-formation* is an attempt to put the "opposite construct pole" in effect when it is the "other pole" which bears the significance for a person.

DEVELOPMENT AS THE DISPERSION OF DEPENDENCY

Kelly did not formulate many time perspective constructs, feeling that the *present* is what counts in behavior. The psychology of personal constructs also turns man's attention forward in time. Even so, some things can be said about development from birth to maturity.

Essentially, this question of maturing constructions extends man's dependencies from one or a few to several persons. Kelly did not favor calling people either "dependent" or "independent," since he believed that everyone is both. We cannot exist without relying upon others. In the earliest months of life a child presumably focuses his rudimentary attention on the mother. He thus formulates a *dependency construct,* by which Kelly meant a preverbal "figure construct" signifying that some one person is essential to personal survival.[113] By "figure" we mean the actual image of a mother or surrogate mothering-one. Kelly notes: "When the child uses a figure in this manner he actually develops two levels of meaning for *Mother*: the one referring to the actual behaviors of his mother, the other referring to *motherliness*."[114] Such preverbal constructs which utilize images tend to be impermeable. They are not very effective in determining interpersonal relations, for they fail to view the other person as a construing organism. In other words, they are not role constructs.

The task of maturing now becomes one of making such basic dependency constructs more permeable, extending the child's reliance for existence upon others. We can be fairly certain that in his initial contacts with them a child assesses other people in terms of preverbal mothering constructs. He will see how other adults (father, uncles, aunts, visitors) are alike and yet also different from his mother. He will begin to acquire language, which Kelly viewed as "a device for anticipating the events that are about to happen to us."[115] This growing sense of awareness will permit the child to begin construing role constructs, to realize that other people are also construing his behavior. This permits interpersonal relations and an even greater extension of dependency upon others as friendships are formed during the school years.

Another important development in everyone's life is the ability to experiment, to predict and control events in order to find avenues for extending the range of one's construct system. In childhood, this is the function of *play*. Kelly observes: "Play is adventure. Its outcomes are always veiled in some delightful uncertainty."[116] Children thus develop skills in their play. The primary constructs an individual formulates can be gleaned from his play and other recreation patterns. For example, does the young person's recreation involve role relationships or are these solitary activities?[117] Kelly emphasizes that in his free-time activity a person is likely to be spontaneously construing what is most important to him.

What one notices in a properly maturing child, therefore, is the accretion of propositional constructs, as well as the more permeable dependency constructs. He moves from the "whole figure" construct—viewing mother as *only* "such and such" a person—to a more flexible trait attribution which recognizes that the same person may be motherly or maternalistic and yet in other respects very *un*motherly. Thus as we grow to adulthood we can confirm or disconfirm our constructs *in part* rather than in their entirety.[118]

SOCIETY AND CULTURE AS A VALIDATIONAL BACKDROP FOR INDIVIDUAL PREDICTION

One's personality patterns are drawn out along lines which tie into his *society* and *culture*, two terms which Kelly wrestled with because they seemingly have much to say about what we become. Is it that man is *nothing but* a product of sociocultural forces? Kelly could not accept this. His approach considered the individual person rather than the society.[119] He insisted that "social psychology must be a psychology of interpersonal understandings, not merely a psychology of common understandings."[120] Society exists, *not* because it is some form of external power, dictating social roles for men to fill but *rather* because men do construe one another as fellow construers and hence can enter into role relationships.[121] We must not be tricked into assigning the responsibility for man's behavior to an impersonal "society" anymore than we must be tricked into assigning it to an impersonal "nature."

Of course, society's cultural mandates are important. A cultural *norm,* for example, may be thought of as "the eyes of society," and it is the unusual person who can ignore the evaluation of such eyes entirely.[122] The quintessence of culture for Kelly is that people "construe their experience in the same way."[123] This means that a group of people can agree on what will *validate* their construction systems, their individual predictions as to life experience, and so forth.[124] Yet this does not mean that man is a simple product of his culture. Since man is the construer he is under the control of culture only when he submits to such control by construing things in this way.[125] Hence, we must think of cultural factors as the background against which man puts his constructs to test, accepting as validators the "common sense" of the community which sees things as he does. For example, in growing to adulthood the individual selects a vocation. Kelly felt that a vocation might be seen in one sense as a body of evidence, to which one's daily anticipations are repeatedly subjected.[126] It is difficult for a person to accept the validity of his construct system if these predictions do not facilitate his life experience "on the job." This is the reason so many of man's constructs seem bound to society's "means of production."

Kelly was not overly awed by the communistic theorists who focus on this aspect of construct validation. He also tended to disparage a great reliance upon the social strata analysis of upper, middle, and lower classes.[127] Though such breakdowns do tell us what advantages large groups of people enjoy, they sidestep the fundamental issue of how the individual person views his world and especially how he varies from his class norm. What Kelly was trying to emphasize here, in disclaiming great reliance on supraindividual conceptions, was his resentment of the "mass man" thinking which he saw as so typical of the academic psychology of his time. Rather than focus on a person the psychologist is happy to use a statistical dragnet procedure, in which he gleans some regularity having little relevance for *a* person. Kelly put his attitude regarding culture quite succinctly when he noted: "Just as we have insisted that man is not necessarily the victim of his biography, we would also insist that man is not necessarily the victim of his culture."[128]

INDIVIDUAL DIFFERENCES CONSTRUCTS

An individual's personality is determined by the kinds of constructs he formulates, so that individual differences in the psychology of personal constructs indicate individual differences in the construct systems of fellow men. How does *he* or *she* typically approach life? When we now begin applying our constructs, as professional psychologists, to the constructs of our "subjects" we begin to subsume the constructs of others. We rise several levels of abstraction and group the subjective construers into some designation.[129] Kelly was aware that this could be done, and in fact he stressed that psychotherapists must have an ability to construe their cases in some such fashion. Yet, he also stressed that such professional constructions must always be propositional and permeable, open to invalidating evidence and held to only speculatively rather than rigidly.

If one now wished to emphasize the typical drift of a person's construct system he could do so—referring to him as dependent[130] or aggressive[131]—but Kelly was not much interested in such designations. He developed a means (Rep Test) for identifying the unique constructs of an individual from *his* slant on things. Kelly could see little profit in pigeonholing other people. What the psychology of personal constructs aims for is to grasp the unique slant of our fellow human beings. This means that by definition we have entered into a role relationship with them and thus can carry out the purposes for which we come together. So far as Kelly was concerned, the major purpose of his theory was to further professional activity in the clinical area, particularly as regards psychotherapy.[132]

Psychopathology and Psychotherapy

THEORY OF ILLNESS

PERSONAL CONSTRUCTS IN ABNORMALITY

Kelly defines psychological disorder as *"any personal construction which is used repeatedly in spite of consistent invalidation."*[133] The construction system is thus not accomplishing its purpose.[134] The individual cannot predict, his experiments are going awry, he is not anticipating events and hence fails to learn. Indeed, one of the ways in which the clinician can be sure that a prospective client is truly abnormal is when even he—the therapist—cannot predict the client's behavior with great accuracy.[135] Of course, therapists have a professional construction system which should always permit prediction of client behavior to some extent. But the error in prediction is greater for the abnormal individual, and there is more behavioral deviation from group norms as well.[136] This suggests that the maladjusted person is beginning to depart from the community of expectations which he earlier had embraced. Caught up in his lack of predictability, the increasingly disturbed individual

begins making assumptions and presumptions greatly at odds with the "common sense" of others.

The typical abnormal individual feels that his troubles result from the elements of his life, rather than his construction of these events.[137] He begins "regressing" to the earlier, less mature dependency constructs.[138] He turns to his parent, marital partner, or physician for validation in all things. When the preverbal dependency constructs are in operation we often witness what the classical analysts called "acting-out" in his behavior.[139]

At this point the therapist is likely to enter the client's life. In the presenting *complaint* which the therapy client proffers we can usually see the locus of his maladjustment. Kelly felt that by having the client carefully elaborate his complaint, the therapist can come to understand the conceptual processes within which the maladjustment has developed and is maintained.[140] Invariably, the clinician will find that a complaint reflects the client's inability to plan and thence enact a role in life. A good picture of the complaint is quite important for it tells a lot about the client's approach to life in general.[141] Kelly did not favor a professional construct of "conflict," saying that this is usually an inappropriate designation for what the client experiences.[142] The client does not feel conflicted but rather feels a greater degree of anxiety than does the normal person.

In normal anxiety the emotion of anxiety heralds a loss of structure in the construct system. The normal person thus revises his constructions, usually avoiding a collapse into total anxiety by relaxing the superordinate constructs and rearranging the more permeable aspects of his system.[143] The increasingly disturbed person, on the other hand, does a poor job of this rearrangement and hence his changes are maladaptive. They do not help him to allay the nagging sense of anxiety which prompted the alteration. He may now loosen all the more, dilating his constructs to some bizarre extreme of plausibility. Or he may swing in the opposite direction and constrict his outlook until everything in life is frozen into the rigidity of a miniscule impermeability. Sometimes he vacillates back and forth between these extremes. The particular style of this changing construction arrangement defines the classical clinical syndromes. Kelly held that no one loses the patterning structure of his construction system *entirely*.[144] Even the most regressed psychotic has some remnant of construction in operation.

Rather than finding a solution to his problems, the severely anxious person is likely to find a symptom, which Kelly defined as "the rationale by which one's chaotic experiences are given a measure of structure and meaning."[145] Symptoms are, therefore, inappropriate ways of adapting to problems.[146] Rather than meet a challenge an individual "gets sick" or "gets drunk" and then feels that his inability to meet challenges is somehow more acceptable. The illness developed need not be free of an organic involvement, for just as an element of a construct is used as a referent for that construct in symbolic form (the "name" of a construct) so too can a bodily organ become the symbol of a construct: "When the client talks about the pain in his chest he may be expressing in his own language a far more comprehensive construct than the psychologist at first suspects."[147] Preverbal constructs are based upon the raw experience of sensation without labels, and so-called "psycho-physiological" disturbances are likely to be expressions of such beginning attempts to construe experience.

In addition to providing a rationale for present behavior, a symptom is also the way a client asks questions about subsequent life events.[148] He is often asking, "Must I go on in this wretched state, being hounded and manipulated by people who do not understand what a good person I really am?" From an external reference this might be viewed as a delusional thought pattern. But from the client's viewpoint it is an admission that he is unable to enter into role relationships, to make himself known, to have a free interpersonal contact with the give-and-take all of us hope to experience with others.

DIAGNOSING PERSONAL CONSTRUCTS: THE REP TEST

Kelly adamantly rejected the Kraepelinian nosological system in psychology, feeling as he did that it tended to categorize mental disturbance.[149] For him, *diagnosis* was the "planning stage of therapy."[150] It was the initial attempts of the clinician to get to know his client by betting which way the client would move, given this or that circumstance in the therapy room or in the life circumstance. Effective diagnosis is thus a matter of making reasonable predictions.[151] The therapist needs a set of coordinate axes within which he can plot and predict his client's behavior.[152] These concepts should be propositional and permeable. Most important of all, the professional construct system of the clinician must be capable of subsuming the personal construct system of the client. In order to facilitate this process of coming to know how the client is viewing his world Kelly designed what he called the *Role Construct Repertory Test,* or simply the *Rep Test.*[153]

The logic of the Rep Test involves getting a prospective therapy client to express his personal role constructs by having him "compare and contrast" a host of people with whom he has had to deal in his life to date.[154] Various "figures" can be drawn from life, as for example: "a teacher you liked," "the most successful person whom you know personally," "the most threatening person whom you know personally," "the most ethical person you know personally." In addition, the client's parents and siblings or proper surrogates are used, and there is usually a reference to the client's self. Through the use of individual cards for each test figure or a specially prepared test form combining all figures on one page the subject is then taken through a number of "sorts" in which he states how person X and person Y are "alike" and yet different from person Z. Thus, a client might be asked: "Compare your mother and your favorite teacher, and tell me (or record in writing) how they are alike and yet *different* from your best friend."

The construct which emerges here—let us say it is "competent"— is considered only one pole. After a series of other comparisons and contrasts of this nature the client is taken back through his lists of constructs and asked for the other pole. Thus, he is asked to name the opposite of "competent." Assume that in this case the client would say "questioning." Note what has happened here: the therapist has encouraged the client to name a personal role construct. One of the ways in which he deals with people interpersonally is in terms of a construct of "competent vs. questioning." Whereas the therapist might have assumed that the opposite of competence was *in*competence, the client has revealed that for him, someone who is competent may be efficient and effective, yet a little close-minded. An open, questioning attitude may not suggest competence, but yet one can have a friendly relationship with such a person and possibly learn along with him. The implication here is also that as one learns and achieves competence he must assume a less permeable, less propositional outlook on life. There are many such hypotheses to be gleaned from a study of the client's construction system, and the point of the Rep Test is to bring therapists into the world of the client's personal construction system.

Kelly also devised a method for "factor analyzing" the construct matrix of the Rep Test.[155] In the test form, for example, a client would be asked to proffer 22 constructs, having sorted some 19 different persons (test figures) as outlined above (i.e., how are X and Y alike and different from Z). Through the (nonparametric) factor analysis of these sorts a clinician can arrive at a much shortened list of "basic" constructs presumably used by the individual in his daily life. Rather than 22 constructs the

therapist might thus end up with four or five construct dimensions which capture most succinctly the world view of his client. Constructs are not always stated in single words. Test subjects often describe their role constructs in brief phrases, as: "I feel good with them" vs. "I don't like being with her." Prepared with such a list of constructs the therapist can now (a) appreciate the client's slant on life; (b) adapt his language level and theoretical formulations to the language of his client; and (c) begin formulating hypotheses concerning which way the client will react when he (the therapist) says this or that or otherwise behaves in some predetermined fashion. This is the proper scientific attitude, the one which Kelly wanted all advocates of personal construct theory to follow.

CLINICAL SYNDROMES AND THE PSYCHOLOGY OF PERSONAL CONSTRUCTS

Although Kelly did not feel we needed to retain the classical syndromes of personal maladjustment, he did make some effort to subsume these well-known distinctions. He took a quantitative view of the distinction between neurosis and psychosis, feeling that the same individual could pass through both patterns of living.[156] The essential difference between these two states centered on the level of anxiety and the kind of solution made to the problems in living. The neurotic is likely to manifest anxiety more consistently, and to show greater variation in pattern, as he is constantly casting about for new constructions.[157] The psychotic has passed through this phase and after possibly going to the heights of anxiety, has now settled on some delusional or hallucinatory solution to his problem.[158]

The neuroses are variations on the theme of construct alteration. The *hysterias* are typified by converting problems from one area (psychological) into another (bodily), along the lines mentioned before.[159] Hysterical and other psychosomatic patients are often people who have construed their worlds dualistically and preemptively—i.e., in terms of either a body or a mind sphere.[160] Having accepted this predicate assumption they can easily symbolize their "mental" problems in terms of a chest pain or an immobile hand. It appears to be "something else" but we can see beneath the subterfuge. The *obsessive-compulsive* client utilizes tightening as a defense against the failure in prediction his construct system is beginning to manifest.[161] When the compulsions begin to trip him up, inefficiently locking him into some ritualistic performance, we witness the end stage of a tightly drawn, impermeable construct. Anxiety neuroses or *panic* states come about when a sudden comprehensive construction is suggested, with no escape in sight.[162] The person in a state of panic is probably as low in predictive power as the human ever gets, and we often see these states popping up just before a psychotic solution is arrived at. Kelly saw the *psychopath* as a person whose style of construction is not truly of a role-relationship variety.[163] That is, a psychopath is interested in manipulating others rather than relating with them in a spontaneous fashion. He thinks only of himself and how he can construe others to manipulate them. Kelly felt that *suicide* was attempted for various reasons—as a dependency reaction, for example—but that in every instance it was a form of problem solution, even if it meant escape from the responsibility of having to go on predicting.[164]

We have already noted that delusions and hallucinations are forms of problem solution. Delusions of grandeur ("I am the most powerful person on earth") or persecution ("Everyone is out to do me harm") are forms of construct dilation.[165] Delusions of world destruction would suggest imminent collapse of the construct system, and a constricted solution might well lead to delusions of self-worthlessness. The *depression* psychotic often has the latter solution to a problem.[166] People commonly constrict their fields when under pressure to solve some problem. A depressed client

simply pursues this procedure until he severely restricts his freedom of movement. At that point he may attempt suicide, or he may vacillate back and dilate into a *manic* state, with florid delusions of grandeur. The loosening of constructs also appears in a manic's "flight of ideas." The *schizophrenic* also shows these flights, but in general his construct system is much looser and he has a long history of such "schizoid" thinking. Kelly did not wish to label people as "schizophrenics."[167] Too often such labels could not be removed after a client improved. Besides, schizoid thought could be helpful in the beginning of the Creativity Cycle, and it was Kelly's view that creative people loosen in this fashion without moving into a psychotic state.[168] Some forms of schizophrenia reveal considerable withdrawal, suggesting a constriction as well as a loosening of thought pattern.[169]

The *paranoiac* reaction, or some less systematized *paranoid* variation on the schizophrenic diagnosis, was seen by Kelly as involving more permeable construction systems than most psychotics. The paranoid has a highly systematized construction system, and the superordinate constructs are sufficiently permeable to account for changes in experience.[170] This is what makes the paranoid so difficult to treat. He can successfully counter virtually anything we think of to shake his delusional system. There is considerable threat in a paranoid case, probably more so than in any other mental disorder.[171] Finally, the *hebephrenic* and *catatonic* variations of schizophrenia may be seen in terms of highly "regressed" or preverbal construction systems.

THEORY OF CURE

CURE AS RECONSTRUCTION AND THE NATURE OF THERAPY

A person is mentally healthy to the extent that he can solve the problems he encounters in life.[172] Kelly was fond of speaking of this process as involving the rotating of "the axes on life."[173] A new set of dimensions comes into play which opens freedom of movement. Kelly once considered calling his therapeutic process "reconstruction" rather than psychotherapy, and he was never very happy with the latter term.[174] He finally settled for a definition emphasizing that "psychotherapy is a reconstruing process."[175]

The therapy relationship is viewed as a kind of running psychological experiment or a laboratory for the testing of ideas and feelings.[176] The therapist effectively asks the client to join him in a controlled investigation of the client's life style.[177] Experiments will be performed and field studies will be carried out, with proper validation sought for the predictions which both the therapist and the client will make. Kelly did not believe that therapy was confined to the four walls of the consulting room.[178] Since reconstruction cures, the therapy will not be successful unless a client begins his reformulations in the actual life setting. Therapy involves the dual task of reviewing present constructs, and then either altering them in some fashion or formulating entirely new ones which might serve the process of life more adequately.

Kelly liked to speak of this process of change in therapy as *movement*. It is a good prognostic sign if the client enters therapy with some preliminary constructs of movement of his own;[179] for example, if he sees himself as changing—even getting worse—rather than being frozen into a situation which somehow changes around him. Such a person recognizes that he is participating in the flux of events. One of the first forms of movement often noted in therapy is *slot movement*.[180] This involves simply moving over to the contrast end of one's constructs, as when the woman who sees her neighbors all as "kindly" begins to think of them as "mean." Kelly considered this a superficial change but a process of movement worthy of note. We can build on this change, extending the client's recognition of alternative constructions to a more comprehensive level. Whether or not neighbors are kindly or mean can then be tested in a series of experiments—such as asking the client to predict what will happen at the next church social.

As the therapist hears the client's opening complaint he is likely to ask the client to expand on the circumstances surrounding such difficulties. Kelly viewed this preliminary as a very fundamental task of the therapist, one he called *elaboration*.[181] The point is: in elaborating the complaint the therapist encourages the client to extend the range of convenience of his constructs, and usually bring other constructs into play as well. Reconstruction often begins in the loosening which elaboration engenders. As the client goes on talking about his problem, dating its arrival in his life, moving backward and forward in his life's course, he naturally begins to loosen his terms.[182] As the therapist helps him by bringing him forward gradually to tighten once again, and then loosen, the Creativity Cycle or the C-P-C Cycle may operate. The therapist's goal is to help the client develop a set of constructs which are permeable and comprehensive.[183] He does this by using properly psychological devices; hence, "Psychotherapy is the intelligent manipulation and organization of various psychological processes."[184]

INTERPRETATION, INSIGHT, AND THE CLIENT'S VIEWPOINT

The most vital point of Kellyian therapy is that the client must cure himself. This is why the therapist takes the client so seriously and engages in a mutual series of experimental efforts with him as co-investigator. Kelly never tired of telling his therapy students: *"If you don't know what's wrong with a client, ask him; he may tell you!"*[185] At the very least, by getting the client's point of view the therapist has a construed point of departure—one which may only lead to the "other side" of his dichotomous construction system but one which gets them moving in any case.

To be effective, a therapist must have (a) a permeable, nonpreemptive set of professional constructs within which he can construe his client, and (b) a facility for making use of the client's construct system in its own sense.[186] The client heals himself by rearranging and reformulating the latter (b), so the therapist must be able to speak to him via the client's personal idiom, even as he subsumes terms by his own, more technical jargon (a). Kelly did not demand that his clients learn the professional terminology of the psychology of personal constructs. Hence, when therapists begin "interpreting" to clients in psychotherapy the insights which result need have no direct bearing on the language of personal construct theory. Kelly was not doctrinaire in making interpretations. In fact, it was his belief that *insight* of the classical variety was not always necessary for a cure to result.[187]

Kelly defined *insight* as "the comprehensive construction of one's behavior."[188] Note that the vantage point of this definition is the client's. The same goes for *interpretation*: " 'Interpretation' is a term for which we have no particularly limited definition. . . . The therapist does not so much present interpretations as attempt to get the client himself to make helpful interpretations."[189] The therapist says such things as "Is this what you mean when you say that you feel people are ignoring you?" or "Let's try this on 'for size' and see if it helps us organize our thinking" but he is not directing the client toward any particular or uniform area of "insight" in so doing. The client has provided the focus of therapy entirely on the basis of his personal constructions, and whatever change takes place is similarly going to take place only on the basis of his personal efforts to reconstruct. It is likely that he will review his past life, but not because it holds any genetically essential data. The past is only relevant because it can shed light on the client's present life and the future he is moving into.[190] Therapy serves a primarily anticipatory function.[191]

Kelly liked to think of the therapist as a source of validation for the client.[192] Hence, he must realize that in reconstruing experience the client will have to begin with his perception of the therapist. He will be trying out old and then new construction on the therapist, looking for a response. As therapy proceeds insight and interpretation can often be more effective if offered as *organized instruction*.[193] By either validating or not validating the client's constructions the therapist—through his reactions—is effectively teaching his client which constructs "fit" and which do not. This process of adjusting construct to experiential reality is then extended beyond the therapy room to the client's real world. Therapy proceeds, like any other scientific venture, through successive approximations.[194] The client does not need "one" insight but a host of increasingly predictive insights to formulate and reformulate. Some will be mundane and unconventional; others will fall into place under the better known theories of personality.[195]

By saying that insight was not always necessary Kelly meant that the individual did not have to feel he had gained any doctrinaire knowledge. Nor did he always have to appreciate the extent of change which had come about in his construing tendencies. Rather than an "insight" into some condition he could simply feel that he had "gotten his thinking straight" and gone ahead on some new tack. In fact, Kelly sometimes felt it was better to *encapsulate* an old problem rather than try to "work it through" and master it via insight.[196] This could be accomplished through a *time-binding* technique, in which the therapist takes the position: "Well, that was a very tough period in your life all right, and I suppose we might be able to find out more about it if we devoted many months to a search. But maybe we can consider that 'past' and begin our search for a happier and more productive time in the present. What do you say?" With an attitude of this sort, the therapist turns the client's attention away from those intricate, soul-searching efforts that classical analysis seems to become engulfed in.

There are other ways in which psychologists use the term "insight" which Kelly would not greatly quarrel with. For example, if the psychologist feels it is desirable for a client to name—that is assign a symbol to—some new construct which is emerging in his repertoire of constructs then Kelly would consider this action a form of insight.[197] Too many therapists seem to want this more for their own needs—as proof of their effectiveness rather than as a necessary aspect of cure—but Kelly was willing to accept the necessity on occasion. If a highly rigid person who has become more propositional and permeable in his thought is made aware that his thinking has "loosened" up he might be spared some later threat when this more liberal outlook now appears in conflict with his religious convictions. This is surely a kind of insight.

RELATIONSHIP FACTORS: ACCEPTANCE, TRANSFERENCE, AND RESISTANCE

When we take up relationship factors in the theory of personal constructs we begin dealing specifically with *role* constructs. Since the therapist is a major validator of client constructs he begins to take on great importance. The therapist, working through his professional constructs, must actually have greater knowledge of relationship factors than the client. As Kelly put it: "A therapist-client relationship is one which exemplifies greater understanding on the part of one member than on the part of the other."[198] Thus, to be effective as a therapist one must understand and utilize the constructs of clients. This is what Kelly meant by *acceptance*.[199] The therapist evidences acceptance when he demonstrates that he understands the client's point of view well enough to rephrase and recapitulate what the client is expressing—even though many of the constructs so expressed are vague, preverbal, and emotionalized. Acceptance is "the readiness to see the world through another person's

eyes."[200] This does not mean the therapist approves of the client's value system, nor does he condone all client behaviors. But he does understand such behaviors intimately. When this attitude is conveyed by the therapist a client senses *support;* he is reassured and more ready to experiment further by trying alternative constructions out on a tentative basis.

This is the fundamental meaning of *rapport* or relationship factors in therapy. Kelly interpreted rapport in terms of his role theory.[201] Rapport is established when the therapist is able to subsume a part of the client's construction system and thereby enter into a role relationship with him. The client's establishment of a true rapport or relationship may occur sometime later. Signs of rapport in clients include increased relaxation, greater spontaneity, flexibility, and the willingness to loosen a construction.[202] One of the aids to a developing rapport in therapy is what Kelly termed the *credulous attitude* assumed by the therapist.[203] He meant by this that the therapist never discards information given by the client merely because it does not conform to what appear to be the facts of the case history. The perceptive clinician always accepts the client's "lies," looking for the predictions therein rather than for misperceptions *per se.* He wants to understand the client in order to further communication between them. When one attempts to communicate with a client, he is attempting to generate certain anticipations in the relationship which strengthen the rapport.[204]

When we realize that constructions entering into the relationship are likely to be nonverbal and then *preverbal* the question of "transference" arises. Transference brings into play all of those early dependency constructs which we spoke of as having been formulated in infancy and childhood. Since these are formulated around parental figures Kelly viewed transference in the following manner: "The psychoanalytic use of the term [transference] seems altogether too loose for our purposes.

We have therefore tightened up our use of the term to refer precisely to the tendency of any person to perceive another prejudicially as a replicate of a third person. In this sense, 'transference' is not necessarily pathological, nor is the prejudgment necessarily antipathetic."[205] The dependency construct which underwrites transference is what we must understand, for it is invariably preemptive and often constricted—focused on some "one" type of person in life. Kelly did not feel that the therapist's task was to make clients nondependent. The task was rather to encourage through reconstruction a greater dispersion of dependency.

Two forms of transference might arise in the relationship. The one we have referred to thus far—as a form of replay of role constructs from out of the past in terms of parental dependencies—Kelly termed *secondary transference*,[206] "secondary" because nothing in the therapist's personal make-up could determine the nature of these particular constructs. However, a *primary transference* may also emerge in the relationship, in which case the client construes the person of the therapist in a preemptive fashion—as someone of extreme importance to him, a hero figure or whatever.[207] The client may idealize the therapist and make the therapy hour a sort of high point of his day. Kelly felt that primary transference was a great hindrance to effective therapy, for it limited construction to the conference room, distorted reality, and was if anything a kind of smokescreen the client threw up in order to avoid true experimentation. He emphasized that the therapist had to begin acting in ways which might disconfirm a primary transference, once it appeared in the relationship.[208] If he begins to feed on the sense of worth and power this primary transference affords him in the relationship then Kelly would view this as signs of *countertransference*.[209]

The therapist who follows personal construct theory does not make himself completely open nor completely "personal" in psy-chotherapy—at least, not until therapy has gone on for some time. He realizes that the client is using him as a source of validation, and what he wants the client to do is begin seeking validation outside the therapy room, to discover on his own that *he* can find methods to validate life. Hence, at times the therapist must begin to play a role in opposition to the role which the client has written for him in the idealization of primary transference. Kelly even suggested that acting skills could be helpful to a prospective therapist.[210] Since cure did not issue from some emotive bond of "genuineness" anymore than it issued from esoteric "insights," Kelly did not feel that a therapist had to bring himself into the relationship personally—that is, in terms of his real and genuine personality. On the other hand, he *did* have to apply constantly a properly professional set of constructs, for: "The therapist who cannot adequately construe his client within a set of professional constructs runs the risk of transferring his own dependencies upon the client."[211]

Kelly felt that a therapist could see his client moving through not one or two phases of transference, but often the series could be seen continuing indefinitely and, to some extent, the number of transferences which might occur depended upon the therapist's attitude. Thus, Kelly liked to speak of *transference cycles*.[212] A transference cycle begins in the typical attribution of dependency constructions to the therapist, and then after a rise in dependency on the therapist, we note a gradual falling off to where the therapist is not the recipient of quite so much deferential concern, until at the close of the cycle the therapist may be playing a rather peripheral role in the current life process. So-called *resistance* in therapy is viewed as the downward swing of a transference cycle.[213] The therapist might, of course, encourage resistance in the client at any point in therapy. For example, by interpreting too early the therapist might threaten the client, bringing about a rapid constriction in the latter's loosening processes which might be viewed by the therapist as an act of resistance.[214]

Kelly would consider such "resistances" normal tightening reactions in the face of threat, and he would chalk them off to errors of therapeutic interpretation. However, the notion of a continuing resistance to the therapist as inevitably taking place was construed by Kelly as the growing freedom of the client, who is now extending his dependencies away from the therapist to other people in his life who are now seen as equally special.[215] The therapist *wants* the client to become resistive at some point, for it heralds his growing sense of confidence, his growing capacity to predict life events free of his therapist. This is, of course, occasionally threatening to the therapist since he is being countered by the client or since the client is not showing the deference he once did. Kelly felt that all *negative transference* amounted to was an unpleasant reaction experienced by the therapist rather than the client.[216]

When a transference cycle has settled and remained stable for some time the therapist considers termination of therapy. At the very mention of termination the client may revert to a more dependent pattern, wanting to rekindle a further transference cycle, but the therapist should have by this time assured himself that such is not necessary and thus carry out his plans for ending the sessions. The therapist never, on the other hand, breaks off therapy at the height of a transference cycle, leaving the client stranded without alternative sources of validation.

THERAPEUTIC TECHNIQUES

ENACTMENT

In the psychology of personal constructs approach to therapy the therapist often concretizes the client's views on life by engaging in a *role play* with him. Kelly defined role playing in the following terms: "The therapist may tentatively present a carefully calculated point of view in such a way that the client, through coming to understand it, may develop a basis for understanding other figures in his environment with whom he needs to acquire skill in playing interacting roles."[217]

If a client is having difficulty with a superior in the job sphere the therapist may enter into a spontaneous role play with the client. This usually begins very abruptly and without fanfare as when the therapist says something like: "When you say your boss 'picks' on you, what do you mean? He says 'Haven't you got that work finished yet?' or something to that effect? Well, when he talks that way what do you say? Answer me in your typical way, 'Haven't you got that work finished yet?'" Kelly did not want to alarm the client, to make him feel threatened because of the introduction of role play in the therapy situation. The client was gradually brought deeper into the technique as the role-play situations grew longer and more involved. Kelly would also insist that when the roles became anything more than simply a clarifying example of the sort just presented the participants (client and therapist) play *both* roles. That is, in one version the therapist would play the boss, and then in a second version he would take the role of the client. The reason for this role reversal was to permit the client to see the other side of this role encounter, thereby encouraging a loosening in his construction of the event.

The technical term for such role playing is *enactment*.[218] Kelly felt that clients would approach this activity with less threat if the therapist was himself not threatened by the procedure. Enactments are usually very brief, not lasting more than a few minutes in ordinary therapy. It is also important to avoid caricatures of people. If the therapist's portrayal of another person is inaccurate, the very corrections which the client makes will assist him in the reconstruction process the therapist is hoping to effect. Extensive role play is yet another Kellyian technique.

SELF-CHARACTERIZATION AND FIXED-ROLE THERAPY

Although a certain insight can be gleaned from enacting roles with the therapist within the consulting room, a far greater potential for reconstruction lies outside therapy, in the life sphere itself. Kelly believed that clients should approach their daily lives with a construct system which was not of their usual choosing —all with a sense of "let's pretend."[219] This could be accomplished by altering the role constructs on the basis of which the client customarily lived. The Rep Test can help here, but in addition Kelly relied upon what he termed a *self-characterization* sketch. After a period of time in therapy he might ask his client, "Harry Brown," to draw up a personal role sketch, as follows: "I want you to write a character sketch of Harry Brown, just as if he were the principal character in a play. Write it as it might be written by a friend who knew him very *intimately* and very *sympathetically*, perhaps better than anyone ever really could know him. Be sure to write it in the third person. For example, start out by saying, 'Harry Brown is. . . .' "[220]

The client will produce a document of from a few paragraphs to possibly several pages of self-description. The next step is for the therapist—usually with the help of other professional therapists—to write out a *fixed role* based upon what the client has said of himself, as well as what he might know of the client otherwise. The point is to discover the major themes in the client's life and then to write a role *in contrast to* these themes,[221] a role which will be radically different. The new role should remove impermeable constructions, consider available validation for the constructs, and include a framework for construing others to aid in establishing role relationships. Roles which include notions of financial wealth for a client

living in near poverty or other wildly unrealistic aspects are pointless. Finally, the client must always be aware that this is "make believe," and that no matter how he may find others responding to his contrived change in behavior, he has the protection of "experimental fantasy" to reassure him.

The point of fixed-role therapy is not to "suggest" subtly and covertly to the client how he ought to behave.[222] When a highly aggressive, interpersonally rigid person is handed a fixed role written around passivity and acceptance, the therapist is not writing unilateral prescriptions for change. The therapist realizes that what happens always depends on the client and how he comes to accommodate his reconstruction attempts with the accidental and unpredictable events which arise in carrying out the fixed role. This person may retain his aggression but add to it a more sensitive understanding of the passive individual's feelings. He can grasp the impact of his manner on others more clearly now for he has played the "other's part," a fact which is essential to understanding and healthy role relationships. The client has written the first script, the clinician the second; the final life plan remains to be worked out. Hence, Kelly defined this technique as follows: *Fixed-role therapy is a sheer creative process in which therapist and client conjoin their talents. Any attempt to make it a* repair *process rather than a* creative *process seems to result in some measure of failure."*[223] His hope is that a "fresh personality," of the client's own choosing will emerge.[224]

Fixed-role therapy is ordinarily conducted for an eight week period, though there is no hard and fast rule to follow here.[225] Clients are often fascinated by the impact their changed roles have upon others. This can be very upsetting to a spouse or other important figures in a person's life, of course. The content of therapy is likely to shift to such reactions, with supplemental role plays carried on during the regular consulting hour. There are marvelous opportunities here for making propositional and permeable constructions of the client's life processes. The first sign of progress is usually evidenced by the client's spontaneously noting that elements are falling into place; he sees now why "such and thus" seems to happen, or he expresses emotional empathy with someone whom before he considered to be unfathomable or frightening.[226] Sometimes the client "finds himself" in the fixed role and actually does take on the values it expresses. This is hardly surprising, since the role was concocted in terms of his own formulations. Occasionally roles need to be rewritten after a few weeks, and here again Kelly thought it advisable to have consultation with peers in the therapy profession.

CONTROLLED ELABORATION

We noted in the discussion of cure that a basic task of the therapist is elaboration of the complaint. However, the general strategy of *controlled elaboration* was important enough in Kelly's thought to be considered a major technique of therapy. The strategy here involves taking up large sections of a client's construction system to make them internally consistent and communicable so that they might be submitted to test. The C-P-C Cycle might enter here. The therapist would be using controlled elaboration if he said to the client: "Let us think through how this would be done and how it would turn out in the end."[227] Although elaboration could be backward in time, Kelly was constantly seeking to orient his client's thinking in a forward direction, to anticipate and predict the future, with clarification and a reorganization of the hierarchical structure of the construct system often the result.[228]

THE USE OF DREAMS

Dreams are viewed as "the most loosened construction that one can put into words,"[229] often prompted by preverbal constructions.[230] Since they are such vague and nebulous aspects of man's behavior Kelly thought it was senseless to think that dreams contained a "given" mean-

ing.[231] It is not unlikely that what Freud had called the "latent" content is actually the submerged pole of a construct. Kelly noted that dreams can sometimes make sense if we interpret the imagery in an oppositional sense.[232] This was analogical to slot movement in that a person is likely to try the other side of his conceptual street when in a dream or even a conscious reverie. This is the reason we are sometimes alarmed by what we spontaneously "think of," even while awake.

Kelly did not have a formal role for the dream, except in this sense of taking it as a sign of the possible beginnings of loosened thinking. Often the therapist gets his first hints of movement in a vivid dream reported by his client. Kelly did not routinely ask the client to report dreams, but he felt that if it were of sufficient impact on the client to be brought up spontaneously in therapy he would at least want to hear the dream story out. He was interested in the loosened construction and not the content of the dream *per se*. He was opposed to those approaches which saw dreams as reflecting *symbols*.[233] If a dream heralded some movement Kelly would interpret this to the client in light of their ongoing discussion as a form of controlled elaboration. For example, a female patient who was beginning to wrestle with her passive approach to life might begin dreaming that she was bound and gagged. This would be a loosening extension of her generally quiet and ineffective manner with others, and Kelly would so inform her.

PROCEDURAL DETAILS

Kelly sometimes found it necessary to get a client moving by threatening him or aggravating his anxiety.[234] As a therapist, he did not attack the client's construct structure completely, of course, but by moving the area of concern in therapy to topics which were questionably subsumed by the client he might get a lackadaisical person moving to find his lost predictability. In the usual practice, however, Kelly did not advocate moving a client into some area of discourse until he had a fundamental construct superstructure on which he could build his new experience.[235] Kelly advised the therapist to sharpen his thinking on each client by predicting what the client would do, from therapy hour to therapy hour.[236] In cases where the client is a child the therapist may find that he must work with the parents in order to help.[237]

Kelly advocated group therapy whenever a problem area which brought people together with a common dilemma might be arranged.[238] Role-play techniques were particularly well suited to group therapy. Occasionally he found it necessary to confront a client sharply, to challenge his construct system in no uncertain terms.[239] We have already mentioned the techniques of encapsulation and time binding. Kelly also spoke of *word binding*, by which he meant tying the client down to some specific term for each of his constructs.[240] This is an aspect of tightening, and it can prove useful in making some item impermeable, as when we wish to encapsulate a paranoid idea with something like: "Yes, that's probably another example of those 'strange happenings' which we spoke of earlier as things which we all experience but can't explain. Let's chalk it up to that and move on to this next point." We can dismiss the significance of the experience by binding it in the already discredited construct bound by the words "strange happenings." This cuts down rumination and turns the client's attention to the more propositional and permeable aspects of his construction system.

Kelly said he had never taken a fee from a client in over 30 years of therapeutic practice.[241] One can only speculate what this means regarding the kind of psychotherapy he was to formulate. It is important to note that Kelly's attitude toward fee taking was somewhat negative. He felt: "The psychologist because he operates within a psychological rather than an economic framework, cannot allow himself to be caught up in such a system of values. As a psychologist he is committed to a more comprehensive viewpoint with respect to human relations. If he makes his fee system the universal basis of his psychotherapeutic relations, he abdicates this more enlightened position at the outset. One cannot always insist upon a monetary exchange as the primary basis of his relations with his client and at the same time hope, as a therapist, to represent values which transcend crass materialism."[242]

Notes

1. Kelly, 1955a, p. 361. 2. Kelly, 1969, p. 49. 3. *Ibid.*, p. 48. 4. *Ibid.*, p. 51. 5. *Ibid.*, p. 52. 6. Kelly, 1955a, p. 363. 7. *Ibid.*, p. 15. 8. *Ibid.*, p. 43. 9. *Ibid.*, p. 11. 10. Kelly, 1955b, p. 613. 11. Kelly, 1955a, p. 15; 1969, pp. 299–300. 12. Kelly, 1955b, pp. 908, 943. 13. Kelly, 1969, p. 29. 14. Kelly, 1955a, p. 48. 15. Kelly, 1955b, p. 744. 16. Kelly, 1969, p. 21. 17. Kelly, 1955a, p. 127. 18. *Ibid.*, p. 75. 19. *Ibid.*, pp. 48–49. 20. *Ibid.*, p. 5. 21. Kelly, 1969, p. 62. 22. Kelly, 1955a, p. 453. 23. *Ibid.*, p. 50. 24. *Ibid.*, p. 76. 25. *Ibid.*, p. 304. 26. *Ibid.*, p. 62. 27. *Ibid.*, p. 61. 28. *Ibid.*, pp. 8–9. 29. Kelly, 1970, p. 40. 30. Kelly, 1955a, p. 72. 31. *Ibid.*, p. 109. 32. *Ibid.*, p. 120. 33. *Ibid.*, p. 128. 34. Kelly, 1969, p. 219. 35. Kelly, 1955a, pp. 16, 110. 36. *Ibid.*, p. 111. 37. *Ibid.*, p. 63. 38. *Ibid.*, p. 116. 39. *Ibid.*, p. 139. 40. *Ibid.*, p. 128. 41. *Ibid.*, p. 136. 42. *Ibid.*, p. 56. 43. *Ibid.*, p. 57. 44. *Ibid.*, p. 68. 45. *Ibid.*, p. 69. 46. *Ibid.*, p. 476. 47. Kelly, 1955b, p. 816. 48. *Ibid.*, p. 1031. 49. *Ibid.*, pp. 854, 1038. 50. Kelly, 1955a, p. 483. 51. Kelly, 1955b, p. 1065. 52. Kelly, 1955a, p. 80. 53. *Ibid.*, p. 229. 54. *Ibid.*, p. 153. 55. *Ibid.*, p. 155. 56. *Ibid.* 57. *Ibid.* 58. *Ibid.*, pp. 477–478. 59. *Ibid.*, p. 67. 60. *Ibid.*, p. 480. 61. *Ibid.*, p. 482. 62. *Ibid.*, p. 466. 63. Kelly, 1969, p. 92. 64. Kelly, 1955a, p. 114. 65. *Ibid.*, p. 133. 66. *Ibid.*, p. 100. 67. Kelly, 1969, p. 221. 68. Kelly, 1955a, p. 503. 69. Kelly, 1969, p. 178. 70. Kelly, 1955a, p. 99. 71. *Ibid.*, p. 503. 72. *Ibid.*, p. 35. 73. *Ibid.*, p. x. 74. *Ibid.*, p. 37. 75. *Ibid.*, p. 68. 76. Kelly, 1955b, p. 888. 77. Kelly, 1969, p. 68. 78. Kelly, 1955a, p. 78. 79. *Ibid.*, p. 83. 80. *Ibid.*, p. 169. 81. *Ibid.*, p. 21. 82. *Ibid.*, p. 78. 83. *Ibid.*, p. 130. 84. Kelly, 1969, p. 9. 85. Kelly, 1970, p. 36.

86. Kelly, 1955a, p. 515. 87. *Ibid.*, p. 516. 88. *Ibid.* 89. *Ibid.*, p. 62. 90. *Ibid.*, p. 528. 91. Kelly, 1955b, p. 1060. 92. Kelly, 1955a, p. 89. 93. Kelly, 1955b, p. 803. 94. Kelly, 1969, p. 54. 95. Kelly, 1955b, p. 1049. 96. *Ibid.*, pp. 643, 699. 97. Kelly, 1955a, p. 489. 98. Kelly, 1955b, p. 792. 99. *Ibid.*, p. 717. 100. Kelly, 1955a, p. 473. 101. Kelly, 1955b, p. 1032. 102. Kelly, 1955a, p. 14. 103. *Ibid.*, p. 484. 104. *Ibid.*, p. 508. 105. *Ibid.*, p. 510. 106. Kelly, 1955b, p. 881. 107. Kelly, 1955a, p. 502. 108. Kelly, 1969, p. 186. 109. Kelly, 1955a, p. 473. 110. Kelly, 1955b, p. 768. 111. *Ibid.* 112. *Ibid.*, p. 887. 113. *Ibid.*, pp. 668–669. 114. Kelly, 1955a, p. 297. 115. Kelly, 1969, p. 148. 116. Kelly, 1955b, p. 998. 117. *Ibid.*, p. 721. 118. Kelly, 1969, p. 223. 119. Kelly, 1955a, p. 94. 120. *Ibid.*, p. 95. 121. Kelly, 1969, p. 28. 122. Kelly, 1955b, p. 779. 123. Kelly, 1955a, p. 94. 124. *Ibid.*, p. 176. 125. Kelly, 1955b, p. 700. 126. *Ibid.*, p. 750. 127. *Ibid.*, p. 694. 128. *Ibid.*, p. 700. 129. Kelly, 1955a, p. 40. 130. *Ibid.*, p. 463. 131. Kelly, 1955b, p. 877. 132. See Kelly, 1955a, pp. 185, 319. 133. Kelly, 1955b, p. 831. 134. *Ibid.*, p. 835. 135. *Ibid.*, p. 781. 136. *Ibid.*, p. 780. 137. *Ibid.*, p. 889. 138. Ibid., p. 760. 139. *Ibid.*, p. 804. 140. *Ibid.*, p. 789. 141. *Ibid.*, p. 797. 142. Kelly, 1955a, p. 118. 143. Kelly, 1955b, p. 896. 144. *Ibid.* 145. Kelly, 1955a, p. 366. 146. Kelly, 1955b, p. 759. 147. *Ibid.*, p. 763. 148. Kelly, 1969, p. 19. 149. Kelly, 1955a, pp. 26–27, 193. 150. *Ibid.*, p. 203. 151. Kelly, 1955b, p. 829. 152. *Ibid.*, p. 836. 153. Kelly, 1955a, Chs. 5 and 6. 154. *Ibid.*, p. 219. 155. *Ibid.*, p. 302. 156. *Ibid.*, p. 456. 157. Kelly, 1955b, p. 895. 158. *Ibid.*, pp. 895–896. 159. *Ibid.*, p. 1081. 160. *Ibid.*, p. 872. 161. Kelly, 1955a, p. 498. 162. Kelly, 1955b, p. 918. 163. Kelly, 1970, p. 55. 164. Kelly, 1955b, p. 846. 165. *Ibid.*, p. 840. 166. *Ibid.*, p. 904. 167. *Ibid.*, p. 866. 168. *Ibid.* 169. *Ibid.*, p. 858. 170. Kelly, 1955a, p. 482; 1955b, p. 938. 171. Kelly, 1955b, p. 840. 172. *Ibid.*, p. 887. 173. Kelly, 1955a, p. 134. 174. Kelly, 1955a, p. 187; 1969, p. 185. 175. Kelly, 1955b, p. 937. 176. *Ibid.*, p. 683. 177. Kelly, 1969, p. 60. 178. Kelly, 1955b, p. 622. 179. Kelly, 1955a, p. 348. 180. Kelly, 1955b, p. 938. 181. *Ibid.*, p. 967. 182. *Ibid.*, p. 850. 183. *Ibid.*, p. 912. 184. *Ibid.*, p. 1071. 185. Kelly, 1955a, p. 201. 186. Kelly, 1955b, p. 673. 187. *Ibid.*, pp. 834–835. 188. *Ibid.*, p. 917. 189. *Ibid.*, p. 1102. 190. *Ibid.*, p. 833. 191. *Ibid.*, p. 649. 192. *Ibid.*, p. 575. 193. Kelly, 1955a, p. 417. 194. Kelly, 1955b, p. 1085. 195.

Kelly, 1969, pp. 82–83. 196. Kelly, 1955b, p. 890. 197. *Ibid.*, p. 1002. 198. Kelly, 1955a, pp. 96–97. 199. Kelly, 1955b, p. 587. 200. *Ibid.*, p. 1160. 201. *Ibid.*, p. 1099. 202. *Ibid.*, p. 1105. 203. Kelly, 1955a, p. 322. 204. Kelly, 1955b, p. 1089. 205. *Ibid.*, p. 1100. 206. *Ibid.*, p. 674. 207. *Ibid.*, p. 675. 208. *Ibid.*, pp. 684–685. 209. *Ibid.*, p. 620. 210. Kelly, 1955a, p. 399. 211. Kelly, 1955b, p. 671. 212. *Ibid.*, p. 681. 213. *Ibid.*, p. 1101. 214. *Ibid.*, p. 1053. 215. *Ibid.*, p. 1050. 216. *Ibid.*, p. 665. 217. Kelly, 1955a, p. 97. 218. Kelly, 1955b, p. 1025. 219. Kelly, 1955a, p. 369. 220. *Ibid.*, p. 323. 221. *Ibid.*, p. 376. 222. *Ibid.*, p. 369. 223. *Ibid.*, p. 380. 224. *Ibid.* 225. *Ibid.*, p. 391. 226. Kelly, 1955b, p. 1092. 227. *Ibid.*, p. 585. 228. *Ibid.*, p. 938. 229. *Ibid.*, p. 1037. 230. Kelly, 1955a, p. 465. 231. Kelly, 1955b, p. 1037. 232. Kelly, 1955a, p. 470. 233. Kelly, 1955b, p. 1041. 234. *Ibid.*, pp. 583, 844. 235. *Ibid.*, p. 917. 236. *Ibid.*, p. 635. 237. *Ibid.*, p. 625. 238. *Ibid.*, p. 1155. 239. *Ibid.*, p. 967. 240. *Ibid.*, p. 1074. 241. Kelly, 1969, p. 54. 242. Kelly, 1955b, p. 610.

12

Theory Construction in the Phenomenological Outlook

The Kantian Criticism and Phenomenological Psychology

At the outset of Chapter 9 we reviewed a series of theorists who could properly be described as issuing a Kantian polemic against the more Lockean psychology of their time. It was only a historical accident which made the gestaltists apply their Husserlian framework in the realm of sensation and perception, for this happened to be the preoccupation of psychology at the time. The so-called "cognitive" tradition in psychology invariably stirs images of "perceptual maps" or "sensory constancies" in the thinking of academic psychology, thanks to the heavy commitment which Wertheimer, Köhler, and Koffka made to this realm of scientific endeavor. Yet surely we must appreciate that the *fundamental* issue dividing gestalt phenomenologists from behaviorists was a Kantian vs. a Lockean image of man.

True to his gestalt tradition, Rogers spoke of the organized perceptual field. He defined perception in Kantian terms as "a construction from our past experience and a hypothesis or prognosis for the future."[1] A perception is thus *transactional*; it not only uses information from the past, but thanks to man's active intellect the perception "orders" this input in such a way that it represents a guess about what the future will hold.[2] Since this ordering is a *subjective* occurrence, with each person framing in his own perceptual (phenomenal) field, there seems little point in speaking of a "true" reality. As Rogers says: ". . . reality is basically the private world of individual perceptions, though for social purposes reality consists of those perceptions which have a high degree of commonality among various individuals."[3] Reality for Rogers—as well as most existentialists—is therefore a matter of *intersubjectivity*.

Although one might view Rogers' position here as idealistic, in fact he does not make a clear distinction between idealism and subjectivity. Though it is possible to take an objective-idealistic view of things, Rogers seems to feel that once one acknowledges subjectivity in knowledge he *cannot* hope to capture objectivity as well: "To put it more briefly, it appears to me that though there may be such a thing as objective truth, I can never know it; all I can know is that some statements appear to me subjectively to have the qualifications of objective truth."[4] Kelly takes a similar stand. This kind of argument rests on a confusion of idealism with subjectivity. Rogers' comments here essentially paraphrase Kant, who said that man could never know the noumena directly but had ever to deal with his phenomena. Yet this did not mean that phenomenal knowledge was not objective. We can be perfectly objective even about chimerical data. Rogers and many other phenomenologically inclined theorists have taken this Kantian insight to mean "all knowledge is ultimately subjective knowledge," surely an overstatement and a simplification of the theoretical issues involved. The position is "true" only in the sense that some *one* person must ultimately take in, record, receive, evaluate, or otherwise "grasp" information. But such singleness of reception does not mean that the information or knowledge received is therefore "subjective" in nature.

Yet Rogers would have it so. He argues that only through *empathy* can man know the meanings being conveyed by his fellows. This would require, in our terms, an objective communication. When we perceive without empathy we never grasp the subjective views of another: "To perceive solely from one's own subjective internal frame of reference without empathizing with the observed person or object, is to perceive from an external frame of reference."[5] Rogers clearly would say that taking an exclu-

sively extraspective perspective as a theorist would negate some of the most vital and sensitive aspects of observation. One loses the subjectivity of the individual in the objectivity of nonempathic extraspection. Most psychologists, laments Rogers, are "committed to seeing the individual solely as an object."[6] They conceptualize the person "over there," as a compendium of stimuli and responses, all arrayed in interlocking action patterns, literally an intricate "atomistic chain of events."[7] Though he does not use the precise term we can see the Lockean model in this description of psychology—a psychology that Rogers clearly rejects.

As he matured, Rogers became increasingly concerned with the philosophy being employed in the behavioral sciences. He recognized that modern psychology was basing its future on the outmoded Newtonian model of science.[8] This model is of course a Lockean one. One can also see the Kantian polemic in Rogerian attacks on modern education, which erroneously assumes that *knowledge is the accumulation of brick upon brick of content information.*"[9] This building-block analogue is based on the Lockean premise that meaning issues from below. Rogers, on the other hand, feels that education is something closer to a Kantian interest and personal commitment, leading to new conceptions "from above." He could never bring himself to accept what he called the "mug and jug" theory of education, which prompts the teacher to ask himself: "How can I make the mug hold still while I fill it from the jug with these facts which I regard as so valuable?"[10] Rogers wants the individual to decide what he wishes to learn and to set out doing it himself.

The existentialists would concur, for they view this as the formulation of "possibilities." The entire thrust of existentialism is to view man as existing uniquely, within his phenomenal experience which is constituted at least as much by his view of things as it is the result of how *he* is structured by experience.[11] Life is meaning, and meaning is endowed or disclosed as a *totality*; it is not constructed from smaller meanings and cannot be reduced from one level of significance to another and yet retain the *same* meaning for Dasein. We find the existentialists constantly exhorting against the reductive attempts of both Freud and the behavioristic scientists to seek "the" Lockean substrate (see Chapters 4 and 8).

Both Binswanger and Boss drew intellectual inspiration from Heidegger, who was in turn influenced by the thought of Kant. Heidegger employed the Kantian term "category" for what we have called the ontological a priori. However, he did not believe these categories literally *created* Dasein for the individual since, as Boss noted, this would imply a division between "category" and "experience," as if the former were *a priori* and the latter *a posteriori*.[12] This parallels the Kantian division of noumena and phenomena, although the expressed purpose of the Heideggerian existentialist is to keep Dasein a totality. *In point of fact*, phenomenological theories in the Husserlian tradition can be seen in precisely this way. It was Binswanger who took this clearly Kantian view in his psychology. He interpreted (Boss would feel he misinterpreted) Heidegger in this way. One finds Binswanger referring to the "Kantian-Copernican turn" or "switch" of existentialistic psychology.[13] His psychology searches for the a priori ontological formulations (world-designs) which in turn "cause" the nature of experience, rather than seeking the Lockean "effects" that have been put into the organism by past experience.

Without entirely rejecting the merits of this interpretation, Boss is concerned that emphasis on ontological factors might subdivide Dasein. Here is why the distinction between the Binswanger emphasis on meaning-endowing and the Boss emphasis on meaning-disclosing features of Dasein is significant. Existential analysis can lean in either direction—toward the self's conceptualization of its experience or, in turn, the experience's impact on the self "as it happens." Both views are clearly Kantian, con-

sidering the Dasein as it appears phenomenally to the individual. The question of *idealism* is suggested here in a somewhat different guise. Existentialism is ordinarily characterized as trending to the idealistic. Binswanger in particular relies on this idealistic bent in proposing that the a priori ontological structures (world-designs) literally create or make experience possible. Boss has called this a *subjectivistic revision* of Heidegger's philosophy,[14] thereby confounding "subjective" with "idealistic" usages in the style of Rogers. Boss contends that neither Heidegger's philosophy nor existentialism in general is an idealistic philosophy. The reality as well as the subjectivity of Dasein is revealed to man as a lumination. Sartre has developed an idealistic brand of existentialism more in line with Binswanger's outlook than is Heidegger.[15] It is not possible for us to decide which emphasis is "best" or the "real" existentialistic position, for, as we noted in Chapter 10, there is no single existential philosophy but only a collection of variations on common themes.

Kelly is much like Binswanger in basic outlook. One could not find a more purely Kantian formulation than the following: "Man looks at his world through transparent patterns or templets which he creates and then attempts to fit over the realities of which the world is composed."[16] The Kantian spectacles in this sense are not "categories" fixed by birth among all men, nor are they ontological a prioris. But the fundamental Kantian model is clearly in Kellyian thought. Kelly's image of man is as an animal with a premising intellect, one which frames in his experience either helpfully or detrimentally. Constructions can be in error, hence distort man's viewpoint.[17] But even so, meaning issues "from above." Kelly actually contrasts our two models in the following quote, emphasizing at the same time that his psychology is *not* Lockean: "This philosophical position we have called *constructive alternativism*, and its implications keep cropping up in the psychology of personal constructs. It can be contrasted with the prevalent epistemological assumption of *accumulative fragmentalism* [i.e., Lockeanism], which is that truth is collected piece by piece."[18]

Kelly specifically mentioned Locke in discussing how man comes to know anything—whether by collating sensory inputs or conceptualizing through active formulations—and he rejected the view that knowledge is transmitted through the senses.[19] Since human thought is constructive in nature, we must not fall into the trap of thinking that all man can do is "respond" to the sensory stimulus input of his environment.[20] Man's behavior is more a formulating hence stimulating experience than a response. He is controlled by inputs without self-directed action only when he construes his circumstances in this way.[21] But he need not be a "victim of his biography" (i.e., determined by past events in the sense of Skinnerian shaping) if he thinks of himself as acting upon sensation—as indeed he can—with a construing and reconstruing capacity to direct himself. We will return to this question when we consider Kelly's use of determinism.

Having argued that man's reality is his construed reality, the question arises: ". . . does not the psychology of personal constructs presume a form of idealism in its philosophical outlook?" Kelly clearly found this a difficult question; but he emphasized that his view was *not* idealistic.[22] Kelly seemed to believe that if a theory was idealistic it would be open to the charge that it was "unreal," an epiphenomenal collection of words which have nothing to say about significant events.[23] It was on essentially such grounds that Kelly spoke negatively of existentialism and other phenomenological positions.[24] He, like Rogers, confounded idealism with subjectivity. But, whereas Rogers extolls the virtues of subjective accounts and the need to empathize with others and come to know their subjective reality, Kelly was unalterably opposed to such "subjective" viewpoints.

For Kelly, a subjective construct would be an *unshared* construct, one that is difficult to communicate and hence not understandable to all who might be asked to deal with it.[25] Since Kelly wished to make his psychology into a science, he felt that phenomenological and existentialistic views were *tainted* by subjectivity of this sort.[26] For example, here is a quote from Henri F. Ellenberger, an advocate of existential psychoanalysis and a peer of Binswanger and Boss:

Whatever the method used for a phenomenological analysis, the aim of the investigation is the reconstruction of the inner world of experience of the subject. Each individual has his own way of experiencing temporality, spatiality, causality, materiality, but each of these coordinates must be understood in relation to the others and to the total inner "world."[27]

Such comments, acceptable to Rogers, disturbed Kelly. Kelly also was not entirely convinced of the value of objectivity in the style of a behaviorist. Objectivity was for Kelly a form of "realism" in the sense of reifying (making palpable) constructions. He was always ready to warn against the "pitfall of so-called objective thinking, the tendency to reify our constructs and treat them as if they were not constructs at all, but actually all the things that they were originally only intended to construe."[28] It is ever clearer that Kelly confounded subjective-objective and idealism-realism as dimensions of classifying theory:

Kelly doubtless wanted to embrace a *sophisticated*—as opposed to a *naive*—form of *realism* (which was Kant's predilection also). The reality of experience was "there," and the individual's constructions of this reality were also "there." What Kelly did as therapist was to change the relationship between these two "real realms." He argued that: ". . . since we insist that man can erect his own alternative approaches to reality, we are out of line with traditional realism, which insists that he is always the victim of his circumstances."[29] Yet, the data of such reconstructed alternatives are always "relatively concrete elements."[30] Hence, something clearly palpable exists independently of one's constructs. Would this not suggest that we have a basic reality after all? Kelly adds fuel to this suggestion, even as he shows his typical ambivalence over the entire question: "For my part, I am quite ready to assume—indeed it seems important to assume— that there is a reality out there, or, if you prefer, a truth deep inside all of us."[31]

The idealist might point out to Kelly that the "truth deep inside all of us" is that "we are all pretty much alike," hence an objective-idealism is possible without presuming an independent, palpable reality. Kelly continues wrestling with the problem of what is real and what ideal, finally suggesting that: ". . . *it is only in terms of his predictions* that man ever touches the real world about him."[32] But can one's predictions be in error? Kelly has already answered this, in the affirmative since constructions can be in error. If this is the case, was not the individual afflicted with erroneous predictions clearly living in an idealistic realm until such time as he failed to retain his predictive capacity and had to alter his construction system? Kelly must answer that a better "fit" between the (real) construction system and the (real) events of his experience is what has changed. But if that is so, does this not say *in principle* that *one* "best fit" is possible, between construction systems and life experiences? Kelly's answer here is clearly "yes," as when he notes in speaking of two constructions of present reality which may be in conflict: "I prefer the more cosmic view which supposes these two progressions [the conflicting constructions] may ultimately join hands, though that auspicious moment may prove to be an infinity of years away."[33] And with this admission Kelly classifies himself as basically realistic in outlook, even though the thrust of constructive alternativism is to infuse views of reality with a respect for the "point of view" being advanced in that typically Kantian way—"from above."

Reluctant Dialectical Formulations

The very fact that Rogers used a self-consistency model implies that he was not much drawn to the image of man as a being wrought with internal contradictions. The clearest use of a dialectic in client-centered theory emerges in the clinical method employed by its founder —at least in the two-person interview. Socrates' use of a dialectical questioning technique was *not* as an instrumental device to manipulate a student's thought in some preselected direction (see p. 6), which would have been *sophistry*. The essence of a Socratic dialogue is nondirectiveness. We see Rogers employing a similar approach to the client in the following, where a mother of a mentally retarded son is having difficulty accepting this fact. One can sense much doubt in her self-questioning, as she tells herself that the son is really more capable than he appears to be when he is given an intelligence test. The therapist picks up on this self-doubt:

Therapist: You think that perhaps he can't learn some of those things that you'd like to have him learn.
Mother: I don't believe that he *can't*. Now, I may be blind from a mother's point of view; understand, I may be blind, but I don't think so. I think that Isaac [son's name] has a little stubborn streak in him. If I could get to the bottom of that I think that he *could,* but I don't know.
Therapist: But you've tried for quite a few years to make him learn, haven't you?
Mother: Maybe I haven't tried hard enough.
Therapist: Maybe you've tried too hard.
Mother: I don't know, I don't know. I went to this baby specialist, and he asked me two questions, and then he said to me, "Well, take him home and let him be," and I said, "If there is something wrong with him, why don't you tell

me the truth?" (*Voice rising to a crescendo.*) I'd like to know the truth, then I would know exactly how to go about it and know that I've got to make up my mind, and I'll hire him out for a carpenter or cement mixer or something! Tell me the truth!
Therapist: (*Sympathetically.*) Don't you know the truth already?
Mother: (*Very quietly—voice very much changed.*) I don't want to know it. I don't want to believe it. I don't want to know it. (*Tears come to her eyes.*)[34]

Reading this exchange on paper might lead one to think that Rogers has subtly and covertly brought this woman around to face the truth—that her son *is* mentally retarded. He, as Socrates before him, has been interpreted in this fashion again and again. Yet, in a *truly* open interview there is little doubt but that a dialectical relationship emerges, with the client as capable of turning things around as is the therapist. When the therapist says to this mother "Maybe you've tried too hard" he has turned her earlier phrase into its opposite in tentative fashion, permitting her to look at the "other side" of what she is contending. Doubtless she could have done this for herself. We all mull things over in this fashion when we are working our way through a wretched life circumstance. But sometimes, due to great desire for a *given* alternative to be true, we fail to explore a dilemma quite this openly. At this time a dialectical exchange with someone else can prove very beneficial.

At this point of internal rumination, the looking of this side over against that side and so forth, we see the clearest manifestation of the Rogerian dialectic. One's emotions are rarely either/or; they do not follow the law of contradiction. One loves and also hates the same person, for example. The client who has suffered guilt over his negative feelings toward his parents may come to say: "I have thought I must feel only love for my parents, but I find that I experience both love and bitter resent-

ment. Perhaps I can be that person who freely experiences both love *and* resentment."[35] Self-consistency is thus achieved by way of a freedom to be "all sides" of what one is. It does not mean feeling only "one way" about things or people in the phenomenal world of experience.

We often find theorists like Rogers who favor dialectical formulations but dislike the conflict-laden image of man which results from a conception of this sort—one which states that man is "all things." And we can see in their resultant theoretical maneuvers an employment of our *one-in-many* thesis. This solution is especially popular in the gestalt-phenomenological camp, where emphasis is so definitely on totalities and wholes. A gestalt is truly that "one" which is also the "many" configured subparts. Hence, inner contradictions are not really contradictory when we take in the totality which is the "person." We see this resolution of opposites in Rogers' presentation of the fully functioning person: "He feels loving and tender and considerate and cooperative, as well as hostile or lustful or angry. He feels interest and zest and curiosity, as well as laziness or apathy. He feels courageous and venturesome, as well as fearful. His feelings, when he lives closely and acceptingly with their complexity, operate in a constructive harmony rather than sweeping him into some uncontrollably evil path."[36]

To live what Rogers sometimes called the "good life" is to invest oneself more fully in the experience of pain *and* pleasure, anger *and* love, or fear *and* courage.[37] The dialectic of the emotions thrusts the fully functioning person to be what he truly "is" in a given moment, only to move him along in the next moment in a process which is ever-changing and growing. Sometimes this process is more akin to a turmoil than a feeling of growth. The therapy client says: "I don't know who I am any more, but sometimes when I *feel* things I seem solid and real for a moment. I'm troubled by the contradictions I find in myself—I act one way and feel another—I think one thing and feel another. It is very disconcerting. It's also sometimes adventurous and exhilarating to be trying to discover who I am. Sometimes I catch myself feeling that perhaps the person I am is worth being, whatever that means."[38] It would be difficult to capture the turmoil and tempo of change reflected here in exclusively demonstrative terms. Speaking of himself as group facilitator Rogers says: "I wish to be as expressive of positive and loving feelings as of negative or frustrated or angry ones."[39]

Rogers also reasoned demonstratively in his many efforts to test his theory of man through experimental study. No personality theorist has been more committed to science than Carl Rogers. He wanted to capture both the introspective and the extraspective features of human behavior in his studies. He once phrased it as follows: "Therapy is the experience in which I can let myself go subjectively. Research is the experience in which I can stand off and try to view this rich subjective experience with objectivity, applying all the elegant methods of science to determine whether I have been deceiving myself."[40] We want to know the person's phenomenal field as best we can (empathically), but we also wish to extract certain empirically verifiable predictions about our ideas and then eventually freeze them into experimental research designs. Rogers thus effectively calls for a more—in our terms—dialectically framed image of man, validated when possible in a demonstrative scientific procedure.

Among the existentialists, Boss is considerably less taken by dialectical strategies than Binswanger. The problem with dialectical formulations is that they permit the theorist to twist Dasein into its opposite, in order to meet the theorist's rather than the client's awareness. As Boss put it, existential analysts do "not try to persuade patients that much of what they feel and mean is only a cloak for opposite wishes and tendencies."[41] If a client dreams of the death of a loved one and senses

great regret, the therapist has no right to turn this into an opposite "wish" that the loved one in question actually die.[42] Freudian concepts such as reaction-formation are merely further "reductive" attempts to make what something existentially "is" into something else. Boss views the contradictions of life as Rogers does; that is, to see the entire picture requires that opposites be subsumed under the totality of a "one" in the many: "Without concealment and darkness, man would not be the world-disclosing being that he is. Light and darkness, concealment and disclosure, belong together inseparably: Freud must have sensed this."[43]

The concept of a "transcendence," which is so central to many existentialistic positions, is also a dialectical formulation. Kant employed this term, and he did so in the context of a "transcendental dialectic" which he viewed man as capable of exercising, to turn back on himself and, riding above routine thought, examine his ways of thinking free of his customary biases. In the same way, the man who surveys his circumstances—his life situation—and sees what is called for given the facts as they are grasps his existential possibilities. Fact A defines not-A, hence the potential is there for changing A into not-A. Man immersed in a problem examines the nature of that problem and in defining it so implies, suggests, identifies the necessary steps to problem solution. Some people feel that the existentialists too often assume that the "possibilities" are always productive ones and that life is growing better and better (vitalism), whereas Dasein might be indicating a harmful direction. It might be self-destructive in the long run, even though over a period of time the individual or nation pursuing "possibilities" may sense considerable uplift and improvement. The sagacious dialectician would not be upset by this decidedly "unproductive" transcendence, feeling that mankind is neither advancing nor regressing except in terms of certain arbitrary criteria. But many existentialistic psychological views seem to imply that advancement is inevitable if man will only turn to the possibilities which Dasein reveals.

Of course, since Dasein is thrown we are always limited in the possibilities open to us. Binswanger speaks of the "dialectical movement" obtaining "between freedom and nonfreedom; nonfreedom and freedom."[44] Dialectical formulations can also be seen in Binswanger's treatment of *shame,* a human emotion which reveals to others precisely what the individual wishes to hide.[45] Clients who wrestle with the problems of life and hope for death often find themselves once again being thrust into a taste for life due to their contemplation of their possible death.[46] Dialectical formulations are typical of dreams, says Binswanger, such as a client who dreamt he was floating "above" the sky, which had a greenish hue, far below him.[47] The uncanny experiences of life are dialectical in tone, and Binswanger also sees in the defensiveness of the client a readiness to oppose himself to others in dialectical friend-enemy fashion.[48]

Although Kelly advocated demonstrative tactics in his Rep Test and emphasized science, the main outlines of constructive alternativism are clearly dialectical. Kelly properly appreciated that meanings are rarely unipolar and that man is incapable of saying merely "one thing" about anything: "Whatever one says about any event gathers its meaning from what contrasting things could otherwise have been said about it, as much as from the other events of which the same might have been said."[49] To say that one event will take place is also to say that various other possible events will *not* take place.[50] Man's meaningful understanding is therefore framed within dialectical, bipolar formulations. Kelly stated flatly that he was ascribing "a dichotomous quality to all human thinking."[51]

The law of contradiction was both accepted and rejected by Kelly in different contexts. He acknowledged the valid application of this law in ordering the hierarchy of a construct system. Hence, a minor (less abstract) structure may be inconsistent with the meaning of a more abstract, overriding major structure in the construct system. The major construct may thus be incapable of subsuming the minor, when in fact the minor should be considered in the major's range of convenience. For example, a person considering himself "friendly" is noticeably cool each time he must interact with a member of some race other than his own. Rather than alter his major construct of friendliness he conveniently "forgets" those instances where this surely does not apply.[52] This would be similar to the "logic-tight compartment" resolution of contradictions which is sometimes cited by the more demonstratively inclined theorists. To retain a demonstratively consistent approach to life people keep their Lockean units free of each other; they do not cement the "many" into a "one" as the gestaltist would have it but rather make tight compartments which do not permit inconsistency. Though Kelly seems to be leaning in this direction at this point, in another context he specifically rejected the necessity of resolving contradictions at every turn:

One of the most exciting aspects of constructive alternativism is its bearing upon the conduct of human inquiry. According to the canons of logic a statement, if meaningful, is either true or not true [law of contradiction]. Indeed, the logical positivists have reversed the logic and argued that the criterion for meaningfulness is whether or not a statement can be proved true or not true. This means, I take it, that we should not ask a question until we have answered it. But constructive alternativism suggests that the canon itself is not fruitful, or at least that it tends to stultify fruitful endeavor.[53]

This is the argument of a dialectician, a thinker who can see merit in contemplating error, who is not chagrined by inconsistency or contradiction. Kelly applied dialectical reasoning and concepts to his clinical method,[54] the understanding of dreams,[55] Hamlet's soliloquy,[56] and the resolutions of moral decisions.[57] Even so, Kelly like Freud was positively unfriendly to the dialectic as metaconstruct. Once, while speaking to Polish communists in Warsaw, Kelly was called upon to admit that his views basically supported dialectical materialism—the Marxian tenet on which communist economic theory rests.[58] Kelly took such attempts to categorize his views in a mood of humorous disdain. He once suggested that Freud had been influenced by Hegelian themes.[59] He would have preferred to stay clear of the term "dialectic" altogether, even though he seems to have appreciated the relevance of this metaconstruct to his outlook. Here is the clearest statement he recorded on the subject:

Stated in Hegelian terms this is to say no thesis is complete without its antithesis. Perhaps I should add that I am aware that this dialectical form goes back a good deal further than Hegel, perhaps as far as the pre-Socratic philosopher Anaximander. Be that as it may, I am not so much concerned with the classical logic of the dialectic as I am with its psychological appropriateness in describing how man characteristically functions.[60]

Kelly was correct about the historical antecedents of the dialectic. Dialectical strategies are as old as thought, as of course they should be if Kelly's thesis on the bipolarity of meaning is to be taken seriously. Kelly thus seems willing to accept—however reluctantly—the designation of a dialectician, if we only add that he is drawn to the psychology of the term rather than to some doctrinaire economic theory about how history is supposedly moved by a Hegelian-Marxian process of force and counterforce. Dialectical materialism was for Kelly another one of those deterministic formulations which locked man into his past, conceptually robbing him of his greatest capacity—to change his future as an individual in his own time and in terms of his unique circumstance. Kelly thus considered *dialectical materialism* "nonsense."[61]

Substance Construct Meanings

We know from Chapter 9 that the gestalt-phenomenological theorist does not wish to reduce behavioral explanations to some presumed underlying "physical" cause. Hence, substance constructs do not play a central role in their formal views. Wertheimer's principle of *isomorphism* (see Chapter 9, p. 406) asserted an identity between gestalt laws and the actual corporeal actions of the atomic structure of the central nervous system. As such, isomorphism would have to be viewed as in part a substance construct meaning. The gestaltists also took a *nativistic* position on such things as the capacity for humans to maintain size constancy in vision. The Kantian categories of understanding were translated by gestalt psychology into inborn frames of reference which each human being carries with him from birth. Whereas the Lockean behaviorists had man a ready-made machine at birth, prepared by nature to mediate inputs into outputs, the Kantian gestaltists conceived of man as a ready-made conceptualizer, prepared by nature to order his experience in certain ways so that he did not simply mediate but literally created aspects of that experience.

Rogers clearly feels that though he could define perception in terms of light rays falling upon certain nerve cells this characterization would not contain what he is out to represent: the *psychological* roots of behavior.[62] Hence, though he constantly refers to emotions or "gut feelings," Rogers does not employ substance construct meanings in the larger theory he espouses. Yet, in curious fashion, when Rogers invokes a naturalistic ethic to say that all men are—as common species types—moving toward a common value structure, he is pointing his theory toward a substance construct usage of sorts.[63] To say "I have seen the 'wisdom of the organism' exhibited at every level from cell to group"[64] is to suggest something about the *structure of matter* that has far-reaching consequences. One gets the distinct impression that man's grasp of experience is more rooted in the "stuff" of which he is constituted than we might have realized.

The problem with substance constructs for the existentialists is that the *meaning* of experience cannot be reduced to this level without great leaps of the imagination. Boss states the typical attitude: "For nobody has ever seen an apparatus of any kind which could perceive anything and understand it as this or that something which it is, much less an apparatus which could love or hate."[65] The meaning of Dasein is not to be found in the stuff of life. Freud erred when he continued in the natural science vein of explaining behavior through energic principles and physicalistic analogues.[66] Explanations of a substantial nature invariably force one's theory into dualisms, which in turn break up Dasein into something which it is not.[67] Indeed, history would suggest that when Dasein is divided into the palpable and the impalpable the latter conceptions—which are the psychological ones—suffer as if they were the lesser of two phenomena. The substance construct is given a status which phenomenal reality untainted by dualisms would *not* afford it. Hence, we might say that the existentialists caution against too easy a reliance upon the substance construct meaning.

And the same goes for Kelly, who was very critical of psychology for its readiness to view man as composed of static material elements, which in turn are "pushed along" by physically based motives.[68] Kelly felt this style of thought was uncritically transferred from physics, and he asked in rebuttal to this view: ". . . what a person does when he is not being motivated. Does he turn into some kind of inert substance? If not—and he won't—should we not follow up our observation with a basic assumption that any person is motivated, motivated for no other reason than that he is alive?"[69] This distinction between what is behavior and what is motivation plays an im-portant role in man's description, and we shall want to keep it in mind as we take up the *time factor* in considering our impetus and pattern metaconstructs.

Impetus Construct Meanings

In line with their rejection of substance construct meanings, the phenomenologists also dislike "reducing" their theories to impetus factors. This attitude crops up in the reluctance Rogers once had to organize a chapter of his for publication. When he was asked to present a detailed exposition of his theory for a publication being sponsored by the American Psychological Association, Rogers reports that the editorial policy asked that such theoretical accounts be written according to a *common* style. This style, which would presumably facilitate absorption of the views for the reader, required that theories be presented in terms of independent, intervening, and dependent variables. Rogers found that he could *not* meet this editorial policy in presenting client-centered theory. As he expressed it: "I regret that I find this terminology somehow uncongenial. I cannot justify my negative reaction very adequately, and perhaps it is an irrational one, for the logic behind these terms seems unassailable. But to me the terms seem static—they seem to deny the restless, dynamic, searching, changing aspects of scientific movement. . . . The terms also seem to me to smack too much of the laboratory, where one undertakes an experiment *de novo,* with everything under control, rather than of a science which is endeavoring to wrest from the phenomena of experience the inherent order which they contain."[70] Rogers went on to say that only after we first put a theory together must we then put our ideas into the "variables" approach in order to test it empirically.

Though he was unable to cite a theory construction reason for his inability to follow the editorial policy of that volume, Rogers found himself being crushed within the pincers of the *S-R bind.* The editorial decision to present theoretical formulations in a methodological way of considering events stacked the cards against a neo-gestaltist like Rogers. He accurately sensed that no matter what he said under the "independent variable" rubric it would be interpreted as an antecedent event, hence a stimulus factor. Similarly, the intervening variables would become mediational factors, and the dependent variables would become responses in the confused thinking of most psychologists who read such accounts gripped by the bias of an impetus construct meaning. The confusion here, of course, is between what is a theory and what is a method.

Furthermore, the phenomenologist knows that such methodological lingo is what sustains an image of man as 100 per cent determined, and he wants to think of man in other terms. So in contrasting his views with Skinner's, Rogers notes: "This [impetus] view is shared by many psychologists and others who feel, as does Dr. Skinner, that all the effective causes of behavior lie outside of the individual and that it is only through the external stimulus that behavior takes place."[71] Rogers, on the other hand, prefers to see man as free from such iron-clad constraints as might be construed once we assume that all dependent variables and independent variables are rigidly cemented by natural law: "I see this freedom of which I am speaking, then, as existing in a different *dimension* than the determined sequence of cause and effect [i.e., impetus construct meaning]. I regard it as a freedom which exists in the subjective person, a freedom which he courageously uses to live his potentialities."[72]

The existentialists specifically reject impetus construct meanings on two grounds. First, they argue that the logic of "antecedent-consequent" thinking splits Dasein along the time dimension and then emphasizes the antece-

dents or the "befores." The stimulus of S-R theory is what brings about events, and invariably this is the determining factor in the past. Yet, for anything meaningful to have relevance it must operate in the *present.*[73] Meanings framed introspectively by the unique individual are all-important to existentialistic thought, and one does not find such meanings in yesterday's time but in the ever active "now." Man must commit himself to the now or he will be lost. Both Freudians and behaviorists erred in searching for man's identity in his past.[74] If man were really functioning in this way he could not actualize his possibilities. He would be *thrown* by circumstance and thus—as Rogers notes—become a determined creature without options or alternatives.[75]

This brings us to the second major objection to an impetus construct meaning. Although Dasein is not to be split up into parts—including a time dimension split of past vs. present—the weight of *phenomenal* evidence is that existence is pitched toward the future. In the future man finds his meaningful possibilities taking root from present understandings. He knows his circumstances in the present but he achieves his possibilities in the henceforth. Boss has carried out an extensive analysis of the strategy of explanation used in natural science, noting that Aristotle's original fourfold theory of causation was gradually reduced so that: "Significantly, only the 'causa efficiens' has remained as causality in general."[76] We have traced this very point in the Introduction. The resulting impetus construct restriction which was employed by natural science necessitated that energies and drives had to be concocted in order to explain how behavior came about.[77] As with Kelly's speculations about motivation vs. behavioral learning, the existentialists question whether behavior should be viewed as being "pushed" over time.[78] What moves man is not pushes but the pull of a meaningful possibility in his future. As Boss sums it up: "We cannot repeat often enough that no amount whatever of 'blind' energies can ever produce and build a lucid human world consisting of meaning-disclosing relationship with what is encountered."[79]

Kelly's attack on the impetus construct meanings of psychology centered on energy conceptions and the S-R model *per se*. He could see no merit in postulating mental energies, as Freud and Jung had done. This style of theorizing worked well enough for physics, but it was a travesty when applied to man. Although he did not term it such, Kelly was very sensitive to the S-R bind which had settled on his discipline. He felt that the antecedent-consequent form of thought advocated by academic psychology was simply one of many possible schemes which could be employed to describe behavior.[80] It therefore irked him to find his scholarly peers behaving as if the S-R model were the *only* one acceptable to a science of psychology.

Kelly's writings are liberally dotted with attacks on the S-R psychology of his time. He liked to show how the S-R psychologist invariably held two theories of man: one applying to his subject and a second applying to his own behavior. Kelly thought this to be the height of scientific insincerity. A few courageous behaviorists, such as Skinner, were willing to cast themselves in the behavioral image. Yet: "Skinner's subjects are not the model of man; Skinner is."[81] If we disregard Skinner's characterization of his own behavior and look at the man, we find a completely different theory of behavior taking shape—one filled with planfulness, decision making, and self-growth. Life, said Kelly, is *anticipatory,* and there is no better example of this fact than the life pattern of B. F. Skinner.[82] There are antecedents and consequents to be noted over time, of course. In fact, the very notion of "time" demands some such recognition of a passage from now to then, sooner to later, before to after. Often such connecting links over time take place "just once." However, to argue that because an antecedent *precedes* its consequent therefore it *causes* its consequent was a step which Kelly did not feel justified to take: "We have intentionally avoided saying that the raw events of the past have themselves *caused* the individual to become the person that he is. Events may be the mile posts in reference to which the individual's progress is timed, yet it is the *construing* that weaves impersonal events into personal experience."[83]

Pattern Construct Meanings

We come now to the construct meaning which is clearly the most important theoretical descriptive terminology employed by the gestalt-phenomenological tradition. It assumes the importance in this tradition that the impetus construct meaning does in behaviorism. In fact, the best way to distinguish between theorists in these two traditions is to examine what they are trying to say in terms of these contrasting meanings. What distinguishes a gestalt-phenomenological-existential thinker from a learning-behavioral thinker is his reliance upon *time* as a principle of explanation. Figure 27 diagrams this distinction.

In Figure 27 we have two time lines: I and II. The first time line (I) symbolizes how a behaviorist or learning theorist is likely to think about behavior. Time moves ahead, from left to right in the figure. Relying now on the impetus construct meaning, it is natural for us to think in terms of antecedents and consequents *across* time. Whether we use the stimulus-response, stimulus-mediation-response, independent-dependent variable, or independent-intervening-dependent variable conceptualization everything falls into line as a "before" and "after" across time. We must answer the question "How is behavior caused?" by saying "It is brought about via changes taking place over time—stimulated, varied, impelled, or

Figure 27
The Role of Time in Stimulus-Response vs. Gestalt Psychology

I. TIME ESSENTIAL TO STIMULUS RESPONSE PSYCHOLOGY: IMPETUS CONSTRUCT MEANING

TIME:

ANTECEDENT TO CONSEQUENT TO ANTECEDENT TO CONSEQUENT . . .
STIMULUS TO RESPONSE TO STIMULUS TO RESPONSE . . .
STIMULUS TO MEDIATIONAL STIMULUS TO RESPONSE TO STIMULUS . . .
INDEPENDENT VARIABLE TO DEPENDENT VARIABLE TO INDEPENDENT VARIABLE . . .
INDEPENDENT VARIABLE TO INTERVENING VARIABLE TO DEPENDENT VARIABLE . . .
BEFORE TO AFTER TO BEFORE TO AFTER TO BEFORE ACROSS TIME . . .

II. TIME IRRELEVANT TO GESTALT-PHENOMENOLOGICAL PSYCHOLOGY: PATTERN CONSTRUCT MEANING

TIME:

CONTINUITY OF DYNAMIC CHANGES OVER TIME

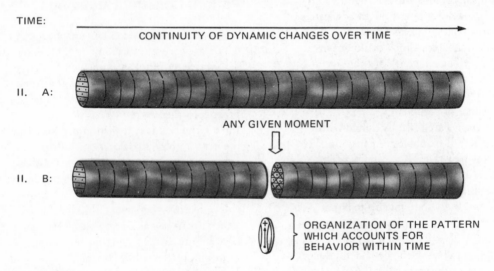

II. A:

ANY GIVEN MOMENT

II. B:

ORGANIZATION OF THE PATTERN
WHICH ACCOUNTS FOR
BEHAVIOR WITHIN TIME

something to that effect." Who can deny that man "behaves" in a time-bound universe? Isn't it therefore certain that his behavior is to be seen as issuing out of *past* influences?

Yet, if one views man as orienting himself toward goals, seeking positive valences (possibilities) off in a future not yet realized how can such a reliance on the past suffice? It cannot, and the story of gestalt-phenomenological psychology is one of trying to explain how behavior comes about with *time parcelled out of the account.*

To achieve this feat the theorists in this line of descent fell back upon a concept of "fields," organizations *within time* which altered values and brought about spatial change entirely on the basis of a *patterning* of relationships. The long, tubular figure in Figure 27 stretching across the time bar at IIA symbolizes this concept. One might think of this as a series of poker chips stacked up and then turned on end. Or, as a continuing "time sausage" of materials packed into a tubular skin with differing hues of meats and contrasting organizations of meat and fat throughout the entire length. We are trying to show here how a different "field" organization could result if we sliced our "total" sausage at some one point and then looked at the end to see the patterned totality at that particular "slice." If each poker chip had an organization of differentiated members painted on it, continuous throughout the stack but changing according to gestalt principles (closure, good continuation, and so forth; see Chapter 9, pp. 404–407) we would have the same dynamic organization of changing "field" relations over the length of the tubular figure. Our chips would be like independent slices of the time sausage—each patterned differently but also "one" with the total (one-and-many thesis).

Now, suppose at point IIB of Figure 27 we were to slice a piece of our sausage or poke one of our chips away from the stack, turning it face up to observe the pattern at *that* point in time. We have placed a gestalt organization on this sliver of time, with a positive valence suggested according to Lewin. It is the organization on *this* "phenomenal field" or "life space" which "causes" behavior in the gestalt-phenomenological tradition. Since the changing relations within the stacked poker chips of time (or the time sausage) follow gestalt principles and *not* S-R principles we cannot find gestalt in S-R. By noting that these gestalt changes within time also take place over time we do not require the gestaltist to alter his position. He does not need to add an "across time" explanation to his dynamic theory within time, any more than a mathematician needs to add time into his statistical proofs simply because it takes time to work out his solutions on the calculating machine. In the same way that a stack of IBM data cards already contains within it the F-test or the correlation coefficient that a subsequent run-through in a computer will print out for us to read, so too can we think of behavioral organizations as already plotted out before time enters in as a secondary factor.

This style of thought is truly a Kantian or Copernican twist on the Lockean formulations of classical learning theory. The reason we find gestalt-phenomenologists (as Kelly and the existentialists) so reluctant to speak of "motivation" is that the behaviorists have so firmly identified learning as something which takes place exclusively along a time dimension. Learning is change, change is time, hence learning *must* involve time. True, a motivational factor may enter in "secondarily" and get the organism moving across time by some drive or empirical law of effect; but only what is "observable" over time can be thought of as learning. For the gestaltist, the Kantian a priori is like the stack of data cards before they enter the computer. Time brings out the order already there. Hence, time catalogues change, but what "learning" is need not be tied to a time factor. Look for the patterns *within* time, argues the gestaltist. Since these patterns are often concerned with valences, judgments of what the individual wishes to do, accomplish, achieve, it would seem that so-called "motivational" factors *are* basic after all. Knowing the perceptual organization we know the behavior to follow without doubt. Behavior over time is thus secondary. Actually, the phenomenologists do *not* wish to order motivation as primary and behavior as secondary. They wish simply to drop the question of motivation altogether—at least this is true of Boss, Binswanger, and Kelly.

In Chapter 4 we distinguished between *sensory* and *logical* phenomenologists, pointing out that Jung falls into the latter designation whereas our classical gestaltists Wertheimer, Koffka, Köhler and Lewin fall into the former (p. 203). The sensory phenomenologist is making a Kantian criticism but more in the realm of how we *literally* see, hear, and orient ourselves by way of the native equipment we have to experience "reality." The early psychologists were much interested in "sensation and perception." Wundt and Helmholtz were drawn to this study because they believed, as Lockeans, that man learned only through inputs; hence, if we begin by studying the mechanisms (eyes, ears, tactile receptors, etc.) we should be able to learn much about what makes man function psychologically as he does. The gestaltists then came along to advance their Kantian argument. Even in the realm of sensation and perception, they said, we can show that man orders his inputs in a way that is simply not discernible in the environment. No completely extraspective theory can capture the individual's "phenomenal" field or life space, which is ever-changing according to gestalt principles. The logical phenomenologist, on the other hand, emphasizes the "conceptual" premises which man employs to frame-in his understanding. He is more in the realm of *logic* than in the realm of bodily sensory equipment. The "sliver of time" of Figure 27 is in this case more like the premise of a syllogism than a "field" of sensory perception (see Chapter 4, p. 223 and p. 203 for examples of this premising intellect in the theories of Freud and Jung).

Yet both the sensory and the logical phenomenologists would concur that behavior receives contributions from *other* than time factors. The major premise of a logician, when combined with the minor premise, leads to a conclusion "seemingly" over time. That is, the process of reasoning seems to take time. However, just as in the case of mathematical proofs or data cards being processed through computing machines, the processes of "mind" are *patterned* and the meanings so patterned are *within* rather than across time. The flow of thought from premise to conclusion receives *no* contribution from the passage of time. Given certain premises (which may be in error) and an ordered mind (logical errors are also possible) the conclusion of a premise is determined before time has a chance to operate. The reasoning sequence—whether inaccurate or accurate—gains nothing from the passage of time *qua* time. It is this *patterned sequence* of logical thought which accounts for the meanings (conclusions) arrived at. Jung was such

a theorist, viewing mind as receiving contributions from supraindividual patterns (archetypes) which acted as premises to force their meaningful import on the person in times of psychic disbalance.

Such patterned conceptions of intellect are difficult, if not impossible, to apply to lower organisms. Though Watson had erased the dividing line between man and brute, and even the gestaltists had attempted to apply their sensory phenomenology to lower animals, the logical phenomenologist finds it literally beyond his capacity as theorist to ascribe a meaning-processing intellect to lower animals. He might like to do so, but since animals do not reason symbolically (meaning expressing) and hence cannot reason to the "opposite" of a meaning, a dark curtain falls between man and brute in contradiction to what Watson claimed. However, in this case the distinction is not made out of a need to elevate man as "spiritual being" above the brute or some such. No elevation is intended. The logical phenomenologist simply finds it technically impossible to describe animal behavior in this timeless fashion. He thus can agree with the behaviorist's theories of how animals learn—over time, through repetitions and associative inputs which are passively collated and then via mediation rechurned into outputs. Tolman's theory fits nicely in this context (see Chapter 6, p. 286). But this is not exclusively the way a human intellect operates say the humanists, existentialists, and other logical phenomenologists.

Among the phenomenologists of the last three chapters, Rogers and Boss are clearly more on the side of sensory phenomenology than Binswanger and Kelly who would better be thought of as logical phenomenologists in the tradition of Jung. The theory of man as finding his truest nature spontaneously by way of his freely occurring emotions (Rogers) or disclosed to him in naive experience (Boss) supports a patterning in sensation. One need not speak of the predicating assumption or premise here. Man "is" such and thus, as can be immediately determined if experience is given free reign to operate through sensation and perception. Binswanger and Kelly, on the other hand, view the human being as logically framing-in his phenomenal world. Their theories are more "mentalistic" (intellectualized), and they place less emphasis on emotions *per se* than do their brethren. When Kelly reacted negatively to phenomenology he was in part reacting to what he took to be the subjectivity of *sensory* phenomenology. And when Boss criticized Heidegger, he was in part reacting to what he took to be the arbitrary (idealistic or subjective) intellectual distinctions of a *logical* phenomenology.

Rogers' reliance upon pattern construct meanings is pervasive. Not only his use of a phenomenal field concept but his notion of self-consistency is in this vein, for to be inconsistent is essentially to be malorganized, like a poorly-constructed puzzle.[84] And, as we know from Chapter 9, Rogers extended this pattern construct to a belief in the *natural* patternings of organic structures. Organic nature takes on patterns, and as an aspect of the "many" organisms in the "oneness" of nature a given man can best sense his truest values as human being. When he does otherwise man suffers *estrangement* from nature. This existentialistic theme of alienation is summarized by Rogers in the following:

This, as we see it, is the basic estrangement in man. He has not been true to himself, to his own natural organismic valuing of experience, but for the sake of preserving the positive regard of others has now come to falsify some of the values he experiences and to perceive them only in terms based upon their value to others.[85]

The existentialists would concur with Rogers here that a man must be what he "is," what his meaning-endowing Dasein makes possible for him to be. He cannot forsake this destiny without risking being *thrown* by the views of others. Kelly would also hold that man must be

permitted to array his behavior as he uniquely sees things. It is up to us as observers to understand what each man is about. If we force our constructs onto another we do him an injustice, literally as an act of hostility. Running through this style of theorizing and stemming particularly from the existentialistic philosophers is what might be termed a *purity criticism*. Rogers' favorite philosopher, Kierkegaard, pressed one of the more famous purity criticisms of modern times when he said that Hegel confused his concepts with reality.[86] In responding to this kind of criticism Hegel effectively defined the purity criticism for us when he noted that a philosopher might indeed bring "reason to bear on the object [of his discussion] from the outside and so to tamper with it."[87] This idea of pressing plausible notions onto an object or person, and thus tampering with or "alienating" the item under description from its true nature is the very heart of most existentialistic formulations.

We have already noted that the tie binding our phenomenological theorists together is their common call for introspective theory. We can now see that in making their purity criticisms the phenomenologists are cautioning against the extraspectionist's tendency to account for behavior as he sees fit—*not* as the subject sees fit (see Kelly's criticism). Rogers re-enacts Kierkegaard's historical role when he argues: "Because science has as its field the 'other,' the 'object,' it means that everything it touches is transformed into an object. . . . When science transforms people into objects . . . it has another effect. The end result of science is to lead toward manipulation."[88] First we convince people that they are objects to be scientifically adjusted to their environments—from which their controlling forces emanate—and then we control them albeit "scientifically." The purity criticism is aimed directly at such sequences of thought (see Chapter 8). But the purity criticism is also contained in Rogers' challenge to all men to be "that self which one truly is." And, as we have already noted, this capacity for self-fulfillment is not to be gained from reading books or studying the results of other people's lives but rather from letting oneself magnify his potentials as an aspect of the totality of nature.

Nature herself is a pattern, a gestalt, and the fully functioning person has the good sense to let his "organic wisdom" settle upon his life and prompt him in directions that he might not intellectually understand from the outset if he lets others do his thinking and talking for him. Therapy sets the nonnatural man free to be a new self; and this new self which emerges "is a pattern drawn from or perceived in experience, rather than a pattern imposed upon experience."[89] This freedom—the freedom of *self*-definition—is the most precious gift one man can give to another.[90]

In discussing the Kantian twist we were entering the topic of *meaning,* for what the existentialists refer to as Dasein is shot through with meaningful ties. The a priori ontological structure organizes one's world, it establishes a matrix of meaning within which understanding, significance, and variations therefrom can take place. A possibility is a meaningful projection, based upon present circumstances. Binswanger observes: "We speak . . . quite generally of a daseinsanalytic order; it is of a purely phenomenological nature. But such an order would not be ascertainable if the Dasein as such did not exhibit a definite ontological structure."[91] Does man, as an aspect of this daseinsanalytic order, structure his existence, or does he merely take the order which is "there" independent of his conceptualizing ability? Binswanger says the former, and Boss the latter. In either case, man is an animal steeped in the *necessity* of meaningful awareness. Without this patterned matrix of understanding he slips into the unpatterned ground of nothingness.

The existentialistic view of *determinism* can be seen taking root here from a pattern meaning. This development is similar to Kelly's, but it requires the addition of our intentional construct meaning to bring all of the theoretical factors to light. However, for now we will note that Binswanger's world-design construct "locks" man into a fixed pattern.[92] As an animal with a premising intelligence, man first accepts a "given" pattern and then is unable to change it without much difficulty (note the similarity here to Adler's theory, see Chapter 2). A person can change his world-design, of course, and in taking this up we would of necessity be moving into our intentional construct meaning section.

It is the complete reliance on pattern construct meanings which permits the existentialist to accept phenomenal evidence so completely. If the natural scientist, sitting off to one side, extraspectively observing one's highly personal (subjective) experiences finds it difficult to capture these in his arbitrary notions, who is to blame? If we find some experience so meaningful at this end and he calls this a "mentalistic" illusion, what are we to do? Should we deny our patterned (meaningful) experience or ask that he change his conceptions of science? The existentialists find it easy to accept delusional and hallucinatory experience as phenomenally "real" in precisely the same way. Boss has gone so far as to suggest that in a hallucinated sun image one of his clients may have had a meaning disclosed to him of "something more profound than the ordinary man is commonly privileged to become aware of."[93]

In line with the existentialistic stress on meaning, the Kellyian "construct" is a stylized pattern of relationships between elements in experience which predetermine how the individual will behave. Patterns recur, hence they can be construed. Even in his most heightened states of anxiety man never sinks into a complete chaos of unpatterned events.[94] To theorize is also to deal with patterns, and Kelly liked to point out that man is "an inveterate collector of paradigms."[95] The behaviorists may conceive of thought as action, as the motility of antecedents pushing consequents through a mediation of stored feedback mechanisms or whatever. But for Kelly, thinking was fundamentally a patterned activity. Theorizing was identical to thought. Theorizing and thinking may take place over time, amid the swirling of events, but the essential feature of both activities is that a pattern was construed and symbolized no matter how crudely and improperly.[96] Once fixed, a theory or construction system could lock a man into a determined sequence, much in the fashion of Adlerian and existentialistic theory.

Intentional Construct Meanings

Rogers has a heavy personal commitment to human teleology. He says: "There is then no such thing as random trial-and-error behavior, no such thing as delusion, except as the individual may apply these terms to his past behavior. In the present, behavior is always purposeful, and in response to reality as it is perceived."[97] Rogerian subjectivity is heavily colored by teleology, by the goal orientation of "subjective choice." Yet, unlike the classical analysts, Rogers does not assign purposiveness to the unconscious. The unconscious is the ground, and man's goals emerge as figures into awareness. The concept of subception is simply a preliminary dawning, a kind of imperfect discrimination which has portent but which is not clearly oriented toward a goal: "But when he is most fully man, when he is his complete organism, when awareness of experience, that peculiarly human attribute, is most fully operating, then he is to be trusted, then his behavior is constructive."[98] Whereas the psychoanalytical tradition has two (or more) identities dialectically vying for control of the psyche, Rogerian theory places no such confrontation of wills *within* man. Man is not naturally at odds with himself. Rogers thought this Freudian image of man was the result of a confusion of poor gestalt with conflicting wishes.

As gestalts emerge they may appear to be in opposition to one another, but given time as they emerge into good figures the consistency of a "one" combining "many" sides can be made clear.

As is true with all of these phenomenologists, concepts of freedom and determinism draw meaning from the pattern and intentional constructs rather than from the impetus construct meaning. What does it mean to Rogers when an individual's behavior can be predicted in a psychological experiment? Does this not prove that man *is* determined and not free after all? Though he made every effort to clarify this problem of "freedom vs. determination" Rogers ended with a position which does not come up to Kelly's sophisticated views and rests ultimately on an appeal to paradox which only the dialectician might appreciate:

I share this conviction that we must live openly with mystery, with the absurd. Let me put the whole theme of my discussion in the form of a contradiction.

A part of modern living is to face the paradox that, viewed from one perspective, man is a complex machine. We are every day moving toward a more precise understanding and a more precise control of this objective mechanism which we call man. On the other hand, in another significant dimension of his existence, man is subjectively free; his personal choice and responsibility account for the shape of his life; he is in fact the architect of himself. A truly crucial part of his existence is the discovery of his own meaningful commitment to life with all of his being.

If in response to this you say, "But these views *cannot* both be true," [note law of contradiction here] my answer is, "This is a deep paradox with which we must learn to live."[99]

This is not the only paradox we can find in Rogerian theory. In the natural ethic of client-centered theory there is also a kind of hard determinism which is quite at variance with the broader philosophy espoused. That is, if somehow nature's gestalt—into which man can slip and find his real being—contains a balanced adjustment for all, does this not imply that any *one* man's individuality is predetermined? Let us go back to the historical precedents of hard determinism, as presented in Chapter 4 (p. 222). Recall that it was the presumption that a "perfect" Deity had chosen to create a world which encouraged the theologians and then earliest scientists to presume that this world would at base be "perfect," hence *not* inconsistent, entirely predictable, and so forth.[100] In terms of our pattern and intentional construct meanings, it was the Divine (perfect) plan (pattern) "for the sake of which" (intention) the world was created that ensured 100 per cent predictability. Later, science dropped this Deity side of the theory but retained the rigid or "hard" determinism—now framed in impetus construct terms. But does not Rogers' return to the "natural gestalt" hark back to this identical style of theorizing, such as when he speaks of the wisdom of the organism and then what is tantamount to the "wisdom of the group"? Here is an excerpt from his writings demonstrating the latter point:

To me the group seems like an organism, having a sense of its own direction even though it could not define that direction intellectually. I am reminded of a medical motion picture which made a deep impression on me. It was a photomicrographic movie which showed the white blood corpuscles moving very randomly through the blood stream, until a disease bacterium appeared. Then, in a fashion which could only be described as purposeful, they moved toward it. When they approached it, they surrounded it and gradually engulfed and destroyed it, and then moved on about their business. In the same way, it seems to me, a group recognizes the unhealthy aspects of its process, focuses on these, clears them up or eliminates them, and moves on toward becoming a healthier group. This is my way of saying that I have seen the "wisdom of the organism" exhibited at every level from cell to group.[101]

The prospect that groups of people behave as groups of blood cells is remarkably un-Rogerian in that we take here an extraspective perspective and threaten to say that groups of people may somehow correct the pattern of individuals within a group. Rogers has faith in the process, of course, and would not believe that anything the "natural and spontaneous" group would do might subvert the "natural and spontaneous" processes of any of its members. Yet, by coming to his natural ethic and its natural teleology—really *vitalism*—Rogers is placing the responsibility on the individual member who sincerely *feels* the group is dead wrong on some issue. Rogers—as Adler before him—is almost naive in his trust of the group at this point. But then, he could well retort, who is at fault in this failure of trust? Is it the "others," or are *we* emotively corrupt and unable to trust our feelings which might dictate the way our behavior "naturally" trends?

Many scholars find this appeal to the naturalness of feelings dangerously anti-intellectual. It is possible to be right on some issue, for example, yet "feel" wretched about the necessity of standing against others whom one might well respect yet disagree with. What do we do in a situation like this? Trust to our emotions or stick to our intellectual guns? By emphasizing the necessity of coming down to his felt meanings, set within the patterns of nature, the wisdom of organic functioning, and so forth, Rogers clearly soft-pedals man's intellectual potentials. For example, in speaking of what it takes to be a therapist in his first book he opined: "The essential qualifications of the psychotherapist lie primarily . . . in the realm of attitudes, emotions, and insight, rather than in the realm of intellectual equipment."[102] Later he was to drop the reference to insight in what he considered was the course of cure: "Several years ago the theory of therapy seemed best phrased in terms of the development of verbalized insight. This type of formulation seems to us today to fall far short of explaining all the phenomena of therapy, and hence occupies a relatively small place in our current thinking."[103] Speaking of what constitutes change Rogers notes: "In order for behavior to change, a change in perception must be *experienced*. Intellectual knowledge cannot substitute for this."[104] Finally, speaking of himself: ". . . I have learned that my total organismic sensing of a situation is more trustworthy than my intellect. . . . I have found that when I have trusted some inner non-intellectual sensing, I have discovered wisdom in the move."[105]

In light of this "phenomenological trust," it is surprising that Rogers makes almost no *formal* effort to define the role of dreams in behavior. Dreaming might be seen as the purest "that for the sake of which" a phenomenal world is manifested; and surely myriad feeling tones are expressed and felt in the dream world. One can show in his writings that at times Rogers falls back on dream contents to explain the nature of a relationship between client and therapist—albeit in informal terms. For example, he once told of a very difficult female client of his, who was apparently driven to destroy Rogers as a person in spite of herself. To illustrate the client's plight Rogers tells his readers: "The situation is best summarized by one of her dreams in which a cat was clawing my guts out, but really did not wish to do so."[106] Despite this helpful reference to the dream world, Rogers' great commitment to awareness (consciousness) negated a major effort on his part to include more fantasy material in his formal theorizing.

We noted above in discussing impetus construct meanings that the existentialists place great emphasis on the pitch of Dasein toward the future. Man is a future-oriented animal, says Binswanger: "The primary phenomenon of the original and authentic temporality is the future, and the future in turn is the primary meaning of existentiality, of the designing of one's self 'for-one's-own-sake.' "[107] This is clearly an intentional construct meaning. Man not only designs himself for himself by pro-

jecting possibilities which are then attained, but he constantly evaluates his circumstance and senses guilt or anxiety when he is *not* meeting possibilities or not meeting *all* of the possibilities he knows are open to him. Our wrenching life decisions are *not* mere illusions, as the natural scientist would have us believe.[108] Man is blindly determined by his past only because natural science has no other way of accounting for his behavior. It is the world-design of natural science which is the *real* determiner of man's wooden, mechanical image. If we believe this erroneous conception and behave accordingly we have, in our own peculiarly human fashion, made ourselves over into "thrown"—that is "determined"—creatures and no more.

But man, thanks to his dialectical reasoning capacities, can reason from what "is" to what "is not" and thence to an "ought" or a "maybe" that impels him to fulfill this possible change in his circumstances. Hence, the behaviorists and the Freudians incorrectly ascribe today's neuroticisms to yesterday. As Boss puts it: ". . . in the strict sense of the term, no event in the life history of a person can ever be the 'cause' of neurotic symptoms. Personal experiences merely initiate inhibitions against fully carrying out all possible interpersonal and interworldly relationships."[109] Hence, what a man "is" today must be accepted as in part due to what *he has done* in relation to his circumstance. What ontological a priori did he accept and further? What possible meaning disclosing challenges which emerged as patterns in his life style did he accept, and which did he avoid? Here is where we find man: a teleological being fixed only by those patterned life's aspirations and challenges "for the sake of which" he *chooses* to *commit* himself to *action*.

It is the same with Kellyian constructs. They are paradigmatic patterns which allow the individual to predict, hence behave "for the sake of which," the meaning they endow to life.[110] Here is where the human being controls his own destiny. As we may recall from Chapter 11, Kelly defined control as an aspect of the relationship between a superordinate and a subordinate construct.[111] If our superordinate construct implies that "authority" must always "repress" then it follows that we shall always see repression in the exercise of authority. Those instances of a nonrepressive exercise of authority fall out of the range of convenience of the authority construct and hence will likely be forgotten by the individual. Furthermore, if a person having such a superordinate-subordinate construction of events one day accepts what is for him a position of authority it is a determined likelihood that he will be seen to behave in a repressive manner with his subordinates.

Man is under the control of his intentions, for "to control behavior, as to predict it successfully, is to put it into a sequence; in the case of control, to make it follow upon intent, and, in the case of prediction, to envision outcomes before they happen."[112] In thus placing man's controls and being-controlled as that which comes about based upon how one construes his reality Kelly frees man from a slavish dependency on "the facts." Of course, if we agree in principle—as Kelly does—that one day a uniform set of constructs will be forthcoming (or is at least possible), then man may find it less and less easy to depart from a common view of reality in the future. We might then wonder if the future holds more determinism for man than can now be had, due to the less perfect fit of constructs to today's reality? This is surely a point for the constructive alternativist to ponder. But at least for the indefinite future in the psychology of personal constructs, the matter of how determined one man becomes is tied to his construction of events rather than to events *per se*.

Kelly properly grasped that a determinism based upon intentional construct meanings resulted in a completely different form of behavioral control than did those determinisms based upon impetus construct meanings. His

treatment of determinism is thus in the classical tradition of Freud and Jung. Anticipating events permitted man to intend, and: "In specifying *ways of anticipating events* as the directive referent for human processes we cut ourselves free of the stimulus-response version of nineteenth century scientific determinism."[113] Man is best described as an animal seeking paradigms, hence, as fundamentally curious.[114] He never tires of putting questions to nature, but once he settles on an answer to his question man is probably more vulnerable to the weight of "tradition" and "fact" than he need be.[115] Because man can arrive at self-fulfilling prophecies and make events come out the way he wants them to he must be seen as the source of change, as the shaper of events, rather than as the passive receiver of environmental change in the Skinnerian sense.[116]

The Motives to Psychotherapy

THE SCHOLARLY MOTIVE

Rogers does not consider the therapeutic relationship as the proper locus for the testing of hypotheses about man. In therapy, we give ourselves over to our subjectivity. We allow the spontaneous patterns to emerge without feeling that they must fit some predetermined scientific scheme (purity criticism). Of course, this does not mean that science cannot relate to a problem of therapy. Speaking of the therapeutic experience, Rogers observes: ". . . I can abstract myself from the experience and look upon it as an observer, making myself and/or others the objects of that observation. . . . I make use of all the canons of science [in so abstracting myself]. A deeper understanding of therapy . . . may come from living it, or from observing it in accordance with the rules of science, or from the communication within the self between the two types of experience."[117] The main danger is confusing the extraspective *observation* of therapy with the introspective *happening* of therapy. Hence, though Rogers has done considerable work of a scholarly nature on the process and outcome of client-centered therapy, he has never considered the therapeutic relationship itself to be a proper methodology in the sense of Freudian psychoanalysis.[118]

Though the existentialists were critical of the Freudian "reductive" explanation, they were not as reluctant to think of therapy as a methodology as was Rogers. Binswanger notes that: ". . . in the mental diseases we face modifications of the fundamental or essential structure and of the structural links of being-in-the-world as transcendence. It is one of the tasks of psychiatry to investigate and establish these variations in a scientifically exact way."[119] Binswanger argued that there were really two types of scientific knowledge. The *discursive inductive* variety describes, explains, and controls "natural events," whereas the phenomenological empirical variety critically and methodically explores phenomenal contents in their own realm.[120] It is typical of natural science to separate experience, breaking it up into pieces rather than capturing it as a phenomenal totality. In doing so, the natural scientist fails to appreciate that phenomenological empirical knowledge is distorted when it is made to conform to discursive inductive principles. The greatest error of natural science is that of *"interpreting existence as natural history."*[121]

To force an inappropriate terminology onto Dasein in this fashion can only result in the poorest form of scientific knowledge, a distortion of cataclysmic proportions. The lower animal will never transcend his circumstances the way a human being can; hence of what merit is it to explain man in rat terms, as the behaviorists do?[122] Animals are "in" nature and can never remove themselves from the natural science description. Man is often above or beyond nature, bending nature to the willful aspirations of his transcending possibilities. We see in this line of argument a reflection of

the purity criticism, which plays such a central role in existential philosophy as well as in existential analysis. Here is an excellent example of this polemic, taken from Boss:

It is fortunate that Daseinsanalytic thinking does not require us to accept a ready-made conceptual framework and to learn it by heart. On the contrary, analysis of *Dasein* urges all those who deal with human beings to start seeing and thinking from the beginning, so that they can remain with what they immediately perceive and do not get lost in "scientific" abstractions, derivations, explanations, and calculations estranged from the immediate reality of the given phenomena. It is of paramount importance to realize from the start that *the fundamental difference which separates the natural science from the Daseinsanalytic of existential science of man is to be found right here.*[123]

Despite such worthy criticisms of the biases of natural science, the existentialists do not escape a heavy reliance on procedural evidence in their theory of knowledge.[124] To speak of a "phenomenal reality" is to speak of the plausible assumptions, biases, and so forth, which guide thought. A world-view or world-design is nestled into place by procedural evidence. The existentialists might argue that a belief in something like "procedural evidence" is itself a world-design and hence requires further study to see what a priori ontological structures presage this view of experience.

But all this serves to demonstrate is that ultimately the *basis* for deciding what is "the" beginning of thought, vision, awareness, and so on, must ever rest on *someone's* plausibility. And just how pure can anyone be in this regard? When one of his clients spoke of feeling ashamed every time he sensed a gentleness in his nature Boss retorted as follows: ". . . each time he confessed to his shame of these gentler feelings, we confined ourselves to asking him whether there was any need actually to feel so ashamed of them."[125] Is not Boss here (dialectically) challenging the phenomenal truth of the client's Dasein? He *does* feel shame. It is of course "possible" for him *not* to feel shame. By asking him questions in this fashion do we not raise possibilities for him to consider, turn over in his mind, and eventually embrace as an alternate phenomenal reality? Boss goes on to say that the stern attitude of this client had been taken over from his father, but: "It took weeks for him to realize, under the consistently kindly and reassuring guidance of the analyst, that the dislike of and contempt for feeling which dominated his parents' world was not universally valid."[126] Without in any way challenging the truth of this statement, we might ask of Boss just how far has he alienated this client from *his* subjective phenomenal reality?

This, of course, is the reason for science. It is flatly unacceptable to rest with plausibilities of this nature—even if they are subjectively true. Science speaks beyond the individual, true enough, but this in itself does not demand that its terminology be destructive of phenomenal truth. Variations on the common or "objective" themes of knowledge will always occur, and they must be appreciated as worthwhile items of knowledge. What science aims to do is decide what are the common factors and what are the variations. It should also appreciate that variations may become the common trend over time and vice versa. Scientific knowledge is alienated knowledge only when that openness which is an integral part of science has been closed. New data, new ideas: these are the essentials of a vital science. This may require adaptations in thought, the reintroduction of teleologies, and so on, as the existentialists themselves call for. But only if we assume from the outset that "the" subjective truth exists someplace—in a phenomenal Garden of Eden unique to each person's Dasein—can we presume that *all* objective knowledge must of necessity become alienated (purity criticism) from subjective description.

Kelly spent the major part of his career trying to bring clinical psychology as a profession into the realm of knowledge known as science. Clinical psychology was thus to be considered a basic science.[127] Kelly emphasized that so far as he was concerned: "I have very little interest in applied psychology . . . . for me the most exciting experimental situation is the therapy room."[128] If every man is a scientist and a theorist then it would follow that life—even a life fouled by neurosis—would lend itself to study in terms of how the human being enacting it perceived and predicted events.[129] It was therefore important for all therapists practicing in the name of the psychology of personal constructs to prepare themselves in the fundamentals of science: "It seems to me that the extensive training of therapists in theory and technique only, and failing to demonstrate scientific methodology as an actual interview-room procedure, is itself unethical."[130]

Kelly's scholarly motive was therefore rather prominent in his approach to the client, though it was not of paramount importance. Kelly believed with great conviction that in order to know man we must get intimately close to him, and this in turn is most possible in a therapeutic contact.[131] The greatest mistake one could make is to feel that the therapy room and the experimental room were based on mere analogy: "We believe there is a fundamental similarity. The discoveries one makes in therapy are similar to the discoveries one makes in the laboratory or in the field."[132]

In pressing his case so adamantly and colorfully, Kelly inspires admiration in those of us who would prefer a more humanistic psychology. Yet, in terms of theory construction factors, it seems clear that he, like the existentialists, confounds procedural with validating evidence. Kelly's definition of validation is as follows: "A person commits himself to anticipating a particular event. If it takes place, his anticipation is validated. If it fails to take place, his anticipation is invalidated. Validation represents the compatibility (subjectively construed) between one's prediction and the outcome he observes. Invalidation represents incompatibility (subjectively construed) between one's prediction and the outcome he observes."[133] This definition of validation would fit our "control and prediction" definition (see p. 16) if it were not for the fact that controls in the life situation are always less certain than controls in the laboratory, and it is always possible for man in the life situation to recall his past "predictions" in a way suitable to his present desires (intentions, hopes, purposes). Kelly has actually said it most succinctly himself, although he seems little concerned about this very likely outcome to validation in the life setting:

One's anticipation of a future incident is scarcely more than a plotted position within a system of personal constructs. If subsequent observations made within the same system seem to coincide with the forecasted plot, one may say, within the referents of his system, that his anticipation has been confirmed. Later, of course, he may devise other reference axes against which the occurrence may take on new meaning. Then he may wonder if what happened is what he would have anticipated if he had been using the new reference axes at the time he made his original forecast. But this is a question he can scarcely hope to answer. The best he can do is make another forecast, this time in terms of his augmented dimensional system.[134]

Since it is up to the individual to decide what his past predictions "really were" and since it is no great problem for man to shift the grounds on the basis of which he now evaluates, or to realign his constructs with the evidence now emerging, this process described by Kelly is surely fraught with potential sophistry and error. Procedural evidence plays a much greater—often exclusive—role in the validations of the life setting than it plays in the validations of the laboratory. Kelly has noted that "group expectancies operate as validators of personal constructs."[135] In the laboratory or any similarly well-designed experiment what

the group expects—even if this group is the "scientific community"—is of no consequence to the outcome of the hypothesis under test. Hence, it is of questionable value to draw such direct parallels as Kelly does between the laboratory and the consulting room.

THE ETHICAL MOTIVE

Rogers is above all an ethical thinker. He makes his strongest case and leaves us with the greatest impression when he speaks of the interpersonal phoniness, insincerity, and manipulation among people. The emphasis on values, the subjectivity of experience, and the absolute necessity for allowing people the freedom to be what they are all add up to an ethical philosophy of life, one which we might term the "ethics of existential freedom." This is why Rogers focuses so on the therapist rather than the client. He does not wish to tell people what they ought to be like in order to find the good life. He *does* wish to find out and then tell therapists what is required of them in order to facilitate the good life in their clients' experience. Invariably, this instruction in "how to" cure comes down to a series of ethical pronouncements: accept, show regard for others, be congruent, and so forth. Note that one cannot simply "affect" these prescriptions. These are not instrumentalities or "techniques" for the more efficient manipulation of a client. One either *is* this sort of person intrinsically or he *is not*.[136] And, if not, then one will never prove a helpful therapist. Recall from Chapter 9 that Rogerian ethics are intrinsic and not instrumental. In a sense, it is more true for client-centered therapy than any other approach that a therapist is either spontaneously "born"—he acquires the proper attitudes through living—or he is simply "not a therapist." Rogers cannot teach others to be accepting or congruent; he can simply show through studies that attitudes such as these promote constructive change in neurotic clients seeking to be cured of nagging conditions.

The well-publicized debate with Skinner in

1956 centered on this issue of intrinsic versus instrumental values.[137] Is not the therapist attitude merely one of the "intervening" factors (variables, when studied empirically) that come between the client and his environment? Or, do we not subtly and covertly influence another person to talk by "reinforcing" (operantly, or whatever) what he says by showing interest, nodding our head, or saying "mmm hmm"? Rogers staunchly denied these allegations, and his denial takes on particular relevance because if he *were to manipulate* a client in this fashion he would be *violating his intrinsic ethic of existential freedom*. Hence, we find him arguing as follows:

Here is the answer to those who question, "Isn't client-centered therapy *really* directive, because the counselor selects the elements he will respond to, and thus subtly guides the client toward certain areas and certain goals?" As indicated here, if the attitude of the therapist is to follow the client's lead, the client not only perceives this, but is quick to correct the counselor when he gets off the track, and comfortable in doing so."[138]

In short, Rogers argues that though the therapist might indeed influence his client through subtleties, by keeping the relationship open and without facade, he can make this control *two-way*. Not only the therapist but the client can contribute to the controls being exerted in the relationship. And, not only the client but the therapist will be affected by such controls. We might concretize this view by imagining one therapist proceeding in therapy on the following value basis: "It is right and good that I, as a psychotherapist, with certain knowledge and training, make decisions for others, and consciously, deliberately influence others' behavior in ways which my researches tell me are good ways, correct ways, or at the very least conventional ways of behaving." A behavior therapist might take such a view, and this would be a good example of an *instrumental* ethic. But another therapist, possibly a Rogerian, would proceed on the following value assumption: "It is right and good that I should try, as best I can, to refrain from making decisions for my client, even though I realize that social conventions, the force of my personality, and my personal values may very well exert a selective influence on him as we move along; in fact, when appropriate, I intend to bring up all of this and talk it over with him."[139]

Now, when critics ask "Doesn't the client-centered therapist have *goals* in mind, which he aims for?" a psychologist of this approach can freely admit to the goal of his intrinsic ethic for existential freedom. There are goals, and then there are goals! By striving to attain this form of open, free, self-enlarging relationship the client-centered therapist need not press *his* selective goals on the client anymore than the client presses goals onto him. There is no covert manipulation in this goal striving attempt of the therapist. One can speak of his controlling the client here only in the sense of a language of description or possibly as a theory of knowledge. But control as a method of social influence has been specifically negated in this intrinsic ethical pronouncement (see pp. 231–233 and p. 396).

The existentialists emphasize the ethical motive to therapy, as witnessed by their call for a commitment to life and a willingness to accept responsibility for one's behavior. Boss probably leans a bit more in this direction than does Binswanger, who probably leans more toward the scholarly motive. It is no accident that Kierkegaard studied for the ministry, was a very devout human being personally, and was primarily responsible for founding a philosophy of personal commitment and responsibility. These themes have remained with the existential thinkers, even those who have since lost a belief in a supreme being. Hence, like Adlerian psychology, existentialism has struck some readers as excessively moralistic.

The insight of existentialism is that man, being capable of formulating a "possibility" in light of what now exists, must of necessity be capable of *evaluating* which of the present circumstances needs improving in Dasein. He can sense immediately what is "best" or "right" or "proper" in awareness because that is his nature. And with this judgmental evaluation the "oughts" begin taking form in his Dasein: things ought to be improved, we ought not treat other people in this or that fashion, we ought to do our best, and so on. Here we have the nagging of conscience. Rather than enslaving man, the existentialist views the conscience as coaxing him to his greatest manifestations of humanity. Freud and the behaviorists would have man's ethical values being deflected into his identity after birth, by way of toilet training routines or the reinforcement schedules of parental figures, but mankind's morality is based on man's a priori capacity to judge: "Mankind's ethics becomes self-evident on the basis of such an understanding of man's essence. No so-called ethical values need be added *a posteriori*."[140]

Hence, the existentialistic cure of neurosis is heavily tinged with ethical considerations. The neurotic is a person who has given in to a narrowed existence, a "thrown" Dasein in which he is not affirming his possibilities. Therapists help him gain or regain his footing in life. Through the relationship he begins to exercise those "oughts" which have slipped by him in the past. He looks at this side and that side of his existence, reasons to the opposite of a maladaptive "given" of today and projects the counterbalancing pattern which can set things straight tomorrow. He begins to live again, to grow again, and to accept the succeeding beckoning goals of his forward-pitched Dasein, reaching into the future where life is constantly unfolding.

Kelly's commitment to ethical considerations was probably the least of his reasons for entering the consulting room. He was not deaf to the obvious role which guilt, feelings of sin —that is, loss of role factors—played in the etiology of mental illness. He once said of those who rely exclusively on "disease models"

of abnormality that they were avoiding: ". . . moral judgments where their patients are concerned. They end up making medical judgments instead!"[141] Nor did Kelly reject religious devotion and belief as one aspect of man's perfectly normal and healthy behavioral side.[142] What he did reject in religious observance was what he took to be its "magical" features.[143] Any person who accepts the challenges of life runs the risk of sinning, of falling out of role and suffering guilt as a consequence.[144] Kelly felt that too often a nonsinner was nothing more than a flaccid personality, an individual who lacks the personal courage to take risks and to engage in life aggressively.

The problem with moralistic theory is that it begins to pre-empt and to reify moral behavior, so that it eclipses the spontaneous side to life. Kelly had observed the chest-beating confessions of both Catholic and Communist peoples in his time, and he found that all such efforts were suppressive of individuality and basically counterproductive.[145] In the final analysis, the search for good and evil is a personal quest, not something to be dictated by doctrinaire, impermeable formulations. This is why it is so important to think of man as controlling rather than as controlled. Those who wish to manipulate behavior, no matter how scientifically, invariably fall into the impermeable trap of the moralists. They must choose *for* their subjects of control. Kelly said that it took him a long time to realize that his clients were just as capable of deciding for themselves as he was of deciding for them how they might conduct their lives.[146] He thought only a psychopathic person could take the behavioral manipulation thesis seriously.[147] Though he did not state it as such, this is surely an ethical question and just as relevant for Kelly as it was for Rogers and the existentialists.

THE CURATIVE MOTIVE

The motive to help others, to remove their self-distortions, and to help set them back on the spontaneous, natural track in life is surely quite prominent in Rogerian theory. However, there is a definite way in which this must be accomplished. Hence, strictly speaking, the Rogerian curative cannot be divorced from the ethical motivation we have already considered. The same goes for the existentialists. Once man has begun affirming his possibilities and meeting the "oughts" of existence he is on the way to health. For both Rogers and the existentialists the client achieves his own cure, and will continue to take over the reins of his life when he leaves therapy.

Kelly attaches more significance to the curative motive *per se* in his writings. He once said that he specifically invented his theory in order to assist psychotherapists.[148] We would conclude that this motive was probably on a par to the scholarly in his thinking about therapy. As he said of the client: "When a client comes to a psychologist for assistance he usually, though not always, believes there is a chance that he can be helped. The psychologist, in accepting him as a client, necessarily concurs in this hope."[149] We enter therapy to accomplish things for our clients.[150] Kelly was not even opposed to a symptomatic approach to therapy, feeling that often basic changes in personality will flow after we have alleviated the presenting symptom.[151] Unfortunately, the therapist sometimes becomes more interested in the details of *his* constructions than he is in the constructions of the client, leading to an ignoring of complaints and consequent misery for the client.[152] Kelly's feelings about such egocentric therapist practices speak for themselves. He greatly appreciates curative motives —possibly more than the scholarly at this point—when he observes that: ". . . the clinical psychologist is in the process of developing hypotheses as he goes along, and . . . the emphasis of the method is on formulating appropriate questions whose answers may have relevance to the client's difficulty, rather than on extracting definitive answers to irrelevant questions."[153]

Notes

1. Rogers, 1959, p. 198. **2.** *Ibid.* **3.** Rogers, 1951, p. 485. **4.** Rogers, 1959, p. 192. **5.** *Ibid.*, p. 211. **6.** Rogers, 1961, p. ix. **7.** Rogers, 1951, p. 487. **8.** Rogers and Hart, 1970, p. 505. **9.** Roger, 1969a, p. 178. **10.** Rogers, 1969b, p. 8. **11.** Boss, 1963, p. 69. **12.** *Ibid.*, p. 40. **13.** Binswanger, 1958, pp. 197, 319. **14.** Boss, 1963, p. 51. **15.** *Ibid.*, pp. 52, 84. **16.** Kelly, 1955a, pp. 8–9. **17.** *Ibid.*, p. 33. **18.** Kelly, 1970, p. 28. **19.** Kelly, 1969, p. 147. **20.** *Ibid.*, p. 71. **21.** Kelly, 1955b, p. 700. **22.** Kelly, 1955a, p. 6. **23.** *Ibid.*, p. 8. **24.** See Kelly, 1969, p. 24. **25.** Kelly, 1955a, p. 116. **26.** Kelly, 1969. **27.** Ellenberger, 1958, p. 116. **28.** Kelly, 1969, p. 85. **29.** Kelly, 1955a, p. 17. **30.** *Ibid.*, p. 174. **31.** Kelly, 1969, p. 210. **32.** *Ibid.*, p. 275. **33.** *Ibid.*, p. 25. **34.** Rogers, 1942, p. 176. **35.** Rogers, 1961, p. 104. **36.** *Ibid.*, p. 177. **37.** *Ibid.*, p. 195. **38.** Rogers, 1970a, p. 204. **39.** Rogers, 1970f, p. 14. **40.** Rogers, 1961, p. 14. **41.** Boss, 1963, p. 235. **42.** *Ibid.*, p. 264. **43.** *Ibid.*, p. 101. **44.** Binswanger, 1963, p. 313. **45.** Binswanger, 1958, p. 338. **46.** *Ibid.*, p. 294. **47.** Binswanger, 1963, p. 234. **48.** *Ibid.*, pp. 309, 323. **49.** Kelly, 1969, p. 11. **50.** Kelly, 1955a, p. 124. **51.** *Ibid.*, p. 109. **52.** *Ibid.*, p. 473. **53.** Kelly, 1970, p. 31. **54.** Kelly, 1955b, p. 857. **55.** Kelly, 1955a, p. 470. **56.** Kelly, 1955b, p. 1062. **57.** Kelly, 1969, p. 11. **58.** *Ibid.*, p. 216. **59.** Kelly, 1955a, p. 38. **60.** Kelly, 1969, p. 169. **61.** *Ibid.*, p. 90. **62.** Rogers, 1959, p. 199. **63.** Rogers, 1970c, p. 440. **64.** Rogers, 1970f, p. 2. **65.** Boss, 1963, pp. 79–80. **66.** *Ibid.*, p. 103. **67.** *Ibid.*, p. 212. **68.** Kelly, 1955a, p. 35. **69.** Kelly, 1969, p. 80. **70.** Rogers, 1959, p. 189. **71.** Rogers, 1969a, p. 260. **72.** *Ibid.*, p. 269. **73.** Binswanger, 1963, pp. 92–93. **74.** *Ibid.*, p. 43. **75.** *Ibid.*, p. 115. **76.** Boss, 1958, p. 50. **77.** *Ibid.*, p. 105. **78.** *Ibid.*, pp. 106, 243. **79.** *Ibid.*, p. 243. **80.** Kelly, 1969, p. 286. **81.** *Ibid.*, p. 136. **82.** *Ibid.*, p. 30. **83.** Kelly, 1955b, pp. 752–753. **84.** Rogers, 1951, pp. 507–513. **85.** Rogers, 1959, p. 226. **86.** Rychlak, 1968, p. 390. **87.** Hegel, 1952, pp. 19–20. **88.** Rogers, 1961, pp. 212–213. **89.** Rogers, 1951, p. 194. **90.** Rogers, 1961, p. 178. **91.** Binswanger, 1963, p. 250. **92.** *Ibid.*, p. 215. **93.** Boss, 1963, p. 225. **94.** Kelly, 1955b, p. 896. **95.** Kelly, 1969, p. 47. **96.** Kelly, 1955a, p. 22. **97.** Rogers, 1951, p. 494. **98.** Rogers, 1961, p. 105. **99.** Rogers, 1969a, p. 275. **100.** Rychlak, 1968, p. 231.

101. Rogers, 1970f, p. 2. **102.** Rogers, 1942, p. 256. **103.** Rogers, 1951, p. 15. **104.** *Ibid.,* p. 222. **105.** Rogers, 1961, p. 22. **106.** Rogers, 1967, p. 367. **107.** Binswanger, 1958, p. 302. **108.** Boss, 1958, p. 105. **109.** Boss, 1963, p. 248. **110.** Kelly, 1955a, p. 14. **111.** Kelly, 1955b, p. 926. **112.** Kelly, 1969, p. 40. **113.** Kelly, 1970, p. 37. **114.** Kelly, 1955b, p. 944. **115.** Kelly, 1969, p. 12. **116.** Kelly, 1955a, p. 19. **117.** Rogers, 1961, p. 278. **118.** Rogers and Dymond, 1954; Rogers, Gendlin, Kiesler, and Truax, 1967. **119.** Binswanger, 1958, p. 194. **120.** *Ibid.,* p. 192. **121.** Binswanger, 1963, p. 175. **122.** Binswanger, 1958, pp. 197–198. **123.** Boss, 1963, pp. 29–30. **124.** *Ibid.,* p. 201. **125.** *Ibid.,* p. 198. **126.** *Ibid.* **127.** Kelly, 1955a, p. 400. **128.** Kelly, 1969, p. 154. **129.** Kelly, 1955b, p. 605. **130.** Kelly, 1969, p. 53. **131.** *Ibid.,* p. 215. **132.** Kelly, 1955b, p. 1123. **133.** Kelly, 1955a, p. 158. **134.** Kelly, 1969, p. 32. **135.** Kelly, 1955a, p. 176. **136.** Rogers, 1951, pp. 21–22. **137.** Rogers and Skinner, 1956. **138.** Rogers, 1951, p. 113. **139.** Rychlak, 1968, pp. 143–144. **140.** Boss, 1963, p. 271. **141.** Kelly, 1969, p. 171. **142.** Kelly, 1955a, p. 127. **143.** Kelly, 1955b, p. 1076. **144.** Kelly, 1969, p. 11. **145.** *Ibid.,* p. 187. **146.** *Ibid.,* p. 18. **147.** Kelly, 1970, p. 55. **148.** Kelly, 1955a, p. 12. **149.** Kelly, 1955b, p. 611. **150.** Kelly, 1969, p. 221. **151.** Kelly, 1955b, pp. 995–996. **152.** *Ibid.,* p. 831. **153.** Kelly, 1955a, pp. 192–193.

REFERENCES

Adler, A. (1930) *The education of children.* London: George Allen & Unwin, Ltd. Quotations by permission of Allen & Unwin, Ltd. Used by permission of Dr. Kurt A. Adler. From *The education of children* by Alfred Adler, © 1930, 1958, by Dr. Kurt A. Adler.

Adler, A. (1954) *Understanding human nature.* New York: Fawcett World Library.

Adler, A. (1958) *What life should mean to you.* New York: Capricorn Books. Used by permission of Dr. Kurt A. Adler. From *What life should mean to you* by Alfred Adler. Copyright © 1931, 1958 by Dr. Kurt A. Adler.

Adler, A. (1963) *The Problem Child.* New York: Capricorn Books.

Adler, A. (1964a) *Problems of neurosis.* New York: Harper & Row. Quotations by permission of the publisher.

Adler, A. (1964b) *Social interest: A challenge to mankind.* New York: Capricorn Books. Used by permission of Dr. Kurt A. Adler. From *Social interest: A challenge to mankind* by Alfred Adler.

Adler, A. (1968) *The practice and theory of individual psychology.* Totowa, N.J.: Littlefield, Adams, & Co. and New York: Humanities Press, Inc. Quotations by permission of the publishers.

Alexander, F. G., and Selesnick, S. T. (1966) *The history of psychiatry: An evaluation of psychiatric thought and practice from prehistoric times to the present.* New York: Harper & Row.

Allport, G. W. (1946) Personalistic psychology as a science: A reply. *Psychological Review,* **53,** 132–135.

Ansbacher, H. L. (1959) The significance of the socio-economic status of the patients of Freud and of Adler. *American Journal of Psychotherapy,* **13,** 376–382.

Ansbacher, H. L., and Ansbacher, R. R. (Eds.). (1956) *The individual psychology of Alfred Adler.* New York: Basic Books, Inc. Quotations by permission of Basic Books, Inc. Used by permission of Dr. Kurt A. Adler. From *The individual psychology of Alfred Adler* by H. L. and R. R. Ansbacher, © 1964, 1970 by Heinz L. and Rowena R. Ansbacher.

Ansbacher, H. L., and Ansbacher, R. R. (Eds.). (1964) *Superiority and social interest.* Evanston, Ill.: Northwestern University Press. Quotations by permission of the publisher.

Aristotle. (1952a) *Physics.* In R. M. Hutchins (Ed.), *Great books of the western world* (Vol. 8). Chicago: Encyclopaedia Britannica, pp. 257–355.

Aristotle. (1952b) *Topics.* In R. M. Hutchins (Ed.), *Great books of the western world* (Vol. 8). Chicago: Encyclopaedia Britannica, pp. 143–223.

Atthowe, J. M., and Krasner, L. (1968) Preliminary report on the application of contingent reinforcement procedures (token economy) on a "chronic" psychiatric ward. *Journal of Abnormal Psychology,* **73,** 37–43.

Bacon, F. (1952) *Advancement of learning.* In R. M. Hutchins (Ed.), *Great books of the western world* (Vol. 30). Chicago: Encyclopaedia Britannica, pp. 1–101.

Barker, J. C., and Miller, M. B. (1968) Recent developments and some future trends in the application of aversion therapy. Unpublished Manuscript.

Becker, H., and Barnes, H. E. (1952) *Social thought from lore to science* (2 vols.). Washington, D.C.: The Harren Press.

Bennet, E. A. (1961) *C. G. Jung.* New York: E. P. Dutton & Co., Inc.

Bercel, N. A. (1960) A study of the influence of schizophrenic serum on the behavior of the spider. Zilla-x-notata. In D. D. Jackson (Ed.), *The etiology of schizophrenia.* New York: Basic Books, Inc., pp. 159–174.

Binswanger, L. (1957) *Sigmund Freud: Reminiscences of a friendship.* New York: Grune & Stratton.

Binswanger, L. (1958) The existential analysis school of thought; Insanity as life-historical phenomenon and as mental disease: The case of Ilse; The case of Ellen West: An anthropological-clinical study. In R. May, E. Angel, and H. F. Ellenberger (Eds.), *Existence: A new dimension in psychiatry and psychology*. New York: Basic Books, Inc., Chs. VII, VIII, and IX.

Binswanger, L. (1963) *Being-in-the-world* (translated and with a critical introduction by J. Needleman). New York: Basic Books, Inc. Quotations by permission of the publisher.

Blackham, H. J. (1959) *Six existentialist thinkers*. New York: Harper & Row.

Boring, E. G. (1946) Mind and mechanism. *American Journal of Psychology, 59,* 179–192.

Boss, M. (1958) *The analysis of dreams*. New York: Philosophical Library.

Boss, M. (1963) *Psychoanalysis and daseinsanalysis*. New York: Basic Books, Inc. Quotations by permission of the publisher.

Bottome, P. (1957) *Alfred Adler: A portrait from life*. New York: The Vanguard Press.

Bridgman, P. W. (1927) *The logic of modern physics*. New York: The Macmillan Co.

Brown, J. F. (1936) *Psychology and the social order*. New York: McGraw-Hill Book Co.

Cassirer, E. (1944) *An essay on man*. Garden City, N.Y.: Doubleday & Co.

Combe, G. (1851) *Lectures on phrenology*. New York: Fowler and Wells.

Cronbach, L. J. (1957) The two disciplines of scientific psychology. *American Psychologist, 12,* 671–684.

Darwin, C. R. (1952a) *The descent of man*. In R. M. Hutchins (Ed.), *Great books of the western world* (Vol. 49). Chicago: Encyclopaedia Britannica, pp. 251–659.

Darwin, C. R. (1952b) *The origin of species*. In R. M. Hutchins (Ed.), *Great books of the western world* (Vol. 49). Chicago: Encyclopaedia Britannica, pp. 1–250.

Dollard, J. (1937) *Caste and class in a southern town*. New Haven, Conn.: Yale University Press.

Dollard, J. (1942) *Victory over fear*. New York: Reynal & Hitchcock.

Dollard, J. (1943) *Fear in battle*. New Haven, Conn.: Yale University Press.

Dollard, J., and Auld, F. (1959) *Scoring human motives*. New Haven, Conn.: Yale University Press.

Dollard, J., Auld, F., and White, A. (1953) *Steps in psychotherapy*. New York: The Macmillan Co.

Dollard, J., Doob, L. W., Miller, N. E., Mowrer, O. H., and Sears, R. R. (1939) *Frustration and aggression*. New Haven, Conn.: Yale University Press.

Dollard, J., and Miller, N. E. (1950) *Personality and psychotherapy: An analysis in terms of learning, thinking, and culture*. New York: McGraw-Hill Book Co. Copyright, 1950, by the McGraw-Hill Book Co., Inc., Quotations by permission of the publisher.

Dulany, D. E. (1961) Hypotheses and habits in verbal "operant conditioning." *Journal of Abnormal and Social Psychology, 63,* 251–263.

Dunham, A. M., Jr. (1938) The concept of tension in philosophy. *Psychiatry, 1,* 79–120.

Ellenberger, H. F. (1958) A clinical introduction to psychiatric phenomenology and existential analysis. In R. May, E. Angel, and H. F. Ellenberger (Eds.), *Existence: A new dimension in psychiatry and psychology*. New York: Basic Books, Inc., pp. 92–124.

Evans, R. I. (1964) *Conversations with Carl Jung*. Princeton, N.J.: D. Van Nostrand Co., Inc.

Evans, R. I. (1968) *B. F. Skinner: The man and his ideas*. New York: E. P. Dutton & Co.

Eysenck, H. J. (1952) The effects of psychotherapy: An evaluation. *Journal of Consulting Psychology, 16,* 319–324.

Feldman, M. P., and MacCulloch, M. J. (1967) Aversion therapy in the management of homosexuals. *British Journal of Medical Psychology, 1,* 560–594.

Ferster, C. B., and Skinner, B. F. (1957) *Schedules of reinforcement*. New York: Appleton-Century-Crofts.

Freud, S. (1954) *The origins of psycho-analysis: The letters to Wilhelm Fliess: Drafts and notes: 1887–1902*. New York: Basic Books, Inc.

Freud, S. (1960) *Letters of Sigmund Freud* (edited by E. L. Freud). New York: Basic Books, Inc.

Freud, S. *The standard edition of the complete psychological works of Sigmund Freud*. London: Hogarth Press:
Vol. I. *Pre–psycho-analytic publications and*

unpublished drafts, 1966. Acknowledgment is made to Sigmund Freud Copyrights, Ltd., The Institute of Psycho-Analysis and the Hogarth Press for permission to quote from Vol. I of the Standard Edition of the Complete Psychological Works of Sigmund Freud, revised and edited by James Strachey.

Vol. II. *Studies on hysteria*, 1955 (coauthor J. Breuer).

Vol. III. *Early psycho-analytic publications*, 1962.

Vol. IV. *The interpretation of dreams* (First part), 1953.

Vol. V. *The interpretation of dreams* (Second part), 1953.

Vol. VI. *The psychopathology of everyday life*, 1960.

Vol. VII. *A case of hysteria and three essays on sexuality*, 1953.

Vol. VIII. *Jokes and their relation to the unconscious*, 1960.

Vol. IX. *Jensen's "Gradiva" and other works*, 1959.

Vol. X. *Two case histories: "Little Hans" and the "rat man,"* 1955.

Vol. XI. *Five lectures on psycho-analysis and Leonardo da Vinci*, 1957.

Vol. XII. *The case of Schreber and papers on technique*, 1958.

Vol. XIII. *Totem and taboo and other works*, 1955.

Vol. XIV. *On the history of the psycho-analytic movement, papers on metapsychology, and other works*, 1957. Acknowledgment is made to Sigmund Freud Copyrights, Ltd., The Institute of Psycho-Analysis and the Hogarth Press for permission to quote from Vol. XIV of the Standard Edition of the Complete Psychological Works of Sigmund Freud, revised and edited by James Strachey, and to Basic Books, Inc., Publishers, New York, 1957.

Vol. XV. *Introductory lectures on psycho-analysis* (Parts I and II), 1963.

Vol. XVI. *Introductory lectures on psycho-analysis* (Part III), 1963.

Vol. XVII. *An infantile neurosis and other works*, 1955.

Vol. XVIII. *Beyond the pleasure principle, group psychology and other works*, 1955.

Vol. XIX. *The ego and the id and other works*, 1961.

Vol. XX. *An autobiographical study, inhibitions, symptoms and anxiety, the question of lay analysis, and other works*, 1959.

Vol. XXI. *The future of an illusion, civilization and it discontents, and other works*, 1961.

Vol. XXII. *New introductory lectures on psycho-analysis*, 1964.

Vol. XXIII. *Moses and monotheism, an outline of psycho-analysis, and other works*, 1964.

Freud, S., and Bullitt, W. C. (1967) *Thomas Woodrow Wilson: A psychological study.* Boston: Houghton Mifflin Co.

Freund, K. (1960) Some problems in the treatment of homosexuality. In H. J. Eysenck (Ed.), *Behaviour therapy and the neuroses.* New York: Pergamon Press, pp. 312–326.

Fromm, E. (1959) *Sigmund Freud's mission.* New York: Harper & Bros.

Fromm, E. (1963) C. G. Jung: Prophet of the unconscious. *Scientific American*, September, 283–290.

Furtmüller, C. (1964) *Alfred Adler: A biographical essay.* In H. L. Ansbacher and R. R. Ansbacher (Eds.), *Superiority and social interest.* Evanston, Ill.: Northwestern University Press, pp. 330–393.

Gayley, C. M. (1965) *The classic myths in English literature and art.* New York: Blaisdell Publishing Co.

Greenspoon, J. (1954) The effect of two nonverbal stimuli on the frequency of members of two verbal response classes (Abstract). *American Psychologist*, **9**, 384.

Greenspoon, J. (1955) The reinforcing effect of two spoken sounds on the frequency of two responses. *American Journal of Psychology*, **68**, 409–416.

Harms, E. (1946) Carl Gustav Jung—Defender of Freud and the Jews. *Psychiatric Quarterly*, **20**, 199.

Hegel, G. W. F. (1952) *The philosophy of right.* In R. M. Hutchins (Ed.), *Great books of the western world* (Vol. 46). Chicago: Encyclopaedia Britannica, pp. 1–150.

Heinemann, F. H. (1958) *Existentialism and the modern predicament.* New York: Harper & Row.

Hilgard, E. R., and Marquis, D. G. (1940) *Conditioning and learning.* New York: Appleton-Century-Crofts.

Hobbes, T. (1952) *Leviathan.* In R. M. Hutchins (Ed.), *Great books of the western world* (Vol. 23). Chicago: Encyclopaedia Britannica, pp. 49–283.

Hofstadter, R. (1955) *Social Darwinism in American thought.* Boston: The Beacon Press.

Hull, C. L. (1937) Mind, mechanism, and adaptive behavior. *Psychological Review,* **44,** 1–32.

Hull, C. L. (1938) The goal-gradient hypothesis applied to some "field-force" problems in the behavior of young children. *Psychological Review,* **45,** 271–299.

Hull, C. L. (1943) *Principles of behavior.* New York: Appleton-Century-Crofts.

Hull, C. L. (1952) *A behavior system.* New Haven, Conn.: Yale University Press.

Husserl, E. (1965) *Phenomenology and the crisis of philosophy* (translated by Q. Lauer). New York: Harper & Row Torchbooks.

Jacobson, E. (1938) *Progressive relaxation.* Chicago: University of Chicago Press.

Janet, P. (1920) *The major symptoms of hysteria* (2nd ed.). New York: The Macmillan Co.

Jones, E. (1953) *The life and work of Sigmund Freud* (Vol. 1). New York: Basic Books, Inc.

Jones, E. (1957) *The last phase* (Vol. 3). New York: Basic Books, Inc.

Jung, C. G. (1946) *Psychological types.* London: Kegan Paul, Trench, Trubner & Co., Ltd., and New York: Harcourt, Brace & Co. (This work appears in the Bollingen Series as Vol. 6.)

Jung, C. G. (1963) *Memories, dreams, reflections.* New York: Pantheon Books, and London: William Collins Sons, Ltd.

Jung, C. G. *The collected works of C. G. Jung* (edited by H. Read, M. Fordham, and G. Adler). Bollingen Series. New York: Pantheon Books, and London: Routledge & Kegan Paul.

Vol. 1. *Psychiatric studies,* 1957.

Vol. 3. *The psychogenesis of mental disease,* 1960.

Vol. 4. *Freud and psychoanalysis,* 1961.

Vol. 5. *Symbols of transformation,* 1956.

Vol. 6. *Psychological types,* 1971. (See Jung, 1946).

Vol. 7. *Two essays on analytical psychology,* 1953.

Vol. 8. *The structure and dynamics of the psyche,* 1960.

Vol. 9i. *The archetypes and the collective unconscious,* 1959.

Vol. 9ii. *Aion,* 1959.

Vol. 10. *Civilization in transition,* 1964.

Vol. 11. *Psychology and religion: West and east,* 1958.

Vol. 12. *Psychology and alchemy,* 1953.

Vol. 13. *Alchemical studies,* 1967.

Vol. 14. *Mysterium coniunctionis,* 1963.

Vol. 15. *The spirit in man, art, and literature,* 1966.

Vol. 16. *The practice of psychotherapy,* 1954.

Vol. 17. *The development of personality,* 1954.

Kant, I. (1952) *The critique of pure reason.* In R. M. Hutchins (Ed.), *Great books of the western world* (Vol. 42). Chicago: Encyclopaedia Britannica, pp. 1–250.

Kaufmann, W. (1956) *Nietzsche: Philosopher, psychologist, antichrist.* New York: Meridian.

Kelly, G. A. (1955a) *The psychology of personal constructs. Volume one: A theory of personality.* New York: W. W. Norton & Co., Inc. Quotations by permission of the publisher.

Kelly, G. A. (1955b) *The psychology of personal constructs. Volume two: Clinical diagnosis and psychotherapy.* New York: W. W. Norton & Co., Inc. Quotations by permission of the publisher.

Kelly, G. A. (1969) *Clinical psychology and personality: The selected papers of George Kelly* (edited by Brendan Maher). New York: John Wiley & Sons, Inc. Quotations from *Clinical Psychology and Personality: The Selected Papers of George Kelly,* edited by Brendan Maher. Copyright © 1969 by John Wiley & Sons, Inc. Reprinted by permission.

Kelly, G. A. (1970) A summary statement of a cognitively-oriented comprehensive theory of behavior. In J. C. Mancuso (Ed.), *Readings for a cognitive theory of personality.* New York: Holt, Rinehart and Winston, Inc., pp. 27–58.

Kety, S. S. (1960) Recent biochemical theories of schizophrenia. In D. D. Jackson (Ed.), *The etiology of schizophrenia.* New York: Basic Books, Inc., pp. 120–145.

Koffka, K. (1935) *Principles of gestalt psychology*. New York: Harcourt, Brace & Co.

Köhler, W. (1961a) Gestalt psychology today. In M. Henle (Ed.), *Documents of gestalt psychology*. Berkeley, Calif.: University of California Press, pp. 1–14.

Köhler, W. (1961b) Psychological remarks on some questions of anthropology. In M. Henle (Ed.), *Documents of gestalt psychology*. Berkeley, Calif., University of California Press, pp. 203–221.

Korzybski, A. (1921) *Manhood of humanity*. New York: E. P. Dutton & Co.

Korzybski, A. (1924) *Time-binding*. New York: E. P. Dutton & Co.

Korzybski, A. (1941) *Science and sanity: An introduction to non-Aristotelian systems and general semantics* (2nd ed.). Lancaster: Science Press.

Krasner, L. (1962) Behavior control and social responsibility. *American Psychologist,* **17,** 199–204.

Krasner, L. (1965) Verbal conditioning and psychotherapy. In L. Krasner and L. P. Ullmann (Eds.), *Research in behavior modification*. New York: Holt, Rinehart and Winston, Inc., pp. 211–228.

Kuhn, T. S. (1962) *The structure of scientific revolutions*. Chicago: University of Chicago Press.

Ladd, G .T. (1899) On certain hindrances to the progress of psychology in America. *Psychological Review,* **6,** 121–133.

Lazarus, A. A. (1961) Group therapy of phobic disorders by systematic desensitization. *Journal of Abnormal and Social Psychology,* **63,** 504–510.

Lecky, P. (1945) *Self-consistency: A theory of personality*. New York: Island Press.

Leff, G. A. (1958) *Medieval thought: St. Augustine to Ockham*. Chicago: Quadrangle Books.

Lewin, K. (1935) *A dynamic theory of personality*. New York: McGraw-Hill Book Co.

Lewin, K. (1947) Group decision and social change. In T. M. Newcomb and E. L. Hartley (Eds.), *Readings in social psychology*. New York: Henry Holt & Co.

Lewin, K. (1951) *Field theory in social science: selected theoretical papers* (edited by D. Cartwright), New York: Harper & Row.

Lewin, K. (1961) Environmental forces in child behavior and development. In C. Murchison (Ed.), *A handbook of child psychology*. Worcester, Mass.: Clark University Press.

Lewin, K., Dembo, T., Festinger, L. and Sears, P. S. (1944) Level of aspiration. In J. McV. Hunt (Ed.), *Personality and the behavior disorders* (Vol. I). New York: The Ronald Press, pp. 333–378.

Lewin, K. Lippitt, R., and White, R. (1939) Patterns of aggressive behavior in experimentally created "social climates." *Journal of Social Psychology,* **10,** 271–299.

Lippmann, W. (1946) *Public opinion*. New York: Penguin Books.

Locke, J. (1952) *An essay concerning human understanding*. In R. M. Hutchins (Ed.), *Great books of the western world* (Vol. 35). Chicago: Encyclopaedia Britannica, pp. 85–395.

McCleary, R. A., and Lazarus, R. S. (1949) Autonomic discrimination without awareness. *Journal of Personality,* **18,** 171–179.

McDougall, W. (1923a) Purposive or mechanical psychology? *Psychological Review,* **30,** 273–288.

McDougall, W. (1923b) *Outline of psychology*. New York: Charles Scribner's Sons.

MacKinnon, D. W. (1944) The structure of personality. In J. McV. Hunt (Ed.), *Personality and the behavior disorders* (Vol. I): New York: The Ronald Press, pp. 3–48.

Marrow, A. J. (1969) *The practical theorist: The life and work of Kurt Lewin*. New York: Basic Books, Inc.

Maslow, A. H., and Mittlemann, B. (1951) *Principles of abnormal psychology: The dynamics of psychic illness* (rev. ed.). New York: Harper and Bros.

Masserman, J. H. (1943) *Behavior and neurosis*. Chicago: University of Chicago Press.

Meyer, A. (1910) The dynamic interpretation of dementia praecox. *American Journal of Psychology,* **21,** 385–403.

Miller, N. E. (1937) Analysis of the form of conflict reactions. *Psychological Bulletin,* **34,** 720.

Miller, N. E. (1944) Experimental studies of conflict. In J. McV. Hunt (Ed.), *Personality and the behavior disorders* (Vol. I). New York: The Ronald Press, pp. 431–465.

Miller, N. E. (1948a) Studies of fear as an acquirable drive. 1. Fear as motivation and fear-reduction as reinforcement in the learning of new responses. *Journal of Experimental Psychology,* **38,** 89–101.

Miller, N. E. (1948b) Theory and experiment relating psychoanalytic displacement to stimulus-response generalization. *Journal of Abnormal and Social Psychology,* **43,** 155–178.

Miller, N. E. (1951) Learnable drives and rewards. In S. S. Stevens (Ed.), *Handbook of experimental psychology.* New York: John Wiley & Sons, Inc., pp. 435–472.

Miller, N. E. (1957) Experiments on motivation: Studies combining psychological, physiological, and pharmacological techniques. *Science,* **126,** 1271–1278.

Miller, N. E. (1959) Liberalization of basic S-R concepts: Extensions to conflict behavior, motivation, and social learning. In S. Koch (Ed.), *Psychology: A study of science* (Vol. II). New York: McGraw-Hill Book Co., pp. 196–292.

Miller, N. E. (1961) Analytical studies of drive and reward. *American Psychologist,* **16,** 739–754.

Miller, N. E. (1963) Some reflections on the law of effect produce a new alternative to drive reduction. In M. R. Jones (Ed.), *The Nebraska symposium on motivation* (No. XI), pp. 65–112.

Miller, N. E. (1964) Some implications of modern behavior theory for personality change and psychotherapy. In P. Worchel and D. Byrne (Ed.), *Personality Change.* New York: John Wiley & Sons, Inc.

Miller, N. E., and Dollard, J. (1941) *Social learning and imitation.* New Haven, Conn.: Yale University Press.

Moore, T. V. (Dom) (1921) The parataxes. *Psychoanalytic Review,* **8,** 252–283.

Mowrer, O. H. (1939) A stimulus-response analysis of anxiety and its role as a reinforcing agent. *Psychological Review,* **46,** 553–566.

Mowrer, O. H. (1948) Learning theory and the neurotic paradox. *American Journal of Orthopsychiatry,* **18,** 571–610.

Mowrer, O. H. (1961) *The crisis in psychiatry and religion.* New York: D. Van Nostrand.

Munsterberg, H. (1900) Psychological atomism. *Psychological Review,* **7,** 1–17.

Nunberg, H., and Federn, E. (Eds.). (1962)

Minutes of the Vienna psycho-analytic society: 1906–1908 (Vol. I). New York: International Universities Press.

Oppenheimer, R. (1956) Analogy in science. *American Psychologist,* **11,** 127–135.

Park, R. E., and Burgess, E. W. (1921) *Introduction to the science of sociology.* Chicago: University of Chicago Press.

Pavlov, I. P. (1927) *Conditioned reflexes: An investigation of the physiological activity of the cerebral cortex* (translated by G. V. Anrep). New York: Oxford University Press.

Plato. (1952) *Sophist.* In R. M. Hutchins (Ed.), *Great books of the western world* (Vol. 7). Chicago: Encyclopaedia Britannica, pp. 85–395.

Pressey, S. L. (1926) A simple apparatus which gives tests and scores—and teaches. *School and Society,* **23,** 373–376.

Rachman, S. (1963) Introduction to behaviour therapy. *Behavioral Research and Therapy,* **1,** 3–15.

Rank, O. (1968) *Will therapy and truth and reality.* New York: Alfred A. Knopf, Inc.

Rivers, W. H. R. (1920) *Instinct and the unconscious: A contribution to a biological theory of the psychoneuroses.* Cambridge: Cambridge University Press.

Rogers, C. R. (1939) *The clinical treatment of the problem child.* Boston: Houghton Mifflin Co.

Rogers, C. R. (1942) *Counseling and psychotherapy.* Boston: Houghton Mifflin Co.

Rogers, C. R. (1951) *Client-centered therapy.* Boston: Houghton Mifflin Co.

Rogers, C. R. (1953) The interest in the practice of psychotherapy. *American Psychologist,* **8,** 48–50.

Rogers, C. R. (1955) Persons or science? A philosophical question. *American Psychologist,* 1955, **10,** 267–278.

Rogers, C. R. (1959) A theory of therapy, personality, and interpersonal relationships, as developed in the client-centered framework. In S. Koch (Ed.), *Psychology: A study of a science. Study I. Conceptual and systematic. Vol. 3: Formulations of the person and the social context.* New York: McGraw-Hill Book Co., pp. 184–256. Copyright © 1959 by the McGraw-Hill Book Company, Inc. Quotations by permission of the publisher.

Rogers, C. R. (1961) *On becoming a person.* Boston: Houghton Mifflin Co.

Rogers, C. R. (1963) Learning to be free. In S. M. Farber and R. H. L. Wilson (Eds.), *Control of the mind. Vol. 2: Conflict and creativity.* New York: McGraw-Hill Book Co., pp. 268–288. Quotations by permission of the publisher.

Rogers, C. R. (1967) Autobiography. In E. G. Boring and G. Lindzey (Eds.), *A history of psychology in autobiography* (Vol. V.). New York: Appleton-Century-Crofts, pp. 343–384.

Rogers, C. R. (1969a) *Freedom to learn.* Columbus, O.: Charles E. Merrill Publishing Co. Quotations by permission of the publisher.

Rogers, C. R. (1969b) Self-directed change: An answer to the educational crisis? Talk given to the Council of Chief State School Officers, Phoenix, Arizona, Nov. 17.

Rogers, C. R. (1970a) The process equation of psychotherapy. In J. T. Hart and T. M. Tomlinson (Eds.), *New directions in client-centered therapy.* Boston: Houghton Mifflin Co., pp. 190–205.

Rogers, C. R. (1970b) The process of the basic encounter group. In J. T. Hart and T. M. Tomlinson (Eds.), *New directions in client-centered therapy.* Boston: Houghton Mifflin Co., pp. 292–313.

Rogers, C. R. (1970c) Toward a modern approach to values: The valuing process in the mature person. In J. T. Hart and T. M. Tomlinson (Eds.), *New directions in client-centered therapy.* Boston: Houghton Mifflin Co., pp. 430–441.

Rogers, C. R. (1970d) The interpersonal relationship in the facilitation of learning. In J. T. Hart and T. M. Tomlinson (Eds.), *New directions in client-centered therapy.* Boston: Houghton Mifflin Co., pp. 468–483.

Rogers, C. R. (1970e) Current assumptions in graduate education: A passionate statement. In J. T. Hart and T. M. Tomlinson (Eds.), *New directions in client-centered therapy.* Boston: Houghton Mifflin Co., pp. 484–501.

Rogers, C. R. (1970f) Can I be a facilitative person in a group? Unpublished Manuscript. Quotations by permission of the author. (This work has been published in slightly different form as Ch. 3 of *Carl Rogers on Encounter Groups,* New York: Harper & Row, 1970.)

Rogers, C. R. (1970g) The person in change: Experiences following an encounter group. Unpublished Manuscript.

Rogers, C. R. (1970h) Change after encounter groups: In persons, in relationships, in organizations. Unpublished Manuscript.

Rogers, C. R., and Dymond, R. F. (1954) *Psychotherapy and personality change.* Chicago. University of Chicago Press.

Rogers, C. R., Gendlin, E. T., Kiesler, D. J., and Truax, C. B. (1967) *The therapeutic relationship and its impact.* Madison, Wis.: University of Wisconsin Press.

Rogers, C. R., and Hart, J. T. (1970) Looking back and ahead: A conversation with Carl Rogers. In J. T. Hart and T. M. Tomlinson (Eds.), *New directions in client-centered therapy.* Boston: Houghton Mifflin Co., pp. 502–534.

Rogers, C. R., and Skinner, B. F. (1956) Some issues concerning the control of human behavior: A symposium. *Science, 124,* 1057–1066.

Russell, B. (1959) *Wisdom of the west.* Garden City, N.Y.: Doubleday & Co., Inc.

Rychlak, J. F. (1968) *A philosophy of science for personality theory.* Boston: Houghton Mifflin Co.

Rychlak, J. F. (1970) The two teleologies of Adler's individual psychology. *Journal of Individual Psychology, 26,* 144–152. (Paper read at the 78th Annual Convention of the American Psychological Association, Miami Beach, Florida, Sept. 7.)

Sapir, E. (1921) *Language, an introduction to the study of speech.* New York: Harcourt, Brace & Co.

Sartre, J.-P. (1956) *Being and nothingness.* New York: Philosophical Library.

Sheldon, W. H. (1944) Constitutional factors in personality. In J. McV. Hunt (Ed.), *Personality and the behavior disorders* (Vol. I). New York: The Ronald Press, pp. 526–549.

Sheldon, W. H., Dupertuis, C. W., and McDermott, E. (1954) *Atlas of men: A guide for somatotyping the adult male at all ages.* New York: Harper & Bros.

Sheldon, W. H., Hartl, E. M., and McDermott, E. (1949) *Varieties of delinquent youth: An introduction to constitutional psychiatry.* New York: Harper & Bros.

Sheldon, W. H., and Stevens, S. S. (1942) *The varieties of temperament: A psychology of constitutional differences.* New York: Harper & Bros.

Sheldon, W. H., Stevens, S. S., and Tucker, W. B. (1940) *The varieties of human physique: An introduction to constitutional psychology.* New York: Harper & Bros.

Sherrington, C. S. (1947) *The integrative action of the central nervous system.* Cambridge: Cambridge University Press.

Shock, N. W. (1944) Physiological factors in behavior. In J. McV. Hunt (Ed.), *Personality and the behavior disorders* (Vol. I). New York: The Ronald Press, pp. 582–618.

Sidgwick, H. (1960) *Outlines of the history of ethics.* Boston: The Beacon Press.

Skinner, B. F. (1938) *The behavior of organisms: An experimental analysis.* New York: Appleton-Century.

Skinner, B. F. (1948) *Walden two.* New York: The Macmillan Co. Copyright, 1948, by B. F. Skinner. Quotations by permission of the publisher.

Skinner, B. F. (1950) Are theories of learning necessary? *Psychological Review, 57,* 193–216.

Skinner, B. F. (1953) *Science and human behavior.* New York: The Macmillan Co.

Skinner, B. F. (1955) The control of human behavior. *Annals of the New York Academy of Science, 17,* 547–551.

Skinner, B. F. (1956) A case history in scientific method. *American Psychologist, 11,* 221–223.

Skinner, B. F. (1957) *Verbal behavior.* New York: Appleton-Century-Crofts.

Skinner, B. F. (1959) *Cumulative record.* New York: Appleton-Century-Crofts.

Skinner, B. F. (1960) Pigeons in a pelican. *American Psychologist, 15,* 28–37.

Skinner, B. F. (1961) The design of cultures. *Daedalus, 90,* 534–546.

Skinner, B. F. (1963a) Operant behavior. *American Psychologist, 18,* 503–515.

Skinner, B. F. (1963b) *Behaviorism at fifty. Science, 140,* 951–958.

Skinner, B. F. (1967a) Autobiography of B. F. Skinner. In E. G. Boring and G. Lindzey (Eds.), *History of psychology in autobiography* (Vol. V). New York: Appleton-Century-Crofts, pp. 387–413.

Skinner, B. F. (1968) *The technology of teaching.* New York: Appleton-Century-Crofts.

Skinner, B. F. (1969) *Contingencies of reinforcement: A theoretical analysis.* New York: Appleton-Century-Crofts.

Skinner, B. F. (1971) *Beyond freedom and dignity.* New York: Alfred A. Knopf, Inc. Copyright © 1971 by B. F. Skinner. Quotations by permission of the publisher.

Skinner, B. F., and Ferster, C. (1957) *Schedules of reinforcement.* New York: Appleton-Century-Crofts.

Skinner, B. F., and Lindsley, O. R. (1954) Studies in behavior therapy, status reports II and III, Office of Naval Research Contract N5 ori-7662.

Skinner, B. F., Solomon, H. C., and Lindsley, O. R. (1954) A new method for the experimental analysis of the behavior of psychotic patients. *Journal of Nervous and Mental Diseases, 120,* 403–406.

Snygg, D., and Combs, A. W. (1949) *Individual behavior: A new frame of reference for psychology.* New York: Harper & Bros.

Spence, K. W. (1956) *Behavior theory and conditioning.* New Haven, Conn.: Yale University Press.

Spielberger, C. D., and DeNike, L. D. (1966) Descriptive behaviorism versus cognitive theory in verbal operant conditioning. *Psychological Review, 73,* 306–327.

Stampfl, T. G. (1966) Implosive therapy: The theory, the subhuman analogue, the strategy, and the technique. In S. G. Armitage (Ed.), *Behavior modification techniques in the treatment of emotional disorders.* Battle Creek, Mich.: Veterans Administration Publication, pp. 12–21.

Stampfl, T. G., and Levis, D. J. (1966) Implosive therapy. Unpublished Manuscript.

Stampfl, T. G., and Levis, D. J. (1967a) Essentials of implosive therapy: A learning-theory—based psychodynamic behavioral therapy. *Journal of Abnormal Psychology, 72,* 496–503.

Stampfl, T. G., and Levis, D. J. (1967b) Phobic patients: Treatment with the learning theory approach of implosive therapy. *Voices,* **3**, 23–27.

Stampfl, T. G., and Levis, D. J. (1968) Implosive therapy—a behavioral therapy? *Behavioral Research and Therapy,* **6**, 31–36.

Stampfl, T. G., and Levis, D. J. (1969) Learning theory: An aid to dynamic therapeutic practice. In L. D. Eron and R. Callahan (Eds.), *The relation of theory to practice in psychotherapy.* Chicago: Aldine Publishing Co., pp. 85–114.

Standal, S. (1954) The need for positive regard: A contribution to client-centered theory. Unpublished doctoral dissertation, University of Chicago.

Stephenson, W. (1953) *The study of behavior.* Chicago: University of Chicago Press.

Stevens, S. S. (1935) The operational definition of psychological concepts. *Psychological Review,* **42**, 517–527.

Storch, A. (1924) *The primitive archaic forms of inner experience and thought in schizophrenia: A genetic and clinical study of schizophrenia* (translated by Clara Willard). New York and Washington, D.C.: Nervous and Mental Disease Publishing Co.

Sullivan, H. S. (1924) Schizophrenia: Its conservative and malignant features. *American Journal of Psychiatry,* **4**, 77–91.

Sullivan, H. S. (1940) *Conceptions of modern psychiatry.* New York: W. W. Norton & Co., Inc. Quotation by permission of the publisher.

Sullivan, H. S. (1953) *The interpersonal theory of psychiatry* (edited by H. S. Perry and M. L. Gawel). New York: W. W. Norton & Co., Inc. Quotations by permission of the publisher.

Sullivan, H. S. (1954) *The psychiatric interview* (edited by H. S. Perry and M. L. Gawel). New York: W. W. Norton & Co., Inc.

Sullivan, H. S. (1956) *Clinical studies in psychiatry* (edited by H. S. Perry, M. L. Gawel, and M. Gibbon). New York: W. W. Norton & Co., Inc. Quotations by permission of the publisher.

Sullivan, H. S. (1962) *Schizophrenia as a human process.* New York: W. W. Norton & Co., Inc. Quotations by permission of the publisher.

Sullivan, H. S. (1964) *The fusion of psychiatry and social science.* New York: W. W. Norton & Co., Inc. Quotations by permission of the publisher.

Thomas, W. I. (1951) The behavior pattern and the situation. In E. H. Volkart (Ed.), *Social behavior and personality: Contributions of W. I. Thomas to theory and social research.* New York: Social Science Research Council, pp. 14–36.

Thorndike, E. L. (1898) Animal intelligence: An experimental study of the associative processes in animals. *Psychological Review Monograph Supplement,* No. 8.

Thorndike, E. L. (1933) *An experimental study of rewards.* New York: Bureau of Publications, Teachers College, Columbia University.

Thorndike, E. L. (1943) *Man and his works.* Cambridge, Mass.: Harvard University Press.

Tolman, E. C. (1960) *Purposive behavior in animals and men.* New York: Appleton-Century-Crofts.

Ullmann, L. P., and Krasner, L. (1965) *Case studies in behavior modification.* New York: Holt, Rinehart and Winston, Inc.

Voegtlin, W., and Lemere, F. (1942) The treatment of alcohol addiction. *Quarterly Journal of Studies on Alcoholism,* **2**, 717–723.

Watson, J. B. (1913) Psychology as the behaviorist views it. *Psychological Review,* **20**, 158–177.

Watson, J. B. (1917) The place of the conditioned reflex in psychology. *Psychological Review,* **24**, 329–352.

Watson, J. B. (1924) *Behaviorism.* New York: W. W. Norton & Co., Inc.

Watson, J. B., and Rayner, P. (1920) Conditioned emotional reactions. *Journal of Experimental Psychology,* **3**, 1–16.

Watson, R. I. (1962) The experimental tradition and clinical psychology. In A. J. Bachrach (Ed.), *Experimental foundations of clinical psychology.* New York: Basic Books, Inc., pp. 3–25.

Wertheimer, M. (1945) *Productive thinking.* New York: Harper & Bros.

Wiener, N. (1954) *The human use of human beings.* Boston: Houghton Mifflin Co.

Wittels, F. (1924) *Sigmund Freud: His personality, his teaching, and his school.* New York: Dodd, Mead.

Wolpe, J. (1948) An approach to the problem of neurosis based on the conditioned response. Unpublished M.D. Thesis: University of Witwatersrand.

Wolpe, J. (1958) *Psychotherapy by reciprocal inhibition*. Stanford, Calif.: Stanford University Press. Quotations by permission of the publisher.

Wolpe, J. (1960) Reciprocal inhibition as the main basis of psychotherapeutic effects. In H. J. Eysenck (Ed.), *Behaviour therapy and the neuroses*. New York: Pergamon Press, pp. 88–113.

Wolpe, J. (1969) *The practice of behavior therapy*. New York: Pergamon Press.

Woodworth, R. S. (1929) *Psychology*. New York: Holt, Rinehart & Winston.

PHOTOGRAPH ACKNOWLEDGMENTS

27   Culver Pictures
92   Historical Pictures Service—Chicago
134 Culver Pictures
240 Courtesy of the William Alanson White Psychiatric Foundation, Inc.
291 Courtesy of Yale University News Bureau
292 Courtesy of Rockefeller University
330 Courtesy of Harvard University Department of Psychology
341 Courtesy of Joseph Wolpe, Temple University Department of Psychiatry
354 Courtesy of Thomas Stampfl
413 Courtesy of Mrs. Frank Coyle, Secretary to Dr. Rogers
447 Courtesy of Sanatorium Bellevue, Zurich
448 Courtesy of Medard Boss, M.D., Zollikon-Zurich
472 Courtesy of Mrs. Gladys T. Kelly; photo by Ralph Norman

INDEX OF NAMES

INDEX OF SUBJECTS

Cue(s) (*Cont.*)
   see also Cue-producing response
Cue-producing response(s)
   Dollard and Miller's definition of, 295
   as response-produced stimuli, Dollard and Miller, 295
   verbal vs. nonverbal, Dollard and Miller, 296
Culture
   belief systems of, 1
   Adler's definition of, 105
   Kelly's views on, 485–486
Curative motive to therapy
   general statement of, 19
   theorists' attitudes toward
      Freud, 225, 233
      Adler, 233–234
      Jung, 234
      Sullivan, 391
      Skinner, Wolpe, and Stampfl, 392
      Rogers, 526
      Binswanger and Boss, 526
      Kelly, 526
Cybernetics, as demonstrative, 368

Dasein
   as used by Heidegger, 445
   as existence, 449
   as being-in-the-world, 449
   definition of, existentialism, 451
   as essentially Mitwelt, Binswanger, 452
   as both thrown and open, existentialism, 452
   as figure-ground, existentialism, 452
   identity in, existentialism, 453
Daydream, Adler, 126
Death instinct, Freud, 42
   see also Eros, Life instinct
Deduction, in abstraction, 5
   see also Induction
Delusion(s)
   as falsification of reality, Freud, 66
   as fictions, Adler, 118
   role of, in theory of
      Dollard and Miller, 316
      Kelly, 490

as subjectively legitimate, existentialism, 463
Demonstrative reasoning
   vs. dialectical, Aristotle, 6
   as an American style, 367
   of cybernetics, 368
   see also Dialectical reasoning
Dependency, Kelly, 485
Depotentiation
   Jungian theory of, 174
   as educating anima or animus, Jung, 180
   confrontation in, Jung, 182
Depression
   as result of harsh superego and guilt, Freud, 68–69
   role of, in theory of
      Adler, 119
      Sullivan, 272
      the existentialists, 464
      Kelly, 490
Derivatives, of repression, Freud, 43
Determinism
   vs. chance, 3
   logical, via syllogism, 5
   role of, in theory of
      Freud, 70, 222–223
      Jung, 153–154
      S-R, 375
      Kelly, 481, 520
   as locked into prototype, Adler, 96–97
   hard, role of God's perfection in, Newton, 222
   Skinner vs. Freud on, 375–376
   hard vs. soft, 376, 518
   hard, and pattern meanings, 379
   as thrown, 451
   as locked in by world-design, Binswanger, 516
   as locked in by constructs, Kelly, 516
   as paradox, Rogers, 517
   see also Chance
Diagnosis
   differential, Freud, 65–66
   in Kraepelinian scheme, 88
   technique of comparison in, Adler, 124
   teleological aspects of, Jung, 173
   as unnecessary, Rogers, 428

reluctance of existentialists to use, 462
   Kellyian view of, 488–489
Dialectic
   as bipolarity in meaning, 5
   in Greek thought, 5–6
   in free thought, Kant, 8
   in psychotherapy, Jung, 190
   attitude of theorists toward
      Freud, 207–209
      Adler, 209–210
      Jung, 210–211
      Sullivan, 367
      Skinner, in informal writings, 369–371
      Rogers, in interviews, 504–505
      Binswanger and Boss, 506–507
      Kelly, 507–508
   and energy concepts, Freud, 215
   transcendence as, 506
   see also Dialectical reasoning
Dialectical reasoning
   vs. demonstrative, Aristotle, 6
   Skinner vs. Whitehead on, 370
   as rationale for teleology, 385
   see also Demonstrative reasoning
Differentiation, Jung
   in theory, 138
   as synonymous with discrimination, 138
   generates libido, 150
   as adjustment mechanism, 156
   see also Principle of opposites
Discriminal theorizing
   definition of, 17
   Freud's approach to, 218
   ascribed to culture by behaviorism, 381
   see also Vehicular theorizing
Discrimination
   in theory of
      Jung, 138
      Dollard and Miller, 296
   in learning, Pavlov, 284
Displacement
   as derived symbolization, Freud, 44
   as the deflection of emotion, Sullivan, 260

as stimulus generalization,
Dollard and Miller, 307
Dissociation
as Janet's term, 60
in theory of
Jung, 139
Sullivan, 257
Distance, Adler, 107
Dream(s)
manifest vs. latent content,
Freud, 78
symbols in, Freud, 78
effect of day residues on,
Freud, 78
wish fulfillment in, Freud, 78
definition of,
Freud, 78
Adler, 126
Jung, 195
Sullivan, 279
related to hallucination, Freud,
78
condensation and displacement
in, Freud, 79
overdeterminism in, Freud, 79
as sleep guardian, Freud, 79
as road to unconscious, Freud,
79
reversal in, Freud, 79
means of representation in,
Freud, 79
as tied to goals, Adler, 125
symbols in, Jung, 143–144
relation to projection, Jung,
170
Jung rejects manifest-latent
content of, 192
big or highly significant, Jung,
195
compensatory, Jung, 195–196
in theory of
existentialists, 468–479
Kelly, 497
Rogers, 519
Drive(s)
aggression vs. affection, Adler,
101
Dollard and Miller's definition
of, 298
primary vs. secondary, Dollard
and Miller, 298
vs. need, Dollard and Miller,
302
rejected by Kelly, 481

Drive reduction
in Dollard and Miller, 298
in Wolpe, 343
Dualism
in theory of
Freud, 29–30, 223
Jung, 148
Sullivan, 242
Kelly, 474
as a pseudo-issue, Jung, 136
and psychosomatic illness,
Kelly, 489
Dynamism(s), Sullivan
definition of, 243
zonal vs. interpersonal, 243
of difficulty, 266
as drive toward mental health,
273

Early recollections, Adler, 125
Education
role in Adlerian therapy, 121–
122
as third stage of Jungian
therapy, 177
Efficient cause, definition of, 3
see also Cause, Impetus construct
Ego
Freud's definition of, 34–35
enlarged, following therapy,
Freud, 74
as a complex, Jung, 140
as identified with archetype,
Jung, 173
as under sway of mana personality, Jung, 183
as higher mental processes,
Dollard and Miller, 297,
308
Ego ideal, Freud, 35
see also Superego
Ego strength, Dollard and Miller,
297
Eigenwelt, existentialism, 449,
452, 459
see also Mitwelt, Umwelt
Elaboration, Kelly, 491
Elucidation, second stage of
therapy, Jung, 176
Emmy von N., case of, Freud, 60
Emotion(s)
and the Freudian psyche, 30,
32
importance of, to cure

in Freud, 74–75
in Adler, 102
as compressing life style,
Adler, 102
inferiority vs. social, Adler,
102
in theory of
Jung, 136
Kelly, 482–483
in Jung, 174
as zonal dynamisms, Sullivan,
243
theorem of reciprocal, Sullivan, 253–254
uncanny, Sullivan, 254, 267
hostility vs. aggression, Kelly,
483–484
Empathy, vs. anxiety, Sullivan,
255
see also Anxiety
Enactment, as role play, Kelly,
495
see also Fixed role therapy
Encapsulation, Kelly, 492
Encounter group(s)
as T-groups, 409
Lewin's role in originating,
409–410
Rogers' behavior in, 431
Rogerian approach to, 439–
441
Entropy, principle of, Jung, 150
Equivalence, principle of, Jung,
150
Era(s) (epoch[s]), in development, Sullivan, 260–265
Eros, Freud, 42
see also Death instinct, Life instinct
Erotogenic zone(s), Freud, 45–
46
see also Libido
Error(s), Adler, 106
Ethic(s)
natural
in Adler, 106, 231
in Rogers, 435–436
intrinsic vs. instrumental,
Adler, 231, 233
and behavior therapy, 393–
399
intrinsic vs. instrumental, behaviorism, 396, 524

Impetus construct (*Cont.*)
  as incompatible with intentional meanings, Jung, 225
  in theory of
    Sullivan, 373–374
    S-R, 374
    Rogers, 509–510
    existentialists, 510
    Kelly, 510
  see also Cause, Efficient cause
Implosion, definition of, Stampfl, 356
  see also Implosive therapy
Implosive therapy, steps in, Stampfl, 358–361
Incorporation, definition of, Freud, 46
  see also Identification
Independence
  in view of
    Rank, 411
    Rogers, 425–426
    existentialists, 459
    Kelly, 485
  lack of, and maladjustment, existentialism, 461
  see also Dependence
Individual psychology, Adler, 93
  importance of goals in, 94
  comparative features of, 97
  meaning of individual, 97
  contact with social psychology, 97
  as not completely social psychological in approach, 123–124
Individuation, Jung
  adjustment mechanism, 157
  in fourth stage of therapy, 178
  quickened maturation, 184
  via rate of the Mass, 186
  via alchemy, 188–189
Induction, via assumptions, 5
  see also Deduction
Inferiority, Adler
  of brain, 98
  feelings of, vs. social, 102
  as spur to compensate, 102
  segmental, 116
Inferiority complex, Adler, 103
Inflation, Jung
  definition of, 152
  positive vs. negative, 156

Inhibition
  of response, Wolpe, 344
  reactive, Hull, 344
  conditioned, Hull, 344
  reciprocal, Sherrington, 344
Insight
  definition of
    Freud, 69, 74
    Rogers, 431
    Kelly, 492
  as rectifying mistakes, Adler, 121
  as central to cure, Adler, 123
  as labeling, Dollard and Miller, 318
  as not essential to cure in Dollard and Miller, 320–321
  Stampfl, 358
  currency emphasis on, existentialism, 465
Instinct(s)
  Freud's definition of, 36
  aim of, Freud, 36
  pressure of, Freud, 36
  source of, Freud, 36, 40
  object of, Freud, 37
  sexual, Freud, 38–39
  number of, Freud, 40
  primal, Freud, 40
  ego vs. object, Freud, 40
  self-preservative vs. sexual, Freud, 40
  as components, Freud, 40, 53
  aim inhibition of, Freud, 51, 53
  relation to archetype, Jung, 144
  tied to unconscious energies, Jung, 147
  Jung's teleological definition of, 148
  as inexplicable, Jung, 148–149
  Freud's arbitrary employment of, 206
  rejected by Dollard and Miller, 293
Instrumental act(s), definition, Dollard and Miller, 295
  see also Cue-producing response
Integration of a situation, Sullivan
  in theory, 251–252
  schematization of, 253

Intentional construct
  definition of, 4
  in Freud's early theory, 60
  in Freud's use of "wish," 64
  involved in mental illness, Freud, 65
  Freud's extensive use of, 221–222
  in Adler's two teleologies, 223–224
  as incompatible with impetus meanings, Jung, 224–225
  rejection of
    by Sullivan, 383
    by behaviorists, 383
  of mind as mediational, behaviorism, 383–385
  Skinner's informal use of, 385–387
  major application in Rogerian theory, 517
  in concept of future, Binswanger, 519
  existentialists emphasis of choice in, 519
  Kellyian theory's reliance on, 519–520
  see also Cause, Final cause, Teleology
Interpersonal relations, Sullivan, 241, 245
Interpersonal situation, Sullivan, 245
Interpretation
  definition of
    Freud, 71
    Kelly, 412
  as maternal re-education, Adler, 121–122
  of symbols, Jung, 193–194
  Jung acknowledged other views in, 196
  Sullivan's active use of, 278
  via successive approximations, Dollard and Miller, 324
  point of, existentialism, 467
  client's role in, Kelly, 491
  see also Insight
Intoxication, alcoholic, as therapy technique, Sullivan, 274
Introjection
  in Freud's theory, 47
  in Jung's theory, 155
  in Sullivan's theory, 258, 259

in Rogers' theory, 423
in existentialism, 458
see also Identification, Incorporation
Introspective theory
definition of, 13
vs. introspective method, 365
as tie binding all phenomenologists, 515
see also Extraspective theory
Introversion, definition of, Jung, 165
see also Attitude, Extraversion
Isolation, definition of, Freud, 45
Isophilic intimacy, Sullivan, 263

Kantian model
schematization of, 11
discussion of, 11–12
mixed, with Lockean, 200–201
theorists' attitude toward
Freud, 202
Adler, 203
Jung, 203
and "critical realism," Kant, 203
as promoting idealism, 203
related to meaning expression, 365
see also Lockean model
Knowledge, definition of, 16

Label, definition of, Dollard and Miller, 296
see also Cue
Language
as important to Sullivan's theory, 247–248
as important to Dollard and Miller's theory, 296–297
as patterning into logic, Dollard and Miller, 296
Latency psychosexual stage, Freud
theory of, 51–52
as not inevitable, 52
diphasic sexual development, 52
Law(s)
definition of, 17
in behaviorism, 365
S-R vs. R-R, Spence, 380
lower vs. higher level, 381
in gestalt psychology, 405–406
see also Method

Law of contradiction
definition of, 7
as demonstrative principle, 15
see also Demonstrative reasoning
Law of effect
coined by Thorndike, 284
via drive-reduction, Hull, 287
empirical, Skinner, 290
Law of exercise, Thorndike, 285
Learning
definition of
Dollard and Miller, 294
Kelly, 474
two-factor theory of, Mowrer, 355
mug and jug theory of, Rogers, 438
Learning dilemma, Dollard and Miller, 312
Lesbianism, Adler, 108
see also Homosexuality
Libidinal anticipatory idea, Freud, 72
Libido
Freud's definition of, 38
Freud vs. Jung on, 41
damming-up of, in fixation, Freud, 54
reflowing of, in regression, Freud, 56
Jung's teleological view of, 147–148
as *hormé*, Jung, 147
as value, Jung, 148
as *élan vital*, Jung, 149
as Will, Jung, 149
free, can constellate, Jung, 150
generated via differentiation, Jung, 150
as numen, Jung, 171
analogue, Jung, 182
Freud's arbitrary employment of, 206
as honest subterfuge, Freud, 215
see also Cathexis, Instinct
Life instinct, definition of, Freud, 42
see also Death instinct, Eros
Life line
vs. life lie, Adler, 117–118
mistakes in, Adler, 121
course of, Jung, 157–160

Life space, Lewin
behavioral function of, 407
as a phenomenal field, 407
path, 408
valence, 408
conflict in, 408
demand character of, 408
topological geometry and, 408
vs. foreign hull (external experience), 408
regions, of, 409
communication vs. locomotion, 409
cell, 409
Little Hans, case of, 77
Lockean model
schematization of, 10
discussion of, 10–11
mixed, with Kantian, 200–201
as predominant in American academic psychology, 365–367
and the founders of experimental psychology, 404
Locus of evaluation, definition of, Rogers, 423
Love
as aim-inhibited lust, Freud, 53
Adler's views on, 114
vs. lust, Sullivan, 262
autophilic, Sullivan, 262, 264
isophilic, Sullivan, 262, 264
heterophilic, Sullivan, 262, 264
Lumination, of Dasein, Boss, 451

Malevolent transformation, Sullivan, 259
Mana, definition of, Jung, 149, 166
Mana personality, Jung
theory of, 166
as taking possession of ego, 183
handling of, in therapy, 183–184
Mandala, Jung
in psychology, 184–189
common examples of, 185
of Christ symbol, 186
Antichrist or Devil as balancing totality, 187

Mania
  Adlerian view of, 119
  Jungian view of, 183
  Sullivanian view of, 271–272
  existentialistic view of, 464
Many and one
  see One and many
Masculine protest, Adler, 117
  see also Fiction
Masturbation, autoerotic, Sullivan, 264
Matched-dependent behavior, Dollard and Miller, 302
Material cause, definition of, 3
  see also Cause, Substance construct
Meaning
  as tied to Kantian model, 365
  bipolarity in, 367
  as most important to phenomenology, 449
  vs. nothingness, existentialism, 456
  bipolarity of, Kelly, 465
  as a pattern construct, 516
Meaning-disclosing, of Dasein, Boss, 451
  see also Lumination, of Dasein
Meaning-endowing, of Dasein, Binswanger, 450
  see also Meaning-disclosing, of Dasein
Mechanism, Watson's definition of, 286
Mediation
  introduced by Tolman, Woodworth, 286
  Dollard and Miller's definition of, 296
Memory, Sullivan's definition of, 242
Mental illness
  three-stage compromise model, Freud, 62–64
  quantitative view of, Freud, 65
  flight into, Freud, 65
  and life's major challenge, Adler, 118
  emotions and, Jung, 136
  in theory of
    Jung, 169
    Sullivan, 266–268
  via lack of conscience, Jung, 170

complex formation in, Jung, 169–170
of modern man, Jung, 189–190
definition of
  in operant theory, Skinner, 335
  in Rogers, 427
  in Kelly, 487
  as constricted Dasein, existentialism, 461
  see also Neurosis, Normal, Psychosis
Metatheory, 2
Method
  definition of, 15
  confused with theory in behaviorism, 376
  see also Procedural evidence, Theory, Validating evidence
Mind
  Freud's early model of, 30
  and Freud's introspective theory, 202
  as tabula rasa, 205
  as intentional, 223
  in Adlerian terms, 224
  as mediational, 383–384
  as teleological via dialectical reasoning, 385
  as needing no energies, Kelly, 481
  see also Idea, Psyche
Mitwelt, social world, existentialism, 452, 459
Model(s)
  causes as, 3
  informal, use of, 3
  definition of, 3, 13
  depth, Freud, 30–33
  dynamic, Freud, 33–36
  adhesive, Jung, 139
  stylized meaning expression, Jung, 143
  see also Theory, Formal theory
Modes of experience, Sullivan, 246–249
Monism
  Sullivan's dislike of, 242
  in Dollard and Miller's view, 293
  Rogerian phenomenal field and, 416

in existential theory, 448–449
  see also Dualism
Mood, as pitch of Dasein, existentialism, 455
Motivation, definition, Dollard and Miller, 298
Motives to psychotherapy, general overview, 17–19
  see also Curative motive, Ethical motive, Scholarly motive
Movement, law of
  as uniting mind-body, Adler, 93
  produced via prototype, Adler, 95
Multiordinality, definition of, 12
Mysticism
  inappropriate Jungian label, 188
  and the dialectic, 211
Myth(s), Jung
  in dreams, 144
  compensatory role of, 185
  and religious rites, 186
  of Job, answer to, 187

Narcissism
  in Greek mythology, 40–41
  definition of, Freud, 41
Nativism
  in Jungian psychology, 205
  in gestalt psychology, 407
Need(s)
  as integrating tendencies, Sullivan, 252
  rejected by Skinner, 289–290
  vs. drive, Dollard and Miller, 302
  as sensory stimulations, Wolpe, 343
  as cause of all behaviors, 420
  organism vs. self, Rogers, 421
Neurosis, Neurotic
  actual vs. proper, Freud, 62
  unresolved Oedipal and, Freud, 62
  transference vs. narcissistic, Freud, 73
  as unfree, Freud, 77
  nailed to cross of fiction, Adler, 118
  as inner cleavage, Jung, 173
  vs. psychosis, Jung, 173–174
  definition of

Pattern construct (*Cont.*)
Rogers, 514, 516
existentialists, 514–515
Kelly, 516
role of, in hard determinism,
378–379
as related to language meaning, 378–379
in concepts of hierarchy,
Wolpe and Stampfl, 381
as major meaning of gestalt-
phenomenological out-
look, 511
as substitute for time in behavior theory, 512
vs. impetus construct in history of psychology, 513–
514
as basic to conceptions of logic,
514
see also Cause, Formal cause
Penis envy, Freud, 48, 50
Permeability, vs. impermeability
of constructs, Kelly, 479
Persona, as a complex, Jung, 140
Personal constructs, psychology
of, Kelly, 471
Personality
theoretical issues and, 1–2
as temperament, 17
as character, 17
Freud's totality conception of,
56–57
as typologizing the life style,
Adler, 97
in the multifaceted Jungian
view, 142–143, 166, 175
definition of
Sullivan, 245, 250–251
Rogers, 424
Kelly, 474–475
warp of, Sullivan, 266
Dollard and Miller's usage of,
293
Personification
through archetypes, Jung, 146
of anima or animus, Jung,
179–180
Sullivan's use of, 244
fantastic, Sullivan, 244
potent, Sulivan, 244
good-me, bad-me, not-me, Sullivan, 244
good vs. bad mother, father,
Sullivan, 244

of self, Sullivan, 250
of self vs. others, Sullivan, 250
supervisory pattern as, 250
"thee," as, Sullivan, 250
Phallic personality, Freud, 58
Phallic psychosexual stage,
Freud, 47–48
Phallus, Freud, 47
Phenomena, Kant
as "categories of understanding," 11
as sensory knowledge, 402
see also Noumena
Phenomenal field
life space as, Lewin, 407
Rogerian concept of, 416–417
Phenomenal movement
Wertheimer's concept of, 404
as nonreductive experience,
405
Phenomenology
sensory vs logical, Jung, 203
father of, Husserl, 402
relation to gestalt psychology,
404
rejects mind-body distinction,
existentialism, 448–449
based on Kantian model, 500
emphasis on sensory, Rogers
and Boss, 514
emphasis on logical, Kelly and
Binswanger, 514–515
Phenotypic description
definition of, 13
in Freudian theory, 40
in natural science, 205
see also Genotypic description
Philosophy, and psychology, 2
Phobia
as learned pattern of anxiety,
Dollard and Miller, 317
as specific anxiety, existentialism, 463
Phrenology, Gall, 85
Pitch, of Dasein, existentialism,
455
Pleasure principle
Freud's definition of, 37
as reinforcement principle,
Dollard and Miller, 298
Pole(s)
similarity vs. contrast, Kelly,
475
and choice, Kelly, 481

Positive regard, definition of,
Rogers, 422
Possibilities
as an aspect of Dasein, existentialism, 452
fulfilling of, as care, 452
as motivational construct, existentialism, 456
positive or negative, 506
Power motive, Sullivan, 252
Preconscious, Freud, 32
Predicament, of men, existentialism, 443
Preemption, Kelly, 479
Prehension, Sullivan, 248
Premise(s)
arriving at, in reason, 6
primary and true, 7
in logical phenomenology, 514
see also Reason
Primal father, Freud, 48
Primal horde, Freud, 48–49
Primary and true
in Aristotelian thought, 7
as unipolar meaning, 7
see also Demonstrative reasoning
Primary process, Freud, 35
see also Secondary process
Procedural evidence
definition of, 15
Freudian confounding of, as
scientific method, 226
Jung's defense of, 229–230
in therapy of
existentialists, 521
Kelly, 523
see also Validating evidence
Process, seven-stage, in therapy,
Rogers, 433–435
Progression
as early Freudian construct,
31, 33
and principle of neuronic
inertia, 36
as used by Jung, 156
see also Regression
*Project, for a scientific psychol-
ogy*
Freud's prompting by Fliess in
conceiving, 29
use of cathexis in, 39
Freud's Lockean efforts in,
201–202

Reinforcement
in Pavlovian theory, 284
as drive reduction
Hull, 287
Dollard and Miller, 298
primary vs. secondary
Hull, 288
Dollard and Miller, 298
immediate vs. delayed, Dollard and Miller, 298
latency in, Dollard and Miller, 299
gradient of, Dollard and Miller, 299, 304
delayed, Dollard and Miller, 299
schedule of, Skinner, 331
negative, vs. punishment, Skinner, 332
Wolpe's definition of, 343
via anticipation of events, Kelly, 481
see also Conditioning
Relationship
in Freudian analysis, 76–77
client-centered, Rogers, 430
genuine, existentialism, 466
Kelly's definition of, 493
Religion
function of
Jung, 149, 170
Adler, 225
mythological features of, Jung, 186–187
role of, in compensation, Jung, 186–188
Jung's attitude toward, 188, 211
Freud's views on, 227, 460
God as reason in, Freud, 233
as next to delusion, Sullivan, 392
as not immature adult pattern, Binswanger, 460
Repertoire
of responses, Watson, 286, 287
in Dollard and Miller's theory, 294–295
Repetition compulsion, Freud
definition of, 41
in transference, 71
Repression
definition of
Freud, 43

Dollard and Miller, 306
Kelly, 484
primal, as fixation, Freud, 43
vs. suppression, Freud, 43
primal vs. proper, Freud, 43–44
continuing (after-repression), as proper, Freud, 62
return of repressed memories, Freud, 64
Adler's modest use of, 107
theory of
Jung, 139, 155
Sullivan, 258
Stampfl, 356
relation of, to sin, Jung, 170–171
relation of, to secrets, Jung, 171
can be positive, Dollard and Miller, 306–307
Freud vs. Dollard and Miller, 387–389
Rogerian interpretation of, 423
existentialistic view of, 458
see also Suppression, Unconscious
Research
related to method, 15
variables in: independent, dependent, and control, 16
Resistance
Freud's definition of, 70
as major facet of cure, Freud, 72
as lack of courage, Adler, 123
in confrontation with Anima, Jung, 179
Sullivan's criticism of, 276
in theory of
Rank, 411
Rogers, 440
existentialists, 466
Kelly, 494
Response(s)
conditioned, Pavlov, 283
internal vs. external, Watson, 285
elicit vs. emit, Skinner, 289
classes of, Skinner, 290
Dollard and Miller's definition of, 294
innate hierarchy of, Dollard and Miller, 294–295

dominant vs. weak, Dollard and Miller, 295
operant, level of, Skinner, 331–332
Role
Kelly's definition of, 480
core constructs of, Kelly, 480
constructs involving, in therapy, Kelly, 493
see also Role construct repertory test
Role construct repertory test, Kelly, 488–489
Role relationship, Kelly, 480

Sadism, Freud
as a fusion of instincts, 42
as prominent in oral stage, 47
Safeguarding tendencies, Adler, 107
Schedule(s), of reinforcement
fixed vs. variable ratio, 331
fixed vs. variable interval, 331
Schizophrenia
simple, paranoid, catatonic, hebephrenic, 88
as dementia praecox, Kraepelin, 88
in theory of
Adler, 119
Jung, 135, 169, 214
Sullivan, 268–271
existentialists, 464
Kelly, 490
see also Mental illness, Psychosis
Scholarly motive to therapy
general statement of, 18
as Freud's major motive, 225–227
theorists' attitudes toward
Adler, 228
Jung, 228
Sullivan, 391
Dollard and Miller, 391
behaviorists, 391
Rogers, 519
existentialists, 521
Kelly, 522
Science
nature of, 7–8
restriction of causal description in, 7–8
Kuhnian paradigms in, 16

Subjective realm, existentialism, 462–463
Sublimation
   definition of
      Freud, 44
      Sullivan, 264
   Sullivan's use of, 259, 261
   Binswanger's criticism of, 458
Subpersonification, Sullivan, 244
Substance construct(s)
   definition of, 4
   limited use of
      Freud, 212–213
      Adler, 213, 214
      Jung, 214–215
      Sullivan, 371
      Stampfl, 373
   emphasis on
      in early behaviorism, 372
      Wolpe, 373
   Dollard and Miller's position on, 372
   rejection of
      Skinner, 373
      existentialists, 509
   as nativism, in gestalt theory, 508
   in Rogers' naturalistic ethic, 509–510
   Kelly highly critical of, 509
   see also Cause, Material cause
Substitution, definition of, Freud, 44
Successive approximation
   in Skinner, 290
   in Dollard and Miller, 324
Superego
   as tantamount to ego-ideal, Freud, 35
   Freud's theory of, 35–36
   heir to the Oedipal complex, Freud, 50
   too harsh, in neurosis, Freud, 68
   Jung's theory of, 170
   as result of cultural training, Dollard and Miller, 297–298
Superiority, Adler
   striving for, 103
   related to inferiority feelings, 103
   see also Emotion, Inferiority

Superiority complex, Adler, 103
Support, Kelly, 493
Suppression
   definition of, 43
   Freud's early use of, 60
   Dollard and Miller's use of, 307
   as therapeutic, Dollard and Miller, 325
Symbol(s)
   definition of
      Freud, 78
      Rogers, 416
   vs. sign, 143
   universal, 144
   role of, in mental illness, Jung, 171
   as bridges, Jung, 171
   of transformation, Jung, 172
   as essential to cure, Jung, 176
   as libido analogue, Jung, 182
   have more than one meaning, Jung, 193
   table of Jungian interpretations of, 194
   as signs of signs, Sullivan, 247
   as identical to signs, Dollard and Miller, 296–297
   Existentialist theory of, 468
   Kelly's views on, 497
   see also Sign
Symbolization, Rogers
   denied, 418
   distorted, 423
Symptom(s)
   conversion in, Freud, 64
   as compromises, Freud, 64–65
   as deceptions, Adler, 118
   as communications, existentialism, 462
   Kelly's definition of, 488
Symptom substitution, and behavioral cures, Wolpe, 352
Synchronicity
   Jung's definition of, 154
   in telepathy, extrasensory perception, Jung, 154
   schematization of, 155
   and the one-in-many thesis, 217
Syntaxic mode, Sullivan, 248–249

Systematic desensitization, Wolpe
   definition of, 344–345
   hypnosis and, 348
   procedure of, 348–351

Tabula rasa, 205
Teaching machine(s), Skinner and Pressy, 333
Teleology
   definition of, 4
   natural, 4
   deity, 4, 7
   organic, in Adlerian theory, 105
   as fundamental to Jungian psyche, 137
   as fundamental to life, Jung, 147
   denied by
      Watson, 286
      Tolman, 286
      Hull, 288
      Dollard and Miller, 293, 296
   rejected by behavior therapists
      Wolpe, 375
      Skinner, 379
   vs. vitalism, 382
   as due to dialectical reasoning, 385
   informally phrased in Skinnerian theory, 385–387
   in Rogerian theory, 417, 422, 517
   and self-growth in existentialistic cure, 465
   in Kelly's views on freedom, 481–482
   see also Final cause, Intentional construct
Tension(s), as energy transformations, Sullivan, 252
Theorotype, vs. stereotype, 14
   see also Stereotype
Theory
   definition of, 2
   and metatheory, 2
   relates to pattern-intentional construct meanings, 5
   objective vs. subjective, 9
   perspective in, 13
   formal vs. informal, 14
   and facts, 16
   as thought, 16